Law and Practice of Investment Treaties

KLUWER LAW INTERNATIONAL

Law and Practice of Investment Treaties

Standards of Treatment

By

Andrew Newcombe

Lluís Paradell

 Wolters Kluwer

Law & Business

AUSTIN   BOSTON   CHICAGO   NEW YORK   THE NETHERLANDS

Published by:
Kluwer Law International
PO Box 316
2400 AH Alphen aan den Rijn
The Netherlands
Website: www.kluwerlaw.com

Sold and distributed in North, Central and South America by:
Aspen Publishers, Inc.
7201 McKinney Circle
Frederick, MD 21704
United States of America
Email: customer.care@aspenpubl.com

Sold and distributed in all other countries by:
Turpin Distribution Services Ltd.
Stratton Business Park
Pegasus Drive, Biggleswade
Bedfordshire SG18 8TQ
United Kingdom
Email: kluwerlaw@turpin-distribution.com

ISBN 978-90-411-2351-0

Printed and bound by CPI Group (UK) Ltd, Croydon, CR0 4YY

Table of Contents

Authors' Preface   xix

Acknowledgements   xxi

List of Abbreviations   xxiii

Guide to Investment Treaty Resources   xxix

Chapter 1
Historical Development of Investment Treaty Law   **1**
    Introduction   1
    §1.1   A unique treaty framework   1

I   Historical Origins of International Investment Law   3
    §1.2   Early history   3
    §1.3   Diplomatic protection   5
    §1.4   Dispute settlement by claims commissions and
            international arbitration   7
    §1.5   Use and abuse of diplomatic protection   8
    §1.6   Colonial territories and extraterritorial jurisdiction   10
    §1.7   The minimum standard of treatment   11
    §1.8   The Calvo Doctrine   13
    §1.9   Early jurisprudence on the minimum standard of treatment   14
    §1.10 Efforts to codify treatment standards in the 1920s and 1930s   15
    §1.11 Convention on the Treatment of Foreigners   16
    §1.12 Seventh International Conference of American States   17
    §1.13 The Hull Rule   18

II   Post-WWII Developments   18
    §1.14 Decolonization and nationalizations   18
    §1.15 The Havana Charter and the International Trade Organization   19

§1.16 Non-governmental initiatives to create a multilateral
      legal framework for investment   20
§1.17 Bilateral and regional initiatives   22
§1.18 Increasing resort to international arbitration post-WWII   24
§1.19 New York Convention   25
§1.20 Permanent Sovereignty Over Natural Resources   26
§1.21 International Centre for Settlement of Investment Disputes   27
§1.22 OECD Convention on the Protection of Foreign Property   30
§1.23 Charter of Economic Rights and Duties of States   31
§1.24 Draft UN Code of Conduct on Transnational Corporations   33
§1.25 OECD Declaration on International Investment and
      Multinational Enterprises   33
§1.26 Lump sum agreements and national claims commissions   34
§1.27 Investment disputes before the International Court of Justice   35
§1.28 Iran-US Claims Tribunal   39
§1.29 Foreign investment insurance   39

III   International Investment Agreements   41
§1.30 The origins of international investment agreements   41
§1.31 The advent of treaty-based investor-state arbitration in BITs   44
§1.32 BITs – the 1970s and 1980s   46
§1.33 BITs – the 1990s   47
§1.34 World Bank Guidelines   49
§1.35 Developments in Latin America   50
§1.36 Developments in Africa, Middle East and Asia   52
§1.37 North American Free Trade Agreement   53
§1.38 Energy Charter Treaty   53
§1.39 World Trade Organization   54
§1.40 Multilateral Agreement on Investment (MAI)   55
§1.41 WTO Working Group on the Relationship between
      Trade and Investment and the Doha Declaration   55
§1.42 Chinese IIAs   56
§1.43 Indian IIAs   57

IV   Current Status of the Network of IIAs   57
§1.44 The expanding network of IIAs   57
§1.45 The increase in investor-state arbitrations   58
§1.46 IIA jurisprudence   59
§1.47 Renegotiation and new model IIAs   61
§1.48 Investment promotion effects of IIAs   62
§1.49 Critiques of IIAs   63

V   Structure and Scope of Application of IIAs   65
§1.50 The structure of IIAs   65
§1.51 The scope of application – investment   65
§1.52 The scope of application – investors   68
§1.53 Dispute settlement   70

Chapter 2
Applicable Substantive Law and Interpretation 75
    Introduction 75
    §2.1 Applicable law and interpretation 75
    §2.2 Meaning of applicable substantive law 75
    §2.3 Relevance of the applicable law 78

I   Choice of Law Clauses 79
    §2.4 Express choice of law clauses 79
    §2.5 Distinction from other clauses 84
    §2.6 Choice of law clauses in arbitration rules 85

II   Relevant Sources of Law in IIA Disputes 86
    §2.7 Laws relevant to IIA disputes 86
    §2.8 Law pleaded and *iura novit curia* 88

III   Role of the IIA 91
    §2.9 The IIA as the primary source of law 91
    §2.10 The need to supplement the IIA 91

IV   Role of Municipal Law 92
    §2.11 Existence of the investment as a domestic law issue 92
    §2.12 Other matters to which domestic law is relevant 93
    §2.13 The *renvoi* of international law to domestic law 95
    §2.14 The relevance of domestic court decisions 95
    §2.15 Domestic law questions as jurisdictional issues 95
    §2.16 Criticism of the attitude of IIA tribunals towards
           domestic law 96
    §2.17 Limitations to the role of domestic law 97
    §2.18 Subsequent changes in the domestic law 98

V   Role of International Law 98
    §2.19 International law as the law applicable to issues of liability 98
    §2.20 IIAs and international law as part of domestic law 100
    §2.21 Domestic law applied alongside international law on
           issues of liability 101

VI   Applicable International Law 102
    §2.22 Sources of international law in IIA disputes 102
    §2.23 Precedents 102
    §2.24 Inconsistent decisions 105
    §2.25 Human rights 107

VII Interpretation of IIAs 109
    §2.26 Treaty interpretation as the process of applying the proper law 109
    §2.27 International law rules on treaty interpretation 110
    §2.28 Methods of interpretation 111

§2.29 Object and purpose, preambles and pro-investor or
       pro-state interpretations   113
§2.30 Interpretations and amendments to IIAs by the
       contracting states   117
§2.31 Interpretation and the adjudicative function
       under IIAs   119

Chapter 3
Promotion, Admission and Establishment Obligations   **121**
       Introduction   121
       §3.1   Overview   121
       §3.2   Customary international law obligations   121
       §3.3   IIA obligations   122

I   Treaty Titles and Preambles   122
       §3.4   Treaty practice   122
       §3.5   The use of the treaty title and preamble in interpreting
              IIA obligations   124

II   Promotion and Encouragement Obligations   126
       §3.6   Promotion and encouragement   126
       §3.7   Favourable conditions   130

III   Admission and Establishment   132
       §3.8   Distinguishing admission and establishment   132
       §3.9   Rationale for freedom of admission and establishment 132
       §3.10 Domestic regulation of foreign investment   133
       §3.11 Treaty models for admission and establishment   134
       §3.12 The post-entry model   134
       §3.13 The pre-entry model   137
       §3.14 WTO General Agreement on Trade in Services (GATS)   140

IV   Other Entry Obligations   142
       §3.15 Entry of personnel   142
       §3.16 Senior management and offices   144
       §3.17 Granting of permits   145
       §3.18 Special formalities for establishment   146

Chapter 4
National Treatment   **147**
       Introduction   147
       §4.1   Non-discrimination in international economic law   147
       §4.2   A relative standard   148
       §4.3   A treaty-based obligation   149

§4.4   IIA prohibitions on discriminatory measures   150
§4.5   Overview of the issues covered in this chapter   150

I   Background on National Treatment in IIAs   150
§4.6   National treatment – purpose and definition   150
§4.7   Historical background and development   152

II   Treaty Practice   156
§4.8   General overview of treaty practice   156
§4.9   Establishment: pre-entry and post-entry models   158

III   Application of National Treatment   159
§4.10 The two elements of national treatment analysis   159

A   The Comparator   159
§4.11 The basis for comparison   159
§4.12 Sequence of analysis   162
§4.13 Relevant factors in comparing investors and investments 164
§4.14 Economic sector and the existence of the competitive
       relationship   164
§4.15 IIA jurisprudence on determining the comparator based
       on economic sector   165
§4.16 The relevance of WTO like products jurisprudence
       to the like circumstances determination   170
§4.17 The existence of protectionist intent or motive   174
§4.18 Regulatory purpose of the measure   176
§4.19 The absence of foreign or domestic comparators   180

B   The Standard of Treatment   181
§4.20 Treaty provisions   181
§4.21 Meaning of 'treatment'   182
§4.22 *De facto* analysis   182
§4.23 Comparisons of treatment   183
§4.24 Examples of less favourable treatment   184
§4.25 Better of national and MFN treatment?   186
§4.26 Best treatment or average treatment?   186
§4.27 Application to sub-state units   188

IV   Exceptions and Reservations   189
§4.28 Exceptions and reservations   189

Chapter 5
Most-Favoured-Nation Treatment   **193**
Introduction   193
§5.1   Principle and rationale   193
§5.2   A conventional not a customary obligation   193

§5.3   IIA prohibitions on discriminatory measures   194
§5.4   Overview of the issues covered in this chapter   194

I   Background on MFN Treatment in IIAs   195
§5.5   MFN treatment – principle and definition   195
§5.6   Historical background and forms of MFN   198

II   Treaty Practice   201
§5.7   General overview of treaty practice   201
§5.8   Meaning of treatment   203

III   The Scope of MFN Treatment   204
§5.9   The subject matter of MFN treatment   204
§5.10 Does MFN treatment apply to investor-state
       arbitration clauses?   205
§5.11 MFN clauses applied to avoid local remedy requirements   208
§5.12 MFN clauses applied to provide subject matter jurisdiction   210
§5.13 Assessment of IIA MFN jurisprudence   216
§5.14 Using MFN to confer more favourable scope of application   222
§5.15 Application of MFN to investment or investors   223
§5.16 The treaty practice response to the application of MFN
       to investor-state arbitration provisions   223

IV   Applying MFN Treatment   224
§5.17 Similarities and differences with the national
       treatment analysis   224
§5.18 The two elements of MFN treatment analysis   225

       A The Comparator   225
§5.19 The basis for comparison   225
§5.20 Comparing the treatment of investors and investments
       under third state IIAs   226
§5.21 Comparing the treatment of investors and investments
       under domestic measures   226
§5.22 The existence of a special legal relationship between
       the host state and investor   227

       B The Standard of Treatment   228
§5.23 Treaty provisions   228
§5.24 Less favourable treatment compared to treatment under
       third state IIAs   228
§5.25 Less favourable treatment under domestic measures   230
§5.26 Better of national and MFN treatment?   231

V   Exceptions and Reservations   231
§5.27 Exceptions and reservations   231

Chapter 6
Minimum Standards of Treatment   **233**
    Introduction   233
    §6.1   Principle and rationale   233
    §6.2   Overview   235

I   The Minimum Standard of Treatment   235
    §6.3   The continued relevance of the minimum standard
            of treatment   235
    §6.4   The content of the minimum standard of treatment   235
    §6.5   Denial of justice   238
    §6.6   Denial of justice and exhaustion of local remedies   241
    §6.7   Due process   244
    §6.8   Due diligence   246
    §6.9   Arbitrariness   246
    §6.10 Discrimination   251
    §6.11 Individuals and international human rights law   252

II   Treatment in Accordance with International Law   253
    §6.12 IIA clauses   253

III   Fair and Equitable Treatment   255
    §6.13 The baseline of investment protection   255
    §6.14 Early treaty practice   255
    §6.15 IIA practice   257
    §6.16 Meaning of treatment   261
    §6.17 No requirement for impairment   262
    §6.18 Scope of fair and equitable treatment – investment
            or investors?   262
    §6.19 Interpretive approaches to fair and equitable treatment   263
    §6.20 Fair and equitable treatment as an independent treaty
            standard with an autonomous meaning   264
    §6.21 Fair and equitable treatment as reflecting the minimum
            standard of treatment   268
    §6.22 Fair and equitable treatment as an independent treaty
            standard and customary international law   270
    §6.23 Interpretation of Article 1105(1), NAFTA   272
    §6.24 General characteristics of the fair and equitable
            treatment standard   275
    §6.25 Specific elements of fair and equitable treatment   279
    §6.26 Legitimate expectations   279
    §6.27 Discrimination   289
    §6.28 Transparency   291
    §6.29 Bad faith, coercion, threats and harassment   294
    §6.30 A requirement to create favourable conditions?   295
    §6.31 The relevance of the conduct of the foreign investor   296

IV	Arbitrary, Unreasonable or Discriminatory Measures	298
	§6.32 Background	298
	§6.33 Treaty practice	299
	§6.34 Elements of the guarantee	300
	§6.35 Relationship with fair and equitable treatment	301
	§6.36 Arbitrary measures	302
	§6.37 Unreasonable or unjustifiable measures	303
	§6.38 Discriminatory measures	304
	§6.39 An effects-based analysis of discrimination	306
	§6.40 Overlap with national and MFN treatment clauses	306
V	Protection and Security Obligations	307
	§6.41 Background	307
	§6.42 IIA practice	308
	§6.43 Physical protection	309
	§6.44 Due diligence, physical protection and the level of host state resources	310
	§6.45 Regulatory and legal protection	311
	§6.46 Breach of protection and security in the administration of justice	314
VI	Compensation for Extraordinary Losses	315
	§6.47 Extraordinary losses	315
VII	Preservation of Rights/More Favourable Treatment Clauses	317
	§6.48 More favourable treatment	317
VIII	Exceptions	319
	§6.49 Exceptions	319
	Chapter 7	
	Expropriation	**321**
	Introduction	321
	§7.1 Expropriation in international law	321
I	What Constitutes Expropriation?	322
	§7.2 Introduction	322
	§7.3 Direct expropriation	324
	§7.4 Indirect expropriation	325
	§7.5 Attempts to develop international standards for expropriation	328
	§7.6 IIA provisions defining expropriation	332
	§7.7 More recent model BITs	334
	§7.8 Express exceptions for specific measures	336
	§7.9 The meaning of the term 'measures'	337
	§7.10 Do IIAs expand the scope of expropriation?	338

§7.11 Direct expropriation   340
§7.12 Key principles relating to indirect expropriation   341
§7.13 The form of measure is not determinative   341
§7.14 State intent to expropriate is not a necessary condition   342
§7.15 Creeping expropriation   343
§7.16 The requirement for a substantial deprivation   344
§7.17 Categorizing the object of the deprivation and the question
       of partial expropriation   348
§7.18 Legitimate and reasonable expectations   350
§7.19 The relationship between domestic law and expropriation   351
§7.20 Breach of contract and expropriation   352
§7.21 Debt contracts and expropriation   355
§7.22 Payments under statutory obligations and expropriation   356
§7.23 Non-expropriatory regulation   357
§7.24 Police powers   358
§7.25 Proportionality and standard of review in assessing
       police powers   363
§7.26 Transparency and due process in police powers   366
§7.27 Burden of proof with respect to police powers   366
§7.28 A case-by-case analysis   366
§7.29 Effect of a finding of expropriation   368
§7.30 Title to expropriated property   369

II   Conditions for Expropriation   369
§7.31 Conditions for a lawful expropriation   369
§7.32 Public purpose   370
§7.33 Non-discrimination   373
§7.34 Due process of law and judicial review   375
§7.35 Contractual undertakings   377

III   Compensation   377
§7.36 IIA provisions on compensation   377

A   Standard of Compensation   377
§7.37 The standard of compensation in customary
       international law   377
§7.38 Legal and illegal expropriation in customary
       international law   379
§7.39 Standard of compensation in IIAs   383
§7.40 MFN and the standard of compensation   385
§7.41 Measuring fair market value – valuation methods   385
§7.42 Going-concern value and discounted cash flow   388
§7.43 Net book value, replacement or liquidation value   390
§7.44 DCF and NBV compared   391
§7.45 Actual investment   391
§7.46 Arm's length transactions or third party offer to purchase   392
§7.47 Market capitalization   392

§7.48 Reductions   392

B   Date for Determining Compensation   393
§7.49 Date of the expropriation   393

C   Transferability and Convertibilility   395
§7.50 Timing   395
§7.51 Transferability and convertibility   396

D   Interest   396
§7.52 Interest   396

E   Judicial Review   398
§7.53 Review   398

Chapter 8
Transfer Rights, Performance Requirements and
Transparency   **399**
    Introduction   399
    §8.1   Overview   399

I   Transfer of Funds   399
    §8.2   Introduction   399
    §8.3   Articles of Agreement of the International Monetary Fund
           (IMF Articles)   401
    §8.4   OECD Liberalization Codes   403
    §8.5   General Agreement on Trade in Services (GATS)   404
    §8.6   Transfer of funds in early investment instruments   404
    §8.7   Transfer of funds in IIAs   405
    §8.8   The scope of transfer rights   406
    §8.9   Types of transfers   407
    §8.10 Convertibility rights   411
    §8.11 Permissible restrictions on transfers   413
    §8.12 Express exceptions to transfer obligations   414
    §8.13 Jurisprudence   416

II   Prohibitions on Performance Requirements   417
    §8.14 Introduction   417
    §8.15 Trade-related investment measures (TRIMs) and the
           WTO TRIMS Agreement   419
    §8.16 Performance requirements in the General Agreement
           on Trade in Services (GATS)   421
    §8.17 Performance requirements in IIAs   422
    §8.18 The relationship between performance requirements
           and national treatment   422
    §8.19 The relationship between performance requirements
           and establishment rights   423

§8.20 Performance requirements and host state nationals and
third parties   423
§8.21 Express exceptions to prohibitions on performance
requirements   423
§8.22 Prohibitions on domestic content, sourcing and trade
balancing requirements   424
§8.23 Prohibitions on restrictions on sales of goods within
host state territory   427
§8.24 Prohibitions on requirements for technology transfer   428
§8.25 Conditions for receipt of advantages   429
§8.26 Other prohibited performance requirements   430
§8.27 Prohibitions on performance requirements in other
IIA standards   430

III   Transparency Related Standards   431
§8.28 Treaty practice   431
§8.29 Publication of laws, regulations and policies   431
§8.30 Notification and due process requirements   432

Chapter 9
Observance of Undertakings   **437**
Introduction   437
§9.1   Umbrella clause and other denominations   437
§9.2   Principle, rationale and interpretive uncertainty   438
§9.3   Contracts in international law   438

I   History and Treaty Practice   440
§9.4   Origins   440
§9.5   Early treaty practice   441
§9.6   Modern treaty practice   443
§9.7   Placement   444
§9.8   Drafting variations   445

II   Applicable Law   448
§9.9   Existence of the obligation to be observed   448
§9.10 Scope and effects of the obligation to be observed   450

III   Undertakings Covered   451
§9.11 Contractual undertakings   451
§9.12 Contracts with a foreign owned company   455
§9.13 Unilateral undertakings   457

IV   Undertakings Attributable to the State   460
§9.14 State entities and attribution of obligations to the state 460

§9.15 The application of international law rules of attribution   461
§9.16 Recognition of separate personality under domestic law   463
§9.17 Contract/treaty claim distinction and international rules
        of attribution   465

V   Substantive Content of the Duty of Observance   466
       §9.18 Doctrinal debate on the substantive content of the
               umbrella clause   466
       §9.19 The *SGS v. Pakistan* restrictive approach   466
       §9.20 The *SGS v. Philippines* literal approach   467
       §9.21 The governmental breach approach   469
       §9.22 The literal approach after *SGS v. Philippines*   470
       §9.23 The correct literal and *effet utile* approach   471

VI   Concurrent Jurisdictions   472
       §9.24 The *SGS v. Philippines* decision to stay proceedings   472
       §9.25 The approach to concurrent jurisdiction after *SGS v. Philippines* 473

VII   Limitations   475
       §9.26 Domestic law limitations   475
       §9.27 Observance of undertakings and stabilization clauses   476

VIII   Distinction from other Clauses   477
       §9.28 Preservation of rights clause   477
       §9.29 Wide dispute resolution clauses   478

Chapter 10
Exceptions and Defences   **481**
Introduction   481
       §10.1 Overview of exceptions and defences   481

I   Express Exceptions in IIAs   482
       §10.2 Introduction   482
       §10.3 The interpretation of exceptions   485

II   Security Exceptions   488
       §10.4 Treaty practice   488
       §10.5 Is the security exception self-judging?   492
       §10.6 Exception or excuse – the relationship between
               security exceptions and necessity   495
       §10.7 The scope of the security exception   497
       §10.8 Distinction from the war and civil disturbance clause   499

III   General Exceptions Modelled on Article XX GATT or
Article XIV GATS   500
§10.9   Treaty practice   500
§10.10 The interpretation of general exceptions   503

IV   Subject Matter and Obligation-Specific Exceptions   506
§10.11 Overview   506
§10.12 Tax measures   507
§10.13 Subsidies and government procurement   508
§10.14 Miscellaneous exceptions   508
§10.15 Exceptions or reservations for non-conforming measures   508

V   Interpretive Guidelines   509
§10.16 Express provisions on environmental measures   509
§10.17 Provisions on relaxation of standards   509

VI   Circumstances Precluding Wrongfulness in Customary
International Law   510
§10.18 Circumstances precluding wrongfulness   510
§10.19 Consent and waiver   510
§10.20 *Force majeure*   514
§10.21 Necessity as a circumstance precluding wrongfulness   516
§10.22 IIA jurisprudence on necessity   517
§10.23 Temporal limitations on preclusion of wrongfulness   522
§10.24 Compensation and preclusion of wrongfulness   523

VII   Other Defences   524
§10.25 Acquiescence   524
§10.26 Extinctive prescription and laches   525
§10.27 Estoppel   526

Table of Cases   **529**

Table of Treaties and Other Instruments   **555**

Index   **599**

Authors' Preface

There have been significant developments in investment treaty law and practice over the past twenty years. Since 1990, the date of the first investor-state arbitral award under a modern investment treaty, the growth in the number of investment treaties and treaty disputes has been exponential. This book, drawing on the authors' academic and professional expertise, examines the origins and evolution of investment treaty law and practice, the law applicable to investment treaty disputes, and substantive investment law issues: standards of treatment and exceptions and defences to treaty obligations. Our aim is to provide a systematic, comprehensive and detailed statement of the law, along with applicable principles and policies, and to analyze critically investment treaty jurisprudence in the subject areas covered by the book.

The book is the product of extensive collaboration between the co-authors. Primary research and writing responsibilities were allocated as follows: Chapters 1, 3-8 and 10, Newcombe; and Chapters 2, 9 and 10, Paradell.

Andrew Newcombe
Victoria, Canada

Lluís Paradell
Rome

July 2008

Acknowledgements

We have benefited greatly from discussions over the past ten years with numerous international law scholars, practitioners and arbitrators, and from their writings and presentations. We thank our colleagues (past and present) at Freshfields Bruckhaus Deringer for their support and contributions to this project. In particular, we thank Jan Paulsson for acting as a mentor to both of us and providing extensive comments on the draft manuscript. We have also received invaluable comments on specific chapters from a number of academics and practitioners: José Alvarez, Andrea Bjorklund, James Crawford, Meg Kinnear, Jürgen Kurtz, Vaughan Lowe, Mark Milford, Martin Paparinskis, Georgios Petrochilos, Michael Reisman, Judge Stephen Schwebel and Todd Weiler. We thank each of them for their time and effort in reviewing draft chapters. The book has been immeasurably improved by their comments. Any errors or omissions remain the sole responsibility of the authors.

Devashish Krishan has been an invaluable resource and has greatly assisted at various stages of the project. We thank him for his significant contributions. We have also benefited from online discussions on the OGEMID e-mail forum. We thank OGEMID participants for sharing their views and insights on investment treaty law.

We also thank our editors at Kluwer, beginning with Gwen de Vries and Bas Kniphorst, who originally supported the project, and more recently, Eleanor Taylor who has worked closely with us to bring the book to publication. Thanks also go to Vincent Verschoor and the production team at Kluwer for taking the project from manuscript to book.

Andrew Newcombe expresses his gratitude for the support he has received from the Faculty of Law, University of Victoria, and its faculty members and staff. Dean Andrew Petter and Associate Dean Cheryl Crane supported the project in a multitude of ways over the past five years. Faculty colleagues, Professors Ted McDorman, Benjamin Berger and Gillian Calder, provided invaluable comments on draft chapters. Professor Jeremy Webber provided wise counsel on academic publishing and much appreciated moral support. Special thanks are due to those in the Law Library – Law Librarian Neil Campbell, Associate Law Librarian Caron Rollins and staff members, including Irene Godfrey, Damaris Simair, Lynne Curry, Carol Shaw, Glenda Lee Jury and Rich McCue – for providing access to a vast array of print and electronic resources consulted while researching for the book. Thanks are also due to Rosemary Garton, who provided secretarial services throughout.

Lluís Paradell wants to thank especially Nigel Blackaby for his support and the extensive exchanges during the preparation of memorials and hearings (and early morning jogging!), which have greatly enriched the book, Lucy Reed for the first opportunity to plead at a hearing and her continued professional guidance, and Robert Volterra for having first introduced him to the subject.

Over the past five years a series of bright and talented University of Victoria law students have assisted with research and editing. Their assistance was invaluable to the success of this project and each of them made a significant contribution. We thank Jennifer Bond, Philippa Estall, Claire Farmer, Anna Johnston, Adam Kay, Sean McGinty, Micah Rankin, Karen Penate and Ania Zbyszewska.

Funding support for Andrew Newcombe's research of this book has come from various sources, including the University of Victoria, Borden Ladner Gervais, LLP, through its Summer Fellowship Program, Miller Thomson LLP, and the Foundation for Legal Research. Their financial support is gratefully acknowledged.

Finally, our greatest thanks are due to our families. We are grateful for their support and encouragement while we have worked on this project over the past five years.

List of Abbreviations

GENERAL

ACP	African, Caribbean and Pacific Group of States
ASEAN	Association of South East Asian Nations
BIT	Bilateral Investment Treaty
BLEU	Belgo-Luxembourg Economic Union
CAFTA-DR	Central America-Dominican Republic-United States Free Trade Agreement
DCF	Discounted Cash Flow
DSB	Dispute Settlement Body
EC	European Community
ECJ	European Court of Justice
ECT	Energy Charter Treaty
EU	European Union
FDI	Foreign Direct Investment
FCN	Treaty of Friendship, Commerce and Navigation
FIPA	Foreign Investment and Protection Agreement
FIRA	Foreign Investment Review Act
FTA	Free Trade Agreement
FTC	Free Trade Commission (NAFTA)
GATS	General Agreement on Trade in Services
GATT	General Agreement on Tariffs and Trade
ICC	International Chamber of Commerce
ICCA	International Council for Commercial Arbitration
ICJ	International Court of Justice
ICSID	International Centre for Settlement of Investment Disputes

ICSID Convention	Convention on the Settlement of Investment Disputes between States and Nationals of Other States 1965
IGO	Intergovernmental Organization
IIA	International Investment Agreement
ILA	International Law Association
ILC	International Law Commission
IPPA	Investment Promotion and Protection Agreement
JSEPA	Japan-Singapore Economic Partnership Agreement
LCIA	London Court of International Arbitration
MAI	Draft Multilateral Agreement on Investment
MERCOSUR	Mercado Común del Sur (Common Market of the South)
MFN	Most-Favoured-Nation
NAFTA	North American Free Trade Agreement
OECD	Organisation for Economic Co-operation and Development
PCIJ	Permanent Court of International Justice
SCC	Stockholm Chamber of Commerce
SLA	Softwood Lumber Agreement
SPS Agreement	Agreement on the Application of Sanitary and Phytosanitary Measures
TBT Agreement	Agreement on Technical Barriers to Trade
TRIMS Agreement	Agreement on Trade-Related Investment Measures
TRIPS Agreement	Agreement on Trade-Related Aspects of Intellectual Property Rights
UAE	United Arab Emirates
UN	United Nations
UNCITRAL	United Nations Commission on International Trade Law
UNCTC	United Nations Centre on Transnational Corporations
UNCTAD	United Nations Conference on Trade and Development
UNGA Res	United Nations General Assembly Resolution
UK	United Kingdom
US	United States
USD	United States Dollars
USSR	Union of Soviet Socialist Republics
Vienna Convention	Vienna Convention on the Law of Treaties 1969
WTO	World Trade Organization
WWI	World War I
WWII	World War II

JOURNALS, REPORTS AND TREATY SERIES

ABAJ	American Bar Association Journal
AULR	American University Law Review
AUILR	American University International Law Review
AIAJ	Asian International Arbitration Journal
AJIL	American Journal of International Law
AJIL Spec Supp	American Journal of International Law Special Supplement
AJCL	American Journal of Comparative Law
AI	Arbitration International
ARIA	American Review of International Arbitration
ASIL Proc	American Society of International Law Proceedings
AYIL	Asian Yearbook of International Law
BCICLR	Boston College International and Comparative Law Review
BLI	Business Law International
BYIL	British Yearbook of International Law
Can-USLJ	Canada-United States Law Journal
CBLJ	Canadian Business Law Journal
CLP	Current Legal Problems
CILJ	Cornell International Law Journal
CJIL	Chicago Journal of International Law
CJICL	Cardozo Journal of International and Comparative Law
CJTL	Columbia Journal of Transnational Law
CLQ	Cornell Law Quarterly
Con TS	Consolidated Treaty Series
CTS	Canadian Treaty Series
CYIL	Canadian Yearbook of International Law
EELR	European Environmental Law Review
EJIL	European Journal of International Law
ELJ	Energy Law Journal
ELR	Environmental Law Reporter
Foreign Aff	Foreign Affairs
Foreign Pol'y	Foreign Policy
FILJ	Fordham International Law Journal
FLR	Fordham Law Review
GYIL	German Yearbook of International Law
GGULR	Golden Gate University Law Review
GBDLJ	Global Business and Development Law Journal
GWJILE	George Washington Journal of International Law and Economics
HICLR	Hastings International and Comparative Law Review

HILJ	Harvard International Law Journal
IALR	International Arbitration Law Review
ICJ Rep	International Court of Justice Reports
ICLQ	International and Comparative Law Quarterly
ICLR	International Community Law Review
ICSID Rep	ICSID Reports
ICSID Rev	ICSID Review - Foreign Investment Law Journal
IFLR	International Financial Law Review
IALR	International Arbitration Law Review
IL	International Lawyer
ILF	International Law Forum
ILM	International Legal Materials
ILR	International Law Reports
ILSA JICL	ILSA Journal of International and Comparative Law
Iran-USCTR	Iran-United States Claims Tribunal Reports
ITBL	International Tax & Business Lawyer
IYBHR	Israel Yearbook on Human Rights
JAIL	Japanese Annual of International Law
JBL	Journal of Business Law
JCE	Journal of Comparative Economics
JDI	Journal de droit international
JENRL	Journal of Energy and Natural Resources Law
JILE	Journal of International Law and Economics
JIA	Journal of International Arbitration
JIEL	Journal of International Economic Law
JPL	Journal of Public Law (now Emory Law Journal)
JWI	Journal of World Investment (now JWIT)
JWIT	Journal of World Investment and Trade
JWT	Journal of World Trade
LCP	Law and Contemporary Problems
LNOJ	League of Nations Official Journal
LN Doc	League of Nations Documents
LNTS	League of Nations Treaty Series
LSI	Law & Social Inquiry
Marq LR	Marquette Law Review
Mich LR	Michigan Law Review
Minn LR	Minnesota Law Review
MJGT	Minnesota Journal of Global Trade
MJIL	Michigan Journal of International Law
NCLR	North Carolina Law Review
NILR	Netherlands International Law Review
NJILB	Northwestern Journal of International Law and Business
NYLJ	New York Law Journal
NYUJIL	New York University Journal of International Law

NYUELJ	New York University Environmental Law Journal
NYULQR	New York University Law Quarterly Review
NYULR	New York University Law Review
RDCADI	Recueil des cours de l' Académie de Droit International de La Haye
RIAA	Reports of International Arbitral Awards
RGD	Revue Générale de Droit
RGDIP	Revue Générale de Droit International Public
SJIL	Stanford Journal of International Law
TDM	Transnational Dispute Management
TILJ	Texas International Law Journal
UCDJILP	UC Davis Journal of International Law and Policy
UCDLR	UC Davis Law Review
UPJIEL	University of Pennsylvania Journal of International Economic Law
UTLJ	University of Toronto Law Journal
UKTS	United Kingdom Treaty Series
UNTS	United Nations Treaty Series
UST	United States Treaties
VJIL	Virginia Journal of International Law
VLR	Virginia Law Review
WCR	World Court Reports
WD	World Development
WILJ	Wisconsin International Law Journal
YJIL	Yale Journal of International Law
VJTL	Vanderbilt Journal of Transnational Law
YBCA	Yearbook of Commercial Arbitration
YBILC	Yearbook of the International Law Commission
YBUN	Yearbook of the United Nations
YWBA	Yearbook of World Affairs

FREQUENTLY CITED DRAFT CONVENTIONS AND OTHER INSTRUMENTS

1929 Draft Convention	*Convention on the Treatment of Foreigners*
1929 Harvard Draft	*Draft Convention on Responsibility of States for Damage done in their Territory to the Person or Property of Foreigners*
1961 Harvard Draft	*Draft Convention on the International Responsibility of States for Injuries to Aliens*
1967 Draft OECD Convention	*Draft Convention on the Protection of Foreign Property*

Abs-Shawcross Draft Convention	*Draft Convention on Investments Abroad*
Charter	*Charter of Economic Rights and Duties of States*
ICC Code	*International Code of Fair Treatment for Foreign Investment*
ILA Statute	*Draft Statutes of the Arbitral Tribunal for Foreign Investment and the Foreign Investment Court*
NIEO Declaration	*Declaration on the Establishment of a New International Economic Order*

NOTE ON REFERENCES TO BILATERAL INVESTMENT TREATIES

For ease of reference, specific bilateral investment treaties in this book are listed by referring to the two treaty parties in alphabetical order, followed by the date the treaty was signed (not the date of ratification). For example, the *Treaty between the United States of America and the Argentine Republic Concerning the Reciprocal Encouragement and Protection of Investment* (signed 14 November 1991, entered into force 20 October 1994) is referred to as Argentina-US (1991).

Guide to Investment Treaty Resources

INTERNATIONAL INVESTMENT AGREEMENTS AND INSTRUMENTS

International investment agreements and instruments are available in two print sources:

> United Nations Conference on Trade and Development, *International Investment Instruments: A Compendium* (New York: United Nations, 1996) in three volumes.

> International Centre for Settlement of Investment Disputes, *Investment Promotion and Protection Treaties*, looseleaf (New York: Oceana Publications, Inc., 1983) in ten volumes.

The United Nations Conference on Trade and Development (UNCTAD) website has two searchable electronic databases – a compilation of bilateral investment treaty texts and a compendium of international investment instruments. In addition, a number of commercially available databases including Kluwer Arbitration and Investment Claims have various treaty materials available online.

INVESTMENT TREATY AWARDS AND DECISIONS

Investment treaty awards and decisions are reproduced in various print sources including ICSID Reports, ICSID Review-Foreign Investment Law Journal, International Law Reports and International Legal Materials.

Online access to current and past investment treaty awards and decisions, along with links to other materials and resources, is available through Professor Andrew Newcombe's Investment Treaty Arbitration website: <http://ita.law.uvic.ca>.

OTHER RESOURCES

A number of specialized websites provide access to current investment treaty decisions, awards and other materials, including links to further resources:

Digest of Investment Treaty Decisions and Awards: <http://arbitration-icca.org>
ICSID: <http://icsid.worldbank.org>
Investment Arbitration Reporter: <http://iareporter.com>
Investment Claims: <http://investmentclaims.com>
Investment Treaty Arbitration: <http://ita.law.uvic.ca>
Investment Treaty News: <http://iisd.org/investment/itn>
Kluwer Arbitration: <http://kluwerarbitration.com>
NAFTA Claims: <http://naftaclaims.com>
Transnational Dispute Management: <http://transnational-dispute management.com>
UNCTAD international investment agreement: <http://unctad.org>

Chapter 1

Historical Development of Investment Treaty Law

INTRODUCTION

§1.1 A unique treaty framework   The international legal framework governing foreign investment consists of a vast network of international investment agreements (IIAs)[1] supplemented by the general rules of international law. Although other international treaties interact with this network in important ways, IIAs are the primary public international law instruments governing the promotion and protection of foreign investment.[2] IIA texts differ in many important respects, but they are also remarkably similar in structure and content: most IIAs combine similar (sometimes identical) treaty-based standards of promotion and protection for foreign investment with an investor-state arbitration mechanism[3] that allows foreign investors to enforce

---

1.   The abbreviation IIAs is used throughout this text to refer to standalone bilateral investment treaties (BITs), bilateral and regional free trade agreements that include foreign investment obligations, such as the *North American Free Trade Agreement* (NAFTA), and sectoral treaties, such as the *Energy Charter Treaty* (ECT), that include investment obligations. The expression 'investment treaties' is sometimes used in the text instead of IIAs.
2.   The interaction between investment promotion and protection under IIAs and the rules imposed by other multilateral economic treaties is addressed throughout the text. Important interactions include market access for service suppliers under the *General Agreement on Trade in Services* (see *infra* Chapter 3 on establishment obligations), prohibitions on restrictions on transfers and convertibility under the International Monetary Fund's *Articles of Agreement* (see *infra* Chapter 8 on transfer rights) and prohibitions on various types of performance requirements, including domestic content requirements, under the WTO's *Agreement on Trade-Related Investment Measures* (see *infra* Chapter 8 on performance requirements).
3.   See generally J.G. Merrills, *International Dispute Settlement*, 4th edn (Cambridge: Cambridge University Press, 2005). On trends in international law regarding the access of private actors (individuals and corporations) to international dispute settlement see F. Orrego Vicuña, *International Dispute Settlement in an Evolving Global Society: Constitutionalization,*

these standards against host states.[4] The network of IIAs provides foreign investors with a powerful and dynamic method of international treaty enforcement. The purpose of this book is to provide a comprehensive explanation of the substantive standards of treatment that states must accord to foreign investors and investment under IIAs.[5]

The uniqueness of the current IIA network is a product of an historical evolution going as far back as the Middle Ages. Prior to the twentieth century, international standards of foreign investment and investor protection developed primarily through the related processes of diplomatic protection and claims commissions. In the late nineteenth and early twentieth centuries, as the world economy became increasingly internationalized, the limits of the diplomatic protection model became apparent, particularly as controversies arose between capital exporting and importing states regarding the customary international law minimum standard of treatment to be accorded to foreign investors and investments.[6] In the aftermath of

---

Accessibility, Privatization (Cambridge: Cambridge University Press, 2004) [Orrego Vicuña, *International Dispute Settlement*], which describes treaties that provide individuals and corporate entities direct access to international courts and tribunals.

4. 'Host' state refers to the state in which a foreign investor or investment is located. 'Home' state refers to the state of which the investor is a national.

5. See *infra* Part V for an overview of the topics covered in this text. As noted in Part V, this book does not address threshold issues of the application of IIAs: to whom they apply (investors), to what they apply (investment), or when they apply (temporal application). Further, the book does not address jurisdictional or procedural issues related to investor-state arbitration or the consequences of breaches of IIA standards of treatment (reparations). A number of other texts consider these issues. See C. McLachlan, L. Shore & M. Weiniger, *International Investment Arbitration: Substantive Principles* (Oxford: Oxford University Press, 2007); R. Dolzer & C. Schreuer, *Principles of International Investment Law* (Oxford: Oxford University Press, 2008); K. Sauvant, ed., *Appeals Mechanism in International Investment Disputes* (Oxford: Oxford University Press, 2008); R.D. Bishop, J. Crawford & W.M. Reisman, *Foreign Investment Disputes: Cases, Materials and Commentary* (The Hague: Kluwer Law International, 2005); N. Rubins & N.S. Kinsella, *International Investment, Political Risk and Dispute Resolution* (Dobbs Ferry, NY: Oceana Publications Inc., 2005) and G. Van Harten, *Investment Treaty Arbitration and Public Law* (Oxford: Oxford University Press, 2007). There are also a number of new and forthcoming texts: P. Muchlinski, F. Ortino & C. Schreuer, *The Oxford Handbook of International Investment Law* (Oxford: Oxford University Press, 2008); A. Reinisch, ed., *Standards of Investment Protection* (Oxford: Oxford University Press, 2008); C. Dugan, D. Wallace, N. Rubins & B. Sabahi, *Investor-State Arbitration* (Oxford: Oxford University Press, 2008); Z. Douglas, *Investment Treaty Arbitration* (Cambridge: Cambridge University Press, forthcoming) and S. Ripinsky *et al.*, *Damages in International Law* (London: British Institute of International and Comparative Law, 2008).

6. Throughout this chapter, the term 'capital exporting' states refers to 'Western', 'developed' or 'industrialized' states – generally those that are now members of the Organization for Economic Co-operation and Development (OECD). The term 'capital importing' states refers to former colonies, 'developing' and 'newly-industrializing' states of Latin America, Asia and Africa. The terms 'capital importing' and 'capital exporting' states are generalizations and misleading in several respects. Many states are both capital importers and exporters. The categories are not static and states may become capital exporters or importers as political and economic circumstances change. Moreover, the capital exports in question are generally those of private

the Second World War (WWII), the process of international economic integration was rekindled, leading to the emergence of the contemporary investment treaty framework. It is crucial to consider this historical development in order to better understand current debates and contentious issues in investment treaty law.[7]

This chapter is divided into five parts. Part I delves into the historical origins of international investment law. Part II then explores developments in the post-WWII period, setting the background for Part III, which discusses the origins and development of IIAs. Part IV provides an overview of the current status of the IIA network. Part V discusses the basic structure of IIAs.

I HISTORICAL ORIGINS OF INTERNATIONAL INVESTMENT LAW

§1.2 Early history   There is no comprehensive history of the treatment of foreigners and their property under international law. However, historical records attest to the fact that early political communities routinely denied legal capacity and rights to those who originated from outside their community.[8] These 'outsiders', often known as aliens, from the Latin word *alius*, meaning 'other', were frequently treated as enemies, barbarians or outcasts. The treatment and the legal status of the alien has markedly improved from ancient times through the Middle Ages to the modern era. In his classic 1915 treatise, *The Diplomatic Protection of Citizens Abroad*, Edwin Borchard wrote that the 'legal position of the alien has in the progress of time advanced from that of complete outlawry, in the days of the early Rome and the Germanic tribes, to that of the practical assimilation with nationals, at the present

---

foreign investors, not the state itself as these expressions may wrongly suggest. Despite these conceptual limitations, the terms are useful since they reflect the tensions that have contributed to the development of the law governing relations between capital exporters and importers, as well as differing views about the nature and role of international investment law. As noted by Van Harten, *ibid.*, at 13-14, capital exporting states can be defined empirically as states whose outward foreign direct investment (FDI) stock exceeds their inward stock or whose outward stock exceeds USD100 billion. Based on data from the United Nations Conference on Trade and Development (UNCTAD), *World Investment Report 2005*, Annex Table B.2, Van Harten identifies 16 major capital exporters with outward stock of over USD100 billion. These are (ranked in order from the largest exporter): US, UK, Germany, France, Netherlands, Hong Kong, Switzerland, Japan, Canada, Spain, Italy, Belgium, Sweden, Luxembourg, Australia and Singapore. Capital importing states can be defined as states whose inward FDI exceeds outward FDI stocks by a ratio of at least 2 to 1. On this measure there are 111 capital importing states (Van Harten, *ibid.*, at 13). See UNCTAD's annual *World Investment Report* for recent statistics on foreign investments flows.

7. Given the breadth of this topic and the varied state practice, only the most important historical developments are highlighted and citations to specialized works in the area are provided.

8. On the status of foreign nationals or aliens in international law see R. Arnold, 'Aliens', in R. Bernhardt, ed., *Encyclopedia of Public International Law*, Vol. I (Amsterdam: North-Holland Pub. Co, 1992) [*Encyclopedia*] at 102.

time.'[9] These developments have continued through the twentieth and twenty-first centuries and are reflected in the current network of IIAs.

By the commencement of the modern era, international legal scholars considered that international law protected the rights of aliens to travel and trade.[10] Francisco de Vitoria argued that under international law foreigners had the right to travel, live and trade in foreign lands.[11] Hugo Grotius treated the status of foreigners under the category 'Of Things That Belong To Men In Common' and asserted a norm of non-discrimination in the treatment of foreigners.[12] However, Emmerich de Vattel was the first modern scholar to address the status of foreigners in detail. In *Law of Nations* (1758), Vattel argued that a state has the right to control and set conditions on the entry of foreigners.[13] Once admitted, foreigners are subject to local laws and the state is under a duty to protect foreigners in the same manner as its own subjects.[14] At the same time, however, foreigners retained their membership in their own state and were not 'obliged to submit, like the subjects, to all the commands of the sovereign.'[15] In Vattel's view, foreigners' membership in their home state extended to their property, which remained part of the wealth of their home nation.[16] As a result, a state's mistreatment of foreigners or their property was an injury to the foreigners' home state.[17] This view eventually coalesced into the international legal principle of diplomatic protection.

---

9. E.M. Borchard, *Diplomatic Protection of Citizens Abroad or The Law of International Claims* (New York: Banks Law Publishing Co., 1915) [Borchard, *Diplomatic Protection*] at 33.
10. See generally H. Neufeld, *The International Protection of Private Creditors from the Treaties of Westphalia to the Congress of Vienna (1648-1815): A Contribution to the History of the Law of Nations* (Leiden: Sijthoff, 1971) at 47-55 for a summary of the views of early international law publicists on the economic interests of aliens.
11. See F. de Vitoria, *De Indis et De Ivre Belli : Relectiones* (1696), E. Nys, ed., J.P. Bate, trans. (Washington, DC: Carnegie Institution of Washington, 1917), s. III. For a critical assessment of Vitoria's work in the context of the colonial origins of international law and the Spanish conquest of the Americas, see A. Anghie, *Imperialism, Sovereignty, and the Making of International Law* (Cambridge: Cambridge University Press, 2005).
12. See H. Grotius, *De Jure Belli Ac Pacis Libri Tres* (1625), J. B. Scott, ed., F.W. Kelsey, trans. (Oxford: Clarendon Press, 1925), Book II, Chapter II, XXII, where Grotius refers to most-favoured-nation treatment: 'A common right by supposition relates to the acts which any people permits without distinction to foreigners; for if under such circumstances a single people is excluded, a wrong is done to it. Thus if foreigners are anywhere permitted to hunt, fish, snare birds, or gather pearls, to inherit by will, or sell property, and even to contract marriages in case there is no scarcity of women, such rights cannot be denied to one people alone, except on account of previous wrong-doing.'
13. E. Vattel, *Law of Nations*, J. Chitty, trans. (Philadelphia: T.&J.W. Johnson & Co., 1858), Book II, Chapter VIII, §100.
14. *Ibid.*, §104.
15. *Ibid.*, §108.
16. *Ibid.*, §109. For this reason, Vattel opposed the 'droit d'aubaine' or right of escheat, by which the property of foreigners passed to the host state at their death. See A.H. Roth, *The International Minimum Standard* (Leiden: Sijthoff, 1949) at 26-27 and Borchard, *Diplomatic Protection*, *supra* note 9 at 35-36.
17. F.V. Garcia-Amador argues that while Vitoria and Grotius viewed foreigners' rights as arising out of their status as members of the human race, and looked to nationality as a way to improve

§1.3 Diplomatic protection   The exercise of diplomatic protection can be traced back to the Middle Ages, if not earlier.[18] The theory underlying the principle of diplomatic protection is that an injury to a state's national is an injury to the state itself, for which it may claim reparation from any responsible state.[19] Through the exercise of diplomatic protection, the home state makes a claim against the host state for an injury to the home state's national.[20] In the vernacular of international claims, a state 'espouses' the claim of its national. States exercised diplomatic protection throughout the eighteenth and nineteenth centuries, and by 1924 the Permanent Court of International Justice (PCIJ) recognized a state's right to exercise diplomatic protection over its nationals as an 'elementary principle of international law.'[21]

Although a comprehensive examination of the rules of diplomatic protection is beyond the scope of this book,[22] for present purposes, it is important to highlight

---

their treatment, under Vattel's approach international legal rights and obligations arose as a result of nationality. See F.V. Garcia-Amador *The Changing Law of International Claims* (Dobbs Ferry, NY: Oceana Publications Inc., 1984) at 46.

18. See I. Brownlie, *Principles of Public International Law*, 6th edn (Oxford: Oxford University Press, 2003) [Brownlie, *Principles of Public International Law*] at 500. In addition to diplomatic protection, claims were also enforced through private means by obtaining letters of marque or reprisal from political authorities. See K.J. Partsch, 'Reprisals' in *Encyclopedia*, *supra* note 8, Vol. IV at 200.

19. Art. 1 of the International Law Commission's (ILC's) Articles on Diplomatic Protection adopted by the ILC at its fifty-eighth session, in 2006, provides that 'diplomatic protection consists of the invocation by a State, through diplomatic action or other means of peaceful settlement, of the responsibility of another State for an injury caused by an internationally wrongful act of that State to a natural or legal person that is a national of the former State with a view to the implementation of such responsibility'. See 'Report on the work of its fifty-eighth session', in *Report of the International Law Commission,* UN GAOR, 61st Sess., Supp. No. 10, UN Doc A/61/10 (2006), at 16.

20. See *supra* note 4 on the terms 'home' and 'host' state.

21. The PCIJ affirmed the principle in *The Mavrommatis Palestine Concessions* (1924) PCIJ Ser. A, No. 2 at 12: 'It is an elementary principle of international law that a State is entitled to protect its subjects, when injured by acts contrary to international law committed by another state, from whom they have been unable to obtain satisfaction through the ordinary channels. By taking up the case of one of its subjects and by resorting to diplomatic action or international judicial proceedings on his behalf, a State is in reality asserting its own rights – its right to ensure, in the person of its subjects, respect for the rules of international law.' Also see *Panevezys-Saldutiskis Railway Case* (1939) PCIJ Ser. A/B, No. 76 at 14.

22. On diplomatic protection and international claims see Borchard, *Diplomatic Protection, supra* note 9; Garcia-Amador, *supra* note 17; C. Eagleton, *Responsibility of States in International Law* (New York: New York University Press, 1928); F.S. Dunn, *The Protection of Nationals: A Study in the Application of International Law* (Baltimore: The Johns Hopkins Press, 1932); A. Freeman, *The International Responsibility of States for Denial of Justice* (New York: Longmans, Green and Co. Ltd, 1938); C.F. Amerasinghe, *State Responsibility for Injuries to Aliens* (Oxford: Clarendon Press, 1967); R.B. Lillich, ed., *International Law of State Responsibility for Injuries to Aliens* (Charlottesville: University Press of Virginia, 1983) and C.F. Amerasinghe, *Diplomatic Protection* (Oxford: Oxford University Press, 2008). In addition, see the various reports of the ILC's and International Law Association (ILA) on diplomatic protection, *supra* note 19 and *infra* notes 23 and 24.

three issues related to the espousal of international claims. First, the state must bring the claim in accordance with the rules relating to international claims, including the nationality of claims. These rules determine the eligibility of persons for whom a state may espouse a claim and address issues such as whether continuous nationality is required from the time of injury to adjudication of the claim.[23] Second, state responsibility for injury to foreign nationals may not be invoked if 'the rule of exhaustion of local remedies applies and any available and effective local remedy has not been exhausted.'[24] Before a state may exercise diplomatic protection, the foreign national must have sought redress in the host state's domestic legal system. Finally, the right to exercise diplomatic protection is at the discretion of the espousing state.[25] A state may decide not to exercise protection for reasons unrelated to the merits of the claim, particularly if the state has other diplomatic, military or geo-political objectives that might be compromised by making a claim. As a result of this discretionary power, absent international treaty rights of action, a foreign investor has no control over the international claim-making process. As will be seen, IIAs provide a treaty-based right to bring claims through investor-state arbitration.[26] The extent to which elements of the

---

23. The issue of nationality of claims has been the subject of extensive study and discussion by the ILA and the ILC. See *Report of the International Law Commission*, UN GAOR, 56th Sess., Supp. No. 10, UN Doc A/59/10 (2004), and F. Orrego Vicuña, *The Changing Law of Nationality of Claims*, Report for the International Law Association Committee on Diplomatic Protection of Persons and Property, 69th Conference, London 2000 at 631-645 [Orrego Vicuña, *The Changing Law of Nationality of Claims*]. Nationality issues have arisen in a series of IIA cases, including *The Loewen Group, Inc. and Raymond L. Loewen v. United States; Tokios Tokelės v. Ukraine* and *Waguih Elie George Siag and Clorinda Vecchi v. Egypt*.

24. Art. 44(b), International Law Commission's Articles on Responsibility of States for Internationally Wrongful Acts, *Official Records of the General Assembly*, UN GAOR, 56th Sess., Supp. No. 10, UN Doc A/56/10 at 11; 2001 YBILC, Vol. II, Part Two. The Articles and commentary are *reprinted in* J. Crawford, *The International Law Commission's Articles on State Responsibility: Introduction, Text, and Commentaries* (Cambridge: Cambridge University Press, 2002) [ILC's Articles on State Responsibility]. The issue of exhaustion of local remedies has been the subject of extensive study and discussion by the ILA and the ILC's. See *Report of the ILC's*, 56th Session (2004), *ibid.*, and Articles on Diplomatic Protection, *supra* note 19. See also J. Kokott, *The Exhaustion of Local Remedies*, Report for the International Law Association Committee on Diplomatic Protection of Persons and Property, 69th Conference, London 2000 at 3-27. Treatises on exhaustion of local remedies include C.F. Amerasinghe, *Local Remedies in International Law*, 2nd edn (Cambridge: Cambridge University Press, 2004) and A.A. Cançado Trindade, *The Application of the Rule of Exhaustion of Local Remedies in International Law* (Cambridge: Cambridge University Press, 1983). For a discussion of the rule in the context of investor-state arbitrations, see W.S. Dodge, 'National Courts and International Arbitration: Exhaustion of Remedies and Res Judicata Under Chapter 11 of NAFTA' (2000) 23 HICLR 357.

25. 'The State must be viewed as the sole judge to decide whether its protection will be granted, to what extent it will be granted, and when it will cease. It retains in this respect a discretionary power the exercise of which may be determined by considerations of a political or other nature, unrelated to the case.' *Barcelona Traction, Light and Power Company Limited (Belgium v. Spain)* [1970] ICJ Rep 4 at para. 79.

26. See *infra* §1.31 *et seq.* regarding the development of investor-state arbitration.

international law relating to diplomatic protection, such as the rules relating to continuous nationality, are relevant to IIA claims remains unsettled.[27]

§1.4 Dispute settlement by claims commissions and international arbitration Early state practice on diplomatic protection took a number of forms. In addition to the diplomatic settlement of claims[28] and settlement through coercive means,[29] states established *ad hoc* commissions and arbitral tribunals to adjudicate specific claims or classes of claims involving a host state's treatment of foreign nationals and their property. This practice dates from the 1794 Treaty of Amity, Commerce and Navigation between Great Britain and United States (Jay Treaty),[30] which, among other things, established a commission to decide claims regarding the treatment of British and US nationals during and after the American Revolution.[31]

From 1840-1940 states established over sixty arbitral commissions to deal with disputes arising from injuries to foreign nationals.[32] In addition, there were various *ad hoc* tribunals established to deal with specific claims[33] and national prize courts that adjudicated claims regarding the capture of property at sea.[34] State practice and the decisions of these commissions and tribunals formed the nascent jurisprudence on state responsibility for injuries to aliens. Although these claims commissions, by hearing claims based on individual losses, were designed to protect the rights of individuals, they generally relied on a model of diplomatic protection, meaning that only states, and not individuals, were party

---

27. For an in-depth discussion of this issue, see Z. Douglas, 'Hybrid Foundations of Investment Treaty Arbitration'(2003) 74 BYIL 151.
28. The volume of diplomatic practice with respect to international claims increased substantially in the 19th century. US practice was collected in F. Wharton, *A Digest of the International Law of the United States* (Washington: Government Printing Office, 1886) and in J.B. Moore, *International Law Digest* (Washington: Government Printing Office, 1906) Vol. VII, both of which were official US government publications. In contrast, European state practice was less accessible and European publicists tended not to cite it. See I. Brownlie, *System of the Law of Nations, State Responsibility – Part I* (Oxford: Oxford University Press, 1986) [Brownlie, *System of the Law of Nations*] at 6.
29. See §1.5.
30. 19 Nov. 1794, 52 Cons TS 243, entered into force 28 Oct. 1795.
31. See B. Legum, 'The Innovation of Investor-State Arbitration Under NAFTA'(2002) 43 HILJ 534. The Jay Commissions issued over 500 awards. See A.M. Stuyt, *Survey of International Arbitrations, 1794-1989*, 3rd edn (Dordrecht: Martinus Nijhoff Publishers, 1990) at 2-3. Also see, D.M. Johnston, *The Historical Foundations of World Order: The Tower and the Arena* (Leiden: Martinus Nijhoff, 2008) at 636.
32. Brownlie, *Principles of Public International Law*, *supra* note 18 at 500. See also J.H. Ralston, *International Arbitration, from Athens to Locarno* (London: Oxford University Press, 1972) and Stuyt, *ibid.*
33. Several of these were established under the auspices of the Permanent Court of Arbitration. See Ralston, *ibid.*, and Stuyt, *ibid.*
34. See Halsbury, *et al.*, *The Principles and Practice of Prize Law* (London: Butterworths, 1914).

to the proceedings.[35] After the First World War (WWI), it became more common for agreements to provide that individual claimants could make claims directly.[36]

In addition to the mixed claims commissions of the nineteenth century, there were several direct investor-state arbitrations. One of the first was between *La Compagnie Universelle du Canal de Suez*, a Turkish company, and Egypt. In 1864, the company sought compensation from Egypt after a law was passed that disrupted a concession agreement to work on the Suez Canal. Although there was no arbitration clause in the original agreement, both parties agreed to use arbitration to resolve the dispute, and jointly agreed on Napoleon III as arbitrator.[37]

§1.5 Use and abuse of diplomatic protection   The evolution and exercise of diplomatic protection should be viewed in its historical context. The espousal of claims developed in an era of colonialism and imperialism.[38] States exercised all possible means – political, economic and military – to protect their nationals' interests abroad. Reflecting on the development of the law of state responsibility for injuries to aliens, Henry Steiner and Detlev Vagts note that:

> The growth of the law of state responsibility reflected the more intense identification of the individual (or later, the corporation) with his country that accompanied the nationalist trends of the 18th to early 20th centuries. That growth would not have taken place but for Western colonialism and economic imperialism which reached their zenith during this period. Transnational business operations centered in Europe, and later in the United States as well, penetrated Asia, Africa and Latin America. Thus security of the person and property of a national inevitably became a concern of his government. That concern manifested itself in the vigorous assertion of diplomatic protection and in the enhanced activity of arbitral tribunals. Often the arbitrations occurred under the pressure of actual or threatened military force by the aggrieved nations, particularly in Latin America.[39]

---

35. R. Dolzer, 'Mixed Claims Commissions' in *Encyclopedia, supra* note 8, Vol. III at 438.
36. Legum, *supra* note 31 at 533, notes that mixed arbitral tribunals were established to address claims by Allied nationals against Germany and the Iran-United States Claims Tribunal permitted direct claims. See *infra* §1.28 on the Iran-United States Claims Tribunal. On trends in international law to allow individual claims see Orrego Vicuña, *The Changing Law of Nationality of Claims, supra* note 23.
37. *Egypt v. Suez Canal Company* (Award, 1864) in Stuyt, *supra* note 31 at 471. For commentary, see Ch. Leben, 'La théorie du contrat d'Etat et l'évolution du droit international des investissements' (2003) 302 RDCADI 197 at 219. See Stuyt, *supra* note 31 at 472 *et seq.,* for lists of other early arbitrations between states and foreign entities. Also see E. Darby, *Modern Pacific Settlements Involving the Application of the Principle of International Arbitration* (London: Peace Society, 1904) on early international arbitrations and dispute resolution.
38. See Anghie, *supra* note 11. For another critical view of the law of state responsibility for injuries to aliens, see S.N. Guha Roy, 'Is the Law of Responsibility of States for Injuries to Aliens a Part of Universal International Law' (1961) 55 AJIL 863.
39. H.J. Steiner & D.F. Vagts, *Transnational Legal Problems: Materials and Text*, 2nd edn (Mineola, N.Y.: Foundation Press, 1976) at 357.

During the nineteenth and early twentieth centuries, the exercise of diplomatic protection by powerful states was often accompanied by 'gun-boat diplomacy' – the threat or the use of force to back up diplomatic protection claims.[40] At the time, the use of force in the exercise of diplomatic protection was not inconsistent with international law.[41] Despite the fact that the 1899 and 1907 *Hague Convention for the Pacific Settlement of International Disputes* (Hague Conventions) provided for state parties 'to use their best efforts to ensure the pacific settlement of international differences,'[42] both the US and the European powers used force and threats of force on numerous occasions to back up and enforce claims of diplomatic protection.[43] For instance, between 1820 and 1914, Great Britain intervened in Latin America at least forty times to enforce British claims for injuries to its nationals and to restore order and protect property.[44] These claims were sometimes based on limited or erroneous evidence and frequently led to reprisals out of proportion to the injury suffered.[45]

Abuses, real and perceived, of diplomatic protection led Latin American states to resist its use, particularly in its more interventionist forms. This opposition solidified after armed English, German and Italian forces intervened in Venezuela in 1902 to enforce claims relating to state-issued bonds.[46] In reaction, Luis Drago, the Argentine foreign minister, authored a diplomatic note to the US in December 1902, arguing that the public debt of Latin American states should

---

40. See D.R. Shea, *The Calvo Clause* (Minneapolis: University of Minnesota Press, 1955); M. Hood, *Gunboat Diplomacy 1895-1905* (London: George Allen & Unwin, 1975) and J. Cable, *Gunboat Diplomacy, 1919-1979: Political Applications of Limited Naval Force*, 2nd edn (London: Macmillan, 1981).
41. Moore, *supra* note 28, Vol. VII at 103-135.
42. Art. 1 of both conventions ((1898-1899) 187 Con TS at 410 and (1907) 205 Con TS at 233).
43. See the discussion of 'nonamicable' modes of redress and the practice of the US in Moore, *supra* note 28, §1089-§1099. Key incidents involving European powers include: French interventions in Mexico in 1838 and 1861 (see Shea, *supra* note 40 at 13); Great Britain threatening naval intervention in the 1836 Sicilian sulphur monopoly dispute (see J. Fawcett (1950) 27 BYIL 355); Italy sending a vessel to Colombia to rescue an Italian national in 1885 and later sending its fleet to enforce an arbitral award regarding the property of an Italian citizen (see W. Benedek, 'Cerrutti Arbitrations' in *Encyclopedia*, *supra* note 8, Vol. I at 555) and the embargo of Venezuelan ports by Great Britain, Germany and Italy in 1902-3 (see M. Silagi, 'Preferential Claims Against Venezuela Arbitration' in *Encyclopedia*, *supra* note 8, Vol. III at 1098). The US intervened in Dominican Republic in 1905 and 1916, Nicaragua in 1911 and Haiti in 1915 (K.J. Vandevelde, *United States Investment Treaties: Policy and Practice* (Boston: Kluwer Law and Taxation, 1992) [Vandevelde, *United States Investment Treaties*] at 8). As Vandevelde notes, US military intervention, while serving to protect US commercial interests, also reflected more general geopolitical considerations.
44. C. Lipson, *Standing Guard: Protecting Foreign Capital in the Nineteenth and Twentieth Centuries* (Berkeley: University of California Press, 1985) at 54.
45. Shea, *supra* note 40 at 12.
46. See Silagi, *supra* note 43 at 1098. On bond defaults and intervention, see Lipson, *supra* note 44 at 37-64. For a discussion of more recent attempts to enforce sovereign bond obligations through international arbitration, see M. Waibel, 'Opening Pandora's Box: Sovereign Bonds in International Arbitration' (2007) 101 AJIL 711.

not give rise to a right of armed intervention.[47] This led to the development of the Drago Doctrine, which was incorporated into the *Hague Convention II of 1907 Respecting the Limitations of the Employment of Force for the Recovery of Contract Debts* (Drago-Porter Convention).[48] Under the Drago-Porter Convention, states agreed not to use armed force for the recovery of state debts unless there was a refusal to submit the claim to arbitration. Thus, even under the Drago-Porter Convention, and despite the general obligations in the Hague Conventions regarding pacific settlement of disputes, force remained a legal means of exercising diplomatic protection should a state fail to accept an offer of arbitration or accept any resulting award.[49] It was not until the *General Treaty for the Renunciation of War 1928* (Briand-Kellogg Pact) that international law prohibited the use of force and required states to resolve disputes only by pacific means.[50]

§1.6 Colonial territories and extraterritorial jurisdiction Much of the expansion of international trade and investment in the eighteenth, nineteenth and twentieth centuries occurred within colonial political and legal regimes. In this

47. See D. Drago, 'State Loans in Their Relation to International Policy' (1907) 1 AJIL 692; E.M. Borchard, 'Limitations on Coercive Protection' (1927) 21 AJIL 303 [Borchard, 'Limitations'] and discussion in Shea, *supra* note 40 at 15.
48. *Hague Convention II of 1907 Respecting the Limitations of the Employment of Force for the Recovery of Contract Debts*, 18 Oct. 1907 [Drago-Porter Convention] in (1907) 205 Con. TS 250.
49. Lipson, *supra* note 44 at 74. As discussed in §1.8, Latin American states' general adherence to the Calvo Doctrine reflected an unwillingness to accept international arbitration. In addition, the Drago-Porter Convention, *ibid.*, only applied to intervention for the purpose of collecting on public debt obligations. It did not address interventions for other types of diplomatic claims. Most Latin American states entered reservations to the Drago-Porter Convention and only Mexico ratified it. See I. Brownlie, *International Law and the Use of Force by States* (London: Oxford University Press, 1963) [Brownlie, *International Law and the Use of Force by States*] at 23-25. Proposals made at the Inter-American Conference for the Maintenance of Peace in 1936 and the Eighth International Conference of American States in 1938 that the Drago Doctrine should be given treaty form were not adopted (Brownlie, *International Law and the Use of Force by States*, *ibid.*, at 226).
50. *General Treaty for the Renunciation of War 1928*, 94 LNTS 57. There was some debate over whether the Briand-Kellogg Pact prohibited armed force that did not amount to war. As of 1945, Art. 2(4), *Charter of the United Nations,* prohibits the threat or use of force. Various types of overt or covert interventions by Western states nevertheless continued, related in part to the protection of economic interests. The Roosevelt Corollary to the Monroe Doctrine authorized the use of force to collect private debts owed to US citizens. See A. Rappaport, *A History of American Diplomacy* (New York: Macmillan, 1975) at 223 *et seq.* Further, commentators have argued that interventions by Western states in Iran (1954), Guatemala (1954), Egypt (1956), Cuba (1961), British Guinea (1973), Brazil (1964), Dominican Republic (1965) and Chile (1973) may have been, or were at least in part, motivated by the desire to protect foreign economic interests. See A. Akinsanya, *Multinationals in a Changing Environment* (New York: Praeger Publishers, 1984) at 252-306 and *The Expropriation of Multinational Property in the Third World* (New York: Praeger Publishers, 1980). It should be noted that the USSR, China and other states with communist and socialist economies also intervened in the affairs of other states and that these interventions were arguably also motivated at least in part by economic reasons.

context, there was no need for colonists to have recourse to international law processes since colonial political and military power protected colonists and their property from local interference or control.[51] In addition, extraterritorial jurisdiction, which allowed foreign powers to apply their laws to their nationals in foreign states, was exercised under treaties.[52] In some cases, these regimes were imposed by force through treaties of capitulation. Extraterritorial jurisdiction in one form or another existed in China, Japan, Thailand, Iran, Egypt, Morocco, Turkey and other parts of the Ottoman Empire.[53] The existence of extraterritorial regimes in Asia and the Far East, but not in Latin America, explains why Latin American states are the source of almost all early jurisprudence and cases on diplomatic protection.[54]

§1.7 The minimum standard of treatment The expansion of trade and investment in the nineteenth and early twentieth centuries directed increased attention to the legal status of foreign nationals abroad and to the protection of their economic interests.[55] By the early 1900s, there was general agreement amongst international lawyers in Europe and the US that there existed a minimum standard of justice in the treatment of foreigners.[56] At the same time, an emerging body of international

---

51. M. Sornarajah, *The International Law on Foreign Investment*, 2nd edn (Cambridge: Cambridge University Press, 2004) at 19-20.
52. See A. Heyking, 'L'exterritorialité et ses applications en Extrême-Orient' (1925) 7 RDCADI 237.
53. See Lipson, *supra* note 44 at 12-16, L.T. Lee, *Consular Law and Practice*, 2nd edn (Oxford: Clarendon Press, 1991) at 7-17 and R. Jennings & A. Watts eds., *Oppenheim's International Law*, 9th edn (London: Longman, 1992), §406 at 911.
54. Dunn, *supra* note 22 at 54.
55. In 1910, Elihu Root, then President of the American Society of International Law and former US Secretary of War and Secretary of State, noted: 'The great accumulation of capital in the money centres of the world, far in excess of the opportunities for home investment, has led to a great increase of international investment extending over the entire surface of the earth, and these investments have naturally been followed by citizens from the investing countries prosecuting and caring for the enterprises in the other countries where their investment are made.' E. Root, 'The Basis of Protection to Citizen's Residing Abroad' (1910) 4 AJIL 517 at 518-519.
56. See Brownlie, *System of the Law of Nations, supra* note 28 at 7 with respect to the emergence of German, French and English language treatises on the principle of state responsibility in the late nineteenth century and early twentieth century. The international standards of treatment applicable to the economic interests of foreign investors were still, however, nascent. International law treatises written in the early 1900s focus on issues such as denial of justice, equality before the law and mob violence, usually in the context of the rights of the individual. J. Westlake's treatise, *International Law* (Cambridge: Cambridge University Press, 1904) devoted an eight page chapter to 'The Protection of Subjects Abroad' and addressed denial of justice and contract claims. In the 1905 first edition of *International Law*, L. Oppenheim touched on the 'Protection to be Afforded to Foreigner's Person and Property' in one page and simply focused on the requirement for the host state to provide equality before the law. L. Oppenheim, *International Law* (London: Longmans, Green, and Co., 1905) at 376. G.G. Wilson, Professor of International Law at Harvard University addressed the treatment of aliens in two pages and focuses on the right to exclude and expel. With respect to property, he wrote: 'Rights of property and inheritance may be determined by local laws.' G.G. Wilson, *Handbook*

law on state responsibility for the treatment of aliens was developing through various commercial treaties,[57] state practice and the decisions of arbitral tribunals and mixed commissions.[58] Most of the practice and jurisprudence in this area related to injuries to individual foreigners arising from the denial of justice or acts of violence. Although the principles applying to the treatment of economic interests were less developed, there was a consensus amongst capital exporting states that expropriation of property required compensation.[59]

In the early twentieth century, the major powers and capital exporting states, including the US and the UK, took the position that foreign nationals and their property were entitled, under customary international law, to a minimum standard of treatment. This minimum standard was essentially similar to standards of justice and treatment accepted by 'civilized states', including the European states and the US.[60] The capital exporting states' approach is reflected in Elihu Root's 1910 address to the American Society of International Law:

> Each country is bound to give to nationals of another country in its territory the benefit of the same laws, the same administration, the same protection, and the same redress for injury which it gives to its own citizen's, and neither more nor less: provided the protection which the country gives to its own citizens conforms to the established standard of civilization.

> There is a standard of justice, very simple, very fundamental, and of such general acceptance by all civilized countries as to form part of the international law of the world. A country is entitled to measure the standard of justice due an alien by the justice it accords its own citizens only when its system of law and administration conforms to this general standard. If any country's system of law and administration does not conform to that standard of justice, although the people of the country may be content or compelled to live under it, no other country can be compelled to accept it as furnishing a satisfactory measure of treatment to its citizens.[61]

---

of International Law (St Paul: West Publishing, 1910) at 145. C.C. Hyde primarily addressed denial of justice and mob violence. C.C. Hyde, *International Law: Chiefly as Interpreted and Applied by the United States* (Boston: Little, Brown and Company, 1922) at 491-496 and 516-524.

57.   See Neufeld, *supra* note 10. On early friendship and commerce treaties, see *infra* §1.17.
58.   See *supra* note 22 for the principal treatises.
59.   See *infra* Chapter 7, §7.5.
60.   The term was used almost exclusively to refer to Western or European states. Westlake, *supra* note 56 at 313, argued that these were rules 'on which the people of European civilization are agreed that legal and administrative procedure ought to be based.' E. Borchard, in 'The "Minimum Standard" of the Treatment of Aliens' (1939) 33 ASIL Proc 51 [Borchard, 'Minimum Standard'] at 53, states that international law is 'composed of the uniform practices of civilized states of the western world who gave birth and nourishment to international law.' These rules included a minimum standard of due process and justice. See the discussion in Anghie, *supra* note 11 at 52 *et seq.*, on the civilized/uncivilized dichotomy.
61.   Root, *supra* note 55 at 521-2. Interestingly, Root's comments focus not only on the delicts of foreign states but also on the breach of international obligations by the US arising out of the mobbing and

§1.8 The Calvo Doctrine   In response to assertions of a minimum standard of treatment, some states, particularly those in Latin America, endorsed a national treatment or equality of treatment standard. This position is most commonly associated with the Argentine jurist Carlos Calvo, who argued as early as 1868 against the exercise of diplomatic protection and the existence of a minimum standard of treatment. In Calvo's view, state equality required that there be no intervention, diplomatic or otherwise, in the internal affairs of other states, and that foreigners were not entitled to better treatment than host state nationals.[62] The Calvo Doctrine has three distinct elements: foreign nationals are entitled to no better treatment than host state nationals; the rights of foreign nationals are governed by host state law; and host state courts have exclusive jurisdiction over disputes involving foreign nationals.[63] The twin pillars of the Calvo Doctrine are the absolute equality of foreigners with nationals and the principle of non-intervention.[64] At its logical extreme, the doctrine would have abolished the principle of diplomatic protection[65] and the concept of the minimum standard of treatment.[66]

The Calvo Doctrine never attained the status of a principle of customary international law.[67] In the early twentieth century, capital exporting states maintained the view that international law requires a minimum standard of treatment. Capital importing states, however, continued to challenge the minimum standard of treatment, particularly with respect to compensation for expropriation. In 1917, the revolutionary government in Russia issued a decree abolishing all private property, including the property of foreign nationals.[68] Although Western states took the position that the decree violated international law, many of the claims

---

lynching of Chinese, Italian and Mexican nationals in various US states between 1880 and 1901.

62.   'It is certain that aliens who establish themselves in a country have the same rights to protection as nationals, but they ought not to lay claim to a protection more extended.' C. Calvo, *Le droit international théorique et pratique*, 5th edn, 1896, Vol. VI at 231 as translated and quoted in Shea, *supra* note 40 at 18. From the Calvo Doctrine rose the Calvo Clause – a contractual clause by which a foreigner purports to waive any right to diplomatic protection vis-à-vis the host state. The clause attempts to ensure equality between foreigners and nationals. If effective, the foreigner, with respect to matters to which the contract applies, would waive any right to the protection of international law. In *North American Dredging Co.* (1926) IV RIAA 26, the US-Mexico Mixed Claims Commission held that a state is not bound by its own national's waiver of diplomatic protection, since the right of diplomatic protection belongs to the state. See Shea, *supra* note 40 at 210. See also M.R. Garcia-Mora, 'The Calvo Clause in Latin American Constitutions and International Law' (1950) 33 Marq L Rev 205 and K. Lipstein, 'The Place of the Calvo Clause in International Law' (1945) BYIL 130.

63.   B.M. Cremades, 'Resurgence of the Calvo Doctrine in Latin America' (2006) 7 BLI 53 at 54.

64.   Shea, *supra* note 40 at 19-29.

65.   *Ibid.*, at 20.

66.   The position of absolute equality between nationals and foreigners was formally adopted by Latin American states at the First International Conference of American States in 1889. See Shea, *supra* note 40 at 75.

67.   See Shea, *ibid.*, at 20.

68.   Lipson, *supra* note 44 at 66-70.

were never formally settled.[69] The Soviet nationalizations of private property were significant because they challenged the assumption that all states were committed to private property, a market economy and limited state control of the economy.[70] Prior to WWI, the need to protect private property had never been seriously challenged; however, after WWI, ideological divisions came to dominate.[71]

§1.9 Early jurisprudence on the minimum standard of treatment   Despite the challenge posed by Russia and continued Latin American resistance to the minimum standard of treatment, the view that international law required a minimum standard of treatment was reaffirmed during the 1920s in several influential decisions of the US-Mexico General Claims Commission (the Commission). The US and Mexico established the Commission in 1923 to address claims by US citizens against Mexico and those of Mexican citizens against the US.[72] Commission decisions rejected Calvo's vision and affirmed the existence of the minimum standard of treatment.[73] For example, in *Harry Roberts*, the Commission stated that:

> Roberts was given the same treatment as that given to all other persons.... Facts with respect to equality of treatment of aliens and nationals may be important in determining the merits of a complaint of mistreatment of an alien. But such equality is not the ultimate test of the propriety of the acts of authorities in the light of international law. That test is, broadly speaking, whether aliens are treated according to ordinary standards of civilization.[74]

In addition to decisions of the Commission, there were other important decisions in the 1920s that reaffirmed the view held by capital exporting states. In 1922, an arbitral tribunal established between Norway and the US declared that international law requires 'just compensation' for the taking of property rights.[75] The

---

69.   See A. Lowenfeld, *International Economic Law* (Oxford: Oxford University Press, 2002) at 392-393. The US recognized the Soviet government and the extraterritorial effect of Soviet expropriation decrees in the Litvinov Assignment Agreement. Under this Agreement, monies due to the former Russian government by US nationals were assigned to the US government, which in turn would use monies collected to pay off claims of the US and its nationals against the USSR. See J.W. Garner, 'Recognition by the United States of The Government of Soviet Russia' (1935) BYIL 171. France and Russia settled claims as recently as 1997. See P. Juillard & B. Stern, *Les emprunts russes: aspects juridiques* (Paris: Pedone, 2002).
70.   Lipson, *supra* note 44 at 70.
71.   *Ibid.*, at 73.
72.   A.H. Feller, *The Mexican Claims Commissions: 1923-1934* (New York: Macmillan Company, 1935). A Special Claims Commission was also established to address claims arising out of revolutionary conditions in Mexico from 1910 to 1920.
73.   Five decisions of the Commission are often cited to support the existence of the minimum standard of treatment: *Neer* (1926) IV RIAA 60, *Faulkner* (1927) 21 AJIL 349, *Harry Roberts* (1927) 21 AJIL 357, *Hopkins* (1927) 21 AJIL 160 and *Way* (1929) 23 AJIL 466. See also Roth, *supra* note 16 at 94-99. See *infra* Chapter 6 on the minimum standard of treatment.
74.   *Harry Roberts, ibid.*, at 360-361.
75.   'Here it must be remembered that in the exercise of eminent domain the right of friendly alien property must always be respected. Those who ought not to take property without making just

tribunal ordered the US to pay compensation for its requisition of Norwegian ships during WWI.

These developments were further reinforced by judgments of the PCIJ. In *The Mavrommatis Palestine Concessions*, the PCIJ affirmed that diplomatic protection is an 'elementary principle of international law.'[76] Two years later, in the *Case Concerning Certain German Interests in Polish Upper Silesia*, the PCIJ confirmed that vested rights of foreign nationals must be respected.[77] The PCIJ also held, in the 1928 *Case Concerning the Factory at Chorzów*, that an illegal seizure of property requires reparation.[78] These judgments reflected the view that states owe a duty to other states to treat foreign nationals and their property according to a minimum standard of treatment.

§1.10 Efforts to codify treatment standards in the 1920s and 1930s   In 1924, the League of Nations established a Committee of Experts for the Progressive Codification of International Law.[79] The Committee reported in 1927, recommending that seven subjects were ripe for codification. On 27 September 1927, the Eighth Assembly of the League of Nations resolved to submit three topics to the First Conference for the Codification of International Law (the 1930 Codification Conference), including the 'Responsibility of States for Damage done in their Territory to the Person or Property of Foreigners.'[80]

In anticipation of the 1930 Codification Conference, a number of organizations, including the Institute of International Law, Association de Droit International du Japon, the American Institute of International Law and the International Commission of Jurists instituted research projects on rules of international responsibility relating to injuries to foreigners.[81] The Harvard Law School undertook a program of research in international law for the purpose of preparing a draft international convention on each of the three topics to be discussed at the 1930 Codification Conference.[82] The reporter for responsibility of states, Edwin Borchard, prepared a *Draft Convention on Responsibility of States for Damage done in their Territory to the Person or Property of Foreigners* (1929 Harvard Draft).[83]

---

      compensation at the time or at least without due process of law must pay the penalty for their action.' *Norwegian Shipowners' Claims (Norway v. US)* (1922) 1 RIAA 307 at 332.

76. *Mavrommatis, supra* note 21.

77. See *Case Concerning Certain German Interests in Polish Upper Silesia (Germany v. Poland)* (1926) PCIJ Ser. A, No. 7 at 22 and 42.

78. *Case Concerning the Factory at Chorzów (Claim for Indemnity) (Germany v. Poland)* (1928) PCIJ Ser. A, No. 17 at 47. With respect to compensation for expropriation, see *infra* Chapter 7.

79. (1925) 5 LNOJ 143.

80. LNOJ Spec Supp 53 at 9. The other two topics were 'Nationality' and 'Territorial Waters'.

81. These projects resulted in various draft codifications, which are reproduced at (1929) 23 AJIL Spec Supp at 219-239.

82. The drafts had no official status. According to the Director of Research, Manley Hudson, the preparation of the drafts 'has been undertaken with the object of placing before the representatives of the various governments at the First Conference on Codification of International Law the collective views of a group of Americans specially interested in the development of international law.' (1929) 23 AJIL Spec Supp at 9.

83. The 1929 Harvard Draft and commentary is reproduced at (1929) 23 AJIL Spec Supp at 133-218.

Divided opinion on standards of treatment, however, was evident at the 1930 Hague Conference, during its proceedings on codifying customary international law rules on the 'Responsibility of States for Damage Caused in Their Territories to the Persons and Properties of Foreigners.'[84] Article 10 of the draft codification provides as follows:

> As regards damage caused to the person or property of foreigners by a private person, the State is only responsible if the damage sustained by the foreigner results from the fact that the State has failed to take the measures which may reasonably be expected of it in the circumstances in order to prevent, remedy or inflict punishment for the damage.[85]

In voting on the article, seventeen states (mainly capital importing states) maintained the position that foreign nationals were only entitled to equality of treatment with nationals, while twenty-one states, including the capital exporting states, maintained the existence of a minimum standard of treatment.[86] Divided opinion on the issue of the minimum standard was a significant factor in the breakdown of the conference's codification efforts in the area of state responsibility.[87] The final version of the codification was not adopted because it failed to receive the requisite support of two-thirds of the states at the conference.

§1.11 Convention on the Treatment of Foreigners In addition to the codification efforts at the 1930 Codification Conference, states also attempted to conclude a *Convention on the Treatment of Foreigners* (1929 Draft Convention), in the late 1920s and early 1930s, under the auspices of the League of Nations.[88] A diplomatic conference – the International Conference on the Treatment of Foreigners – was held in Paris in late 1929 with forty-seven states participating.[89] The origin for the conference lay in Article 23 of the *Covenant of the League of Nations*,

---

84. See S. Rosenne, *League of Nations Conference for the Codification of International Law (1930)* (Dobbs Ferry, NY: Oceana Publications Inc., 1975), Vol. II at 423-702 for a collection of the documents relating to this topic. See also S. Rosenne, *League of Nations Committee of Experts for the Progressive Codification of International Law (1925-1928)* (Dobbs Ferry, NY: Oceana Publications Inc., 1972), Vol. 2 at 118 for the Report of the Sub-Committee of Experts by Guerrero, Rapporteur and Wang Chung-Hui. For commentary, see G.H. Hackworth, 'Responsibility of States for Damage Caused in Their Territories to the Persons and Properties of Foreigners' (1930) 24 AJIL 500 and E. Borchard, 'Responsibility of States at the Hague Codification Conference' (1930) 24 AJIL 517 [Borchard, 'Responsibility of States'].
85. See Hackworth, *ibid.,* at 513-514; Borchard, 'Responsibility of States', *ibid.,* at 533-537 and Roth, *supra* note 16 at 68-80.
86. See Hackworth, *ibid.,* at 514 and Roth, *ibid.,* at 74.
87. J.W. Cutler, 'The Treatment of Foreigners in Relation to the Draft Convention and Conference of 1929' (1933) 27 AJIL 225 at 230.
88. The text of the 1929 Draft Convention is reproduced in *International Conference on the Treatment of Foreigners, Preparatory Documents*, L.N. Doc. C.36.M. 21.1929.II. The conference proceedings are reproduced in L.N. Doc. C.97.M. 23.1930.II. For commentary see A.K. Kuhn, 'The International Conference on the Treatment of Foreigners' (1930) 24 AJIL 570 and Cutler, *ibid.*
89. See *Final Protocol of the First Session of the Conference on the Treatment of Foreigners* (Paris, 5 Dec. 1929), (1930) 11 LNOJ 171.

under which states undertook to 'secure and maintain equitable treatment for the commerce of all members of the League.'[90] At the World Economic Conference in Geneva in 1927, the International Chamber of Commerce (ICC) had submitted a report on the treatment of foreigners, recommending that the Council of the League hold a diplomatic conference.[91] The Council entrusted the Economic Committee of the League of Nations to prepare a draft convention to serve as a basis for discussions at the conference.[92]

The twenty-nine articles of the draft convention were far-reaching.[93] They accorded foreigners equality with nationals (national treatment) in almost all respects, including the right of establishment, freedom in relation to fiscal matters, freedom to travel, carry on a business and engage in all occupations, and the ability to exercise civil, judicial and succession rights.[94] The conference, however, revealed significant differences of opinion between capital exporting and importing states on the principle of equality. The report of the President of the Conference, M. Devèze, highlighted that:

> ... after three weeks' discussion, the draft Convention has been so profoundly modified and its essential provisions so attenuated that the delegations with liberal tendencies stated their intention of not signing a convention which, in their view, would have constituted, not the progress they wished to achieve, but, on the contrary, a retrograde step as compared with the present situation.[95]

§1.12 Seventh International Conference of American States Overwhelming Latin American support for the equality of treatment standard was also evident a few years later at the Seventh International Conference of American States in Montevideo, where states concluded the 1933 *Convention on the Rights and Duties of States* (Montevideo Convention).[96] Article 9 of the Montevideo Convention provides, in part, that: 'Nationals and foreigners are under the same protection of the law and the national authorities and the foreigners may not claim rights other or more extensive than those of the nationals.' The Convention was

---

90. *Covenant of the League of Nations*, 28 Jun. 1919 (1920) 1 LNOJ 3 (entered into force 10 Jan. 1920).
91. Kuhn, *supra* note 88 at 571.
92. *Ibid.*
93. See *Work of the International Conference on the Treatment of Foreigners: Report by M. Devèze, President of the Conference*, Geneva, 14 Jan. 1930, L.N. Doc. C.10.1930.II [Report by M. Devèze].
94. The draft convention also provided a number of exceptions to the national treatment obligation, for example, the exclusion of certain professions (lawyers and stockbrokers), government contracts, exploitation of minerals and hydraulic power and limitation on ownership of land and business for national security purposes. National treatment extended to foreign companies (Art. 16(8)).
95. Report by M. Devèze, *supra* note 93.
96. *Convention on the Rights and Duties of States*, 26 Dec. 1933, 165 LNTS 19 (1933) (entered into force 26 Dec. 1924).

adopted, but with reservations deposited by the US and other capital exporting states.[97]

§1.13 The Hull Rule   The disagreement between capital exporting and importing states over the minimum standard of treatment came to a head in an exchange of correspondence between Mexico and the US in 1938 regarding the standard of compensation for expropriation. The US insisted on the Hull Rule, named after US Secretary of State Cordell Hull, who, in response to the expropriation of American-held oil interests by Mexico in 1938,[98] argued that 'adequate, effective and prompt payment for the properties seized'[99] was required under international law. By contrast, Mexico argued that, in the case of general and impersonal expropriation for the purpose of redistribution of land, it was only required to pay compensation in accordance with its national laws. In Mexico's view, international law distinguished between expropriations resulting from a 'modification of the juridical organization and which affect equally all the inhabitants of the state and those otherwise decreed in specific cases and which affect interests known in advance and individually determined.'[100] General social reforms imposed no international obligation to provide immediate compensation, as foreigners were only entitled to the same treatment as Mexican citizens.[101] Thus, although the Hull Rule focuses on the required standard of compensation under international law, the actual dispute between Mexico and the US that gave rise to the articulation of the rule concerned the types of measures affecting property that are compensable under international law. The standard of compensation for expropriation continued to be a source of significant disagreement in the post-WWII era.

II   POST-WWII DEVELOPMENTS

§1.14 Decolonization and nationalizations   Disputes over the treatment of foreign investment increased and intensified after WWII as the process of decolonization resulted in colonial territories becoming states. Many of these newly independent states, along with the Eastern European communist states, adopted socialist economic policies, including large scale nationalizations of key sectors of their economies.[102] Notable examples include the nationalizations of major

---

97. For a discussion of Art. 9, see Borchard, 'Minimum Standard', *supra* note 60 at 69.
98. See J.L. Kunz, 'The Mexican Expropriations' (1940) 17 NYULQR 327.
99. US Secretary of State to Mexican Ambassador, 22 Aug. 1938, reproduced in 'Mexico-United States: Expropriation by Mexico of Agrarian Properties Owned by American Citizens' (1938) 33 AJIL Supp at 191-201.
100. Mexican Minister of Foreign Affairs to US Ambassador, 1 Sep. 1938, *supra* note 99 at 201-207.
101. See discussion by Lowenfeld, *supra* note 69 at 397-403.
102. See I. Foighel, *Nationalization: A Study in the Protection of Alien Property in International Law* (London: Stevens & Sons Limited,1957); G. White, *Nationalisation of Foreign Property* (London: Stevens & Sons Limited, 1961); R.B. Lillich, ed., *The Valuation of Nationalized Property in International Law* (Charlottesville: University Press of Virginia, 1972); M. Sornarajah, *The Pursuit of Nationalized Property* (Dordrecht: Martinus Nijhoff Publishers,

industries in Eastern European states, China, Cuba, and Latin America (Argentina, Bolivia, Brazil, Chile, Guatemala and Peru); the Indonesian nationalization of Dutch properties; the Egyptian nationalization of the Suez Canal; and the nationalizations of the oil industry throughout the Middle East and Northern Africa (Algeria, Iran, Iraq, Libya, Kuwait and Saudi Arabia).[103] The foreign investment disputes that ensued focused on two principal issues: the extent to which acquired rights, including natural resource concessions granted by colonial powers, were to be respected; and the standard of compensation for the expropriation of those acquired rights. In a series of cases, newly independent and developing states asserted that, upon independence, states were entitled to review concession agreements that had been granted by colonial powers, and, furthermore, maintained that compensation for the expropriation of property would be based on national laws.[104]

§1.15 The Havana Charter and the International Trade Organization The post-WWII political and economic climate stimulated a series of initiatives with the goal of establishing a multilateral legal framework for investment.[105] The first attempt arose during the negotiations for the proposed International Trade Organization (ITO), an institution intended as the third pillar of the new international financial system alongside the International Monetary Fund (IMF) and the International Bank for Reconstruction and Development (the Word Bank).[106] The initial US proposal for the ITO contained no investment provisions. This reflected the US preference for bilateral commercial treaties with high standards of protection, rather than a multilateral agreement that reflected the 'lowest common denominator of protection.'[107] During the ITO negotiations, articles on investment protection with provisions for national treatment, most-favoured-nation (MFN) treatment and just compensation for expropriation were introduced. States, however, were unable to agree on the standards.[108] As a result, the final draft of the

---

1986) and A.A. Akinsanya, *The Expropriation of Multinational Property in the Third World*, *supra* note 50.

103. See Lowenfeld, *supra* note 69 at 405. In the period from 1960 to 1977, there were on average ninety-eight cases of expropriation of foreign property a year. See F.N. Burton & H. Inoue, 'Expropriation of Foreign-Owned Firms in Developing Countries: A Cross National Analysis' (1984) 18 JWTL 396 at 397.

104. See *infra* §1.23.

105. For a comprehensive bibliography of works on multilateral approaches to foreign investment current to the early 1990s, see (1992) 7 ICSID Rev 504. See, in particular, the review of international instruments by F. Tschofen, 'Multilateral Approaches to the Treatment of Foreign Investment' (1992) 7 ICSID Rev 384.

106. On the investment aspects of the IMF and World Bank, see T.L. Brewer & S. Young, *The Multilateral Investment System and Multinational Enterprises* (Oxford: Oxford University Press, 1998) at 70-73. The role of the IMF *Articles of Agreement* with respect to transfer of funds is addressed at Chapter 8, §8.3.

107. C. Wilcox, *A Charter for World Trade* (New York: Macmillan, 1949) at 146.

108. See Brewer & Young, *supra* note 106 at 66-68.

Havana Charter for the International Trade Organization (Havana Charter)[109]
only briefly addressed the issue of investment protection by providing a prohibition on 'unreasonable or unjustifiable action' and permitting the ITO to make
recommendations for bilateral or multilateral investment agreements.[110] The
Havana Charter never came into force and the ITO was never established, chiefly
because the US Senate would not approve US ratification.[111] As a result, the
General Agreement on Tariffs and Trade (GATT),[112] which had been negotiated to
liberalize trade, was applied provisionally without an overarching ITO framework.[113] Thus, although international trade and investment are economically
intertwined,[114] the absence of investment from the purview of the GATT meant
that after 1947, international investment and trade law developed independently of
one another.

**§1.16 Non-governmental initiatives to create a multilateral legal framework
for investment**   From the 1940s to the early 1960s there were four important
non-governmental initiatives designed to create a multilateral legal framework for
foreign investment. In 1949, the ICC proposed an *International Code of Fair
Treatment for Foreign Investment* (ICC Code).[115] The ICC Code reflected high
standards of treatment for foreign investment by providing national treatment and
MFN treatment for investments, prohibiting restrictions on transfers of funds,
ensuring 'fair compensation according to international law' in the event of expropriation, and providing binding state-to-state dispute resolution before the ICC

---

109.   *Havana Charter for an International Trade Organization*, 24 Mar. 1948, UN Conference on
        Trade and Employment, U.N. Doc. E/CONF.2/78, Sales No. 1948.II.D.4.
110.   Art. 11(1)(b) of the Havana Charter provides: 'No Member shall take unreasonable or unjus-
        tifiable action within its territory injurious to the rights or interests of nationals of other
        Members in the enterprise, skills, capital, arts or technology which they have supplied.' Art.
        11(2) provides, in part, that: 'The Organization may, in such collaboration with other inter-
        governmental organizations as may be appropriate: (a) make recommendations for and pro-
        mote bilateral or multilateral agreements on measures designed: (i) to assure just and equitable
        treatment for the enterprise, skills, capital, arts and technology brought from one Member
        country to another....'
111.   J.H. Jackson, *The World Trading System Law and Policy of International Economic
        Relations*, 2nd edn (Cambridge, MA: MIT Press, 1997) at 38.
112.   *General Agreement on Tariffs and Trade*, 30 Oct. 1947, 55 UNTS 814 (applied provisionally
        as from 1 Jan. 1948 pursuant to the Protocol of Provisional Application).
113.   Jackson, *supra* note 111 at 39.
114.   Where there are import barriers, a producer may decide to set up a local subsidiary to produce
        goods locally, thereby 'jumping' the trade barrier. In many cases, trade and investment are
        substitutes. Whether a producer decides to engage in trade or investment will depend on both
        economic factors and the regulatory environment, including the comparative legal barriers to
        trade and investment. See M. Trebilcock & R. Howse, *The Regulation of International Trade*,
        3rd edn (London: Routledge, 2005) at 439-446.
115.   International Chamber of Commerce, *International Code of Fair Treatment of Foreign
        Investment*, ICC Pub. No. 129 (Paris: Lecraw Press, 1948), *reprinted in* UNCTAD, *International
        Investment Instruments: A Compendium*, Vol. 3 (New York: United Nations, 1996)
        [*IIA Compendium*] at 273. The compendium is available online on the UNCTAD website.

International Court of Arbitration. States were reticent to accept such a broad ranging investment regime and the ICC Code was never adopted.

The next initiative was the International Law Association (ILA) *Draft Statutes of the Arbitral Tribunal for Foreign Investment and the Foreign Investment Court* (ILA Statute).[116] The purpose of the proposed tribunal and court was to provide an impartial forum for the resolution of foreign investment disputes rather than to establish specific standards of treatment for foreign investment. States never adopted the ILA Statute.

Although the ICC Code and the ILA Statute were not adopted, the initiatives were significant in signaling both a conceptual and semantic change from the traditional notions of protection of aliens and their property. Instead of state responsibility for injuries to aliens and their property, the primary concern had become the protection of foreign investment with the object of promoting economic development.[117] The change reflected a shift in emphasis from the protection of private property as an end in itself to a policy of promoting conditions upon which the private foreign investment necessary for economic development could occur. This shift from the language of property to investment took place at the same time that newly independent states were beginning to challenge the system of acquired rights (concessions, contracts and other forms of tangible and intangible property) and could be seen as an attempt to reground the protection of private property in the language of international economic development.[118] This conceptual and semantic change would be reflected in future developments in the international legal framework for investment.

The third non-governmental initiative was the 1959 *Draft Convention on Investments Abroad* (Abs-Shawcross Draft Convention).[119] The Draft Convention was prepared under the leadership of Hermann Abs, the Director-General of Deutsche Bank, and Lord Shawcross, former Attorney General of the UK. The draft had its origins partly in a 1957 draft document entitled the *International*

---

116. *Reprinted in IIA Compendium, ibid.*, at 259.
117. For example, the preamble to the ICC Code, *supra* note 115, notes that 'an ample flow of private investments is essential to the economic and industrial growth of their countries and to the welfare of their peoples ...'
118. See T. Wälde, 'The Specific Nature of Investment Arbitration – Report of the Director of Studies of the English-speaking Section of the Centre,' *New Aspects of International Investment Law*, eds P. Khan & T. Wälde (Leiden: Matinus Nijhoff Publishers, 2007) at 43.
119. *IIA Compendium, supra* note 115, Vol. 5 at 395. The draft was first published in (1960) 9 JPL 116. See also H. Shawcross, 'The Problems of Foreign Investment in International Law' (1961) 102 RDCADI 334 and Chapter 8 of G. Schwarzenberger, *Foreign Investments and International Law* (New York: Frederick A. Praeger, 1969) for a history of and commentary on the Abs-Shawcross Draft Convention. For contemporary discussions of proposals for multilateral foreign investment protection, see A.S. Miller, 'Protection of Private Foreign Investment by Multilateral Convention' (1959) 53 AJIL 371; R. Gardner, 'International Measures for the Promotion and Protection of Foreign Investment' (1959) ASIL Proc 255; A.A. Fatouros, 'An International Code to Protect Private Investment-Proposals and Perspectives' (1961) 14 UTLJ 77; E. Snyder, 'Protection of Private Foreign Investment: Examination and Appraisal' (1961) 10 ICLQ 469 and D.A.V. Boyle, 'Some Proposals for a World Investment Convention' (1961) JBL 18 and 155.

Convention for the Mutual Protection of Private Property Rights in Foreign Countries, published by a group of German business people called the Society to Advance the Protection of Foreign Investments.[120] The Abs-Shawcross Draft Convention provided for a minimum standard of treatment (defined as 'fair and equitable treatment'),[121] protection against 'unreasonable or discriminatory measures,' observance of undertakings, and 'just and effective' compensation for expropriation. Importantly, the Abs-Shawcross Draft Convention was the first instrument that expressly provided for direct investor-state arbitration.[122]

Two years later, the 1961 *Draft Convention on the International Responsibility of States for Injuries to Aliens*[123] (1961 Harvard Draft) was prepared by Louis Sohn and Richard Baxter at the request of the UN Secretariat in an attempt to codify the international law on state responsibility. The 1961 Harvard Draft is an updated version of the 1929 Harvard Draft.[124] Early drafts of the 1961 Harvard Draft were presented to the International Law Commission (ILC).[125] The draft has been cited by a number of IIA tribunals as an authoritative statement of certain aspects of the minimum standard of treatment.[126]

§1.17 Bilateral and regional initiatives   In the post-WWII era, several states, including the UK, US and Japan, entered into bilateral treaties on commerce and navigation.[127] These treaties were often called Treaties of Friendship, Commerce

---

120. This document is also known as the *Köln Draft Convention*. See Tschofen, *supra* note 105 at 389.
121. See *infra* Chapter 6, §6.14, for a discussion of early treaty practice on fair and equitable treatment.
122. Art. VII states that nationals may make claims for a breach of the convention before an arbitral tribunal established under the convention provided the state had consented to the arbitral jurisdiction through a special agreement or unilateral declaration.
123. (1961) 55 AJIL 545. The text of the 1961 Harvard Draft is accompanied by extensive commentary.
124. See *supra* §1.10.
125. (1961) 55 AJIL 545 at 546.
126. The Harvard Draft has been cited in several cases in the context of expropriation: *Saluka Investments BV v. Czech Republic* (Partial Award, 17 Mar. 2006) at paras 256-257; *Pope & Talbot Inc v. Canada* (Interim Award, 26 Jun. 2000) at para. 102; *Wena Hotels Limited v. Egypt* (Award, 8 Dec. 2000) at note 242, as well as in *United Parcel Service America Inc v. Canada* (Award on Jurisdiction, 22 Nov. 2002) at paras 90-91 on the issue of anti-competitive behaviour, and in *Mondev International Ltd. v. United States* (Award, 11 Oct. 2002) at footnote 57 on fair and equitable treatment. See also *The Loewen Group, Inc. and Raymond L. v. United States* (Award, 26 Jun. 2003) at para. 167 and *Tokios Tokelès Group, Inc. and Raymond L. v. Ukraine* (Award, 29 Apr. 2004) at para. 92. In *United Parcel Service, ibid.* at paras 89-89, the tribunal characterized it as 'something of a high water mark in the statement of the law for the protection of aliens.'
127. See generally D. Blumenwitz, 'Treaties of Friendship, Commerce and Navigation' in Encyclopedia, *supra* note 8, Vol. IV at 953. For British treaty practice, see G. Schwarzenberger, *Foreign Investments and International Law*, *supra* note 119. For US practice, see R.R. Wilson, *United States Commercial Treaties and International Law* (New Orleans: Hauser Press, 1960) and H. Walker, Jr. 'Treaties for the Encouragement and Protection of Foreign Investment: Present United States Practice' (1956) 5 AJCL 229. For Japanese practice, see L. Jerold Adams,

and Navigation, or FCN treaties.[128] Although traditionally the focus of FCN treaties had been to promote trade and commercial relationships,[129] in the post-WWII era the investment protection function of these treaties came to dominate.[130] FCN treaties, designed to facilitate post-war reconstruction in Europe, provided significant investment protections.[131] In addition, the implementation of the GATT in 1947 reduced the need for trade provisions in FCN treaties amongst GATT Contracting Parties.[132] In Europe the most significant development was the creation of the common market in 1957.[133]

One of the earliest post-war examples of a regional initiative was the Ninth International Conference of American States (1948), which adopted the *Economic Agreement of Bogotá*.[134] The Agreement was signed by twenty Latin American states, but never entered into force. Although certain provisions of the *Economic Agreement of Bogotá* could be viewed as providing for a minimum standard of treatment,[135] many Latin American states made reservations providing that standards of treatment were governed by the state constitution.[136]

In 1961, the then twenty Member States of the Organization for Economic Co-operation and Development (OECD) liberalized capital transfers and investment

---

'Japanese Treaty Patterns' (1972) 12 Asian Survey 242 and L. Jerod Adams, *Theory, Law and Policy of Contemporary Japanese Treaties* (New York: Oceana Publications Inc., 1974).

128. From 1946 to 1966, the US entered into twenty-one FCN treaties. Two of the treaties were subject to proceedings before the International Court of Justice: *Military and Paramilitary Activities In and Against Nicaragua* (*Nicaragua v. US*) [1984] ICJ Rep 392 and [1986] ICJ Rep 14, and *Elettronica Sicula S.p.A. (ELSI) (US v. Italy)* [1989] ICJ Rep 15 [*ELSI*].

129. The US entered into numerous FCNs with Latin American, Asian and African states in the nineteenth century. See Wilson, *supra* note 127, and Vandevelde, *United States Investment Treaties, supra* note 43.

130. Vandevelde, *ibid.,* at 15-16 and K.J. Vandevelde, 'A Brief History of International Investment Agreements' (2005) 12 UCDJILP [Vandevelde, 'A Brief History'] at 162.

131. In 1956 Herman Walker, Jr., a former advisor on commercial treaties for the US State Department wrote that the 'FCN treaty as a whole is an investment treaty'. H. Walker, Jr. 'Treaties for the Encouragement and Protection of Foreign Investment: Present United States Practice' (1956) 5 AJCL 229 at 244-245.

132. See Wilson, *supra* note 127. Post-WWII US FCN treaties generally provided national and MFN treatment, the rights of foreign nationals to enter and stay in the host state, guarantees regarding freedom of conscience, fair and/or equitable treatment, a constant protection guarantee, compensation for expropriation, transfer of funds and freedom of navigation. Disputes regarding the interpretation or application of the treaties were to be resolved by the ICJ. Vandevelde, 'A Brief History', *supra* note 130 at 17.

133. P. Craig and G. De Búrca, *EU Law: Texts, Cases, and Materials*, 3rd edn (Oxford; New York: Oxford University Press, 2002) [*EU Law*] at 11-12.

134. Organization of American States Treaty Series No. 21, available on the OAS website.

135. In particular, Art. 25 provides: 'Los Estados no tomarán acción discriminatoria contra las inversiones por virtud de la cual la privación de los derechos de propiedad legalmente adquiridos por empresas o capitales extranjeros se lleve a cabo por causas o en condiciones diferentes a aquellas que la Constitución o las leyes de cada país establezcan para la expropiación de propiedades nacionales. Toda expropiación estará acompañada del pago del justo precio en forma oportuna, adecuada y efectiva.'

136. See Brownlie, *International Law and the Use of Force by States, supra* note 49. See C.G. Fenwick, 'The Ninth International Conference of American States' (1948) 42 AJIL 562.

in major service industries through codes on the liberalization of capital movements and current invisible operations.[137]

§1.18 Increasing resort to international arbitration post-WWII   In the post-WWII era, the use of international arbitration to resolve foreign investment disputes significantly increased.[138] The assertion of economic sovereignty by capital importing states and the implementation of socialist economic policies in the 1950s augmented the risks for foreign investment of expropriations, nationalizations, the imposition of new regulatory controls, and breaches of contract.[139] Although many developing countries viewed international arbitration with distrust,[140] foreign investors generally preferred it to submitting disputes to local courts where decisions might be affected by bias, corruption and inefficiency. Investors began to use various contractual mechanisms, including stabilization, choice of law and international arbitration clauses in order to mitigate political risks.[141] Other risk management mechanisms, such as political risk insurance, also began to be available at this time.[142]

Many international arbitrations in the period immediately after WWII were the result of the cancellation or nationalizations of oil concessions.[143] In these

---

137. The codes are legally binding on OECD Member States under the convention on the *Organisation for Economic Co-operation and Development* (14 Dec. 1960), 888 UNTS 179 (entered into force 30 Sep. 1961). As of 1 May 2008, thirty states have ratified the Convention. See *infra* Chapter 8, §8.4, for discussion of the codes on the liberalisation of capital movements and current invisible operations.

138. Prior to WWII, almost all arbitral tribunals or mixed commissions created to address foreign investment claims were established by agreement between the home and host state *after* a dispute had arisen. For example, see *The Jaffa-Jerusalem Railway Arbitration*, reproduced in S. Rosenne, 'The Jaffa-Jerusalem Railway Arbitration (1922)' (1998) 28 IYBHR 239. Also see M.R. Reynolds, 'The Jaffa-Jerusalem Railway Company Arbitration 1922' (1991) 57 Arbitration 42. There were a number of arbitrations arising out of concession agreements made in the 1920s between Western companies and the Soviet Union. See V.V. Veeder, 'Lloyd George, Lenin and Cannibals: The Harriman Arbitration' (2000) 16 AI 115 and V.V. Veeder, 'The 1921-1923 North Sakhalin Concession Agreement: The 1925 Court Decisions Between the US Company Sinclair Exploration and the Soviet Government' (2002) 18 AI 185. Also see the award in the *Lena Goldfields Arbitration* and commentary by A. Nussbaum in (1950) 36 CLQ 31 and V.V. Veeder, 'The *Lena Goldfields* Arbitration: The Historical Roots of Three Ideas' (1998) 47 ICLQ 747. See also S.M. Schwebel & J.G. Wetter, 'Some Little Known Cases on Concessions' *reprinted in* S.M. Schwebel, *Justice in International Law* (Cambridge: Grotius Publications/Cambridge University Press, 1994) at 436.

139. See generally Rubins & Kinsella, *supra* note 5.

140. See J. Paulsson, 'Third World Participation in International Investment Arbitration' (1987) 2 ICSID Rev 19 and A.A. Shalakany, 'Arbitration and the Third World: A Plea for Reassessing Bias under the Specter of Neoliberalism' (2000) 41 HILJ 419.

141. See Rubins & Kinsella, *supra* note 5 at 43-68 and Sornarajah, *supra* note 51 at 404-415.

142. See *infra* §1.29.

143. See *Petroleum Development Ltd. v. The Sheikh of Abu Dhabi* (1951) 18 ILR 144; *Ruler of Qatar v. International Marine Oil Co.* (1953) 20 ILR 534; *Saudi Arabia v. Arabian American Oil Co.* (ARAMCO) (1963) 27 ILR 117; *Sapphire International Petroleums Ltd. v. National Iranian Oil Co.* (1963) 35 ILR 136; *BP Exploration Company Ltd. v. Libya* (1979) 53 ILR

arbitrations, tribunals had to consider the applicable law and the extent to which the proper law of the contract included general principles of international law, such as the observance of commitments in good faith and respect for acquired rights.[144] The cases gave rise to a continuing debate in international law regarding the extent to which state responsibility arises for a breach of a contract between a foreign national and a host state.[145]

§1.19 New York Convention   The increased use of international arbitration to settle foreign investment and commercial disputes exposed the practical difficulties involved in enforcing international arbitral awards. A key development in the evolving international legal framework for international arbitration was the conclusion and widespread ratification of the *1958 New York Convention on the Recognition of Foreign Arbitral Awards* (the New York Convention),[146] which provides for the recognition and enforcement of foreign arbitral awards and limits the grounds upon which local courts may refuse to recognize and enforce awards.[147] Importantly, the New York Convention makes respect of arbitration agreements a treaty obligation. Although the New York Convention provides the foundation for international arbitration, it does not address the issue of state immunity; thus, even if a foreign investor obtains a favourable arbitral award and seeks to enforce it against state assets located in another state, the assets may be

---

297; *Texaco Overseas Petroleum Co. (TOPCO) and Californian Asiatic Oil Co. v. Libya* (1977) 104 JDI 350 (French original), (1979) 53 ILR 389 (English translation); *Libyan American Oil Co. (LIAMCO) v. Libya* (1981) 20 ILM 1; *Kuwait v. American Independent Oil Company (AMINOIL)* (1982) 21 ILM 976; *Elf Aquitaine Iran v. NIOC* (1982) 11 YCA 112. For commentary on the cases and further sources see Lowenfeld, *supra* note 69 at 416-431 and D.W. Bowett. 'State contracts with aliens: contemporary developments on compensation for termination or breach' (1988) 59 BYIL 49-74. For a critical assessment of the arbitral treatment of state contracts, see Anghie, *supra* note 11 at 226-244.

144.   See Lowenfeld, *supra* note 69 at 417-430 and Paulsson, *supra* note 140. See *infra* Chapter 2 for discussion of applicable law in IIAs.

145.   See P. Weil, 'Problèmes relatifs aux contrats passés entre un Etat et un particulier' (1969) 128 (III) RDCADI 95; P. Weil, 'Droit international et contrats d'Etat' in D. Bardonnet *et al.* eds., *Mélanges offerts à Paul Reuter: le droit international: unité et diversité*, (Paris: Pedone, 1981) at 549; S.J. Toope, *Mixed International Arbitration: Studies in Arbitration between States and Private Persons* (Cambridge: Grotius, 1990); T.E. Carbonneau, ed., *Lex Mercatoria and Arbitration: A Discussion of the New Merchant Law* (Dobbs Ferry, N.Y.: Transnational Juris Publications, 1990) and Sornarajah, *supra* note 51 at 416-433. This issue has also arisen under IIA provisions providing for the observance of undertakings. See *infra* Chapter 9.

146.   *Convention on the Recognition and Enforcement of Foreign Arbitral Awards*, 10 Jun. 1958, 330 UNTS 38 (entered into force 7 Jun. 1959).

147.   A.J. van den Berg, *The New York Arbitration Convention of 1958: Towards a Uniform Judicial Interpretation* (Boston: Kluwer Law and Taxation, 1981) and E. Gaillard & J. Savage, eds, *Fouchard, Gaillard, Goldman on International Commercial Arbitration* (The Hague; Boston: Kluwer Law International, 1999) at 966-997. See the *Yearbook of Commercial Arbitration* for discussion of court decisions applying the Convention. As of 10 May 2008, there were 142 parties to the New York Convention.

subject to immunity from execution under the law of the state where the asset is located.

§1.20 Permanent Sovereignty Over Natural Resources   Confronted with the legacy of colonialism and continued foreign control over resources, throughout the 1950s developing states sought to affirm their economic independence. One avenue for the assertion of economic independence was through the United Nations General Assembly, which in 1952, passed the first of seven resolutions on Permanent Sovereignty Over Natural Resources.[148] In the late 1950s the UN Commission on Permanent Sovereignty over Natural Resources was established to study the question of national control over resources. In 1962, the General Assembly passed Resolution 1803, which declares that the 'right of peoples and nations to permanent sovereignty over their natural wealth and resources must be exercised in the interest of their national development and of the well-being of the people of the State concerned.'[149] The Resolution reaffirmed that the admission of foreign investment was subject to the authorization, restriction or prohibition of the state.[150] Once admitted, however, foreign investment was to be treated in accordance with national and international law.[151] Paragraph 4 of the Resolution addresses expropriation as follows:

> Nationalization, expropriation or requisitioning shall be based on grounds or reasons of public utility, security or the national interest which are recognized as overriding purely individual or private interests, both domestic and foreign. In such cases the owner shall be paid appropriate compensation, in accordance with the rules in force in the State taking such measures in the exercise of its sovereignty and in accordance with international law. In any case where the question of compensation gives rise to a controversy, the national jurisdiction of the State taking such measures shall be exhausted. However, upon agreement by sovereign States and other parties concerned, settlement of the dispute should be made through arbitration or international adjudication.

Paragraph 4 affirms that appropriate compensation *shall* be paid for expropriation, thereby confirming the customary international law requirement of compensation

---

148.   GA Res. 626 (VII), (1952) YBUN at 387.
149.   GA Res 1803, 14 Dec. 1962, *reprinted in* (1963) 2 ILM 223. The resolution was passed by eighty-seven votes in favour, two against (France and South Africa) and twelve abstentions (Communist states, Ghana and Burma). For a discussion of the drafting of the resolution, see S.M. Schwebel, 'The Story of the UN's Declaration on Permanent Sovereignty Over Natural Resources' (1963) 49 ABAJ 463 *reprinted in* Schwebel, *Justice in International Law, supra* note 138 and K. Gess, 'Permanent Sovereignty Over Natural Resources' (1974) 13 ICLQ 398. For a critical commentary on the resolution and K. Gess' article, see A. Anghie, *Imperialism, Sovereignty and the Making of International Law* (Cambridge: Cambridge University Press, 2005) at 216-220.
150.   *Ibid.*, at para. 2.
151.   *Ibid.*, at para. 3.

for expropriation.[152] The US had proposed that appropriate compensation be defined as 'prompt adequate and effective compensation,' but this proposal was withdrawn because it lacked support. An amendment by the USSR proposing that national law ought to govern the standard of compensation was defeated.[153] Thus, the reference to 'appropriate compensation,' without elaboration, was a compromise between the US position and the position of states advocating a national treatment standard.

Resolution 1803 also provides that 'foreign investment agreements freely entered into by or between sovereign States shall be observed in good faith,' but does not expressly address foreign investment contracts entered into before a state had acquired independence.

§1.21 International Centre for Settlement of Investment Disputes The establishment in 1965 of the International Centre for Settlement of Investment Disputes (ICSID) under the auspices of the World Bank was the next important step in the creation of the international legal framework for foreign investment protection.[154] Discussions on the standard of investment protection in multilateral fora, including the United Nations, had revealed the divided state of opinion on substantive standards. In 1961, Aron Broches, General Counsel of the World Bank, proposed creating a mechanism for the impartial settlement of international investment disputes, rather than seeking agreement on substantive standards of treatment.[155] The ICSID was the result, and was designed to provide a neutral forum for the settlement of investment disputes[156] with the desired consequence of creating 'an atmosphere of mutual confidence and thus stimulating a larger flow of private international capital into those countries which wish to attract it.'[157] Ibrahim

---

152. It should be noted, however, that the preamble to the resolution expressly provides that 'nothing in paragraph 4 below in any way prejudices the position of any Member State on any aspect of the question of the rights and obligations of successor States and Governments in respect of property acquired before the accession to complete sovereignty of countries formerly under colonial rule.'

153. See Lowenfeld, *supra* note 69 at 408; Gess, *supra* note 149 at 420-429 and Schwebel, *supra* note 149 at 465-466.

154. *Convention on the Settlement of Investment Disputes between States and Nationals of Other States*, 18 Mar. 1965, (1965) 4 ILM 524. The convention is commonly called the ICSID or Washington Convention. As of 4 Nov. 2007, 155 states have signed and 143 have ratified the ICSID Convention. For legal commentary on the Convention and references to other sources see: C. Schreuer, *The ICSID Convention: A Commentary* (Cambridge: Cambridge University Press, 2001) [Schreuer, *ICSID Commentary*]; E. Gaillard, *La Jurisprudence du CIRDI* (Paris, Pedone, 2004); L. Reed, J. Paulsson & N. Blackaby, *Guide to ICSID Arbitration* (The Hague: Kluwer Law, 2004); and S. Manciaux, *Investissements étrangers et arbitrage entre Etats et ressortissants d'autres Etats, Trente années d'activité du CIRDI* (Paris: Litec, 2004). The ICSID website contains an extensive bibliography of works on the ICSID.

155. E. Lauterpacht, foreword in Schreuer, *ICSID Commentary, ibid.*, at xi.

156. I.F.I. Shihata, *Towards a Greater Depoliticization of Investment Disputes: The Roles of ICSID and MIGA* (Washington: ICSID, 1993).

157. Report of the Executive Directors of the International Bank for Reconstruction and Development on the Convention of the Settlement of Investment Disputes between States and

Shihata noted in his well-known article, 'Towards a Greater Depoliticization of Investment Disputes,' that the ICSID provides:

> A forum for conflict resolution in a framework that carefully balances the interests and requirements of all the parties involved, and attempts in particular to 'depoliticize' the settlement of investment disputes.[158]

The ICSID is not a permanent arbitral tribunal; rather it provides a legal and organizational framework for the arbitration of disputes between Contracting States and investors who qualify as nationals of other Contracting States. The ICSID Convention makes the agreement to arbitrate an investment dispute before the ICSID a treaty obligation. Thus, an arbitration agreement providing for ICSID proceedings engages the state's international responsibility. The ICSID allows investment disputes to be arbitrated without interference from domestic political or judicial organs in the same manner as a dispute between states can be made subject to international adjudication by an international court or tribunal.

Arbitration under the ICSID is subject to four conditions: (1) the parties must have agreed to submit their dispute to dispute settlement under the ICSID; (2) the dispute must be between a Contracting State to the ICSID (or a subdivision or agency of that state) and the national of another Contracting State; (3) the dispute must be a legal dispute; and (4) the dispute must arise directly out of an investment made in the host Contracting State.[159] The ICSID Convention provides that, where the parties have consented to ICSID arbitration, the consent operates to exclude any other forum or remedy.[160] In particular, states may not exercise diplomatic protection once a claim has been submitted to the ICSID, except where there is a failure to comply with an award.[161] In addition, where a state has consented to arbitration, it cannot withdraw consent unilaterally nor, require that there be an exhaustion of local remedies unless this has been made an express condition of its consent to arbitration.[162]

One of the purposes of the ICSID is to 'delocalise' disputes by making ICSID arbitration and awards subject solely to the ICSID Convention, rather than national law. This does not mean that national law is irrelevant to the resolution of disputes under ICSID arbitration.[163] Rather, the substantive law applicable to the investment dispute will largely depend on the relationship between the host state and the investor in question (e.g., the dispute might arise out of a contract,

---

Nationals of Other States, 1 ICSID Rep 23 [Report of the Executive Directors on the Convention].

158. I.F.I. Shihata, 'Towards a Greater Depoliticization of Investment Disputes' (1986) 1 ICSID Rev 1. Shihata became the Secretary General of the ICSID in 1983, serving in that role and as General Counsel of the World Bank until 1998.

159. The conditions for the jurisdiction of ICSID are set out in Art. 25(1) of the ICSID Convention. See *supra* note 154 for commentary on the jurisdiction of ICSID tribunals.

160. Art. 26, *ibid.*

161. Art. 27, *ibid.*

162. Art. 25(1) and 26, *ibid.*

163. See *infra* Chapter 2 for a discussion of applicable law in the context of IIAs.

foreign investment code or an IIA).[164] However, the ICSID Convention provisions govern the conduct of the arbitration. Awards made by ICSID tribunals are binding on the parties and can only be annulled by an *ad hoc* committee established under the ICSID Convention.[165] This is designed to prevent national courts from reviewing the merits of ICSID awards.

Another important innovation under the ICSID Convention is the definition of 'nationals of another Contracting State.' Under the principles of diplomatic protection in customary international law, states espouse the claims of their nationals.[166] In the foreign investment context, however, local laws may require that a foreign investment be made using a locally incorporated company, which is technically the national of the host state. The ICSID Convention addresses this issue by providing that the host state can agree to treat legal entities created under its jurisdiction as nationals of another party if those entities are under foreign control.[167] As a result, a locally incorporated company controlled by foreign investors can begin ICSID arbitration against the state in which it is incorporated, even though technically the company is not a foreign national.

In 1978, ICSID created an Additional Facility that allows the ICSID Secretariat to administer arbitration proceedings where one of the parties is not a Contracting State to the ICSID Convention or a national of a Contracting State.[168] The Additional Facility allows the ICSID Secretariat to administer arbitrations not otherwise falling within the purview of the ICSID Convention. An important difference between arbitrations under the ICSID Rules and the Additional Facility Rules is that national laws, rather than the ICSID Convention, apply to the enforcement of awards made under the Additional Facility Rules. Article 19 of the Additional Facility Rules provides that arbitration proceedings are to be held only in states that are parties to the New York Convention. Many IIAs now provide for arbitrations under the both the ICSID Arbitration Rules and the Additional Facility Rules.

---

164. Art. 42(1), ICSID Convention provides that: 'The Tribunal shall decide a dispute in accordance with such rules of law as may be agreed by the parties. In the absence of such agreement, the Tribunal shall apply the law of the Contracting State party to the dispute (including its rules on the conflict of laws) and such rules of international law as may be applicable.'

165. See Art. 50, *ibid.* On annulment, see *supra* note 154 for commentary, and E. Gaillard & Y. Banifatemi, eds, *Annulment of ICSID Awards,* IAI International Arbitration Series No.1 (New York: Juris Publishing, 2004). If an award is annulled, the claimant may still resubmit the claim. A number of IIA awards have been subject to annulment proceedings, including: *CMS Gas Transmission Company v. Argentina; Compañía de Aguas del Aconquija, & Compagnie Générale des Eaux v. Argentina; Consortium R.F.C.C. v. Morocco; Empresas Lucchetti, S.A. and Lucchetti Peru, S.A. v. Peru; Mr. Patrick Mitchell v. Congo; MTD Equity Sdn. Bhd. & MTD Chile S.A. v. Chile*; and *Wena Hotels Limited v. Egypt.*

166. See *supra* §1.3 for a discussion of diplomatic protection.

167. Art. 25(1), *supra* note 154.

168. Rules Governing the Additional Facility for the Administration of Proceedings By the Secretariat of the International Centre for Settlement of Investment Disputes. The original rules are published in 1 ICSID Reports 213. The rules were revised effective 1 Jan. 2003.

§1.22 OECD Convention on the Protection of Foreign Property   In 1962 the OECD released the *Draft Convention on the Protection of Foreign Property*,[169] which was revised and approved by the OECD in 1967 (1967 Draft OECD Convention).[170] Given the membership of the OECD,[171] it is not surprising that the 1967 Draft Convention generally reflects the views of the major capital exporting states on the minimum standard of treatment. The 1967 OECD Council Resolution approving the Draft Convention highlights that it 'embodies recognised principles relating to the protection of foreign property' and that it 'will be a useful document in the preparation of agreements on the protection of foreign investment.'[172] The 1967 Draft OECD Convention sets out the minimum standards of treatment as follows:

> Each Party shall at all times ensure fair and equitable treatment to the property of the nationals of the other Parties. It shall accord within its territory the most constant protection and security to such property and shall not in any way impair the management, maintenance, use, enjoyment or disposal thereof by unreasonable or discriminatory measures. The fact that certain nationals of any State are accorded treatment more favourable than that provided for in this Convention shall not be regarded as discriminatory against nationals of a Party by reason only of the fact that such treatment is not accorded to the latter.[173]

With respect to compensation for expropriation, the 1967 Draft OECD Convention reflects the Hull Rule requirement for prompt, adequate and effective compensation. Taking of property is to be:

> … accompanied by provision for the payment of just compensation. Such compensation shall represent the genuine value of the property affected, shall be paid without undue delay, and shall be transferable to the extent necessary to make it effective for the national entitled thereto.[174]

Although the 1967 Draft OECD Convention failed to gain sufficient support among OECD countries for adoption as a multilateral convention,[175] its substantive provisions have served as an important model for bilateral investment treaties (BITs).[176] It should be noted that the 1967 Draft OECD Convention, although

---

169.   (1963) 2 ILM 241.
170.   (1968) 7 ILM 117.
171.   *Supra* note 137.
172.   Resolution of the OECD Council, 12 Oct. 1967, (1968) 7 ILM 117.
173.   Art. 1(a), *ibid.*, at 119. See *infra* Chapter 6, §6.4 *et seq.*, on the development of the minimum standard of treatment.
174.   Art. 3, *ibid.*
175.   This was due, in part, to the reluctance of some less developed members, including Greece, Portugal and Turkey, to be bound by the provisions. See, UNCTC, *Bilateral Investment Treaties* (New York: United Nations, 1988) (Doc. No. ST/CTC/65) at 7.
176.   R. Dolzer & M. Stevens, *Bilateral Investment Treaties* (The Hague: Martinus Nijhoff Publishers, 1995) at 2.

setting out a mechanism for investor-state arbitration, conditions arbitration on a separate declaration of consent to arbitral jurisdiction by the state.[177]

§1.23 Charter of Economic Rights and Duties of States Throughout the late 1960s and 1970s, developing states sought to reconstruct the legal framework for international economic relations. In the UN, these efforts culminated in a series of General Assembly resolutions, including the 1974 *Declaration on the Establishment of a New International Economic Order* (NIEO Declaration) and the 1974 *Charter of Economic Rights and Duties of States* (Charter).[178] The NIEO Declaration asserts that the international economic system, including neo-colonialism and the inequitable distribution of income, are obstacles to developing states. While reaffirming the principle of permanent sovereignty over resources and economic activities, it sets out principles for a new system of economic relations, including such items as: terms of trade for raw materials and primary commodities; the reform of the international monetary system; the financing of development; the transfer of technology; and the regulation of transnational corporations.

The Charter elaborates on the principles in the NIEO Declaration and contains specific measures concerning foreign investment.[179] It affirms the right

---

177. See Art. 7, 1967 Draft OECD Convention, *supra* note 170.
178. 'General Assembly Resolution on Permanent Sovereignty over Natural Resources', GA Res 3171, 17 Dec. 1973, (1974) 13 ILM 238; 'Declaration on the Establishment of a New International Economic Order', GA Res 3201, 1 May 1974, (1974) 13 ILM 715; 'Charter of Economic Rights and Duties of States', GA Res 3281, 12 Dec. 1974, (1975) 14 ILM 251. For commentary, see M. Bedjaoui, *Towards a New International Economic Order* (New York: Holmes & Meier, 1979); I. Brownlie, 'Legal Status of Natural Resources In International Law (Some Aspects)' (1979) 162 RDCADI 245 [Brownlie, 'Legal Status of Natural Resources'] and N. Schrijver, *Sovereignty Over Natural Resources: Balancing Rights and Duties* (Cambridge: Cambridge University Press, 1997). See *supra* §1.20 on the 1962 Resolution 1803.
179. Section 2.2 of the Charter provides:

1. Every State has and shall freely exercise full permanent sovereignty, including possession, use and disposal, over all its wealth, natural resources and economic activities.
2. Each State has the right:
   a. To regulate and exercise authority over foreign investment within its national jurisdiction in accordance with its laws and regulations and in conformity with its national objectives and priorities. No State shall be compelled to grant preferential treatment to foreign investment;
   b. To regulate and supervise the activities of transnational corporations within its national jurisdiction and take measures to ensure that such activities comply with its laws, rules and regulations and conform with its economic and social policies. Transnational corporations shall not intervene in the internal affairs of a host State. Every State should, with full regard for its sovereign rights, co-operate with other States in the exercise of the right set forth in this subparagraph;
   c. To nationalize, expropriate or transfer ownership of foreign property in which case appropriate compensation should be paid by the State adopting such measures, taking into account its relevant laws and regulations and all circumstances that the State considers pertinent. In any case where the questions of compensation give rise to a controversy, it shall be settled under the domestic law of the nationalizing State and by its tribunals, unless it is freely and mutually agreed by all States concerned that other

of states to regulate foreign investment within their jurisdictions and provides that no state can be compelled to grant 'preferential treatment' to foreign investment.[180] The Charter also states that transnational corporations are not to intervene in the internal affairs of states and affirms the right of states to regulate transnational corporations. Simultaneously, the Charter encourages states to co-operate in regulating the activities of transnational corporations.[181] In contrast to the 1962 General Assembly Resolution 1803 on Permanent Sovereignty over National Resources, which recognized that there is an international law standard of compensation for expropriation ('appropriate compensation'),[182] the Charter provides that compensation for expropriation is to be determined in accordance with national laws and omits any reference to international law or a minimum international standard in determining compensation.[183]

The Charter, like the NIEO Declaration, was an assertion of national sovereignty by developing states. Although the Charter was adopted by an overwhelming majority as a result of the numerical preponderance of developing states in the General Assembly, most developed states either voted against its adoption or abstained from voting.[184] In his influential arbitral award, *Texaco Overseas Petroleum Co. (TOPCO) and Californian Asiatic Oil Co. v. Libya*,[185] René-Jean Dupuy observed that although the 1962 Resolution 1803 on Permanent Sovereignty over Natural Resources was assented to 'by a great many states representing not only all geographic areas but also all economic systems,'[186] the NIEO resolutions – 3171, 3201 and 3281[187] – were supported 'by a majority of states but not any of the developed countries with market economies which carry on the largest part of international trade.'[188]

Although the Charter and NIEO Declaration were strong political and programmatic statements, as General Assembly resolutions, they have no binding force and did not purport to be restatements of existing law. Further, they had little long-term impact on state practice relating to foreign investment protection.

---

        peaceful means be sought on the basis of the sovereign equality of States and in accordance with the principle of free choice of means.

180. Subparagraph (a) was approved by 113 states and opposed by ten. Four states abstained from voting. See (1975) 14 ILM 251 at 264.
181. Subparagraph (b) was approved by 119 states and opposed by four. Six states abstained from voting. *Ibid.*
182. See *supra* §1.20.
183. Subparagraph (c) was approved by 104 states and opposed by sixteen. Six states abstained from voting. *Ibid.*
184. The Charter was adopted by a vote of 120 in favour to six against with ten abstentions. *Supra* note 180 at 251. Belgium, Denmark, Federal Republic of Germany, Luxembourg, UK and US voted against the Charter. Austria, Canada, France, Ireland, Israel, Italy, Japan, The Netherlands, Norway and Spain abstained from voting.
185. *Texaco Overseas Petroleum Co. (TOPCO) and Californian Asiatic Oil Co. v. Libya* (1977) 104 JDI 350 (French original), (1979) 53 ILR 389 (English translation).
186. *Ibid.*, 53 ILR at 487, para. 84.
187. *Supra* note 178.
188. *Supra* note 185, 53 ILR at 491, para. 86.

During the following decades, developing states entered into IIAs to promote and protect investments on terms that departed significantly from the principles reflected in the Charter and the NIEO Declaration.[189]

§1.24 Draft UN Code of Conduct on Transnational Corporations One of the clear objectives of the NIEO Declaration and the Charter was more stringent regulation of multinational enterprises.[190] In 1974, the UN Economic and Social Council established the Commission on Transnational Corporations, the primary purpose of which was to draft a Code of Conduct on Transnational Corporations (TNC Code of Conduct).[191] From the earliest discussions, disagreement emerged between capital exporting and importing states as to whether the Code would only apply to the conduct of transnational corporations or whether it would extend also to the treatment of TNCs by host states. In 1980, the Economic and Social Council decided the Code would address both issues.[192] For the next ten years the drafting of the Code's substantive provisions was characterized by continued disagreements over its content, inclusion of references to the minimum standard of treatment and compensation for expropriation, and its legal status.[193] Negotiations were suspended in 1992.[194]

§1.25 OECD Declaration on International Investment and Multinational Enterprises The 1976 OECD *Declaration on International Investment and Multinational Enterprises* (OECD Declaration)[195] was a response by OECD member states to the NIEO Declaration and Charter and the draft TNC Code of Conduct.[196] The OECD Declaration highlights the importance of international investment to economic development, commits the OECD states to national treatment of foreign enterprises,[197] and includes the *OECD Guidelines on Multinational Enterprises* (the Guidelines). In the OECD Declaration, the OECD

---

189. T. Wälde, 'A Requiem for the "New International Economic Order": The Rise and Fall in International Economic Law and a Post-Mortem with Timeless Significance,' in G.L.G. Hafner *et al.*, eds, *Liber Amicorum Professor Siedl-Hohenveldern*, (The Hague: Kluwer Law International, 1998) 771.
190. *Supra* note 178.
191. See P. Muchlinski, *Multinational Enterprises and the Law*, 2nd edn (Oxford: Oxford University Press, 2007) [Muchlinski (2007)] at 660 and W. Spröte, 'Negotiations on a United Nations Code of Conduct for Transnational Corporations' (1990) 33 GYIL 331.
192. See P. Muchlinski, *Multinational Enterprises and the Law* (Cambridge, Mass: Blackwell Publishers, 1995) [Muchlinski (1995)] at 593.
193. The draft code is available in (1984) 23 ILM 626.
194. Muchlinski (1995), *supra* note 192 at 661. The last draft of the text of the code is dated 31 May 1990. In addition to the draft code, in 1977 the International Labour Organization adopted the *Tripartite Declaration of Principles Concerning Multinational Enterprises and Social Policy* setting out principles with respect to employment, training, conditions of work and life and industrial relations (1978) 17 ILM 422. See Muchlinski (1995), *ibid.*, at 473-506.
195. The *OECD Declaration and Decisions on International Investment and Multinational Enterprises*, DAFFE/IME(2000)20, available on the OECD website.
196. Muchlinski (2007), *supra* note 191 at 658.
197. See *infra* Chapter 4, §4.6 *et seq.*, with respect to the OECD National Treatment Instrument.

states recommend that multinational enterprises operating in or from their territories observe the Guidelines. The Guidelines provide voluntary principles and
standards for responsible business conduct and encourage 'the positive contributions which multinational enterprises can make towards economic and social
progress.'[198] The Guidelines set out standards for multinational enterprises in areas
including disclosure, employment, environment, corruption, consumers, science
and technology, competition and taxation. The Guidelines affirm that states have
the right to regulate multinational corporations, subject to international law standards, although they do not elaborate on the content of those standards.[199]

§1.26 Lump sum agreements and national claims commissions A lump sum
agreement is a settlement agreement whereby claimant and respondent states
agree to settle claims through lump sum compensation. The claimant state then
distributes the lump sum settlement amongst its nationals who have made claims,
typically by establishing special domestic tribunals or claims commissions to
adjudicate the merits of its nationals' claims.[200] In the past sixty years, states have
concluded more than 200 lump sum agreements,[201] making them the primary
method for settling international claims concerning the treatment of nationals and
their property.[202] Lump sum agreements have been popular because they provide
for a final settlement of claims between states and thus resolve the diplomatic,
political and economic frictions caused by outstanding claims, while at the same
time allowing states to avoid binding dispute settlement mechanisms and adjudication of the merits of any particular claim.

Despite the extensive practice involving lump sum agreements, there is a
division of opinion on the jurisprudential significance of lump sum agreements.[203]
Do lump sum agreements simply reflect negotiated resolutions of claims motivated by extra-legal considerations, or do they represent a source of customary

---

198. Para. 2. The original guidelines are reproduced at (1976) 15 ILM 967. The Guidelines have
      been reviewed four times since 1976 and were last updated in 2000. See OECD, The OECD
      Guidelines for Multinational Enterprises: Text, Commentary and Clarification,
      31 Oct. 2001, DAFFE/IME/WPG(2000)15/FINAL.
199. Para. 8 of the Guidelines provides: 'Governments adhering to the Guidelines set them forth
      with the understanding that they will fulfil their responsibilities to treat enterprises equitably
      and in accordance with international law and with their contractual obligations.'
200. The US has been a predominant practitioner in this area. The United States Foreign Claims
      Settlement Commission and predecessor US agencies have adjudicated more than 660,000
      claims under forty-three claims programs. See online: <http://usdoj.gov/fcsc>.
201. See R.B. Lillich, 'Lump Sum Agreements' in *Encyclopedia, supra* note 8, Vol. III at 268.
202. D.J. Bederman, *Lump Sum Agreements and Diplomatic Protection*, Report for the International
      Law Association Committee on Diplomatic Protection of Persons and Property, 70th
      Conference, New Delhi 2002.
203. See R.B. Lillich & B. H. Weston, *International Claims: Their Settlement by Lump Sum
      Agreements* (Charlottesville: University Press of Virginia, 1975); R.B. Lillich & B.H. Weston,
      International Claims: Contemporary European Practice (Charlottesville, VA: University
      Press of Virginia, 1982); B. H. Weston, R.B. Lillich & D.J. Bederman, *International Claims:
      Their Settlement by Lump Sum Agreements, 1975-1995* (New York: Transnational Publishers,
      1999); and D.J. Bederman, *Lump Sum Agreements and Diplomatic Protection, ibid.*

international law reflecting legal determinations of claims? With respect to the admissibility of claims and claims involving state responsibility, there has been significant uniformity between the practices under lump sum agreements, the results of claims commissions and customary international law. Thus, although lump sum agreements are clearly influenced by extra-legal considerations, the international law relating to diplomatic protection and state responsibility has had a significant impact on the agreements and claims commission practice.[204]

One of the most controversial issues regarding lump sum agreements is the jurisprudential significance of the standard of compensation for expropriation. On the one hand, since most lump sum agreements provide for less than full compensation for large scale nationalizations, some international publicists argue that state practice supports the position that only partial compensation is required for large scale nationalizations.[205] On the other hand, others argue that it is difficult to generalize about the standard of compensation because different views on the amount of compensation for an expropriation may simply reflect different views of the merits of specific claims.[206] Further, settlements are often driven by political objectives and may not reflect general rules on standards of compensation.

§1.27 Investment disputes before the International Court of Justice   Despite the intense conflict over the past sixty years regarding the standards that apply to foreign investment under customary international law, the International Court of Justice (ICJ) has played a minimal role in resolving foreign investment disputes and in the development of jurisprudence on substantive standards of foreign investment protection. Since the Court's creation in 1945, only six foreign investment related cases have been brought before it.[207] In three of these cases the ICJ held that it did not have jurisdiction to deal with the complaint, while the fourth

---

204.   See R.J. Bettauer, 'International Claims: Their Settlement by Lump Sum Agreements, 1975-1995. (Review)' (2000) 94 AJIL 810. In his ILA report, *supra* note 202, Professor Bederman puts the position as follows: 'The jurisprudential significance of lump sum settlement lies not in their discount of the face value of claims, but, rather, in the substantive rules they articulate for such matters as claimant eligibility, attribution of State conduct, the nature of compensable claims, and the general standard and modalities of prompt, adequate and affective compensation.'
205.   See discussion in Professor Bederman's ILA Report, *ibid.*
206.   *Ibid.*
207.   As of 1 Jun. 2008.

was denied on the merits. The fifth (*Ahmadou Sadio Diallo*)[208] and sixth (*Pulp Mills on the River Uruguay*)[209] claims are currently before the Court.

The first investment dispute before the ICJ was the 1952 *Anglo-Iranian Co. Case*,[210] which arose out of Iran's nationalization of its oil industry in 1951. The Court held that it lacked jurisdiction because Iran's 1930 declaration accepting the jurisdiction of the Court did not apply to treaties made prior to the declaration. The second dispute, the *Case of Certain Norwegian Loans*,[211] involved a claim by France that Norway had breached its obligations under a series of state bonds. Here the Court also held that it did not have jurisdiction based on the scope of Norway's declaration accepting the jurisdiction of the Court.

The *Barcelona Traction* case (1970)[212] was also one where the ICJ ultimately determined it did not have jurisdiction, but it remains both a controversial and important decision respecting international investment law. Belgium alleged that the acts and omissions of the Spanish courts in placing Barcelona Traction into bankruptcy constituted a denial of justice and an expropriation of the Barcelona Traction shares held by Belgian nationals. Spain objected to the ICJ's jurisdiction on the basis that Barcelona Traction was incorporated in Canada and that Belgium was not entitled to exercise diplomatic protection on behalf of a Canadian company, even if owned by Belgian shareholders. In a much criticized judgment,[213] a majority of the

---

208. *Ahmadou Sadio Diallo* (*Republic of Guinea v. Democratic Republic of the Congo*). The case arose out of the 1995 expulsion of Mr. Diallo from Zaire (the predecessor to the Democratic Republic of the Congo (DRC)). Mr. Diallo was the shareholder in several companies doing business in the DRC and incorporated in the DRC. In its Judgment on Preliminary Objections of 24 May 2007, the ICJ held that Guinea could not exercise diplomatic protection 'by substitution' on behalf of two private limited liability companies created under DRC law but held that Guinea had standing to bring a claim on behalf of Mr. Diallo as an individual and as majority shareholder (para. 65). At para. 61, the Court affirmed that: 'only the State of nationality may exercise diplomatic protection on behalf of the company when its rights are injured by a wrongful act of another State. In determining whether a company possesses independent and distinct legal personality, international law looks to the rules of the relevant domestic law.'

209. In *Pulp Mills on the River Uruguay* (*Argentina v. Uruguay*), Argentina has brought a claim against Uruguay alleging that the government of Uruguay unilaterally authorized the construction of two pulp mills along the River Uruguay, without the compulsory notification and consultation required under the Statute of the River Uruguay signed by both states in 1975. Argentina claims that the mills would have a deleterious effect on the biodiversity of the river and constitute a health hazard to the residents of the area. The pulp mills are to be built by two different foreign investors.

210. *Anglo-Iranian Oil Co. Case* (*UK v. Iran*), [1952] ICJ Rep 93.

211. *Case of Certain Norwegian Loans* (*France v. Norway*), [1957] ICJ Rep 9.

212. *Supra* note 25. For a fascinating discussion of the political and legal context of the case, see J. Brooks, 'Annals of Finance – Privateer' *The New Yorker*, 21 and 28 May 1979. Also see F.A. Mann, 'Protection of Shareholders' Interests in the Light of the Barcelona Traction Case' in F.A. Mann, *Further Studies in International Law* (Oxford: Clarendon Press, 1990) at 217.

213. See F.A. Mann, 'The Protection of Shareholders' Interests in Light of the Barcelona Traction Case' (1973) 67 AJIL 259; R.B. Lillich, 'Two Perspectives on the Barcelona Traction Case: The Rigidity of Barcelona' (1971) 65 AJIL 522; R. Higgins, 'Aspects of the Case Concerning

Court held that 'where it is a question of an unlawful act committed against a company representing foreign capital, the general rule of international law authorizes the national State of the company alone to make a claim.'[214] As a result, Canada, not Belgium, was the proper party to bring a claim before the Court. This, however, was not possible as the Court did not have jurisdiction for disputes between Canada and Spain. In determining that it did not have jurisdiction, the Court highlighted that there had been an 'intense conflict of systems and interests'[215] concerning the protection of foreign investment and that states 'ever more frequently'[216] were providing foreign investment protection through bilateral and multilateral agreements. It noted that no such instrument was in force between Belgium and Spain.[217] By making these statements the ICJ signalled that progressive developments in international investment law would mainly be treaty-based.

The only case involving foreign investment that the ICJ has addressed on the merits to date is the *Elettronica Sicula S.p.A. (ELSI)* case (1982).[218] This case was brought under the 1948 Italy-US *Treaty of Friendship, Commerce and Navigation* (FCN), which provided for ICJ jurisdiction for disputes arising under the treaty.[219] Elettronica Sicula S.p.A. (ELSI) produced electronic components in Italy and was a subsidiary of two American corporations. ELSI's board of directors decided to shut down operations and liquidate ELSI to minimize ongoing losses. In order to protect employment, the local mayor issued a requisition order under which the town took temporary control of ELSI's factory. ELSI appealed this order and subsequently made a bankruptcy petition. The requisition order was later annulled by the Italian courts and the trustee in bankruptcy brought a suit for damages, arguing that the requisition order had caused the bankruptcy. In the case before the ICJ, the US claimed that the requisition, and the delay in overturning it, interfered with the American corporations' management and control of ELSI, as well as their interests in it, and causing the bankruptcy. The ICJ, however, found that

---

the Barcelona Traction, Light and Power Company, Ltd.' (1970) 11 VJIL 327; F. Orrego Vicuña, 'Changing Approaches to the Nationality of Claims in the Context of Diplomatic Protection and International Dispute Settlement' (2000) 15 ICSID Rev 340; and Orrego Vicuña, *The Changing Law of Nationality of Claims*, *supra* note 23.

214. *Supra* note 25 at para. 88.
215. *Ibid.*, at para. 89.
216. *Ibid.*, at para. 90.
217. *Ibid.*
218. *Supra* note 128. The decision was made by a Chamber of the ICJ consisting of Judges Ruda, Oda, Ago, Schwebel and Jennings. For commentary on the case see: F.A. Mann, 'Foreign Investment in the International Court of Justice: The *ELSI* Case' (1992) 86 AJIL 92; S.D. Murphy, 'The ELSI Case: An Investment Dispute at the International Court of Justice' (1991) 16 YJIL 391 and K.J. Hamrock, 'The *ELSI* Case: Toward an International Definition of 'Arbitrary Conduct', (1992) TILJ 837.
219. The factory was owned by ELSI, an Italian company, which was in turn wholly owned by two US corporations. The US claimed that Italy had breached the 1948 Italy-US FCN Treaty, a 1951 Supplementary Agreement to the FCN Treaty and customary international law. Art. I of the Supplementary Agreement provided protection against 'arbitrary or discriminatory measures ... resulting particularly in: (a) preventing ... effective control and management of enterprises ... or, (b) impairing ... other legally acquired rights and interests ...'.

ELSI's bankruptcy was caused not by the requisition order, but rather by the company's precarious financial situation. The Court denied the US's claim that Italy's actions were covered by the FCN Treaty as the mayor's order did not cause or trigger the bankruptcy. It also denied the US's claim that ELSI's shareholders were deprived of their rights to dispose of property, holding that the mayor's action was not the cause of the property loss.[220] Of particular importance with respect to the minimum standard of treatment, the Court addressed the meaning of 'arbitrariness' in international law.[221]

The majority judgment in *ELSI* largely avoided the issue of whether the US was entitled to bring the claim under the FCN Treaty and proceeded on the basis that the property protected under the treaty was not ELSI's plant and equipment (its property), but ELSI itself (the company).[222] In his Separate Opinion, Judge Oda addressed the treaty rights afforded to US nationals with respect to shareholdings in Italian companies. In his view, the treaty did not augment the rights of shareholders and the US shareholders of ELSI could only claim those rights guaranteed to them as shareholders under Italian law.[223] In contrast, in his Dissenting Opinion, Judge Schwebel stated that the treaty protected shareholders' rights. In his view, the treaty's guarantees with respect to the organization, control and management of corporations protected the US shareholders' interests in ELSI.[224]

In its jurisprudence the ICJ has addressed few of the controversial legal issues relating to foreign investment, such as the responsibility of states to foreign investors under customary international law and the standard of compensation for the expropriation of foreign investment. The *Barcelona Traction* and *ELSI* cases, however, highlighted some of the procedural and substantive inadequacies with the diplomatic protection model in safeguarding shareholder interests. These uncertainties and inadequacies may have provided compelling rationales for the development of IIAs. The *Barcelona Traction* case demonstrated

---

220. See Hamrock, 'The *ELSI* Case: Toward an International Definition of 'Arbitrary Conduct' *supra* note 218 for a discussion of the case.
221. See *infra* Chapter 6, §6.9.
222. *Supra* note 128 at 64, para. 106. The issue of shareholder's rights in *ELSI* is discussed in V. Lowe, 'Shareholders' Rights to Control and Manage: From Barcelona Traction to ELSI,' in N. Ando, E. McWhinney & R. Wolfrum, eds, *Liber Amicorum Judge Shigeru Oda* (The Hague: Kluwer Law International, 2002).
223. *Supra* note 128 at 87-88.
224. Judge Schwebel noted: 'it was maintained that the Treaty was essentially irrelevant to the claims of the United States in this case, since the measures taken by Italy (notably, the requisition of ELSI's plant and equipment) directly affected not nationals or corporations of the United States but an Italian corporation, ELSI, whose shares happened to be owned by United States corporations whose rights as shareholders were largely outside the scope of the protection afforded by the Treaty. The Chamber did not accept this argument. Nor did it accept the contention that the right to organize, control and manage a corporation was limited to the founding of a Company and the election of its directors and did not include its continuing management; nor that the right to control and manage was unaffected by the requisition of that corporation's plant and equipment.' *Supra* note 128 at 94-95. See also *ibid.*, at 100: 'the foreign investor shall enjoy the benefits of the Treaty and its Supplement, whether he invests in a corporation of his or the other party's nationality.'

that, depending on the place of incorporation of the investment vehicle, a home state may be unable to espouse the claims of its nationals. In addition, the Court signalled that clarification of the law in the area of foreign investment would need to be treaty-based given the intense conflict in the area. The opposing opinions of Judges Oda and Schwebel in *ELSI* highlighted the need for IIAs to address the extent to which investors holding shares in a corporation incorporated in a host state are entitled to claim for breaches of an IIA where the state measures in question are directed at the locally incorporated company. Finally, both *Barcelona Traction* and *ELSI* demonstrated that the diplomatic protection model was slow and cumbersome.[225]

§1.28 Iran-US Claims Tribunal The Iran-United States Claims Tribunal was established in 1981 to address claims by US and Iranian nationals arising out of the 1979 Iranian revolution.[226] This tribunal was the first international tribunal since WWII to consider a large number of investment claims. Its decisions have contributed substantially to international jurisprudence on state responsibility for injuries to foreigners.[227] Not surprisingly, the tribunal's jurisprudence has been cited extensively by investment treaty tribunals.[228]

§1.29 Foreign investment insurance Foreign investment insurance developed in the post-WWII era to provide foreign investors a mechanism to manage the inherent political risks of investing abroad.[229] National agencies were established by many capital exporting states to provide foreign investment insurance against political risks, including expropriation, restrictions on transfer of funds and political

---

225. The events giving rise to *Barcelona Traction* occurred between 1948 and 1952. Belgium's first ICJ application was filed in 1958. The final court judgment was delivered in 1970. The events giving rise to *ELSI* began in 1968. The US application to the ICJ was made in 1987 and the Chamber of the ICJ formed to deal with the case delivered its judgment in 1989.
226. The tribunal was established under the Claims Settlement Declaration, 19 Jan. 1981 (1981) 1 Iran-US CTR 9. See generally G.H. Aldrich, *The Jurisprudence of the Iran-United States Claims Tribunal* (Oxford: Clarendon Press, 1996); C.N. Brower & J.D. Brueschke, *The Iran-United States Claims Tribunal* (The Hague: Martinus Nijhoff Publishers, 1998); D. Caron & J. Crook, *The Iran-United States Claims Tribunal and the Process of International Claims Resolution: A Study by the Panel on State Responsibility of the American Society of International Law* (Ardsley, New York: Transnational, 2000) and C. Gibson & C. Drahozal, *The Iran-U.S. Claims Tribunal at 25: The Cases Everyone Needs to Know for Investor-State and International Arbitration* (Oxford: Oxford University Press, 2007).
227. As of 11 Jul. 2007, the tribunal had made final awards, decisions or orders in 3,936 cases. See Office of the Secretary-General of the Iran-United Stated Claims Tribunal, Communiqué, 25 Apr. 2008, No. 08/2.
228. See C. Gibson & C. Drahozal, 'Iran-United States Claims Tribunal Precedent in Investor-State Arbitration' (2006) 23 JIA 521.
229. See generally Chapter 3, 'Investment Insurance', in Rubins & Kinsella, *supra* note 5. Most private and public foreign investment insurers are members of the International Union of Credit & Investment Insurers (Berne Union). See online: <http://berneunion.org.uk>.

violence.[230] In 1985, the *Multilateral Investment Guarantee Agency* (MIGA) was created under the auspices of the World Bank to encourage foreign direct investment (FDI) flows between Member States and less developed countries by providing foreign investment insurance, technical assistance and policy advice.[231]

Foreign investment insurance mechanisms interact with investment treaty law in three important ways. First, in deciding whether to offer investment guarantees, insurers will look to whether a state has signed an IIA. In some cases, the existence of an IIA may be a precondition for providing political risk insurance.[232] For example, MIGA's Operational Regulations provide that, in considering the investment conditions of a host state for the purposes of assessing risks, an 'investment will be regarded as having adequate legal protection if it is protected under the terms of a bilateral investment treaty between the Host Country and the Home Country of the investor.'[233] Second, IIAs often provide for subrogation in investment treaty claims, thereby allowing the insurer who has paid a claim under a foreign investment policy to take up an investor's treaty claim.[234] Third, foreign investment insurance regularly covers risks such as expropriation and restrictions on transfers. A claims determination concerning foreign investment insurance, although based on the terms of a specific insurance contract, may address questions of state responsibility, such as attribution of responsibility or the types of conduct amounting to expropriation in international law.[235] Although foreign investment claim

---

230. As of 1992, the US, German and Japanese state agencies accounted for over 80% of national political risk insurance. See M.D. Rowat, 'Multilateral Approaches to Improving the Investment Climate of Developing Countries: The Cases of ICSID and MIGA' (1992) 22 HILJ 103 at 119 as quoted by Rubins & Kinsella, *supra* note 5 at 70. The US government's program is run by the Overseas Private Insurance Corporation (OPIC). Japan's insurer is Nippon Export and Investment Insurance (NEXI). In Germany, foreign investment insurance was formally provided through Treuarbeit. In early 2003, the German Government appointed a consortium formed by PricewaterhouseCoopers and Euler Hermes to manage its investment guarantee scheme. See Rubins & Kinsella, *ibid.*, at 94.

231. *Convention Establishing the Multilateral Investment Guarantee Agency* (1985) 24 ILM 1605 [*MIGA Convention*]. As of 28 Apr. 2008, MIGA had 172 members. Online: <miga.org>. For commentary, see P. Chatterjee, 'The Convention Establishing the Multilateral Investment Guarantee Scheme' (1987) 36 ICLQ 76 and I.F.I. Shihata, *MIGA and Foreign Investment: Origins, Operations, Policies, and Basic Documents of the Multilateral Investment Guarantee Agency* (Dordrecht: Martinus Nijhoff Publishers, 1988).

232. See UNCTAD, *supra* note 175 at 4.

233. Para. 3.16, MIGA, Operational Regulations, as amended by the Board of Directors through 27 Aug. 2002.

234. Subrogation agreements may also appear in separate agreements. For example, the US has investment guarantee agreements with a number of states that provide the right of OPIC to make a claim against the state where it has paid out on a political risk insurance policy. For example, see US-Poland Investment Guaranty Agreement, dated 13 Oct. 1989, TIAS 12039. In addition, MIGA is empowered to enter into investment guarantee agreements with states. See Art. 23(b)(ii), MIGA Convention, *supra* note 231.

235. For example, V.R. Koven, 'Expropriation and the "Jurisprudence" of OPIC' (1981) 22 HILJ 269. OPIC publishes its Memoranda of Determinations on its website.

determinations are based on contractual obligations, IIA tribunals have referred to claims determinations for guidance on legal issues arising under IIAs.[236]

III INTERNATIONAL INVESTMENT AGREEMENTS

§1.30 The origins of international investment agreements[237] The development of IIAs was primarily a response to the uncertainties and inadequacies of the customary international law of state responsibility for injuries to aliens and their property.[238] In addition, capital exporting states sought to obtain better market access commitments from capital importing states for investors and investment, and to obtain progressive development in the standards of investment protection. As already noted, although there were early efforts to create an international framework for foreign investment, disagreement between capital exporting and importing states about standards of treatment for foreign investors derailed the conclusion of a multilateral treaty. As a result, capital exporting states began concluding BITs dedicated to foreign investment promotion and protection.[239]

Prior to the development of the investment-focused BITs, treaty-based investment protection was available under some general economic treaties. As discussed above, after WWII numerous states, including the US and the UK, entered into FCN treaties that focused on the protection of property rights and the business interests of foreigners.[240] For example, the 1956 *Treaty of Friendship, Commerce and Navigation* between Nicaragua and the US, although not formally called a BIT, essentially served the same function – the treaty's preamble highlights the contribution to be made by 'mutually beneficial investments' between the two states. Indeed, the 1956 Nicaragua-US FCN Treaty might be considered as providing

---

236. For example, several IIA tribunals, in discussing the meaning of expropriation in international law, have referred to the determination made in the arbitration *In the Matter of Revere Copper and Brass, Inc. and Overseas Private Investment Corporation* (Award, 24 Aug. 1978) 17 ILM 1321 and 56 ILR 258.

237. For a bibiliography of articles on books on BITs current to 1996, see the ICSID website. An earlier version of this bibliography is available in (1992) 7 ICSID Rev 497.

238. See UNCTC, *supra* note 175 at 1.

239. For an overview of treaty practice, see the following three comprehensive studies: UNCTC, *ibid.*; UNCTAD, *Bilateral Investment Treaties in the Mid-1990s* (New York and Geneva: United Nations, 1998) (Doc. No. UNCTAD/ITE/IIT/7) and UNCTAD, *Bilateral Investment Treaties 1995-2006* (New York and Geneva: United Nations, 2007) (Doc. No. UNCTAD/ITE/IIT/2006/5). Also see the overview of BIT practice as of 1995 by Dolzer & Stevens, *supra* note 176. For the texts of specific BITs see the compilation of investment treaties in ICSID, *Investment Promotion and Protection Treaties*, looseleaf (Dobbs Ferry, New York: Oceana Publications Inc., 1983) [*Investment Protection Treaties*]. UNCTAD also has two comprehensive online databases on its website: one for BITs and one for other investment instruments.

240. See *infra* §1.17.

more comprehensive substantive standards of investment protection than many of the early European BITs.

Germany is commonly cited as the first state to develop a BIT program and to sign the first BIT, with Pakistan, in 1959.[241] The *Treaty between the Federal Republic of Germany and Pakistan for the Promotion and Protection of Investments* (Germany-Pakistan (1959)) contains many of the substantive provisions that have become common in subsequent BITs. The term investment is defined broadly.[242] The contracting states undertake a general obligation to encourage foreign investment, although the right of admission is determined by national law. The parties are obliged to refrain from discrimination based on the nationality of the investor and there is to be no discrimination against investment activities. Investments are to enjoy protection and security.[243] Provision is made for compensation due in the event of an expropriation and a right of subrogation may be exercised where the investor has been compensated under an insurance arrangement. There are guarantees on the transfer of capital and investment returns, as well as a general guarantee that the state will observe any obligation it has undertaken. Finally, the BIT provides for state-to-state dispute settlement before the ICJ if the parties agree, or if they do not agree, to an arbitration tribunal upon the request of either party.[244] This recourse to state-to-state arbitration before a three person arbitral tribunal, as an alternative to ICJ jurisdiction, represents one of the major differences between early post-WWII agreements such as the Nicaragua-US FCN and the BITs that were developed in the early 1960s.

Germany's efforts to conclude BITs were quickly followed by other capital exporting states: Switzerland in 1961,[245] The Netherlands in 1963,[246] Italy[247] and

---

241. On the development of German BITs, see J. Alenfeld, *Die Investitionsförderungsverträge der Bundesrepublik Deutschland* (Frankfurt, Antenäum Verlag, 1970) as cited in UNCTC, *supra* note 175 at iii. For a more recent discussion, see J. Karl, 'The Promotion and Protection of German Foreign Investment Abroad' (1996) 11 ICSID Rev 1.
242. A letter dated the same day as the BIT clarifies that the coverage of the BIT applies only to 'investments' that have been specifically approved by government agencies. See documents in *Investment Protection Treaties, supra* note 239.
243. Later German BITs included provisions on national treatment and MFN treatment. See Germany-Liberia (1961).
244. Art. 11(2), Germany-Pakistan (1959).
245. The first Swiss BIT was Switzerland-Tunisia (1961). On the Swiss BIT program, see Gattiker, 'Behandlung und Rolle von Auslandsinvestitionen im modernen Völkerrecht' (1981) 27 Schweizerisches Jahrbuch für internationales Recht 25; N. Huu-Tru, 'Le Réseau suisse d'accords bilatéraux d'encouragement et de protection des investissements' (1988) 92 RGDIP 577; M. Kraft, 'Les accords bilatéraux sur la protection des investissements conclus par la Suisse', in D. Dicke, ed., *Foreign Investment in the Present and a New International Economic Order* (Fribourg: University Press, 1987) at 72 and J. Liebeskind, 'The Legal Framework of Swiss International Trade and Investments, Part I: Promotion' (2006) JWIT 331. Part II on Protection is published in the subsequent issue at 469.
246. Netherlands-Tunisia (1963). M. Bos, 'The Protection of Foreign Investments in Dutch Court and Treaty Practice,' in H.F. van Panhuys, W.P. Heere *et al.*, eds, *International Law in The Netherlands* (Alphen aan den Rijn: Sijthoff & Noordhoff; Dobbs Ferry, NY: Oceana Publications, 1978-1980), Vol. 3 at 221.
247. Guinea-Italy (1964).

the Belgo-Luxembourg Economic Union (BLEU)[248] in 1964, Sweden[249] and Denmark[250] in 1965, Norway in 1966,[251] France in 1972,[252] the UK in 1975,[253] Austria in 1976[254] and Japan in 1977.[255] BITs in this period were generally quite short – approximately five to six pages and focused on core protections such as national treatment, MFN treatment, a general minimum standard of treatment, compensation for expropriation and rights to transfer capital and returns. Many of the BITs in this period were based on the 1962 and 1967 OECD Draft Conventions.

A characteristic of BITs during this period was the asymmetrical economic and political relationship that existed between capital exporting and importing states. Although the obligations on the state parties to BITs were formally reciprocal, BITs were developed by capital exporting states to protect the economic interests of their nationals abroad. Until Romania began concluding BITs with developing states in 1978,[256] the Iraq-Kuwait (1964) was the only one that did not fall within the developed-developing state paradigm.[257] It is also noteworthy that several major developing states did not conclude BITs until much later.

---

248. BLEU-Tunisia (1964). See W. Van de Voorde, 'Belgian Bilateral Investment Treaties as a Means for Promoting and Protecting Foreign Investment' (1991) 44 Studia Diplomatica 87.
249. Côte d'Ivoire-Sweden (1965).
250. Denmark-Madagascar (1965).
251. Madagascar-Norway (1966).
252. France-Tunisia (1972). See P. Juillard, 'Les conventions bilatérales d'investissements conclues par la France' (1979) 106 JDI 274; 'Les conventions bilatérales d'investissement conclues par la France avec des pays n'appartenant pas à la zone franc' (1982) 28 Annuaire Français de Droit International 760; 'Le réseau français des conventions bilatérales d'investissement: à la recherche d'un droit perdu?' (1987) 13 Droit et Pratique du Commerce International 9 and 'La Convention entre la France et la Roumanie sur l'encouragement, la protection et la garantie réciproque des investissements' (1988) 22 Revue Roumaine d'Etudes Internationales 211.
253. Egypt-UK (1975). On the UK BIT program, see F.A. Mann, 'British Treaties for the Promotion and Protection of Investments' (1981) 52 BYIL 241 and E. Denza & S. Brooks, 'Investment Protection Treaties: United Kingdom Experience' (1987) 36 ICLQ 910.
254. Austria-Czechoslovakia (1974). For a description of Austrian BIT practice, see Maschke, 'Investitionsabkommen' (1986) 37 Österreichische Zeitschrift für öffentliches Recht and Völkerrecht 201 and H.H. Haschek, 'Austrian Foreign Investments and Investment Protection Agreements', in D. Dicke, ed., *Foreign Investment in the Present and a New International Economic Order, supra* note 245 at 3.
255. Egypt-Japan (1977). On Japanese BITs, see Y. Matsui, 'Japan's International Legal Policy for the Protection of Foreign Investment' (1989) 32 JAIL 1 and S. Yanase, 'Bilateral Investment Treaties of Japan and Resolution of Disputes with Respect to Foreign Direct Investment', in ICCA Congress Series No. 11 (The Hague: Kluwer, 2003) at 426.
256. Romania concluded a BIT with Pakistan in 1978 and one with Sudan in 1979.
257. The one other exception is the 1970 Agreement on Investment and Free Movement of Arab Capital Among Arab Countries. See discussion in T. Pollan, *Legal Framework for the Admission of FDI* (Utrecht: Eleven International Publishing, 2006) at 146.

China, for example, did not conclude its first BIT until 1982;[258] Brazil[259] and India[260] not until 1994.

§1.31 The advent of treaty-based investor-state arbitration in BITs   The traditional form of consent to arbitration between a foreign investor and a host state was through an arbitration clause in a contract, such as a natural resource concession or a foreign investment agreement.[261] During discussions of the 1965 ICSID Convention it was recognized that states could consent to arbitrate future disputes by making an offer to arbitrate in a foreign investment code or law, or by means of a treaty. The investor would accept this offer to arbitrate by submitting a claim.[262] Therefore, unlike the typical form of consent to international arbitration through an arbitration clause in a contract, investor-state arbitration under a foreign investment law or IIA can occur where there is no pre-existing formal contractual relationship between the foreign investor and the state. Because the consent to arbitration does not occur in an investment contract or concession, this form of arbitration has been referred to as 'arbitration without privity.'[263] In this form of arbitration, the claimant's acceptance of the offer to arbitrate in a foreign investment law or treaty will normally occur upon submission of a request for arbitration.

Until 1968, BITs only provided for state-to-state dispute resolution through the establishment of an arbitral tribunal or submission of the dispute to the ICJ. It appears that the first BIT that expressly incorporates provisions for investor-state arbitration, though with qualifications, is Indonesia-Netherlands (1968).[264]

---

258. China-Sweden (1982). See note in (1985) 24 ILM 537 on China's BIT program. For a discussion of early Chinese BIT practice, see L. Shishi, 'Bilateral Investment Promotion and Protection Agreements: Practice of the People's Republic of China,' in *International Law and Development*, eds de Waart *et al.* (Dordrecht: Martinus Nijhoff, 1988) at 163-84 and Mo, 'Some Aspects of the Australia-China Investment Protection Treaty' (1991) 25 JWTL 43. See *infra* §1.42 for more recent developments.
259. Brazil-Chile (1994).
260. India-UK (1994). See §1.43 for further discussion.
261. See *supra* §1.18.
262. See Schreuer, *ICSID Commentary*, *supra* note 154 at paras 257-8. The possibility of unilateral state consent to arbitration was specifically contemplated in the Report of the Executive Directors on the Convention (*supra* note 157) noting that the consent of both parties need not be expressed in a single instrument and that a host state 'might in its investment promotion legislation offer to submit disputes arising out of certain classes of investments to the jurisdiction of the Centre, and the investor might give his consent by accepting the offer in writing.' (1 ICSID Rep at 28). See also the definition of 'date of consent' in ICSID Arbitration Rule 2(3) which highlights that acts of consent may occur at different times.
263. J. Paulsson, 'Arbitration Without Privity' (1995) 10 ICSID Rev 232. For an in-depth discussion of the nature of investment treaty arbitration see Douglas, *supra* note 27, and the various texts referenced *supra* note 5.
264. The effect of the ICSID investor-state arbitration clause in this BIT is, however, unclear. Art. 11 of Indonesia-Netherlands (1968) provides that: 'The Contracting Party in the territory of which a national of the other Contracting Party makes or intends to make an investment, *shall assent to any demand* on the part of such national and any such national shall comply

In 1969, ICSID published a series of model BIT arbitration clauses for use in BITs.[265]

Chad-Italy (1969) appears to be the first BIT that provides for investor-state arbitration with unqualified state consent.[266] This BIT, rather than Germany-Pakistan (1959), marks the true beginning of modern BIT practice because it combines substantive investment promotion and protection obligations with binding investor-state arbitration to address alleged breaches of those obligations.

The validity of a unilateral arbitration clause ('arbitration without privity') was first upheld in 1985 in *SPP v. Egypt*.[267] In this case, an ICSID tribunal found that

---

with any request of the former Contracting Party, to submit, for conciliation or arbitration, to the Centre established by the Convention of Washington of 18 Mar. 1965, any dispute that may arise in connection with the investment'. [Emphasis added.] The effect of the article is unclear. On one hand, it could be viewed as a binding offer to the investor to arbitrate. On the other hand, it could be viewed as a binding obligation on the state to agree to arbitrate if an investment dispute arises. Under this interpretation, if the state fails to assent to a demand to arbitration, this failure could be subject to state-to-state arbitration under Art. 22, which provides that disputes 'shall be submitted' to arbitration. The provision is also unusual because it provides that the investor 'shall comply' with a request for arbitration. It is difficult to see how this provision could be enforced. If the investor failed to consent to arbitration, the host state could proceed with state-to-state arbitration, but it is unclear how a private party's failure to consent to arbitration could be attributable to its home state.

265. See *Model Clauses Relating to the Convention on the Settlement of Investment Disputes Designed for Use in Bilateral Investment Agreements* (Sep. 1969) (1969) 8 ILM 1341.

266. Art. VII, Chad-Italy (1969), provides: 'Tout différend relative aux investissements faisant l'objet du présent Accord, qui pourrait surgir entre l'une des Parties contractantes (ou l'une quelconque des institutions ou organisations relevant de ladite Partie ou contrôlée par ladite Partie) et une personne physique ou morale ayant la nationalité de l'autre Partie, est soumis à la juridiction du Centre International pour le Règlement des Différends Relatifs aux Investissements, conformément à la Convention Internationale de Washington du 18 mars 1965. Toute contestation et tout différend entre les deux Parties contractantes, portant sur l'interprétation ou sur l'application du présent Accord sont réglés par la voie diplomatique.' Also see Art. VII, Côte d'Ivoire-Italy (1969), which provides a slightly different formulation: 'Tout différend concernant les investissements, objet du présent accord, qui s'élèverait entre un Etat contractant (ou n'importe quelle institution ou organisation dependantes ou contrôlées par le même Etat) et une personne physique ou morale, ayant la nationalité de l'autre Etat, sera réglé par la voie diplomatique. Si un différend ne peut être réglé de cette façon il sera soumis à la juridiction du Centre international pour le règlement des différends relatifs aux investissements, conformément à la Convention internationale de Washington du 18 mars 1965. Toute contestation ou tout différend entre les deux Etats, portant sur l'interprétation ou l'application du présent accord, seront réglés par la voie diplomatique.' Art. X, Belgium-Indonesia (1970), provides consent in very clear language: 'Each Contracting Party hereby irrevocably and anticipatory gives its consent to submit to conciliation and arbitration any dispute relating to a measure contrary to this Agreement, pursuant to the Convention of Washington of 18 March 1965, at the initiative of a national or legal person of the other Contracting Party, who considers himself to have been affected by such a measure. This consent implies renunciation of the requirement that the internal administrative or judicial resorts should be exhausted.'

267. *Southern Pacific Properties (Middle East) Limited v. Egypt* (Decision on Jurisdiction, 27 Nov. 1985) 3 ICSID Rep 112.

Egypt's foreign investment law provided consent for ICSID arbitration and that, as a result of the investor's notification of acceptance,[268] the tribunal had jurisdiction over the dispute. Five years later, in 1990, an arbitral tribunal established under the investor-state arbitration provisions of Sri Lanka-UK (1980) issued the first ICSID award where jurisdiction was based on an arbitration clause in a BIT.[269] Investment treaty arbitration had begun and, in that case, it had proven to be successful for the foreign investor.

§1.32 BITs – the 1970s and 1980s   States entered into only a small number of BITs through the 1970s – by 1979 states had entered into approximately 100 BITs.[270] As discussed above, the early 1970s were characterized by differences in views among capital exporting and importing states about the standards of treatment for foreign investment, as evidenced by the NIEO Declaration and the *Charter of Economic Rights and Duties of States*. Thus, capital importing states had little interest in, or perceived need for, BITs. Although oil-importing developing states suffered balance-of-payments deficits on current accounts as a result of the combined effect of rising import prices and falling commodity prices,[271] recycled petrodollars in the form of bank loans provided large amounts of capital for most developing states' industrialization and infrastructure programs. As a result, however, developing states' external debt ballooned.[272] By the early 1980s many developing states were unable to service their debt levels and defaulted.[273]

Other major capital exporting states became engaged in negotiating BITs through the 1970s and 1980s.[274] A significant development was the US BIT program.[275] Prior to the 1980s the US had relied on its FCN treaties as its primary

---

268.   The investor had sent a letter to Egyptian authorities expressly accepting ICSID jurisdiction over the dispute. See *ibid.*, at 120.
269.   *Asian Agricultural Products Ltd (AAPL) v. Sri Lanka* (Final Award, 27 Jun. 1990).
270.   Between 1970 and 1974, thirty-nine BITs were concluded. Between 1975 and 1979, sixty BITs were concluded. The numbers are determined by collating results from both the UNCTAD and ICSID databases.
271.   UNCTC, *supra* note 175 at 1.
272.   External debt in Latin America quadrupled from USD75 billion in 1975 to USD315 billion in 1983. See Institute of Latin American Studies, *The Debt Crisis in Latin America* (Stockholm: Nalkas Gruppen, 1986) at 69.
273.   See J. Amuzegar, 'Dealing with Debt' (1987) 68 Foreign Pol'y 140; S. Britain, 'A Very Painful World Adjustment' (1983) 61 Foreign Aff 541 and P. Kucynski, 'Latin American Debt' (1982) 61 Foreign Aff 344.
274.   UNCTC, *supra* note 175 at 7.
275.   On the US BIT program, see generally Vandevelde, *United States Investment Treaties, supra* note 43. Also see J.E. Pattison, 'The United States-Egypt Bilateral Investment Treaty: A Prototype for Future Negotiation' (1983) 16 CILQ 305; P.M. Robin, 'The BIT Won't Bite: The American Bilateral Investment Treaty Program' (1984) 33 AULR Rev 931; P.B. Gann, 'The U.S. Bilateral Investment Treaty Program' (1985) 21 SJIL 373; S. Gudgeon, US Bilateral Investment Treaties: Comments on Their Origins, Purposes and General Treatment Standards' (1986) 4 ITBL 111; K.J. Vandevelde, 'The Bilateral Investment Treaty Program of the United States' (1988) 21 CILQ 201; K.J. Vandevelde, 'U.S. Bilateral Investment Treaties: The Second Wave' (1993) 14 MJIL 621; K.J. Vandevelde, 'Of Politics and Markets:

means of investment protection.[276] In the 1970s, the US business community began lobbying the US government to conclude BITs as a means to provide to US investors protections similar to those available to investors from other capital exporting states.[277] The US government began its BIT program in 1977.[278] The primary purpose of the US program was to create a legal framework with high standards of investment protection. A secondary purpose was to depoliticize investment disputes.[279] The US BIT program, however, was not expressly designed to promote foreign investment, since US labour organizations generally opposed promoting outward investment flows.[280] Nevertheless, from the beginning, US BITs provided entry and establishment rights.[281] The US developed a model BIT in 1982 and concluded its first BIT with Egypt that same year. The US model BIT changed throughout the 1980s as the text was refined.[282]

By 1987, 265 BITs had been concluded, the majority of which continued to be between developed and developing states.[283] Developed states concluded BITs with over seventy developing states worldwide, the majority of which were in Africa and South-East Asia.[284] China signed its first BIT in 1982.[285] The 1980s also saw newly-industrializing states conclude BITs with other developing states.[286]

§1.33 BITs – the 1990s   The end of the 1980s and the 1990s witnessed an exponential growth in the conclusion of international investment and trade treaties. BITs quintupled during the 1990s.[287] Importantly, BITs were being concluded

---

the Shifting Ideology of the BITs' (1993) ITBL 159; K.J. Vandevelde, 'The Political Economy of a Bilateral Investment Treaty' (1998) 92 AJIL 621; K.J. Vandevelde, 'The Economics of Bilateral Investment Treaties' (2000) 41 HILJ 469; and Vandevelde, 'A Brief History', *supra* note 130.

276. Between 1946 and 1966, the US entered into twenty-one FCNs. Vandevelde, *United States Investment Treaties, supra* note 43 at 19.

277. Vandevelde, *United States Investment Treaties, ibid.*, noting that the US business groups including the International Chamber of Commerce and the State Department's Advisory Committee on Transnational Enterprises recommended that the State Department commence a BIT program.

278. Vandevelde, *United States Investment Treaties, ibid,* at 19-22.

279. See the description of the Hickenlooper Amendment to the United States Foreign Assistance Act, denial of preferential trade treatment under the US Trade Act of 1974 and opposition to international financial assistance by international financial institutions. Akinsanya, *supra* note 50 at 284-300 and Vandervelde, *United States Investment Treaties, ibid.,* at 13-14 and 22-28.

280. Vandevelde, *United States Investment Treaties, ibid.,* at 22.

281. *Ibid.,* at 72.

282. *Ibid.,* at 29-43.

283. UNCTC, *supra* note 175 at 6.

284. *Ibid.*

285. *Ibid.,* at 39.

286. By 1987, twelve of the 265 BITs had been concluded between developing states. *Ibid.,* at 6.

287. UNCTAD Press Release, 'Bilateral Investment Treaties Quintupled During the 1990s', 15 Dec. 2000, TAD/INF/2877. The press release notes that there were 1857 BITs by the end of the 1990s, up from 385 at the end of the 1980s.

between non-industrialized states.[288] By the end of the 1990s, 1857 BITs had been concluded.[289] Several industrializing states, including India,[290] Argentina, Brazil and Chile signed their first BITs,[291] and OECD states such as Canada[292] and Australia[293] followed the US in creating BIT programs.

The explosion in IIA practice had two major causes.[294] First, there was an increased political commitment by governments in both developed and developing states to economic liberalism and the freer international flow of goods, services and investment. The economic success of the several Asian economies, which had promoted private investment and export production, was viewed as discrediting import substitution policies that had been the dominant economic development model in the immediate post-WWII era. IIAs were regarded as aiding the flow of the investment required for development. The positive economic development role to be played by IIAs was reinforced by the Washington Consensus – a consensus between the IMF, the World Bank and the US Treasury on the policies for developing states' economic development and stabilization.[295] The pillars of the Washington Consensus were fiscal austerity, privatization and market liberalization. The original 1989 consensus included the promotion of FDI and the enforcement of property rights.[296]

The second main cause of the BIT boom was the lack of developing state alternatives to FDI. International lending and aid, both important sources of development financing in the 1970s and early 1980s, became increasingly scarce. Lending was curtailed as developing state indebtedness and defaults increased. The economic recession of the early 1980s in developed states also contributed to

---

288. By the end of the 1990s, 833 of the total of 1857 were between developing states and states in transition. *Ibid.*
289. *Ibid.*
290. India's first BIT was India-UK (1994). India had signed an exchange of notes with Germany in 1964 with respect to investment. See *Investment Protection Treaties, supra* note 239.
291. Argentina's first BIT was with Italy in 1990. Brazil's first BIT was with Portugal in 1994. Chile's first BIT was with Argentina in 1991. Brazil has not ratified any of its BITs.
292. Canada signed its first BIT in 1989 with the former Soviet Union. Canada calls its BITs Foreign Investment Promotion and Protection Agreements (FIPAs). On Canadian FIPAs, see R.K. Paterson, 'Canadian Investment Promotion and Protection Treaties' (1991) 29 CYIL 373 and J. MacIlroy, 'Canada's New Foreign Investment Protection and Promotion Agreement: Two Steps Forward, One Step Back?' (2004) 5 JWI 621.
293. Australia signed its first BIT in 1988, with China. See P.T.B. Kohona, 'Investment Protection Agreements: An Australian Perspective' (1987) 21 JWTL 79 and P. Turner, M. Mangan & A. Baykitch 'Investment Treaty Arbitration: An Australian Perspective' (2007) 24 JIA 103.
294. Vandevelde, 'A Brief History' *supra* note 130 at 177. See also Vandevelde, *supra* note 275; J. Salacuse & N. Sullivan, 'Do BITs Really Work? An Evaluation of Bilateral Investment Treaties and their Grand Bargain' (2006) HILJ 67 and Van Harten, *supra* note 5 at 38-44.
295. The term 'Washington Consensus' is attributed to economist John Williamson. See 'What Washington Means by Policy Reform' in J. Williamson, ed., *Latin American Adjustment: How Much Has Happened?* (Washington: Institute for International Economics, 1990). For a critical commentary on the Washington Consensus, see J.E. Stiglitz, *Globalization and Its Discontents* (New York: W.W. Norton, 2002).
296. Williamson, *ibid.*

a declining willingness to increase official aid, which forced developing states to look to FDI as a means of encouraging economic development.

The competition for FDI coupled with an increasing acceptance of liberal economic policies provided the fertile ground for the conclusion of IIAs. IIAs proliferated at the same time as FDI to developing states expanded.[297]

§1.34 World Bank Guidelines In 1992 the World Bank issued its *Guidelines on the Treatment of Foreign Direct Investment* (the Guidelines), which emphasized the importance and benefits of FDI and set out the policy for and legal framework governing FDI.[298] The Guidelines were part of the World Bank's wider work on the role of good governance in economic development and the Bank's promotion of the importance of the legal framework for economic development.[299] The Guidelines were created not as binding rules but as part of the evolution of generally acceptable international standards, complementing, but not substituting for, BITs. They are based on the general premise that 'equal treatment of investors in similar circumstances and free competition among them are prerequisites of a positive investment environment.'[300] The Guidelines identify a set of best practices with respect to admission, treatment, expropriation, contracts, the prevention and control of corrupt business practices, the promotion of accountability and transparency in dealings with foreign investors, and settlement of disputes. IIA tribunals have subsequently occasionally referred to the Guidelines in interpreting IIA obligations.[301]

---

297. In 1982, FDI inflows were USD59 billion and total FDI inward stock amounted to USD0.647 trillion. In 2005, FDI inflows amounted to USD916 billion and total FDI inward stock amounted to USD10.13 trillion. Inflows peaked in 2000 at USD1.4 trillion (United Nations Conference on Trade and Development, *World Investment Report 2006* (New York and Geneva: United Nations, 2006) at xvi and 9 [WIR 2006]). In the 1990's, developing states increased their share of FDI inflows from USD34 billion in 1990 (17% of global inflows) to USD149 billion in 1997 (37% of global inflows). See *World Investment Report 1998: Trends and Determinants – Overview* (New York and Geneva: United Nations, 1998) at 1-12. Of the USD916 billion world FDI inflows in 2005, inflows to developed states were USD542 billion (59%) and inflows to developing state were USD334 billion (36%). The share of South-East Europe (SEE) and the Commonwealth of Independent States (CIS) was 4%. There have been significant increases in FDI *outflows* from developing states, which totaled USD133 billion – or 17% of world outflows – in 2005 (WIR 2006, *ibid.*, at xvi). For current FDI statistics, see UNCTAD's annual *World Investment Report*.
298. Foreword, *World Bank Guidelines on the Treatment of Foreign Direct Investment*, in World Bank, *Legal Framework for the Treatment of Foreign Investment* (Washington DC: The World Bank, 1992). The Guidelines are *reprinted in* (1992) 31 ILM 1379. See, generally, I.F.I. Shihata, *Legal Treatment of Foreign Investment: The World Bank Guidelines* (Washington DC: The World Bank, 1993) and C. Wendrich, 'The World Bank Guidelines as a Foundation for a Global Investment Treaty: A Problem-Oriented Approach' (2005) 2 TDM.
299. See World Bank, *Governance and Development* (Washington DC: The World Bank, 1992).
300. Guideline I(3), *supra* note 298.
301. See *Fedax N.V. v. Venezuela* (Decision of the Tribunal on Objections to Jurisdiction, 11 Jul. 1997) at para. 35; *Mr. Patrick Mitchell v. Congo* (Decision on the Application for Annulment of the Award, 1 Nov. 2006) at para. 33; and *CME Czech Republic B.V. v. Czech Republic* (Final Award, 14 Mar. 2003) at para. 161.

§1.35 Developments in Latin America   Throughout the 1960s and 1970s, Latin American states maintained their general opposition to the minimum standard of treatment and supported the NIEO *Declaration and the Charter of Economic Rights and Duties of States*. Latin American states remained uncomfortable with international investment arbitration, with no Latin American state becoming a party to the ICSID Convention in the 1960s or 1970s. The general approach to foreign investment in Latin America in the 1970s is reflected in Decision 24 of the Andean Common Market (ANCOM) – the *Andean Investment Code*.[302] The Code provided for stringent regulation of foreign investment and incorporated the Calvo Doctrine by providing that Member States would not accord foreign investors more favourable treatment than national investors[303] and that states would not enter into investment instruments limiting the jurisdiction of national courts over investment disputes.[304] In the 1980s, however, Latin American states began liberalizing their foreign investment policies, and in 1987 and 1991 there was a substantial liberalization of the treatment of foreign investment as a result of two Andean Group Commission decisions.[305] By the 1990s, Latin American states were signing BITs *en masse*[306] and began to accede to the ICSID Convention[307] leaving behind the Calvo Doctrine and resistance to the minimum standards of treatment as well as to international adjudication of investment disputes.[308]

The Common Market of the Southern Cone was established in 1991 by Argentina, Brazil, Paraguay and Uruguay under the *Treaty of Asunción* (MERCOSUR).[309] In 1994, the MERCOSUR Council approved the Colonia

---

302.   ANCOM was created in 1969 by Bolivia, Chile, Ecuador and Peru under the *Cartegena Agreement*. Venezuela joined in 1973 and Chile withdrew in 1976. The *Andean Investment Code* originally appeared in 1970 (1972) 11 ILM 126 and was amended in 1976 (1977) 16 ILM 138. See L. Valdez, 'The Andean Foreign Investment Code: An Analysis' (1972) 7 JILE 1.

303.   See Muchlinski (2007), *supra* note 191 at 575-577 and Rubins & Kinsella, *supra* note 5 at 158.

304.   Arts. 50 and 51 (1977) 16 ILM 138.

305.   See *Andean Group: Commission Decision 220 Replacing Decision 24, the Common Foreign Investment and Technology Licensing Code* (1988) 27 ILM 974 and *Andean Group: Commission Decision 291 (Common Code for the Treatment of Foreign Capital and on Trademarks, Patents, Licenses and Royalties)* (1991) 30 ILM 1283.

306.   There were a handful of early BITs between European and Latin American states, namely, Colombia-Germany (1965); Costa Rica-Switzerland (1965); Ecuador-Switzerland (1968); El Salvador-France (1978); Paraguay-UK (1981); Belize-UK (1982); Costa Rica-UK (1982) and Panama-US (1982). Argentina, Chile and Brazil did not conclude their first BITs until the 1990s (see *supra* note 291).

307.   The first Latin American country to ratify the ICSID Convention was El Salvador in 1984. Significant numbers ratified in the 1990s.

308.   P. Peters & N. Schrijver, 'Latin America and International Regulation of Foreign Investment: Changing Perceptions' (1992) 39 NILR 368.

309.   The treaty is *reprinted in* (1991) 30 ILM 1041.

Protocol,[310] which provides BIT-like protections to nationals of MERCOSUR,[311] and the Buenos Aires Protocol, which provides similar protections to non-nationals.[312] However, neither of these protocols has entered into force. The *Group of Three Treaty* (between Colombia, Mexico and Venezuela), concluded in 1994, is a comprehensive free trade agreement (FTA) that, like the *North American Free Trade Agreement* (NAFTA),[313] has a chapter on investment.[314] In addition, Chile entered into an FTA with an investment chapter with Canada in 1996. Other agreements that included investment chapters have been completed in the 2000s.[315]

More recently, IIA claims and awards against Latin American states, and the renewed interest in nationalizing energy industries, have led some Latin American states to reconsider their commitment to investor-state arbitration under IIAs.[316]

---

310. See N. Rubins, 'Investment Arbitration in Brazil' (2003) 4 JWI 1071.

311. *Colonia Protocol on the Reciprocal Promotion and Protection of Investments within MERCOSUR*, signed on 17 Jan. 1994.

312. *Buenos Aires Protocol on the Promotion and Protection of Investments Made by Countries that are not Parties to MERCOSUR*, signed on 8 Aug. 1994. As of 1 Jun. 2008 neither protocol was in force.

313. *North American Free Trade Agreement Between the Government of Canada, the Government of Mexico and the Government of the United States*, 17 Dec. 1992, CTS 1994 No. 2; (1993) 32 ILM 289 (Chapters 1-9), 32 ILM 605 (Chapters 10-22) (entered into force 1 Jan. 1994) [NAFTA].

314. *Treaty on Free Trade Between the Republic of Colombia, the Republic of Venezuela and the United Mexican States*, signed on 13 Jun. 1994 available online: <http://sice.oas.org>. Chapter XVII covers investment and provides similar protections as in other modern BITs.

315. US FTAs with Latin American states include Central America-Dominican Republic-US FTA (CAFTA-DR) (2004); Chile-US FTA (2003); Colombia-US FTA (2006); Panama-US FTA (2007) and Peru-US FTA (2006).

316. Prominent manifestations of this concern are Bolivia's notice of denunciation of the ICSID Convention in May 2007 and Ecuador's notification to ICSID in Dec. 2007 that it will not consent to investment disputes regarding natural resources. See ICSID website. Further, the constitutionality of IIAs has been questioned in some countries. See, H. Rosatti, 'Los Tratados Bilaterales de Inversión, el Arbitraje Internacional Obligatorio y el Sistema Constitucional Argentino' (2003) La Ley 1; and C.S. Fayt, *La Constitución Nacional y los Tribunales Internacionales de Arbitraje* (Buenos Aires: La Ley, 2007). In Bolivia, the laws approving several BITs were challenged before the Constitutional Tribunal which dismissed the application on the basis that the constitutionality of treaties in Bolivia can only subject to an *ex ante* review (before approval) and not to an *ex post* review. See *Wilson Beimar Magne Hinojosa, Diputado Nacional contra Eduardo Rodríguez Veltzé, Presidente Constitucional de la República de Bolivia, y otro* (Sentencia TC 0031/2006, 10 May 2006). The constitutionality of NAFTA Chapter 11 has been questioned in Canada before the provincial superior court. The Ontario Court of Appeal rejected the challenge in 2006 (see *Council of Canadians et al. v. Attorney General of Canada*, Ontario Court of Appeal (Judgment, 30 Nov. 2006)).

§1.36 Developments in Africa, Middle East and Asia Many African, Middle Eastern and Asian states were early signatories to BITs. As already noted, these early BITs were generally based on model agreements prepared by capital exporting states. In the early 1980s, the Asian-African Legal Consultative Organization (AALCO)[317] published three draft BITs, which provided different models of investment liberalization and protection.[318] In 1980, the *United* treaties *Agreement for the Investment of Arab Capital in the Arab States* was signed creating an Arab Investment Court.[319] A number of other regional investment have been concluded in the Middle East and Africa.[320] In addition, the European Economic Community (EEC) and certain African, Caribbean and Pacific (ACP) states concluded the *Lomé III and Lomé IV* Conventions, both of which had sections addressing investment.[321] In 2007, the Common Market for Eastern and Southern Africa (COMESA) adopted an *Investment Agreement for the COMESA Common Investment Area.*[322]

In 1987, the Association of South East Asian Nations (ASEAN) created the *Agreement for the Promotion and Protection of Investments* (ASEAN Investment Agreement) applicable to ASEAN investors.[323] The ASEAN Investment Agreement was amended by the Jakarta Protocol in 1996. In 1998, the *Framework Agreement on the ASEAN Investment Area* (Framework Agreement) was concluded. The aim

---

317. AALCO was formed in 1956, a tangible outcome of the 1955 Bandung Conference, which forged the non-aligned movement (see <aalco.int>). The question of promotion and protection of investments was first discussed at the Jakarta Session held in Apr. 1980, in the context of regional co-operation in the field of industry among the countries of the Asian-African region. At this time, the AALCO was called Asian African Legal Consultative Committee.

318. Model A provides the highest standards of investment protection. Model B provides for more restrictive investment promotion and protection provisions. Model C provides protection similar to Model A but the protections apply to specific types of investments. The models are *reprinted in* (1984) 23 ILM 237. Online: <http://aalco.int>.

319. The first Arab Investment Court decision is *Tanmiah v. Tunisia*, 12 Oct. 2004. For a discussion of the case, see W. Ben Hamida, 'The First Arab Investment Court Decision' (2006) 7 JWIT 699. For a discussion of BITs with Arab states, see R.T. Greig, C. Annacker & R. Ziandé 'How Bilaeral Investment Treaties Can Protect Foreign Investors in the Arab World or Arab Investors Abroad' (2008) 25 JIA 257.

320. These treaties include the *Agreement on Promotion, Protection and Guarantee of Investments Among Member States of the Organisation of Islamic Conference* (1981) and *the Community Investment Code of the Economic Community of the Great Lakes Countries* (1982) (See UNCTAD IIA Compendium Vol. 9, Nos 38 and 39).

321. *Third ACP-EEC Convention* of 8 Dec. 1984 [Lomé III] (1985) 24 ILM 571 and *Fourth ACP-EEC Convention* of 15 Dec. 1989 [Lomé IV] (1990) 29 ILM 783. Lomé III and Lomé IV provide for investor-state arbitration in limited circumstances. For a discussion of the investment provisions in the Lomé Conventions see J. Paulsson, *supra* note 263 at 241-246.

322. *Investment Agreement for the COMESA Common Investment Area*, adopted at the Twelfth Summit of COMESA Authority of Heads of State and Government, held in Nairobi, Kenya, 22-23 May 2007.

323. (1988) 27 ILM 612. The ASEAN Investment Agreement was considered in *Yaung Chi Oo Trading Pte. Ltd. v. Myanmar* (Award, 31 Mar. 2003).

of the Framework Agreement is to create an ASEAN Investment Area by 2010 where all ASEAN investors would benefit from national treatment.[324]

§1.37 North American Free Trade Agreement   A significant development in the 1990s was the conclusion of the NAFTA in 1992.[325] The NAFTA is a comprehensive free trade agreement between Canada, Mexico and the US covering, among other things, goods, services, government procurement and investment. Chapter Eleven, the investment chapter, was unique at the time because of the breadth of its coverage and its provision for investor-state arbitration between an OECD Member State and nationals of another OECD Member State. Although the investor-state arbitration provisions were originally included in NAFTA at US insistence in order to protect US investors in Mexico, a number of high profile claims have been made against the US and Canada. Over forty-five claims have been commenced under NAFTA Chapter Eleven,[326] resulting in a series of important IIA orders, decisions and awards addressing procedural and jurisdictional issues, as well as the substantive scope of investment protections.[327] NAFTA investment practice and jurisprudence is considered in detail in subsequent chapters.

§1.38 Energy Charter Treaty   The *Energy Charter Treaty* (ECT) was concluded in 1994 and covers multilateral co-operation in the areas of energy transit, trade, investments, environmental protection and energy efficiency.[328] The ECT's

---

324. For a discussion of the ASEAN investment protection framework and more generally for developments in Asia, see J. Savage, 'Investment Treaty Arbitration and Asia: Survey and Comment' (2005) 1 AIAJ 3 and 'Investment Treaty Arbitration and Asia: Recent Developments in 2005 and 2006' (2007) 3 AIAJ 1.
325. NAFTA, *supra* note 313.
326. Documents relating to NAFTA claims are available on the official Canadian, Mexican and US NAFTA websites and naftaclaims.org.
327. For a comprehensive negotiating history of Chapter Eleven and analysis of Chapter Eleven jurisprudence, see M. Kinnear, A.K. Bjorklund & J. Hannaford, *Investment Disputes Under NAFTA: An Annotated Guide to NAFTA Chapter 11* (The Netherlands: Kluwer Law International, 2006); H.C. Alvarez, 'Arbitration under the North American Free Trade Agreement' (1999) 16 AI 393; C. Brower, II, 'Investor-State Disputes Under NAFTA: The Empire Strikes Back' (2001) 40 CJTL 43; J.C. Thomas, 'A Reply to Professor Brower' (2002) 40 CJTL 433; C. Brower, II, 'Beware the Jabberwock: A Reply to Mr. Thomas' (2002) 40 CJTL 465; G.A. Alvarez & W.W. Park, 'The New Face of Investment Arbitration: NAFTA Chapter 11' (2003) 28 YJIL 365; C.H. Brower, II, 'Structure, Legitimacy, and NAFTA's Investment Chapter.' (2003) 36 VJTL 37; J. Coe, 'Taking Stock of NAFTA Chapter 11 in Its Tenth Year: An Interim Sketch of Selected Themes, Issues, and Methods' (2003) VJTL 36. Also see the collection of papers in L.R. Dawson, ed., *Whose Rights?: The NAFTA Chapter 11 Debate* (Ottawa: Centre for Trade Policy and Law, 2002) and T. Weiler, ed., *NAFTA Investment Law and Arbitration: Past Issues, Current Practice, Future Prospects* (Ardsley: Transnational Publishers, 2004).
328. The treaty, reprinted at (1995) 34 ILM 360, was concluded in 1994 and entered into force in 1998. As of 1 Jun. 2008, forty-six states and the EC have ratified the ECT, including most European states. Australia, Belarus, Iceland, Norway and Russia have signed the treaty but not yet ratified it. A number of other states, including Canada, China, a number of Middle Eastern states and the US are observers. See online <http://encharter.org>. For background

investment protection provisions are similar to those found in other BITs, although they only apply to investments in the energy sector. To date, eighteen investor-state claims have been commenced under the ECT, resulting in a number of awards.[329]

§1.39 World Trade Organization   The World Trade Organization (WTO) was established on 1 January 1998 as a result of the Uruguay Round trade negotiations.[330] Under pre-WTO GATT law, the GATT applied only to a limited number of trade-related investment measures (TRIMs), primarily those that link foreign investment to a requirement to use domestic goods.[331] During the Uruguay Round (1986-1994), the US pushed for greater discipline on TRIMs and sought a code that would further liberalize market access for investment.[332] The majority of the GATT members, however, rejected this proposal, preferring to clarify the types of measures that breached the existing GATT obligations.[333] The accord attained as part of the Uruguay Round, *Agreement on Trade-Related Investment Measures* (TRIMS Agreement),[334] reaffirms that WTO Members may not apply investment measures that are inconsistent with GATT national treatment obligations or that otherwise violate the general prohibition on quantitative restrictions on imports and exports of goods.

In addition to the TRIMS Agreement, the Uruguay Round produced the *General Agreement on Trade in Services* (GATS), which liberalizes trade in services. The GATS includes a commitment with respect to commercial presence, essentially creating rights for foreign investors to invest in service sectors covered

---

on the ECT, see T. Wälde., ed., *The Energy Charter Treaty: An East-West Gateway for Investment and Trade* (London: Kluwer Law, 1996); R. Happ, 'Dispute Settlement under the Energy Charter Treaty' (2003) 45 GYIL 331; T. Wälde, 'Energy Charter Treaty-based Investment Arbitration – Controversial Issues' (2004) 5 JWIT 373 and C. Ribeiro, *Investment Arbitration and the Energy Charter Treaty* (New York: Juris, 2007). See also P. Cameron, *International Energy Investment Law* (Oxford: Oxford University Press, forthcoming).

329.   As of 14 Jun. 2008, the Energy Charter Secretariat listed eighteen ECT investor-state dispute settlement cases on its website. Thirteen of the cases were pending, two had been settled by the parties and in three cases tribunals had made a final award. The three final awards are: *Nykomb Synergetics Technology Holding AB v. Latvia* (Award, 16 Dec. 2003); *Petrobart Limited v. Kyrgyz Republic* (Award, 29 Mar. 2005) and *Limited Liability Company Amto v. Ukraine* (Award, 26 Mar. 2008). In addition, there are two decisions on jurisdiction: *Plama Consortium Limited v. Bulgaria* (Decision on Jurisdiction, 8 Feb. 2005) and *Ioannis Kardassopoulos v. Georgia* (Decision on Jurisdiction, 6 Jul. 2007).

330.   See *The Legal Texts: Results of the Uruguay Round of Multilateral Trade Negotiations* (Cambridge: Cambridge University Press, 1994) [Legal Texts].

331.   See *infra* Chapter 8, §8.15.

332.   See T. Stewart, 'Trade Related Investment Measures' in T. Stewart, ed., *The GATT Uruguay Round: A Negotiating History* (Boston: Kluwer Law International, 1994) at 2348. See also *infra* Chapter 8, §8.15.

333.   P. Civello, 'The TRIMS Agreement: A Failed Attempt at Investment Liberalization' (1999) 8 MJGT 97.

334.   *Agreement on Trade-Related Investment Measures*, Apr. 15, 1994, Marrakesh Agreement Establishing the World Trade Organization, Annex 1A, reproduced in Legal Texts, *supra* note 330.

by GATS commitments.[335] For this reason, the GATS can be considered as being the first multilateral investment liberalization treaty.

§1.40 Multilateral Agreement on Investment (MAI)   Although states have been willing to create a network of IIAs in a piece-meal way, states have been unable agree on investment issues at a multilateral level. Following the failure to obtain investment protection in the Uruguay Round agreements, the US promoted negotiations for a *Multilateral Agreement on Investment* (MAI) within the OECD. The strategy was to conclude a multilateral agreement with high standards of protection amongst OECD members and other willing states, and then to open the agreement to other states.[336] Negotiations for the *MAI* were conducted by OECD Member States between 1995 and 1998.[337] However, MAI negotiations were commenced at the same time that several NAFTA investment claims attained a high public profile. This and disagreements between the negotiating states on a broad range of issues, as well as concerns raised by non-governmental organizations (NGOs) about the procedural and substantive protections afforded by investment treaties, resulted in the abandonment of the draft MAI.[338]

§1.41 WTO Working Group on the Relationship between Trade and Investment and the Doha Declaration   As a result of the 1996 WTO Singapore Declaration, a Working Group on the Relationship between Trade and Investment (Working Group) was established, which began studying the nexus between trade and investment. The abandonment of the MAI negotiations in 1998 led to renewed interest amongst some states to provide the WTO a role in international investment rules. In the 2001 *Doha Declaration*, WTO members recognized 'the case for a multilateral framework to secure transparent, stable and predictable conditions for long-term cross-border investment.'[339] The Declaration directed the Working Group to focus on several investment issues,[340] with the formal decision on the

---

335. See *infra* Chapter 3, §3.14.
336. For commentary see J.W. Salacuse, 'Towards a Global Treaty on Foreign Investment: The Search for a Grand Bargain' in N. Horn, ed., *Arbitrating Foreign Investment Disputes* (The Hague: Kluwer Law International, 2004) at 51.
337. The Multilateral Agreement on Investment: Draft Consolidated Text, DAFFE/MAI(98)7/REV1; The Multilateral Agreement on Investment: Commentary to the Consolidated Text, DAFFE/MAI(98)8/REV1. See also the database containing documents from the negotiations, online: <http://www1.oecd.org/daf/mai/index.htm>.
338. See S. Picciotto, 'Linkages in International Investment Regulation: The Antinomies of the Draft Multilateral Agreement on Investment' (1998) UPJIEL 731; R. Geiger, 'Towards a Multilateral Agreement on Investment' (1998) 31 CILQ 467; C. Schittecatte, 'The Politics of the MAI – On the Social Opposition of the MAI and its Role in the Demise of the Negotiations' (2000) 1 JWI 329; J. Kurtz, 'A General Investment Agreement in the WTO? Lessons from Chapter 11 of NAFTA and the OECD Multilateral Agreement on Investment' (2002) 23 UPJIEL 713 and P. Sauve 'Multilateral Rules on Investment: Is Forward Movement Possible' (2006) 9 JIEL 325.
339. Para. 20, *Doha Declaration,* 14 Nov. 2001, 41 ILM 746 [*Doha Declaration*].
340. These were scope and definition; transparency; non-discrimination; modalities for pre-establishment commitments based on a GATS-type, positive list approach; development

beginning of negotiations on a possible text to be taken at the next WTO Ministerial Conference in 2003. In the lead-up to the 2003 Ministerial Conference, developing state members opposed negotiation of the 'Singapore Issues' (trade and investment, trade and competition, transparency in government procurement and trade facilitation).[341] Disagreement between WTO members on including investment in the Doha Round is seen as a major factor in the breakdown of the Doha negotiations. At the 2003 Ministerial Conference, the EC Trade Commissioner agreed to drop investment from the Doha agenda, a decision later supported by the US. As a result, there is unlikely to be any comprehensive discussion of investment disciplines within the WTO in the foreseeable future.[342]

§1.42 Chinese IIAs   Although China did not enter its first BIT until 1982,[343] over the past twenty five years, China has signed a significant number of BITs. With over 120 BITs, it ranks only second to Germany in the numbers of BITs concluded.[344] Although China is the largest recipient of FDI among developing economies,[345] it has increasingly become a major source of FDI, with significant Chinese investment in Africa and Asia.[346] Since 1998, Chinese BIT policy has increasingly addressed the protection of Chinese overseas FDI.[347] Importantly, beginning with Barbados-China (1998), China changed its practice of limiting investor-state arbitration to disputes concerning the amount of compensation resulting from expropriation and consented generally to the arbitration of IIA disputes.[348] Current Chinese BIT practice is reflected in China's BITs with The Netherlands (2001) and Germany (2003). Unlike early Chinese BITs, which provided for significant limitations in substantive and procedural protections,[349] China's most recent BITs provide

---

provisions; exceptions and balance-of-payments safeguards; consultation; and the settlement of disputes between members (*Doha Declaration, ibid.*, at para. 22).

341. See M. Trebilcock & R. Howse, *The Regulation of International Trade*, 3rd edn (London: Routledge, 2005) at 498.

342. *Ibid.*, at 461.

343. China-Sweden (1982).

344. UNCTAD, *Recent Developments in* international investment agreement, *IIA Monitor No. 3 (2007)*, UNCTAD/WEB/ITE/IIA/2007/6 [IIA Monitor No. 3 (2007)] at 2. Germany ranks first with BITs concluded (134), followed by China (120) and Switzerland (114).

345. UNCTAD, *World Investment Report 2007* (United Nations: Geneva: 2007) [WIR 2007] at 41.

346. WIR 2007, *ibid.*, at 41-44.

347. See C. Congyan, 'Outward Foreign Direct Investment Protection and the Effectiveness of Chinese BIT Practice' (2006) 7 JWIT 621. See also Savage, *supra* note 324; A. Chen 'Should the Four Great Safeguards in Sino-Foreign Bits Be Hastily Dismantled – Comments on Provisions Concerning Dispute Settlement in Model U.S. and Canada Bits' (2006) 7 JWIT 899; S. Schill, 'Tearing Down the Great Wall: The New Generation Investment Treaties of the People's Republic of China' (2007) 15 CJICL 73; P. Turner, 'Investor-State Arbitration' in M. Moser, ed., *Managing Business Disputes in Today's China: Duelling with Dragons* (Hague: Kluwer Law International, 2007) and W. Shan & N. Gallagher, *Chinese Investment Treaties: Policies and Practice* (Oxford: Oxford University Press, forthcoming).

348. See Congyan, *ibid.*, at 638.

349. Older Chinese BITs limit (i) the scope of national treatment to treatment in accordance with domestic laws and regulations; (ii) transfer rights; and (iii) recourse to investor-state

substantive and procedural protections generally similar to capital exporting state BITs.[350] China has also begun to conclude free trade agreements with wide-ranging procedural and substantive investment obligations.[351]

§1.43 Indian IIAs The US proposed concluding an FCN Treaty with India shortly after Indian independence in 1947.[352] These talks floundered because of India's inward looking economic policy, a policy that continued until the 1980s.[353] Between 1988 and 1991, India began to embrace the prescriptions of economic liberalization.[354] This policy change led to the rapid development an IIA program. India signed the MIGA Convention in 1992. In 1993, it signed a *Third-Generation Cooperation Agreement on Partnership and Development* with the EU, which called for the development of India's IIAs. India signed its first IIA with the UK in 1994.[355] As of December 2006, India had signed sixty-one IIAs, of which forty-nine were ratified, and was in negotiations with forty-one other countries.[356] In addition, India has entered into economic co-operation agreements that contain investment chapters.[357] All of India's IIAs adopt the principle of direct investor-state arbitration.

IV   CURRENT STATUS OF THE NETWORK OF IIAS

§1.44 The expanding network of IIAs The current international legal framework governing foreign investment consists of a network of over 2800 IIAs.[358] By the end of 2006, this network comprised some 2573 BITs[359] (of which 75% had

---

arbitration to the determination of compensation for expropriation. Congyan, *ibid.,* at 638.

350. There are some important exceptions. For example, national treatment does not apply to existing non-conforming measures and the investor must have exhausted a domestic administrative review procedure before submission of the claim (see China-Netherlands (2001)). For a comparison of older and newer model Chinese BITs see articles cited *supra* at note 347.

351. See Chapter 11 (Investment), *China-New Zealand Free Trade Agreement* (2008).

352. See D. Krishan, 'India and International Investment Laws' in B. Patel, ed., *India and International Law* Vol. 2 (London: Brill, 2008) 277.

353. *Ibid.,* at 291-294.

354. *Ibid.,* at 294-295.

355. *Ibid.,* at 297. India based its model BIT upon a not very significant adaptation of the UK Model BIT. The UK Model BIT, in turn, was created in the mid-1970s and was based on the 1967 Draft OECD Convention, the ICSID Convention and German and Swiss BIT practice. See, for example, Egypt-UK (1975).

356. Krishan, *supra* note 352 at 298. India has since signed an IIA with China. Negotiations with the US and Canada are ongoing.

357. See *India-Singapore Comprehensive Economic Co-operation Agreement* (2005).

358. Note by the UNCTAD Secretariat, 'International Investment Rulemaking', 22 May 2007, TD/B/COM.2/EM.21/2 [International Investment Rulemaking]. For earlier statistics see UNCTAD, *World Investment Report 2006* (Geneva: United Nations, 2006) at xix. Current statistics are available on the UNCTAD webpage on IIAs.

359. International Investment Rulemaking, *ibid.* at 3.

entered into force[360]) and 241 bilateral or trilateral free trade and investments agreements.[361] The network also includes a number of important regional and sectoral agreements that include investment protection provisions, notably NAFTA, the ECT and the *Framework Agreement on the ASEAN Investment Area*.[362] In addition, there is a network of 2,651 double taxation treaties.[363]

Although historically BITs developed in an asymmetrical context in which developing states exported capital and developing states imported capital, in recent years developing states have been concluding IIAs between themselves. In 1990, there were 42 BITs between developing states. This number jumped to 679 by the end of 2006 – 26% of existing BITs.[364] Further, there were over 90 south-south free trade and investment agreements by the end of 2006.[365] This reflects the economic reality that developing states are increasingly capital exporters.[366] As a result, there is a global, decentralized and overlapping network of IIAs that protect foreign investment.[367]

§1.45 The increase in investor-state arbitrations   Despite the fact that investor-state arbitration provisions had been included in IIAs since 1968, until 1990 there were no reported IIA arbitrations. The first reported IIA award was *Asian Agricultural Products Ltd v. Sri Lanka (AALP)* a claim under the Sri Lanka-UK BIT arising from the destruction of a shrimp farm by Sri Lankan security forces.[368] The tribunal ultimately awarded the investor USD460,000 in damages for the destruction of the farm. The *AAPL* award was followed by an award against Poland in 1995 that is not publicly available,[369] an award against Zaire in 1997 under the

---

360. UNCTAD, 'The Entry into Force of Bilateral Investment Agreements (BITs),' IIA Monitor No. 3 (2006), UNCTAD/WEB/ITE/IIA/2006/9.
361. International Investment Rulemaking, *supra* note 358 at 4.
362. Others include the Colonia and Buenos Aires Investment Protocols of MERCOSUR; the *Unified Agreement for the Investment of Arab Capital in the Arab States*; and the *Agreement on Promotion, Protection and Guarantee of Investments Among Member States of the Organisation of Islamic Conference*. See *infra* §§1.35 to 1.38.
363. International Investment Rulemaking, *supra* note 358 at 3. On double taxation treaties see, UNCTAD, *Taxation*, UNCTAD Series on issues in international investment agreements (New York and Geneva: United Nations, 2000) (UNCTAD/ITE/IIT/16). Also see the OECD's extensive publications and analysis of taxation treaties.
364. International Investment Rulemaking, *supra* note 358 at 6. Also see UNCTAD, *Recent Developments in International Investment Agreements,* IIA Monitor No. 2 (2005) (New York and Geneva: United Nations, 2005) at 4.
365. *Ibid.*
366. There have been significant increases in FDI outflows from developing states, which totaled USD133 billion – or 17% of world outflows – in 2005.
367. International Investment Rulemaking, *supra* note 358 at 6.
368. *Asian Agricultural Products Ltd (AAPL) v. Sri Lanka* (Final Award, 27 Jun. 1990).
369. *Saar Papier Vertriebs GmbH v. Poland.* See Investment Law and Policy Weekly News Bulletin, 5 Jan. 2004.

US-Zaire BIT,[370] and a decision on jurisdiction under Netherlands-Venezuela (1991).[371]

According to UNCTAD, by the end of 2007, there were 290 known IIA arbitrations, the majority of which had been commenced under BITs.[372] Over two-thirds of the claims have been filed since 2001[373] – 182 of these claims were filed with ICSID,[374] 80 under the UNCITRAL Rules and 14 under the Stockholm Chamber Commerce Rules.[375] The remaining claims were filed under other international and regional arbitral rules.[376] Of the ICSID claims, 46 have been brought against Argentina, 44 of which relate to the measures taken by Argentina in the early 2000s to address its economic crisis.[377] Recent studies have begun to empirically analyze trends in IIA awards.[378]

§1.46 IIA jurisprudence The growing body of IIA arbitration decisions has created a specialized body of jurisprudence. Although there is no formal doctrine

---

370. *American Manufacturing & Trading, Inc. v. Zaire* (Final Award, 21 Feb. 1997).
371. *Fedax N.V. v Venezuela* (Decision of the Tribunal on Objections to Jurisdiction, 11 Jul. 1997).
372. See UNCTAD, *Latest Developments in Investor-State Dispute Settlement*, IIA Monitor No. 1 (2008), UNCATD/WEB/ITE/IIA/2008/3 [IIA Monitor No. 1 (2008)]. For earlier reports, see International Investment Rulemaking, *supra* note 358 at 5 and UNCTAD, 'Investor State Disputes Arising from Investment Treaties: A Review', UNCTAD/ITE/IIT/2005/4. [UNCTAD, 'Investor-State Disputes']. A 2007 International Institute for Sustainable Development report highlights, however, that the number of non-ICSID IIA claims may be significantly higher since claims may proceed under arbitration rules that require no public disclosure. See L.E. Peterson 'Investment Treaty News: 2006 – A Year in Review' (Winnipeg: IISD, 2007).
373. *Supra* note 358.
374. See International Investment Rulemaking, *supra* note 358 at 5. Also see UNCTAD, 'Investor-State Disputes', *supra* note 372 at 4.
375. IIA Monitor No. 1 (2008), *supra* note 372. The UNICTRAL Arbitration Rules were adopted by the United Nations Commission on International Trade Law in 1976 as a comprehensive set of procedural rules to govern international commercial arbitrations. For commentary on the rules in the context of foreign investment see D. Caron, *The UNCITRAL Arbitration Rules: A Commentary* (Oxford: Oxford University Press, 2006) and S. Baker & M. Davis, *The UNCITRAL Arbitration Rules in Practice: The Experience of the Iran-United States Claims Tribunal* (Deventer: Kluwer Law and Taxation Publishers, 1992). Despite their widespread use, there is concern that the 30 year old UNCITRAL Rules need to be updated to reflect developments and changes in international arbitral practice. UNCITRAL is considering revisions to the rules. See UNCITRAL, Secretariat Note, 'Settlement of commercial disputes: Revisions of the UNCITRAL Arbitration Rules' (20 Jul. 2006) A/CN.9/WG.II/WP.143. UNCITRAL commissioned Jan Paulsson and Georgios Petrochilos to report on recommendations for revisions. See J. Paulsson & G. Petrochilos, 'Revisions of the UNCITRAL Rules' (2006), available on the UNCITRAL website.
376. IIA Monitor No. 1 (2008), *supra* note 372.
377. IIA Monitor No. 1 (2008), *ibid.* For a summary of events see J.F. Hornbeck, 'The Argentine Financial Crisis: A Chronology of Events' US Congressional Research Service Report No. RS21130, 31 Jan. 2002.
378. See S.D. Franck, 'Empirically Evaluating Claims About Investment Treaty Arbitration' (2007) 86 NCLR 1 and 'Empiricism and International Law: Insights from Investment Treaty Dispute Resolution' (2008) 48 VJIL 767. Also see Van Harten, *supra* note 5 at 30-34.

of *stare decisis* or precedent in public international law,[379] in practice IIA tribunals refer to and rely on previous IIAs awards and decisions to support their interpretation of IIAs.[380] The tribunal in *ADC Affiliate Limited and ADC & ADMC Management Limited v. Hungary*, noted:

> The Parties to the present case have also debated the relevance of international case law relating to expropriation. It is true that arbitral awards do not constitute binding precedent. It is also true that a number of cases are fact-driven and that the findings in those cases cannot be transposed in and of themselves to other cases. It is further true that a number of cases are based on treaties that differ from the present BIT in certain respects. However, cautious reliance on certain principles developed in a number of those cases, as persuasive authority, may advance the body of law, which in turn may serve predictability in the interest of both investors and host States.[381]

A recent empirical study on the incidence of citation to previous awards highlights that the jurisprudence has been facilitated by: the publication and ready availability of IIA awards and decisions; the similarity between provisions amongst IIAs; and the comparatively small number of arbitrators many of whom sit on multiple cases.[382] As noted by a leading IIA practitioner and arbitrator:

> That a special jurisprudence is developing from the leading awards in the domain of investment arbitration can only be denied by those determined to close their eyes.[383]

The existence of a growing body of IIA case law has not necessarily resulted in a consistent jurisprudence. As will be explored throughout this book, there are

---

379. Art. 59, *Statute of the International Court of Justice* provides that '[t]he decision of the Court has no binding force except between the parties and in respect of that particular case.' Art. 38 states that judicial decisions constitute only 'subsidiary means for the determination of rules of law.' See A. Zimmermann *et al.*, eds, *Statute of the International Court of Justice: A Commentary* (Oxford: Oxford University Press, 2006) at 1244. Art. 53 of the ICSID Convention provides that the '[t]he award shall be binding on the parties,' which has been interpreted 'as excluding the applicability of the principle of binding precedent to successive ICSID cases.' C. Schreuer, *ICSID Commentary, supra* note 154 at 1082. See *infra* Chapter 2, §2.23.
380. See J. Commission, 'Precedent in Investment Treaty Arbitration: A Citation Analysis of a Developing Jurisprudence' (2007) 24 JIA 129 for an in-depth survey of this phenomenon. For statements by tribunals on the use of previous IIA awards and decisions see *CMS Gas Transmission Company v. Argentina* (Decision of the Tribunal on Objections to Jurisdiction, 17 Jul. 2003); *El Paso Energy International Company v. Argentina* (Decision on Jurisdiction, 27 Apr. 2006); *Suez, Sociedad General de Aguas de Barcelona S.A., and InterAgua Servicios Integrales del Agua S.A. v. Argentina*, (Decision on Jurisdiction, 16 May 2006); and *Jan de Nul N.V., Dredging International N.V. v. Egypt* (Decision on Jurisdiction, 16 Jun. 2006). Also see *infra* T. Cheng, 'Precedent and Control in Investment Treaty Arbitration' (2007) 30 FILJ 1014. See *infra* Chapter 2, §2.23 on the use of precedent in IIA arbitrations.
381. Award of the Tribunal, 2 Oct. 2006, at para. 293.
382. *Ibid.*, at 136 *et seq.*
383. J. Paulsson, 'International Arbitration and the Generation of Legal Norms: Treaty Arbitration and International Law,' in ICCA Congress Series No. 13 (The Hague: Kluwer, 2007).

inconsistencies in the IIA case law. One of the purposes of this book is to examine critically the emerging jurisprudence and, where possible, provide a statement of applicable principles.

§1.47 Renegotiation and new model IIAs The rapid developments in IIA practice and jurisprudence has led states to renegotiate older IIAs and to develop new model IIAs to address issues of concern.[384] By June 2007, a total of 109 BITs had been renegotiated. Germany, the state that initiated the first BIT program, led this development with thirteen renegotiated BITs, followed by China and Morocco with twelve renegotiated BITs each.[385]

The experience of the US and Canada as respondents in NAFTA investment arbitrations has lead these states to create new Model BITs that clarify the scope and meaning of investment obligations, including the minimum standard of treatment, expropriation and MFN treatment. The new model treaties also address various issues related to investor-state arbitration, including the ability of non-disputing parties to participate in the proceedings.[386] The Canadian (2003),[387] US (2004)[388] and Norwegian (2007)[389] Model BITs, along with the investment chapters in recent free trade and investment agreements,[390] suggest that the IIA regime is continuing to evolve.[391]

---

384. See UNCTAD, Investor-State Dispute Settlement and Impact on Investment Rulemaking, UNCTAD/ITE/IIA/2007/3 (United Nations, Geneva, 2007) [UNCTAD, Investor-State Dispute Settlement and Impact on Investment Rulemaking] for a discussion of the impact of IIA arbitrations on IIA practice.

385. IIA Monitor No. 3 (2007), *supra* note 344.

386. UNCTAD, Investor-State Dispute Settlement and Impact on Investment Rulemaking, *supra* note 384.

387. See J. MacIlroy, *supra* note 292.

388. For commentary see G.A. Alvarez & W.W. Park, *supra* note 327; C.H. Brower, II, 'Investor-State Arbitration, and the Law of State Immunity' (2005) 20 AUILR 907; J. Coe Jr., 'The State of Investor-State Arbitration-Some Reflections on Professor Brower's Search for Sensible Principles' (2005) 20 AUILR 931; W.S. Dodge, 'Investor-State Dispute Settlement Between Developed Countries: Reflections on the Australia-United States Free Trade Agreement' (2006) 39 VJTL 1; D. Gantz, 'The Evolution of FTA Investment Provisions: From NAFTA to the United States-Chile Free Trade Agreement' (2004) 19 AUILR 679; B. Legum, 'Lesson Learned from the NAFTA: The New Generation of U.S. Investment Treaty Arbitration Provisions' (2004) 19 ICSID Rev 344 and S.M. Schwebel, 'The United States 2004 Model Bilateral Investment Treaty: An Exercise in the Regressive Development of International Law,' in G. Aksen *et al.*, eds, *Reflections on International Law, Commerce and Dispute Resolution, Liber Americorum in honour of Robert Briner*, (Paris: International Chamber of Commerce, 2005) 815.

389. The 2007 Norwegian Model BIT and commentary is available on <http://ita.law.uvic.ca>.

390. For example, see Chapter 6 (Investment), *India-Singapore Comprehensive Economic Co-operation Agreement* (2005) and Chapter 11 (Investment), *China-New Zealand Free Trade Agreement* (2008).

391. For an overview of developments in IIA practice in the context of sustainable development, see A. Newcombe, 'Sustainable Development and Investment Treaty Law' (2007) 8 JWIT 357.

§1.48 Investment promotion effects of IIAs   Although there is little commentary or jurisprudence on legal obligations arising from promotion clauses in IIAs,[392] there is a growing body of literature on the effects of IIAs on FDI flows. Given the rate at which states have concluded BITs, it is perhaps surprising that the empirical literature is inconclusive on the extent to which BITs result in increased FDI. Commentators have highlighted the polarized views of 'Treaty Protagonists' and 'Market Protagonists.'[393] 'Treaty Protagonists' argue that IIAs attract FDI, while 'Market Protagonists' suggest that market factors are determinative. The 2003 UNCTAD World Investment Report (WIR) concluded – with a 'Market Protagonist' argument – that 'BITs play a minor role in influencing global FDI flows.'[394] The WIR nevertheless highlights, with a 'Treaty Protagonist' argument, the 'enabling' function of IIAs in allowing a state's economic determinants to assert themselves:

> The policy framework is at best enabling, having by itself little or no effect on FDI flows. It has to be complemented by economic determinants that attract FDI, especially market size and growth, skills, abundant competitive resources and good infrastructure. As a rule, IIAs tend to make the regulatory framework more transparent, stable, predictable and secure – that is, they allow the economic determinants to assert themselves. And when IIAs reduce obstacles to FDI and the economic determinants are right, they can lead to more FDI. But it is difficult to identify the specific impact of the policy framework on FDI flows, given the interaction and relative importance of individual determinants.[395]

Although later studies provide support for a more robust relationship between IIAs and FDI levels,[396] the existence of a causal relationship and the strength of that

---

392. See *infra* Chapter 3, §3.6.
393. S. Franck, 'Foreign Direct Investment, Investment Treaty Arbitration and the Rule of Law' (2005) 19 Pacific McGeorge GBDLJ 337.
394. UNCTAD, *World Investment Report 2003* (UNCTAD: Geneva, 2003) at 89 [WIR 2003]. This conclusion is based on a 1998 aggregate statistical analysis conducted by UNCTAD. See also M. Hallward-Driemeier, 'Do Bilateral Investment Treaties Attract Foreign Direct Investment? Only a Bit ... and They Could Bite', World Bank Policy Research Working Paper Series No. 3121. Online: <http://ssrn.com/abstract=636541>; S. Rose-Ackerman & J. Tobin, 'Foreign Direct Investment and the Business Environment in Developing Countries: The Impact of Bilateral Investment Treaties', Yale Law & Economics Research Paper No. 293, May 2, 2005. Online: http://ssrn.com/abstract=557121 [Rose-Ackerman & Tobin, 'Foreign Direct Investment']; and J.W. Yackee, 'Sacrificing Sovereignty: Bilateral Investment Treaties, International Arbitration, and the Quest for Capital' (2006) USC CLEO Research Paper No. C06-15. Online: <http://ssrn.com/abstract=950567>. Also see R. Bubb & S. Rose-Ackerman, 'BITs and Bargains: Strategic Aspects of Bilateral and Multilateral Regulation of Foreign Investment' (2007) 27 IRLE 291.
395. WIR 2003, *ibid.* at 91.
396. J. Salacuse & N. Sullivan, 'Do BITs Really Work: An Evaluation of Bilateral Investment Treaties and their Grand Bargain' (2005) 46 HJIL 67; E. Neumayer & L. Spess, 'Do Bilateral Investment Treaties Increase Foreign Direct Investment to Developing Countries?' (2005) 33 WD 1567; P. Egger & M. Pfaffermayr, 'The Impact of Bilateral Investment Treaties on

relationship remain disputed.[397] For example, despite the fact that Brazil has ratified neither a BIT nor the ICSID Convention, it was the largest recipient of FDI in South America in 2005.[398] Nevertheless, even if empirical evidence of a causal relationship is inconclusive, there remains strong competitive pressure for developing states to enter into IIAs and thereby signal to foreign investors that an enabling environment for foreign investment exists.[399] In addition, firms from developing states are increasingly investing abroad, providing an incentive for these states to enter into IIAs to protect their nationals' FDI. This trend will likely continue as more developing states become FDI exporters.[400]

§1.49 Critiques of IIAs Criticisms of IIAs by NGOs and academics are wide ranging.[401] Some liken IIAs to a neo-imperialist regime designed to protect multinational capital,[402] or a form of global economic constitutionalism that subverts democratic decision making.[403] Other critics re-assert the Calvo Doctrine and reject the development of international standards and adjudication in the area of investment. There are also focused legal critiques about the scope of investment guarantees and the investor-state arbitration process.[404] These critiques typically

---

Foreign Direct Investment' (2004) 32 JCE 788 and S. Kim, 'Bilateral Investment Treaties, Political Risk, and Foreign Direct Investment' (2006), online: <http://ssrn.com>abstract=909760>.

397. S. Rose-Ackerman & J. Tobin, 'When BITS Have Some Bite: the Political-Economic Environment for Bilateral Investment Treaties' (2006), online: <http://law.yale.edu/documents/pdf/When_BITs_Have_Some_Bite.doc> [Rose-Ackerman & Tobin, 'When BITS Have Some Bite']. The authors find, in contrast to their earlier paper, *supra* note 394, that there is a positive relationship between BITs and FDI. However, the marginal impact of BITs decreases as the number of BITs worldwide grows. The study also highlights the importance of the political, economic and institutional features of the host state.

398. WIR 2006, *supra* note 297 at 69.

399. Z. Elkins, A. Guzman & B. Simmons, 'Competing for Capital: The Diffusion of Bilateral Investment Treaties, 1960-2000', UC Berkeley Public Law Research Paper No. 578961, online: <http://ssrn.com/abstract=578961>. On the motivations for signing IIAs, see A. Guzman, 'Why LDCs Sign Treaties That Hurt Them: Explaining the Popularity of BITs' (1998) 38 VJIL 639 and L. Swenson, 'Why Do Developing Countries Sign BITs' (2005) UCDJILP 131.

400. See IIA Monitor No. 3 (2007), *supra* note 344 at 4, highlighting that as of Jun. 2007, 27% of BITs are between developing states. See also WIR 2006, *supra* note 297 at 228 highlighting the expansion of FDI from developing states.

401. See J. Atik, 'Legitimacy, Transparency and NGO Participation in the NAFTA Chapter 11 Process' in T. Weiler, ed., *supra* note 327 at 135, for an overview of the concerns and issues. Also see M. Sornarajah, 'A Coming Crisis: Expansionary Trends in Investment Treaty Arbitration' in K. Sauvant, ed., *supra* note 5 at 39 and Van Harten, *supra* note 5.

402. S. Gill. 'Globalisation, Market Civilisation, and Disciplinary Neoliberalism' (1995) 24 Millennium 399 and K. Jayasuriya, 'Globalization, Sovereignty, and the Rule of Law: From Political to Economic Constitutionalism' (2001) 8 Constellations 442.

403. See D. Schneiderman, *Constitutionalizing Economic Globalization: Investment Rules and Democracy's Promise* (New York: Cambridge University Press, 2008).

404. The International Institute for Sustainable Development (IISD) has published a number of reports on the IIA regime raising concerns about IIAs. IISD's early work focused primarily on NAFTA investment obligations. For example, see H. Mann, *Private Rights, Public*

highlight three core concerns.[405] The first is that investment liberalization and treatment standards are too wide and indeterminate and their interpretation has been too expansive and pro-investment. The second broad critique focuses on the process of investor-state arbitration.[406] It is argued that investor-state arbitration is an inappropriate mechanism for what are, in essence, public regulatory disputes. Some critics recommend the wholesale replacement of investor-state arbitration with an international investment court. Alternatively, it has been suggested that an appeal mechanism should be developed to review IIA awards.[407] Still other critics focus on how arbitration rules and practices need to be changed to make the investor-state arbitration process more transparent and to address conflicts of interest. The third broad critique concerns the asymmetry of obligations in IIAs.[408] IIAs impose obligations on host states with respect to investments and investors; there are no corresponding international obligations imposed on foreign investors in the operation of investments, or on the investors' home state to require that its nationals comply with standards of conduct in their operations abroad. These criticisms are typically linked to debates about corporate social responsibility and whether international economic actors have international obligations.[409]

    Problems (Winnipeg: International Institute for Sustainable Development, 2001). Its more recent work focuses more generally on investment and sustainable development including the proposal of a *Model International Agreement on Investment for Sustainable Development*. See online: <http://iisd.org/investment>.

405.   See generally, Atik, *supra* note 401 and Van Harten, *supra* note 5. For a very critical perspective on IIAs, see S. Anderson & S. Grusky, *Challenging Corporate Investor Rule* (Washington, DC: Institute for Policy Studies and Food and Water Watch, Apr. 2007). For a recent paper highlighting a number of concerns with IIAs, see H. Mann, 'International Investment Agreements, Business and Human Rights: Key Issues and Opportunities' (Feb. 2008), online: <http://reports-and-materials.org/IISD-Ruggie-Feb-2008.pdf>.

406.   See generally Van Harten, *supra* note 5 for an in-depth analysis of the use of arbitration as a regulatory dispute settlement mechanism between foreign investors and states.

407.   For a discussion of this issue see K. Sauvant, *supra* note 5; K. Yannaca-Small, 'Improving The System Of Investor-State Dispute Settlement: An Overview' OECD Working Papers On International Investment Number 2006/1; D. Gantz, 'An Appellate Mechanism for Review of Arbitral Decisions in Investor-State Disputes: Prospects and Challenges' (2006) 39 VJTL 49; S. Franck, 'The Legitimacy Crisis in Investment Treaty Arbitration: Privatizing Public International Law Through Inconsistent Decisions' (2005) 73 FLR 1521 and S. Franck, 'Integrating Investment Treaty Conflict and Dispute Systems Design' (2007) 92 Minn LR 161.

408.   See, for example, IISD's work on a *Model International Agreement on Investment for Sustainable Development*, *supra* note 404.

409.   The question whether multinational enterprises have human rights responsibilities has been particularly controversial and is the subject of debate. See *UN Norms on the Responsibilities of Transnational Enterprises and Other Business Enterprises with regard to Human Rights* ECOSOC, Sub-Commission on Promotion and Protection of Human Rights, UN Doc E/CN.4/Sub.2/2003/12/Rev.2 (2003). For a detailed account of the provenance of the norms see D. Weissbrodt & M. Kruger, 'UN Norms on the Responsibilities of Transnational Corporation and Other Business Entities with Regard to Human Rights' (2003) 97 AJIL 901. The norms have been controversial and the ECOSOC has not accepted them. A special representative, John Ruggie, has been appointed to study the matter. See *Report of the Special Representative of the Secretary-General on the Issue of Human Rights and Transnational Corporations and Other Business Entities* (Apr. 2008) UN Doc. A/HRC/8/5. Other recent initiatives include the Global

V   STRUCTURE AND SCOPE OF APPLICATION OF IIAS

§1.50 The structure of IIAs   IIAs have a recognizable look, starting from their titles, which tend to be similar, and continuing with their structure and content. BITs in particular are often named alike. For example a common title is 'Treaty between [one contracting party] and [the other contracting party] concerning the encouragement and reciprocal protection of investment.'[410] Preambles are also often similar, providing a short statement of purposes such as 'desiring' to promote greater economic co-operation, 'recognising' that an agreement on the treatment of investment will stimulate the flow of private investment, and 'agreeing' in this context on the importance of a stable framework for investment.[411] The actual content of IIAs also follows a pattern.[412] It typically includes: (i) initial provisions establishing the scope of coverage of the IIA defining who are the 'investors' and what are the 'investments' benefiting from treaty protections, as well as often defining the notion of territory of the contracting parties, so that investments made in that territory of a contracting party by investors of another contracting party qualify as protected 'foreign' investments; (ii) clauses establishing the substantive protections accorded to those investors and/or investments; (iii) dispute resolution mechanisms both for disputes between the contracting parties and between an investor of a contracting party and another contracting party (investor-state arbitration); (iv) provisions on subrogation and on the preservation of more favourable rules to the investors (the preservation of rights clause);[413] and (v) final provisions on entry into force and termination. The following sections briefly highlight some of the above issues as an introduction to the substantive protections analysis addressed in this book.[414]

§1.51 The scope of application – investment   IIAs usually provide a definition of what constitutes an investment protected by the treaty in their initial clauses. Definitions are broad, often referring to 'every kind of asset'[415] or 'every kind of investment in the territory,'[416] and then adding a specific non-exhaustive list of

---

Compact, which the UN Secretary General launched in 2000, and the Principles for Responsible Investment launched in 2005. See A. Newcombe, *supra* note 391. See *infra* Chapter 2, §2.25, and Chapter 6, §6.11, on human rights in the IIA context.

410. For example, 1994 US Model BIT.
411. *Ibid.* On the interpretive issues that arise from IIA titles and preambular language, see *infra* Chapter 2, §2.29, Chapter 3, §3.5, and Chapter 6, §6.20 and §6.30.
412. For an overview of IIA practice, see the three comprehensive studies cited supra note 239
413. See *infra* Chapter 6, §6.48, and Chapter 9, §9.28.
414. The sections below are developed on the basis of the introductory work to IIAs in N. Blackaby & L. Paradell, 'Investment Treaty Arbitration' in *Bernstein's Handbook of Arbitration Practice* (London: Sweet & Maxwell, 2003) part 10.
415. Art. 1(a), UK-USSR (now UK-Russia) (1989), and Art. 1(6), ECT.
416. Art. I(1)(a), Argentina-US (1991).

examples. Typical in this respect is UK-USSR (1989), which provides in Article 1(a):

> the term 'investment' means every kind of asset and in particular, though not exclusively, includes:
>
> (i)   movable and immovable property and any other related property rights such as mortgages;
> (ii) shares in, and stock, bonds and debentures of, and any other form of participation in, a company or business enterprise;
> (iii) claims to money, and claims to performance under contract having a financial value;
> (iv) intellectual property rights, technical processes, know-how and any other benefit or advantage attached to a business;
> (v)   rights, conferred by law or under contract, to undertake any commercial activity, including the search for, or the cultivation, extraction or exploitation of natural resources.

With small variations, similar definitions bringing into the scope of treaties almost all possible forms of investment are found in most IIAs. These definitions cover direct, as well as indirect, investments and modern contractual and other transactions having economic value.[417] This is confirmed by decisions of tribunals in IIA arbitrations. In *Fedax N.V. v. Venezuela*, for example, the tribunal found that promissory notes issued by Venezuela, and acquired by the claimant from the original holder in the secondary market by way of endorsement, were an investment under Netherlands-Venezuela (1991).[418] The tribunal engaged in an extensive analysis of the notion of investment under IIAs, which it refused to limit to the classic forms of direct investment, i.e., 'the laying out of money or property in business ventures, so that it may produce a revenue or income,' as argued by the respondent state. Further, another ICSID tribunal has found that transactions that, taken into isolation might not qualify as investments, may nevertheless be so considered if the overall operation of which they are part, or to which they are connected, constitutes an investment.[419]

While extensive, the notion of investments obviously has limitations. In 1985, for example, the ICSID Secretary-General refused to register a case on the basis that the dispute related to a mere commercial sale and could not be qualified

---

417. See A. Parra, 'The Scope of New Investment Laws and International Instruments,' in R. Pritchard, ed., *Economic Development, Foreign Investment and the Law* (The Hague: Kluwer, 1996) at 35. UNCTAD, *Scope and Defintion*, UNCTAD Series on issues in international investment agreements (New York and Geneva: United Nations, 1999) UNCTAD/ITE/IIT/11 (Vol. II).

418. *Fedax N.V. v. Venezuela* (Decision on Jurisdiction, 11 Jul. 1997) at para. 19 *et seq.* The definition contained in the applicable BIT was substantially the same as the one quoted above.

419. *Československá Obchodní Banka, A.S. v. Slovak Republic* (Decision of the Tribunal on Objections to Jurisdiction, 24 May 1999) at para. 72 *et seq.*

as an investment.[420] Another example is the award declining jurisdiction in *Mihaly International Corporation v. Sri Lanka.* There the tribunal found that expenses incurred in preparation for obtaining a public contract, including sums spent in planning the financial and economic modeling necessary for the negotiation and finalization of the contract, were not an investment under the applicable BIT. The tribunal attached great importance to the fact that the respondent state had taken care to point out, throughout the negotiations, that these created no rights and obligations between the parties.[421] Thus, the claimant had not acquired any asset, right or interest that could fall within the notion of investment. It remains to be seen whether a different conclusion could be reached in different circumstances, for example where expectations are raised or not adequately averted by a negotiating state.

An investment is protected under a treaty, obviously, only if made by a covered investor. The point is clear and thus very few treaties provide this expressly. The exception are US BITs which provide that they apply to investments 'owned or controlled directly or indirectly' by covered investors.[422] While the principle is incontrovertible, its practical application, i.e., determining whether a particular investment can be regarded as belonging to a given investor, may be a difficult question in certain circumstances. In *Philippe Gruslin v. Malaysia,* for example, the question arose whether investors in an investment fund that held foreign shares could actually be said to own or control an investment in the territory of the foreign state where the shares were traded, so as to benefit from the BIT between that state

---

420. ICSID 1985 Annual Report at 6. It is important to distinguish between the meaning of investment for the purposes of ICSID jurisdiction under Art. 25, ICSID Convention, and the definition of investment for the purposes of an IIA. It is argued that the fact that an asset qualifies as an investment under the IIA in question does not necessarily mean that it qualifies as an investment for the purposes of the ICSID Convention. Further, there is conflicting ICSID jurisprudence on the meaning of investment under the ICSID convention. In *Salini Costruttori S.p.A. and Italstrade S.p.A. v. Morocco* (Decision on Jurisdiction, 23 Jul. 2001) the tribunal set out a test based on: (i) the existence of contributions in capital or otherwise; (ii) a certain duration; (iii) an element of risk; and added that 'the contribution to the economic development of the host state of the investment as an additional condition' for there being an investment for the purposes of the ICSID Convention (para. 52). In contrast, in *L.E.S.I. S.p.A. et ASTALDI S.p.A. v. Algeria* (Decision, 12 Jul. 2006) another ICSID tribunal found that there is no requirement under the ICSID Convention for the investment to promote economic development (para. 72). The *ad hoc* annulment committee in *Mr. Patrick Mitchell v. Congo* (Decision on the Application for the Annulment of the Award, 1 Nov. 2006) followed *Salini* and stated that the 'existence of a contribution to the economic development of the host State as an essential – although not sufficient – characteristic' of an investment for the purposes of the ICSID Convention (para. 33). For discussion of Art. 25, ICSID Convention, see Schreuer and other reference sources, *supra* note 154 at 82 *et seq.* For an analysis of the conflicting ICSID jurisprudence, see D. Krishan, 'A Notion of ICSID Investment' in T. Weiler, ed., *Investment Treaty Arbitration: A Debate and Discussion* (New York: Juris, 2008).
421. *Mihaly International Corporation v. Sri Lanka* (Award, 15 Mar. 2002) at paras 58-61.
422. See Art. I(1)(a), Argentina-US (1991).

and the investor's state.[423] The question was difficult. Formally, investment funds do not 'own' investments but just 'manage' them on behalf of their unit-holders which, on the other hand, cannot be said to control them in any meaningful (perhaps proprietary) way. Further, the case had huge potential implications. A decision favourable to the investor could have opened the door to innumerable BIT claims brought by countless disappointed partakers of investment funds, pension funds, or investment savings accounts. Ultimately the tribunal declined jurisdiction on other grounds, leaving the question unanswered.

§1.52 The scope of application – investors   IIAs typically include also a provision specifying the requirements of nationality, location, place of incorporation, etc., for a person or entity making an investment to be protected by, and thus to be able to rely on, the IIA. Together with the definition of 'investment,' this is usually found in the initial article of the treaty which, *inter alia*, defines who are the 'investors' or 'nationals' benefiting from treaty protections. Although in this, as well as in other issues, treaties vary substantially, the following provision of Bolivia-Netherlands (1992) is quite representative:

> For the purposes of the present agreement:
>   [...]
>
>   (b) the term 'nationals' shall comprise with regard to either Contracting Party:
>   (i)   natural persons having the nationality of that Contracting Party in accordance with its laws;
>   (ii) without prejudice to the provisions of (iii) hereafter, legal persons constituted in accordance with the law of that Contracting Party;
>   (iii) legal persons controlled directly or indirectly, by nationals of that contracting Party, but constituted in accordance with the law of the other Contracting Party.

Natural persons that are nationals of a state party to the IIA, and entities incorporated or constituted under the laws of such state, are thus able to rely on the treaty against the other state party to it. Some IIAs add the requirement that entities also have their seat and/or actually carry out business in the relevant state.[424]

Most IIA may be relied upon either by the entity that makes the investment directly or, when this is a separate host state entity, by the direct or indirect foreign controller of that entity, or the controlled entity itself. In this way, the obligation frequently imposed by host states on foreign investors to incorporate

---

423. *Philippe Gruslin v. Malaysia* (Award, 27 Nov. 2000).
424. See Art 1(b), Argentina-Netherlands (1992): 'the term "investor" shall comprise with regard to either Contracting Party: .... (ii) ... legal persons constituted under the law of that Contracting Party and actually doing business under the laws in force in any part of the territory of that Contracting Party in which a place of effective management is situated; and (iii) legal persons, wherever located, controlled, directly or indirectly, by nationals of that Contracting Party.'

a local entity as a vehicle for their investment does not weaken the effectiveness of the IIA, which can still be relied upon by the controlling foreign investor, or its local subsidiary. Some treaties go further, and encompass investing entities *wherever located* which are directly or indirectly controlled by investors of a state party to the IIA.[425] Control, under international law, is a flexible and broad concept, referring not only to majority shareholding, but also to other 'reasonable' criteria such as managerial responsibility, voting rights, nationality of board members, etc.[426]

In permitting to look behind strict formal criteria, to determine an entity's 'nationality' on the basis of where control or ownership is located, these IIA provisions may extend treaty coverage more vastly than it would appear at first sight. The complexities of some corporate organizations and investment vehicles may effectively allow companies to claim several foreign nationalities. Some IIAs appear to restrain this laxity by specifying that their protections extend to 'effectively' controlling entities.[427] The question arises whether a similar effective control test may be read into treaty provisions on foreign control, even absent explicit language. There is still no reported case law on this point. Nor is there a clear indication of the criteria that may be used in defining the required level of control.[428] IIA tribunals so far have been flexible and willing to uphold the rights of any legitimate investor under an applicable treaty, including where the investor is an intermediate company in the investment structure.[429] Some tribunals have expressed concern that this allows for 'treaty shopping,' i.e., it permits claimants to select as the 'investor' a company in the investment structure (or even constitute a new company, often a 'shell') simply to benefit from the provisions of a particular IIA.[430]

---

425. See, *ibid.* In any case, the foreign shareholder of a host state or third country entity would normally be able to invoke the treaty at least in relation to its participation in that entity, assuming that participation qualifies as a protected investment. See *CMS Gas Transmission Company v. Argentina* (Decision of the Tribunal on Objections to Jurisdiction, 17 Jul. 2003).

426. *Aguas del Tunari, S.A. v. Bolivia* (Decision on Respondent's Objections to Jurisdiction, 21 Oct. 2005) at paras 225 *et seq.*; *Autopista Concesionaria de Venezuela, C.A. v. Venezuela* (Decision on Jurisdiction, 27 Sep. 2001) [*Autopista*] at paras 110-125; and *Vacuum Salt Products Ltd. v. Ghana* (Award 16 Feb. 1994) at paras 38 *et seq.*

427. See Art. 1(2), Argentina-France (1991), which reads: 'The term "investors" means: ... c) legal persons effectively controlled directly or indirectly by nationals of one of the contracting Parties, or by legal persons having their seat on the territory of one of the contracting Parties and constituted in conformity with its legislation' (authors' translation from French original).

428. In a non-IIA case, an ICSID tribunal has refused the notion of effective control, suggesting instead that any reasonable criteria of control is valid under international law. The tribunal seemed to suggest, however, that a more restrictive approach could be applied in certain circumstances to prevent abuse by 'corporations of convenience exerting a purely fictional control for jurisdictional purposes.' See *Autopista, supra* note 426 at paras 110-125.

429. *Ibid.*

430. See *Saluka Investments BV v. Czech Republic* (Partial Award, 17 Mar. 2006) at para. 240: 'The Tribunal has some sympathy for the argument that a company which has no real connection with a State Party to a BIT, and which is in reality a mere shell company controlled by another

§1.53 Dispute settlement   A few early IIAs do not provide any direct right of investor action at all,[431] or they limit access to arbitration to certain specific treaty breaches, such as issues of expropriation and repatriation of profits.[432] The great majority of IIAs, however, do provide aggrieved investors with a direct right to resort to arbitration with regard to any disputes arising from alleged treaty breaches or more generally with regard to investments.

Some treaties contain the so-called 'fork in the road' provision, that is, the stipulation that if the investor submits a dispute to the local courts of the host state, or to any other agreed dispute settlement procedures, it losses the right to submit it to arbitration. This provision is, for example, contained in Article VII(2) and (3), Argentina-US (1991):

> In the event of an investment dispute, the parties to the dispute should initially seek a resolution through consultation and negotiation. If the dispute cannot be settled amicably, the national or company concerned may choose to submit the dispute for resolution:
>
> (a) to the courts or administrative tribunals of the Party that is a party to the dispute; or
> (b) in accordance with any applicable, previously agreed dispute-settlement procedures; or
> (c) in accordance with the terms of paragraph 3.
>
> Provided that the national or company concerned has not submitted the dispute for resolution under ... (a) or (b) [above] and that six months have elapsed from the date on which the dispute arose, the national or company concerned may choose to consent in writing to the submission of the dispute for settlement by binding arbitration ...

The case law seems to suggest that IIA arbitration would not be precluded by the submission to domestic courts of grievances, framed as breaches of contract, arising out of the same host state acts;[433] in order to constitute a 'fork in the road' choice, it would seem to be required that the court action raised the same IIA

---

company which is not constituted under the laws of that state, should not be entitled to invoke the provisions of that BIT. Such a possibility lends itself to abuses of the arbitral procedure, and to practices of "treaty shopping" which can share many of the disadvantages of the widely criticized practice of "forum shopping".' Although the tribunal found that Saluka fell within the broad definition of 'investor' provided by Czechoslovakia- Netherlands (1991), the tribunal's expression of 'sympathy' is a hallmark of the increasing concern displayed by IIA tribunals about 'treaty shopping' by claimants. See also the dissenting opinion of the President of the tribunal in *Tokios Tokelès v. Ukraine* (Decision on Jurisdiction, 29 Apr. 2004) and *The Rompetrol Group N.V. v. Romania* (Decision on Respondent's Preliminary Objections on Jurisdiction and Admissibility, 18 Apr. 2008) at paras 79 *et seq.*

431.   See Germany-Pakistan (1959).
432.   See Art. 8(1), UK-USSR (1989).
433.   *Compañía de Aguas del Aconquija, S.A. & Compagnie Générale des Eaux v. Argentina* (Award, 21 Nov. 2000) at para. 55.

claims, e.g., breach of 'fair and equitable' treatment or no expropriation without compensation, that are the subject of the IIA arbitration.[434]

A similar approach has been applied to the question of whether the investor may be held to have waived its right to resort to IIA arbitration, simply by agreeing, in a contract with the host state, to a dispute resolution clause providing for local or other international remedies. Tribunals have held that as long as the arbitration claims allege a cause of action under the treaty, they are not subject to the jurisdiction of the local courts as provided by the contract.[435]

Typically IIA dispute resolution clauses establish the conditions that must be fulfilled before such arbitration pursuant to the IIA can be commenced. These can vary widely from treaty to treaty but typically include a negotiation or consultation period, usually between three months and six months from the date when the dispute arose or was formally notified by the investor to the host state authorities. For example, Article 9, Bolivia-Netherlands (1992) provides, in the relevant part, as follows:

> For the purpose of resolving disputes that may arise from investments between one Contracting Party and a national of the other Party to the present Agreement, consultation will be held with a view to settling amicably the conflict between the parties to the dispute.
>
> If a dispute cannot be settled within a period of six months from the date on which the interested national shall have formally notified it, the dispute shall, at the request of the interested national, be submitted to an arbitral tribunal.

Usually there are no required formalities to be followed either in the notification or eventual ensuing negotiations.[436] As a matter of practice the negotiating periods are triggered by letters to the authorities of the host state (e.g., the Head of State and Government and the Minister in charge of foreign investment) notifying the existence of the dispute, a basic summary of its nature and a request to commence negotiations (the so-called 'trigger' letter). Upon expiry of the negotiation period, the arbitration may be instituted. In *Ronald S. Lauder v. Czech Republic*, the tribunal rejected a formalistic approach to the negotiation period requirement of the applicable BIT. The tribunal found that, provided the host state had an opportunity

---

434. See *Eudoro Armando Olguín v. Paraguay* (Award, 26 Jul. 2001) at para. 30.
435. For the first decision on this point, see *Lanco International Inc. v. Argentina* (Preliminary Decision on the Jurisdiction of the Arbitral Tribunal, 8 Dec. 1998) at paras 31 *et seq.* There is abundant case law in this regard. See *Salini Costruttori S.p.A. and Italstrade S.p.A. v. Morocco* (Decision on Jurisdiction, 23 Jul. 2001) at paras 59-63; *CMS Gas Transmission Company v. Argentina* (Decision of the Tribunal on Objections to Jurisdiction, 17 Jul. 2003) at paras 72 and 76; *Azurix Corp v. Argentina* (Decision on Jurisdiction, 8 Dec. 2003) at paras 76-77, and generally paras 75-85; *SGS Société Générale de Surveillance S.A. v. Pakistan* (Decision of the Tribunal on Objections to Jurisdiction, 6 Aug. 2003) at para. 154; *Impregilo S.p.A. v. Pakistan* (Decision on Jurisdiction, 22 Apr. 2005) at paras 286-290; and *Eureko B.V. v. Poland* (Partial Award, 19 Aug. 2005) at paras 92-114. On the admissibility issues that arise in umbrella clause claims see *infra* Chapter 9, §9.24-9.25.
436. See, however, Art. 9.1, BLEU-Venezuela (1998), providing for a 'sufficiently detailed memorandum to be presented by the investors to the state with its formal notification of the dispute.

to engage in negotiations, the investor could initiate arbitration without waiting until the end of the negotiation period.[437]

Some IIAs require the aggrieved investor to make use of host state courts and only subsequently, if the courts do not issue a decision within the specified period of time, or the decision is rendered but the dispute subsists, the investor is entitled to resort to arbitration. This sort of provision has been by-passed in a number of cases on the basis of most-favoured-nation arguments,[438] and in one case on the basis of the host state measures arguably foreclosing local remedies.[439]

IIAs often present the investor with a choice of dispute resolution mechanisms. This choice usually includes more than one type of arbitration, alongside local court litigation and other agreed dispute settlement procedures. By way of example, Article IX, Azerbaijan-US (1997), provides:

> (2) A national or company that is a party to an investment dispute may submit the dispute for resolution under one of the following alternatives:
>   (a) to the courts of administrative tribunals of the Party that is a party to the dispute; or
>   (b) in accordance with any applicable, previously agreed dispute-settlement procedures; or
>   (c) in accordance with the terms of paragraph 3.
> (3) Provided that the national or company concerned has not submitted the dispute for resolution under paragraph 2 (a) or (b), and that three months have elapsed from the date on which the dispute arose, the national or company concerned may submit the dispute for settlement by binding arbitration:
>   (i) to the Centre, if the Centre is available; or
>   (ii) to the Additional Facility of the Centre, if the Centre is not available; or
>   (iii) in accordance with the UNCITRAL Arbitration Rules; or
>   (iv) if agreed by both parties to the dispute, to any other arbitration institution or in accordance with any other arbitration rules.

The institutional form of arbitration, i.e., arbitration under the auspices of an arbitration institution that assists in the initiation of the arbitration, constitution of the tribunal and subsequent proceedings, most frequently mentioned in investment treaties is ICSID arbitration (sometimes referred to just as 'ICSID' or 'the Centre'). In order for ICSID arbitration to be available, the host State and the investor's state must be parties to the ICSID Convention. If only one of the states

---

437. *Ronald S. Lauder v. Czech Republic* (Final Award, 3 Sep. 2001 at para. 187. See also *Bayindir Insaat Turizm Ticaret Ve Sanayi A.Ş. v. Pakistan* (Decision on Jurisdiction 14 Nov. 2005) at paras 88-103) *Cf. Antoine Goetz et consorts v. Burundi* (Award, 10 Feb. 1999) at paras 91-93; *Generation Ukraine, Inc. v. Ukraine* (Award, 16 Sep. 2003) at paras 14.1-14.6 and *Western NIS Enterprise Fund v. Ukraine* (Order, 16 May 2006).
438. See *infra* Chapter 5, Part III.
439. *BG Group Plc. v. Argentina* (Final Award, 24 Dec. 2007) at paras 147-157.

is party to the Convention, then the ICSID Additional Facility is available, and sometimes also offered in investment treaties as an option.[440] Two other forms of institutional arbitration are also often mentioned. These are arbitration under the International Chamber of Commerce Rules of Arbitration (usually abbreviated 'ICC Arbitration'), and arbitration under the Arbitration Rules of the Arbitration Institute of the Stockholm Chamber of Commerce (principally in investment treaties implicating Eastern European countries). Alongside institutional arbitration, investment treaties usually provide also for the possibility of *ad hoc* arbitration, i.e., arbitration without an administering institution. The most common form of *ad hoc* arbitration is arbitration under the 1976 Arbitration Rules of the United Nations Commission on International Trade Law (UNCITRAL), which are designed for *ad hoc* or non-institutional proceedings.

---

440. See *supra* §1.21.

Chapter 2

Applicable Substantive Law and Interpretation

INTRODUCTION

§2.1 Applicable law and interpretation   Two preliminary questions arise when international investment agreement (IIA) obligations are to be applied: what is the law to be used to establish the content of the legal rules on a given issue (i.e., the question of applicable law) and what is the process and criteria to ascertain that content (i.e., the question of interpretation). These questions arise primarily before tribunals that apply IIAs in specific disputes.

This chapter begins by introducing the meaning and relevance of applicable law and then considers questions of applicable law and interpretation in seven parts. Part I addresses the various types of choice of law clauses in IIAs. Part II turns to the relevant sources of law for IIA disputes. The role of the IIA as the primary source of law is considered in Part III. Part IV addresses the role of domestic law in IIA disputes. Part V examines the role of international law as the law applicable to issues of state responsibility. Sources of applicable international law, including the role of precedent, are considered in Part VI, and Part VII addresses the interpretation of IIAs.

§2.2 Meaning of applicable substantive law   IIA disputes may be brought before three different fora: (i) international arbitration pursuant to the dispute resolution mechanisms in the IIA; (ii) domestic courts if the IIA is part of the relevant municipal law system; or (iii) a contractually agreed forum in the case of an investor-state contract. Domestic or contract IIA litigation has been uncommon because IIAs provide their own effective system of dispute resolution.[1] In any case, with regard to the question of applicable law, the same issues that are relevant to an international tribunal (i.e., what law is applicable to the different aspects of the dispute) should be equally relevant to domestic courts applying an IIA.[2]

IIAs contain two types of dispute resolution mechanisms: international arbitration for inter-state disputes, i.e., disputes between the contracting parties regarding the interpretation and application of the IIA; and international arbitration for investor-state disputes, i.e., disputes between a protected investor of a contracting party and another contracting party. Inter-state disputes under IIAs are disputes between subjects of international law concerning an international agreement governed by international law (as established in Article 2(1)(a), *Vienna Convention on the Law of Treaties*)[3] and are, by definition, disputes in which public international law is the applicable law.[4] However, as discussed below in relation to investor-state disputes, when the dispute relates to a specific underlying investment some factual and legal investigation into domestic law may be required.[5]

---

1. For an example of domestic IIA litigation, see the Argentine court decision in *Desarrollos en Salud S.A S/Concurso preventivo/ S/ Incidente de Revisión* (N.V. NISSHO IWAI S.A. (BENELUX)) (Juzgado Comercial 26, Secretaría 51, 10 Nov. 2003). See, also on the possibility of domestic IIA litigation, *Occidental Exploration & Production Company v. Ecuador* (English Court of Appeal, 9 Sep. 2005) at para. 56.

2. If litigation proceeds under domestic law, other complex related issues may arise as to the status of the IIA and applicable international law in domestic law, and whether these sources of law are self-executing and can be invoked directly by individuals before courts.

3. *Vienna Convention on the Law of Treaties*, done at Vienna, 23 May 1969, entered into force, 27 Jan. 1980, 1155 UNTS 331, *reprinted in* (1969) 8 ILM 679 [Vienna Convention].

4. Some IIAs provide explicitly for the application of the IIA itself and international law as the proper law in disputes between contracting parties. See, for example, the 1994 US Model BIT (Art. X(1)); the Danish Model BIT (Art. 10(6)); and the Greek Model BIT (Art. 9(5)). Conversely, some BITs provide only that such disputes shall be resolved 'in respect for the law' without indicating the legal sources to be applied. This clause is present for example in some Dutch BITs (Art. 10(5), Lebanon-Netherlands (2002)), and seems to have its origins in Art. 37 of the 1907 *Hague Convention for the Pacific Settlement of International Disputes*, (1907) 205 Con TS at 233 [1907 Hague Convention] (under Part IV 'International Arbitration', Chapter I 'The System of Arbitration'), which reads: 'International arbitration has for its object the settlement of disputes between States by Judges of their own choice and on the basis of respect for law.' This clause cannot be considered a proper choice of law clause because it does not spell out the applicable law. The intention of the drafters appears to have been to exclude the resolution of disputes *ex aequo et bono*. *Cf.* H.-J. Schlochauer stating that this provision in the Hague Convention is intended to permit arbitrators to base their decisions upon equity. See H.-J. Schlochauer, 'Arbitration' in R. Bernhardt, ed., *Encyclopedia of Public International Law*, Vol. I (Amsterdam: North-Holland Pub. Co, 1992) at 224. This view is questionable. For example, the Dutch BITs that incorporate this type of clause then provide for the possibility of decisions *ex aequo et bono* only if specifically agreed to between the parties. See Art. 10(5), Lebanon-Netherlands (2002); Art. 12(5), Gambia-Netherlands (2002); and Art. 12(5), Costa Rica-Netherlands (1999).

5. In this case, the applicable law will be similar, if not identical, to that concerning investor-state disputes, i.e., a combination of international and domestic law sources. Indeed, a dispute

Investor-state disputes are more complex. Three different questions arise as to applicable law in this type of dispute: (i) what is the law applicable to the substance of the dispute, that is, the law that applies to determining the content of the rights and obligations that the investor seeks to enforce; (ii) what is the law applicable to jurisdictional issues, that is, the law that applies to determining the scope of the arbitration agreement; and (iii) what is the law applicable to the procedure, that is, the law that regulates the arbitration process and the validity and enforceability of the award. This chapter deals with the first of these questions – the law applicable to the substance of disputes. Nevertheless, this also involves considering the law applicable to some jurisdictional issues, which, in practice, are often inseparable from the merits of a given case, such as the existence of a protected investment under the relevant IIA.

In determining the law applicable to the substance of disputes, a further distinction is required. In IIA claims the investor normally brings proceedings relying on rights conferred by the IIA. But if the IIA's investor-state dispute resolution clause is widely formulated, thereby permitting purely contractual and domestic law disputes to be referred to an IIA tribunal, the investor may also seek to enforce its contractual and/or domestic law rights, or some combination of these with treaty rights, through the IIA's jurisdiction clause.[6] In pure contractual claims, the law applicable to the substance of the dispute will be the contract and the law governing the contract. In domestic law claims it will be the relevant domestic law system. However, where the investor relies on rights conferred directly by the IIA (e.g., fair and equitable treatment, non-discrimination, no expropriation without compensation or observance of commitments), the applicable law is a composite. In addition to the municipal law under which the investment was made, and any underlying contract, the applicable law includes, first and foremost, the IIA itself and general international law as the proper law of the IIA. The role of the IIA and general international law is unassailable since the question will be whether the host state has breached the standards of investment protection provided by the treaty beyond any question of strict contractual or domestic law breach or liability. The focus of this chapter is on the law applicable to the substance of these IIA disputes.

---

concerning whether a contracting party is liable for breach of an IIA for government measures allegedly adversely affecting a particular investment or investor could be the object of either, or both, investor-state or a state-to-state arbitration, with no reason for different choices of law potentially leading to conflicting decisions.

6. See *SGS Société Générale de Surveillance S.A. v. Philippines* (Decision of the Tribunal on Objections to Jurisdiction, 29 Jan. 2004) [*SGS v. Philippines*] at paras 130-135 and *Salini Costruttori S.p.A. and Italstrade S.p.A. v. Morocco* (Decision on Jurisdiction, 23 Jul. 2001) [*Salini*] at para. 59. *Cf. SGS Société Générale de Surveillance S.A. v. Pakistan* (Decision of the Tribunal on Objections to Juridiction, 6 Aug. 2003) [*SGS v. Pakistan*] at paras 160-161. On the *SGS* cases, see E. Gaillard, 'Investment Treaty Arbitration and Jurisdiction Over Contract Claims – the SGS Cases Considered' in T. Weiler, ed., *International Investment Law and Arbitration: Leading Cases from the ICSID, NAFTA, Bilateral Treaties and Customary International Law* (London: Cameron May, 2005) at 331. See also *infra* Chapter 9.

§2.3 Relevance of the applicable law The applicable law is an essential element of the agreement to arbitrate since it constitutes the parameters of any arbitral tribunal's activity. Hence, applying the wrong law or no law at all may amount to a derogation from the terms of reference within which the tribunal has been authorized to function. Ultimately, the failure to apply the proper law may result in the nullification or non-recognition of the award. Under Article 52(1)(b) (excess of powers) of the *ICSID Convention*,[7] and many national legal systems,[8] disregarding the applicable law (as opposed to a mistake in applying the law) may be a valid ground for annulment or non-recognition of an award. It could hardly be otherwise since the proper resolution of the case is at stake. In the *ELSI* case, the International Court of Justice (ICJ) highlighted that: 'what is a breach of treaty may be lawful in the municipal law and what is unlawful in the municipal law may be wholly innocent of violation of a treaty provision.'[9] This point was also emphasized by the tribunal in *Antoine Goetz et consorts v. Burundi.*[10] The tribunal

---

7. Art. 52 of the ICSID Convention provides, in the relevant part: '(1) Either party may request annulment of the award by an application in writing addressed to the Secretary-General on one or more of the following grounds: [...] (b) that the Tribunal has manifestly exceeded its powers.' On the application of this standard to failure to apply the proper law, see E. Gaillard, 'The Extent of Review of the Applicable Law in Investment Treaty Arbitration,' in E. Gaillard & Y. Banifatemi, eds, *Annulment of ICSID Awards*, IAI International Arbitration Series No. 1 (New York: Juris Publishing, 2004) at 223; C. Schreuer, *The ICSID Convention: A Commentary* (Cambridge: Cambridge University Press, 2001) at 943 *et seq.*; A. Broches, 'Observations on the Finality of ICSID Awards' (1991) 6 ICSID Rev 92. See also *Klöckner Industrie-Anlagen GmbH and others v. Cameroon (Klöckner I)* (Decision on Annulment, 3 May 1985) at paras 3, 60 and 83; *Amco Asia Corporation and Others v. Indonesia (Amco I)* (Decision on the Application for Annulment, 16 May 1986) at para. 23; *Maritime International Nominees Establishment v. Guinea* (Decision on Annulment, 22 Dec. 1999) at para. 4.04; *Wena Hotels Limited v. Egypt* (Decision on the Application by the Arab Republic of Egypt for Annulment, 22 Jan. 2002) [*Wena Annulment*] at paras 21 *et seq.*; *Mr. Patrick Mitchell v. Congo* (Decision on the Application for Annulment of the Award, 1 Nov. 2006) at paras 55 *et seq.*; *CDC Group Plc. v. Seychelles* (Decision of the *Ad Hoc* Committee on the Application for the Annulment of the Republic of Seychelles, 29 Jun. 2005) at paras 44 *et seq.*; *MTD Equity Sdn Bhd. & MTD Chile S.A. v. Chile* (Decision on Annulment, 21 Mar. 2007) [*MTD Annulment*] at paras 44-48 and 58 *et seq.*; *Hussein Nuaman Soufraki v. United Arab Emirates* (Decision of the *Ad Hoc* Committee on the Application for Annulment of Mr. Soufraki, 5 Jun. 2007) at paras 83 *et seq.*; *Industria Nacional de Alimentos S.A., and Indalsa Perú, S.A. v. Peru* (Decision on Annulment, 5 Sep. 2007) at paras 97 *et seq.* and *CMS Gas Transmission Company v. Argentina* (Decision of the *Ad Hoc* Committee on the Application for Annulment of the Argentina Republic, 25 Sep. 2007) [*CMS Annulment*] at paras 48 *et seq.*
8. Under US law a 'manifest disregard' of the applicable law may be a ground to vacate an award even if this is not expressly provided for under the Federal Arbitration Act, 9 UCS §10(a). See *LaPrade v. Kidder, Peabody & Co.*, 246 F.3d 702, 706 (D.C. Cir. 2001); *DiRussa v. Dean Witter Reynolds, Inc.*, 121 F.3d 818, 821 (2d Cir. 1997); and *International Thunderbird Gaming Corporation v. United Mexican States*, 473 F.Supp.2d 80, 83 (D.D.C. 2007). For other IIA awards challenged on applicable law grounds before national courts see, e.g., *Czech Republic v. CME Czech Republic B.V.* (Judgment of the Svea Court of Appeal, 15 May 2003) at 54 *et seq.*
9. *Elettronica Sicula S.p.A (ELSI) (US v. Italy)* [1989] ICJ Rep 15 [*ELSI*] at 51, para. 73.
10. *Antoine Goetz et consorts v. Burundi* (Award, 10 Feb.1999) [*Goetz*] at para. 99, where the tribunal states: 'la question de la licéité des actes d'un Etat n'appelle pas nécessairement la même réponse selon qu'on l'envisage au regard du droit interne de cet Etat ou au regard du droit international.'

examined the measures complained of both under Burundian law and the applicable BIT, and found that they were in breach of the latter but not the former.[11] Thus, determining the proper law is a necessary precondition for a correct resolution of a dispute.

I   CHOICE OF LAW CLAUSES

§2.4 Express choice of law clauses   Some IIAs contain clauses providing an express choice of law for the resolution of IIA disputes. There are generally six types of clauses.

The first and most common type of clause calls for the application of a variety of legal sources, including the law of the host state. The majority of these clauses refer to four sources of law: (1) the IIA itself; (2) the municipal law of the host state; (3) the provisions of any investment agreement or contract relating to the investment; and (4) general principles of international law. An example of this choice of law clause is that of most Argentine BITs, including Argentina-UK (1990), which provides as follows at Article 8(4):

> The arbitral tribunal shall decide the dispute in accordance with the provisions of this Agreement, the laws of the Contracting Party involved in the dispute, including its rules on conflict of laws, the terms of any specific agreement concluded in relation to such an investment and the applicable principles of international law. The arbitration decision shall be final and binding on both Parties.[12]

Some IIAs add other sources of applicable law, such as any rules agreed to by the parties to the dispute,[13] or any other agreements between the contracting parties.[14] Others shorten the list to three sources, omitting the reference to any underlying investment agreement or contract.[15]

Among the abundant differences in wording in this type of clause, the most curious aspect is the great diversity of expressions used to designate international law: 'rules,' 'principles,' 'norms,' sometimes with the qualifications 'applicable,' 'basic,' 'general,' 'relevant,' 'generally recognized,' 'universally accepted' and/ or 'adopted by both Contacting Parties,' of 'public,' 'general' or 'customary' inter-

---

11. *Ibid.*, at paras 119, 130-133.
12. This choice of law clause is also common in Belgo-Luxembourg Economic Union (BLEU) BIT practice. A similar clause is present in Art. 9(5), 1994 *Colonia Protocol on the Reciprocal Promotion and Protection of Investments within MERCOSUR*, and Art. H(4), 1994 *Buenos Aires Protocol on the Promotion and Protection of Investments made by Countries that are not Parties to MERCOSUR*.
13. E.g., Art. 9(5), Netherlands-Venezuela (1991).
14. E.g., Art. 8(6), Czechoslovakia-Netherlands (1991).
15. E.g., Art. 9(4), China-Netherlands (2001).

national law.[16] A 'veritable confusion of tongues' as one author has put it,[17] with countless combinations and permutations and abundant room for interpretation. It is not clear what influenced these choices of terms, and whether a specific choice must be deemed intentional or rather the result of confusion regarding how to refer to international law, especially considering that the expressions used often make no logical sense. For example, the preference in this type of clause for the concept of 'principles' rather than 'rules' of international law is difficult to understand: principles tend to be identified with more elusive and vague norms than those usually referred to as rules; if the purpose of referring to principles was to use a comprehensive notion, then the expression 'international law' without more would be adequate. In reality, the reference to principles may well have a historical explanation. Its roots may be traced to the applicable law clauses of state contracts in the early and mid twentieth century, which referred to a relevant applicable municipal law system and added 'general principles of law.' That reference prompted the so-called 'internationalization' of state contracts: it was used as a justification to apply international law alongside domestic law to contractual disputes.[18]

However peculiar and whatever the motives for the specific references to international law in treaty choice of law clauses, they have been understood as calling for the application of all sources of international law without restriction,[19] unless there is clear evidence of a contrary intention by treaty drafters. That said, to avoid confusion and interpretive difficulties, it would be better for IIA choice

---

16. See examples cited in P. Peters, 'The Semantics of Applicable Law Clauses and the Arbitrator' in M. Sumampouw *et al.*, eds, *Law and Reality: Essays on National and International Procedural Law* (The Hague: TMC Asser Institute, 1992), 231.
17. *Ibid.*, at 242.
18. See, e.g., *Lena Goldfields Arbitration*, (1939) 5 Annual Digest 3 at 3; *reprinted in* (1950) 36 CLQ 42 at para. 22. See also the comment on this arbitration, V.V. Veeder, 'The Lena Goldfields Arbitration: The Historical Roots of Three Ideas' (1998) 47 ICLQ 747 at 772. See generally for the role of 'principles of international law' in the internationalisation of contracts, O. Spiermann, 'Applicable Law,' in P. Muchlinski, F. Ortino & C. Schreuer, eds, *The Oxford Handbook of International Investment Law* (Oxford: Oxford University Press, 2008). See *supra* Chapter 1, §1.18, for further references.
19. See W. Ben Hamida, *L'arbitrage transnational unilatéral* (Doctoral Thesis presented at the Université Panthéon-Assas (Paris II), 24 Jun. 2003) (on file with the authors) at 509, citing the PCIJ's holding in the *Lotus* case that 'the words "principles of international law," as ordinarily used, can only mean international law as applied between all nations belonging to the community of States.' *The Case of the S.S. 'Lotus' (France v. Turkey)* (1927) PCIJ Ser. A, No. 10 at 16. Ben Hamida notes also that Art. 42 of the French version of the ICSID Convention refers to 'principes de droit international' which the Report of the Executive Directors of the World Bank on the ICSID Convention interprets as covering all international law sources as established in Art. 38(1) of the *Statute of the International Court of Justice*. See the Report of the Executive Directors of the International Bank for Reconstruction and Development on the Convention on the Settlement of Investment Disputes between States and Nationals of Other States, 1 ICSID Rep 23 at para. 40. *Cf.*, B. Goldman, 'La *lex mercatoria* dans les contrats et les arbitrages internationaux: Réalités et perspectives' (1979) JDI 481.

of law clauses to simply refer to 'international law,' without distinguishing between principles and rules or adding further qualifications.

Another curious element of express choice of law clauses is the explicit inclusion, in many cases, of the 'rules on the conflict of laws' in the reference to host state law. This explicit mention seems superfluous. Private international law or conflict rules would be applicable as part of the host state law. Their specific mention may be an instance of abundance of caution. It may respond to the concern of the contracting states that a plain reference to host state law may overlook the relevance of the law of the investor's home state (or even the law of a third state) in cases and for matters sufficiently connected with that law, for example, the nationality of the investor.[20] In any case, even if specific reference to conflict rules is omitted, these rules are still applicable unless there is evidence that their omission was intended.

A second type of choice of law clause also refers to a list of legal sources but provides, in somewhat looser language, that the tribunal shall 'take into account' those sources of law and, further, that the list of legal sources is non-exhaustive. An example is Article 8(6), Czechoslovakia-Netherlands (1991):

> The arbitral tribunal shall decide on the basis of the law, taking into account in particular though not exclusively: the law in force in the Contracting Party concerned; the provisions of this Agreement, and other relevant Agreements between the Contracting Parties; the provisions of special agreements relating to the investment; the general principles of international law.

In *CME Czech Republic B.V. v. Czech Republic*, the tribunal noted that this clause 'is broad and grants to the Tribunal a discretion' since it 'instructs the Tribunal to *take into account* (not: to apply) the above mentioned sources of law, in particular *though not exclusively.*'[21] It was, *inter alia,* on the basis of this provision, that the tribunal rejected the respondent's argument that the measures complained of be first examined under Czech law and then, the result thereby obtained, checked for compliance with international law. According to the tribunal, the treaty provided no specific order in which the listed legal sources would apply, nor did the provision require the application of domestic law, but simply to take it into account.[22] The tribunal's conclusion rejecting the respondent's two step analysis seems correct, although arguably that results neither from the wording of the specific clause nor from any discretion in applying domestic law, but rather from the specific and

---

20. Peters, *supra* note 16 at 245 and Ben Hamida, *supra* note 19 at 507.
21. *CME Czech Republic B.V. v. Czech Republic* (Final Award, 14 Mar. 2003) [*CME*] at para. 402 [emphasis in original]. Criticising the tribunal's conclusion on discretion, see C. Schreuer, 'Comments relating to Applicable Law of the Stockholm Tribunal's Final Award of 14 March 2003' (2005) 2 TDM (Schreuer provided expert testimony on this case on behalf of the respondent). Prior to the *CME* final award, the governments of Czech Republic and The Netherlands had issued 'Agreed Minutes' indicating *inter alia* that under Art. 8(6) of the BIT the tribunal 'must … take into account as far as they are relevant to the dispute' the sources of law set out in Art. 8(6), thereby indicating that resort to those sources was mandatory, not discretionary. *CME, ibid.,* at paras 87-93.
22. *CME, ibid.,* at paras 396-413.

distinct roles that domestic law and international law play in IIA disputes as discussed below.[23]

A third type of clause refers to the application of the treaty itself and interna-
tional law. This clause is present in a small number of BITs;[24] Article 26(6),
Energy Charter Treaty (ECT);[25] Article 17-20(1) ('Applicable Law'), *Group of
Three Treaty*;[26] and Article 1131, *North American Free Trade Agreement*
(NAFTA) ('Governing Law') which reads:

> A tribunal established under this section shall decide the issues in dispute in
> accordance with this agreement and applicable rules of international law.

A fourth type of clause is that found in Indian BIT practice, where the choice of
law, which provides for the application of the treaty itself, refers only to disputes
to be submitted to *ad hoc* United Nations Commission on International Trade Law
(UNCITRAL) arbitration and not to the alternative arbitration option, ICSID arbitration.[27] Presumably this is because ICSID arbitration has its own choice of law
clause at Article 42(1), ICSID Convention.

A fifth type of clause is that found in the most recent IIAs concluded by the
US,[28] and in the 2004 US Model BIT, which provides for two different choices of
law. For claims relating to breaches of the treaty's investment protections, the
sources of applicable law are the treaty itself and international law. For claims
relating to investment authorizations and investment agreements, the source of
applicable law is that which is specified in the authorizations and agreements or has
been otherwise agreed to by the parties, or, if no law has been specified or agreed
on, a combination of the law of the respondent state, the terms of the investment
authorizations and agreements, international law and the treaty itself.[29] This type of
twofold clause reflects a greater concern for applicable law issues, and thus, the
perceived need to define with precision the sources of law applicable to investment
disputes.

---

23. See Parts III, IV and V below.
24. E.g., Canadian BITs such as Art. XII(7), Canada-El Salvador (1999), and Art. XII(7), Canada-
    Uruguay (1997); Mexican BITs such as Art. 14(1), Korea-Mexico (2000), and Art. 17, Austria-
    Mexico (1998); and Art. 9(3), France-Hungary (1986).
25. This reads: 'A tribunal established under para. 4 shall decide the issues in dispute in accordance
    with this Treaty and applicable rules and principles of international law.'
26. Agreement between Colombia, Mexico and Venezuela. See *supra* Chapter 1, §1.35. Art.
    17-20(1) reads:

    > Any tribunal constituted under this Section shall decide the disputes submitted for its review
    > in accordance with this Treaty and with the applicable rules of international law.

27. See Art. 9(2)(c)(iii), Denmark-India (1995).
28. See US-Uruguay (2005), the investment chapters of recent US FTAs with Chile (2003) and
    Morocco (2004), and the 2004 Central America-Dominican Republic-US FTA (CAFTA-DR).
29. Art. 10.21(2), Chile-US FTA (2003), provides for the default application of all these sources.
    Art. 10.22(2), CAFTA-DR (2004), and Art. 10.21(2), Morocco-US FTA (2004), provide for
    the default application of only the law of the respondent state and international law.

A sixth and final type of clause is that which provides a list of sources of applicable law, and then adds, usually in a separate paragraph, that an interpretation of a provision of the IIA jointly made by the treaty contracting parties shall be binding on a tribunal resolving an IIA dispute.[30] For example, Article 15.21 of the investment chapter of the 2003 Singapore-US Free Trade Agreement (FTA) reads:

(1) Subject to paragraph 2, a tribunal shall decide the issues in dispute related to an alleged breach of an obligation in Section B in accordance with this Agreement and applicable rules of international law.

(2) A decision of the Joint Committee declaring its interpretation of a provision of this Agreement under Article 20.1.2 (Joint Committee) shall be binding on a tribunal established under this Section, and any award must be consistent with that decision.

Certain of these clauses limit the time period in which any such interpretation may be made with binding effects. For example, Article 8(2) of the Schedule of Mexico-Netherlands (1998) reads:

An interpretation jointly formulated and agreed by the Contracting Parties of a provision of this Agreement shall be binding on any tribunal established under this Schedule. If the Contracting Parties fail to submit an interpretation within sixty days of the date of the request of either Contracting Party, the tribunal shall decide the issue.

Another variation is to provide that a tribunal must, at the request of a state party, ask for a joint interpretation. For example, Article 155, China-New Zealand FTA (2008), provides:

1. The tribunal shall, on request of the state party, request a joint interpretation of the Parties of any provision of this Agreement that is in issue in a dispute. The Parties shall submit in writing any joint decision declaring their interpretation to the tribunal within 60 days of delivery of the request.

2. A joint decision issued under paragraph 1 by the Parties shall be binding on the tribunal, and any award must be consistent with that joint decision. If the Parties fail to issue such a decision within 60 days, the tribunal shall decide the issue on its own account.

---

30. This provision is common in Mexican BITs. See Art. 16, Greece-Mexico (2000), which reads: '(1) A tribunal established under this Part shall decide the submitted issues in dispute in accordance with this Agreement and the generally acknowledged rules and principles of international law. (2) An interpretation jointly formulated and agreed upon by the Contracting Parties of a provision of this Agreement shall be binding on any tribunal established under this Part.'

§2.5 Distinction from other clauses Express choice of law clauses for investment disputes must be distinguished from two other types of clauses sometimes present in IIAs: the clause on the law applicable to the investment and the preservation of rights clause.[31]

Clause on the law applicable to the investment. The clause on the law applicable to the investment does not prescribe the proper law to investment disputes but the law applicable to the everyday operation of the investment. This clause is sometimes called the 'Sri Lanka clause' because it is found mainly in Sri Lanka BIT practice,[32] although it seems to have originated in BLEU-Singapore (1978).[33] Article 9, Korea-Sri Lanka (1980), entitled 'Laws,' provides, for example, as follows:

> For the avoidance of any doubt, it is declared that all investments shall, subject to this Agreement, be governed by the laws in force in the territory of the Contracting Party in which such investments are made.

Variations of this clause are the omission of the 'for the avoidance of any doubt' language,[34] and the addition of international law to the 'subject to this agreement' caveat,[35] or to the host state law as governing law.[36] The clause, in its common reference only to host state law, seeks to make the obvious, though superfluous, point that investments, and the property or commercial rights associated with them, are generally subject to the law of the state in which they are made. This is different from the law by which an arbitral tribunal should be guided when settling an IIA dispute, which must necessarily include international law. IIAs and international law cannot govern the everyday business actions related to an investment, even if they become applicable once remedies under the IIA are pursued. Hence the caveat 'subject to this agreement' and (sometimes accompanied by 'international law') usually present in the clause, aimed at confirming the application of the IIA's substantive protections and remedies to protected investment.

Preservation of rights clause. The preservation of rights clause is a common IIA clause, often headed 'Application of other Rules,'[37] providing for the application to a given investor or investment of any rule of law more favourable than the provisions of the IIA.[38] This sort of clause does not contain a choice of law. It establishes a criterion to articulate the different legal sources that may be applicable as a result of the relevant choice of law rule. The principle is the primacy of the rule more favourable to the investor. Thus, the clause does not designate the

---

31. See on this distinction, Ben Hamida, *supra* note 19 at 504-5.
32. Peters, *supra* note 16 at 239.
33. Art. 3, BLEU-Singapore (1978), provides that 'an investment ... shall be subject to the laws in force in the territory of the [host country].'
34. Art. 8, Finland-Sri Lanka (1985).
35. Art. 8, Sri Lanka-Switzerland (1981).
36. Art. 8, Finland-Sri Lanka (1985).
37. Art. 11, 1991 UK Model BIT.
38. See *supra* Chapter 6, §6.48, and *infra* Chapter 9, §9.28, on preservation of rights provisions.

applicable law, but certainly has an impact on the way the relevant applicable legal sources are combined and applied by a tribunal to resolve a given dispute.[39]

§2.6 Choice of law clauses in arbitration rules Provisions on applicable law for the resolution of IIA disputes are also found in the arbitration rules governing the IIA arbitral proceedings. Article 42(1) of the ICSID Convention,[40] for example, provides:

> The Tribunal shall decide a dispute in accordance with such rules of law as may be agreed by the parties. In the absence of such agreement, the Tribunal shall apply the law of the Contracting State party to the dispute (including its rules on the conflict of laws) and such rules of international law as may be applicable.[41]

It may be argued that unless the relevant IIA contains an express choice of law clause (an agreement of the contracting parties as to applicable law), the second sentence of Article 42(1) provides the choice of law rule for IIA disputes submitted to ICSID arbitration. Some tribunals, however, have inferred an agreement of the parties on the applicable law arising from their consent to arbitration under the IIA and the rules of law invoked in their submissions. Thus, tribunals have found the IIA, international law and municipal law applicable under Article 42(1), first sentence, even in the absence of an express choice of law clause.[42] These same sources are applicable under Article 42(1), second sentence. In this context, little practical difference seems to exist, therefore, between the first and the second sentences of Article 42(1) with regard to the applicable law in IIA disputes.[43]

---

39. See *Middle East Cement Shipping and Handling Co. S.A. v. Egypt* (Award,12 Apr. 2002) [*Middle East Cement*] at para. 87 (finding that this provision gives primacy to the BIT since it 'does not permit the application of provisions of national law limiting any claims found by the Tribunal to exist under the BIT'). See also on this type of clause, *Goetz, supra* note 10 at paras 95 and 99.

40. On Art. 42(1) of the ICSID Convention, see Schreuer, *supra* note 7 at 549 *et seq.*, and references therein. See also E. Gaillard & Y. Banifatemi, 'The meaning of "and" in Art. 42(1), Second Sentence, of the Washington Convention: The Role of International Law in the ICSID Choice of Law Process' (2003) 18 ICSID Rev 375; W.M. Reisman, 'The Regime for Lacunae in the ICSID Choice of Law Provision and the Question of its Threshold' (2000) 15 ICSID Rev 362; I.F.I. Shihata & A.R. Parra, 'Applicable Substantive Law in Disputes Between States and Private Foreign Parties: The Case of Arbitration under the ICSID Convention'(1994) 9 ICSID Rev 183; and A. Broches, 'Convention on the Settlement of Investment Disputes between States and Nationals of Other States of 1965: Explanatory Notes and Survey of its Application' (1993) 18 YBCA 627.

41. Art. 54, ICSID Additional Facility Rules, provides, similarly, as follows: 'The Tribunal shall apply the rules of law designated by the parties as applicable to the substance of the dispute. Failing such designation by the parties, the Tribunal shall apply (a) the law determined by the conflict of laws rules which it considers applicable and (b) such rules of international law as the Tribunal considers applicable.'

42. See *Asian Agricultural Products Ltd (AAPL) v. Sri Lanka* (Final Award, 27 Jun. 1990) [*AAPL*] at paras 18-24 and *MTD Equity Sdn. Bhd. and MTD Chile S.A. v. Chile* (Award, 25 May 2004) [*MTD* Award] at paras 86-87.

43. *Cf.* The dissenting opinion of arbitrator Asante in *AAPL, ibid.*, criticising the majority's inference of an agreement as to applicable law under Art. 42(1), first sentence, and regretting that that resulted in an insufficient full argumentation of the case on Sri Lankan law.

The ICC Rules of Arbitration provide, in Article 17, that 'the parties shall be free to agree upon the rules of law to be applied by the tribunal to the merits of the dispute.' 'In the absence of such agreement,' which is arguably the case if the IIA provides no express choice of law rule, the tribunal 'shall apply the rules of law which it determines to be appropriate,' and 'in all cases take account of the provisions of the contract and the relevant trade usages.' Article 33 of the UNCITRAL Rules similarly provides that the tribunal shall apply the law designated by the parties, failing which it shall apply the law determined by the conflict of law rules that it considers applicable, and the terms of the contract and trade usages. Article 24(1) of the Rules of the SCC Institute provides that 'the Arbitral Tribunal shall decide the merits of the dispute on basis of the law or rules of law agreed by the parties' or, 'in the absence of such an agreement,' 'apply the law or rules of law which it considers to be most appropriate.' Under any of these clauses, whether an implicit agreement on applicable law is found to exist or not, the applicable law would still consist of the IIA, international law and domestic law, which are the laws relevant and thus 'appropriate' to the resolution of IIA disputes.

II   RELEVANT SOURCES OF LAW IN IIA DISPUTES

§2.7 Laws relevant to IIA disputes   Whichever choice of law rule is ultimately applied by the arbitral tribunal, there are four sources of substantive legal rules relevant, and thus to be applied, to the resolution of any IIA dispute: the treaty itself, the law of the host state of the investment, the terms of any underlying contract relating to the investment, and general international law.[44] *First*, as IIA disputes concern IIA protections (see above §2.2), the treaty itself necessarily applies. *Second*, since the treaty is an international agreement 'governed by international law' (Article 2(1)(a) of the Vienna Convention), general rules and principles of international law must also apply to supplement the treaty. *Third*, the underlying private, commercial and property rights and interests that constitute the protected investments are governed by the law of the state where the investment is made, and/or the terms of any contract relating to the investment including any choice of law provisions. Hence, domestic law and any contracts related to the investment also apply. As a result, the applicable law in IIA disputes is a hybrid of international and municipal law.

This explains why most express choice of law clauses in IIAs refer to a combination of international and municipal legal sources. Even in clauses referring only to the treaty itself and international law, municipal law and contract terms should be deemed applicable by effect of a *renvoi* from international law to those sources,

---

44.   See Z. Douglas, 'The Hybrid Foundations of Investment Treaty Arbitration' (2003) 74 BYIL 151 at 194.

for the determination of issues relating to the commercial and property rights and interests that form the investment protected by the IIA and international law.[45]

The majority of IIA tribunals do not provide, in their awards, explicit expositions on the law applicable to the dispute at hand, although generally speaking a combination of domestic and international legal rules are usually resorted to in resolving the dispute.[46] When the issue is expressly referred to, tribunals recognize the hybrid nature of the applicable law.[47] The first tribunal to rule on an IIA dispute, for example, stated that the BIT on which the arbitration was based provided the 'primary source of applicable legal rules.' This was, in turn, to be complemented 'by direct reference to certain supplementary rules, whether of international law character or of domestic law nature.'[48] In *Fedax N.V. v. Venezuela*, the tribunal referred to the 'broad framework of the applicable law,' which included the application of municipal and international law, as confirmed by the express choice of law clause of the BIT calling for the application of various legal sources.[49] In *Goetz*, the tribunal highlighted the hybrid nature of the applicable law, finding that the reference to the treaty and international law in an express choice of law clause could not have the effect of totally excluding the application of municipal law:

> Il n'est pas sans intérêt a cet égard de noter que la référence assez fréquente, dans des clauses de *choice of law* insérés dans des conventions de protection des investissements, aux dispositions de la convention elle-même – et, plus largement, aux principes et règles du droit international – provoque, après un certain reflux dans la pratique et la jurisprudence, un retour remarquable du droit international dans les relations juridiques entre les Etats d'accueil

---

45. See, e.g., *EnCana Corporation v. Ecuador* (Award, 3 Feb. 2006) [*EnCana*] at para. 184 (domestic law applies to determine the existence of the rights affected even if the applicable law clause refers only to the BIT and applicable rules of international law). On choice of law clauses see *supra* §2.4.

46. *American Manufacturing and Trading, Inc. v. Zaire* (Award, 21 Feb. 1997); *Mr. Franz Sedelmayer v. Russia* (Arbitration Award, 7 Jul. 1998); *Robert Azinian, Kenneth Davitian, & Ellen Baca v. Mexico* (Award, 1 Nov. 1999) [*Azinian*]; *Pope & Talbot Inc. v. Canada* (Interim Award, 26 Jun. 2000); *Metalclad Corporation v. Mexico* (Award, 30 Aug. 2000) [*Metalclad*]; *SwemBalt AB, Sweden v. Latvia* (Decision by the Court of Arbitration, 23 Oct. 2000); *Emilio Augustín Maffezini v. Spain* (Award, 13 Nov. 2000) [*Maffezini*]; and *S.D. Myers, Inc. v. Canada* (Partial Award, 13 Nov. 2000).

47. *Cf. Alex Genin, Eastern Credit Limited, Inc. and A.S. Baltoil v. Estonia* (Award, 18 Jun. 2001) [*Genin*] at para. 350, holding that on the basis of Art. 42(1), second sentence, of the ICSID Convention, 'in the absence of any agreement by the parties to the contrary, it is the law of the Republic of Estonia that applies,' which would appear an incorrect conclusion; but adding that in any case 'there is no basis on which to conclude that the application of rules of international law would effect a result any different than that reached on the basis of Estonian law'.

48. *AAPL, supra* note 42 at paras 20-21.

49. *Fedax N.V. v. Venezuela* (Award, 9 Mar. 1998) at para. 30. Art. 9(5), Netherlands-Venezuela (1991), reads: 'The arbitral award shall be based on: (i) the law of the Contracting Party concerned; (ii) the provisions of this Agreement and other relevant Agreements between the Contracting Parties; (iii) the provisions of special agreements relating to the investments; (iv) the general principles of international law; and (v) such rules of law as may be agreed by the parties to the dispute.'

et les investisseurs étrangers. Cette internationalisation des rapports d'investissement – qu'ils soient contractuels ou non – ne conduit certes pas à une 'dénationalisation' radicale des relations juridiques nées de l'investissement étranger, au point que le droit national de l'Etat hôte serait privé de toute pertinence ou application au profit d'un rôle exclusive du droit international. Elle signifie seulement que ces relations relèvent simultanément – en parallèle, pourrait-on dire – de la maîtrise souveraine de l'Etat d'accueil sur son droit national et des engagements internationaux auxquels il a souscrit.[50]

In this case, the relevant BIT contained an express choice of law clause providing for the application of municipal law, the treaty, contract terms and international law.[51] But the reasoning of the tribunal appears equally applicable to clauses calling for the application only of the treaty and international law, such as Article 1131, NAFTA.

The hybrid nature of the law applicable to IIA disputes was also underlined by the tribunal in *CMS Gas Transmission Company v. Argentina*:

> More recently, however, a more pragmatic and less doctrinaire approach has emerged, allowing for the application of both domestic law and international law if the specific facts of the dispute so justifies. It is no longer the case of one prevailing over the other and excluding it altogether. Rather, both sources have a role to play.[52]

The tribunal rightly found that there was a 'close interaction between the legislation and the regulation' of Argentina, governing the industry in question, the underlying license contract, and international law 'as embodied both in the Treaty and in customary international law.' It then, however, failed to explain how the different sources would interact and what role each would play. It simply said: 'all these rules are inseparable and will, to the extent justified, be applied by the Tribunal.'[53]

§2.8 Law pleaded and *iura novit curia*   In determining the applicable law, tribunals have accorded relevance to the law pleaded by the parties in their submissions. These have been used to support an implicit agreement on choice of law,[54] but more often to confirm the tribunal's determination on applicable law which was arrived at independently from the parties' legal submissions.[55]

The question arises whether failure by the parties to plead a particular legal proposition of principle justifies not applying it. Often the question arises in relation to domestic law issues. Both counsel and tribunals in IIA arbitrations

---

50.   *Goetz, supra* note 10 at para. 69.
51.   Art. 9(5), BLEU-Burundi (1989).
52.   *CMS Gas Transmission Company v. Argentina* (Award, 12 May 2005) [*CMS Award*] at para. 116.
53.   *Ibid.*, at para. 117.
54.   *AAPL, supra* note 42 at paras 20-21.
55.   *CMS Award, supra* note 52 at para. 118.

(normally international lawyers) tend to consider the IIA and general international law as applicable law, and relegate national law to a factual issue on which evidence is to be provided. In *CME*, the tribunal found that it was not 'bound to research, find and apply national law which has not been argued or referred to by the parties and has not been identified by the parties and the Tribunal to be essential to the Tribunal's decision.'[56] Yet, the contrary would seem required under the basic principle in national and international law of *iura novit curia*,[57] according to which a court should, of its own motion, apply any rule of law relevant to the facts to resolve a given dispute, irrespective of whether such a rule is pleaded. In the words of Jan Paulsson:

> One fundamental issue appears not yet to have been considered in the depth it obviously deserves: whenever they are created by treaties which refer to the applicability of international law, are international tribunals in investment disputes organs of the international legal system and therefore bound to apply international law whether or not it is pleaded by the parties? The parallel with the ICJ and its Article 38 is obvious, and the implications are equally clear, as the ICJ put it in the Fisheries Jurisdiction cases:
>> 'The Court ... as an international judicial organ is deemed to take judicial notice of international law, and is therefore required ... to consider on its own initiative all rules of international law which may be relevant to the settlement of the dispute. It being the duty of the Court itself to ascertain and apply the relevant law in the given circumstances of the case, the burden of establishing or proving rules of international law cannot be imposed upon any of the parties for the law lies within the judicial knowledge of the Court.'
> In other words, a tribunal in an investment dispute cannot content itself with inept pleadings, and simply uphold the least implausible of the two. Furthermore, as the PCIJ put it in Brazilian Loans, an international tribunal 'is deemed itself to know what law is,' ...[58]

While referring to international law, Paulsson's remarks appear equally applicable to domestic law as part of the law applicable to investment disputes. In this context, ICSID *ad hoc* committees hearing annulment cases have uniformly rejected

56. *CME, supra* note 21 at para. 411. See also, noting that the respondent itself 'devoted little attention to Czech law during the ... proceedings' and 'presented no evidence regarding Czech law,' *Czech Republic v. CME Czech Republic B.V.* (Judgment of the Svea Court of Appeal, 15 May 2003) at 54-55.
57. See discussion on the concept in R. Kolb, 'General Principles of Procedural Law,' in A. Zimmermann *et al.* eds *Statute of the International Court of Justice: A Commentary* (Oxford: Oxford University Press, 2006) at 820-822. For an instance of application of the principle of *iura novit curia* in an IIA case, albeit under Swedish law as the law applicable to the proceedings, see *Iurii Bogdanov, Agurdino-Invest Ltd and Agurdino-Chimia JSC v. Moldova* (Arbitral Award, 22 Sep. 2005) at 9-10.
58. J. Paulsson, 'International Arbitration and the Generation of Legal Norms: Treaty Arbitration and International Law', in ICCA Congress Series No. 13 (The Hague: Kluwer, 2007), at 879.

the idea that tribunals, in drafting their awards, were restricted to the legal arguments presented to them by the parties.[59]

That said, *iura novit curia* cannot extend to the point that arguments not made, claims not advanced or defences not raised should be supplemented by the tribunal. As stated by the *ad hoc* committee in *Mr. Patrick Mitchell v. Congo*, referring to the failure by the tribunal to apply the so-called 'non-precluded measures clause' of the relevant BIT (a clause arguably exempting from liability measures required to protect essential security interests[60]):

> It is entirely conceivable that, in view of the specific circumstances of the intervention of the military forces against the [investor], the well known state of war in Congo, and the DRC's contestation of the qualification of the measures under dispute as an expropriation, the Arbitral Tribunal would have been welcome to address *ex proprio motu* the other provisions of the Treaty, which might potentially excuse taking such measures against the Claimant. A comparable approach would have been along the lines of the adage *jura novit curia* – on which the DRC leaned during the Annulment Proceedings – but this could not truly be required of the Arbitral Tribunal, as it is not, strictly speaking, subject to any obligation to apply a rule of law that has not been adduced; this is but an option – and the parties should have been given the opportunity to be heard in this respect – for which reason it is not possible to draw any conclusions from the fact that the Arbitral Tribunal did not exercise it.[61]

It is suggested that the committee reached the right conclusion here, although its reasoning is questionable. Discretion in applying the proper law is not germane to the judicial function. The point is that the tribunal could not be expected to raise a defence that had not been put forward by the respondent. *Iura novit curia* demands the application of the proper law to claims or defences made; it does not require, and indeed cannot lead to, supplementing *ex oficio* the parties' claims or defences: arguments not raised cannot be entertained and thus no law should be applied to it; simply there is no role of *iura novit curia* in this context.[62]

---

59. See *Wena Hotels Limited. v. Egypt* (Award, 8 Dec. 2000) [*Wena*] at para. 70; *Compañía de Aguas del Aconquija S.A. and Vivendi Universal (formerly Compagnie Générale des Eaux) v. Argentina* (Decision on Annulment, 3 Jul. 2002) [*Vivendi Annulment*] at paras 82-85.
60. See *infra* Chapter 10.
61. *Mr. Patrick Mitchell v. Congo* (Decision on the Application for Annulment of the Award, 1 Nov. 2006) at para. 57.
62. This stems from the rule that judgments should not be *ultra petita*. See, e.g., the ICJ decision in *Request for the interpretation of the Judgment of November 20th, 1950, in the Asylum Case (Colombia v. Peru)* [1950] ICJ Rep 395 at 402 ('it is the duty of the Court not only to reply to the questions as stated in the final submissions of the parties, but also to abstain from deciding points not included in those submissions').

III   ROLE OF THE IIA

§2.9 The IIA as the primary source of law   The substantive provisions of an IIA are the primary source of applicable law in IIA disputes. IIAs grant foreign investors access to arbitration in order for those investors to be able to claim the substantive protections of the IIA itself.[63] IIA arbitration claims are based on IIA provisions; they are grounded in the investor rights and host state obligations granted by IIAs. Accordingly, the substantive standards of the IIA are *lex specialis* and the primary source of applicable law.

Tribunals have consistently underlined the central role of the IIA as applicable substantive law in IIA disputes. In *AAPL*, for example, the tribunal stated that the BIT on which the arbitration was based provided the 'primary source of applicable legal rules.'[64] The same principle is reflected in the award in *Wena*. The tribunal found that, as the case 'turns on an alleged violation' by Egypt of the BIT, 'the Tribunal considers the IPPA [Investment Promotion and Protection Agreement or BIT] to be the primary source of applicable law.'[65]

Antonio Parra, former Deputy Secretary General of ICSID, writing about the rules of law applicable to the substance of disputes brought under BITs, states:

> These mainly have been the rules set out in the substantive provisions of the treaties themselves. In most instances, this follows simply from the investor's invocation of those rules in bringing the claim, such reliance on the rules being explicitly or implicitly authorized by the investor-to-State dispute settlement provisions of the treaty.[66]

The primacy of the IIA is also implicit in the preservation of rights clause which is common in IIAs and provides investors the right to claim the application of any rule of law more favourable than the provisions of the IIA.[67] On this clause, the tribunal in *Middle East Cement* found that 'by argumentum *a contrario* it does not permit the application of provisions of national law limiting any claims found by the Tribunal to exist under the BIT.'[68] The same reasoning would appear to apply to any contrary and not more favourable provisions of international law. The IIA is the starting point, and in principle prevails over domestic and international law rules, except where those are more favourable.

§2.10 The need to supplement the IIA   IIAs, however, contain only a basic set of state obligations and do not aim to exhaustively define all aspects of the

---

63.   Some dispute resolution clauses in IIAs have a wider scope. See *supra* §2.2.
64.   *AAPL, supra* note 42 at paras 20-21.
65.   *Wena, supra* note 59 at paras 78-79.
66.   A. Parra, 'Applicable Substantive Law in ICSID Arbitrations Initiated Under Investment Treaties' (2001) ICSID Rev 20 at 21.
67.   See *supra* §2.6 and *infra* Chapter 6, § 6.48 on preservation of rights provisions.
68.   *Middle East Cement, supra* note 39 at para. 87.

investor-state relationship. For example, the tribunal in *AAPL* found that the BIT was the primary source and added:

> ... the Bilateral Investment Treaty is not a self-contained closed legal system limited to provide for substantive material rules of direct applicability, but it has to be envisaged within a wider juridical context in which rules from other sources are integrated through implied incorporation methods or by direct reference to certain supplementary rules, whether of international law character or of domestic law nature.[69]

Similarly, after defining the BIT, as 'the primary source of applicable law,' the *Wena* tribunal added: 'however, the IPPA is a fairly terse agreement of only seven pages containing thirteen articles.' Thus Egyptian law and international law applied alongside the BIT.[70]

IV   ROLE OF MUNICIPAL LAW

§2.11 Existence of the investment as a domestic law issue   As stated by a commentator: 'Investments disputes are about investments, investments are about property, and property is about specific rights over things cognisable by the municipal law of the host state.'[71] That is, whether a particular right, interest or asset held in the territory of a state party to an IIA is an investment protected by the IIA is a matter for the IIA not municipal law; but in order for a particular asset to be able to qualify as an investment under the IIA, it must first exist and such existence is owed to the law of the territory in which such asset is allegedly held. Thus, while IIAs designate which assets are to be considered investments for the purposes of the treaty, typically defining investment as 'any kind of asset' and providing a non-exhaustive enumeration of certain categories or types of assets, the preliminary question as to whether one of these types of investments exists is a matter primarily for the municipal law of the host state, not international law.

---

69. *AAPL, supra* note 42 at paras 20-21.
70. *Wena, supra* note 59 at para. 79, applying Art. 42(1) of the ICSID Convention.
71. Douglas, *supra* note 44 at 197. See also on this point C. Staker, 'Public International Law and the *Lex Situs* Rule in Property Conflicts and Foreign Expropriations' (1987) 58 BYIL 151 at 169-170.

The point was well made by the tribunal in *EnCana* stating that the substantial protections offered by IIAs apply to investments that exist under the domestic legal system:

> … for there to have been an expropriation of an investment or return (in a situation involving legal rights or claims as distinct from the seizure of physical assets) the right affected must exist under the law which creates them, in this case, the law of Ecuador.[72]

Some IIAs make this explicit. For example, Article I(2) second paragraph, Argentina-Spain (1991) provides:

> The content and scope of the rights corresponding to the various categories of assets shall be determined by the laws and regulations of the Party in whose territory the investment is situated.[73]

Other IIAs make the same point by adding to the definition of protected investments a provision that investments must be duly made in accordance with the municipal law of the host state.[74] This does not mean that host state law determines or limits what qualifies as an investment for the purposes of the IIA. Rather, the existence of the asset that may qualify as an investment under the IIA, as well as its validity, is a matter of domestic law.[75]

§2.12 Other matters to which domestic law is relevant   In addition to the existence of an investment, host state law is also relevant to a number of related threshold issues.[76] For example, municipal law governs matters such as whether

---

72. *EnCana, supra* note 45 at para. 184.
73. Similar clauses, though with different wording, are found in many BITs. Art. 1(a), Argentina-UK (1990) provides '"Investment" means every kind of asset defined in accordance with the laws and regulations of the Contracting Party in whose territory the investment is made admitted.…'
74. E.g., Art. 1(1), second paragraph, Bolivia-France (1989), which, after defining the term 'investment' adds: 'It being understood that the said assets shall be or shall have been invested in accordance with the legislation of the Contracting Party in whose territory or maritime zone the investment is made.…'
75. *Desert Line Projects LLC v. Yemen* (Award, 6 Feb. 2008) at 102-105; *Saipem S.p.A. v. Bangladesh* (Decision on Jurisdiction and Recommendation of Provisional Measures, 21 Mar. 2007) [*Saipem*] at para. 79 and note 11; *Inceysa Vallisoletana, S.L. v. El Salvador* (Award, 2 Aug. 2006) at paras 190 *et seq.*; *LESI S.p.A. et ASTALDI S.p.A. v. Algeria* (Decision, 12 Jul. 2006) at para. 83 (iii); *Salini, supra* note 6 at para. 46; *Bayindir Insaat Turizm Ticaret Ve Sanayi A.Ş. v. Pakistan* (Decision on Jurisdiction, 14 Nov. 2005) [*Bayindir*] at paras 105-110.
76. Domestic law will also be relevant to determining the nationality of the investor, though this issue is typically a jurisdictional one and not a point of applicable substantive law. For an application of domestic law on nationality, see *Hussein Nuaman Soufraki v. United Arab Emirates* (Award, 7 Jul. 2004) at paras 55 *et seq.*; *Hussein Annulment, supra,* note 7 at paras 83 *et seq.* On issues of nationality, see also *Champion Trading Company, Ameritrade International, Inc., James T. Wahba, John B. Wahba, Timothy T. Wahba v. Egypt* (Decision on Jurisdiction, 21 Oct. 2003) and *Waguih Elie George Siag and Clorinda Vecchi v. Egypt* (Decision on Jurisdiction, 11 Apr. 2007).

the investment is held in the territory of the host state,[77] its validity,[78] the nature and the scope of the rights making up the investment and whether they vest on a protected investor,[79] the conditions imposed or assurances granted by national law for the operation of the investment,[80] as well as the nature and scope of the government measures allegedly in breach of the IIA.[81]

These issues constitute the circumstances against which the host state conduct allegedly in breach of international law is to be assessed. The relevance of municipal law in this regard is well expressed in the *MTD Award*:

> The breach of an international obligation will need, by definition, to be judged in terms of international law. To establish the facts of the breach, it may be necessary to take into account municipal law.[82]

Hence, the tribunal applied Chilean law to establish whether there had been a breach of contract under that law, which could in turn constitute a breach of the BIT:

> The Tribunal accepts that the authorisation to invest in Chile is not a blanket authorization but only the initiation of a process to obtain the necessary permits and approvals from the various agencies and departments of the Government. It also accepts that the Government has to proceed in accordance with its own laws and policies in awarding such permits and approvals. Clause Four of the Foreign Investment Contracts would be meaningless if it were otherwise. Therefore, the Tribunal finds that Chile did not breach the BIT on account of breach of the Foreign Investment Contracts.[83]

The ICSID *ad hoc* annulment committee in this same case agreed with the tribunal's approach to applicable law, stating:

> In considering the implications of the Foreign Investment Contracts for fair and equitable treatment, the Tribunal faced a hybrid issue. The meaning of

---

77. See *Philippe Gruslin v. Malaysia* (Award, 27 Nov. 2000), at paras 14.1 *et seq.*, noting the parties' pleadings on whether investment by a Belgian national in a Luxembourg investment fund holding investments in the Kuala Lumpur Stock Exchange could be considered an investment in Malaysia, on the basis of Luxembourg law and contractual documents relating to ownership of the units in the fund and underlying investments (although the tribunal decided on other grounds). See also *SGS v. Pakistan, supra* note 6 at paras 136 *et seq.*; and *SGS v. Philippines, supra* note 6 at paras 99 *et seq.*, resolving the issue on the basis of contractual documents and the facts rather than domestic law rules.

78. See *Tokios Tokelės v. Ukraine* (Decision on Jurisdiction, 29 Apr. 2004) at paras 83-86; *Fraport AG Frankfurt Airport Services Worldwide v. Philippines* (Award, 16 Aug. 2007) at paras 344 *et seq.*; *Ioannis Kardassopoulos v. Georgia* (Decision on Jurisdiction, 6 Jul. 2007) at paras 142 *et seq.*

79. See *William Nagel v. Czech Republic* (Award, 10 Sep. 2003) at 158-162; and *CMS Award, supra* note 52 at paras 127-144.

80. See *Genin, supra* note 47 at paras 348 *et seq.*; and *Maffezini, supra* note 46 at paras 66-71.

81. See *Azinian, supra* note 46 at paras 105 and 120.

82. *MTD Award, supra* note 42 at para. 204.

83. *Ibid.*, at para. 118. See *infra* Chapter 6, §6.26, with respect to the tribunal's finding that there was a breach of fair and equitable treatment.

a Chilean contract is a matter of Chilean law; its implications in terms of an international law claim are a matter for international law.[84]

§2.13 The *renvoi* of international law to domestic law The role of domestic law in defining and regulating the investor's acquired rights is entirely logical. IIAs and general international law do not purport to regulate the complex problems of proprietary and contractual rights, or the legal nature of state measures. Further, the investment rights and state conduct at issue in IIA disputes arise in the context of legal relationships governed by domestic law. Hence the IIA and international law leave these questions to be decided, in principle, by the law of the host state. This may, at first sight, differ little from the well-established principle of international law that, before an international tribunal, the host state's domestic law is relevant only with respect to factual issues.[85] An important difference, however, is that being part of the proper law, a treaty tribunal may not treat domestic law as a fact that must be proven by the parties. The principle of *iura novit curia* requires a tribunal to establish, interpret and apply any legal rules relevant to the case before it, including any domestic law rules.[86]

§2.14 The relevance of domestic court decisions Along with domestic law, any relevant decisions of national courts should be taken into consideration, as instances of interpretation and application of the domestic law, but cannot bind an IIA tribunal.[87] As noted by the ICJ in *ELSI*, 'where the determination of a question of municipal law is essential to the Court's decision in a case, the Court will have to weigh the jurisprudence of the municipal courts.'[88]

§2.15 Domestic law questions as jurisdictional issues Domestic law questions often arise at the jurisdictional phase of IIA arbitration proceedings, as they are relevant to establishing the existence of the protected investment or the specific disputed contractual or proprietary right, and thus a tribunal's jurisdiction *ratione*

---

84. *MTD Annulment, supra* note 7 at para. 75. The *ad hoc* committee, however, stated that whether the tribunal properly interpreted Chilean law was not a matter falling within the jurisdiction of the committee. *Ibid.*

85. See R. Jennings & A. Watts, eds, *Oppenheim's International Law*, 9th edn (London: Longman, 1992), Vol. 1, at 83 ('From the standpoint of international law, a national law is generally regarded as a fact with reference to which rules of international law have to be applied, rather than as a rule to be applied on the international plane as a rule of law; and insofar as the International Court of Justice is called upon to express an opinion as to the effect of a rule of national law it will do so by treating the matter as a question of fact to be established as such rather than as a question of law to be decided by the court'). See also, *Case Concerning Certain German Interests in Polish Upper Silesia (Germany v. Poland)* (1926) P[1] Ser. A, No. 3 at 19. See note 101.

86. See *supra* §2.8 above.

87. *Azinian, supra* note 46 at para. 86 and *Čexskoslovenská Obchodní Banka, A.S. v. Slovak Republic* (Decision of the Tribunal on Respondent's Further and Partial Objection to Jurisdiction, 1 Dec. 2000) at para. 35.

88. *ELSI, supra* note 9 at 47.

materiae. But, as has been suggested by commentators,[89] if the pleadings reveal complex and contentious issues of fact and law regarding the existence and scope of the investment or investment rights, then the matter is better left for the merits phase, when the tribunal will have been fully briefed by the parties on these points. In these instances, the domestic law analysis is incorporated into the examination of the host state's liability and forms part of the factual background against which the proper law on matters of state responsibility apply (the IIA and international law). To avoid confusion, some tribunals have thus rightly treated the preliminary domestic law issues in a separate section of the merits awards preceding the merits analysis itself. For example, in the *CMS Award* the tribunal stated first (and somewhat confusingly) that Argentine and international law were 'inseparable' and should be applied in conjunction; then proceeded to confine its Argentine legal analysis regarding the currency for the calculation of gas transportation tariffs and conditions for their adjustment in the initial part of the award, separate from the analysis regarding the application of the standards of protection of the BIT to the circumstances of the case, which was fully based on international law.

§2.16 Criticism of the attitude of IIA tribunals towards domestic law It has been argued that IIA tribunals have not always paid sufficient attention to the relevant provisions of domestic law when faced with disputed issues as to the existence and scope of investment rights or the nature of the host state measures.[90] The award in *CME*, for example, has been criticized for assuming, rather than examining under Czech law, that certain changes in the joint venture agreement between the foreign investor and its local partner, imposed by a government agency, had weakened the position of the foreign investor thereby somehow paving the way for the local partner to terminate the agreement.[91]

In *Wena*, the tribunal found that the seizure of two hotels by an Egyptian governmental entity amounted to expropriation and other BIT breaches by Egypt. Neither the tribunal nor the subsequent ICSID annulment committee considered the fact that the termination of two hotel leases by the Egyptian entity had been upheld as valid under Egyptian law in contractual arbitration proceedings. The question whether in these circumstances Wena's contractual rights could be expropriated, considering that it had previously, and regularly under Egyptian law, lost the right to continue operating the hotels, was never addressed. No doubt the

---

89. Douglas, *supra* note 44 at 212.
90. *Ibid.*, at 197-211.
91. See *CME*, *supra* note 21 and *CME Czech Republic B.V. v. Czech Republic* (Partial Award, 13 Sep. 2001). Although the tribunal has the responsibility to apply the proper law, it is also incumbent on the respondent states to fully brief the tribunal on applicable domestic law. In the *CME* case, the Svea Court of Appeal, noted that the respondent state 'devoted little attention to Czech law during the ... proceedings' and 'presented no evidence regarding Czech law', *supra* note 56. See *infra* Chapter 6, §6.26, for further discussion of the *CME* case.

tribunal was influenced by the government's self-help take over and physical eviction of Wena's personnel from the hotels.[92]

§2.17 Limitations to the role of domestic law   Although some tribunals may have failed in sufficiently examining domestic law on the existence and scope of investment rights or the nature of the host state measures, it is important to note the limitations to the implicit *renvoi* of international law to domestic law, and thus of role of domestic law in IIA disputes.

Domestic law has a different role depending on the investment allegedly adversely affected and the treaty standard invoked by the claimant. Thus, the scope of the tribunal's duty to apply domestic law varies from case to case. The *Eureko v. Poland* case illustrates this point.[93] In this case, the claimant had acquired shares in 1999 in the partial privatization of the leading insurance group in Poland allegedly in the expectation, and arguably under the commitment later confirmed in certain contractual documents, of the State Treasury to complete the privatization in a public offering (the IPO) before the end of 2001. This completion of the privatization never took place. The tribunal found that Poland had disregarded Eureko's contractual rights to an IPO in breach of the umbrella clause of the BIT, and had been treated unfairly and inequitably as well as indirectly expropriated. The dissent and subsequent commentary highlights the failure of the tribunal to discuss the contractual rights in question under domestic law.[94] But if the claim and the decision, instead of framing the issue as the scope of contractual rights under domestic law (as protected investments) and contractual obligations (to be observed under the umbrella clause), had focussed on the initial shares acquired (as protected investment), the value of which had been adversely affected by political interferences and arbitrary acts (particularly in view of the various assurances as to the completion of the privatization), arguably the domestic law analysis required would have been of a different (and possibly more limited) scope altogether.

Further, the *renvoi* of international law to domestic law in matters pertaining to the existence and scope of investment rights, or the nature of host state measures, is not without limitations. Domestic law will apply provided it is not wholly unreasonable or leads to a result abhorrent to international law.[95] For example, having formally or *de facto* recognized the validity of an investment

---

92.   See *Wena, supra* note 59. See also *infra* Chapter 7, §7.29, for further discussion of the *Wena* case.

93.   *Eureko B.V. v. Poland* (Partial Award, 19 Aug. 2005) [*Eureko*].

94.   See dissenting opinion by arbitrator Jerzy Rajski in *Eureko, ibid.*, For commentary, see Z. Douglas, 'Nothing if Not Critical for Investment Treaty Arbitration: *Occidental, Eureko* and *Methanex*' (2006) 22 AI 27 at 38 *et seq.*

95.   The same principle applies in other areas in which international law leaves certain questions to be decided by municipal law. Thus, for example, in order to determine whether an individual is a national of a state, international law normally looks first at the law of that state, provided it is not wholly unreasonable. See P. Malanczuk, *Akehurst's Modern Introduction to International Law* (New York; London: Routledge, 2007) at 64.

contract by benefiting from it for a certain time, international law precludes a host state from denying, without more, its validity under domestic law and thus escape liability for breach or unilateral termination.[96] It is difficult to imagine that a domestic legal system would permit such a result, and recognize in these circumstances no intangible property rights including an acquired right to the operation of the contract or adequate compensation. In any case, it is suggested that such domestic law analysis will not be determinative. The IIA tribunal may reject such invalidity arguments by having direct recourse to well-established international law principles of good faith and estoppel.[97]

§2.18 Subsequent changes in the domestic law   The domestic law applicable in an IIA claim will be the law existing at the time the investment is made and any subsequent changes to that law. Naturally, subsequent changes in the domestic law may have a detrimental impact on the investment and these changes are often the subject of IIA claims.[98] These may be changes in taxation, minimum wages, environmental standards and other aspects of the regulatory framework for the investor's operations. Other changes may go as far as causing the complete termination of a contract, or the total destruction of the investment. In addition, changes applied to the investment may breach stabilization clauses agreed to between the investor and the host state, according to which the host state undertakes to leave the investor unaffected by subsequent changes of the local law. Although the host state law at the time of the investment and normal regulatory changes apply to determine the existence and scope of investment rights, subsequent adverse changes are likely to be relevant only as evidence of state measures that the IIA tribunal must assess against the standards of protection in the IIA. It will thus be open to the tribunal to find that the host state's law changes constitute a breach of the IIA[99] as interpreted under general international law, to which we now turn.

V   ROLE OF INTERNATIONAL LAW

§2.19 International law as the law applicable to issues of liability International law as embodied in the IIA applies to determine whether host state conduct breaches the IIA and creates international responsibility. The principal matter in an IIA dispute, the issue of the liability of the host state for measures that breach the IIA, is a matter for international law, not domestic law.

---

96.   See, e.g., the *Shufeldt Claim* (1930) II RIAA 1079 at 1094; T. Meron, 'Repudiation of Ultra Vires State Contracts and the International Responsibility of States' (1957) 6 ICLQ 273. See also *Ioannis Kardassopoulos v. Georgia* (Decision on Jurisdiction, 6 Jul. 2007) at paras 171 *et seq.* and *Repsol YPF Ecuador S.A. v. Empresa Estatal Petróleos del Ecuador* (Award, 20 Feb. 2004) at para. 166.
97.   See *infra* Chapter 9, §9.27, and Chapter 10, §10.27.
98.   See *infra* Chapter 6, §6.26, on legitimate expectations with respect to regulatory treatment.
99.   See *ibid.*

Although domestic law is relevant at the first stage of analysis (to determine the existence and scope of the investment, any governmental guarantees and commitments regarding the investment, and host state measures), these issues then need to be analyzed through the lens of international law. At this second stage of analysis the IIA regime and international law take over – the host state conduct must be assessed against the standards of protection in the IIA, and international law. That assessment determines first whether the host state has incurred international responsibility vis-à-vis the claimant investor by breaching the IIA. Second, it determines the content of international responsibility – the legal consequences of the IIA breach, such as reparation and compensation, which are also governed by international law. This is because the breach of an IIA standard by the host state creates a new obligation (a so-called secondary obligation) upon that state (i.e., essentially the obligation to provide reparation). That obligation arises in the international plane; it stems from the principle that a state's breach of an international obligation engages its international responsibility. Domestic law plays no part in any of these respects.

This role for international law follows from fundamental principles of public international law. IIAs are treaties and thus, according to the Vienna Convention, are 'governed by international law' and must be interpreted *inter alia* in the light of 'any relevant rules of international law applicable.'[100] Further, national law cannot excuse a breach of an international obligation, including a treaty obligation. Article 27 of the Vienna Convention provides that 'a party may not invoke the provisions of its internal law as justification for its failure to perform a treaty.' Article 3 of the International Law Commission (ILC) Articles on State Responsibility provides that 'the characterization of an act of a State as internationally wrongful is governed by international law. Such characterization is not affected by the characterization of the same act as lawful by internal law.'[101]

The decision by the ICSID *ad hoc* annulment committee in the *Vivendi* case rightly described the role of international law in IIA disputes in the following terms:

> … in respect of a claim based upon a substantive provision of that BIT […] the inquiry which the […] tribunal is required to undertake is one governed by […] the BIT and by applicable international law. Such an inquiry is neither in principle determined, nor precluded, by any issue of municipal law […][102]

---

100. Arts. 2(1)(a) and 31(3)(c), Vienna Convention. See *infra* §2.26.
101. International Law Commission's Articles on Responsibility of States for Internationally Wrongful Acts, *Official Records of the General Assembly,* UN GAOR, 56th Sess., Supp. No. 10, UN Doc A/56/10 at 11; 2001 YBILC, Vol. II, Part Two. The Articles and commentary are *reprinted in* J. Crawford, *The International Law Commission's Articles on State Responsibility: Introduction, Text, and Commentaries* (Cambridge: Cambridge University Press, 2002). See also, e.g., *Treatment of Polish Nationals and Other Persons of Polish Origin or Speech in the Danzig Territory* (1932) PCIJ Ser. A/B, No. 44 at 4 (municipal law, including the constitution of the state, in itself cannot form the basis for an international claim, nor can it form a defence to international liability; it merely constitutes the state actions that may violate the state's obligations under international law). See also *Greco-Bulgarian 'Communities'* (1930) PCIJ Sec. B, No. 17 at 32; *Case of the Free Zones of Upper Savoy and the District of Gex* (1930) PCIJ Sec. A, No. 24 at 12, and (1932) PCIJ Sec. A/B, No. 46 at 167.
102. *Vivendi Annulment, supra* note 59 at para. 102.

The tribunal found that international law is 'the proper or applicable law,' i.e., the law that determines whether the conduct of the host state has breached the IIA.[103] Similarly, in the *MTD Award* the tribunal found that '[...] the parties have agreed to this arbitration under the BIT. This instrument being a treaty, the agreement to arbitrate under the BIT requires the Tribunal to apply international law,'[104] and that 'the breach of an international obligation will need, by definition, to be judged in terms of international law.'[105] Tribunals are consistent in applying the IIA itself, as *lex specialis*, complemented by customary international law where necessary, to adjudge the liability of the host state in IIA disputes.[106] Professor Prosper Weil, referring to this jurisprudence states:

> ... [these] cases are noteworthy illustrations of the trend – which can only grow stronger – toward ICSID arbitration governed by international law by virtue of the fact that the BIT implicitly or explicitly provides that disputes must be settled not only on the basis of the provisions of the treaty itself, but also, and more generally, on the basis of the principles and rules of international law.[107]

Other commentators agree. Antonio Parra, former Deputy Secretary General of ICSID, for example, writing about the rules of law applicable to the substance of disputes brought under BITs, states that the BIT is the primary applicable source of law and the 'treaty being an instrument of international law, it is I think also implicit in such cases that the arbitrators should have recourse to the rules of general international law to supplement those of the treaty.'[108]

§2.20 IIAs and international law as part of domestic law   Some tribunals have justified the application of the IIA and customary international law on the basis that the host state's legal order would, in any case, incorporate the IIA and international law as part of domestic law with priority over ordinary legislation on the basis of the hierarchy of legal sources or as *lex specialis*.[109]

---

103. *Ibid.*, at para. 96.
104. *MTD Award, supra* note 42 at para. 87.
105. *Ibid.*, at para. 204. See also *Consorzio Groupement L.E.S.I. – Dipenta v. Algeria* (Award, 10 Jan. 2005) at para. 24; *Técnicas Medioambientales Tecmed S.A. v. Mexico* (Award, 29 May 2003) [*Tecmed*] at para. 120 (citing J. Crawford, *The International Law Commission's Articles on State Responsibility: Introduction, Text and Commentaries* (2002) at 84). See also K.J. Vandevelde, *United States Investment Treaties: Policy and Practice* (Boston: Kluwer Law and Taxation, 1992), at 78 ('because treatment of investment [under BITs] must never be less than that required by international law, international law provides the governing rules of decision, except where national law is more favourable').
106. E.g., *Compañía de Aguas del Aconquija S.A. & Compagnie Générale des Eaux v. Argentina* (Award, 21 Nov. 2000) and *Middle East Cement, supra* note 39 at paras 85-87.
107. P. Weil, 'The State, the Foreign Investor, and International Law: The No Longer Stormy Relationship of a Ménage à Trois' (2000) 15 ICSID Rev 401 at 412.
108. A. Parra, 'Applicable Substantive Law in ICSID Arbitrations Initiated Under Investment Treaties' (2001) 16 ICSID Rev 20 at 21.
109. *Wena Annulment, supra* note 7 at paras 42 *et seq.*; *Goetz, supra* note 10 at para. 98.

An example of the effects of IIAs in domestic law is the decision of an Argentine lower court in the *Desarrollos en Salud* case.[110] The court refused the conversion of the currency of a private contract from US dollars to Argentine pesos, as prescribed by the Argentine January 2002 Emergency Law, holding that that would breach the rights of the claimant as a foreign investor in Argentina under Argentina-BLEU (1990) which is part of Argentine law with primacy over legislation.

There are risks, however, in relying exclusively on domestic law to justify the pre-eminence of IIAs and international law on issues of liability in IIA arbitrations. The status of treaties and general international law varies in each legal system. Domestic issues, such as the need for transformation of international law into domestic law or the doctrine of non-self-executing treaties, may compromise the role of the IIA and international law in a given case.[111] First and foremost, the application of international law in IIA disputes is required by fundamental principles of international law, even it is also consistent with principles of domestic law. Thus, nothing is gained by relying solely upon the incorporation of international law into domestic law, and it may well lead to unnecessary confusion and controversy.

§2.21 Domestic law applied alongside international law on issues of liability Some IIA tribunals appear to have examined the merits of claims not only on the basis of international law, but also domestic law.[112] This seems to arise out of comity or a perceived need for courtesy towards the host state legal system, rather than a real requirement or duty to apply domestic law in matters of liability. Professor Prosper Weil states:

> The reference to the domestic law of the host State, even if designed only to ascertain whether it is, or is not, compatible with international law, is indeed a pointless exercise, the sole raison d'être of which is to avoid offending the sensibilities of the host State.[113]

In this approach, the exercise would be 'pointless' because, under fundamental principles of public international law, national law would be irrelevant in case of conflict with international law. Thus, if it is international law that provides the rule

---

110. *Desarrollos en Salud S.A. S/Concurso preventivo/ S/ Incidente de Revisión* (N.V. NISSHO IWAI S.A. (BENELUX)) (Juzgado Comercial 26, Secretaría 51, 10 Nov. 2003).
111. Lluís Paradell-Trius, 'International Law in National Legal Systems: Constitutional Obstacles and Opportunities' (2005) 2 TDM.
112. E.g., *Goetz, supra* note 10.
113. P. Weil, *supra* note 107 at 409. ICSID practice under Art. 42(1), second sentence, of the ICSID Convention clearly indicates that in ICSID cases international law is fully applicable and prevails over municipal law. In *Compañía de Desarrollo de Santa Elena, S.A. v. Costa Rica*, for example, the tribunal found that under Art. 42(1), international law would prevail over municipal law: it was 'controlling,' and governed the arbitration. *Compañía del Desarrollo de Santa Elena, S.A. v. Costa Rica* (Final Award, 17 Feb. 2000), at paras 64-65.

of decision in IIA disputes, it would seem to be the law that must generally apply and cannot be reduced to a gap filling law.[114]

VI   APPLICABLE INTERNATIONAL LAW

§2.22 Sources of international law in IIA disputes   IIA tribunals determine the liability of the host state by applying the specific terms of the IIA under which the claim is brought and other sources of international law to supplement the IIA. The sources of international law are set out in Article 38 of the *Statute of the International Court of Justice*: international conventions, whether general or particular; international custom; the general principles of law recognized by civilized nations; and judicial decisions and teachings of the most highly qualified publicists, as subsidiary means for the determination of rules of law.[115]

IIA tribunals have applied all these sources. Treaty provisions aside from those of the IIA have been often invoked and applied,[116] as have customary international law rules,[117] and general principles of international law.[118] Tribunals also make abundant reference to prior IIA decisions (as set out in the following section), ICJ and Permanent Court of International Justice (PCIJ) case law,[119] as well as decisions of inter-state arbitral commissions and mixed commissions.[120] The same is true for the writing of publicists.[121]

§2.23 Precedents   Counsel and tribunals in IIA cases regularly refer to and rely on IIA case law.[122] Although it is well-established that there is no doctrine of

---

114.   See, e.g., *Eastern Sugar B.V. v. Czech Republic* (Partial Award, 27 Mar. 2007) at para. 196.
115.   For commentary, see A. Pellet, 'Art. 38,' in A. Zimmermann *et al.*, eds, *Statute of the International Court of Justice: A Commentary* (Oxford: Oxford University Press, 2006) at 676.
116.   *Metalclad, supra* note 46 at paras 75 *et seq.* on transparency obligations under NAFTA, not in Chapter Eleven.
117.   *Compañía de Aguas del Aconquija S.A. and Vivendi Universal S.A. v. Argentina* (Award, 20 Aug. 2007) [*Vivendi II*] at para. 8.2.5 on the principle of full compensation in lieu of restitution as a customary international law rule.
118.   *Tecmed, supra* note 105 at para. 124 on the principle of good faith.
119.   *Maffezini, supra* note 46 at paras 43-50, referring to the *Rights of Nationals of the United States of America in Morocco* on the scope of MFN protection; *Hussein Nuaman Soufraki v. United Arab Emirates* (Award, 17 Jul. 2004) at para. 45, referring to the *Nottebohm* case on nationality of the claimant; *Tokios Tokelès v. Ukraine* (Decision on Jurisdiction, 29 Apr. 2004) at paras 53-56 and 66 referring to *Barcelona Traction* on piercing the corporate veil; *CMS Gas Transmission Company v. Argentina* (Decision of the Tribunal on Objections to Jurisdiction, 17 Jul. 2003) at para. 44 on the *ELSI* case for the standing of shareholders.
120.   *Maffezini, ibid.*, referring to the *Ambatielos* case when deciding on the scope of MFN protection.
121.   *Vivendi II, supra* note 117 at para 7.4.8 quoting one of the most commonly cited works on BITs, that of F.A. Mann, 'British Treaties for the Promotion and Protection of Investments' (1981) 52 BYIL 241.
122.   On precedent in IIA disputes see G. Kaufmann-Kohler, 'Arbitral Precedent: Dream Necessity or Excuse?' (2007) 23 AI 357; P. Duprey, 'Do Arbitral Awards Constitute Precedents? Should Commercial Arbitration Be Distinguished in this Regard from Arbitration Based on Investment Treaties?' in P. Pinsolle, A.V. Schlaepfer & L. Degos, eds, *Towards a Uniform International*

precedent in international law (*stare decisis*),[123] and this is expressly stated in some IIAs,[124] and possibly in the ICSID Convention,[125] tribunals often refer to previous decisions as providing guidance. Although not always explicit in tribunal decisions, previous decisions appear to be taken into account as determinative or authoritative statements of the rules or principles of law applicable (rather than their establishment), as examples of how similar issues have been resolved in previous instances, or to highlight consistency between the tribunal's reasoning and previous decisions. As stated by the tribunal in *Enron Corporation and Ponderosa Assets, L.P. v. Argentina* (Ancillary Claim), referring to earlier decisions:

> ... the conclusions of the Tribunal follow the same line of reasoning, not because there might be a compulsory precedent but because the circumstances of the various cases are comparable, and in some respects identical.[126]

The use of prior decisions as guidance has become an issue in the Argentine IIA cases relating to Argentina's 2002 emergency legislation.[127] This has occurred mainly in the jurisdictional decisions, as Argentina has raised identical objections to jurisdiction in most of the cases. In *AES Corporation v. Argentina*, the claimant requested that the tribunal dismiss Argentina's jurisdictional objections out of hand as moot given the prior case law. The tribunal rejected this radical approach though not the value of previous decisions as guidance:

> Each tribunal remains sovereign and may retain, as it is confirmed by ICSID practice, a different solution for resolving the same problem; but decisions on jurisdiction dealing with the same or very similar issues may at least indicate some lines of reasoning of real interest; this Tribunal may consider them in order to compare its own position with those already adopted by its predecessors and, if it shares the views already expressed by one or more of these tribunals on an specific point of law, it is free to adopt the same solution.[128]

Arbitration Law, IAI International Arbitration Series No. 3 (New York: Juris Publishing, 2005), at 251; and D. Di Pietro, 'The Use of Precedents in ICSID Arbitration: Regularity or Certainty?' (2007) 10 IALR 92; *Special Issue on Precedent in Investment Arbitration* (2008) 5 TDM.

123. E.g., M. Shahabuddeen, *Precedent in the World Court* (Cambridge: Cambridge University Press, 1996). See Art. 59 of the ICJ Statute. For a statement in IIA case law see *SGS v. Philippines*, *supra* note 6 at para. 97.

124. E.g., Art. 1136(1) NAFTA Chapter Eleven. See D.M. Price, 'Chapter 11-Private Party vs. Government, Investor-State Dispute Settlement: Frankenstein or Safety Valve?' (2000) 26 Can-USLJ 107 at 111.

125. Art. 53(1), ICSID Convention. See Schreuer, *supra* note 7 at 1082. *Cf. SGS v. Philippines*, *supra* note 6 at para. 97 (arguing that this provision refers to res judicata rather than precedent).

126. *Enron Corporation and Ponderosa Assets, L.P. v. Argentina* (Ancillary Claim) (Decision on Jurisdiction, 2 Aug. 2004) [*Enron Jurisdiction*] at para. 25.

127. See discussion of the cases *infra* at Chapter 6, §6.26, and Chapter 10, §10.21-§10.23.

128. *AES Corporation v. Argentina* (Decision on Jurisdiction, 26 Apr. 2005) at para. 30, and see generally the analysis at paras 17-33.

The tribunal added that 'precedents may also be rightly considered, at least as a matter of comparison and, if so considered by the Tribunal, of inspiration.'[129] In *SGS v. Philippines*, the tribunal underlined concerns regarding the consistency of decisions, while plainly rejecting the notion of compulsory precedent:

> In the Tribunal's view, although different tribunals constituted under the ICSID system should in general seek to act consistently with each other, in the end it must be for each tribunal to exercise its competence in accordance with the applicable law, which will by definition be different for each BIT and each Respondent state. Moreover, there is no doctrine of precedent in international law, if by precedent is meant a rule of the binding effect of a single decision. There is no hierarchy of international tribunals, and even if there were, there is no good reason for allowing the first tribunal in time to resolve issues for all later tribunals.[130]

The tribunal in *Saipem* explained the role of precedent in light of 'a duty to adopt solutions established in a series of consistent cases' and 'a duty to seek to contribute to the harmonious development of investment law and thereby to meet the legitimate expectations of the community of States and investors towards certainty of the rule of law.'[131] This approach echoes that of the ICJ in the *Libya/Malta Continental Shelf* case, referring to 'justice of which equity is a manifestation ... should display consistency and a degree of predictability.'[132]

All this indicates that when (as is often the case) legal issues already addressed by a tribunal reappear in a subsequent case, litigating parties may rely on case law to support their legal arguments and tribunals may follow it as grounds for their findings.[133] This is inevitable and arguably desirable for reasons of consistency and predictability. However, it still remains that the circumstances under which international decisions may be used as precedents, in the absence of a hierarchy or clear relationship between the organs that produce them, are unclear and may consequently be subject to misuse. As noted by Jan Paulsson, 'there are awards and awards, some destined to become ever brighter beacons, others to flicker and die near-instant deaths' and noting that the legal status of the corpus of decided cases 'will also doubtless turn out to be subject to the same Darwinian imperative:

---

129. *Ibid.*, at para. 31.
130. *SGS v. Philippines*, *supra* note 6 at para. 97.
131. *Saipem*, *supra* note 75 at para. 67. See also, *Gas Natural SDG, S.A. v. Argentina* (Decision of the Tribunal on Preliminary Questions on Jurisdiction, 17 Jun. 2005) [*Gas Natural*] at paras 36 and 52 (noting that the tribunal arrived at its conclusions independently but then checked them for consistency with other decisions) and *Bayindir*, *supra* note 75 at para. 76.
132. *Continental Shelf (Libyan Arab Jamahiriya v. Malta)* [1985] ICJ Rep 13 at para. 45.
133. One author has identified the publication of awards and decisions, the existence of specialized scholarly journals, academic and professional fora and committees dedicated to IIA arbitration and email discussion lists (like OGEMID) as factors for the increase in the use of precedent. See C. McLachlan, 'Investment Treaties and General International Law' (2008) 57 *ICLQ* 361 at 379.

the unfit will perish.'[134] But while this natural selection occurs, wrong law may be in the making by an uncritical reliance on precedent.

§2.24 Inconsistent decisions   In some cases, tribunals have critically reviewed, and disagreed with, precedents relevant to their decisions. The classical example is the *SGS v. Philippines* case, where the tribunal discussed the earlier *SGS v. Pakistan* case and expressed its disagreement with some of the holdings in that case, in particular those on the interpretation of the umbrella clause:

> As it will become clear, the present Tribunal does not in all respects agree with the conclusions reached by the *SGS v. Pakistan* Tribunal on issues of the interpretation of arguably similar language in the Swiss-Philippines BIT. This raises the question whether, nonetheless, the present tribunal should defer to the answers given by the *SGS v. Pakistan* Tribunal. [...] In the Tribunal's view, although different tribunals constituted under the ICSID system should in general seek to act consistently with each other, in the end it must be for each tribunal to exercise its competence in accordance with the applicable law, which will by definition be different for each BIT and each Respondent State. Moreover, there is no doctrine of precedent in international law, if by precedent is meant a rule of the binding effect of a single decision. There is no hierarchy of international tribunals, and even if there were, there is no good reason for allowing the first tribunal in time to resolve issues for all later tribunals. It must be initially for the control mechanisms provided for under the BIT and the ICSID Convention, and in the longer term for the development of a common legal opinion or *jurisprudence constante*, to resolve the difficult legal questions discussed by the *SGS v. Pakistan* Tribunal and also in the present decision.[135]

There are other examples of decisions refusing to follow or distancing themselves from earlier decisions, such as on the interpretation of most-favoured-nation clauses in relation to dispute resolution matters.[136]

---

134.   Paulsson, *supra* note 58 at 881.
135.   *SGS v. Philippines*, *supra* note 6 at para. 97.
136.   See *infra* Chapter 5 on MFN clauses. See also the different approaches (albeit not plain contradiction) between *EnCana*, *supra* note 45 and *Occidental Exploration and Production Company v. Ecuador* (Final Award, 1 Jul. 2004) [*Occidental*]. Of course, decisions may contradict themselves inadvertently in case of parallel proceedings, as the classical examples of the *CME* and *Lauder* cases demonstrates: *CME Czech Republic B.V. v. Czech Republic* (Partial Award, 13 Sep. 2001); *Ronald S. Lauder v. Czech Republic* (Final Award, 3 Sep. 2001). On inconsistent decisions, see J. Gill, 'Inconsistent Decisions: An Issue to be Addressed or a Fact of Life?,' in F. Ortino, A. Sheppard & H. Warner, eds *Investment Treaty Law-Current Issues*, Vol. 1 (London: BIICL, 2006) at 23; S. Franck, 'The Legitimacy Crisis in Investment Treaty Arbitration: Privatising Public International Law Through Inconsistent Decisions' (2005) 73 FLR 1521.

Even if a tendency can be observed where '[t]he award becomes a showcase for legal erudition,'[137] and there is perhaps unnecessary acrimonious criticism of earlier decisions by some tribunals, this critical approach to precedent is unavoidable as well as desirable. As stated by Jan Paulsson, '[t]he corpus of decided cases in the field of international investment arbitration is of recent vintage.' Often a tribunal is on untested ground, faced with novel issues and sometimes not ideally equipped to address them; hence quality control is required.

An example in which critical appraisal of precedents would have been welcome is with regard to the law of necessity in the Argentine emergency cases. For instance, the *LG&E* award is at least partly inconsistent with the *CMS* award in relation to the express treaty exception and customary law defences of necessity and their operation, although the two cases concerned identical factual backgrounds (the Argentine 2002 crisis and related emergency legislation interfering with the tariff regime of privatized gas utilities), and the same applicable law (the Argentina-US BIT). Hence one would have expected the *LG&E* tribunal to refer to *CMS* and explain its disagreement. Yet there is not a single citation or allusion.[138] The same is true for the subsequent award in *Enron*, which is consistent with *CMS* but not with *LG&E*, yet cites neither.[139] Only the fourth award in this line of cases the *Sempra* case, referred to the prior conflicting decisions as follows:

> The Tribunal has examined with particular attention the recent decision on liability and subsequent award on damages in the *LG&E* case as they have dealt with mostly identical questions concerning emergency and state of necessity. The decision on liability has been contrasted with the finding of the tribunal in *CMS*. While two arbitrators sitting in the present case were also members of the tribunal in the *CMS* case the matter has been examined anew. This Tribunal must note, first, that in addition to differences in the legal interpretation of the Treaty in this context, an important question that distinguishes the *LG&E* decision on liability from *CMS*, and for that matter also from the recent award in *Enron*, lies in the assessment of the facts. While the *CMS* and *Enron* tribunals have not been persuaded by the severity of the Argentine crisis as a factor capable of triggering the state of necessity, *LG&E* has considered the situation in a different light and justified the invocation of emergency and necessity, albeit for a limited period of time. This Tribunal

---

137. N. Blackaby, 'Investment Arbitration and Commercial Arbitration,' in L.A. Mistelis & J. Lew, eds, *Pervasive Problems in International Arbitration* (Amsterdam: Kluwer, 2006) at 228.

138. *LG&E Energy Corp., LG&E Capital Corp. and LG&E International Inc. v. Argentina* (Decision on Liability, 3 Oct. 2006) [*LG&E*] and *CMS Award, supra* note 52. See *infra* Chapter 10, §10.21 *et seq.,* for a discussion of the necessity defence. For commentary on this inconsistency see, e.g., A. Reinisch, 'Necessity in International Investment Arbitration – An Unnecessary Split of Opinions in Recent ICSID Cases? Comments on *CMS v. Argentina and LG&E v. Argentina*' (2007) 8 JWIT 191.

139. *Enron Corporation and Ponderosa Assets, L.P. v. Argentina* (Award, 22 May 2007) [*Enron*].

however, is not any more persuaded than the *CMS* and *Enron* tribunals about the crisis justifying the operation of emergency and necessity, although it also readily accepts that the changed economy conditions have an influence on the questions of valuation and compensation, as will be examined further below.[140]

More was to be expected given the critical issue at stake. Also, the *Sempra* award was issued three days after the decision on annulment in the *CMS* case, which was critical of the *CMS* award on the point.[141] However, the award in *Sempra* does not refer to the *CMS* annulment decision, and is unclear as to whether it took on board some of the criticism of the *CMS* award contained in that decision. Given the relevance of the *CMS* annulment case, the tribunal in *Sempra* presumably could have delayed its award to assess that decision. It is open to question whether the overlap of some arbitrators in these cases inhibited tribunals from criticising or openly endorsing prior decisions, or to the contrary should have helped or prompt tribunals to explain different approaches.[142] Perhaps the desire not to influence the *CMS* annulment proceedings pending around the same time also played a role.[143] Be that as it may, the net unfortunate result is that, by tribunals ignoring each other, several opportunities to clarify the law on necessity were missed.

§2.25 Human rights As part of international law, human rights law may be applicable in IIA disputes. It may be possible for human rights claims to be brought to IIA tribunals, which may have jurisdiction over them depending on the terms of the IIA and, presumably, the extent to which such claims are connected to an underlying investment dispute. This point was well made by the tribunal in *Biloune and Marine Drive Complex Ltd. v. Ghana*, a contractual arbitration:

> In the final cause of action asserted, the claimant seeks recovery for alleged violation by the Government of Ghana of Mr Biloune's human rights. The Claimants assert that the Government's allegedly arbitrary detention and expulsion of Mr Biloune and violation of his property and contractual rights constitute an actionable human rights violation for which compensation may

---

140. *Sempra Energy International v. Argentina* (Award, 28 Sep. 2007) [*Sempra*] at para. 46. In the one other award against Argentina to date, *BG Group Plc. v. Argentina* (Final Award, 24 Dec. 2007) [*BG*] at paras 407-412, the tribunal summarily rejected the defence of necessity, with an approving reference to *Enron* and distinguishing *LG&E* on the basis that the BIT at stake did not contain a treaty emergency clause which arguably was the basis of the *LG&E* award.
141. *CMS Annulment, supra* note 7.
142. The tribunal in *CMS* was Orrego Vicuña (president), and Lalonde and Rezek (arbitrators); in *LG&E*: de Maekelt (president), and Rezek and van den Berg (arbitrators); in *Enron*: Orrego Vicuña (president), van den Berg and Tschanz (arbitrators); and in *Sempra*: Orrego Vicuña (president), and Lalonde and Morelli Rico (arbitrators).
143. *CMS* annulment proceedings took place between 27 Sep. 2005 (date of registration of the application) and 25 Sep. 2007 (date of decision). The *LG&E* and *Enron* awards came out during that period.

be required in a commercial arbitration pursuant to the GIC Agreement. They assert that the Tribunal should consider this portion of the claim because this is the only forum in which redress for these alleged injuries may be sought.

Long-established customary international law requires that a State accord foreign nationals within its territory a standard of treatment no less than that prescribed by international law. Moreover, contemporary international law recognizes that all individuals, regardless of nationality, are entitled to fundamental human rights (which, in the view of the Tribunal, include property as well as personal rights), which no government may violate. Nevertheless, it does not follow that this Tribunal is competent to pass upon every type of departure from the minimum standard to which foreign nationals are entitled, or that this Tribunal is authorized to deal with allegations of violations of fundamental human rights.

This Tribunal's competence is limited to commercial disputes arising under a contract entered into in the context of Ghana's Investment Code. As noted, the Government agreed to arbitrate only disputes 'in respect of' the foreign investment. Thus, other matters – however compelling the claim or wrongful the alleged act – are outside this Tribunal's jurisdiction. Under the facts of this case it must be concluded that, while the acts alleged to violate the international human rights of Mr. Biloune may be relevant in considering the investment dispute under arbitration, this Tribunal lacks jurisdiction to address, as an independent cause of action, a claim of violation of human rights.[144]

The claims in *Biloune* were brought under a contract arbitration clause and the arbitration was formally a commercial one. However, the considerations of the tribunal are equally transposable to a case brought under an IIA: the jurisdiction of the tribunal to address human rights violations will largely depend on their relevance to the underlying investment dispute and on the terms of the IIA itself.

More often, however, human rights law may be invoked by respondent states to justify the measures complained of, and thus as defences against liability under the applicable IIA. The question is whether, and if so how, tribunals may balance IIA protections against human rights considerations.[145] So far human rights arguments have been rare, and the impact of human rights law in IIA

144. *Biloune and Marine Drive Complex Ltd. v. Ghana Investments Centre and the Government of Ghana* (Award on Jurisdiction and Liability, 27 Oct. 1989) 95 ILR 184 at 203.
145. U. Kriebaum, 'Privatizing Human Rights – The Interface Between International Investment Protection and Human Rights' (2006) 3 TDM; M. Hirsch, 'Interactions between Investment and Non-Investment Obligations in International Investment Law' (2006) Research Paper No. 14-06, Faculty of Law of the Hebrew University of Jerusalem, submitted to the ILA Committee on International Law on Foreign Investment 31 Mar. 2006; L.E. Peterson & K.R. Grey, 'International Human Rights in Bilateral Investment Treaties and in Investment Arbitration' (2003) Research Paper of the International Institute for Sustainable Development (IISD) for the Swiss Department of Foreign Affairs (Apr. 2003).

disputes is yet to be considered by tribunals.[146] In principle, human rights concerns may be treated as any other public purpose pursued by state measures. State measures taken to fulfill international human rights concerns may not, for this reason alone, be exempted from IIA obligations. Measures may still give rise to liability where contrary to specific commitments granted to investors. Thus the scope of the measures, and of the commitments at play in the context of human rights' considerations, is bound to be of significant importance, as will be in other cases the proportionality and reasonableness of the measures (i.e., the balancing of human rights' considerations and the protection of foreign investments).[147]

VII   INTERPRETATION OF IIAS

§2.26 Treaty interpretation as the process of applying the proper law   Issues of applicable law and interpretation are obviously interconnected. Having determined the applicable law, tribunals interpret it in adjudicating on the underlying dispute. In IIA claims the applicable law on the merits is the IIA itself and international law, supplemented by municipal law. But the identification of international law as the proper law is not the end of the enquiry; international law is then to be applied to resolve the underlying dispute. The question is when and how to resort to general international law. In this context, it has been suggested that international law be introduced into the analysis of the IIA claim in the first place through treaty interpretation mechanisms. This ensures that the IIA is the centre of the enquiry and that general international law assists in the interpretation of the IIA under Article 31(3)(c) of the Vienna Convention, which establishes that, in interpreting a treaty:

> There shall be taken into account, together with the context:
> [...]
> (c) Any relevant rules of international law applicable in the relations between the parties

The suggestion is that this approach ensures that the IIA supplies the primary rule, which takes precedence over custom or general principles if those provide a

---

146. See, e.g., only a reference in passing to this issue in *Azurix Corp. v. Argentina* (Award, 14 Jul. 2006) [*Azurix*] at paras 254 and 261. For arguments of a somewhat human rights' nature see the Argentine emergency cases *BG, supra* note 140; *Sempra, ibid.*; *Enron, supra* note 139; *LG&E, supra* note 138; *CMS Award, supra* note 52. Human rights arguments have been raised in the pending Argentine water cases: *Suez, Sociedad General de Aguas de Barcelona S.A., and InterAgua Servicios Integrales del Agua S.A. v. Argentina* (ICSID Case No. ARB/03/17); *Suez, Sociedad General de Aguas de Barcelona S.A. and Vivendi Universal S.A., v. Argentina* (ICSID Case No. ARB/03/19); *AWG Group Ltd. v. Argentina* (UNCITRAL Arbitration), and in other pending cases, such as *Piero Foresti, Laura de Carli and others v. South Africa* (ICSID Case No. ARB(AF)/07/1).
147. See *infra* Chapter 6, §6.11.

different rule or test; but also that IIAs are not regarded as self-contained with the risks of fragmentation in international law, but rather systemically integrated within the international legal system according to the 'constitutional norm' and 'fundamental principle' enshrined in Article 31(3)(c).[148]

§2.27 International law rules on treaty interpretation   IIA tribunals regularly begin the interpretation process by invoking Articles 31 and 32[149] of the Vienna Convention,[150] often adding that those provisions reflect customary international law.[151] For example, in *Noble Ventures, Inc. v. Romania*, the tribunal stated:

---

148.   McLachlan, *supra* note 133 at 365, 371 and 399. See also C. McLachlan, 'The Principle of Systemic Integration and Art. 31(3)(c) of the Vienna Convention' (2005) 54 ICLQ 279; D. French, 'Treaty Interpretation and the Incorporation of Extraneous Legal Rules', (2006) 55 ICLQ 281 and A. van Aaken, 'Fragmentation in International Law: The Case of International Investment Protection' Working Paper No. 2008-1, Law and Economics Research Paper Series, University of St Gallen Law School.
149.   Arts 31 and 32, Vienna Convention, read as follows:

Article 31 General rule of interpretation

(1) A treaty shall be interpreted in good faith in accordance with the ordinary meaning to be given to the terms of the treaty in their context and in the light of its object and purpose.
(2) The context for the purpose of the interpretation of a treaty shall comprise, in addition to the text, including its preamble and annexes:
    (*a*) any agreement relating to the treaty which was made between all the parties in connection with the conclusion of the treaty;
    (*b*) any instrument which was made by one or more parties in connection with the conclusion of the treaty and accepted by the other parties as an instrument related to the treaty.
(3) There shall be taken into account, together with the context:
    (*a*) any subsequent agreement between the parties regarding the interpretation of the treaty or the application of its provisions;
    (*b*) any subsequent practice in the application of the treaty which establishes the agreement of the parties regarding its interpretation;
    (*c*) any relevant rules of international law applicable in the relations between the parties.
(4) A special meaning shall be given to a term if it is established that the parties so intended.

Article 32 Supplementary means of interpretation

Recourse may be had to supplementary means of interpretation, including the preparatory work of the treaty and the circumstances of its conclusion, in order to confirm the meaning resulting from the application of article 31, or to determine the meaning when the interpretation according to article 31:

(*a*) leaves the meaning ambiguous or obscure; or
(*b*) leads to a result which is manifestly absurd or unreasonable.
150.   E.g., *AAPL, supra* note 42 at paras 38-42; *MTD Award, ibid.* at para. 112; *Enron Jurisdiction, supra* note 126 at para. 32; *Plama Consortium Limited v. Bulgaria* (Decision on Jurisdiction, 8 Feb. 2005) [*Plama*] at paras 117 and 147-165; *Eureko, supra* note 93 at para. 247 and *Aguas del Tunari, S.A. v. Bolivia* (Decision on the Respondent's Objections to Jurisdiction, 21 Oct. 2005) [*Aguas del Tunari*] at paras 88-93, 226, 230, 239.
151.   See *Tokios Tokelès v. Ukraine* (Decision on Jurisdiction, 29 Apr. 2004) at para. 27.

reference has to be made to Arts. 31 *et seq.* of the Vienna Convention on the Law of Treaties which reflect the customary international law concerning treaty interpretation. Accordingly, treaties have to be interpreted in good faith in accordance with the ordinary meaning to be given to the terms of the treaty in their context and in the light of the object and purpose of the Treaty, while recourse may be had to supplementary means of interpretation, including the preparatory work and the circumstances of its conclusion, only in order to confirm the meaning resulting from the application of the aforementioned methods of interpretation. Reference should also be made to the principle of effectiveness (*effet utile*), which, too plays an important role in interpreting treaties.[152]

§2.28 Methods of interpretation   The starting point of any analysis must be the ordinary meaning of the terms, as required by Article 31(1), Vienna Convention.[153] While this may prove sufficient in some cases, in others 'it may result in little more than an exchange of synonyms.'[154] When interpreting the standard of fair and equitable treatment, for example, the tribunal's decision in *MTD* began quoting the Oxford Concise English Dictionary and then noted that '[i]n their ordinary meaning, the terms "fair" and "equitable" … mean "just," "even handed," "unbiased," "legitimate." '[155] That did not appear to take the tribunal very far.[156]

Sometimes, tribunals have resorted to special principles or presumptions as supplementary means to determine ordinary meaning.[157] An example is the principle *expressio unius est exclusio alterious*, i.e., specific mention of an item excludes others. In *National Grid Plc v. Argentina*, for example, the tribunal referred to this rule as a starting point for the interpretation of the most-favoured-nation (MFN) clause of the applicable BIT and whether it covered dispute resolution.[158] The tribunal noted that the BIT enumerated certain exceptions to the clause, which did not include dispute resolution: 'dispute resolution is not included among the exceptions to the application of the clause. As a matter of interpretation, specific mention of an item excludes others: *expressio unius est exclusio*

---

152.   *Noble Ventures, Inc. v. Romania* (Award, 12 Oct. 2005) [*Noble Ventures*] at para. 50.
153.   On treaty interpretation, see I.M. Sinclair, *The Vienna Convention on the Law of Treaties*, 2nd edn (Manchester: Manchester University Press, 1984). See also A. Aust, *Modern Treaty Law and Practice*, 2nd edn (Cambridge: Cambridge University Press, 2007) and *Oppenheim's International Law*, *supra* note 85 at §629-634.
154.   McLachlan, *supra* note 133 at 371.
155.   *MTD Award, supra* note 42 at para. 105.
156.   See *infra* Chapter 6, §6.26, on the *MTD* tribunal's approach to the interpretation of fair and equitable treatment.
157.   *Oppenheim's International Law*, *supra* note 85 at §633, referring to a series of maxims and principles as supplementary means of interpretation. See also Aust, *supra* note 153 at 248-249.
158.   See *infra* Chapter 5, Part III, applying MFN treatment to investor-state arbitration procedures.

alterius.[159] However, this rule of logic has its limitations. As noted by a commentator: 'whether the mention of one item or a list of items in a provision really excludes the relevance of other items depends very much on the particular circumstances and cannot be answered in a generalized way.'[160]

Another principle of textual interpretation is the *ejusdem generis* doctrine, i.e., 'general words following or perhaps preceding special words are limited to the genus indicated by the special words.'[161] The principle derives from the fundamental rule of contract construction that the 'meaning of a term is determined not in the abstract but in its context.'[162] This principle has been followed by some international tribunals,[163] and could be used, for example, to interpret the so-called 'war and civil disturbance' or 'losses due to war' clause, present in some BITs.[164] These typically contain a list of situations covered by the clause including fairly specific and easily understandable expressions such as 'war or other armed conflict, revolution [...], revolt, insurrection or riot,' but which interject other terms of a more elusive nature such as 'state of national emergency.'[165] Arguably, the latter general expression could be interpreted as referring to another type of civil disturbance situation in the context of the former, more specific ones. Techniques of interpretation, including *expressio unius* and *ejusdem generis* and others, however, need to used with caution. They are guides to interpretation and should not be followed slavishly.[166]

Apart from focusing on the text and related rules of logical presumptions and grammar, other means of interpretation are available and are often resorted to by tribunals. Interpretation in accordance with the object and purpose of the IIA has been the most prevalent, and is dealt with in the following section. Another method that may be used, given the large number of BITs often containing similar

---

159. *National Grid Plc v. Argentina* (Decision on Jurisdiction, 20 Jun. 2006) *[National Grid]* at para. 82.
160. C. Schreuer, 'Diversity and Harmonization of Treaty Interpretation in Investment Arbitration' (2006) 3 TDM at 7.
161. I. Brownlie, *Principles of Public International Law*, 6th edn (Oxford: Oxford University Press, 2003), at 604; A. McNair, *The Law of Treaties* (Oxford: Clarendon, 1961), at 393. The principle is regarded also as a basic principle for the interpretation of MFN clauses, according to which the clause operates only in matters covered by the basic treaty. See, e.g., *Emilio Agustín Maffezini v. Spain* (Decision of the Tribunal on Objections to Jurisdiction, 25 Jan. 2000) *[Maffezini Jurisdiction]* at paras 41-56. See *infra* Chapter 5 on MFN clauses.
162. *Oppenheim's International Law, supra* note 85 at 1273.
163. See, e.g., *Grimm v. Iran*, Case No. 71, Award, 18 Feb. 1983, 71 ILR 650, 652 (1986); *Payment of Various Serbian Loans Issued in France; Payment in Gold of the Brazilian Federal Loans Issued in France* (1929) PCIJ Ser. A, Nos. 20/21.
164. See *infra* Chapter 6, §6.47 and Chapter 10, §10.8.
165. E.g., Art. 4, Argentina-UK (1990), headed 'Compensation for Losses' reads in part: 'Investors of one Contracting Party whose investments in the territory of the other Contracting Party suffer losses owing to war or other armed conflict, revolution, state of national emergency, revolt, insurrection or riot [...] shall be accorded [...] treatment, as regards restitution, indemnification, compensation or other settlement, no less favourable than that which the latter Contracting Party accords to its own investors or to investors of any third State. [....].'
166. Aust, *supra* note 153 at 249.

or identical provisions and the fact that many BITs are based on model treaties, is a comparative approach between the BIT in question and other BITs concluded by the host state, or the model BIT. For example, in the *National Grid* case, the tribunal examined whether the MFN clause in Argentina-UK (1990) extended to dispute resolution matters *inter alia* by comparing the language of the clause with that in UK Model BITs and signed UK BITs. Some of these provided the same MFN language but added 'for the avoidance of doubt it is confirmed that the treatment [...] shall apply to the provisions of Articles 1 to 11 of this Agreement,'[167] i.e., also dispute resolution. The terms 'for the avoidance of doubt' and 'it is confirmed' arguably demonstrated that even in BITs where such clarification was not specifically provided, the same MFN treatment language intended to cover all investment protection matters, including dispute resolution between investors and host states.[168] Further, in deciding on the irrelevance of the requirement of prior submission of disputes to local courts provided for in the BIT at hand, the tribunal examined other Argentine BITs and noted that 'the Argentine Republic has dispensed with it in its investment treaties concluded since 1994.'[169] In *CMS*, comparing the language of the emergency (or non-precluded measures) clause of the applicable BIT with other treaties and the US Congress debates on other BITs, helped the tribunal defeat the allegation that such a clause was self-judging.[170]

The use of *travaux prépartoires* has been scarce.[171] The reason may be that 'the negotiating history of BITs is typically not documented,' and thus *travaux* are not readily available.[172] In *Aguas del Tunari*, the tribunal requested the parties to provide such material but was disappointed with the result: 'This sparse negotiating history thus offers little additional insight into the meaning of the aspects of the BIT at issue, neither particularly confirming nor contradicting the Tribunal's interpretation.'[173]

§2.29 Object and purpose, preambles and pro-investor or pro-state interpretations Many tribunals have sought to interpret IIAs on the basis of their object and purpose, typically by looking at their titles and preambles.[174] IIA

---

167. See, e.g., Albania-UK (1994).
168. *National Grid supra* note 159 at para. 85.
169. *Ibid.*, at 91. For other examples of such comparative interpretation see *Telenor Mobile Communications A.S. v. Hungary* (Award, 13 Sep. 2006) at paras 96-97; *Maffezini Jurisdiction, supra* note 161 at paras 58-66.
170. *CMS Award, supra* note 52 at paras 368-373.
171. But see *Inceysa Vallisoletana, S.L. v. El Salvador* (Award, 2 Aug. 2006) at paras 192-200.
172. Schrever, *supra* note 160 at 9. The exception is Chapter Eleven NAFTA, where the NAFTA parties have published online the trilateral negotiating draft texts. On the negotiating history of Chapter Eleven NAFTA, see M. Kinnear, A.K. Bjorklund & J. Hannaford, *Investment Disputes under NAFTA: An Annotated Guide to NAFTA Chapter 11* (The Netherlands: Kluwer Law International, 2006).
173. *Aguas del Tunari, supra* note 150 at para. 274.
174. E.g., *Ronald S. Lauder v. Czech Republic* (Final Award, 3 Sep. 2001) at para. 292; *SGS v. Philippines, supra* note 6 at para. 116; *MTD Award, supra* note 42 at para. 113; *Siemens A.G. v. Argentina* (Decision on Jurisdiction, 3 Aug. 2004) at paras 80-81; *CMS Award, supra* note 52

preambles have been particularly influential in the development of the jurisprudence on fair and equitable treatment, requiring host states to maintain a stable investment environment and to create favourable conditions for investment. The first tribunal to make that link was that in the *Lauder* case, which noted that the preamble of the relevant BIT stated that the contracting parties agree 'that fair and equitable treatment of investment is desirable in order to maintain a stable framework for investment.'[175] This sort of preambular language was later noted by the tribunal in *Occidental* concluding that 'the stability of the legal and business framework is thus an essential element of fair and equitable treatment.'[176] The tribunal in *CMS* reached the same conclusion on the basis of the same type of statement in the preamble.[177] Other tribunals have followed suit.[178]

In looking at object and purpose and, with it, the title and preamble of BITs, tribunals have noted that the purpose of BITs is to protect investments and investors:

> The Tribunal shall be guided by the purpose of the Treaty as expressed in its title and preamble. It is a treaty 'to protect' and 'to promote' investments. The preamble provides that the parties have agreed to the provisions of the Treaty for the purpose of creating favourable conditions for the investments of nationals or companies of one of the two States in the territory of the other State. Both parties recognize that the promotion and protection of these investments by a treaty may stimulate private economic initiative and increase the well-being of the peoples of both countries. The intention of the parties is clear. It is to create favourable conditions for investments and to stimulate private initiative.[179]

Linked to the interpretation of IIA provisions in light of the protection of investments as its object and purpose, is the principle of effectiveness or *effet utile* of treaty provisions. This means that the interpretation which accords practical content to a treaty provision will be favoured over one that deprives it of such effect.[180] This principle has been used in particular in the context of the interpretation of the

---

at para. 274; *Eureko, supra* note 93 at para. 248; *Noble Ventures, supra* note 152 at para. 52; *Aguas del Tunari, supra* note 150 at paras 240-241 and 247; *Continental Casualty Company v. Argentina* (Decision on Jurisdiction, 22 Feb. 2006) at para. 80; *Saluka Investments BV v. Czech Republic* (Partial Award, 17 Mar. 2006) at paras 299-300; *Azurix, supra* note 146 at paras 307 and 360.

175. *Ronald S. Lauder v. Czech Republic* (Final Award, 3 Sep. 2001) at para. 292.
176. *Occidental,* supra note 136 at para. 183. Also see *MTD Award, supra* note 42 at para. 113.
177. *CMS Award, supra* note 52 at para. 274.
178. E.g., *Azurix, supra* note 146 at para. 360 and *Siemens A.G. v. Argentina* (Award, 6 Feb. 2007) at para. 81.
179. *Siemens A.G. v. Argentina* (Decision on Jurisdiction, 3 Aug. 2004) at para. 81.
180. E.g., *Salini Costruttori S.p.A. and Italstrade S.p.A. v. Jordan* (Decision on Jurisdiction, 29 Nov. 2004) at para. 95; *Continental Casualty Company v. Argentina* (Decision on Jurisdiction, 22 Feb. 2006) at para. 80.

umbrella clause, in order to reject restrictive interpretations which arguably leave the umbrella clause inoperative.[181]

Sometimes, it has been expressly stated that a teleological interpretation of IIAs leads to a principle of interpretation in favour of protected investors and investments:

> The object and purpose of the BIT supports an effective interpretation [...]. The BIT is a treaty for the promotion and reciprocal protection of investments. According to the preamble it is intended 'to create and maintain favourable conditions for investments by investors of one Contracting Party in the territory of the other.' It is legitimate to resolve uncertainties in its interpretation so as to favour the protection of covered investments.[182]

Commenting on this case law, it has been argued that the determination of object and purpose may be deceptive, and that the fact that IIAs commonly contain preambles stating that their purpose is to promote and protect investment should not be conflated with a general preference to protect the interests of the foreign investor over those of the host state.[183] To some extent this would seem correct: the object and purpose of a treaty are realized by its provisions; an interpretation that would result in the implementation of a treaty's purpose in a fashion not contemplated by the parties would be contrary to their intentions and, thus, should be rejected. As put by the tribunal in *Plama*:

> [T]he Tribunal is mindful of Sir Ian Sinclair's warning of the 'risk that the placing of undue emphasis on the "object and purpose" of a treaty will encourage teleological methods of interpretation [which], in some of its more extreme forms, will even deny the relevance of the intentions of the parties.'[184]

In this context, attempts have also been made to temper this pro-investor inclination by reading a more balanced statement of aims in the preamble of IIA's:

> The 'object and purpose' of the Treaty may be discerned from its title and preamble. These read [...].

This is a more subtle and balanced statement of the Treaty's aims that is sometimes appreciated. The protection of foreign investments is not the sole aim of the Treaty, but rather a necessary element alongside the overall aim of encouraging foreign investment and extending and intensifying the parties' economic relations. That in turn calls for a balanced approach to the interpretation of the Treaty's substantive provisions for the protection of investments, since an interpretation which exaggerates the protection to be accorded to foreign investments may serve

---

181. E.g., *SGS v. Philippines, supra* note 6 at para. 116; *Eureko, supra* note 93 at para. 248; and *Noble Ventures supra* note 152 at para. 52.
182. *SGS v. Philippines, ibid.,* at para. 116.
183. Douglas, *supra* note 44 at 51 and McLachlan, *supra* note 133 at 371.
184. *Plama, supra* note 150 at para. 193.

to dissuade host States from admitting foreign investments and so undermine the overall aim of extending and intensifying the parties' mutual economic relations.[185]

Some tribunals have expressly opted for a restrictive interpretation on the basis that treaty commitments are a derogation of sovereignty and thus the interpretation implying a lesser obligation should be favoured:

> The appropriate interpretive approach [...] is the prudential one summed up in the literature as *in dubio pars mitio est sequenda*, or more tersely, *in dubio mitius*.[186]

But the better view is that there is no such principle of restrictive interpretation of treaties. The classic authority is the *Wimbledon Case* in the following, often quoted, passage:

> The Court declines to see in the conclusion of any Treaty by which a State undertakes to perform or refrain from performing a particular act an abandonment of its sovereignty. No doubt any convention creating an obligation of this kind places a restriction upon the exercise of the sovereign rights of the State, in the sense that it requires them to be exercised in a certain way. But the right of entering into international engagements is an attribute of State sovereignty.[187]

With regard to teleological interpretations, it is clear that many IIAs 'have been drafted in narrow, uni-dimensional terms, with treaty preambles hailing the need to enhance economic cooperation and create a favourable investment climate, and often little else in the way of broader policy objectives.'[188] Thus, at the end of the day, pro-investor interpretations on the basis of the object and purpose of IIA would seem to be defensible readings. Critics must admit, as has been noted, that for their concerns 'the blame lies with governments which have negotiated treaties.'[189] In particular, a more balanced approach would be favoured by preambles which recognize not only the protection of investment but also the prerogative of states to regulate in the public interest.[190]

---

185. *Saluka Investments BV v. Czech Republic* (Partial Award, 17 Mar. 2006) at paras 299-300. See also *Azurix, supra* note 146 at para. 307 and *El Paso Energy International Company v. Argentina* (Decision on Jurisdiction, 27 Apr. 2006) at paras 68-70.
186. *SGS v. Pakistan, supra* note 6 at para. 171.
187. *Case of the S.S. 'Wimbledon'* (1923) PCIJ Ser. A, No. 1 at 25. See J. Crawford, 'Treaty and Contract in Investment Arbitration' (2008) TDM at 4.
188. L.E. Peterson, 'Bilateral Investment Treaties and Development Policy-Making' (Winnipeg: International Institute for Sustainable Development, 2004) at 23.
189. *Ibid.*, at 24.
190. See A. Newcombe, 'Investment Treaty Law and Sustainable Development' (2007) 8 JWIT 357, reviewing new model IIAs that incorporate references to sustainable development in their preambles.

§2.30 Interpretations and amendments to IIAs by the contracting states Occasionally, state parties to an IIA may issue interpretations or clarifications of an IIA provision during the pendency of arbitral proceedings. Some choice of law provisions provide explicitly for the binding nature of those interpretations.[191] In any case, those interpretations may constitute evidence of a 'subsequent agreement between the parties regarding the interpretation of the treaty or the application of its provisions,' which, under Article 31(3)(a) of the Vienna Convention, must be taken into account when interpreting a treaty provision.

An example of such interpretive agreement is the NAFTA Free Trade Commission's Notes of Interpretation of 31 July 2001, which effectively interpreted or recast several NAFTA Chapter Eleven provisions.[192] These included Article 1105 on 'fair and equitable treatment', which early tribunals had found to have been breached by NAFTA states and viewed that standard as independent from the minimum standard required by customary international law, affording greater protection.[193] The NAFTA Commission's interpretation provided that Article 1105 prescribed the customary minimum standard of treatment and that 'fair and equitable treatment' and 'full protection and security' did not require treatment beyond or in addition to that customary standard. Not without some initial reluctance,[194] tribunals in pending NAFTA proceedings and in future cases have applied the interpretation which, in any case, left considerable leeway to tribunals insofar as the content of the customary standard still needed to be defined.[195]

Similarly, after the Partial Award in *CME*, the government of the Czech Republic and that of The Netherlands entered into consultations with regard to the correct interpretation of certain provisions of Czechoslovakia-Netherlands (1991).[196] The common positions reached by the two governments were then taken into consideration by the tribunal in its Final Award.[197]

Tribunals have rejected arguments by respondent states that their position is implicitly agreed to by the other contracting party to the BIT in question. For example, in *Aguas del Tunari*, the tribunal rejected the argument that the apparent coincidence between certain statements made by Dutch Ministers to Parliament in The Netherlands and Bolivia's own arguments in the arbitration formed an

---

191. See *supra* §2.4.
192. As provided under Art. 2001, NAFTA, the NAFTA Free Trade Commission is composed of one representative of each NAFTA state and its functions include providing interpretations of the NAFTA provisions. Art. 1131 ('Governing Law') provides at para. (2) that '[A]n interpretation by the Commission of a provision of this Agreement shall be binding on a Tribunal established under this Section.' See *infra* Chapter 6, §6.22 *et seq.*
193. *S.D. Myers, Inc. v. Canada* (Partial Award, 13 Nov. 2000); *Metalclad, supra* note 46; *Pope and Talbot Inc. v. Canada* (Award on the Merits of Phase 2, 10 Apr. 2001).
194. *Pope & Talbot Inc. v. Canada* (Award in respect of Damages, 31 May 2002) [*Pope & Talbot*] at paras 8-69.
195. See *infra* Chapter 6.
196. Art. 9 of the BIT contemplates the possibility of the contracting parties 'to consult on any matter concerning the interpretation or application of the Agreement.'
197. *CME, supra* note 21 at paras 87-93.

agreement regarding the scope of certain provisions in Bolivia-Netherlands (1992):

> The coincidence of several statements does not make them a joint statement. And, it is clear that in the present case, there was no intent that these statements be regarded as an agreement.[198]

In *Gas Natural*, the tribunal found that Argentina's position in the case and Spain's position as a defendant in another case could not reflect 'practice establishing agreement between the parties to a treaty within the meaning of Article 31(3)(b) of the Vienna Convention on the Law of Treaties' with regard to the Argentina-Spain BIT.[199] A similar Argentine argument, based on the position taken by the US in some NAFTA cases with regard to provisions equivalent to those in Argentina-US (1991), was dismissed in *Sempra Energy International v. Argentina*, finding that:

> Counsel representing the State in arbitration proceedings have the duty to put forward all the arguments they deem appropriate to defend their position, but a tribunal could not presume that each of those arguments constitutes the expression of a unilateral act that obligates the State.[200]

Later in the case, Argentina submitted a letter from a US official at the US Department of State, dated 15 September 2006, to a former official authorizing him to testify in another pending Argentine BIT case, at the request of the claimant in that case, on the issue of whether essential security clauses in US BITs were 'self-judging.' The letter stated, in passing, that the US position was that those clauses were indeed self-judging. The tribunal noted that the letter did not address any specific BIT, and stated:

> Not even if this is the interpretation given to the clause today by the United States would this necessarily mean that such an interpretation governs the Treaty. The view of one State does not make international law, even less so when such a view is ascertained only by indirect means of interpretation or in a rather remote or general way as far as the very Treaty at issue is concerned. What is relevant is the intention which both parties had in signing the Treaty, and this does not confirm the self-judging interpretation.[201]

As opposed to interpretations, amendments of IIA provisions may not be given effect in pending disputes (but the distinction between amendment and interpretation may not be easy to draw in practice[202]). The *Sempra* tribunal made this point as a follow up to the above-quoted holding:

---

198. *Aguas del Tunari, supra* note 150 at para. 251.
199. *Gas Natural, supra* note 131 at note 12.
200. *Sempra Energy International v. Argentina* (Decision on Objections to Jurisdiction, 11 May 2005) at para. 146.
201. *Sempra, supra* note 140 at para. 385.
202. *Pope & Talbot, supra* note 194 at paras 8-47.

Moreover, even if this interpretation were shared today by both parties to the Treaty, it still would not result in a change of its terms. States are of course free to amend the Treaty by consenting to another text, but this would not affect rights acquired under the Treaty by investors or other beneficiaries.[203]

§2.31 Interpretation and the adjudicative function under IIAs The way in which arbitration tribunals approach interpretive issues may reveal (or in fact derive from) their views as to the nature and scope of their adjudicative function. In this context, it has been argued that tribunals act in three different ways in this respect: as commercial arbitrators; public international law adjudicators; or through the lens of individual (perhaps human) rights protection. It is also argued that a public law framework should be adopted, one that does not relegate public law and regulatory concerns to the hands of a pure commercial arbitration approach, or to the politics of inter-state public international law, or to the exaggerated emphasis on individual right protection resulting in a pro-investor approach to interpretation of IIA obligations. The public law framework would recognize instead the essentially regulatory character of IIA adjudication, by reference to the principles and practices of national administrative law adjudication. The proponents of this view essentially predict (and perhaps desire) a result that moderates state liability in order to preserve governmental discretion.[204]

Whether or not these approaches reveal a particular policy agenda and whether these categorizations accord to reality, and account sufficiently for the more fine-grained analysis that each case requires, may be open to question. However, they provide a useful framework as to the direction in which IIA case law may tend to develop, one in which the specific nature of this area of international law, which in many cases effectively substitutes national administrative law, is acknowledged, and with it the specific role that IIA arbitrators are bound to perform.

---

203. *Sempra, supra* note 140 at para. 386.
204. See G. Van Harten, *Investment Treaty Arbitration and Public Law* (Oxford: Oxford University Press, 2007) at Chapter 6; and G. Van Harten & M. Loughlin, 'Investment Treaty Arbitration as a Species of Global Administrative Law' (2006) 17 EJIL 150.

Chapter 3

Promotion, Admission and Establishment Obligations

INTRODUCTION

§3.1 Overview   This chapter begins by highlighting the customary international law with respect to the admission of foreign investors and investment and how international investment agreements (IIAs)[1] impose promotion, admission and establishment obligations. Part I then briefly considers the purposes of IIAs as expressed in treaty titles and preambles. Part II turns to a more detailed examination of IIA promotion, admission and establishment obligations. In Part III, a series of ancillary obligations with respect to the entry of personnel, establishment of offices and granting of permits are covered.

§3.2 Customary international law obligations   Under customary international law, states have the sovereign right to control the admission of foreign investors and investments into their respective territories.[2] A state is not required to admit

---

1. See supra §1.30 on the use of this term.
2. *Barcelona Traction, Light and Power Company Limited (Belgium v. Spain)* [1970] ICJ Rep 4 at para. 33 and *Mihaly International Corporation v. Sri Lanka* (Award, 15 Mar. 2002) [*Mihaly*] at para. 60. See also I. Brownlie, *Principles of Public International Law*, 6th edn (Oxford: Oxford University Press, 2003) at 498; R. Jennings & A. Watts, eds, *Oppenheim's International Law*, 9th edn (London: Longman, 1992) at 896-900; I. Seidl-Hohenveldern, *International Economic Law*, 3rd edn (Dordrecht: Kluwer Law International, 1999) at 99-126; P. Juillard & D. Carreau, *Droit International Économique*, 4th edn (Paris: L.G.D.J., 1998) at 379; P. Muchlinski, *Multinational Enterprises and the Law*, 2nd edn (Oxford: Oxford University Press, 2007) at 177-214; M. Sornarajah, *The International Law on Foreign Investment*, 2nd edn (Cambridge: Cambridge University Press, 2004) at 98-108; I. Shihata, 'Recent Trends Relating to Entry of Foreign Investment' (1994) 9 ICSID Rev 47; R. Dolzer & M. Stevens, *Bilateral Investment Treaties* (The Hague: Martinus Nijhoff Publishers, 1995) at 50; G. Sacerdoti, 'The Admission and

foreign investors or investments, or otherwise allow foreigners to engage in commercial activities in its territory unless it has made an express commitment to do so. However, after admission, a host state is required to treat foreign investors and investments in accordance with local laws and the customary international law minimum standard of treatment.[3] Likewise, a state is under no general obligation to promote foreign investment within its territory or to encourage foreign investment by its nationals in other states. In the absence of a treaty or other legal obligation (such as a foreign investment contract), a state is not required to promote, engage in, or allow any particular investment relationship.[4]

§3.3 IIA obligations   The express purpose of IIAs, as expressed in treaty titles, preambles and through their specific obligations, is to promote and protect investment. The greater emphasis, however, is on protection. Most IIAs have weak promotion, admission and establishment (pre-entry) obligations. With the exception of a small number of agreements,[5] IIAs typically do not provide national treatment or most-favoured-nation treatment (MFN treatment) with respect to the admission or establishment of foreign investors or investment or provide other general rights of entry for foreign investors or investment. Most IIAs provide protections only *after* foreign investors or investments have been admitted into the host state in accordance with local law.

I   TREATY TITLES AND PREAMBLES

§3.4 Treaty practice[6]   Most BITs are formally called agreements for the promotion and protection of investment.[7] In some agreements, the title refers to reciprocal or mutual protection.[8] Treaty titles are normally followed by short preambles, which typically focus on the objective of promoting and protecting

---

Treatment of Foreign Investment under Recent Bilateral and Regional Treaties' (2000) 1 JWI 105 at 105 and United Nations Conference on Trade and Development (UNCTAD), *Admission and Establishment*, UNCTAD Series on issues in international investment agreements (New York and Geneva: United Nations, 1999) (UNCTAD/ITE/IIT/10) at 7 [UNCTAD, *Admission and Establishment*].

3.   See *infra* Chapter 6, Minimum Standards of Treatment.
4.   See *Military and Paramilitary Activities In and Against Nicaragua* (*Nicaragua v. US*), [1986] ICJ Rep 14 [*Nicaragua*] at 138.
5.   See *infra* §3.9.
6.   For an overview of treaty practice, see the three comprehensive studies: United Nations Centre on Transnational Corporations (UNCTC), *Bilateral Investment Treaties* (New York: United Nations, 1988) (Doc. No. ST/CTC/65); UNCTAD, *Bilateral Investment Treaties in the Mid-1990s* (New York and Geneva: United Nations, 1998) (Doc. No. UNCTAD/ITE/IIT/7) and UNCTAD, *Bilateral Investment Treaties 1995-2006* (New York and Geneva: United Nations, 2007) (Doc. No. UNCTAD/ITE/IIT/2006/5) [together *UNCTAD BIT Studies*]. Also see Dolzer & Stevens, *supra* note 2 at 20-25. See also *supra* Chapter 1, §1.50.
7.   Some early treaties refer simply to protection and not promotion (Egypt-Sweden (1978).
8.   See Bolivia-Netherlands (1992) and Ecuador-US (1993).

investment and providing favourable conditions for foreign investment. This practice is common in older BITs and continues to be reflected in current treaty practice. China-Germany (2003) is a recent example of a typical preamble:

> Intending to create favourable conditions for investment by investors of one Contracting Party in the territory of the other Contracting Party,
> Recognizing that the encouragement, promotion and protection of such investment will be conducive to stimulating business initiative of the investors and will increase prosperity in both States,
> Desiring to intensify the economic co-operation of both States[9]

Preambles are usually short and highlight the treaty parties' desire to increase economic co-operation, stimulate economic growth, and create favourable conditions for investment.[10] Some BITs make specific reference to the desirability of fair and equitable treatment.[11] A small number refer to other objectives including: the importance of technology transfer;[12] the importance of contractual protection of investment;[13] or the need to respect the sovereignty and laws of the state parties.[14]

In a number of more recent BITs, preambles have highlighted that investment promotion and protection are to be achieved in a manner consistent with other public policy objectives,[15] including a commitment to observing internationally recognized labour rights[16] and to achieving the treaty's objectives 'without relaxing health, safety and environmental measures of general application.'[17] The 2003 Canadian Model BIT expressly refers to 'sustainable development,'[18] whereas the 2004 US Model BIT speaks of achieving the agreement's objectives 'in a manner consistent with the protection of health, safety, and the environment, and the

---

9. Preamble, China-Germany (2003). See A. Newcombe, 'Investment Treaty Law and Sustainable Development' (2007) 8 JWIT 357, reviewing the preambles of 71 IIAs signed between 2000 and 2005.
10. See *UNCTAD BIT Studies*, *supra* note 6 and I. Tudor, *The Fair and Equitable Treatment Standard in the International Law of Foreign Investment* (Oxford: Oxford University Press, 2008) at 20-22 citing examples of IIA preambles referring to fair and equitable treatment.
11. Argentina-Netherlands (1992) and Armenia-US (1992).
12. France-Hungary (1986) and Brunei Darussalam-Korea (2000).
13. Chile-Germany (1991).
14. Australia-Egypt (2001) and Korea-Trinidad and Tobago (2002).
15. See Newcombe, *supra* note 9, and *Bilateral Investment Treaties 1995-2006*, *supra* note 6 at 4.
16. For example, the preambles to several Austrian BITs reaffirm the parties 'commitment to the observance of internationally recognized labour standards.' See Austria-Azerbaijan (2000) and Austria-Belize (2001).
17. Mozambique-Netherlands (2001); Korea-Trinidad and Tobago (2002); Namibia-Netherlands (2002); US-Uruguay (2005) and Netherlands-Suriname (2005).
18. The 2003 Canadian Model BIT states: 'Recognizing that the promotion and the protection of investments of investors of one Party in the territory of the other Party will be conducive to the stimulation of mutually beneficial business activity, to the development of economic co-operation between them and to the promotion of sustainable development.' See Canada-Peru (2006).

promotion of consumer protection and internationally recognized labor rights.'[19] The 2007 Norwegian Model BIT goes even further, enumerating numerous public policy objectives.[20]

The inclusion of a broader set of policy objectives in these new model BITs would appear to be motivated by these states' concerns that the preambles of older model BITs fail to provide a balance between investment promotion and protection and other public policy objectives.[21]

§3.5 The use of the treaty title and preamble in interpreting IIA obligations Although treaty titles and preambles do not create rights or obligations,[22] their use to interpret a treaty is a well accepted approach to treaty interpretation.[23] Article 31(2), *Vienna Convention on the Law of Treaties* (Vienna

---

19. The US Model forms the basis for US-Uruguay (2005).
20. The model provides:
    '*Desiring* to develop the economic co-operation between the Parties;
    Desiring to encourage, create and maintain stable, equitable, favourable and transparent conditions for investors of one Party and their investments in the territory of the other Party on the basis of equality and mutual benefit;
    Desiring to achieve these objectives in a manner consistent with the protection of health, safety, and the environment, and the promotion of internationally recognized labour rights;
    Desiring to contribute to a stable framework for investment in order to maximize effective and sustainable utilization of economic resources and improve living standards;
    Conscious that the promotion and reciprocal protection of investments in accordance with this Agreement will stimulate the business initiative;
    Emphasising the importance of corporate social responsibility;
    Recognising that the development of economic and business ties can promote respect for internationally recognised labour rights;
    Reaffirming their commitment to democracy, the rule of law, human rights and fundamental freedoms in accordance with their obligations under international law, including the principles set out in the United Nations Charter and the Universal Declaration of Human Rights;
    Recognising that the promotion of sustainable investments is critical for the further development of national and global economies as well as for the pursuit of national and global objectives for sustainable development, and understanding that the promotion of such investments requires cooperative efforts of investors, host governments and home governments;
    Recognising that the provisions of this agreement and provisions of international agreements relating to the environment shall be interpreted in a mutually supportive manner;
    Determined to prevent and combat corruption, including bribery, in international trade and investment;
    Recognising the basic principles of transparency, accountability and legitimacy for all participants in foreign investment processes.'
21. See, for example, Norway's 'Comments on the Model for Future Investment Agreements.' See *supra* Chapter 2, §2.29.
22. In *Bayindir Insaat Turizm Ticaret Ve Sanayi A.Ş v. Pakistan* (Decision on Jurisdiction, 14 Nov. 2005) [*Bayindir*], the tribunal noted at para. 230 that 'it is doubtful that, in the absence of a specific provision in the BIT itself, the sole text of the preamble constitutes a sufficient basis for a self-standing fair and equitable treatment obligation under the BIT.'
23. I.M. Sinclair, *The Vienna Convention on the Law of Treaties*, 2nd edn (Manchester: Manchester University Press, 1984) at 128. On interpretation, also see A. Aust, *Modern Treaty Law and Practice*, 2nd edn (Cambridge: Cambridge University Press, 2007) at 230-255. See *supra* Chapter 2, §2.29.

Convention),[24] provides that the preamble forms part of the context of the treaty for the purposes of interpretation.

IIA tribunals have regularly relied on the titles and preambles of IIAs in interpreting treaty obligations.[25] For example, in *Siemens A.G. v. Argentina*, the tribunal referred to the title and preamble of Argentina-Germany (1991) and noted that:

> The Tribunal shall be guided by the purpose of the Treaty as expressed in its title and preamble. It is a treaty 'to protect' and 'to promote' investments. The preamble provides that the parties have agreed to the provisions of the Treaty for the purpose of creating favorable conditions for the investments of nationals or companies of one of the two States in the territory of the other State. Both parties recognize that the promotion and protection of these investments by a treaty may stimulate private economic initiative and increase the well-being of the peoples of both countries. The intention of the parties is clear. It is to create favorable conditions for investments and to stimulate private initiative.[26]

Care must be exercised, however, in not giving preambles undue weight. In *Plama Consortium Limited v. Bulgaria*,[27] the tribunal noted that it 'is mindful of Sir Ian Sinclair's warning of the *"risk that the placing of undue emphasis on the 'object and purpose' of a treaty will encourage teleological methods of interpretation [which], in some of its more extreme forms, will even deny the relevance of the intentions of the parties"'* [28] This point was also made by the *Saluka Investments BV v. Czech Republic* tribunal, which noted with respect to the preamble[29] in Czechoslovakia-Netherlands (1991):

> The 'object and purpose' of the Treaty may be discerned from its title and preamble. These read [...].

---

24. *Vienna Convention on the Law of Treaties*, done at Vienna, 23 May 1969, entered into force, 27 Jan. 1980, 1155 UNTS 331, *reprinted in* (1969) 8 ILM 679 [Vienna Convention]. Art. 31(2) provides: 'The context for the purpose of the interpretation of the treaty shall [include] the text, including its *preamble* and annexes ...' [Emphasis added.]
25. *Bayindir, supra* note 22; *SGS Société Générale de Surveillance S.A. v. Philippines* (Decision of the Tribunal on Objections to Jurisdiction, 29 Jan. 2004) at para. 116; *Occidental Exploration and Production Company v. Ecuador* (Final Award, 1 Jul. 2004) at para. 183; *MTD Equity Sdn. Bhd. & MTD Chile S.A. v. Chile* (Award, 25 May 2004) at para. 113; *Siemens A.G. v. Argentina* (Decision on Jurisdiction, 3 Aug. 2004) [*Siemens*] at para. 81; *Enron Corporation and Ponderosa Assets, L.P. v. Argentina* (Award, 22 May 2007) at para. 259 and *Compañiá de Aguas del Aconquija S.A. and Vivendi Universal S.A. v. Argentina* (Award, 20 Aug. 2007) at para. 7.4.4. For commentary, see O.E. García-Bolívar, 'The Teleology of International Investment Law' (2005) 6 JWIT 751.
26. *Siemens, ibid.*, at para. 81.
27. Decision on Jurisdiction, 8 Feb. 2005.
28. *Ibid.*, at 193, quoting from Sinclair, *supra* note 23 at 130. See also discussion *supra* at Chapter 2, §2.29.
29. The preamble states, in part, 'Desiring to extend and intensify the economic relations between them particularly with respect to investments by the investor of one Contracting Party in the territory of the other Contracting Party' and 'Recognizing that agreement upon the treatment to be accorded to such investments will stimulate the flow of capital and technology and the economic development of the Contracting Parties and that fair and equitable treatment is desirable.'

This is a more subtle and balanced statement of the Treaty's aims than is sometimes appreciated. The protection of foreign investments is not the sole aim of the Treaty, but rather a necessary element alongside the overall aim of encouraging foreign investment and extending and intensifying the parties' economic relations. That in turn calls for a balanced approach to the interpretation of the Treaty's substantive provisions for the protection of investments, since an interpretation which exaggerates the protection to be accorded to foreign investments may serve to dissuade host States from admitting foreign investments and so undermine the overall aim of extending and intensifying the parties' mutual economic relations.[30]

The interpretation of IIAs is covered in more detail above in Part VII, Chapter 2, Applicable Law and Interpretation.

II   PROMOTION AND ENCOURAGEMENT OBLIGATIONS

§3.6 Promotion and encouragement   Most IIAs contain a general obligation on the state parties to 'promote' or otherwise 'encourage' investment.[31] There is a wide range of different formulations, including 'shall encourage';[32] 'shall promote and encourage';[33] 'shall promote as far as possible'[34] and 'shall accept, encourage and provide legal protection.'[35] The scope of this general obligation is typically circumscribed by two conditions: promotion obligations are subject to the host state's domestic laws or foreign investment policies;[36] and the obligation applies

---

30. *Saluka Investments BV v. Czech Republic* (Partial Award, 17 Mar. 2006) at para. 300.

31. See *UNCTAD BIT Studies*, *supra* note 6 and Dolzer & Stevens, *supra* note 2 at 49-57.

32. See Art. 2(1), Chile-China (1994); Art. 2(1), China-Romania (1994); Art. 8(1), Ethiopia-Tunisia (2000); Art. 2(1), Algeria-Denmark (1999); Art. 2(1), Denmark-Mongolia (1996); Art. 2(1), Cyprus-USSR (1997); Art. 2(1), Egypt-USSR (1997); Art. 2(1), Bahrain-China (1999) and Art. 2, BLEU-Rwanda (1983).

33. See Art. 3, Estonia-Norway (1992); Art. 3, Australia-Uruguay (2001) and Art. 2(1), Portugal-Turkey (2001).

34. See Art. 2(1), Bolivia-Germany (1987); Art. 2, Burundi-Germany (1984) and Art. 2, Egypt-Ukraine (1992).

35. See Art. 2(1), Egypt-Thailand (2000).

36. For example, Art. 2(1), Argentina-Sweden (1991), provides: 'Each Contracting Party shall, subject to its general policy in the field of foreign investment, promote in its territory investments by investors of the other Contracting Party and shall admit such investments in accordance with its legislation.' Also see Art. 3(1), Australia-Romania (1993); Art. 2(1), Cuba-Ghana (1999); Art. 2, Netherlands-Romania (1994) and Art. 3, Chile-New Zealand (1999). Other IIAs use similar language. Variations include: (i) 'shall, having regards to its plans and policies, encourage and facilitate investments': Art. 3(1), Hungary-Thailand (1991); Art. 3(1), Peru-Thailand (1991); Art. 3(1), Cambodia-Thailand (1995) and Art. 2(1), Israel-Thailand (2000); (ii) 'Each Contracting Party promotes in its territory investments by investors of the other Contracting Party and admits such investments in accordance with its legislation': Art. 2(1), Estonia-Greece (1997). Some model IIAs identify specific steps that the host state might take to promote investments, such as offering incentives like tax concessions. See, for example, Art. 2,

to promoting inward foreign direct investment (FDI) in the host state and not to promoting outward FDI by its nationals. For example, Article 2, Argentina-Netherlands (1992), provides:

> Either Contracting Party shall, within the framework of its laws and regulations, promote economic co-operation through the protection in its territory of investment of investors of the other Contracting Party. Subject to its right to exercise powers conferred by its laws or regulations, each Contracting Party shall admit such investments.

Article 3(1), Australia-Egypt (2001), also reflects these two conditions:

> Each Party shall encourage and promote investments in its territory by investors of the other Party and shall, in accordance with its laws and investment policies applicable from time to time, admit investments.

Other variations in treaty practice relating to promotion include provisions for the exchange of information in order to promote foreign investment.[37] For example, Article 7, Argentina-Mexico (1996), provides:

> With the intention to increase significantly the reciprocal participation in investments, the Contracting Parties will inform each other in a detailed manner concerning especially
>
> a. investment opportunities;
> b. laws, regulations and decrees that directly or indirectly concern foreign investments, including, among others, exchange controls, monetary and fiscal regimes; and
> c. performance of foreign investments in their respective countries.

Although most BITs are called foreign investment promotion and protection agreements, promotion obligations in BITs generally are weak and subject to host state laws.[38] In most BITs, promotion and encouragement are the presumed by-products of specific substantive and procedural investment protections. General promotion and encouragement obligations do not liberalize admission and establishment, nor require states to adopt specific measures to promote FDI.[39]

Asian-African Legal Consultative Committee, Revised Draft of Model Agreements for the Promotion and Protection of Investments, Model A, reproduced in UNCTC, *Bilateral Investment Treaties, supra* note 6 at 132.

37. Art. 2(2), Finland-Kuwait (1996), provides: 'Each Contracting State shall endeavour to take the necessary measures for granting of appropriate facilities, incentives and other forms of encouragement for investments made by investors of the other Contracting State.'

38. These comments apply primarily to post-entry IIAs, rather than pre-entry IIAs and comprehensive free trade and investment agreements that provide for admission and establishment rights on a non-discriminatory basis. See §3.8 *et seq.* below on admission and establishment.

39. Sacerdoti, *supra* note 2 at 108. See *supra* Chapter 1, §1.48, on the relationship between IIAs and FDI flows. UNCTAD's most recent study (UNCTAD, *Bilateral Investment Treaties 1995-2006, supra* note 6) notes at 26: 'The approach to promotion of foreign investment taken by

In contrast to the majority of BITs that focus on the role of *host* states in promoting and protecting inward foreign investment, a small number of BITs expressly provide for *home* states to promote outward foreign investment by its nationals. For example, Article 2(3), Belgo-Luxembourg Economic Union (BLEU)-Cameroon (1980) provides:

> Aware of the importance of investments for the promotion of its development co-operation, the Belgo-Luxembourg Economic Union shall adopt measures to encourage its economic agents to participate in the development effort of the United Republic of Cameroon, in accordance with its priority objectives.

There is little guidance in IIAs or legal authorities regarding the specific legal obligations that might flow from host state's commitment to 'promote' or 'encourage' investment.[40] The obligation would appear particularly weak where the host state's admission and establishment obligations are expressly subject to its laws and policies (as is the case in post-entry model IIAs).[41] The same uncertainty applies to obligations on home states to promote outward foreign investment by its nationals.

Although promotion language might be considered hortatory,[42] promotion obligations may, in some contexts, impose justiciable constraints on state conduct. In particular, international authorities support the view that a promotion clause should be interpreted as restricting the right of IIA state parties to take certain types of economic measures against its IIA treaty partners, unless expressly permitted to do so in accordance with its obligations under a specific treaty regime, such as by the United Nations Security Council or the World Trade Organization (WTO). In the *Nicaragua* case,[43] the International Court of Justice (ICJ) considered whether the Nicaragua-US FCN Treaty imposed an obligation on one party to abstain from any act toward the other party that could be classified as an unfriendly act, even where the act in question did not breach an international obligation. Although the ICJ noted there was no customary international law rule to that effect, it found that in an FCN Treaty there is a distinction between a broad category of unfriendly acts and a narrow category that defeat the object and purpose of the FCN Treaty:

BITs is mainly indirect, relying in the first place on their protection provisions to create a favourable investment climate.'

40.   There appears to be no substantive difference between an obligation 'to promote' and one 'to encourage.' It could be argued that an obligation 'to promote' connotes a higher standard of conduct than 'to encourage' and that the rule of effectiveness in treaty interpretation requires that each word be given an independent meaning. In our view, the literal meanings of 'promote' and 'encourage' as defined in leading dictionaries are essentially interchangeable. Some treaties impose an obligation to 'promote' and 'encourage,' such as 'promote, encourage, and create favourable conditions' in Art. 2(1), Philippines-Romania (1994), and 'promote and encourage' in Art. 3, Estonia-Norway (1992).

41.   See §3.11.

42.   A view expressed in UNCTAD, *Bilateral Investment Treaties 1995-2006, supra* note 6 at 26.

43.   *Supra* note 4.

[The] object and purpose is the effective implementation of friendship in the specific fields provided for in the Treaty, not friendship in a vague general sense.[44]

Since a core object and purpose of IIAs is investment promotion and co-operation and IIAs typically impose general obligations to encourage or promote investment, a strong case can be made that investment restrictions imposed for political ends or as reprisals are inconsistent with an IIA's investment promotion obligation.[45]

Further, to the extent that there are justiciable promotion and encouragement obligations, the obligation is one of means, not of result. IIA promotion obligations cannot be read as providing guarantees of quantitative increases in investment. The obligation is, at most, one of means – to facilitate investment.[46]

If promotion obligations apply to a home state whose nationals invest abroad, they might limit the range of measures that the home state might take to restrict foreign investment abroad by its nationals. For example, home state restrictions on exports of technology or prohibitions on outsourcing might breach investment promotion and co-operation obligations.

Although a general promotion obligation should not be interpreted as requiring host states to adopt specific investment policies that liberalize admission or establishment, a breach of promotion obligations would likely occur where a host state engages in a concerted and systematic campaign of discouraging foreign investment or creating an inhospitable climate for foreign investment.[47] Further, some treaties might be interpreted as requiring positive consideration of the interests of foreign investors. For example, Article 2(1), Denmark-Hong Kong (1994), requires the host state to 'promote [investment] as far as possible.'

To date, there have been no publicly reported IIA claims relating to breaches of promotion and encouragement obligations. The provisions have nonetheless been important in providing a context for the interpretation of other investment protection provisions, notably fair and equitable treatment.

---

44. *Ibid.*, at 136-137. See also, *ibid.*, at 138 as to the sort of acts which could fall within the narrow category.
45. State responsibility, however, might be precluded on one of several bases, including countermeasures. See *infra* Chapter 10, Exceptions and Defences. On IIAs as a mechanism to depoliticize investment issues, see I.F.I. Shihata, *Towards a Greater Depoliticization of Investment Disputes: The Roles of ICSID and MIGA* (Washington: ICSID, 1993) and K.J. Vandevelde, 'Of Politics and Markets: the Shifting Ideology of the BITs' (1993) ITBL 159.
46. For a brief discussion of this point, see P. Juillard, 'Variation in the Substantive Provisions and Interpretation of International Investment Agreements' in K. Sauvant, ed., *Appeals Mechanism in International Investment Disputes* (Oxford: Oxford University Press, 2008) 81 at 84-86. See Vandevelde, *ibid.,* at 162, noting the US position that the purpose of BITs was to protect not promote investment.
47. This follows from the basic principle of international law that treaty obligations must be performed in good faith as codified in Art. 26, Vienna Convention, *supra* note 24. Further, such conduct would also likely breach a fair and equitable treatment obligation with respect to investments already made.

§3.7 Favourable conditions IIAs often provide that, in addition to promotion and encouragement, the host state is to 'create favourable conditions' for investment.[48] For example, Article 2(1), Azerbaijan-UK (1997), provides:

> Each Contracting Party shall encourage and create favourable conditions for nationals and companies of the other Contracting Party to invest capital in its territory, and, subject to its right to exercise powers conferred by its laws, shall admit such capital.

Other IIAs use similar language: 'shall promote and create favourable conditions';[49] 'shall promote, encourage, and create favourable conditions';[50] 'shall encourage and provide suitable conditions';[51] 'shall encourage and create favourable conditions'[52] and 'shall, as far as possible, encourage and create favourable conditions.'[53]

As with promotion and encouragement obligations, there is little guidance in international authorities regarding the meaning of creating 'favourable conditions.' Some commentators have noted that BITs oblige the host state to create normative 'favourable conditions' for investment:

> The 'favourable conditions' established by BITs consist, not merely of natural phenomena such as climate, resources, and access to the sea, nor even of an educated population in the host state receptive to and eager to participate in the benefits of foreign investment; they also contemplate, more significantly and innovatively, an effective *normative* framework: impartial courts, an efficient and legally restrained bureaucracy, and the measure of transparency in decision that has increasingly been recognized as a control mechanism over governments and as a vital component of the international standard of governance. Hence, in a BIT regime, the host state must do far more than open its doors to foreign investment and refrain from overt expropriation. It must establish and maintain an appropriate legal, administrative, and regulatory framework, the legal environment that modern investment theory has come to recognize as a *conditio sine qua non* of the success of private enterprise. This is not to say, of course, that every governmental adjustment to this normative framework that adversely affects the conditions for foreign investment

---

48. Other examples of similar provisions include Art. 3(1), Australia-Romania (1993); Art. 3(1), Chile-Egypt (1999); Art. 3(1), Chile-Tunisia (1998); Art. 3, Chile-Turkey (1998); Art. 2(1), Cuba-Ghana (1999); Art. 2(1), Cuba-Lebanon (1995); Art. 2(1), Czech Republic-Romania (1993); Art. 1(1), Egypt-Romania (1976); Art. 2(1), Czech Republic-Estonia (1994); Art. 1(1), Germany-Romania (1979); Art. 3(1), Hong Kong-New Zealand (1995); Art. 3(1), Indonesia-Thailand (1987); Art. 2(1), Korea-Mexico (2000); Art. 2, Netherlands-Romania (1994); Art. 2(1), Oman-UK (1995). Other IIAs use similar language.
49. Art. 1, Bangladesh-Germany (1981).
50. Art. 2(1), Philippines-Romania (1994).
51. Art. 2(1), Jordan-Syria (2001).
52. Art. 2(1), Canada-Uruguay (1997); Art. 2(1), Croatia-Ukraine (1997); Art. 2(1), Belarus-Egypt (1997); Art. 2(1), Indonesia-Ukraine (1996) and Art. 2(1), Belarus-South Korea (1997).
53. Art. 2(1), Denmark-Hong Kong (1994).

will constitute an expropriatory act, but that an appropriately operational governmental framework must be in place.[54] [footnotes omitted]

Although these views are elaborated in discussing indirect expropriation and other IIA standards – the corpus of standards of treatment imposed by the IIA framework – they are suggestive of how an obligation to 'create favourable conditions' might be viewed as having a substantive content that focuses on the creation of 'the minimal legal, administrative, and regulatory framework that fosters and sustains investment in industrialized capital-exporting states.'[55] Unlike fair and equitable treatment, which focuses on the actual treatment of a specific investment, creating favourable conditions might refer more broadly to the legal, administrative, and regulatory framework necessary for private investment. For example, a systemic failure in a state's legal and regulatory system that substantially impedes a financial company's ability to enforce security interests might be viewed as breaching the obligation to create favourable conditions. This type of claim would likely, however, overlap substantially with a claim that the host state has breached fair and equitable treatment.[56]

The requirement to 'create favourable conditions' is often in addition to the obligation to encourage investment. For example, Article 3(1), Hungary-India (2003), provides that:

> Each Contracting Party shall encourage and create favourable conditions for investors of the other Contracting Party to make investments in this territory and admit such investments in accordance with its laws and regulations.

As in UK BITs, the requirement in this formulation is to create favourable conditions *for investors to make investments*. This might refer to creating an investment climate that is amenable to foreign investment, for example, by having a government agency that provides information to foreign investors. In other BITs, the requirement appears alongside other treatment standards and provides an obligation to maintain favourable conditions for investments (a post-entry obligation) rather than focusing on favourable conditions for the making of investments (a pre-entry obligation).[57] For example, Article II(1), Panama-US (1982), provides:

> Each Party shall maintain favorable conditions for investment in its territory by nationals and companies of the other Party.

This requirement might be interpreted as requiring host states to take active steps in creating a regulatory framework conducive for investment activities – elements that are often reflected in the term 'good governance,' such as the rule of law, protection of property rights, an independent judiciary and transparency in

---

54. W.M. Reisman & R.D. Sloane, 'Indirect Expropriation and Its Valuation in the BIT Generation' (2004) 74 BYIL 115 at 117.
55. *Ibid.*, at 118.
56. See *infra* Chapter 6, §6.15 *et seq.*
57. See *supra* §3.11, on the distinction between pre and post-entry IIA obligations.

decision-making.[58] Favourable conditions thus might be interpreted as 'the minimal legal, administrative, and regulatory framework that fosters and sustains investment in industrialized capital-exporting states.'[59] Indeed, tribunals have relied on references to creating favourable conditions when interpreting fair and equitable treatment as requiring host states to provide a stable and predictable legal framework for investment protection.[60]

The requirement to 'create favourable conditions,' however, should not be viewed as requiring specific types of market-based regulatory policies, such as an obligation to privatize state-owned enterprises or to deregulate. Although IIAs are intended to provide an overall stable and predictable environment for investment, there is no basis for interpreting the obligation to create favourable conditions as compelling a host state to adopt specific types of market or economic reforms.

III   ADMISSION AND ESTABLISHMENT

§3.8 Distinguishing admission and establishment   In international investment law, the term admission refers to the right of foreign investors and investments to enter into a host state.[61] Admission or entry rights without corresponding rights of establishment may be sufficient for economic activities that simply require a short-term presence, such as negotiating a contract or transferring investment funds into a host state bank account. However, if the economic activity in question requires regular interaction between the foreign investor and the host state economy, then the foreign investor may need to establish a more permanent economic presence in the host state. In such a case, the foreign investor may also require a right of establishment. This entails not only a right to carry out business trans-actions in the host country, but also the right to set up a permanent business presence.[62]

§3.9 Rationale for freedom of admission and establishment   The general rationale for granting admission and establishment rights is economic. Liberalizing restrictions on foreign investment is said to allow for 'the efficient allocation of productive resources across countries through the operation of market forces by

58. For a discussion of changing ideology in BIT practice, see K.J. Vandevelde, 'Of Politics and Markets: the Shifting Ideology of the BITs,' *supra* note 45.
59. Reisman & Sloane, *supra* note 54.
60. See *infra* Chapter 6, §6.26.
61. UNCTAD, *Admission and Establishment*, *supra* note 2.
62. One commentator has defined freedom of establishment as 'the right for nationals of one country to set up a permanent presence within the territory of another country for the purpose of conducting economic activities other than activities of a salaried character.' See P. Juillard, 'Freedom of Establishment, Freedom of Capital Movements, and Freedom of Investment' (2000) 15 ICSID Rev 322 at 323. Since not all investments require a physical presence, establishment rights are not necessarily a precondition to making an investment. For example, financial instruments such as shares and bonds can be purchased usually without a physical presence.

avoiding policy-induced barriers to the international flow of investment.'[63] The argument for allocative efficiency, however, often yields to other policy objectives, including: national security; promoting macro-economic policy goals; creating and supporting local industries; and protecting local industries from foreign control and competition.[64] Although the trend since the early 1980s has been increasingly to liberalize national foreign investment regimes (with some recent exceptions),[65] even IIAs with the most liberal admission and establishment provisions maintain exceptions and restrictions. No existing IIA provides an unfettered right of admission and establishment. IIAs with pre-entry obligations typically limit rights to invest in some sectors.[66] Even the European Union – the world's most integrated regional economic system – provides limited exceptions to establishment rights.[67]

§3.10 Domestic regulation of foreign investment   Since most IIAs do not provide a general right of admission or establishment, the host state's foreign investment regime generally governs not only whether foreign investment is permitted to operate, but also the conditions applying to the entry of foreign investments. Host states control the entry and operation of foreign investment through a variety of regulatory mechanisms.[68] These can range from a complete ban on foreign investment to other forms of regulation, such as limiting the form or amount of foreign investment, or restricting the sectors and geographical areas in which

---

63.   UNCTAD, *Admission and Establishment, supra* note 2 at 11. See also Sornarajah, *supra* note 2 at 34-168; Shihata, *supra* note 2 at 47; M. Trebilcock & R. Howse, *The Regulation of International Trade*, 3rd edn (London: Routledge, 2005), Chapter 14, Trade and Investment; and T. Pollan, *Legal Framework for the Admission of FDI* (Utrecht: Eleven International, 2006).
64.   Sornarajah, *ibid.*
65.   UNCTAD, *World Investment Report 1998: Trends and Determinants – Overview* (New York and Geneva: United Nations, 1998) at 1-12. See also UNCTAD, *World Investment Report 2006* (New York and Geneva: United Nations, 2006) at xviii which notes that 'the bulk of regulatory changes have facilitated FDI' but highlights the rise of economic protectionist and nationalist policies in a number of high profile cases. See also, *ibid.*, at 23-25. For a general discussion of trends, see K. Sauvant, 'The Rise of International Investment, Investment Agreements and Investment Disputes' in Sauvant, ed., *supra,* note 46 at 3. However, there are an increasing number of challenges to foreign investment liberalization, particularly by Latin American States. See The Economist Intelligence Unit Ltd and Columbia Program on International Investment, *World Investment Prospects to 2011: Foreign Direct Investment and the Challenge of Political Risk* (New York: The Economist Intelligence Unit Ltd, 2007); OECD, *International Investment Perspectives 2007: Freedom of Investment in a Changing World* (Paris: OECD, 2007) noting the increase in discriminatory practices; and the Apr. 2008 issue of Transnational Dispute Management highlighting the 'battle' between contract sanctity and resource sovereignty.
66.   See *infra* §3.13.
67.   See P. Craig & G. De Búrca, *EU Law: Text, Cases, and Materials*, 3rd edn (Oxford: Oxford University Press, 2003), Chapter 19 for a discussion of establishment rights in the EU.
68.   See Chapter 5, 'Control of Inward Investment by Host States' in P. Muchlinski, *Multinational Enterprises and the Law, supra* note 2; Chapter 3, 'Controls by the Host State' in Sornarajah, *supra* note 2 and Shihata, *supra* note 2 at 49-54. See also the discussion on performance requirements in Chapter 8 *infra*.

investment is permitted.[69] Some host states regularly screen foreign investments and may make admission and establishment conditional upon fulfilling specific requirements.[70]

§3.11 Treaty models for admission and establishment   There are two dominant IIA models with respect to admission and establishment: post-entry and pre-entry.[71] Sometimes referred to as post-establishment and pre-establishment, or the admission clause model and the right of establishment model, the major difference between these models is whether they provide national treatment and MFN treatment with respect to admission and establishment.[72] Most IIAs, including European model BITs, follow the post-entry model and provide no admission and establishment rights. In contrast, the pre-entry model provides admission and establishment rights that allow market access for foreign investors and investment. Pre-entry model BITs, therefore, move beyond investment promotion and protection, and contain obligations with respect to the liberalization of host state regulatory controls over foreign investment.

§3.12 The post-entry model   The post-entry model provides no general right of admission or establishment. Admission of investments under post-entry model IIAs is contingent upon their conformity with local laws.[73] The specific provisions in post-entry models vary significantly. Some have no provisions on the admission of investments.[74] Some require that the investment be admitted in conformity with the constitution or legislation of the host state.[75] Some IIAs supplement the requirement of admitting investments in accordance with local laws with the

---

69.   See, for example, the Annex to Bolivia-US (1998), which, like other US BITs that provide national treatment with respect to admission and establishment, allows the parties to maintain exceptions in various sectors.

70.   For an overview on various types of controls and requirements, see UNCTAD, *Admission and Establishment, supra* note 2 at 7-14. Provisions in IIAs prohibiting certain types of host state measures relating to the operation of foreign investment, such as performance requirements, are considered in Chapter 8 *infra*.

71.   For treaty practice see *UNCTAD BIT Studies, supra* note 6 and Dolzer & Stevens, *supra* note 2.

72.   For ease of reference this chapter uses the terms pre- and post-entry to refer to the different approaches.

73.   Where an investment is not made in accordance with local laws as required by the IIA, it might be denied protection under the IIA in question. For consideration of this issue, see *Inceysa Vallisoletana, S.L. v. El Salvador* (Award, 2 Aug. 2006); *Fraport AG Frankfurt Airport Services Worldwide v. Philippines* (Award, 16 Aug. 2007) and *Desert Line Projects LLC v. Yemen* (Award, 6 Feb. 2008). See also *supra* Chapter 2, §2.11 and §2.12.

74.   Malta-Netherlands (1984) and Germany-Malta (1973). For commentary, on this issue, see R. Dolzer & C. Schreuer, *Principles of International Investment Law* (Oxford: Oxford University Press, 2008) at 84-88.

75.   Art. 2(2), Philippines-Romania (1994): 'Investments shall be admitted in accordance with the Constitution ...' and Art. 2(1), Germany-Guyana (1989): 'Each Contracting Party shall in its territory promote as far as possible the investments by nationals or companies of the other Contracting Party and admit such investments in accordance with its legislation.'

obligation that they conform to local administrative practices.[76] Some refer to the need to admit investments not only in accordance with local laws, but also in conformity with national objectives.[77] Still others have the added requirement of admitting investments in accordance with international obligations.[78] Some require that investments receive the written approval of the host state.[79] Some combine the reference to the requirement of admitting investments in conformity with local laws with the reference to the granting of 'fair and equitable treatment' to such investments.[80]

In the post-entry model, admission and establishment rights are subject to local laws, which may be as liberal or restrictive as the host state's foreign investment regime dictates. Accordingly, refusal to permit an investment based on local laws would not normally breach IIA obligations.[81] An IIA breach, however, might occur if the host state's refusal is in breach of local law because it would have failed to admit the investment in accordance with its own laws.[82] The post-entry model reflects the host state's sovereign prerogative to control admission and establishment in accordance with domestic policy.

---

76. Art. 2, Egypt-Ukraine (1992), and Art. 2(1), Czech Republic-United Arab Emirates (1994).
77. See, for example, Art. 2(1), Belize-UK (1982). Others, particularly Singaporean BITs, allow the host state to make such determinations in consideration of its 'general economic policy.' See, for example, Art. 3(1), Mongolia-Singapore (1995), and Art. 3(1), Singapore-Vietnam (1992). Some early BITs stipulated that investments must fit into national development plans with specific approval by the host country, among other restrictive conditions. See, for example, Ad Art. 2, Germany-Mali (1977). After the increasing liberalization of FDI policies, most BITs today do not contain such restrictions. See Sacerdoti, *supra* note 2 at 108. Whether national law imposes specific criteria with respect to the admission of investment should be distinguished from question whether investment must contribute to the economic development of the host state for purposes of Art. 25, ICSID Convention. See *supra* Chapter 1, §1.51, and at note 420.
78. Art. 2(8), Italy-Jordan (1996).
79. Thai BITs follow this model. See, for example, Art. II(5) and Annex II, Canada-Thailand (1997); Art. 2, Bangladesh-Thailand (1988); Art. 2(2), Egypt-Thailand (2000); Art. 2(1), Hungary-Thailand (1991) and Art. 2, Peru-Thailand (1991). See *Yaung Chi Oo Trading Pte. Ltd. v. Myanmar* (Award, 31 Mar. 2003) regarding the requirement for approval in writing in the ASEAN context. This requirement also appears in a number of other IIAs. See, for example, Art. 1(2), Singapore-Switzerland (1978), and Art. 2(1), Nigeria-UK (1990). Approval requirements sometimes appear within the definition of 'investment.' See, for example, Art. 1(1), Malaysia-Sweden (1979), and Art. 1(2), Chile-Tunisia (1998).
80. Art. 3, Estonia-Norway (1992); Art. 2(1), Bulgaria-Thailand (2003); Art. 2(1), Bolivia-Germany (1987); Art. 2, Burundi-Germany (1984); Art. 2(1), Germany-Jamaica (1992); Art. 2(1), Austria-Cape Verde (1991); Art. 2(1), Bulgaria-Finland (1997); Art. 2(1), Germany-Kenya (1996), and Art. 1, Germany-Zambia (1966).
81. See *Antoine Goetz et consorts v. Burundi* (Award, 10 Feb. 1999) at para. 123. Since an investment would not have yet been made, post-entry treatment obligations would not apply. However, see *infra* Chapter 5, §5.14, with respect to the application of MFN treatment to establishment obligations.
82. Some Turkish BITs make the admission of investments subject to the laws and regulations of the host state and combine this requirement with MFN treatment (but not national treatment). See, for example: Art. II(1), Algeria-Turkey (1997); Art. 3, Chile-Turkey (1998), and Art. II(1), Latvia-Turkey (1997).

In *Aguas del Tunari, S.A. v. Bolivia*,[83] the tribunal considered a post-entry admission clause in Article 2 of Bolivia-Netherlands (1992), which provides as follows:

> Either Contracting Party shall, within the framework of its law and regulations, promote economic co-operation through the protection in its territory of investments of nationals of the other Contracting Party. Subject to its right to exercise powers conferred by its laws or regulations, each Contracting Party shall admit such investments.

Bolivia argued that the fact that protection and admission of investment were subject to domestic law precluded the tribunal's jurisdiction over Aguas del Tunari's claim that Bolivia had breached its IIA obligations with respect to its conduct relating to the rescission of a water and sewage services concession. Bolivia argued that Aguas del Tunari's claim was subject to the exclusive jurisdiction of the Bolivian courts.[84] The tribunal rightly rejected Bolivia's submission on the meaning of the admission clause, noting that the clause was a standard admission clause that subjected the entry and establishment of foreign investment to local requirements, such as using a locally incorporated company. The tribunal stated that to read the clause as subjecting investment to the exclusive jurisdiction of the Bolivian courts would defeat the object and purpose of the treaty.[85]

Where a state refuses admission and establishment to a foreign investor based on restrictions in local law, there may be no IIA protection available to the investor. Many IIAs provide protection to *investments* and not to *investors*, who may have been denied the opportunity to make an investment. However, if the host state's obligation is to admit investments in accordance with its legislation, the foreign investor may be able to pursue available local remedies under the domestic foreign investment regime in order to challenge the refusal. If there is a discriminatory application of local law or a denial of justice in the local courts, this may give rise to a breach of relative or minimum standards of treatment in the IIA, provided the IIA covers investors and not just investments.

Since some IIAs provide foreign investors with admission and establishment rights and others do not, the question arises as to whether an investor can avail itself of an MFN treatment clause in a post-entry model BIT to obtain the benefits of the admission and establishment rights in a pre-entry model BIT.[86] Some BITs address this issue expressly. For example, Article 2(2), Bangladesh-Japan (1998), provides:

> Investors of either Contracting Party shall within the territory of the other Contracting Party be accorded treatment no less favorable than that accorded to investors of any third country in respect of matters relating to the admission of investment.

---

83. *Aguas del Tunari, S.A. v. Bolivia* (Decision on Respondent's Objections to Jurisdiction, 21 Oct. 2005).
84. *Ibid.*, at para. 139.
85. *Ibid.*, at para. 153.
86. See *infra* Chapter 5, §5.14.

Considering that Japan has entered into other BITs providing establishment rights, it would appear that Bangladeshi investors are entitled to establishment rights under Article 2(2). Where there is no express provision providing MFN with respect to establishment rights, the issue will be whether the subject matter of the MFN clause extends to establishment. This is dealt with elsewhere.[87]

§3.13 The pre-entry model   The pre-entry model typically accords national and MFN treatment with respect to admission and establishment, subject to a series of enumerated exceptions.[88] This approach is used by several states, including the United States, Japan and Canada and is common in regional trade agreements and recent bilateral free trade agreements that include investment obligations.[89] For example, the *North American Free Trade Agreement* (NAFTA) provides national and MFN treatment to both investors and investments with respect to establishment, acquisition and management.[90] Other IIAs, rather than expressly referring to establishment, require the host state to 'permit' investment as part of national and MFN treatment obligations. BITs based on the US Model follow this approach. For example, the Panama-US BIT (1982), provides as follows:

> Each Party shall maintain favorable conditions for investment in its territory by nationals and companies of the other Party. Each Party shall permit and treat such investment, and activities associated therewith, on a basis no less

---

87. See *infra* Chapter 5, §5.14 *et seq.*
88. Although recognizing the state's right to govern admission, the World Bank Guidelines advocate a pre-entry model whereby foreign investment is provided national treatment with respect to establishment rights, subject to a 'negative listing' approach that identifies sectors or activities that are restricted or subject to additional requirements. The Guidelines note that exceptions to national treatment might apply for the purposes of national security and for sectors reserved to nationals based on the state's economic development objectives. See I. Shihata, *Legal Treatment of Foreign Investment: The World Bank Guidelines* (Washington, DC: World Bank, 1993). On the World Bank Guidelines see *supra* Chapter 1, §1.34
89. NAFTA, the Group of Three Treaty (1994) (Colombia-Mexico-Venezuela FTA), the Bolivia-Mexico FTA (1994), the Costa Rica-Mexico FTA (1994) and the Canada-Chile FTA (1996) follow this model. Art. 2 of the Colonia Protocol, which provides for the promotion and protection of investments in MERCOSUR (the common market between Argentina, Brazil, Paraguay and Uruguay), also provides a right of establishment. See also *Framework Agreement on the ASEAN Investment Area* (1998). The draft MAI followed the NAFTA model of providing national treatment with respect to establishment and contemplated exceptions to be listed in annexes. Regional treaties that create customs unions or common markets also provide rights of establishment. Freedom of establishment is a core element of the *Treaty Establishing the European Community*. On freedom of establishment in the EU see Craig & De Búrca, *supra* note 67 at Chapter 19. For a discussion of the liberalization of investment access model in the EU as compared to a managed foreign direct investment regime, see J. Atik, 'Fairness and Managed Foreign Direct Investment' (1994) 32 CJTL 1.
90. Art. 1102(1), NAFTA, includes a general right of establishment: 'Each Party shall accord to investors of another Party treatment no less favorable than it accords, in like circumstances, to its own investors with respect to the establishment, acquisition, expansion, management, conduct, operation, and sale or other disposition of investments.' Limitations to this right are set out in annexes.

favorable than that accorded in like situations to investment or associated activities of its own nationals or companies, or of nationals or companies of any third country, whichever is more favorable.[91]

Another recent example is Article 3(1), Finland-Nigeria (2005), which provides:

1. Each Contracting Party shall accord to investors of the other Contracting Party and to their investments, a treatment no less favourable than the treatment it accords to its own investors and their investments with respect to the acquisition, expansion, operation, management, maintenance, use, enjoyment and sale or other disposal of investments.
2. Each Contracting Party shall accord to investors of the other Contracting Party and to their investments, a treatment no less favourable than the treatment it accords to investors of the most favoured nation and to their investments with respect to the establishment, acquisition, expansion, operation, management, maintenance, use, enjoyment, and sale or other disposal of investments.

Where national and MFN treatment are accorded with respect to admission and establishment, the standard practice is to annex a list of exceptions or reservations to these obligations.[92] This is often referred to as a negative listing approach since all sectors are covered unless specifically excluded. The practice contrasts with the positive listing approach under the General Agreement on Trade in Services (GATS), under which national treatment obligations only apply to specific commitments made in a WTO member's schedule.[93]

Reservations to IIA admission and establishment obligations are made in a number of ways. Certain sectors, subsectors or activities may be entirely excluded for admission and establishment obligations. This is often the case in economic sectors with particular strategic, political or economic significance to the state. Reservations may be made for existing or future non-conforming measures.[94] States may thus maintain existing measures, or adopt new and more restrictive

---

91. Art. II(1), Panama-US (1982). In *Mihaly, supra* note 2 at para. 60, the tribunal noted that 'while the US-Sri Lanka BIT contains provisions regarding the definition of investment and conditions for its admission, they recognize the Parties' prerogative in this respect.' This statement is not entirely accurate. The BIT in question accords national and MFN treatment with respect to admission and establishment but subjects that right to a number of annexed exceptions.
92. See Sacerdoti, *supra* note 2 at 109. For examples, see annexes to Japan-Vietnam (2003); US-Uruguay (2005); Canada-Peru (2006) and *Japan-Malaysia Economic Partnership Agreement* (2005). Also see *infra* Chapter 10, Defences and Exceptions.
93. See *infra* §3.14 on GATS.
94. See Art. 1108(1), NAFTA, and Annex 1 entitled 'Reservations for Existing Measures and Liberalization Requirements.' Canada annexed measures with respect to foreign investment screening and foreign ownership restrictions that would have violated national treatment. Art. 1108(1)(c) further provides a 'standstill' obligation with respect to amendments to non-conforming measures. Reservations apply to amendments to non-conforming measures provided they do not decrease the conformity of the measure with the applicable obligation. For certain non-conforming measures, the parties agreed to phase them out over time.

ones that do not conform to IIA obligations.[95] Reservations may also be made to allow for specific social policies, such as development considerations[96] or the protection of disadvantaged groups.[97]

Pre-entry model IIAs also sometimes expressly carve out exceptions to the national treatment obligation for special establishment formalities, including requirements that: (i) investors or board members reside in the host state;[98] (ii) certain information be disclosed, including the need to report currency transfers;[99] and (iii) investments be legally constituted under the laws of the host state.[100] However, it is important to note that these carve-outs are typically subject to the caveat that the formalities in question do not 'materially impair' other protections afforded under the IIA.[101]

Another model of investment liberalization is the *Framework Agreement on the ASEAN Investment Area*, which provides for each member state to 'open immediately all its industries for investments by ASEAN investors,'[102] subject to temporary exclusion lists. In addition, the Agreement provides that states may take emergency safeguard measures where, as a result of the implementation of the liberalization obligation, a member state suffers or is threatened by serious injury or threat.[103]

Finally, some treaties provide for entry rights to be established in the future. A leading example is the *Energy Charter Treaty* (ECT),[104] which couches entry obligations in more permissive terms by calling upon the contracting parties to 'endeavour to accord' national and MFN treatment to foreign investors and

---

95. See Art. 1108(3), NAFTA, and Annex II entitled 'Reservations for Future Measures.' The US Schedule included measures with respect to the ownership of oceanfront land, communications, social services, legal services, newspaper publishing, maritime transportation services and preferences to economically disadvantaged minorities.
96. Protocol, Indonesia-Switzerland (1974); Art. 3, Jamaica-Switzerland (1990); Art. 3(6), Jamaica-Netherlands (1991) and Art. 3(3), Italy-Morocco (1990).
97. In NAFTA, the parties made reservations for Aboriginal Affairs or Minority Affairs. See Annex II, Reservations for Future Measures, NAFTA, *supra* note 95.
98. See, for example, Art. 1111(1), NAFTA; Art. 15(1), US-Uruguay (2005), and Art. 6(2), Canadian Model (2003).
99. See, for example, Art. 1111(2), NAFTA, and Art. 15(2), US-Uruguay (2005). These provisions, however, are made subject to the protection of confidential business information.
100. See, for example, Art. 14(2), Bahrain-US (1999), and Art. 15(2), US-Uruguay (2005).
101. See, for example, Art. 15(1), US-Uruguay (2005); Art. 15, US Model BIT (2004) and Art. 6(2), Canadian Model (2003).
102. Art. 7(1), *Framework Agreement on the ASEAN Investment Area*, online: <www.aseansec. org>.
103. Art. 14, *ibid.* See *infra* Chapter 10, Exceptions and Defences with respect to measures to safeguard essential interests.
104. *Energy Charter Treaty*, opened for signature on 17 Dec. 1994, (1995) 34 ILM 360 [ECT]. See *supra* Chapter 1, §1.38.

investments.[105] More stringent requirements are to be laid down in a supplementary treaty.[106]

§3.14 WTO General Agreement on Trade in Services (GATS)   Not all foreign investment liberalization obligations are contained in IIAs. Under the GATS, the subject matter of which is the international trade in services, WTO members have undertaken specific commitments to liberalize investment in some service sectors.[107] The GATS defines four modes of supply through which international trade in services may occur: (i) cross-border supply;[108] (ii) overseas consumption;[109] (iii) commercial presence abroad;[110] and (iv) temporary entry of natural persons into a foreign market.[111] Market access commitments under the third mode of supply – commercial presence abroad – provides sector-specific admission and establishment rights for service suppliers by allowing them to establish both offices and a commercial presence in the country of delivery. In addition, the fourth mode of supply – temporary entry – liberalizes restrictions on the entry of foreign investors and personnel. In this respect, the GATS may be described as the first multilateral agreement on FDI, at least with regards to the supply of services.[112]

Under the GATS, WTO members have made specific market access commitments in their respective GATS schedules. A member's schedule lists its market access commitments under each of the four modes of supply, as well as any

---

105. Art. 10(2), ECT, *ibid.*
106. *Ibid.*, Art. 10(4). Negotiations on the supplementary treaty were commenced but to date have not been concluded. See S. Elshibabi, 'The Difficulty Behind Securing Sector-Specific Investment Establishment Rights: The Case of the Energy Charter Treaty,' (2001) IL 35: 137. Member states put negotiations on the supplementary treaty on hold in 2002 pending the outcome of discussions at the WTO on a multilateral framework for FDI. See online: Energy Charter Treaty Blue Book <www.encharter.org>. The 2004 formal review of the ECT states that: 'We will also continue our work on non-discriminatory treatment in the pre-investment phase, i.e., on the 'making of investments'. The Investment Group should continue to monitor exceptions to this principle, with a view to their reduction and removal. We will also periodically review the possibility of making progress on this issue on a legally binding basis, as foreseen by the Energy Charter Treaty.' (Conclusions of the Review Conducted under Art. 34(7) of the Energy Charter Treaty as Adopted by the Energy Charter Conference at its 15th Meeting on 14 Dec. 2004).
107. For a general overview of the GATS, see Trebilcock & Howse, *The Regulation of International Trade*, *supra* note 63; WTO Trade in Services Division, *Handbook on the GATS Agreement* (Cambridge: Cambridge University Press, 2005) and WTO Secretariat, *Guide to the GATS: An Overview of Issues for Further Liberalization of Trade in Services* (Hague: Kluwer Law International, 2001).
108. GATS, Art. II(a).
109. *Ibid.*, Art. II(b).
110. *Ibid.*, Art. II(c). Art. XXVIII(d) provides as follows: ' "commercial presence" means any type of business or professional establishment, including through (i) the constitution, acquisition or maintenance of a juridical person, or (ii) the creation or maintenance of a branch or a representative office, within the territory of a Member for the purpose of supplying a service". '
111. *Ibid.*, Art. II(d).
112. Sacerdoti, *supra* note 2 at 113.

exceptions or qualifications that may extend to both national[113] and MFN[114] treatment obligations. The GATS represents a hybrid between the pre- and post-entry models because establishment rights are only provided where specific market access commitments have been made.[115] As previously noted, the GATS adopts a positive listing approach, as opposed to the negative listing approach in IIAs that adopt a pre-entry model.

GATS market access commitments are protected by prohibiting quantitative restrictions on services, including limits on the total number of service providers,[116] the total value of service transactions,[117] the quantity of service imports,[118] and the number of people that may be employed in a particular service sector.[119] Prohibitions on measures that restrict the legal form through which services are supplied[120] or limit the percentage of foreign shareholding[121] are particularly important aspects of foreign investment liberalization achieved through the GATS.

The GATS was drafted in contemplation of future rounds of multilateral negotiations to further liberalize trade in services.[122] Just as successive rounds of the *General Agreement on Tariffs and Trade* (GATT) negotiations have improved market access for goods by lowering tariffs, successive rounds of GATS negotiations are intended to promote market access for services. This is to be achieved by improving market access in sectors listed on members' GATS schedules, as well as by adding further commitments for new service sectors. Since 1995, there have been negotiations and further commitments made in areas such as financial services, telecommunication services, the movement of natural persons and maritime services.[123]

If a WTO member breaches one of its GATS commitments, any other member can seek a ruling from the WTO Dispute Settlement Body (DSB) with respect to the consistency of the state measure in question. Individual investors do not have standing to bring a complaint before the DSB, since the mechanism is designed only for state-to-state dispute resolution. Nonetheless, obligations under the various WTO agreements may still be important to foreign investors in making a claim against a host state for an alleged breach of an IIA.[124]

---

113. GATS, Art. XVII.
114. *Ibid.*, Art. II.
115. UNCTAD, *International Investment Agreements: Key Issues*, Vol. 1 (Geneva and New York: UNCTAD, 2004) at 169.
116. GATS, Art. XVI(2)(a).
117. *Ibid.*, Art. XVI(2)(b).
118. *Ibid.*, Art. XVI(2)(c).
119. *Ibid.*, Art. XVI(2)(d).
120. *Ibid.*, Art. XVI(2)(e).
121. *Ibid.*, Art. XVI(2)(f).
122. *Ibid.*, Art. XIX.
123. See online: WTO, Services: Negotiations <http://wto.org/english/tratop_e/serv_e/s_negs_e.htm>.
124. On the interaction between WTO law and minimum standards of treatment, see *infra* Chapter 6, §6.12, and G. Verhoosel, 'The Use of Investor-State Arbitration under Bilateral Investment Treaties to Seek Relief for Breaches of WTO Law' (2003) 6 JIEL 493. See also F. Ortino & A. Sheppard, 'International Agreements Covering Foreign Investment in Services: Patterns and Linkages,' in L. Bartels & F. Ortino, eds, *Regional Trade Agreements and the WTO Legal*

Article II of the GATS provides a general MFN treatment obligation as follows:

> With respect to any measure covered by this Agreement, each Member shall accord immediately and unconditionally to services and service suppliers of any other Member treatment no less favourable than that it accords to like services and service suppliers of any other country.

Where a WTO member has provided establishment rights in its IIAs that include commercial presence in services, the state may be in breach of its WTO obligations if it does not extend these establishment rights unconditionally to other WTO members.[125]

IV   OTHER ENTRY OBLIGATIONS

§3.15 Entry of personnel   In contrast to the liberalization of foreign investment and international trade in goods and services, there has been little liberalization in the international movement of natural persons.[126] States stringently control the entry of foreign nationals through national immigration policies. There are few international obligations with respect to the entry of foreign workers. In the context of the GATS, states have undertaken obligations for the temporary entry of natural persons relating to the trans-border supply of services and have established a protocol with respect to the movement of natural persons.[127] In the context of Free Trade Agreements (FTAs) and other regional economic integration agreements,

---

System (Oxford: Oxford University Press, 2006) at 201. On the potential of the GATS MFN clause applying to IIA dispute settlement mechanisms, see W. Ben Hamida, 'Clause de la nation la plus favorisée et mécanismes de règlement des différends : que dit l'histoire' (2007) 134 JDI 1127 at 1159-1162.

125. See Ortino & Sheppard, *ibid.* See also Statement by the Russian Federation, 'Main Provisions within the Framework of Further Work on Regulation of Investment Issues by The Russian Federation,' UNCTAD Expert Meeting on Development Implications of International Investment Rule Making, 28-29 Jun. 2007, highlighting at 3 that '[if] the treatment accorded to the investment under BITs does not correspond to the WTO provisions, in particular to the obligations of the Parties under the GATS, and no cross-reference with those obligations under the WTO is made in respective BITs, a legal collision may arise.' Online: <www.unctad.org/sections/wcmu/docs/c2em21p01_en.pdf>.

126. See Trebilcock & Howse, *The Regulation of International Trade*, *supra* note 107 at 611. Some early US FCN treaties provide obligations with respect to entry. For example, Belgium-US FCN (1961) provides that the nationals of either party be permitted to 'enter the territories of the other party and reside therein: (a) for the purpose of carrying on trade between the two countries and engaging in related commercial activities; or (b) for the purpose of developing and directing the operations of an enterprise in which they have invested, or are actively in the process of investing, a substantial amount of capital.'

127. See *Third Protocol to the General Agreement on Trade in Services*, WTO Document S/L/12, 24 Jul. 1995 and WTO Council for Trade in Services, Secretariat Background Note, 'Presence of Natural Persons (Mode 4)' 8 Dec. 1998 (S/C/W/75).

there are a range of liberalization obligations.[128] The EU model, under which there is free internal movement of peoples, and obligations with respect to the recognition of professional and vocational qualifications, is the most liberal.[129] In contrast, Chapter 16, NAFTA, provides only for a system of temporary entry visas for business persons.

Despite the fact that foreign investors will often need or want to employ foreign individuals, IIAs do not typically address entry rights or immigration requirements or restrictions.[130] The small number of IIAs that address the entry of foreign personnel typically do so in provisions that subject entry to host state law.[131] In post-entry model BITs, the provisions are typically framed as requirements to provide consideration that is 'sympathetic,'[132] 'well meaning,'[133] or otherwise to provide 'favourable conditions'[134] to applications for the entry and residence of personnel who will perform activities related to the investment.[135] A few IIAs

---

128. Art. 10.4(a)(iv), Australia-US FTA (2004); Art. 10.4(a)(iv), Bahrain-US FTA (2004); Art. 11.4(a)(iv), Chile-US FTA (2003); Chapter 11, Singapore-US FTA (2003); Art. 3, Jordan-US FTA (2000); Art. H (Cross-Border Trade in Services), Canada-Chile FTA (1996); Art. K (Temporary Entry for Business Persons), *ibid.*; Art. VIII(3), Canada-Costa Rica FTA (2002); Chapter X, *ibid.*, and Art. 4.8, Canada-Israel FTA (1997).

129. Craig & De Búrca, *supra* note 67 at Chapter 17.

130. On the international movement of persons, see Chapter 19, Trebilcock & Howse, *The Regulation of International Trade*, *supra* note 63.

131. For example, the agreement might provide an affirmative obligation to permit nationals to 'enter, stay or leave its territory' in accordance with state law. See, for example, Art. 2(7), Italy-USSR (1989), and Art. 7, Bahrain-US (1999).

132. See, for example, Art. 2(3), Finland-Philippines (1998); Ad Art. 3(c), Bolivia-Germany (1987); Ad Art. 3(c), Bosnia-Germany (2001); Ad Art. 3(c), Germany-Nigeria (2000); Art. 8, Japan-Vietnam (2003); Art. 4, French Model BIT (no date provided); Ad Art. 3(c), German Model BIT (1991); Art. 8, Jamaican Model BIT (no date provided); Art. III(3), Turkish Model BIT (no date provided); Art. 7(1)(a), US Model BIT (2004); Art. 3, Bolivia-France (1989); and Art. 2(2), Finland-Lebanon (1997). Model BITS are available on the online UNCTAD IIA Compendium database.

133. See, for example, Art. 1, China-Finland (1984).

134. For example, the French Model BIT provides: 'Les Parties contractantes examineront avec bienveillance, dans le cadre de leur législation interne, les demandes d'entrée et d'autorisation de séjour, de travail, et de circulation introduites par des nationaux d'une Partie contractante, au titre d'un investissement réalisé sur le territoire ou dans la zone maritime de l'autre Partie contractante.' See, for example, Art. II, Canada-South Africa (1995), and Art. 3, Ugandan Model BIT (no date provided).

135. Some model BITs provide obligations with respect to the entry of personnel. Art. 3(iii), Asian-African Model (1985), provides that the parties: 'shall facilitate the implementation and operation of the investment through ... expeditious clearance of authorizations or permits for ... employment of consultants and technicians of foreign nationality.' Art. II(6), Italian Model BIT (2003), provides that each party 'shall regulate as favourably as possible the problems connected with the entry, stay, work and movement in its territory of [nationals of the other party].' In contrast, others provide for consideration of the use of local resources. See, for example, Art. 2(2), Jamaican Model BIT (no date provided), which states that the parties 'shall endeavour to encourage the use of local resources both human and material for the promotion of investment.'

provide for the entry into the host state of managers 'who are essential' to the foreign investor.[136]

An important distinction in these types of provisions is whether entry rights apply only to nationals of the home state[137] or more broadly to personnel already under the employment of the investor (who might be third state nationals).[138]

By contrast, pre-entry model IIAs tend to have more expansive obligations – obligations that are consistent with the right of establishment based on national treatment.[139] For example, Article II(3), Argentina-US (1991), provides:

> Subject to the laws relating to the entry and sojourn of aliens, nationals of either Party shall be permitted to enter and to remain in the territory of the other Party for the purpose of establishing, developing, administering or advising on the operation of an investment to which they, or a company of the first Party that employs them, have committed or are in the process of committing a substantial amount of capital or other resources.

Further, some US BITs prohibit the host state from imposing numerical quotas or labour certifications for personnel.[140]

§3.16 Senior management and offices   A small number of IIAs require the host state to allow the investor to appoint individuals of any nationality to senior management positions.[141] For example, Article II(5), Estonia-US (1994), provides:

> Companies which are legally constituted under the applicable laws or regulations of one Party, and which are investments, shall be permitted to engage top managerial personnel of their choice, regardless of nationality.[142]

Some agreements, including the NAFTA, go further and provide that, although parties may require that a majority of the board of directors be of a particular nationality or a resident, such requirements are not to materially impair the ability of investors to exercise control of their investment.[143]

Some IIAs also require the host state to encourage or otherwise facilitate the establishment of representative offices. Danish BITs provide that the parties

---

136. Art. 12(2), Bosnia-Finland (2000).
137. Art. 2, Botswana-China (2000), and Art. 4, France-Mexico (1998).
138. Art. 5, Australia-India (1999).
139. Art. II(3), Russia-US (1992).
140. Art. VII, Nicaragua-US (1995). Compare Art. 8, Japan-Korea (2002).
141. See Art. 1107(1), NAFTA; Art. 9(1), US-Uruguay (2005); Art. II(6), Italian Model BIT (2003); Art. 9(1), US Model BIT (2004); Art. V(1), Canada-Costa Rica (1998); Art. V(1)(a), Canada-South Africa (1995); Art. V(1)(a), Canada-Thailand (1997) and Art. 6(1), Canadian Model FIPA (2003).
142. See also Art. 5, Australia-Egypt (2001).
143. Art. 1107, NAFTA. See also Art. II(4), Russia-US (1992); Art. V(2), Canada-Costa Rica (1998); Art. V(1)(b), Canada-South Africa (1995); Art. G-07, Canada-Chile FTA (1996); Art. V(1)(b), Canada-Thailand (1997); Art. 6(2), Canadian Model BIT (2003); Art. 9(2), US Model BIT (2004); Art. 9(2), US-Uruguay (2005) and Art. 4(1)(f), Japan-Vietnam (2003).

shall admit investments in accordance with their legislation and administrative practice and encourage such investments, 'including facilitating the establishment of representative offices.'[144] Finally, some IIAs also prohibit the host state from requiring a foreign investor to locate its headquarters in a specific region.[145]

§3.17 Granting of permits   Some IIAs provide ancillary rights once an investment has been admitted, such as the granting of the necessary business permits to carry out the investment.[146] In some cases, the obligation is that of good faith in reviewing applications for necessary permits in accordance with local law. For example, Article 3(2), China-Switzerland (1986), provides:

> Chaque Partie Contractante examinera avec bienveillance, dans le cadre de sa législation interne, les demandes d'autorisations et de licences nécessaires pour toutes les activités relatives à la gestion, à la promotion, à l'exécution et aux besoins de main-d'oeuvre de tels investissements.

On the other hand, some IIAs appear to provide a right to necessary permits once an investment has been admitted. For example, Article 2, Bolivia-Korea (1996), provides:

> When a Contracting Party shall have admitted an investment on its territory, it shall grant the necessary permits in connection with such an investment and with the carrying out of licensing agreements and contracts for technical, commercial or administrative assistance. Each Contracting Party shall, whenever needed, issue, as far as possible, the necessary authorizations concerning the activities of consultants and other qualified persons of foreign nationality related to investment.[147]

The above provision might suggest that where an investment has been admitted it is entitled to necessary permits, even where granting the permit is contrary to local law. This issue arose in *MTD Equity Std. Bhd and MTD Chile S.A. v. Chile.*[148] Chile had approved an investment for a real estate development under its foreign investment legislation. It transpired that the project was not permitted under the

---

144. Art. 2(1), Danish Model BIT; Art. 2(1), Denmark-India (1995); Art. 2, Denmark-Lithuania (1992); Art. 2(1), Denmark-Pakistan (1996); Art. 2, Czechoslovakia-Denmark (1991) and Art. 2, Denmark-Vietnam (1993).
145. Art. 75(1)(g), Japan-Singapore Economic Partnership Agreement (2002).
146. This is common in Swiss BITs. For example, see Art. 3(2), Switzerland-Paraguay (1992). See generally Dolzer & Stevens, *supra* note 2 at 52-53.
147. See also Art. 3(2), Pakistan-Switzerland (1995), which provides: 'Lorsqu'elle aura admis un investissement sur son territoire, chaque Partie Contractante délivrera les autorisations qui seraient nécessaires en relation avec cet investissement, y compris avec l'exécution de contrats de licence, d'assistance technique, commerciale ou administrative. Chaque Partie Contractante veillera à délivrer, chaque fois que cela sera nécessaire, les autorisations requises pour ce qui a trait aux activités de consultants ou d'autres personnes qualifiées de nationalité étrangère.'
148. Award, 25 May 2004 [*MTD Award*]. See *infra* Chapter 6, §6.26, for discussion of the case.

applicable land use planning regulations. The investor claimed that it was entitled to development permission based on Article 3(2), Chile-Croatia (1994), which provides:

> When a Contracting Party has admitted an investment in its territory, it shall grant the necessary permits in accordance with its laws and regulations.

The claimant argued that the IIA requirement to grant 'the necessary permits in accordance with its laws and regulations'[149] meant that applicable permits for its real estate development must be issued as long as doing so was lawful. In addressing this claim, the tribunal drew a distinction between permits granted in accordance with the laws and regulations of the state and actions that require a change in laws and regulations. In the tribunal's view, the provision only required that a permit be granted if an application for a permit met the requirements of the domestic law. It did not 'entitle an investor to a change in the normative framework.'[150] The tribunal found there was no breach of the obligation because the claimant's development depended on an actual change in the applicable land use planning regulations rather than the simple issuance of a permit, although the tribunal went on to hold Chile responsible for breaching fair and equitable treatment.[151]

§3.18 Special formalities for establishment   Pre-entry model IIAs with establishment rights often provide that the host state may impose special formalities in connection with the establishment of investments, provided the formalities do not materially impair the protections afforded to a party. For example, Article 1111(1), NAFTA, provides two examples of special formalities: a requirement that investors be resident, or that investments be legally constituted under the law or regulations of the host state.[152]

---

149.   In *MTD Award, ibid.*, the tribunal held that the Malaysian investor was entitled to the protection afforded by Art. 3(2), Chile-Croatia (1994), by virtue of the MFN clause in Chile-Malaysia (1992). See *infra* Chapter 6 on MFN clauses.
150.   *Ibid.*, at para. 205.
151.   See *infra* Chapter 6, §6.20 and §6.26.
152.   See K.J. Vandevelde, *United States Investment Treaties: Policy and Practice* (Boston: Kluwer Law and Taxation, 1992) at 69-72 and, with respect to NAFTA, the discussion on special formalities in M. Kinnear, A.K. Bjorklund & J. Hannaford, *Investment Disputes under NAFTA: An Annotated Guide to NAFTA Chapter 11* (The Netherlands: Kluwer Law International, 2006).

Chapter 4

National Treatment

INTRODUCTION

§4.1 Non-discrimination in international economic law One of the main objectives of international trade and investment law is to limit state measures that discriminate based on the nationality of the foreign individual, entity, good, service or investment in question.[1] The rationales for prohibiting nationality-based discrimination are economic and political. The traditional economic justification for non-discrimination is that it promotes efficient economic exchange.[2] Neoclassical economic theory argues that state measures that distort capital allocation, such as performance requirements and barriers to the admission of foreign direct investment, are welfare reducing.[3] From this perspective, non-discriminatory treatment of goods and services ensures that domestic markets are not insulated from international price competition through protectionist barriers. The commitment to non-discrimination has also important political rationales,

---

1. See M. Trebilcock & R. Howse, *The Regulation of International Trade*, 3rd edn (London: Routledge, 2005) at 1-112 for an overview of the arguments for and against free trade, as well as a discussion of non-discrimination as a foundational principle of international economic law. See also E. Laing, 'Equal Access/Non-Discrimination and Legitimate Discrimination in International Economic Law' (1995) 14 WILJ 246 and G. Wang, 'The Globalized Economy in Quest of Globalization of the Rule of Law – From the Perspective of the National Treatment Principle' (2001) 2 JWI 21.
2. Trebilcock & Howse, *ibid.*; J. Jackson, *The World Trading System: Law and Policy of International Economic Relations*, 2nd edn (Cambridge, MA: MIT Press, 1999) [*World Trading System*]; and J. Jackson, W. Davey & A. Sykes, eds, *Legal Problems of International Economic Relations*, 4th edn (St. Paul: West Group, 2002) [*Legal Problems*].
3. See Trebilcock & Howse, *ibid.*, at 441-6. The economic case for investment liberalization remains contested. See *supra* Chapter 3, §3.8 *et seq.*, regarding admission and *infra* Chapter 8, §8.14 *et seq.*, regarding performance requirements.

including the promotion of multilateralism and the prevention of conflicts that might arise due to discriminatory economic policies.[4] Many historians argue that high tariffs and related protectionist economic policies in the 1930s exacerbated the Great Depression and were a contributing cause of the Second World War (WWII).[5] International economic treaties concluded after WWII, namely the *General Agreement on Tariffs and Trade* (GATT)[6] and the *Articles of Agreement of the International Monetary Fund*,[7] aimed at creating a legal framework for international trade and monetary relations. Disciplining nationality-based discrimination is a guiding principle and pillar of both treaties.

International economic treaties limit nationality-based discrimination through two distinct non-discrimination treatment obligations: national and most-favoured-nation (MFN) treatment.[8] As its name suggests, a national treatment obligation requires non-discrimination between similarly-situated domestic and foreign persons, entities, goods, services or investments. In contrast, an MFN treatment obligation requires that state conduct does not discriminate between similarly-situated foreign persons, entities, goods, services or investments. National treatment affords non-discrimination between the national and the foreign. MFN treatment affords non-discrimination between the foreign and the foreign. This chapter addresses national treatment. MFN treatment is addressed in the next chapter. General prohibitions on discriminatory measures are addressed at Chapter 6, §6.10. Non-discrimination as a requirement for a legal expropriation is addressed at Chapter 7, §7.33.

§4.2 A relative standard   A national treatment obligation accords a relative or contingent standard of treatment: it does not bestow an absolute or minimum standard of treatment.[9] The national treatment standard is an empty shell that obtains substantive content in relation to the treatment afforded to someone or something else. The legal analysis involves a comparison between the host state's treatment

---

4. See *World Trading System, supra* note 2 at 36, and *Legal Problems, supra* note 2 at 415 *et seq.* Also see P. Ala'i, T. Broude & C. Picker, *Trade as Guarantor of Peace, Liberty and Security? – Critical, Empirical and Historical Perspectives* (Washington, DC: The American Society of International Law, 2006). More broadly, the commitment to prohibiting nationality-based discrimination can also be viewed as progressive development in the creation of a 'constitutionalized' international economic legal order. For example, see Ernst-Ulrich Petersmann's work on the constitutionalization of international economic law: 'The WTO Constitution and Human Rights' (2000) 3 JIEL 19 and more recent works. For a critical perspective on IIAs as a constitutional order, see D. Schneiderman, *Constitutionalizing Economic Globalization: Investment Rules and Democracy's Promise* (New York: Cambridge University Press, 2008).
5. *World Trading System, ibid.*
6. Art. III, *General Agreement on Tariffs and Trade*, 30 Oct. 1947, 55 UNTS 194.
7. Art. VIII (General Obligations) of the *Amended Articles of Agreement of the International Monetary Fund* (1992) 31 ILM 1309 [IMF Articles]. The IMF Articles prohibit discriminatory currency practices and provide for the convertibility of foreign currency. See *infra* Chapter 8, §8.3 *et seq.*
8. *World Trading System, supra* note 2 at 157, and *Legal Problems, supra* note 2 at 417. Also see C. Crépet Daigremont, 'Traitement national et traitement de la nation la plus favorisée dans la jurisprudence arbitrale récente relative à l'investissement international' in Ch. Leben, ed., *Le contentieux arbitral transnational relatif à l'investissement* (Paris: Anthemis, 2006) at 107.
9. See *infra* Chapter 6, Minimum Standards of Treatment.

of domestic and foreign investors or domestic and foreign investments. Unlike an absolute or minimum standard of treatment provision (e.g., expropriation and fair and equitable treatment), the national treatment standard does not have any intrinsic substantive content. The required standard of treatment depends on the treatment of the applicable treaty-defined comparator.

§4.3 A treaty-based obligation   In international investment law, national treatment is a treaty-based obligation.[10] Although the prevalence of national treatment provisions in international investment agreements (IIAs) might suggest consistent and general state practice sufficient for the formation of a customary international law obligation, the scope and content of the provisions vary widely and the obligations are subject to myriad exceptions.[11] Even if sufficient state practice existed to satisfy the requirements for establishing a customary international law obligation, there is little evidence that national treatment in IIAs is accorded out of a sense of legal obligation (*opinio juris*). At present, the more persuasive view is that national treatment obligations with respect to the treatment of foreign investment arise only on the basis of an express treaty obligation.[12]

In *Methanex v. United States*, the tribunal noted:

> As to the question of whether a rule of customary international law prohibits a State, in the absence of a treaty obligation, from differentiating in its treatment of nationals and aliens, international law is clear. In the absence of a contrary rule of international law binding on the States parties, whether of conventional or customary origin, a State may differentiate in its treatment of nationals and aliens. As the previous discussion shows, no conventional rule binding on the NAFTA Parties is to the contrary with respect to the issues raised in this case.[13]

The tribunal's discussion highlights that although there is no blanket prohibition in customary international law against differentiating between nationals and foreigners, there may be specific conventional and customary non-discrimination obligations. For example, it is contrary to the minimum standard of justice to discriminate in the administration of justice based on nationality.[14] Expropriations

---

10.   For the view that, in the investment context, national and MFN treatment are not customary international law obligations, see arbitrator Asante's dissenting opinion in *Asian Agricultural Products Ltd. (AAPL) v. Sri Lanka* (Final Award, 27 Jun. 1990) [*AAPL*] at paras 642-643; and E. Denza & S. Brooks, 'Investment Protection Treaties: United Kingdom Experience' (1987) 36 ICLQ 910 at 911.

11.   See *infra* Chapter 4, §4.8, regarding variations in treaty practice.

12.   See R. Jennings & A. Watts, eds, *Oppenheim's International Law*, 9th edn (London: Longman, 1992), §409 at 933: 'a degree of discrimination in the treatment of aliens as compared with nationals is, generally, permissible, as a matter of customary international law.'

13.   *Methanex Corporation v. United States* (Final Award of the Tribunal on Jurisdiction and Merits, 3 Aug. 2005) [*Methanex*] at Part IV – Chapter C, para. 25. See also paras 14 and 15.

14.   See *infra* Chapter 6, §6.10.

directed solely against foreigners breach customary international law.[15] Further, prohibitions on some other forms of non-nationality-based discrimination, including racial discrimination, are generally viewed as international customary rules.[16]

§4.4 IIA prohibitions on discriminatory measures   In addition to national treatment provisions, some IIAs contain a general prohibition on discriminatory measures. Other IIAs have no express national treatment provision and only contain a general prohibition against discriminatory measures. In both cases, IIAs usually do not clarify the content, extent or meaning of a general prohibition against discriminatory measures. IIA tribunals have, however, held that discriminatory measures include those 'directed specifically against a certain investor by reason of his, her or its nationality.'[17] General prohibitions on discriminatory measures are addressed at Chapter 6, §6.10.

§4.5 Overview of the issues covered in this chapter   Part I covers the background and evolution of national treatment provisions. IIA practice is covered in Part II. Although national treatment provisions are common in IIAs, specific provisions vary significantly – whether the national treatment provision applies to investors, investments or both; whether it extends to admission or establishment; and whether it contains an express comparator such as 'in like circumstances.' Part III covers the application of national treatment, which gives rise to two issues. First, the basis of national treatment is that a comparison must be made between the treatment of domestic and foreign investors or investments. Hence, identifying the appropriate comparator is key in the national treatment analysis. Second, the application of national treatment requires an evaluation of whether the host state accorded less favourable treatment to the foreign investor or investment compared to the domestic comparator. Part IV addresses exceptions and reservations to national treatment obligations. States may desire to provide special or differential treatment to domestic investors and investment. As a result, national treatment provisions often are subject to exceptions and reservations.

I   BACKGROUND ON NATIONAL TREATMENT IN IIAS

§4.6 National treatment – purpose and definition   The purpose of the national treatment obligation in IIAs is to prohibit nationality-based discrimination by the host state between the host states' investors and investments and those of another

---

15. See *infra* Chapter 7, §7.33.
16. See I. Brownlie, *Principles of Public International Law*, 6th edn (Oxford: Oxford University Press, 2003) at 546.
17. *Noble Ventures, Inc. v. Romania* (Award, 12 Oct. 2005) at para. 180.

IIA party.[18] From an economic perspective, the prohibition of nationality-based discrimination serves to ensure that foreign investors and investments benefit from equality of competitive opportunities. As noted by one commentator with respect to the national treatment provision in Chapter Eleven, *North American Free Trade Agreement* (NAFTA): 'it promises equality of competitive opportunity for comparable investors operating in like circumstances.'[19] From a legal perspective, national treatment guarantees equality before the law and equal administration of the law (administrative equality) and equal protection of the law (formal equality).

Although the exact scope and application of national treatment varies from one IIA to another, the Organization of Economic Co-operation and Development's (OECD) definition of national treatment in the 1976 *Declaration on International Investment and Multinational Enterprises* (the Declaration) provides a useful starting point for analysis of the principle:

> adhering governments should, consistent with their needs to maintain public order, to protect their essential security interests and to fulfil commitments relating to international peace and security, accord to enterprises operating in their territories and owned or controlled directly or indirectly by nationals of another adhering government (hereinafter referred to as 'Foreign-Controlled Enterprises') treatment under their laws, regulations and administrative practices, consistent with international law and no less favourable than that accorded in like situations to domestic enterprises.[20]

The Declaration's definition highlights four central elements of national treatment. The first is that the prohibited discrimination is between foreigners and nationals. To this end, the Declaration uses the terminology of domestic enterprises and foreign-controlled enterprises to identify the subjects for comparison. Second, the applicable subjects must be in like situations. Third, a foreign enterprise in a like situation to a domestic enterprise is to receive no less favourable treatment than the national enterprise. Finally, national treatment obligations are not absolute. Legitimate, non-protectionist rationales may justify differential treatment.

Although arguably the purpose of national treatment provisions in IIAs is to prohibit nationality-based discrimination, a literal interpretation of some IIA national treatment provisions might suggest that they apply to prohibit less

---

18. IIA tribunals have confirmed that national treatment is directed at nationality-based discrimination. See *The Loewen Group, Inc. and Raymond L. Loewen v. United States* (Award, 26 Jun. 2003) [*Loewen*] at para. 40; *Técnicas Medioambientales Tecmed S.A. v. Mexico* (Award, 29 May 2003) at para. 181 [*Tecmed*]; *S.D. Myers, Inc. v. Canada* (Partial Award, 13 Nov. 2000) [*S.D. Myers*] at paras 252-253; and *Methanex, supra* note 13 at Part IV-Chapter B, para. 12. For a comprehensive elaboration of the rationale for national treatment, see J. Kurtz, 'National Treatment, Foreign Investment and Regulatory Autonomy: The Search for Protectionism or Something More?,' in P. Kahn & T. Wälde, eds, *New Aspects of International Investment Law* (Leiden: Martinus Nijhoff Publishers, 2007) at 311.
19. T. Weiler, 'Methanex Corp. v. U.S.A. Turning the Page on NAFTA Chapter Eleven' (2005) 6 JWIT 903 at 915.
20. Art. II.1, OECD, *Declaration on International Investment and Multinational Enterprises,* Jun. 1976 (Paris: OECD, 1976).

favourable treatment unrelated to nationality-based discrimination. For example, national treatment provisions might be viewed as applying to a broader range of disparate impacts and more generally as serving to liberalize regulatory restrictions on foreign investors.[21] In *Occidental Exploration and Production Company v. Ecuador*,[22] the tribunal found a breach of national treatment where exporters of flowers, mining and seafood products were entitled to receive value added tax (VAT) refunds but oil exporters were not. In its reasoning, the tribunal appears to identify national treatment with an economically disadvantageous distinction, not necessarily related to nationality-based discrimination.[23] In contrast, in the NAFTA national treatment cases, the search for nationality-based discrimination appears as central elements of the analysis.[24]

IIA national treatment jurisprudence does not provide a consistent approach to articulating the purpose of national treatment. The majority of the IIA jurisprudence to date suggests that the purpose of national treatment is to prohibit *de jure* and *de facto* nationality-based discrimination.[25] Functionally, this serves to ensure that there is equality of competitive opportunities between competing local and non-local investors or investment. In other words, an essential element of the national treatment analysis is whether there is a competitive relationship between the investors and investments in question. However, as discussed below, depending on the government measure in question, a competitive relationship is neither a sufficient nor necessary element of establishing a breach of national treatment.[26] Further, while national treatment serves to discipline nationality-based discrimination, the investor need not demonstrate protectionist intent or motive.[27]

§4.7 Historical background and development Legal scholars have traced national treatment provisions to the Hanseatic League treaties of the twelfth and thirteenth centuries and earlier.[28] Comprehensive trade treaties including national treatment began to appear in the seventeenth and eighteenth centuries. By the nineteenth and twentieth centuries, national treatment had become a standard provision in trade treaties. In the late nineteenth century, national treatment also began to appear in other types of treaties, such as the 1883 *Paris Convention for*

---

21. For a discussion on this issue, see Kurtz, *supra* note 18 at 333-335.
22. *Occidental Exploration and Production Company v. Ecuador* (Final Award, 1 Jul. 2004) [*Occidental*]. For general commentary on the decision see S.D. Franck, 'International Decision: Occidental Exploration & Production Co. v. Republic of Ecuador' (2005) 99 AJIL 675 and Z. Douglas, 'Nothing if Not Critical for Investment Treaty Arbitration: Occidental, Eureko and Methanex' (2006) 22 AI 27.
23. See *infra* §4.15 for a discussion of the case.
24. Kurtz, *supra* note 18 at 335 *et seq.*
25. *Ibid.*
26. See *infra* §4.14.
27. See *infra* §4.17.
28. See P. Verloren van Themaat, *The Changing Structure of International Economic Law* (The Hague: Martinus Nijhoff, 1981) 19-21 and G. Schwarzenberger, 'The Principle and Standards of International Economic Law' (1966) 117 RDCADI 1 at 18-52.

the Protection of Industrial Property.[29] After WWII, national treatment was incorporated into the GATT as a pillar of the international trading system, serving to ensure that GATT Contracting Parties did not avoid their market access commitments (tariff concessions) by providing less favourable regulatory or tax treatment to 'like products' of foreign origin.

Historically, the term national treatment has been used in two quite different ways: the first to limit the rights of foreigners and the second to expand those rights.[30] National treatment was endorsed by many Latin American states in the nineteenth century in response to claims by capital exporting states that foreigners were entitled to an international minimum standard of treatment. This position, known as the Calvo Doctrine, provides that the treatment of foreigners is to be equal to that of nationals under relevant domestic law.[31] Under the doctrine, foreigners cannot lay claim to greater protections than offered to nationals. This formulation of national treatment, although promising equal treatment under domestic law, serves as a rejection of the international minimum standard of treatment.

In contrast, national treatment has also been promoted as a means to expand the rights of traders and investors. For example, the *Draft Convention on the Treatment of Foreigners* (1929 Draft Convention), considered at the 1929 Paris International Conference on the Treatment of Foreign Nationals (Paris Conference), would have provided wide-ranging national treatment obligations.[32] Under Article 1, foreign nationals would be entitled 'to conduct commercial transactions of every kind' on the same terms as nationals. Subject to a number of exceptions, foreigners were to be 'placed on terms of complete equality, de jure and de facto.'[33] There were specific provisions guaranteeing the same treatment with respect to legal and property rights[34] as well as fiscal treatment.[35] In addition, many of the equal treatment guarantees were extended to foreign companies.[36] Given the broad formulation of these equality guarantees, and worsening economic conditions worldwide in late 1929, it is not surprising that the Paris Conference ended in failure. Indeed, the President of the Conference noted that 'the majority ... seemed more bent on retaining as extensive a freedom of action as possible without accepting any limitation on their full sovereignty.'[37]

---

29. See Art. 2, *Paris Convention for the Protection of Industrial Property* (1883) 828 UNTS 305.
30. M. Kinnear, A.K. Bjorklund & J. Hannaford, *Investment Disputes under NAFTA: An Annotated Guide to NAFTA Chapter 11* (The Netherlands, Kluwer Law International, 2006) at 1102-12.
31. See *supra* Chapter 1, §1.8 *et seq.*, for a discussion of the Calvo Doctrine, named after the Argentine jurist, Carlos Calvo.
32. The text of the 1929 Draft Convention is reproduced in *International Conference on the Treatment of Foreigners, Preparatory Documents*, L.N. Doc. C.36.M. 21.1929.II. See *supra* Chapter 1, §1.11, for further discussion of the 1929 Draft Convention.
33. *Ibid.*, Art. 7, 1929 Draft Convention.
34. *Ibid.*, Arts. 9 and 10.
35. *Ibid.*, Art. 12.
36. *Ibid.*, Part II.
37. See *Work of the International Conference on the Treatment of Foreigners: Report by M. Devèze, President of the Conference*, Geneva, Jan. 14, 1930, L.N. Doc. C.10.1930.II.

The discussions at the Paris Conference also illustrate two different conceptions of non-discrimination between nationals and foreigners. The narrow approach is to provide non-discrimination simply in the application of domestic law, while still allowing domestic law to restrict the entry and establishment of foreign investment and distinguish between nationals and foreigners with respect to regulatory or tax treatment. The broader approach, as represented by the 1929 Draft Convention, is to provide equality of treatment extending to establishment rights and the same *de jure* and *de facto* treatment across a broad range of state regulatory and tax measures.

Various formulations of the non-discrimination principle were included in the post-WWII initiatives to create an international legal framework for investment.[38] The first of these, the International Chamber of Commerce's *International Code of Fair Treatment for Foreign Investment,* included broad national treatment provisions, extending to entry and establishment, with a limited national defence exception.[39] A much different approach was taken in the 1959 *Draft Convention on Investments Abroad* (Abs-Shawcross Draft Convention), which did not expressly provide for national treatment. Rather it provided that the property of foreign nationals 'shall not be impaired by unreasonable or discriminatory measures.'[40] Contemporaneous commentary highlights uncertainty over the meaning of 'discriminatory' and, in particular, whether it was intended as a relative or minimum standard or both.[41] Similarly, the 1961 *Draft Convention on the International Responsibility of States for Injuries to Aliens* (1961 Harvard Draft) had no express national treatment provision. This is not surprising, however, as the purpose of the draft was to codify customary international law for the protection of aliens. Professors Sohn and Baxter's commentary to the 1961 Harvard Draft notes that state responsibility arises if treatment falls below minimum standards, such as where there is a discriminatory violation of domestic law, but that generally the rights and remedies accorded to nationals can only be enjoyed by foreigners if expressly granted to them.[42] For example, they note that the fact that states commonly reserve many occupations and professions to domestic nationals is 'unexceptionable from the point of view of international law'[43] and that state responsibility arises only where aliens are deprived of their existing means of livelihood without reasonable notice.

In 1967, the OECD approved the *Draft Convention on the Protection of Foreign Property* (1967 Draft OECD Convention) as a model for future IIAs.[44]

---

38. See *supra* Chapter 1, §1.14 *et seq.,* for discussion of post-WWII initiatives.
39. International Chamber of Commerce, *International Code of Fair Treatment for Foreign Investment,* ICC Pub. No. 129 (Paris: Lecraw Press, 1948), Articles 3-7.
40. Art. II, Abs-Shawcross Draft Convention.
41. The Abs-Shawcross Draft Convention does not define discrimination and, in particular, specify whether discrimination is shorthand for national treatment or whether it is intended to apply more widely to other forms of disparate impact. See *infra* Chapter 6, §6.10, regarding discriminatory measures.
42. (1961) 55 AJIL 545 at 547.
43. *Ibid.,* at 564.
44. OECD *Draft Convention on the Protection of Foreign Property,* (1968) 7 ILM 117 [OECD Draft]. See *supra* Chapter 1, §1.22.

Like the Abs-Shawcross Draft Convention and the 1961 Harvard Draft, the 1967 Draft OECD Convention does not expressly refer to national treatment. Rather, Article 1(a) prohibits impairment by discriminatory measures:

> Each Party shall at all times ensure fair and equitable treatment to the property of the nationals of the other Parties. It shall accord within its territory the most constant protection and security to such property and shall not in any way impair the management, maintenance, use, enjoyment or disposal thereof by unreasonable or discriminatory measures.

The commentary accompanying the OECD draft suggests that discriminatory treatment of property can take four forms, namely, differentiation between the property of: (i) nationals of the same foreign state party; (ii) nationals of different foreign state parties; (iii) nationals of a foreign state party and a third state; (iv) nationals of a foreign state party and domestic nationals.[45] This fourfold typology suggests that the reference to 'discriminatory' measures in the 1967 Draft OECD Convention is intended to provide both national treatment ((iv) above) and MFN treatment ((ii) and (iii) above).[46] This interpretation is supported by the fact that Article 1(b) establishes an exception to national treatment by allowing the host state to restrict acquisitions of property by foreign nationals.[47]

In addition to the post-WWII model investment instruments, the US, the UK, Japan and other states entered into bilateral treaties on commerce and navigation containing national treatment provisions.[48]

Finally, national treatment is a guiding principle in the 1961 OECD *Code of Liberalization of Current Invisible Operations* and the *Code of Liberalization of Capital Movements*, both of which liberalize foreign investment between OECD members by requiring national treatment.[49] The 1976 OECD *Declaration on International Investment and Multinational Enterprises* establishes further requirements regarding national treatment.[50]

---

45. *Ibid.*, at 122.
46. See *infra* Chapter 6, §6.10.
47. Art. 1(b) provides: 'The provisions of this Convention shall not affect the right of any Party to allow or prohibit the acquisition of property or the investment of capital within its territory by nationals of another Party.'
48. For UK treaty practice, see G. Schwarzenberger, *Foreign Investments and International Law* (New York: Praeger, 1969). For US practice, see R.R. Wilson, *United States Commercial Treaties and International Law* (New Orleans: Hauser Press, 1960). For Japanese practice, see L. Jerold Adams, 'Japanese Treaty Patterns' (1972) 12 *Asian Survey* at 242 and *Theory, Law and Policy of Contemporary Japanese Treaties* (New York: Oceana Publications Inc., 1974) by the same author.
49. The Codes are discussed at Chapter 1, §1.17 *supra*.
50. OECD member obligations with respect to the treatment of foreign-controlled enterprises are contained in the Declaration, *supra* note 20 and the *Third Revised Decision on National Treatment* (Dec. 1991), as amended. National treatment obligations are subject to state-specific exceptions. See the most recent edition of *National Treatment for Foreign-Controlled Enterprises* on the OECD website. For discussion, see P. Muchlinski, *Multinational Enterprises and the Law*, 2nd edn (Oxford: Oxford University Press, 2007) at 626-628.

II TREATY PRACTICE

§4.8 General overview of treaty practice[51]   Although express national treatment obligations appear in almost all IIAs,[52] there are significant variations between clauses, including whether the obligation: (i) is expressly subject to national law; (ii) appears in the same clause with MFN treatment; (iii) applies to establishment; (iv) applies to both investors and investments; (v) specifies the types of activities to which it applies; and (vi) contains an express comparator, such as 'in like circumstances.' These variations are discussed in more detail below.

A small number of IIAs make national treatment expressly subject to domestic laws. For example, Article 4(3), India-Indonesia (1999), provides:

> Each Contracting Party shall, subject to its laws and regulations, accord to investment of investors of the other Contracting Party treatment no less favorable than that which is accorded to investments of its investors.

This provision makes national treatment expressly subject to national laws and regulation. This suggests that laws and regulations can provide for *de jure* distinctions in treatment between domestic and foreign investments but that foreign investment should not receive less favourable treatment in the application of laws and regulations.

In most IIAs, national and MFN treatment are combined into one provision. Article 4(2), Chile-Egypt (1999), is representative in this regard:

> Each Contracting Party shall accord investments of the investors of [*sic.*] other Contracting Party in its territory a treatment which is no less favourable than that accorded to investments made by its own investors or by investors of any third country, whichever is more favourable.[53]

Early US bilateral investment treaties (BITs) also follow the model of combining national and MFN treatment into one provision. Article II (2), Ecuador-US (1993), provides:

---

51. For an overview of treaty practice, see UNCTAD's three comprehensive studies: United Nations Centre on Transnational Corporations (UNCTC), *Bilateral Investment Treaties* (New York: United Nations, 1988) (Doc. No. ST/CTC/65); UNCTAD, *Bilateral Investment Treaties in the Mid-1990s* (New York and Geneva: United Nations, 1998) (Doc. No. UNCTAD/ITE/ IIT/7) and UNCTAD, *Bilateral Investment Treaties 1995-2006* (New York and Geneva: United Nations, 2007) (Doc. No. UNCTAD/ITE/IIT/2006/5) [together *UNCTAD BIT Studies*]. Also see UNCTAD, *National Treatment*, UNCTAD Series on issues in international investment agreements (New York and Geneva: United Nations, 1999) (UNCTAD/ITE/IIT/11) [UNCTAD National Treatment] and R.. Dolzer & M. Stevens, *Bilateral Investment Treaties* (The Hague: Martinus Nijhoff Publishers, 1995).

52. *Bilateral Investment Treaties 1995-2006, ibid.*, at 133 at note 44 states that fifty-two BITs between 1995-2006 contain no national treatment provision. Early Chinese BITs did not provide national treatment. Later BITs, such as China-Japan (1988), include national treatment (see *supra* Chapter 1, §1.42, on Chinese BITs). Early Swedish BITs did not contain a national treatment provision either (*Bilateral Investment Treaties in the Mid-1990s, ibid.*, at 60).

53. Also see Art. 4(1), India-Ghana (2000), and Art. III(2), Cuba-Lebanon (1995).

> Each Party shall permit and treat investment, and activities associated
> therewith, on a basis no less favorable than that accorded in like situations
> to investment or associated activities of its own nationals or companies, or of
> nationals or companies of any third country, whichever is the most favorable,
> subject to the right of each Party to make or maintain exceptions falling within
> one of the sectors or matters listed in the Protocol to this Treaty.

Three elements distinguish the approach in the US BIT from that in the Chile-
Egypt BIT. The US BIT provides establishment rights by specifying that each
party 'shall permit' investment.[54] Second, it expressly subjects national treatment
to sectoral or subject matter exceptions to be listed in a Protocol. Third, it provides
an express basis for comparing investments by including the expression 'in like
situations.'[55]

Article IV, Philippines-Switzerland (1997), provides another model, where
national and MFN treatments extend to both investments and investors and, in
addition, lists a series of investment activities to which the standards apply.

> 2. Each Contracting Party shall in its territory accord investments or returns
> of investors of the other Contracting Party treatment not less favourable
> than that which it accords to investments or returns of its own investors or
> to investments or returns of investors of any third State, whichever is more
> favourable to the investor concerned.
> 3. Each Contracting Party shall in its territory accord investors of the other
> Contracting Party with respect to the management, maintenance, use,
> enjoyment or disposal of their investments, treatment not less favourable
> than that which it accords to its own investors or investors of any third
> State, whichever is more favourable to the investor concerned.[56]

Article 3, US-Uruguay (2005), headed 'National Treatment,' reflects the approach
in the 2004 Model US BIT.

> 1 Each Party shall accord to investors of the other Party treatment no less
> favorable than that it accords, in like circumstances, to its own investors
> with respect to the establishment, acquisition, expansion, management, con-
> duct, operation, and sale or other disposition of investments in its territory.
> 2 Each Party shall accord to covered investments treatment no less favorable
> than that it accords, in like circumstances, to investments in its territory
> of its own investors with respect to the establishment, acquisition, expan-
> sion, management, conduct, operation, and sale or other disposition of
> investments.

A comparison of the Chile-Egypt and US-Uruguay BITs highlights five salient
differences. Unlike in the Chile-Egypt BIT, the national treatment provision in the

---

54. See *infra* §4.9.
55. See other contemporaneous US BITs, for example, Art. II(1), Argentina-US (1991), and Art.
    II(1), Romania-US (1992).
56. Authors' translation from French original.

US-Uruguay BIT: (i) is in a separate clause from MFN treatment; (ii) expressly applies to both investors and investments; (iii) applies to establishment; (iv) specifies a range of activities to which the obligation applies; and (v) provides an express comparator. The significance of these differences is addressed in the sections below.[57]

Some IIAs provide that national treatment applies to specific obligations, including to the free transfer of investment returns[58] and compensation for losses.[59]

With respect to the meaning of like circumstances, a footnote to the national treatment provision of the 2007 Norwegian Model BIT clarifies that:

> The Parties agree/ are of the understanding that a measure applied by a government in pursuance of legitimate policy objectives of public interest such as the protection of public health, safety and the environment, although having a different effect on an investment or investor of another Party, is not inconsistent with national treatment and most favoured nation treatment when justified by showing that it bears a reasonable relationship to rational policies not motivated by preference of domestic over foreign owned investment.

The commentary to the Model states that the clarification is intended to reflect an interpretation in accordance with the most recent developments in practice and reflects the need to balance non-discrimination and national regulatory interests.

§4.9 Establishment: pre-entry and post-entry models   The majority of IIAs do not provide foreign investors or investments the right of entry or establishment into the host state.[60] National treatment obligations are typically limited to investments made in accordance with domestic laws, which may limit the ability of foreign investors to invest in the first place and stringently regulate the manner in which any permitted investments may be made. Most national treatment obligations arise only after a foreign investment has been made. This is often referred to as the post-entry or post-establishment model. Nonetheless, a number of IIAs – notably US BITs and FTAs, recent Canadian BITs and FTAs, as well as a number of regional IIAs including the NAFTA and the MERCOSUR – establish pre-entry national treatment obligations. Under these IIAs, the host state must allow foreign investors and investments access to its markets on terms no less favourable than

---

57.   See *infra* §4.13 on application to investors and investments; §4.9 with respect to establishment and the range of activities to which the provisions apply; and §4.11 with respect to 'in like circumstances.'

58.   This is common in UK BITs. See *infra* Chapter 8 on transfer rights.

59.   For example, Art. IV(3), Argentina-US (1991), provides: 'Nationals or companies of either Party whose investments suffer losses in the territory of the other Party owing to war or other armed conflict, revolution, state of national emergency, insurrection, civil disturbance or other similar events shall be accorded treatment by such other Party no less favorable than that accorded to its own nationals or companies or to nationals or companies of any third country, whichever is the more favorable treatment, as regards any measures it adopts in relation to such losses.' See *infra* Chapter 6, §6.47, and Chapter 10, §10.8, on these clauses.

60.   See *supra* Chapter 3 on admission and establishment obligations.

those enjoyed by national investors. These are often referred to as establishment rights. IIAs that provide national treatment establishment rights typically do so subject to important exceptions and reservations.[61]

Although the pre-entry national treatment obligation generally extends to both the investment and the investor, the majority of IIAs that provide only for post-entry national treatment obligations extend the obligation only to investments or activities associated with investments and not to investors.[62] One explanation for this difference is that the existence of substantive obligations is premised on an investment having been made in accordance with local laws.[63] The omission of the reference to 'investor' in a post-entry provision means that national treatment does not apply to investors wishing to make investments. In the post-entry provision, national treatment only applies to investments already made in accordance with domestic law.[64]

III   APPLICATION OF NATIONAL TREATMENT

§4.10 The two elements of national treatment analysis   Despite significant variation in national treatment provisions, two common issues arise in the application of national treatment: (i) identifying the relevant comparator (the comparator); and (ii) comparing the treatment received by the foreign investor or investment and the domestic comparator to determine whether there has been less favourable treatment (the standard of treatment). Since national treatment is a relative standard, its application always turns on making the appropriate comparison between two different entities or things. In the case of national treatment, the comparison will be between domestic and foreign investors or domestic and foreign investments. The less favourable treatment analysis then looks at whether the effect of the state conduct in question results in the foreign investment in like circumstances being in a less favourable situation than the local investment.[65]

A   THE COMPARATOR

§4.11 The basis for comparison   The majority of IIAs provide no guidance regarding the basis of comparison when applying national treatment. The national treatment provisions in Chile-Egypt (1999) and Philippines-Switzerland (1997), reproduced above at §4.8, are typical in not specifying the basis for comparing the

---

61. See *supra* Chapter 3, §3.9, for further discussion.
62. *Bilateral Investment Treaties in the Mid-1990s*, *supra* note 51 at 61.
63. On IIA requirements that investments comply with domestic law, see *Inceysa Vallisoletana, S.L. v. El Salvador* (Award, 2 Aug. 2006); *Fraport AG Frankfurt Airport Services Worldwide v. Philippines* (Award, 16 Aug. 2007); and *Desert Line Projects LLC v. Yemen* (Award, 6 Feb. 2008). See *supra* Chapter 2, §2.11 and §2.12, and Chapter 3, §3.12.
64. *Supra* Chapter 3, §3.12.
65. See §4.20 *et seq.* on the standard or treatment.

investments in question.[66] A small number of treaties, of which the NAFTA is the most prominent example, clarify that national treatment applies to investors and investments in 'like circumstances.'[67] For example, US, Canadian and Turkish BITs also refer to 'like circumstances' in their national treatment provisions. Other IIAs use expressions such as 'like situations,'[68] 'similar situations'[69] and 'same circumstances.'[70]

A threshold question is whether the absence of an express comparator clause, such as 'in like circumstances' or 'in like situations,' is legally significant. To date, IIA tribunals have not squarely addressed the significance of the absence of a comparator clause. In *Occidental*, the claimant argued that a national treatment obligation not qualified by the reference to 'in like situations' was less restrictive, but this claim was not addressed.[71] In examining a discrimination claim under Article 10(1) of the *Energy Charter Treaty* (ECT), the tribunal in *Nykomb Synergetics Technology Holding AB v. Latvia* stated that in 'evaluating whether there is discrimination in the sense of the Treaty one should only "compare like with like."'[72] Although this comment was made in the context of applying the prohibition on 'discriminatory measures,' the reasoning applies equally to national treatment.[73] In *Consortium RFCC v. Morocco*, in commenting on the interpretation of the national and MFN treatment provisions in Italy-Morocco (1990) (which did not expressly provide a basis for comparison), the tribunal noted that the interpretation of relative standards clauses does not give rise to any particular problem. According to the tribunal, the principal difficulty resides in determining whether the situation of the foreign investor was identical ('identique') to that of the national investor or that of the investor from the third state.[74]

---

66. Recent Austrian, Chilean, Chinese, Danish, French, German, Swiss and UK BITs do not provide an express basis for comparison. See, for example, Art. 3(1), Austria-Egypt (2001); Art. 3(1), Kyrgyzstan-UK (1999); Art. 4(2), Chile-Tunisia (1998); Art. 4(1), China-Jordan (2001); Art. 3(2), Brazil-Netherlands (1998); Art. 4, Cambodia-France (2000); Art. 3(1), Bosnia-Herzegovina-Germany (2001); and Art. 4(3), Armenia-Switzerland (2003).
67. See *supra* §4.8.
68. Art. II(2), Senegal-US (1983).
69. Art. 3(1), Ethiopia-Turkey (2000).
70. Art. 3(1), Belize-UK (1982).
71. Occidental argued that the absence of 'in like situations' in the MFN clause in Ecuador-Spain (1996) resulted in a less restrictive standard of national treatment than that found in the Ecuador-US BIT, which refers to 'in like situations.' The tribunal did not address this issue, having found a national treatment breach in any event under Ecuador-US (1993). See *Occidental*, *supra* note 22 at para. 170.
72. *Nykomb Synergetics Technology Holding AB v. Latvia* (Award, 16 Dec. 2003) at 34.
73. Art. 10(3) of the ECT clarifies that the treatment required by Art. 10(1) means national and MFN treatment.
74. *Consortium RFCC v. Morocco* (Arbitral Award, 22 Dec. 2003) [*Consortium RFCC*]. The full para. 53 from the French original states that: 'Le contenu de cette disposition qui se rencontre systématiquement dans les traités de protection des investissements ne pose pas de problème d'interprétation particulier. La principale difficulté réside dans son application et plus spécifiquement dans la nécessité de déterminer *si la situation de l'investisseur étranger était identique à celle de l'investisseur national ou à celle de l'investisseur d'un pays tiers* avec lequel l'Etat d'accueil a conclu un traité similaire de protection des investissements, afin de

The OECD commentary on the *Draft Multilateral Agreement on Investment* (MAI) is also instructive. The draft negotiating text of the MAI included, in the national treatment provision, the term 'in like circumstances' in brackets. The commentary to the draft text notes that:

> National treatment and MFN treatment are comparative terms. Some delegations believed that the terms for national treatment and MFN treatment implicitly provide the comparative context for determining whether a measure discriminates against foreign investors and their investments; they considered that the words "in like circumstances" were unnecessary and open to abuse. Other delegations believed that the comparative context should be spelled out …'[75]

The absence of a comparator clause, such as in like situations, is arguably not legally significant. This follows from both the logic and structure of national treatment provisions, which prohibit nationality-based discrimination. The relevant inquiry is whether differences in treatment are attributable directly or indirectly to the nationality of the investor or investment. This necessarily requires a comparison of investors or investments that are in like circumstances – the logic of any discrimination analysis being to compare like with like.

Though the *Consortium RFCC* tribunal was correct to imply a basis of comparison into the treaty text, 'identical' is not the appropriate standard, if that term is interpreted strictly. Given the wide ranging differences amongst investors and investments (location, number of employees, manufacturing processes, corporate and management structure etc.), it is unlikely that any two investors or investments are ever strictly identical, even if, for the purposes of applying relative standards of treatment, they may be very similar.

The reference by the *Consortium RFCC* tribunal to 'identical' as the basis of comparison raises a further issue. Are there substantive differences in the various standards of comparison used in treaty practice? Is there a substantive difference between the terms 'like' and 'similar' circumstances and 'like' and 'similar' situations'? The more persuasive view is that there is no legally significant distinction between the terms 'situations' and 'circumstances' on the one hand, and 'similar' and 'like' on the other. These words are interchangeable with no substantive differences in their usage or meaning.[76] Moreover, situational comparisons are highly-fact

---

pouvoir affirmer que la différence de traitement appliquée par l'État d'accueil était ou non justifiée. Cette analyse sera faite au moment de l'examen détaillé des réclamations du Consortium.' [Emphasis added.]

75. OECD, The Multilateral Agreement on Investment: Commentary to the Consolidated Text, 22 Apr. 1998, DAFFE/MAI(98)8/REV1 at 11. Available online: <http://www1.oecd.org/daf/mai/toc.htm>.

76. According to the *Oxford English Dictionary* (OED) online edition, 'situation' is a 'position of affairs; combination of circumstances,' while a 'circumstance' is a 'condition or state of affairs surrounding and affecting an agent.' The OED states that 'situation is expressed by "in the circumstances."' While the 'same circumstances' might suggest a higher degree of affinity than 'like circumstances,' in practice, it is unlikely that this subtle distinction would result in a different outcome. Nor, in our view, is there any rationale for a different outcome based on the

contingent. Where investors or investments are in like or similar situations, the underlying purpose of national treatment protection – to prohibit nationality-based discrimination and ensure effective equality of competitive opportunities – will be a more significant consideration than whether the treaty drafters have used the terms 'like', 'same' and, perhaps, even 'identical.'[77] From a practical perspective, how tribunals characterize the subjects to be compared will likely be determinative of whether they are in like circumstances or same circumstances, regardless of whether one type of comparator clause arguably has a slightly wider or narrower scope.

§4.12 Sequence of analysis   IIAs do not provide a required method for applying national treatment. In analyzing national treatment, NAFTA investment tribunals have considered three distinct issues. First, tribunals have identified the relevant subjects for comparison – are they in like circumstances? Second, they have considered the relative treatment each subject received and whether one received less favourable treatment. Finally, they have considered whether there are legitimate, non-protectionist rationales to justify differences in treatment.[78] Although not treaty-mandated, this three-step process provides a logical coherence to the national treatment analysis. Certain caveats, however, need to be kept in mind.

First, steps one and three of the analysis are interconnected since both relate to the question of whether the subjects are in like circumstances. In the first step, the claimant must establish that it is in like circumstances with the domestic comparator. In the third step, the burden shifts to the respondent state to establish that there is a legitimate rationale for differential treatment unrelated to nationality-based discrimination. Some commentators suggest that, rather than speaking of two separate like circumstances, analyses should be broken into two parts. It is clearer to consider the third step of the analysis as a requirement that the respondent state provide a rational basis for the differential treatment.[79]

---

use of 'same' or 'like.' *In the Matter of Cross Border Trucking Services* (NAFTA Chapter 20 Panel Decision, Final Report, 6 Feb. 2001) [*Trucking Case*], the US argued (and Mexico did not dispute) that the phrase 'in like circumstances' is not substantively different from the phrase 'in like situations.' *Trucking Case* at para. 249.

77.   No two investments are likely ever to be completely identical in all respects. In light of the regulatory purpose of the distinction at issue, however, they might be viewed as identical for the purpose of applying national treatment. In this sense, there would appear to be little substantive difference between the terms 'same' and 'identical' for the purpose of applying national treatment.

78.   For commentary on and elaboration of the NAFTA approach see T. Weiler, 'Prohibitions Against Discrimination in NAFTA Chapter 11' in T. Weiler, ed., *NAFTA Investment Law and Arbitration: Past Issues, Current Practice, Future Prospects* (Ardsley: Transnational Publishers, 2004). Also see J.R. Johnson, 'Essential Disciplines on the National Treatment Obligation Under NAFTA Chapter Eleven,' 2001, online: <http://dfait-maeci.gc.ca/tna-nac/treatment-en. asp> and Kinnear *et al.*, *Investment Disputes Under NAFTA*, *supra* note 30 at 1102-1 to 1102-53.

79.   Kinnear *et al.*, *ibid.*, at 1102-26.

Second, in the first step, the identification of the relevant subject for comparison must take into account the regulatory purpose of the treatment in question and who or what is affected. In other words, determining the appropriate comparator for the like circumstances analysis cannot be divorced from the reasons for the treatment in question. For example, if the less favourable treatment in question relates to pollution emission standards in urban areas, the applicable comparator may be other emitters in the geographical area, rather than a direct competitor in the same sector that operates in a less environmentally sensitive area.

A third issue is the threshold requirement that the claimant must establish to satisfy its *prima facie* burden of a breach of national treatment. In some cases, tribunals appear to have applied a low threshold. For example, in *Pope & Talbot Inc v. Canada*,[80] the tribunal stated that the first step in the national treatment analysis is essentially a comparison of whether the investments are in the same business or economic sector. It then found that if a difference in treatment is established, there is a presumptive violation of national treatment, which can then be justified by rational government policies that do not discriminate on the basis of nationality and that do not unduly undermine the liberalizing objectives of the NAFTA.[81] Commentators have highlighted that this approach applies a very low threshold to the first step of the like circumstances analysis because like circumstances is equated with the investors or investments being in the same widely defined business or economic sector. This approach will often fail to reflect the significant regulatory differences between the investments or investors in question.[82]

Since the NAFTA tribunals' three-step analysis is not treaty-mandated, its application must not result in an unjustifiable shifting or reversal of the burden of proof. International and domestic practice[83] requires the claimant to establish a *prima facie* case that it is in like circumstances and has received less favourable treatment.[84] Thus, with respect to a purported breach of national treatment, the claimant must identify the relevant subjects for comparison, demonstrate how it is in comparable circumstances in light of the purpose of the measure at issue, and demonstrate that it received less favourable treatment than the applicable comparator. If the claimant makes out a *prima facie* case that the host state has accorded differential treatment to investments in like circumstances, the burden arguably shifts to the state to justify the measure based on legitimate non-nationality based public policy considerations.

---

80. *Pope & Talbot Inc v. Canada* (Award on the Merits of Phase 2, 10 Apr. 2001) [*Pope & Talbot*].
81. *Ibid.*, at para. 78. See *supra* §4.6 on this point.
82. Kinnear *et al.*, *supra* note 30 at 26-1102. For further discussion on this point see *infra* §4.14 .
83. See *Middle East Cement Shipping and Handling Co. S.A. v. Egypt* (Award, 12 Apr. 2002) at paras. 89-91 and *Marvin Feldman v. Mexico* (Award, 16 Dec. 2002) [*Feldman*] at para. 177. See also S. Rosenne, *The Law and Practice of the International Court, 1920-1996*, Vol. III (The Hague; Boston: M. Nijhoff, 1997) at 1083: 'Generally, in application of the principle *actori incumbit probation* the Court will formally require the party putting forward a claim to establish the elements of fact and of law on which the decision in its favour might be given.'
84. See *United Parcel Service of America Inc. v. Canada* (Award on the Merits, 24 May 2007) at para. 84 [*UPS*].

The NAFTA tribunals' three-step process in assessing national treatment, if properly applied, provides a sound analytical framework that other IIA tribunals may wish to adopt. There should be no objection in principle to the three-step process in analyzing national treatment. It has a logical progression and is animated by the underlying purpose of relative standards of treatment, that of prohibiting nationality-based discrimination.

§4.13 Relevant factors in comparing investors and investments   Determining the proper comparator for the purposes of national treatment is highly fact-specific and context-dependent.[85] The application of national treatment requires an 'evaluation of the entire fact setting'[86] and of 'all the relevant circumstances.'[87] A number of factors are relevant to whether investments or investors are in like circumstances. They include the economic sector involved and the existence of a competitive relationship, the existence of protectionist intent or motive and whether legitimate policy reasons exist for having the distinction in question. These factors are addressed in turn below.

§4.14 Economic sector and the existence of the competitive relationship   National treatment issues most often arise where the domestic and foreign investments are in the same economic sector and the foreign investment has received less favourable treatment than the domestic investment. When investments are in the same economic sector, there will usually be some degree of competitive relationship between them – often direct competition. As a result, the foreign investor will claim to be at a competitive disadvantage as a result of host state measures.[88]

In assessing whether investments are in like circumstances, an analysis of the competitive relationship is often critical.[89] The existence of a competitive relationship or that the investments are in the same sector (narrowly or broadly defined), however, does not mean they are necessarily in like circumstances for the purposes of applying national treatment. The separate statement of Ronald Cass in *United Parcel Service of America Inc. v. Canada* is instructive in this regard:

> It is not sufficient for a complaining investor to show that that the investor or investment is in the same economic sector as, or competes with, an investor or investment of the NAFTA Party charged with violating its national treatment obligation. Sharing the same economic sector may be evidence that two businesses are in like circumstances. So, too, being in competition, even if businesses might be classified in different economic sectors, may be evidence of like circumstances. Yet, neither showing is conclusive of like circumstances.

---

85. *S.D. Myers, supra* note 18 at paras 244-251. See also *Pope & Talbot, supra* note 80.
86. *Pope & Talbot, ibid.*
87. *UPS, supra* note 84 at para. 86.
88. For example, in *S.D. Myers, supra* note 18, the tribunal found that nationals and foreign investors were providing PCB remediation services.
89. See *infra* §4.16 regarding the relevance of GATT Art. III like products jurisprudence.

> It is possible for two investor or enterprises to be in the same sector or to be in competition and nonetheless be quite unlike in respect of some characteristic critical to a particular treatment.[90]

This statement highlights that investment might be in the same sector or in a competitive relationship yet not be in like circumstances. The statement, however, then proceeds to argue that the existence of a competitive relationship, establishes a *prima facie* case of like circumstances in all cases.[91] This approach is questionable. A competitive relationship may be sufficient to establish like circumstances in some cases, but not in others. The central issue is whether the investors or investments are like or unlike with respect to *a particular regulatory treatment* – which will normally result from the purpose of the regulatory distinction in the measure at issue. For example, consider two manufacturing businesses that have very similar business operations with the exception of their locations. One is located in an urban area and is subject to stricter air pollution emission standards. If the focus of the like circumstances analysis is simply on whether the investments are in a competitive relationship then the two investments might be said to be in like circumstances. However, the more appropriate comparator in these circumstances might be another urban based manufacturer in a completely different economic sector but which has similar pollution emissions.[92] The claimant should not be able to shift the burden of proof upon showing a competitive relationship. Rather, it would have to prove that it is in like circumstances in light of all of the facts, which include the particular regulation or measure at issue. This will normally require the claimant to demonstrate why it is in like circumstances in light of the regulatory treatment being challenged.

§4.15 IIA jurisprudence on determining the comparator based on economic sector IIA tribunals have taken inconsistent approaches in determining the appropriate comparator for the purposes of the national treatment analysis. The NAFTA national treatment cases generally illustrate a tendency to narrowly define the comparator to similarly situated domestic investments, i.e., in the same economic sector, where there is a high degree of competition between the investments in question.[93] In contrast, in *Occidental*, the tribunal compared investments in very different economic sectors that were not in a competitive relationship.

---

90. *United Parcel Service of America Inc. v. Canada* (Separate Statement of Dean Ronald A. Cass, Award on Merits, 24 May 2007) [*UPS Cass Separate Statement*] at para. 16.
91. *UPS Cass Separate Statement, ibid.*, at para. 17: 'A showing that there is a competitive relationship and that two investors or investments are similar in that respect establishes a *prima facie* case of like circumstances. Once the investor has established the competitive relationship between two investors or investments, the burden shifts to the respondent Party to explain why two competing enterprises are not in like circumstances.'
92. See *infra* §4.18 on the relevance of regulatory purpose.
93. *S.D. Myers, supra* note 18 at para. 250 and *Pope & Talbot, supra* note 80 at para. 73.

Looking in more detail at NAFTA national treatment jurisprudence, the tribunals in *S.D. Myers* and *Pope & Talbot* relied on the OECD's 1993 interpretation of national treatment, which states that:

> As regards the expression 'in like situations', the comparison between foreign-controlled enterprises established in a Member country and domestic enterprises in that Member country is valid only if it is made between firms operating in the same sector.[94]

The OECD statement highlights that the relevant comparison is one between businesses in the same sector. The *S.D. Myers* tribunal found that the US and Canadian investments in question were in like circumstances because they competed for customers in the provision of PCB remediation services based on price, experience and credibility.[95]

In *Pope & Talbot*, despite starting with a broad sectoral comparison, the tribunal ultimately concluded that the underlying economic conditions of the Canadian softwood lumber industry meant that the claimant's investment in British Columbia was not in like circumstances with those in other Canadian provinces, despite the fact that other Canadian and coastal British Columbian softwood lumber producers were in a competitive relationship with Pope & Talbot's operations. [96] Further, the tribunal held that differences in treatment between coastal and interior lumber producers within British Columbia were justified as was the differential treatment between Pope & Talbot and new entrants into the market.[97] According to the tribunal, a decisive consideration was that there was a legitimate rationale for the regulatory distinction made between producers in different regions of Canada, namely the good faith implementation of the Canada-US Softwood Lumber Agreement in order to prevent the US from applying trade remedy laws against Canadian softwood lumber.

The NAFTA tribunal in *Feldman* found that the foreign and domestic investments in question were in like circumstances based on the relatively narrow criterion that they were in the business of reselling/exporting cigarettes but held that other firms that also engaged in exports, including Mexican cigarette producers, were not in like circumstances.[98] The tribunal stated that there were rational bases for treating producers and re-sellers differently, including better control over tax revenues, discouraging smuggling, protecting intellectual property rights and prohibiting gray market sales.[99]

---

94. OECD, *National Treatment for Foreign-Controlled Enterprises, supra* note 50 at 22. The OECD *Declaration on International and Multinational Enterprises, ibid.*, states that investors and investments should receive treatment that is '...no less favorable than that accorded in like situations to domestic enterprises.'
95. *S.D. Myers, supra* note 18 at para. 251.
96. See *Pope & Talbot, supra* note 80.
97. *Ibid.*, at paras. 84-104.
98. *Feldman, supra* note 83 at paras. 171-172.
99. *Ibid.*, at para. 170.

In another NAFTA case, *UPS*, the claimant, a courier company, argued that goods imported using its courier services received less favourable treatment than goods imported by mail through the services of Canada Post, a Crown corporation with a monopoly on postal services.[100] The majority of the tribunal concluded that the different characteristics of goods imported by mail and courier required different customs treatment, justifying the differential treatment.[101]

Pope & Talbot, *Feldman* and *UPS* illustrate situations where, despite investments being in a competitive relationship, tribunals found that they were not in like circumstances. In these cases, the tribunals found that there were legitimate rationales for different treatment of investments within the same broad sector.

The role competition plays in the like circumstances analysis was a key issue in *Methanex*.[102] Methanex alleged that California's ban on MTBE, a fuel additive, breached the NAFTA's national treatment obligation because Methanex's product, methanol, a primary feedstock in MTBE, received less favourable treatment than other gas additives including ethanol. Methanex submitted that it was in like circumstances to the US ethanol industry because ethanol and methanol were in a competitive relationship. In Methanex's view, the key consideration of likeness

---

100. *UPS, supra* note 84. The tribunal rejected several of UPS' national treatment claims on the basis that there are special rules applying to state enterprise under the NAFTA (paras. 45-79).

101. *Ibid.*, at paras. 98-120. In particular, the majority found that customs authorities worldwide view postal and courier streams as different. There is a high degree of automation in the courier stream, and these distinctions are reflected in international conventions. The tribunal stated that 'postal administration and expert consignment operators have different objects, mandates and transport and deliver goods in different ways and under different circumstances.' (para. 117). UPS also claimed that a Canadian publications assistance program (PAP) that provides postal subsidies to Canadian periodical publishers violated national treatment because the subsidy is available only to cover postal services supplied by Canada Post, the state run monopoly mail service, and not to pay for delivery through private couriers. The majority of the tribunal held that UPS was not in like circumstances with Canada Post as it could not offer universal delivery services throughout Canada, and that UPS was unable to assume this obligation (*ibid.*, at paras. 173-181). In contrast, in his separate statement, Cass found that both enterprises are capable of making deliveries of periodicals but rejected UPS's claim that the design of governmental programs must comply with a stringent least restrictive means test. *UPS Cass Separate Statement, supra* note 90 at paras. 101-116. The *UPS* tribunal also addressed whether NAFTA's government procurement, subsidies and cultural industries exceptions applied to the PAP. See *infra* Chapter 10, §10.3.

102. It should be noted that the *Methanex* tribunal's discussion of national treatment in Art. 1102, NAFTA, is technically *obiter dicta*. In the *Methanex* tribunal's Partial Award, 7 Aug. 2002, the tribunal held that it did not have jurisdiction based on Methanex's pleadings because Methanex had not established that the Californian measures in question were 'relating to' its investment for the purposes of Art. 1101, NAFTA. The tribunal's jurisdiction in the subsequent proceedings was therefore premised on Methanex's amended pleadings that the California measures were applied with an intent to favour the US ethanol industry and to harm MTBE producers. In its Final Award, the *Methanex* tribunal concluded that Methanex had failed to establish that California intended to harm foreign methanol producers, including Methanex (Part IV - Chapter E - Para. 18) and, therefore, the measures did not relate to Methanex or its investment as required under Art. 1101 (*ibid.*, at para. 22). See Kinnear *et al.*, *Investment Disputes Under NAFTA, supra* note 30 at 1101.

was competition – if investments compete for the same business they are in like circumstances.[103] Relying on GATT like products jurisprudence, Methanex argued that methanol and ethanol were like products because they served similar end uses and were treated as alternatives.[104] According to Methanex, ethanol and methanol were both oxygenates used in manufacturing reformulated gasoline and that, prior to the ban, integrated oil refineries bought either ethanol or methanol. As a result of the Californian ban, these refineries could only buy ethanol.

In contrast to Methanex's competition-based analysis, the US proposed a different approach, under which national treatment was viewed as a protection against nationality-based discrimination:

> ... the function of the national treatment provision is to address discrimination on the basis of nationality of ownership of an investment. The function of addressing nationality-based discrimination is served by comparing the treatment of the foreign investor to the treatment accorded to a domestic investor that is most similarly situated to it. In ideal circumstances, the foreign investor or foreign-owned investment should be compared to a domestic investor or domestically-owned investment that is like it in all relevant respects, but for nationality of ownership. When nationality is the only variable, such a comparison serves the Article's purpose of ascertaining whether the treatment accorded differed on the basis of nationality.[105]

Accordingly, the US argued that the proper comparator was the US methanol industry, the domestic industry most similarly situated to Methanex.

In the view of the tribunal, domestic methanol producers were in an identical situation to Methanex and it would be inappropriate to ignore them.[106] The Californian ban had precisely the same effect on American methanol producers (47% of the industry) as the Canadian investor, Methanex. The tribunal therefore concluded that: 'The fact stands – Methanex did not receive less favourable treatment than the identical domestic comparators, producing methanol.'[107] Further, the tribunal rejected the argument that ethanol and methanol were like products in competition, reasoning that, unlike ethanol, methanol was not a gasoline additive but a feedstock in the production of MTBE.

A question arising from the approach adopted by the *Methanex* tribunal is whether the appropriate comparator is always the identical domestic comparator, particularly where there is a significant competitive relationship between different investments and the ownership structure is segmented between domestic and foreign investors. For example, assume that ethanol and methanol were considered to be substitutable for more uses and that there was a significant degree of competition between the products. Depending on ownership and market structures

---

103. *Supra* note 13 at para. 5, Part IV-Chapter B.
104. *Ibid.*, at para. 7, Part IV-Chapter B. See *infra* §4.16 for discussion of GATT like products jurisprudence.
105. *Ibid.*
106. *Ibid.*, at para. 17-18.
107. *Ibid.*, at para. 19, Part IV-Chapter B.

(e.g., if 98% of ethanol production was in domestic hands and 98% of methanol production was in foreign hands) there could be a situation where, despite there being an identical domestic industry comparator (the 2% of methanol production in domestic hands), state measures predominantly favour the competing domestic industry. In this type of case, it may be that differential treatment results from nationality-based discrimination and the appropriate comparator group might not be the domestic investment in identical circumstances, but another competitor in like circumstances.

In contrast to the predominantly narrow like circumstances analysis in the NAFTA cases, the tribunal in *Occidental* took a broad interpretation of like situations in the national treatment provision of Ecuador-US (1993),[108] holding that all exporters in a number of diverse sectors were in like situations.[109] Further, unlike in *Methanex*, in *Occidental* the domestic comparator, Petroecuador, which had also been denied VAT refunds, was ignored. Occidental had entered into a contract with Petroecuador, a state-owned corporation, to undertake oil exploration and production. A dispute arose as to whether Occidental was entitled to VAT refunds. Occidental claimed a breach of the national treatment obligation in Ecuador-US (1993) on the basis that other exporting companies, including exporters of flowers, mining and seafood products, were entitled to receive VAT refunds, but oil exporters were not. According to Occidental, it was in a like situation to other exporters even if it was not in the same economic sector. Ecuador argued that the like situation analysis was sector-based and relied on the fact that other oil exporters, including Petroecuador, were also denied VAT refunds, which demonstrated that there was no intention to discriminate against foreign companies.

The tribunal concluded that there was a breach of national treatment. First, it stated that the purpose of national treatment is to protect investors as compared to local producers. In the view of the tribunal, this could not be done by addressing 'exclusively the sector in which that particular activity is undertaken.'[110] Second, the tribunal held that the purpose of national treatment is to avoid 'exporters being placed at a disadvantage in foreign markets because of the indirect taxes paid in the country of origin.'[111] The tribunal reasoned that no exporter ought to be put in a disadvantageous position as compared to other exporters.[112]

The *Occidental* tribunal interpreted like situations very broadly and appears to have conflated national treatment with any kind of disadvantageous distinction, unrelated to nationality-based discrimination. If flower exporters are granted a tax preference that is not extended to oil exports, there is disadvantageous tax

---

108. Art. II(1), Ecuador-US (1993), provides: 'Each party shall permit and treat investment, and activities associated therewith, on a basis no less favorable than that accorded in like situations to investment or associated activities of its own nationals or companies of any third country, whichever is most favorable, subject to the right of each Party to make or maintain exceptions falling within one of the sectors or matters listed in the Protocol to this Treaty.'
109. *Occidental, supra* note 22.
110. *Ibid.*, at para. 60.
111. *Ibid.*, at para. 175.
112. *Ibid.*, at para. 175.

treatment between the two sectors. However, the mere existence of disadvantage or different treatment between different sectors does not establish that there is nationality-based discrimination. The tribunal's reasoning that no exporter ought to be put in a disadvantageous position as compared to other exporters fails to consider whether the distinction between exporters is any way connected to discrimination based on nationality. Further, in proceeding in this way, the tribunal failed to address the third part in the national treatment analysis: are there legitimate, non-discriminatory rationales for distinguishing between oil and seafood exporters?[113] The tribunal also failed to address whether the effect of the VAT rebate policy was to segment the economy into domestically owned sectors that received favourable VAT treatment and foreign-owned sectors that received less favourable treatment. In short, the award never expressly addressed the key issue – whether the distinction between Occidental and other exporters was nationality-based. The unstated assumption and inference in the award appears to be that the denial of VAT refunds was *de facto* nationality-based discrimination. The weakness in the award's reasoning, however, is that this was never expressly discussed. In particular, there was no discussion of the significance of state ownership of Petroecuador and whether it was an inappropriate comparator because payment of taxes by a state owned entity may well be revenue neutral, assuming tax payments reduce the profits that would have accrued to the state in any event.

Although the *Occidental* tribunal's national treatment analysis is questionable, this does not mean the tribunal was incorrect in finding a breach of the national treatment obligation. The tribunal noted that the Ecuadorian Supreme Court has found that the imposition of VAT depends not on the source of the goods, but rather on their final destination.[114] The relevant regulatory distinction was therefore not the type or source of goods, but their destination. From this perspective, for the purposes of VAT, oil, flower and seafood exporters are in a like situation. The reasoning in the award assumes, however, that the *de facto* discrimination between Occidental and other exporters was based on nationality, without considering whether the flower and seafood exporters in question were foreign or domestically owned.[115]

§4.16 The relevance of WTO like products jurisprudence to the like circumstances determination   In several IIA national treatment cases, claimants have relied on Article III, GATT, national treatment and like products jurisprudence to support arguments that investments are in like circumstances. GATT national treatment jurisprudence has been invoked to support arguments that

---

113.   Since the pleadings in the case are not publicly available, it is unclear whether Ecuador provided rationales for the distinction.
114.   *Occidental, supra* note 22 at para. 142.
115.   In his Partial Dissenting Opinion in *EnCana Corporation v. Ecuador* (Award, 3 Feb. 2006), another case involving VAT refunds in Ecuador, Dr. Horacio Grigera Naón found at para. 40 that the 'oil and gas sector adversely affected by [the VAT interpretation] is exclusively and entirely composed of foreign companies, a situation that is not shared by the other non-manufacturing export sector.'

investments are in like circumstances where there is a competitive relationship between the products produced by the investments in question.[116]

Claimants have drawn on two related aspects of GATT national treatment jurisprudence. First, claimants have argued that GATT jurisprudence is relevant to determining whether investments are in like circumstances. For example, in *Methanex*, the claimant argued that since methanol and ethanol are like products,[117] producers of methanol and ethanol should be considered to be in like circumstances for the purposes of the national treatment analysis in the investment chapter of the NAFTA. Second, claimants have argued that national treatment in the investment context has the same overriding purpose as it has in the trade context – to provide effective equality of treatment to investments that are in a competitive relationship. These two related aspects of GATT national treatment jurisprudence are addressed in turn.

In examining likeness, GATT like products jurisprudence has looked at four categories of characteristics that products might share: (i) the physical properties of the products; (ii) the extent to which the products are capable of serving the same or similar end-uses; (iii) the extent to which consumers perceive and treat the products as alternative means of performing particular functions in order to satisfy a particular want or demand; and (iv) the classification of the products for tariff purposes.[118] The WTO Appellate Body has confirmed that these categories are not treaty-mandated[119] and that the interpretation and application of like products is a discretionary decision that must be made considering the various characteristics of products in individual cases. No one approach to exercising judgment will be appropriate for all cases.[120] For example, in *Asbestos*, the WTO Appellate Body found that in determining whether asbestos fibres were like polyvinyl, cellulose and glass fibres, health risks associated with asbestos fibres were a relevant consideration in determining likeness.

In *Methanex*, the US disputed the applicability of GATT national treatment jurisprudence to the interpretation of like circumstances because of differences in

---

116. See N. DiMascio & J. Pauwelyn, 'Nondiscrimination in Trade and Investment Treaties: Worlds Apart or Two Sides of the Same Coin?' (2008) 102 AJIL 48 for a comparison on trade and investment national treatment jurisprudence.
117. In *Methanex*, the claimant argued that Methanex and other methanol producers were in like circumstances with US domestic ethanol producers because they both produced oxygenates used in manufacturing reformulated gasoline and because they competed for customers in the oxygenate market. Methanex submitted an expert legal opinion of former WTO Appellate Body Member, Dr. Claus-Dieter Ehlermann, to this effect. See Opinion of Professor Claus-Dieter Ehlermann, 4 Nov. 2002.
118. *EC-Measures Affecting Asbestos and Asbestos-Containing Products,* WT/DS135/AB/R (adopted 5 Apr. 2001) [*Asbestos*] at para. 101. On national treatment in the WTO, see Trebilcock & Howse, *supra* note 1; *World Trading System, supra* note 2; *Legal Problems, supra* note 2 and G. Verhoosel, *National Treatment and WTO Dispute Settlement: Adjudicating the Boundaries of Regulatory Autonomy* (Oxford: Hart, 2002).
119. *Asbestos, ibid.,* at para. 102.
120. *Japan – Taxes on Alcoholic Beverages,* WT/DS8/AB/R, WT/DS10/AB/R, & WT/DS11/AB/R (adopted 1 Nov. 1996) at 7.

the texts, contexts, objects and purposes of Article III, GATT, and the investment chapter of the NAFTA.[121] The US submitted that, even if the likeness of the products in question might be part of the relevant circumstances, ethanol and methanol were not like products.[122]

The second element of the GATT like products jurisprudence is the purpose of national treatment. The WTO Appellate Body has stated that the Article III, GATT, likeness analysis 'is, fundamentally, a determination about the nature and extent of the competitive relationship between and among products.'[123] Claimants have drawn on this because it narrows the range of factors to be assessed in making the like circumstances determination to one: the existence of a competitive relationship between the investments in question.

This approach to national treatment analysis is similar to the approach in Article III(1), GATT, which specifically refers to measures not being 'applied ... so as to afford protection....'[124] GATT national treatment jurisprudence has highlighted that the requirement for no less favourable treatment serves to ensure that once products have been imported, and paid any applicable tariffs and other border charges, domestic measures do not modify the conditions of competition between local and foreign products.[125] The requirement for no less favourable treatment serves to ensure that there is effective equality of opportunity between domestic and imported products.[126] For example, Methanex argued that 'the most accurate and widely recognised test of "likeness" is competition'[127] and that 'if two or more investors or their investments compete for the same business, they are in like circumstances' for the purposes of national treatment.[128]

---

121. See *Amended Statement of Defence of Respondent United States of America*, 5 Dec. 2003 at paras. 300-308.
122. The US submitted that methanol and ethanol have different physical characteristics, have different end uses, do not compete with each other and have different tariff classifications. Further, it submitted that MTBE and ethanol are not like products. *Amended Statement of Defence of Respondent United States of America, ibid.*, at paras. 300-343.
123. In *Asbestos, supra* note 118 at para. 99.
124. It should be noted, however, that IIA national treatment provisions do not have express textual references to protectionism. Unlike GATT Art. III, IIAs do not provide that measures should not be 'applied.... so as to afford protection....'
125. In the international trade regime, national treatment serves to protect the 'tariff bargain' by prohibiting differential treatment once goods have been imported. See Chapter 3, Trebilcock & Howse, *supra* note 1.
126. In GATT jurisprudence the 'less favourable treatment' analysis focuses on whether the treatment in question modifies conditions of competition. See, for example, *Korea – Measures Affecting Imports of Fresh, Chilled and Frozen Beef*, AB-2000-8, 1 Dec. 2000 at para. 144, where the Appellate Body addressed whether a Korean measure that required domestic and imported beef to be sold in separate locations provided less favourable treatment to imported beef. The Appellate Body held that the determination depended on whether or not the measure modified conditions of competition.
127. *Methanex, supra* note 13 at Part IV - Chapter B - Page 3, para. 5.
128. *Ibid.*, at para. 5.

The use of GATT like products jurisprudence by claimants in IIA cases has been met with resistance from states and tribunals.[129] The tribunal in *Methanex* stated that GATT like products jurisprudence should not be 'transported' into NAFTA's investment provisions.[130] The tribunal reasoned that the drafters of the NAFTA were well aware of the term like products and had used it in other parts of the NAFTA with the result that if a GATT-type approach had been intended, it could have been expressly adopted.[131] The tribunal stated that, unlike like circumstances, the GATT criteria leave little discretionary scope to the state.[132]

Although it is clear that GATT like products national treatment jurisprudence should not be uncritically transported into international investment law, in certain cases it might be useful for a tribunal in assessing whether the goods produced by an investor are like those of another investor. The same may be said of *General Agreement on Trade in Services* (GATS) jurisprudence on 'like services and service suppliers.'[133] Depending on the context, this analysis may be a relevant factor in assessing whether the investments or investors in question are in like circumstances. For example, if a government provided a tax rebate to manufacturers of a certain type of machinery, but not another, it could be argued that one of the factors that a tribunal should assess in determining whether the investments are in like circumstances is the extent to which the different machines are like products. That said, it is important to keep in mind that even if the manufacturers produce identical products, they will not necessarily be in like circumstances for investment reasons, since the purpose of the measures is key in assessing like circumstances. Depending on the measure challenged, differential treatment of the two manufacturers might still be justified on the basis of various factors, such as location, size or how the products are produced.[134]

In the IIA context, although the existence of a competitive relationship may often be relevant in assessing like circumstances, it is not necessary for a claimant to establish a competitive relationship between investments. Where a foreign investment produces the same types of goods or services as a domestic investment and

---

129. See *Occidental, supra* note 22 and *UPS, supra* note 84.
130. *Methanex, supra* note 13 at Part IV-Chapter B, para. 37.
131. *Ibid.*, at para. 33.
132. *Ibid.*, at para. 30.
133. On the GATS, see *supra* Chapter 3, §3.14.
134. There is a lively debate on the extent to which process and production methods (PPMs), such as labour conditions and environmental degradation, can and should be taken into account in Art. III, GATT, like products analysis. Traditionally there is reluctance to view PPMs as relevant to the like products determination. This is another reason why care must be taken in applying GATT national treatment jurisprudence in an investment context. Unlike imported products, foreign investment has potentially a very significant effect on local labour and environmental conditions. Such conditions may be very relevant in making a like circumstances determination in an investment dispute. On Art. III, GATT, national treatment, see Chapter 3, Trebilcock & Howse, *supra* note 1 and R. Howse & D. Regan, 'The Product/Process Distinction-An Illusory Basis for Disciplining 'Unilateralism' in Trade Policy' (2000) 11 EJIL 249 regarding the product versus process distinction. Also see S. Charnovitz, 'The Law of Environmental "PPMs" in the WTO: Debunking the Myth of Illegality' (2002) 27 YJIL 59.

there is a competitive relationship between these goods and services, the investments will invariably be in the same economic sector or subsector. This may be an important factor (and in some cases a determinative one) in establishing that the investments are in like circumstances. However, the absence of a competitive relationship between the investments in question does not conclude the analysis. For example, consider a situation where a separate domestic court system is established for debt collection by foreign investors in the electrical distribution sector (which is 100% foreign-controlled) and that collection procedures, including filing fees, procedural protections and timelines for court decisions, were less favourable than those available to domestic utilities in other sectors, such as water or gas.[135] Assuming the state could not justify the differential treatment, it may well be that there would be a breach of national treatment notwithstanding there was no direct competition between the utilities in question. Systemic nationality-based discrimination against foreign investors of this type would likely breach national treatment.

§4.17 The existence of protectionist intent or motive   Host state measures motivated by protectionism will normally involve either *de jure* or *de facto* discrimination between nationals and foreign investors. Where a foreign investor is able to demonstrate that the less favourable treatment was motivated by protectionism, a breach of national treatment will usually follow.

However, proof of protectionist intent is neither a necessary nor a sufficient condition for a finding that there has been a breach of national treatment. The analysis focuses on the objective effect of the treatment in question. The *Feldman* tribunal stated the rationale as follows:

> … requiring a foreign investor to prove that discrimination is based on his nationality could be an insurmountable burden to the Claimant, as that information may only be available to the government. It would be virtually impossible for any claimant to meet the burden of demonstrating that a government's motivation for discrimination is nationality rather than some other reason.[136]

The focus on the objective treatment in question is consistent with the approach in WTO national treatment jurisprudence,[137] where there is no requirement to prove subjective intent to discriminate.[138]

---

135.   The 1961 Harvard Draft, *supra* note 42, suggests that foreigners can be required to pay higher security cost fees because of the possibility of flight and attaching assets.
136.   *Feldman, supra* note 83 at para. 183.
137.   In *Japan-Taxes on Alcoholic Beverages, supra* note 120 at 27-28 the Appellate Body declined to inquire into the subjective motivations of government decision-makers. As the Appellate Body observed in analogous circumstances, in *Chile-Taxes on Alcoholic Beverages*, WT/DS87/AB/R (adopted 12 Jan. 2000) at para. 62: 'The *subjective* intentions inhabiting the minds of individual legislators or regulators do not bear upon the inquiry, if only because they are not accessible to treaty interpreters. It does not follow, however, that the statutory purposes or objectives – that is, the purpose or objectives of a Member's legislature and government as a whole – to the extent that they are given *objective* expression in the statute itself, are not pertinent.'
138.   The WTO Appellate Body's approach has been followed by the NAFTA tribunals. See, for example, in *Trucking Case, supra* note 76 at para. 214.

Further, the existence of evidence of protectionist intent does not necessarily mean that there has been a breach of national treatment obligations. In order for there to be a breach of national treatment obligations, there must also be less favourable treatment. As noted by the tribunal in *S.D. Myers*:

> Intent is important, but protectionist intent is not necessarily decisive on its own. The existence of intent to favour nationals over non-nationals would not give rise to a breach of Chapter 1102 of the NAFTA if the measure in question were to produce no adverse effect on the non-national complainant. The word 'treatment' suggests that practical impact is required to produce a breach of Article 1102, not merely a motive or intent that is in violation of Chapter 11.[139]

This approach is also supported by *Siemens A.G. v. Argentina*,[140] where the tribunal stated that:

> The Tribunal concurs that intent is not decisive or essential for a finding of discrimination, and that the impact of the measure on the investment would be the determining factor to ascertain whether it had resulted in non-discriminatory treatment.[141]

A number of IIA tribunals have referred to the OECD's 1992 statement on national treatment, *National Treatment for Foreign-Controlled Enterprises,* which provides:

> In any case, the key to determining whether a discriminatory measure applied to foreign-controlled enterprises constitutes an exception to National Treatment is to ascertain whether the discrimination is motivated, at least in part, by the fact that the enterprises concerned are under foreign control.[142]

Although the reference to the 'motivation' for the discrimination in question might be read as requiring evidence of intent, the better view is that motivation refers to the regulatory purpose of the measure. The existence of less favourable treatment resulting from nationality-based discrimination may be apparent from an objective assessment of the design of the measure or inferred where the host state is unable to justify differential treatment.

In practice, host state regulatory measures rarely result from one decision-maker whose motives and intent are clearly identifiable.[143] A state regulatory

---

139. *S.D. Myers, supra* note 18 at para. 254.
140. *Siemens A.G. v. Argentina* (Award, 6 Feb. 2007).
141. *Ibid.*, at para. 321.
142. OECD, *National Treatment for Foreign-Controlled Enterprises* (Paris: OECD, 1992) at 22. This statement is referred to in *Pope & Talbot, supra* note 80 at para. 77, note 73.
143. *S.D. Myers, supra* note 18. In some cases, however, public statements by senior ministers or government officials will provide convincing evidence that the measure is designed for protectionist purposes. In *S.D. Myers, ibid.*, at para. 116, the tribunal noted that the Canadian Minister of the Environment, responsible for banning exports of PCB wastes, stated in the Canadian Parliament: 'It is still the position of the government that the handling of PCBs should be done in Canada by Canadians.'

measure that affects foreign investments may be the result of a large number of competing and overlapping interests. Bureaucrats, legislators and the executive may support a specific measure for a variety of reasons. The fact that there is evidence that some government actors had protectionist motives does not necessarily condemn a measure. In a case where there is some evidence of discriminatory intent, the investor must still establish a *prima facie* case of like circumstances and less favourable treatment. The claim will then turn on whether there is a legitimate rationale to justify the distinction being made. Where there is evidence that the treatment was motivated by nationality-based discrimination, tribunals are apt to subject claims by the respondent host state that there are legitimate policy rationales for the treatment to a heightened degree of scrutiny. Nevertheless, the mere fact that, for example, one of the relevant government officials was motivated by protectionism is not decisive if the measure can be otherwise justified by a legitimate, non-protectionist rationale.

§4.18 Regulatory purpose of the measure   An assessment of the regulatory purpose of a challenged measure or measures is fundamental to a like circumstances analysis.[144] As noted above, regulatory purpose is relevant at the first step of analysis in determining the appropriate comparators (where the investor has the *prima facie* burden of proof) and in the third step in assessing whether there are legitimate, non-protectionist rationales to justify differences in treatment (when the host state has the burden of proof).[145] Whether any two investors or investments are in like circumstances will necessarily change in light of the regulatory purpose of the measure. As discussed in the previous section, even if firms are in a competitive relationship and are in the same business or economic sector, they may not be in like circumstances because of a legitimate policy basis for distinguishing between them.[146] A firm subject to different pollution emission standards because it is located in an environmentally sensitive area is not necessarily in like circumstances to an otherwise similar firm located in a different area. However, if differential tax rates (unrelated to environmental issues) apply to these two otherwise similarly-situated firms, then they may be in like circumstances for the purposes of the treatment in question.

Relative standards of treatment serve to prohibit *de jure* and *de facto* nationality-based discrimination. A necessary element of any like circumstances analysis is a consideration of whether there is a non-discriminatory rationale or

---

144. *Pope & Talbot, supra* note 80 at paras. 75-76.
145. As discussed above at §4.12, the investor has the burden of proof to demonstrate that its investment is in like circumstances with domestic investments. This burden of proof is not satisfied simply by demonstrating a competitive relationship. The investor must demonstrate it is in like circumstances based on the type of regulatory treatment in question.
146. DiMascio & Pauwelyn, *supra* note 116 at 75-76, highlight that although GATT jurisprudence has generally applied a 'competition test' to determine likeness, IIA jurisprudence has favoured a test that focuses on whether the discrimination is nationality-based rather than grounded on some other policy reason (a 'regulatory context test').

purpose for regulatory distinctions that result in less favourable treatment.[147] In considering this issue, the *Pope & Talbot* tribunal stated that the like circumstances analysis must address '*any* difference in treatment, demanding that it be justified by showing that it bears a reasonable relationship to rational policies not motivated by preference of domestic over foreign owned investments.'[148] The tribunal also referred to the requirement that there be a 'reasonable nexus to rational government policies that (1) do not distinguish, on their face or *de facto* between foreign-owned and domestic companies, and (2) do not otherwise unduly undermine the investment liberalizing objectives of NAFTA.'[149] The tribunal in *GAMI* took a similar view and stated that the differential treatment must be 'plausibly connected with a legitimate goal of policy ... and ... applied neither in a discriminatory manner nor as a disguised barrier to equal opportunity.'[150] In essence, both the *Pope & Talbot* and *GAMI* awards emphasize that protectionism – whether *de jure* or *de facto* – is not a valid basis for discriminating between investors or investments.[151] This is consistent with the primary goal of the national treatment obligation: it is a safeguard against nationality-based discrimination.

In this context, the *Occidental* award did not expressly address whether there was nationality-based discrimination based on the regulatory purpose of the measure.[152] In *Occidental*, the tribunal stated that the purpose of national treatment in the particular case was 'to avoid exporters being placed at a disadvantage in foreign markets because of the indirect taxes paid in the country of origin'[153] and that 'no exporter ought to be put in a disadvantageous position as compared to other exporters.'[154] Although it was true that the foreign oil company received less favourable treatment than locally owned floral export companies with respect to VAT refund treatment, the relevant issue was whether there was a legitimate rationale for differential regulatory treatment between different categories of exporters. The tribunal's assertion that the national treatment provision prohibits differential regulatory treatment between exporters *qua* exporters significantly expands the scope of like circumstances. This approach makes differential treatment

---

147. The OECD's statement on national treatment is instructive in this regard: 'More general considerations, such as the policy objectives of Member countries, could be taken into account to define the circumstances in which comparison between foreign-controlled and domestic enterprises is permissible inasmuch as those objectives are not contrary to the principle of National Treatment,' OECD, *National Treatment for Foreign-Controlled Enterprises, supra* note 142, cited in *S.D. Myers, supra* note 18 at para. 248.
148. *Pope & Talbot, supra* note 80 at para. 79.
149. *Pope & Talbot, ibid.*, at para. 78. The *Pope & Talbot* tribunal found that the exclusion of some provinces and different quota provisions for new entrants had a reasonable nexus with a rational policy and was not discriminatory. See paras. 88 and 93.
150. *GAMI Investments, Inc. v. Mexico* (Final Award, 15 Nov. 2004) at para. 114 [*GAMI*]. In this case, the rationale was ensuring that the sugar industry was in the hands of solvent enterprises.
151. The same rationale applies in the context of MFN treatment to nationality-based discrimination between foreigners.
152. *Occidental, supra* note 22.
153. *Ibid.*, at para. 175.
154. *Ibid.*, at para. 175.

synonymous with a breach of national treatment, conflating the difference between nationality-based discrimination prohibited by relative standards of treatment and other forms of discrimination. The *Occidental* tribunal's national treatment analysis should have highlighted that, for the purposes of VAT, the place of export was the relevant distinction, not the type or source of goods. The tribunal failed to consider whether there was *de facto* discrimination between exports of different nationalities.[155]

Investment treaty jurisprudence to date does not provide clear guidance on the standards to be met by treatment rationally connected to legitimate policy rationales. Since there will normally be a range of measures a state can implement to address a particular policy goal, one unanswered question is whether the state is to impose the measure that minimizes less favourable treatment. In other words, in choosing different policy responses to a legitimate policy goal, is there a requirement to take the least-investment-restrictive measure? Must the measure be both necessary and proportionate? Should tribunals apply a margin of appreciation when assessing proportionality?[156] To date, there is little investment treatment jurisprudence on these questions.[157]

The *GAMI* and *Pope & Talbot* awards both highlight the need for a rational connection between the government measures and the differential treatment. The *GAMI* award states that the measures should be 'plausibly connected with a legitimate goal' whereas *Pope & Talbot* refers to a 'reasonable relationship to rational policies.'[158] The reference in *Pope & Talbot* to policies that 'do not otherwise unduly undermine the investment liberalizing objectives of NAFTA' might suggest the policies chosen are subject to a proportionality requirement that compares the importance of the policy goal in question with the differential treatment. The reference in *GAMI* to 'plausibly connected' might suggest a slightly more deferential standard in assessing government measures than that in *Pope & Talbot*. Further, the reference in *Pope & Talbot* to the NAFTA objectives, highlights that in making this assessment tribunals are likely to be guided by IIA purposes and objectives.

---

155. See *supra* §4.15 for further discussion.
156. On the margin of appreciation doctrine, see Y. Shany, 'Toward a General Margin of Appreciation Doctrine in International Law' (2005) 16 EJIL 907. Also see G. Van Harten, *Investment Treaty Arbitration and Public Law* (Oxford: Oxford University Press, 2007) who argues at 144-145 that tribunals 'should afford a margin of appreciation to the discretionary policy choices of domestic institutions and defer to governmental decisions that are not specifically abusive or discriminatory.'
157. In this context, future IIA tribunals might be guided by Art. XX GATT jurisprudence on general exceptions, where the WTO Appellate Body has developed a balancing test with respect to whether a measure is necessary to achieve a legitimate objective. The Appellate Body has stated that the required degree of nexus between a measure and a legitimate objective will based on the relative importance of the interest or value furthered by the challenged measure. For example, more deference might be afforded where the measure relates to the protection of human health. See *infra* Chapter 10, §10.9 *et seq.*
158. *Pope & Talbot, supra* note 80 at para. 79 and *GAMI, supra* note 150 at para. 114.

The NAFTA *Trucking Case*[159] suggests that the differential treatment in question should be no greater than necessary for legitimate regulatory reasons. In the *Trucking Case*, a state-to-state dispute under Chapter Twenty of the NAFTA, Mexico argued that the US had breached its NAFTA national treatment obligations with respect to services and investment because of its refusal to lift a moratorium on the processing of applications authorizing Mexican-owned trucking firms to operate in US border states. The US argued that the Mexican truck transportation regulatory system did not maintain the same rigorous standards as the US system and that, as a result, Mexican service providers were not in like circumstances and could be treated differently in order to address a legitimate regulatory objective – road safety.[160] In addressing this issue, the panel highlighted that one of the NAFTA's objectives is to facilitate cross-border economic activity. It stated that in light of this purpose, the differential treatment in question should be 'no greater than necessary for legitimate regulatory reasons such as safety, and that such different treatment be equivalent to the treatment accorded to domestic service providers.'[161] The tribunal concluded that there was not a legally sufficient basis for a blanket moratorium on all Mexican trucking firms.[162] With respect to investment, the tribunal stated that even though Mexico had not identified a specific Mexican national that the US had rejected, the refusal to permit Mexicans to establish trucking services resulted in less favourable treatment.[163]

The issue of deference to how the government implements regulatory policy choices (the standard of review for the public policy rationales) was directly addressed in an arbitrator's separate statement in *UPS*, respecting whether Canada's publications assistance program (PAP) violated the NAFTA's national treatment obligation.[164] Canada had designed the PAP so that Canadian periodicals would be delivered by one entity nationwide. The only entity which had the capacity to do so was Canada Post, the national mail service. UPS argued that there was no reasonable basis for designing the program so that delivery had to be made by one entity capable of delivering nationwide to all residential addresses. UPS claimed that the national treatment obligation requires any government program to be tailored so that it discriminates as little as possible between national investors and foreign investors; in essence, UPS argued for a least restrictive means test.

The separate statement expressly rejected UPS's argument stating that, although there were limits on the reach of the host state policy justifications, 'those limits should not be imposed through an overly critical examination of

---

159. *Trucking Case, supra* note 76 at para. 258.
160. *Ibid.*, at para. 242.
161. *Ibid.*, at para. 258.
162. *Ibid.*, at para, 278.
163. The tribunal also held that the US breached its MFN treatment obligations because no similar moratorium applied to Canadian service providers or investors.
164. *UPS, supra* note 84. See *infra* Chapter 10, §10.3, for discussion of the case with respect to exceptions to NAFTA obligations. This issue did not arise for the majority as it determined that UPS and Canada Post were not in like circumstances (see *supra* §4.15).

governmental policy choices by arbitral tribunals.'[165] In particular, the separate statement rejected UPS's position which would have required that Canada 'assemble a collection of enterprises that together can assure such delivery and to bear the burden of monitoring and coordinating the coverage areas to produce the same end.'[166] This approach arguably reflects a standard similar to that adopted in *Pope & Talbot* – that of reasonable relationship to rational policies in the substantive review of government measures and program design.[167]

The separate statement commented that:

> Canada may be free to adopt any reasonable design to implement its policy of promoting widespread distribution of Canadian periodicals, but it is not free to assert for the first time during a dispute resolution proceeding an ex post rationalization that would limit availability of a government benefit to a single (domestic) recipient.[168]

It further noted that Canada had never publicly articulated the rationales for limiting benefits to Canada Post and that Canadian publishers wanted a choice of delivery providers. Canada 'used a procedure for constructing this aspect of the PAP that on its face seemed only to ask how to give PAP benefits to Canada Post, not why that was important to broader public policy goals.'[169] The statement rejected Canada's argument that the tribunal's inquiry should end as soon as Canada advanced a public policy rationale, noting that this would mean that the NAFTA Parties 'would not be required to articulate in advance a rationale for treating firms differently, but would be able to craft rationales during the course of a dispute that would be tailored to the legal issues arising in the proceeding.'[170]

The above reasoning is attractive. While providing substantial deference to policy objectives and program design, it ensures that states must articulate *ex ante* rationales to justify their actions. This contributes to transparency in the design and implementation of government measures and guards against states developing self-serving *ex post facto* rationalizations for discriminatory conduct. Where there is no contemporaneous evidence of a rationale, it might be reasonable for a tribunal to doubt the *bona fides* of the proffered rationale. At the same time, the absence of a fully elaborated *ex ante* rationale does not necessarily condemn a measure. Particularly in cases of *de facto* discrimination, it may be that the less favourable treatment in question was an unanticipated consequence of a legitimate and non-protectionist regulatory policy choice.

§4.19 The absence of foreign or domestic comparators   The national treatment analysis requires a tribunal to compare the treatment of one foreign investor or

---

165.   *UPS Cass Separate Statement, supra* note 90 at para. 120.
166.   *Ibid.*, at para. 119.
167.   The separate statement did not offer a 'precise formula for the degree of justification required of the Party.' *Ibid.*, at para. 121.
168.   *Ibid.*, at para. 124.
169.   *Ibid.*, at para. 130.
170.   *Ibid.*, at para. 132.

investment with at least one domestic investor or investment. Some national treatment provisions refer to 'investments' and 'investors' rather than the singular 'investment' and 'investor'.[171] In *Pope & Talbot*, Canada argued that national treatment did not apply where there is only a single foreign investor because the provision refers 'to investors of another Party' and that this required a comparison amongst many similarly-situated foreign investors. The tribunal rejected this argument and found that an individual foreign investor can maintain a claim based on a comparison of treatment with only one host state investor.[172] The same logic applies to domestic investment. Generally, the national treatment obligation will apply where a foreign investor or investment can identify at least one domestic investor or investment that is, or could be, in like circumstances.[173]

B   THE STANDARD OF TREATMENT

§4.20 Treaty provisions   IIAs vary in how they describe the applicable standard of treatment. Some call for the 'same' or 'as favourable as' treatment.[174] Others provide that the foreign investment be entitled to national treatment or the treatment accorded to other foreign investments, 'whichever is more favourable.'[175] More commonly, the requirement is for 'no less favourable treatment'[176] or prohibiting 'treatment less favourable'[177] than domestic investors or investments. In all of these formulations, the protection afforded by the national treatment clause involves a relative comparison between the treatment accorded to foreign investors or investments and the domestic investors or investments.

---

171.   For example, Art. 1102(2), NAFTA, provides: 'Each Party shall accord to investments of investors of another Party treatment no less favorable than that it accords, in like circumstances, to investments of its own investors with respect to the establishment, acquisition, expansion, management, conduct, operation, and sale or other disposition of investments.'

172.   *Pope & Talbot, supra* note 80 at para. 38.

173.   This was an issue in *Loewen, supra* note 18, a claim arising from the treatment Loewen received in the Mississippi courts when it was sued by Mississippian based O'Keefe. The tribunal considered that the applicable comparator was domestic defendants in local courts, rather than the plaintiff O'Keefe. The tribunal rejected Loewen's submission that Loewen and O'Keefe were in like circumstances as a result of being litigants in the same case. This reasoning is not particularly convincing given that the less favourable treatment in question related to whether there was nationality-based discrimination between the litigants in a particular case. The better view is that Loewen and O'Keefe were in like circumstances for the purposes of determining whether there was less favourable treatment of the foreigner.

174.   UNCTAD National Treatment, *supra* note 51 at 35.

175.   See, for example, the following BITs: Art. 4(2), Chile-Egypt (1999); Art. 4(3), China-Jordan (2001); Art. 3(2), Cuba-Lebanon (1995); Art. 3(2), Egypt-Jordan (1996); and Art. 3(2), Netherlands-Romania (1994).

176.   See, for example, Art. 1103, NAFTA, and Art. 3, Canadian Model FIPA (2003). Also see the following BITs: Art. 4, Australia-Romania (1993); Art. IV(2), Chile-Egypt (1999); Art. 4(2), Chile-Tunisia (1998); Art. 4(1), India-Ghana (2000); Art. 3(2), Netherlands-Romania (1994); and Art. 3(1), Ethiopia-Turkey (2000).

177.   Art. 3(1), Egypt-Greece (1993), and Art. 3(2), (1975) Egypt-UK.

A small number of IIAs define the meaning of less favourable treatment to include limitations on the buying, production and exploitation of raw materials and restrictions on the sale of products, while at the same time establishing that measures taken for reasons of public security and order as well as public health do not result in less favourable treatment.[178]

§4.21 Meaning of 'treatment'   IIAs do not define the term treatment. Treatment is a broad term that the Oxford English Dictionary defines as 'Conduct, behaviour; action or behaviour towards a person.' In *Siemens*, the tribunal stated that 'treatment' ordinarily means 'behaviour in respect of an entity or a person.'[179]

In *Canfor*, the claimants drew a distinction between conduct and treatment, not adopted in the tribunal's decision, arguing that conduct is what officials do and treatment is the manner in which the officials direct conduct to a specific investor or claimant.[180] This distinction is potentially misleading because it suggests that the state must 'direct' conduct to a specific investor, which might imply either a requirement of specificity or intent. The better view is that conduct consists of an action or omission,[181] whereas treatment refers to the effect or result of the conduct on the investment or investor in question. 'Treatment' can be further contrasted with the term 'measures' which focuses on the state 'conduct' in question.

§4.22 *De facto* analysis   Once a tribunal has determined the applicable comparator, the application of the standard of treatment is usually straightforward: Has the claimant or its investment received less favourable treatment than the applicable comparator(s)? The focus of the analysis is the *de facto* result of the impugned treatment; thus, the concern is the effect of the state conduct in question on a particular investor or investment. The standard of treatment does not differ

---

178.   This is common in German BITs. For a recent example, see para. 4, Protocol to China-Germany (1993).

179.   *Siemens, supra* note 140 at para. 85. Also see *Suez, Sociedad General de Aguas de Barcelona S.A., and InterAgua Servicios Integrales del Agua S.A. v. Argentina* (Decision on Jurisdiction, 16 May 2006) at para. 55: 'The word 'treatment' is not defined in the treaty text. However, the ordinary meaning of that term within the context of investment includes the rights and privileges granted and the obligations and burdens imposed by a Contracting State on investments made by investors covered by the treaty.'

180.   *Canfor Corporation v. United States and Terminal Forest Products Ltd. v. United States* (Consolidated Proceedings) (Decision on Preliminary Question, 6 Jun. 2006) at para. 150.

181.   State conduct constituting an international wrong may be either an action or omission: 'There is an internationally wrongful act of a State when conduct consisting of an action or omission: (a) Is attributable to the State under international law; and (b) Constitutes a breach of an international obligation of the State.' Art. 2, International Law Commission's Articles on Responsibility of States for Internationally Wrongful Acts, *Official Records of the General Assembly,* UN GAOR, 56th Sess., Supp. No. 10, UN Doc A/56/10 at 11; 2001 YBILC, Vol. II, Part Two. The Articles and commentary are *reprinted in* J. Crawford, *The International Law Commission's Articles on State Responsibility: Introduction, Text, and Commentaries* (Cambridge: Cambridge University Press, 2002) [ILC's Articles on State Responsibility].

depending on whether the nationality-based discrimination is *de facto* or *de jure*.[182] For example, in *Feldman* the issue was not whether Mexican law authorized tax rebates in the circumstances, but whether tax rebates had in fact been provided to other domestic cigarette exporters. The tribunal stated that a '*de facto* difference in treatment is sufficient to establish a denial of national treatment.'[183] Further, in *Bayindir*, the tribunal noted that the fact that an investor had always been subject to the same legal and regulatory framework as every other investor did not mean it had been treated in the same way.[184]

As noted above, proof of protectionist intent is neither a necessary nor a sufficient condition for a finding that there has been a breach of national treatment.[185] There is no requirement that the claimant prove that less favourable treatment is due to nationality. In the absence of a legitimate rationale for discrimination between investors in like circumstances, a tribunal will presume – or at least infer – that the differential treatment was a result of the claimant's nationality. In *Feldman*, the tribunal held that:

> However, it is not self-evident ... that any departure from national treatment must be *explicitly* shown to be a result of the investor's nationality. There is no such language in Article 1102. Rather, Article 1102 by its terms suggests that it is sufficient to show less favorable treatment for the foreign investor than for domestic investors in like circumstances.... For practical as well as legal reasons, the Tribunal is prepared to assume that the differential treatment is a result of the Claimant's nationality, at least in the absence of any evidence to the contrary.[186]

§4.23 Comparisons of treatment As already noted, most IIAs do not provide that investors must be given identical treatment; rather the requirement is to ensure that the treatment is no less favourable.[187] Treatment is more or less favourable where the effect on the investment or investor is to impose advantages or burdens. In *Pope & Talbot*, Canada argued that *de facto* discrimination does not in and of itself constitute a breach of national treatment, and that such a breach can only flow from a 'disproportionate disadvantage' accorded to foreign investors. The tribunal rejected this submission on the basis that there is no textual basis for the distinction.[188] This requirement would, in any event, be inconsistent

---

182. *Pope & Talbot, supra* note 81 at para. 70.
183. *Feldman, supra* note 83 at para. 169.
184. *Bayindir Insaat Turizm Ticaret Ve Sanayi A.Ş. v. Pakistan* (Decision on Jurisdiction, 14 Nov. 2005) [*Bayindir*] at para. 206.
185. See *infra* Chapter 6, §6.24.
186. See *Feldman, supra* note 83 at para. 181.
187. Even where the national treatment or MFN treatment provision provides for the 'same treatment,' different treatment may be justifiable if the investments are not in the same or similar circumstances.
188. *Pope & Talbot, supra* note 80 at para. 72. It should be added, however, that there is little textual basis for much of the *Pope & Talbot* tribunal's national treatment analysis, in particular the

with the rationale of national treatment – prohibiting nationality-based discrimination to protect equality of competitive opportunities.

Formal or technical differences in treatment do not necessarily result in less favourable treatment. For example, the fact that investors from State A have to fill out one type of form whereas investors from State B or nationals have to fill out a different form does not necessarily entail less favourable treatment. It may be difficult for tribunals to determine whether there is less favourable treatment where foreign investors or investments are subject to different administrative processes or requirements that are not on their face more time-consuming, complex or expensive. Conversely, cases that involve some type of quantitative discrimination, such as differential tax rates, are likely to be straightforward.

The term treatment is wide enough to cover both substantive and procedural requirements and, arguably, does not necessarily imply that there is a direct financial disadvantage. For instance, less favourable administrative or court procedures to enforce rights might give rise to a breach of national treatment obligations. The GATT *Section 337* case is instructive in this respect. The *Section 337* case involved an assessment of whether different administrative and court procedures for challenging patent infringements depending on whether the goods were domestic or foreign violated GATT national treatment obligations. The panel highlighted six significant differences between the procedures and held that foreign goods were subject to less favourable procedures because of those differences.[189] The same reasoning applies to other administrative processes. In *UPS*, the tribunal rejected Canada's submission that the processing of couriered materials by customs authorities did not constitute treatment of an investment. It highlighted that processing decisions affects demand for services and changes in demand for the services affect the returns associated with the business.[190]

§4.24 Examples of less favourable treatment   Less favourable treatment most commonly arises from state conduct in the form of the application of laws, regulations, procedures or policies or the actions of state officials. National treatment claims have arisen where it is alleged the host state has favoured domestic investments or investors over foreign investments or investors including: in the provision of tax rebates;[191] the conduct of a trial judge in court proceedings;[192]   domestic

---

reading in of an implied exception for non-discriminatory policy measures. See *supra* §4.6.

189. *United States – Section 337 of the Tariff Act of 1930* (GATT Panel, 7 Nov. 1989) 36th Supp. BISD 345 [*Section 337*]. The differences in procedures included the non-availability of a choice of forum; tighter and fixed time limits; the inability to bring counterclaims; differences in the available remedies; the possibility of having to defend claims in multiple fora (see para. 5.20).

190. *UPS, supra* note, 84 at para. 86.

191. In *Feldman, supra* note 83, and *Occidental, supra* note 22, the tribunals found less favourable treatment.

192. In *Loewen, supra* note 18, despite evidence that the trial judge allowed prejudicial nationality-based comments by counsel, the tribunal stated that this did not evidence more favourable treatment accorded to a person in a like situation to that of the claimant (who had

fabrication requirements;[193] imposition export bans;[194] the processing of items by customs authorities and the procurement of postal services;[195] and the selective tendering and contract administration practice.[196]

The *ADF* case highlights the interaction between the characterization of the investment and the issue of less favourable treatment. It also raises questions about proving less favourable treatment. *ADF*, a Canadian company, challenged US measures requiring that only US-fabricated steel be used in a federally-funded highway project. ADF had a contract to supply fabricated steel to the project. It planned to buy US-origin steel, fabricate the steel in its Canadian facilities and then ship the finished steel to the construction site. The US measures in question, however, essentially required that the steel be 100% produced and fabricated in the US. In addressing the national treatment claim, the tribunal stated that the question was whether ADF's investment – which it defined as ADF's steel in the US – was treated less favourably than the US-origin steel of US investors.[197] The tribunal found that steel from US producers and ADF's steel was in like circumstances and that the steel fabricated in the US was not treated differently based on the nationality of the investor owning the steel – all steel was required to be fabricated in the US.[198]

ADF had argued that it was treated less favourably because it was prevented from using its production facilities located in Canada, whereas US producers were able to use their US production facilities. According to the tribunal, 'less favourable treatment' would have required 'evidence concerning the comparative economics of the situation,' such as the comparative costs of steel fabrication in the US and Canada.[199] In the tribunal's view, the claimant had failed to prove that the US measures resulted in less favourable treatment.[200]

The result in *ADF* flows logically from the tribunal's finding that ADF's investment was its steel in the US rather than its contractual rights to provide

---

been the defendant in the local proceedings). The tribunal appears to have considered that the applicable comparison was that of the treatment of other plaintiffs in local courts, rather than a comparison of the treatment of plaintiffs and defendants.

193. *ADF Group Inc. v. United States* (Award, 9 Jan. 2003) [*ADF*].
194. The *S.D. Myers* tribunal found less favourable treatment. See *supra* note 18.
195. The tribunal in *UPS* rejected the claim of breach of national treatment on the basis that the investors in question were not in like circumstances (see *supra* note 84). In a separate statement, Dean Ronald Cass held there was less favourable treatment (*UPS Cass Separate Statement, supra* note 90).
196. The *Bayindir* tribunal, *supra* note 184, addressed less favourable treatment in the context of its jurisdictional decision. It held that practices including selective tendering and providing more favourable construction timetables, if proven on the facts, could in principle breach relative standards of treatment.
197. *Ibid.*, at para. 155.
198. *Ibid.*, at para. 156.
199. *Ibid.*, at para. 157. T. Weiler, 'Prohibitions Against Discrimination in NAFTA Chapter 11,' *supra* note 78 at 36 criticizes the decision: 'the tribunal appeared to ignore the *de facto* results of the decision to refuse ADF to use steel fabricated in its Canadian facility ... Given that the business model of ADF's investment was naturally predicated on the use of its parent company's facilities when necessary, it seems absurd to arrive at this conclusion.'
200. *Ibid.*

fabricated steel. If the investment had been characterized as the contractual right to provide fabricated steel, then the tribunal might have found there had been less favourable treatment. ADF's treatment was arguably less favourable because ADF was not allowed to fabricate the steel in its own facilities in Canada, whereas US competitors could source fabricated steel from their own facilities, which were likely to be based in the US. Even if ADF could have fabricated the steel in the US, a requirement that effectively required out-sourcing to local competitors arguably would have constituted less favourable treatment[201] and a performance requirement.[202] Indeed, the NAFTA has express exceptions from national treatment obligations for government procurement to allow governments to source from local suppliers.[203] Thus, even if a breach of national treatment had been found, the end result in *ADF* was justified because of the express exception to national treatment for government procurement in Article 1108(7), NAFTA.

§4.25 Better of national and MFN treatment?   Faced with the situation where either national or MFN treatment is more favourable, the investor or investment is entitled to the more favourable treatment. As a general rule, international obligations are cumulative – an investor can rely on each treatment standard independently. Although some treaties expressly provide that an investor is entitled to the better treatment afforded in the circumstances,[204] these provisions would appear to have been added for greater clarification and certainty. As the International Law Commission (ILC) has noted with respect to MFN treatment:

> The right of the beneficiary State, for itself or for the benefit of persons or things in a determined relationship with it, to MFN treatment under a MFN clause is without prejudice to national treatment or other treatment which the granting State has accorded to that beneficiary State with respect to the same subject-matter as that of the MFN clause.[205]

§4.26 Best treatment or average treatment?   References to 'no less favourable' treatment in IIAs do not clarify whether the investor is entitled to the best treatment afforded to any other investor, national or foreign, or the average treatment afforded

---

201. *ADF, supra* note 193, argued that the only difference between ADF and US steel fabricators was the physical location of their facilities (which is similar to the *S.D. Myers* situation where Myers' PCB facilities were in the US).
202. See *infra* Chapter 8, §8.14 *et seq.*
203. See *infra* Chaper 10, §10.13.
204. See, for example, ECT, Art. 10(3): 'For the purposes of this Article, 'Treatment' means treatment accorded by a Contracting Party which is no less favourable than that which it accords to its own Investors or to Investors of any other Contracting Party or any third state, whichever is the most favourable.' See also NAFTA, Art. 1104: 'Each Party shall accord to investors of another Party and to investments of investors of another Party the better of the treatment required by [national treatment] and [MFN].' See also Art. 1(9), Italy-Jordan (1996).
205. ILC's *Draft Articles on Most-Favoured-Nation Clauses, infra* Chapter 5, §5.2, Art. 19(2).

to a group of like investors. In *Feldman*, the tribunal noted that the national treatment provision in the NAFTA is:

> ... on its face unclear as to whether the foreign investor must be treated in the most favorable manner provided for any domestic investor, or only with regard to the treatment generally accorded to domestic investors, or even the least favorably treated domestic investor. There is no 'most-favored investor' provision in Chapter 11, parallel to the most favored nation provision in Article 1103, that suggests that a foreign investor must be treated no less favorably than the most favorably treated national investor, if there are other national investors that are treated less favorably, that is, in the same manner as the foreign investor. At the same time, there is no language in Article 1102 that states that the foreign investor must receive treatment equal to that provided to the most favorably treated domestic investor, if there are multiple domestic investors receiving differing treatment by the respondent government.[206]

The *Pope & Talbot* tribunal, relying in part on GATT jurisprudence,[207] concluded that the national treatment obligation in the NAFTA provides for the best treatment afforded to any one national.[208] If a national investor in like circumstances is provided preferential treatment (i.e., better than other nationals), the foreigner is entitled to no less favourable treatment, even if other similarly situated national investors are not provided comparable treatment. This approach means that a state cannot aggregate the favourable and non-favourable treatment that it accords to national investors and then compare the average treatment afforded to nationals with the treatment afforded to foreign investors.[209] Nor would the state be able to pick a national champion and provide it super-preferential treatment, while according less favourable treatment to domestic and foreign investors. This approach is consistent with the purpose of protecting the individual foreign investor or investment from injury caused by nationality-based discrimination.[210]

---

206. *Feldman, supra* note 83 at para. 185.
207. *Pope & Talbot, supra* note 80 at para. 68 cited the GATT Panel decision in *Section 337, supra* note 189. The Panel in *Section 337* at para. 5.14, 'rejected any notion of balancing more favourable treatment of some imported products against less favourable treatment of other imported products. If this notion were accepted, it would entitle a contracting party to derogate from the no less favourable treatment obligation in one case, or indeed in respect of one contracting party, on the ground that it accords more favourable treatment in some other case, or to another contracting party. Such an interpretation would lead to great uncertainty about the conditions of competition between imported and domestic products and thus defeat the purposes of Article III.'
208. *Pope & Talbot, ibid.,* at para. 42: 'The Tribunal also interprets both standards to mean the right to treatment equivalent to the 'best' treatment accorded to domestic investors or investments in like circumstances. The Tribunal thus concludes that 'no less favorable' means equivalent to, not better or worse than, the best treatment accorded to the comparator.' See also *Methanex, supra* note 13 at Part IV-Chapter B, para. 21.
209. In contrast, GATT national treatment jurisprudence evaluates less favourable treatment upon the entire group of like foreign products. See DiMascio & J. Pauwelyn, *supra* note 116 at 82.
210. *Ibid.*

Unlike international trade law where the focus is to ensure non-discrimination between foreign and domestic products as a whole, non-discrimination in IIAs protects the individual investor that may have a significant and immobile investment from targeted action that disrupts equality of competitive opportunities.[211]

Relative standards provisions apply to any form of less favourable treatment between different nationals, suggesting that preferences cannot be given to one category of investors but not another, assuming all are in like circumstances. It might be argued that preferences to one category of investors (the national champion) might be justified on other bases, such as trying to create first mover advantages in strategic sectors, a policy which might dictate choosing one investor or investment for special treatment. The problem with this argument is that the creation of a national champion (if tied to domestic ownership or control) is inherently premised on some form of nationality-based discrimination.[212] Nevertheless, if there were an open competition to obtain special advantages and competition criteria were not tied to the nationality of the investment, an argument could be made that the investment or investor chosen by the state for special treatment was not in like circumstances to other investors.

§4.27 Application to sub-state units   A further standard of treatment issue arises where a subdivision of a state provides preferential treatment to its residents. In federal states, a subdivision (i.e., a state, province or region) may have regulatory authority over certain economic activities within its territory. A subdivision may provide preferential treatment to its residents' investments. In this case, is the foreign investor entitled to the best treatment afforded to the investor from the subdivision in question, or only to the best treatment accorded to nationals from other subdivisions?

Most national treatment provisions do not address this issue expressly. Where the national treatment obligation is unqualified, one view is that the foreign investment is entitled to no less favourable treatment without qualification; that is, the best treatment of any investment in that subdivision. This is sometimes referred to as 'best in-state treatment' because the foreign investment is entitled to the best treatment that the subdivision provides to any other investment (including those of its own residents). Best in-state treatment stands in contrast to best out-of-state treatment, which requires treatment by a subdivision that is no less favourable than that which it accords to national investors from other subdivisions. A best out-of-state treatment provision allows the subdivision to discriminate in favour of residents of the subdivision.

---

211.   *Ibid.*, at 56, 82 and 88-89.
212.   In *UPS*, Dean Ronald Cass's separate statement noted that national treatment requires an effective parity of foreign and domestic investors and investments and that parity does not exist where a party favours a national champion: 'The violation is not mitigated by the existence of discrimination against other domestic investors and investments as well as against foreign investors and investments' (*UPS Cass Separate Statement, supra* note 90 at para. 60).

It may be argued that best-in-state treatment is more consistent with the overriding rationale of the relative treatment standards: to prohibit differential treatment of comparable investors on the basis of nationality. It is also consistent with a general presumption that a treaty applies to the whole territory of the state regardless of whether it contains subdivisions.[213] The opposing view is that the foreign investment is only entitled to no less favourable treatment than domestic investors from other subdivisions. Since national treatment is a discipline on nationality-based discrimination, discrimination based on residency in a particular subdivision is not within the purview of national treatment.

A small number of IIAs specifically address this issue. For example, Article 1102(3) (national treatment), NAFTA, provides:

> The treatment accorded by a Party under paragraphs 1 and 2 means, with respect to a state or province, treatment no less favorable than the most favorable treatment accorded, in like circumstances, by that state or province to investors, and to investments of investors, of the Party of which it forms a part.

NAFTA tribunals have interpreted this provision to mean best in-state treatment.[214] In contrast, Article 3(3), 2004 US Model BIT, expressly provides for best out-of-state treatment:

> The treatment to be accorded by a Party ... means, with respect to a regional level of government, treatment no less favorable than the treatment accorded, in like circumstances, by that regional level of government to natural persons resident in and enterprises constituted under the laws of other regional levels of government of the Party of which it forms a part, and to their respective investments.[215]

IV   EXCEPTIONS AND RESERVATIONS

§4.28 Exceptions and reservations   IIAs commonly provide express exceptions and reservations to relative standards of treatment, often in annexes or protocols to the main treaty text.[216] In addition, a number of express general exceptions and

---

213. Art. 27, *Vienna Convention on the Law of Treaties*, done at Vienna, 23 May 1969, entered into force, 27 Jan. 1980, 1155 UNTS 331, *reprinted in* (1969) 8 ILM 679.

214. For example, in *Loewen, supra* note 18 at para. 139, the tribunal stated that 'What Article 1102(3) requires is a comparison between the standard of treatment accorded to a claimant and the most favourable standard of treatment accorded to a person in like situation to that claimant.' In the context of *Loewen* this meant that 'a Mississippi court shall not conduct itself less favourably to Loewen, by reason of its Canadian nationality, than it would to an investor involved in similar activities and in a similar lawsuit from another state in the United States *or from another location in Mississippi itself...*' (at para. 139) [Emphasis added.] See also *Pope & Talbot, supra* note 80 at paras. 39-42.

215. This Model forms the basis for US-Uruguay (2005).

216. On the distinction between exceptions and reservations see *infra* Chapter 10.

customary international law defences may apply to relative standards of treatment.[217]

Since state measures are more likely to discriminate between nationals and foreigners, reservations and exceptions to national treatment may be extensive, particularly where national treatment extends to admission and establishment.[218] National treatment reservations are made in a number of ways. First, certain sectors, subsectors or activities may be entirely excluded. This is often the case with respect to sectors of the economy with particular strategic, political, social or economic significance to the state, such as petroleum, defence and cultural industries.[219] Another common exception is to exclude government procurement and the provision of subsidies and grants from IIA obligations.[220] Second, reservations may be made for existing non-conforming measures.[221] For example, the Protocol to China-Germany (2003) provides that the national treatment obligation does not apply to:

(a) any existing non-conforming measures maintained within its territory;
(b) the continuation of any such non-conforming measure;
(c) any amendment to any such non-conforming measure to the extent that the amendment does not increase the non-conformity of these measures.

The Protocol then provides that China 'will take all appropriate steps in order to progressively remove the non-conforming measures.' Third, reservations may be made for future non-conforming measures. This allows states to adopt new and more restrictive measures that are not in conformity with their national treatment obligation.[222] Fourth, reservations may be made to allow for specific social

---

217. See *infra* Chapter 10.
218. For treaty practice, see UNCTAD National Treatment, *supra* note 51 at 43-54 and *UNCTAD BIT Studies*, *supra* note 51. See *supra* Chapter 3, §3.13, on reservations to admission and establishment obligations.
219. Reservations are often industry specific, such as the exception for cultural industries in NAFTA, Annex 2106. See *infra* Chapter 10, §10.3, on the *UPS* tribunal's interpretation of the cultural exception in NAFTA. See J. Karl, 'The Promotion and Protection of German Foreign Investment Abroad' (1996) 11 ICSID Rev 1 at 12-13 for a discussion of various limitations to national treatment that occur in German BITs.
220. See *infra* Chapter 10, §10.1 *et seq.,* for a discussion of government procurement, subsidies and exceptions.
221. China-Germany (2003). See Art. 1108(1), NAFTA, and Annex 1 entitled 'Reservations for Existing Measures and Liberalization Requirements.' For example, Canada annexed measures with respect to foreign investment screening and foreign ownership restrictions that would have violated national treatment. Art. 1108(1)(c) further provides a 'standstill' obligation with respect to amendments to non-conforming measures. Reservations apply to amendments to nonconforming measures provided they do not decrease the conformity of the measure with the applicable obligation. For certain non-conforming measures, the parties agreed to phase-out the measures over time.
222. See Art. 1108(3), NAFTA, and Annex II entitled 'Reservations for Future Measures.' The US Schedule included measures with respect to the ownership of oceanfront land, communications, social services, preferences to economically disadvantaged minorities, legal services, newspaper publishing and maritime transportation services.

policies, such as development considerations[223] or the protection of disadvantaged groups.[224]

Nonetheless, certain IIAs incorporate particular provisions guarding against discrimination on the basis on nationality. For example, Article 1108(4), NAFTA, specifically prohibits forced dispositions on the grounds of nationality.[225]

---

223. Protocol, Indonesia-Switzerland (1974); Art. 3, Jamaica-Switzerland (1990); Art. 3(6), Jamaica-Netherlands (1991); Art. 3(3), Italy-Morocco (1990); and Protocol, Germany-Papua New Guinea (1980).

224. See Art. 3(4)(c), Mauritius-South Africa, which provides that national treatment and MFN treatment 'shall not be construed so as to oblige one Contracting Party to extend to the investors of the other Contracting Party the benefit of any treatment, preference or privilege resulting from ... Any law or measure in pursuance of any law, the purpose of which is to promote the achievement of equality in its territory, or designed to protect or advance persons, or categories of persons, disadvantaged by unfair discrimination in its territory. In NAFTA, the parties made reservations for Aboriginal Affairs or Minority Affairs. (See Annex II, Reservations for Future Measures, NAFTA). See also Art. 24(2)(b)(iii), ECT.

225. Art. 1108(4), NAFTA, reads as follows: 'No Party may, under any measure adopted after the date of entry into force of this Agreement and covered by its Schedule to Annex II, require an investor of another Party, by reason of its nationality, to sell or otherwise dispose of an investment existing at the time the measure becomes effective.'

Chapter 5

Most-Favoured-Nation Treatment

INTRODUCTION

§5.1 Principle and rationale As discussed in the chapter on national treatment, international economic treaties prohibit nationality-based discrimination through two distinct treatment standards: national and most-favoured-nation (MFN) treatment.[1] MFN treatment obligations require that state conduct does not discriminate between similarly situated persons, entities, goods, services or investments of different foreign nationalities. As with national treatment, MFN treatment is a relative standard – the required standard of treatment in international investment agreements (IIAs) depends on the treatment of similarly situated foreign investors or investments.[2] MFN treatment ensures that, within a host state, there is equality of competitive opportunities between investors and investments from different states.[3]

§5.2 A conventional not a customary obligation Entitlement to MFN treatment arises from the existence of an MFN clause in a treaty.[4] Although some

---

1. See *supra* Chapter 4, §4.1, for a general discussion and introduction to nationality-based discrimination.
2. See *supra* Chapter 4, §4.2.
3. United Nations Conference on Trade and Development (UNCTAD), *Most-Favoured-Nation Treatment*, UNCTAD Series on issues in international investment agreements (New York and Geneva: United Nations, 1999) (UNCTAD/ITE/IIT/10) [UNCTAD, *MFN Treatment*] at 8.
4. Arts 7 and 8 of the International Law Commission's *Draft Articles on Most-Favoured-Nation Clauses*, in *Report of the International Law Commission on its Thirtieth Session*, (1978) 2 YBILC 8, (pt. 2) (U.N. Doc. A/33/10) [*Draft MFN Articles*], provide that the entitlement to MFN treatment is treaty-based. See also OECD, *Working Papers on International Investment Law*, Most-Favoured-Nation Treatment in International Investment Law, Working Papers No. 2004/2 (Paris: OECD, 2004) at note 23, *reprinted in* OECD, *International Investment Law: A Changing Landscape* (OECD: Paris, 2005) and E. Denza & S. Brooks, 'Investment

commentators have suggested that MFN treatment is required under customary international law based on the principle of the sovereign equality of states,[5] there is little state practice or *opinio juris* to support this contention. Although the prevalence of MFN provisions in IIAs might suggest consistent and general state practice sufficient for the formation of a customary international law obligation, the scope and content of the provisions varies widely and the obligations are subject to myriad exceptions. Even if sufficient state practice existed to satisfy the requirements for establishing a customary international law obligation, there is little evidence that MFN treatment in IIAs is accorded out of a sense of legal obligation (*opinio juris*). At present, the more persuasive view is that MFN treatment obligations with respect to foreign investment and investors arise only on the basis of an express treaty obligation.

§5.3 IIA prohibitions on discriminatory measures   In addition to national and MFN treatment provisions, some IIAs contain a general prohibition on discriminatory measures. Other IIAs have no express national and MFN treatment provisions and only contain a general prohibition against discriminatory measures. In both cases, IIAs usually do not clarify the content, extent or meaning of a general prohibition against discriminatory measures. IIA tribunals have, however, held that discriminatory measures include those 'directed specifically against a certain investor by reason of his, her or its nationality.'[6] Non-discrimination as an element of minimum standards of treatment is considered below at Chapter 6, §6.10. Non-discrimination as a specific requirement for a legal expropriation is considered below at Chapter 7, §7.33.

§5.4 Overview of the issues covered in this chapter   This chapter is divided into five parts. Part I covers the background and evolution of MFN clauses. IIA treaty practice is covered in Part II. Part III turns to the scope of the MFN clause and examines whether MFN treatment extends to investor-state arbitration procedures. Part IV considers the application of MFN treatment. Part V addresses exceptions and reservations to MFN treatment.

Protection Treaties: United Kingdom Experience' (1987) 36 ICLQ 910 at 911. For the view that, in the IIA context, national and MFN treatment are not customary international law obligations, see arbitrator Asante's dissenting opinion in *Asian Agricultural Products Ltd. (AAPL) v. Sri Lanka* (Final Award, 27 Jun. 1990) [*AAPL*] (1991) 30 ILM 577 at 642-643. For authorities and discussion on MFN clauses generally, see R. Jennings & A. Watts, eds, *Oppenheim's International Law*, 9th edn (London: Longman, 1992) at 669.

5.   This view was generally rejected before WWI. It gained favour amongst some Eastern European scholars during the 1950's. For discussion of this issue see J. Hazard, 'Commercial Discrimination and International Law' (1958) 52 AJIL 495 and G. Schwarzenberger, 'Equality and Discrimination in International Economic Law (I)' (1971) 25 YBWA 162 at 164-165.
6.   *Noble Ventures, Inc. v. Romania* (Award, 12 Oct. 2005) at para. 180.

I   BACKGROUND ON MFN TREATMENT IN IIAS

§5.5 MFN treatment – principle and definition   MFN treatment provisions in IIAs prohibit host states from discriminating amongst foreigners or foreign investment of different nationalities.[7] In the *Case Concerning Rights of Nationals of the United States of America in Morocco*, the International Court of Justice (ICJ) stated that the purpose of the MFN clauses at bar was 'to establish and to maintain at all times fundamental equality without discrimination among all of the countries concerned.'[8]

States have traditionally used MFN clauses in trade treaties to ensure that they obtain any advantages, privileges and concessions that the granting state has accorded or accords in the future to third states. As noted by Georg Schwarzenberger, the overall effect of an MFN treaty regime is that 'anybody's advantage accrues to everybody's profit':

> Assuming that States are prepared to exchange a condition of unceasing vigilance and never-ending uneasiness for the safer and more dignified position in which anybody's advantage accrues to everybody's profit, the standard of MFN treatment is the very means to this end. It generalizes automatically the advantages granted by one state to any other included in the MFN arrangement. Thus its main function consists in forming an agency of equality. It prevents discrimination and establishes equality of opportunity on the highest possible plane: the minimum of discrimination and the maximum of favours conceded to any third State. . . . It is clear that MFN clauses serve as insurance against incompetent draftsmanship and lack of imagination on the part of those who are responsible for the conclusion of international treaties.[9]

As noted by Schwarzenberger, in addition to minimizing discrimination, an MFN clause also acts as an insurance policy against oversights and errors in treaty drafting and changing conditions. If the state granting MFN treatment provides more favourable treatment to a third state in the future and that treatment is within the scope of the MFN clause, the beneficiaries of an MFN clause will obtain the advantage of that treatment. An added benefit of the MFN clause is that it allows less powerful states to obtain the benefits and advantages that more powerful states might be able to obtain in treaty negotiations.

---

7.   IIA MFN clauses differ in whether they cover investment, investors or both. See *infra* §5.15.
8.   *Case Concerning Rights of Nationals of the United States of America in Morocco (France v. US)* (1952) ICJ Rep 176 [*Rights of US Nationals in Morocco*] at 192. Also see J. Kurtz, 'The MFN Standard and Foreign Investment: An Uneasy Fit?' (2004) 5 JWIT 861 [Uneasy Fit] for a discussion that contrasts the role MFN plays in tariff discrimination under international trade law with its application in the context of IIAs.
9.   G. Schwarzenberger, 'The Most-Favoured Nation Standard in British State Practice' (1945) 22 BYIL 96 at 99-100.

The International Law Commission's (ILC) definition of MFN treatment in its *Draft Articles on Most-Favoured-Nation Clauses* provides a useful starting point for analysis of the concept:

> Most-favoured-nation treatment is treatment accorded by the granting State to the beneficiary State, or to persons or things in a determined relationship with that State, not less favourable than treatment extended by the granting State to a third State or to persons or things in the same relationship with that third State.[10]

The ILC's definition highlights three elements of MFN treatment. First, MFN treatment prohibits the granting state from discriminating between 'persons or things' of the beneficiary state and a third state. In the IIA context, these persons are 'investors' and the things are 'investments.' Second, MFN treatment applies where the comparators (the investors or investments) from the beneficiary and third state are in the same relationship with the granting state. In other words, they must be in like circumstances. Third, the investor or investment from the beneficiary state (the home state) is to receive no less favourable treatment than the treatment the granting state (the host state) provides to the investor or investment from the third state.

The ILC's definition reflects the basic structure and legal effect of MFN clauses as elaborated by the ICJ. In *Anglo-Iranian Oil Co.*,[11] the ICJ referred to the treaty between the granting and beneficiary states containing the MFN clause as the 'basic treaty.'[12] The basic treaty establishes the juridical link between the beneficiary state and the third-party treaty and confers the rights enjoyed by the third party on the beneficiary state. Absent the MFN clause, the third-party treaty 'independent of and isolated from the basic treaty, cannot produce any legal effect as between . . . [the beneficiary state] . . . and . . . [the granting state]: it is *res inter alios acta.*'[13]

In IIAs, MFN clauses provide that foreign investors and investments are entitled to the same or no less favourable treatment than the host state provides to foreign investors and investments from third-party states.[14] Thus, in IIA claims, the issue is whether the host state (the granting state) has provided less favourable treatment to investments or investors of the home state (the beneficiary state) than it has accorded to investments or investors from a third state. This gives rise to two questions of application: whether the investments or investors in question are comparable ('in the same relationship') and whether there has been less favourable treatment.[15]

---

10.   Art. 5, *Draft MFN Articles, supra* note 4.
11.   *Anglo-Iranian Oil Co. Case (UK v. Iran)* (1952) ICJ Rep 93 [*Anglo-Iranian Oil*].
12.   *Ibid.*, at 109.
13.   *Ibid.*, at 109. In *Anglo-Iranian Oil*, the ICJ did not consider the meaning and scope of the MFN clause at issue because it held that it did not have jurisdiction to hear the merits of the case. On this point, see *Siemens A.G. v. Argentina* (Decision on Jurisdiction, 3 Aug. 2004) at para. 96 [*Siemens*].
14.   MFN clauses vary in whether they afford protection to investors, investments or to both. See *infra* §5.15 regarding the significance of different treaty formulations.
15.   See Part IV, *infra.*

There is, however, a crucial threshold question to be addressed before applying MFN treatment, namely, what is the subject matter of the MFN clause – to what does the clause apply? The ILC's *Draft MFN Articles* highlights that the beneficiary of the MFN clause acquires 'only those rights which fall within the limits of the subject matter of the clause.'[16] In IIA cases, there has been significant disagreement about the subject matter of particular MFN clauses and, in particular, whether the subject matter of the MFN clause in question applies to dispute settlement.[17]

An MFN clause in a basic treaty does not technically incorporate by reference the provisions of the third-party treaty. As noted by the ICJ in *Anglo-Iranian Oil Co.*,[18] the MFN clause confers the rights enjoyed by the third party on the beneficiary. The MFN clause can confer no benefit if the third party's rights come to an end, for example, where the third-party treaty has been terminated.[19] In other words, an MFN clause does not, as soon as it becomes applicable, crystallize or incorporate by reference the more favourable treatment afforded by a third-party treaty. Access to more favourable treatment is available only so long as the third party is able to obtain the advantage in question.[20] As observed by the tribunal in *Siemens A.G. v. Argentina*, the '[b]enefits available due to an MFN clause last as long as the treaty that grants them is in effect, but they do not become incorporated into the treaty containing the MFN clause.'[21]

Since an MFN clause permits an investor or investment to claim the benefits that a state affords to investors or investments from third-party states, the MFN clause multilateralizes investment protections by creating an 'integrated network'[22] of IIAs. Commentators, respondent states and tribunals have raised concerns that a broad interpretation of MFN clauses will give rise to expansive treaty rights never intended by the state parties.[23] One concern is that MFN clauses have the potential

---

16. Art. 9, *Draft MFN Articles, supra* note 4.
17. See Part III, *infra.*
18. *Anglo-Iranian Oil, supra* note 11.
19. It should be noted that under most IIAs, treaty obligations continue to exist after treaty termination. For example, Art. 13(3), Czechoslovakia-Netherlands (1991), provides: 'In respect of investments made before the date of the termination of the present Agreement the foregoing Articles thereof shall continue to be effective for a further period of fifteen years from that date.'
20. In *Rights of US Nationals in Morocco, supra* note 8, the US claimed that MFN provisions provided it the benefits of British and Spanish treaty provisions providing for consular jurisdiction in all cases involving their nationals. However, since the UK and Spain had renounced their capitulatory rights, the US could not claim such rights. See *Siemens, supra* note 13 at paras 98-99. For a more nuanced discussion of the arguments in *Rights of US Nationals in Morocco*, see M. Paparinskis, 'MFN Clauses in Investment Arbitration Between *Maffezini* and *Plama*: The Third Way?' ICSID Rev, forthcoming (manuscript on file with authors).
21. *Siemens, supra* note 13 at para. 99.
22. F. Orrego Vicuña, 'Bilateral Investment Treaties and the Most-Favored-Nation-Clause: Implications for Arbitration in the Light of a Recent ICSID Case' Paper delivered at ASA Swiss Arbitration Association Conference: Investment Treaties and Arbitration, 25 Jan. 2002.
23. For commentary on cases dealing with MFN treatment see Orrego Vicuña, *ibid.*; Kurtz, 'Uneasy Fit,' *supra* note 8; R. Dolzer & T. Myers, 'After *Tecmed*: Most-Favored-Nation

to accord treaty rights without the corresponding limitations or exceptions that apply in the basic treaty. On the other hand, IIA claimants and commentators have argued that the very purpose of MFN clauses is to ensure that the favourable treatment afforded by other IIAs is extended without discrimination. The claim is made that the purpose of IIA MFN clauses is to ensure, as Georg Schwarzenberger argued over fifty years ago, 'the minimum of discrimination and the maximum of favours conceded to any third State.'[24] This debate has played out in several IIA awards, beginning with *Emilio Agustin Maffezini v. Spain*,[25] and led to significant developments in treaty practice and IIA jurisprudence on MFN treatment.

§5.6 Historical background and forms of MFN   MFN clauses have a long history that can be traced back to at least the eleventh century.[26] A reciprocal form of

---

Clauses in Investment Protection Agreements' (2004) 19 ICSID Rev 49: 49; E. Gaillard, 'Establishing Jurisdiction Through a Most-Favoured-Nation Clause' 233 NYLJ 105 (2 Jun. 2005); B. Appleton, 'MFN and International Investment Treaty Arbitration: Have We Lost Sight of the Forest Through the Trees?' (2005) 1 Appleton's International Investment Law & Arbitration News 10; S. Fietta, 'Most Favoured Nation Treatment and Dispute Resolution under Bilateral Investment Treaties' (2005) 8 IALR 131; R. Teitelbaum, 'Who's Afraid of *Maffezini*? Recent Developments in the Interpretation of Most Favored Nation Clauses' (2005) 22 JIA 225; D.H. Freyer & D. Herlihy, 'Most-Favored-Nation Treatment and Dispute Settlement in Investment Arbitration: Just How "Favored" is "Most-Favored"?' (2005) 20 ICSID Rev 58; L. Hsu, 'MFN and Dispute Settlement: When the Twain Meet' (2006) 6 JWIT 25; N. Gallus, '*Plama v. Bulgaria* and The Scope of Investment Treaty MFN Clauses' (2005) TDM; B. Poulain, 'Clauses de la nation la plus favorisée et clauses d'arbitrage investisseur-Etat: est-ce la fin de la jurisprudence Maffezini?' (2007) 25 ASA Bulletin 279; S. Vesel, 'Clearing a Path Through a Tangled Jurisprudence: Most-Favoured-Nation Clauses and Dispute Settlement Provisions in Bilateral Investment Treaties' (2007) 32 YJIL 125; C. Crépet Daigremont, 'Traitement national et traitement de la nation la plus favorisée dans la jurisprudence arbitrale récente relative à l'investissement international' in Ch. Leben, ed., *Le contentieux arbitral transnational relatif à l'investissement* (Anthemis, 2006) at 107; Y. Radi, 'Application of the Most-Favoured-Nation Clause to the Dispute Settlement Provisions of Bilateral Investment Treaties' (2007) 18 EJIL 757; W. Ben Hamida, 'Clause de la nation la plus favorisée et mécanismes de réglement des différends: que dit l'histoire' (2007) 134 JDI 1127; N. Rubins, 'MFN Clauses, Procedural Rights, and a Return to the Treaty Text' in T. Weiler, ed., *Emerging Issues in International Investment Law*, (New York: Juris, 2008); P. Acconci, 'The Most-Favoured-Nation Treatment and International Law on Foreign Investment,' in P. Muchlinski, F. Ortino & C. Schreuer, eds, *The Oxford Handbook of International Investment Law*, (Oxford: Oxford University Press, 2008); A.F. Rodriguez, 'The Most-Favoured-Nation Clause in *international investment agreements*: A Tool for Treaty Shopping?' (2008) 25 JIA 89 and Paparinskis, *supra* note 20.

24.   *Supra* note 8.
25.   (Decision of the Tribunal on Objections to Jurisdiction, 25 Jan. 2000) [*Maffezini*]. See Part III for a discussion of *Maffezini* and subsequent awards on the scope of MFN treatment.
26.   P. Verloren van Themaat, *The Changing Structure of International Economic Law* (The Hague: Martinus Nijhoff, 1981) at 19-21 and G. Schwarzenberger, 'The Principle and Standards of International Economic Law' (1966) 117 RDCADI 1 at 19. For a general history of MFN clauses in international treaties, S.K. Hornbeck, 'The Most-Favoured-Nation Clause' (1909) 3 AJIL 395; B. Nolde, 'La Clause de la Nation la Plus Favorisé et les Tarifs Preferentiels' (1932) 39 RDCADI 1; 'Most-Favoured-Nation Clause' by Special Rapporteur Mr Endre Ustor

an MFN clause appears in a treaty dated 17 August 1417 between England and Burgundy under which each party's vessels were granted the right to use harbours in the same way as certain specified nations. The use of MFN clauses increased in the fifteenth and sixteenth centuries with commercial expansion. By the eighteenth and nineteenth centuries MFN clauses had become common in commercial treaties and most MFN clauses provided the benefit of the favourable treatment of any third state, rather than a limited number of named states.

The increasing treaty practice gave rise to variations in MFN clauses and, in particular, between conditional and unconditional forms of MFN treatment.[27] Under a conditional MFN clause, if the granting state provides a benefit to a third state and has received a concession in return, the beneficiary state only obtains the same benefit upon providing a corresponding concession.[28] On the other hand, an MFN clause in its unconditional form provides that advantages extended to third states are automatically extended to the beneficiary state as a right and are not subject to corresponding concessions. The Cobden Treaty of 1860 between England and France served to popularize the unconditional form of the MFN clause championed by early free trade advocates.

Although early MFN clauses came in the form of unilateral grants,[29] modern MFN clauses are typically reciprocal: each state party is both a granting and beneficiary state. One of the best-known modern examples of a reciprocal and unconditional MFN clause is found in Article I(1) of the 1947 *General Agreement on Tariffs and Trade* (GATT),[30] which provides that:

> . . . any advantage, favour, privilege or immunity granted by any contracting party to any product originating in or destined for any other country shall be accorded immediately and unconditionally to the like product originating in or destined for the territories of all other contracting parties.

The GATT MFN clause served to multilateralize tariff and trade concessions between GATT Contracting Members and is considered one of the cornerstones of the international trading system.[31]

As noted in the historical background to national treatment, various formulations of the non-discrimination principle were included in initiatives to create an international legal framework for investment.[32] The draft *Convention on the*

(UN Doc. A/CN.4/213) YBILC 1969, Vol. 2, at 157-186 [Ustor ILC's Report]; Schwarzenberger, *supra* note 9, and *Oppenheim's International Law, supra* note 4 at 669.

27. See Ustor ILC's Report, *ibid.*, at 161.
28. A form of conditional MFN treatment was used by European states between 1830 and 1860 and by the United States until 1923. See Ustor ILC's Report, *ibid.*, at 161 *et seq*. On early US practice, see E.J. Conroy, 'The American Interpretation of the Most Favored Nation Clause' (1926-1927) 12 CLQ 327.
29. Ustor ILC's Report, *ibid.*, at 159.
30. Art. I(1), *General Agreement on Tariffs and Trade*, 30 Oct. 1947, 55 UNTS 194.
31. See M. Trebilcock & R. Howse, *The Regulation of International Trade*, 3rd edn (London: Routledge, 2005).
32. See *supra* Chapter 4, §4.7.

Treatment of Foreigners (1929 Draft Convention) considered at the 1929 Paris International Conference on the Treatment of Foreign Nationals (Paris Conference), although focused on guaranteeing wide-ranging national treatment rights, would have also provided for an 'unconditional granting of MFN treatment,' subject to a number of exceptions including one for bilateral agreements for the avoidance of double taxation.[33] The International Chamber of Commerce's 1948 *International Code of Fair Treatment for Foreign Investment* also included an MFN treatment provision.[34] The 1959 Abs-Shawcross Draft Convention and 1967 Organization for Economic Co-operation and Development (OECD) Draft Convention refer to 'discrimination' generally without specifically providing for national or MFN treatment.[35] In addition, early Friendship, Commerce and Navigation (FCN) Treaties included MFN clauses.[36]

The ILC began to study MFN clauses in the late 1967 and adopted final draft articles in 1978, which it submitted to the General Assembly with a recommendation that an international convention be signed on the subject.[37] The diversity of MFN clauses and practice, however, made codification in any one form a controversial issue. The General Assembly did not take any substantive action to adopt the ILC's draft articles,[38] due in part to criticism of the draft.[39]

---

33. Arts 17 and 18, 1929 Draft Convention. See *supra* Chapter 1, §1.10, and Chapter 4, §4.7, for background and references to the 1929 Draft Convention.
34. Art. 4, *ICC International Code of Fair Treatment for Foreign Investment.* See *supra* Chapter 1, §1.16, for discussion of the ICC Code.
35. See *supra* Chapter 4, §4.7.
36. See *supra* Chapter 1, §1.17, on FCN Treaties.
37. The ILC's reports provide useful analyses of MFN treatment. See Ustor ILC's Report, *supra* note 28; 'Report on the most-favoured-nation clause' by Special Rapporteur Mr Nikolai Ushakov (UN Doc. A/CN.4/309 and ADD.1 and 2) YBILC 1978, Vol. 2, pt 1, 1-30 and 'Report of the International Law Commission on the work of its thirtieth session 8 May – 28 Jul. 1978' (UN doc. A/33/10) (1978) YBILC, Vol. II(2), 1-73 [ILC's MFN Report]. The draft articles are available online on the ILC's website. The ILC considered the draft articles to be both a codification and progressive development of international law (ILC's MFN Report, *ibid.*, at para. 72).
38. See *Oppenheim's International Law, supra* note 4 at 30, note 43, referring to GA Res. 33/139 (1978), 35/161 (1980), 36/111 (1981) and 40/65 (1985), and Decision 43/429 (1988).
39. See Doc. A/CN.4/308 ('Comments of Member States, organs of the United Nations, specialized agencies and other intergovernmental organizations on the draft articles on the most-favoured-nation clause adopted by the International Law Commission at its twenty-eighth session') in (1978) YBILC, Vol. II(2) 161.

II TREATY PRACTICE

§5.7 General overview of treaty practice[40] Although express MFN treatment obligations appear in almost all IIAs, there is significant variation in how specific provisions are drafted. As discussed in the previous chapter on national treatment, MFN and national treatment often appear in the same clause and a number of common issues arise with respect to the interpretations of the two obligations.[41] In particular, MFN and national treatment clauses often vary in whether they: (i) apply to establishment;[42] (ii) apply to both investors and investments; (iii) specify the activities to which the obligations apply; and (iv) contain an express comparator such as 'in like circumstances'.

In most IIAs, national and MFN treatment are combined in one provision. Article 4(2), Chile-Egypt (1999), is representative in this regard:

> Each Contracting Party shall accord investments of the investors of other Contracting Party in its territory a treatment which is no less favourable than that accorded to investments made by its own investors or by investors of any third country, whichever is more favourable.[43]

Early US BITs follow the model of combining national and MFN treatment in one provision. Article II(1), Ecuador-US (1993), provides:

> Each Party shall permit and treat investment, and activities associated therewith, on a basis no less favorable than that accorded in like situations to investment or associated activities of its own nationals or companies, or of nationals or companies of any third country, whichever is the most favorable, subject to the right of each Party to make or maintain exceptions falling within one of the sectors or matters listed in the Protocol to this Treaty.

For the purposes of MFN treatment, three elements distinguish this early 1990s US BIT from the Chile-Egypt BIT. The US BIT provides establishment rights by specifying that each party 'shall permit' investment. It also provides an express basis for comparing investments by including the term in like situations.[44] Finally,

---

40. For an overview of treaty practice, see UNCTAD's three comprehensive studies: United Nations Centre on Transnational Corporations (UNCTC), *Bilateral Investment Treaties* (New York: United Nations, 1988) (Doc. No. ST/CTC/65); UNCTAD, *Bilateral Investment Treaties in the Mid-1990s* (New York and Geneva: United Nations, 1998) (Doc. No. UNCTAD/ITE/IIT/7) and UNCTAD, *Bilateral Investment Treaties 1995-2006* (New York and Geneva: United Nations, 2007) (Doc. No. UNCTAD/ITE/IIT/2006/5) [together *UNCTAD BIT Studies*]. Also see UNCTAD, *Most-Favoured Nation Treatment, supra* note 3; and R. Dolzer & M. Stevens, *Bilateral Investment Treaties* (The Hague: Martinus Nijhoff Publishers, 1995).
41. See *supra* Chapter 4, §4.8.
42. See *supra* Chapter 4, §4.8 and Chapter 3.
43. Also see Art. 4(1), India-Ghana (2000), and Art. III(2), Cuba-Lebanon (1995).
44. See other contemporaneous US BITs, for example, Art. II(1), Argentina-US (1991), and Art. II(1), Romania-US (1992).

as is common for IIAs that provide for establishment rights, the US BIT excludes certain economic sectors or measures from non-discrimination obligations.[45]

Article IV, Philippines-Switzerland (1997), provides another model, where national and MFN treatment extend to both investments and investors, but the clause covers investment and investors in different parts. Further, with respect to investors, the provision enumerates a series of investment activities to which the standard of treatment applies:

> 2. Each Contracting Party shall in its territory accord investments or returns of investors of the other Contracting Party treatment not less favourable than that which it accords to investments or returns of its own investors or to investments or returns of investors of any third State, whichever is more favourable to the investor concerned.

> 3. Each Contracting Party shall in its territory accord investors of the other Contracting Party with respect to the management, maintenance, use, enjoyment or disposal of their investments, treatment not less favourable than that which it accords to its own investors or investors of any third State, whichever is more favourable to the investor concerned.[46]

US-Uruguay (2005) reflects the approach in the 2004 Model US BIT, and like *North American Free Trade Agreement* (NAFTA) Chapter Eleven, has separate national and MFN treatment clauses:[47]

> Article 4: Most-Favoured-Nation Treatment

> 1. Each Party shall accord to investors of the other Party treatment no less favorable than that it accords, in like circumstances, to investors of any non-Party with respect to the establishment, acquisition, expansion, management, conduct, operation, and sale or other disposition of investments in its territory.
> 2. Each Party shall accord to covered investments treatment no less favorable than that it accords, in like circumstances, to investments in its territory of investors of any non-Party with respect to the establishment, acquisition, expansion, management, conduct, operation, and sale or other disposition of investments.

A comparison of the Chile-Egypt and the US-Uruguay BITs highlight five salient differences between the provisions. Unlike the Chile-Egypt BIT, the US-Uruguay BIT's national and MFN treatment provisions are: (i) in separate clauses; (ii) expressly

---

45. See *supra* Chapter 3, §3.13.
46. Authors' translation.
47. See M. Kinnear, A. K. Bjorklund & J. Hannaford, *Investment Disputes under NAFTA: An Annotated Guide to NAFTA Chapter 11*, (The Netherlands: Kluwer Law International, 2006) at 1103 for an in-depth discussion of Art. 1103, NAFTA.

apply to both investors and investments;[48] (iii) apply to establishment;[49] (iv) specify a range of activities to which the provisions apply; and (v) provide an express comparator.[50] The significance of these differences is discussed below.

Some IIAs expressly apply MFN treatment to specific investment obligations. This is common with respect to returns[51] and compensation for losses.[52] For example, Article IV(3), Argentina-US (1991), provides:

> Nationals or companies of either Party whose investments suffer losses in the territory of the other Party owing to war or other armed conflict, revolution, state of national emergency, insurrection, civil disturbance or other similar events shall be accorded treatment by such other Party no less favorable than that accorded to its own nationals or companies or to nationals or companies of any third country, whichever is the more favorable treatment, as regards any measures it adopts in relation to such losses.

As discussed at §5.16 below, as a result of developments in IIA jurisprudence, some states have expressly provided that MFN treatment does not apply to dispute settlement provisions.

§5.8 Meaning of treatment   IIAs do not define the term treatment. Treatment is a broad term that the Oxford English Dictionary defines as '[c]onduct, behaviour; action or behaviour towards a person.' In *Siemens*, the tribunal stated that 'treatment' ordinarily means 'behaviour in respect of an entity or a person.'[53]

In *Canfor*, the claimants drew a distinction between conduct and treatment, not adopted in the tribunal's decision, arguing that conduct is what officials do and treatment is the manner in which the officials direct conduct to a specific investor or claimant.[54] This distinction is potentially misleading because it suggests that the state must 'direct' conduct to a specific investor, which might imply either a requirement of specificity or intent. The better view is that conduct consists of an action or omission,[55] whereas treatment refers to the effect or result of the conduct

---

48. See *infra* §5.15.
49. See *infra* §5.14.
50. See *infra* §5.19.
51. This is common in UK BITs.
52. See *infra* Chapter 6, §6.47.
53. *Siemens, supra* note 13 at para. 85. Also see *Suez, Sociedad General de Aguas de Barcelona S.A., and InterAgua Servicios Integrales del Agua S.A. v. Argentina* (Decision on Jurisdiction, 16 May 2006) at para. 55: 'The word 'treatment' is not defined in the treaty text. However, the ordinary meaning of that term within the context of investment includes the rights and privileges granted and the obligations and burdens imposed by a Contracting State on investments made by investors covered by the treaty.'
54. *Canfor Corporation v. United States and Terminal Forest Products Ltd. v. United States* (Consolidated Proceedings) (Decision on Preliminary Question, 6 Jun. 2006) at para. 150.
55. State conduct constituting an international wrong may be either an action or omission: 'There is an internationally wrongful act of a State when conduct consisting of an action or omission: (a) Is attributable to the State under international law; and (b) Constitutes a breach of an international obligation of the State. Art. 2, ILC's Articles on State Responsibility: 'Responsibility of States

on the investment or investor in question. Treatment can be further contrasted with
the term *measures*, which focuses on the state conduct in question.

III   THE SCOPE OF MFN TREATMENT

§5.9 The subject matter of MFN treatment   MFN treatment applies to the
subject matters to which the MFN clause applies. MFN clauses in IIAs typically
provide that the investments of investors of one state are to receive treatment
which is not less favourable than that accorded to investments by investors of third
states.[56] What remains unclear in most IIA texts is whether MFN clauses confer
rights under investor-state arbitration clauses in other IIAs and, if so, to what
extent.

The starting point for analysis is the subject matter of the MFN clause. Since
the basic treaty between the host and home state contains the MFN clause, the
beneficiary's rights are determined by the clause's subject matter. This is a reflection of the *ejusdem generis* principle – literally 'of the same kind or class,' a
general rule of treaty interpretation that limits the scope of a term in a treaty to
the same genus or category.[57] The principle is also reflected in the ILC's *Draft
MFN Articles*, which provide that:

> Under a most-favoured-nation clause the beneficiary State acquires, for itself
> or for the benefit of persons or things in a determined relationship with it, only
> those rights which fall within the limits of the subject-matter of the clause.[58]

This principle, like many general principles, is easy to state and difficult to
apply because the scope of the subject matter of IIA MFN clauses are open to
varying interpretations. Further, it is difficult to generalize as MFN clauses vary
substantially.[59] Arnold McNair's statement that 'speaking strictly, there is no

---

for Internationally Wrongful Acts,' in *Official Records of the General Assembly,* UN GAOR, 56th
Sess., Supp. No. 10, UN Doc A/56/10, at 11, *reprinted in* J. Crawford, *The International Law
Commission's Articles on State Responsibility: Introduction, Text, and Commentaries* (Cambridge:
Cambridge University Press, 2002) [ILC's Articles on State Responsibility].

56. See Art. 3(1), Bulgaria-Cyprus, considered in *Plama v. Bulgaria, infra* note 98, which
     provides: 'Each Contracting Party shall apply to the investments in its territory by investors of
     the other Contracting Party a treatment which is not less favourable than that accorded to
     investments by investors of third states.'

57. See OECD, *Working Papers on International Investment Law*, Most-Favoured-Nation Treatment
     in International Investment Law, *supra* note 4 at Section 3.2 for a discussion of the *ejusdem
     generis* principle. This use of *ejusdem generis* should be distinguished from its meaning in
     some domestic systems, where it applies as a rule of interpretation when several words precede
     a general word. Under the rule, the meaning of the general word is governed by the preceding
     words and the meaning of the general word is not to be expanded beyond the subjects or classes
     of the preceding words. On the use of the term, see M. Paparinskis, *supra* note 20. See also
     supra Chapter 2, §2.28.

58. Art. 9(1), ILC's *Draft MFN Articles, supra* note 4.

59. For example, Art. 3(2) China-Romania (1994), provides that MFN treatment applies only to
     the fair and equitable treatment guarantee. In contrast, the UK model BIT provides expressly

such thing as the MFN clause: every treaty requires independent examination'[60] is as true for MFN clauses in IIAs as in other treaties. As a result it is difficult to make generalizations about MFN clauses.

For the purposes of analyzing the scope of IIA MFN clauses, it is useful to identify four different models: (i) clauses that expressly apply to dispute settlement;[61] (ii) clauses that refer broadly to 'treatment' without any specific reference to dispute settlement; (iii) clauses that refer to treatment in the context of certain activities (establishment, maintenance, etc.); and (iv) clauses that expressly exclude dispute settlement.[62] Most IIA MFN clauses follow models (ii) and (iii) and do not expressly state whether dispute settlement comes within the scope of the clause.

§5.10 Does MFN treatment apply to investor-state arbitration clauses?   The contrasting IIA jurisprudence on whether MFN treatment applies to investor-state arbitration provisions highlights the difficulty of applying the *ejusdem generis* principle in the context of MFN clauses. In a series of cases, IIA tribunals have given conflicting answers to this question. Although some of the differences in result might be explained by variations in the drafting of the clauses, a comparison of the reasoning in the various decisions and awards highlights that tribunals have approached the interpretation of MFN clauses in very different ways. Some tribunals have operated from a presumption that the MFN clause applies to dispute settlement unless the IIA expressly excludes its application, whereas others have applied the opposite presumption. The present analysis begins with an extended description of *Emilio Agustín Maffezini v. Spain*, the first IIA award to address the issue, followed by a discussion of the subsequent cases.[63]

In *Maffezini v. Spain*, an Argentine investor submitted an investor-state arbitration claim against Spain under Article X, Argentina-Spain (1991), which required that disputes be submitted to local courts for a period of eighteen months before the investor could commence arbitration.[64] Maffezini did not submit the dispute to local courts and claimed that the MFN clause in Argentina-Spain (1991) accorded him the more favourable procedural treatment in Chile-Spain (1991), which had no corresponding requirement for submission of disputes to the local

---

that MFN applies to dispute settlement. The protocol to Czechoslovakia-Sweden provides that MFN does not apply to national treatment granted under earlier Swedish agreements. See Dolzer & Stevens, *Bilateral Investment Treaties, supra* note 40 at 72.

60. A. McNair, *The Law of Treaties* (New York: Columbia University Press, 1938) at 285, note 1.

61. Only a small number of BITs expressly provide that MFN treatment applies to dispute settlement. See Art. 3(3), UK-Albania (1994); Art. 8(2), Argentina-Korea (1994) and Art. 59 (Note 3), *Japan-Mexico Economic Partnership Agreement* (2004). See *infra* §5.13 on treaty developments resulting from IIA MFN jurisprudence.

62. See S. Vesel, *supra* note 23 at 184-185 for this typology.

63. For commentary on cases dealing with MFN see articles listed, *supra* note 23.

64. Art. X(3) of the Argentina-Spain BIT provides that a dispute may be submitted to international arbitration if no decision of the local court has been rendered on the merits of the claim after the expiration of a period of eighteen months or if a decision has been rendered but the dispute persists.

courts. Relying on the ICJ's reasoning in *Anglo-Iranian Oil Co.*,[65] the tribunal stated that the scope of the MFN clause in the basic treaty between the home and host state governs the extent to which the investor obtains the protections in the third-party treaty. The tribunal therefore turned to the MFN provision in the basic treaty, Argentina-Spain (1991), which provides that:

> *In all matters subject to this Agreement*, this treatment shall be no less favorable than that extended by each Party to the investments made in its territory by investors of a third country.[66] [Emphasis added.]

Thus, the question before the tribunal was whether the subject matter of the MFN clause in the basic treaty (Argentina-Spain (1991)) encompassed the more favourable treatment accorded by the investor-state arbitration provisions of the third-party treaty (Chile-Spain (1991)).

To answer this question, the tribunal drew on the analysis in *Ambatielos*.[67] In *Ambatielos*, Greece claimed that by virtue of the MFN clause in Article X of the 1886 Anglo-Greek *Treaty of Commerce and Navigation*, Ambatielos, a Greek shipowner, was entitled to claim certain guarantees with respect to the administration of justice that the UK had accorded to nationals of other states in later treaties.[68] In response, the UK argued that MFN obligations could only apply to matters belonging to the same subject matter as the basic treaty. According to the UK, since Article X related only to 'commerce and navigation,' protections afforded to nationals of other states with respect to the administration of justice fell outside the subject matter scope of the MFN clause. Although the Commission of Arbitration agreed that 'The MFN clause can only attract matters belonging to the same category of subject as that to which the clause itself relates,'[69] the Commission stated that administration of justice related to commerce and navigation because both involve the rights of traders:

> It is true that the 'administration of justice,' when viewed in isolation, is a subject-matter other than 'commerce and navigation,' but this is not necessarily so when it is viewed in connection with the protection of the rights of traders. Protection of the rights of traders naturally finds a place among the matters dealt with by treaties of commerce and navigation. Therefore it cannot be said that the administration of justice, in so far as it is concerned with the protection of these rights, must necessarily be excluded from the field of application of

---

65. See *Anglo-Iranian Oil, supra* note 11.
66. Art. 4(2), Argentina-Spain (1991).
67. *The Ambatielos Claim between (Greece, United Kingdom of Great Britain and Northern Ireland)* (Final Award, 6 Mar. 1956)), (1963) XII UNRIAA 91 [*Ambatielos Claim*].
68. Article X provided: 'The Contracting Parties agree that, in all matters relating to *commerce and navigation*, any privilege, favour, or immunity whatever which either Contracting Party has actually granted or may hereafter grant to the subjects or citizens of any other state shall be extended immediately and unconditionally to the subjects or citizens of the other Contracting Party; it being their intention that the trade and navigation of each country shall be placed, in all respects, by the other on the footing of the most favoured nation.' [Emphasis added.]
69. *Ambatielos Claim, supra* note 67 at 107.

the most-favored-nation clause, when the latter includes 'all matters relating to commerce and navigation.' The question can only be determined in accordance with the intention of the Contracting Parties as deduced from a reasonable interpretation of the Treaty.[70]

Administration of justice therefore fell within the subject matter of 'commerce and navigation' because commercial rights are ultimately enforced and protected through domestic judicial proceedings.[71]

The *Maffezini* tribunal concluded that even though the Argentina-Spain BIT MFN clause did not specifically refer to dispute resolution, the investor-state arbitration provisions were a fundamentally important aspect of the substantive investment protections. In the view of the tribunal, they were essential to the protection of the treaty rights and were 'closely linked to the material aspects of the treatment accorded.'[72] The tribunal also looked to subsequent Spanish BIT practice which, with one exception, provided for arbitration without prior recourse to local courts. In addition, the tribunal highlighted the exceedingly broad formulation of the MFN clause, which applied to 'all matters subject to this Agreement.'[73] Accordingly, the tribunal concluded that it was fully compatible with the *ejusdem generis* principle for Maffezini to obtain the benefit of the dispute settlement provisions in Chile-Spain (1991) and not be subject to the requirement to submit the dispute to local courts for eighteen months before bringing the claim.[74]

Although it found that procedural advantages under the dispute resolution provisions of the third-party treaty were within the scope of the MFN clause, the *Maffezini* tribunal also stated that:

> As a matter of principle, the beneficiary of the clause should not be able to override public policy considerations that the contracting parties might have envisaged as fundamental conditions for their acceptance of the agreement in question[75]

---

70. *Ibid.*
71. In the prior proceedings before the ICJ regarding whether the matter had to be submitted to arbitration, some of the dissenting judges took the view that the MFN treatment clause only related to matters of commerce and navigation and could not be applied to the administration of justice. See (1953) ICJ Rep 10 at 34. The tribunal in *Salini Costruttori S.p.A. and Italstrade S.p.A. v. Jordan* (Decision on Jurisdiction, 29 Nov. 2004) [*Salini v. Jordan*] distinguished *Ambatielos* on the basis that the MFN clause had been invoked to secure substantive protections (guarantees with respect to administration of justice in local courts), as opposed to procedural provisions such as those relating to the settlement of disputes. Accordingly, it held that the approach used in *Ambatielos* could not be transposed (para. 112). See M. Paparinskis, *supra* note 20, for a discussion of the use of the *Ambatielos Claim* as a precedent in the very different context of investor-state arbitration.
72. *Maffezini, supra* note 25 at para. 55.
73. *Ibid.*, at paras 57-61.
74. See *supra* note 57 on *ejusdem generis*.
75. *Ibid.*, at para. 62. See *Siemens, supra* note 13 at para. 109. In *Siemens*, the tribunal stated that there were no applicable public policy considerations to negate the application of the MFN clause.

The tribunal provided four examples of these fundamental conditions: (i) where consent to arbitration is conditioned on prior exhaustion of local remedies; (ii) there is a fork in the road clause between submission to domestic courts and arbitration and the choice is made final and irreversible; (iii) the treaty provides for a specific forum for arbitration; or (iv) there is a highly institutionalized system of arbitration with precise procedural rules, such as in NAFTA.[76]

The tribunal further noted that:

> ... a distinction has to be made between the legitimate extension of rights and benefits by means of the operation of the clause, on the one hand, and disruptive treaty-shopping that would play havoc with the policy objectives of underlying specific treaty provisions, on the other hand.[77]

The tribunal found that, in the case before it, public policy considerations were not fundamental conditions because Spain had provided a similar right in its subsequent treaties and the right sought was simply the relaxation of a time limit.

Post-*Maffezini* cases addressing the scope of MFN clauses can be divided into two categories. The first line of cases, similar to *Maffezini*, applies MFN clauses to avoid local remedy requirements (submission of the claim to local courts for an eighteen-month period before commencing arbitration). In all these cases, tribunals have applied the MFN clause to allow the investor to take advantage of the more favourable procedural treatment available under the investor-state arbitration provisions of another BIT. The second line of cases raises a different issue. In these cases investors have attempted to rely on the MFN clause as a basis for expanding the scope of a tribunal's subject matter jurisdiction. The two lines of cases are considered below.

§5.11 MFN clauses applied to avoid local remedy requirements   In a series of cases against Argentina subsequent to *Maffezini*, tribunals have found that claimants could rely on MFN clauses to avoid requirements that disputes be submitted to local courts for a period of eighteen months prior to commencing arbitration.[78] These cases provide strong authority for the principle that an MFN treatment

---

76. *Ibid.*, at para. 63.
77. *Ibid.*
78. *Siemens, supra* note 13; *Gas Natural SDG, S.A. v. Argentina* (Decision of the Tribunal on Preliminary Questions on Jurisdiction, 17 Jun. 2005) [*Gas Natural*]; *National Grid Plc. v. Argentina* (20 Jun. 2006); *Suez, Sociedad General de Aguas de Barcelona S.A., and InterAgua Servicios Integrales del Agua S.A. v. Argentina* (Decision on Jurisdiction, 16 May 2006) [*Suez/ InterAgua*]; *Suez, Sociedad General de Aguas de Barcelona S.A., and Vivendi Universal S.A. v. Argentina* (Decision on Jurisdiction, 3 Aug. 2006) [*Suez/Vivendi*] and *AWG Group Ltd. v. Argentina* (Decision on Jurisdiction, 3 Aug. 2006) [*AWG*]. In *BG Group Plc. v. Argentina* (Final Award, 24 Dec. 2007) [*BG*], the tribunal held that the local remedies requirement was inapplicable because Argentina had effectively impeded them through its emergency legislation. As a result, the tribunal found it unnecessary to address the MFN clause (paras 140-157).

clause can be used to avoid a procedural requirement to submit a dispute to domestic courts for a minimum time period.

The MFN clause in four of the cases (*Maffezini, Gas Natural, Suez/InterAgua* and *Suez/Vivendi*[79]) was Article 4(2), Argentina-Spain (1991), which expressly refers to 'all matters':

> In all matters subject to this Agreement, this treatment shall be no less favorable than that extended by each Party to the investments made in its territory by investors of a third country.

The MFN clause considered in *Camuzzi*[80] has a similarly wide application, but covers investors, not investments:

> En todas las materias regidas por el presente Convenio, los inversores de cada Parte Contratante gozarán, en el territorio de la otra Parte, del tratamiento a la nación más favorecida. Este tratamiento no será en ningún caso menos favorable que el reconocido por el derecho internacional.[81]

The MFN clause considered in *Siemens*[82] does not expressly refer to all matters but covers investors and investments:

(1) None of the Contracting Parties shall accord in its territory to the investments of nationals or companies of the other Contracting Party or to investments in which they hold shares, a less favorable treatment than the treatment granted to the investments of its own nationals or companies or to the investments of nationals or companies of third States.

(2) None of the Contracting Parties shall accord in its territory to nationals or companies of the other Contracting Party a less favorable treatment of activities related to investments than granted to its own nationals and companies or to the nationals and companies of third States.[83]

Finally, the MFN clause considered in *AWG* and National Grid does not expressly refer to all matters and, with respect to investors, applies to the management, maintenance, use, enjoyment or disposal of their investments:

(1) Neither Contracting Party shall in its territory subject investments or returns of investors of the other Contracting Party to treatment less favorable than that which it accords to investments or returns of its own investors or to investments or returns of investors of any third state.

(2) Neither Contracting Party shall in its territory subject investors of the other Contracting Party, as regards their management, maintenance, use, enjoyment or disposal of their investments, to treatment less favorable

---

79. *Ibid.*
80. *Camuzzi International S.A. v. Argentina* (Decision of the Arbitral Tribunal on Objections to Jurisdiction, 10 Jun. 2005) [*Camuzzi*]
81. Art. 4(1), Argentina-BLEU (1990).
82. *Supra* note 78.
83. Art. 3, Argentina-Germany (1991).

than that which it accords to its own investors or to investors of any third state.[84]

The decisions in this line of cases highlight several relevant considerations regarding whether claimants may obtain the more favourable treatment under investor-state arbitration provisions in third-party IIAs. Tribunals have found that the absence an express reference to dispute settlement is not determinative in assessing the scope of the MFN clause. Tribunals have emphasized that the term 'treatment' in the MFN clause 'is so general that the Tribunal cannot limit its application except as agreed by the parties.'[85] Tribunals have noted that although IIAs often specifically excluded certain matters from the scope of MFN treatment, including treatment under tax treaties and free trade agreements, IIAs do not typically exclude the resolution of disputes from the scope of the MFN clause.[86] These tribunals have also tended to highlight the importance of investor-state arbitration to the protections granted under IIAs, calling it a 'crucial element – indeed perhaps the most crucial element'[87] of investor protection and an 'integral part'[88] of IIAs. As discussed below, in a second line of cases, tribunals have approached the interpretation of MFN clauses differently.

§5.12 MFN clauses applied to provide subject matter jurisdiction   In the second line of cases, claimants have attempted to rely on MFN clauses as a basis for expanding the scope of a tribunal's subject matter jurisdiction beyond that provided in the basic treaty's investor-state arbitration provisions. In the majority of these cases, tribunals have found that the MFN clause at issue could not be applied to ground jurisdiction beyond that in the basic treaty. Further, these tribunals have disapproved of the *Maffezini* approach in principle or confined it to its particular facts.[89] By contrast, in *RosInvestCo UK Ltd. v. Russia*, the tribunal held that it had jurisdiction on the basis of an MFN clause.

The first of the cases post-*Maffezini* taking a more restrictive view of an MFN clause is *Salini Costruttori S.p.A. and Italstrade S.p.A. v. Jordan.*[90] In this case, the jurisdictional issue was whether a breach of contract claim resulting from a dam construction project in Jordan was within the jurisdiction of a tribunal

---

84.   Art. 3, Argentina-UK (1990). A similar clause was considered in *RosInvestCo UK Ltd. v. Russia* (Award on Jurisdiction, Oct. 2007) [*RosInvestCo*]. See *infra* §5.12
85.   *Siemens, supra* note 13 at para. 106.
86.   *Gas Natural, supra* note 78 at para. 30. See *infra* §5.27 on exceptions to MFN.
87.   *Ibid.*, at para. 29.
88.   See *Suez/InterAgua, supra* note 78 at para. 57 and *Suez/Vivendi, supra* note 78 at para. 59.
89.   See discussion *infra* of *Telenor Mobile Communications A.S. v. Hungary* (Award, 13 Sep. 2006) [*Telenor*]. In *Yaung Chi Oo Trading Pte. Ltd. v. Myanmar* (Award, 31 Mar. 2003), the claimant argued that the MFN clause in the *Framework Agreement on the ASEAN Investment Area* could be used as a basis for attracting investor-state arbitration under the Myanmar-Philippines BIT (1998). At para. 83, the tribunal rejected the claim as having been brought too late in the proceedings and stated that, in any event, the tribunal would not have jurisdiction under any of the BITs entered into by Myanmar in force at the relevant time.
90.   *Supra* note 71.

established under Italy-Jordan (1996). The dam construction contract required the submission of disputes to local courts and Article 9(2) of the BIT provided that where there is an investment contract the dispute resolution provision in the contract applies.[91] Despite these express provisions in the contract and the BIT, the investor argued that, by virtue of the MFN clause in Italy-Jordan (1996),[92] it was entitled to the more favourable treatment under Jordan-US (1997), which it argued provides the right to submit investment disputes to investor-state arbitration regardless of any clause in a contract providing for a different dispute settlement mechanism.[93]

The *Salini v. Jordan* tribunal, although not expressly rejecting *Maffezini*, noted its concern with the *Maffezini* MFN analysis and with the fact that the exceptions identified by the *Maffezini* tribunal are difficult to apply.[94] The tribunal highlighted the importance of ascertaining the common intention of the parties and examining the treaty practice of the states in question. It then distinguished the case from *Maffezini* on three grounds. First, the MFN clause in question did not expressly extend to dispute settlement. Nor, unlike the clause considered in *Maffezini*, did it expressly apply to 'all matters' subject to the BIT.[95] Second, there was no evidence that the common intention of the parties was to extend MFN treatment to dispute settlement. The tribunal noted that the BIT expressly excluded investor-state arbitration under the BIT where there was a dispute settlement provision under an investment contract. Third, no Jordanian or Italian treaty practice was cited to support the claim that MFN treatment extended to dispute settlement.[96] The tribunal concluded that the MFN clause did not apply to dispute

---

91. See Art. 9.2, Italy-Jordan (1996). The investor's primary argument was that the tribunal had jurisdiction because Italy-Jordan (1996) contained an umbrella clause guaranteeing compliance with contractual undertakings and that Art. 9(2) did not apply. This argument was rejected by the tribunal. See *infra* Chapter 9 for a discussion of the jurisprudence on umbrella clause.

92. Art. 3, Italy-Jordan (1996), provides:

    (1) Both Contracting Parties, within the bounds of their own territory, shall grant investments effected by, and the income accruing to, investors of the other Contracting Party, no less favourable treatment than that accorded to investments effected by, and income accruing to, its own nationals or investors of Third States.

    (2) In case, from the legislation of one of the Contracting Parties, or from the international obligations in force or that may come into force in the future for one of the Contracting Parties, should come out a legal framework according to which the investors of the other Contracting Party would be granted a more favourable treatment than the one foreseen in this Agreement, the treatment granted to the investors of such other Parties will apply also for outstanding relationships.

93. Art. IX, Jordan-US (1997).

94. *Salini v. Jordan, supra* note 71 at para. 115.

95. The tribunal noted that some UK BITs expressly extend MFN treatment to dispute settlement. See *supra* note 61.

96. *Salini v. Jordan, supra* note 71 at para. 118.

settlement and that contractual disputes were to be settled in accordance with the procedure set out in the Italy-Jordan (1996) BIT.[97]

The subsequent four cases involved a slightly different MFN issue. In each of these the claimant was confronted by an investor-state arbitration clause that provided limited subject matter jurisdiction. The BITs in question were Soviet era BITs that limited investor-state arbitration to issues related to expropriation. In each case, the claimant relied on an MFN clause to expand the subject matter jurisdiction of the tribunal. This attempt was rejected in three cases (*Plama Consortium Limited v. Bulgaria*;[98] *Telenor Mobile Communications A.S. v. Hungary*[99] and *Vladimir Berschader and Moïse Berschader v. Russia*[100]) and accepted in one (*RosInvestCo UK Ltd. v. Russia*[101]).

In *Plama*, the investor made a claim under both the *Energy Charter Treaty* (ECT) and Bulgaria-Cyprus (1987) relating to an oil refinery project. As the scope of investor-state arbitration in Bulgaria-Cyprus (1987) was limited to determining compensation for expropriation,[102] the investor claimed that the MFN clause in the BIT[103] entitled it to the more favourable investor-state arbitration provisions available in later Bulgarian BITs, which provided for investor-state arbitration on a broader range of investment protection guarantees. Bulgaria objected to this claim on three bases. First, an MFN clause cannot create a basis for jurisdiction where none already exists. Second, the subject matter of the MFN clause in the Bulgaria-Cyprus BIT did not include dispute resolution. Third, echoing the reasoning in the *Maffezini*, the MFN clause could not be used to override fundamental policy considerations reflected in the BIT.[104]

The *Plama* tribunal found that the MFN clause could not be interpreted as providing consent to investor-state arbitration. First, in analyzing the BIT under principles of treaty interpretation, the tribunal found that there were competing interpretations of the MFN clause. The tribunal placed significant emphasis on

---

97. *Ibid.*, at para. 119.
98. *Plama Consortium Limited v. Bulgaria* (Decision on Jurisdiction, 8 Feb. 2005) [*Plama*].
99. *Supra* note 89.
100. *Vladimir Berschader and Moïse Berschader v. Russia* (Award, 21 Apr. 2006) [*Berschader*].
101. *Supra* note 84.
102. Art. 4.1, Bulgaria-Cyprus (1987), provides: 'The legality of the expropriation shall be checked at the request of the concerned investor through the regular administrative and legal procedure of the Contracting Party that had taken the expropriation steps. In cases of dispute with regard to the amount of the compensation, which disputes were not settled in an administrative order, the concerned investor and the legal representatives of the other Contracting Party shall hold consultations for fixing this value. If within three months after the beginning of the consultations no agreement is reached, the amount of the compensation at the request of the concerned investor shall be checked either in a legal regular procedure of the Contracting Party which had taken the measure on expropriation or by an international "Ad Hoc" Arbitration Court.'
103. Art. 3(1), Bulgaria-Cyprus (1987) provides: 'Each Contracting Party shall apply to the investments in its territory by investors of the other Contracting Party a treatment which is not less favourable than that accorded to investments by investors of third states.'
104. *Plama, supra* note 98 at para. 37.

evidence that negotiations between Bulgaria and Cyprus to revise their BIT had failed and these negotiations suggested that the parties did not consider that the MFN clause extended to the dispute settlement provisions in other BITs.[105] Second, drawing on authorities with respect to international arbitral agreements, the tribunal suggested that the intention to incorporate dispute settlement provisions must be 'clearly and unambiguously expressed' and the expression 'with respect to all matters' does not alleviate the doubt about the parties' intentions.[106] The tribunal also raised questions about the practical application of MFN treatment to investor-state arbitration. For example, by what standard would a tribunal determine that arbitration under the International Centre for Settlement of Investment Disputes (ICSID) Arbitration Rules is more or less favourable than one under the United Nations Commission on International Trade Law (UNCITRAL) Arbitration Rules?[107] The tribunal emphasized that there were no precedents for the dispute settlement provisions in one treaty being replaced by the dispute settlement provisions of another.[108] Although the tribunal noted that there were 'exceptional circumstances'[109] in *Maffezini* justifying the result, it disagreed in principle with the *Maffezini* approach to the application of MFN treatment to dispute settlement provisions:

> … the principle with multiple exceptions as stated by the tribunal in the *Maffezini* case should instead be a different principle with one, single exception: an MFN provision in a basic treaty does not incorporate by reference dispute settlement provisions in whole or in part set forth in another treaty, unless the MFN provision in the basic treaty leaves no doubt that the Contracting Parties intended to incorporate them.[110]

In *Telenor Mobile Communications A.S. v. Hungary*,[111] the subject matter of the investor-state arbitration clause in Hungary-Norway (1991) was expressly limited to compensation for expropriation, losses due to armed conflict and repatriation of investments.[112] It did not include claims for breaches of fair and equitable

---

105. *Ibid.*, at para. 195-197.
106. *Ibid.*, at paras 204-205.
107. *Ibid.*, at para. 208.
108. *Ibid.*, at para. 210.
109. The tribunal noted at para. 224: 'The decision in *Maffezini* is perhaps understandable. The case concerned a curious requirement that during the first eighteen months the dispute be tried in the local courts. The present Tribunal sympathizes with a tribunal that attempts to neutralize such a provision that is nonsensical from a practical point of view. However, such exceptional circumstances should not be treated as a statement of general principle guiding future tribunals in other cases where exceptional circumstances are not present.'
110. *Plama, supra* note 98 at para. 223.
111. *Telenor, supra* note 89.
112. Art. XI, Hungary-Norway (1991), provides: 'This Article shall apply to any legal disputes between an Investor of one Contracting Party and the other Contracting Party in relation to an investment of the former either concerning the amount or payment of compensation under Article V [Compensation for Losses] and VI [Expropriation and Compensation] of the present Agreement, or concerning any other matter consequential upon an act of expropriation in

treatment. Telenor relied on the MFN clause[113] in Hungary-Norway (1991) to argue that it could avail itself of the wider arbitration clause in other Hungarian BITs. The tribunal in *Telenor*, following *Plama*, rejected this contention (and implicitly the *Maffezini* line of reasoning) in very strong terms:

> In the absence of language or context to suggest the contrary, the ordinary meaning of 'investments shall be accorded treatment no less favourable than that accorded to investments made by investors of any third state' is that the investor's *substantive* rights in respect of the investments are to be treated no less favourably than under a BIT between the host State and a third State, and there is no warrant for construing the above phrase as importing *procedural* rights as well.[114]

The tribunal stated that where consent to arbitration is limited to specific categories of disputes, the state has made its intention clear and the jurisdiction of the tribunal is to be limited and not inferentially extended by an MFN clause.[115]

In the third case, *Berschader*,[116] the investor claimed under BLEU-USSR (1989), which limited investor-state arbitration to the amount or mode of compensation for expropriation. The investor relied on the MFN clause, which accorded MFN treatment to investors 'on all matters covered by the present Treaty'[117] and argued that it benefited from the broader scope of investor-state arbitration in Denmark-Russia (1993). The tribunal agreed with the *Plama* tribunal that particular care must be exercised in finding an arbitration agreement based on incorporation by reference in an MFN clause.[118] The tribunal then stated that for an MFN clause to have this effect, the terms of the BIT must be clear and unambiguous.[119] Even though the MFN clause expressly applied to 'all matters covered by the present Treaty,' the tribunal found that since MFN treatment was in principle inapplicable to certain obligations (including state to state dispute settlement), the term

---

accordance with Article VI of the present Agreement or concerning the consequences of the non-implementation or of the incorrect implementation of Article VII [Repatriation of Investments] of the present agreement.'

113. Art. IV(1) provides: 'Investments made by Investors of one Contracting Party in the territory of the other Contracting Party, as also the returns therefrom, shall be accorded treatment no less favourable than that accorded to investments made by Investors of any third State.'

114. *Telenor, supra* note 89 at para. 92.

115. *Telenor, ibid.*, at para. 95. At para. 91, the tribunal states that an MFN clause should not be construed 'as extending the jurisdiction of the arbitral tribunal to categories of dispute beyond those set out in the BIT itself in the absence of clear language that this is the intention of the parties.'

116. *Supra* note 100.

117. Art. 2 provides: 'Each Contracting Party guarantees that the most favoured nation clause shall be applied to investors of the other Contracting Party in all matters covered by the present Treaty, and in particular in Articles 4, 5 and 6, with the exception of benefits provided by one Contracting Party to investors of a third country on the basis – of its participation in a customs union or other international economic organisations, or – of an agreement to avoid double taxation and other taxation issues.'

118. *Supra* note 100 at para. 178.

119. *Ibid.*, at para. 181.

'does not really mean that the MFN provision extends to all matters covered by the Treaty.'[120] In a separate opinion, Todd Weiler rejected the tribunal's MFN analysis. In his view, the fact that certain treaty provisions do lend themselves to an MFN analysis, simply meant that all matters means 'all matters from which one may be capable of deriving more or less favourable treatment.'[121]

The last MFN case to be examined is *RosInvestCo UK Ltd. v. Russia*,[122] in which the tribunal found that the MFN clause could be applied to provide arbitral jurisdiction. In *RosInvestCo*, the claimant made a claim under UK-USSR (1989) alleging that Russia had expropriated its investment in the Russian oil company, Yukos. The tribunal held that it did not have jurisdiction under the investor-state arbitration clause in UK-USSR (1989) because the subject matter of the clause did not extend to whether an expropriation had occurred.[123] The tribunal, however, held that it had jurisdiction under Denmark-USSR (1993) by operation of the MFN clause in UK-USSR (1989).[124] Unlike UK-USSR, the investor-state arbitration in Denmark-USSR (1993) applied to any dispute in connection with an investment.[125]

The MFN clause in Article 3, UK-USSR (1989), provides:

(1) Neither Contracting Party shall in its territory subject investments or returns of investors of the other Contracting Party to treatment less favourable than that which it accords to investments or returns of investors of any third State.

(2) Neither Contracting Party shall in its territory subject investors of the other Contracting Party, as regards their management, maintenance, use, enjoyment or disposal of their investments, to treatment less favourable than that which it accords to investors of any third State.

The tribunal noted that although protection of an investment is a highly relevant aspect of treatment, arbitration is a procedural right of an investor, not of an investment. Article 3(1) was therefore inapplicable as it applies to the treatment of investments and returns of investors.[126] The tribunal then turned to Article 3(2) and stated that submission to arbitration 'forms a highly relevant part of the corresponding protection for the investor by granting him, in case of interference with

---

120. *Ibid.*, at para. 194.
121. (Separate Opinion, 7 Apr. 2006) at para. 22.
122. *RosInvestCo, supra* note 84.
123. *Ibid.*, at paras 114 and 118. The clause generally only applies to determining the amount of compensation. See Art. 8, UK-USSR (1989), which provides in part: '(1) This Article shall apply to any legal disputes between an investor of one Contracting Party and the other Contracting Party in relation to an investment of the former either concerning the amount or payment of compensation under Articles 4 or 5 of this Agreement, or concerning any other matter consequential upon an act of expropriation in accordance with Article 5 of this Agreement, or concerning the consequences of the non-implementation, or of the incorrect implementation, of Article 6 of this Agreement.'
124. *Ibid.*, at para. 151.
125. Art. 8, Denmark-USSR (1993).
126. *RosInvestCo, supra* note 84 at para. 128.

his '*use*' and '*enjoyment*,' procedural options of obvious and great significance compared to the sole option of challenging such interference before the domestic courts of the host state.'[127] The tribunal further noted that its conclusion was confirmed by the lack of an express exception for arbitration in the listing of exceptions from MFN treatment in the UK-USSR BIT.[128] The tribunal concluded:

> Thus, at the end of its analysis of the relevant factors, the Tribunal concludes, on the basis of the MFN clause in Article 3(2) of the UK-Soviet BIT in conjunction with Article 8 of the Denmark-Russia BIT, that it has jurisdiction extending beyond that granted by Article 8 of the UK-Soviet BIT and covering the issues whether Respondent's actions have to be considered as expropriations and were valid.[129]

§5.13 Assessment of IIA MFN jurisprudence IIA tribunals have consistently applied MFN clauses to allow investors to avoid requirements that disputes be submitted to local courts before resorting to arbitration. On the other hand, to date, all tribunals except one have rejected the use of an MFN clause in a basic treaty to confer greater subject matter jurisdiction provided for in a third-party treaty.

As the overview of the jurisprudence in §5.10-§5.12 above highlights, tribunals have adopted conflicting approaches to the application of MFN clauses to investor-state arbitration provisions. The *Telenor* tribunal proceeded on the basis that the ordinary meaning of an IIA MFN clause is that it only applies to substantive rights, unless there is express provision otherwise. Likewise, *Salini v. Jordan* and *Plama* proceeded on the basis that an MFN clause does not apply to dispute settlement unless there is evidence of specific intention to the contrary. The majority of the tribunal in *Berschader* agreed with the *Plama* tribunal that particular care must be exercised conferring arbitral jurisdiction on the basis on an MFN clause. In contrast to these decisions, in *Gas Natural*, the tribunal proceeded on the basis than an IIA MFN clause applies to dispute settlement unless there is express intention to the contrary:

> Unless it appears clearly that the state parties to a BIT or the parties to a particular investment agreement settled on a different method for resolution of disputes that may arise, most-favored-nation provisions in BITs should be understood to be applicable to dispute resolution.[130]

The conflicting approaches adopted by tribunals raise a number of different interpretive issues. IIA MFN clauses like other treaty provisions, including those dealing with dispute settlement, are to be construed in accordance with rules of treaty interpretation. In accordance with these rules, it would appear inappropriate for tribunals to adopt presumptions about the scope of the MFN clause – one way or

---

127. *Ibid.*, at para. 130.
128. *Ibid.*, at para. 135.
129. *Ibid.*, at para. 139.
130. *Gas Natural, supra* note 78 at para. 49.

the other. In particular, the *Maffezini* tribunal's reference to 'fundamental conditions' and 'public policy' limitations to an IIA MFN clause[131] is not supported by reference to the rules of treaty interpretation. The rules in the *Vienna Convention on the Law of Treaties* (VCLT)[132] do not provide special rules for 'fundamental conditions' and 'public policy' limitations to the scope of treaty obligations.[133]

There appears to be agreement that, in principle, an MFN clause can confer consent to arbitration. For example, tribunals have referred to the UK practice of expressly providing that MFN treatment applies to dispute settlement.[134] Tribunals have, however, stated that an agreement to arbitrate must be clear and unambiguous[135] and that doubts may well exist where consent to arbitrate is obtained through incorporation by reference by means of an MFN clause.[136]

As a matter of treaty interpretation, it is not self-evident that an agreement to arbitrate only arises if it is clear and unambiguous, if this is taken to mean that different rules of interpretation should apply to investor-state arbitration clauses compared to other treaty clauses.[137] Although some commentators have argued for a strict interpretation doctrine in case of uncertainty, i.e., *in dubio mitius*,[138] neither the rules of treaty interpretation nor general principles with respect to the interpretation of arbitration agreements[139] support a rule of strict, or for that matter, of favourable interpretation (*in favorem validitatis* or *in favorem jurisdictionis*). Rather, the appropriate principle was stated by the tribunal in *Amco Asia Corporation v. Indonesia* in the context of the ICSID Convention:

> In the first place, like any other conventions, a convention to arbitrate is not to be construed *restrictively*, nor, as a matter of fact, *broadly* or *liberally*. It is to be construed in a way which leads to find out and to respect the common will of the parties: such a method of interpretation is but the application of the fundamental principle *pacta sunt servanda*, a principle common, indeed, to all systems of internal law and to international law.

---

131. The *Maffezini* tribunal provided four examples: (i) where consent to arbitration is conditioned on prior exhaustion of local remedies; (ii) where there is a fork in the road clause between submission to domestic courts and arbitration, and the choice is made final and irreversible; (iii) where the treaty provides for a specific forum for arbitration; or (iv) where there is a highly institutionalized system of arbitration with precise procedural rules, such as in NAFTA. *Maffezini, supra* note 25 at para. 63.
132. *Vienna Convention on the Law of Treaties*, done at Vienna, 23 May 1969, entered into force, 27 Jan. 1980, 1155 UNTS. 331, *reprinted in* (1969) 8 ILM 679 [VCLT].
133. See M. Paparinskis, *supra* note 20 for a discussion of this issue.
134. For example, see *Berschader, supra* note 100 at para. 179.
135. *Ibid.*, at para. 177, and *Plama, supra* note 98 at para. 223.
136. *Berschader, ibid.*, at para. 178.
137. *Ibid.*, at para. 177.
138. See C. McLachlan, L. Shore & M. Weiniger, *International Investment Arbitration: Substantive Principles* (Oxford: Oxford University Press, 2007) at 7.168 arguing that the ambit of state consent should be construed strictly. Also see G. Van Harten, *Investment Treaty Arbitration and Public Law* (Oxford: Oxford University Press, 2007) at 133 and 135.
139. E. Gaillard & J. Savage, eds., *Fouchard, Gaillard, Goldman on International Commercial Arbitration* (The Hague: Kluwer, 1999) at paras 471-482.

Moreover – and this is again a general principle of law – any convention, including conventions to arbitrate, should be construed in good faith, that is to say by taking into account the consequences of their commitments the parties may be considered as having reasonably and legitimately envisaged.[140]

In attempting to discern the common intention of the parties as expressed in the IIA MFN clause and treaty text, those tribunals and commentators favouring the application of MFN clauses to dispute settlement have emphasized a number of points: the promotion and protection purposes of IIAs as expressed in their pre-ambles; the role and purpose of MFN clauses in creating a multilateral system where all benefit from treaty developments and more favourable treatment; the breadth of the term 'treatment'; the breadth of MFN clauses that expressly apply to 'all matters'; express exclusions from MFN clauses as an affirmation that the MFN clause applies to anything not excluded; World Trade Organization (WTO) jurisprudence applying MFN treatment to procedural treatment;[141] and practice under the *General Agreement on Trade in Services* (GATS) suggesting that states were aware of the potential of the MFN clause in the GATS applying to IIA dispute settlement mechanisms.[142]

On the other hand, those that view MFN treatment as limited to substantive protections have emphasized: the lack of evidence of an intention that MFN would apply to dispute settlement; that the application of MFN would disrupt the balance achieved in the treaty text and lead to treaty shopping; the need for clear and unambiguous consent; and the practice of states such as the UK that have expressly provided for MFN treatment to cover dispute resolution.

For the reasons identified above, it would seem that a generally worded MFN treatment clause can apply to confer consent to arbitrate and extend the scope of subject matter jurisdiction.[143] However, given the ambiguity in most MFN clauses, a tribunal can reasonably come to the opposite view. This uncertainty is likely to continue until states clarify the scope of MFN clauses.

Assuming that a general MFN clause in an IIA can confer consent to arbitration, there are a number of interpretive issues that are not completely addressed

---

140.	*Amco Asia Corporation v. Indonesia* (Decision on Jurisdiction, 25 Sep. 1983) [*Amco*] at para. 14, *reprinted in* 1 ICSID Rep 377 at 394.
141.	The WTO Appellate Body applied MFN treatment to procedural matters in *EC-Regime for the Importation, Sale and Distribution of Bananas*, WT/DS27/AB/R at paras 205-207. See also earlier GATT decisions, including *United States-Section 337 of the Tariff Act of 1930* (GATT Panel, 7 Nov. 1989) 36th Supp. BISD 345 [*Section 337*]. On the application of MFN treatment in the context of international trade to IIAs see J. Kurtz, *The MFN Standard and Foreign Investment: An Uneasy Fit?*, *supra* note 8; W. Ben Hamida, 'MFN Clause and Procedural Rights: Seeking Solutions from WTO Experiences' in T. Weiler, ed., *Emerging Issues in International Investment Law* (New York: Juris, 2008) and M. Paparinskis, *supra* note 20 for a discussion of this issue.
142.	Ben Hamida, 'Clause de la nation la plus favorisée et mécanismes de règlement des différends: que dit l'histoire,' *supra* note 23 at 1159-1162.
143.	Emmanuel Gaillard has suggested that MFN treatment could be applied as a basis for consent to arbitration. See E. Gaillard, *Chronique des sentences arbitrales*, 133 JDI 219 at 286-287.

in the jurisprudence to date. First, the MFN clauses considered in the various cases discussed above differ in one arguably important respect. Some IIAs accord MFN treatment only to investments,[144] others only to investors,[145] whereas still others accord it to both investments and investors.[146] The MFN clauses considered in *Siemens, Camuzzi, Berschader* and *RosInvestCo* applied MFN treatment to investors. In the other cases, the MFN clause applied only to investment. Two tribunals have stated that they do not attach particular significance to the use of these different terms.[147] However, the *RosInvestCo* tribunal correctly noted that although protection of an investment is a highly relevant aspect of treatment, arbitration is a procedural right of an investor, not an investment. It therefore held that the MFN clause in Article 3(1) of the relevant BIT was inapplicable as it refers to the treatment of investments.[148] The distinction between investment and investor is arguably very significant – rights relating to investment are property rights whereas the right to invoke arbitration is a personal right – a right which must be held by an investor, not an investment.[149] In other words, less favourable arbitration provisions afford less favourable treatment to investors with respect to the protection of their investments. They do not technically afford less favourable treatment of the investment (i.e., a contract or piece of real property cannot commence arbitration and cannot therefore be treated less favourably). Accordingly, where MFN treatment is accorded specifically to 'investors,' there is more scope for arguing that MFN treatment applies to investor-state arbitration provisions. But, of course, the intention of the parties as assessed by other means can provide otherwise. Once again, generalizations on this topic are not without risk.

A second interpretive issue is the role of a host state's IIA practice. Subsequent IIA practice has been invoked by both claimants and host states to support arguments both for and against applying MFN clauses to confer consent to arbitration. Unless this practice relates to the specific IIA in question, however, it is of limited relevance to the interpretation of the MFN clause at issue. Other host state's IIAs are not context within the meaning of Article 31(2), Vienna Convention, because they do not relate to the conclusion of the treaty at issue nor are they instruments related to that treaty. Further, they are not subsequent agreements or practice relating to the treaty within the meaning of Article 31(3).[150]

A third interpretive issue involves the particular situation that arises with IIAs that limit the scope of investor-state arbitration to issues related to expropriation. The interpretation of the various MFN clauses by the tribunals in *Plama, Telenor, Berschader* and *RosInvestCo* might be objected to because the tribunals did not

---

144. For example, see Art. 10(7), ECT; Art. 3(2), Austria-Chile (1997); Art. 3(2), Netherlands-Romania (1994).
145. Art. 4, Argentina-France (1991).
146. NAFTA Chapter 11, some German, Swiss and UK BITs, and BITs based on the new US and Canadian Models.
147. *Plama, supra* note 98 at 190 and *Siemens, supra* note 13 at 92.
148. *RosInvestCo, supra* note 122 at para. 128.
149. See Gallus, *supra* note 23 at 3, citing D. Krishan on this point. Online: TDM.
150. For a discussion of this issue, see Paparinskis, *supra* note 20, and Vesel, *supra* note 23.

have jurisdiction to interpret the MFN clauses in the first place. The arbitration clauses under which the tribunals were constituted limit their jurisdiction to some issues related to expropriation. For example, in *RosInvestCo,* the jurisdiction of the tribunal constituted under Article 7, UK-USSR (1989), is limited to:

> ... legal disputes [...] in relation to an investment of the [investor] either concerning the amount or payment of compensation under Articles 4 or 5 of this Agreement, or concerning any other matter consequential upon an act of expropriation in accordance with Article 5 of this Agreement, or concerning the consequences of the non-implementation, or of the incorrect implementation, of Article 6 of this Agreement.[151]

The investor-state arbitration clause does not apply to disputes about the scope of MFN treatment and whether MFN treatment applies to dispute resolution procedures.

On the one hand, it can be argued that the tribunal has jurisdiction to decide its own jurisdiction on the basis of Kompetenz-Kompetenz[152] and that this includes the jurisdiction to assess whether the MFN clause confers it jurisdiction. Further, it can be argued that the subject matter jurisdiction of a tribunal constituted under Article 7, UK-USSR (1989), is expanded by the MFN clause in the BIT, which has the effect of conferring the wider subject matter jurisdiction under Denmark-USSR (1993).

In *RosInvestCo,* the tribunal stated that:

> Thus, at the end of its analysis of the relevant factors, the Tribunal concludes, on the basis of the MFN clause in Article 3(2) of the UK-Soviet BIT in conjunction with Article 8 of the Denmark-Russia BIT, that it has jurisdiction extending beyond that granted by Article 8 of the UK-Soviet BIT and covering the issues whether Respondent's actions have to be considered as expropriations and were valid.[153]

The *RosInvestCo* tribunal does not expressly address what rights the MFN clause is conferring. Does the MFN clause in the basic treaty simply confer consent to the wider subject matter jurisdiction in the Denmark-Russia BIT so that the tribunal is in all other respect operating under the arbitration provisions of the UK-USSR BIT, or does the MFN clause confer the benefit of the entire arbitration clause in Denmark-USSR? The difference is significant as it determines whether the tribunal in question is operating under the rules provided in the UK-USSR BIT (the basic treaty) or the Denmark-Russia BIT (the third-party treaty). This funda-mental issue remains unanswered and may have practical significance where the basic treaty and the third-party treaty provide for different arbitral rules.

It might be suggested that the conflicting approaches of tribunals to the appli-cation of MFN clauses can be explained by the distinction between questions of

---

151.   Art. 8(1), UK-USSR (1989).
152.   As noted by the tribunal at para. 35.
153.   *Supra* note 84 at para. 139.

admissibility and jurisdiction.[154] Under this approach, a procedural pre-condition to arbitration, such as the domestic litigation requirements in the *Maffezini* line of cases, is an issue of admissibility, not of jurisdiction. The admissibility/jurisdiction distinction suggests a middle ground can be reached between the two lines of jurisprudence. MFN clauses that do not expressly refer to dispute settlement could be applied to provide more favourable treatment with respect to procedural issues relating to the admissibility of a claim, but not to fundamental matters of consent.

Although this argument is appealing on its surface, there would not appear to be a principled basis upon which to decide that an MFN clause applies to issues of admissibility but not jurisdiction. Further, from a practical standpoint, the distinction between admissibility and jurisdiction is very difficult to apply. Indeed, the *Maffezini* tribunal stated that failure to comply with the local remedies requirement, if applicable, would mean that the tribunal lacked jurisdiction. In contrast, in *BG*, the tribunal viewed the local remedies requirement as an issue of admissibility.[155]

The use of MFN treatment to obtain the more favourable procedural treatment in other investor-state arbitration provisions has been criticized on the basis that it amounts to 'cherry picking'. In *Siemens*, the investor, claiming under Argentina-Germany (1991) sought the more favourable terms of Argentina-Chile (1991) – terms that allowed for direct recourse to arbitration, rather than having to submit the dispute to local courts for a certain time period. Argentina argued that the foreign investor could not use the MFN clause to take advantage of other IIAs in a piecemeal fashion, and that it would have to assume the associated disadvantages in pursuing any claim under the other IIA.

The tribunal noted that there was some merit to the position that the various provisions of an IIA constitute an entire package, but it rejected Argentina's argument on the grounds that the MFN obligation 'relates only to more favorable treatment,' noting that 'even if the MFN clause is of a general nature, its application will be related only to the benefits that the treaty of reference may grant and to the extent that benefits are perceived to be such.'[156] The tribunal reasoned that the 'indivisible package' interpretation put forth by Argentina would 'defeat the intended result of the [MFN] clause which is to harmonize benefits agreed with a party with those considered more favorable granted to another party.'[157]

The reasoning of the *Siemens* tribunal has been criticized on the basis that Argentina is bound by a dispute settlement provision to which Argentina never consented. It is said that the German investor obtained direct access to arbitration

---

154. Emmanuel Gaillard has suggested that MFN treatment could be applied as a basis for consent to arbitration. See E. Gaillard, *Chronique des sentences arbitrales*, 133 JDI 219 at 286-287.
155. See *BG, supra* note 78.
156. *Siemens, supra* note 13 at para. 120. The tribunal's conclusion is consistent with the commentary to Art. 19 of the ILC's *Draft MFN Articles*: 'Whenever the beneficiary State is accorded different types of treatment with respect to the same subject-matter, it shall be entitled to whichever treatment or combination of treatments it prefers in any particular case.' ILC's MFN Report at p. 52, cited in *Siemens* at para. 65.
157. *Siemens, ibid.*

under the Argentina-Chile BIT without being bound by the fork in the road provision in the same IIA.[158] This, however, misapprehends the result in *Siemens* because the investor never submitted the dispute to the local courts and was not trying to avoid a fork in the road provision. It simply sought direct access to arbitration (an advantage in the third-party treaty) rather than having to wait eighteen months to begin the process. The *Siemens* tribunal rejected the 'indivisible package' argument as fundamentally inconsistent with MFN treatment, which is the conferral of the advantages accorded under other IIAs. Nevertheless, where a third-party IIA imposes express obligations or conditions with respect to obtaining the treatment in question, there is merit to the argument that the investor can only obtain that treatment if the investor has complied with the obligations or conditions for obtaining it.

Finally, even if MFN treatment in principle applies to dispute settlement, a clause normally applies only where there is less favourable treatment of investments or investors in like circumstances. This issue is considered in Part IV below.

§5.14 Using MFN to confer more favourable scope of application   To date IIA jurisprudence has focused primarily on applying MFN clauses to confer the benefits of more favourable investor-state arbitration provisions in other IIAs. It remains unclear the extent to which an MFN clause might be applied to confer more favourable treatment with respect to subject matters or persons not contemplated in the basic treaty or to change the temporal application of the treaty. For example, if the third-party treaty has a wider definition of investment than the basic treaty, does the definition of investment in the basic treaty circumscribe the application of MFN treatment, or can the MFN clause be applied to confer the benefit of the wider definition? In this case, whether the MFN clause applies to investments, investors or both might be decisive because an investor might argue that it receives less favourable treatment where 'investment,' in the basic treaty, is defined more narrowly than 'investment' in the third-part treaty. Thus, if the MFN clause applies to investors, the investor might argue that it is entitled to the more favourable treatment in the third-party treaty – the wider definition of investment.

In *Tecmed*, the claimant argued that by virtue of the MFN clause in Mexico-Spain (1995),[159] it was entitled to the retroactive application of the BIT's protections because, unlike Mexico-Spain (1995), Austria-Mexico (1998) applied to investments made before its entry into force.[160] The *Tecmed* tribunal rejected the claim, stating:

> The Arbitral Tribunal will not examine the provisions of such Treaty in detail in light of such principle, because it deems that matters relating to the application over time of the Agreement, which involve more the time dimension of

---

158. See Vesel, *supra* note 23 at 168. Also see Fietta, *supra* note 23.
159. The treaty had entered into force on 18 Dec. 1996.
160. *Técnicas Medioambientales Tecmed, S.A. v. Mexico* (Award, 29 May 2003) [*Tecmed*] at paras 69 and 74.

application of its substantive provisions rather than matters of procedure or jurisdiction, due to their significance and importance, go to the core of matters that must be deemed to be specifically negotiated by the Contracting Parties. These are determining factors for their acceptance of the Agreement, as they are directly linked to the identification of the substantive protection regime applicable to the foreign investor and, particularly, to the general (national or international) legal context within which such regime operates, as well as to the access of the foreign investor to the substantive provisions of such regime. Their application cannot therefore be impaired by the principle contained in the most favored nation clause.[161]

The tribunal's above statement that the temporal dimension of the BIT 'go to the core of matters that must be deemed to be specifically negotiated by the Contracting Parties' is open to question. It is unclear that rules of treaty interpretation direct the treaty interpreter to distinguish between matters that must be deemed to be specifically negotiated and those that do not. The applicable treaty principle with respect to non-retroactivity is Article 28, Vienna Convention, which states: 'Unless a different intention appears from the treaty or is otherwise established, its provisions do not bind a party in relation to any act or fact which took place or any situation which ceased to exist before the date of the entry into force of the treaty with respect to that party.' It is arguable that an MFN clause that applies to all matters in the treaty could be applied to establish the intention of the parties to confer better temporal protection.[162]

§5.15 Application of MFN to investment or investors   As noted above, some IIAs accord MFN treatment only to investments,[163] others only to investors,[164] whereas still others accord it to both investments and investors.[165] Two tribunals have stated that they do not attach particular significance to the use of different terms.[166] Where MFN treatment applies to 'investors' and not just 'investment', claimants might argue that they are entitled to treatment as favourable as any other foreign investor, which might include more favourable temporal application of investment protections, broader definition of investments and admission and establishment rights. Further, as noted above, where the MFN clause applies to investors, there may be greater scope for arguing that MFN treatment applies to dispute settlement.

§5.16 The treaty practice response to the application of MFN to investor-state arbitration provisions   In recent IIA practice, some states have reacted to the IIA

---

161. *Ibid.*, at para. 69.
162. See also *M.C.I. Power Group L.C. and New Turbine, Inc. v. Ecuador* (Award, 31 Jul. 2007) at paras 118-128 regarding temporal application.
163. Art. 10(7), ECT; Art. 3(2); Austria-Chile (1997); Art. 3(2) Netherlands-Romania (1994).
164. Art. 4, Argentina-France (1991).
165. NAFTA Chapter 11, some German, Swiss and UK BITs and BITs based on the new US and Canadian Models.
166. *Plama, supra* note 98 at 190, and *Siemens, supra* note 13 at 92.

MFN jurisprudence by expressly limiting the scope of MFN treatment. In particular, some recent treaties have expressly excluded dispute settlement from the MFN clause.[167] The US approach has been to record in its investment negotiations that MFN is not intended to extend to dispute settlement provisions.[168] With respect to existing treaties, some states have agreed that the MFN clause in an existing treaty does not apply to dispute settlement.[169] A more drastic approach has been to conclude agreements without an MFN clause applying to investment, as in the *India-Singapore Comprehensive Economic Co-operation Agreement* (2005).[170]

IV   APPLYING MFN TREATMENT

§5.17 Similarities and differences with the national treatment analysis   MFN and national treatment are both relative standards that prohibit discrimination between investors and/or investment. In both cases, the comparison made between the treatment of two investors or investments requires the identification of the applicable comparator and an assessment of whether the investor or investment at issue has been accorded less favourable treatment. As a result, MFN treatment analysis shares many similarities with the national treatment analysis.

Despite similarities in analysis, there are also fundamental differences. National treatment cases typically involve state measures that accord more favourable *de jure* or *de facto* treatment to domestic investors. National treatment cases usually arise as the result of protectionist domestic measures that deprive foreign investors or investments of equality in competitive opportunities. As

---

167. See, for example, 2005 *New Zealand - Thailand Comprehensive Economic Cooperation Agreement*, Article 9.8 Most Favoured Nation Treatment with respect to the Promotion and Protection of Investments. Online: <http://mfat.govt.nz>. The Norwegian 2007 Model BIT provides in Art. 4(3) that MFN treatment 'does not encompass dispute resolution mechanisms provided for in this Agreement or other International Agreements.'

168. The final draft text of the CAFTA-DR dated 28 Jan. 2004 records the parties' intentions as follows in a footnote to the MFN treatment clause: 'The Parties note the recent decision of the arbitral tribunal in *Maffezini (Arg.) v. Kingdom of Spain*, which found an unusually broad most-favoured-nation clause in an Argentina-Spain agreement to encompass international dispute resolution procedures. See Decision of Jurisdiction §§38-64 (Jan. 25, 2000), *reprinted in* 16 ICSID Rev 212 (2002). By contrast the Most-Favoured-Nation Treatment Article of this Agreement is expressly limited in scope to matters 'with respect to the establishment, acquisition, expansion, management, conduct, operation, and sale or other disposition of investments.' The Parties share the understanding and intent that this clause does not encompass international dispute resolution mechanisms such as those contained in Section C of this Chapter, and therefore could not reasonably lead to a conclusion similar to that of the *Maffezini* case.' ASIL, International Law In Brief, 6 Feb. 2004. See online: <http://asil.org/search.cfm?displayPage=702#t1>.

169. Argentina and Panama have exchanged diplomatic notes with an 'interpretive declaration' of the MFN clause in their 1996 BIT to the effect that the MFN clause does not extend to dispute resolution clauses, and that this has always been their intention. See *National Grid plc v. Argentina* (Decision on Jurisdiction, 20 Jun. 2006) [*National Grid*] at para. 85.

170. See Chapter 6 (Investment) *India-Singapore Comprehensive Economic Co-operation Agreement* (29 Jun. 2005).

discussed in Chapter 4 above, a key issue in the national treatment analysis is the determination of whether the foreign investor or investment in question is in like circumstances with a domestic competitor and whether differences in treatment can be justified on non-protectionist and rational policy grounds.[171]

In contrast, MFN cases raise different issues. Although host states often seek to provide more favourable treatment to their own investors, it is less common for states to differentiate between foreign investors and investments of different nationalities in their domestic measures. To date, the majority of IIA cases involving the application of MFN treatment involve questions of whether third parties receive more favourable treatment under other IIAs and not whether they are receiving more favourable treatment under domestic measures. As discussed below, the application of MFN treatment raises distinct issues if the question is treatment under a third-party treaty as compared to treatment under domestic measures.

§5.18 The two elements of MFN treatment analysis Despite the variation between MFN clauses, two common issues arise in their application: (i) identifying the relevant comparator; and (ii) comparing the treatment received by the foreign investor or investment and the comparator to determine if there is less favourable treatment. Since MFN treatment is a relative standard, its application always turns on making the appropriate comparison between two different entities or things. In the case of MFN treatment, the comparison will be between third state investors or investments and the foreign investors or investments benefiting under the basic treaty between the home and host state. Identifying the appropriate comparator is a key element in the analysis. Second, there must be a comparison of the treatment afforded to the applicable investors or investments to assess whether the host state accorded less favourable treatment.

A   THE COMPARATOR

§5.19 The basis for comparison The majority of IIAs provide no guidance regarding the basis of comparison when applying MFN treatment. Chile-Egypt (1999) and Philippines-Switzerland (1997), reproduced above at §5.7, are typical in not specifying the basis for comparing the investments in question.[172] A small number of treaties, of which NAFTA is the most prominent example, clarify that MFN treatment applies to investors and investments in 'like circumstances.'[173] US,

---

171. See, *supra* Chapter 4, §4.11 *et seq.*, on the assessing of whether investors or investments are in like circumstances.
172. Recent Austrian, Chilean, Chinese, Danish, French, German, Swiss and UK BITs do not use a comparator. See, for example, Art. 3(1), Austria-Egypt (2001); Art. 3(1), Kyrgyzstan-UK (1999); Art. 4(2), Chile-Tunisia (1998); Art. 4(1), China-Jordan (2001); Art. 3(2), Brazil-Netherlands (1998); Art. 4, Cambodia-France (2000); Art. 3(1), Bosnia and Herzegovina-Germany (2001); and Art. 4(3), Armenia-Switzerland (2003).
173. Art.1103, NAFTA.

Canadian and Turkish BITs also often refer to 'like circumstances' in their MFN treatment clauses. Other IIAs use terms such as 'like situations,'[174] 'similar situations'[175] and 'same circumstances.'[176]

§5.20 Comparing the treatment of investors and investments under third state IIAs   In principle, determining the appropriate comparator where the treatment in question is that under a third state IIA is straightforward. The MFN clause will apply where any third state investment or investor is entitled to more favourable treaty protections than those afforded to an investment or investor under the basic treaty. In these cases, the fact that *any* third state investors or investments *are* or *could* be entitled to more favourable treaty protections is sufficient to put the investors or investments in like circumstances for the purpose of applying the MFN clause. For example, in cases involving the application of MFN treatment to avoid local remedy requirements, the threshold issue has been whether any third-party investor or investment would be entitled to avoid the local remedy requirement. The availability of the better treatment did not depend on the investor or investment demonstrating that they were in the same economic sector as third state investors or investments, or indeed that any third state investors or investments existed. These cases support the proposition that the existence of an actual or potential competitive relationship between the investors or investments in question is not a necessary prerequisite to obtaining the benefit of MFN treatment. To recall the words of Georg Schwarzenberger, the MFN clause in this case is operating to provide the maximum of favours conceded to any third State.[177] In this case, a foreign investor is in like circumstances with a third state investor simply by coming within the scope of IIA protection.

§5.21 Comparing the treatment of investors and investments under domestic measures   In contrast to comparisons of treatment under different IIAs, where the issue is the treatment of different foreign investors or investments under domestic measures, the MFN treatment like circumstances analysis will be similar to the national treatment analysis discussed in Chapter 4 above. The question will be whether the investors or investments in question are in like circumstances, determining the appropriate comparator and whether there are legitimate grounds for distinguishing between investors or investments.

A good example of this type of analysis is *Parkerings-Compagniet AS v. Lithuania*,[178] where the Norwegian claimant alleged a breach of MFN treatment in Lithuania-Norway (1992)[179] on the basis that a Dutch firm, Pinus Proprius, had

---

174.   Art. 2(2), Senegal-United States (1983).
175.   Art. 3(1), Ethiopia-Turkey (2000).
176.   Art. 3(1), Belize-UK (1982).
177.   *Supra* note 9.
178.   *Parkerings-Compagniet AS v. Lithuania* (Award, 11 Sep. 2007).
179.   Art. IV(1) provides: 'Investments made by Investors of one Contracting Party in the Territory of the other Contracting Party, as also the Returns therefrom, shall be accorded treatment no less favourable than that accorded to investments made by Investors of any third state.'

obtained more favourable treatment with respect to the building of a parking complex. Despite the fact that the MFN clause did not provide an express basis for comparison, the tribunal stated that, for the purpose of applying the MFN clause, the investors must be in like circumstances.[180] According to the tribunal, a less favourable treatment: 'is acceptable if a State's legitimate objective justifies such different treatment in relation to the specificity of the investment.'[181] This analysis is generally consistent with the approach that tribunals have taken in the national treatment context.[182] The tribunal found that one of Parkerings' projects was not in like circumstances because it was larger and extended significantly more into a sensitive heritage area. As a result, there were legitimate grounds to distinguish the project on the basis of historical and archaeological preservation and environmental protection reasons.[183]

§5.22 The existence of a special legal relationship between the host state and investor Where the host state is in a special legal relationship with an investor (e.g., an investment or concession agreement), other investors will not normally be in 'like circumstances,' as any differential treatment that arises may be due to the existence of the special legal relationship with the investor or investment. The prototypical example would be a foreign investment contract under which a foreign investor receives the rights to certain resources or certain tax exemptions. An investor might build a section of a highway and in return obtain special incentives, such as a relaxation on zoning requirements to allow for a commercial development. The state would not thereby breach MFN treatment by failing to provide similar benefits to another foreign investor, since the two investors would not be in 'like circumstances.' As noted in the UNCTAD's commentary on MFN treatment in IIAs: 'The reason is that a host country cannot be obliged to enter into an individual investment contract. Freedom of contract prevails over the MFN standard.'[184]

Although states may enter contracts providing special advantages, a state cannot use contractual mechanisms to avoid its national and MFN treatment obligations. The general principle that 'freedom of contract prevails over the MFN standard' is not absolute. Where the state provides special advantages through contractual mechanisms, the fact that the treatment is provided under contract rather than through a public regulatory measure will not shield the state from a breach of MFN treatment. As noted by the tribunal in *Bayindir*:

> ... the very fact that these questions are governed by specific contractual provisions does not necessarily mean that they have no relevance in the framework of a treaty claim. One cannot seriously dispute that a State

---

180. *Parkerings, supra* note 178 at para. 369. See *supra* Chapter 4, §4.11, on this point in the context of national treatment.
181. *Ibid.*, at para. 371.
182. See *supra* Chapter 4, §4.11 *et seq.*
183. *Parkerings, supra* note 178 at para. 396.
184. UNCTAD, *MFN Treatment, supra* note 3.

can discriminate against an investor by the manner in which it concludes an investment contract and/or exercises the rights there under. Any other interpretation would consider treaty and contract claims as mutually exclusive, which would be at odds with the well-established principles deriving from the distinction between treaty and contract claims as discussed above.[185]

If state contracts favour one set of nationals over another in like circumstances, a breach of MFN or national treatment may well arise. For example, a state would likely breach MFN treatment if it charged foreigners of different nationalities different lease rates for government owned office space and the difference in lease rates could not be objectively justified by reference to normal market considerations.

B   THE STANDARD OF TREATMENT

§5.23 Treaty provisions   IIAs vary in how they describe the applicable standard of MFN treatment. Some call for the 'same' or 'as favourable as' treatment.[186] Others provide for treatment 'whichever is more favourable.'[187] More commonly, the requirement is for 'no less favourable treatment'[188] or a prohibition on according investments 'treatment less favourable.'[189] In all of these formulations, the protection afforded by the MFN treatment clause involves a comparison between the treatment accorded to the foreign investor or investments from one state and the investor or investments of third states.[190]

A small number of IIAs define the meaning of less favourable treatment to include limitation on the buying, production and exploitation of raw materials and restrictions on the sale of products, while at the same time establishing that measures taken to ensure security, maintain order, and protect public health and morality do not result in 'less favourable treatment.'[191]

§5.24 Less favourable treatment compared to treatment under third state IIAs   Foreign investors have relied on MFN treatment clauses to obtain the more

---

185. *Bayindir Insaat Turizm Ticaret Ve Sanayi A.Ş. v. Pakistan* (Decision on Jurisdiction, 14 Nov. 2005) [*Bayindir*] at para. 215.
186. UNCTAD, *MFN Treatment, supra* note 3 at 35.
187. See, for example, the following BITs: Art. 4(2), Chile-Egypt (1999); Art. 4(3), China-Jordan (2001); Art. 3(2), Cuba-Lebanon (1995); Art. 3(2), Egypt-Jordan (1996); and Art. 3(2), Netherlands-Romania (1994).
188. See, for example, Art. 1103, NAFTA, and Art. 3, Canadian Model FIPA (2003). Also see the following BITs: Art. IV, Australia-Romania (1993); Art. IV(2), Chile-Eygpt (1999); Art. 4(2), Chile-Tunisia (1998); Art. 4(1), Ghana-India (2000); Art. 3(2), Netherlands-Romania (1994) and Art. 3(1) Ethiopia-Turkey (2000).
189. Art. 3(1), Egypt-Greece (1993), and Art. 3(2), Egypt-UK (1975).
190. Or investors if the provision so provides.
191. See Art. 1, Protocol to Egypt-Romania (1976).

favourable substantive and procedural protections in other host state's IIAs.[192] For example, with respect to substantive investment protections, in *MTD* the tribunal found that an MFN clause in Chile-Malaysia (1992)[193] allowed the claimant the benefit of guarantees in Chile-Croatia (1994) and Chile-Denmark (1993),[194] both of which contained an obligation to award permits subsequent to the approval of an investment.[195] Likewise, in *CME*, the majority of the tribunal noted that the MFN clause would entitle the investor to a more favourable compensation standard for expropriation in other IIAs.[196]

It is also established that less favourable treatment may arise as a result of more or less cumbersome investor-state arbitration procedures. As discussed above, in a series of cases, claimants have relied on MFN treatment to argue that they can avoid an eighteen-month domestic litigation period prior to commencing investor-state arbitration.[197] After holding that the MFN clause applies to dispute settlement, tribunals have agreed that the eighteen-month period provides 'a less favorable degree of protection than access to arbitration immediately upon expiration of the negotiation period.'[198]

---

192. In *AAPL, supra* note 4; *ADF Group Inc v. United States* (Award, 9 Jan. 2003) and *MTD Equity Sdn. Bhd. and MTD Chile S.A. v. Ecuador* (Award, 25 May 2004) [*MTD*] the investors relied on the MFN clauses of the respective IIAs to obtain the benefits of the minimum standard of treatment guarantees in other IIAs. In all three cases the tribunals nevertheless rejected the investors' claims on the basis that the third party treaty in question did not provide more favourable protection than the basic treaty. In *ADF*, the claimant argued that, by virtue of Art. 1103, NAFTA, it was entitled to the more favourable treatment in the Estonia-US and Albania-US BITs. Although in principle the tribunal appears to have accepted that the claimant was entitled to the benefit of the other BITs, the tribunal found that the claimant had not proven that standards in those BITs were different than the NAFTA's fair and equitable treatment standard (Art. 1105). It also found that, even if the other BITs did provide a more stringent standard of treatment, the US had not breached it. See *ADF, ibid.*, at paras 193-198. In *AAPL, supra* note 4 ((1990) 4 ICSID Reports 246 at page 272), the investor argued that the MFN clause in the Sri Lanka-UK BIT entitled the investor to the more favourable treatment in the Sri Lanka-Switzerland BIT. The tribunal rejected the claim on the basis that the claimant had not proven that the Sri Lanka-Switzerland BIT provided more favourable treatment. Similarly, see *MTD, ibid.*, at paras 203-206.
193. Article 3(1): 'Investments made by investors of either Contracting Party in the territory of the other Contracting Party shall receive treatment which is fair and equitable, and not less favourable than that accorded to investments made by investors of any third State.'
194. *MTD, supra* note 192 at paras 100-104.
195. On this point see also *Pope & Talbot Inc v. Canada* (Award on the Merits of Phase 2, 10 Apr. 2001) at para. 117.
196. *CME Czech Republic B.V. v. Czech Republic* (Final Award, 14 Mar. 2003) [*CME*] at para. 500. In a separate opinion, Professor Ian Brownlie suggested that MFN treatment does not apply to compensation provisions because MFN treatment only applies to treatment of an investment and not the process of dispute settlement. *CME* (Separate Opinion on the Issues at the Quantum Phase, 14 Mar. 2003) at paras 11-13. But, arguably reparation is not a procedural matter relating to the conduct of arbitral proceedings – it could be considered as part of the substantive treatment to which an investor is entitled. See above Part III on the scope of MFN treatment.
197. See above Part III on the scope of MFN treatment.
198. *Gas Natural, supra* note 78 at para. 31. See also *Suez/Vivendi, supra* note 78 at para. 57.

Where MFN clauses are applied to dispute settlement procedures difficult questions will arise with respect to what constitutes less favourable treatment. As noted by the tribunal in *Plama*, it may be difficult for a tribunal to apply the standard to determine that arbitration under the ICSID Arbitration Rules is more or less favourable than one under the UNCITRAL Arbitration Rules.[199]

In this context, one commentator has criticized the lack of analysis with respect to whether submission to local courts is in fact less favourable treatment than direct recourse to investor-state arbitration:

> The *Maffezini* approach is to simply assume that access to the Spanish courts in the eighteen-month period is 'less favourable treatment' than direct arbitral proceedings. This view in itself seems almost reflective of an epistemological belief in the superiority of investment arbitration. The lack of a rigorous comparison between the two forms of adjudication is a serious flaw in the Tribunal's reasoning and one which should (but most likely will not) weaken its influence amongst later arbitral tribunals.[200]

Although the *Maffezini* line of cases fails to provide a rigorous analysis of less favourable treatment, the issue of less favourable treatment in question is not an 'epistemological belief in the superiority of investment arbitration', but rather the ability to choose between local courts or arbitration. On its face, the ability of an investor to be able to choose between proceeding to local court or to international arbitration immediately is more favourable than not having that choice, but being obliged to submit instead to local remedies for eighteen months.

§5.25 Less favourable treatment under domestic measures   The analysis of whether a foreign investor or investment has received less favourable treatment, under domestic measures, than a third state investor or investment in like circumstances is similar to that under the national treatment analysis. Treatment has a wide meaning and includes the effect of any type of state conduct.[201] In *Parkerings*, if the tribunal were to have found that the investments in question were in like circumstances, the fact that one received government approval and the other did not would have amounted to less favourable treatment.[202] 'Treatment' is wide enough to cover both substantive and procedural requirements and arguably does not necessarily imply that there is a direct financial disadvantage.[203] For example, less favourable treatment likely extends to the unavailability of an opportunity available to another third state investor or investment.

---

199.   *Plama, supra* note 98 at para. 208.
200.   Kurtz, *supra* note 8 at 880.
201.   See *supra* Chapter 4, §4.21.
202.   See discussion on this case above at §5.21.
203.   See *supra* Chapter 4, §4.21.

§5.26 Better of national and MFN treatment? Faced with the situation where either national or MFN treatment is more favourable, the investor or investment is entitled to the more favourable treatment. As a general rule, international obligations are cumulative – an investor can rely on each treatment standard independently. Although some treaties expressly provide that the investor is entitled to the better treatment afforded in the circumstances,[204] these provisions would appear to have been added for greater clarification and certainty. As the ILC has noted with respect to MFN treatment:

> The right of the beneficiary State, for itself or for the benefit of persons or things in a determined relationship with it, to most-favoured-nation treatment under a most-favoured-nation clause is without prejudice to national treatment or other treatment which the granting State has accorded to that beneficiary State with respect to the same subject-matter as that of the most-favoured-nation clause.[205]

V EXCEPTIONS AND RESERVATIONS

§5.27 Exceptions and reservations IIAs commonly provide express exceptions and reservations to relative standards of treatment, often in annexes or protocols to the main treaty text.[206] For example, US-Uruguay (2005), excludes from the MFN treatment obligation '[all] existing non-conforming measures of all states of the United States, the District of Columbia, and Puerto Rico.'[207] In addition, a number of express general exceptions and customary international law defences may apply.[208]

IIAs normally exempt advantages granted under regional economic integration organization agreements,[209] trade agreements and tax treaties from MFN

---

204. See, for example, Art. 10(3), ECT: 'For the purposes of this Article, 'Treatment' means treatment accorded by a Contracting Party which is no less favourable than that which it accords to its own Investors or to Investors of any other Contracting Party or any third state, whichever is the most favourable.' See also Art. 1104, NAFTA: 'Each Party shall accord to investors of another Party and to investments of investors of another Party the better of the treatment required by [national treatment] and [MFN].' See also Art. 1(6), Italy-Jordan (1996).
205. Art. 19(2), *Draft MFN Articles, supra* note 4.
206. See *infra* Chapter 10.
207. Annex 1-US.
208. See *infra* Chapter 10.
209. See UNCTAD, *The REIO Exception in MFN Treatment Clauses* (Geneva: UNCTAD, 2004). (UNCTAD/ITE/IIT/2004/7).

treatment.[210] In addition, foreign aid programs to promoteeconomic development are sometimes expressly exempted from MFN treatment.[211]

The approach under NAFTA and the 2003 Canadian Model BIT is to provide that MFN does not apply to treatment under any prior treaties.[212]

---

210. See UNCTAD, *MFN Treatment, supra* note 3 at 17-23, and UNCTAD BIT Studies, *supra* note 40. For example, see Art. 2(3), Cuba-Lebanon (1995): 'If a Contracting Party accords special advantages to investors of any third State by virtue of an agreement establishing a free trade area, a customs union, a common market or a similar regional organization or by virtue of an agreement on the avoidance of double taxation, it shall not be obliged to accord such advantages to investors of the other Contracting Party.' Also see Art. 3(a), Chile-Malaysia (1992), and Art. 3, Argentina-Germany (1991).

211. Annex III, Canada-Peru (2006), provides the following express exceptions from MFN treatment:
    (1) Art. 4 shall not apply to treatment accorded under all bilateral or multilateral international agreements in force or signed prior to the date of entry into force of this Agreement.
    (2) Art. 4 shall not apply to treatment by a Party pursuant to any existing or future bilateral or multilateral agreement: (a) establishing, strengthening or expanding a free trade area or customs union; or (b) relating to (i) aviation; (ii) fisheries; (iii) maritime matters, including salvage.
    (3) For greater certainty, Art. 4 shall not apply to any current or future foreign aid programme to promote economic development, whether under a bilateral agreement, or pursuant to a multilateral arrangement or agreement, such as the OECD Agreement on Export Credits.

212. In Annex IV, NAFTA, each NAFTA state has made an exception for MFN treatment with respect to 'treatment accorded under all bilateral or multilateral international agreements in force or signed prior to the date of entry into force of this Agreement.' See also Annex III, Canada-Peru (2006).

Chapter 6
Minimum Standards of Treatment

INTRODUCTION

§6.1 Principle and rationale International investment agreements (IIAs) provide a series of general and specific minimum standards of treatment. General minimum standards, including treatment in accordance with international law, fair and equitable treatment, the prohibition of arbitrary and discriminatory measures, full protection and security, compensation for extraordinary losses and more favourable treatment clauses are covered in this chapter. Other specific minimum standards on expropriation, transfer rights, performance requirements and observance of undertakings are covered separately in Chapters 7-9.

Unlike the national and most-favoured-nation (MFN) obligations considered in the previous two chapters, in which the standard of treatment is contingent on the treatment of a comparator,[1] the substantive content of minimum standards is not determined by reference to the treatment of other investors or investments.[2] With the exception of the prohibition on discriminatory measures, which involves a comparative analysis,[3] minimum standards of treatment measure state conduct

---

1. National and MFN treatment prohibit nationality-based discrimination by providing that foreign investors and investment cannot be treated less favourably than host state nationals and their investments and investors and investments from third states. See *infra* Chapter 4, National Treatment; and *infra* Chapter 5, Most-Favoured-Nation Treatment.
2. Minimum standards of treatment usually apply only to 'investments of investors' and not to 'investors' individually. See *infra* §6.18.
3. A prohibition on impairment by discriminatory measures, while technically a relative standard because it involves an unreasonable distinction being made between things that should be treated alike, is considered in this chapter as this prohibition typically appears in the same IIA provision as the prohibition on arbitrary measures. In addition, there is overlap between minimum and relative standards as IIA tribunals have interpreted fair and equitable treatment as prohibiting certain forms of discrimination. See *infra* §6.27.

against non-contingent, objective standards.[4] Minimum standards of treatment therefore provide a treaty-defined baseline or, in the words of one IIA tribunal, 'a floor below which treatment of foreign investors must not fall, even if a government were not acting in a discriminatory manner.'[5] Minimum standards of treatment serve a key role in promoting and protecting foreign investment by assessing government conduct based on internationally accepted standards of good governance. Standards such as fair and equitable treatment can be viewed as reflecting elements of the rule of law and as serving to restrain abuses of governmental power.[6]

Six types of general minimum standard provisions commonly appear in IIAs, with most IIAs having one or more of these provisions. First, the IIA may require treatment in accordance with the customary international law minimum standard of treatment of aliens and their property.[7] The substantive content of the minimum standard, however, is usually not specified in any detail. Further, the content of the minimum standard has been and remains contentious.[8] In spite of this, it is now generally accepted that a minimum standard of treatment exists in customary international law.[9] IIAs sometimes refer more generally to treatment in accordance with international law. As discussed below, this requires the state to accord, at the very least, the minimum standard of treatment. Second, and more commonly, IIAs guarantee 'fair and equitable treatment' in some shape or form. There remain significant variations in how the fair and equitable treatment standard is drafted. In some cases it appears as an independent standard, whereas in other cases it is expressly associated with the minimum standard of treatment. Often it appears in the same sentence with other standards. Third, some treaties provide a guarantee against impairment by arbitrary or discriminatory measures. This standard often appears in IIAs that also call for fair and equitable treatment, raising interpretive issues about whether there is a substantive difference between the two standards. Fourth, most IIAs require host states to accord investments 'full

---

4. See A. A. Fatouros, *Government Guarantees to Foreign Investors* (New York; London: Columbia University Press, 1962) at 136.
5. *S.D. Myers, Inc. v. Canada* (Partial Award, 13 Nov. 2000) [*Myers*] at para. 259.
6. See *infra* §6.24.
7. The customary standard is sometimes referred to as *the* minimum standard of treatment. Confusion sometimes arises between references to *the* minimum standard and references to treaty-based minimum standards of treatment. References in this book to *the* minimum standard of treatment are to the customary international law minimum standard of treatment of aliens and their property.
8. See *supra* Chapter 1, §1.2 to §1.13, for an overview of the historical debate.
9. See generally, *Barcelona Traction, Light and Power Company, Limited* (*Belgium v. Spain*) [1970] ICJ Rep 3 [*Barcelona Traction*] at 32; A.H. Roth, *The International Minimum Standard* (Leiden: A.W. Sijthoff's Uitgeversmaatschappij N.V., 1949); E. Borchard, 'The "Minimum Standard" of the Treatment of Aliens' (1940) 3 Mich LR 445; I. Brownlie, *Principles of Public International Law*, 6th edn (Oxford: Oxford University Press, 2003) at 502-505 and R. Jennings & A. Watts, eds, *Oppenheim's International Law*, 9th edn (London: Longman, 1992) [*Oppenheim's International Law*] at 903-939. Also see J.C. Thomas, 'Reflections on Article 1105 of NAFTA: History, State Practice and the Influence of Commentators' (2002) 17 ICSID Rev 21 for a comprehensive discussion of authorities on the minimum standard of treatment.

protection and security' of some kind. Fifth, IIAs often provide for compensation standards that apply to extraordinary losses. Finally, some IIAs have more favourable treatment clauses, sometimes also called 'preservation of rights' or 'non-derogation clauses'. This chapter addresses each of these standards and the complex interrelationships amongst them.[10]

§6.2 Overview   The chapter is divided into eight parts. Part I discusses the minimum standard of treatment in customary international law. Part II considers IIA provisions that accord treatment in accordance with international law. The main part of the chapter, Part III, addresses fair and equitable treatment. Provisions on impairment by arbitrary, unreasonable or discriminatory measures are considered in Part IV. Part V addresses obligations of protection and security. Part VI discusses compensation for extraordinary losses. More favourable treatment clauses are considered in Part VII. Part VIII highlights that IIAs normally do not provide specific exceptions to minimum standards of treatment.

I   THE MINIMUM STANDARD OF TREATMENT

§6.3 The continued relevance of the minimum standard of treatment   States are required under customary international law to accord aliens and their property the minimum standard of treatment. In the absence of an IIA, the minimum standard of treatment remains the relevant treatment standard in diplomatic protection claims.[11] In IIA treaty-based claims, the minimum standard of treatment remains highly relevant to the interpretation of IIA obligations. First, some treaties expressly incorporate the minimum standard of treatment as the treaty-based standard or require treatment in accordance with international law. Second, fair and equitable treatment has been interpreted to include, at the very least, the protections afforded by the minimum standard of treatment.[12] Further, other general minimum standards, such as full protection and security, reflect elements of the minimum standard of treatment. As a result, the minimum standard of treatment informs the interpretation of other general minimum standards of treatment in IIAs. Further, some commentators have argued that IIA practice has resulted in the evolution of the minimum standard of treatment and that fair and equitable treatment is now a, or the, customary international law standard.[13]

§6.4 The content of the minimum standard of treatment   Respondent states in a series of early IIA cases have cited the 1926 *Neer* case,[14] a decision of the

---

10. A small number of IIAs have no general minimum standard of treatment provisions. See Albania-Egypt (1993).
11. See *supra* Chapter 1, §1.3 on diplomatic protection.
12. See *infra* §6.21.
13. See *infra* §6.22.
14. *Neer* (1926) IV RIAA 60 at 61-62. See also Commissioner Nielsen's separate opinion at 65.

Mexico-US General Claims Commission, as reflecting the minimum standard of treatment.[15] In *Neer*, the US claimed that Mexico had failed to properly investigate and prosecute those responsible for the murder of one of its nationals. Although the Commission ultimately held that Mexico had not violated the minimum standard of treatment because its officials had been duly diligent in the criminal investigation,[16] it also stated that:

> ... the propriety of governmental acts should be put to the test of international standards ... the treatment of an alien, in order to constitute an international delinquency, should amount to an outrage, to bad faith, to wilful neglect of duty, or to an insufficiency of governmental action so far short of international standards that every reasonable and impartial man would readily recognize its insufficiency. Whether the insufficiency proceeds from the deficient execution of an intelligent law or from the fact that the laws of the country do not empower the authorities to measure up to international standards is immaterial.[17]

Although respondent states have referred to this statement as reflecting the minimum standard of treatment (at least as of 1926),[18] care must be taken in identifying the minimum standard of treatment with a one or two line definition.[19] Rather, the minimum standard of treatment consists of a series of interconnecting and overlapping elements or standards that apply to both the treatment of

---

15. In a number of early NAFTA cases, Canada submitted that *Neer* reflected the international minimum standard. The Czech Republic took a similar position in *Saluka Investments BV v. Czech Republic*. As discussed below, tribunals have, on the whole, rejected this submission. For the discussion of *Neer* as reflecting the minimum standard of treatment, see *Pope & Talbot Inc v. Canada* (Award in Respect of Damages, 31 May 2002) at para. 57; *Mondev International Ltd. v. United States* (Award, 11 Oct. 2002) at para. 114 [*Mondev*]; *United Parcel Services of America Inc. v. Canada* (Award on Jurisdiction, 22 Nov. 2002) at para. 78; *ADF Group Inc. v. United States* (Award, 9 Jan. 2003) [*ADF*] at para. 180; *Waste Management, Inc. v. Mexico* (Award, 30 Apr. 2004) [*Waste Management II*] at para. 93; *GAMI Investments, Inc. v. Mexico* (Final Award, 15 Nov. 2004) at para. 95 [*GAMI*]; and *Saluka Investments BV v. Czech Republic* (Partial Award, 17 Mar. 2006) [*Saluka*] at para. 290.
16. See *infra* §6.8 on due diligence.
17. See also *Harry Roberts* (1926) IV RIAA 77 arising from the physical treatment of a US citizen, Harry Roberts, during his detention by Mexican authorities. The Commission stated, *ibid.*, at 80, that national treatment 'is not the ultimate test of the propriety of the acts of the authorities in the lights of international law. That test is, broadly speaking, whether aliens are treated in accordance with ordinary standards of civilization.' Thus, even where a state has the sovereign right to expel an alien, the minimum standard can be invoked with respect to the manner in which the right is exercised. See also *Boffolo* (1903) X RIAA 528, *Chevreau* (1931) 27 AJIL 153, *Hopkins* (1926) 21 AJIL 160 at 166-167 and discussion in *Oppenheim's International Law*, *supra* note 9 at 903-948.
18. *Supra* note 15. Despite citation in early IIA cases, *Neer* does not appear to have been cited in the voluminous jurisprudence of the Iran-US Claims Tribunal. For a discussion of early references to *Neer*, see Thomas, *supra* note 9 at 31-39.
19. In *Pope & Talbot Inc v. Canada* (Award on the Merits of Phase 2, 10 Apr. 2001) [*Pope & Talbot*] Canada suggested that the minimum standard of treatment is breached where the state acts 'egregiously.' See *Pope & Talbot, ibid.*, at para. 109.

foreigners and their property.[20] Further, the *Neer* case involved the question of state conduct in response to criminal acts of private parties, and not the treatment by the state itself of foreigners or their property.[21] In *Neer*, the Commission did not purport to provide an exhaustive definition of the minimum standard of treatment. The *Neer* decision is therefore of little value as an articulation of the minimum standard for the purpose of IIA claims. It importance lies more in its articulation of the now well-accepted principle that state treatment of aliens and their property is to be measured against an international minimum standard.

IIA tribunals have confirmed that the minimum standard of treatment is constantly in the 'process of development'[22] and has continued to evolve since 1926.[23]

---

20. At the Hague Codification Conference in 1929, delegates considered the *Draft Convention on Responsibility of States for Damage Done in their Territory to the Person or Property of Foreigners* prepared by Professor Edwin Borchard. The draft identifies a number of elements of the minimum standard of treatment including a requirement that redress for injuries to aliens be no less adequate than those afforded to its nationals, responsibility for denial of justice and a requirement for due diligence to prevent injuries. See *supra* Chapter 1, §1.10, regarding the Hague Codification Conference and the draft convention. In 1949, Roth, *supra* note 9 at 185-186, identified the eight following rules that general international law imposes on states with regard to the treatment of aliens: '(1) An alien, whether a natural person or a corporation, is entitled by international law to have his juridical personality and legal capacity recognized by the receiving state. (2) The alien can demand respect for his life and protection for his body. (3) International law protects the alien's personal and spiritual liberty within socially bearable limits. (4) According to general international law, aliens enjoy no political rights in their State of residence, but have to fulfil such public duties as are not incompatible with allegiance to their home state. (5) General international law gives aliens no right to be economically active in foreign States. In cases where national economic policies of foreign States allows aliens to undertake economic activities, however, general international law assures aliens equality of commercial treatment among themselves. (6) According to general international law, the alien's privilege of participation does not go so far as to allow him to acquire private property. The State of residence is free to bar him from ownership of all certain property, whether movables or realty. (7) Where an alien enjoys the privilege of ownership of property, international law protects his rights in so far as his property may not be expropriated under any pretext, except for moral or penal reasons, without adequate compensation. Property rights are to be understood as rights to tangible property which have come into concrete existence according to the municipal law of the alien's State of residence. (8) International law grants the alien procedural rights in his State of residence as primary protection against violation of his substantive rights. These procedural rights amount to freedom of access to court, the right to a fair, non-discriminatory and unbiased hearing, the right to full participation in any form in the procedure, the right to a just decision rendered in full compliance with the laws of the State within a reasonable time.'
21. In *Mondev, supra* note 15, the tribunal stated at para. 115 that '... there is insufficient cause for assuming that provisions of bilateral investment treaties, and of NAFTA, while incorporating the *Neer* principle in respect of the duty of protection against acts of private parties affecting the physical security of aliens present on the territory of the State, are confined to the *Neer* standard of outrageous treatment where the issue is the treatment of foreign investment by the State itself.'
22. *ADF, supra* note 15 at para. 179.
23. *Mondev, supra* note 15 at para. 116; *ADF, ibid.*, at para. 179; and *The Loewen Group, Inc. and Raymond L. Loewen v. United States* (Award, 26 Jun. 2003) [*Loewen*] at para. 132.

This evolution includes the thousands of IIAs concluded amongst states.[24] In its 2004 final award in *Waste Management II*, a *North American Free Trade Agreement* (NAFTA) investment tribunal stated that the minimum standard of treatment is infringed by conduct:

> ... attributable to the State and harmful to the claimant if the conduct is arbitrary, grossly unfair, unjust or idiosyncratic, is discriminatory and exposes the claimant to sectional or racial prejudice, or involves a lack of due process leading to an outcome which offends judicial propriety – as might be the case with a manifest failure of natural justice in judicial proceedings or a complete lack of transparency and candour in an administrative process. In applying this standard it is relevant that the treatment is in breach of representations made by the host State which were reasonably relied on by the claimant.[25]

The above statement highlights a number of specific elements of the minimum standard of treatment where state responsibility may arise for mistreatment of foreign investors and investment, including, but not exhaustively: denial of justice, lack of due process, lack of due diligence, and instances of arbitrariness and discrimination. Each of these elements of the minimum standard is considered below in more detail.

Although the following sections discuss the elements of the minimum standard of treatment in customary international law, reference is sometimes made to IIA cases, in which the tribunals in question are interpreting IIA provisions. In these cases tribunal statements can be read as reflecting the minimum standard of treatment. In particular, with respect to NAFTA, the NAFTA Free Trade Commission (FTC) has equated Article 1105, NAFTA, with the customary international law minimum standard of treatment.[26] NAFTA tribunal interpretations of Article 1105 therefore address the minimum standard of treatment.

§6.5 Denial of justice   Denial of justice is a long recognized element of the minimum standard of treatment. Indeed, many of the classic minimum standard of treatment cases arise out of claims with respect to the host state's misadministration or maladministration of justice.[27]

---

24.   *Ibid.*, at para. 117.
25.   *Waste Management II, supra* note 15 at para. 98. The tribunal referred to the 'the minimum standard of treatment of fair and equitable treatment' as it was interpreting Art. 1105, NAFTA. The NAFTA Free Trade Commission in its 31 Jul. 2001 interpretation equated Art. 1105 with the minimum standard of treatment and stated that for the purposes of Art. 1105, 'The concepts of "fair and equitable treatment" and "full protection and security" do not require treatment in addition to or beyond that which is required by the customary international law minimum standard of treatment of aliens.' On Art. 1105, NAFTA, see *infra* §6.23. See also *Myers, supra* note 5 at para. 263 and *Mondev, supra* note 15 at para. 127.
26.   NAFTA Free Trade Commission, *ibid.*
27.   See, generally, C. Eagleton, 'Denial of Justice in International Law' (1928) 22 AJIL 538; J.W. Garner, 'International Responsibility of States for Judgments of Courts and Verdicts of Juries Amounting to a Denial of Justice' (1929) 10 BYIL 181; G.G. Fitzmaurice, 'The Meaning of the Term "Denial of Justice"' (1932) 13 BYIL 93; C. De Visscher, 'Le deni de justice en droit international' (1935) 52 RDCADI 367; A.V. Freeman, *The International*

The term denial of justice has been used to identify a wide variety of international wrongs. As a result, its use has given rise to much confusion.[28] The term has sometimes been used to refer generally to any breach of international law that entails state responsibility for the treatment of foreigners. This formulation is too broad as it equates denial of justice with the minimum standard of treatment. On the other hand, denial of justice is sometimes used narrowly to refer to a denial of access to courts or to the failure of the courts to pronounce a judgment. This approach is too narrow because it does not encompass the variety of ways in which the justice system may fail. A better and more accurate approach is to associate denial of justice with minimum standards of administration of justice.[29] A denial of justice relates to serious inadequacies in the state's judicial or administrative system with respect to the judicial protection of foreigners and their rights.[30] Irrespective of the treatment that a state affords its own nations, foreigners are entitled to a minimum standard of justice.

In 1929, the Harvard Law School prepared a draft codification of international law relating to the treatment of foreigners called *The Law of Responsibility of States for Damages Done in Their Territory to the Person or Property of Foreigners*[31] (1929 Harvard Draft), which codified the principle of denial of justice as follows:

> Denial of justice exists where there is a denial, unwarranted delay or obstruction of access to courts, gross deficiency in the administration of judicial or remedial process, failure to provide those guaranties which are generally considered indispensable to the proper administration of justice or

---

Responsibility of States for Denial of Justice (London: Longman, Green and Company, 1938); H. W. Spiegel, 'Origin and Development of Denial of Justice' (1938) 32 AJIL 63; E. Borchard, 'The "Minimum Standard" of the Treatment of Aliens' (1940) 3 Mich LR 445; F.V. García-Amador, Louis B. Sohn & R.R. Baxter, *Recent Codification of the Law of State Responsibility for Injuries to Aliens* (Dobbs Ferry, New York: Oceana Publications, 1974); A. Bjorklund, 'Reconciling State Sovereignty and Investor Protection in Denial of Justice Claims,' (2005) 45 VJIL 809 and J. Paulsson, *Denial of Justice in International Law* (Cambridge: Cambridge University Press, 2005) [Paulsson].

28. See D. Wallace, 'Fair and Equitable Treatment and Denial of Justice: Loewen v. US and Chattin v. Mexico,' in T. Weiler, ed., *International Investment Law and Arbitration: Leading Cases from the ICSID, NAFTA, Bilateral Treaties and Customary International Law* (London: Cameron May, 2005) 669 at 671-685 for a discussion of the terminological confusion.

29. On this point see commentary to Article 9, *The Law of Responsibility of States for Damages Done in Their Territory to the Person or Property of Foreigners* (1929) 23 AJIL Spec Supp 173 [1929 Harvard Draft] at 174.

30. Jan Paulsson's recent treatise *Denial of Justice in International Law* provides the following succinct definition 'a state incurs responsibility if it administers justice to aliens in a fundamentally unfair manner.' Paulsson, *supra* note 27 at 4.

31. 1929 Harvard Draft, *supra* note 29. See *supra* Chapter 1, §1.10, for historical background on the 1929 Harvard Draft.

a manifestly unjust judgment. An error of a national court which does not produce manifest injustice is not a denial of justice.[32]

Denial of justice can therefore arise from procedural irregularities in judicial proceedings, such as undue delays, lack of due process, failure to provide a fair hearing or the non-execution of a judgment.[33] This is sometimes referred to as procedural denial of justice.[34] These elements of denial of justice were highlighted in *Robert Azinian, Kenneth Davitian, & Ellen Bacca v. Mexico*, the first NAFTA investment award, and the first IIA award to address denial of justice. The tribunal noted that a denial of justice could be pleaded 'if the relevant courts refuse to entertain a suit, if they subject it to undue delay, or if they administer justice in a seriously inadequate way.'[35] In addition, the *Azinian* tribunal noted that the fact that the national tribunal made an error of law does not constitute denial of justice.[36] IIA tribunals have stated that refusal of access to the courts, undue delay in court proceedings, serious inadequacies in the administration of justice and clearly improper and discreditable court decisions constitute denials of justice.[37]

States can also be held responsible for gross defects in the substance of judicial decisions. Although state responsibility does not arise for an erroneous judgment, it may arise where a court ruling is manifestly unjust.[38] In *Mondev,* the NAFTA tribunal stated that, with respect to judicial decisions, the:

> ... test is not whether a particular result is surprising, but whether the shock or surprise occasioned to an impartial tribunal leads, on reflection, to justified concerns as to the judicial propriety of the outcome, bearing in mind on the

---

32.   Art. 9, *ibid.* The commentary to the Harvard Draft 1929, *ibid.*, at 175, notes that an 'exact definition seems neither possible nor advisable.' The commentary provides a number of examples based on authorities: 'the failure to apprehend a criminal, denial of free access to the courts, failure to render a decision or undue delay in rendering judgment, corruption in the judicial proceedings, discrimination or ill-will against the alien as such, or as a national of a particular state, the refusal in bad faith to apply the local law, executive interference with the freedom or impartiality of the judicial process, failure to execute judgment, denial of an appeal where local law ordinarily permits it, negligently permitting a prisoner to escape, refusal to prosecute the guilty, or premature pardon of a convicted person, have all been deemed, under particular circumstances, instances of "denial of justice." '

33.   A small number of IIAs have specific provisions guaranteeing access to courts. See *infra* Chapter 8, §8.30.

34.   See *Mondev, supra* note 15 at para. 136; *Loewen, supra* note 23 at para. 189 and *Saluka, supra* note 15 at paras 492-493. With respect to procedural irregularities amounting to a denial of justice, see discussion in *Amco Asia Corporation v. Indonesia* (Award, 31 May 1990), 1 ICSID Rep 569 at 597-605.

35.   *Robert Azinian, Kenneth Davitian, & Ellen Baca v. Mexico* (Award, 1 Nov. 1999) [*Azinian*] at para. 102.

36.   *Azinian, ibid.*, at para. 99.

37.   See *Azinian, ibid.*, at paras 97-103. See also *Mondev, supra* note 15 at para. 127; *Loewen, supra* note 23 at paras 57-58; *Waste Management II, supra* note 15 at para. 98; and *Compañía de Aguas del Aconquija, S.A. and Compagnie Générale des Eaux v. Argentina* (Award, 21 Nov. 2000) [*Vivendi I*] at para. 80. This award was later annulled on other grounds.

38.   See Freeman, *supra* note 27 at 326 *et seq.*

one hand that international tribunals are not courts of appeal, and on the other hand that Chapter 11 of NAFTA (like other treaties for the protection of investments) is intended to provide a real measure of protection. In the end the question is whether, at an international level and having regard to generally accepted standards of the administration of justice, a tribunal can conclude in the light of all the available facts that the impugned decision was clearly improper and discreditable, with the result that the investment has been subjected to unfair and inequitable treatment.[39]

Although denial of justice for manifestly unjust judgments is sometimes referred to as substantive denial of justice,[40] this term might be considered a misnomer and potentially confusing because it suggests that IIA tribunals sit in international appellate review of national law. In *Denial of Justice in International Law*, Jan Paulsson rejects the concept of substantive denial of justice, arguing that denial of justice in the form of a manifestly unjust domestic judgment is properly viewed as a deficiency in the process. The manifestly unjust judgment is evidence that the state has failed to provide a judicial system that meets international standards:[41]

> Denial of justice is always procedural. There may be extreme cases where the proof of the failed process is that the substance of a decision is so egregiously wrong that no honest or competent court could possibly have given it. Such cases would sanction the state's failure to provide a decent system of justice. They do not constitute international appellate review of national law.[42]

In other words, the substantive absurdity evidences the procedural defect. It bears emphasizing that customary international law requires states to maintain a judicial system that meets international minimum standards of due process in its treatment of foreigners. These due process protections do not serve to guarantee that final judicial outcomes are reviewable by international tribunals based on a standard of reasonableness. The fact that an international tribunal would have decided a case differently or made different findings of fact or that it considers that the national court made an error of law, is not sufficient to prove denial of justice.

§6.6 Denial of justice and exhaustion of local remedies   One of the significant procedural benefits of investor-state arbitration is that, under most IIAs, there is no need to exhaust local remedies.[43] There must be exhaustion of local remedies, however, to claim denial of justice.[44] Denial of justice arises where a national legal

---

39.   *Mondev, supra* note 15 at para. 127. Also see *Loewen, supra* note 23 at para. 132.
40.   For a recent restatement of the distinction between procedural and substantive denial of justice, see Bjorklund, *supra* note 27.
41.   Paulsson, *supra* note 27, at 82–88.
42.   *Ibid.*, at 98.
43.   See *supra* Chapter 5, §5.11 *et seq.,* on the use of MFN clauses to circumvent local remedy requirements as a condition of proceeding to arbitration.
44.   Some tribunals have, nevertheless, questioned whether this is invariably the case. In *Mondev, supra* note 15 at para. 96, the tribunal stated that: 'under NAFTA it is not true that the denial

system fails to provide justice – not where there is a single procedural irregularity or misapplication of the law at some level of the judicial system.[45] States have an obligation to create a system of justice that allows errors in the administration of justice to be corrected.[46] Since a denial of justice occurs only where 'there is no reasonably available national mechanism to correct the challenged action,'[47] the exhaustion of local remedies becomes an inherent and material element of every denial of justice claim.[48]

The requirement for exhaustion of local remedies was at issue in *Loewen*, where a NAFTA tribunal determined that a Mississippi trial proceeding fell short of international standards of due process.[49] In a much criticized decision,[50] the NAFTA tribunal held that it did not have jurisdiction over Loewen's claim because, as a result of a corporate reorganization, the corporate investor had not maintained continuous Canadian nationality.[51] The *Loewen* tribunal also refused jurisdiction (by way of extended *obiter dictum*) on the basis that Loewen had failed to exhaust local remedies because it failed to apply to the US Supreme Court to review the Mississippi proceedings.[52]

The *Loewen* decision has given rise to a lively debate on the need to exhaust local remedies in the context of IIA denial of justice claims. Jan Paulsson has made a strong case that local remedies should be considered exhausted in this context only where they 'provide no reasonable possibility of an effective remedy,'[53] one of the alternate formulations proposed by Special Rapporteur John Dugard in his *Second Report on Diplomatic Protection* to the International

---

of justice rule and the exhaustion of local remedies rule 'are interlocking and inseparable.' In *Mondev*, the claimant had exhausted local remedies because its petition for *certiorari* to the US Supreme Court was denied (see, *ibid.*, at para. 1).

45. The tribunal in *Loewen, supra* note 23, after surveying various international authorities at paras 151-155 concluded at para. 156 that: 'The purpose of the requirement that a decision of a lower court be challenged through the judicial process before the State is responsible for a breach of international law constituted by judicial decision is to afford the State the opportunity of redressing, through its legal system, the inchoate breach of international law occasioned by the lower court decision.' See also Paulsson, *supra* note 27 at 36.

46. Paulsson, *ibid.*, at 109.

47. Paulsson, *ibid.*, at 100.

48. For a contrary view, however, see Wallace, *supra* note 28 questioning the requirement for exhaustion in the context of IIAs.

49. *Loewen, supra* note 23 at 138. Loewen was sued in Mississippi by O'Keefe for breach of a funeral services contract worth some USD 4 million. The Mississippi jury awarded O'Keefe some USD 500 million in damages. Loewen then sought to appeal the verdict but was required to post an appeal bond for 125% of the judgment as a condition of staying execution. The Mississippi Supreme Court refused to reduce the appeal bond, which effectively foreclosed Loewen's appeal rights because obtaining such a large appeal bond was practically impossible. Loewen eventually settled with O'Keefe for USD 175 million.

50. See, Wallace, *supra* note 28 and N. Rubins, '*Loewen v. United States*: The Burial of an Investor-State Arbitration Claim' (2005) 21 AI 1.

51. See J. Paulsson, 'Continuous Nationality in Loewen' (2004) 20 AI 213.

52. In contrast, in *Mondev, supra* note 15, local remedies had been exhausted as the US Supreme Court denied certiorari.

53. Paulsson, *supra* note 27 at 118.

Law Commission.[54] In *Loewen*, the tribunal found that seeking review of the Mississippi proceedings by the US Supreme Court provided 'at most a reasonable prospect or possibility of success'[55] and that Loewen had failed to present evidence to justify the decision to settle with O'Keefe rather than pursuing other local remedies.[56] Yet, in the subsequent request by Raymond Loewen, in his personal capacity, for a supplemental decision[57] it became clear that the claimants had submitted evidence on the rationale for not seeking Supreme Court review. Despite this evidence and the practical difficulties the claimants faced, the NAFTA tribunal stated that it was not satisfied that Loewen's agreement to settle the original claim had been the only option available to Loewen. The *Loewen* tribunal's reasoning and conclusions on the availability of local remedies can be seriously questioned, despite the undoubted eminence of the tribunal members.[58] In light of the expert evidence that the prospects of a successful appeal to the US Supreme Court were 'illusory,' the better view is that Loewen had exhausted local remedies.[59]

The requirement to exhaust local remedies in order to claim denial of justice in an IIA proceeding has also been criticized by some commentators as inconsistent with the purpose of investor-state arbitration.[60] It is argued that IIA investor-state arbitration mechanisms, having dispensed with procedural requirements for the exhaustion of local remedies, are being interpreted to require exhaustion as a substantive element for denial of justice claims,[61] introducing the exhaustion requirement through the proverbial back door. Further, if investors are required to exhaust judicial appeals of judicial decisions, should not the same rationale apply to administrative and regulatory decisions (such as the denial of an operating permit by a regulatory agency), which are invariably subject to review by some state judicial authority? Andrea Bjorklund has identified the issue as follows:

> From a policy perspective, however, it is difficult to distinguish the desirability of requiring a decision of the highest body within a court system from requiring a final decision from the highest official in an administrative system. Thus, if a lower-level official denies a request for a permit, why not require an applicant to appeal to the official's superiors for a different decision, or to an administrative body with supervisory or appellate oversight? If the *Loewen* tribunal finds that only a final act of a judicial system may give rise

---

54. *Ibid.*, at 115-119.
55. *Loewen, supra* note 23 at 122.
56. *Ibid.*, at 123.
57. The claim had been brought by The Loewen Group, Inc. and Raymond L. Loewen [Loewen]. See *The Loewen Group, Inc. and Raymond L. Loewen v. United States* (Decision on Respondent's Request for a Supplementary Decision, 6 Sep. 2004).
58. Paulsson, *supra* note 27 at 185.
59. See Wallace, *supra* note 28 at 692-693, on this point.
60. See Wallace, *ibid.*
61. C. McLachlan, L. Shore & M. Weiniger, *International Investment Arbitration: Substantive Principles* (Oxford: Oxford University Press, 2007) at 7.97.

to a NAFTA claim, the logical extension of that concept to requiring 'appeals' within different hierarchical structures may lead to claims by states party to NAFTA that eviscerate any waiver of the local remedies rule.[62]

In principle, however, the requirement to exhaust remedies within the judicial system is not inconsistent with the fact that investors are not required to exhaust administrative appeal mechanisms to bring an IIA claim. The reason is that there is a fundamental difference in the type of claim being made. The basis for a claim of denial of justice is that the judicial system has failed to provide justice. Special considerations apply to judicial systems in terms of international minimum standards of procedural due process. Further, a judicial system is specifically designed to allow for review and the correction of due process errors. A due process failure can only be made out where the judicial system has been tested and exhausted. An IIA claim arising as a result of the conduct of the executive branch, for example the denial of a business permit by a government department, gives rise to a categorically different type of claim, which may arise based on various IIA standards, such as national treatment, fair and equitable treatment or expropriation. Finally, a court may also violate an IIA standard – not as a denial of justice – but as a direct breach of the IIA attributable to the respondent state with no requirement to exhaust local remedies. For example, a court decree freezing assets is a measure attributable to the state and an IIA claim might be made without the requirement to exhaust local remedies. An unjustified, complete and permanent freezing order on assets, for example, might well amount to an expropriation, for which the state would be responsible.

On a practical level, where there is state conduct that an investor wishes to challenge, under most IIAs the investor will have a choice. It can challenge the state conduct directly in investor-state arbitration under an applicable IIA or it can engage in administrative processes and ultimately judicial processes for reviewing the conduct. Most reasonable business persons are unlikely to proceed directly to investor-state arbitration if there are low cost and effective options for review by local authorities.[63] Further, although investors should generally be required to exhaust local remedies where claims are made based on denial of justice (and not bring claims based on an alleged breach of due process by a lower magistrate in a district court), IIA tribunals should adopt a flexible approach to whether the investor had exhausted local remedies.

§6.7 Due process   Due process is required in the administration of justice. If a breach of due process is not corrected by the judicial system, a denial of justice will result. The requirement for due process under customary international law, however, applies also to other forms of government decision-making in which host

---

62. Bjorklund, *supra* note 27 at 858.
63. A further practical consideration is that in the absence of some genuine attempt to resolve a domestic law dispute at the local level, there may be insufficient evidence that the state has breached the investment standard in question. See *Generation Ukraine, Inc. v. Ukraine* (Award, 16 Sep. 2003) [*Generation Ukraine*] at para. 20.30.

state decisions affect the rights of the investor or investment. For example, a breach of the minimum standard of treatment might occur if there is a complete lack of candour or transparency and unfairness in an administrative process, such as the revocation of a business license without notice and without the possibility for the licensee to be heard.[64] Further, there may be a lack of due process when a decision-maker bases a decision on inappropriate or irrelevant considerations.[65] However, at least one tribunal has stated that the requirements of administrative due process are less than those of a judicial process.[66]

In a number of cases, IIA tribunals have found a lack of due process sufficient to breach fair and equitable treatment. Yet it appears that an application of the customary minimum standard of treatment would yield the same results. In *Pope & Talbot*, the tribunal found a breach of the minimum standard of treatment in Article 1105, NAFTA, owing to Canada's treatment of the investor during an administrative review process.[67] In *Middle East Cement,* the tribunal held that a failure to provide notification of the seizure and auctioning of property (even when there was apparently no domestic law requirement to do so) breached fair and equitable treatment.[68] On the other hand, in *Genin*, although the tribunal criticized the Central Bank of Estonia for not providing notice that a banking license might be revoked or providing an opportunity for the licensee to be heard, the tribunal concluded that there was no breach of fair and equitable treatment in part because of the investor's own lack

---

64. *Metalclad Corporation v. Mexico* (Award, 30 Aug. 200) [*Metalclad*] at para. 91.
65. *Técnicas Medioambientales Tecmed S.A. v. Mexico* (Award, 29 May 2003) [*Tecmed*] at para. 209 and *Metalclad, ibid.*, at paras 92-93.
66. *International Thunderbird Gaming Corporation v. Mexico* (Arbitral Award, 26 Jan. 2006) [*Thunderbird*] at para. 200: 'The Tribunal does not exclude that the SEGOB proceedings may have been affected by certain irregularities. Rather, the Tribunal cannot find on the record any administrative irregularities that were grave enough to shock a sense of judicial propriety and thus give rise to a breach of the minimum standard of treatment. As acknowledged by Thunderbird, the SEGOB proceedings should be tested against the standards of due process and procedural fairness applicable to administrative officials. The administrative due process requirement is lower than that of a judicial process.'
67. The tribunal in *Pope & Talbot, supra* note 19 at para. 181 stated: 'Against that background, within the context of the verification review process, the treatment of the Investment stands in stark contrast. The relations between the SLD [the Canadian government's Softwood Lumber Division] and the Investment during 1999 were more like combat than co-operative regulation, and the Tribunal finds that the SLD bears the overwhelming responsibility for this state of affairs. It is not for the Tribunal to discern the motivations behind the attitude of the SLD; however, the end result for the Investment was being subjected to threats, denied its reasonable requests for pertinent information, required to incur unnecessary expense and disruption in meeting SLD's requests for information, forced to expend legal fees and probably suffer a loss of reputation in government circles. While administration, like legislation, can be likened to sausage making, this episode goes well beyond the glitches and innocent mistakes that may typify the process. In its totality, the SLD's treatment of the Investment during 1999 in relation to the verification review process is nothing less than a denial of the fair treatment required by NAFTA Article 1105, and the Tribunal finds Canada liable to the Investor for the resultant damages.'
68. See *Middle East Cement Shipping and Handling Co. S.A. v. Egypt* (Award, 12 Apr. 2002) [*Middle East Cement*] at para. 143.

of forthrightness to Central Bank enquiries.[69] Further, as noted above, in *Waste Management II*, a NAFTA tribunal stated that the minimum standard of treatment would be infringed by 'a complete lack of transparency and candour in an administrative process.'[70]

§6.8 Due diligence   The requirement to act with due diligence in the protection of foreigners is a well-accepted element of the minimum standard of treatment.[71] The requirement arises in two contexts. First, the host state must use due diligence to protect foreign nationals and their property from the injurious acts of private parties, including mobs and insurgents. Many early minimum standard of treatment cases involved the failure of host states to protect foreign nationals from physical violence.[72] Second, the state must exercise due diligence in the administration of justice, for example, by investigating or prosecuting those responsible for criminal acts against foreign nationals.[73] State responsibility arises from failure to exercise due diligence to prevent crime or in the pursuit, arrest and bringing to justice of the accused.[74]

§6.9 Arbitrariness   Various elements of the minimum standard of treatment protect the foreign investor and investment from arbitrary host state conduct. Responsibility for denial of justice, requirements for due process, prohibitions on racial and other forms of discrimination and respect for acquired rights, including the requirement to pay compensation for expropriation, all serve to discipline arbitrary and abusive government conduct. More generally, an overriding obligation to refrain from arbitrary conduct that impairs the acquired rights of aliens is sometimes grounded on the principle of abuse of rights and the requirement of good

---

69.   See *Alex Genin, Eastern Credit Limited, Inc. and A.S. Baltoil v. Estonia* (Award, 18 Jun. 2001) [*Genin*] at paras 357-358 and 362. On due process see also *Myers, supra* note 5 at para. 134: 'Article 1105 of the NAFTA requires the Parties to treat investors of another Party in accordance with international law, including fair and equitable treatment. Article 1105 imports into the NAFTA the international law requirements of due process, economic rights, obligations of good faith and natural justice.'
70.   *Waste Management II, supra* note 15 at para. 98. See also *Myers, supra* note 5 at para. 263 and *Mondev, supra* note 15 at para. 127.
71.   See I. Brownlie, *System of the Law of Nations: State Responsibility Part I* (Oxford: Clarendon Press, 1983) at 159-166 regarding responsibility for the acts of private persons and 167-179 regarding responsibility in case of insurrection and civil war. See also *Oppenheim's International Law, supra* note 9 at 549-554. Requirements for due diligence are reflected in the 1929 Harvard Draft, *supra* note 31. Arts 10-12 address cases of state responsibility for the failure of the state to exercise due diligence to prevent injury, including cases of acts of an individual or from mob violence and insurgents. Requirements for due diligence are also reflected in Art. 13 of the 1961 Harvard Draft (1961) 55 AJIL 545. For a recent overview of public international law relating to due diligence, see R.B. Barnidge, 'The Due Diligence Principle Under International Law' (2006) 8 ICLR 81.
72.   *Youmans* (1926) IV RIAA 110.
73.   *Janes* (1926) IV RIAA 82.
74.   See *Oppenheim's International Law, supra* note 9 at 549, note 4.

faith.[75] An abuse of rights may occur when a state exercises its rights in a manner that prevents other states from exercising their rights, exercises rights for a purpose other than that for which the right exists, or arbitrarily exercises rights and causes injury to another state but does not clearly violate its rights.[76] The concept of abuse of rights is an expression of the principle of good faith. In *Case Concerning Rights of Nationals of the United States of America in Morocco*,[77] which dealt with the Nazi practice of imposing flight taxes, the International Court of Justice (ICJ) found an abuse of rights where the state did not exercise its power to value property for the purposes of taxation reasonably and in good faith. Limits on the right of a state to expel aliens is another example of the application of customary international law prohibitions on arbitrariness and abuse of rights.[78]

It is unclear whether, historically, the prohibition on arbitrariness was confined to specific types of due process protections, physical integrity of the individual and respect for acquired rights, or whether the specific instances reflected a more generalized obligation to refrain from arbitrary conduct with respect to the treatment of aliens and their property. In his 1931 Hague lectures Alfred Verdross suggested that a state may not arbitrarily impair the acquired rights of a foreigner.[79] Further, §712 of the *Restatement (Third) of the Foreign Relations Law of the United States* provides that a state is responsible under international law for injury resulting from … 'other arbitrary or discriminatory acts or omissions by the state that impair property or other economic interests of a national of another state.' The commentary to §712 notes that 'arbitrary' refers 'to an act that is unfair and unreasonable, and inflicts serious injury to established rights of foreign nationals, though falling short of an act that would constitute an expropriation.'[80]

On the other hand, if there was a general prohibition on arbitrary conduct as an overarching principle in customary international law, it is surprising that neither the 1929 nor the 1961 Harvard Draft Conventions attempted to codify it. Rather, both draft instruments identify specific elements of the minimum standard of treatment where arbitrary conduct may give rise to responsibility.[81]

What, then, amounts to arbitrariness in the context of the treatment of foreign investors and investment? Different approaches to the meaning of arbitrary conduct in the foreign investment treaty context are reflected in *Elettronica Sicula*

---

75. See B. Cheng, *General Principles of Law* (London: Stevens & Sons, Ltd, 1953) at 121-136 and A.C. Kiss, *L'abus de droit en droit international* (Paris: Librairie générale de droit et de jurisprudence, 1952).

76. A. Kiss, 'Abuse of Rights,' in *Encyclopedia of Public International Law*, ed. R. Bernhardt, Vol. 1 (Amsterdam: North-Holland Pub. Co., 1992) at 4-5.

77. [1952] ICJ Rep 176 at 212.

78. See Memorandum by the International Law Commission Secretariat, Expulsion of Aliens (10 Jul. 2006) A/CN.4/565.

79. A. Verdross, *Les règles internationales concernant le traitement des étrangers* (1931-III) 37 RDCADI 323 at 358-59.

80. *The American Law Institute's Restatement (Third) of the Foreign Relations Law of the United States* (Washington: American Law Institute Publishers, 1987).

81. See *supra* note 20. Roth's enumeration of the elements of the minimum standard of treatment in his comprehensive 1949 treatise, *ibid.*, contains no general prohibition on arbitrariness.

S.p.A (ELSI).[82] In *ELSI*, one of the issues in dispute was whether the requisition of a foreign-owned factory by the local mayor was an arbitrary measure under the Italy-US *Treaty of Friendship, Commerce and Navigation* (FCN Treaty).[83] The Italian courts had found the mayor's requisition of the ELSI plant to have been unlawful and beyond the administrative powers of the mayor. The US argued that arbitrary measures include an unreasonable or unfair exercise of government authority.[84] In contrast, Italy argued that an arbitrary measure is one for which there is a complete lack of justification, in the sense that there is no lawful basis for the exercise of power.[85] In Italy's view, the mayor had the power to requisition under Italian law and the fact that the requisition had been found to be illegal did not make his conduct arbitrary. The majority of the Chamber of the ICJ agreed with Italy's position and held that illegality under local law was not sufficient to make the mayor's conduct 'arbitrary' under international law:

> To identify arbitrariness with mere unlawfulness would be to deprive it of any useful meaning in its own right. Nor does it follow from a finding by a municipal court that an act was unjustified, or unreasonable, or arbitrary, that that act is necessarily classed as arbitrary in international law, though the qualification given to the impugned act by a municipal authority may be a valuable indication ... [86]
>
> Arbitrariness is not so much something opposed to a rule of law, as something opposed to the rule of law. This idea was expressed by the Court in the *Asylum* case, when it spoke of 'arbitrary action' being 'substituted for the rule of law' (*Asylum, Judgment, I.C.J. Reports 1950*, p. 284). It is a wilful disregard of due process of law, an act which shocks, or at least surprises, a sense of juridical propriety.[87]

In his dissent, Judge Stephen Schwebel found that the Italian measures were arbitrary. He based this finding on three factors: (i) the local courts had found the requisition to be arbitrary; (ii) the requisition was unreasonable and capricious because, among other things, it was illegal, issued to assuage public opinion and

---

82. *Elettronica Sicula S.p.A. (ELSI) (US v. Italy)* [1989] ICJ Rep 15 [*ELSI*]. The decision was made by a Chamber of the ICJ consisting of Judges Ago, Jennings, Oda, Ruda and Schwebel. For further background, see *supra* Chapter 1, §1.27.
83. The factory was owned by ELSI, an Italian company, which was in turn wholly owned by two US corporations. The US claimed that Italy had breached the 1948 Italy-US FCN Treaty, a 1951 Supplementary Agreement to the FCN and customary international law. Article I of the Supplementary Agreement provided protection against 'arbitrary or discriminatory measures ... resulting particularly in: (a) preventing ... effective control and management of enterprises ... or, (b) impairing ... other legally acquired rights and interests ... .'
84. International Court of Justice Verbatim Record, C 3/CR 89/3 at 51 (15 Feb. 1989) as cited by S.D. Murphy, 'The ELSI Case: An Investment Dispute at the International Court of Justice' (1991) 16 YJIL 391 at note 175.
85. International Court of Justice Verbatim Record, C 3/CR 89/7 at 42-43 (22 Feb. 1989) as cited by S.D. Murphy, *ibid.*, at note 177.
86. *ELSI, supra* note 82 at para. 124.
87. *Ibid.*, at para. 128.

incapable of achieving its purported purpose; and (iii) a review of the mayor's order by the Italian courts could not correct the arbitrariness of the mayor's act.[88] Judge Schwebel found that since the treaty in question prohibited arbitrary measures, Italy was required to achieve a specified result – that of relieving ELSI from the effects of the arbitrary measure.[89] On this last point, Judge Schwebel distinguished between whether the protection from arbitrary or discriminatory measures' was an obligation of conduct or an obligation of result.[90] In Judge Schwebel's view, arbitrariness for the purposes of the FCN Treaty was an obligation of result. The appeal to the Italian courts and the annulment of the requisition order sixteen months later, did not remedy the initial wrongdoing, or otherwise fully compensate ELSI for the effect of the original act.[91]

The majority's approach has been criticized because its interpretation of arbitrariness suggests that an investor is not treated arbitrarily as long as the state asserts a lawful basis for its actions and provides due process in local courts.[92] This approach arguably confines the concept of arbitrariness to procedural due process. On the other hand, Judge Schwebel's approach imports a more substantive review by focusing on whether the government measure in question was

---

88. *Ibid.*, at paras 108-121.
89. *Ibid.*, at 118.
90. Judge Schwebel refers to the then draft Arts 20 and 21 of the ILC's *Draft Articles on State Responsibility* which originally made a distinction between obligations of conduct and obligations of result. Obligations of conduct refer to obligations requiring a state to adopt a particular course of conduct. Obligations of result refer to obligations requiring a state to achieve, by means of its own choice, a specified result. He categorized the prohibition on arbitrary measures as an obligation of result, not of means or conduct. The final version of the ILC's *Articles on State Responsibility* does not include draft Arts 20 and 21. The Articles now provide in Art. 12 that '[t]here is a breach of an international obligation by a State when an act of that State is not in conformity with what is required of it by that obligation, regardless of its origin or character.' The commentary to Art. 12 notes that the distinction between obligations of conduct and obligations of result is commonly made and this distinction may be helpful in ascertaining whether a breach has occurred. See International Law Commission's Articles on Responsibility of States for Internationally Wrongful Acts, *Official Records of the General Assembly,* UN GAOR, 56th Sess., Supp. No. 10, UN Doc A/56/10 at 11; 2001 YBILC, Vol. II, Part Two. The Articles and commentary are *reprinted in* J. Crawford, *The International Law Commission's Articles on State Responsibility: Introduction, Text, and Commentaries* (Cambridge: Cambridge University Press, 2002) [ILC's Articles on State Responsibility] at 129.
91. *ELSI, supra* note 82 at 121: 'the equivalent result was not attained by Italian administrative and judicial processes, however estimable they were.' The majority found that at the time of the requisition, ELSI was technically insolvent and therefore was not entitled under Italian law to control its own liquidation. Since the majority concluded that ELSI had no right to control its liquidation under Italian law, the requisition did not deprive ELSI of any rights or impair ELSI's rights. In other words, ELSI's precarious financial situation – not the requisition – was the cause of its losses. Judge Schwebel dissented on this point. See *ELSI, supra* note 82 at 100-108. In his view, since ELSI's original position was characterized by the right to manage its own liquidation, the requisition had resulted in the loss of that right. The success of subsequent appeals did not compensate for this loss.
92. See S.D. Murphy, *supra* note 84 at 433-434. Also see K. J. Hamrock, 'The *ELSI* Case: Toward an International Definition of "Arbitrary Conduct"' (1992) TILJ 837.

clearly unreasonable. In this respect, Judge Schwebel's view of arbitrariness is closer to the US pleadings in *ELSI* and the position in the US *Third Restatement* that arbitrary refers to an act that is 'unfair and unreasonable.'[93]

As discussed below, IIA jurisprudence to date, although interpreting treaty provisions, suggests more generally that the customary minimum standard of treatment is breached by arbitrary conduct.[94] Respondent states do not appear to have contested that, at least within the IIA framework, the minimum standard of treatment is breached by arbitrary treatment of foreign investment. Further, IIA tribunals have confirmed that conduct that is arbitrary in international law is a breach of the 'fair and equitable treatment' standard.[95] With respect to illegality, IIA tribunals have confirmed that something more than simple illegality or lack of authority (*ultra vires* acts) under domestic law is necessary to breach the minimum standard of treatment.[96]

It is not clear what amounts to arbitrariness under the current international minimum standard. In defining arbitrariness, a number of IIA tribunals have referred to the definition in *ELSI*, quoted above. The literal meaning of 'arbitrary' suggests a decision that is derived from opinion or preference, a capricious and unrestrained exercise of power. In contrast, an unreasonable decision is one not based on sound reasoning, inequitable or unfair.[97] The tribunal in *Waste Management II* stated that the minimum standard of fair and equitable treatment in the NAFTA is breached by conduct that is arbitrary, grossly unfair, unjust or idiosyncratic.[98] It did not equate unreasonableness with arbitrariness. Thus, although the minimum standard of treatment and the fair and equitable treatment standard are both (if indeed they are at all different) breached by arbitrary acts, there is less authority for the proposition that 'arbitrary' is to be equated with 'unreasonable.'[99]

Finally, it may be useful to distinguish between two types of arbitrariness. The discussion of arbitrariness above focuses on whether the government measures in question fail to meet some yardstick of rationality or proportionality. This could

---

93.   *Third Restatement,* §712 and Reporters' Note 11, *supra* note 80.
94.   See *Waste Management II, supra* note 15.
95.   *CMS Gas Transmission Company v. Argentina* (Award, 12 May 2005) [*CMS*] at para. 290; *Waste Management II, supra* note 15 at para. 98, and *Myers, supra* note 5 at para. 263.
96.   This view was endorsed in *ADF, supra* note 15 at para. 190 with respect to whether domestic illegality was a breach of the minimum standard of treatment: 'The Tribunal would emphasize, too, that even if the U.S. measures were somehow shown or admitted to be *ultra vires* under the internal law of the United States, that by itself does not necessarily render the measures grossly unfair or inequitable under the customary international law standard of treatment embodied in Article 1105(1). An unauthorized or *ultra vires* act of a governmental entity of course remains, in international law, the act of the State of which the acting entity is part, if that entity acted in its official capacity. But something more than simple illegality or lack of authority under the domestic law of a State is necessary to render an act or measure inconsistent with the customary international law requirements of Article 1105(1).'
97.   See Oxford English Dictionary, online edition.
98.   *Waste Management II, supra* note 15 at para. 98.
99.   See *infra* §6.36 on this issue.

be referred to as substantive arbitrariness. The second type of arbitrariness is procedural and overlaps with denial of justice, lack of due process and lack of due diligence.

§6.10 Discrimination   Discrimination is a relative standard, involving a comparison between two things or situations. The use of the terms 'discrimination' and 'discriminatory' give rise to confusion in the IIA context because IIA texts and tribunals often use the terms generically without specifying what type or types of discrimination are prohibited. Since host state regulatory frameworks typically depend on drawing distinctions of some kind, discrimination cannot be the same as distinction. Discrimination in the IIA context involves a type of illegitimate distinction between persons or things that are in a similar situation.

At least four different types of discrimination claim might arise in the IIA context. The first is discrimination prohibited by international human rights law with respect to individuals, if it is based on factors such as race, sex and religion, unless there is an objective and legitimate justification for the distinction.[100] Racial discrimination and other forms of discrimination contrary to international human rights breach the minimum standard of treatment. For example, in *Waste Management II* the tribunal included conduct that 'is discriminatory and exposes the claimant to sectional or racial prejudice' as prohibited by the minimum standard of treatment.

Second, there may be other forms of discrimination not prohibited under customary international law that relate to the status of the investor or investment. In particular, it is well-accepted that, subject to treaty obligations, a state may in its legislative measures discriminate on the basis of nationality.[101] For example, foreigners generally have neither the right to vote, nor to political affiliation nor to receive state aid.[102] A state law that limits eligibility to state funding to host state nationals does not breach customary international law. Typically, IIA national and MFN treatment obligations address nationality-based discrimination of this kind by requiring that foreign investors or investments receive no less favourable treatment than either nationals or investments of the host state itself or third party

---

100.   The main instruments in international human rights law consist of the *Universal Declaration of Human Rights*, GA Res. 217 (III) A, U.N. Doc. A/811 (1948), the *International Covenant on Civil and Political Rights*, 16 Dec. 1966, 999 U.N.T.S. 171 [ICCPR] and the *International Covenant on Economic, Social and Cultural Rights*, UNGAOR, 21st Sess., U.N. Doc. A/6316 (1966). These, plus the Optional Protocol to the ICCPR constitute what has been called the 'International Bill of Human Rights.' See, generally, H.J. Steiner, P. Alston & R. Goodman, *International Human Rights in Context: Law, Politics, Morals*, 3rd edn (Oxford: Oxford University Press, 2007). Other key international human rights treaties include the *International Convention on the Elimination of All Forms of Racial Discrimination* (CERD), the *International Convention on the Elimination of Discrimination Against Women*, the *Convention Against Torture and Other Cruel, Inhuman or Degrading Treatment or Punishment* (CAT), and the *Convention on the Rights of the Child* (CRC).
101.   See *supra* Chapter 4, §4.3 and Chapter 5, §5.2.
102.   See Brownlie, *Principles of Public International Law, supra* note 9 at 546-549.

states.[103] As discussed below, some IIAs do not have express national and MFN treatment provisions and refer more generally to discriminatory measures. IIA tribunals have interpreted these provisions as including nationality-based discrimination.[104]

Third, foreigners are entitled to the non-discriminatory application of host state law. Although under customary international law may distinguish between foreigners and nationals (e.g., with respect to entitlement to state aid), domestic law must be *applied* without distinction on nationality, unless the distinction in question is expressly provided in the law. If domestic courts apply domestic law in a discriminatory manner (e.g., if a foreigner is denied the right to commence a claim in domestic courts based on the foreigner's nationality), the foreign investor will have grounds for claiming a breach of the customary minimum standard based on a denial of justice.[105]

Fourth, discrimination may occur where the state makes an arbitrary or unreasonable distinction between similarly situated investors or investments. Discrimination in this sense overlaps substantially with concepts of arbitrariness, unreasonableness and unfairness.[106]

§6.11 Individuals and international human rights law   The pre-World War II (WWII) jurisprudence on the minimum standard of treatment with respect to the treatment of individuals (e.g., denial of justice claims) has to a large extent been eclipsed by the post-WWII development of international human rights law. State measures that affect individual foreign investors may well violate international human rights law and give rise to a claim under regional and international human rights instruments. Violations of international human rights may also give rise to a violation of minimum standard of treatment provisions in IIAs.[107] With respect to procedural rights, there may be significant overlap between claims of human rights violations on the one hand, and claims of denial of justice and due process on the other.[108]

---

103. See *supra* Chapters 4 and 5.
104. See *infra* §6.38.
105. See *supra* §6.5.
106. See *supra* §6.9 above on arbitrariness. Prohibitions in IIAs on arbitrary, unreasonable or discriminatory measures are discussed below in Part V.
107. See Brownlie, *Principles of Public International Law, supra* note 9 at 537 and *Declaration on the Human Rights of Individuals Who are not Nationals of the Country in Which They Live*, G.A. Res. 40/144 (13 Dec. 1985). In *Barcelona Traction, supra* note 9 the ICJ referred to the 'principles and rules concerning the basic rights of the human person' as obligations *erga omnes* (at 32).
108. On the interaction between IIAs and international human rights, see International Institute for Sustainable Development, *International Human Rights in Bilateral Investment Treaties and in Investment Arbitration* (Winnipeg: IISD, 2003); T. Weiler, 'Balancing Human Rights and Investor Protection: A New Approach for a Different Legal Order' (2004) BCICLR 429; R. Suda, 'The Effect of Bilateral Investment Treaties on Human Rights Enforcement and Realization,' in O.D. De Schutter, ed., *Transnational Corporations and Human Rights*, (Oxford: Hart, 2006); and H. Mann, 'International investment agreements, Business and Human Rights: Key Issues and Opportunities' (Feb. 2008). Online: <http://reports-and-materials.org/

The extent to which an individual investor may be able to claim a breach of an IIA for human rights violations is unclear. International human rights generally protect the human being and not corporate entities or commercial interests. Furthermore, most minimum standard of treatment provisions only apply to *investments* made by investors and not to individual investors. Depending on the IIA in question, an individual investor may be able to rely on breaches of international human rights obligations to found a breach of the treaty's minimum standards of treatment. Conduct directed at the individual investor, such as arbitrary detention, may also result in the impairment of the investment.[109] Finally, it is important to note that a host state might also rely on its international human rights obligations to justify measures that it has taken.[110]

II TREATMENT IN ACCORDANCE WITH INTERNATIONAL LAW

§6.12 IIA clauses IIAs sometimes provide for treatment 'in accordance with international law'.[111] For example, Article 2(1), Bosnia and Herzegovina-Sweden (2000), provides that neither party 'shall award treatment less favourable than that required by international law.' Article II(2)(a), US-Argentina (1991), provides:

> Investment shall at all times be accorded fair and equitable treatment, shall enjoy full protection and security and shall in no case be accorded treatment less than that required by international law.

Finally, Article 1105(1), NAFTA, entitled 'Minimum Standard of Treatment,' provides:

> Each Party shall accord to investments of investors of another Party treatment in accordance with international law, including fair and equitable treatment and full protection and security.

IISD-Ruggie-Feb-2008.pdf>. With respect to human rights protections during the conduct of arbitrations, see G. Petrochilos, *Procedural Law in International Arbitration* (Oxford: Oxford University Press, 2004) and A. Jaksic, *Arbitration and Human Rights*, Comparative and International Law Studies, No. 59 (Frankfurt: Peter Lang). See *supra* Chapter 2, §2.25, on the relevance of human rights in interpreting IIAs.

109. See *Biloune and Marine Drive Complex Ltd v. Ghana Investments Centre and the Government of Ghana* (Award on Jurisdiction and Liability, 27 Oct. 1989) 95 ILR 184. In *Biloune,* the tribunal stated that while the state conduct in question could constitute a violation of fundamental human rights, the tribunal lacked jurisdiction to address human rights issues because its jurisdiction was limited to commercial disputes (*ibid.*, at 202-203). See *supra* Chapter 2, §2.25.

110. The decision on *amicus curiae* in *Suez, Sociedad General de Aguas de Barcelona S.A. and Vivendi Universal S.A. v. Argentina* noted that the dispute involved the water distribution and sewage systems of a large metropolitan area which provides basic public services to millions of people, and 'as a result may raise a variety of complex public and international law questions, including human rights considerations.' *Ibid.* (Order in Response to a Petition for Transparency and Participation as *Amicus curiae*, 19 May 2005) at para. 19.

111. This provision is common in Belgian, Canadian, French, Japanese, Swiss, UK and US BITs.

Although treatment in accordance with international law means at least and by definition the minimum standard of treatment,[112] it could also mean other sources of international law, such as treaty obligations or general principles of law. In the NAFTA context, the parties have clarified that the reference to international law means the minimum standard of treatment and not conventional norms.[113]

There does not appear to be any state treaty practice or *travaux préparatoires* to suggest that references to treatment in accordance with international law in IIAs were intended to extend to a host state's treaty obligations. Further, the implication of this interpretation would be very far reaching – it would provide investors a direct recourse against the state for *any* breach of a state's myriad international treaty obligations. This would mean, for example, that investors could seek damages for a breach of a state's World Trade Organization (WTO) obligations. If states intended to provide this novel and extremely broad right, it would be surprising that it does not appear to be reflected in *travaux préparatoires* or government statements about the meaning of 'international law.'

The better view is that where states have intended to guarantee treatment in accordance with other general treaty obligations they have done so expressly. For example, Article 10(1), Energy Charter Treaty (ECT), provides:

> In no case shall such Investments be accorded treatment less favourable than that required by international law, *including treaty obligations*. Each Contracting Party shall observe any obligations it has entered into with an Investor or an Investment of an Investor of any other Contracting Party. [Emphasis added.]

This formulation is uncommon in IIAs. On its face it suggests that an investor is entitled to claim a breach whenever a Member State of the ECT breaches any international treaty obligations, including for example obligations under the *General Agreement on Tariffs and Trade* and the *General Agreement on Trade in Services*.[114]

Recent US, Canadian and Norwegian Model BITs clarify that references to treatment in accordance with international law means treatment in accordance

---

112. In considering the meaning of an IIA clause providing for treatment 'which conforms to principles of international law,' the tribunal in *Ronald S. Lauder v. Czech Republic* (Award, 3 Sep. 2001) stated at para. 209 that acts or omissions that fall below the minimum standard or treatment violate the obligation to provide 'fair and equitable treatment.' Art. II(2)(a) of the Czechoslovakia-US BIT reads as follows: 'Investment shall at all times be accorded fair and equitable treatment, shall enjoy full protection and security and shall in no case be accorded treatment less than that which conforms to principles of international law.'

113. As discussed above at *supra* note 25, the NAFTA Free Trade Commission has issued an interpretive statement equating Art. 1105 with the customary international law minimum standard of treatment. In *Azinian*, in reference to a claim of breach of Art. 1105(1), the tribunal stated that the substantive principle is that a NAFTA investor should not be dealt with in a 'manner that contravenes international law.' *Azinian*, *supra* note 35 at para. 92.

114. G. Verhoosel, 'The Use of Investor-State Arbitration under Bilateral Investment Treaties to Seek Relief for Breaches of WTO Law' (2003) 6 JIEL 493.

with the minimum standard of treatment.[115] The US and Canadian Models also provide that a breach of another provision of the IIA or a separate international agreement does not establish that there has been a breach of the minimum standard of treatment provision.[116]

III   FAIR AND EQUITABLE TREATMENT

§6.13 The baseline of investment protection   Fair and equitable treatment has emerged as perhaps the most important standard of treatment in IIAs. Fair and equitable treatment clauses appear in most IIAs. Further, even where there is no express fair and equitable treatment clause in the IIA, the standard is likely to be applicable based on an MFN clause. As discussed below, IIA tribunals have interpreted fair and equitable treatment as providing a wide range of procedural and substantive protections, including the protection of legitimate expectations.[117] Given the breadth of the treatment standard, claims of a breach of fair and equitable treatment can succeed where claims under more specific standards might fail.

§6.14 Early treaty practice   The term fair and equitable treatment has its provenance in post-WWII economic treaties. It was not a term of art in public

---

115. Art. 5, 2003 Canadian Model BIT; Art. 5, 2004 US Model BIT; and Art. 5, 2007 Norwegian Model BIT.

116. Art. 5(3), 2003 Canadian Model BIT; and Art. 5(3), 2004 US Model BIT.

117. For commentary on fair equitable treatment, see S. Vasciannie, 'The Fair and Equitable Treatment Standard in International Investment Law and Practice'(1999) 70 BYIL 99; UNCTAD, '*Fair and Equitable Treatment*,' UNCTAD Series on issues in international investment agreements (New York and Geneva: United Nations, 1999) (UNCTAD/ITE/ IIT/11); J.C. Thomas, 'Reflections on Article 1105 of NAFTA: History, State Practice and the Influence of Commentators' (2002) 17 ICSID Rev 21; C. Yannaca-Small, 'Fair and Equitable Treatment Standard in International Investment Law,' in OECD, *International Investment Law: A Changing Landscape* (Paris: OECD, 2005); R. Dolzer, 'Fair and Equitable Treatment: A Key Standard in Investment Treaties' (2005) 39 IL 87 [*Dolzer*]; C. Schreuer, 'Fair and Equitable Treatment in Arbitral Practice' (2005) 6 JWIT 357; B. Choudhury, 'Evolution or Devolution? – Defining Fair and Equitable Treatment in International Investment Law' (2005) 6 JWIT 297 (2005); S. Schill, 'Fair and Equitable Treatment under Investment Treaties as an Embodiment of the Rule of Law,' Institute for International Law and Justice, New York University School of Law Working Paper 2006/6; T. Westcott, 'Recent Practice on Fair and Equitable Treatment' (2007) 8(3) JWIT 409; G. Mayeda, 'Playing Fair: The Meaning of Fair and Equitable Treatment in Bilateral Investment Treaties' (2007) 41 JWT 273; C. McLachlan, L. Shore & M. Weiniger, *International Investment Arbitration: Substantive Principles* (Oxford: Oxford University Press, 2007); R. Dolzer & C. Schreuer, *Principles of International Investment Law* (Oxford: Oxford University Press, 2008); L. Paradell, 'The BIT Experience of the Fair and Equitable Treatment Standard', in F. Ortino, L. Liberti, A. Sheppard & H. Warner, eds, *Investment Treaty Law, Current Issues II* (London: BIICL, 2007) 117; and I. Tudor, *The Fair and Equitable Treatment Standard in the International Law of Foreign Investment* (Oxford: Oxford University Press, 2008).

international law before WWII.[118] The term 'just and equitable treatment' appears in the investment provisions[119] of the 1948 *Havana Charter*, the treaty which would have established the proposed International Trade Organization.[120] The *Economic Agreement of Bogotá* (1948) provided that foreign investment should receive 'equitable treatment.' References to 'equitable' or 'fair and equitable' appear in numerous post-WWII FCN treaties.[121] Fair and equitable treatment was included as a term in post-WWII draft investment conventions including the 1959 *Draft Convention on Investments Abroad*[122] and the 1963 and 1967 drafts of the Organization for Economic Co-operation and Development (OECD) *Draft Convention on the Protection of Foreign Property*.[123] The term is now commonly used in multilateral,[124] regional,[125] sectoral[126] and bilateral[127] treaties.

---

118. By 1996, however, a judge of the International Court of Justice referred to fair and equitable treatment as a term of art. In *Oil Platforms (Iran v. United States)* [1996] ICJ Rep at 858, para. 39, Judge Higgins in her separate opinion stated that ' "fair and equitable treatment to nationals and companies" and "unreasonable and discriminatory measures" are legal terms of art well known in the field of overseas investment protection, which is what is there addressed.'

119. Art. 11(2), *Havana Charter for an International Trade Organization*, 24 Mar. 1948, UN Conference on Trade and Employment, UN Doc. E/CONF.2/78, Sales No. 1948.II.D.4.

120. See *supra* Chapter 1, §1.15.

121. US FCN treaties with Belgium, Luxembourg, Greece, Ireland, Israel, France and Pakistan provided for 'equitable treatment,' while treaties with the Federal Republic of Germany, Ethiopia and The Netherlands called for 'fair and equitable treatment.' Kenneth Vandevelde, a former US BIT treaty negotiator, argues that the terms 'fair and equitable treatment' and 'equitable treatment' are synonymous. See K. Vandevelde, 'The Bilateral Treaty Program of the United States' (2001) 21 CILQ 201 at 221.

122. *Draft Convention on Investments Abroad* (1960) 9 JPL 116 [Abs-Shawcross Draft Convention]. See *supra* Chapter 1, §1.16, for background.

123. OECD *Draft Convention on the Protection of Foreign Property* (1963) 2 ILM 241 [1963 Draft Convention] and (1968) 7 ILM 118 [1967 Draft OECD Convention]. See *supra* Chapter 1, §1.30, for background.

124. See Art. 12(d), *Convention Establishing the Multilateral Investment Guarantee Agency* (1985) 24 ILM 1605, which provides that the Multilateral Investment Guarantee Agency must be satisfied that the host country provides 'fair and equitable treatment and legal protection for the investment' before it will provide investment guarantees (1988) 27 ILM 1228. See *supra* Chapter 1, §1.29, for background on the MIGA Convention.

125. See Art. 258, *Fourth Convention of the African, Caribbean and Pacific Group of States and the European Economic Community* (EEC) [*Lomé IV*] (1989) 29 ILM 809; Art. IV, *ASEAN Treaty for the Promotion and Protection of Investments* (1987) 27 IILM 612; Art. 3, *Colonia Protocol on Reciprocal Promotion and Protection of Investments, reprinted in* UNCTAD, *International Investment Instruments: A Compendium*, Vol. 2 (New York: United Nations, 1996) at 513 and Art. 159, *Common Market for Eastern and Southern Africa (COMESA)* (1994) 33 ILM 1072.

126. *Energy Charter Treaty* [ECT], Art. 10(1), (1995) 34 ILM 373.

127. See §6.15 below.

§6.15 IIA practice Although the fair and equitable treatment standard is included in the majority of IIAs,[128] there are important variations among IIA texts. The most common practice is for fair and equitable treatment to appear by itself, unqualified by any other terms.[129] This formulation is common in Dutch, German, Swedish, Swiss and US BITs.[130] In many cases, although the requirement for fair and equitable treatment is unqualified, it is combined with other treatment standards in the same sentence. For example, Article II(2)(a), Argentina-US (1991), provides:

> Investment shall at all times be accorded fair and equitable treatment, shall enjoy full protection and security and shall in no case be accorded treatment less than that required by international law.

Another example is Article 3(1), Czechoslovakia-Netherlands (1991), which provides:

> Each Contracting Party shall ensure fair and equitable treatment to the investments of investors of the other Contracting Party and shall not impair, by unreasonable or discriminatory measures, the operation, management, maintenance, use, enjoyment or disposal thereof by those investors.[131]

Rather than using the exact term 'fair and equitable treatment,' there are slight variations in the terms used, including 'equitable and reasonable treatment.'[132] For example, Article III, Lithuania-Norway (1992), provides:

> Each contracting party shall promote and encourage in its territory investments of investors of the other contracting party and accept such investments in accordance with its laws and regulations and accord them equitable and reasonable treatment and protection ...

---

128. For an overview of treaty practice, see the three comprehensive studies: United Nations Centre on Transnational Corporations (UNCTC), *Bilateral Investment Treaties* (New York: United Nations, 1988) (Doc. No. ST/CTC/65); UNCTAD, *Bilateral Investment Treaties in the Mid-1990s* (New York and Geneva: United Nations, 1998) (Doc. No. UNCTAD/ITE/IIT/7) and UNCTAD, *Bilateral Investment Treaties 1995-2006* (New York and Geneva: United Nations, 2007) (Doc. No. UNCTAD/ITE/IIT/2006/5) [together *UNCTAD BIT Studies*]. Also see R. Dolzer & M. Stevens, *Bilateral Investment Treaties* (The Hague: Martinus Nijhoff Publishers, 1995) and Tudor, *supra* note 117, Chapter 1, which reviews in detail various drafting formulations.
129. Treaties in French refer to 'juste et équitable' and treaties in Spanish refer to 'justo y equitativo.' While it could be argued that 'just' and 'fair' are different standards, the French and Spanish versions of NAFTA Art. 1105(1) refer to 'fair and equitable treatment' as 'un traitement juste et équitable' and 'un tratamiento justo y equitativo' respectively. See G. Sacerdoti, 'Bilateral Treaties and Multilateral Instruments' (1997) 269 RDCADI 251 [*Sacerdoti*] at 345.
130. See *Dolzer, supra* note 117 at 90.
131. See also 3(1), Cuba-Lebanon (1995).
132. See also Art. 1, Italy-Korea (1989).

The tribunal in *Parkerings-Compagniet AS v. Lithuania* regarded the terms 'equitable and reasonable treatment' and 'fair and equitable treatment' as synonymous.[133]

The reference to fair and equitable treatment is sometimes combined with a reference to international law.[134] For example, Article 3, Argentina-France (1991), provides:

> Each of the Contracting Parties undertakes to grant, within its territory and its maritime area, fair and equitable treatment according to the principles of international law to investments made by investors of the other Party, and to do it in such a way that the exercise of the right thus recognized is not obstructed *de jure* or *de facto*.[135]

Another approach is to grant treatment in accordance with international law and specify that this includes fair and equitable treatment. NAFTA Article 1105(1) adopts this approach:

> Each Party shall accord to investments of investors of another Party treatment in accordance with international law, including fair and equitable treatment and full protection and security.

As discussed below, this formulation has given rise to significant debate in NAFTA cases regarding whether Article 1105 provides treatment guarantees beyond the minimum standard of treatment.[136]

A more recent approach is to define fair and equitable treatment expressly as the customary international minimum standard of treatment applicable to aliens and their property. The 2004 US and 2003 Canadian Model BITs, as well as recent US bilateral free trade agreements (FTAs) adopt this approach.[137] For example, Article 5, US-Uruguay (2005), provides:

Minimum Standard of Treatment

1. Each Party shall accord to covered investments treatment in accordance with customary international law, including fair and equitable treatment and full protection and security.

---

133. *Parkerings-Compagniet AS v. Lithuania* (Award, 11 Sep. 2007) [*Parkerings*] at para. 198.
134. The US and French BITs include references to international law, although with slightly different wording, as do some Japanese, Swedish, Swiss and UK BITs.
135. As translated in *Compañiá de Aguas del Aconquija S.A. and Vivendi Universal S.A. v. Argentina* (Award, 20 Aug. 2007) [*Vivendi II*] at para. 7.4.1. The French original of Art. 3 provides: Chacune des Parties contractantes s'engage a'assuser, sur son territoire et dans sa zone maritime, un traitement juste et équitable, conformément aux principes du droit international, aux investissements effectués par des investisseurs de l'autre Partie et à faire en sorte que l'exercice du droit ainsi reconnu ne soit entravé ni en droit, ni en fait.
136. See *infra* §6.23.
137. Recent US FTAs follow this model, including those with Australia, Central America, Chile, Morocco and Singapore. Current treaties and information are available on the website of the US Trade Representative.

2. For greater certainty, paragraph 1 prescribes the customary international law minimum standard of treatment of aliens as the minimum standard of treatment to be afforded to covered investments. The concepts of 'fair and equitable treatment' and 'full protection and security' do not require treatment in addition to or beyond that which is required by that standard, and do not create additional substantive rights. The obligation in paragraph 1 to provide:

    (a) 'fair and equitable treatment' includes the obligation not to deny justice in criminal, civil, or administrative adjudicatory proceedings in accordance with the principle of due process embodied in the principal legal systems of the world; and

    (b) 'full protection and security' requires each Party to provide the level of police protection required under customary international law.

3. A determination that there has been a breach of another provision of this Treaty, or of a separate international agreement, does not establish that there has been a breach of this Article.

US-Uruguay (2005) further provides that Article 5 shall be interpreted in accordance with Annex A as follows:

> Customary International Law
> The Parties confirm their shared understanding that 'customary international law' generally and as specifically referenced in Article 5 and Annex B results from a general and consistent practice of States that they follow from a sense of legal obligation. With regard to Article 5, the customary international law minimum standard of treatment of aliens refers to all customary international law principles that protect the economic rights and interests of aliens.

Although this formulation clarifies that fair and equitable treatment does not go beyond the minimum standard of treatment, it does not exhaustively define the current content of the minimum standard.[138]

Some provisions clarify the interaction between fair and equitable treatment and other treatment standards. For example, Article 4(1), India-Thailand (2000), provides that fair and equitable treatment shall not be less favourable than national and MFN treatment:

> Investments of investors ... shall receive treatment which is fair and equitable and not less favourable than that accorded in respect of the investments and returns of the investor of the latter Contracting Party or of any third State.[139]

---

138. See *infra* §6.21.
139. A similar clause appears in Art. 4(1) of the Swiss-Ghana (1991) BIT: 'Chaque Partie Contractante assurera sur son territoire un traitement juste et équitable aux investissements des investisseurs de l'autre Partie Contractante. Ce traitement ne sera pas moins favorable que celui accordé par chaque Partie Contractante à des investissements effectués sur son territoire par ses propres investisseurs ou que celui accordé par chaque Partie Contractante à des investissements effectués sur son territoire par les investisseurs d'un Etat tiers, si ce dernier

Article 10(1), ECT, combines fair and equitable treatment with a host of other standards:

> Each Contracting Party shall, in accordance with the provisions of this Treaty, encourage and create stable, equitable, favourable and transparent conditions for Investors of other Contracting Parties to make Investments in its Area. Such conditions shall include a commitment to accord at all times to Investments of Investors of other Contracting Parties fair and equitable treatment. Such Investments shall also enjoy the most constant protection and security and no Contracting Party shall in any way impair by unreasonable or discriminatory measures their management, maintenance, use, enjoyment or disposal. In no case shall such Investments be accorded treatment less favourable than that required by international law, including treaty obligations. Each Contracting Party shall observe any obligations it has entered into with an Investor or an Investment of an Investor of any other Contracting Party.

Article 10(3) clarifies that treatment means 'treatment accorded by a Contracting Party which is no less favourable than that which it accords to its own Investors or to Investors of any other Contracting Party or any third state, whichever is the most favourable.' This suggests that, for the purposes of the ECT, national and MFN treatment are subsumed within fair and equitable treatment.

Some IIAs, particularly French BITs,[140] provide that all restrictions on the purchase or transport of raw materials, fuel, machinery or restrictions on the sale or transport of products amount to a breach of fair and equitable treatment. The reference to 'all restrictions' is very broad and it is unclear the extent to which the provision might prevent a state from imposing non-discriminatory restrictions in cases of shortages or for other regulatory reasons.

A small number of IIAs impose the additional qualification that government conduct be necessary to maintain public order. Article 2(2), Morocco-Pakistan (2001), provides that:

> Each Contracting Party shall at all times ensure fair and equitable treatment and subject to strictly necessary measures to maintain public order...

A few IIAs appear to define fair and equitable treatment in relation to domestic law. For example, Article IV, Caribbean Common Market-Cuba (1997), provides:

---

traitement est plus favorable.' See also Art. 3, Denmark-Egypt (1999), and Art. 3 and Protocol, Netherlands-Venezuela (1991).

140. See, for example, Art. 3, France-Zimbabwe (2001): 'En particulier, bien que non exclusive- ment, sont considérées comme des entraves de droit ou de fait au traitement juste et équitable, toute restriction à l'achat et au transport de matières premières et de matières auxiliaires, d'énergie et de combustibles, ainsi que de moyens de production et d'exploitation de tous genres, toute entrave à la vente et au transport des produits à l'intérieur du pays et à l'étranger, ainsi que toutes autres mesures ayant un effet analogue.' Also see Art. 4, French Model BIT; Art. 3, Bolivia-France (1989); Art. 3, Cambodia-France (2000); Art. 3, France-Venezuela (2001); Art. 3, France-Ukraine (1994); Art. 3, France-Zimbabwe (2001); and Art. 3, France- Madagascar (2003).

Each Party shall ensure fair and equitable treatment of Investments of Investors of the other Party under and subject to national laws and regulations.

The meaning of this provision is unclear. It appears that fair and equitable treatment is qualified by treatment 'under and subject to national laws and regulations.' If so, the provision only requires treatment in accordance with domestic law – not international law.

Finally, in some IIAs, there is no provision for fair and equitable treatment. For example, *India-Singapore Comprehensive Economic Cooperation Agreement* (2005) has no fair and equitable treatment clause. A study on fair and equitable treatment clauses found that of 365 BITs surveyed, nineteen did not provide for fair and equitable treatment.[141]

Although the above survey of fair and equitable treatment provisions suggests that there is a fair degree of variation among texts, in practice there are two dominant approaches. The first is to provide for fair and equitable treatment of investment without limitation. The second is to provide for fair and equitable treatment and equate it with the minimum standard of treatment. As discussed below, if the minimum standard of treatment now requires fair and equitable treatment then this is a distinction without a difference. Alternatively, even if fair and equitable treatment goes beyond the minimum standard of treatment, in most cases the application of the two standards is unlikely to result in a different result. Further, where an investment is entitled to MFN treatment and fair and equitable treatment is available in a third state IIA, any potential difference between different formulations of the fair and equitable treatment will likely be moot.[142]

§6.16 Meaning of treatment Although the term treatment is used in both national and MFN treatment and fair and equitable treatment provisions, IIAs do not define the term. Treatment is an expansive term that the Oxford English Dictionary defines as '[c]onduct, behaviour; action or behaviour towards a person.' In *Siemens*, in the context of discussing national and MFN treatment, the tribunal stated that 'treatment' ordinarily means 'behaviour in respect of an entity or a person.'[143] In *Suez, Sociedad General de Aguas de Barcelona S.A., and InterAgua Servicios Integrales del Agua S.A. v. Argentina*, in the context of discussing MFN treatment, the tribunal noted that:

> The word 'treatment' is not defined in the treaty text. However, the ordinary meaning of that term within the context of investment includes the rights and privileges granted and the obligations and burdens imposed by a Contracting State on investments made by investors covered by the treaty.[144]

---

141. Tudor, *supra* note 117 at 23. This practice is most prevalent in Romanian and Japanese BITs. See, *ibid.*, at 246.
142. See *supra* Chapter 5 on MFN clauses.
143. *Siemens A.G. v. Argentina* (Award, 6 Feb. 2007) [*Siemens*] at para. 85.
144. *Suez, Sociedad General de Aguas de Barcelona S.A., and InterAgua Servicios Integrales del Agua S.A. v. Argentina* (Decision on Jurisdiction, 16 May 2006) at para. 55.

In *Canfor*, the claimants drew a distinction between 'conduct' and 'treatment', arguing that 'conduct' is what officials do and 'treatment' is the manner in which the officials direct conduct to a specific investor or claimant.[145] This distinction is potentially misleading because it suggests that the state must 'direct' conduct to a specific investor, which might imply either a requirement of specificity or intent. The better view is that, in accordance with the ILC's Articles on State Responsibility, 'conduct' consists of an action or omission,[146] whereas treatment refers to the effect or result of the conduct on the investment or investor in question. 'Treatment' can be further contrasted with the term 'measures' used in expropriation provisions and that focuses on the state conduct in question.[147]

§6.17 No requirement of impairment   In contrast to minimum standards that prohibit arbitrary or discriminatory measures that impair investment,[148] the fair and equitable treatment standard can be breached without evidence of impairment of the investment. For example, an investment might be subject to an arbitrary decision or process, such as a politically motivated or malicious investigation into the investment's industrial practices. Although the government's actions might breach the standard of fair and equitable treatment, there might be no actual impairment of the investment. For example, in the context of an administrative review by Canadian authorities with respect to exports of softwood lumber, the *Pope & Talbot* tribunal cited a lack of forthrightness in communications, questionable statements and misrepresentations in internal communications as constituting a breach of 'fair and equitable treatment.'[149] Although Canada's action breached fair and equitable treatment, the episode does not appear to have impaired the operation of the investment. Another example might be a situation similar to *ELSI*, in which a state mistreats a business that turns out to be worthless. Despite the fact that the business has no market value, state conduct could be sanctioned by a tribunal finding a breach of fair and equitable treatment, with no or nominal damages awarded for the taking.

§6.18 Scope of fair and equitable treatment – investment or investors?   The fair and equitable treatment standard in IIAs typically applies only to 'investments' or 'investments of investors' but not to investors alone.[150] It is unlikely that an

---

145.   *Canfor Corporation v. United States and Terminal Forest Products Ltd. v. United States* (Consolidated Proceedings) (Decision on Preliminary Question, 6 Jun. 2006) at para. 150.

146.   State conduct constituting an international wrong may be either an action or omission: 'There is an internationally wrongful act of a State when conduct consisting of an action or omission: (*a*) Is attributable to the State under international law; and (*b*) Constitutes a breach of an international obligation of the State.' Art. 2, ILC's Articles on State Responsibility, *supra* note 90.

147.   See *infra* Chapter 7, §7.9.

148.   See *infra* Part IV.

149.   See *infra* §6.28 on transparency and *supra* note 67 with respect to the tribunal's findings.

150.   There is some variation. For example, Art. 258(1)(b), *Lomé IV*, *supra* note 125, provides 'fair and equitable treatment' to investors. Art. 5, 2007 Model Norwegian BIT, provides: 'Each

individual investor would be able to claim a breach of fair and equitable treatment for measures that affect the individual investor personally with no concomitant effect on the investment. IIAs are designed to promote and protect investment and not to protect the individual human rights of the foreign investor, who generally will have to seek recourse under other applicable mechanisms. Although the fair and equitable treatment guarantee is normally limited to the investment, in many situations it will be extremely difficult to separate the treatment of the investor from that of the investment, particularly where the investor participates in the management of the investment. For example, if the individual foreign investor, who also acts as the managing director of the investment, is placed under house arrest on spurious criminal charges, the effect may be that the investment cannot be effectively managed or operated. In this situation, there might be a sufficiently close link between the investor and the investment that mistreatment of the investor significantly affects the investment. The distinction also has remedial consequences. While compensation might be claimed for the unfair treatment of the investment, the individual investor would not be able to obtain personal damages.

When the investor is a legal person, the application of fair and equitable treatment will depend in part on how the investment is structured. If the corporate investor has a locally incorporated subsidiary, the investment will be the subsidiary, which under some IIAs may also qualify as an investor in its own right.

§6.19 Interpretive approaches to fair and equitable treatment The ubiquity of fair and equitable treatment provisions in IIAs has not been accompanied by certainty, clarity or agreement with respect to their meaning. As noted previously, historically fair and equitable treatment was not a term of art in public international law. It does not refer to a well defined juridical concept and, as noted by one commentator, does not 'connote a clear set of legal prescriptions.'[151] The irony is that the substantial interpretive uncertainty inherent in the meaning of treatment that is *fair and equitable* may well be one of the reasons for its successful adoption. Unlike the minimum standard of treatment, which some states have historically viewed with suspicion because of the legacy of gun-boat diplomacy and imperialism,[152] the term fair and equitable treatment is not accompanied by unwanted political baggage. Furthermore, in principle no state is likely to oppose fair and equitable treatment – for which state would contend that international law should admit unfair and inequitable treatment of foreign investment?[153] For capital exporting states that traditionally supported the minimum standard, fair and equitable treatment represented a high standard of treatment, reflecting at least the

---

Party shall accord to *investors of the other Party, and their investments* treatment in accordance with customary international law, including fair and equitable treatment and full protection and security.' [Emphasis added.]
151. Vasciannie, *supra* note 117 at 101. While this may have been true in 1999, as discussed below, it is now possible to identify core elements of the standard in the evolving jurisprudence.
152. See *infra* Chapter 1, §1.5.
153. Sacerdoti, *supra* note 129 at 341.

minimum standard of treatment. On the other hand, for capital importing states fair and equitable treatment might well have served as an empty vessel reflecting a new era of state equality and regulatory sovereignty. In commenting in 1960 on the requirement of equitable treatment in the Abs-Shawcross Draft Convention, Georg Schwarzenberger highlighted that in relations between heterogeneous communities the standard provides 'equality on a footing of commendable elasticity.'[154]

There are three general approaches to the interpretation of a general and unqualified obligation of 'fair and equitable treatment'. First, fair and equitable treatment can be viewed as an independent treaty standard that has an autonomous meaning and provides treatment protections above and beyond the minimum standard of treatment. Second, fair and equitable treatment can be viewed as reflecting the minimum standard of treatment. Since the minimum standard of treatment is a customary standard, it evolves in light of state practice and *opinio juris* (a sense of legal obligation).[155] From this perspective, fair and equitable treatment is an element of the currently existing minimum standard of treatment, which has continued to evolve. Third, assuming fair and equitable treatment is an independent treaty standard beyond the traditional requirements of the minimum standard of treatment, it has been argued that pervasive and consistent treaty practice favours the view that the independent treaty standard of fair and equitable treatment has now emerged as customary international law. In addition, it has been argued that fair and equitable treatment is a general principle of law and therefore legitimized by a defined source of law under Article 38(1)(c), *Statute of the International Court of Justice*.

Before considering each of these views in more detail below, it is important to emphasize two points. As highlighted above in §6.15 on IIA practice, there are significant variations in the drafting of the fair and equitable treatment standard. For example, some IIAs clarify that the governing standard is the minimum standard of treatment and that fair and equitable treatment is not to be interpreted as an autonomous standard. Thus, the interpretation of a specific fair and equitable treatment provision depends, first and foremost, on the interpretation of the actual text of the IIA in question under principles of treaty interpretation. Second, whatever approach is taken, definitions of fair and equitable treatment do not affect the state's duty to accord the current minimum standard of treatment under customary international law.

§6.20 Fair and equitable treatment as an independent treaty standard with an autonomous meaning The dominant approach by tribunals[156] and

---

154. G. Schwarzenberger, 'The Abs-Shawcross Draft Convention on Investments Abroad: A Critical Commentary' (1960) JPL 147 at 152.
155. See Brownlie, *Principles of Public International Law, supra* note 9 at 7-12 on state practice and *opinio juris et necessitatis* as elements to establish customary international law.
156. See *MTD Equity Sdn. Bhd. & MTD Chile S.A. v. Chile* (Award, 25 May 2004) [*MTD*] at paras 110-112; *Occidental Exploration and Production Company v. Ecuador* (Final Award, 1 Jul. 2004) [*Occidental*] at paras 188-190; *CMS, supra* note 95 at paras 282-284; *Saluka, supra* note 15 at paras 286-295; *LG&E Energy Corp., LG&E Capital Corp.,* and *LG&E International*

commentators[157] has been to interpret fair and equitable treatment as an independent treaty standard with an autonomous meaning. In a series of cases, IIA tribunals have held that fair and equitable treatment has a meaning independent of the minimum standard of treatment. Interpretation has been guided by a textual interpretation based on the specific wording of the fair and equitable treatment provision, with significant reliance on the expressed purpose of the IIA in question, which in almost all cases is explicitly to promote and protect investment.[158]

Principles of treaty interpretation provide the primary argument in favour of fair and equitable treatment as an independent treaty standard. Article 31(1) of the *Vienna Convention on the Law of Treaties* provides that: 'A treaty shall be interpreted in good faith in accordance with the ordinary meaning to be given to the terms of the treaty in their context and in the light of its object and purpose.' Article 31(1) suggests that 'fair and equitable' should be given its ordinary meaning, in the context of other treatment standards and consistent with the overall promotion and protection purpose of the IIA. Since IIA drafters were well aware of the minimum standard of treatment as a term of art and instead chose to use fair and equitable treatment, an ordinary meaning approach supports an interpretation that fair and equitable treatment is an autonomous standard and not the same as the minimum standard of treatment.[159]

The argument in favour of fair and equitable treatment as an independent treaty standard is often attributed to F.A. Mann who argued in an influential article in 1981 that fair and equitable treatment envisages conduct:

> … which goes far beyond the minimum standard and afford[s] protection to a greater extent and according to a much more objective standard than any previously employed form of words. A tribunal would not be concerned with a minimum, maximum or average standard. It will have to decide whether in all circumstances the conduct in issue is fair and equitable or unfair and inequitable. No standard defined by other words is likely to be material. The

---

Inc. v. Argentina (Decision on Liability, 3 Oct. 2006) [*LG&E*] at paras 125-131; *PSEG Global Inc. and Konya Ilgin Elektrik Üretim ve Ticaret Limited Şirketi v. Turkey* (Award, 19 Jan. 2007) at para. 239 and *Siemens, supra* note 143 at paras 291-299.

157. Dolzer & Stevens, *Bilateral Investment Treaties, supra* note 128 at 60; UNCTAD, '*Fair and Equitable Treatment*,' *supra* note 117 at 10-16; Vasciannie, 'The Fair and Equitable Treatment Standard in International Investment Law and Practice,' *supra* note 117 at 70; P. Muchlinski, *Multinational Enterprises and the Law*, 2nd edn (Oxford, New York: OUP, 2007) at 635-647; C. McLachlan, L. Shore & M. Weiniger, *International Investment Arbitration: Substantive Principles* (Oxford: Oxford University Press, 2007) at 226-247; Dolzer & Schreuer, *Principles of International Investment Law, supra* note 117 at 119-149 and Tudor, *supra* note 117 at 53-104.

158. *SGS Société Générale de Surveillance S.A. v. Philippines* (Decision of the Tribunal on Objections to Jurisdiction, 29 Jan. 2004) [*SGS v. Philippines*] at para. 116; *Occidental, supra* note 156 at para. 183; *MTD, supra* note 156 at para. 113; *Siemens A.G. v. Argentina* (Decision on Jurisdiction, 3 Aug. 2004) at para. 81; and *Enron Corporation and Ponderosa Assets, L.P. v. Argentina* (Award, 22 May 2007) [*Enron*] at para. 259. See also O.E. García-Bolívar, 'The Teleology of International Investment Law' (2005) 6 JWIT 751.

159. See UNCTAD, '*Fair and Equitable Treatment*,' *supra* note 117 at 13.

terms are to be understood and applied independently and autonomously to be material.[160]

In interpreting fair and equitable treatment, tribunals have tended to rely heavily on treaty preambles to highlight the object and purpose of given IIAs.[161] This is part of the general tendency to rely on treaty titles and preambles in interpreting treaty obligations.[162] For example, in *Siemens,* the tribunal referred to the title and preamble of Argentina-Germany (1991) and noted that:

> The Tribunal shall be guided by the purpose of the Treaty as expressed in its title and preamble. It is a treaty 'to protect' and 'to promote' investments. The preamble provides that the parties have agreed to the provisions of the Treaty for the purpose of creating favorable conditions for the investments of nationals or companies of one of the two States in the territory of the other State. Both parties recognize that the promotion and protection of these investments by a treaty may stimulate private economic initiative and increase the well-being of the peoples of both countries. The intention of the parties is clear. It is to create favorable conditions for investments and to stimulate private initiative.[163]

In *Azurix v. Argentina,* the tribunal stated that:

> It follows from the ordinary meaning of the terms fair and equitable and the purpose and object of the BIT that fair and equitable should be understood to be treatment in an even-handed and just manner, conducive to fostering the promotion of foreign investment. The text of the BIT reflects a positive attitude towards investment with words such as 'promote' and 'stimulate.' Furthermore, the parties to the BIT recognize the role that fair and equitable treatment plays in maintaining 'a stable framework for investment and maximum effective use of economic resources.'[164]

---

160. F.A. Mann, 'British Treaties for the Promotion and Protection of Investments' (1981) 52 BYIL 241 [Mann] at 244. Despite this widely quoted statement, in a nearly contemporaneous publication (*The Legal Aspects of Money,* 1982), Mann appears to have taken a more restrictive approach: 'In some cases, it is true, treaties merely repeat, perhaps in slightly different language, what in essence is a duty imposed by customary international law; the foremost example is the familiar provision whereby states undertake to accord fair and equitable treatment to each other's nationals and which in law is unlikely to amount to more than a confirmation of the obligation to act in good faith, or to refrain from abuse or arbitrariness.' See the discussion of Mann's views and influence in Thomas, *supra* note 9.

161. See *supra* Chapter 2, §2.29 and Chapter §3.5, on the use of IIA preambles in the interpretation of the fair and equitable treatment standard.

162. See *supra* Chapter 3, §3.4 and §3.5, on treaty preambles.

163. *Siemens A.G. v. Argentina, supra* note 158 at para. 81. See also *Vivendi II, supra* note 135 at para. 7.4.4: 'As to the object and purpose of the BIT, the Tribunal notes the parties' wish, as stated in the preamble, for the Treaty to create favourable conditions for French investments in Argentina, and *vice versa,* and their conviction that the protection and promotion of such investments is expected to encourage technology and capital transfers between both countries and to promote their economic development. In interpreting the BIT, we are thus mindful of these objectives.'

164. *Azurix Corp. v. Argentina* (Award, 14 Jul. 2006) [*Azurix*] at para. 130.

The *MTD* award is representative of the general interpretive approach to the fair and equitable treatment standard. The tribunal began with the interpretation rules of the *Vienna Convention on the Law of Treaties*, after having referred to an expert opinion on the meaning of the standard.[165] The tribunal next turned to the ordinary meaning of 'fair' and 'equitable' as defined in the *Concise Oxford Dictionary of Current English*, as 'just,' 'even-handed,' 'unbiased,' 'legitimate.' The tribunal then referred to the object and purpose of the BIT as expressed in the preamble, highlighting the parties' desire to create favourable conditions for investment and the need to protect investment. The tribunal then stated that:

> ... in terms of the BIT, fair and equitable treatment should be understood to be treatment in an even-handed and just manner, conducive to fostering the promotion of foreign investment. Its terms are framed as a pro-active statement –'to promote,' 'to create,' 'to stimulate'- rather than prescriptions for a passive behavior of the State or avoidance of prejudicial conduct to the investors.[166]

The tribunal then compared the meaning it attributed to fair and equitable treatment with that attributed by another tribunal that was faced with a 'similar task.'[167] After a detailed review of the facts, the tribunal concluded that Chile treated the claimants unfairly and inequitably by authorizing an investment that could not take place for reasons of existing urban policy.[168]

The use of ordinary meaning however does little to elucidate the meaning of fair and equitable treatment. Substituting the terms 'just' or 'even-handed' does not clarify the content of the standard.[169] It simply results in words of 'almost equal vagueness.'[170] Second, it has been argued that interpretations that focus on the object and purpose of IIAs as creating favourable conditions for investment should not lead to interpretations that are exclusively in favour of investors.[171] The interpretation of fair and equitable treatment needs to balance the legitimate interests of investors and states. In interpreting Czechoslovakia-Netherlands (1991), the *Saluka* tribunal noted with respect to the preamble:

> This is a more subtle and balanced statement of the Treaty's aims than is sometimes appreciated. The protection of foreign investments is not the

---

165. The tribunal referred to an Opinion of Judge Stephen Schwebel, who states that fair and equitable treatment is 'a broad and widely-accepted standard encompassing such fundamental standards as good faith, due process, non-discrimination, and proportionality.' See *MTD*, *supra* note 156 at para. 109.
166. *MTD, ibid.*, at para. 113.
167. *Ibid.*, at para. 114. See *supra* Chapter 2, §2.23, on the use of IIA awards as precedents.
168. *Ibid.*, at para. 166 and 188.
169. Stephen Schill refers to this as the semantics of fair and equitable treatment. See S. Schill, 'Fair and Equitable Treatment under Investment Treaties as an Embodiment of the Rule of Law,' Institute for International Law and Justice, New York University School of Law Working Paper 2006/6.
170. *Saluka, supra* note 15 at para. 297.
171. See *Noble Ventures, Inc. v. Romania* (Award, 12 Oct. 2005) [*Noble*] at para. 52. See *supra* Chapter 2, §2.29, regarding interpretation and the principle of *in dubio mitius*.

sole aim of the Treaty, but rather a necessary element alongside the overall aim of encouraging foreign investment and extending and intensifying the parties' economic relations. That in turn calls for a balanced approach to the interpretation of the Treaty's substantive provisions for the protection of investments, since an interpretation which exaggerates the protection to be accorded to foreign investments may serve to dissuade host States from admitting foreign investments and so undermine the overall aim of extending and intensifying the parties mutual economic relations.[172]

The interpretation of fair and equitable treatment must take into account legitimate public interests in regulating investments to achieve national objectives and the enforcement of the laws. At the same time, it must be recognized that the express purpose of IIAs is to promote and protect investments and that fair and equitable treatment must be read in this context.

§6.21 Fair and equitable treatment as reflecting the minimum standard of treatment   There is some state practice amongst major capital exporting states suggesting that fair and equitable treatment was viewed as reflecting, and as synonymous with, the minimum standard of treatment. For example, some elements of US, UK, Swiss[173] and Canadian treaty practice[174] suggest that these states considered that fair and equitable treatment reflected the minimum standard of treatment.[175] For example, the US State Department official description of the US Model BIT of February 1992 notes that the reference in Article II(2)(a) ('Investment shall at all times be accorded fair and equitable treatment, shall enjoy full protection and security and shall in no case be accorded treatment less than that required by international law') sets out 'a minimum standard of treatment based on

---

172. *Saluka*, *supra* note 15 at para. 300.
173. Statement by the Swiss Foreign Office, quoted in (1980) 36 Annuaire Suisse de droit international at 178 referring to fair and equitable treatment: 'On se réfère ainsi au principe classique du droit des gens selon lequel les Etats doivent mettre les étrangers se trouvant sur leur territoire et leurs biens au bénéfice du "standard minimum" international, c'est-à-dire leur accorder un minimum de droits personnels, procéduraux et économiques.'
174. It should be noted that unilateral statements by one state party to a treaty are not 'subsequent practice' under Art. 31(3)(b), *Vienna Convention on the Law of Treaties*. Art. 31(3)(b) provides that that the subsequent practice in question must establish the agreement of the parties regarding the interpretation of the treaty. See *supra* Part VII, Chapter 2 on interpretation.
175. See US Department of State Letter of Submittal for BITs, referred to in Thomas, *supra* note 9 at 50. With respect to NAFTA, see Canada's Statement on the Implementation, Canada Gazette, Part I, 1 Jan. 1994 at 149. As noted by Thomas, Canada formally transmitted the Statement of Implementation to the US and Mexico and it has been endorsed by Mexico and the US in later Chapter Eleven proceedings. See Thomas, *supra* note 9 at footnote 98. With respect to NAFTA Art. 1105, see discussion by one of its negotiators: D. Price, 'An Overview of the NAFTA Investment Chapter: Substantive Rules and Investor-State Dispute Mechanism' (1993) 27 IL 727. For commentary on US practice, see P. Gann, 'The U.S. Bilateral Investment Treaty Program' (1985) 21 SJIL 373. For UK practice, see E. Denza & S. Brooks, 'Investment Protection Treaties: United Kingdom Experience' (1987) 36 ICLQ 908.

customary international law.'[176] Further, there is a distinct lack of conclusive evidence of state practice clearly indicating that it was the intention of *any* state entering an IIA that fair and equitable treatment would be a new and autonomous standard of conduct.[177]

The commentary to the 1967 Draft OECD Convention – the model for many subsequent IIAs – states that fair and equitable treatment 'indicates the standard set by international law for the treatment due by each State with regard to the property of foreign nationals' and that it 'conforms in effect to the "minimum standard" which forms part of customary international law.'[178] This view was reconfirmed by the OECD's Committee on International Investment and Multinational Enterprises in 1984.[179] Accordingly, it is arguable that when incorporating the fair and equitable treatment standard into their BITs, OECD states were guided by the meaning ascribed to that language by the intergovernmental organization (IGO) of which they were members.

In answer to the argument that: '[as] a matter of textual interpretation it is inherently implausible that a treaty would use an expression such as "fair and equitable treatment" to denote a well known concept like the "minimum standard of treatment in customary international law,"'[180] it can be argued that the use of a different and more politically neutral term might be explained by the historical political sensitivities regarding the minimum standard of treatment. Fair and equitable treatment may simply have been viewed as a convenient, neutral and acceptable reference to the minimum standard of treatment.[181]

---

176. Description of the United States Model Bilateral Investment Treaty (BIT) – Feb. 1992, Submitted by the State Department, 30 Jul. 1992, in Hearing Before the Committee on the Foreign Relations, United States Senate, 102nd Congress, Second Session, 4 Aug. 1992, S. HRG. 102-795 at 62.

177. One exception is the position taken in 1992 by European Communities (EC). The EC issued investment protection principles that state that, '"fair and equitable treatment" is an "overriding concept" that comprises other investment protection principles including: transparency and stability of investment conditions, full protection and security, MFN treatment, NT and observance of undertakings.' *Community Position on Investment Protection Principles in the ACP States*, Council of the European Communities, ACP-CEE 2172/92. The position was set out in response to the *Lomé IV*, *supra* note 125. Art. 258(1)(b) of *Lomé IV* requires state parties to 'accord fair and equitable treatment to investors.' It should be noted that the document is referred to as 'position' and not a definitive statement of the technical meaning of fair and equitable treatment.

178. 1967 Draft OECD Convention, *supra* note 123 at 120. See OECD, Committee on International Investment and Multinational Enterprises, 'Intergovernmental Agreements Relating to Investment in Developing Countries,' Doc. No. 84/14 (27 May 1984), at para. 36 as quoted by Thomas, *supra* note 9 at 48.

179. Thomas, *supra* note 9 at 48. See also UNCTC, *Bilateral Investment Treaties*, *supra* note 128 at 30 stating that it is a 'classical international law standard.'

180. C.H. Schreuer, 'Fair and Equitable Treatment (FET): Interactions with Other Standards' (2007) 4 TDM at 10. See also Vasciannie, *supra* note 117.

181. See discussion *supra* at §6.19. Indeed, the underlying political assumption of the 1974 *Charter of Economic Rights and Duties of States* was that there was no minimum standard of treatment with respect to compensation for expropriation. See K. Vandevelde, 'U.S. Bilateral Investment Treaties: The Second Wave' (1993) 14 MJIL 621 at 625.

Respondent states have relied on *Genin*,[182] an early decision on fair and equitable treatment, as equating fair and equitable treatment with the *Neer* standard.[183] In *Saluka*,[184] the tribunal noted, however, that the *Genin* tribunal merely stated that a BIT standard of 'fair and equitable' treatment provides 'a basic and general standard which is detached from the host States' domestic law.' In the view of the *Saluka* tribunal, fair and equitable treatment is *an* international minimum standard, not *the* international minimum standard.[185] As noted above, on the whole, IIA jurisprudence supports the view that fair and equitable is an independent treaty standard.

§6.22 Fair and equitable treatment as an independent treaty standard and customary international law   Since treaties are evidence of state practice, some commentators have suggested that the pervasive and consistent practice of including fair and equitable treatment and other minimum standards of treatment in IIAs has shaped the body of customary international law on the treatment of foreign investment.[186] In *Mondev*, the tribunal noted that:

> ... [on] a remarkably widespread basis, States have repeatedly obliged themselves to accord foreign investment such treatment. In the Tribunal's view, such a body of concordant practice will necessarily have influenced the content of rules governing the treatment of foreign investment in current international law.[187]

However, even if general and consistent state practice is proven,[188] there is little evidence that states provide treatment beyond the minimum standard of treatment

---

182.   *Genin*, *supra* note 69.
183.   In *Genin*, *ibid.*, the tribunal at para. 367 stated: 'Acts that would violate this minimum standard would include acts showing a wilful neglect of duty, an insufficiency of action falling far below international standards, or even subjective bad faith.' See discussion at *supra* notes 15 and 18 on references to *Neer* in early IIA awards.
184.   *Saluka*, *supra* note 15. Yves Fortier, the president of the *Genin* tribunal, was also a member of the *Saluka* tribunal.
185.   *Ibid.*, at para. 295.
186.   S.M. Schwebel, 'The Influence of Bilateral Investment Treaties on Customary International Law' (2004) ASIL Proceedings 27-30 and Tudor, *supra* note 117 at 53-84. See also Brownlie, *Principles of Public International Law*, *supra* note 9 at 520 noting that, in the context of provisions in BITs addressing compensation for expropriation, a pattern of agreement with a consistent standard constitutes evidence of an international standard.
187.   *Mondev*, *supra* note 15 at para. 117.
188.   The argument that there is general and consistent state practice is difficult to make. As noted in the review of IIA provisions above, there is a fair degree of variation in IIA provisions. Further, new model IIAs and current state practice demonstrate increasing diversity, not less, including agreements that do not contain a fair and equitable treatment standard. Tudor, *supra* note 117 at 84 suggests that the 'customary' fair and equitable treatment clause could consist of the following elements: 'Each State shall accord, at all times to the foreign investors and their investments in its territory, fair and equitable treatment in accordance with international law.' This formulation, however, cannot be justified in light of IIA provisions that apply almost uniformly to investments but not to investors (see *supra* §6.18).

out of a sense of legal customary obligation.[189] Rather, economic interests motivate states to enter into IIAs.[190]

In response to the lack of evidence of *opinio juris*, some commentators have suggested either that the practice of states may be understood as confirmation of *opinio juris* or that *opinio juris* has become obsolete for the formation of custom in many areas of law.[191]

An alternative argument is that the various elements of fair and equitable treatment, including good faith, due process, estoppel, unjust enrichment and *pacta sunt servanda* are recognized as general principles of law. Although national legal systems may not use the term fair and equitable treatment, the content of the standard – the procedural and substantive guarantees accorded to foreign investment – are found in domestic law.[192]

A number of tribunals have suggested that, at least in some respects, fair and equitable treatment is not different from the minimum standard of treatment. In *Occidental*, the tribunal stated that the fair and equitable treatment standard in Ecuador-US 'is not different from that required under international law concerning both the stability and the predictability of the legal and business framework of the investment.'[193] Similarly, in *CMS*, the tribunal stated that:

> While the choice between requiring a higher treaty standard and that of equating it with the international minimum standard might have relevance in the context of some disputes, the Tribunal is not persuaded that it is relevant in this case. In fact, the Treaty standard of fair and equitable treatment and its connection with the required stability and predictability of the business environment, founded on solemn legal and contractual commitments, is not different from the international law minimum standard and its evolution under customary law.[194]

On a practical level, the question of whether fair and equitable treatment has become customary international law is unlikely to be determinative in the majority of IIA cases. Most IIAs already provide fair and equitable treatment as a treaty-based standard in some form. If an IIA has a different treatment standard that the

---

189. For discussion, see B. Kishoiyian, 'The Utility of Bilateral Investment Treaties in the Formulation of Customary International Law' (1994) 14 NJILB 327 and S. Hindelang, 'Bilateral Investment Treaties, Custom and a Healthy Investment Climate? The Question of Whether Bits Influence Customary International Law Revisited' (2004) 5 JWIT 767.
190. A. Guzman, 'Why LDCs Sign Treaties That Hurt Them: Explaining the Popularity of BITs,' VJIL 38 (1998): 639 at 686.
191. Tudor, *supra* note 117 at 80-85.
192. *Ibid.,* at 85-104. Tudor further argues that fair and equitable treatment is a customary standard independent of the minimum standard of treatment (at 68). It would appear, however, quite artificial to postulate that there are two distinct customary standards – fair and equitable treatment and the international minimum standard of treatment. If fair and equitable treatment is a customary standard, the better view is that it forms part of the international minimum standard of treatment of aliens and their property.
193. *Occidental, supra* note 156 at para. 190.
194. *CMS, supra* note 95 at para. 294.

respondent state argues is less onerous than fair and equitable treatment, fair and equitable treatment will likely apply in any event as a result of an MFN clause. Therefore, in practice, the question simply does not arise. Further, the trend in the jurisprudence suggests that there are few, if any, differences between the current minimum standard of treatment and the fair and equitable standard of treatment.[195] This issue is considered in more detail in this chapter following a discussion of the elements of fair and equitable treatment.

§6.23 Interpretation of Article 1105(1), NAFTA   The question of whether fair and equitable treatment is an independent treaty standard has been the subject of much discussion and jurisprudence in the specific context of Article 1105(1), NAFTA.[196] The first NAFTA investment awards diverged in their interpretation of Article 1105(1). In *Myers*, the tribunal equated 'fair and equitable treatment' with the minimum standard of treatment.[197] Shortly thereafter, the *Pope & Talbot* tribunal stated that fair and equitable treatment is a higher standard than the minimum standard of treatment. According to that tribunal, the fairness element in Article 1105(1) adds to – and is not simply part of – the minimum standard of treatment. More specifically, it stated that investments are entitled to 'the benefits of the

---

195.   In *Saluka*, *supra* note 15 at para. 291, the tribunal stated: 'Whatever the merits of this contro-versy between the parties may be, it appears that the difference between the Treaty standard laid down in Article 3.1 and the customary minimum standard, when applied to the specific facts of a case, may well be more apparent than real. To the extent that the case law reveals different formulations of the relevant thresholds, an in-depth analysis may well demonstrate that they could be explained by the contextual and factual differences of the cases to which the standards have been applied.' In *BG Group Plc. v. Argentina* (Final Award, 24 Dec. 2007) [*BG*] at paras 289-310 the tribunal found that Argentina's conduct would in any event have breached the minimum standard of conduct.

196.   Art. 1105 is entitled 'Minimum Standard of Treatment.' It provides that '[e]ach Party shall accord to investments of investors of another Party treatment in accordance with international law, including fair and equitable treatment and full protection and security.' For detailed dis-cussion of Art. 1105, see M. Kinnear, A. K. Bjorklund & J. Hannaford, *Investment Disputes under NAFTA: An Annotated Guide to NAFTA Chapter 11*, looseleaf (Kluwer Law International, 2005) at 1102. Also see P. Dumberry, 'The Quest to Define "Fair and Equitable Treatment" for Investors under International Law: The Case of the NAFTA Chapter 11 Pope & Talbot Awards' (2002) 3 JWI 657; P. Foy & R. Deane, 'Foreign Investment Protection under Investment Treaties: Recent Developments Under Chapter 11 of the North American Free Trade Agreement' (2001) 16 ICSID Rev 299; Thomas, *supra* note 9; and I. Laird, 'Betrayal, Shock and Outrage-Recent Developments in NAFTA Article 1105,' in T. Weiler, ed., *NAFTA Investment Law and Arbitration: Past Issues, Current Practice, Future Prospects* (Ardsley: Transnational Publishers, 2004).

197.   The tribunal stated that a breach 'occurs only when it is shown that an investor has been treated in such an unjust or arbitrary manner that the treatment rises to the level that is unac-ceptable from the international perspective. That determination must be made in the light of the high measure of deference that international law generally extends to the right of domes-tic authorities to regulate matters within their own borders.' See *Myers*, *supra* note 5 at para. 263. The majority of the tribunal then went on to find at para. 266 that, in the circumstances, the breach of national treatment also amounted to a breach of fair and equitable treatment.

fairness elements under ordinary standards applied in the NAFTA countries, without any threshold limitation that the conduct complained of be "egregious," "outrageous," "shocking," or "otherwise extraordinary."'[198] According to the *Pope & Talbot* tribunal, the purpose of NAFTA is to provide investors a 'hospitable climate that would insulate them from political risks or incidents of unfair treatment.'[199] Consequently, the tribunal held that the fair and equitable treatment guarantee is an additive requirement to be 'ascertained free of any threshold that might be applicable to the evaluation of measures under the minimum standard of international law.'[200]

In response to the *Pope & Talbot* ruling, the NAFTA FTC[201] issued a binding interpretation of Article 1105(1).[202] This interpretation equated the reference to fair and equitable treatment in Article 1105(1) with the minimum standard of treatment.[203] This position reflected the pleadings of all three NAFTA parties before various NAFTA Chapter Eleven tribunals. In this regard the US submission to the *Pope & Talbot* tribunal is representative:

> from its first use in investment agreements, 'fair and equitable treatment' was no more than a shorthand reference to elements of the developed body of customary international law governing the responsibility of a State for its treatment of the nationals of another State. It is in this sense, moreover, that the United States incorporated 'fair and equitable treatment' into its various bilateral investment treaties ('BITs').[204]

---

198. *Pope & Talbot, supra* note 19 at para. 118.
199. *Ibid.*, at para. 116.
200. *Ibid.*, at para. 111.
201. The Commission consists of cabinet-level representatives of Canada, Mexico and the US. See Art. 2001, NAFTA.
202. Art. 1131 of NAFTA provides that the FTC's interpretation of a NAFTA provision is binding on a tribunal established under Chapter 11. The FTC's 'Notes of Interpretation of Certain Chapter 11 Provisions,' issued on 31 Jul. 2001, provide:

    1. Art. 1105(1) prescribes the customary international law minimum standard of treatment of aliens as the minimum standard of treatment to be afforded to investments of investors of another Party.
    2. The concepts of 'fair and equitable treatment' and 'full protection and security' do not require treatment in addition to or beyond that which is required by the customary international law minimum standard of treatment of aliens.
    3. A determination that there has been a breach of another provision of the NAFTA, or of a separate international agreement, does not establish that there has been a breach of Art. 1105(1).

203. It also clarified that a breach of another provision of NAFTA or another international treaty does not in-and-of-itself amount to a breach of NAFTA Art. 1105(1).
204. *Pope & Talbot, Inc., v. Canada* (Fourth Submission of the United States of America, 1 Nov. 2000). US submissions to NAFTA tribunals are available on the US Department of State website. See also discussion of the NAFTA parties' views on fair and equitable treatment in *Mondev, supra* note 15 at paras 100-125.

The FTC's interpretation, however, has been criticized. Claimants have argued that the interpretation amounted to an unauthorized amendment of the NAFTA and was therefore beyond the FTC's authority.[205] NAFTA tribunals have accepted, however, that the interpretation is binding on them.[206]

The FTC interpretation has not brought any finality to the debate about the meaning of fair and equitable treatment within the NAFTA since it does not clarify the content of the minimum standard of treatment and, in particular, whether it is what other IIA tribunals have found to be required by fair and equitable treatment. NAFTA tribunals, while accepting that Article 1105(1), NAFTA, provides at least *the* minimum standard of treatment,[207] have rightly noted that the minimum standard of treatment evolves over time. Its content has been shaped by the considerable developments in substantive and procedural rights since the 1920s, as well as the substantial state practice manifested in the conclusion of thousands of IIAs.[208] As noted by the tribunal in *Mondev*, '[t]o the modern eye, what is unfair or inequitable need not equate with the outrageous or the egregious.'[209] The tribunal in *Waste Management II*, after reviewing the jurisprudence as of 2004, stated that:

> Taken together, the *S.D. Myers*, *Mondev*, *ADF* and *Loewen* cases suggest that the minimum standard of treatment of fair and equitable treatment is infringed

---

205. See, for example, *Mondev, ibid.*, at paras 100-125. In particular, at para. 102 the tribunal states: 'The Claimant professed to be "somewhat bewildered" by the interpretations. It maintained that the Respondent saw fit "to change the meaning of a NAFTA provision in the middle of the case in which that provision plays a major part" and questioned whether it could do so in good faith. It contended that the FTC's decision was "more than a matter of amendment" to the text of NAFTA than an interpretation of it ... .' See also *Methanex Corporation v. United States* (Letter by the Claimant to the Tribunal, 18 Sep. 2001) at 17; and *ADF Group Inc v. United States* (Investor's Reply to the Counter-Memorial of the United States of America on Competence and Liability, 28 Jan. 2002) at paras 213 *et seq.* The objections of Methanex were also echoed in the expert opinion of Sir Robert Jennings. See *Methanex* (Second Opinion of Sir Robert Jennings, 5 Nov. 2002). However, even experts disagree on this matter, as evidenced by the opinion of Christopher Greenwood in the context of the *Loewen* case. See *Loewen v. United States* (Appendix to US Counter Memorial: Opinion of Christopher Greenwood, 30 Mar. 2001). Also see discussion in articles cited at *supra* note 196.
206. See, in particular, *Methanex Corporation v. United States* (Final Award, 3 Aug. 2005) [*Methanex*]. The *Methanex* tribunal sidestepped the issue of whether the FTC interpretation was an amendment or not and held that the interpretation was binding either under Art. 39 of the Vienna Convention (providing for amendment by agreement) or Art. 31(3)(a) (providing for subsequent agreement between the parties regarding the interpretation of a treaty to be taken into account). It noted, however, that an interpretation contrary to *jus cogens* would not be binding on it. See *ibid.*, Part IV-Chapter C, paras 20-24.
207. See, for example, *Mondev, supra* note 15 at para. 125. Also see *United Parcel Service of America Inc. v. Canada* (Award on Jurisdiction, 22 Nov. 2002) at para. 96; *ADF, supra* note 15 at paras 176 and 178; *Loewen, supra* note 23 at para. 128; *Waste Management II, supra* note 15 at paras 90-91; *Methanex, supra* note 206, Part IV, Chapter C, paras 17-24; and *Thunderbird, supra* note 66 at paras 192-193.
208. *Mondev, supra* note 15 at paras 116 and 125 and *ADF, supra* note 15 at para. 179.
209. *Mondev, ibid.*, at para. 116. Quoted with approval in *Tecmed, supra* note 65 at para. 153.

by conduct attributable to the State and harmful to the claimant if the conduct is arbitrary, grossly unfair, unjust or idiosyncratic, is discriminatory and exposes the claimant to sectional or racial prejudice, or involves a lack of due process leading to an outcome which offends judicial propriety – as might be the case with a manifest failure of natural justice in judicial proceedings or a complete lack of transparency and candour in an administrative process. In applying the standard it is relevant that the treatment is in breach of representations made by the host State which were reasonably relied on by the claimant.[210]

This restatement of the content of Article 1105, NAFTA, comprises elements similar to those identified by tribunals in interpreting the fair and equitable treatment standard in other IIAs. Thus, even if it were accepted that in principle the standards are different, the trend appears to be towards convergence, not divergence. Further, tribunals have noted that any differences between the standards are more apparent than real.[211]

§6.24 General characteristics of the fair and equitable treatment standard IIA jurisprudence and commentary have identified a series of specific elements of fair and equitable treatment, which are discussed in the next section. A number of more general observations can be made about the requirement for fair and equitable treatment.[212]

A legal standard. Fair and equitable treatment is not a subjective standard based on the idiosyncratic view of the tribunal. The fair and equitable treatment standard does not confer upon a tribunal the right to determine the case before it *ex aequo et bono* (according to what is equitable and fair).[213] As noted by the *Saluka* tribunal:

> This does not imply, however, that such standards as laid down in Article 3 of the Treaty would invite the Tribunal to decide the dispute in a way that resembles a decision *ex aequo et bono*. This Tribunal is bound by Article 6 of the Treaty to decide the dispute on the basis of the law, including the provisions of the Treaty. Even though Article 3 obviously leaves room for judgment and appreciation by the Tribunal, it does not set out totally subjective standards which would allow the Tribunal to substitute, with regard to the Czech Republic's conduct to be assessed in the present case, its judgment on the choice of solutions for the Czech Republic's. As the tribunal in *S.D. Myers* has said, the 'fair and equitable treatment' standard does not create an 'open-ended mandate to second-guess government decision-making.' The standards formulated in Article 3 of the

---

210. *Waste Management II, supra* note 15 at para. 98.
211. See *supra* notes 194 and 195.
212. For general commentary on the fair and equitable treatment standard see references *supra* notes 117 and 157.
213. See M. Habicht, *The Power of the International Judge to Give a Decision Ex Aequo Et Bono* (London: Constable & Co., 1935). See also A. Zimmerman, C. Tomuschat & K. Oellers-Frahm, eds, *The Statute of the International Court of Justice: A Commentary* (Oxford: Oxford University Press, 2006) at 730-735.

Treaty, vague as they may be, are susceptible of specification through judicial practice and do in fact have sufficient legal content to allow the case to be decided on the basis of law. Over the last few years, a number of awards have dealt with such standards yielding a fair amount of practice that sheds light on their legal meaning.[214]

An IIA tribunal must make its decision based on the IIA in question and principles of international law, including rules of treaty interpretation.[215] Statements in some early awards to the effect that fair and equitable treatment is subjective are misleading.[216] Although a tribunal must exercise its judgment in applying the standard to a specific factual context, the tribunal applies a legal standard interpreted in accordance with international law. In this context, it is confusing to refer to the application of the standard to the facts of the case as subjective, as suggested in a recent treatise on the standard.[217] Application of general standards to facts is inherent in judicial decision-making. Referring to this process as subjective may improperly suggest that it is based on individual intuition rather than reason.

Fair and equitable treatment is a broad legal standard. While it 'does not provide a tribunal an open-ended mandate to second-guess government decision-making,'[218] it does allow tribunals to assess whether state conduct was clearly unreasonable. Although traditionally state conduct had 'to display a relatively higher degree of inappropriateness' to breach the minimum standard, to breach the fair and equitable treatment standard 'it may be sufficient that States' conduct displays a relatively lower degree of inappropriateness.'[219]

One standard. Tribunals and commentators have treated fair and equitable treatment as a single standard. Although it could be argued that there are two separate standards – fair treatment and equitable treatment – tribunals have not interpreted the

---

214. *Saluka, supra* note 15 at para. 284.
215. In this regard, see *Mondev, supra* note 15 at para. 119: 'Article 1105(1) did not give a NAFTA Tribunal an unfettered discretion to decide for itself, on a subjective basis, what was "fair" or "equitable" in the circumstances of each particular case … It may not simply adopt its own idiosyncratic standard of what is "fair" or "equitable" without reference to established sources of law.' See also *ADF, supra* note 15 at para. 184. While this statement was made in the NAFTA context, which directs tribunals to apply the customary minimum standard of treatment, the same considerations apply to fair and equitable treatment provisions in other IIAs.
216. See *Lauder, supra* note 112 at para. 292: 'In the context of bilateral investment treaties, the "fair and equitable" standard is subjective and depends heavily on a factual context.' This position should either be rejected outright or interpreted as meaning that whether the standard has been breached will necessarily depend on the specific facts of the case.
217. Tudor, *supra* note 117 at 144, argues that there are two elements of the fair and equitable treatment standard, an objective element based upon the interpretation of treaty in question and a subjective element where the arbitrator proceeds to the application of the standard to the facts.
218. *Myers, supra* note 5 at para. 261. See also *Marvin Feldman v. Mexico* (Award, 16 Dec. 2002) *Feldman* at para. 139: 'not just any denial of due process or of fair and equitable treatment … constitutes a violation of international law,' and, quoting *Azinian, supra* note 35 at para. 103, 'there must be a clear and malicious misinterpretation of the law.'
219. *Saluka, supra* note 15 at paras 292 and 293.

term in this way and commentators have argued that there is no substantive difference between 'fair and equitable treatment' and 'equitable treatment'.[220]

No requirement of bad faith or intent to injure. Bad faith or the intention to injure is not a necessary condition for establishing a breach of fair and equitable treatment.[221] By contrast, bad faith or intent to injure is likely a sufficient condition for establishing a breach of fair and equitable treatment. State conduct that is intended to harm a foreign investment is not fair and equitable treatment.

Good faith. The commitment to fair and equitable treatment is an expression of the principle of good faith,[222] though it has been argued that good faith 'adds only negligible assistance' in interpreting the scope and meaning of fair and equitable treatment.[223] In any case, the various elements of fair and equitable treatment, including due process, due diligence and the protection of legitimate expectations, are manifestations of the more general principle of good faith.

Fair and equitable treatment requires at least the minimum standard of treatment. At a minimum, fair and equitable treatment of investments requires treatment in accordance with the minimum standard of treatment.[224] No IIA awards nor any commentator have suggested that fair and equitable treatment provides less favourable treatment than the minimum standard of treatment.[225] For example, in their interpretation of fair and equitable treatment some tribunals have recognized due diligence and due process as an element of the standard.[226] On the

---

220. See Vandevelde, *supra* note 121.
221. *CMS, supra* note 95 at para. 280. See also *Azurix, supra* note 164 at para. 372. Except for *Genin*, which *might* be read as requiring bad faith (although see *supra* note 184 and discussion in text), IIA jurisprudence suggests there is no requirement for bad faith or malicious intention for a breach of fair and equitable treatment. As stated in *CMS, supra* note 95 at para. 280: it is an objective standard 'unrelated to whether the Respondent has had any deliberate intention or bad faith in adopting the measures in question. Of course, such intention and bad faith can aggravate the situation but are not an essential element of the standard.' Also see *Loewen, supra* note 207 at para. 132: 'Neither State practice, the decisions of international tribunals nor the opinion of commentators support the view that bad faith or malicious intention is an essential element of unfair and inequitable treatment or denial of justice amounting to a breach of international justice.' Although the tribunal's statement is made in the context of discussing denial of justice, the principle applies equally to minimum standards of treatment generally. See also *Mondev, supra* note 15 at para. 116; *Loewen, supra* note 23 at para. 132; *Occidental, supra* note 156 at para. 186; *Tecmed supra* note 65 at para. 153; *Waste Management, Inc. v. Mexico* (Award, 2 Jun. 2000) at para. 93; *LG&E, supra* note 156 at para. 129.
222. *Tecmed, supra* note 65 at para. 153.
223. In *ADF*, the claimant maintained that the US had failed to comply with obligations under NAFTA Art. 1105(1) in good faith, thereby breaching its duty under customary international law. The tribunal stated in this regard that '[a]n assertion of breach of a customary law duty of good faith adds only negligible assistance in the task of determining or giving content to a standard of fair and equitable treatment.' See *ADF, supra* note 15 at para. 191.
224. See *Sempra Energy International v. Argentina* (Award, 28 Sep. 2007) [*Sempra*] at para. 302.
225. For example, treatment that constitutes a denial of justice in international law would *ipso facto* violate a fair and equitable treatment guarantee.
226. In *Lauder, supra* note 112 the tribunal noted at para. 292 that 'fair and equitable treatment is related to the traditional standard of due diligence.'

other hand, not every violation of the minimum standard of treatment of aliens will breach the standard of fair and equitable treatment. Fair and equitable treatment does not usually apply directly to individual investors but, rather, only to investments of investors.[227] For example, it is unclear whether mistreatment of an individual foreign investor in police detention would result in a breach of fair and equitable treatment of an investment. In this case, there might be a sufficient nexus if the foreign investor is detained because of activities related to the investment, rather than his or her private activities.

Substantive and procedural treatment. The scope of fair and equitable treatment is not limited to the *process* of state decision-making in terms of ensuring due process and natural justice. State decision-making processes that meet due process and transparency requirements may still lead to treatment that breaches fair and equitable treatment. The fair and equitable treatment standard allows tribunals to assess the substantive fairness of state treatment.[228] Legitimate expectations with respect to fairness and due process in decision-making are protected, as well as legitimate expectations with respect to substantive treatment.[229]

A highly fact and context dependent assessment. The determination of whether there has been a breach of fair and equitable treatment is highly fact and context dependent: 'A judgment of what is fair and equitable cannot be reached in the abstract; it must depend on the facts of the particular case.'[230] Furthermore, the tribunal must assess the entire context of investor and state conduct. As noted by the tribunal in *GAMI*: 'It is the record as a whole – not dramatic incidents in isolation – which determines whether a breach of international law has occurred.'[231]

Although the application of fair and equitable treatment is highly fact and context dependent, some awards have done no more than set out the facts in detail and then conclude that there has been a breach of fair and equitable treatment, without sufficient legal analysis.[232] Alternatively, some tribunals posit fair and equitable treatment as an abstract standard and then conclude that there has been a breach of the standard after a review of the facts without specifying what aspect of the standard would have been breached.[233]

---

227. See *supra* §6.18.
228. See *infra* §6.26.
229. McLachlan, Shore & Weiniger, *International Investment Arbitration: Substantive Principles,* *supra* note 117 at 7.182 suggest that the fair and equitable treatment standard 'is concerned with the *process* of decision-making as it affects the rights of the investor, rather than with the protection of substantive rights (the latter being the function of the protection against expropriation and the guarantee of full protection and security).' In our view, this statement is not supported by IIA jurisprudence.
230. *Mondev, supra* note 15 at para. 118. *Accord, Saluka, supra* note 15 at 285.
231. *GAMI, supra* note 15 at para. 103.
232. An example is the majority decision in *Eastern Sugar B.V. v. Czech Republic* (Final Award, 12 Apr. 2007) [*Eastern Sugar*].
233. See Schill, *supra* note 117 at 6-7 on this point and *Dolzer, supra* note 107 at 93.

§6.25 Specific elements of fair and equitable treatment Fair and equitable treatment is a broad, overarching standard, that contains various elements of protection, including those elements commonly associated with the minimum standard of treatment,[234] the protection of legitimate expectations, non-discrimination, transparency and protections against bad faith, coercion, threats and harassment. As discussed below, there is a substantial degree of overlap among the various elements.

The analysis that follows eschews providing a single conceptual theory for the normative content of fair and equitable treatment. Fair and equitable treatment, and minimum standards more broadly, have been analyzed as an embodiment of the rule of law,[235] as protecting against the abuse of government power, as a manifestation of the principle of good faith, as good governance norms,[236] and as reflecting general principles of law.[237] Although it would appear that fair and equitable treatment promotes these various objectives, it cannot be explained readily by one concept alone. For example, state responsibility to foreign investment under the fair and equitable treatment standard does not arise from sheer bad governance. In our view, while reference to general normative concepts may assist in some cases in elucidating the broad contours of the treatment guarantee, the content of fair and equitable treatment is best addressed by reference to the particular and often overlapping elements of the standard as elaborated in international jurisprudence.

§6.26 Legitimate expectations Tribunals have identified the protection of legitimate expectations as a key element of fair and equitable treatment.[238] Indeed, one tribunal has referred to it as the 'dominant element' of the standard.[239] References to legitimate expectations have become ubiquitous in IIA claims and awards. These ubiquitous references, however, might give rise to confusion because the term 'legitimate expectations' is used in at least three ways. In its most specific form, legitimate expectations refers to expectations arising from the foreign investor's reliance on specific host state conduct, usually oral or written representations or commitments made by the host state relating to an investment. Reliance typically takes the form of making an initial investment or the expansion of an existing one. Protection of legitimate expectations in this sense is closely related to the principle of estoppel and state responsibility under public international law for unilateral acts.[240] Second, tribunals have referred to legitimate

---

234. Elements of the minimum standard of treatment are discussed *supra* at §6.4 *et seq.*
235. Schill, *supra* note 117.
236. See Wälde, Separate Opinion (Dec. 2005), *Thunderbird, supra* note 66 at para. 13.
237. Tudor, *supra* note 117.
238. *Tecmed, supra* note 65 at para. 154; *Waste Management II, supra* note 15 at para. 98; and *Occidental, supra* note 156 at para. 183. See the analysis in Paradell, *supra* note 117.
239. *Saluka, supra* note 15 at para. 302.
240. On unilateral acts, see W.M. Reisman & M.H. Arsanjani, 'The Question of Unilateral Government Statements as Applicable Law in Investment Disputes' (2004) 19 ICSID Rev 32. See *infra* Chapter 10, §10.27, on estoppel.

expectations of a stable and predictable legal and administrative framework that
meets certain minimum standards, including consistency and transparency in
decision-making.[241] Third, at the most general level, legitimate expectations can
be used to refer to the 'expectation that the conduct of the host State subsequent
to the investment will be fair and equitable.'[242] This would appear to be simply
another way of stating that the investor has a reasonable expectation that the host
state will comply with its IIA obligations.

In developing the concept of legitimate expectations as an element of fair and
equitable treatment, tribunals and commentators have drawn on a number of
sources: the principle of good faith,[243] abuse of rights, estoppel,[244] the jurisprudence of the European Court of Human Rights (ECtHR),[245] and general principles
of law, including the development of the legitimate expectations doctrine in
domestic law.[246] Whereas in some legal regimes, the principle of legitimate expectations applies only to expectations of due process in decision-making,[247] IIA tribunals have applied the concept to protect substantive expectations about the treatment of an investment. Legitimate expectations with respect to fairness and due
process in decision-making are protected, as well as the expectations with respect
to the use and benefit of economic rights and interests forming part of the
investment.[248]

Legitimate expectations as a result of investor reliance on state conduct.
Legitimate expectations may arise as a result of specific state conduct directed at
the investor upon which the investor relies. Any form of state conduct can, in principle, give rise to legitimate expectations. Typically, the conduct giving rise to the
legitimate expectations will be in the form of oral or written representations,
undertakings or commitments, various types of administrative acts such as licenses
or permits or providing an official opinion or view. Legitimate expectations will
also arise where the investor has a contract with the state. An example of the

---

241. *Tecmed, supra* note 65 at para. 154. In *EnCana Corporation v. Ecuador* (Award, 3 Feb. 2006),
the tribunal noted at para. 158 that '[u]nder standards such as those in Article II [fair and
equitable treatment] of the BIT the State must act with reasonable consistency and without
arbitrariness in its treatment of investments. One arm of the State cannot finally affirm what
another arm denies to the detriment of a foreign investor.'
242. *Saluka, supra* note 15 at para. 301.
243. See E. Zoller, *La bonne foi en droit international public* (Paris, Éditions A. Pedone, 1977).
Also see M. Panizzon, *Good Faith in the Jurisprudence of the WTO* (Oxford: Hart Publishing,
2006).
244. See *infra* Chapter 10, §10.27, on estoppel.
245. *Tecmed, supra* note 65 relies, on ECtHR jurisprudence.
246. See, generally, Wälde, Separate Opinion (Dec. 2005), *Thunderbird, supra* note 66; and E.
Snodgrass, 'Protecting Investors' Legitimate Expectations and Recognizing and Delimiting a
General Principle' (2006) 21 ICSID Rev 1 at 53. On a comparative review of legitimate
expectations as a principle of administrative law, see S. Schønberg, *Legitimate Expectations
in Administrative Law* (Oxford: Oxford University Press, 2000).
247. This is the case, for example, in Canadian administrative law.
248. See discussion below on the Argentine cases.

protection of investment expectations (in a non-IIA context) is the *SPP case* in which the tribunal held that certain acts of Egyptian officials were:

> ... cloaked with the mantle of Governmental authority and communicated as such to foreign investors who relied on them in making their investments. Whether legal under Egyptian law or not, the act ... created expectations protected by established principles of international law.[249]

In the NAFTA context, the *Waste Management II* tribunal stated that the minimum standard of treatment is breached where the state has reneged on a representation upon which the foreign investor reasonably relied.[250] The NAFTA tribunal in *Thunderbird* describes the elements of legitimate expectations as follows:

> Having considered recent investment case law and the good faith principle of international customary law, the concept of 'legitimate expectations' relates, within the context of the NAFTA framework, to a situation where a Contracting Party's conduct creates reasonable and justifiable expectations on the part of an investor (or investment) to act in reliance on said conduct, such that a failure by the NAFTA Party to honour those expectations could cause the investor (or investment) to suffer damages.[251]

Legitimate expectations about the treatment of investments will arise 'based on the conditions offered by the host State at the time of the investment.'[252] IIA jurisprudence highlights that, to create legitimate expectations, state conduct needs to be specific and unambiguous.[253] Encouraging remarks from government officials do not of themselves give rise to legitimate expectations.[254] There must be an 'unambiguous affirmation'[255] or a 'definitive, unambiguous and repeated' assurance.[256] The conduct must be targeted at a specific person or identifiable

---

249. *Southern Pacific Properties (Middle East) Limited v. Egypt* (Award on the Merits, 20 May 1992) [*SPP*] 3 ICSID Rep 208 at paras 82-83.
250. *Waste Management II, supra* note 15 at para. 98: '... In applying this standard it is relevant that the treatment is in breach of representations made by the host State which were reasonably relied on by the claimant.' In our view, there is no substantive difference between reasonable and legitimate expectations. An unreasonable expectation is not legitimate and vice versa.
251. *Thunderbird, supra* note 66 at para. 147. While the tribunal refers to 'the reasonable and justifiable expectations on the part of an investor (or investment),' it should be noted that Art. 1105(1) applies to investments only.
252. *LG&E, supra* note 156 at para. 130. See also, *Enron, supra* note 158 at para. 262.
253. In *Metalclad, supra* note 64, the tribunal noted at para. 148 that the 'assurances received by the investor from the Mexican government in *Metalclad* were definitive, unambiguous and repeated.'
254. *Nagel v. Czech Republic* (Award, 2003) at 164.
255. *GAMI, supra* note 15 at para. 76, noting that the 'Mexican regulatory regime did not contain an unambiguous affirmation to the effect that *the Government shall announce annually individual export quotas for all mills and shall promptly enforce any non-compliance.*'
256. *Feldman, supra* note 218 at para. 148. Wälde, Separate Opinion (Dec. 2005), *Thunderbird, supra* note 66 at para. 30, to the contrary, suggests that the risk of ambiguity should be

group.[257] For example in *Tecmed, CMS, LG&E, Enron, Azurix, BG, Sempra* and *Siemens* there were specific representations that were crystallized into the terms of licenses or concession contracts under which the foreign investment operated.

The expectations in question must be legitimate – justifiable and reasonable based on objective criteria. State representations, commitments or undertakings that were obtained by fraud, bribery, coercion or by providing incomplete or inaccurate information do not give rise to legitimate expectations.[258] For example, in *Thunderbird*, the majority of the tribunal held that a foreign investor could not rely on the opinion of the Mexican gambling regulator about the legality of gambling operations because the information the investor presented to the regulator was incomplete and inaccurate.[259] Although legitimate expectations may still arise where host states representations are not consistent with local law (for example where a government regulatory agency represents to the investor that a specific regulatory requirement does not apply to investment activities and local courts later find that it does), a key issue will be whether the investor had clean hands and if the investor's reliance on the representation was reasonable in light of all the circumstances.[260]

Whether expectations are legitimate and should be protected involves balancing investor interests in maintaining stability and certainty with the likelihood that regulatory regimes change over time. Expectations are not 'not un-conditional and ever-lasting.'[261] As noted by the tribunal in *Saluka*:

> No investor may reasonably expect that the circumstances prevailing at the time the investment is made remain totally unchanged. In order to determine whether frustration of the foreign investor's expectations was justified and reasonable, the host State's legitimate right subsequently to regulate domestic matters in the public interest must be taken into consideration as well.[262]

This statement, however, must be read in its specific context. All investors must reasonably assume that the regulatory environment, like the business environment, is subject to change (absent a specially negotiated stabilization clause). Where, however, an investment is made based on specific representations by the host state

---

allocated to the government that made the statement and that a 'government agency can not rely on intentionally inserted obfuscation to extract itself from the key message the investor relied upon and that the drafter and the public authority in a position of superiority over the foreign investor has to be clear, unambiguous and consistent.'

257. See discussion in Snodgrass, *supra* note 246 at 53.
258. *Ibid.*
259. *Thunderbird, supra* note 66 at paras 151-155.
260. See *SPP, supra* note 249. In *MTD*, the tribunal found that there were legitimate expectations as a result of a foreign investment approval despite the fact that the development could not proceed under existing local laws. But see *Thunderbird, supra* note 66 at paras 164-166 where the tribunal notes that the claimant knew that certain forms of gaming were illegal and failed to disclose fully information about its planned activities to the regulator. As a result, the tribunal found there were no legitimate expectations created by a government statement, which suggested that the claimant's planned activities would not breach local gaming laws.
261. Wälde, Separate Opinion (Dec. 2005), *Thunderbird, supra* note 66 at para. 30.
262. *Saluka, supra* note 15 at para. 305.

regarding the stability of the regulatory regime, radical changes in the regime will likely breach the fair and equitable treatment standard, provided the disappointment of legitimate expectations is sufficiently serious and material.[263]

The failure to satisfy legitimate expectations as an element of the breach of fair and equitable treatment has been identified in a series of IIA awards. In *MTD*, the tribunal found that Chile had breached its fair and equitable treatment guarantee by authorizing a development project under a foreign investment contract for a project that could not proceed on the basis that it ran afoul of predetermined urban development policies.[264] The tribunal found that the government actions were contrary to the investor's 'basic assumptions.'[265] In *CME*, the tribunal found that changes to the business relationship between CME and its Czech partner resulted in CME losing 'its legal protection' for the investment.[266] In the end, it concluded that there had been a breach of fair and equitable treatment[267] 'by evisceration of the arrangements in reliance upon which the foreign investor was induced to invest.'[268]

The terms 'basic assumptions,' 'reasonable reliance' and 'legitimate expectations' of the *investor*, however, must be used with caution when assessing whether the state has been fair and equitable in its treatment of an *investment*. Fair and equitable treatment provisions normally apply only to investments. Investors have legitimate expectations about the enjoyment of investments because they have acquired rights under domestic law. Normally an investment consists of a bundle of rights, both tangible and intangible. These might include leases of property, licenses and permits, contracts, inventory and other assets. As a consequence, investors have a legitimate expectation that these acquired rights will be protected and treated in accordance with state representations upon which the investor has relied.

The *Tecmed* case provides a good illustration of the protection of legitimate expectations based on acquired rights. Tecmed, through its subsidiary, Cytrar, had acquired by public auction rights to operate a hazardous waste landfill in Mexico in 1996. The official 1994 authorization to operate the landfill and the subsequent permits granted by Mexican environmental authorities had projected that the landfill would have a ten year life. Cytrar's acquisition included the landfill's tangible assets and permits. The necessary permit to operate the landfill, with an infinite duration, was subsequently transferred to Cytrar. Mexican environmental

---

263. Wälde, Separate Opinion (Dec. 2005), *Thunderbird, supra* note 66 at para. 14.
264. *MTD, supra* note 156 at paras 188-189.
265. *Ibid.*, at para. 188.
266. *CME Czech Republic B.V. v. Czech Republic* (Partial Award, 13 Sep. 2001) [*CME*] at paras 505-527.
267. Art. 3(1), Czechoslovakia-Netherlands (1991) provides that: 'Each Contracting Party shall ensure fair and equitable treatment to the investments of investors of the other Contracting Party and shall not impair, by unreasonable or discriminatory measures, the operation, management, maintenance, use, enjoyment or disposal thereof by those investors.'
268. *CME, supra* note 266 at para. 611. At para. 517, the tribunal referred to the D.F. Vagts, 'Coercion and Foreign Investment Rearrangements' (1978) 72 AJIL 17 at 28: 'The threat of cancellation of the right to do business might well be considered coercion … Such coercion might be found, even where a "clean" waiver of rights is signed.' Also see para. 526.

authorities thereafter replaced the original permit with a one-year renewable permit. This amendment was part of a larger general regulatory change by Mexican authorities to facilitate enforcement actions against non-compliant sites. Owing to community opposition to the continued operation of the site, in 1998 Cytrar and the Mexican authorities agreed that Cytrar would relocate the existing site. Cytrar's agreement to the relocation was premised on the continued operation of the existing site until the relocation. Before the relocation occurred, however, Mexican authorities refused to renew Cytrar's permit for its existing facility.[269] The tribunal found that the denial of the permit was not based on any misconduct on the part of Cytrar but, rather, on community opposition to the continued operation of the site. Accordingly, it held that Mexico's conduct amounted to a breach of fair and equitable treatment.[270] The tribunal stated that fair and equitable treatment:

> ... in light of the good faith principle established by international law, requires the Contracting Parties to provide to international investments treatment that does not affect the basic expectations that were taken into account by the foreign investor to make the investment. The foreign investor expects the host State to act in a consistent manner, free from ambiguity and totally transparency in its relations with the foreign investor, so that it may know beforehand any and all rules and regulations that will govern its investments, as well as the goals of the relevant policies and administrative practices or directives, to be able to plan its investment and comply with such regulations. Any and all State actions conforming to such criteria should relate not only to the guidelines, directives or requirements issued, or the resolutions approved there under, but also to the goals underlying such regulations. The foreign investor also expects the host State to act consistently, i.e. without arbitrarily revoking any pre-existing decisions or permits issued by the State that were relied upon by the investor to assume its commitments as well as to plan and launch its commercial and business activities.[271]

In *MTD*, the tribunal found a breach of fair and equitable treatment because, at the time the host state approved the investment under a foreign investment contract, the investment in question (an urban development project) was inconsistent with government urban planning policies. The land MTD acquired could not be developed under the development and zoning laws in force at the time of acquisition. In the tribunal's view, the breach of fair and equitable treatment occurred as a result of the host state authorizing the investment when it was contrary to established government policy. The tribunal, however, failed to address the exact nature of the investment in question, that is, the legally protected rights that the tribunal

---

269. See *Tecmed, supra* note 65 at paras 158-160.
270. Art. 4(1), Mexico-Spain (1995), provides: 'Each Contracting Party will guarantee in its territory fair and equitable treatment, according to International Law, for the investments made by investors of the other Contracting Party.'
271. *Tecmed, supra* note 65 at para. 154.

found had been subject to unfair and inequitable treatment. Nor did the tribunal identify the specific legal rights arising from the foreign investment contract. Of particular note, clause four of the contract made the approval in question subject to other necessary authorizations. MTD had not acquired a right or promise to an amendment of zoning or development laws.[272] Even if MTD had a basic assumption that it could proceed with the development, basic assumptions – or legitimate expectations for that matter – alone do not constitute investments. It is clear that MTD was under a mistaken assumption regarding its rights. The fundamental question in *MTD*, as in all cases of mistaken assumptions, is who should bear the risk of the mistaken assumption? While the tribunal held that MTD was fifty percent responsible for the loss, it failed to clearly identify what rights MTD had acquired that amounted to an investment. If the foreign investment contract did not bind the government to allow the project to proceed (which it did not) then, arguably, MTD's entire loss was the result of its own conduct.[273] The tribunal, on the other hand, found that fair and equitable treatment requires the state to engage in coherent and consistent acts. In its view, one organ of state cannot authorize an investment while, at the same time, the investment is contrary to the urban development laws of the state.[274] However, the finding of inconsistency is questionable where the foreign investment contract was clear that the approval to admit the foreign investment was subject to the necessary regulatory approvals. But it could be otherwise when the government consistently reassured the investor in this regard, or was aware of the important investments being made by the claimant and did not warn the investor accordingly.

The *MTD* case highlights another unsatisfactory element in some IIA awards. In the majority of IIAs, the fair and equitable treatment standard applies to investments, not to investors.[275] Strictly speaking, there is no direct obligation under most IIAs to treat foreign investors fairly and equitably.[276] Although tribunals sometimes refer to the basic assumptions or legitimate expectations of *investors*, caution must be exercised in this regard. Investors have legitimate expectations with respect to the fair and equitable treatment of their investments first and foremost because legitimate expectations crystallize in an acquired right or investment. As noted above, in a series of cases against Argentina (*BG, CMS, Enron, LG&E* and *Sempra*), tribunals have found a breach of fair and equitable treatment because of the evisceration of the investors' rights under gas licenses. In this type of case, investors have legitimate expectations about the use and enjoyment of their investments because they have legitimately acquired rights under domestic or international law. Another example is *M.C.I. Power Group L.C. and New Turbine, Inc. v. Ecuador*, in which the tribunal found that the investor could not have

---

272. *MTD, supra* note 156 at para. 514.
273. See §6.31.
274. *MTD, supra* note 156 at para. 164.
275. See *supra* §6.18.
276. Tribunals sometimes do not make this distinction clear. See *MTD, supra* note 156 at para. 166.

legitimate expectations as to the outcome of negotiations because the contract in question did not give rise to an obligation to resolve disputes.[277] A breach of fair and equitable treatment is more likely to arise where the state has made specific representations about the use or enjoyment of the rights that the investor has acquired and where the investor has detrimentally relied on those representations.

Assessing legitimate expectations. Whether reliance by a foreign investor upon host state conduct is 'reasonable' is a highly contextual inquiry. Tribunals and commentators have identified a number of factors that are potentially relevant in assessing an investor's reasonable reliance. These include: (i) the timing and specificity of the representation; (ii) whether there were any disclaimers by the state; (iii) the position of the person making the representation within the government hierarchy; (iv) the relative skills and expertise of the parties; (v) the foreseeability of reliance; (vii) changes in circumstances or conditions upon which the representations were based; (viii) the extent to which there were mistaken assumptions; (ix) the extent to which the investor sought to protect itself for a specific risk; (x) the conduct of the investor.

Stability and predictability of the legal framework. Tribunals have found that the stability and predictability of the legal framework is an essential element of fair and equitable treatment.[278] When investors acquire rights under domestic law, the fair and equitable treatment standard will protect legitimate expectations about the use and enjoyment of these rights. This requires a basis level of stability and predictability in the legal framework. Fundamental changes in the legal framework that eviscerate legitimately acquired rights are likely to violate fair and equitable treatment.

In a series of claims against Argentina, tribunals have found that the changes Argentina made to its gas regime in the early 2000s to address severe economic conditions breached the fair and equitable treatment guarantee, because the changes destroyed the stability and predictability of the regulatory regime governing the gas sector. In the first of these cases, *CMS v. Argentina*, the tribunal found that investors have a legitimate expectation of a certain level of stability and predictability.

The dispute, like other claims, arose out of Argentina's privatization program in the 1990s. CMS – a US company – became a minority shareholder in TGN, a gas distribution company. CMS claimed that its investment was based on a gas tariff regime calculated in dollars and adjusted every six months based on a dollar price index. This regime was specifically established in Argentine law through the Gas Decree and was protected contractually through TGN's license. The license provided, among other things, that its terms could not be changed without the licensee's

---

277.   *M.C.I. Power Group L.C. and New Turbine, Inc. v. Ecuador* (Award, 31 Jul. 2007) at para. 279.

278.   In *Metalclad, supra* note 64, the tribunal stated at para. 99: 'Mexico failed to ensure a transparent and predictable framework for Metalclad's business planning and investment.' See also *CMS, supra* note 95 at para. 276; *LG&E, supra* note 156 at paras 124-125 and 131; *Enron, supra* note 158 at para. 259-260; and *Occidental, supra* note 156 at para. 183.

consent. The crux of the dispute between the parties was whether there was a binding commitment that tariffs would be calculated in US dollars with biannual adjustments or whether the obligation was to provide a fair and reasonable tariff. The tribunal concluded that the license and Gas Decree guaranteed a tariff regime in dollars. The tribunal then turned to whether Argentine measures reforming the currency exchange system and suspending price adjustments were consistent with Argentina's obligations under the US-Argentina BIT which provides in Article II(2)(a):

> Investment shall at all times be accorded fair and equitable treatment, shall enjoy full protection and security and shall in no case be accorded treatment less than that required by international law.

The *CMS* tribunal stated that 'fair and equitable treatment is inseparable from stability and predictability.'[279] Likewise, the *LG&E, Enron, Sempra* and *BG* tribunals found that the abrogation of the specific guarantees granted to the investors violated the stability and predictability underlying the standard of fair and equitable treatment.[280]

While some awards to date might suggest that the requirement for a stable and predictable framework for investment is an independent element of fair and equitable treatment, caution should be exercised in referring to freestanding obligations of stability and predictability. The majority of cases where tribunals have invoked the element of stability and predictability have arisen in contexts where there was reliance on specific representations or undertakings and the investors in question had acquired investments with those legitimate expectations. In these cases, tribunals have found that the legal framework cannot 'be dispensed

---

279. *CMS, ibid.,* at para. 276. The tribunal had noted two paragraphs earlier that 'The Treaty Preamble makes it clear, however, that one principal objective of the protection envisaged is that fair and equitable treatment is desirable "to maintain a stable framework for investments and maximum effective use of economic resources." There can be no doubt, therefore, that a stable legal and business environment is an essential element of fair and equitable treatment.' This echoed the statement of the *Metalclad* tribunal that 'Mexico failed to ensure a transparent and predictable framework for Metalclad's business planning and investment. The totality of these circumstances demonstrates a lack of orderly process and timely disposition in relation to an investor of a Party acting in the expectation that it would be treated fairly and justly in accordance with the NAFTA.' See *Metalclad, supra* note 64 at para. 99. In *CMS, ibid.,* the tribunal also stated in *obiter dicta* at para. 284 that 'the Treaty standard of fair and equitable treatment and its connection with the required stability and predictability of the business environment, founded on solemn legal and contractual commitments, is not different from the international law minimum standard and its evolution under customary law.'

280. *LG&E, supra* note 156 at para. 133; *Enron, supra* note 158 at paras 260-267; and *Sempra, supra* note 224 at para. 300. In *BG, supra* note 195 at para. 307, the tribunal stated that: 'Argentina, however, entirely altered the legal and business environment by taking a series of radical measures, starting in 1999, as described in Chapter III.D above. Argentina's derogation from the tariff regime, dollar standard and adjustment mechanism was and is in contradiction with the established Regulatory Framework as well as the specific commitments represented by Argentina, on which BG relied when it decided to make the investment. In so doing, Argentina violated the principles of stability and predictability inherent to the standard of fair and equitable treatment.'

with altogether when specific commitments to the contrary have been made.'[281] When the host state has made no specific assurances or guarantees linked to specific acquired rights, such as in a license or permit, tribunals are less likely to find there is a legitimate expectation that the legal framework will not change.

Further, tribunals have noted that stability and predictability are never absolute. In *Parkerings* the tribunal noted:

> It is each State's undeniable right and privilege to exercise its sovereign legislative power. A State has the right to enact, modify or cancel a law at its own discretion. Save for the existence of an agreement, in the form of a *stabilization* clause or otherwise, there is nothing objectionable about the amendment brought to the regulatory framework existing at the time an investor made its investment. As a matter of fact, any businessman or investor knows that laws will evolve over time. What is prohibited however is for a State to act unfairly, unreasonably or inequitably in the exercise of its legislative power.[282]

The *Parkerings* award highlights that the legal regime regulating any particular investment will evolve over time. In assessing legitimate expectations regarding stability and predictability, tribunals will also consider the political environment at the time of the investment. For states in transition, legislative changes are more likely to occur compared to other states.[283] The legal and commercial risks that were known by the investor, or could have been known with reasonable due diligence at the time the investment was made, are a significant factor in assessing legitimate expectations. As noted by the tribunal in *Generation Ukraine*:

> … it is relevant to consider the vicissitudes of the economy of the state that is host to the investment in determining the investor's legitimate expectations, the protection of which is a major concern of the minimum standards of treatment contained in bilateral investment treaties. The Claimant was attracted to the Ukraine because of the possibility of earning a rate of return on its capital in significant excess to the other investment opportunities in more developed

---

281. *CMS, supra* note 95 at para. 277.
282. *Parkerings, supra* note 133 at para. 332. Also see para. 334, where the tribunal stated: 'Neither is it contested that the Republic of Lithuania gave no specific assurance or guarantee to Parkerings that no modification of law, with possible incidence on the investment, would occur. The legitimate expectations of the Claimant that the legal regime would remain unchanged are not based on or reinforced by a particular behaviour of the Respondent. In other words, the Republic of Lithuania did not give any explicit or implicit promise that the legal framework of the Agreement would remain unchanged.'
283. In *Parkerings, ibid.*, at para. 335, the tribunal noted that: 'In 1998, at the time of the Agreement, the political environment in Lithuania was characteristic of a country in transition from its past being a part of the Soviet Union to being a candidate for European Union membership. Thus, legislative changes, far from being unpredictable, were in fact to be regarded as likely. As any businessman would, the Claimant was aware of the risk that changes of laws would probably occur after the conclusion of the Agreement. The circumstances surrounding the decision to invest in Lithuania were certainly not an indication of stability of the legal environment. Therefore, in such a situation, no expectation that the laws would remain unchanged was legitimate.'

economies. The Claimant thus invested in the Ukraine on notice of both the prospects and the potential pitfalls. Its investment was speculative.[284]

Although the dismantling of legal protections will breach fair and equitable treatment, general regulatory changes to address changing public policy needs generally will not. The issue as stated by the tribunal in *Parkerings* at paragraph 332 is whether in modifying the regulatory regime, the state has acted 'unfairly, unreasonably or inequitably in the exercise of its legislative power.' As noted in *Saluka*, this requires a detailed weighing of the Claimant's legitimate and reasonable expectations on the one hand and the Respondent's legitimate regulatory interests on the other:

> A foreign investor protected by the Treaty may in any case properly expect that the Czech Republic implements its policies bona fide by conduct that is, as far as it affects the investors' investment, reasonably justifiable by public policies and that such conduct does not manifestly violate the requirements of consistency, transparency, even-handedness and non-discrimination. In particular, any differential treatment of a foreign investor must not be based on unreasonable distinctions and demands, and must be justified by showing that it bears a reasonable relationship to rational policies not motivated by a preference for other investments over the foreign-owned investment.
>
> Finally, it transpires from arbitral practice that, according to the 'fair and equitable treatment' standard, the host State must never disregard the principles of procedural propriety and due process and must grant the investor freedom from coercion or harassment by its own regulatory authorities.[285]

§6.27 Discrimination   IIA tribunals have stated that discriminatory measures violate fair and equitable treatment.[286] Although intuitively it appears reasonable to assume that discriminatory treatment is neither fair nor equitable, it is useful to distinguish five types of discrimination that may arise with respect to the treatment of foreign investors and investment: (i) discrimination contrary to international human rights, such as discrimination based on race or sex;[287] (ii) unjustifiable or arbitrary regulatory distinctions made between things that are alike or treating unlike things in the same way;[288] (iii) conduct targeted at specific persons or things motivated by bad faith or with an intent to injure or harass;[289] (iv) discrimination in the application of domestic law;[290] and (v) nationality-based discrimination.

---

284. *Generation Ukraine, supra* note 63 at para. 20.37.
285. *Saluka, supra* note 15 at paras 307-308.
286. *CMS, supra* note 95 at para. 290.
287. See §6.10.
288. Where this type of discrimination is alleged, there will be substantial overlap with the prohibition of arbitrary measure. See *infra* §6.33 *et seq.*
289. See *infra* §6.29.
290. In *Loewen, supra* note 23 at para. 135, the tribunal states that a decision which is in breach of municipal law and is discriminatory against the foreign litigant amounts to manifest injustice according to international law.

The first four forms of discrimination described above would violate the minimum standard of treatment and fair and equitable treatment.[291] The more difficult issue is whether nationality-based discrimination is contrary to fair and equitable treatment. If so, then arguably fair and equitable treatment provisions subsume national and MFN treatment clauses. This view was taken by F.A. Mann, who argued that 'fair and equitable treatment' is an overarching standard of which specific investment guarantees, including national and MFN treatment, are merely expressions.[292]

A number of awards support the view that nationality-based discrimination is contrary to fair and equitable treatment. In *Eureko B. V. v. Poland*, the tribunal found a breach of fair and equitable treatment because Poland acted for 'purely arbitrary reasons linked to the interplay of Polish politics and nationalistic reasons of a discriminatory character.'[293] In *Eastern Sugar*, the tribunal found a breach of fair and equitable treatment where the state failed to provide a rational explanation for a regulatory regime. The tribunal drew the inference that the system was designed to appease local economic interests to the detriment of foreign investors.[294]

The argument against interpreting fair and equitable treatment as including nationality-based discrimination is that it would make national and MFN treatment provisions redundant, contrary to an *effet utile* interpretation. Second, the prevailing view is that national and MFN treatment are treaty-based obligations that do not arise under customary international law. If fair and equitable treatment is viewed as synonymous with the minimum standard of treatment, national treatment and MFN treatment would have become customary international law obligations. Third, national and MFN treatment obligations are often subject to a number of exceptions and reservations.[295] These reservations typically do not apply to fair and equitable treatment. Since the overwhelming IIA treaty practice is to prohibit nationality-based discrimination through specific national and MFN treatment provisions, the intent to do so through general fair and equitable treatment provisions should not lightly be inferred without specific evidence of the parties' intentions. Accordingly, the better view is that a general fair and equitable treatment clause does not encompass relative standard of treatment guarantees.[296] This general conclusion is subject to the caveat that each IIA must be assessed on the

---

291. See *supra* §6.10.
292. Mann, *supra* note 160 at 243 states that: 'it is submitted that the right to fair and equitable treatment goes much further than the right to most-favored-nation and to national treatment ... so general a provision is likely to be almost sufficient to cover all conceivable cases, and it may well be that provisions of the Agreements affording substantive protection are not more than examples of specific instances of this overriding duty.'
293. *Eureko B. V. v. Poland* (Partial Award, 19 Aug. 2005) at para. 233. Also in *Waste Management II*, *supra* note 25 at para. 98, the tribunal referred to conduct that is discriminatory and exposes the claimant to sectional or racial prejudice.
294. *Eastern Sugar*, *supra* note 232 at para. 314.
295. See *supra* Chapter 4, §4.28, and Chapter 5, §5.27.
296. In *Myers*, the tribunal split on this issue. A majority of the tribunal held that the breach of national treatment with respect to a ban on PCB exports established a breach of fair and equitable treatment. Arbitrator Chiasson disagreed and stated that breach of national treat-

basis of its particular text and negotiating history. If an IIA has no other specific provisions on discrimination or national and MFN treatment, it may be that the treaty parties did not agree to protect against discrimination, or to the contrary intended fair and equitable treatment to be an all encompassing treatment standard that would include nationality-based discrimination.

§6.28 Transparency   There is broad agreement among states that transparency is an important element in creating a predictable, stable and secure climate for foreign investment.[297] Despite broad agreement as to the desirability of transparency in principle, the meaning of transparency in the context of IIAs is less clear.

Given that transparency is such an ambiguous concept, it is useful to identify core elements or obligations that might be said to arise by a requirement for a government to act transparently. International trade law provides some guidance in this respect distinguishing four distinct transparency obligations: (i) the publication of applicable laws, regulations and policies (publication obligations); (ii) notification requirements with respect to laws, regulations and policies and amendments (notification obligations); (iii) requirements to provide a reasonable opportunity to comment on new laws, regulations or policies (comment obligations); and (iv) the fair and transparent administration of laws, regulations and policies (administration obligations).[298] As discussed in Chapter 8 below, a number of IIAs have express publication, notification, comment and administration obligations.

Some IIA awards have stated that fair and equitable treatment imposes a publication obligation with respect to laws, regulations and policies applicable to foreign investment and investors.[299] In *Tecmed*, the tribunal stated that in order to plan, an investor expects to:

---

ment did not establish a breach of fair and equitable treatment. See *Myers, supra* note 5 at para. 266.

297. WTO, Working Group on the Relationship between Trade and Investment, Transparency, Note by Secretariat, WT/WGTI/W/109, 27 Mar. 2002 [WTO Transparency] at 4. On the evolution of the concept of transparency in international economic law, see C.-S. Zoellner, 'Transparency: An Analysis of an Evolving Fundamental Principle in International Economic Law' (2006) 27 MJIL 579.

298. See WTO Transparency, *ibid.* Various WTO Agreements provide examples of these obligations. Transparency obligations in the WTO system include: (i) publication of laws, regulations and administrative rulings (Art. X, GATT; Art. III, GATS, and Art. 63, TRIPS Agreement). Some agreements require the establishment of 'enquiry points' to respond to questions (Art. 10, TBT Agreement; Art. III(4), GATS; and Art. 63(3), TRIPS Agreement); (ii) the requirement to notify other WTO member of changes to laws and regulations or the application of trade remedies (Arts 2.9-10, TBT Agreement, and Annex B, SPS Agreement); (iii) The WTO Agreements also include provisions on procedural transparency. Art. X, GATT, provides that rules and regulations must be administered in a uniform, impartial and reasonable manner and that there be a right of appeal and review. Also see Art. VI, GATS, and Arts 41-42 and 62, TRIPS Agreement. On WTO obligations, see M. Trebilcock & R. Howse, *The Regulation of International Trade*, 3rd edn (London: Routledge, 2005).

299. *Tecmed, supra* note 65 at para. 154; *Metalclad, supra* note 64 at paras 76 and 88; and *Waste Management II, supra* note 15 at para. 98. The review of the *Metalclad* award in the British Columbia Supreme Court (*Mexico v. Metalclad Corp.,* Judgment of the Supreme Court of

... know beforehand any and all rules and regulations that will govern its investments, as well as the goals of the relevant policies and administrative practices or directives, to be able to plan its investment and comply with such regulations. Any and all State actions conforming to such criteria should relate not only to the guidelines, directives or requirements issued, or the resolutions approved there under, but also to the goals underlying such regulations.[300]

Given the centrality of publication of laws, regulations and policies to the rule of law and the administration of justice, the conclusion that fair and equitable treatment includes an obligation on host states to publish applicable law, regulations and policies would appear sound.

The position with respect to notification and comment obligations, however, is less clear. In the trade context, notification and comment obligations arise as a result of specific treaty commitments. Even if these obligations appear in some international trade treaties, trade commitments cannot be simply transposed into the investment context through the fair and equitable treatment standard.[301] There is little state practice to suggest that states have a general duty to specifically notify foreign investors of laws or changes to laws that might affect them. *A fortiori*, there is even less authority for the proposition that governments have an obligation to provide foreign investors with an opportunity to comment on changes to state regulation before changes are implemented. That said, a failure by a government to notify foreign investors of changes to laws, regulations and policies and to allow comments may well be one factor in determining whether there has been a breach of fair and equitable treatment.

Although the existence of a general notification or comment obligation arising from fair and equitable treatment may be questionable, the situation is different where the investor has relied on specific government representations about state regulation. Depending on the circumstances, the conduct or representations of the government may give rise to legitimate expectations.[302] In addition, where

---

British Columbia, 2 May 2001) found that the *Metalclad* tribunal's finding of a breach of fair and equitable treatment based on transparency was an excess of jurisdiction because transparency obligations are contained in other NAFTA chapters. Neither the award nor the judicial review, however, expressly addresses the extent to which transparency is an independent element of fair and equitable treatment.

300. *Tecmed, supra* note 65 at para. 154.
301. The discussion within the Working Group on the Relationship between Trade and Investment on Transparency suggests that while there is general agreement between WTO members for the need for transparency in the investment context, there is little agreement on the exact scope of that obligation, particularly for developing members. See WTO, Working Group on the Relationship Between Trade and Investment, Communication from China, Transparency, WT/WGTI/W/160, 15 Apr. 2003. See also the concurring opinion by B. Schwartz in *Myers, supra* note 5 at paras 247-255. Professor Schwartz notes that '[i]t is far from obvious, in the absence of evidence, that basic GATT norms like transparency and procedural fairness have been accepted by states throughout the world and so have passed into the body of general (or "customary") international law.'
302. Bin Cheng argues that where a state has knowingly led another state to believe that it will pursue a certain policy, the state has a duty to notify the other state of changes in its policy.

changes to the legal framework would result in changing the terms of an acquired right (such as a business license or permit or changing a royalty rate under a concession), due process requirements of notification and an opportunity to be heard will apply.

Finally, fair and equitable treatment most certainly imposes an obligation with respect to the impartial administration of state regulation.[303] For example, in the context of an administrative review, the *Pope & Talbot* tribunal cited a lack of forthrightness in communications, questionable statements and misrepresentations in internal communications as constituting a breach of fair and equitable treatment.[304] IIA tribunals have cited haphazard, opaque, contradictory and inconsistent decisions and decision-making as not being transparent.[305] This element of transparency overlaps substantially with requirements for due process.

In addition to these core elements of transparency, the term is also sometimes used in a general way to refer to the totality of government measures that have negatively affected the investment. For example, in *Metalclad*, the tribunal stated that Mexico had:

> … failed to ensure a transparent and predictable framework for Metalclad's business planning and investment. The totality of these circumstances demonstrated a lack of orderly process and timely disposition in relation to an investor acting in the expectation that it would be treated fairly and justly.[306]

In *Metalclad*, the lack of transparency arose from the inconsistency between government representations that Metalclad would receive all necessary approvals for the project and the actions of local authorities opposed to the project (in particular the denial of a construction permit for reasons outside their jurisdiction and without providing the investor a right to be heard). The use of transparency in this sense overlaps significantly with the protection of legitimate expectations and due process.[307]

See B. Cheng, *General Principles of International Law, supra* note 75 at 137. Also see Reisman & Arsanjani, *supra* note 240.

303. See, for example, *Emilio Agustín Maffezini v. Spain* (Award, 13 Nov. 2000) [*Maffezini*] at para. 83: 'the lack of transparency with which this loan transaction was conducted is incompatible with Spain's commitment to ensure the investor a fair and equitable treatment …' See also *Waste Management II, supra* note 15 at para. 98.

304. *Pope & Talbot, supra* note 19 at paras 177-179.

305. *Petrobart Ltd. v. Kyrgyz Republic* (Award, 29 Mar. 2005) at 25 and *Tecmed, supra* note 65 at paras 162 and 164.

306. *Metalclad, supra* note 64 at para. 99. This part of the *Metalclad* award was eventually set aside by the Supreme Court of British Columbia because the court concluded that the tribunal had exceeded its jurisdiction in finding that Art. 1105 of NAFTA included a duty of transparency. *Mexico v. Metalclad Corp.* (Judgment of the Supreme Court of British Columbia, 2 May 2001). In addressing the question of whether lack of transparency breaches Art. 1105 of NAFTA, the *Feldman* tribunal found the court's decision 'instructive.' *Feldman, supra* note 218 at para. 133.

307. See also *Maffezini supra* note 303 at para. 83 where the tribunal refers to the lack of transparency in a loan transaction, where the core issue was that the state failed to obtain the investor's

Tribunals should exercise caution in asserting – as the *Tecmed* tribunal did – that states have an obligation to act 'in a consistent manner, free from ambiguity and totally transparently in its relations with the foreign investor.'[308] In the case of a large investment that involves the jurisdiction of several government ministries and agencies and multiple levels of government, a host state cannot be held to a standard of strict or absolute liability whereby any degree of inconsistency, ambiguity or lack of transparency breaches fair and equitable treatment.[309] Indeed, in federal states it is common for there to be uncertainties regarding administrative competencies. In addition, the fact that there is a certain lack of transparency because regulation is complex, perhaps even arcane or unwieldy, does not mean that a government has breached its obligation to provide fair and equitable treatment.[310] Further, fair and equitable treatment does require a duty of disclosure of all documents in the possession of the state relating to the investment.[311]

§6.29 Bad faith, coercion, threats and harassment Bad faith, coercion,[312] threats, public denunciation and harassment of an investment by a host state are in most situations likely to result in a breach of fair and equitable treatment. A breach occurs when a state fails to act in good faith and its conduct is sufficiently severe. In *Pope & Talbot*, the tribunal found a breach of fair and equitable treatment due to state conduct during an administrative review process when the investor was subject to inappropriate treatment including threats.[313] In *Tecmed*, the tribunal found that the denial of a permit renewal was coercive and inconsistent with fair and equitable treatment.[314]

Politically motivated harassment may amount to a breach of fair and equitable treatment where regulatory powers are used for an improper purpose or the host state's reaction is irresponsible, unreasonable and disproportionate.[315] In *Vivendi II*, the tribunal found that the state had imposed charges and fines on the investment in order to coerce negotiation. The tribunal stated that the 'charges and fines

---

          consent to transfer funds from its bank account.
308. *Tecmed, supra* note 65 at para. 154. While the unofficial English translation uses 'totally transparently,' the original Spanish version refers simply to 'transparente.'
309. It has been argued that where the ambiguity arises as a result of a government representation, the risk falls on the government (*Thunderbird*, the Separate Opinion, *supra* note 256). While this may be appropriate in some circumstances, a hard and fast rule or presumption should not apply in this area. The tribunal will have to assess whether the investor's reliance was reasonable based on all of the circumstances and whether the risk of the ambiguity should fall on the investor or host state.
310. *Feldman, supra* note 218 at paras 132-133.
311. In *Parkerings*, the tribunal stated that non-disclosure of a legal opinion did not breach the fair and equitable treatment standard. *Parkerings, supra* note 133 at para. 307.
312. The classic article is Vagts, *supra* note 268.
313. See *Pope & Talbot, supra* note 19 at paras 177-179.
314. *Tecmed, supra* note 65 at para. 163.
315. *Vivendi II, supra* note 135 at para. 7.4.24.

constitute a blatant misuse of the Province's regulatory powers for illegitimate purposes' and that:

> Under the fair and equitable standard, there is no doubt about a government's obligation not to disparage and undercut a concession (a 'do no harm' standard) that has properly been granted, albeit by a predecessor government, based on falsities and motivated by a desire to rescind or force a renegotiation.[316]

State conduct amounting to duress and harassment will call into question whether investor conduct was voluntary and may vitiate the consent of the investor.[317] For example, in *Desert Line Projects LLC v. Yemen*,[318] the tribunal found a breach of fair and equitable treatment where the investor was coerced into a settlement agreement. The settlement agreement provided that Yemen would pay approximately fifty percent of the amount that it was liable to pay under a final and binding arbitral award. The tribunal found that the claimant had no realistic choice but to enter into the settlement agreement given the physical and financial duress it faced:

> The settlement agreement according to which the prevailing party in an arbitral proceeding renounces half of its rights without due consideration can only be valid if it is the result of an authentic, fair and equitable negotiation.[319]

In *SGS v. Philippines*, the tribunal noted that 'an unjustified refusal to pay sums admittedly payable under an award or a contract'[320] raises arguable issues with respect to a breach of fair and equitable treatment. Particularly where the claimant is able to show that a refusal to pay a sum due is being used coercively, a claim of fair and equitable treatment is likely to be successful. However, it is unlikely that a refusal to pay sums owing breaches fair and equitable treatment provided judicial enforcement remedies are not denied to the investor.[321]

§6.30 A requirement to create favourable conditions? The perambulatory language in many IIAs is framed proactively.[322] IIA preambles often provide

---

316. *Vivendi II, ibid.*, at para. 7.4.39.
317. See generally, Vagts, *supra* note 268, referred to in *Tecmed* at para. 163 and *CME, supra* note 266 at paras 517-538. Whether the conduct of the Czech Media council was coercive or not was at the heart of the *Lauder* and *CME* cases. The *Lauder* tribunal characterized the Czech Media Council's conduct as that of requiring clarification of the relationship between the parties, not enforcing changes. In addition, since the investor acquiesced to this process, the *Lauder* Tribunal held that it was barred from arguing that the change was coerced (*Lauder, supra* note 112 at para. 272). In contrast, the *CME* tribunal found the Czech Media Council's actions were coercive.
318. *Desert Line Projects LLC v. Yemen* (Award, 6 Feb. 2008).
319. *Ibid.*, at para. 179.
320. *SGS v. Philippines, supra* note 158 at para. 162.
321. See *infra* Chapter 7, §7.21, regarding the issue of whether non-payment of debts is expropriatory.
322. *CMS, supra* note 95 at para. 274. See *supra* Chapter 2, §2.29, Chapter 3, §3.5, and Chapter 6, §6.20, on IIA preambles.

expressly that the treaty is to create favourable conditions for foreign investment. In *MTD*, the tribunal stated that fair and equitable treatment is intended to promote, create and stimulate investment rather than to provide 'prescriptions for a passive behaviour of the State or avoidance of prejudicial conduct to the investors.'[323] The tribunal in that case noted that these favourable conditions contemplate 'an effective normative framework; impartial courts, an efficient and legally restrained bureaucracy, and the measure of transparency in decisions that has increasingly been recognized as a control mechanism over governments.'[324] Accordingly, the host state must 'establish and maintain an appropriate legal, administrative, and regulatory framework that modern investment theory has come to recognize as a *conditio sine qua non* of the success of private enterprise.'[325]

There is a distinction between the favourable conditions for foreign investment provided by a stable and predictable legal framework based on the rule of law and favourable conditions based on a certain view of appropriate economic policies. Fair and equitable treatment does not require that governments adopt specific types of economic policies. It does not require host states to liberalize, privatize, deregulate, lower taxes or engage in other economic policies that might be viewed as creating favourable conditions for private investment.

The situation is more complicated where a state represents that it is going to undertake regulatory reforms and, in reliance, the investor invests. For example, in *GAMI* the tribunal addressed whether there was a breach of Article 1105, NAFTA, resulting from Mexico's failure to implement a regulatory program in the sugar industry. The tribunal concluded that the claimant had not proven that the failure to implement the program was attributable to the government. Further, the tribunal stated that the investor 'has not shown that the government's self-assigned duty in the regulatory regime was simple and unequivocal. It is impossible to conclude that the failures in the Sugar Program were both directly attributable to the government and directly causative of GAMI's alleged injury.'[326]

One might ask whether an investor can have legitimate expectations where a state makes general statements about regulatory reforms. In such cases, there is no acquired right to a specific type of regulatory framework and changes in government policy remain a business risk. Further, legitimate expectations arise only where there is specific and unambiguous conduct directed at a specific actor or a defined group of actors.[327] Thus, a stronger claim might be made where government officials make specific and direct promises to an investor about changes to the regulatory framework. Whether reliance is reasonable and should be protected will remain a highly fact contingent determination.

§6.31 The relevance of the conduct of the foreign investor A factor in assessing fair and equitable treatment is the conduct of the investor, particularly

---

323.   *MTD, supra* note 156 at para. 113.
324.   *Ibid.,* at para. 117.
325.   *Ibid.*
326.   *GAMI, supra* note 15 at para. 110.
327.   Snodgrass, *supra* note 246 at 56.

where the state treatment in question is in response to the misconduct of the foreign investor.[328] The conduct of the foreign investor (whether malfeasance, misfeasance and non-feasance)[329] cannot be separated from the issue of legitimate or reasonable expectations and reasonable reliance. Malfeasance, fraud, bribery, misrepresentation or other unlawful acts may be sufficient to destroy any basis for legitimate expectations or reasonable reliance.[330] For example, when a license is obtained through bribery, revoking it on the basis that it was obtained illegally would probably not give rise to a breach of fair and equitable treatment. Contracts obtained on the basis of fraudulent misrepresentation[331] or bribery may be void or voidable based on the governing law of the contract.[332] Further, when investments are not made in compliance with local law, they might be denied protection, *ratione materiae*, under the specific IIA in question.[333]

Illegal activity by the investor does not, however, provide a license for the state to act illegally, particularly where the illegality is technical. Further, even if a state were entitled to revoke a license or permit based on fraudulent misrepresentation, a revocation of the license without due process might amount to an independent breach of fair and equitable treatment. A discriminatory revocation might also give rise to a breach, such as where other license holders in the same circumstances as the investor also obtained their licenses through misconduct but the state failed to revoke their licenses as well.

Misfeasance or non-feasance by the foreign investment might also be relevant to the fair and equitable treatment analysis. In assessing whether states have

---

328. See generally P. Muchlinski, '"Caveat Investor"? The Relevance of the Conduct of the Investor under the Fair and Equitable Treatment Standard' (2006) 55 ICLQ 567. Also see I. Brownlie, 'Treatment of Aliens: Assumption of Risk and The International Standard,' in W. Flume, H.J. Hahn, G. Kegel & K.R. Simmonds, eds, *International Law and Economic Order: Essays in Honour of F.A. Mann* (Munich: Verlag C.H. Beck, 1977) at 309.

329. W.M. Reisman & R.D. Sloane, 'Indirect Expropriation and Its Valuation in the BIT Generation' (2003) 74 BYIL 115 at 121 using these categories with respect to state conduct.

330. In *Feldman, supra* note 218, the tribunal found a breach of national treatment on the basis that the foreign investor had not, like a national, received tax rebates, even though the tax rebates were not authorized under Mexican law. The dissenting member of the tribunal, stated that the investor's business was based on illegal rebates and would not have found a breach of national treatment absent 'extremely clear and convincing evidence' of discrimination.

331. See *Azinian, supra* note 35 at paras 104-105.

332. See *SPP, supra* note 249 at 219 and dissenting opinion of Dr El Mahdiat at 305. Generally see H. Raeschke-Kessler, 'Corrupt Practice in the Foreign Investment Context: Contractual and Procedural Aspects,' in N. Horn & S. Kröll, eds, *Arbitrating Foreign Investment Disputes* (The Hague: Kluwer, 2004); R.H. Kreindler, 'Aspects of Illegality in the Formation and Performance of Contracts', in ICCA Congress Series No. 11 (The Hague: Kluwer, 2003) 209; A. Court de Fontmichel, *L'arbitre, le juge et les pratiques illicites du commerce international* (Paris: Éditions Panthéon Assas, 2004); International Chamber of Commerce, Institute of World Business Law, *Arbitration – Money Laundering, Corruption and Fraud* (Paris: ICC, 2003); and M. Scherer, 'Circumstantial Evidence in Corruption Cases Before International Arbitral Tribunals' (2002) 5 IALR 29.

333. See *Inceysa Vallisoletana, S.L. v. El Salvador* (Award, 2 Aug. 2006) and *Fraport AG Frankfurt Airport Services Worldwide v. Philippines* (Award, 16 Aug. 2007). See *supra* Chapter 2, §2.11 and §2.12.

treated investments in accordance with the treaty standards, tribunals have referred to omissions and a lack of due diligence by the investor relating to the regulatory environment,[334] a failure to obtain legal protection for business risks,[335] relying on misleading advice from professional advisors,[336] failure to assess properly the quality of investment assets,[337] a lack of candour with regulatory authorities[338] and a failure to seek any redress from national authorities.[339]

IIAs do not provide blanket insurance against all forms of business risk.[340] A tribunal will consider whether someone in the situation of the investor would normally take steps to protect the investment from common types of business and legal risks. A failure to take reasonable steps towards self protection may result in a finding of no breach or a reduction in damages.[341]

IV ARBITRARY, UNREASONABLE OR DISCRIMINATORY MEASURES

§6.32 Background   A number of post-WWII investment instruments prohibit impairment of legally acquired rights by arbitrary, unreasonable or discriminatory measures. Prohibitions on these types of measures are common in post-WWII FCN treaties.[342] Provisions similar to those in US FCN treaties were included in

---

334. *MTD, supra* note 156 at para. 117. The tribunal stated at para. 164 that 'it is the responsibility of the investor to assure itself that it is properly advised, particularly when investing abroad in an unfamiliar environment.' In *MTD*, the Tribunal found that MTD incurred costs as a result of bad business judgment irrespective of the breach of fair and equitable treatment. In particular, they did not obtain appropriate legal protection for a land purchase, the price of which was based on the assumption that all applicable development permits would be obtained (*ibid.*, at para. 242).
335. *MTD, ibid.*, at 164.
336. *ADF, supra* note 15 at para. 189.
337. *Genin, supra* note 69 at para. 345.
338. *Ibid.*, at para. 362.
339. *Generation Ukraine, supra* note 63 at para. 20.30.
340. *MTD, supra* note 156 at para. 178: 'BITs are not an insurance against business risk'. *Maffezini, supra* note 303 at para. 69: 'the Tribunal must emphasize that Bilateral Investment Treaties are not insurance policies against bad business judgments.' See also, *LG&E, supra* note 156 at para. 130.
341. As was the case in *MTD*. See discussion *supra* at §6.26.
342. In *ELSI, supra* note 82, a Chamber of the ICJ considered Art I of the Supplementary Agreement to the 1948 Italy-US FCN Treaty (404 UNTS 326). Art. I provides: 'The nationals, corporations and associations of either High Contracting Party shall not be subjected to arbitrary or discriminatory measures within the territories of the other High Contracting Party resulting particularly in: (a) preventing their effective control and management of enterprises which they have been permitted to establish or acquire therein; or, (b) impairing their other legally acquired rights and interests in such enterprises or in the investments which they have made, whether in the form of funds (loans, shares or otherwise), materials, equipment, services, processes, patents, techniques or otherwise. Each High Contracting Party undertakes not to discriminate against nationals, corporations and associations of the other High

Article I, Abs-Shawcross Draft Convention,[343] and Article 1, 1967 Draft OECD Convention.[344]

§6.33 Treaty practice IIAs establish guarantees against impairment of investments by arbitrary, unreasonable or discriminatory measures. The guarantee frequently appears in the same clause providing for fair and equitable treatment. For example, after calling for investments to be accorded fair and equitable treatment, Article II(1)(b), Argentina-US (1991), states:

> Neither Party shall in any way impair by arbitrary or discriminatory measures the management, operation, maintenance, use, enjoyment, acquisition, expansion, or disposal of investments.[345]

Rather than 'arbitrary or discriminatory', other BITs refer to 'unreasonable or discriminatory'[346] or 'unjustifiable or discriminatory' measures.[347] For example, Article 3(1), Czechoslovakia-Netherlands (1991), provides:

> Each Contracting Party shall ensure fair and equitable treatment to the investments of investors of the other Contracting Party and shall not impair, by unreasonable or discriminatory measures, the operation, management, maintenance, use, enjoyment or disposal thereof by those investors.

Similarly, Article 10(1) of the ECT refers to 'unreasonable or discriminatory measures.'

Although most IIAs use the disjunctive 'or,' some IIAs use the conjunctive 'and.' The conjunctive formulation is reflected in the April 1994 US Model BIT, which refers to impairment by 'unreasonable and discriminatory' measures and appears in Article II(2)(b), Czechoslovakia-US (1991), which provides:

> Neither Party shall in any way impair by arbitrary and discriminatory measures the management, operation, maintenance, use, enjoyment, acquisition, expansion, or disposal of investment. For the purpose of dispute resolution

---

Contracting Party as to their obtaining under normal terms the capital, manufacturing processes, skills and technology which may be needed for economic development.' See also Art. V(3), Germany-US FCN, *reprinted in* R. Wilson, *United States Commercial Treaties and International Law* (New Orleans: Hauser Press, 1960) at 397.

343. Art. 1 provides: 'the management, use and enjoyment [of the property] shall not in any way be impaired by unreasonable or discriminatory measures.' UNCTAD, *International Investment Instruments: A Compendium*, Vol. 5 (New York: United Nations, 1996) at 395. The Draft was first published in (1960) 9 JPL 116 (now Emory Law Journal). See *supra*, Chapter 1, §1.16, for an overview of the historical background.

344. Art. 1 provides: 'Each Party ... shall not in any way impair the management, maintenance, use, enjoyment or disposal ... by unreasonable or discriminatory measures.' (1968) 7 ILM 117. See *supra*, Chapter 1, §1.22, for an overview of the historical background.

345. See also Art. 3(3), Germany-Nigeria (2000), and Art. 2(3), Argentina-Germany (1991).

346. The model BITs of Austria, Denmark, Egypt, Indonesia, The Netherlands and the UK use this formulation.

347. The model BITs of the Belgo-Luxembourg Economic Union (BLEU) and Italy use this formulation.

under Articles VI and VII, a measure may be arbitrary and discriminatory notwithstanding the fact that a party has had or has exercised the opportunity to review such measure in the courts or administrative tribunals of a Party.[348]

The *Lauder* tribunal, in interpreting this provision, relied on the conjunctive wording to find that the measure must be arbitrary *and* discriminatory to breach the treaty.[349] On the other hand, where the disjunctive 'or' is used, the IIA will be breached by a measure that is either arbitrary or discriminatory.[350]

§6.34 Elements of the guarantee   Despite differences in drafting, most provisions share three common elements. First, the standard typically applies to investments and not to investors. Thus, in common with most fair and equitable treatment provisions, the protection afforded by the clause does not extend to protect individual investors.[351] Second, the standard applies to measures rather than to treatment.[352] Third, the standard is breached by measures that 'impair' the investment. The term 'impair' has not been subject to extensive discussion in IIA awards. The Oxford English Dictionary defines 'impair' as follows: 'To make worse, less valuable, or weaker; to lessen injuriously; to damage, injure.' The ordinary meaning of 'impair' suggests that there has to be a detrimental impact on the investment. The commentary to the 1967 Draft OECD Convention notes that the requirement for impairment means that it is insufficient to prove that the measure is unreasonable or discriminatory, it must also be established that, as a consequence of the measure, 'actual possibilities for the exercise of the right in question are reduced.'[353] In *CMS*, the tribunal rejected the claim with respect to arbitrary

---

348. See also Art. II(3)(b), Albania-US (1995); Art. 3(1), Croatia-Zimbabwe (2000), and Art. 2(3), Korea-Trinidad and Tobago (2002).
349. See *Lauder*, *supra* note 112 at para. 219.
350. *Azurix*, *supra* note 164 at para. 391.
351. See *supra* §6.18.
352. See *supra* §6.16 on the term treatment and Chapter 7, §7.9 on the term measures.
353. Note 6 to Art. 1 in Commentary on 1967 Draft OECD Convention, *supra* note 123 at 121 reads:

  '(a) ... Article 1 provides that "management, maintenance, use, enjoyment or disposal" of property of nationals of other Parties shall not "in any way" be impaired by unreasonable or discriminatory measures. "Maintenance" is probably implicit in the concept of "management" and, moreover, as a precondition, in "use" and "enjoyment." The term is added for the sake of clarity. It is more doubtful whether 'disposal' is implicit in these notions. Yet knowledge alone of measures taken that prevent or limit the "disposal" of the property reduces its value and interferes with its "enjoyment." The term indicates therefore with greater precision the limits to which, under the Convention, the exercise of rights arising out of property is protected. It cannot, on the other hand, be assumed that the rights to "enjoyment" of property implies for the Party concerned that obligation to permit automatically transfers in connection with that property.

  (b) Exercise of the rights quoted in the preceding paragraph shall not in any way be "impaired" by unreasonable or discriminatory measures. This means that a breach of the obligation is established if it can be shown that a certain measure:
  (i)   is "unreasonable" or "discriminatory" ...;

measures on the basis that there had been no impairment in the management or operation of the investment.[354] On the other hand, the tribunal found that other forms of impairment were already covered by the claim of breach of fair and equitable treatment, which the tribunal upheld.

In order to establish impairment by an arbitrary or discriminatory measure, an investor need not exhaust local remedies. This is made express is some IIAs, such as Article II(2)(b), Czechoslovakia-US (1991), reproduced above. Government conduct may be arbitrary or discriminatory under the IIA despite that fact that the investor has exercised the opportunity to review the measure in the courts or administrative tribunals of the host state. The US practice on this point may be explained by reference to the *ELSI* case where the US argued that review of the mayor's order (which the US considered arbitrary) by the Italian courts could not correct the arbitrariness of the mayor's act.[355] In other words, international responsibility arose from the mayor's conduct, notwithstanding subsequent corrective action taken by the Italian state.[356] What remains unclear is whether arbitrariness or discrimination by a judicial authority, would automatically breach the standard, or whether, as in claims involving denial of justice, there would be a requirement to exhaust local remedies before the action of judicial authorities would be considered arbitrary or discriminatory for the purposes of the IIA.[357]

§6.35 Relationship with fair and equitable treatment   Where an IIA accords fair and equitable treatment (expressly or where the treatment guarantee is conferred based on an MFN clause), a separate prohibition on impairment by unreasonable, unjustifiable or arbitrary measures appears to be superfluous. A measure that involves impairment of this kind will breach fair and equitable treatment.[358] On the other hand, tribunals have found a breach of fair and equitable treatment without finding that the conduct in question was arbitrary or discriminatory.[359] As discussed below, the relationship between fair and equitable treatment and discrimination is less clear, owing to the variety of ways in which discrimination can occur.[360]

      (ii) may be attributed to the Party against whom complaint is made- see Article 5; and that it

     (iii) impairs the exercise of any of the rights quoted. Thus it is insufficient to prove- as in the case of "fair and equitable treatment" … that the measure complained of is contrary to a standard set by international law; it must also be established that, as its consequence, actual possibilities for the exercise of the right in question are reduced.'

354.   *CMS, supra* note 95 at para. 292. See also, *Occidental, supra* note 156 at para. 161 on the requirement for impairment.
355.   See discussion of *ELSI* at Chapter 1, §1.27, and §6.9, above.
356.   *ELSI, supra* note 82 at paras 108-121.
357.   See *supra* §6.5-6 discussing denial of justice and exhaustion of local remedies, and §6.46 in the context of other protection and guarantee standards.
358.   *CMS, supra* note 95 at para. 290. See also *MTD, supra* note 156 at para. 196.
359.   See *supra* §6.36-§6.38.
360.   See *supra* §6.38.

§6.36 Arbitrary measures   IIA tribunals have consistently held that the threshold for what constitutes arbitrariness is high. In interpreting the meaning of arbitrary, tribunals have referred to the *Neer* standard[361] and the definition of arbitrariness set out in *ELSI*.[362] In *Azurix*, the tribunal stated that:

> In its ordinary meaning, 'arbitrary' means 'derived from mere opinion,'
> 'capricious,' 'unrestrained,' 'despotic.' Black's Law Dictionary defines the term,
> *inter alia*, as 'done capriciously or at pleasure,' 'not done or acting according
> to reason or judgment,' 'depending on the will alone.' ... The Tribunal finds
> that the definition in *ELSI* is close to the ordinary meaning of arbitrary since it
> emphasizes the element of wilful disregard of the law.[363]

In *Enron*, the tribunal found that Argentina's measures to address its economic
crisis were not arbitrary because they were based on:

> ... what the Government believed and understood was the best response to
> the unfolding crisis. Irrespective of the question of intention, a finding of
> arbitrariness requires that some important measure of impropriety is manifest,
> and this is not found in a process which although far from desirable is
> nonetheless not entirely surprising in the context it took place.[364]

The requirement that some important measure of impropriety be manifest suggests
a high standard. Other tribunals, including other tribunals considering claims arising out of the Argentine financial crisis, have applied a similarly high standard.[365]

In *LG&E*, the tribunal highlighted that determining whether a measure is
arbitrary involves an assessment of the decision-making process involved in
implementing the measure:

> It is apparent from the Bilateral Treaty that Argentina and the United States
> wanted to prohibit themselves from implementing measures that affect the
> investments of nationals of the other Party without engaging in a rational
> decision-making process. Such process would include a consideration of the
> effect of a measure on foreign investments and a balance of the interests of
> the State with any burden imposed on such investments. Certainly a State that
> fails to base its actions on reasoned judgment, and uses abusive arguments
> instead, would not 'stimulate the flow of private capital.'[366]

---

361. In *Neer, supra* note 14, the Mexico-US General Claims Commission referred to the standard as:
      'an insufficiency of governmental action so far short of international standards that every reason-
      able and impartial man would readily recognize its insufficiency.' See discussion *supra* at §6.4.
362. *ELSI, supra* note 82.
363. *Azurix, supra* note 164 at para. 392.
364. *Enron, supra* note 158 at para. 281.
365. See also *Siemens, supra* note 143 at para. 318; *LG&E, supra* note 156 at para. 157; *Sempra,
      supra* note 224 at para. 318; *Lauder, supra* note 112 at para. 221; *Noble, supra* note 171 at
      paras 176-177.
366. *LG&E, supra* note 156 at para. 158.

A measure is likely to be found arbitrary when motivated by inappropriate considerations, as was the case in *Lauder*,[367] or not based on reason, as the tribunal found
in *Siemens*.[368]

The high threshold of impropriety required to establish arbitrariness is highlighted by a series of cases, including *Enron*, in which tribunals have found the
state to have breached the fair and equitable treatment standard, but have not
found states measures to be arbitrary.[369] A fourfold cumulative test for arbitrative-
ness has been suggested by one commentator: whether the measures were taken
by the proper authority, for the proper purpose, because of relevant circumstances
and were not patently unreasonable.[370] To date this has not been reflected in the
case law.

A slightly lower threshold for establishing arbitrariness is suggested by the
award in *Occidental*, where the tribunal found that confusion and lack of clarity
in the Ecuadorian tax system 'resulted in some form of arbitrariness, even if not
intended....'[371] This finding appears to equate arbitrariness with the fair and equitable treatment requirement for predictability and clarity in regulatory regimes.

Although some commentators have suggested that there do not appear to be
relevant distinctions between the terms 'arbitrary,' 'unjustified' and 'unreasonable'
and the terms are used interchangeably,[372] IIA awards predominantly suggest that
arbitrary is not to be equated with 'unjustified' or 'unreasonable.'[373] Rather, arbitrariness involves a manifest impropriety, such as the absence of a legitimate purpose, capriciousness, bad faith, or a serious lack of due process.

§6.37 Unreasonable or unjustifiable measures   There is little IIA jurisprudence on what constitutes an unreasonable or unjustifiable measure. Although it
is clear that an arbitrary measure could also be categorized as unreasonable or
unjustifiable, it is less clear whether unreasonable or unjustifiable should be

---

367.   *Lauder, supra* note 112 at paras 222-232. In *Lauder*, the tribunal found arbitrary and discriminatory measures as the result of the Czech Media Council's requirement that the foreign
investment not hold shares in a Czech company that would hold a television broadcasting
licence. The Media Council took this position due to local concerns with foreign control over
television broadcasting. The tribunal referred to the Black's *Law Dictionary* definition of
'arbitrary' as 'depending on individual discretion; ... founded on prejudice or preference
rather than on reason or fact.' (at para. 221) It held that the measure in question was indeed
'arbitrary,' because it was neither founded on reason, fact, nor law, but rather on 'mere fear
reflecting national preference.' (at para. 232).

368.   *Siemens, supra* note 143 at para. 319.

369.   See *LG&E, supra* note 156 at para. 162: 'though unfair and inequitable, were the result of
reasoned judgment rather than simple disregard of the rule of law.'; *Sempra, supra* note 224
at para. 318; *CMS, supra* note 95 at para. 292.

370.   This four part test for assessing whether a measure is arbitrary is set out in Hamrock,
supra note 92.

371.   *Occidental, supra* note 156 at para. 163.

372.   See C. Schreuer, 'Protection against Arbitrary or Discriminatory Measures' in R.P. Alford & C.A.
Rogers, eds, *The Future of Investment Arbitration* (Oxford: University Press, forthcoming).

373.   In *BG, supra* note 195 at para. 341, the tribunal stated that it would be inappropriate to equate
unreasonableness and arbitrariness.

equated with the same type of conduct that breaches fair and equitable treatment.

In a number of cases, tribunals have equated 'unreasonable' with 'unfair.' In *MTD*, the tribunal, having concluded there was a breach of fair and equitable treatment, proceeded to find that an approval of an investment contrary to predetermined government urban policy was unreasonable.[374] In *CME*, the tribunal found a breach of fair and equitable treatment. It then held that the conduct of the Czech Media Council had also been unreasonable on the basis that it had the intention of depriving the foreign investor of the exclusive use of its television license.[375] In *BG*, the tribunal stated that unreasonableness should be measured against the expectations of the parties to the BIT, rather than as a function of the means chosen by a state to achieve its goals. In the view of the tribunal, the unilateral withdrawal of undertakings and assurances given in good faith to investors as an inducement to their making of investment is 'by definition' unreasonable.[376]

Although the IIA jurisprudence is not clear on this point, where an IIA has a general fair and equitable treatment standard, a separate prohibition on impairment by unreasonable or unjustifiable measures would to some extent appear to be superfluous. Measures that impair investment by unreasonable or unjustifiable measures are likely to breach the fair and equitable treatment standard as they did in *BG*.

§6.38 Discriminatory measures   IIAs commonly prohibit impairment of the investment by discriminatory measures without providing any guidance on the type or types of prohibited discrimination. This leaves the scope of the obligation unclear. An ordinary meaning approach would suggest that the prohibition applies to all forms of discrimination. As discussed above at §6.27, discrimination with respect to the treatment of foreign investors and investment could involve: (i) discrimination contrary to international human rights, such as discrimination based on race or sex; (ii) unjustifiable or arbitrary regulatory distinctions made between things that are like or treating unlike things in the same way; (iii) conduct targeted at specific persons or things motivated by bad faith or with an intent to injure or harass; (iv) discrimination in the application of domestic law; and (v) nationality-based discrimination.

With respect to the first four types of discrimination, discriminatory measures will often overlap with the prohibition on unreasonable, unjustifiable or arbitrary measures. The fifth type overlaps with national and MFN treatment. The overlap is illustrated by the *Lauder* case. In *Lauder*, the tribunal found arbitrary *and* discriminatory measures as the result of the Czech Media Council's requirement that the foreign investment not hold shares in a Czech company that would hold a television broadcasting license. The Media Council took this position due to local

---

374.   *MTD, supra* note 156 at para. 196.
375.   *CME, supra* note 266 at para. 612.
376.   *BG, supra* note 195 at paras 342-343.

concerns with foreign control over television broadcasting.[377] The tribunal found that the Media Council had discriminated against the foreign investment on the basis of nationality.[378]

Tribunals have confirmed that different treatment of similarly situated investments is discriminatory unless the state can establish a reasonable basis for the differential treatment. In *Nykomb Synergetics Technology Holding AB v. Latvia*, the tribunal found the investment was subject to discriminatory measures where higher prices were paid to two other electricity companies but not to the claimant. The tribunal stated:

> The *Arbitral Tribunal* accepts that in evaluating whether there is discrimination in the sense of the Treaty one should only 'compare like with like'... all of the information available to the Tribunal suggests that the three companies are comparable, and subject to the same laws and regulations ... In such a situation, and in accordance with established international law, the burden of proof lies with the Respondent to prove that no discrimination has taken or is taking place.[379]

Likewise, in *Saluka*, the tribunal found discrimination where there was dissimilar treatment among four similarly situated banks. The tribunal stated that '[s]tate conduct is discriminatory, if (i) similar cases are (ii) treated differently (iii) and without reasonable justification.'[380]

Discrimination has also been an issue in a number of cases against Argentina. In *LG&E*, the tribunal found that although Argentina had treated the gas distribution companies in a discriminatory manner by imposing stricter measures on them than other public-utility sectors, LG&E had not proven that the measures were targeted at foreign investments, even though gas distribution was primarily in foreign hands.[381] Nevertheless, the tribunal found that discrimination 'against gas distribution companies vis-à-vis other companies, such as water supply and electricity companies, is evident.'[382] In contrast, in *Enron*, the tribunal found that there were important differences between the sectors and that there was no 'capricious, irrational or absurd differentiation in the treatment accorded to the Claimants as compared to other entities or sectors.'[383] Similarly, in *CMS*,[384] *Sempra*,[385] and

---

377. *Lauder, supra* note 112 at para. 227-231 (although those measures were held not to have caused the alleged destruction of the investment). It is unclear why this claim was not made expressly on the basis of a breach of national treatment, since the national treatment obligation in Czechoslovakia-US (1991) extends to establishment.

378. *Lauder, supra* note 112 at para. 231.

379. *Nykomb Synergetics Technology Holding AB v. Latvia* (Award 16 Dec. 2003) at 64.

380. *Saluka, supra* note 15 at para. 313.

381. *LG&E, supra* note 156 at para. 147.

382. *Ibid.*, at para. 148.

383. *Emron, supra* note 158 at para. 282.

384. *CMS, supra* note 95, at para. 293.

385. *Sempra, supra* note 224 at para. 319.

BG^{386} the respective tribunals held there was no discrimination between similarly situated groups.

§6.39 An effects-based analysis of discrimination   In addressing the meaning of discrimination, at least one tribunal has suggested that discrimination requires proof of intention.[387] The better position is that discrimination is an effects-based analysis. As noted in *LG&E*: 'a measure is considered discriminatory if the intent of the measure is to discriminate or if the measure has a discriminatory effect.'[388] As in the case of national treatment and fair and equitable treatment, subjective intention is not a necessary element for breach of an IIA treatment standard.[389]

§6.40 Overlap with national and MFN treatment clauses   When the discrimination at issue is nationality-based, there may well be overlap with national and MFN treatment clauses. Whether this is the case will depend on the particular IIA in question. Some IIAs, such as Czechoslovakia-Netherlands (1991) considered in *Saluka* and *CME*, do not have separate national and MFN treatment provisions. In this type of IIA, a general reference to discrimination should be interpreted to include nationality-based discrimination.[390]

On the other hand, where an IIA has specific national and MFN treatment provisions, an *effet utile* interpretation might suggest that a reference to 'discriminatory measures' should not be interpreted to cover nationality-based discrimination but other forms of discrimination. Some support for this position comes from the decision in *Genin*. In *Genin*, the tribunal discussed Article II(3)(b), Estonia-US (1994), which provided for non-impairment by arbitrary or discriminatory measures. The tribunal noted:

> Customary international law does not, however, require that a state treat all aliens (and alien property) equally, or that it treat aliens as favourably as nationals. Indeed, 'even unjustifiable differentiation may not be actionable.' In the present case, of course, any such discriminatory treatment would not

---

386.   *BG, supra* note 195 at paras 354-359.
387.   *Genin, supra* note 69 at para. 370. In support of this finding, the tribunal referred to I. Brownlie, *Principles of Public International Law*, 5th edn (Oxford: Clarendon Press, 1998) at 541, footnote 96: 'The test of discrimination is the intention of the government.'
388.   *LG&E, supra* note 156 at para. 146. See also *Siemens,* where the tribunal stated that: 'intent is not decisive or essential for a finding of discrimination, and that the impact of the measure on the investment would be the determining factor to ascertain whether it had resulted in non-discriminatory treatment.' See also *Siemens, supra* note 143 at para. 321 and *Eastern Sugar, supra* note 232 at para. 338.
389.   See *supra* §6.24 and Chapter 4, §4.17.
390.   In the cases of Czechoslovakia-Netherlands (1991), this would appear to be the case because Art. 3(3) provides exclusions for MFN treatment, suggesting that the reference in Art. 3(1) to 'discriminatory' includes more favourable treatment of investments from third states. Further, see *supra* §6.21 on the commentary to the 1967 Draft OECD Convention, suggesting that the reference to discrimination indicates nationality-based discrimination.

be permitted by Article II(1) of the BIT, which requires treatment of foreign investment on a basis no less favourable than treatment of nationals.[391]

In *BG*, the tribunal noted that, although the Claimant was relying on national treatment cases, its discrimination claim was based on the prohibition of discriminatory measures of Argentina-UK (1990),[392] rather than the national and MFN treatment provision in Article 3. The tribunal, nevertheless, accepted for the sake of its analysis that a breach of Article 3 would 'unavoidably also be "discriminatory"' for the purposes of the discriminatory measures provision.[393] Drawing on national treatment cases, the tribunal concluded, however, that the claimant had not proven that BG, a gas distribution company, was in like circumstances to companies operating in the transmission and distribution of electricity.[394]

As suggested by the tribunal in *BG*, where the discrimination is question is nationality-based there would appear to be overlap between a general prohibition on discriminatory measures and national and MFN treatment provisions. If the claim is framed as a question of nationality-based discrimination, tribunals should follow the approach of the *BG* tribunal and analyze the claim in accordance with national and MFN treatment jurisprudence.

V   PROTECTION AND SECURITY OBLIGATIONS

§6.41 Background   The minimum standard of treatment requires the host state to exercise due diligence to protect foreigners and their property from physical harm.[395] Nineteenth century FCN treaties commonly had clauses providing for protection and security.[396] Clauses providing for protection and security are also common in post-WWII investment instruments, including FCN treaties.[397] For example, the Italy-US FCN considered in *ELSI* guarantees foreign nationals 'the most constant protection and security for their persons and property' and 'the full

---

391.   *Genin, supra* note 69 at para. 368.
392.   Art. 2(2), second sentence, provides: 'Neither Contracting Party shall in any way impair by unreasonable or discriminatory measures the management, maintenance, use, enjoyment or disposal of investments in its territory of investors of the other Contracting Party.'
393.   *BG, supra* note 195 at para. 355.
394.   *Ibid.*, at para. 357 and 358.
395.   See *supra* §6.8 on due diligence as an element of the minimum standard of treatment. On protection obligations, see *Sambiaggio* (1903) X RIAA at 499 and Judge Huber's statement in *British Claims in the Spanish Zone of Morocco* (1925) II RIAA 615 at 642 *et seq.* For commentary, see A.V. Freeman, 'Responsibility of States for Unlawful Acts of their Armed Forces' (1955-II) 88 RDCADI 263. With respect to state enterprises, see A. Cohen Smutney, 'State Responsibility for the Acts of State Enterprises? *Emilio Agustín Maffezini v. The Kingdom of Spain*' in T. Weiler, ed., *International Investment Law and Arbitration: Leading Cases from the ICSID, NAFTA, Bilateral Treaties and Customary International Law* (London: Cameron May, 2005).
396.   For example, Art. 4 of the 1861 Treaty between Italy and Venezuela cited in *Sambiaggio, ibid.*, provided for 'the fullest measure of protection and security of person and property.'
397.   Wilson, *supra* note 342.

protection and security required by international law.'[398] In *ELSI*, the ICJ stated that the 'constant protection and security' guarantee did not provide a 'warranty that property shall never in any circumstances be occupied or disturbed.'[399]

Article I, Abs-Shawcross Convention, and Article 1, 1967 Draft OECD Convention, both provide that property is to receive the 'the most constant protection and security.' The commentaries on both conventions highlight that the clause is based on the provisions in US FCNs.[400]

§6.42 IIA practice Most IIAs provide a guarantee of protection and security to investments. The drafting of the clause varies widely. Typical clauses provide guarantees of 'protection,'[401] 'full protection,'[402] 'protection and security,'[403] 'full protection and security,'[404] 'full physical security and protection,'[405] 'adequate protection and security,'[406] 'full and constant protection and security,'[407] 'complete and adequate protection and security,'[408] 'constant protection and security,'[409] or 'the most constant protection and security.'[410] A small number of IIAs refer to 'full protection and legal security.'[411]

A number of more recent IIAs clarify that the protection and security obligation is not to be given an autonomous meaning, equating it with the obligation imposed under the minimum standard of treatment. For example, Article 5, US-Uruguay (2005), provides that:

1. Each Party shall accord to covered investments treatment in accordance with customary international law, including fair and equitable treatment and full protection and security.

---

398. Art. V, para. 1, *supra* note 83. The US alleged a breach of this standard as a result of the occupation of the plant by ELSI's employees and also a sixteen-month delay in obtaining a ruling on an appeal. See *supra* Chapter 1, §1.27, and §6.9 for discussion of *ELSI*.
399. *ELSI*, *supra* note 82 at para. 108.
400. On the Abs-Shawcross Convention, see 'Comment on the Draft Convention by Its Authors' (1960) 9 JPL 119 at 119. On the 1967 Draft OECD Convention, see *supra* note 123 at 120.
401. Art. III, Lithuania-Norway (1992). See also Art. 2(1), Bulgaria-Croatia (1996); Art. 3(1), Cuba-Spain (1994); and Art. 3(1), Jordan-Poland (1997).
402. Art. 3(1), Marshall Islands-Taiwan (1999).
403. Art. II(4), US-Zaire BIT (1984).
404. Art. 2(2), Sri Lanka-UK (1980), and Art. 2(2) Egypt-UK (1975), considered respectively in *Asian Agricultural Products Ltd. (AAPL) v. Sri Lanka* (Final Award, 27 Jun. 1990) [*AAPL*] and *Wena Hotels Limited v. Egypt* (Award, 8 Dec. 2000) [*Wena*]. This is the most widely used formulation.
405. Art. 3(1), Eritrea-Netherlands (2003); and Art. 3(2), Hungary-Netherlands (1987).
406. Art. 2(2), Indonesia-Syria (1997).
407. Art. 2(2), China-Djibouti (2003); and Art. 10(1), Japan-Korea (2002).
408. Art. 2(2), Jordan-Yemen (1996).
409. Early US FCN treaties refer to 'the most constant protection.' Later FCN treaties refer to 'the most constant protection and security.' Thomas, *supra* note 9 at 39-40.
410. Art. 3(2), Thailand-Vietnam (1991); Art. 5(1), Bangladesh-Japan (1998); and Art. 3(2), Hungary-Thailand (1991).
411. See Art. 4(1), Argentina-Germany (1991), considered in *Siemens*, *supra* note 143.

2. For greater certainty, paragraph 1 prescribes the customary international law minimum standard of treatment of aliens as the minimum standard of treatment to be afforded to covered investments. The concepts of 'fair and equitable treatment' and 'full protection and security' do not require treatment in addition to or beyond that which is required by that standard, and do not create additional substantive rights. The obligation in paragraph 1 to provide:

…

  (b) 'full protection and security' requires each Party to provide the level of police protection required under customary international law.

A few IIAs make no express mention of protection obligations.[412]

§6.43 Physical protection Due diligence in the physical protection of aliens and their property is required under the minimum standard of treatment.[413] IIA awards have consistently found that protection and security obligations in IIAs impose on the host state an obligation of due diligence or vigilance with respect to the physical protection of foreign investment.[414] Tribunals have rejected arguments that full protection and security obligations provide a guarantee against injury or impose strict liability.[415] The obligation with respect to physical protection is one of due diligence – the same standard as that under customary international law.

In *AAPL,* the first IIA award, the tribunal interpreted a clause providing that investments shall enjoy 'full protection and security' in the context of the destruction of a shrimp farm during a conflict between Tamil rebels and Sri Lankan forces.[416] The issue before the tribunal was whether the requirement for full protection and security represents a codification of customary international law, or imposes strict liability on the host state. In line with previous authorities,[417] the tribunal held that the term could not be construed as giving rise to strict liability.[418] The majority concluded that there had been a breach of full protection and security

---

412. Estonia-Sweden (1992); Egypt-Kazakhstan (1993); India-Kazakhstan (1996); Argentina-New Zealand (1999); and Iran-Kazakhstan (1996).
413. See §6.8 above.
414. See *AAPL, supra* note 404 at paras 72-86; *American Manufacturing and Trading, Inc. v. Zaire* (Award, 21 Feb. 1997) [*AMT*] at paras 6.05-6.19; *Wena, supra* note 404 at paras 84-95 and *Lauder, supra* note 112 at para. 308. Certain portions of the *AMT* award suggest that the tribunal was applying a strict liability standard. For example, at paras 6.05 and 6.06, the tribunal states that Zaire had the obligation to take 'all measures' to protect the investment. Further, at para. 6.14, it states that Zaire had an obligation to 'prevent the occurrence of any act of violence.' These excerpts should, however, be read in the context of the overall obligation of 'vigilance,' which suggest an obligation of conduct, not of result.
415. *Tecmed, supra* note 65 at para. 177.
416. For commentary on *AAPL, supra* note 404, see S. Vasciannie, 'Bilateral Investment Treaties and Civil Strife: The AAPL/Sri Lanka Arbitration' (1992) 39 NILR 332.
417. See *Sambiaggio* (1903) X RIAA at 499 and *ELSI, supra* note 82, discussed in *AAPL, supra* note 403 at paras 47-50 and other authorities discussed at paras 72-78.
418. *AAPL, supra* note 404 at para. 49.

because of the failure of Sri Lankan authorities to take precautionary measures before launching an armed attack and because the farm was destroyed while under the exclusive control of government forces.[419]

§6.44 Due diligence, physical protection and the level of host state resources   The relevance of the host state's level of development and resources to the application of physical protection and security obligations is unclear.[420] The standard of due diligence has been expressed by Alwyn Freeman as: 'nothing more nor less than the reasonable measures of prevention which a well-administered government could be expected to exercise under similar circumstances.'[421] The reference to reasonable measures might suggest that host states are required to provide an objective minimum standard of physical protection to foreign investors and investment. International authorities, however, suggest that the applicable standard depends on the situation of the host state. In *British Claims in the Spanish Zone of Morocco*, arbitrator Max Huber, in discussing the diligence required of a state in the protection of aliens, noted that a state is 'obliged to exercise only that degree of vigilance which corresponds to the means at its disposal' and that the 'vigilance which from the point of view of international law a state is obliged to exercise, may be characterized as *diligentia quam in suis*.'[422] *Diligentia quam in suis*, a principle of Roman law, requires a level of care that one applies in one's own affairs. In his work on state responsibility, Ian Brownlie has argued that the *diligentia quam in suis* principle applies to due diligence. The standard calls for an objective national treatment standard that measures conduct based on what could be reasonably expected of the state in question in light of its resources.[423] The extent of due diligence an investor may expect will vary, therefore, according to local conditions. This means that due diligence is limited by a state's capacity to act – a state will not be responsible when action would have been impossible.

Although the host state is required to exercise an objective minimum standard of due diligence, the standard of due diligence is that of a host state in the circumstances and with the resources of the state in question. This suggests that due diligence is a modified objective standard – the host state must exercise the level of due diligence of a host state in its particular circumstances. In practice, tribunals will likely consider the state's level of development and stability as relevant circumstances in determining whether there has been due diligence. An investor investing in an area with endemic civil strife and poor governance cannot have the same expectation of physical security as one investing in London, New York or Tokyo.

---

419.   *Ibid.*, at para. 85.
420.   N. Gallus, 'The Influence of the Host State's Level of Development on International Investment Treaty Standards of Protection' (2005) 6 JWIT 711.
421.   Freeman, *supra* note 395 at 277-278.
422.   (1925) II UNRIAA 639 at 644 (as translated by B. Cheng, *General Principles of Law as Applied by International Courts and Tribunals*, *supra* note 75 at 220).
423.   See Brownlie, *Principles of Public International Law*, *supra* note 9 at 504.

§6.45 Regulatory and legal protection A number of IIAs awards have suggested that protection and security obligations include a guarantee of regulatory and legal security for investments. This issue has arisen in a number of the claims by foreign investors against Argentina. Claimants have argued that protection and security extends beyond physical protection of an investment's officials, employees or facilities, and extends more generally to protections afforded by the legal system. Some tribunals, while not disagreeing in principle that protection and security obligations can extend beyond physical security, have expressed reluctance with this approach and suggested that this interpretation would result in equating the standard with fair and equitable treatment.[424]

In *CME*, the tribunal interpreted the full security and protection guarantee in Article 3(2), Czechoslovakia-Netherlands (1991), as including legal security:

> The host State is obligated to ensure that neither by amendment of its laws nor by actions of its administrative bodies is the agreed and approved security and protection of the foreign investor's investment withdrawn or devalued.[425]

The tribunal found a breach of full security and protection due to the actions of the Czech Media Council in undermining the claimant's contractual rights.[426] In contrast, the *Saluka* tribunal, interpreting the same provision, found that it 'applies essentially when the foreign investment has been affected by civil strife and physical violence.'[427] Further, it stated that the 'practice of arbitral tribunals seems to indicate … that the "full security and protection" clause is not meant to cover just any kind of impairment of an investor's investment, but to protect more specifically the physical integrity of an investment against interference by use of force.'[428] The *Saluka* tribunal appears to have accepted that the guarantee would apply with respect to police searches of premises.[429]

In *Lauder,* although the tribunal did not find a breach of full protection and security, the tribunal suggested that in the context of a dispute between two private parties, the clause prescribes a duty to provide a judicial system in which disputes can be resolved.[430] This suggests that protection and security includes an obligation to provide a judicial system where private rights can be vindicated. Further, support for the position that protection and security obligations extend to judicial

---

424. *Enron, supra* note 158 at para. 286, and *Sempra, supra* note 224 at para. 323.
425. *CME, supra* note 266 at para. 613. This sentence was quoted with approval in *Vivendi II, supra* note 135 at para. 7.4.16.
426. See *Československá Obchodní Banka, A.S. v. Slovak Republic* (Award, 29 Dec. 2004) at para. 170.
427. *Saluka, supra* note 15 at para. 484.
428. *Saluka, ibid.*
429. *Saluka, ibid.*, at para. 494-496. The tribunal also applied the guarantee to a Czech Securities Commission's suspension in trading of shares and a police order prohibiting transfer of shares, finding that the Czech conduct did not breach the guarantee. However, the tribunal had assumed for the sake of argument that the State conduct was within the scope of the 'full security and protection' clause (see paras 486-493).
430. *Lauder, supra* note 112 at para. 314.

proceedings can also be found in *ELSI*, in which the US argued that a sixteen month delay of the Italian courts in ruling on the lawfulness of the requisition of a manufacturing plant was a denial of procedural justice that amounted to a breach of the most constant protection and security provision in the Italy-US FCN.[431] The decision of the Chamber of the ICJ holding that the delay in question did not amount to a treaty breach suggests that in principle the clause applies to judicial procedures.[432]

The reasoning of tribunals on the scope of the protection and security obligation is often unclear because of the tendency to interpret the obligation as part of the fair and equitable treatment guarantee, rather than as an independent treatment standard. Awards, while suggesting that protection and security provisions extend beyond physical protection, often do so in the context of finding that there was an independent breach of fair and equitable treatment. For example, in *Azurix*, the tribunal stated:

> The Tribunal is persuaded of the interrelationship of fair and equitable treatment and the obligation to afford the investor full protection and security. The cases referred to above show that full protection and security was understood to go beyond protection and security ensured by the police. It is not only a matter of physical security; the stability afforded by a secure investment environment is as important from an investor's point of view. The Tribunal is aware that in recent free trade agreements signed by the United States, for instance, with Uruguay, full protection and security is understood to be limited to the level of police protection required under customary international law. However, when the terms 'protection and security' are qualified by 'full' and no other adjective or explanation, they extend, in their ordinary meaning, the content of this standard beyond physical security. To conclude, the Tribunal, having held that the Respondent failed to provide fair and equitable treatment to the investment, finds that the Respondent also breached the standard of full protection and security under the BIT.[433]

The *Azurix* tribunal suggests that 'full' protection and security goes beyond physical security, and found that since there was a breach of fair and equitable treatment, there was also a breach of full protection and security. But the cases that the *Azurix* tribunal refers to as authority – *Occidental* and *Wena* – do not support the argument that full protection and security go beyond physical protection and security. In *Occidental*, the question of whether the full protection and security clause was breached was moot because the tribunal had found a breach of fair and

---

431. See *ELSI, supra* note 82 at paras 111-112.
432. *Vivendi II, supra* note 135 at para. 7.4.16.
433. *Azurix, supra* note 164 at para. 408. In contrast to the *Azurix* tribunal's suggestion that the reference to 'full' is meaningful, another tribunal has suggested there is no substantive difference between 'protection' and 'full protection and security.' *Parkerings, supra* note 133 at para. 354.

equitable treatment.[434] In *Wena*, the breach of full protection and security resulted from the failure of the police to take any action relating to the physical seizure of Wena's hotels.[435]

In some cases, the treaty itself expressly subsumes protection and security within fair and equitable treatment. For example, Article 5(1), Argentina-France (1991), guarantees that '... investments ... shall enjoy ... protection and full security in accordance with the principle of fair and equitable treatment referred to in Article 3 of this Agreement.' In *Vivendi II*, the tribunal, in interpreting this provisions, stated that:

> In the absence of such words of limitation, the scope of the Article 5(1) protection should be interpreted to apply to reach any act or measure which deprives an investor's investment of protection and full security, providing, in accordance with the Treaty's specific wording, the act or measure also constitutes unfair and inequitable treatment. Such actions or measures need not threaten physical possession or the legally protected terms of operation of the investment.[436]

Some treaties expressly extend the scope of protection and security beyond physical protection. In *Siemens*, the tribunal addressed Argentina-Germany (1991), which includes a requirement for 'legal security.'[437] The tribunal highlighted that since investment includes tangible and intangible assets, the obligation to provide full protection and security extends beyond physical protection of tangible things.[438] On the other hand, the 2004 Model US BIT adopts a narrower approach, stating that full protection and security only requires each Party to provide the level of police protection required under customary international law.

In *BG*,[439] the tribunal rejected BG's argument that Argentina breached the obligation to ensure that investments 'shall enjoy protection and constant security'[440] and stated that the obligation has traditionally been associated with 'situations where the physical security of the investor or its investment is compromised.'[441] Although the tribunal notes that other tribunals have interpreted the obligation more broadly to provide a secure investment environment, the tribunal found that it was inappropriate to depart from the 'originally understood standard.'[442]

The above discussion illustrates that IIA jurisprudence has adopted conflicting views on the scope of protection and security obligations. As highlighted

---

434. *Occidental, supra* 156 at para. 187.
435. *Wena, supra* note 404 at paras 84-95.
436. *Vivendi II, supra* note 135 at para.7.4.15.
437. See *supra* §6.42.
438. *Siemens, supra* note 143 at para. 303.
439. *BG, supra* note 195.
440. Art. 2(2), Argentina-UK (1990).
441. *BG, supra* note 195 at para. 324.
442. *Ibid.*, at para. 326.

by the *Azurix* tribunal, the ordinary meaning of a full protection and security obligation arguably extends beyond physical security, particularly since investment is typically defined to include intangible assets. Various forms of legal and judicial protection may therefore be elements of the protection and security obligation. Further, as suggested by the *Vivendi II* tribunal, the obligation may extend to protection against harassment where there is no physical harm.[443]

In practice, since most IIAs already accord fair and equitable treatment, whether protection and security obligations extend to legal security and the stability and predictability of the regulatory framework is unlikely to affect the outcome of a case. Further, since fair and equitable treatment includes treatment in accordance with the minimum standard, it would appear that a general fair and equitable treatment clause includes the protection and security obligation.

§6.46 Breach of protection and security in the administration of justice   When there has been a breach of protection or security due to deficiencies in the administration of justice, it is arguable that the delict in question is a denial of justice. IIA tribunals, consistent with international authorities, have stated that local remedies must be exhausted (to a degree of reasonableness) in order to claim a denial of justice.[444] If relief is obtained in the domestic judicial system, then no denial of justice would have occurred. This appears to have been the unstated approach taken by the *Saluka* tribunal. In *Saluka*, the claimant complained that a police search of offices and seizure of documents was illegal, violated privacy rights and breached the Czech Republic's full protection and security obligation. The tribunal rejected the claim on the basis that there had been a successful petition to the Czech Constitutional Court and the claimant could 'no longer be aggrieved.'[445]

One may question whether this is the proper approach. If a police search and seizure were to be found to be a breach of another minimum standard – for example arbitrary, discriminatory, or unfair and inequitable treatment – an investor may well want to seek damages – particularly if the police conduct were malicious. Even if the investor had obtained a local remedy, as in *Saluka*, and subject to double compensation issues, this would not appear to bar it from seeking damages – perhaps moral damages – for the breach of the state's international obligation. The same reasoning arguably applies if there is a breach of protection and security.

---

443.   *Vivendi II, supra* note 135 at para. 7.4.17 citing *Rankin v. Iran*, Award No. 326-10913-2, Award of 3 Nov. 1987, 17 Iran-US CTR 135 at para. 30 (c), where the Iran-US Claims Tribunal found that statements that could 'have reasonably been expected to initiate or prompt' harassment suffered by a foreigner were inconsistent with the requirement to accord protection and security.
444.   See *supra* §6.5.
445.   *Saluka, supra* note 15 at para. 475.

VI COMPENSATION FOR EXTRAORDINARY LOSSES

§6.47 Extraordinary losses   Host states are not generally responsible for losses attributable to war, armed conflict, state of national emergency, revolution or insurrection where the loss in question is caused by the host state's own armed forces, acting with reasonable necessity in the circumstances.[446] State responsibility arises only if there has been a lack of due diligence, or if the destruction could not be justified by the exigencies of the situation.[447]

IIAs usually address compensation for losses in one of two ways.[448] The first type of provision provides an entitlement to compensation in the event of requisition or when losses are suffered that are not justified by the exigencies of the circumstances. Second, IIAs often expressly provide for national and MFN treatment in case the host state compensates other investors for extraordinary losses.

An example of the first type of provision appears in Article 4(2), Sri Lanka-UK (1980), which states:

.... nationals and companies of one Contracting Party who in any of the situations referred to in that paragraph suffer losses in the territory of the other Contracting Party resulting from

(a) requisitioning of their property by its forces or authorities, or
(b) destruction of their property by its forces or authorities which was not caused in combat action or was not required by the necessity of the situation,

shall be accorded restitution or adequate compensation. Resulting payments shall be freely transferable.

Under Article 4(2), there is a right to compensation for losses resulting from the requisition or destruction of investments by armed forces where the measures were neither caused in combat, nor required by the exigencies of the circumstances. In these situations, IIAs usually require restitution or adequate compensation.[449]

Second, even though customary international law and IIAs do not generally impose an obligation on the host state to compensate foreign investors for these types of extraordinary losses, a host state might as a matter of domestic law or policy provide compensation for these losses. As a result many IIAs have specific

---

446. See *AAPL, supra* note 404 at para. 63. See generally Freeman, *supra* note 395.
447. In this case, a tribunal must assess whether persons in the circumstances of the commanding officers in question would have reasonably believed the impugned action to be necessary. In these situations, international tribunals are likely to provide a margin of appreciation to the decision-maker given the realities of armed conflict.
448. For an overview of treaty practice, see *UNCTAD BIT Studies, supra* note 128. Also see Dolzer & Stevens, *Bilateral Investment Treaties, supra* note 128 at 83 and K.J. Vandevelde, *US Investment Treaties: Policy and Practice* (Boston: Kluwer Law and Taxation, 1992) at 212.
449. See Art 4(2), Sri Lanka-UK (1980) and Art. IV(2), US-Zaire (1984).

provisions that require that, in such as case, compensation be granted on a non-discriminatory basis. For example, Article 4, Argentina-UK (1990), provides that:

> Investors of one Contracting Party whose investments in the territory of the other Contracting Party suffer losses owing to war or other armed conflict, revolution, a state of national emergency, revolt, insurrection or riot or resulting from arbitrary action by the authorities in the territory of the latter Contracting Party shall be accorded by the latter Contracting Party treatment, as regards restitution, indemnification, compensation of other settlement, no less favourable than that which the latter Contracting Party accords to its own investors or to investors of any third State. Resulting payments shall be freely transferable.[450]

This provision clarifies that national and MFN treatment apply to compensation payments for these types of losses. Some provisions only expressly provide for MFN treatment.[451]

Tribunals have rejected the argument that this type of provision establishes an exception to IIA obligations. In *BG*, the tribunal rejected Argentina's argument that Article 4, Argentina-UK (1990), provides that non-discriminatory measures taken in cases of national emergencies do not breach IIA protections. The tribunal stated that Article 4 provides for a 'specific expression of the national treatment and MFN treatment standard in relation to compensation' and not an excuse from liability.[452] Similarly, in *CMS*, in interpreting Article IV(3), Argentina-US (1991),[453] the tribunal noted:

> The plain meaning of the Article is to provide a floor treatment for the investor in the context of the measures adopted in respect of the losses suffered in the emergency, not different from that applied to nationals or other foreign investors. The Article does not derogate from the Treaty rights but rather ensures that any measures directed at offsetting or minimizing losses will be applied in a non-discriminatory manner.[454]

The relationship between extraordinary loss provisions and necessity defences is discussed further at Chapter 10, §10.8, below.

---

450.   Other examples include Art. 6(1), Austria-Bosnia (2000); Art. 6(1), Bosnia-Spain (2002); Art. 7, Bosnia-Netherlands (1998); Art. 6(1), Austria-Macedonia (2001); Art. 5, China-Cote d'Ivoire; Art. 4(1), Haiti-UK (1985); Art. 4(1), Sri Lanka-UK (1980); Art. 6, Chile-Nicaragua (1996); Art. 4(1), Estonia-Israel (1994); and Art. 3(3), South Africa-Turkey (2000).

451.   Art. 4, Ethiopia-Malaysia (1998).

452.   *BG, supra* note 195 at para. 382.

453.   Art. IV(3) provides: 'Nationals or companies of either Party whose investments suffer losses in the territory of the other Party owing to war or other armed conflict, revolution, state of national emergency, insurrection, civil disturbance or other similar events shall be accorded treatment by such other Party no less favorable than that accorded to its own nationals or companies or to nationals or companies of any third country, whichever is the more favorable treatment, as regards any measures it adopts in relation to such losses.'

454.   *CMS, supra* note 95 at para. 375. See also *LG&E, supra* note 156 at paras 243 and 261.

VII   PRESERVATION OF RIGHTS/MORE
             FAVOURABLE TREATMENT CLAUSES

§6.48 More favourable treatment   Some IIAs clarify that the IIA obligations do
not prevail over more favourable laws or agreements and that foreign investors or
investments are to receive the more favourable treatment provided in other
international agreements or in domestic laws.[455] More favourable treatment clauses,
also called preservation of rights or non-derogation clauses, appear in early investment instruments including the Abs-Shawcross Draft Convention[456] and the 1967
Draft OECD Convention.[457] As noted by Georg Schwarzenberger in his commentary on the Abs-Shawcross Draft Convention, the purpose of the provision is to
clarify that what are intended as minimum standards of treatment are not interpreted
as 'constituting an upper ceiling for the treatment of foreign nationals.'[458]

An example of clause entitled 'Preservation of Rights' is Article IX, US-Zaire
(1984), considered in *AMT*:[459]

> This Treaty shall not supersede, prejudice, or otherwise derogate from:
>
> (a) laws and regulations, administrative practices or procedures, or adjudica-
>   tory decisions of either Party;
> (b) international legal obligations; or
> (c) obligations assumed by either Party, including those contained in an
>   investment agreement or an investment authorization,
>
> whether extant at the time of entry into force of this Treaty or thereafter, that
> entitle investments, or associated activities, of nationals or companies of the
> other Party to treatment more favorable than that accorded by this Treaty in
> like situations.

Article 3(5), China-Netherlands (2001), provides a typical example of a more
favourable treatment clause:

> If the provisions of law of either Contracting Party or obligations under
> international law existing at present or established hereafter between the
> Contracting Parties in addition to the present Agreement contain a regulation,
> whether general or specific, entitling investments by investors of the other

---

455. For an overview of treaty practice, see *UNCTAD BIT Studies*, *supra* note 128. Also see Dolzer &
      Stevens, *Bilateral Investment Treaties*, *supra* note 128.
456. Art.VI provides: 'The provisions of this Convention shall not prejudice the application of any
      present or future treaty or municipal law under which more favourable treatment is accorded
      to nationals of any of the Parties.'
457. Art. 8 entitled 'Other International Agreements' provides: 'Where a matter is covered both by
      the provisions of this Convention and any other international agreement nothing in this
      Convention shall prevent a national of one Party who holds property in the territory of another
      Party from benefiting by the provisions that are most favourable to him.'
458. G. Schwarzenberger, *supra* note 154 at 161.
459. See *AMT supra* note 414 at paras 5.33-5.37.

Contracting Party to a treatment more favourable than is provided for by the present Agreement, such regulation shall, to the extent that it is more favourable, prevail over the present Agreement.

The clause serves to ensure that the investment is entitled to the more favourable treatment that may exist under domestic or international law, or that may arise in the future. At first glance, the clause might be viewed as a particularly widely worded MFN clause that could apply to extend the scope of IIA protections available under other host state IIAs. This interpretation, however, would overlook the fact that the more favourable treatment in question is that of 'obligations under international law ... between the Contracting Parties.'[460] It does not extend to more favourable treatment accorded by the host state to third-state investments.

Article 16, US-Uruguay (2005), provides a slightly different formulation by framing the rule as one of non-derogation. Under this provision, the BIT does not derogate from more favourable treatment available to an investor or investment.

Article 16: Non-Derogation
This Treaty shall not derogate from any of the following that entitle an investor of a Party or a covered investment to treatment more favorable than that accorded by this Treaty:

1. laws or regulations, administrative practices or procedures, or administrative or adjudicatory decisions of a Party;
2. international legal obligations of a Party; or
3. obligations assumed by a Party, including those contained in an investment authorization or an investment agreement.

In *Siemens*, the claimant relied upon the more favourable treatment clause in Article 7(1), Argentina-Germany (1991),[461] to buttress its argument that host state law may prevail over the provisions of the BIT only to the extent that it provides treatment to the investment more favorable than the BIT. By contrast, those provisions of domestic law that provide less favorable treatment do not derogate from IIA obligations.[462]

---

460. For the interpretation of a similar clause, see *Vladimir Berschader* and *Moïse Berschader v. Russia* (Award, 21 Apr. 2006) at para. 190 interpreting Art. 8(1), BLEU-USSR (1989), which provides: 'The present Treaty shall not prevent investors from benefiting from more favourable terms provided by the laws applicable to them in the country in which the investments are made, or by international treaties concluded by the Contracting Parties at present or in the future.'
461. Art. 7(1) provides: 'If the laws and regulations of either Contracting Party or obligations under international law existing at present or established hereafter between the Contracting Parties in addition to this Treaty contain a regulation, whether general or specific, entitling investments by nationals or companies of the other Contracting Party to a treatment more favorable than is provided for by the Treaty, such regulation shall to the extent that it is more favorable prevail over this Treaty.'
462. *Siemens, supra* note 143 at para. 71.

Preservation of rights clauses should not be confused with observance of undertakings clauses (see below Chapter 9, §9.28) and applicable law clauses (see above Chapter 2, §2.5).

VIII   EXCEPTIONS

§6.49 Exceptions   IIAs typically do not provide specific reservations or exceptions to general minimum standards of treatment. A state may, however, be able to rely on express general reservations, exceptions or defences under customary international law.[463]

---

463. See *infra* Chapter 10.

Chapter 7

Expropriation

INTRODUCTION

§7.1 Expropriation in international law International expropriation law
mediates between two general principles of international law: (i) that states
exercise permanent sovereignty over their territories and natural resources;[1] and
(ii) that states must respect the acquired rights of foreigners.[2] The exercise of
permanent sovereignty means that private property, is not inviolable. Subject to
specific commitments to the contrary, states have a right to regulate and tax
property as well as to expropriate it.[3] International expropriation law, however,
generally imposes four conditions on the expropriation of foreign-held property:
the expropriation must be for a public purpose, in accordance with due process,[4]
non-discriminatory, and accompanied by compensation.

Throughout the twentieth century there was significant disagreement between
capital importing and exporting states over the existence and content of the

---

1. See N. Schrijver, *Sovereignty Over Natural Resources* (Cambridge: Cambridge University
   Press, 1997); R. Jennings & A. Watts, eds, *Oppenheim's International Law*, 9th edn (London:
   Longman, 1992) [*Oppenheim's International Law*] at §106 and I. Brownlie, *Principles of Public
   International Law*, 6th edn (Oxford: Oxford University Press, 2003) [Brownlie, *Principles of
   Public International Law*] at 512-520.
2. See *Case Concerning Certain German Interests in Polish Upper Silesia (Germany v. Poland)*
   (1926) PCIJ Ser. A, No. 7 at 42; *Norwegian Shipowners' Claims (Norway v. US)* (1922) I RIAA
   307 at 332; and F.V. García-Amador, 'Fourth Report of the Special Rapporteur – Responsibility
   of the State for Injuries Caused in its Territory to the Persons or Property of Aliens – Measures
   Affecting Acquired Rights' (1959) 2 YBILC 1 [García-Amador, Fourth Report] at 4. Also see
   F.V. García-Amador *et al.*, *Recent Codification of the Law of State Responsibility for Injuries to
   Aliens* (New York: Oceana Publications, Inc., 1974) and *Oppenheim's International Law*, *ibid.*,
   at §407.
3. García-Amador, Fourth Report, *ibid.*, at para. 41.
4. Not all authorities accept that due process is a requirement for a lawful expropriation under
   customary international law. See §7.34 below.

customary international law minimum standard of treatment, including the rules applicable to expropriation.[5] Three issues in international expropriation law have been particularly contentious.[6] First, what are the economic interests capable of being subject to expropriation? Second, when do government measures amount to expropriation? Third, what is the standard of compensation payable upon expropriation? International investment agreements (IIAs) address, with greater or lesser specificity, each of these issues. The range of economic interests that IIAs protect turns on the definition of 'investment,' which most IIAs define expansively.[7] In contrast, most IIAs do not define what constitutes expropriation with any significant degree of specificity. Finally, many IIAs contain provisions (some more detailed than others) on the standard and manner of compensation. Given the long standing disagreement over the standard of compensation, IIAs have served an important role in clarifying the applicable compensation standard.

IIA obligations with respect to expropriation are discussed below in two parts. Part I addresses the meaning of expropriation. Part II addresses the four conditions for an expropriation, common to almost all IIAs: public purpose, non-discrimination, due process and compensation.

I   WHAT CONSTITUTES EXPROPRIATION?

§7.2 Introduction   Under customary international law, a state must pay compensation to a foreign national if the state expropriates its property.[8] International

---

5. See *supra* Chapter 1, §1.2 *et seq.*
6. R. Dolzer, 'Indirect Expropriation of Alien Property' (1988) 1 ICSID Rev 41 at 41.
7. Under customary international law, both tangible (i.e., land, equipment and inventory) and intangible property (i.e., company shares, dividends, bank accounts, contract rights, intellectual property and goodwill) can be expropriated. See collection of authorities in R.D. Bishop, J. Crawford & W.M. Reisman, *Foreign Investment Disputes: Cases, Materials and Commentary* (The Hague: Kluwer Law, 2005) at 849-881. The investments protected by IIAs are wide ranging. For example, in *Eureko B.V. v. Poland* (Partial Award, 19 Aug. 2005) [*Eureko*] at paras 147-160, the right to an initial public offering was found to be an investment on the theory that this was an acquired and vested right, and not a contingent one. It emerges from this jurisprudence that, at least in some cases, expectations of profit may also be protected by expropriation provisions in IIAs. See *supra* §1.51 on the definition of investment in IIAs.
8. *Norwegian Shipowners' Claims, supra* note 2 (compensation due to the shipowners under international law based on the respect for private property) and *Case Concerning Certain German Interests in Polish Upper Silesia, supra* note 2 (where the PCIJ held that under international law, property rights must be respected). See generally García-Amador, Fourth Report, *supra* note 2. International law supports the principle of respect for private property in a number of areas other than expropriation: state recognition of pre-existing private property claims in territory that no state has previously claimed (*terra nullius*); the principle that acquired rights survive state succession and must be respected by the successor state; and, in cases of military occupation, the principle that immovable private property must be respected. See L.B. Ederington, 'Property as a Natural Institution: The Separation of Property from Sovereignty in International Law' (1997) 13 AUILR 262. On state succession and international responsibility,

authorities establish that expropriation can occur in myriad ways.[9] The primary distinction in customary international law is between: (i) direct forms of expropriation in which the state openly and deliberately seizes property, and/or transfers title to private property to itself or a state-mandated third party;[10] and (ii) indirect forms of expropriation in which a government measure, although not on its face effecting a transfer of property, results in the foreign investor being deprived of its property or its benefits.[11] Although some IIAs use the term expropriation and

---

see P. Dumberry, *State Succession to International Responsibility* (Leiden: Martinus Nijhoff, 2007).

9. See OECD, "Indirect Expropriation" and the "Right to Regulate" in International Investment Law' in *International Investment Law: A Changing Landscape* (OECD: Paris, 2005) at 43 for a comprehensive overview of indirect expropriation in international law.

10. See J.H. Herz, 'Expropriation of Foreign Property' (1941) 35 AJIL 243; S. Friedman, *Expropriation in International Law* (London: Stevens & Sons Limited, 1953) and B.A. Wortley, *Expropriation in Public International Law* (Cambridge: Cambridge University Press, 1959). With respect to third parties see *Amco Asia Corporation v. Indonesia* (Award, 20 Nov. 1984) at para. 158 (1 ICSID Rep 413 at 455) where the tribunal states 'a case of expropriation exists not only when a state takes over private property but also when the expropriating state transfers ownership to another legal or natural person. Expropriation in international law also exists merely by the state withdrawing the protection of its courts from the owner expropriated, and tacitly allowing a *de facto* possessor to remain in possession of the thing seized ... .'

11. For commentary on indirect expropriation see G.C. Christie, 'What Constitutes a Taking of Property under International Law' (1962) 33 BYIL 307; B.H. Weston, "Constructive Takings' under International Law: A Modest Foray into the Problem of Creeping Expropriation' (1975) 16 VJIL 103 [Constructive Takings]; D.F. Vagts, 'Coercion and Foreign Investment Rearrangements' (1978) 72 AJIL 17; and R. Higgins, 'The Taking of Property by the State: Recent Developments in International Law' (1982) 176 RDCADI 259. For more recent discussions, see V. Been & J. C. Beauvais, 'The Global Fifth Amendment: NAFTA's Investment Protections and the Misguided Quest for an International 'Regulatory Takings' Doctrine' (2003) 78 NYULR 30; M. Brunetti, 'Iran-United States Claims Tribunal, NAFTA Chapter 11, and the Doctrine of Indirect Expropriation' (2000) 2 CJIL 203; D. Clough, 'Regulatory Expropriations and Compensation under NAFTA' (2005) 6 JWIT 553; R. Dolzer, 'Indirect Expropriation of Alien Property' (1988) 1 ICSID Rev 41 [Dolzer, Indirect Expropriation of Alien Property]; R. Dolzer, 'New Foundations of the Law of Expropriation of Alien Property' (1981) 75 AJIL 553 [Dolzer, New Foundations]; R. Dolzer, 'Indirect Expropriations: New Developments?' (2003) 11 NYUELJ 64 [New Developments]; R. Dolzer & F. Bloch, 'Indirect Expropriation: Conceptual Realignments?' (2003) 5 ILF 155 [Conceptual Realignments]; L.Y. Fortier & S.L. Drymer, 'Indirect Expropriation in the Law of International Investment: I Know It When I See It, or Caveat Investor' (2004) 19 ICSID Rev 293; E.M. Graham, 'Regulatory Takings, Supernational Treatment, and the Multilateral Agreement on Investment: Issues Raised by Nongovernmental Organizations' (1998) 31 CILQ 599; K. Hobér, *Investment Arbitration in Eastern Europe: In Search of a Definition of Expropriation* (New York: Juris, 2007); A. Hoffmann, 'Indirect Expropriation,' in A. Reinisch, ed., *Standards of Investment Protection* (Oxford: Oxford University Press, 2008); U. Kriebaum, 'Partial Expropriation' (2007) 8 JWIT 69; U. Kriebaum, 'Regulatory Takings: Balancing the Interests of the Investor and the State' (2007) 8 JWIT 717; Ch. Leben 'La liberté normative de l'etat et la question de l'expropriation indirecte' in C. Leben, ed., *Le contentieux arbitral transnational relatif à l'investissement* (Anthemis, 2006); C. Lévesque, 'Les fondements de la distinction entre l'expropriation et la réglementation en droit international' (2003) 33 RGD 39; V. Lowe, 'Regulation or Expropriation?' (2002) 55 CLP 447; I. Madalena, 'Foreign Direct Investment and the Protection of the Environment: the Border between National Environmental Regulation

others deprivation, IIA jurisprudence has interpreted these two terms as having a similar meaning.[12]

§7.3 Direct expropriation The majority of expropriation cases in international law have involved a deprivation of a foreign investor's acquired rights and a corresponding acquisition, or appropriation, of those acquired rights by the state or a state-mandated third party.[13] The classic forms of direct expropriation fall into this category – nationalizations of strategic industries or expropriations for public infrastructure, such as roads or parks. A variety of terms are used to describe direct expropriations. Expropriations of entire industries or sectors of the economy are called nationalizations.[14] Expropriations of property during wartime or national emergency are often called requisitions.[15] Confiscation is used to describe compulsory acquisitions of property where the acquisition is not accompanied by compensation, for example in the case of forfeiture of property acquired by crime or left

---

and Expropriation' (Mar. 2003) EELR 70; T.W. Merrill, 'Colloquium Article: Incomplete Compensation for Takings' (2002) 11 NYUELJ 110 at 116; Y. Nouvel, 'Les mesures équivalent à une expropriation dans la pratique récente des tribunaux arbitraux' (2002) 106 RGDIP 79; A. Newcombe, 'The Boundaries of Regulatory Expropriation' (2005) 20 ICSID Review 1 [Newcombe, Boundaries]; J. Paulsson & Z. Douglas, 'Indirect Expropriation in Investment Treaty Arbitrations,' in N. Horn & S. Kröll, eds, *Arbitrating Foreign Investment Disputes: Procedural and Substantive Legal Aspects*, (The Hague: Kluwer Law International, 2004) at 145; A. Reinisch, 'Expropriation,' in P. Muchlinski, F. Ortino & C. Schreuer, eds, *The Oxford Handbook of International Investment Law*, (Oxford: Oxford University Press, 2008); A. Reinisch, 'Legality of Expropriation,' in A. Reinisch, ed., *Standards of Investment Protection* (Oxford: Oxford University Press, 2008); G.H. Sampliner, 'Arbitration of Expropriation Cases Under US Investment Treaties – A Threat to Democracy or the Dog that Didn't Bark?' (2003) 18 ICSID Rev 1; A. Sedigh, 'What Level of Host State Interference Amounts to a Taking under Contemporary International Law' (2002) 2 JWI 631; T. Wälde & A. Kolo, 'Environmental Regulation, Investment Protection and 'Regulatory Taking' in International Law' (2001) 50 ICLQ 811; and J.M. Wagner, 'International Investment, Expropriation and Environmental Protection' (1999) 29 GGULR 465. See also the collection of papers from the *Colloquium on Regulatory Expropriations in International Law* published in (2003) 11 NYUELJ and the collection of papers in (2003) 5 ILF.

12. See for example, *Saluka Investments BV v. Czech Republic* (Partial Award, 17 Mar. 2006) [*Saluka*] at paras 254-275. See below at §7.24.

13. See *De Sabla v. Panama* (1934) 28 AJIL 602; (1933) VI RIAA 358, a case involving government grants of title and cultivation licenses to third parties on land owned by the claimant.

14. In 1952, the Institut de Droit International defined nationalization as: 'the transfer to the State, by a legislative act and in the public interest, of property or private rights of a designated character, with a view to their exploitation or control by the State, or to their direction to a new objective by the State,' as quoted by M. Domke in 'Foreign Nationalizations: Some Aspects of Contemporary International Law' (1961) 55 AJIL 585 at 588. On nationalization of foreign-held property, see I. Foighel, *Nationalization: A Study in the Protection of Alien Property in International Law* (London: Stevens, 1957); G. White, *Nationalisation of Foreign Property* (London: Stevens & Sons Limited, 1961); R.B. Lillich, *The Valuation of Nationalized Property in International Law* (Charlottesville: University Press of Virginia, 1972); and M. Sornarajah, *The Pursuit of Nationalized Property* (Dordrecht: Martinus Nijhoff Publishers, 1986).

15. The classic case of wartime requisition is *Norwegian Shipowners' Claims*, *supra* note 2.

intestate.[16] The term spoliation is sometimes used to describe takings of property without compensation.[17] Notwithstanding the various forms that state conduct can take or the terminology used to describe them, in all these cases the government measures in question result in a state sanctioned compulsory transfer of property from the foreigner to either the government or a state-mandated third party.[18]

State responsibility for acquisition or appropriation of property will arise unless the taking can be justified as a legitimate use of state police powers, such as taxation or forfeiture for crime.[19] These are non-compensable takings.[20]

§7.4 Indirect expropriation   An array of adjectives is used to describe indirect expropriation: equivalent, tantamount, *de facto*,[21] creeping,[22] constructive, disguised, consequential, regulatory or virtual.[23] No matter how the expropriation

---

16. See M. Sornarajah, *The International Law on Foreign Investment*, 2nd edn (Cambridge: Cambridge University Press, 2004) at 346 on the association of confiscation with takings for the personal gain of dictators or oligarchies.
17. UNCTC, *Bilateral Investment Treaties* (New York: United Nations, 1988) [UNCTC, BITs] at 49.
18. In *Amoco International Finance Corporation v. Iran* (1987) 15 Iran-US CTR 189 the Iran-US Claims Tribunal referred to expropriation at para. 108 as a 'compulsory transfer of property rights.'
19. See *infra* §7.24.
20. See generally *Saluka, supra* note 12 at paras 255-262. Influential contemporary jurisprudence considers the taking of property as not necessarily always being compensable. See J. Penner, *The Idea of Property in Law* (Clarendon: Oxford University Press, 2000).
21. In *Técnicas Medioambientales Tecmed S.A. v. Mexico* (Award, 29 May 2003) [*Tecmed*] the tribunal stated at para. 113: 'Although formally an expropriation means a forcible taking by the Government of tangible or intangible property owned by private persons by means of administrative or legislative action to that effect, the term also covers a number of situations defined as *de facto* expropriation, where such actions or laws transfer assets to third parties different from the expropriating State or where such laws or actions deprive persons of their ownership over such assets, without allocating such assets to third parties or to the Government.'
22. The term creeping expropriation refers to a series of separate government measures that, although not expropriatory when considered as separate and distinct measures, are expropriatory when considered cumulatively. See Weston, Constructive Takings, *supra* note 11; and E.P. Mendes, 'The Canadian National Energy Program: An Example of Assertion of Economic Sovereignty or Creeping Expropriation in International Law' (1981) 14 VJTL 475. The tribunal in *Generation Ukraine Inc. v. Ukraine,* (Award, 16 Sep. 2003) [*Generation Ukraine*] at para. 20.22 defined creeping expropriation as follows: 'Creeping expropriation is a form of indirect expropriation with a distinctive temporal quality in the sense that it encapsulates the situation whereby a series of acts attributable to the State *over a period of time* culminate in the expropriatory taking of such property.' In *Waste Management Inc. v. Mexico,* Keith Highet noted that: 'a 'creeping expropriation' is comprised of a number of elements, none of which can – separately – constitute the international wrong. These constituent elements include non-payment, non-reimbursement, cancellation, denial of judicial access, actual practice to exclude, non-conforming treatment, inconsistent legal blocks, and so forth. The 'measure' at issue is the expropriation itself; it is not merely a sub-component part of expropriation. A nationalization or expropriation – in particular a 'creeping expropriation' comprised of numerous components – must logically be more than the mere sum of its parts.' (Dissenting Opinion of K. Highet, 2 Jun. 2000) at paras 17 and 18.
23. *Waste Management Inc v. Mexico (*Award, 30 Apr. 2004) at para. 163 [*Waste Management II*].

is described, international law looks to the effect of the government measures on the investor's property. This approach is reflected in the writings of jurists,[24] the decisions of tribunals,[25] as well as the texts of investment instruments[26] and has been referred to as the 'sole effect doctrine' because the focus of the analysis is the effect of the state measure on the investment.[27] The effects-based approach is reflected in commonly cited definitions of expropriation, including decisions of the Iran-US Claims Tribunal in *Starrett Housing Corporation v. Iran* and *Tippetts, Abbett, McCarthy, Stratton and TAMS-AFFA Consulting Engineers of Iran v. Iran.*[28] In *Starrett* the tribunal held that:

> ... [it] is recognized in international law that measures taken by a state can interfere with property rights to such an extent that these rights are rendered so useless that they must be deemed to have been expropriated, even though the state does not purport to have expropriated them and the legal title to the property formally remains with the original owner.[29]

And in *Tippetts*:

> The Tribunal prefers the term 'deprivation' to the term 'taking,' although they are largely synonymous, because the latter may be understood to imply that the Government had acquired something of value, which is not required.

---

24. See studies at *supra* note 11.
25. See *infra* §7.16 *et seq.*
26. See Art. III of the 1959 *Draft Convention on Investments Abroad* (Abs-Shawcross Draft Convention), reproduced in G. Schwarzenberger, *Foreign Investments and International Law* (New York: Frederick A. Praeger, 1969); Art 10 of Professors L. B. Sohn's and R.R. Baxter's 1961 *Draft Convention on the International Responsibility of States for Injuries to Aliens* (1961) 55 AJIL 545 [1961 Harvard Draft]; the definition of 'taking' in §192, American Law Institute, *Restatement (Second) of the Foreign Relations Law of the United States* (Washington: American Law Institute Publishers, 1965) and Art. 3 of the 1967 OECD's *Draft Convention on the Protection of Foreign Investment* (1968) 7 ILM 117. See *supra* Chapter 1 for a discussion of the development of the draft conventions.
27. See Dolzer's articles New Developments and Conceptual Realignments, *supra* note 11.
28. Iran-US Claims Tribunal decisions need to be approached with some caution as the tribunal's jurisdiction extended to 'expropriation or other measures affecting property rights' (Art. II, Claims Settlement Declaration, 19 Jan. 1981 in (1981) 1 Iran-US CTR 9 at 11). Thus, decisions do not always clearly distinguish whether state responsibility arose because the government measure amounted to an expropriation or whether it was a measure affecting property rights. See *Pope & Talbot Inc v. Canada* (Interim Award, 26 Jun. 2000) [*Pope & Talbot*] at para. 104.
29. *Starrett Housing Corporation v. Islamic Republic of Iran* (1983) 4 Iran-US CTR 122 [*Starrett*] at 154 per Lagergren. For a discussion of the expropriation jurisprudence of the Iran-US Claims Tribunal see A. Mouri, *The International Law of Expropriation as Reflected in the Work of the Iran-U.S. Claims Tribunal* (Dordrecht: Kluwer Academic, 1994); G.H. Aldrich, *The Jurisprudence of the Iran-United States Claims Tribunal* (Oxford: Clarendon Press, 1996), C.N. Brower & J.D. Brueschke, *The Iran-United States Claims Tribunal* (The Hague: Martinus Nijhoff Publishers, 1998); and C. Gibson & C. Drahozal, *The Iran-U.S. Claims Tribunal at 25: The Cases Everyone Needs to Know for Investor-State and International Arbitration* (Oxford: Oxford University Press, 2007). See *supra* Chapter 1, §1.28, on the Iran-US Claims Tribunal.

A deprivation or taking of property may occur under international law through interference by a state in the use of that property or with the enjoyment of its benefits, even where legal title to the property is not affected.

While assumption of control over property by a government does not automatically and immediately justify a conclusion that property has been taken by the government, thus requiring compensation under international law, such a conclusion is warranted whenever events demonstrate that the owner was deprived of fundamental rights of ownership and it appears that this deprivation is not merely ephemeral. The intent of the government is less important than the effects of the measures on the owner, and the form of the measures of control or interference is less important than the reality of their impact.[30]

As the above statements from *Starrett* and *Tippetts* highlight, the focus of the expropriation analysis is on the extent of the deprivation that the investor suffers and, to a far lesser degree, on the form or content of the state measure or the intent of the state.[31]

Diverse types of government measure may give rise to an indirect expropriation. For example, international tribunals have found states responsible for indirect expropriations in a wide variety of circumstances[32] including: requisition of land;[33] forced sales;[34] exorbitant or arbitrary taxation,[35] deprivation of profits;[36] measures substantially interfering with the management or control of a business enterprise;[37] annulment and

---

30. The majority of the Tribunal found that the claimants were entitled to compensation for their 50% interest in a joint venture, as the Iranian government had appointed a manager for the business and the claimant was deprived of the control and benefit of its property. Whether the Tribunal decided that property had been expropriated is slightly unclear because the Tribunal held that the claimant was subjected to measures affecting property rights. See *Tippetts, Abbett, McCarthy, Stratton and TAMS-AFFA Consulting Engineers of Iran v. Islamic Republic of Iran* (1984) 6 Iran-US CTR 219 [*Tippetts*] at 225.

31. See §7.14 below.

32. See *Oppenheim's International Law, supra* note 1 at §407 for an extensive list of literature and authorities relating to expropriation.

33. *Reverend Jonas P. King* in M.M. Whiteman, *Damages in International Law*, Vol. II (Washington DC, 1937) at 1387-91 and *De Sabla, supra* note 13. See also Christie, *supra* note 11 at 312-313.

34. See *Gowan and Copland (US v. Venezuela)* in J.B. Moore, *History and Digest of the International Arbitrations*, Vol. 4, 3354 (United States-Venezuelan Claims Commission); *Nazi cases* described in Christie, *supra* note 11 at 324-329, *Fedordchak Claim* (1962) 40 ILR 96; *Reineccius v. Bank of International Settlements*, Arbitral Tribunal of the Bank of International Settlements (8 Jan. 2001). Also see discussion by Sornarajah, *supra* note 16 at 359-364.

35. *Corn Products Refining Company Claim* (1955) 22 ILR 333; *Revere Copper & Brass, Inc. v. Overseas Private Investment Corporation* (1978) 17 ILM 1321, (1980) 56 ILR 258 [*Revere Copper*]; and I. Brownlie, *General Course on Public International Law* (1995) 255 RDCADI at 143 stating that international law recognizes a presumption of lawfulness for taxation.

36. *Corn Products Refining Company Claim, ibid.* See also Sornarajah, *supra* note 16 at 284 and Christie, *supra* note 11.

37. *Starrett, supra* note 29 and *Tippetts, supra* note 30. *Benvenuti and Bonfant Srl v. Congo* (1980) 21 ILM 740 [*Benvenuti et Bonfant*] at 757. Also see authorities in *Oppenheim's International Law, supra* note 1 at 917. See *Revere Copper, supra* note 35. Revere Copper had developed a

cancellation of property rights, contractual rights, debts or licenses,[38] the total prohibition on the sale or occupancy of a property,[39] the harassment of employees, blocking
of access to a plant and government take-over of a key supplier,[40] the prohibition on
re-export of equipment,[41] the creation of state monopolies,[42] and other forms of
arbitrary conduct depriving the investor of the benefits of its property.[43]

§7.5 Attempts to develop international standards for expropriation   As
described in Chapter 1, in addition to developments at the United Nations, there
were a number of attempts after World War II to develop international rules of
expropriation.[44] The first of these was the 1959 *Draft Convention on Investments
Abroad* (the Abs-Shawcross Draft Convention). Article III provides that states
must pay just and effective compensation for direct or indirect deprivations of
property:

---

bauxite mining and processing operation in Jamaica through a wholly owned subsidiary,
Revere Jamaica Alumina, Limited (RJA) under a twenty-five-year agreement made in 1967
with the Government of Jamaica (Agreement). The Agreement governed the payments of taxes
and royalties to Jamaica for twenty-five years. In 1972, the newly elected government of
Michael Manley initiated a review of the bauxite industry. As a result of this review, in 1974
the Jamaican government imposed new requirements on RJA including increases in royalties
and levies, extraction quotas, exchange controls and export controls.

38.   *Felix Claim* (1961) 42 ILR 161; *Henke Claim* (1958-II) 26 ILR 276; *General Electric Company
      Claim* (1959) 30 ILR 140; *Pietrzak Claim* (1962) 56 AJIL 1110.
39.   *Albert Bela Root* (1958) United States Foreign Claims Settlement Commission, Decision
      No. Hung-1625. See Christie, *supra* note 11 at 314.
40.   See V.R. Koven, 'Expropriation and the "Jurisprudence" of OPIC' (1981) 22 HILJ 269.
41.   *Petrolane Inc. v. Iran* (1991) 27 Iran-US CTR 64.
42.   See discussion of *Italian Insurance Monopoly* case in Friedman, *supra* note 10 at 53,
      International Law Association, Report of the Thirty-seventh Conference (1932), Report of the
      Committee on Private Property, and in A.P. Fachiri, 'Expropriation and International Law'
      (1925) 6 BYIL 159. The creation of a state monopoly for life insurance would not seem to be
      a justifiable exercise of state police powers by which obligation to pay compensation may be
      avoided (Christie, *supra* note 11 at 335). On the other hand, a broad reading of *Oscar Chinn*
      (1934) PCIJ Rep Ser. A/B No 63, might suggest that state subsidization that makes it unprofit-
      able to engage in business does not amount to an expropriation. See Brownlie, *Principles of
      Public International Law*, *supra* note 1 at 509. For a discussion of *Oscar Chinn*, see T. Weiler,
      'Saving Oscar Chinn: Non-Discrimination in International Investment Law,' in Horn & Kröll,
      eds, *Arbitrating Foreign Investment Disputes*, *supra* note 11 at 159.
43.   *Biloune and Marine Drive Complex Ltd v. Ghana Investments Centre and the Government of
      Ghana* (Award on Jurisdiction and Liability, 27 Oct. 1989) [*Biloune*] is representative of this
      type of scenario. Biloune made an investment agreement with the Ghana Investments Centre,
      a government entity, for the development of a resort complex. After work had begun, the gov-
      ernment issued a stop work order and partially demolished the work in progress. Biloune was
      then arrested, detained and deported. The tribunal found that there was no justification for any
      of these actions. See Herz, *supra* note 10 at 250.
44.   Art. III, Abs-Shawcross Draft Convention, *supra* note 26; Art. 10(3)(a), 1961 Harvard Draft,
      supra note 26; and Art. 3, 1967 OECD *Draft Convention on the Protection of Foreign
      Investment*, *supra* note 26. See *supra* Chapter 1 for a discussion of these instruments.

No Party shall take any measures against nationals of another Party to deprive them directly or indirectly of their property except under due process of law and provided that such measures are not discriminatory or contrary to undertakings given by that Party and are accompanied by the payment of just and effective compensation ...[45]

The 1961 *Draft Convention on the International Responsibility of States for Injuries to Aliens*[46] (1961 Harvard Draft), which was intended as a codification of customary international law, provides that all takings are to be compensated and defines a taking as follows:

A 'taking of property' includes not only an outright taking of property but also any such unreasonable interference with the use, enjoyment, or disposal of property as to justify an inference that the owner thereof will not be able to use, enjoy, or dispose of the property within a reasonable period of time after the inception of such interference.[47]

Article 10(5) of the 1961 Harvard Draft further provides that uncompensated takings as a result of the exercise of state police powers[48] are not wrongful:

An uncompensated taking of property of an alien or a deprivation of the use or enjoyment of property of an alien which results from the execution of the tax laws; from a general change in the value of currency; from the action of the competent authorities of the State in the maintenance of public order, health, or morality; or from the valid exercise of belligerent rights; or is otherwise incidental to the normal operation of the laws of the State shall not be considered wrongful, provided:

(a) it is not a clear and discriminatory violation of the law of the State concerned;

(b) it is not the result of a violation of any provisions of Articles 6 to 8 of this Convention[49]

(c) it is not an unreasonable departure from the principles of justice recognized by the principal legal systems of the world; and

(d) it is not an abuse of the powers specified in this paragraph for the purpose of depriving an alien of his property.

---

45. *Ibid.*, at 117.
46. (1961) 55 AJIL 545. This citation includes the history and text of the Harvard Draft and is accompanied by extensive commentary.
47. Art. 10(3)(a). According to the commentary accompanying the 1961 Harvard Draft, a state can employ a wide variety of measures for the purpose of making it impossible for an investor to use or enjoy its property. For example, a state may make it impossible for an investor to operate a factory by blocking the factory gates on the grounds of maintaining public order; through labour legislation it may set wages at a prohibitively high level; or it may deny visas for required technical staff. *Ibid.*, at 559.
48. See §7.24 *et seq.* below regarding police power exceptions.
49. These articles provide procedural protections.

Article 3 of the 1967 Organization for Economic Co-operation and Development (OECD) *Draft Convention on the Protection of Foreign Property*,[50] like the Abs-Shawcross Draft Convention, refers to direct or indirect deprivations of property:

> No Party shall take any measures depriving, directly or indirectly, of his property a national of another Party unless the following conditions are complied with:
>
> (i)   The measures are taken in the public interest and under due process of law;
> (ii) The measures are not discriminatory or contrary to any undertaking which the former Party may have given; and
> (iii) The measures are accompanied by provisions for the payment of just compensation[51]

The American Law Institute has codified the international law governing expropriation in §712 of its *Restatement of the Law Third, The Foreign Relations Law of the United States* (Third Restatement).[52] The Third Restatement refers to state responsibility arising from a 'taking' of property and provides, in part, that:

> A state is responsible under international law for injury resulting from:
>
> (1) a taking by the state of the property of a national of another state that:
>   (a) is not for a public purpose, or
>   (b) is discriminatory, or
>   (c) is not accompanied by provision for just compensation;
>   . . . .
>
> (3) other arbitrary or discriminatory acts or omissions by the state that impair property or other economic interests of a national of another state.

'Taking' is defined in the *Restatement of the Law Second The Foreign Relations Law of the United States*[53] (Second Restatement) as:

> Conduct attributable to a state that is intended to, and does, effectively deprive an alien of substantially all benefit of his interest in property, constitutes a

---

50. *Supra* note 26.
51. The commentary to the 1967 Draft OECD Convention remarks that measures that are otherwise lawful can be applied in such as a way as to deprive the investor of its property. It suggests that excessive or arbitrary taxation, prohibition of dividend redistribution coupled with compulsory loans, imposition of administrators, prohibition of dismissal of staff, refusal of access to raw materials, or the denial of essential export or import licenses may amount to a taking. *Ibid.*, at 126.
52. See §712, American Law Institute, *Restatement of the Law Third, The Foreign Relations Law of the United States* (Washington: American Law Institute Publishers, 1987) [Third Restatement].
53. American Law Institute, *Restatement of the Law Second, The Foreign Relations Law of the United States* (Washington: American Law Institute Publishers, 1965).

taking of the property ... even though the state does not deprive him of his entire legal interest in the property.[54]

But, according to the Third Restatement, a state is not responsible for loss of property or other economic disadvantage resulting from *bona fide* general taxation, regulation, forfeiture from crime, or other action of the kind that is commonly considered as within the police powers of states.[55]

The expropriation and compensation provisions of Article IV.2.1 of the draft *Multilateral Agreement on Investment* (MAI)[56] provide:

2.1. A Contracting Party shall not expropriate or nationalise [directly or indirectly][57] an investment in its territory of an investor of another Contracting Party or take any measure or measures having equivalent effect (hereinafter referred to as 'expropriation') except:

a) for a purpose which is in the public interest,
b) on a non-discriminatory basis,
c) in accordance with due process of law, and
d) accompanied by payment of prompt, adequate and effective compensation in accordance with Articles 2.2 to 2.5 below.

In response to criticisms of the MAI, a number of interpretive notes were added to the text. These included a clarification of the expropriation provision as follows:

Articles – on General Treatment, and – on Expropriation and Compensation, are intended to incorporate into the MAI existing international legal norms. The reference in Article IV.2.1 to expropriation or nationalisation and 'measures tantamount to expropriation or nationalisation' reflects the fact that international law requires compensation for an expropriatory taking without regard to the label applied to it, even if title to the property is not taken. It does not establish a new requirement that Parties pay compensation for losses which an investor or investment may incur through regulation, revenue raising and other normal activity in the public interest undertaken by governments. Nor would such normal and non-discriminatory government activity contravene the standards in Article –.1 (General Treatment).

In addition to Article IV.2.1, an interpretive note on taxation measures states that the imposition of taxes does not generally constitute expropriation but accepts that

---

54. This definition does not appear in the Third Restatement although it is reflected in the Reporters' Notes. The Third Restatement adopts the same approach as the Second Restatement to the definition of taking.
55. Third Restatement, *supra* note 52 at §712(g).
56. The MAI Negotiating Text and Commentary (as of 24 Apr. 1998). See *supra* Chapter 1, §1.40.
57. The chair's package of proposals for text on environment and labour would have eliminated 'directly or indirectly' from the provision and included the interpretive note reproduced in the text below.

some taxation measures may constitute expropriation, though not if the measure is 'within the bounds of internationally recognized tax policies and practices.'[58]

§7.6 IIA provisions defining expropriation   IIAs uniformly have provisions that require the host state to pay compensation if it expropriates a foreign investment. This requirement is consistent with customary international law.[59] What constitutes expropriation is expressed in a variety of ways.[60] Some IIAs refer simply to investments that are expropriated.[61] Other IIAs refer to expropriation or nationalization or similar measures.[62] The most common formulation in recent IIAs is to refer to expropriation and nationalization, through direct or indirect means, and to government measures that have an effect that is 'similar',[63] 'same',[64] 'equivalent'[65] or 'tantamount'[66] to expropriation or nationalization. These IIAs expressly equate measures that have an expropriatory effect with more traditional forms of direct expropriation. For example, Article 13(1), Energy Charter Treaty (ECT),[67] provides:

> Investments of Investors of a Contracting Party in the Area of any other Contracting Party shall not be nationalized, expropriated or subjected to a measure or measures having effect equivalent to nationalization or expropriation (hereinafter referred to as 'Expropriation').

58. MAI, *supra* note 56 at 87.
59. It also serves as a rejection of the view advanced by Communist states in the early 1960s. See S.M. Schwebel, 'The Story of the UN's Declaration on Permanent Sovereignty Over Natural Resources' (1963) 49 ABA J 463 *reprinted in Justice in International Law: Selected Writings of Stephen M Schwebel* (Cambridge: Cambridge University Press, 1994) at 401-415. See *supra* Chapter 1, §1.20.
60. For in-depth surveys of treaty practice, see the three comprehensive studies: UNCTC, BITs, *supra* note 17; UNCTAD, *Bilateral Investment Treaties in the Mid-1990s* (New York and Geneva: United Nations, 1998) (Doc. No. UNCTAD/ITE/IIT/7) and UNCTAD, *Bilateral Investment Treaties 1995-2006* (New York and Geneva: United Nations, 2007) (Doc. No. UNCTAD/ITE/IIT/2006/5) [together *UNCTAD BIT Studies*]. Also see R. Dolzer & M. Stevens, *Bilateral Investment Treaties* (The Hague: Martinus Nijhoff Publishers, 1995) and UNCTAD, *Taking of Property*, UNCTAD Series on issues in international investment agreements (New York and Geneva United Nations, 2000) (UNCTAD/ITE/IIT/15) [UNCTAD, Taking of Property] for a review of various formulations.
61. Art. 4, Austria-Egypt (2001).
62. Art. 4, Chile-China (1994), and Art. 4, China-Romania (1994).
63. Art. 5, Bahrain-Jordan (2000), and Art. 5, China-Netherlands (2001).
64. Art. 5, Australia-Romania (1993); Art. 5, Chile-Turkey (1998); and Art. 4, Lebanon-Switzerland (2000).
65. Art. 6, Chile-Tunisia (1998); Art. 5, China-Jordan (2001); Art. 5, Austria-Azerbaijan (2000); Art. 4, Bosnia and Herzegovina-Sweden (2000); Art. 5, Chile-China (1994); Art. 5, India-Portugal (2000); and Art. 5, Bosnia and Herzegovina-UK (2002).
66. For example, Art. 1110(1), NAFTA, provides: 'No Party may directly or indirectly nationalize or expropriate an investment of an investor of another Party in its territory or take a measure tantamount to nationalization or expropriation of such an investment ('expropriation').' See also Art. 5, Cuba-Ghana (1999); Art. III, Romania-US (1992); and Art. 5, Egypt-Japan (1977).
67. See *supra* Chapter 1, §1.38, on the *Energy Charter Treaty*.

A smaller number of IIAs refer to measures that deprive investors of their investments, directly or indirectly, rather than expressly using the term expropriation.[68] For example, Article 5, Czechoslovakia-Netherlands (1991), provides:

> Neither Contracting Party shall take any measures depriving, directly or indirectly, investors of the other Contracting Party of their investments …

Others refer to measures that effect a dispossession of an investment.[69] For example, Article 5(2), Argentina-France (1991), provides:

> The Contracting Parties shall not adopt, directly or indirectly, measures of expropriation or nationalization or any other equivalent measure having an effect similar to dispossession, except for public purpose and provided that such measures are not discriminatory or contrary to a specific commitment.

A small minority of BITs refer more generally to a 'deprivative or restrictive measure or any other measure having a similar effect'[70] or measures that interfere with an investment.[71]

Some older BITs, including early US BITs,[72] enumerate specific types of measures that can be expropriatory, including taxation, the freezing or blocking of assets or funds, compulsory sales and deprivation of management, control or

---

68. Recent Dutch BITs follow this model. See, for example, Art. 6, Netherlands-Panama (2000): 'Neither Contracting Party shall take any measures depriving, directly or indirectly, investors of the other Contracting Party of their investments.' Also see Art. 6, Chile-Egypt (1999). Art. 10(1), *Agreement for Promotion, Protection and Guarantee of Investment Among Members States of the Organisation of Islamic Conference* (1981) provides one of the most detailed provisions in this respect: 'The host state shall undertake not to adopt or permit the adoption of any measure – itself or through one of its organs, institutions or local authorities – if such a measure may directly or indirectly affect the ownership of the investor's capital or investment by depriving him totally or partially of his ownership or of all or part of his basic rights or the exercise of his authority on the ownership, possession or utilization of his capital, or of his actual control over the investment, its management, making use out of it, enjoying its utilities, the realization of its benefits or guaranteeing its development and growth.'
69. This provision was considered in *Compañiá de Aguas del Aconquija S.A. and Vivendi Universal v. Argentina* (Award, 20 Aug. 2007) [*Vivendi II*]. The French original reads: 'Les parties contractantes ne prennent pas, directement ou indirectement, de measures d'expropriation ou de nationalization, ni tout autre measure équivalente ayant un effect similaire de dépossession …' For similar provisions see Art. 5, France-Pakistan (1983); Art. 4, Gabon-Lebanon (2001); Art. 6, Kuwait-Netherlands (2001); and Art. VI, Chile-Indonesia (1999).
70. Art. 4, Belgo-Luxembourg Economic Union (BLEU)-Burundi (1989) (authors' translation). Art. 4 of the treaty provides: '… ne prendre aucune mesure privative ou restrictive de propriété, ni aucune autre mesure ayant un effet similaire.' See *Antoine Goetz et consorts v. Burundi* (Award, 10 Feb. 1999)[*Goetz*].
71. Art. 4, Germany-USSR (1989), refers to 'dispossession.' The Protocol to the BIT provides that '[an] investor shall also be entitled to compensation if the other Contracting Party interferes with the economic activities of an enterprise in which he is participating, if his investment is significantly reduced by such interference.' As translated by the tribunal in Mr. *Franz Sedelmayer v. Russia* (Arbitration Award, 7 Jul. 1998) [*Sedelmayer*] at 11.
72. See K.J. Vandevelde, *United States Investment Treaties: Policy and Practice* (Boston: Kluwer Law and Taxation, 1992) at 117-138 on early US practice.

economic value.[73] Others clarify that the expropriation provisions apply where the state expropriates the assets of a company and the foreign investor owns shares in the company.[74]

§7.7 More recent model BITs   Canada in 2003 and the US in 2004 published new model BITs that, unlike previous IIAs, provide detailed guidance to tribunals on the interpretation of expropriation.[75] Although the main expropriation provisions in both models[76] are similar to other IIAs, they provide that expropriation shall be interpreted in accordance with an annex. The new approach is reflected in US-Uruguay (2005) and investment chapters in several US bilateral free trade agreements.[77] Article 6, similarly to other US BITs, provides that 'Neither Party may expropriate or nationalize a covered investment either directly or indirectly through measures equivalent to expropriation or nationalization ("expropriation")' followed by the four conditions for a legal expropriation common with other BITs. The annex elaborates on the meaning of expropriation:

The Parties confirm their shared understanding that:

1. Article 6(1) is intended to reflect customary international law concerning the obligation of States with respect to expropriation.
2. An action or a series of actions by a Party cannot constitute an expropriation unless it interferes with a tangible or intangible property right or property interest in an investment.
3. Article 6(1) addresses two situations. The first is known as direct expropriation, where an investment is nationalized or otherwise directly expropriated through formal transfer of title or outright seizure.

---

73. Art. 5, Protocol to Democratic Republic of Congo-US (1984), provides that: ' "Direct or indirect measures tantamount to expropriation" as used in Article III(1) may include the levying of taxes equivalent to indirect expropriation, the compulsory sale of all or part of an investment, or the impairment or deprivation of the management, control, or economic value of an investment.'
74. See, for example, Art. 5(2), Argentina-UK (1990), and Art. III(2), Senegal-US (1983).
75. See, for example, Annex 10-D, *Chile-US FTA (2003)*, and Annex B, 2004 US Model BIT, both available on the website of the Office of the US Trade Representative. Canada refers to its BITs as Foreign Investment Protection Agreements. See Annex B.13(1) to Canadian 2003 Model *Foreign Investment Protection Agreement*, available on the website of the Canadian Department of Foreign Affairs. The impetus for elaborating on the meaning of expropriation was US and Canadian experience of indirect expropriation claims under NAFTA and the concern that an investment tribunal might find various types of non-discriminatory regulation to be expropriatory.
76. Art. 6, US Model (2004), provides: 'Neither Party may expropriate or nationalize a covered investment either directly or indirectly through measures equivalent to expropriation or nationalization ("expropriation").' Art. 13, Canadian Model (2003), provides: 'Neither Party shall nationalize or expropriate a covered investment either directly, or indirectly through measures having an effect equivalent to nationalization or expropriation (hereinafter referred to as "expropriation").'
77. For example the FTAs with Australia, Chile, Dominican Republic and Morocco. For a complete listing see the website of the Office of the US Trade Representative.

4. The second situation addressed by Article 6(1) is known as indirect expropriation, where an action or series of actions by a Party has an effect equivalent to direct expropriation without formal transfer of title or outright seizure.

(a) The determination of whether an action or series of actions by a Party, in a specific fact situation, constitutes an indirect expropriation, requires a case-by-case, fact-based inquiry that considers, among other factors:

(i) the economic impact of the government action, although the fact that an action or series of actions by a Party has an adverse effect on the economic value of an investment, standing alone, does not establish that an indirect expropriation has occurred;

(ii) the extent to which the government action interferes with distinct, reasonable investment-backed expectations; and

(iii) the character of the government action.

(b) Except in rare circumstances, non-discriminatory regulatory actions by a Party that are designed and applied to protect legitimate public welfare objectives, such as public health, safety, and the environment, do not constitute indirect expropriations.

The interpretive statement provides that the expropriation provisions are intended to 'reflect customary international law concerning the obligation of States with respect to expropriation.' As discussed below, the case-by-case, fact-based inquiry for indirect expropriation focusing on economic impact, legitimate expectations and the character of the government action is generally consistent with customary international law authorities on the scope of expropriation and the developing IIA jurisprudence on the scope of expropriation under IIAs.[78]

The 2007 Norwegian Model BIT provides another variation on expropriation:

1. A Party shall not expropriate or nationalise an investment of an investor of the other Party except in the public interest and subject to the conditions provided for by law and by the general principles of international law.

2. The preceding provision shall not, however, in any way impair the right of a Party to enforce such laws as it deems necessary to control the use of property in accordance with the general interest or to secure the payment of taxes or other contributions or penalties.

The commentary to the BIT notes that:

The expropriation provision must provide effective and intentional investor protection, while safeguarding the regulatory freedom of the state. The aim of an expropriation provision is to protect established investments from open or camouflaged expropriation. The provision must at the same time safeguard the state's right to implement general regulations and administrative decisions

---

78. See Newcombe, Boundaries, *supra* note 11.

without incurring liability to pay compensation. The challenge involves finding the correct point of intersection between regulation/intervention by the authorities that is deemed to be expropriation (and thus gives rise to claims for compensation) and the measures that fall outside this category.[79]

§7.8 Express exceptions for specific measures   A small number of IIAs clarify that certain types of measures are not expropriatory. For example, the 2003 Canadian Model provides that the expropriation provisions:

> ... shall not apply to the issuance of compulsory licenses granted in relation to intellectual property rights, or to the revocation, limitation or creation of intellectual property rights, to the extent that such issuance, revocation, limitation or creation is consistent with the WTO Agreement.[80]

US and Canadian BITs commonly have an express general exception for taxation measures,[81] but allow claims for expropriatory taxation.[82] Further, claims asserting that taxation measures are expropriatory are subject to a screening mechanism. For example, the *North American Free Trade Agreement* (NAFTA) provides that the investor may arbitrate a claim only if the tax authorities 'do not agree to consider the issue or, having agreed to consider it, fail to agree that the measure is not an expropriation.'[83] If there is consensus between the tax authorities of the home and host state that the tax measure is not expropriatory, then arbitration of the expropriation claim is barred.[84] The 2004 US Model provides a similar screening mechanism. Although the expropriation provisions apply to taxation measures, a claim that a taxation measure is expropriatory may not be submitted to arbitration unless the claimant has: (i) referred the question of whether that taxation measure involves an expropriation to the competent tax authorities of both state parties; and

---

79. 'Comments on the Model for Future Investment Agreements,' 19 Dec. 2007 at 21. Available online on <http://ita.law.uvic.ca>.

80. Art. 13(5). Earlier Canadian BITs follow this approach. See, for example, Art. VI, Barbados-Canada (1997).

81. See *infra* Chapter 10. On tax measures generally see *Pan American Energy LLC, and BP Argentina Exploration Company v. Argentina* (Decision on Preliminary Objections, 27 Jul. 2006) at paras 117-139; *El Paso Energy International Company v. Argentina* (Decision on Jurisdiction, 27 Apr. 2006) at paras 101-1116; *EnCana Corporation v. Ecuador* (Award, 3 Feb. 2006) [*EnCana*] at paras 141-145, 177; *Enron Corporation and Ponderosa Assets, L.P. v. Argentina* (Decision on Jurisdiction, 14 Jan. 2004) at paras 25-32; *United Parcel Service of America Inc. v. Canada* (Award on Jurisdiction, 22 Nov. 2002) at paras 116-117; and *Link-Trading Joint Stock Company v. Moldova* (Final Award, 18 Apr. 2002) at paras 63-92.

82. See *Occidental Exploration and Production Company v. Ecuador* (Final Award, 1 Jul. 2004) [*Occidental*] and *EnCana, ibid.*

83. Art. 2103(6), NAFTA.

84. See W. Park, 'Expropriation and Taxation in the NAFTA,' in T. Weiler, ed., *NAFTA Investment Law and Arbitration: Past Issues, Current Practice, Future Prospects*, (Ardsley: Transnational Publishers, 2004) at 93. The scope of Art. 2103(6) was considered in *Marvin Feldman v. Mexico* in the Interim Decision on Preliminary Jurisdictional Issues, 6 Dec. 2000, and Award 16 Dec. 2002.

(ii) within 180 days after the date of such referral, the competent tax authorities of both state parties fail to agree that the taxation measure is not an expropriation.[85]

§7.9 The meaning of the term 'measures' The majority of IIAs refer to 'measures' that are expropriatory.[86] This term has generally been given a wide interpretation in public international law and by IIA tribunals.[87] In the *Fisheries Jurisdiction Case*, the International Court of Justice (ICJ) stated that 'in its ordinary sense the word is wide enough to cover any act, step or proceeding, and imposes no particular limit on their material content or on the aim pursued thereby.'[88] It is, however, unclear whether measure is synonymous with conduct in Article 2 of the International Law Commission (ILC's) *Articles on State Responsibility*, such that any state action or omission can be considered a measure.[89] In *Ronald S. Lauder v. Czech Republic*, the tribunal found that statements by the Czech Media Council did not constitute measures and that a letter issued by the Czech Media Council was not a measure but a 'general opinion of a regulatory body' which had no legal effect.[90]

At least one IIA tribunal has suggested that an expropriation cannot occur through an omission.[91] This approach should not be followed. Although expropriation

---

85. Art. 21(2).
86. In contrast, other IIA provisions refer to treatment (national treatment, MFN treatment and fair and equitable treatment). See *supra* Chapters 4, 5 and 6.
87. On 'measures' generally, see *Canfor Corporation v. United States and Terminal Forest Products Ltd. v. United States* (Decision on Preliminary Question, 6 Jun. 2006) at paras 148-150; *Eureko, supra* note 7 at paras 185-189; *The Loewen Group Inc. v. United States* (Decision on Hearing of Respondent's Objection to Competence and Jurisdiction, 5 Jan. 2001) at paras 39-74; *Pope & Talbot, supra* note 28 at para. 103; *Fireman's Fund Insurance Company v. Mexico* (Decision on the Preliminary Question, 17 Jul. 2003) at paras 96-99 [*Fireman's Fund*]; *ADF Group Inc. v. United States* (Arbitral Award, 9 Jan. 2003) at paras 56-59; and *Methanex Corporation v. United States* (Partial Award, 7 Aug. 2002) at paras 89, 127-147. On the interpretation of 'measures' in the context of expropriation, see *CME Czech Republic B.V. v. Czech Republic* (Partial Award, 13 Sep. 2001) at paras 591-609 [*CME* Partial Award]; *EnCana, supra* note 81 at para. 177; *Consortium RFCC v. Morocco* (Arbitral Award, 22 Dec. 2003) [*Consortium RFCC*] at paras 63-68; *Tecmed, supra* note 21 at paras 113-115; *Metalclad Corporation v. Mexico* (Award, 30 Aug. 2000) at paras 105-107 [*Metalclad*]; and *Goetz, supra* note 70 at paras 121-133.
88. *Fisheries Jurisdiction Case* (*Spain v. Canada*) [1998] ICJ Rep 432 at para. 66. See also *Ethyl Corporation v. Canada* (Award on Jurisdiction, 24 Jun. 1998) at paras 65-69.
89. International Law Commission's Articles on Responsibility of States for Internationally Wrongful Acts, *Official Records of the General Assembly*, UN GAOR, 56th Sess., Supp. No. 10, UN Doc A/56/10 at 11; 2001 YBILC, Vol. II, Part Two. The Articles and commentary are *reprinted in* J. Crawford, *The International Law Commission's Articles on State Responsibility: Introduction, Text, and Commentaries* (Cambridge: Cambridge University Press, 2002) [ILC's Articles on State Responsibility].
90. *Ronald S. Lauder v. Czech Republic* (Final Award, 3 Sep. 2001) [*Lauder*] at paras 282-283.
91. The tribunal in *Mr. Eudoro Armando Olguín v. Paraguay* (Final Award, 26 Jul. 2001) at para. 84 states 'Expropriation therefore requires a teleologically driven action for it to occur; omissions, however egregious they may be, are not sufficient for it to take place.' See C. McLachlan, L. Shore & M. Weiniger, *International Investment Arbitration: Substantive Principles* (Oxford: Oxford University Press, 2007) at para. 8.73 who state that the reasoning in *Olguín* is to be preferred.

normally arises due to a positive act of a state, rather than an omission, such as a failure to pay a debt or to provide full security and protection, in principle an omission is conduct attributable to the state and can be an expropriatory measure. For example, if an investor were to build a chemical production facility in accordance with host state laws and the host state refused to issue the applicable operational, business or work permits or other regulatory approvals in order to allow the plant to operate, that could be considered expropriatory. The better view is that conduct consisting of an action or omission can be an expropriatory measure.

For responsibility to arise under public international law, the measures in question must be attributable to the state. In cases where the expropriation is effected by some form of government legislation or decree, attribution will not be an issue. Issues of attribution have generally arisen in cases of physical take-over of properties.[92] As in all cases of state responsibility, the claimant must prove 'that the ultimate result was the consequence of the acts or omissions' of state authorities.[93]

§7.10 Do IIAs expand the scope of expropriation?   Since most IIA expropriation provisions do not define expropriation, IIA tribunals have had to address whether IIA expropriation provisions codify customary international law or expand the scope of expropriation. In the NAFTA context, the *Pope & Talbot* and *Myers* tribunals held that the phrase 'a measure tantamount to nationalization or expropriation' in Article 1110, NAFTA does not broaden the ordinary concept of expropriation: tantamount means equivalent.[94] In *Generation Ukraine*,[95] discussing Ukraine-US (1994), the tribunal noted that:

> It is plain that several of the BIT standards, and the prohibition against expropriation in particular, are simply a conventional codification of standards that have long existed in customary international law.[96]

---

92. See discussion in *Tradex Hellas S.A. v. Albania* (Award, 29 Apr. 1999) [*Tradex*] at paras 165 and 200. Also see *Otis Elevator Company v. Iran* (1991) 84 ILR 618.
93. For an overview of principle of attribution in the IIA context see R. Dolzer & C. Schreuer, *Principles of International Investment Law* (Oxford: Oxford University Press, 2008) at 195-205 and McLachlan, Shore & Weiniger, *supra* note 91 at para. 8.73. Also see A. Cohen Smutny, 'State Responsibility and Attribution: When Is a State Responsible for Acts of State Enterprises: Emilio Agustín Maffezini v. The Kingdom of Spain,' in T. Weiler, ed., *International Investment Law and Arbitration: Leading Cases from the ICSID, NAFTA, Bilateral Treaties and Customary International Law* (London: Cameron May, 2005) at 17.
94. *Pope & Talbot, supra* note 28 at para. 104. The tribunal in *S.D. Myers, Inc. v. Canada* (Partial Award, 13 Nov. 2000) [*S.D. Myers*] agreed with this interpretation at para. 286. But see W. M. Reisman & R. D. Sloane, 'Indirect Expropriation and Its Valuation in the BIT Generation' (2003) 74 BYIL 115, who argue at 118-119 that the 'tantamount clause extends the concept of indirect expropriation. The major achievement of the 'tantamount' clause, found in substance in almost all BITs, ... consists in extending the scope of indirect expropriation to an egregious failure to create or maintain the normative 'favourable' conditions in the host state.'
95. *Generation Ukraine, supra* note 22.
96. *Ibid.*, at para. 11.3.

In practice, IIA tribunals have equated IIA expropriation provisions with the scope of expropriation in customary international law.[97] References to 'equivalent,' 'tantamount to expropriation' or 'measures having similar effect' do not expand the scope of expropriation beyond that accepted in customary international law.[98]

Some commentators have argued that IIAs extend the scope of indirect expropriation to an egregious failure to create or maintain normative favourable conditions in the host state.[99] This teleological approach views IIA expropriation provisions as creating new norms. However, in the absence of clear state practice supporting this interpretation, the better view is that the expropriation provisions that appear in the vast majority of IIAs, represent state parties' restatements, of varying brevity, of the customary international law position that expropriation can occur directly or indirectly and in myriad forms.

Formulations such as 'tantamount,' 'equivalent' or 'deprivation' reflect the customary international law position that the analysis focuses on the effect of the government measures, not its form.[100] Further, there is no evidence in state practice that states intended to expand the meaning of expropriation beyond that ascribed to it under customary international law.[101] Rather, in light of uncertainty about the scope of expropriation in customary international law, effects-based definitions have been used out of an abundance of caution to ensure that all potential forms of indirect expropriation are caught.

It would appear that where states have intended to expand the discipline on state measures, they have done so expressly. For example, the Protocol to Germany-USSR (1989), considered in *Sedelmayer*,[102] provides that '[an] investor shall also be entitled to compensation if the other Contracting Party interferes with the economic activities of an enterprise in which he is participating, if his investment is significantly reduced by such interference.'[103] Belgo-Luxembourg Economic Union (BLEU)-Burundi (1989) provides that the state may not take 'any deprivative or restrictive measure or any other measure having a similar effect.'[104] Measures that are restrictive of investment would appear to be broader than those that are expropriatory under customary international law. The formulation in BLEU-Burundi (1989) is arguably exceedingly broad.[105] By definition, almost any government regulation restricts property rights. The treaty provides no

---

97. See *Telenor Mobile Communications A.S. v. Hungary* (Award, 13 Sep. 2006) [*Telenor*] at para. 63.
98. *Ibid.*
99. Reisman & Sloane, *supra* note 94.
100. See §7.13.
101. The 2004 US Model BIT provides in Annex B that the definition of expropriation, 'is intended to reflect customary international law concerning the obligation of States with respect to expropriation.'
102. *Sedelmayer, supra* note 71.
103. *Ibid.*
104. Authors' translation. Art. 4 of the treaty provides: '... ne prendre aucune mesure privative ou restrictive de propriété, ni aucune autre mesure ayant un effet similaire.' See *Goetz, supra* note 70 interpreting this provision.
105. See Paulsson & Douglas, *supra* note 11 at 156.

guidance on the type of restrictions that give rise to compensation and those that are non-compensable regulatory activities.

§7.11 Direct expropriation Direct expropriation arises where there is a forced transfer of property from the investor to the state, or a state-mandated beneficiary.[106] Direct expropriation involves the investor being deprived of property and a corresponding appropriation by the state, or state-mandated beneficiary, of specific property rights.[107]

The most common form of direct expropriation is state acquisition of property for public infrastructure or to pursue national economic policies. A state will be responsible for expropriation where it appropriates an investor's property, unless the taking may be justified in some cases by the legitimate use of state police powers, such as confiscation for breach of criminal law.[108] As highlighted by the tribunal in *Compañiá del Desarrollo de Santa Elena, S.A. v. Costa Rica*,[109] mere public purpose (e.g., the creation of a new national park to preserve an ecologically sensitive area) does not justify uncompensated appropriations.

> Expropriatory environmental measures – no matter how laudable and beneficial to society as a whole – are, in this respect, similar to any other expropriatory measures that a state may take in order to implement its policies: where property is expropriated, even for environmental purposes, whether domestic or international, the state's obligation to pay compensation remains.[110]

A state may not rely on environmental regulations as a way of acquiring and enhancing public infrastructure without payment of compensation.[111] Public purpose is a condition for a legal expropriation; it does not provide an excuse for an uncompensated taking.[112] The fact that government measures indirectly benefit a specific group, such as consumers, or the society generally, however, is insufficient

---

106. *Sempra Energy International v. Argentina* (Award, 28 Sep. 2007) [*Sempra*] at para. 280 and *Enron Corporation and Ponderosa Assets, L.P. v. Argentina* (Award, 22 May 2007) [*Enron*] at para. 243.
107. In *LG&E Energy Corp., LG&E Capital Corp., LG&E International Inc. v. Argentina* (Decision on Liability, 3 Oct. 2006) [*LG&E*], the tribunal referred, at para. 187, to a direct expropriation 'understood as the forcible appropriation by the State of the tangible or intangible property of individuals by means of administrative or legislative action.'
108. See *infra* §7.24.
109. *Compañiá del Desarrollo de Santa Elena, S.A. v. Costa Rica* (Final Award, 17 Feb. 2000) [*Santa Elena*].
110. *Ibid.*, at para. 72.
111. Newcombe, Boundaries, *supra* note 11. See also *Tecmed, supra* note 21 at paras 148-151; *Emilio Agustín Maffezini v. Spain* (Award, 13 Nov. 2000) [*Maffezini*] at paras 65-71; and *Myers, supra* note 94.
112. The tribunal in *Vivendi II, supra* note 69 at para. 7.5.21 made this point succinctly: 'If public purpose automatically immunises the measure from being found to be expropriatory, then there would never be a compensable taking for a public purpose.'

to ground a direct expropriation.[113] A direct expropriation involves appropriation of a tangible or intangible property interest.

Few IIA cases have involved claims of direct expropriation.[114] One of the few is *Sedelmayer*,[115] in which the tribunal held that Russia had expropriated a joint venture's long-term right to use a building by means of a Presidential Decree that ordered the transfer of the property to a government procurement department. The property was subsequently sealed and taken over by Russian authorities. The tribunal held that Russia was required to compensate the investor for the loss of the premises and for the confiscation of business equipment located on the premises even though the Presidential Decree did not extend to movable property.

§7.12 Key principles relating to indirect expropriation IIA jurisprudence to date has identified a series of key principles relevant to analyzing whether there has been indirect expropriation. First, the form of the measure is not determinative nor is the intent of the state. Second, the claimant must establish that the measure in question results in a substantial deprivation. Third, the character of the government measures in question must be taken into account in determining whether a police powers exception applies. Fourth, the investment-backed legitimate expectations of the investor are relevant in assessing whether there has been an indirect expropriation. Finally, the indirect expropriation analysis is context and fact specific. Each of these principles is addressed in turn below.

§7.13 The form of measure is not determinative International expropriation law takes a functional, effects-based approach, to the expropriation analysis: the 'form of the measures of control or interference is less important than the reality of their impact.'[116] The formal status of a government measure will not insulate a measure from scrutiny: there are no blanket exceptions for certain types of state measures. The tribunal in *Pope & Talbot* rightly rejected Canada's argument that non-discriminatory regulations cannot be expropriatory, holding that a blanket exception for regulatory measures would create a 'gaping loophole in international protections against expropriation.'[117] States are not permitted to evade responsibility for *de facto* expropriations simply by characterizing the measure as regulation in the public interest. Equally, it is no defence for the state to characterize its measure as commercial or mercantile rather than a sovereign act; so far as the conduct is attributable to the state, its characterization is not determinative.

---

113. *Sempra, supra* note 106 at para. 280.
114. At the time of writing, visible direct expropriation programmes were being followed by the governments of Venezuela, Ecuador and Bolivia.
115. *Supra* note 71. See K. Hobér, 'Investment Arbitration in Eastern Europe: Recent Cases on Expropriation' (2003) 14 ARIA 377 and K. Hobér, *Investment Arbitration in Eastern Europe: In Search of a Definition of Expropriation, supra* note 11 at 46 *et seq.*
116. *Tippetts, supra* note 30 at 225.
117. *Pope & Talbot, supra* note 28 at para. 99.

§7.14 State intent to expropriate is not a necessary condition   Intent to expropriate is not a necessary element of expropriation.[118] In *Compañiá de Aguas del Aconquija S.A. and Vivendi Universal S.A. v. Argentina*, the tribunal noted that:

> While intent will weigh in favour of showing a measure to be expropriatory, it is not a requirement, because the *effect* of the measure on the investor, not the state's intent, is the critical factor.[119]

In cases of direct expropriation, nationalization or requisition, there is necessarily a convergence of intent and result. The government intends to expropriate and the measure in question carries out the government policy. In *Sempra*,[120] the tribunal noted that cases of direct expropriation involving a transfer of property and ownership require direct intent.[121] By contrast, in cases of indirect expropriation, there may be no discernible intent to expropriate, even though expropriation is an inevitable result of the government measure. Moreover, it might well be impossible for the investor to prove or establish intent on behalf of the state. The essence of the test is whether the measures are attributable to the state under international law. There is no requirement for malice or *culpa*.[122]

Intent, however, is not wholly irrelevant to the judicial determination of whether or not a government measure is expropriatory.[123] A tribunal is more likely to find an expropriation where there is clear evidence of intent to expropriate.[124] Where there is evidence of intent to expropriate, it is unlikely that a state could rely on the good faith exercise of its police powers as justification for non-compensation. Further, where the state relies upon its police powers regulations to justify a deprivation, and no prior specific commitments are being reneged, the regulatory purpose of the measure will be vitally important in assessing whether a non-compensable taking can be justified. Furthermore, the

---

118.   See *Biloune, supra* note 43 at 209 where the tribunal notes that it 'need not establish [the government's] motivations to come to a conclusion in the case.' *Phillips Petroleum Company Iran v. Iran* (Award, 29 Jun. 1989) [*Phillips Petroleum*] at 115. In *Metalclad, supra* note 87, the Tribunal stated, at para. 111, that it 'need not decide or consider the motivation or intent of the adoption of the Ecological Decree.' In *Waste Management II, supra* note 23 at para. 79, the Tribunal notes that there is no general requirement of *mens rea* or intent in Section A, Chapter Eleven, NAFTA (the substantive investment protections) that include national treatment, expropriation and the minimum standard. Also see discussion of intent by Reisman & Sloane, *supra* note 94.

119.   *Vivendi II, supra* note 69 at para. 7.5.20, referring to *Tippetts, supra* note 30 at 225-226; *Phillips Petroleum, ibid.*, at 97-98; *Tecmed, supra* note 21; *Occidental, supra* note 82 at para. 186; *Metalclad, supra* note 87 at para. 111; and *Pope & Talbot, supra* note 28 at para. 181.

120.   *Sempra, supra* note 106.

121.   *Ibid.*, at para. 282.

122.   R. Higgins, *Problems and Process: International Law and How We Use It* (New York; Oxford: Oxford University Press, 1994) at 159-165.

123.   On this point see C. Lévesque, *supra* note 11 at 66.

124.   Evidence of intent has been an issue in many indirect expropriation cases. See K. Byrne, 'Regulatory Expropriation and State Intent' (2000) CYIL 89.

absence or presence of intent or motive can be a relevant factor when assessing damages.[125]

§7.15 Creeping expropriation The term creeping expropriation is used to refer to an indirect expropriation that occurs as a result of a series of measures taken over time that cumulatively have an expropriatory effect, rather than a single measure or group of measures that occur at one time. The tribunal in *Generation Ukraine* defined creeping expropriation as:

> … a form of indirect expropriation with a distinctive temporal quality in the sense that it encapsulates the situation whereby a series of acts attributable to the State *over a period of time* culminate in the expropriatory taking of such property.[126]

State responsibility for creeping expropriation is reflected in the concept of a composite act, defined in Article 15(1) of the ILC's Articles on State Responsibility as follows:

> The breach of an international obligation by a State through a series of actions or omissions defined in aggregate as wrongful occurs when the action or omission occurs which, taken with the other actions or omissions, is sufficient to constitute the wrongful act.[127]

Unlike direct or indirect expropriations that might occur through one clearly identifiable and discrete measure, creeping expropriations are often identified only with hindsight:

> Discrete acts, analyzed in isolation rather than in the context of the overall flow of events, may, whether legal or not in themselves, seem innocuous vis-à-vis a potential expropriation. Some may not be expropriatory in themselves. Only in retrospect will it become evident that those acts comprised part of an accretion of deleterious acts and omissions, which in the aggregate expropriated the foreign investor's property rights.[128]

---

125. For example, in *Desert Line Projects LLC v. Yemen* (Award, 6 Feb. 2008) [*Desert Line*], the tribunal ordered moral damages as a corollary to its finding of malicious acts by the state.
126. *Generation Ukraine, supra* note 22 at para. 20.22. The tribunal continued at para. 20.26: 'A plea of creeping expropriation must proceed on the basis that the investment existed at a particular point in time and that subsequent acts attributable to the State have eroded the investor's rights to its investment to an extent that is violative of the relevant international standard of protection against expropriation.' In *Telenor*, the tribunal defined creeping expropriation as 'involving a series of acts over a period of time none of which is itself of sufficient gravity to constitute an expropriatory act but all of which taken together produce the effects of expropriation.' *Telenor, supra* note 97 at para. 63.
127. See *Siemens A.G. v. Argentina* (Award, 6 Feb. 2007) [*Siemens*] at paras 262-266, and *Enron, supra* note 106.
128. Reisman & Sloane, *supra* note 94 at 123-124.

IIA tribunals tend to ascertain creeping expropriation by reference to the cumulative effect of distinct acts and omissions or a totality of evidence.[129]

§7.16 The requirement for a substantial deprivation A substantial deprivation is a necessary *factual* predicate for a determination of *legal* liability for expropriation.[130] IIA tribunals, in common with customary international law authorities, have adopted an effects-based substantial deprivation requirement for a finding of expropriation.[131] The deprivation of property must be severe, fundamental or substantial and not ephemeral. This will necessarily be a case-by-case analysis.[132]

The analysis is complicated by three factors. First, although tribunals have consistently held that the deprivation must be severe and not ephemeral, cases have eschewed numerical thresholds. This is understandable – saying that a deprivation of 90% of the value of an investment is expropriatory, but that an 89% deprivation of the value is not expropriatory, would simply be arbitrary. Second, how the investment is characterized can be determinative to the deprivation analysis. Whether there has been a deprivation or not may well depend on how widely or narrowly the tribunal characterizes the investment in question.[133] Third, even a severe deprivation may be justified on the basis of police powers.[134]

IIA tribunals have consistently highlighted the requirement for a substantial deprivation, as the following statements attest:

- under international law, expropriation requires a 'substantial deprivation';[135]
- *the affected property* must be impaired to such an extent that it must be seen as 'taken';[136]
- a lasting removal of the ability of an owner to make use of its economic rights;[137]
- open, deliberate and acknowledged takings of property, such as outright seizure or formal or obligatory transfer of title in favour of the host State, but also covert or incidental interference with the use of property which has the effect of depriving the owner, in whole or in significant part, of the use

---

129. See *Eureko, supra* note 7 at paras 222 and 227; *Saluka, supra* note 12 at paras 497-505.
130. Paulsson & Douglas, *supra* note 11.
131. *M.C.I. Power Group L.C. and New Turbine, Inc. v. Ecuador* (Award, 31 Jul. 2007) at para. 300. See *Telenor, supra* note 97 at para. 65; *LG&E, supra* note 107 at paras 188-191; *Enron, supra* note 106 at para. 245.
132. See *infra* §7.28.
133. For example, assume that an investment involves both manufacturing and distribution but that distribution activities account for only 10% of the entire investment. Is a government measure that destroys the distribution business expropriatory?
134. See *infra* §7.24.
135. *Pope & Talbot, supra* note 28 at para. 102.
136. *GAMI Investment, Inc. v. Mexico* (Final Award, 15 Nov. 2004) at para. 126.
137. *Myers, supra* note 94 at paras 282 and 283.

or reasonably-to-be-expected economic benefit of property even if not necessarily to the obvious benefit of the host State;[138]

- substantial deprivation of the entire investment or a substantial part of the investment;[139]
- substantial deprivation of rights;[140]
- radically deprived of the economical use and enjoyment of its investments, as if the rights related thereto ... had ceased to exist;[141]
- effectively neutralize the benefit of the property of the foreign owner;[142]
- the negative effect of government measures on the investor's property rights, which does not involve a transfer of property but a deprivation of the enjoyment of the property;[143]
- that the investor no longer be in control of its business operation, or that the value of the business have been virtually annihilated.[144]

The deprivation in question must amount to a lasting removal of the ability of an owner to make use of its economic rights.[145] The deprivation must be intense and enduring.[146] The degree of permanence required is fact specific. In *Wena Hotels Limited v. Egypt*, exclusion from management of a hotel for a period of a year, despite the subsequent re-entry into the hotel by the investor, was held to be expropriatory.[147] In *Middle East Cement Shipping and Handling Co. S.A. v. Egypt*, the revocation of a license that deprived the investor of rights granted under the license for four months, was held to be expropriatory.[148] In contrast, in *Myers*, the tribunal found that a ban on exports for eighteen months did not amount to an expropriation.[149] IIA jurisprudence has not established a formula for temporal duration of measures – each case will depend on its particular facts.[150]

Many IIA expropriation claims have been rejected because the claimant has failed to establish that, as a matter of fact, it suffered a substantial deprivation.[151]

---

138. *Metalclad, supra* note 87 at para. 103.
139. *Eastern Sugar B.V. v. Czech Republic* (Partial Award, 27 Mar. 2007).
140. *Sempra, supra* note 106 at para. 284.
141. *Tecmed, supra* note 21 at para. 115.
142. *CME* Partial Award, *supra* note 87 at para. 604.
143. *Parkerings-Compagniet AS v. Lithuania* (Award, 11 Sep. 2007) [*Parkerings*].
144. *Sempra, supra* note 106 at para. 285.
145. *Myers, supra* note 94 at para. 283.
146. *LG&E, supra* note 107 at para. 190.
147. *Wena Hotels Limited v. Egypt* (Award, 8 Dec. 2000) [*Wena*]. It is unclear from the facts in *Wena* the extent to which the investor was able to obtain any economic benefit from its subsequent re-entry.
148. *Middle East Cement Shipping and Handling Co. S.A. v. Egypt* (Award, 12 Apr. 2002) [*Middle East*].
149. *Myers, supra* note 94.
150. See Hoffman, *supra* note 11.
151. *CMS Gas Transmission Company v. Argentina* (Award, 12 May 2005) at 260-264 [*CMS*], concluding that the company where CMS invested was able to continue operations; *Azurix Corp. v. Argentina* (Award, 14 Jul. 2006) [*Azurix*] at para. 320-321 concluding that management of the concession company had been affected, but not sufficiently for a finding of

Tribunals have found that there is no substantial deprivation where the investment is impaired, but the investor maintains overall control of its investment.

IIA tribunals have only found indirect expropriations in a handful cases, including the following:

- In *Wena*,[152] the tribunal found an expropriation based on Egypt's forcible seizure of Wena's two hotels, followed by its illegal possession of the hotels for nearly a year during which time it stripped them of fixtures and furniture;[153]
- In *Goetz*, the tribunal found that the government's revocation of a certificate of 'zone franche' was expropriatory;[154]
- In *Metalclad*,[155] the investor had obtained the necessary federal permits to operate a waste landfill. The local municipality subsequently denied a construction permit to the investor and the facility was forced to close. Later, the state governor issued an ecological decree that had the effect of barring the operation of the facility.[156] The tribunal held that there had been an expropriation on two distinct grounds. First, the federal authorities had granted the necessary approvals for the facility and the municipality had acted outside its authority and inconsistently with clear representations by not issuing a building permit.[157] Thus, Metalclad's investment had been subject to arbitrary interference because Mexican authorities had represented that Metalclad would obtain all necessary approvals. Second, the tribunal found in the alternative that the ecological decree itself was expropriatory.
- In *Tecmed*,[158] the tribunal found that the Mexican government's failure to renew the hazardous waste landfill permit held by the investor's subsidiary was expropriatory. As a result of the non-renewal of the permit, the 'economic and commercial operations in the landfill after such denial have been fully and irrevocably destroyed.'[159]

---

expropriation. Also see *LG&E, supra* note 107 at paras 188-191; *Enron, supra* note 106 at paras 258-272; and *BG Group Plc. v. Argentina* (Final Award, 24 Dec. 2007) at para. 269.

152. *Wena, supra* note 147.
153. *Wena, ibid.*, at para. 99. See Z. Douglas, 'The Hybrid Foundations of Investment Treaty Arbitration' (2003) 74 BYIL 151 [Douglas, Hybrid Foundations] at 206-207 criticizing the tribunal's failure to address the legal status of the hotel leases under Egyptian law and noting that if Egypt were entitled to terminate the leases because of breaches by Wena, there would have been no investment to expropriate because the leases were governed by Egyptian law. See *supra* Chapter 2 on the applicability of domestic law in defining investment rights.
154. *Goetz, supra* note 70.
155. *Metalclad, supra* note 87.
156. In its petition to the British Columbia Supreme Court to set aside the *Metalclad* award, Mexico disputed many of the tribunal's factual findings. See *Mexico v. Metalclad* (2001) 5 ICSID Rep 236.
157. *Metalclad, supra* note 87 at paras 106 and 107.
158. *Tecmed, supra* note 21.
159. *Ibid.*, at para. 117.

- In *Middle East*,[160] the tribunal found an expropriation as the result of the annulment of a ten year authorization for the import and storage of bulk cement,[161] as well as the seizure and auction of a ship.[162]
- In *CME*,[163] the tribunal found that changes to a business joint venture resulted from government coercion and that the changes caused the destruction of the investment's commercial value.[164] In particular, the loss occurred because the investor was deprived of a business arrangement under which it was to have the exclusive use of a broadcasting license.[165]
- In *Eureko*,[166] the tribunal held that Poland had deprived the investor of the benefits of its contractual right to acquire a controlling stake in an insurance company.[167]

Where an investor claims indirect expropriation as a result of a measure or the cumulative effect of a series of measures – a creeping expropriation[168] – it may be very difficult for the tribunal to make a factual determination of the extent to which there has been a deprivation. This is particularly true where the claimant has not used any local remedies. In *Generation Ukraine*, the tribunal noted that:

> The fact that an investment has become worthless obviously does not mean that there was an act of expropriation; investment always entails risk. Nor is it sufficient for the disappointed investor to point to some governmental initiative, or inaction, which might have contributed to his ill fortune. Yet again, it is not enough for an investor to seize upon an act of maladministration, no matter how low the level of the relevant governmental authority; to abandon his investment without any effort at overturning the administrative fault; and thus to claim an international delict on the theory that there had been an uncompensated virtual expropriation. In such instances, an international tribunal may deem that the failure to seek redress from national authorities disqualifies the international claim, not because there is a requirement of *exhaustion* of local remedies but because the very reality of conduct tantamount to expropriation is doubtful

---

160. *Middle East, supra* note 148.
161. *Ibid.*, at para. 104.
162. *Ibid.*, at para. 131.
163. *CME* Partial Award, *supra* note 87.
164. *CME* Partial Award, *ibid.*, at paras 599 and 609.
165. The tribunal's decision is based on the fact that the investor's right to the exclusive use of the broadcasting license was replaced with the 'use of the know-how of the License.' According to the tribunal, this resulted in the destruction of the legal basis for CME's investment (*ibid.*). In Hybrid Foundations, *supra* note 153 at 202-205, Douglas criticizes the tribunal's finding that use of the know-how was worthless. The agreement was governed by Czech law and the tribunal failed to consider and apply domestic law to the interpretation of 'use of the know-how.' See *supra* Chapter 2 on the applicability of domestic law in defining investment rights.
166. *Eureko, supra* note 7.
167. *Ibid.*, at paras 240-241.
168. See *supra* §7.15.

in the absence of a *reasonable* – not necessarily exhaustive – effort by the investor to obtain correction.[169]

§7.17 Categorizing the object of the deprivation and the question of partial expropriation   Determining whether there has been a substantial or significant deprivation will necessarily depend on the categorization of what has been taken and whether it is possible to divide the investment into identifiable, distinct property rights or investments.[170] This determination is relatively straight forward in cases of physical property. If a transportation company has 100 trucks and 10 are taken as a result of a government measure, there will have been a complete deprivation of 10 trucks. The issue is not whether the taking of 10 trucks is a substantial deprivation of the entire investment of 100 trucks. In this case, each truck may be a separate investment that can be expropriated.

Situations involving the deprivation of intangible rights or of one of the bundle of rights associated with tangible property are conceptually much more difficult. For example, to what extent can a zoning restriction on land, be characterized as a taking of the use of the land in question? In the context of US domestic takings jurisprudence, Margaret Radin has referred to this issue as 'conceptual severance':

> To apply conceptual severance one delineates a property interest consisting of just what the government action has removed from the owner, and then asserts that that particular whole thing has been permanently taken. Thus, this strategy hypothetically or conceptually 'severs' from the whole bundle of rights just those strands that are interfered with by the regulation, and then hypothetically or conceptually construes those strands in the aggregate as a separate whole thing.[171]

In other words, if a tribunal finds that the right affected by a government measure is an investment, then *ipso facto* there is a substantial deprivation of that investment. US takings jurisprudence has adopted the 'parcel as a whole rule,' which provides that the property owner cannot divide its bundle of property rights and argue that the strand affected by the regulation has been taken.[172] For instance, in the truck example above, an individual truck would qualify as an investment. A case of conceptual severance would involve postulating that a pollution emissions regulation that prevents trucks from being operated on a highway amounts to a

---

169. *Generation Ukraine, supra* note 22 at para. 20.30.
170. In *Fireman's Fund, supra* note 87 at para. 176, the tribunal noted that an expropriation involves: 'a substantially complete deprivation of the economic use and enjoyment of the rights to the property, or of identifiable distinct part thereof (i.e., it approaches total impairment).'
171. M.J. Radin, 'The Liberal Conception of Property: Crosscurrents in the Jurisprudence of Takings,' in *Reinterpreting Property*, ed. M.J. Radin (Chicago: The University of Chicago Press, 1993) at 127-128.
172. *Tahoe-Sierra Preservation Council, Inc. v. Tahoe Regional Planning Agency* (2002) 122 S. Ct 1465.

deprivation of the use of the trucks. If this approach is used, any regulation that restricts the use of an investment in some way can be characterized as a taking.

The characterization of what has been taken is therefore a key and sometimes a conceptually difficult part of substantial deprivation analysis, particularly where an investment can be segregated into discrete economic activities (production, distribution, marketing etc.). A foreign enterprise will often consist of a number of discrete investments (e.g., land, equipment, inventory and contracts) capable of expropriation. Tribunals have noted that an expropriation may involve the enterprise as a whole or the expropriation of an identifiable part of the enterprise:

> It is open to the Tribunal to find a breach of Article 1110 in a case where certain facts are relied on to show the wholesale expropriation of an enterprise but the facts establish the expropriation of certain assets only. Accordingly the Tribunal will consider first the standard set by Article 1110, in particular for conduct tantamount to an expropriation, then whether the enterprise as a whole was subjected to conduct in breach of Article 1110, and finally whether (even if there was no wholesale expropriation of the enterprise as such) the facts establish a partial expropriation.[173]

In *GAMI*, the tribunal referred to the statement by the tribunal in *Pope & Talbot* that an impairment of economic value is only expropriatory if the degree of impairment is equivalent to expropriation.[174] It then asked:

> Should *Pope & Talbot* be understood to mean that property is taken only if it is so affected in its entirety? That question cannot be answered properly before asking: *what property*? The taking of 50 acres of a farm is equally expropriatory whether that is the whole farm or just a fraction. The notion must be understood as this: *the affected property* must be impaired to such an extent that it must be seen as 'taken.'[175]

Thus, a fundamental issue in the expropriation analysis is the characterization of the affected property. This, in turn, requires an analysis of the extent to which the affected property can be severed or segregated into distinct parts from the rest of the investment. This analysis will necessarily be context specific.[176] Relevant facts will include whether the applicable law recognizes the right or interest in question as a distinct property right, how the investment is legally structured and operated, the extent to which elements of the investment are treated as distinct in the applicable law (e.g., for the purposes of regulation and taxation) and, as discussed below, the purpose of the measure and the investor's legitimate investment-backed

---

173. *Waste Management II, supra* note 23 at para. 141. Also see *Myers, supra* note 94 at para. 283.
174. *GAMI, supra* note 135 at para. 125.
175. *Ibid.*, at para. 126.
176. A parallel may be drawn from the conceptual categories made in many IIAs, especially in the context of fair and equitable treatment and freedom from arbitrary or discriminatory impairment. There, many IIAs distinguish between different investment operations – from establishment, acquisition and expansion, to operation, use and management, to disposal, sale or alienation of the investment.

expectations. The tendency has been for tribunals to consider that the investment must be viewed as a whole.[177] In contrast, if there has been a taking of a specific asset, such as a ship in *Middle East*, or specific contractual right, such as in *Eureko*, that qualified as investment in its own right, tribunals have found that there was an expropriation of the specific investment in question.[178]

§7.18 Legitimate and reasonable expectations   In addition to an assessment of the character of the government measure, the legitimate expectations of the investor are an important element in assessing whether government action is expropriatory. Legitimate expectations will primarily be manifested in the investor's concrete investment. The investor will expect to be able to exercise its acquired rights as crystallized in the tangible and intangible interests acquired under host state law.[179] The interests acquired will be subject to the law of the *lex situs* and the scope and nature of the legitimate expectations have to be assessed accordingly. Although legitimate expectations are an important factor, as noted by the tribunal in *Sempra*, they do not make the test for indirect expropriation less stringent.[180]

The legitimate expectations of the investor must also be assessed in the context that investments are made for commercial returns and inevitably involve risk. IIAs are not insurance policies.[181] In *Waste Management II*, the tribunal noted that, with respect to the expropriation provision in NAFTA, its function was not to 'compensate for failed business ventures, absent arbitrary intervention by the State amounting to a virtual taking or sterilizing of the enterprise.'[182] In *Fireman's Fund*, the tribunal found that the investor's investment in debentures was almost valueless, not because of government conduct, but because of the economic circumstances prevailing at the time.[183]

In certain cases, the investment in question may have been made on the basis of express state representations or commitments. If the government subsequently takes action contrary to those commitments, is that action to be considered expropriatory? There is authority for this proposition. The *Methanex* award highlights the importance of government undertakings and assurances in assessing the reasonable expectations of investors:

> ... as a matter of general international law, a non-discriminatory regulation for a public purpose, which is enacted in accordance with due process and,

---

177.   See *Telenor, supra* note 97 at para. 67 and *Azurix Corp v. Argentina* (Decision on Jurisdiction, 8 Dec. 2003) at para. 65.
178.   See U. Kriebaum, 'Partial Expropriation' (2007) 8 JWIT 69 and U. Kriebaum, 'Regulatory Takings: Balancing the Interests of the Investor and the State' (2007) 8 JWIT 717.
179.   See *supra* Chapter 2 on domestic law as applicable law.
180.   *Sempra, supra* note 106 at para. 288.
181.   *MTD Equity Sdn. Bhd.* and *MTD Chile S.A. v. Chile* (Award, 25 May 2004) at para. 178. and *Maffezini, supra* note 111 at para. 69.
182.   *Waste Management II, supra* note 23 at 160. Also see *General Ukraine, supra* note 22 at para. 20.30 and *Robert Azinian, Kenneth Davitian, & Ellen Baca v. Mexico* (Award, 1 Nov. 1999) [*Azinian*] at paras 83, 87 and 90-91.
183.   *Fireman's Fund, supra* note 87 at para. 199.

which affects, inter alios, a foreign investor or investment is not deemed expropriatory and compensable *unless specific commitments had been given by the regulating government to the then putative foreign investor contemplating investment that the government would refrain from such regulation.* [Emphasis added.][184]

In *EnCana*, the investor claimed that a denial of a tax refund was itself expropriatory (a direct expropriation claim) and also had an equivalent effect to the expropriation of the investment (an indirect expropriation). The tribunal denied the claim and stated that in the 'absence of a specific commitment from the host state, the foreign investor has neither the right nor any legitimate expectation that the tax regime will not change, perhaps to its disadvantage....'[185] The question of whether the denial of a statutory right to refund is expropriatory is considered at §7.22 below.

Although state commitments or representations with respect to an investment are an important aspect of the expropriation analysis, legitimate expectations based on these commitments or representations would not normally be, in and of themselves, acquired rights under host state laws. Where the state fails to honour its commitments or representations, but there is no substantial deprivation of the underlying acquired rights, the investor's claim is better framed as a denial of fair and equitable treatment or breach of another minimum standard.[186]

§7.19 The relationship between domestic law and expropriation The rights associated with any investment are normally determined by local law.[187] Thus, the nature and scope of property rights are determined by the law of the state in which the property is located (the *lex situs*). Conceptually, property can only be expropriated if it exists. If a right was never acquired or has been otherwise extinguished under local law, it cannot be expropriated. *Azinian*, the first NAFTA investment arbitration, addressed this issue.[188] In *Azinian*, Mexican courts had held that a municipality's cancellation of a waste disposal concession was valid on a number of grounds, including misrepresentations by the investor and non-performance. The NAFTA tribunal found there was no basis for an expropriation claim as the contract was governed by Mexican law and the Mexican courts had determined that the concession was invalid. As the investor did not claim that the Mexican courts had committed a denial of justice or that the Mexican law governing public service concessions under which the concession was held invalid was itself expropriatory, there simply was no breach of Mexico's investment guarantees.

Azinian underlines a fundamental issue. Where the investment in question is a contract governed by host state law and the contract is invalid or otherwise nullified based on the host state law, in principle there can be no expropriation

---

184. *Methanex, supra* note 87 at para. 7, Part IV-Chapter D.
185. *EnCana, supra* note 81 at para. 173.
186. See *supra* Chapter 6 on minimum standards of treatment.
187. See *supra* Chapter 2 for a discussion of domestic law as applicable law in IIA disputes.
188. *Azinian, supra* note 182.

because there has been a judicial determination that there is no contract to expropriate. The investor will either have to show that the judicial determination of the contract rights amounted to a denial of justice or that the law in question cancelling or nullifying the contract was itself expropriatory. In this context, the awards in *Wena*, *CME* and *Eureko,* in which tribunals found investments were expropriated, might be criticized for failing to address adequately the specific nature of the contractual rights in question under domestic law.[189] For example, the *CME* tribunal held that the replacement of the 'license-holder's contribution of the License by the worthless "use of the know-how of the License" is nothing else than the destruction of the legal basis ... of the Claimant's investment.'[190] Yet, arguably this conclusion was reached without a proper analysis of why this would necessarily be the case under Czech law. If the right to the 'use of the know-how of the License' was an actionable right under Czech law, the finding of expropriation is questionable.[191]

§7.20 Breach of contract and expropriation[192]   A breach of contract unaccompanied by other government measures does not amount to an expropriation.[193] A foreign investor contracting with a state assumes a risk of breach of contract as with any other commercial actor. However, where the state acts in its capacity as a sovereign and not merely as a contractual party,[194] the question of expropriation arises. In order to establish an expropriation of contractual rights, some form of sovereign conduct, such as a decree or law, is required that nullifies or eviscerates the contractual rights.[195] For example, if the state enacts a law providing that it has no contractual liability under a contract that it has previously entered into notwithstanding the fact that the contract would otherwise be valid under local law, then the state is exercising legislative powers to essentially repudiate contractual obligations. This type of government measure, as in *Middle East*, is expropriatory.[196]

---

189. Douglas, Hybrid Foundations, *supra* note 153 and Z. Douglas, 'Nothing if Not Critical for Investment Treaty Arbitration: Occidental, Eureko and Methanex' (2006) 22 AI 27.
190. *CME, supra* note 87 at para. 593.
191. In *EnCana*, the dissenting arbitrator suggested that the IIA determines the scope of investment, not local law. *Supra* note 81. See *supra* Chapter 2 for analysis on domestic law as applicable law in IIA disputes.
192. See generally, García-Amador, Fourth Report, *supra* note 2, which opines that if the contract is governed by international law, non-performance of its obligations gives rise to state responsibility. Further, see S.M. Schwebel, 'On Whether Breach of Contract With an Alien is a Breach of International Law' *reprinted in Justice in International Law: Selected Writings of Stephen M Schwebel* (Cambridge: Cambridge University Press, 1994) at 425.
193. *Parkerings, supra* note 143 at paras 440-447; *Azurix, supra* note 151 at para. 314; *Phillips Petroleum, supra* note 118 at para. 75; *Southern Pacific Properties (Middle East) Limited v. Egypt* (Award on the Merits, 20 May 1992) [*SPP*]; *Sempra, supra* note 106 at para. 281; and *Vivendi II, supra* note 69 at para. 7.5.4.
194. *Consortium RFCC, supra* note 87 at para. 65.
195. *SGS Société Générale de Surveillance v. Philippines* (Decision of the Tribunal on Objections to Jurisdiction, 29 Jan. 2004) [*SGS*] at para. 161.
196. *Middle East, supra* note 160.

Where the government, however, breaches or fails to perform a contract under local law acting as any other commercial party might under a contract, the foreign investor's remedy is arguably that which would exist for a breach of contract.

In *Waste Management II*, involving various alleged state breaches of a waste disposal concession, the tribunal stated:

> … it is one thing to expropriate a right under a contract and another to fail to comply with the contract. Non-compliance by a government with contractual obligations is not the same thing as, or equivalent or tantamount to, an expropriation. In the present case the Claimant did not lose its contractual rights, which it was free to pursue before the contractually chosen forum. The law of breach of contract is not secreted in the interstices of Article 1110 of NAFTA. Rather it is necessary to show an effective repudiation of the right, unredressed by any remedies available to the Claimant, which has the effect of preventing its exercise entirely or to a substantial extent.[197]

Where the investor's complaint is essentially that the state has breached its contract, but contractual rights have not been denied by a sovereign government measure or otherwise (e.g., by a persistent bad faith failure to comply) and the investor is able to pursue its contractual rights in the contractually agreed forum, then arguably an expropriation has not occurred. As noted by the tribunal in *EnCana*: 'Like private parties, governments do not repudiate obligations merely by contesting their existence.'[198] A repudiation may exist where a state persistently refuses or fails to comply and there is no good faith underlying dispute on the existence of the contractual right in question, but rather a political decision not to honour the contract.

In *Vivendi II*, the tribunal found that rights under a water and waste concession had been expropriated where there was a destructive, state-initiated campaign against the investment. In the words of the tribunal, there were a series of 'sovereign acts designed illegitimately to end the concession or to force its renegotiation.'[199] The tribunal found that the investment's principal contractual right was to invoice customers for services provided in accordance with the concession. Various state acts, including persistent steps taken by the Province of Tucumán to prevent the collection of payments due for services from customers,[200] deprived the investor of the right to operate the concession and be compensated in accordance with the concession's established tariffs. The tribunal found an expropriation notwithstanding that the concession had been terminated by the concessionaire. The tribunal found that, even before termination, the contractual rights had been rendered worthless and losses would only continue to mount. In other words, the termination of the contract was a reasonable step to avoid further losses.

---

197.   *Waste Management II, supra* note 23 at para. 175.
198.   *EnCana, supra* note 81 at para. 192.
199.   *Vivendi II, supra* note 69 at para. 7.5.22.
200.   *Ibid.*, at para. 7.6.2. The tribunal refers to this as the 'most important of the Province's breaches.'

In *Siemens*, the tribunal found that an Argentine decree terminating a contract was an expropriatory act.[201] The tribunal found that this was an exercise of public power, not the action of a contracting party terminating a contract for mere non-performance.

The normal remedy for breach of contract will be for the claimant to sue in the contractually agreed forum. In *Parkerings*, the tribunal suggested that investors faced with a breach of contract should, as a general rule, sue the state in the appropriate forum.[202] If the claimant is denied the right to seek remedies before local courts, this might amount to a denial of justice.[203] There is, however, no general requirement to seek remedies before a local court.[204] Indeed, where a state, acting in its sovereign capacity, has expressly nullified contractual rights under local law, local proceedings may well be fruitless. In any case, in such a scenario, a treaty claim would have arisen for which treaty remedies would be available.

In *Eureko*, the tribunal did not distinguish between breach of contract and expropriation. It found that Eureko held the right to acquire a controlling interest in an insurance company that was under state control. The government then changed its privatization strategy, essentially deciding to maintain the company under national control. On these facts, and without an analysis of Polish contract law governing the contract, the tribunal found that the government's refusal to proceed with the sale to be expropriatory, despite the fact that the tribunal did not identify Eureko's rights under domestic law that would have been eviscerated or destroyed. For the tribunal, Poland 'decided to violate the investment of Eureko ... by refusing to honour its legal commitments.'[205] Hence, the tribunal appeared to equate breach of contract with expropriation, when the breach is a conscious refusal to honour contractual obligations motivated not by a contractual dispute, but for political reasons. However, the tribunal noted that the 'Statement of Claim does not allege expropriation as such'[206] and the claimant does not appear to have argued that the Polish measures had destroyed its contractual rights. The *Eureko* tribunal's finding of expropriation may be viewed as an application of expropriation law to a situation where other investment treaty protections, namely the umbrella clause,[207] may have been more apposite.[208]

Although the jurisprudence tends to dissimilate the basis for international responsibility in cases of breaches of contract from expropriation, there is assimilation in the analysis related to reparation. When a breach of contract amounts to an internationally

---

201. *Siemens, supra* note 127 at para. 271.
202. *Parkerings, supra* note 143 at para. 448.
203. *Azinian, supra* note 182 at para. 100.
204. See, however, statement in *Generation Ukraine, supra* note 169.
205. *Supra* note 7 at para. 224.
206. *Ibid.*, at para. 238.
207. See *infra* Chapter 9, Observance of Undertakings.
208. It is a separate question whether a discriminatory or arbitrary breach of contract, or a breach of contract for non-commercial reasons, gives rise to international responsibility under minimum standards such as fair and equitable treatment. See *supra* Chapter 6, Minimum Standards of Treatment.

wrongful act,[209] then reparation under international law will be due and payable: 'breaches of development or concession contracts are similar to, and often allied with, expropriations ... and international law tends to treat the two similarly.'[210]

§7.21 Debt contracts and expropriation   The mere refusal to pay a debt based on contract unaccompanied by other government measures is not expropriatory. Something more than mere refusal is required. In *SGS Philippines*, the tribunal noted that:

> In the Tribunal's view, on the material presented by the Claimant no case of expropriation has been raised. Whatever debt the Philippines may owe to SGS still exists; whatever right to interest for late payment SGS had it still has. There has been no law or decree enacted by the Philippines attempting to expropriate or annul the debt, nor any action tantamount to an expropriation. The Tribunal is assured that the limitation period for proceedings to recover the debt before the Philippine courts under Article 12 has not expired. A mere refusal to pay a debt is not an expropriation of property, at least where remedies exist in respect of such a refusal. A fortiori a refusal to pay is not an expropriation where there is an unresolved dispute as to the amount payable.[211]

Where a state measure cancels a pre-existing liability to an investor, however, an expropriation may arise.[212] However, a mere denial to pay a liability is not expropriatory:

> Under a bilateral investment treaty executive agencies must be able to take positions on disputable questions of local law, provided that they act in good faith, the courts are available to resolve the resulting dispute, and judicial decisions adverse to the executive are complied with.[213]

> The mere non-performance of a contractual obligation is not to be equated with a taking of property, nor (unless accompanied by other elements) is it tantamount to expropriation ... [T]he normal response by an investor

---

209.   See *Waste Management II*, *supra* note 23 at para. 145 *et seq.* Section 712 of the Third Restatement, *supra* note 52, provides that: 'A state is responsible under international law for injury resulting from: ... (2) a repudiation or breach by the state of a contract with a national of another state (a) where the repudiation or breach is (i) discriminatory; or (ii) motivated by noncommercial considerations, and compensatory damages are not paid; or (b) where the foreign national is not given an adequate forum to determine his claim of repudiation or breach, or is not compensated for any repudiation or breach determined to have occurred ... .'

210.   Third Restatement, *ibid.*, Reporter's Note 9. This assimilation of breach of contract to expropriation has remained mainly unchallenged: D.W. Bowett, 'State Contracts with Aliens: Contemporary Developments on Compensation for Termination or Breach' (1988) 59 BYIL 49. See *Československá Obchodní Banka A.S. v. Slovak Republic* (Award, 29 Dec. 2004) [*CSOB*] at paras 219-368, which awarded full compensation for breach of contract.

211.   *SGS, supra* note 195.

212.   *EnCana, supra* note 81 at para. 183.

213.   *EnCana, ibid.*, at para. 200, footnote 138.

faced with a breach of contract by its governmental counter-party (the breach not taking the form of an exercise of governmental prerogative, such as a legislative decree) is to sue in the appropriate court to remedy the breach. It is only where such access is practically or legally foreclosed that the breach could amount to an outright denial of the right, and the protection of Article 1110 would be called into play.[214]

Thus, where the state repudiates its liability or the investor has no local remedies to challenge the breach, there will be a strong case for expropriation. A refusal by the state to pay an established liability will be evidence of the substantial deprivation necessary for an expropriation. The question is whether there was a 'final refusal to pay (combined with effective obstruction and denial of legal remedies)'[215] or the refusal to pay is accompanied by bad faith or other elements permitting refusal to be equated with a repudiation of contractual obligations.

§7.22 Payments under statutory obligations and expropriation   An investor may claim that it is entitled under host state law to a payment, such as a subsidy, a tax refund or other financial benefit, and that non-payment constitutes an expropriation. For example, in *EnCana*, the investor claimed that it was entitled to a refund of value added tax (VAT) and that the refusal by Ecuadorian taxation authorities to refund the amount claimed amounted to an expropriation. The majority of the tribunal rejected the claim, stating that:

> ... there is nonetheless a difference between a questionable position taken by the executive in relation to a matter governed by the local law and a definitive determination contrary to law. In terms of the BIT the executive is entitled to take a position in relation to claims put forward by individuals, even if that position may turn out to be wrong in law, provided it does so in good faith and stands ready to defend its position before the courts. Like private parties, governments do not repudiate obligations merely by contesting their existence. An executive agency does not expropriate the value represented by a statutory obligation to make a payment or refund by mere refusal to pay, provided at least that (a) the refusal is not merely willful, (b) the courts are open to the aggrieved private party, (c) the courts' decisions are not themselves overridden or repudiated by the State.[216]

In his dissenting opinion, Dr Horacio Grigera Naón stated that the right to a VAT return was a right protected by the IIA in question and that the entitlement crystallizes once the investment has been made.[217] According to Grigera Naón, EnCana was denied a tax refund, a distinct return on its investment and an asset within the meaning of the investment, protected by the IIA. In his view 'a return

---

214. *Waste Management II, supra* note 23 at para. 174.
215. *Ibid.,* at para. 176.
216. *EnCana, supra* note 81 at para. 194.
217. *Ibid.,* Dissenting Opinion at para. 23.

is expropriated when adversely affected in a substantial way by a measure or string of measures.'[218]

In response, the majority of the tribunal commented:

> ... the question is the narrow one, whether the denial of an incidental public law right (in an unclear, nascent domestic taxation regime) by an executive organ acting in good faith amounts to the expropriation of that right.... Under a bilateral investment treaty executive agencies must be able to take positions on disputable questions of local law, provided that they act in good faith, the courts are available to resolve the resulting dispute, and judicial decisions adverse to the executive are complied with.[219]

The disagreement between the majority and dissenting arbitrator focuses, in part, on the role of national law in IIA disputes. The opinion of the dissenting arbitrator highlights that the investor's legitimate expectations are embedded in the BIT, not local law.[220] One difficulty with this analysis is that it suggests that once investments are made, entitlements are crystallized forever. It is difficult to see how this is a legitimate economic expectation, given that there may well be uncertainty in the application of tax laws and that tax and other regulatory laws are often subject to change. If a foreign investor seeks to be protected from the economic effect of tax and regulatory changes, this would normally be obtained through a stabilization clause.

§7.23 Non-expropriatory regulation   In the majority of cases, host state regulatory activity has been found not to be expropriatory for the simple reason that it does not result in a substantial deprivation of the investment – the factual predicate for a claim of expropriation simply does not exist. For example, in a number of the cases against Argentina to date, arising out of measures taken to address its financial crisis, tribunals have denied claims of expropriation on the basis that investors did not suffer a substantial deprivation.[221] Although regulatory measures designed to protect the environment, health, safety or ensure fair competition frequently impose regulatory and compliance costs on an investment, these will not normally reach the threshold of a substantial deprivation. As noted by the *Telenor* tribunal:

> It is well established that the mere exercise by government of regulatory powers that create impediments to business or entail the payment of taxes or other levies does not of itself constitute expropriation.[222]

---

218.   *Ibid.*, at para. 73.
219.   *Ibid.*, at para. 198 at note 138.
220.   *Ibid.*, Dissenting Opinion at para. 23. See *supra* Chapter 2, Applicable Law.
221.   See *supra* note 151. The tribunals in those cases did, however, find breaches of minimum standards of treatment. See *supra* Chapter 6, Minimum Standards of Treatment.
222.   See *Telenor*, *supra* note 97 at para. 64. This fact is reflected in the 2004 US Model BIT, which states that: 'Except in rare circumstances, non discriminatory regulatory actions by a Party that are designed and applied to protect legitimate public welfare objectives, such as public health, safety, and the environment, do not constitute indirect expropriations.'

Similarly, the tribunal in *Waste Management II* noted that: '[the] loss of benefits or expectations is not a sufficient criterion for an expropriation, even if it is a necessary one.'[223]

§7.24 Police powers   Under customary international law, not all deprivations of property are expropriatory. Property may be forfeited under a state's criminal law. Property might be destroyed for reasons of public health. General taxation is not expropriation. In all these cases, a state does not incur responsibility for the legitimate and *bona fide* exercise of sovereign police powers subject to specific commitments or an analysis of proportionality and reasonableness. International law authorities have regularly concluded that no right to compensation arises for reasonably necessary regulations passed for the 'protection of public health, safety, morals or welfare'[224] or for government regulations that are 'non-discriminatory and ... within the commonly accepted taxation and police powers of states.'[225] This view is reflected in international investment instruments such as the MIGA Convention,[226] IIA practice[227] and codifications such as the US Third Restatement[228] and the 1961 Harvard Draft.[229] IIA awards have confirmed that states may justify deprivations based on the exercise of what are called the state's 'police powers,'[230] a term that has historically been used in the context of US takings law.

International authorities recognize three broad categories of police power regulation that might justify non-compensation where there is a deprivation: (i) public order and morality; (ii) protection of human health and the environment; and (iii) state taxation.

---

223.   *Waste Management II, supra* note 23 at para. 159.
224.   Christie, *supra* note 11 at 338.
225.   G.H. Aldrich 'What Constitutes a Compensable Taking of Property? The Decisions of the Iran-United States Claims Tribunal' (1994) 88 AJIL 585 at 609.
226.   Art. 11(a)(ii), *Convention Establishing the Multilateral Investment Guarantee Agency* (1985) 24 ILM 1605 [*MIGA Convention*]: 'with the exception of non-discriminatory measures of general application which governments normally take for the purpose of regulating economic activity in their territories.' See *supra* Chapter 1, §1.29, on MIGA.
227.   See *supra* §7.6.
228.   *Supra* note 52.
229.   *Supra* note 26.
230.   *Saluka, supra* note 12 at paras 253 *et seq.*; *Methanex, supra* note 87 at para. 410; *Myers, supra* note 94 at para. 281-288; *Lauder, supra* note 90 at para. 198; *Tecmed, supra* note 21 at para. 115. In *Saluka, ibid.*, the tribunal noted that the treaty provision on expropriation was drafted very broadly ('Neither Contracting Party shall take any measures depriving, directly or indirectly, investors of the other Contracting Party of their investments'). However, it stated that 'in using the concept of deprivation, Article 5 imports into the Treaty the customary international law notion that a deprivation can be justified if it results from the exercise of regulatory actions aimed at the maintenance of public order.' (para. 254). As noted *supra* in §7.6, some treaties, including the Dutch model, refer to measures that deprive investors directly or indirectly of their investments.

(i) Public order and morality In order to enforce its laws, a state may take property without compensation. Property might be seized and subject to forfeiture if it arises from criminal activities such as smuggling or drug trafficking. In many states it is illegal to possess certain types of goods, such as pornography, drugs, or weapons and no compensation would be due if a state seizes such goods to enforce local laws. [231] Indeed, it is unlikely that any municipal legal systems would even recognize that a person can hold an enforceable property right in illegal goods.[232] Property might also be seized for non-payment of taxes, fines or duties.[233] Further, it may be destroyed or subject to restrictions in times of civil unrest or war.[234]

The tribunal in *Saluka* stated that a 'deprivation can be justified if it results from the exercise of regulatory actions aimed at the maintenance of public order.'[235] It further noted that:

> It is now established in international law that States are not liable to pay compensation to a foreign investor when, in the normal exercise of their regulatory powers, they adopt in a non-discriminatory manner *bona fide* regulations that are aimed at the general welfare.[236]

The *Saluka* tribunal went on to say that:

> ... international law has yet to identify in a comprehensive and definitive fashion precisely what regulations are considered 'permissible' and 'commonly accepted' as falling within the police or regulatory power of States and, thus, noncompensable. In other words, it has yet to draw a bright and easily

231. Not all confiscations or destructions of property can be justified. For example, see *The Case of The 'Phare,'* J.B. Moore, *History and Digest of International Arbitrations* (1898), Vol. V at 4870.
232. See Wortley, *supra* note 10 at 40-45 and *Case of the 'Robert Wilson'* (1841) in J.B. Moore, *History and Digest of International Arbitrations* (1898), Vol. IV at 3373.
233. See *Chazen v. Mexico* (1930) IV RIAA 586 (judicial auction for non-payment of duties) and *Too v. Greater Modesto* (1989) 23 Iran-US CTR 378 [*Too*] (seizure and sale of liquor license to pay overdue withheld taxes). In *Too,* the Tribunal referred to the general principle in §712 of the Third Restatement, *supra* note 52, that a state is not responsible for regulation, forfeiture from crime, or other action of the kind that is commonly considered as within the police powers of states or for loss of property or any other economic disadvantage resulting from *bona fide,* non-discriminatory general taxation.
234. *Parsons (Great Britain v. United States)* (Award, 30 Nov. 1925). In *Parsons,* the destruction of 'poisonous liquors' was held to be within the police power of the government during a rebellion in the Philippines. In *Sea-Land Service Inc. v. Iran* (1984) 6 Iran-US CTR 149, the Iran-US Claims Tribunal held that restrictions on the type of cargo that Sea-Land could unload were a reasonable and legitimate measure during a time of civil unrest. See also Brownlie, *Principles of Public International Law, supra* note 1 at 511-512. But see *De Garmendía* in J.H. Ralston, *Venezuelan Arbitrations of 1903* (Washington, 1904) where compensation was ordered for the destruction of a structure that blocked the customs officials' view of the port, even though the Venezuelan authorities viewed the destruction as necessary as an act of public utility. The destruction in this case could be viewed as the compulsory acquisition of a view easement or servitude on land, for which compensation should be granted.
235. *Saluka, supra* note 12 at para. 254.
236. *Ibid.,* at para. 255.

distinguishable line between non-compensable regulations on the one hand and, on the other, measures that have the effect of depriving foreign investors of their investment and are thus unlawful and compensable in international law.

It thus inevitably falls to the *adjudicator* to determine whether particular conduct by a state 'crosses the line' that separates valid regulatory activity from expropriation. Faced with the question of *when, how and at what point an otherwise valid regulation becomes, in fact and effect, an unlawful expropriation*, international tribunals must consider the circumstances in which the question arises. The context within which an impugned measure is adopted and applied is critical to the determination of its validity.[237]

In *Saluka*, the tribunal found that the investor had been deprived of its investment as a result of the forced administration of a bank. Nevertheless, it found that the Czech National Bank was entitled to take this measure given the critical financial condition of the bank and the potential destabilization that would occur in the Czech Republic.[238]

Although the extent to which regulatory powers may be used to deprive investors of their investments is unclear, there are several key restraints on the use of state regulatory powers. The measure in question must be non-discriminatory,[239] *bona fide* and aimed at the general welfare.[240] More generally, police power regulation will have to conform to minimum standards of treatment. For example, a police powers deprivation could not be justified by a government measure that is arbitrary or breaches international human rights law.

There is likely to be widespread state practice and *opinio juris* with respect to the use of police powers in core areas of criminal law. The scope of police powers in the area of public morality and order, however, are particularly difficult to define. The types of property restrictions that could be supported on the basis of public morality may substantially diverge from state to state. Although the boundary is by no means easy to determine (and there is a paucity of cases in this area), in many situations reference to international standards will be of assistance in determining whether the state measure is reasonable in the circumstances.[241] In the absence of accepted international standards, evidence of consistent and general comparative practice in a variety of states is likely to be relevant, for example, the

---

237. *Ibid.*, at paras 263, 264.
238. *Ibid.*, at paras 266-275.
239. Discrimination might be used in at least three senses: (i) the types of discrimination prohibited under customary international law, such as racial discrimination; (ii) an arbitrary or unjustifiable distinction based on irrelevant criteria (particularly one that favours nationals over foreigners); or (iii) disparate impact or effect. See *supra* Chapter 6 on discriminatory measures.
240. *Fireman's Fund, supra* note 87 at para. 176.
241. For example, a state is unlikely to be able to justify confiscation of a foreign investor's publishing equipment on the basis of the police powers. The scope of legitimate exercise of police powers is limited by customary human rights law and international human rights protections with respect to freedom of expression would be relevant in this type of case.

prevalence of competition laws to ensure fair market practices or consumer protection laws with respect to the safety of consumer products.

(ii) Protection of human health and the environment There are no international expropriation law cases that provide express guidance on when measures designed to protect human health or the environment might justify non-compensation.[242] International legal authorities recognize that governments may need to prohibit and severely regulate certain types of property in order to protect the environment.[243] Property may be confiscated during an epidemic of an infectious disease[244] and presumably destroyed if the situation so requires. For example, in 1894, Brazilian authorities destroyed several lots of watermelons due to an outbreak of cholera. The watermelon producers appealed to Brazilian authorities for compensation. When this claim was dismissed, several of the US producers requested the US government make a claim on their behalf. The US Department of State stated that the measures were justified in the circumstances and that compensation could not be demanded.[245]

(iii) Taxation Taxation is, by definition, an appropriation of property for which there can be no of compensation.[246] International authorities are clear that a significant tax burden may be imposed on an investment. Taxes of fifty percent to sixty percent are common in some countries. At some point, however, international authorities are also clear that taxation can be expropriatory.[247] As noted by the tribunal in *EnCana*:

> In principle a tax law creates a new legal liability on a class of persons to pay money to the State in respect of some defined class of transactions, the money

242. See commentary, *supra* note 11. See also J.M. Wagner, 'International Investment, Expropriation and Environmental Protection' (1999) 29 GGUL Rev 465; H. Mann & K. von Moltke, *NAFTA's Chapter XI and the Environment* (Winnipeg: International Institute for Sustainable Development, 1999) at 39-40; J. Soloway, 'Environmental Regulation as Expropriation' (1999) 33 CBLJ 92; and D. Gantz, 'Reconciling Environmental Protection and Investor Rights Under Chapter 11 of NAFTA' (2001) 31 ELR 10646.

243. In *International Bank*, a tribunal interpreting an Overseas Private Investment Corporation contract held that forest conservation restrictions were a legitimate exercise of government authority and not expropriatory. *International Bank of Washington – Overseas Private Investment Corporation: Arbitration of Dispute Involving U.S. Investment Guaranty Program* (Award, 8 Nov. 1972) [*International Bank*], (1972) 11 ILM 1216. It is important to note, however, that in *International Bank* there was no acquired right to log and it is unclear whether on the facts there was a substantial deprivation.

244. *Bischoff Case* in Ralston, *supra* note 234 at 580. See also *Booker Aquaculture Ltd. & Hydro Seafood GSP Ltd. v. Scottish Ministers* [2003] ECR-1-7411 (finding no deprivation of property rights for destruction of contaminated fish stocks).

245. See J.B. Moore, *International Law Digest*, Vol. VI, Section 1003.

246. The *Oxford English Dictionary* defines 'tax' as 'A compulsory contribution to the support of government, levied on persons, property, income, commodities, transactions, etc., now at fixed rates, mostly proportional to the amount on which the contribution is levied.'

247. See generally A. Kolo & T. Wälde, 'Confiscatory Taxation under Customary International Law and Modern Investment Treaties' (1999) 4 CEPMLP Internet Journal; W. Park, *supra* note 84 at 93; and W. Park, 'Arbitration and the fisc: NAFTA's "tax veto"' (2001) 2 CJIL 231.

to be used for public purposes. In itself such a law is not a taking of property; if it were, a universal State prerogative would be denied by a guarantee against expropriation, which cannot be the case. Only if a tax law is extraordinary, punitive in amount or arbitrary in its incidence would issues of indirect expropriation be raised. In the present case, in any event, the denial of VAT refunds in the amount of 10% of transactions associated with oil production and export did not deny EnCana 'in whole or significant part' the benefits of its investment.[248]

In *Link-Trading Joint Stock Company v. Moldova*, the tribunal, in addressing a claim that changes in customs and tax regulations were expropriatory, held that fiscal measures become expropriatory when they amount to an 'abusive taking.' It then defined abusive in terms of unfairness, arbitrariness and discrimination or the violation of a state undertaking.[249] In *EnCana*, the tribunal split on whether the denial of VAT refunds was expropriatory.[250]

In assessing whether taxation is expropriatory, the interpretive notes to the draft MAI highlight a series of elements to consider:

a) The imposition of taxes does not generally constitute expropriation. The introduction of a new taxation measure, taxation by more than one jurisdiction in respect to an investment, or a claim of excessive burden imposed by a taxation measure are not in themselves indicative of an expropriation.

b) A taxation measure will not be considered to constitute expropriation where it is generally within the bounds of internationally recognised tax policies and practices. When considering whether a taxation measure satisfies this principle, an analysis should include whether and to what extent taxation measures of a similar type and level are used around the world.

c) While expropriation may be constituted even by measures applying generally (e.g., to all taxpayers), such a general application is in practice less likely to suggest an expropriation than more specific measures aimed at particular nationalities or individual taxpayers. A taxation measure would not be expropriatory if it was in force and was transparent when the investment was undertaken.

d) Taxation measures may constitute an outright expropriation, or while not directly expropriatory they may have the equivalent effect of an expropriation (so-called 'creeping expropriation'). Where a taxation measure by itself does not constitute expropriation it would be extremely unlikely to be an element of a creeping expropriation.[251]

---

248. *EnCana, supra* note 81 at para. 177.
249. *Link-Trading Joint Stock Company v. Moldova* (Final Award, 18 Apr. 2002) at paras 64-91.
250. See *supra* §7.22.
251. *MAI, supra* note 56.

§7.25 Proportionality and standard of review in assessing police powers A significant consideration in assessing police power regulations, absent a breach of specific commitments which arguably (if clear and unambiguous) may give rise to a duty to compensate, is the proportionality[252] between the harm that the government measure aims to address and its effect on the investor, in light of the investor's legitimate investment-backed expectations.[253] Are the means applied proportional to the purpose to be achieved? Did the state have less restrictive measures available to it that could have achieved the same result? The tribunal in *Tecmed* stated the issue as follows:

> After establishing that regulatory actions and measures will not be initially excluded from the definition of expropriatory acts, in addition to the negative financial impact of such actions or measures, the Arbitral Tribunal will consider, in order to determine if they are to be characterized as expropriatory, whether such actions or measures are proportional to the public interest presumably protected thereby and to the protection legally granted to investments, taking into account that the significance of such impact has a key role upon deciding the proportionality. Although the analysis starts at the due deference owing to the State when defining the issues that affect its public policy or the interests of society as a whole, as well as the actions that will be implemented to protect such values, such situation does not prevent the Arbitral Tribunal, without thereby questioning such due deference, from examining the actions of the State in light of Article 5(1) of the Agreement to determine whether such measures are reasonable with respect to their goals, the deprivation of economic rights and the legitimate expectations of who suffered such deprivation. There must be a reasonable relationship of proportionality between the charge or weight imposed to the foreign investor and the aim sought to be realized by any expropriatory measure. To value such charge or weight, it is very important to measure the size of the ownership deprivation caused by the actions of the state and whether such deprivation was compensated or not. On the basis of a number of legal and practical factors, it should be also considered that the foreign investor has a reduced or nil participation in the taking of the decisions that affect it, partly because the investors are not entitle [sic] to exercise political rights reserved to the nationals of the State, such as voting for the authorities that will issue the decisions that affect such investors.[254]

---

252. The principle of proportionality is incorporated in many areas of international law. See E. Kussbach, 'Proportionality,' in R. Bernhardt, ed., *Encyclopedia of Public International Law*, Vol. III (Amsterdam: North-Holland Pub. Co., 1992). IIA arbitrations applying the principle include: *The Loewen Group Inc and Raymond L. Loewen v. United State* (Award, 26 Jun. 2003) at paras 104-118; *Tecmed, supra* note 21 at paras 128-133, 148-151; *Pope & Talbot Inc v. Canada* (Award on the Merits on Phase 2, 10 Apr. 2001) at paras 43-72. See U. Kriebaum, 'Regulatory Takings: Balancing the Interests of the Investor and the State' (2007) 8 JWIT 717.
253. *LG&E, supra* note 107 at para. 195. Also see *Tecmed, supra* note 21 at para. 122.
254. *Tecmed, ibid.*

The *Tecmed* award explicitly draws on the concept of proportionality under the European Court of Human Rights' (ECtHR) jurisprudence on Protocol No. 1 of the *Convention for the Protection of Human Rights and Fundamental Freedoms* (Protocol No. 1).[255] In the first sentence of the above quote, the tribunal highlighted three factors to be assessed: (i) the goals and reasonableness of the government measures; (ii) the deprivation of economic rights; and (iii) the legitimate expectations of the investor. These three factors are reflected in the 2004 US Model BIT and the 2003 Canadian Model BIT.[256]

Other IIA tribunals have highlighted the importance of proportionality:

> With respect to the power of the State to adopt its policies, it can generally be said that the State has the right to adopt measures having a social or general welfare purpose. In such a case, the measure must be accepted without any imposition of liability, except in cases where the State's action is obviously disproportionate to the need being addressed.[257]

In addressing whether a regulation goes too far and amounts to an expropriation, a tribunal must essentially assess whether, given a particular threat to public welfare, the means the state has used to address that threat can be justified in light of the legitimate investment-backed expectations of the investor.[258]

Although the tribunal is mandated to assess state measures against international law, a threshold question is the standard by which this assessment should be made. Christie puts the matter this way:

> If, however, such prohibition can be justified as being reasonably necessary to the performance by a State of its recognized obligations to protect the public health, safety, morals or welfare, then it would normally seem that there has been no 'taking' of property.[259]

---

255. Protocol No. 1, *Convention for the Protection of Human Rights and Fundamental Freedoms* provides:

    Every natural or legal person is entitled to the peaceful enjoyment of his possessions. No one shall be deprived of his possessions except in the public interest and subject to the conditions provided for by law and by the general principles of international law.

    The preceding provisions shall not, however, in any way impair the right of a State to enforce such laws as it deems necessary to control the use of property in accordance with the general interest or to secure the payment of taxes or other contributions or penalties.

    For commentary, see H. Mountfield, 'Regulatory Expropriations in Europe: The Approach of the European Court of Human Rights' (2003) 11 NYUELJ 136 and H. Ruiz Fabri, 'The Approach Taken by the European Court of Human Rights to the Assessment of Compensation for 'Regulatory Expropriations' of the Property of Foreign Investors' (2003) 11 NYUELJ 148. Generally see, P. van Dijk, F. van Hoof , A. van Rijn & L. Zwaak, eds, *Theory and Practice of the European Convention on Human Rights*, 4th edn (Antwerp: Intersentia, 2006).
256. See *supra* §7.7.
257. *LG&E, supra* note 107 at para. 195.
258. See *supra* §7.18.
259. Christie, *supra* note 11 at 338.

In making the assessment of whether the measure in question was reasonably necessary, the state will enjoy a margin of appreciation. In *Saluka*, the tribunal stated that, in determining whether to impose forced administration, the regulator 'enjoyed a margin of discretion'[260] and that '[i]n the absence of clear and compelling evidence that the CNB erred or acted otherwise improperly in reaching its decision, which evidence has not been presented to the Tribunal, the Tribunal must in the circumstances accept the justification given by the Czech banking regulator for its decision.'[261]

In *Tecmed*, the tribunal referred to a 'reasonable relationship of proportionality' between a legitimate government aim and the measure in question.[262] This standard appears to lie somewhere between the requirement that there be a plausible basis for the measure and the requirement that the measure be the least restrictive necessary in order to meet the objectives of the government.

The *Methanex* award provides some guidance with respect to the assessment of scientific evidence in the context of IIA claims. In *Methanex*, the tribunal assessed the evidence upon which California banned MTBE, a gasoline additive. California's decision to ban MTBE was primarily based on a research report by the University of California (the UC Report), which concluded, among other things, that there are significant risks and costs associated with water contamination due to the use of MTBE.[263] In its findings on the scientific evidence, the tribunal found that the UC Report reflected a 'serious, objective and scientific approach.'[264] The existence of scientific disagreement about MTBE did not warrant a conclusion that the UC Report was a political sham, particularly as the research report involved public hearings and testimony and was subject to peer-review. Moreover, the tribunal was not persuaded that the UC Report was scientifically incorrect and accepted without reservation the conclusions of the US's scientific expert witnesses. In conclusion, the tribunal held that the Californian ban was 'motivated by the honest belief, held in good faith and on reasonable scientific grounds, that MTBE contaminated groundwater and was difficult to clean up.'[265] The tribunal did not elaborate on the meaning of 'reasonable scientific grounds.'

The *Methanex* tribunal applied a standard of review based on honest belief, good faith and reasonable scientific grounds. Although the *Methanex* tribunal found that the UC report was not 'scientifically incorrect,'[266] the tribunal did not suggest that 'scientifically correct' is the standard for assessing the legitimacy of an environmental measure. Nor did it suggest that there was a requirement for California to use the least investment restrictive measure to address the risk of ground water

---

260. *Saluka*, *supra* note 12 at para. 272.
261. *Ibid.*, at para. 273.
262. *Tecmed*, *supra* note 21 at para. 122.
263. *Methanex*, *supra* note 87 at para. 9, Part III-Chapter A.
264. *Ibid.*, at para. 101.
265. *Ibid.*, at para. 102.
266. *Ibid.*, at para. 101, Part III-Chapter A.

contamination. This is significant as Methanex had argued that MTBE was present in groundwater because of leaking underground fuel tanks and the appropriate risk management technique was to address the leaky fuel tank problem.

§7.26 Transparency and due process in police powers   Transparency and due process will be another important factor is assessing government measures. In *Methanex*, the tribunal noted that the UC Report was subject to public hearings, testimony and peer-review and that its 'emergence as a serious scientific work from such an open and informed debate is the best evidence that it was not the product of a political sham.'[267]

§7.27 Burden of proof with respect to police powers   The claimant has the burden of proving its expropriation claim. It will have to prove that it suffered a substantial deprivation and the measures in question caused the deprivation. Assuming the state defends the measure on the basis of the police powers, the question arises – who bears the burden of proof? On the one hand, it could be argued that the claimant has the burden to prove all material elements of the expropriation – namely that it has suffered a substantial deprivation and the deprivation is not justified by *bona fide* regulation within the ambit of the police powers. On the other hand, it could be argued that once the deprivation has been proven, the burden shifts to the state to justify the need for the measure. In our view, once substantial deprivation has been proven, the state will have to make a *prima facie* case to justify the regulatory measure as a non-compensable taking. Absent a justification, the state measure should be presumed to be a compensable expropriation. The state has taken the measure for a reason and it lies to the state to justify the measure based on the threat to public welfare at issue. This shifting of burden also appears justified on policy grounds as the state will have the information relating to the measure at its disposal. If the state makes a *prima facie* case of justification, the burden would then shift back to the claimant to show that the measure cannot be justified because, *inter alia*, it lacks a public purpose, was not enacted in good faith, is contrary to local law, is discriminatory or grossly disproportionate to the investor's rights and expectations. In practice, international tribunals have shifted the burden of proof to the state to justify measures where the claimant has established a deprivation. For example, in *Biloune*, the tribunal found that acts of the Ghanaian authorities would constitute constructive expropriation unless the state 'can establish by persuasive evidence sufficient justification for these events.'[268]

§7.28 A case-by-case analysis   Although the legal test for expropriation or deprivation under IIAs may be summarized as requiring measures effecting a substantial deprivation of an investment unless the limited police powers exception applies, the application of the legal text to given facts remains very case specific.

---

267.   *Ibid.*, at para. 101, Part IV-Chapter D.
268.   *Biloune, supra* note 43 at 209.

Indirect expropriation cases involve case-by-case determinations based on the measures in question, the effect on the investment and the overall factual and legal context. G.C. Christie made this point in his well-known article on indirect expropriation over forty years ago when he advocated using the common law method of case development as the appropriate method of legal analysis.[269] Though international tribunals have afforded no dearth of bright line legal tests for expropriation, expropriation cases are, in the end, very fact specific. This is in no way to discount the usefulness of the developing IIA jurisprudence on expropriation. The importance of the jurisprudence rests, however, not in short-hand definitions of what constitutes expropriation that can be applied as a template case-by-case. Rather, its importance lies in identifying a number of legally significant factors that must be assessed in deciding an expropriation claim. The issue was aptly summarized by the IIA tribunal in *Generation Ukraine* as follows:

> Predictability is one of the most important objectives of any legal system. It would be useful if it were absolutely clear in advance whether particular events fall within the definition of an 'indirect' expropriation. It would enhance the sentiment of respect for legitimate expectations if it were perfectly obvious why, in the context of a particular decision, an arbitral tribunal found that a governmental action or inaction crossed the line that defines acts amounting to an indirect expropriation. But there is no checklist, no mechanical test to achieve that purpose. The decisive considerations vary from case to case, depending not only on the specific facts of a grievance but also on the way the evidence is presented, and the legal bases pleaded. The outcome is a judgment, *i.e.* the product of discernment, and not the printout of a computer programme.[270]

Similarly, the tribunal in *Saluka* found:

> ... international law has yet to identify in a comprehensive and definitive fashion precisely what regulations are considered 'permissible' and 'commonly accepted' as falling within the police or regulatory power of States and, thus, non-compensable. In other words, it has yet to draw a bright and easily distinguishable line between non-compensable regulations on the one hand and, on the other, measures that have the effect of depriving foreign investors of their investment and are thus unlawful and compensable in international law.
>
> It thus inevitably falls to the *adjudicator* to determine whether particular conduct by a state 'crosses the line' that separates valid regulatory activity from expropriation. Faced with the question of *when, how and at what point an otherwise valid regulation becomes, in fact and effect, an unlawful expropriation*, international tribunals must consider the circumstances in

---

269. Christie, *supra* note 11.
270. *Generation Ukraine*, *supra* note 22 at para. 20.29.

which the question arises. The context within which an impugned measure is adopted and applied is critical to the determination of its validity.[271]

§7.29 Effect of a finding of expropriation   In cases of direct expropriation, state measures transfer the legal interest in the investment to the state or a third party. As a matter of domestic law, the investor no longer owns the investment. However, in the case of indirect expropriation, although the effect of the measure is expropriatory, the investor may still remain the legal owner of the investment under local law. For example, in the case of land, the investor may retain formal legal title to the land, even though the measure in question has effectively deprived the investor of any use or enjoyment of the land. Two issues arise in this context. First, an investor might incur further liabilities with respect to an investment that a tribunal has found to be expropriated. Taking the case of land, could the investor, as holder of legal title of the land, be liable for property taxes on the land after the date of the expropriation? Second, is an investor required to transfer title to the expropriated assets as a condition of obtaining compensation for the expropriated assets?

In *Wena*, the tribunal, interpreting the original award, found that the determination that Egypt's action amounted to expropriation precluded subsequent legal actions by Egypt with respect to a hotel lease which 'presume the contrary' to the original award.[272] The tribunal found, however, that it did not have the power to address whether a party expropriated from a given right can incur liability associated with that right.[273] In particular, it could not decide on the consequences of the expropriation on the legal relationship between Wena and the Egyptian Hotel Company, in particular the demand for the payment of rent under the hotel lease, which has been found to have been expropriated.[274] The *Wena* scenario is perhaps unique because, despite the fact that the tribunal held Wena's investment had been expropriated as of 1 April 1991, Wena re-entered the hotel on 28 April 1992, until its final eviction on 14 August 1997.[275] Since there had been a determination of expropriation as of 1 April 1991, the *Wena* tribunal determined that Wena did not have any substantial benefit of its hotel lease for over five years. Yet, as a matter of domestic law, the lease may have remained a valid domestic legal obligation.[276]

In a *Wena* type situation, and subject to the manner in which compensation has been calculated, it is difficult to see why the investor should be responsible for lease payments or other liabilities attendant on property ownership such as utility bills, taxes and the like after the date of expropriation unless the investor was deriving the economic benefit from the property. If the state

---

271.   *Saluka, supra* note 12 at paras 264-265.
272.   *Wena Hotels Limited v. Egypt* (Decision on Interpretation, 31 Oct. 2005) at para. 125.
273.   *Ibid.*, at para. 127.
274.   *Ibid.*, at para. 128.
275.   *Ibid.*, at para. 121.
276.   See *ibid.*, at para. 62 with respect to the award.

has expropriated the property, as a matter of international law, it should become responsible for it as of that date. Any costs incurred by the investor after the date of the expropriation, based on local law obligations, could be claimed against the state as consequential damages related to the expropriation.

§7.30 Title to expropriated property In cases of indirect expropriation, if the investor is paid full compensation and retains title to the property, there may be a risk of double recovery. Where full compensation is awarded, a tribunal may make the payment of compensation conditional on the investor relinquishing title and interest in the expropriated property.[277] With respect to transfer of title of the expropriated assets, there appears to be no rule requiring that the investor transfer the title as a condition of obtaining compensation.[278] In practice, in cases involving real property, tribunals have required that legal title be transferred as a condition of payment of compensation.[279] In other cases, tribunals have deducted the residual value of the investment from the compensation payment.[280] In *CMS*, the tribunal fashioned a remedy which envisaged that the investor transfer title over the property to the state upon the payment of its residual value, apparently on the theory that, as there was not a finding of expropriation, the title did not transfer by operation of law but this had to be effected by positive action of the parties.[281]

II   CONDITIONS FOR EXPROPRIATION

§7.31 Conditions for a lawful expropriation IIAs almost uniformly establish four requirements or conditions for a lawful expropriation: the expropriation must be for a public purpose, in accordance with due process of law, non-discriminatory and accompanied by compensation. Some treaties include the additional requirement that the expropriation not be contrary to contractual undertakings. The most important, and historically the most contested requirement, is the standard of compensation.[282] Where the requirements or conditions for an expropriation are not satisfied, the expropriation is illegal. Whether reparation should differ depending on whether or not the expropriation is categorized as legal or illegal is discussed below.[283]

---

277. See *Metalclad, supra* note 87 at para. 127. For commentary, see N. Rubins, 'Must the Victorious Investor-Claimant Relinquish Title to Expropriated Property' (2003) 4 JWI 481. In *ADC Affiliate Limited and ADC & ADMC Management Limited v. Hungary* (Award of the Tribunal, 2 Oct. 2006) [*ADC*], the tribunal ordered ADC to undertake to return the shares in question upon payment of the sum awarded.
278. Rubins, *ibid.*
279. *Metalclad, supra* note 87 at para. 102. See also *Santa Elena, supra* note 109 and *Tecmed, supra* note 21 at para. 201.
280. *CME, supra* note 87 at para. 513.
281. *CMS, supra* note 151 at paras 395-471.
282. See discussion *supra* in Chapter 1 at §1.13 *et seq.*
283. *Supra* §7.38.

§7.32 Public purpose IIAs almost uniformly impose a public purpose requirement for expropriation.[284] The requirement, although sometimes framed as 'public purpose,'[285] appears in a variety of forms including 'public interest,'[286] 'public benefit,'[287] 'public utility,'[288] 'a purpose which is in the public interest,'[289] 'public use, public interest, or in the interest of national defense,'[290] 'public or national interest or security'[291] and 'legal purpose.'[292] Given the margin of appreciation that tribunals, in practice, accord to states in defining what is in the social or public interest, it is unlikely that any potential different shades of meaning in these various formulations would be significant.[293]

In contrast, some BITs, notably UK BITs, specifically narrow the scope of permissible public purposes: 'the public purpose must be related to the internal needs' of the state.[294] This formulation is intended to prevent the host state from justifying an expropriation on the basis of foreign policy reasons.[295] Thus, in principle a state cannot use the threat of expropriation as a political tool in foreign affairs.[296] It may be queried whether this qualification provides any substantive limitations not already inherent in the concept of public purpose. Internal needs necessarily include elements of economic, political and military security related to foreign relations.

Under customary international law, an expropriation must also be for a public purpose.[297] Since the underlying rationale for expropriation is that the public welfare requires that private property be taken, the exercise of the right is dependant on genuine public need and the exercise of good faith.[298] Authorities suggest

---

284. An exception is Art. 3, France-Malaysia (1975). For in-depth surveys of treaty practice, see studies *supra* note 60.
285. Art. 1110(1)(a), NAFTA; Art. 4(1), Austria-Egypt (2001); and Art. 4(1), Afghanistan-Turkey (2004).
286. Art. 5(1), Austria-Azerbaijan (2000).
287. Art. XI, Netherlands-Sudan (1979).
288. Art. 5(2), France-Pakistan (1983).
289. Art. 13(1)(a), ECT.
290. Art. V(1) Philippines-UK (1980).
291. Art. 4(2), BLEU-Cameroon (1980).
292. Art. 4(1), Bahrain-Jordan (2000).
293. Further, if one of the terms were to provide less favourable treatment, an investor would be likely be able to rely on MFN treatment to obtain the more favourable treatment in another host state IIA.
294. Art. V(1), Costa Rica-UK (1982). See also Art. 5(1), Panama-UK (1983); Art. 5(1), Bolivia-UK (1988); Art. 4(1), Bosnia and Herzegovina-Sweden (2000); Art. 5, Israel-Thailand (2000); Art. 7(1), Australia-Egypt (2001); and Art. 6(1)(a), Kuwait-Netherlands (2001).
295. Dolzer & Stevens, *supra* note 60 at 105 and UNCTAD, BITs, *supra* note 17 at 54.
296. For example, Venezuelan president Hugo Chavez threatened to expropriate Colombian investments in Venezuela as retaliation for a border incident and allegations of Chavez's support for rebels that threaten the territorial integrity of Colombia. See Reuters, 'Chavez said could nationalize Colombian firms,' 6 Mar. 2008. Available online <http://uk.reuters.com/article/topNews/idUKN0510446320080306>.
297. For a discussion of the authorities, see A. Reinisch, 'Legality of Expropriation,' *supra* note 11.
298. Bin Cheng, *General Principles of Law as Applied by International Courts and Tribunals* (London: Stevens, 1953) at 40. It may also be noted that the public welfare aspect creates the

that the public purpose requirement would be breached if property were seized for the personal use of a dictator or third party[299] or as a reprisal for another state's conduct.[300] Expropriations in furtherance of acts that violate *jus cogens* norms, such as crimes against humanity, genocide or slavery are contrary to public purpose.[301]

In practice, the public purpose requirement has rarely arisen in international expropriation cases and states have been afforded a wide margin of appreciation in determining whether an expropriation serves a public purpose.[302] Thus, the public purpose requirement has generally not been a significant issue in IIA jurisprudence. IIA tribunals have confirmed that states are accorded deference in determining what is in the public interest.[303] Given the degree of appreciation provided to states in the determination of the public interest in this matter, it might

---

basis for distinction between property and human rights, with the former being alienable and the latter being inalienable.

299. See commentary on §712, Third Restatement, *supra* note 52 at 200 and 209-210. In *Walter Fletcher Smith Claim* (1929) II RIAA 915 the expropriation was held to be not in good faith or for the purposes of public utility because Smith's property was turned over to a private company 'for purposes of amusement and private property, without any reference to public utility' (*ibid.*, at 917-918). In *Liberian Eastern Timber Corporation (LETCO) v. Liberia* (Award, 31 Mar. 1986) (1987) 26 ILM 647 [*LETCO*], a claim relating to the breach of a forestry concession, the tribunal held that taking of LETCO's property was not for a *bona fide* public purpose because it was granted to other foreign companies that were 'good friends' of the Liberian authorities (*ibid.*, at 664-667). A transfer of expropriated property to third parties, however, does not necessarily mean the expropriation lacks public purpose. See *James and Others*, 75 ILR 397 at 415-419. An international tribunal would likely accept that a state may expropriate property to facilitate private economic development projects for the purpose of urban revitalization, as did the US Supreme Court in *Kelo v. New London* (2005) 545 US 469.

300. *Oppenheim's International Law, supra* note 1 at 920. The issue of reprisals arose in the case of the Libyan oil nationalizations. The US and UK protested against the nationalizations on the basis that they were not motivated by reasons of public utility (see US protest *reprinted in* (1974) 13 ILM 767 at 771 and British protest cited in *B.P. v. Libya* 53 ILR 297 at 317. *Cf.*, see *LIAMCO v. Libya* (1981) 20 ILM 1, where the sole arbitrator, Dr Mahmassani, found that public utility determination was for the state alone and public utility was not a prerequisite for the legality of a nationalization (*ibid.*, at 58-59). He, however, went on to assess whether the nationalization was discriminatory. Where property is expropriated as a reprisal, the expropriation might be challenged as discriminatory. See *infra* §7.33.

301. Brownlie, *Principles of International Law, supra* note 1 at 514.

302. See *Amoco International Finance Corporation v. Iran, supra* note 18 at para. 145. On the margin of appreciation doctrine, see Y. Shany, 'Toward a General Margin of Appreciation Doctrine in International Law' (2005) 16 EJIL 907. See also G. Van Harten, *Investment Treaty Arbitration and Public Law* (Oxford: Oxford University Press, 2007) who argues at 144-145 that tribunals 'should afford a margin of appreciation to the discretionary policy choices of domestic institutions and defer to governmental decisions that are not specifically abusive or discriminatory.'

303. See *Goetz, supra* note 70 at para. 126 where the tribunal found that: 'In the absence of an error of fact or of law, of an abuse of power or of a clear misunderstanding of the issue, it is not the Tribunal's role to substitute its own judgment for the discretion of the Government of Burundi of what are imperatives of public need ... or of national interest.'

be questioned whether the requirement is empty of any operative legal content.[304] Broad discretion, however, does not make the condition subjective or self-judging. At the very least, there must be some demonstrable public interest and the determination must be made in good faith. The absence of such a showing may make a finding of malice or *culpa* on the part of the state possible.[305] In this scenario, a state will find it impossible to rely upon any exclusion from liability drawn from the police powers exception, as that doctrine is predicated upon there being a valid and legitimate public purpose, which such powers are meant to protect and further.

In two recent decisions, IIA tribunals have suggested that a state must provide evidence to justify that its actions are in the public interest and that tribunals will scrutinize that evidence. In *ADC*,[306] a 2001 Hungarian decree voided the investors' contracts for the operation and management of the Budapest airport. The airport was subsequently taken over by the state in 2002, but then privatized in 2005. The investor argued that Hungary never articulated a public interest justification for its conduct, other than a general strategic interest. In contrast, the government argued that its measures were part of the harmonization process for Hungary's access to the EU and also served the strategic interests of the state.

In discussing the public interest standard, the *ADC* tribunal noted that:

> ... a treaty requirement for '*public interest*' requires some genuine interest of the public. If mere reference to '*public interest*' can magically put such interest into existence and therefore satisfy this requirement, then this requirement would be rendered meaningless since the Tribunal can imagine no situation where this requirement would not have been met.[307]

The tribunal concluded that it was not satisfied that the taking was in the public interest and stated that '[the] subsequent privatization of the airport involving BAA and netting Hungary USD 2.26 billion renders any public interest argument unsustainable.'[308]

In our view, the *ADC* tribunal was correct in stating that the public interest requirement must mean something. Public interest conditions are not completely self-judging.[309] However, the tribunal's conclusion that there was no public interest served is open to serious questioning. The fact that a host state changes its economic policy from one favouring nationalization to one favouring privatization does not make the earlier public interest any less compelling (particularly where there has been a change of government). Any fiscal benefit accruing to the state through the public purse would, by definition, add to public welfare. Further, the existence of a

---

304. Sohn & Baxter, 1961 Harvard Draft, *supra* note 27 at 555-556.
305. See *Desert Line*, *supra* note 125.
306. *ADC*, *supra* note 277.
307. *Ibid.*, at para. 432.
308. *Ibid.*, at para. 304.
309. See *infra* Chapter 10 on self-judging provisions in the context of essential security interests provisions.

public purpose is to be determined as of the date of the expropriation. The fact that the government's determination of public purpose later changes does not prove that the earlier determination was not made in good faith.

In *Siemens A.G. v. Argentina*,[310] the tribunal found that there was no evidence of a public purpose for a series of Argentine measures relating to a concession contract for the provision of national identity cards because the measures were simply an exercise of public authority to reduce the costs of a contract.[311] Although the tribunal confirmed that the termination of a contract due to a fiscal crisis would be a public purpose, the tribunal suggested that the existence of a public purpose for the termination was questionable in light of the circumstances.[312]

The *Siemens* and *ADC* awards demonstrate a much less deferential stance to the interpretation of the public interest condition for expropriation. Although in both cases the actions of the state were rightly subject to criticism, tribunals should exercise caution in asserting that state measures do not meet the public purpose requirement. The public interest condition is justiciable and not self-judging but it is appropriate for tribunals to provide the host state a margin of appreciation in determining public purpose.

§7.33 Non-discrimination IIAs generally impose a condition that expropriation be on a 'non-discriminatory basis'[313] or a similar requirement, such as 'not discriminatory.'[314] A smaller number of treaties expressly make expropriation subject to national and most-favoured-nation (MFN) treatment.[315]

Customary international law also forbids discriminatory expropriations. Expropriations solely on the basis that the foreign national in question belongs to a specific racial, religious, cultural, ethnic or national group are prohibited.[316] Where one national or ethnic group owns all of a particular industry, nationalization of that industry for a public purpose, however, is not necessarily discriminatory.[317] The fact that only one racial or national group is affected might be the

---

310. *Supra* note 127.
311. *Ibid.*, at para. 273.
312. *Ibid.*
313. Art. 5(1), Turkey-UK(1991); Art. 5(1) Austria-Azerbaijan (2000); and Art. 4(1) Bosnia and Herzegovina-Sweden (2000).
314. Art. 5(2), Chile-Japan (2007); Art. 4(1)(c), Chile-China (1994); and Art. 13(1), ECT. For in-depth surveys of treaty practice, see *supra* note 60.
315. Czechoslovakia-Germany (1990).
316. See *Libyan American Oil Co. (LIAMCO) v. Libya* (1981) 20 ILM 1; *Elettronica Sicula S.p.A. (ELSI) (US v. Italy)* [1989] ICJ Rep 15 [*ELSI*] at 72-73; *LETCO, supra* note 299 at 664-667; B.H. Weston, 'The Charter of Economic Rights and Duties of States and the Deprivation of Foreign-Owned Wealth' (1981) 75 AJIL 447; Sornarajah, *supra* note 16 at 398-399. See also Chapter 6 on discriminatory measures contrary to minimum standards of treatment.
317. See authorities cited in *Oppenheim's International Law, supra* note 1 at 920, note 34 and *Third Restatement, supra* note 52, Reporters' Note 5 at 210.

result of historic ownership patterns (often related to a colonial past), rather than discrimination.[318] This determination is highly context specific.[319]

IIA tribunals have found a violation of the condition that an expropriation be non-discriminatory where the state has discriminated against foreign nationals. In *Eureko*, the tribunal found that the deprivation in question (measures with respect to an agreement to sell shares) was discriminatory because the state acted to keep the insurance company at issue under majority Polish control.[320] Similarly, in *ADC*, the tribunal found discrimination because the government measures prohibited foreigners from operating the airport. The finding of discrimination in *ADC*, however, may be questioned as there was only one private airport operator and the operator was foreign. The tribunal reasoned that a 'comparison of different treatments is made here between that received by the Respondent-appointed operator and that received by foreign investors as a whole.'[321] This reasoning suggests that whenever there is a nationalization of a unique foreign-held business, the nationalization is by definition discriminatory because other foreign businesses were not nationalized.[322] This reasoning is not entirely convincing. There would only be discrimination based on nationality if the different foreign businesses were in like situations. In *ADC*, the other foreign investors were not airport operators and thus the comparison appears as inapposite.

Other tribunals have highlighted that not all distinctions between different types or classes of investors are discriminatory. In *Feldman*, the tribunal cast doubt on whether NAFTA's expropriation discrimination provision covered discrimination among different classes of investors, such as between producers and resellers of tobacco products, provided there is a rational basis for the distinction being made.[323]

---

318. See Brownlie, *Principles of Public International Law*, *supra* note 1 at 515, note 95 stating the test of discrimination is the intention of the government. IIA tribunals have, however, found that claimants are not required to prove state intent to discriminate. Although intent is relevant, discrimination analysis in IIAs focuses on discriminatory impacts or effects. On the effects-based approach to discrimination see *supra* Chapter 4, §4.22 and Chapter 6, §6.38.

319. In some situations, racial discrimination programs might be specifically targeted in order to advance the public interest. Such is the case in South Africa's 'Black Empowerment' policies (at issue in the pending case *Piero Foresti, Laura de Carli, and others v. South Africa*, ICSID Case No. ARB/(AF)/07/1). On the other hand, some racial discrimination programs are specifically intended to disempower defined segments of the populace without a corresponding empowerment of a disenfranchised class (see *Kahane (Successor)/Parisi and the Austrian State*, Case No. 131, Annual Digest 5 (1929-1930) at 213).

320. See §7.19 above for a critique of the tribunal's finding on expropriation.

321. *Eureko*, *supra* note 7 at para. 442.

322. For a discussion of the reasoning in the *ADC* case, see A. Reinisch, 'Legality of Expropriation,' *supra* note 11.

323. *Marvin Feldman* (Award, 16 Dec. 2002) [*Feldman*] at para. 137, note 26.

§7.34 Due process of law and judicial review Most IIAs impose a requirement that expropriations be in accordance with 'due process' of law.[324] Some IIAs tie due process to national law, such as 'under due process of national law.'[325] Rather than referring to due process, a number of IIAs specify that expropriation must occur in accordance with domestic law.[326] This formulation provides less protection, as domestic laws may fail to meet international standards. BITs based on the UK Model do not impose express due process requirements in the expropriation provision.[327]

Due process might be breached in a variety of ways, including failure to provide notice or a fair hearing, non-compliance with local law, or failure to provide a means for legal redress.[328] In *ADC*, the tribunal stated that due process of law requires:

> Some basic legal mechanisms, such as reasonable advance notice, a fair hearing and an unbiased and impartial adjudicator to assess the actions in dispute, are expected to be readily available and accessible to the investor to make such legal procedure meaningful. In general, the legal procedure must be of a nature to grant an affected investor a reasonable chance within a reasonable time to claim its legitimate rights and have its claims heard. If no legal procedure of such nature exists at all, the argument that '*the actions are taken under due process of law*' rings hollow.[329]

It is unclear whether due process of law imports an obligation of conduct, rather than result.[330] If it is an obligation of conduct, any defect in process, even if reviewable or correctable, amounts to a breach of due process. For example, if a state fails to provide an investor notice of an expropriation, the state's conduct would breach due process, even if the investor found out through other means.[331] In *Middle East*, the tribunal held that the seizure and auction of a ship was not in

---

324. Some BITs do not have an express due process requirement: Art. 5, Israel-Thailand (2000), and Art. 6(1)(a), Bahrain-Thailand (2002). For in-depth surveys of treaty practice, see *supra* note 60.
325. Art. 4(1), China-Poland (1998).
326. Art. VI(1), Lithuania-Norway (1992), and Art. 5(1), China-Netherlands (2001).
327. See Art. 5(1), Bosnia and Herzegovina-UK (2002), and Art. 5(1), UK-Vietnam (2002).
328. See G. Schwarzenberger, *International Law as Applied by International Courts and Tribunals*, Vol. I (London: Stevens, 1957) at 206.
329. *ADC*, *supra* note 277 at para. 435.
330. See *supra* Chapter 6, §6.9, on this distinction.
331. In UNCTAD, Taking of Property, *supra* note 60, it is suggested that the due process requirement in IIAs applies after the taking, so as to impose a requirement for some independent review of government actions. The authors claim that where proper procedural standards are not followed the issue becomes one of denial of justice (*ibid.*, 32). The better view, however, is that the due process requirements in IIAs apply to the process of expropriation – before and after the date of the expropriation. Failure to follow proper procedures in expropriating may give rise to a breach of due process. See *infra*, *Middle East*.

accordance with due process of law because there was a failure to provide direct notification of the seizure and auction to the investor.[332]

In contrast, if due process is an obligation of result, a state accords due process provided local remedies are available to correct defects in process. Some support for this position might be garnered from the *Feldman* award. In considering the requirement in Article 1110(1)(c), NAFTA, that the expropriation be 'in accordance with due process of law' and Article 1105(1), a minimum standards provision, the tribunal appeared to equate a denial of due process with a denial of justice. The tribunal noted that since the courts and administrative procedures were available to the claimant there was no denial of due process or denial of justice that would rise to the level of a violation of international law.[333]

The better view is that due process is properly viewed as an obligation of conduct. Due process requires, first and foremost, compliance with local law. Breaches of local procedural laws are *prima facie* breaches of due process. Second, the international standard or due process may be breached by serious procedural irregularities,[334] even if these are later corrected. However, if the basis of the entire expropriation claim is purely due process violations, it is an open question as to what, if any, compensation is payable.[335]

A due process requirement in an IIA could be viewed as having two components. On the one hand, due process of law could mean nothing more than adherence to the principles of natural justice. If this is the case, the executive branch of a state can expropriate without legislative fiat provided an opportunity to be heard is given before an impartial body. On the other hand, due process of law could be interpreted as requiring a procedure established by law. In this situation, the executive branch can only expropriate if the property is earmarked for expropriation by legislative fiat which also lays down the procedure for expropriation. On balance, it seems that due process imports a requirement that an expropriation be in accordance with the law of the host state as well as an international minimum standard of due process, including notice, a fair hearing and non-arbitrariness.[336]

---

332. *Middle East, supra* note 160 at para. 143. The tribunal found that inadequacies in the notification procedure breached fair and equitable treatment.
333. *Feldman, supra* note 323 at para. 140.
334. See the section on fundamental breaches of due process in J. Paulsson, *Denial of Justice in International Law* (Cambridge: Cambridge University Press, 2005).
335. *Amco Asia v. Indonesia, supra* note 10 and Paulsson, *Denial of Justice, ibid.*, at 218-227 where he argues that pecuniary compensation awarded for revocation of an operating permit without fair hearing is in the nature of a penalty if substantive grounds existed for the revocation and the only international delict is the denial of process.
336. The expropriation process may not be arbitrary. In *ELSI, supra* note 316, the ICJ defined arbitrariness to include a willful disregard of due process of law. See *supra* Chapter 6 §6.9, for a discussion of arbitrariness. See also *Arbitration Between Valentine Petroleum & Chemical Corporation and Agency for International Development* (1967) 44 ILR 79 at 89, holding that the cancellation of a concession without notice or reasons was arbitrary.

§7.35 Contractual undertakings   Some IIAs, particularly US and French BITs, require that expropriations not violate contractual undertakings.[337] Other treaties incorporate a provision relating to the observance of specific investment undertakings into the expropriation provision.[338] Where the state expropriates contrary to a contractual commitment, the expropriation will be in breach of the treaty. Such a commitment must be specific and is not easily implied.

III   COMPENSATION

§7.36 IIA provisions on compensation   IIA provisions on compensation for expropriation typically address four issues: the standard of compensation and valuation methods; the date for determining compensation; convertibility and transferability; and payment of interest.[339] In addition, some IIAs have provisions for a right to judicial review of expropriations.

A   STANDARD OF COMPENSATION

§7.37 The standard of compensation in customary international law   The standard of compensation for expropriation has been one of the most controversial issues in international investment law.[340] Capital exporting states have generally espoused a full fair market value compensation standard reflected in US Secretary of State Cordell Hull's statement that compensation must be prompt, adequate and effective.[341] On the other hand, capital importing states have historically espoused a national treatment standard or a standard that provides something less than full fair market value, providing more flexibility in the amount, manner and timing of payment.[342]

The inability of states to agree on the standard of compensation was evident in the 1962 UN General Assembly *Resolution on Permanent Sovereignty Over Natural Resources*[343] (Resolution 1803). Paragraph 4 of Resolution 1803 affirms

---

337. See Art. III(1)(e), Egypt-US (1982); Art. 5(2), Bulgaria-France (1989); and Art. 6, Mozambique-Netherlands (2001).
338. Art. II(3), Tunisia-US (1990). See *infra* Chapter 9 for analysis of observance of undertakings, provisions.
339. For in-depth surveys of treaty practice, see *supra* note 60.
340. See P.M. Norton, 'A Law of the Future or a Law of the Past? Modern Tribunals and the International Law of Expropriation' (1991) 85 AJIL 474; C.F. Amerasinghe, 'Issues of Compensation for the Taking of Alien Property in Light of Recent Cases and Practice' (1992) 4 ICLQ 22; J.A. Westberg, 'Applicable Law, Expropriatory Takings and Compensation in Cases of Expropriation; ICSID and Iran-United States Claims Tribunal Case Law Compared' (1993) 8 ICSID Rev 1; and E. Lauterpacht, 'Issues of Compensation and Nationality in the Taking of Energy Investments' (1990) 8 JENRL 241.
341. See *supra* Chapter 1, §1.13.
342. See *supra* Chapter 1, §1.7.
343. GA Res 1803, 14 Dec. 1962 *reprinted in* (1963) 2 ILM 223. See §1.20.

that 'appropriate compensation' shall be paid for expropriation. The meaning of appropriate was nevertheless contested, with some states suggesting that it meant fair market value and others suggesting it allowed for less than full compensation.[344] The compromise position of appropriate compensation broke down in early 1970s. The 1974 *Charter of Economic Rights and Duties of States* (the Charter) provides that compensation for expropriation is to be determined based on state law and omits any reference to international law or a minimum international standard in determining compensation.[345]

The standard of compensation for expropriations in customary international law remains disputed. A considerable body of international jurisprudence[346] and scholarly writing[347] supports the view that where a state expropriates property, it is required under customary international law to pay full compensation measured by the fair market value of the property that has been taken. This position is arguably reflected in the ILC's Articles on State Responsibility, which provide that states are obliged to pay for damages caused by internationally wrongful acts and specify that compensation 'shall cover any financially assessable damage including loss of profits.'[348] The commentary to the Articles on State Responsibility states that '[c]ompensation reflecting the capital value of property taken

---

344. For discussion on this issue, see O. Schachter, 'Compensation for Expropriation' (1985) 78 AJIL 121 and Lauterpacht, *supra* note 340.
345. See *supra* Chapter 1, §1.23.
346. *Delagoa Bay Railway Case, reprinted in* Whiteman, *Damages in International law*, Vol. III (Washington DC, 1937) at 1694; *Selwyn Case* (1903) IX RIAA 380; *Norwegian Shipowners' Claims, supra* note 2; *British Claims in the Spanish Zone of Morocco* (1925) II RIAA 615; *Goldenberg Case* (1928) II RIAA 901; *Lena Goldfields Arbitration* (1930) *reprinted in* (1950) 56 CLQ 42; *Shufeldt Claim* (1930) II RIAA 1079; and *De Sabla, supra* note 13, are commonly cited as supporting the full compensation standard.
347. See the study by Norton, *supra* note 340, arguing that international jurisprudence until WWII uniformly supports the full compensation standard and discussing post WWII jurisprudence. Also see M. H. Mendelson, 'What Price Expropriation, Compensation for Expropriation: The Case Law' (1985) 79 AJIL 414-420 and O. Schachter's reply 'Compensation Cases – Leading and Misleading', *ibid.*, at 420-422 and his previous article, *supra* note 344. The majority opinions of the Iran-US Claims Tribunal generally support the full compensation standard, although it is necessary to distinguish between cases where the tribunal is commenting on the compensation standard in customary international law and those in which it is applying Art. IV(2) of the *Treaty of Amity, Economic Relations and Consular Rights* between the United States of America and Iran, signed 15 Aug. 1955, entered into force 16 Jun. 1957, 284 UNTS 93. See *INA Corporation v. Iran* (1985) 8 Iran-US CTR 373 at 380, *Sola Tiles, Inc. v. Iran,* (1987) 14 Iran-US CTR 223 at para. 42 and *Amoco International Finance Corp. v. Iran*, 21 Iran-US CTR 79 at para. 207.
348. Art. 36, ILC's Articles on State Responsibility, *supra* note 89. It is generally accepted that lost profits are an element of determining full compensation. ICSID tribunals in *AGIP S.p.A v. Congo* (1982) 21 ILM 726 [*AGIP*]; *Benvenuti et Bonfant, supra* note 37, *LETCO, supra* note 299 and *SPP, supra* note 193, have stated that in principle non-speculative future profits may be claimed. Traditionally, in assessing damages there has been a distinction between *damnum emergens* (actual losses) and *lucrum cessans* (loss of profits). In the case of a factory, *damnum emergens* might include an amount for lands, buildings, and equipment, whereas *lucrum cessans* would reflect lost profits from the ongoing business.

or destroyed as the result of an internationally wrongful act is generally assessed on the basis of the "fair market value" of the property lost.'[349] The World Bank *Guidelines on the Treatment of Foreign Direct Investment* (the World Bank Guidelines) also reflect a fair market value standard.[350]

Other commentators suggest that customary international law does not invariably require full market value compensation in all circumstances, and that the international customary standard of just or appropriate compensation provides flexibility for the consideration of factors such as the financial burden on the expropriating state.[351] The appropriateness of the distinction between 'full' and 'just' compensation, however, may be questioned.[352] Some argue that, even if full compensation is the customary standard, there is support for the view that there are exceptions to the standard in extraordinary circumstances such as for national programs of agricultural land reform,[353] large scale nationalizations,[354] war, and where payment would be an overwhelming financial burden.[355] In support of something less than a full compensation standard, some commentators note the state practice of accepting less than full compensation under lump sum settlements.[356] It is argued that, arbitral awards providing full compensation are distinguishable on various grounds including that they are based on domestic law, involved illegal expropriations, or breach of treaty or contractual obligations.

§7.38 Legal and illegal expropriation in customary international law A further issue with respect to the standard of compensation for expropriation is whether the requirement for reparation differs depending on whether the

---

349. ILC's Articles on State Responsibility, *supra* note 89 at 225. This section of the commentary was cited in *CME, supra* note 87 at para. 501.
350. See *supra* Chapter 1, §1.34. Art. IV provides: '2. Compensation for a specific investment taken by the State will, according to the details provided below, be deemed 'appropriate' if it is adequate, effective and prompt; 3. Compensation will be deemed 'adequate' if it is based on the fair market value of the taken asset as such value is determined immediately before the time at which the taking occurred or the decision to take the asset became publicly known.'
351. Schachter, *supra* note 344 at 129.
352. In *CME Czech Republic B.V. v. Czech Republic* (Final Award, 14 Mar. 2003), the majority of the tribunal found that the standard of just compensation in The Netherlands' BIT practice is the same as full compensation under the Hull formula. Professor Brownlie, in dissent, however, found that there was a distinction, with the just compensation standard being lower and based on subjective proof. In that case, full compensation was calculated by the majority as the objective going value of the undertaking, whereas Professor Brownlie found that just compensation was ascertainable by reference to the investor's contemporaneous expectation as embodied in a business plan. However, this debate may well be otiose as it is likely that the most-favored-nation clause would operate to have the full compensation standard replace any lower 'just' compensation if the country has differing IIAs.
353. §712 of the Third Restatement, *supra* note 52, comment (d) at 199.
354. See *INA Corporation v. Iran, supra* note 347 at 378 and Judge Lagergren's separate opinion at 390.
355. Sohn and Baxter, 1961 Harvard Draft, *supra* note 26 at 560.
356. Sornarajah, *supra* note 16 at 442-443. See *supra* Chapter 1, §1.26, on lump sum agreements.

expropriation is legal or illegal.[357] As noted above, there are four generally recognized conditions on the state's right to expropriate: the expropriation must be for a public purpose, non-discriminatory, in accordance with due process of law and accompanied by compensation. In order to be lawful, an expropriation must comply with all four conditions.[358] In addition, an expropriation contrary to an express international obligation not to expropriate is illegal.

The starting point for this debate, indeed generally for any discussion of reparations in international law, is the Permanent Court of International Justice's (PCIJ) decision in *Chorzów Factory*,[359] which suggests that there are different standards of compensation depending on whether the expropriation is legal or illegal. In *Chorzów Factory*, the PCIJ stated that:

> The essential principle contained in the actual notion of an illegal act – a principle which seems to be established by international practice and in particular by the decisions of arbitral tribunals – is that reparation must, as far as is possible, wipe out consequences of the illegal act and reestablish the situation which would, in all probability, have existed if that act had not been committed. Restitution in kind, or, if that is not possible, payment of a sum corresponding to the value which a restitution in kind would bear; the award, if need be, of damages for loss sustained which would not be covered by restitution in kind or payment of it – such are the principles which should serve to determine the amount of compensation due for an act contrary to international law.

Although this statement is often cited to support the full compensation standard for expropriation, the PCIJ was addressing an illegal seizure of property contrary to a treaty obligation. In the previous paragraph, the PCIJ had noted that:

> The action of Poland which the Court has judged to be contrary to the Geneva convention is not an expropriation – to render which lawful only the payment of *fair* compensation would have been wanting ...
>
> It follows that the compensation due to the German Government is not necessarily limited to the value of the undertaking at the moment of the dispossession, plus interest to the date of payment. This limitation would only be admissible if the Polish Government had the right to expropriate and if its wrongful act consisted merely in not having paid to the two Companies the *just* price of what was expropriated.[360]

---

357. See generally A. Sheppard, 'The Distinction Between Lawful and Unlawful Expropriation,' in *Investment Arbitration and the Energy Charter Treaty*, ed. C. Ribeiro (New York: Juris, 2007); A. Reinisch, 'Legality of Expropriation,' *supra* note 11; and I. Marboe, 'Compensation and Damages in International Law, The Limits of "Fair Market Value"' (2006) 7 JWIT 723.

358. *Mondev International Ltd. v. United States* (Award, 11 Oct. 2002) at paras 71-72.

359. *Case Concerning the Factory at Chorzów (Claim for Indemnity) (Germany v. Poland)* (1928) PCIJ Ser. A., No. 17 at 47 [*Chorzów Factory*].

360. *Ibid.*, at 46.

The PCIJ went on to state that providing the same amount of compensation would be 'tantamount to rendering lawful liquidation and unlawful dispossession indistinguishable in so far as their financial results are concerned.' The PCIJ therefore distinguished between an illegal expropriation which requires reparation to re-establish the *status quo ante* and legal expropriations requiring fair and just compensation equal to the 'value of the undertaking at the moment of dispossession.' On its face *Chorzów Factory* suggests that there is a difference between full reparation which includes lost profits and the 'value of the undertaking.'

Subsequent commentators have highlighted that the distinction between reparation including lost profits and value of the undertaking is illusory.[361] The distinction fails to reflect modern business valuation techniques that accept that property and investments have no intrinsic value – the market attributes value based on the revenue making capacity of the asset in question.[362] If the market value of an undertaking cannot be determined without assessing profit-making capacity then the PCIJ's distinction (if such it be) is illusory. As noted above, numerous international authorities confirm that non-speculative lost profits can (perhaps should) be assessed as part of an investment's value. In other words, as the object of the valuation exercise is to ascertain an objective value of the property, different methodologies should lead to consistent results as there is only one objective value of the property.

Although the PCIJ's distinction between 'full reparation which includes lost profits' and the 'value of the undertaking' cannot be maintained in principle, the difference between legal and illegal expropriation remains significant. Where an expropriation is legal, compensation is calculated as of the date of the expropriation in accordance with the provisions of the IIA. Where an expropriation is illegal, however, it has been argued that the tribunal, in applying a reparation standard, might award compensation as of the date of the award (assuming that the treaty-mandated compensation provisions for a lawful expropriation do not apply and the tribunal applies the customary international law reparation standard). In most cases this distinction will not be significant, particularly where the government measures in question have destroyed the value of the assets. Nevertheless, the distinction is significant where the expropriated investment has appreciated in value since the date of the illegal expropriation. In *Siemens*, the tribunal noted that:

> The key difference between compensation under the Draft Articles and the *Factory at Chorzów* case formula, and Article 4(2) of the Treaty is that under the former, compensation must take into account 'all financially assessable

---

361. J. Paulsson, 'Ghosts of Chorzów: *Maha Nuñez-Schultz v. Republic of the Americas*' in Weiler, ed., *International Investment Law and Arbitration, supra* note 93 at 789. Higgins, *supra* note 122 at 144.

362. As noted by Lauterpacht, *supra* note 340 at 244: 'the issue is whether account should be taken only of some notional intrinsic value of the physical assets of an enterprise or whether, on the other hand, the revenue or profit-earning capacity of such assets is to be treated as an element in their value.'

damage' or 'wipe out all the consequences of the illegal act' as opposed to compensation 'equivalent to the value of the expropriated investment' under the Treaty. Under customary international law, Siemens is entitled not just to the value of its enterprise as of May 18, 2001, the date of expropriation, but also to any greater value that enterprise has gained up to the date of this Award, plus any consequential damages.[363]

In *Vivendi II*, the tribunal noted that the:

> Treaty thus *mandates* that compensation for *lawful* expropriation be based on the *actual value* of the investment, and that interest *shall* be paid from the date of dispossession. However, it does not purport to establish a *lex specialis* governing the standards of compensation for *wrongful* expropriations.[364]

After referring to the *Chorzów Factory* case, the tribunal continued and noted that the standard espoused in *Chorzów Factory* 'permits, if the facts so require, a higher rate of recovery than that prescribed in Article 5(2) for *lawful* expropriations.'[365] Arguably, the distinction between legal and illegal expropriations is misleading. IIA expropriation cases relate to alleged breaches of the prohibition of expropriation without compensation enshrined in IIAs. Thus, they are cases about alleged breaches of international law, to which the standards of compensation for illegal acts under international law should apply.

In *ADC*, the tribunal stated that the BIT stipulates only the standard of compensation payable in the case of a lawful expropriation, and that this standard 'cannot be used to determine the issue of damages payable in the case of an unlawful expropriation since this would be to conflate compensation for a lawful expropriation with damages for an unlawful expropriation.'[366] The tribunal, relying on *Chorzów Factory*, applied the customary international law standard for the assessment of damages resulting from an unlawful act. As noted by the tribunal in *ADC*, there were unique circumstances:

> The present case is almost unique among decided cases concerning the expropriation by States of foreign owned property, since the value of the investment after the date of expropriation (1 January 2002) has risen very considerably while other arbitrations that apply the *Chorzów Factory* standard all invariably involve scenarios where there has been a decline in the value of the investment after regulatory interference.[367]

The tribunal accordingly awarded compensation based on the market value of the expropriated investments as of the date of the award.[368]

---

363. *Siemens, supra* note 127 at para. 352.
364. *Vivendi II, supra* note 69 at para. 8.2.3.
365. *Ibid.*, at para. 8.2.5.
366. *ADC, supra* note 277 at para. 481.
367. *Ibid.*, at para. 496.
368. *Ibid.*, at para. 499. See M.A. Abdala & P. Spiller, '*Chorzów's* Standard Rejuvenated: Assessing Damages in Investment Treaty Arbitrations' (2008) 25 JIA 103; M.A. Abdala, P.

Compensation determined as of the date of the award may allow the investor to claim for consequential damages incurred after the expropriation.[369] This may be important in some cases, such as in *Wena*, where the investor incurs post-expropriation liabilities with respect to the expropriated property.[370] Another important distinction is that if property is illegally expropriated, international law will not recognize the expropriator as having a valid title to the property[371] and (subject to double recovery issues) the original owner might seek to recover the property through national court processes.[372] For example, if a state illegally expropriates an oil company's oil concession, the company may seek to take possession of the exported oil.[373]

No matter what standard of compensation is chosen, tribunals still have significant discretion in how they apply valuation techniques. In practice, a tribunal might indirectly censure illegal state activity by using more generous valuation assumptions.[374] Illegal conduct may also be taken into account in the tribunal's determination of costs in the arbitration. Similar results may be obtained by the utilization of compound interest.

§7.39 Standard of compensation in IIAs IIAs, as a whole, adopt the full compensation standard.[375] The majority of IIAs set a standard of full compensation based on 'market value,'[376] 'actual market value'[377] or 'fair market value'[378] or restitution.[379] A number of treaties expressly adopt the Hull standard of 'prompt, adequate and effective' compensation.[380] Other treaties refer to 'genuine'[381] or

---

Spiller & S. Zuccon, 'Chorzów's Compensation Standard as Applied *in ADC v. Hungary*' (2007) 21 News and Notes from The Institute for Transnational Arbitration.

369. *Siemens, supra* note 127 at para. 387.
370. See *supra* §7.29.
371. See F.A. Mann, 'The Consequences of an International Wrong in International and National Law' (1977) 48 BYIL 1 and Brownlie, *Principles of Public International Law, supra* note 1 at 515.
372. See N. Rubins & N.S. Kinsella, *International Investment, Political Risk and Dispute Resolution* (Dobbs Ferry, NY: Oceana, 2005) at 428-433 for a discussion of the approach of various states to the issue of invalidation of title.
373. See *Anglo-Iranian Oil Co. Ltd. v. Jaffrate (The Rose Mary)* [1953] 1 WLR 246, 20 ILR 316 (Supreme Court, Aden, 1953). Also see Statement by the Department of State on Policy of 'Hot' Libyan Oil, (1974) 13 ILM 767.
374. See §7.41 below regarding valuation methods.
375. For in-depth surveys of treaty practice, see studies *supra* note 60.
376. Art. 5(2), India-Portugal (2000).
377. Art. 4(1), Austria-Belarus (2001).
378. Art. 5(2), China-Netherlands (2001).
379. See China-Japan (1988).
380. Art. 5(2), Egypt-Japan (1977); Art. 6, Sri Lanka-Switzerland (1981); and Art. V(2), Egypt-US (1982).
381. Art. 5(1), UK-Vietnam (2002).

'true'[382] value, simply 'value'[383] or 'equivalent to the value.'[384] Formulations that use 'value' suggest a fair market value standard as modern valuation techniques recognize that economic assets have no intrinsic or inherent monetary value. A 'genuine' or 'true' value is one based on an assessment of market comparables.

The reference to 'just compensation' is less clear as it may suggest that non-market value considerations might apply to the determination of compensation. In many cases, this standard is followed by additional descriptors. For example, Article 5, Czechoslovakia-Netherlands (1991), refers to the payment of 'just compensation' and then clarifies that the compensation shall represent 'the genuine value of the investments affected.'[385]

A smaller number of IIAs adopt formulations that may suggest less than full compensation. For example, the term 'appropriate value'[386] or 'be adequate'[387] may be less than full compensation.[388] Other treaties simply refer to compensation.[389] Where the treaty language does not refer to terms that indicate market value, significant uncertainty will remain. In practice, the application of MFN treatment will, in many cases, mean that the investor is entitled to a market value compensation standard in other IIA.[390]

IIA tribunals have interpreted 'equivalent to the actual value,'[391] 'prompt, adequate and effective compensation' (further defined as market value),[392] 'fair market value,'[393] 'just compensation' (further defined as representing genuine value)[394] and 'actual value'[395] and 'value'[396] as requiring full compensation – in the sense of the fair market value of the expropriated investments.

---

382.   Art. 5(1), Bahrain-Jordan (2000).
383.   Art. 4(2), Argentina-Germany (1991), discussed in *Siemens, supra* note 127.
384.   Art. 4, German Model BIT.
385.   This provision was interpreted in the *CME* awards, *supra* note 87 and 352.
386.   Art. 5(1)(a), China-Thailand (1985). Also see China-France (1984).
387.   Art. 6(1)(a) Bahrain-Thailand(2002).
388.   Lauterpacht, *supra* note 340.
389.   China-New Zealand (1988).
390.   See next section, §7.40.
391.   Art. 4(2), Germany-USSR (1989) in *Sedelmayer, supra* note 71.
392.   Art. 4(c), Egypt-Greece (1993), in *Middle East, supra* note 160; and Art. 5, Egypt-UK (1975), in *Wena, supra* note 41.
393.   Art. 1110, NAFTA, in *Metalclad, supra* note 87 and Art. 5(2), Mexico-Spain (1995), in *Tecmed, supra* note 21.
394.   Art. 5, Czechoslovakia-Netherlands (1991), in *CME* Partial Award, *supra* note 87 at para. 624. In a separate opinion to the Final Award, 14 Mar. 2003, Professor Brownlie stated that 'just compensation' must be subject to legitimate expectations and actual conditions. It is not necessarily equated with fair market value and could be reduced to account for damages to a natural resource (para. 31). Professor Brownlie argued that compensation was premised on the concept of legitimate expectations and that an investor was entitled to a reasonable rate of return (para. 58). Professor Brownlie referred to the 1993 business plan as 'reliable evidence' of the investor's reasonable expectations (para. 64) (Separate Opinion, 13 Mar. 2003).
395.   *Vivendi II, supra* note 69 at para. 8.2.10.
396.   *Siemens, supra* note 127 at para. 353.

§7.40 MFN and the standard of compensation   Where an IIA does not provide expressly for a fair market value standard of compensation, an investor will often be able to rely on an MFN clause to obtain the benefit of a better standard of compensation in another IIA. In practice this is likely to mean that the investor will be entitled to a full compensation measured by the fair market value of the investment as of the date of expropriation.

In *CME*, the tribunal noted that should 'just compensation' in Czechoslovakia-Netherlands (1991) be interpreted as less than 'fair market value,' the investor would be entitled to rely on the Czechoslovakia-US BIT, which provides that compensation shall be equivalent to the fair market value.[397] In his Separate Opinion, Professor Brownlie rejected this argument and argued that applying MFN treatment to the compensation clause would render the express choice of the parties 'nugatory' and that the presumption must be that MFN treatment does not apply to the process of dispute settlement.[398] But it is difficult to see why MFN treatment does not apply because the parties have expressly chosen a standard. The purpose of MFN is to ensure the benefit of better standards whether or not the standard provided for initially was expressly negotiated. Second, even if the view were taken that the scope of MFN treatment does not apply to dispute settlement, the standard of compensation is a matter of substantive treatment, not a procedural issue relating to dispute settlement.[399]

§7.41 Measuring fair market value – valuation methods   No matter what standard of compensation is chosen, a method of valuation is required to calculate the value of the investment. The starting point of a claim for compensation will be the fair market value of the investment, either at the date of the expropriation, or in cases of illegal expropriation where the value of the investment has appreciated, a later date that may well be the date of the award. Even if the IIA were interpreted to require something less than fair market value, that amount will reflect certain elements of fair market value. These claims will often be based on expert opinions by financial and valuation specialists.[400]

In *Starrett Housing Corp. v. Iran*, the Iran-US Claims Tribunal defined fair market value as:

> … the price that a willing buyer would pay to a willing seller in circumstances in which each had good information, each desired to maximize his financial gain, and neither was under duress or threat, the willing buyer being a reasonable businessperson.[401]

---

397.   *CME*, Final Award, *supra* note 352 at para. 500.
398.   *CME*, Professor Brownlie's Separate Opinion, *supra* note 394 at para. 6.
399.   See *supra* Chapter 5 on MFN clauses.
400.   See the discussion of experts opinion in *Santa Elena*, *supra* note 109; *CME*, *supra* note 352; *ADC*, *supra* note 277; and *Sempra*, *supra* note 106.
401.   *Starrett Housing Corp. v. Iran*, Final Award, 16 Iran-US CTR 112 at 201.

The difficulty with valuing expropriated assets is that there often is no comparable market value.[402] A variety of methods is commonly used to determine fair market value. There is a rich literature on this topic.[403] As there are many specialized works, the analysis below focuses on a general overview of common valuation methods and IIA expropriation cases to date.

Although the majority of IIAs do not identify specific valuation methods for determining fair market value, a number of IIAs, particularly the ones to which the US is a party, provide explicit guidance on valuation methods.[404] For example, Article 1110(2), NAFTA, provides that compensation shall be the equivalent of the 'fair market value of the expropriated investment immediately before the expropriation took place' and further provides that '[v]aluation criteria shall include going-concern value, asset value including declared tax value of tangible property, and other criteria, as appropriate, to determine fair market value.' Austrian BITs provide that if fair market value cannot be ascertained then compensation 'shall be determined in accordance with the generally recognized principles of valuation and on equitable principles taking into account, *inter alia*, the capital invested, depreciation, current returns, capital already repatriated, replacement value, goodwill and other relevant factors.'[405]

Typically, IIA tribunals support their valuation method with corroborating evidence in the form of mature income streams; audited, verifiable reserves analysis (possibly as submitted to regulatory authorities such as the US Securities and Exchange Commission); analyses of the capital assets of the investor; analyses of the investment prepared by, or on behalf of, the host state; business plans (preferably prepared by, or provided to, the host state); and expert asset valuations prepared by or for both the investor and the host state.

When considering how to determine compensation for a taking, fair market value of property means 'the price that a willing buyer would pay to a willing seller in circumstances in which each had good information, each desired to

---

402. *Amoco International Finance Corporation v. Iran, supra* note 347 ('market value is an ambiguous concept, to say the least ... when an open market does not exist for the expropriated asset or for goods identical or comparable to it'). See *supra* Chapter 1, §1.28, for references to work on the Iran-Us Claims Tribunal.

403. See S. Ripinsky *et al., Damages in International Law* (London: British Institute of International and Comparative Law, 2008); M. Kantor, *Valuation for Arbitration* (The Hague: Kluwer, 2008); R.A. Brealey & S.C. Myers, *Principles of Corporate Finance*, 7th edn (Boston, Mass: McGraw-Hill/Irwin, 2003); M. Ball, 'Assessing Damages in Claims by Investors Against States' (2001) 16 ICSID Rev 408; P.D. Friedland & E. Wong, 'Measuring Damages for the Deprivation of Income Producing Assets: ICSID Case Studies' (1991) 6 ICSID Rev 400; C.N. Brower & J. Wong, 'General Principles of Valuation: The Case of Santa Elena' in Weiler, ed., *International Investment Law and Arbitration, supra* note 93 at 747; and I. Marboe, 'Compensation and Damages in International Law, The Limits of "Fair Market Value"' (2006) 7 JWIT 723.

404. See Panama-US (1982); Haiti-US (1983); and Israel-Romania (1991).

405. Art. 4(2)(a), Austria-Oman (2001).

maximize his financial gain, and neither was under duress or threat.'[406] Further, one must recall the legal rule that one must assume away any impact on value of the state's expropriatory conduct. In other words, if there were no expropriatory conduct and if this property was going to be purchased – what would the hypothetical purchase price be? Difficult issues of valuation arise when the property taken is a business, a socalled going concern, or contract rights to a long-term concession contract, for which a stream of income was expected.

As a helpful summary, the United Nations Compensation Commission, set up to remedy violations to person and property caused by Iraq's invasion of Kuwait in 1990, outlines in a Resolution the various methodologies that can be utilized:[407]

> Depending on the type of asset and the circumstances of the case, one of several valuation methods may be used. Methods typically used to value tangible assets are book value and replacement value. Book value is considered to mean value at which an asset is carried on a balance sheet. Book value at any time is cost of an item minus accumulated depreciation. Replacement value is considered to mean the amount required to obtain an asset of the same kind and status as the asset damaged or lost. Replacement value would not normally allow for replacement of an old item with a new one ...
>
> For the valuation of income-producing properties there are several alternative concepts. One is to measure by reference to costs, which leads to the determination of book value. Another is to determine the value of the property as a going concern. This is often done by reference to the market value of similar properties. Where such market value cannot be ascertained, the economic or current value of that asset can be ascertained by the discounted cash flow (DCF) method or by the price/earnings (P/E) method. The DCF method calculates the value at one specified time of cash flows that are to be received at a different time by discounting the yearly net cash flows to present value, with the discount rate including cost of capital and risk components. The price/earnings method takes as a basis past periods' business results and then capitalises them by the application of a multiple (P/E ratio) which reflects expectations about future performance and growth, or lack of it.
>
> In principle, the economic value of a business may include loss of future earnings and profits where they can be ascertained with reasonable certainty.

---

406. See *INA Corporation v. Iran, supra* note 347 at 380. See also World Bank Guidelines, Guideline IV(5), *supra* note 350: 'fair market value will be acceptable if determined by the State according to reasonable criteria related to the market value of the investment, i.e., in an amount that a willing buyer would normally pay to a willing seller after taking into account the nature of the investment, the circumstances in which it would operate in the future and its specific characteristics, including the period in which it has been in existence, the proportion of tangible assets in the total investment and other relevant factors pertinent to the specific circumstances of each case.'

407. UN Security Council Document S/AC.26/1992/9 of 6 Mar. 1992 at paras 15, 18-19.

§7.42 Going-concern value and discounted cash flow[408]   Fair market value is often calculated by reference to the business as a going concern.[409] Normally, the fair market value of a going concern that has a history of profitable operations may be based on an estimate of future profits subject to a discounted cash flow (DCF) analysis.[410] The DCF method involves calculating the present value of future profits and assets to estimate the value that a willing purchaser would pay for the business. Present value requires that a discount factor be used to account for the fact that these are future profits. The World Bank Guidelines note that the use of DCF value is reasonable for a going concern with a proven record of profitability. It defines DCF at Guideline IV.6:

> *'discounted cash flow value'* means the cash receipts realistically expected from the enterprise in each future year of its economic life as reasonably projected minus that year's expected cash expenditure, after discounting this net cash flow for each year by a factor which reflects the time value of money, expected inflation, and the risk associated with such cash flow under realistic circumstances. Such discount rate may be measured by examining the rate of return available in the same market on alternative investments of comparable risk on the basis of their present value;

In order to value an enterprise by the DCF method, one has to calculate the cash receipts realistically expected from an enterprise in each future year of its economic life (or contractual life, if there are arrangements for its transfer at certain point in time) and then subtract the amount of anticipated expenditures in each corresponding year in order to obtain the net cash flow of the enterprise for that period. The net cash flow then has to be discounted at a rate that reflects: (i) the time value of the money; (ii) expected inflation; and (iii) the risk associated with such cash flow under realistic circumstances.[411] The discount rate is calculated by examining the rate of return available in the same market on alternative investments of comparable risk on the basis of their present value.[412] Some recent cases, such as *CMS*, have utilized a discount of 14.5% due to the high volatility of that relevant market.[413]

---

408.   S. Ripinsky *et al.*, *Damages in International Law* and M. Kantor, *Valuation for Arbitration*, *supra* note 403 for in-depth treatment.
409.   The World Bank Guidelines, *supra* note 350, define a going concern as 'an enterprise consisting of income-producing assets which has been in operation for a sufficient period of time to generate the data required for the calculation of future income and which could have been expected with reasonable certainty, if the taking had not occurred, to continue producing legitimate income over the course of its economic life in the general circumstances following the taking by the State.'
410.   *Metalclad, supra* note 87 at para. 119 citing *Benvenuti et Bonfant, supra* note 37. See also *AGIP supra* note 348.
411.   Ball, *supra* note 403 at 419.
412.   *Ibid.*
413.   *CMS, supra* note 151 at para. 453.

The inherent difficulty with the DCF method is that it requires an assessment of various forward looking factors. These include: (i) the projected future revenue of the enterprise; (ii) the projected future expenses of the enterprise; (iii) the opportunity cost of keeping funds tied up in the given enterprise and not reinvesting them elsewhere, i.e. a comparative assessment of other available investment opportunities; (iv) the projected future effects of inflation on the future income stream, as inflation over time lowers the net present value of such an income stream; and (v) the probability that the projected revenue in fact will be realized.

Such analysis requires assessments about the future – and in some circumstances, those assessments can be difficult to make reliably; while in others they can be made reasonably well. Thus, reliability of this approach has to be assessed on a case-by-case basis with an appreciation of the elements of the analysis and what they represent. For example, in the case of regulated utilities the DCF analysis may be particularly reliable given the 'asset base' approach to tariff setting often applied by regulators, which means that future income through tariffs be sufficient to recover efficient investments made plus a reasonable rate of return.

The DCF method is relatively new in the world of arbitration.[414] Although historically there was some reluctance to apply DCF analyses,[415] IIA tribunals have increasingly accepted that the approach may be used to calculate fair market value,[416] provided the investment is profitable and has operated for a sufficient period.[417] Where the enterprise has not operated for a long enough time to establish a performance record or where it has failed to make a profit, tribunals have found that future earnings cannot be used to determine going concern or fair market value as an award based on such future profits could be speculative.[418] In *Vivendi II*, the tribunal stated that the absence of a history of demonstrated profitability does not absolutely preclude the use of DCF valuation methodology, but that the claimant would have to lead convincing evidence of its ability to produce profits.[419] In *Middle East*, the tribunal found that Egypt had expropriated a long-term license to supply cement. The tribunal awarded lost profits under three

---

414. See discussion in Ball, *supra* note 403 at 420-421, who noted in 2001, that although the DCF method in not new in the world of finance it is relatively new in the history of international arbitration.
415. See Ball, *ibid.*
416. *Vivendi II, supra* note 69 at para. 8.3.3; *Metalclad, supra* note 87 at para. 120 citing *Asian Agricultural Products Ltd v. Sri Lanka* (Final Award, 27 Jun. 1990) [*AAPL*] at 292, in which the tribunal observed that, in dealing with the comparable problem of the assessment of the value of good will, its ascertainment 'requires the prior presence on the market for at least two or three years, which is the minimum period needed in order to establish continuing business connections.' The Iran-US Claims Tribunal has used this approach in applying Art. IV(2) of the Iran-US Treaty of Amity of 1955 which provides for 'just compensation' defined as 'the full equivalent of the property taken.' See *Starrett Housing, supra* note 401.
417. *Vivendi II, supra* note 69 at para. 8.3.3 citing *Levitt v. Iran*, (1987) 14 Iran-US CTR 191 at 209-10.
418. *Metalclad, ibid.*, at para. 121.
419. *Vivendi II, supra* note 69 at para. 8.3.8. The tribunal stated that the claimant failed to establish with a sufficient degree of certainty that the concession would have been profitable.

cement supply contracts. Although it recognized in principle that the expropriation also deprived Middle East of the opportunity to earn other future profits and that this 'earning capacity' could be considered for the purposes of determining market value,[420] it found that the claimant had the burden to prove lost opportunities and that it had not satisfied the burden of proof.[421]

DCF analyses can result in widely divergent values depending on the assumptions used to calculate future profits and discount values. In *CME*, the valuation gap between the parties' experts was over USD 200 million. As a result the tribunal conducted detailed analysis to explore the assumptions in the DCF valuations. It then confirmed its conclusions by reference to a third party offer to buy the investment.[422]

§7.43 Net book value, replacement or liquidation value   Net book, replacement and liquidation valuations can be used to calculate value based on the difference between assets and liabilities. Replacement value is the amount necessary to replace the investment prior to the injurious acts. Liquidation value is the amount a willing buyer would pay a willing seller for the investment in a liquidation process. Net book value (NBV) is the difference between an enterprise's assets and liabilities as recorded on its financial statements or the value of the tangible assets which are the subject of the claim on the balance sheet, representing their cost after deducting accumulated depreciation in accordance with generally accepted accounting principles.[423] This method is inherently backward looking. One potential virtue is that it is based on attestable documents generated for some purpose other than supporting a claim.[424] As a result, it is less likely to be viewed as favouring a particular party in the arbitration. However, since it bases the valuation on historical data, it may not reflect the present value of the property,[425] especially in periods of high inflation[426] and where there has been a considerable lapse of time between the date of the purchase of the asset and the date of the balance sheet.[427] Furthermore, the balance sheet fails to reflect certain intangible assets and other important elements of a firm that may contribute importantly to its success; these include contractual rights, management skills, technical expertise, and relationships with customers and suppliers.[428] Finally, perhaps the harshest criticism, that has caused some commentators to call the method nonsense and a misnomer,[429] is

---

420.   *Middle East, supra* note 160 at para. 126-127.
421.   *Ibid.*, at para. 128.
422.   *CME, supra* note 87 at para. 604.
423.   T. R. Stauffer, 'Valuation of Assets in International Takings' (1996) 17 ELJ 459 at 461.
424.   *Ibid.* See also T. Weiler & L. M. Diaz, 'Causation and Damages in NAFTA Investor-State Arbitration' in Weiler., ed., *NAFTA Investment Law supra* note 84, 179 at 199.
425.   W.C. Lieblich, 'Determining the Economic Value of Expropriated Income-Producing Property in International Arbitrations' (1991) 8 IA 59 at 69.
426.   Weiler & Diaz, *supra* note 425 at 199.
427.   Friedland & Wong, *supra* note 403 at 406.
428.   Lieblich, *supra* note 425 at 69.
429.   *Ibid.*

that it does not reflect the future cash-generating ability of the enterprise, which is the essence of economic value.[430] Thus, often NBV may fail to reflect an investment's value at the time of the expropriation.[431]

In *Middle East*, the tribunal found the seizure of the ship and its subsequent sale by public auction to be expropriatory. The tribunal rejected the auction price (USD 91,000) as reflecting the true measure of the market value because of deficiencies in the auction procedure. The claimant argued for a price based on a sale contract for the ship (USD 1.3 million) or alternatively based on its scrap value (USD 865,000). The tribunal determined the ship had a market value of USD 478,000, the average between the auction and scrap price. The tribunal stated that given the amount is dispute it would be too time consuming and costly to seek an independent expert opinion.[432]

§7.44 DCF and NBV compared　The DCF and NBV methods are not necessarily inconsistent. Indeed, each method is suitable for enterprises that are in different stages of development. Although DCF is suitable for an entity that has an earning history and has attained the status of a going concern, NBV can be used for valuation of recent investments that have not had the time to earn goodwill and reach profitability. It has even been suggested that the two measures of valuation are not only linked but that they may also yield similar results, provided certain adjustments are made in the NBV value in order to update it.[433] This updated value can be used as a 'reality check' on the DCF valuations of enterprises, especially in the litigation context where parties' valuations are often regarded with suspicion.

If the factors needing to be assessed for a DCF valuation are too difficult to discern reliably, tribunals tend to conclude that DCF should not be used because it is too speculative. In circumstances where, for example, there is no history of profitability, tribunals opt for other measures of fair market value. Strictly speaking, the DCF method could still be used where there is uncertainty, but IIA tribunals may be reluctant to apply it.

§7.45 Actual investment　Fair market value may be determined by the investor's actual investment.[434] Tribunals often adopt this method where, as in *Metalclad*,[435]

---

430. *Ibid.*
431. Ball, *supra* note 403 at 421. In high risk investments, in which the 1/50 successful investment covers the costs of the other 49 unsuccessful investments, the investor will be under compensated if the state can expropriate the successful investment at NBV.
432. *Middle East, supra* note 160 at para. 150.
433. See Stauffer, *supra* note 423 at 466-469.
434. *Metalclad, supra* note 87 at para. 122 citing *Phelps Dodge Corp. v. Iran*, (1986) 10 Iran-US CTR 121 and *Biloune, supra* note 43 at 228-229. See also *Wena, supra* note 41 at para. 123, which cited *SPP, supra* note 193 at 381.
435. In *Metaclad*, the tribunal accorded substantial weight to Metalclad's tax filings and independent audit documents supporting those tax filings, but discounted certain expenses that were 'too far removed' from the investment and not related to the specific investment. *Ibid.*, at paras 124-126.

the investment did not have a profit-making history,[436] or in *Wena*,[437] where one of the hotels had operated for eighteen months and renovations had not been completed on the other. In *Sedelmayer*, the tribunal found that actual investments included in-kind contribution of chattels to a company's capital and money spent on improvements to premises.[438] The tribunal in *Vivendi II* considered investment value as the closest proxy to eliminate the consequences of the IIA breaches.[439]

§7.46 Arm's length transactions or third party offer to purchase   An indicator of fair market value may be a prior (but recent) arm's length transaction for part of the investment (such shares in a company), or what an actual arm's length buyer was willing to pay for the investment. The commentary to the ILC's Articles on State Responsibility notes that where property is freely traded in an open market, asset-based valuation methods based on market data are generally unproblematic.[440] This might be determined by an offer to purchase by a third party buyer or what the claimant paid for the investment prior to the expropriation.[441] In *CME*, the tribunal based its valuation of CME's investment on the basis of an interested third party's valuation, subject to deductions to reflect other relevant circumstances.[442]

§7.47 Market capitalization   Another method for determining fair market value is market capitalization – the value of a firm's shares on the stock market based on the share price multiplied by the number of outstanding shares. Market capitalization, however, may not be appropriate, particularly where the market is illiquid and few shares are traded, or where markets are highly volatile.[443]

§7.48 Reductions   In determining the fair market value of an investment, a tribunal may deduct any residual value in the investment[444] and account for future liabilities related to the investments. For example, in calculating compensation, the *Metalclad* tribunal took into account the cost of remediating a waste disposal site.[445]

In *CSOB*, the respondent state argued that the amount of compensation should be reduced to take account of a tax windfall that would accrue to the investor.[446] Two

---

436.   *Metalclad, ibid.*, at paras 119-130.
437.   *Wena, supra* note 41 at paras 122-125.
438.   *Sedelmayer, supra* note 71.
439.   *Vivendi II, supra* note 69 at para. 8.3.17.
440.   ILC's Articles on State Responsibility, *supra* note 89 at 226.
441.   See *INA Corp. v. Iran, supra* note 347 at 382-383 and *Saghi v. Iran*, 29 Iran-US CTR 20 at 49 referred to in *CME*, Final Award, *supra* note 352 at para. 140.
442.   See *CME, ibid.*, at paras 528 and 549.
443.   See *CME, ibid.*, for a discussion of market capitalization.
444.   See *CME, ibid.*, at para. 612.
445.   *Metalclad, supra* note 87 at para. 127.
446.   See S. Ripinsky *et al.*, *Damages in International Law, supra* note 403 for discussion of taxation and compensation.

reasons were advanced for an alleged tax advantage brought about by the harmful event. First, that of interest capitalization, meaning that if the investor had received its income from the investment over the life of the investment, it would have paid greater taxes on that income when it accrued (rather than a lump sum at the end of a dispute). Second, to take account of changes in the tax regime between the moment the compensation became due and the date of actual payment. The Tribunal rejected the idea that a floating tax rate should be a reduction and stated that:

> ... on the contrary, there is no link between the harmful event and the rate at which the injured party's compensation is taxed as income ... income taxes ... are consequential to the compensation and do not affect its determination. Compensation will not increase or decrease according to whether the amount of income tax rates is increased or decreased.[447]

B   DATE FOR DETERMINING COMPENSATION

§7.49 Date of the expropriation   The date for determining compensation is normally the time immediately before the occurrence of the expropriation or before the expropriation became public knowledge.[448] In either case the purpose of the provision is clear: the amount of the compensation is not to reflect the adverse effect of the expropriatory measure or measures on the value of the investment. Article 5(1), UK-Vietnam (2002), is characteristic in this respect. The date for determining compensation is that:

> ... immediately before the expropriation or before the impending expropriation became public knowledge, whichever is the earlier.

Some treaties expressly provide that the fair market value shall not reflect any change in value occurring because the expropriation had become publicly known earlier.[449]

The date of expropriation is a legal determination to be made by the tribunal; the tribunal need not defer to the claimants' choice as to the valuation date.[450]

Determining the date of the expropriation will normally be straightforward in the case of a direct expropriation. The expropriation will become public knowledge as a result of some government measure that institutes the process of expropriation.[451] Cases of indirect expropriation raise significant difficulties because the government typically disclaims that an expropriation has occurred. In cases where the tribunal finds an indirect expropriation resulting from a single measure, such as

---

447.   *CSOB, supra* note 210 at paras 360-368.
448.   For in-depth surveys of treaty practice, see *supra* note 60.
449.   Art. 5(2)(b), Austria-Azerbaijan (2000).
450.   *Sempra, supra* note 106 at para. 210.
451.   See Egypt-UK (1975) discussed in *Wena, supra* note 41.

in *Tecmed*, the date for determining compensation will be the date the measure took effect or became public knowledge.[452]

The most difficult cases for determining the date for expropriation are cases of creeping expropriation, where no one measure is in and of itself expropriatory, but the overall effect is expropriatory.[453] In this context, Professor Reisman and Robert Sloane have noted that it may:

> ... be useful and appropriate to disaggregate the moment of expropriation and the moment of valuation – to distinguish the 'moment of expropriation,' which goes to the question of *liability* (i.e., whether an accretion of measures *has* ripened into a compensable expropriation), from the 'moment of valuation,' which goes to the question of *damages*.[454]

Further, in cases of indirect expropriation, the question of the legality of the expropriation because of non-payment of compensation will often be an issue. As noted by Judge Brower:

> ... it is difficult to envision a de facto or 'creeping' expropriation ever being lawful, for the absence of a declared intention to expropriate almost certainly implies that no contemporaneous provision for compensation has been made. Indeed, research reveals no international precedent finding such an expropriation to have been lawful.[455]

Where the expropriation is illegal, some tribunals have awarded full reparation by calculating compensation as of the date of the award or another date.[456] Whether a tribunal is permitted to do this or is bound by the compensation standard set out in the IIA remains contentious. Where the IIA provision is mandatory and provides that compensation is to be determined as of the date of the expropriation, the tribunal may have no discretion to apply customary international law reparation standards. As discussed at §7.38 above, the counter-argument is that IIA compensation provisions only apply to legal expropriations. A consequence of the latter approach would be that all cases of indirect expropriation would *ipso facto* be illegal expropriations because the state has failed to pay compensation to the investor. Another approach would be to make a distinction, similar to that in ECtHR jurisprudence, between a wrongful failure to pay compensation and an inherently illegal expropriation (one that is discriminatory or lacks public purpose).[457]

In any case, if an IIA indirect expropriation claim is successful, then the host state will invariably be held to have breached the treaty, with the ensuing duty to

---

452. *Tecmed, supra* note 21. In *Metalclad*, the tribunal found the expropriation occurred on the date of denial of municipal construction permit (*Metalclad, supra* note 87 at para. 128).
453. Reisman & Sloane, *supra* note 94. See *supra* §7.15 on creeping expropriation.
454. *Ibid.*, at 150. See also Abdala & Spiller, *supra* note 368.
455. *Sedco, Inc. v. National Iranian Oil Co.* 10 Iran-US CTR 180; (1986) 25 ILM 629 at 649.
456. *Supra* §7.38.
457. See *Case of the Former King of Greece v. Greece* judgment, (28 Nov. 2002) at para. 78.

provide full compensation for breach of an international obligation under customary international law principles of state responsibility. In this context, the issue will be how best to assess the real value of the property affected, including the necessary flexibility in determining the valuation/expropriation date in order to give effect to the principle of full reparation. For example, it is one thing to value property in an outright and classic direct expropriation, or in a single act indirect expropriation in which the asset changes hands or is destroyed on a given date, but another to do so in the context of a creeping or consequential expropriation. In the latter scenario, the real loss caused by the measures might not be properly assessed if valuation is fixed at the date of the first adverse measure in the series of wrongful acts without any consideration for subsequent events. Nor might it be assessed by choosing the date of the last measure wiping out the residual value of the investment without considering the detrimental and aggregate impact of prior measures. If the cumulative impact of the state's previous interferences, which in retrospect form part of the treaty breach, is ignored, most of the damage caused by the wrongful conduct might go unrecovered. In these cases, to enable the tribunal to give full effect to *Chorzów Factory's* imperative, that reparation must, as far as possible wipe out all the consequences of the illegal act, i.e. undo all (but no more than) the material harm inflicted by the measures, sticking to a rigid principle of valuation at the date of expropriation without more would simply distort reality and would not permit an assessment of the real loss caused by the measures.

Hence, it would seem appropriate, mainly in cases of indirect creeping expropriations, to adopt as the valuation date that of the first adverse measure, but then use hindsight information (i.e. subsequent developments) to determine the value of the asset had the expropriatory measures not been adopted. This approach permits isolating the impact of the adverse measures by formulating a 'without measures' or 'but for' scenario, in which the value of the asset in a hypothetical scenario without measures is established, and then comparing it with the 'actual' value of the asset in light of the measures. The difference between the two values is the amount due as compensation.

C   TRANSFERABILITY AND CONVERTIBILILITY[458]

§7.50 Timing   IIAs normally require that payment of compensation for expropriation be made 'promptly,'[459] 'without delay,'[460] 'without undue delay'[461] or 'without unreasonable delay.'[462] In some IIAs, a specific time period is mentioned.[463] A few treaties provide that payments may be made in instalments in case

---

458. For in-depth surveys of treaty practice, see studies *supra* note 60.
459. Art. 4(1), Austria-Belarus (2001).
460. Art. 4(2), Bosnia and Herzegovina-Sweden (2000).
461. Art. 5(2), India-Portugal (2000).
462. Art. 6(1), India-Thailand (2000).
463. German BITs generally provide a maximum of two months.

of a balance of payment crisis.[464] IIAs therefore clarify that compensation need not be provided before the expropriatory measure.[465]

§7.51 Transferability and convertibility IIAs generally require that payments be made transferable and in a fully convertible currency:[466]

- paid and made freely transferable to a foreign bank account and in currency of the country of which claimants are nationals or any freely convertible currency agreed upon by the parties;[467]
- paid in a freely convertible currency and made transferable to the country designated by the claimants concerned;[468]
- be effectively realizable and be freely transferable.[469]

Tribunals have found that claimants ought not to be prejudiced by the effects of a currency devaluation that takes place between the date of the wrongful act and the determination of the amount of compensation.[470]

D INTEREST

§7.52 Interest Most compensation for expropriation provisions expressly require the payment of interest on compensation. Interest is typically payable from either the date of the expropriation or within a set time period from the date of expropriation until the date of payment of the award.[471] Some IIAs also provide guidance on the interest rate to be applied: 'commercial rate,'[472] 'normal market rate,'[473] 'reasonable market rate'; or 'on the LIBOR basis.'[474]

In the absence of a treaty provision, interest is payable from the date of expropriation.[475] Interest normally accrues until payment of the award.[476]

---

464. Sierra Leone-UK (1981).
465. It remains unclear, however, at what point non-payment of compensation will render the expropriation illegal. For example, if the government accepts liability for expropriation and offers to pay compensation, but fails to do so, or there is an undue delay, then arguably the conditions for a lawful expropriation are not met.
466. Art. 5(c), Czeckoslovakia-Netherlands (1991).
467. Art. 5(2)(c), Austria-Azerbaijan (2000).
468. Art. 4(2), Bosnia and Herzegovina-Sweden (2000).
469. Art. 5, Israel-Thailand (2000).
470. *Vivendi II, supra* note 69 at para. 8.4.5, referring to the *The Lighthouses Arbitration (France v. Greece)* (1956) XII RIAA 155, 23 ILR 659.
471. In *Sedelmayer, supra* note 71 the claimant claimed, and was granted, interest from two weeks after the Statement of Claim was sent to the Respondent.
472. Art. 4(2), Bosnia and Herzegovina-Sweden (2000).
473. Art. 5(2), India-Portugal (2000).
474. Art. 4(1), Austria-Belarus (2001).
475. In *AAPL, supra* note 416 at para. 114, the tribunal found that 'interest becomes an integral part of the compensation itself, and should run consequently from the date when the State's international responsibility became engaged.'
476. See para. 178, *Middle East, supra* note 160.

In *CME*, the tribunal noted that the treaty provided that the compensation was to be paid without 'undue delay' and with interest from the date when the principal sum should have been paid. In determining this date, the tribunal took into account that Czech law provides that an amount is due at the date following the request for payment.[477] It therefore granted interest from the date of the notice of arbitration, over six months later than the date of the expropriation.

In the case of interest rates derived from national law, the situation becomes complicated where the award is in a major currency. In *Sedelmayer,* the tribunal considered the Germany-USSR BIT, which provides that interest shall be paid 'at the rate that is in effect in the territory of the respective Contracting Party.' The Claimant argued that this meant the rate in fact applied in Russia and proffered evidence that the rate in Russia on USD credits at the applicable time was thirty percent. Russia argued that the rate 'in effect' in its territory was that applied under its laws, which under the Russian Civil Code referred to the place of residence of the creditor (i.e. Germany). The tribunal accepted Russia's interpretation as more plausible.

IIA tribunals have regularly awarded interest to successful claimants.[478] In expropriation cases, IIA tribunals have often awarded compound interest as the most appropriate because it mirrors what the investor would normally receive commercially.[479]

---

477. *CME, supra* note 352 at para. 632.
478. In *Vivendi II, supra* note 69, the tribunal stated at note 432 that 'the award of compound interest is no longer the exception to the rule' noting that 'a non-exhaustive review of previous investment arbitration cases and found seven awards granting compound interest and three granting simple interest.'
479. In *Middle East, supra* note 160 at para. 174 the tribunal found that 'international jurisprudence and literature have recently, after detailed consideration concluded that interest is an integral part of the compensation due after the award and that compound (as opposed to simple) interest is at present deemed appropriate as the standard of international law in such expropriation cases ... [T]his Tribunal concludes that in this case, annually compounded interest and, in view of the rates in financial markets during the relevant period, a rate of 6% p.a. is appropriate.' In *Wena, supra* note 147 at para. 128, the tribunal awarded 9% compounded quarterly stating: 'To this [compensation] should be added an appropriate sum for interest. Claimant has claimed interest but neither specified a rate nor whether interest should be compounded. Moreover, the IPPA, the lease agreements, and the ICSID Convention and Rules are all silent on the subject of interest. The Panel is of the view that in this case interest should be awarded and that it would be appropriate to adopt a rate of 9%, to be compounded quarterly.' In *Metalclad, supra* note 79 at para. 131 the tribunal stated: 'So as to restore the claimant to a reasonable approximation of the position in which it would have been if the wrongful act had not taken place, interest has been calculated at 6% p.a., compounded annually.' See also *ADC, supra* note 277 at para. 522. For discussion of interest as a element of damages see J. Y. Gotanda, *A Study of Interest*, VI Dossiers of the ICC Institute of World Business Law (ICC Publications, forthcoming, 2008); J.Y. Gotanda, *Awarding Compound Interest in International Disputes*, Oxford University Comparative Law Forum 2004; J.Y. Gotanda, 'Awarding Interest in International Arbitration' (1996) 90 AJIL 40; F.A. Mann, 'Compound Interest as an Item of Damages in International Law' (1988) 21 UCDLR 577; and J. Gillis Wetter, 'Interest as an Element of Damages in the Arbitral Process,' (1986) 5 IFLR 20.

E   JUDICIAL REVIEW

§7.53 Review   Many IIAs specify that the legality of an expropriation and the amount of compensation must be subject to prompt review by a judicial authority or another competent and independent authority.[480] Some authors have argued that due process requires judicial review.[481] The right to judicial review may also require that the reviewing authority determine whether the expropriation conforms to principles of international law.[482] It is important to note that, under fork in the road provisions in IIA investor-state dispute resolution clauses, seeking review of expropriation decisions before domestic tribunals may foreclose a right to inves- tor-state arbitration.[483]

In *Siemens,* Argentina argued that a treaty stipulation that the legality of expro- priation and the amount of indemnification 'should be reviewable through ordinary legal proceedings' entitled the Argentine courts to review any future decision of the tribunal in connection with the alleged expropriation.[484] The tribunal rejected this claim rightly noting that it is the expropriation or nationalization or compensation that is subject to the review of the ordinary courts, not a tribunal's decision.[485]

---

480.   Art. 4(3), Bosnia and Herzegovina-Sweden (2000); Art. 5(3), Austria-Azerbaijan; and Art. 4(1), Denmark-Hungary (1988). For in-depth surveys of treaty practice, see *supra* note 60.

481.   Vandevelde, *supra* note 72 at 121 citing Art. 3, Comment 6, 1967 OECD Draft Convention (1968) 7 ILM 117.

482.   Art. III(2), Tunisia-US (1990).

483.   See McLachlan, Shore & Weiniger, *supra* note 91 at para. 4.75 on fork in the road provisions.

484.   Article 4(2), Argentina-US (1991), provides: 'The legality of the expropriation, nationaliza- tion or similar measure, and the amount of the indemnification should be reviewable through ordinary legal proceedings.'

485.   *Siemens, supra* note 127 at para. 261.

Chapter 8

Transfer Rights, Performance Requirements and Transparency

INTRODUCTION

§8.1 Overview In addition to the minimum standards of treatment considered in the previous two chapters, international investment agreements (IIAs) contain a number of standards tailored to address particular issues. This chapter covers IIA provisions on transfer of funds (Part I), performance requirements (Part II) and transparency (Part III).

I   TRANSFER OF FUNDS

§8.2 Introduction The ability to transfer funds into and out of home and host states is a fundamental concern of foreign investors.[1] Foreign investors want the ability to transfer funds *into* host states in order to establish, maintain and expand their investments. Foreign investors want to be able to transfer funds *out of* host states to repatriate profits, pay for business expenses and engage in other investment activities. The freedom to transfer funds ensures that investors can reap the financial rewards of a successful investment or exit the host state if an investment is unsuccessful. If transfers out of the host state are subject to restrictions or are frozen, the economic value of the investment can be significantly affected. Indeed, if transfer restrictions are so severe that the funds are frozen within the host state

---

1. See generally UNCTAD, *Transfer of Funds*, UNCTAD Series on issues in international investment agreements New York and Geneva: United Nations, 2000) (UNCTAD/ITE/IIT/20) [*Transfer of Funds*] and G. Sacerdoti, 'The Admission and Treatment of Foreign Investment under Recent Bilateral and Regional Treaties' (2000) 1 JWI 105 [Sacerdoti] at 117.

for an extended period, the transfer restrictions might be expropriatory.[2] Although discussion of transfer rights tends to focus on host state restrictions on outward transfers, restrictions on transferring funds from home states to host states can also impede the investment promotion purpose of IIAs and the ability of foreign investors to establish or maintain the investment in the host state.

There are a number of legitimate reasons why a state may want or need to restrict transfers. In the event of a financial crisis, states may need to take temporary measures that restrict transfers of funds in order to address balance of payment problems.[3] Moreover, states may need to restrict transfers to protect creditors' rights, ensure payment of taxes and enforce anti-corruption measures. The need to regulate and restrict transfers of funds in specified circumstances is recognized in international monetary, trade and investment law.[4]

Although under customary international law states exercise almost absolute monetary sovereignty,[5] there exists a complex international regime that regulates fund transfers and convertibility. The *Articles of Agreement of the International Monetary Fund* regulate currency convertibility and transfers for current transactions, such as payments for trade in goods. In 1961, Organization for Economic Co-operation and Development (OECD) Member States agreed to additional free transfer commitments in two codes.[6] More recently, the international trade regime, through the *General Agreement on Trade in Services* (GATS),[7] established rules regarding transfers of funds to ensure that trade in services is not impeded by transfer restrictions.[8] Transfer provisions in IIAs supplement this regime, providing important protections with respect to capital transfers, among other things. Each of these topics is covered below.

---

2. See *supra* Chapter 7, §7.4 *et seq.*
3. On balance of payments, see A.F. Lowenfeld, *International Economic Law* (Oxford: Oxford University Press, 2002) [Lowenfeld] at 15-18 and Chapter 5, Trade, Exchange Rates and Balance of Payments in M. Trebilcock & R. Howse, *The Regulation of International Trade*, 3rd edn (London: Routledge, 2005) [*Regulation of International Trade*].
4. *Ibid.*
5. See M.R. Shuster, *The Public International Law of Money* (Oxford: Oxford University Press, 1973) at 1-91; C. Proctor, *Mann on the Legal Aspect of Money*, 6th edn (Oxford: Oxford University Press, 2005) at 500-509; R. Dolzer & M. Stevens, *Bilateral Investment Treaties* (The Hague: M. Nijhoff, 1995) at 85. Subject to customary international law rules protecting the rights of foreigners and specific treaty or contractual commitments, states are free to impose restrictions on foreign exchange transactions involving the transfer of funds across their respective borders. State restrictions must comply with customary international law rules regarding the property of foreigners, and state currency valuation and exchange restriction measures may give rise to expropriation and discrimination claims. See Shuster, *ibid.*, at 47-91 for a discussion of pre-International Monetary Fund legal authorities.
6. See §8.4 below.
7. *General Agreement on Trade in Services*, 15 Apr. 1994, Marrakesh Agreement Establishing the World Trade Organization, Annex 1B, reproduced in *The Legal Texts: Results of the Uruguay Round of Multilateral Trade Negotiations* (Cambridge: Cambridge University Press, 1994) [GATS]. The text is also reprinted at 33 ILM 46 (1994).
8. See §8.5 below.

§8.3 Articles of Agreement of the International Monetary Fund (IMF Articles)[9]   The International Monetary Fund (IMF), along with the International Bank for Reconstruction and Development (the World Bank), were conceived in 1944 at the Bretton Woods Conference.[10] These two international economic organizations – the IMF focusing on financial and monetary stability and the World Bank focusing on economic reconstruction and development – were intended to be the central pillars of future international economic cooperation. The third pillar, the International Trade Organization, was never created.[11]

The IMF Articles establish the legal framework for an international system of payments, fund transfers and exchange transactions. One of the central purposes of the IMF is to:

> ... assist in the establishment of a multilateral system of payments in respect of current transactions between members and in the elimination of foreign exchange restrictions which hamper the growth of world trade.[12]

With its nearly universal membership,[13] the IMF system is of central importance to the regulation of international fund transfers.

The IMF system is vital to foreign traders and investors because it prohibits Member States from imposing restrictions on the making of payments and transfers for current international transactions. This prohibition includes government measures that restrict currency exchange. Article VIII, Section 2(a), IMF Articles provides:

> ... no member shall, without the approval of the Fund, impose restrictions on the making of payments and transfers for current international transactions.[14]

This section, in essence, requires states to ensure that their currency is convertible. The rule applies unless specific national restrictions are either approved by the IMF or the restriction in question is subject to the transitional arrangements contained in the IMF Articles.[15] Temporary derogations from obligations may be

---

9. *Amended Articles of Agreement of the International Monetary Fund* (1992) 31 ILM 1309 [IMF Articles]. The Articles entered into force in 1945 and the IMF began to operate in 1946. The IMF Articles have been amended three times since 1944. The 1976 amendments were the most significant because they abolished the par value system of exchange rates and allowed members to have floating currencies. See A.F. Lowenfeld, *supra* note 3, Part VII, The International Monetary System. On the IMF generally see J. Gold, *Legal and Institutional Aspects of the International Monetary System: Selected Essays* (Washington: International Monetary Fund, 1979). Sir Joseph Gold served as a member of the IMF from 1946 to 1960 and as General Counsel and Director of the Legal Department from 1960 to 1979.
10. IMF Articles, *ibid.*
11. See *supra* Chapter 1, §1.15.
12. Art. I(iv), IMF Articles, *supra* note 9.
13. As of 1 Jun. 2008, the IMF had 185 member states. Non-members include North Korea and Cuba.
14. Art. VIII, Section 2(a), IMF Articles, *supra* note 9.
15. Art. XIV, Transitional Arrangements, allows a member to maintain restrictions that were in effect on the date it became a member. Members are required to take measures to withdraw the restrictions. See Art. XIV, Section 2, *ibid.*

approved where a member suffers balance of payments difficulties.[16] In practice, the IMF requires that any exchange restrictions be temporary (usually less than a year) and non-discriminatory.[17]

Under Article VIII, Section 3, IMF Articles, members agree not to engage in discriminatory currency arrangements or multiple currency practices. This means that members may not apply different exchange rates for different purposes (i.e., one for foreign investors and one for nationals).[18]

On the other hand, Member States are allowed to impose restrictions on international capital movements.[19] Therefore, for IMF members, whether financial transfer restrictions are permitted depends on whether the transfer is categorized as a *current transaction* or a *capital movement*. As noted by the Iran-US Claims Tribunal in *Hood v. Iran*, the distinction between capital and current transactions is not 'an easy one.'[20]

The IMF Articles define payments for current transactions as:

> … payments which are not for the purpose of transferring capital, and includes, without limitation:

> (1) all payments due in connection with foreign trade, other current business, including services, and normal short-term banking and credit facilities;
> (2) payments due as interest on loans and as net income from other investments;
> (3) payments of moderate amount for amortization of loans or for depreciation of direct investments; and
> (4) moderate remittances for family living expenses.[21]

The definition of current transactions covers normal business payments and profits and extends to transactions including amortization of loans. It also covers depreciation of direct investments, which would be considered capital transactions in other contexts.[22] Members may, however, restrict capital transfers, including

---

16. Art. VIII, Section 2(a) and Art. VIII, Section 3, IMF Articles, *ibid.*
17. The criteria applied by the IMF Executive Board for approvals are set out in Executive Board Decisions 1034-(60/27), 1 Jun. 1960 and 6790-(81/43), 20 Mar. 1981, as amended. See Lowenfeld, *supra* note 3 at 508-511 and *Transfer of Funds, supra* note 1 at 17.
18. See Lowenfeld, *ibid.*, 510.
19. Art. VI, Section 3, IMF Articles, *supra* note 9, provides that: 'Members may exercise such controls as are necessary to regulate international capital movements, but no member may exercise these controls in a manner which will restrict payments for current transactions or which will unduly delay transfers of funds in settlement of commitments, except as provided in Article VII, Section 3(b) and in Article XIV, Section 2.'
20. 7 Iran-US CTR 36 at 45. On the Iran-US Claims Tribunal jurisprudence on international monetary law see J. Gold, 'The Iran-U.S. Claims Tribunal and the Articles of Agreement of the IMF' (1984) 18 GWJILE 537; A. Mori, 'The Treatment of the Rules of the International Monetary Fund by the Iran-US Claims Tribunal,' (1993) 3 AYIL 71; and G.H. Aldrich, *The Jurisprudence of the Iran-United States Claims Tribunal* (Oxford: Clarendon Press, 1996) at 388-396.
21. See Art. XXX(d), IMF Articles, *supra* note 9. The definition also provides that the IMF 'may, after consultation with the members concerned, determine whether certain specific transactions are to be considered current transactions or capital transactions.'
22. D. Siegel, 'Using Free Trade Agreements to Control Capital Account Restrictions: Summary of Remarks on the Relationship to the Mandate of the IMF' (2004) 10 ILSA JICL 297. At the

transfers of the proceeds from the liquidation or sale of an investment, as well as gains deriving from capital appreciation.[23]

There are three important limitations to the prohibition on imposing restrictions on payments and transfers for current transactions. First, as noted above, the prohibition does not apply where the restrictions are either approved by the IMF or the state in question is subject to the transitional arrangements contained in the IMF Articles. Second, the IMF Articles apply to the 'making of payments' and are essentially concerned with outward flows; they do not regulate transfers for capital investments or additional capital infusions to an established investment.[24] Third, the prohibition applies to *international* transactions and does not cover transactions between a locally incorporated investment vehicle and other local companies. From the perspective of the foreign investor wishing to transfer funds, the IMF Articles provide important, but incomplete, protections.[25] As noted above, the IMF Articles do not prohibit a host state from restricting capital transfers, including transfers of the proceeds from the liquidation or sale of an investment.

§8.4 OECD Liberalization Codes   The OECD has adopted two legally binding codes that liberalize investments and transfers of funds between OECD Member States: (i) the *Code of Liberalization of Capital Movements* (the Capital Movements Code); and (ii) the *Code of Liberalization of Current Invisible Operations* (the Current Invisibles Code).[26] The Capital Movements Code provides for the progressive liberalization of capital movements and liberalizes both the making of investments and capital transfers.[27] It applies to outward investment and requires that residents be permitted to transfer funds abroad to make investments.[28] The Current Invisibles Code liberalizes investment in major services industries (including services related to business, industry and foreign trade, transport, insurance, banking and finance, cinema and television, and travel and tourism) and served as a precursor to the GATS. Together, the Codes cover all income, proceeds and other amounts relating to investments, thereby according broader subject matter

---

time of writing the article, Ms. Siegel was Senior Counsel in the IMF Legal Department.

23.   Further guidance on the distinction between current and capital transfers is available in the IMF's *Balance of Payments Manual*. Although the manual does not establish binding interpretations of the IMF articles, it reflects the considered opinions of the IMF and state officials. See J. Gold, *supra* note 20 at 568.

24.   *Transfer of Funds*, *supra* note 1 at 13.

25.   In addition, the IMF Articles do not provide any direct rights against the state by private parties. State measures that are inconsistent with the IMF Articles could, nevertheless, be a factor in assessing whether a state has breached general minimum standards of treatment including fair and equitable treatment.

26.   The Codes were adopted by the OECD Council on 12 Dec. 1961. See Shuster, *supra* note 5 at 246-259 and P. Muchlinski, *Multinational Enterprises and the Law*, 2nd edn (Oxford: Oxford University Press, 2007) [Muchlinski] at 248-250. The Codes are supplemented by Decisions of the OECD Council. The Codes, Council Decisions and country reservations are available on the OECD website.

27.   *Transfer of Funds*, *supra* note 1 at 19.

28.   *Transfer of Funds*, *ibid.*, at 21.

coverage with respect to transfers than the IMF Articles.[29] In addition to liberalizing payments, the Codes provide a right of establishment between OECD states,
subject to the reservations set out in the schedule for each state.[30]

§8.5 General Agreement on Trade in Services (GATS)   Under the GATS,
World Trade Organization (WTO) members have undertaken specific market
access commitments for the cross-border supply of services. In order to guarantee market access rights for services, the GATS provides that a WTO member
may not impose restrictions on international transfers and payments for current
transactions relating to its specific market commitments.[31] The GATS further
provides that if a member undertakes market access commitments in relation to
the supply of a service, it is required to allow related transfers of capital.[32] For
example, if a host state has undertaken establishment obligations with respect to
insurance services, it must allow foreign investors to transfer capital in order to
establish the service in question.[33] The GATS does not prohibit all restrictions on
transfers. Restrictions for the purpose of safeguarding balance of payments are
permissible.[34] Nonetheless, the GATS imposes stringent requirements on restrictions: they must be consistent with the IMF Articles, temporary, non-discriminatory,
and not adopted or maintained for the purpose of protecting a particular service
sector.[35]

§8.6 Transfer of funds in early investment instruments   The 1949 International
Chamber of Commerce (ICC) *International Code of Fair Treatment for Foreign*

---

29.   The codes are subject to reservations and have provisions for temporary derogations. Unlike
      the codes, IIAs do not expressly liberalize outward investment, although investment promotion
      obligations might be viewed as limiting a state's right to impose controls on outward investment. In addition, since most IIAs do not provide establishment rights, they do not liberalize
      inward transfers to make investments (See *supra* Chapter 3 on admission and establishment).
      In this respect, the coverage of the codes with respect to transfers is broader than most IIAs.
30.   Muchlinski, *supra* note 26 at 249. See §3.8 *et seq.* regarding establishment.
31.   Art. XI, GATS, *supra* note 7. This provision is discussed in *United States - Measures Affecting
      the Cross-Border Supply of Gambling and Betting Services*, WT/DS285/R at paras 6.438-
      6.442. At para. 6.442, the panel emphasized that: 'Article XI plays a crucial role in securing
      the value of specific commitments undertaken by Members under the GATS. Indeed, the value
      of specific commitments on market access and national treatment would be seriously impaired
      if Members could restrict international transfers and payment for service transactions in scheduled sectors. In ensuring, *inter alia*, that services suppliers can receive payments due under
      services contracts covered by a Member's specific commitment, Article XI is an indispensable
      complement to GATS disciplines on market access and national treatment. At the same time,
      the Panel is of the view that Article XI does not deprive Members from regulating the use of
      financial instruments, such as credit cards, provided that these regulations are consistent with
      other relevant GATS provisions, in particular Article VI.'
32.   See Art. XVI, footnote 8, GATS, *supra* note 7.
33.   *Transfer of Funds, supra* note 1 at 25.
34.   See Art. XII, GATS, *supra* note 7.
35.   *Ibid.*

Investment[36] contained an extensive freedom of funds transfer provision covering profits, payments, and the proceeds of sale or liquidation. On the other hand, the 1959 *Draft Convention on Investments Abroad* (Abs-Shawcross Draft Convention)[37] did not have a specific provision on transfers, with the exception of the requirement that compensation for expropriations be made in a transferable form.[38] Further, the 1961 *Draft Convention on the International Responsibility of States for Injuries to Aliens* (1961 Harvard Draft), intended as a restatement or codification of customary international law, only addresses exchange issues obliquely by noting that general changes in the value of currency are not expropriatory.[39] Early bilateral investment treaties (BITs), beginning with Article 4, Germany-Pakistan (1959), provided guarantees with respect to capital transfers:

> Either Party shall in respect of all investments guarantee to nationals or companies of the other Party the transfer of the invested capital, of the returns there-from and in the event of liquidation, the proceeds of such liquidation.

Despite this early BIT practice and the OECD's implementation of the Capital Movements Code and Current Invisibles Code, Article 4 of the 1967 OECD *Draft Convention on the Protection of Foreign Property* only contained a non-binding recommendation on transfers:

> Each Party recognises, with respect to property in its territory owned by a national of another Party, the principles of the freedom of transfer of the current income from, and proceeds upon liquidation of, such property, to such national of a Party as is entitled to them. While this Recommendation does not contain any obligation in this respect, each Party will endeavour to grant the necessary authorisations for such transfers to the country of the residence of that national and in the currency thereof.

§8.7 Transfer of funds in IIAs Most IIAs include provisions dealing specifically with the transfer of funds.[40] In general, IIAs provide that transfers associated

---

36. International Chamber of Commerce, *International Code of Fair Treatment for Foreign Investment,* ICC Pub. No. 129 (Paris: Lecraw Press, 1948), *reprinted in* UNCTAD, *International Investment Instruments: A Compendium,* Vol. 3 (New York: United Nations, 1996) at 273. See *supra* Chapter 1, §1.16 *et seq.* on post World War II international investment instruments.
37. (1960) 9 JPL 116. See *supra* Chapter 1, §1.16.
38. See *supra* Chapter 7, §7.51 *et seq.* on transfer requirements with respect to compensation for expropriation.
39. Art. 10(5), 1961 Harvard Draft, (1961) 55 AJIL 545. See *supra* Chapter 1, §1.16.
40. For an overview of treaty practice, see UNCTAD's three comprehensive studies: United Nations Centre on Transnational Corporations (UNCTC), *Bilateral Investment Treaties* (New York: United Nations, 1988) (Doc. No. ST/CTC/65); UNCTAD, *Bilateral Investment Treaties in the Mid-1990s* (New York and Geneva: United Nations, 1998) (Doc. No. UNCTAD/ITE/IIT/7) and UNCTAD, *Bilateral Investment Treaties 1995-2006* (New York and Geneva: United Nations, 2007) (Doc. No. UNCTAD/ITE/IIT/2006/5) [together *UNCTAD BIT Studies*]. Also see *Transfer of Funds, supra* note 1 and Dolzer & Stevens, *supra* note 5 at 85-95. For early US BIT practice,

with an investment may be made without delay or restriction, in a convertible currency and at the prevailing market exchange rate. Thus, although IIAs provide protection with respect to convertibility and transferability risks, they do not provide a guarantee against normal exchange rate risks.[41] Five distinct issues arise in relation to transfer rights under IIAs: (i) the scope of the transfer provision; (ii) the type of funds covered by the transfer provision; (iii) convertibility rights; (iv) permissible restrictions on transfers; and (v) express exceptions to transfer rights. These issues are addressed in turn in the following five sections.

§8.8 The scope of transfer rights   The scope of most transfer provisions is limited to transfers with respect to investments held by a foreign investor in a host state. The focus is on the right of the foreign investor to transfer funds both into and out of the host state. Article 7, Denmark-Egypt (1999), is typical in this respect:

> Each Contracting Party shall with respect to investments in its territory by investors of the other Contracting Party allow the free transfer into and out of its territory.[42]

The provision covers the principal risk that foreign investors face – host state restrictions on outward transfers of funds. In addition, the provision covers transfers into the host state. This is important because a foreign investor may need to transfer funds into the host state to make the initial investment or pay for investment-related expenses.[43]

Other BITs do not expressly provide the right to transfer funds into the host state. For example, Article 7(1), India-Ghana (2000), entitled 'Repatriation of Investment and Returns,' in its relevant part reads:

> Each Contracting Party shall permit all funds of an investor of the other Contracting Party related to an investment in its territory to be freely transferred.

This provision appears to apply only to funds already in the territory of the host state and not to additional transfers of capital. As the title of the provision suggests, it provides repatriation rights and not broader transfer rights.[44] This

---

see K.J. Vandevelde, *United States Investment Treaties: Policy and Practice* (Boston: Kluwer Law and Taxation, 1992) at 139-155.

41. Sacerdoti, *supra* note 1 at 118. Exchange rate risk is endemic to almost all foreign investment and can be mitigated by entering into foreign currency swaps and options. A state might, however, make commitments with respect to exchange rates or conversion, which may give rise to breaches of other IIA obligations including fair and equitable treatment and observance of undertakings.

42. See also Art. 7(1), Australia-Romania (1993), and Art. 12, Japan-Vietnam (2003).

43. IMF obligations will also apply if the transfer is a payment for a current transaction. See §8.3 above.

44. On the other hand, the transfer rights apply to funds including 'capital and additional capital amounts used to maintain and increase investments,' which might suggest that transfer rights also apply to transfers of capital.

approach is made explicit in Article 6(1), Belgo-Luxembourg Economic Union (BLEU)-Hong Kong (1996):

> Each Contracting Party shall in respect of investments guarantee to investors of the other Contracting Party the unrestricted right to transfer their investments and returns abroad.

In contrast, transfer provisions may be more open-ended, arguably applying to transfer into and out of both the home and host state. For example, Article 4, Czechoslovakia-Netherlands (1991), provides:

> Each Contracting Party shall guarantee that payments related to an investment may be transferred.

The provision expressly applies to funds necessary for the development of an investment, which would include fund transfers from the home state to the host state. Although IIAs do not typically impose obligations on states with respect to its own nationals, broad free transfer provisions, such as in the Dutch IIAs, might be interpreted to apply to outward transfers by home state nationals. Further, it could be argued that IIA investment promotion objectives are undermined if home states restrict the ability of their nationals to invest abroad.[45]

Transfer provisions normally focus on restrictions on the transfer of funds, but some IIA provisions appear to apply more generally to restrictions on the investment itself. For example, Article VII, Canada-Venezuela (1996), guarantees to investors 'the unrestricted transfer of investments.' Domestic restrictions on the sale or other disposition of the investment that prevent the investor from liquidating its investment would appear to be covered by this type of provision, and not simply the transfer of funds after liquidation.

§8.9 Types of transfers   Transfers of funds into the host state may be required to make the initial investment, to maintain and develop the investment and to make payments related to the investment. Transfers of funds out of the host state may be required to repatriate returns on the investment, to allow remittances from foreign employees and to transfer the proceeds from the partial or full liquidation or sale of the investment. Finally, in the event of an investment dispute, the investor may want to transfer compensation payments.

IIA transfer provisions are typically drafted to cover the wide variety of transfers associated with an investment. IIAs normally provide a general obligation to allow transfers related to an investment, followed by a non-exclusive list of illustrative transfers, which usually includes an expansive definition of the term 'returns.' For example, Article V, Argentina-US (1991), provides:

> Each Party shall permit all transfers related to an investment to be made freely and without delay into and out of its territory. Such transfers include: (a) returns; (b) compensation pursuant to Article IV; (c) payments arising

---

45. See *supra* Chapter 3, §3.6.

out of an investment dispute; (d) payments made under a contract, including amortization of principal and accrued interest payments made pursuant to a loan agreement directly related to an investment; (e) proceeds from the sale or liquidation of all or any part of an investment; and (f) additional contributions to capital for the maintenance or development of an investment.[46]

Other IIAs have similarly broad provisions. Article 4, Czechoslovakia-Netherlands (1991), provides:

> Each Contracting Party shall guarantee that payments related to an investment may be transferred. The transfers shall be made in a freely convertible currency, without undue restriction or delay. Such transfers include in particular though not exclusively:
>
> (a) profits, interests, dividends, royalties, fees and other current income;
> (b) funds necessary
>   i. for the acquisition of raw or auxiliary materials, semi-fabricated or finished products, or
>   ii. for the development of an investment or to replace capital assets in order to safeguard the continuity of an investment;
> (c) funds in repayment of loans;
> (d) earnings of natural persons;
> (e) the proceeds of sale or liquidation of the investment.

A smaller number of IIAs provide a list of specific types of funds that may be transferred without a general reference to funds related to an investment. For example, Article 8, Cuba-Denmark (2001), provides:

> Transfer of capital and returns
>
> (1) Each Contracting Party shall with respect to investments in its territory by investors of the other Contracting Party allow the free transfer in and out of its territory of:
>   (a) the initial capital and any additional capital for the maintenance and development of the investment;
>   (b) the investment capital or the proceeds from the sale or liquidation of all or any part of an investment;
>   (c) interests, dividends, profits and other returns realized;
>   (d) payments made for the reimbursement of the credits for investments, and interests due;
>   (e) payments derived from rights enumerated in Article 1, section 1, v of this Agreement;
>   (f) unspent earnings and other remunerations of personnel engaged in connection with an investment;

---

46. Returns is further defined in Art. I(d) as: 'an amount derived from or associated with an investment, including profit; dividend; interest; capital gain; royalty payment; management, technical assistance or other fee; or returns in kind.'

(g) compensation, restitution, indemnification or other settlement pursuant to Articles 6 and 7.

In practice the difference between the two approaches is unlikely to be significant because the listing of specific types of funds is broad and exhaustive.

Initial Investment. Since IMF obligations cover 'current transactions,' one of the primary purposes of IIA provisions is to cover capital transfers. IIAs guarantee the transfer of the 'investment,'[47] or 'capital.'[48] For example, Article 6, UK-Vietnam (2002), provides that:

> Each Contracting Party shall in respect of investments guarantee to nationals or companies of the other Contracting Party the unrestricted transfer of their investments and returns.

Some older BITs, although guaranteeing free transfer of returns, subject transfers of capital to host state laws.[49]

Additional Investment, Capital Gains and Reinvestment. IIA protection typically extends to additional investment, capital gains and reinvestment. Additional investments of capital made after the initial investment would come within the definition of investment. Some transfer provisions address this issue expressly by providing transfer rights for additional capital for the maintenance and development of an investment.[50] Capital gains on investments are typically included within the definition of 'returns,' or would, together with reinvested earnings, normally come within the definition of returns as amounts yielded by, derived from or associated with an investment. Some IIAs include, within their definitions of investment, returns that are reinvested.[51]

Payments. IIAs often provide transfer rights with respect to certain types of payments, most notably repayment of loans related to the investment[52] and payments under a contract.[53] As noted above, IMF rules already prohibit host state restrictions on the making of payments and transfers for current international

---

47. See also Arts 6(1) and 1(6), BLEU-Hong Kong (1996) and Arts 6(1) and 1(4), Hong Kong-Netherlands (1992).
48. Art. 6, Sri Lanka-UK (1980).
49. Art. 6, Egypt-UK (1975).
50. Danish BITs use this approach. See Arts 1 and 7, Denmark-Egypt (1999). See also Art. IV, Armenia-US (1992); Art. 7(a), Ghana-India (2000); Art. 5(a), Botswana-Germany (2000); Art. VII(a), Indonesia-Spain (1995); Art. 7(1), BLEU-Pakistan (1998); Art. 9(1)(a), Argentina-Australia (1995); Art. IV(1)(f), Armenia-US (1992); and Art. 7(1)(a), US-Uruguay (2005).
51. Danish BITs use this approach. See Arts 1 and 7, Denmark-Egypt (1999). See also Art. IV, Armenia-US (1992).
52. See Art. IV, Armenia-US (1992); Art. 5(1)(b), Chile-Tunisia (1998); Art. 5(c), Botswana-Germany (2000); Art. 5(b), Hungary-Spain (1989); Art. VII(c), Indonesia-Spain (1995); Art. 5(1)(4), BLEU-China (1984); Art. 5(1)(c), BLEU-Saudi Arabia (2001); Art. 9(1)(c), Argentina-Australia (1995); Art. VIII(1)(a), Canada-Venezuela (1996); and Art. XII(iii), Caribbean-Dominican Republic FTA (1998).
53. See Art. 5(c), Morocco-Spain (1989); Art. IV(1)(d), Armenia-US (1992); Art. 80(1)(d), Japan-Singapore Economic Partnership Agreement (2002) [JSEPA]; and Art. 17-07(1)(c), Colombia-Mexico-Venezuela FTA (1994).

transactions, which include payments due in current business as interest on loans and 'of moderate amount for amortization of loans.' The benefit of IIA coverage for investors is twofold. First, unlike the IMF definition, repayment of loans is typically not limited to a 'moderate amount for amortization.' Second, there is a direct IIA obligation that can be enforced by the investor.

Returns. In addition to transfers of capital, transfer provisions cover a broad range of returns on investments.[54] Most IIAs provide an expansive definition of 'returns' as amounts yielded by or derived from an investment, including profits, dividends, interest, capital gains, royalty payments, management or technical assistance fees or payments in connection with intellectual property rights and all other lawful income.[55] For example, Article 1(b), UK-Vietnam (2002), provides that:

> ... 'returns' means the amounts yielded by an investment and in particular, though not exclusively, includes profit, interest, capital gains, dividends, royalties and fees.

Many US BITs define the term return broadly as 'an amount derived from or associated with an investment irrespective of the form....,'[56] followed by a similar list. Other IIAs refer to returns and other amounts yielded by the investment.[57]

Remittances by Foreign Employees. The list of funds that may be transferred usually includes remittances by foreign employees.[58] In some cases, this right extends to earnings of natural persons[59] or any personnel engaged from abroad.[60] Other IIAs extend the right only to citizens of the home state.[61]

Proceeds from Sale or Liquidation of the Investment. Transfer provisions typically expressly apply to the proceeds from the total or partial sale or liquidation of the investment.[62]

---

54. For a discussion of returns in the context of a claim for the expropriation of a tax refund, see *EnCana Corporation v. Ecuador* (Award, 3 Feb. 2006).
55. See Art. 1(b), Australia-Romania (1993); Art. 1, Denmark-Egypt (1999). These may include license fees or royalty payments for the use of intellectual property. See, for example, Art. 5(d), Germany-Swaziland (1990); Art. 5(c), Hungary-Spain (1989); Art. 5(b), Morocco-Spain (1989) and Art. X(1)(c), Australia-China (1988).
56. See Art. I(d), Romania-US (1992); Art. I(d), Czechoslovakia-US (1991); Art. I(d), Russia-US (1992); Art. I(d), Ukraine-US (1994); Art. I(d), Poland-US (1994); Art. I(d), Lithuania-US (1998); Art. I(d), Latvia-US (1995); Art. I(d), Jamaica-US (1994); Art. I(f), Panama-US (1982) and Art. I(f) Haiti-US (1983).
57. Art. 5(1)(a), Chile-Tunisia BIT (1998), refers to 'interests, dividends, profits and other returns.'
58. See Art. 7(1)(h), China-Jordan (2001); Art. VII(i), Indonesia-Spain (1995); Art. 5(2), BLEU-Saudi Arabia (2001); Art. XIII(1)(c), Argentina-Canada (1991); Art. 80(1)(e), JSEPA (2002); and Art. XII(iv), Caribbean-Dominican Republic FTA (1998). Note, however, that this obligation is sometimes limited to a 'moderate' or 'adequate' portion of the earnings.
59. Art. 4(d), Czechoslovakia-Netherlands (1991).
60. Art. 7(1)(f), Denmark-Egypt (1999).
61. Art. VIII(1)(c), Canada-Venezuela (1996).
62. See, for example, Art. 5, Chile-Tunisia (1992); Art. 5(1), Germany-Kenya (1996); Art. 6(1), Czechoslovakia-Spain (1990); Art. 7(1), BLEU-Pakistan (1998); Art. 9(1)(e), Argentina-

Compensation Payments for Breach of the IIA. Most transfer provisions also cover the payments a host state may be required to make to an investor as a result of investment disputes,[63] including any compensation due as a result of expropriation and/or losses incurred as a result of conflict in the host state.[64]

Non-monetary Transfers. Although transfer provisions in many IIAs relate only to transfers of funds, other provisions, such as Article V, Argentina-US (1991), which applies to 'all transfers related to an investment,' might extend to transfers of tangible goods, such as industrial machinery or inventory. Article 1109(1)(a), *North American Free Trade Agreement* (NAFTA), specifically refers to 'returns in kind.' Although the term is not defined, commentators suggest that it includes payment in the form of actual goods.[65]

§8.10 Convertibility rights The issue of convertibility involves two separate but related issues: (i) the type of foreign currency available for exchange; and (ii) the exchange rate applicable to the transfer.[66] With respect to the type of currency, IIAs normally require that transfers be made in a currency that is convertible[67] or freely convertible.[68] These terms are usually not defined.[69] By contrast, the IMF Articles use the term 'freely usable currency' and define this as a currency that the

---

Australia (1995); Art. IV(1)(e), Armenia-US (1992); Art. 80(1)(c), JSEPA (2002); and Art. 17-07(1)(b), Colombia-Mexico-Venezuela FTA (1994).

63. See Art. IV(1)(c), Armenia-US (1992); Art. 80(1)(g), JSEPA (2002), and Art. 17-07(1)(e), Colombia-Mexico-Venezuela FTA (1994). Some provide that such payments may be made in installments where the award is particularly large. See Art. 7(3), Netherlands-Philippines (1985), and Art. 6(2), China-Thailand (1985).

64. These obligations sometimes appear in the provisions on expropriation and compensation for losses. See *supra* Chapter 7 on expropriation.

65. M. Kinnear, A. K. Bjorklund & J. Hannaford., *Investment Disputes under NAFTA: An Annotated Guide to NAFTA Chapter 11* (The Netherlands: Kluwer Law International, 2005) at 1109-9 [*Investment Disputes under NAFTA*].

66. Treaty standards on the exchange rates applicable to a transfer of funds should be distinguished from the question of the relevant date and exchange rate for converting domestic currencies to foreign currencies when assessing damages due for other treaty breaches.

67. See Art. 7(3), Ghana-India (2000), and Art. VIII(2), Canada-Venezuela (1996).

68. See Art. 4, Netherlands-Romania (1994); Art. VII, Indonesia-Spain (1995); Art. 7, Peru-Thailand (1991); Art. 6(2), Czechoslovakia-Spain (1990); Art. 7(3), BLEU-Pakistan (1998); Art. V(2)(a), Cameroon-US (1986); and Art. IV(2), Congo-US (1990).

69. There are some exceptions. For example, Art. 1(5), Hong Kong-Netherlands (1992), defines 'freely convertible' to mean 'free of all currency exchange controls and transferable abroad in any currency.' Further, Art. 1(1)(f), Argentina-Australia (1995); Art. 1(b), Australia-India (1999); and Art. 1(1)(f), Australia-Peru (1995), define it as 'a convertible currency as classified by the IMF or any currency that is widely traded in international foreign exchange markets.' Finally, Art. X(2), Australia-China (1988), says that transfers 'shall be permitted in freely convertible currencies as classified by the IMF ...'

IMF deems to be 'widely used to make payments for international transactions.'[70] Some US BITs also use this formulation.[71] In other IIAs, the foreign investor has the right to transfer funds in the same currency as the original investment.[72] In order to avoid interpretive uncertainty, the better treaty practice would be to incorporate the definition of 'freely usable currency' from the IMF Articles.

With regard to the second issue, IIAs often specify the exchange rate as 'the market exchange rate at the time of transfer.'[73] Some IIAs specifically provide that most-favoured-nation (MFN) treatment applies.[74] Some Chinese BITs refer not to the market rate, but rather to the 'official exchange rate of the Contracting Party receiving the investment on the date of transfer.'[75] Some German BITs refer to the IMF rate of the currency for special drawing rights as at the date of payment.[76] Other BITs make reference to a rate in accordance with procedures of 'international financial centres.'[77] Finally, certain treaties provide that, failing other means of determining an appropriate exchange rate, the rate chosen is to be 'fair and equitable.'[78] As these examples suggest, IIAs are not consistent in defining the applicable exchange rate. Again, in order to avoid interpretive uncertainty, the better treaty practice would be to refer to the IMF rate of the currency for special drawing rights.

A related question arises with the application of discriminatory exchange rates. Although IMF rules generally prohibit multiple currency practices (discriminatory exchange rates), this prohibition does not apply to capital transfers.[79] As a result, some IIAs specifically provide for non-discriminatory

---

70. Art. XXX(f), IMF Articles, *supra* note 9. The IMF considers the US Dollar, the Japanese Yen, the British Pound and the Euro to be 'freely usable currencies.' See *Transfer of Funds, supra* note 1 at 33. The term 'freely useable currency' is used in some US BITs. See, for example, Art. IV(2), Armenia-US (1992), and Art. IV(2), Kyrgyzstan-US (1993). These BITs, however, do not define the terms by reference to the IMF Articles.
71. See Art. 7(2), US-Uruguay (2005), and Art. V(2), Argentina-US (1991).
72. See Art. 6, Egypt-Romania (1976), and Art. 6, Germany-Romania (1979).
73. See Art. IV, Russia-US (1992).
74. Art. 6(2), BLEU-Singapore (1978).
75. Art. 6(2), China-Uruguay (1993).
76. See Art. 6, Germany-Romania (1979); Art. 6(2), Benin-Germany (1978); Art. 6(2), Bangladesh-Germany (1981); Art. 6(1), Ethiopia-Germany (1964); Art. 6(2), Germany-Haiti (1973); Art. 6(1), Germany-Turkey (1962) and Art. 6(2), Germany-Zimbabwe (1995). See also Art. 5(3), BLEU-Saudi Arabia (2001); Art. V(2), Cameroon-US (1986); and Art. 6(3), China-Kuwait (1985). Older German BITs refer to the US Dollar and/or gold: see, for example, Art. 6(3), Chad-Germany (1967), and Art. 6(2), Germany-Turkey (1962).
77. Art. 7(4), BLEU-Pakistan (1998). These centres are not defined.
78. See Art. 6(2), Benin-Germany (1978); Art. 6(2), Bangladesh-Germany (1981); Art. 6(2), Ethiopia-Germany (1964); Art. 6(3), Germany-Haiti (1973) (referring to treatment that is 'just and equitable'); Art. 5(3), Germany-Philippines (1998); Art. 6(2), Germany-Turkey (1962); and Art. 6(2), BLEU-China (1984) (referring to treatment that is 'equitable').
79. *Transfer of Funds, supra* note 1 at 15.

treatment with respect to transfers[80] or MFN treatment with respect to transfers.[81] If an IIA does not have this type of provision, the investor might be able to rely on national and MFN treatment provisions or other general non-discrimination provisions in the IIA if it encounters discriminatory exchange rates.

§8.11 Permissible restrictions on transfers Most IIAs seek to minimize the scope and number of delays and restrictions that states may impose on the transfer of funds by foreign investors. They do this in a number of ways. First, some IIAs simply provide that states must allow transfers 'without restriction.'[82] In general, however, the concern centres on time delays. Most IIAs expressly condemn 'delays;' but the manner in which they phrase such condemnation varies. Some IIAs require a host state to allow for fund transfers promptly;[83] others expressly forbid delays, that can be described as 'undue,'[84] 'unreasonable,'[85] or 'excessive,'[86] or impose requirements that transfers be made 'on an expeditious basis.'[87] Indeed, a number of treaties specify a maximum period beyond which a delay may not extend, typically within a range of between one and six months.[88] In contrast, certain IIAs provide that capital (but not returns) can only be repatriated after it has remained in the host state for a specific time. Certain Chilean BITs, for example, provide that capital may only be transferred one year after it has entered the host state, unless legislation provides for a more favourable treatment.[89]

Although these provisions provide a certain level of predictability, they do not necessarily prevent the host state from imposing other types of restrictions – restrictions that may be unforeseen at the time the investment is made. Accordingly, some IIAs make use of a catch-all mechanism, or stabilization clause, to mitigate the risk of such unforeseen regulation. These clauses provide that currency transfers are either governed by the laws of the host state existing at the time the treaty

---

80. Some: Art. 7(1), Ghana-India (2000); Art. 5(3), Egypt-Jordan (1996); Art. V(3), Jordan-Tunisia (1995); Art. 6(4), Czechoslovakia-Spain (1990); Art. 5(3), Bangladesh-BLEU (1981); and Art. 7(5), BLEU-Pakistan (1998).
81. Art. 5(3), Cuba-Lebanon (1995).
82. See Art. 7(1), India-Netherlands (1995); Art. 7(1), Netherlands-Philippines (1985); and Art. 6(1), Hong Kong-Netherlands (1992).
83. Art. 6(1), Ugandan Model BIT, and Art. 6(1), Germany-Turkey (1962).
84. See, for example, Art. 5, Hungary-Spain (1989); Art. 5, Morocco-Spain (1989); Art. 5(2), BLEU-China (1984); Art. X(1), Australia-China (1988) and Art. 9(1), Australia-India (1999).
85. See Art. 6(1), Malaysian Model BIT, and Art. VI, Cambodian Model BIT.
86. See Art. VII, Indonesia-Spain (1995), and Art. 6(5), Czechoslovakia-Spain (1990).
87. Art.7(1), India-Sweden (2000).
88. The Italian Model BIT limits a potential transfer delay to one month. Illustrations of provisions that limit a possible delay to two months include: Art. 5(2), Germany-Thailand (2002); Art. 7(3), Australia-Romania (1993); Art. 5(2) Burundian Model BIT, and Art. 7(4), Germany-India (1995). Instances of BITs that limit a delay to three months include: Art. 5, Hungary-Spain (1989); Art. VII, Indonesia-Spain (1995); Art. 6, Morocco-Spain (1989); Art. 6(5), Czechoslovakia-Spain (1990); and Art. 7(4), BLEU-Pakistan (1998). Finally, a limit of six months appears in Art. 8, Italy-Mongolia (1993).
89. See, for example, Ad Art. VII, Chile-Turkey (1998), and Art. 6(5), Chile-China (1994).

in question entered into force, or, alternatively, by more favourable legislation if subsequently enacted.[90]

On the other hand, a small number of treaties provide simply that transfers are subject to host state laws. For example, Article 6, China-Kuwait (1985), provides for transfers in accordance with host state law and regulations. This provides substantially less protection than the dominant model of providing a standing obligation on transfers.

§8.12 Express exceptions to transfer obligations Though many older IIAs provide open-ended transfer rights, newer IIAs tend to provide express exceptions to permit certain types of host state restrictions including those for: (i) bankruptcy, insolvency or the protection of creditors' rights; (ii) regulation of the issuance, trading or dealing of securities; (iii) enforcement of criminal or penal offences; (iv) reporting of transfers of currency or other monetary instruments; (v) the satisfaction of judgments in adjudicatory proceedings; and (vi) tax collection.[91] The use of exceptions is often disciplined by the requirement that restrictions may only be imposed in a manner that is equitable, non-discriminatory and in good faith.[92]

In the event of a balance of payments crisis where large amounts of capital flow out of the host state (capital flight), the host state may wish to impose temporary restrictions on this outflow.[93] These restrictions, even if temporary, would likely violate most IIA transfer provisions.[94] In contrast, balance of payment provisions are common in other international economic treaties. The IMF

---

90. See, for example, Art. 6, Lesotho-UK (1981). On the other hand, some provide that the parties may still 'impose exchange rate restrictions in accordance with [their] applicable laws and regulations.' See also Art. 6(3), Chile-China (1994). Art. 8(2), China-Japan (1988), is similar.
91. See Art. VIII(4)(a), Canada-Venezuela (1996); Art. 80(3)(a), JSEPA (2002); Art. XII(3)(a), Caribbean-Dominican Republic FTA (1998); Art. 17-07(3)(a), Colombia-Mexico-Venezuela FTA (1994); Art. 7(4)(a), US-Uruguay (2005), Art. 5(2), BLEU-China (1984); Art. IV(3), Romania-US (1992) and Art. 7(4), US Model (2004). Some IIAs allow for limits on transfers to be made for the protection of financial institutions: Art. VIII(6), Canada-Venezuela (1996); Art. XIV(6), Canadian Model (2003). The Canadian Model (2003) also has a provision that allows for transfer restrictions that would otherwise be allowed under WTO rules. See Art. XIV. Some IIAs specifically allow for mandatory reports of currency transfers. See Art. IV(3), Romania-US (1992), and Art. 7(4), US Model (2004).
92. IIAs that are particularly comprehensive in this regard include Art. 7(3), Chile-Turkey (1998), and Art. 7(4), US-Uruguay (2005).
93. This concern is reflected in Guideline III.6(1)(d), World Bank Guidelines on the Treatment of Foreign Direct Investment, which provide that 'in the exceptional cases where the State faces foreign exchange stringencies, such transfer may as an exception be made in installments within a period which will be as short as possible and will not in any case exceed five years from the date of liquidation or sale.' See generally WTO Working Group on the Relationship between Trade and Investment, Note by Secretariat, Exceptions and Balance-of-Payment Safeguards, WT/WGTI/W/137, 26 Aug. 2002 [WTO Note on Balance of Payments].
94. Responsibility may nevertheless be precluded on the basis of necessity. See infra Chapter 10.

Articles, the General Agreement on Tariffs and Trade (GATT) and the GATS all contain balance of payment provisions.[95]

Balance of payment provisions are rare in IIAs.[96] Where they exist, they normally provide that transfer restrictions are only permissible on the condition that the power not be used to impede the transfer of profits, interest, dividends, royalties or fees (transfers that would be considered current transactions under the IMF Articles) and with the further proviso that limits be placed on the extent of the restrictions.[97] For example, balance of payment provisions often provide for transfers of capital to be made in instalments of at least 20% a year.[98] In other IIAs, the WTO balance of payment obligations are incorporated into the IIA.[99] Several US BITs have an 'escape clause' that permits transfers to be delayed if foreign exchange reserves are at a 'very low level.'[100]

Some recent IIAs include provisions that explicitly allow for restrictions on fund transfers in the case of a balance of payments or other external financial crisis.[101] France-Uganda (2003), a typical example, provides that either party may temporarily restrict transfers on condition that the restrictions are communicated without delay to the other party, are compatible with the IMF Articles and are not imposed for longer than six months. Some agreements allow transfer restrictions if movements of capital may cause, or threaten to cause, serious difficulties for macroeconomic management, particularly monetary and exchange rate policies.[102]

Balance of payment provisions that allow for temporary derogation from obligations are best characterized as safeguard measures, rather than as general exceptions or reservations to IIA obligations.[103] If there is no express provision for a temporary derogation from transfer rights, a state facing a severe balance of payments crisis may be able to invoke the defence of necessity to justify a temporary derogation from its obligations.[104] The requirements to establish necessity are,

---

95. Arts VIII and XIV, IMF Articles, Articles XII and XVIII:B, GATT and the Marrakesh Understanding on the Balance-of-Payments Provisions of the GATT 1994, and Article XII, GATS.

96. *Transfer of Funds*, *supra* note 1 at 36 and WTO Note on Balance of Payments, *supra* note 93. Whether they are necessary is another question. Some studies on the relationship to balance of payment of FDI in the context of the Asian financial crisis found that FDI had been very stable. On the other hand, foreign portfolio investment and investment in debt securities are more volatile. Also see Trebilcock & Howse, *Regulation of International Trade*, *supra* note 3 at 171-173 discussing capital controls.

97. See Art. 6(1), UK-USSR (1989); Art. 6(4), China-Kuwait (1985); Art. 8(3), China-Sri Lanka (1986) and Art. 6(2), China-Thailand (1985).

98. See Art. 6(1), UK-USSR (1989) provides that 'transfer of a minimum of 20% a year is guaranteed.' By contrast, the Chinese BITs mentioned, *ibid.*, provide a limit of 50%.

99. Art. V, Jordan-US (1997).

100. Protocol to Egypt-US BIT (1982).

101. See Art. 6, France-Uganda (2003); Art. 6, France-Madagascar (2003); Ad Art. 7, France-Iran (2003); Ad Art. 4, Korea-Netherlands (2003); Art. 6, Bahrain-France (2004).

102. Ad Art. 4, Korea-Netherlands (2003); Art. 10.12, Korea-Singapore FTA (2005).

103. See *infra* Chapter 10.

104. *Ibid.*

however, very strict and express provisions for balance of payment crises are less restrictive.

The lack of balance of payment provisions in IIAs signed by some EU members has led to questions of the compatibility of IIA transfer rights with European law, which allows the Council of the European Union to adopt measures on the movement of capital.[105] Under Art. 307 of the *Treaty Establishing the European Community*, Member States are obliged to take all appropriate steps to eliminate possible incompatibilities contained in prior international agreements. BITs between new EU members and non-member countries have come under scrutiny by the European Commission, concerned that the bilateral treaties lack sufficient restrictions on capital flows, particularly in the event of a balance of payment or other financial crisis. In response, in 2003 the United States agreed to amend its BITs with eight Eastern European countries in order to limit the reach of national and MFN treatment.[106]

By contrast, balance of payment safeguard clauses are more common in Free Trade Agreements (FTAs) that contain investment chapters.[107] Article 2104, NAFTA, provides a general exception for balance of payment measures. Specifically, it stipulates that any restriction on transfers must be: temporary and progressively phased out; consistent with the IMF Articles of Agreement by avoiding unnecessary damage to the economic interests of the other state party; no more burdensome than necessary; and applied on a national and MFN treatment basis. In addition, the party imposing the measure must: (a) submit any current account exchange restrictions to the IMF for review; (b) enter into good faith consultations with the IMF on economic adjustment measures to address the fundamental underlying economic problems causing the difficulties; and (c) adopt or maintain economic policies consistent with such consultations. Other recent FTAs have similar provisions.[108]

The absence of balance of payment provisions in many older BITs may lead to inconsistencies. Restrictions to address balance of payment problems that are fully consistent with IMF and GATS obligations may nevertheless be inconsistent with BIT obligations. Further, if the state complies with its BIT obligations and does not impose restrictions, it might not be eligible for temporary balance of payment financing.[109]

§8.13 Jurisprudence   Despite the importance of transfer rights, it appears that only one investment treaty award has specifically addressed breach of transfer

---

105. Arts 57(2), 59 and 60, *Consolidated Version of the Treaty Establishing the European Community*, O.J. 2002/C 325/01. See European Commission announcement Press Release IP/04/618 (10 May 2004).
106. Online: International Institute for Sustainable Development <http://iisd.org/pdf/2003/investment_investsd_sep19_2003.pdf> and <http://iisd.org/pdf/2004/investment_investsd_oct13_2004.pdf>.
107. Art. 20-06, Mexico-Northern Triangle (2000); Art. O-04, Canada-Chile FTA (1996).
108. See 6(6), India-Singapore Comprehensive Economic Cooperation Agreement (2005) [India-Singapore CECA]; Art. O-04.2, Canada-Chile FTA (1996); and Art. 68, JSEPA (2002).
109. Siegel, *supra* note 22 at 301-302.

obligations and, in that case, the claim was denied.[110] Investors have claimed breach of transfer rights in two other cases, but the claims were not addressed in tribunal awards. The 2001-2002 Argentine crisis has given rise to a large number of IIA claims. Although some claimants have argued that the restrictions imposed by Argentina violate the transfer provisions in IIAs, the issue has not yet been considered on the merits, except briefly in *Metalpar S.A. y Buen Aire S.A. v. Argentina*.[111]

A number of Iran-United States Claims Tribunal awards have considered the consistency of Iranian exchange controls with the IMF Articles and Article VII(1) of the *Treaty of Amity between the United States and Iran*.[112] In *Hood Corp. v. Iran*, the tribunal addressed whether a payment for a transfer of rights in a joint venture was a capital transfer or a current transaction. The majority of the Tribunal held that it was a capital transfer and that the IMF Articles provide for freedom to exercise exchange controls with respect to capital transfers.[113] In a dissenting opinion, Judge Mosk stated that exchange controls that are confiscatory should be denied recognition and that the transaction in question was arguably a current transaction that could not be restricted.[114] In *Sea-Land Service v. Iran*,[115] the tribunal addressed whether there was interference with Sea-Land's bank account because of a refusal to allow conversion to US Dollars and Transfer. Although the majority of the tribunal rejected the claim for lack of proof, in a dissenting opinion, Judge Holtzmann reviewed the international legal authorities and determined that the refusal to allow conversion and transfer resulted in the account having been expropriated.

II   PROHIBITIONS ON PERFORMANCE REQUIREMENTS

§8.14 Introduction   The term performance requirements is used to describe requirements that host states impose on investments to achieve various economic and social objectives. These might include increasing employment levels, augmenting foreign exchange reserves, promoting the use of domestically

---

110. *Metalpar S.A. y Buen Aire S.A. v. Argentina* (Award, 6 Jun. 2008).
111. *Ibid.* See also *Pan American Energy LLC, and BP Argentina Exploration Company v. Argentina* (Decision on Preliminary Objections, 27 Jul. 2006) with respect to a transfer of funds claim. In *CMS Gas Transmission Company v. Argentina*, the Claimant withdrew its claim against Argentina related to restrictions on transfers of funds (Award, 12 May 2005) at para. 88.
112. These include *Dallal v. Iran*, 3 Iran-US CTR 10; *Schering v. Iran*, 5 Iran-US CTR 361 and *Hood Corp. v. Iran*, 7 Iran-US CTR 36. See G.H. Aldrich, *The Jurisprudence of the Iran-United States Claims Tribunal* (Oxford: Clarendon Press, 1996) at 388-396. For more in-depth discussion see J. Gold, *supra* note 20, and A. Mouri, *supra* note 20.
113. *Hood Corp. v. Iran*, 7 Iran-US CTR 36 at 45-6.
114. *Ibid.*
115. *Sea-Land Service v. Iran*, 6 Iran-US CTR 149.

manufactured products and protecting local industries from foreign competition.[116] The application of performance requirements to foreign investment by developing states increased substantially in the 1970s, although states at all levels of development have at one time or another used performance requirements.[117]

Whether, when and how performance requirements should be used as part of a state's economic development remains a matter of controversy in economic theory.[118] The World Bank *Guidelines on the Treatment of Foreign Direct Investment* highlights that:

> States will note that experience suggests that certain performance requirements introduced as conditions of admission are often counterproductive and that open admission ... is a more effective approach.[119]

---

116. UNCTAD refers to these as 'operational measures.' Operational measures fall into several broad categories: (1) *measures restricting methods of production* (sourcing/local content performance requirements and manufacturing performance requirements); (2) *measures restricting human resources* (restrictions on employment; special requirements on professional qualifications; employment performance requirements; and training requirements); (3) *measures restricting access to resources* (restrictions on access to local credit facilities; restrictions on access to foreign exchange; restrictions or conditions on access to local raw materials, spare parts and inputs; and restrictions on access to telecommunications networks); (4) *import/export restrictions* (export requirements; trade balancing requirements; import restrictions, local sales requirements; linking export quotas to domestic sales and export/foreign exchange earning requirements; and restrictions on imports of capital goods, spare parts and manufacturing inputs); (5) *measures on capital mobility* (restrictions on repatriation of capital and profits; operational permits and licenses (e.g., to transfer funds); ceilings on royalties and technical assistance fees or special taxes; and technology transfer requirements); (6) *measures restricting physical mobility* (requirements on location of headquarters; restrictions to relocate operations within a country; and restrictions on long-term leases of land and real property); (7) *measures restricting conditions of competition* (requirements to establish a joint venture with domestic participation; requirements for a minimum level of domestic equity participation; restrictions relating to monopolies or participation in public companies; 'cultural' restrictions, mainly in relation to educational or media services; special requirements on foreign firms in certain sectors/activities (e.g., on branches of foreign banks); and advertising restrictions for foreign firms). See UNCTAD, *Host Country Operational Measures*, UNCTAD Series on issues in international investment agreements (New York and Geneva: United Nations, 2001) (UNCTAD/ITE/IIT/26) [*Host Country Operational Measures*] at 8-9.

117. See UNCTAD, Foreign Direct Investment and Performance Requirements: New Evidence from Selected Countries, UNCTAD/ITE/IIA/2003/7 [Foreign Direct Investment and Performance Requirements]. On the various types of host state regulation on foreign investment, see Muchlinski, *supra* note 26, and M. Sornarajah, *The International Law on Foreign Investment*, 2nd edn (Cambridge: Cambridge University Press, 2004).

118. For a review of the empirical evidence on the impacts of performance requirements on growth, development and trade and investment flows, see Foreign Direct Investment and Performance Requirements, *ibid.*; papers collected in UNCTAD, The Development Dimension of FDI: Policy and Rule-Making Perspectives, UNCTAD/ITE/IIA/2003/4; WTO and UNCTAD Joint Study, 'Trade-Related Investment Measures and Performance Requirements,' Part II WTO Doc. G/C/W/307/add.1 (8 Feb. 2002); D. Guisinger, 'Do Performance Requirements and Investment Incentives Work' (1986) 9 World Economy 81 and D. Rodrik, 'The Economics of Export-Performance Requirements' (1987) 102 Quarterly Journal of Economics 633.

119. Guideline II(3), (1992) 31 ILM 1363.

Some experts view performance requirements as costly, counterproductive and investment-diverting whereas others see them as essential to achieving development objectives.[120] The primary justification for prohibiting performance requirements is that they impede the efficient allocation of resources.[121] For example, local content requirements often force the manufacturer to use more expensive domestic inputs than those available on the international market. On the other hand, the economic and social benefits of local content requirements may outweigh any efficiency losses.

International trade law – as well as a small number of IIAs – prohibit certain types of performance requirements. The following sections address WTO prohibitions on trade-related investment measures (TRIMs) and similar prohibitions in IIAs.

§8.15 Trade-related investment measures (TRIMs) and the WTO TRIMS Agreement TRIMs is a term of art in international trade law indicating an investment-related measure that has an impact on international trade. In the past, TRIMs have often been based on an economic policy of import-substitution that encourages the creation of domestic manufacturing capacity and limited market access by foreign products. The quintessential TRIM is a requirement that local manufacturers use a certain proportion of local products in their manufacturing. TRIMs, however, often fall afoul of international trade law obligations because they effectively discriminate against imported goods on the basis of nationality. In addition, TRIMs may also act as quantitative restrictions on imports and exports, for example, where only a certain quantity of a foreign good may be imported. The overall effect of these sorts of TRIMs is to limit the market access of foreign goods.

The use of TRIMs was considered in the 1984 GATT panel decision, *Canada–Administration of the Foreign Investment Review Act* (*FIRA Panel*).[122] Under the *Foreign Investment Review Act* (FIRA), the Canadian government established a government agency to screen foreign investment and allowed foreign investors to make voluntary undertakings when they applied for investment approvals.[123] Although such undertakings were not mandatory, they would become legally binding if the proposed investment was approved. The US argued that the undertakings regarding local content were contrary to the GATT national treatment obligation because imported goods were treated less favourably than domestic goods.[124] The *FIRA Panel* agreed, finding that the undertakings to purchase Canadian goods – even if voluntary – violated Canada's GATT national treatment

---

120. Foreign Direct Investment and Performance Requirements, *supra* note 117, at 2.
121. See Trebilcock & Howse, *Regulation of International Trade*, *supra* note 3.
122. *Canada–Administration of the Foreign Investment Review Act*, GATT BISD 30th Supp. 140 (1984). The FIRA decision was considered in *S.D. Myers, Inc. v. Canada* (Partial Award Merits, 13 Nov. 2000) at para. 274.
123. For example, an investor could undertake to use a certain percentage of local inputs.
124. *Supra* note 122 at para. 3.1.

obligations.[125] The *FIRA Panel* also addressed whether export undertakings – for example a requirement to export a certain amount or value of production – violated the GATT.[126] The *FIRA Panel* found that the GATT did not prohibit a state from requiring that goods be sold in foreign markets as opposed to domestic markets.[127] Continued uncertainty about the GATT-consistency of various types of TRIMs provided the incentive to address the issue of TRIMs during the Uruguay Round.

During the Uruguay Round, the United States pushed for greater discipline on TRIMs and promoted adoption of a code to further liberalize market access for investment.[128] However, the majority of the GATT Contracting Parties rejected the proposal, preferring instead to clarify the specific types of TRIMs that violate GATT's national treatment or quantitative restriction obligations. The resulting instrument is the *Agreement on Trade-Related Investment Measures* (TRIMS Agreement),[129] which reaffirms that WTO Members may not apply investment measures that are inconsistent with the principle of national treatment,[130] or otherwise violate the general prohibition on quantitative restrictions on imports and exports.[131] The Annex to the TRIMS Agreement sets out an illustrative list of prohibited measures. The list includes local content or sourcing requirements, as well as trade balancing obligations that limit amounts of imports and exports based on the use of local products.[132]

---

125. *Ibid.*, at para. 6.1.
126. This part of the case addressed the issue of obligations under Art. XVII, GATT, with respect to state trading enterprises and non-discriminatory treatment for government measures affecting imports and exports.
127. *Supra* note 122 at para. 6.2.
128. See T. Stewart, 'Trade Related Investment Measures,' in T. Stewart, ed., *The GATT Uruguay Round: A Negotiating History*, (Boston: Kluwer, 1994) and D. Greenaway, 'Why Are We Negotiating on TRIMS?,' in D. Greenaway *et al.*, eds, *Global Protectionism* (Basingstoke, Hampshire: Macmillan, 1991).
129. *Agreement on Trade-Related Investment Measures*, 15 Apr. 1994, Marrakesh Agreement Establishing the World Trade Organization, Annex 1A, reproduced in *The Legal Texts: Results of the Uruguay Round of Multilateral Trade Negotiations* (Cambridge: Cambridge University Press, 1994) [TRIMS Agreement].
130. Art. III, GATT (1994).
131. *Ibid.*, Art. XI.
132. The illustrative list in the Annex to the TRIMS Agreement provides as follows:

   1. TRIMs that are inconsistent with the obligation of national treatment provided for in paragraph 4 of Art. III of GATT 1994 include those which are mandatory or enforceable under domestic law or under administrative rulings, or compliance with which is necessary to obtain an advantage, and which require: (a) the purchase or use by an enterprise of products of domestic origin or from any domestic source, whether specified in terms of particular products, in terms of volume or value of products, or in terms of a proportion of volume or value of its local production; or (b) that an enterprise's purchases or use of imported products be limited to an amount related to the volume or value of local products that it exports.
   2. TRIMs that are inconsistent with the obligation of general elimination of quantitative restrictions provided for in paragraph 1 of Art. XI of GATT 1994 include those which are mandatory or enforceable under domestic law or under administrative rulings, or those

The TRIMS Agreement essentially codifies the finding of the *FIRA Panel* that voluntary undertakings amount to 'requirements' under Article III, GATT (national treatment).[133] This interpretation was confirmed in *Indonesia–Autos*, which involved various Indonesian measures, including tax incentives and customs duty benefits linked to local content requirements.[134] Japan, the European Community and the US challenged these measures as being inconsistent with the TRIMS Agreement. The WTO panel agreed, holding that an advantage, conditional on the use of domestic goods, violates the TRIMS Agreement, even if the local content rule is not binding.

§8.16 Performance requirements in the General Agreement on Trade in Services (GATS)   The GATS is the services companion to the GATT and sets out market liberalization commitments with respect to services.[135] The GATS prohibits six types of host state measures if a WTO member has made market access commitments: (i) limitations on the number of service suppliers; (ii) limitations on the total value of service transactions or assets; (iii) limitations on the total number of service operations or on the total quantity of service output expressed; (iv) limitations on the total number of natural persons that may be employed in a particular service sector or that a service supplier may employ; (v) measures which restrict or require specific types of legal entity or joint venture through which a service supplier may supply a service; and (vi) limitations on the participation of foreign capital.[136] These prohibitions, like the commitments in the TRIMS Agreement, ensure that a state does not subvert its market access commitments through indirect means. From an economic perspective, they serve to maintain the price mechanism under competitive conditions.

---

with which compliance is necessary to obtain an advantage, and which restrict: (a) the importation by an enterprise of products used in or related to its local production, generally or to an amount related to the volume or value of local production that it exports; (b) the importation by an enterprise of products used in or related to its local production by restricting its access to foreign exchange to an amount related to the foreign exchange inflows attributable to the enterprise; or (c) the exportation or sale for export by an enterprise of products, whether specified in terms of particular products, in terms of volume or value of products, or in terms of a proportion of volume or value of its local production.

133. The Annex to the TRIMS Agreement (*ibid.*) refers to measures 'compliance with which is necessary to obtain an advantage.' Prohibited TRIMs therefore include voluntary undertakings.
134. *Indonesia – Certain Measures Affecting the Automobile Industry* (WT/DS44/R, report adopted 23 Jul. 1998), Panel Report at 14.90. The US also claimed violations of the TRIMS Agreement in *EC-Bananas III* (WT/DS27) and *Canada – Autos* (WT/DS139 and WT/DS142). In both cases, the panels did not specifically address the violations of the TRIMS Agreement because they were able to base their findings on other WTO Agreements.
135. See discussion of the GATS *supra* at Chapter 3, §3.14 and Chapter 8, §8.5.
136. Art. XVI, GATS, *supra* note 7.

§8.17 Performance requirements in IIAs   Only a small number of BITs expressly prohibit performance requirements.[137] Treaty practice in this area appears to begin with US BITs.[138] Article II(7) of the 1983 US Model BIT provided:

> Neither Party shall impose performance requirements as a condition for the establishment, expansion or maintenance of investments owned by nationals or companies of the other Party, which require or enforce commitments to export goods produced, or which specify that goods or services must be purchased locally, or which impose any other similar requirements, and which potentially or actually have an adverse effect on the trade and/or investments of the nationals or companies of the other Party.[139]

Until relatively recently, with a few exceptions,[140] only US,[141] Canadian[142] and Japanese[143] BITs have prohibited performance requirements. The practice has become more common in recent FTAs with investment chapters.[144] If IIAs prohibit performance requirements, the prohibitions are usually circumscribed by carefully drafted exceptions.

§8.18 The relationship between performance requirements and national treatment   Prohibitions on performance requirements are minimum standards of treatment. The prohibition applies even if the performance requirement does not distinguish between foreign and domestic investors. Although local content requirements may violate WTO national treatment obligations because preference is given to local over foreign goods, performance requirements do not necessarily violate national treatment obligations in IIAs. A domestic content requirement

---

137. See *Host Country Operational Measures, supra* note 116 at 34 *et seq.* See also WTO and UNCTAD Joint Study, 'Trade-Related Investment Measures and Performance Requirements,' Part I (WTO Doc. G/C/W/307 (1 Oct. 2001)).
138. See Vandevelde, *supra* note 40 at 110-112.
139. Vandevelde, *ibid.*, at Appendix A-1.
140. See for example, Art. 2(g), Malaysia-UAE (1991), which provides that the parties shall 'seek as far as practicable to avoid performance requirements.' Also, Art. 75, JSEPA, prohibits certain performance requirements.
141. See, for example, Art. II(6), Egypt-US (1982); Art. II(7), Turkey-US (1985); Art. II(5), US-Zaire (1984); and Art. 8, US-Uruguay (2005).
142. See, for example, Art. G-06, Canada-Chile FTA (1996); Art. 1106, NAFTA (1992); Arts 7(1) and 7(3), Canadian Model FIPA (2003); Art. V(2), Canada-Ukraine (1995); Art. VI, Canada-Croatia (1997); and Art. VI, Canada-Uruguay (1997).
143. Japan-Korea (2002) and Japan-Vietnam (2003).
144. See, for example, Mexican free trade agreements with Costa Rica (1994), Chile (1998), Bolivia (1994) and Nicaragua (1997), which follow the NAFTA model of prohibiting performance requirements. See also Protocol of Colonia for the Reciprocal Promotion and Protection of Investments in Mercosur, 17 Jan. 1994, Mercosur/CMC/Dec. No. 11/93 [Colonia Protocol], Art. 3(4).

applying to all manufacturers in a host state would not normally breach IIA national treatment obligations.[145]

§8.19 The relationship between performance requirements and establishment rights Prohibitions on performance requirements are more common in IIAs that provide for establishment rights. The concern is that establishment rights might be adversely affected if performance requirements were imposed as a condition of establishment or at any time thereafter. For example, the right to establishment may be of little interest to the foreign investor if it is required to export 100% of its production. Prohibitions on performance requirements serve to protect market access and investment liberalization. Accordingly, they are more common in IIAs that contain establishment rights.[146] Further, in IIAs with establishment rights, the prohibition on performance requirements extends to the establishment of investments, as well as to their operation.

§8.20 Performance requirements and host state nationals and third parties IIAs that follow the NAFTA model prohibit the imposition or enforcement of performance requirements on 'an investment of an investor of a Party or of a non-Party in its territory.'[147] The prohibition therefore extends to all potential investors – those from host, home and third states. Commentators note that this broad application serves to ensure that parties do not use performance requirements to distort the investment decisions of commercial parties.[148]

§8.21 Express exceptions to prohibitions on performance requirements IIAs that contain prohibitions on performance requirements typically also provide a limited number of carefully crafted exceptions. Prohibitions on performance requirements do not normally apply to export promotion and foreign aid programs;[149] government procurement;[150] or qualification requirements for preferential tariffs and quotas.[151] In some cases they do not apply to subsidies and grants.[152] A number of IIAs provide an exception for transfers of technology or for

---

145. A national treatment issue might arise if there were *de facto* less favourable treatment, for example, where the investor's competitor was a national of the host state and also the monopoly producer of the required domestic content. See *supra* Chapter 4 on national treatment obligations.
146. See, for example, Art. V(2), Armenia-Canada (1997); Art. II(6), Estonia-US (1994); Art. II(5), Jamaica-US (1994); Art. II(5), Kazakhstan-US (1994); Art. II(6), Latvia-US (1995); and Art. 13, Israel-US FTA (1985).
147. Art. 1106(1), NAFTA (1992).
148. *Investment Disputes under NAFTA, supra* note 65 at 1106-1111.
149. See, for example, Art. 5(3), ECT (1994); Art. 11.9(3)(d), Australia-US FTA (2004); and Art. G-08(7)(a), Canada-Chile FTA (1996).
150. See, for example, Art. 11.9(3)(e), Australia-US FTA (2004); Art. G-08(7)(b), Canada-Chile FTA (1996); and Art. 17-04(2)(b), Colombia-Mexico-Venezuela FTA (1994).
151. See Art. 1108(8), NAFTA (1992); Art. 5(3), ECT (1994); and Art. VI, Canada-Philippines (1996).
152. See Art. VI, Canada-Philippines (1996).

court, administrative tribunal or competition authority enforcement orders designed to remedy a practice determined to be anti-competitive under a party's laws on the prevention of anti-competitive behaviour.[153]

Although host states might impose performance requirements for protectionist purposes, such requirements might also be used for non-economic purposes, such as fostering higher levels of human health or environmental protection. Accordingly, some IIAs provide an exception to the prohibition of certain performance requirements, as long as they are not applied in an arbitrary or unjustifiable manner, or do not otherwise constitute a disguised restriction on international trade or investment. For example, a state might impose requirements for the use of certain types of environmental technologies to reduce pollution.[154]

§8.22 Prohibitions on domestic content, sourcing and trade balancing requirements   A number of IIAs prohibit TRIMs-like performance requirements regarding domestic content,[155] sourcing[156] and trade balancing requirements linking export and import levels.[157] Some agreements incorporate TRIMS Agreement prohibitions directly by cross-reference,[158] whereas others set out the prohibitions in the IIA. For example, Article 1106(1)(b) and (c), NAFTA, prohibit measures intended to achieve a given level or percentage of domestic content, which have the effect of according a preference to goods produced or services

---

153. See, for example, Art. 11.9(3)(b)(ii), Australia-US FTA (2004); and Art. 75(1)(f)(i), JSEPA (2002).
154. See, for example, Art. 1106(6), NAFTA (1992), which provides that such measures include environmental measures (a) necessary to secure compliance with laws and regulations that are not inconsistent with the provisions of this Agreement; (b) necessary to protect human, animal or plant life or health; or (c) necessary for the conservation of living or non-living exhaustible natural resources. See also Art. 11.9(3)(c), Australia-US FTA (2004); Art. G-06(2) and (6), Canada-Chile FTA (1996); Art. 83(1)(b) and (f), JSEPA (2002), and Arts 7(2) and 10, Canadian Model (2003). See §8.22 below discussing performance requirements in *Myers, supra* note 122.
155. For example, Art. 11.9(1)(b), Australia-US FTA (2004); Art. G-06(1)(b), Canada-Chile FTA (1996); Art. V(1)(a), Trinidad and Tobago-US (1994); Art. 1106(1)(b), NAFTA (1992); Art. 75(1)(b), JSEPA (2002); Art. 17-04(1)(a), Colombia-Mexico-Venezuela (1994) [Group of Three FTA].
156. These include prohibitions on purchase, use or according a preference to goods produced in its territory: Art. 11.9(1)(c), Australia-US FTA (2004); Art. G-06(1)(c), Canada-Chile FTA (1996); Art. 1106(1)(c), NAFTA (1992); Art. 75(1)(c), JSEPA (2002); and Art. 17-04(1)(b), Group of Three FTA (1994).
157. These include prohibitions on: (1) *export levels*: Art. 11.9(1)(a), Australia-US FTA (2004); Art. G-06(1)(a), Canada-Chile FTA (1996); Art. VI(1)(c), Trinidad and Tobago-US (1994); Art. 1106(1)(a), NAFTA (1992); Art. 75(1)(a), JSEPA (2002); and Art. 17-04(1)(d), Group of Three FTA (1994); (2) *relating imports to exports or foreign exchange inflows*: Art. 11.9(1)(d), Australia-US FTA (2004); Art. G-06(1)(d), Canada-Chile FTA (1996); Art. VI(1)(b), Trinidad and Tobago-US (1994); Art. 1106(1)(d), NAFTA (1992); Art. 75(1)(d), JSEPA (2002); and Art. 17-04(1)(c), Group of Three FTA (1994); and (3) *restricting local sales by relating them to exports*: Art. 11.9(1)(e), Australia-US FTA (2004); Art. G-06(1)(e), Canada-Chile FTA (1996); Art. VI(1)(d), Trinidad and Tobago-US (1994); Art. 1106(1)(e), NAFTA (1992); and Art. 75(1)(e), JSEPA (2002).
158. See, for example, Art. VI, Canada-Costa Rica (1998), and Art. 5, ECT (1994).

provided in the territory, or impose requirements on the purchase of goods or services from persons in its territory. Article 1106(1)(a) and (d) similarly prohibit measures requiring the export of a given level or percentage of goods or services that relate in any way to the volume or value of imports or exports, or to the amount of foreign exchange inflows associated with such investment.[159]

Two cases under Chapter 11 of NAFTA have addressed prohibitions on domestic content requirements and their relationship to export restrictions.[160] In *S.D. Myers, Inc. v. Canada*, the tribunal considered whether a Canadian ban on the export to the US of polychlorinated biphenyls (PCBs) violated NAFTA's prohibitions on performance requirements. S.D. Myers argued that the ban required it to undertake PCB waste disposal in Canada, rather than in its US facilities, and that this constituted a violation of the prohibitions on domestic content and purchasing requirements.[161] In other words, the export ban required it to use Canadian goods and services to carry out the physical disposal of PCB waste. The majority of the tribunal, although stating that it was required to look to the substance – not the form – of the ban, held that no 'requirements' were imposed with respect to the conduct or operation of S.D. Myers' investment.[162] In a separate opinion, Bryan Schwartz stated that the practical effect of the export ban was to require S.D. Myers to carry out a major step of the PCB remediation process – physical destruction – in Canada. In his opinion, the ban was effectively a requirement to achieve domestic content and was, therefore, contrary to Article 1106(1)(b), NAFTA.[163] Further, he

---

159. Art. 1106(1) provides 'No Party may impose or enforce any of the following requirements, or enforce any commitment or undertaking, in connection with the establishment, acquisition, expansion, management, conduct or operation of an investment of an investor of a Party or of a non-Party in its territory:

    (a) to export a given level or percentage of goods or services;
    (b) to achieve a given level or percentage of domestic content;
    (c) to purchase, use or accord a preference to goods produced or services provided in its territory, or to purchase goods or services from persons in its territory;
    (d) to relate in any way the volume or value of imports to the volume or value of exports or to the amount of foreign exchange inflows associated with such investment;
    (e) to restrict sales of goods or services in its territory that such investment produces or provides by relating such sales in any way to the volume or value of its exports or foreign exchange earnings;
    (f) to transfer technology, a production process or other proprietary knowledge to a person in its territory, except when the requirement is imposed or the commitment or undertaking is enforced by a court, administrative tribunal or competition authority to remedy an alleged violation of competition laws or to act in a manner not inconsistent with other provisions of this Agreement; or
    (g) to act as the exclusive supplier of the goods it produces or services it provides to a specific region or world market.

160. On performance requirements in NAFTA, see *Investment Disputes under NAFTA, supra* note 65 at 1106-1–1106-18.

161. *S.D. Myers, Inc. v. Canada* (Statement of Claim, 30 Oct. 1998) at paras 43-47.

162. *S.D. Myers, Inc. v. Canada* (Partial Award, 13 Nov. 2000) [*Myers*] at para. 277.

163. *S.D. Myers, Inc. v. Canada*, Separate Opinion of B. Schwartz, 13 Nov. 2000 at paras 188-201. Professor Schwartz also suggested that Art. 1106(1)(c), which prohibits preferences for local

reasoned that Canada's export ban on PCBs could not be justified under Article 1106(6) as the ban was a disguised barrier to trade intended to protect the local waste disposal industry. The ban was arbitrary because it was both discriminatory and unjustifiable.[164]

In our view, the reasoning in the separate opinion is persuasive. The tribunal found that the motivation for the export ban was to protect and assist the domestic waste disposal industry. The effect of the measure was to require 100% domestic content. Although Canada argued that Article 1106(1) only prohibits *de jure* performance requirements,[165] such an interpretation allows states to do indirectly what they cannot do directly. As in the case of national and MFN treatment, the prohibition on performance requirements should be interpreted to apply to measures that result in both *de jure* and *de facto* requirements.

Shortly after this initial attempt to claim a breach of the performance requirements provisions of the NAFTA, a second claim was made.[166] In *Pope & Talbot Inc. v. Canada*, the investor claimed that the export control regime that Canada used to implement the Canada-US Softwood Lumber Agreement (SLA) was a prohibited performance requirement because it implemented a quota system for the export of certain levels of softwood.[167] Individual investors could export a certain amount of softwood lumber to the United States on a duty-free basis; however, investors that wished to export lumber in quantities that exceeded this duty-free amount would have to pay to do so, and they would not be able to carry the difference of their shortfall forward to increase their duty-free levels in future years.[168] As in *S.D. Myers*, Canada argued that Article 1106(1) would only apply to a requirement imposed by Canada to export goods and services and that the SLA imposed no such requirement to export.[169] The tribunal concluded that the export control regime did not impose or enforce requirements. The tribunal characterized the SLA as a 'tariff-rate export restraint regime fixing only the level up to which covered products may be exported fee-free ..., then at a lower fee ... up

---

goods and services, might only apply with respect to purchases from third parties, but made no conclusion on this issue because of lack of evidence. See para. 197.

164. *Ibid.*, at para. 200.

165. Canada based this argument partly on Art. 1106(5), which provides that 'Paragraphs 1 and 3 do not apply to any requirement other than the requirements set out in those paragraphs.' See Statement of Defence, 18 Jun. 1999 at paras 50-51.

166. In a third case, *ADF Group Inc. v. United States*, the investor was required to use steel manufactured in the US in a highway project in Virginia. It argued that this amounted to a requirement to achieve a given level of domestic content by according preference to domestic goods – a requirement that ran contrary to Arts 1106(1)(b) and (c) of NAFTA (Investor's Memorial, 1 Aug. 2005, para. 275). While the US did not dispute this assertion, it argued the government procurement exceptions in NAFTA applied (Award, 9 Jan. 2003 at para. 159). The tribunal agreed with the US on this point (*ibid.*, at para. 170). See *supra* Chapter 4 for discussion of the claimant's national treatment argument.

167. *Pope & Talbot Inc* (Statement of Claim, 25 Mar. 1999) at paras 83-87.

168. *Pope & Talbot Inc v. Canada* (Interim Award, 26 June 2000) [*Pope & Talbot*] at paras 27-40.

169. Statement of Defence, 8 Oct. 1999 at paras 145-146.

to a given higher level, and thereafter in unlimited quantities at a higher fee.'[170] According to the tribunal, although a deterrent to higher level of exports, the SLA did not impose a 'requirement' *per se* for conducting business in Canada, and therefore fell outside the ambit of NAFTA Article 1106(1).

§8.23 Prohibitions on restrictions on sales of goods within host state territory States sometimes implement economic policies to increase exports or foreign exchange reserves. They may try to achieve these objectives through various regulatory measures, including linking levels of domestic sales to the volume or value of exports. These types of measures effectively amount to a performance requirement that restricts the sales of goods and services within the host state.[171] Some IIAs expressly prohibit the imposition of such measures.[172] For example, Article 1106(1)(e), NAFTA, provides:

1. No Party may impose or enforce any of the following requirements, or enforce any commitment or undertaking, in connection with the establishment, acquisition, expansion, management, conduct or operation of an investment of an investor of a Party or of a non-Party in its territory:

    ...

    (e) to restrict sales of goods or services in its territory that such investment produces or provides by relating such sales in any way to the volume or value of its exports or foreign exchange earnings.

Although few claims have arisen in this area, the central issue in the context of NAFTA jurisprudence has been how to characterize restrictions. In *Pope & Talbot*, the investor argued that the Canadian export control regime required it to restrict sales of lumber bound for the US by relating sales to the volume of exports at which no fee would be charged.[173] Canada responded by arguing, *inter alia,* that the investor had misinterpreted the restrictions – that the applicable NAFTA provisions[174] apply to restrictions on sales in the host state's territory, not to restrictions on exports to another country. The tribunal sided with Canada on this issue and held that the export control regime did not impose restrictions or limitations on domestic sales of softwood.[175] This result appears to be justified as there were no limits on the amount of softwood that a producer could sell in Canada. In other

---

170. *Pope & Talbot, supra* note 168 at para. 75.
171. This type of measure would not necessarily violate the TRIMS Agreement provided no distinction was made between imported and domestic goods. The TRIMS Agreement does not prohibit non-discriminatory export promotion policies. See *supra* note 133.
172. See Art. 1106(1)(e), NAFTA. Post-NAFTA US and Canadian IIAs often contain this obligation.
173. *Pope & Talbot, supra* note 168, at para. 45. It was common ground between the parties (para. 73) that the granting of fee-free export quotas was an advantage within the meaning of Art. 1106(3), NAFTA.
174. Articles 1106(1)(e) and 3(d), NAFTA.
175. *Pope & Talbot, supra* note 168 at para. 80.

words, in *Pope & Talbot*, there were no restrictions on sales of goods within the host state.

§8.24 Prohibitions on requirements for technology transfer   As part of their development strategies, states sometimes impose requirements on foreign investors with respect to technology transfer and dissemination.[176] If technology is proprietary, such requirements may violate international intellectual property laws and the WTO *Agreement on Trade-Related Aspects of Intellectual Property* (TRIPS Agreement).[177]

Most IIAs do not specifically address host state measures that may relate to technology transfer.[178] However, prohibitions on technology transfer requirements do appear in NAFTA, as well as many post-NAFTA Canadian[179] and US[180] BITs and bilateral FTAs.[181] For example, Article V(2)(e) of Canada-Trinidad and Tobago (1995), based on the NAFTA model, prohibits requirements:

> ... to transfer technology, a production process or other proprietary knowledge to a person in its territory unaffiliated with the transferor, except when the

---

176.   See Chapter 11, 'Technology Transfer' in Muchlinski, *supra* note 26; UNCTAD, *Transfer of Technology*, UNCTAD Series on issues in international investment agreements (New York and Geneva: United Nations, 2001) (UNCTAD/ITE/IIT28) [*Transfer of Technology*] and UNCTAD, *Facilitating Transfer of Technology to Developing Countries: A Survey of Home-Country Measures*, UNCTAD Series on Technology Transfer and Development (New York and Geneva: United Nations, 2004) (UNCTAD/ITE/IPC/2004/5).

177.   *Agreement on Trade-Related Aspects of Intellectual Property Rights*, 15 Apr. 1994, Marrakesh Agreement Establishing the World Trade Organization, Annex 1C, reproduced in *The Legal Texts: Results of the Uruguay Round of Multilateral Trade Negotiations* (Cambridge: Cambridge University Press, 1994), *reprinted in* (1994) 33 ILM 81. The Agreement has specific rules on compulsory licensing of patents. Some international environmental agreements contain technology transfer obligations. See *Transfer of Technology*, *ibid.*, at 108-111.

178.   In contrast, the Asian-African Legal Consultative Committee Draft Model Agreement 'B' for Promotion and Protection of Investments takes a permissive approach. Article 3(ii) provides 'The investment shall be received subject to the terms and conditions specified in the letter of authorization. Such terms and conditions may include the obligation or requirement concerning employment of local personnel and labour in the investment projects, organization of training programmes, transfer of technology and marketing arrangements for the products.' There do not appear to be any IIAs that adopt this approach.

179.   Examples of Canadian IIAs that include such provisions include: Art. V(2)(e), Armenia-Canada (1997); Art. V(2)(e), Barbados-Canada (1996); Art. VI, Canada-El Salvador (1999); Art. V(2)(e), Canada-Latvia (1995); Art. V(2)(e), Canada-South Africa (1995); Art. VI(3) Canada-Uruguay (1997); Art. VI(e), Canada-Croatia (1997); Art. V(2)(e), Canada-Ecuador (1996); Art. V(2)(e), Canada-Egypt (1996); Art. VI(e), Canada-Lebanon (1997); Art. V(2)(e), Canada-Panama (1996); Art. V(2)(e), Canada-Ukraine (1994); Art. V(2)(b), Canada-Thailand (1997); and Art. V(2)(e), Canada-Trinidad and Tobago (1995).

180.   US IIAs began incorporating such provisions in 1994, when the US developed a new model BIT. Examples of such IIAs include: Art. VI(e), Azerbaijan-US (1997); Art. VI(e), Bolivia-US (1998); Art. VI(e), Mozambique-US (1998); and Art. 10.8(1)(f), Morocco-US FTA (2004).

181.   Art. 10.5(1)(f), Chile-US FTA (2003); Art. 15.8(1)(f), Singapore-US FTA (2003); Art. 11.9(1)(f), Australia-US FTA (2004); Art. G-06(1)(f), Canada-Chile (1996); Art. 1106(1)(f), NAFTA (1992); Art. 75(1)(f), JSEPA (2002).

requirement is imposed or the commitment or undertaking is enforced by a court, administrative tribunal or competition authority, either to remedy an alleged violation of competition laws or acting in a manner not inconsistent with other provisions of this Agreement.[182]

The 2003 US Model BIT and BITs based on that model provide that requirements for technology transfers are permitted, so long as they are consistent with the TRIPS Agreement.[183]

§8.25 Conditions for receipt of advantages   States occasionally impose performance requirements in exchange for certain advantages, such as tax concessions, infrastructure development or subsidies.[184] When IIAs prohibit performance requirements, they also typically address the relationship between the imposition of performance requirements and the receipt of advantages. Agreements that follow the NAFTA model prohibit the conditioning of receipt of advantages in certain cases but not others. For example, Article 1106(3), NAFTA, provides that a host state may not condition the receipt of an advantage on domestic content or trade balancing requirements.[185] However, it does not prohibit host states from conditioning receipt of advantages on three other performance requirements: to export a given level or percentage of goods and services; to transfer technology; or to act as an exclusive supplier.[186] Furthermore, it also expressly permits host states to furnish foreign investors with advantages in exchange for locating production, providing services, training or employing workers, constructing or expanding particular facilities, or carrying out research and development within the host state.[187]

---

182. The corresponding prohibition in the NAFTA (Art. 1106(1)(f)) is qualified by Art. 1103, which states that 'A measure that requires an investment to use a technology to meet generally applicable health, safety or environmental requirements shall not be construed to be inconsistent with paragraph 1(f).'
183. See Art. 8(3)(b)(i), US-Uruguay (2005).
184. International trade law prohibits subsidies contingent upon export performance or the use of domestic goods over imported goods. See Trebilcock & Howse, *Regulation of International Trade, supra* note 3 on restrictions on subsidies under the WTO.
185. See similar provisions in Art. 11.9(2), Australia-US FTA (2004); Art. G-06(3), Canada-Chile FTA (1996) and Art. 8(2), US-Uruguay (2005).
186. Art. 1106(3)(a) to (d) reproduces the prohibitions in 1106(1)(b) to (e) with some minor variations. Art. 1106(3)(b), unlike Art. 1106(1)(c), does not refer to services. There are three prohibited performance requirements under 1106(1) that are not included in 1106(3), which thus can be made conditional upon the receipt of an advantage. These are: (a) to export a given level or percentage of goods and services, (f) to transfer technology, and (g) to act as an exclusive supplier.
187. See, for example, Art. 1106(4), NAFTA (1992); Art. 11.9(3)(a), Australia-US FTA (2004); Art. 17-04(3), Colombia-Mexico-Venezuela FTA (1994) and Art. 7(4), Canadian Model FIPA (2003).

Another approach found in IIAs is to provide expressly that the host state may condition the receipt of advantages on performance requirements.[188] For example, Trinidad and Tobago-US (1994) provides that the prohibition on performance requirements does not preclude the host state from 'providing benefits and incentives conditioned upon such requirements.'[189]

§8.26 Other prohibited performance requirements A number of other prohibited performance requirements also appear in IIAs, particularly in US[190] and Canadian[191] BITs. These include prohibitions on host states from imposing requirements on foreign investors to: (i) act as an exclusive supplier of goods or services;[192] (ii) carry out a particular type, level or percentage of research and development in the Party's territory;[193] and (iii) dispose of an investment by reason of nationality.[194]

§8.27 Prohibitions on performance requirements in other IIA standards Some IIAs, rather than having a separate provision on performance requirements, link the prohibition on performance requirements to unreasonable and discriminatory effects or fair and equitable treatment. For example, Article 4(2), Azerbaijan-Finland (2003), under the heading 'Promotion and Protection of Investments' provides:

> Each Contracting Party shall not impose mandatory measures on investments by investors of the other Contracting Party concerning purchase of materials, means of production, operation, transport, marketing of its products or similar orders having unreasonable or discriminatory effects.

Some French BITs[195] provide that restrictions on the purchase or transport of raw materials, fuel, machinery or restrictions on the sale or transport of products amount to a breach of fair and equitable treatment.

---

188. See also Art. VI, Bolivia-US (1998); Art. VI, Mozambique-US (1998); Art. 6, Bahrain-US (1999); Art. 7(4), Canadian Model FIPA (2003); Art. 8(3)(a), US Model (2004); and Art. 8(3)(a), US-Uruguay (2005).
189. Art. VI(2).
190. See, for example, Art. VII, Trinidad and Tobago-US (1994); Bolivia-US (1998); Art. VI, Mozambique-US (1998) and Art. 6, Bahrain-US (1999).
191. See, for example, Art. V(2), Barbados-Canada (1996); Art. V(2), Canada-Philippines (1996); V(2), Canada-Trinidad and Tobago (1995) and Art. V(2), Canada-Egypt (1996).
192. Art. 1106(1)(g), NAFTA (1992); Art. 8(1)(g), US-Uruguay (2005); Art. 7(1)(g), Canadian Model FIPA (2003) and Art. G-06(1)(g), Canada-Chile FTA (1996).
193. Art. VII (f), Trinidad and Tobago-US (1994); Art. 75(1)(h), JSEPA (2002); Art. 11.9(1)(f), Australia-US FTA (2004) and Art. 1106(1)(g), NAFTA (1992).
194. See, for example, Art. 1108(4), NAFTA (1992); Art. 1108(4) and Art. G-08(3), Canada-Chile FTA (1996).
195. See, for example, Art. 3, France-Zimbabwe (2001): 'En particulier, bien que non exclusivement, sont considérées comme des entraves de droit ou de fait au traitement juste et équitable, toute restriction à l'achat et au transport de matières premières et de matières auxiliaires, d'énergie et de combustibles, ainsi que de moyens de production et d'exploitation de tous

III   TRANSPARENCY RELATED STANDARDS

§8.28 Treaty practice   Most IIAs do not have specific transparency related standards.[196] Some early BITs, notably US model BITs, contain provisions requiring state parties to publicize all laws, regulations and other measures affecting investments and to provide for exchange of information.[197] Some early BITs also have access to court provisions obligating states to provide effective means for asserting investor claims and enforcing rights.[198] Transparency and due process standards have become more common in IIAs concluded after 2000.

Transparency standards in IIAs generally contain three elements: to make information on laws, regulations and policies publicly available; to notify parties of changes in the laws; and to ensure that the laws are applied in a non-discriminatory and impartial fashion. In addition, some IIAs have more general provisions requiring transparency, although the term remains undefined. For example, Article 2(1), Bosnia-Finland (2000), provides that the parties 'shall encourage ... transparent conditions....' Article 10, *Energy Charter Treaty* (ECT), requires the parties to 'create stable, equitable, favourable and transparent conditions.'

Even if an IIA does not have express obligations with respect to transparency, state conduct that is non-transparent might be regarded as a breach of fair and equitable treatment or other minimum standards.[199]

§8.29 Publication of laws, regulations and policies   The most common transparency standard is a requirement to publish laws, regulations and policies. For example, Article 16, Bosnia-Finland (2000), provides:

> Each Contracting Party shall promptly publish, or otherwise make publicly available, its laws, regulations, procedures and administrative rulings and judicial decisions of general application as well as international agreements which may affect the investments of investors of one Contracting Party in the territory of the other Contracting Party.

---

genres, toute entrave à la vente et au transport des produits à l'intérieur du pays et à l'étranger, ainsi que toutes autres mesures ayant un effet analogue.' Also see Art. 4, French Model BIT; Art. 3, Bolivia-France (1989); Art. 3, Cambodia-France (2000); Art. 3, France-Venezuela (2001); Art. 3, France-Ukraine (1994); Art. 3, France-Zimbabwe (2001); and Art. 3, France-Madagascar (2003).

196.   Due process requirements are included within other absolute standards, including minimum standards (*supra* Chapter 6, §6.7) and expropriation (*supra* Chapter 7, §7.34). See *supra* Chapter 6, §6.28 on transparency as a minimum standard of treatment.

197.   Vandevelde, *supra* note 40 at 207-209.

198.   See Art. II(2), Senegal-US (1983). A more recent example is Art. 2(4), Algeria-Sweden (2003), which provides that '[e]ach Contracting Party shall provide effective means of asserting claims and enforcing rights with respect to investments covered by this Agreement.'

199.   See *supra* Chapter 6.

Article XIV, entitled 'Transparency', of Canada-Croatia (1997) provides:

> Each Contracting Party shall, to the extent practicable, ensure that its laws, regulations, procedures, and administrative rulings of general application respecting any matter covered by this Agreement are promptly published or otherwise made available in such a manner as to enable interested persons and the other Contracting Party to become acquainted with them.

In general, transparency provisions in IIAs are less detailed and comprehensive than those found in multilateral trade agreements.[200] More recent IIAs, however, have more extensive publication requirements. For example, Article 10, US-Uruguay (2005), provides:

1. Each Party shall ensure that its:
    (a) laws, regulations, procedures, and administrative rulings of general application; and
    (b) adjudicatory decisions respecting any matter covered by this Treaty are promptly published or otherwise made publicly available.
2. For purposes of this Article, 'administrative ruling of general application' means an administrative ruling or interpretation that applies to all persons and fact situations that fall generally within its ambit and that establishes a norm of conduct but does not include:
    (a) a determination or ruling made in an administrative or quasi-judicial proceeding that applies to a particular covered investment or investor of the other Party in a specific case; or
    (b) a ruling that adjudicates with respect to a particular act or practice.

§8.30 Notification and due process requirements   A number of recent IIAs have included provisions on notice of regulatory changes and the identification of contact points. These IIAs provide for contacts to facilitate communications between the state parties and afford 'interested persons and the other Party a reasonable opportunity to comment on such proposed measures.'[201] Some

---

200.   Art. X GATT sets out comprehensive provisions relating to the publication of laws. Art. X(1) provides that laws must be published promptly, and in a manner that allows interested parties to become acquainted with them. Art. X(2) further provides that regulations cannot be enforced until they have been published officially. The GATS requires that where publication is not practicable, information should be made 'otherwise publicly available.' (GATS, Arts III(1) and 2). The TRIPS Agreement provides that 'all laws and regulations, and final judicial decisions and administrative rulings of general application ... shall be made publicly available, in a national language, in such a manner as to enable governments and rights holders to become acquainted with them.' Art. 63(1), the TRIPS Agreement. See C.S. Zoellner, 'Transparency: An Analysis of an Evolving Fundamental Principle in International Economic Law,' (2006) 27 MJIL 579.

201.   See Art. 11(2), US-Uruguay BIT (2005). These provisions are similar to those appearing in the new generation of US and Canadian FTAs. See for example: Chapter 20, Chile-US FTA (2003); Chapter 17, Bahrain-US FTA (2004); Chapter 20, Australia-US FTA (2004); Chapter L, Canada-Chile FTA (1996); Art. 8, Canada-Israel FTA (1997); and Chapter 12,

agreements require that each party promptly respond to questions and provide requested information to the other party respecting matters in the agreement.[202] Others also require each party to provide routine information needed for statistical or other informational purposes.[203] Confidential business information is protected in the event that disclosure would jeopardize the competitive position of the investor.

Procedural requirements can include prompt notification of decisions concerning applications, the right to file a complaint and the right of review and appeal. US-Uruguay (2005) provides for a number of due process requirements to be met in administrative proceedings, including providing reasonable notice of the proceedings, an opportunity to be heard and an independent and impartial system for the review of administrative actions.[204] Article 11, US-Uruguay (2005), reproduced below, reflects these innovations:

Article 11: Transparency

1. Contact Points
   (a) Each Party shall designate a contact point or points to facilitate communications between the Parties on any matter covered by this Treaty.
   (b) On the request of the other Party, the contact points shall identify the office or official responsible for the matter and assist, as necessary, in facilitating communication with the requesting Party.
2. Publication
   To the extent possible, each Party shall:
   (a) publish in advance any measure referred to in Article 10(1)(a) that it proposes to adopt; and
   (b) provide interested persons and the other Party a reasonable opportunity to comment on such proposed measures.
3. Notification and Provision of Information
   (a) To the maximum extent possible, each Party shall notify the other Party of any proposed or actual measure that the Party considers might materially affect the operation of this Treaty or otherwise substantially affect the other Party's interests under this Treaty.
   (b) On request of the other Party, a Party shall promptly provide information and respond to questions pertaining to any actual or proposed

---

Canada-Costa Rica FTA (2002), which typically have specific requirements with respect to publication of measures, notification of changes in measures, reasonable opportunities to comment on changes in provision of contact or enquiry points for information.

202. Art. 6.15, India-Singapore CECA (2005), and *supra* note 108, Art. 14(6), *Japan-Malaysia Economic Partnership Agreement* (2005). See also Art. 63(3), the TRIPS Agreement.
203. Art. 6.14(2), India-Singapore CECA (2005); Art. 15, US-Uruguay (2005); Art. G-11.2, Canada-Chile FTA (1996); and Art. 10.16(2), Korea-Singapore FTA (2005).
204. *Ibid.*, Art. 11.4-5.

measure referred to in subparagraph (a), whether or not the other Party has been previously notified of that measure.

    (c) Any notification, request, or information under this paragraph shall be provided to the other Party through the relevant contact points.

    (d) Any notification or information provided under this paragraph shall be without prejudice as to whether the measure is consistent with this Treaty.

4.   Administrative Proceedings

With a view to administering in a consistent, impartial, and reasonable manner all measures referred to in Article 10(1)(a), each Party shall ensure that in its administrative proceedings applying such measures to particular covered investments or investors of the other Party in specific cases that:

    (a) wherever possible, persons of the other Party that are directly affected by a proceeding are provided reasonable notice, in accordance with domestic procedures, when a proceeding is initiated, including a description of the nature of the proceeding, a statement of the legal authority under which the proceeding is initiated, and a general description of any issues in controversy;

    (b) such persons are afforded a reasonable opportunity to present facts and arguments in support of their positions prior to any final administrative action, when time, the nature of the proceeding, and the public interest permit; and

    (c) its procedures are in accordance with domestic law.

5.   Review and Appeal

    (a) Each Party shall establish or maintain judicial, quasi-judicial, or administrative tribunals or procedures for the purpose of the prompt review and, where warranted, correction of final administrative actions regarding matters covered by this Treaty. Such tribunals shall be impartial and independent of the office or authority entrusted with administrative enforcement and shall not have any substantial interest in the outcome of the matter.

    (b) Each Party shall ensure that, in any such tribunals or procedures, the parties to the proceeding are provided with the right to:

        (i) a reasonable opportunity to support or defend their respective positions; and

        (ii) a decision based on the evidence and submissions of record or, where required by domestic law, the record compiled by the administrative authority.

    (c) Each Party shall ensure, subject to appeal or further review as provided in its domestic law, that such decisions shall be implemented by, and shall govern the practice of, the office or authorities responsible for the administrative action at issue.

Due process provisions are also common in FTAs with investment chapters. For instance, the India-Singapore CECA and Korea-Singapore Free Trade Agreement require that each party provide investors of the other party the same access to courts of justice and administrative tribunals as it accords to its own investors.[205]

---

205. Art. 6.18, India-Singapore CECA, *supra* note 108, and Art. 10.6, Korea-Singapore FTA (2005). See also Art. 8(2), Korea-Netherlands (2003).

Chapter 9

Observance of Undertakings

INTRODUCTION

§9.1 Umbrella clause and other denominations   Some international investment agreements (IIAs) require that host states observe any obligations or commitments undertaken towards investments. This type of clause is often referred to as the 'umbrella clause,' because obligations undertaken by the host state in contracts or other arrangements are brought under the umbrella of protection of the treaty. Other metaphors used are 'elevator,' 'mirror' or 'parallel' effect clause, because, by its application, breaches of those obligations or commitments are automatically elevated to, mirrored into, or give rise to parallel treaty breaches. More explicit terms are also used to refer to this sort of provision, such as 'observation of commitments,' '*pacta sunt servanda,*' 'sanctity of contract,' or 'respect for contract' clause.[1] For the purposes of this chapter the terms 'observance of undertakings clause' and 'umbrella clause' are used interchangeably.

Observance of undertakings clauses are discussed below in eight parts. Part I addresses the history and treaty practice. Part II examines the applicable law. The undertakings covered by the clause are addressed in Part III while undertakings attributable to the state are addressed in Part IV. Part V looks at the substantive

---

1.   See generally *SGS Société Générale de Surveillance S.A. v. Pakistan* (Decision of the Tribunal on Objections to Jurisdiction, 6 Aug. 2003) [*SGS v. Pakistan*] at para. 163; T. Wälde, 'The "Umbrella" Clause in Investment Arbitration: A Comment on Original Intentions and Recent Cases' (2005) 6 JWIT 183 at 185; A. Sinclair, 'The Origins of the Umbrella Clause in International Law of Investment Protection' (2004) 20 AI 411 at 411; K. Yannaca-Small, 'Interpretation of the Umbrella Clause in Investment Agreements,' OECD Working Papers on International Investment Number 2006/3 at 3 [*OECD Working Paper*]; and W. Ben Hamida, 'La clause relative au respect des engagements dans les traités d'investissement' in Ch. Leben, ed., *Le contentieux arbitral transnational relative à l'investissement* (Paris: Anthemis, 2006) at 53-54.

content of the duty of observance. Concurrent jurisdictions and limitations are addressed in Parts VI and VII respectively. The chapter concludes by examining the distinction between observance of undertakings clauses and other clauses.

§9.2 Principle, rationale and interpretive uncertainty   Observance of undertakings clauses in IIAs reflect a principle common and familiar to most, if not all, legal systems: the obligation to honour legal commitments. The clause thus enshrines the principle of '*pacta sunt servanda,*' a cornerstone of the legal security of economic transactions and the basis for contract law in national and international law. In this context, the rationale for the clause lies in the liberal internationalist approach that developed in the 1950s: namely, that there should be effective international protection of contracts in order to achieve peace and prosperity through international trade, investment and economic integration.[2] Whether these or other principles may be read into the clause largely depends on the precise wording of the particular provision and the structure of the treaty at issue.

There is uncertainty and debate on the scope and effect of the clause and its underlying principles. This is partly because tribunals and commentators have voiced concerns regarding the implications of expansive interpretations of the clause, including the risk of elevating a multitude of ordinary commercial transactions into potential international disputes, and of tilting the balance of IIAs too much in favour of the foreign investor to the detriment of the host state. In essence, despite the broad drafting of many umbrella clauses, there is some unease in interpreting them as radically departing from the more restrictive principles of customary international law on state responsibility for contract breaches.

§9.3 Contracts in international law   It is controversial whether the non-fulfilment of a contractual obligation by a state in and of itself gives rise to international responsibility, or whether there must be a distinct breach of a separate international obligation owed by the state (e.g., either under an IIA or under customary international law).

In principle, the host state and foreign investor may expressly provide that international law is applicable to the contract: the sovereign by its act of agreement to international law governing the contract confers upon the private party the capacity to receive international obligations. Additionally, some contracts might be of a manifestly international character, removing them from a given system of municipal law; these contracts are deemed subject to international law because of their inherent nature and not because the parties' intention confers internationality upon such agreements.[3] In these circumstances, some tribunals have found that because

---

2.   Wälde, *ibid.*, at 201.
3.   See e.g., *Revere Copper and Brass Inc. v. Overseas Private Investment Corporation* (1978) 56 ILR 258 at 271-279; *Government of Saudi Arabia v. The Arabian American Oil Company* (1958) 27 ILR 117 at 153-156; *Texaco Overseas Petroleum Company and California Asiatic Oil Company v. Libya* (1977) 53 ILR 389 at 20-36.

international law is the law applicable to the contract, the mere non-performance of a contractual obligation gives rise to state responsibility under international law without need for a distinct breach of a separate international obligation such as denial of justice.[4] For example, in the *Singer Sewing* case it was held that 'if a Government agrees to pay money for commodities and fails to make payment, the view may be taken that the purchase price of the commodities has been confiscated, or that the commodities have been confiscated.'[5] Also, state responsibility can arise if the state deliberately or negligently fails to comply with a contractual obligation to assist in ensuring the collection of dues payable under a concession to be collected by a concessionaire in the government's name, if the concessionaire is not able to claim compensation for losses from the government (which in fact could be an instance of denial of justice).[6] Similarly, refusal to accept goods under a contract of delivery without giving reasons may give rise to state responsibility.[7] A sovereign's unilateral declaration that a contract is void, or an unjustifiable unilateral alteration of the investor-contractor's benefit may also be internationally wrongful.[8] The state is liable for payment of works performed by an investor under contract with the executive branch if the work is stopped by order of the public authorities.[9]

In contrast, the prevalent view in the second half of the twentieth century was that non-fulfilment of a contractual obligation not governed by international law by itself does not engage state responsibility, unless there is a separate breach of a treaty obligation or a customary international law obligation governing the treatment of a foreigner and foreign property.[10] Hence, the view dominating the

---

4. See *supra* Chapter 6, §6.5 on denial of justice. As one tribunal has noted, there is no general rule 'according to which mere non-performance of contractual obligations by a Government in its civil capacity withholds jurisdiction, whereas it grants jurisdiction when the non-performance is accompanied by some feature of the public capacity of the Government as an authority.' *Illinois Central Railroad Company Case* (1926) IV RIAA 21 at 22; *Lighthouses Concession Case* (1956), *Protocole des Séances, Ordonnances de Procédure et Sentences avec Annexes du Tribunal d'Arbitrage constitué en vertu du compromis signé à Paris le 15 juillet 1931 entre la France et la Grèce, Bureau international de la Cour Permanente d'Arbitrage*, 100-101, Claim No. 5 [*Lighthouses Concession Case* (see summary in the Digest of the Decisions of International Tribunals relating to State Responsibility, 1964 YBILC, Vol. II, 136)]; *Deutz* (1929) IV RIAA 472; *Hemming* (1920) VI RIAA 51 at 53; *German Settlers in Poland* (1923) PCIJ Ser. B, No. 6 at 19-20, 35-38; *Aboilard* (1905) XI RIAA 71 at 79-81; *George W. Cook* (1927) IV RIAA 213 at 214-215; *Joseph E. Davies* (1927) IV RIAA 139 at 141, 143-144; and *Hopkins* (1926) IV RIAA 41 at 42-47.
5. *Singer Sewing Machine Company Arbitration (United States v. Turkey)* reported in F.K. Nielsen, ed., *American-Turkish Claims Settlement under the Agreement of December 24, 1923, Opinions and Report* (Washington: US Government, 1937) at 491.
6. *Lighthouses Concession Case, supra* note 4.
7. *Deutz, supra* note 4.
8. *Landreau* (1922) I RIAA 347 at 356.
9. *Rudloff* (1903) IX RIAA 244 at 257-258; and *Shufeldt Claim* (1930) II RIAA 1079 at 1098.
10. S.M. Schwebel, 'On Whether the Breach by a State of a Contract with an Alien is a Breach of International Law,' in Zanardi *et al.*, eds, *International Law at the Time of its Codification: Essays in Honour of Roberto Ago* (Milano: A. Giuffrè, 1987), *reprinted in* S.M. Schwebel, *Justice in International Law: Selected Writings of Stephen M. Schwebel* (Cambridge: Grotius,

international law debate at present is that, 'while a mere breach by a state of a contract with an alien (whose proper law is not international law) is not a violation of international law, a "non-commercial" act of a State contrary to such a contract may be.'[11] Examples of governmental breaches of this kind are arbitrary or repudiatory measures, in which the state seeks to abrogate a contractual obligation by use of its sovereign authority.[12]

The application of these principles to investor-state contracts has obvious implications. If a contract is governed by international law, it follows that the existence and imputability of international responsibility derives solely from the mere non-performance of the contractual obligation in question. This is because non-fulfilment of a treaty obligation constitutes an internationally wrongful act. Here, as with a breach of treaty, there would be no further need to explain the basis for international responsibility. This would dramatically reduce a private claimant's burden of proof in litigation seeking to establish an internationally wrongful act in relation to a contract. Further, it would automatically entitle the investor's home state to espouse the private contractor's claim for the very same reason: it is simply not necessary to establish any other basis for the host state's international responsibility. Finally, the remedy available to the private contractor for breach or non-performance of the contract would not derive from a municipal system of law, but rather from the international law of state responsibility. Many commentators have viewed these implications as too expansive. As discussed below, this concern has impacted the debate about the effects of the umbrella clause.

I   HISTORY AND TREATY PRACTICE

§9.4 Origins   Some commentators have suggested that the use of umbrella clauses to protect particular state undertakings towards foreign investors can be traced back to the 1920s.[13] The idea is also clearly enshrined in Elihu Lauterpacht's advice in 1954 to the Anglo-Iranian Oil Company that the settlement agreement for the Iranian oil nationalization dispute be 'incorporated or referred to in a treaty

---

1994) at 425; and C.F. Amerasinghe, *State Responsibility for Injuries to Aliens* (Oxford: Clarendon Press, 1967) at 66-69.

11.   Schwebel, *ibid.*, at 431.

12.   E.g., *Jalapa Railroad and Power Co. (US v. Mexico)* (1948) reported in M. Whitman, ed., *Digest of International Law*, Vol. 8 (Washington: US Government, 1976) at 909-909; *Sempra Energy International v. Argentina* (Award, 28 Sep. 2007) [*Sempra*] at para. 310; and *Impregilo S.p.A. v. Pakistan* (Decision on Jurisdiction, 22 Apr. 2005) [*Impregilo*] at para. 260.

13.   Sinclair, *supra* note 1 at 413-14; and P. Weil, 'Problèmes relatifs aux contrats passés entre un État et un particulier' (1969-III) 128 RDCADI 95 at 131. The examples usually cited are: the 1921 Agreement between the United Kingdom and Peru, Respecting the Mineral Property 'La Brea y Pariñas' and the 1922 Geneva Convention between Poland and Germany. The 1921 UK-Peru Agreement, however, dealt with the resolution of an existing contract dispute and the 1922 Geneva Convention related to takings rather than the obligation to respect commitments.

between Iran and the United Kingdom in such a way that a breach of the contract or settlement shall be *ipso facto* deemed a breach of the treaty ... .'[14]

Observance of undertakings clauses originated in the late 1950s. They came about as a result of dissatisfaction with the ambiguous international law protection accorded to long-term investment contracts, particularly in light of the expropriations and contract revocations in the inter-war period, as well as the failure of traditional public international law processes to provide protection, as reflected in cases like the *Anglo-Iranian Oil Company Case*.[15] These events prompted a scholarly debate on the sanctity of concession agreements under international law,[16] and efforts were made to provide treaty protection for those contracts as a subset of property rights.

§9.5 Early treaty practice These efforts crystallized in the 1959 *Draft Convention on Investments Abroad* (Abs-Shawcross Draft Convention). Article II of the draft text, which constitutes the first occurrence of an observance of undertakings clause, reads as follows:

> Each Party shall at all times ensure the observance of any undertakings which it may have given in relation to investments made by nationals of any other Party.[17]

---

14. Elihu Lauterpacht's opinion to the *Anglo-Iranian Oil Company* (1954), cited in Sinclair, *supra* note 1 at 415. The purpose was to internationalise the agreement, preventing its exclusive subjection to Iranian law and the risk of unilateral variation by the government, as well as to provide an interstate remedy for breaches of the agreement. The umbrella treaty never materialized.

15. Wälde, *supra* note 1 at 200-201. Voicing these concerns and motivations see H. J. Abs, *Proposals for Improving the Protection of Private Foreign Investments* (Institut International d'Études Bancaires: Rotterdam, 1958) at 24-25; and H. Shawcross, 'The Problems of Foreign Investment in International Law' (1961-I) 102 RDCADI 335 at 341. In *Anglo-Iranian Oil Company Ltd (UK v. Iran)* [1952] ICJ Rep. 93 [*Anglo Iranian Oil Company Case*], the ICJ declined jurisdiction on the basis that claims under customary international law rather than treaties were not covered by Iran's acceptance of compulsory jurisdiction under the Optional Clause. See *supra* Chapter 1 for historical background.

16. Among those favourable to an international law principle on the sanctity of contracts, see 'Report of the Committee on Nationalization of Property of the American Branch of the International Law Association,' *Proceedings and Committee Reports of the American Branch of the International Law Association 1957-1958* at 61; K.S. Carlston, 'Concession Agreements and Nationalization' (1958) 52 AJIL 260; H. Wehberg, '*Pacta Sunt Servanda*' (1959) 53 AJIL 775; and S.M. Schwebel, 'International Protection of Contractual Agreements' (1959) ASIL Proc. 273. For a more nuanced view, see F.A. Mann, 'State Contracts and State Responsibility' (1960) 54 AJIL 572.

17. Abs-Shawcross Draft Convention (1960) 9 JPL, *reprinted in* UNCTAD, *International Investment Instruments: A Compendium*, Vol. V (New York: United Nations, 2000) at 395. No similar provision can be found in any of the earlier efforts to draft rules for the protection of foreign property such as the 1929 Harvard Draft (1929) 23 AJIL Supp.133; 1948 Havana Charter; or the 1948 Economic Agreement of Bogotá. See *supra* Chapter 1, §1.10-§1.11 and §1.15- §1.17 on these early efforts.

Commentators at the time agreed that the clause covered unilateral as well as consensual undertakings, including contractual commitments.[18] Less clear, however, was the degree of contract protection afforded by the clause.[19] The general concern may have been to counter the all-too-frequent governmental revocation of concession contracts, arguably already covered by customary international law rules.[20] The broad wording of the clause suggests, however, that any strict limitations on state conduct targeted by the clause were deliberately avoided.[21] The risk of opening the floodgates to contract claims framed under international law might have been considered sufficiently countered by the restraint implicit in the state-to-state enforcement mechanism.[22]

The observance of undertakings clause appeared simultaneously in Article 7, Germany-Pakistan (1959), providing as follows:

> Either party shall observe any other obligation it may have entered into with regard to investments by nationals or companies of the other party.

A clause, with a different formulation, was also included in Article 2, 1962 OECD *Draft Convention on the Protection of Foreign Property* and in the revised draft reissued in 1967 (1967 Draft OECD Convention), entitled 'Observance of Undertakings':

> Each Party shall at all times ensure the observance of undertakings given by it in relation to property of nationals of any other Party.[23]

---

18. G. Schwarzenberger, 'The Abs-Shawcross Draft Convention on Investments Abroad: A Critical Commentary' (1960) 9 JPL 147 at 154; and A.A. Fatouros, 'An International Code to Protect Private Investment – Proposals and Perspectives' (1961) 14 UTLJ 77 at 86.

19. The clause was presented as merely affirming and clarifying accepted general international law principles on respect for contractual commitments. See the third recital of the Preamble of the Abs-Shawcross Draft Convention. See also: H. J. Abs & H. Shawcross, 'Comment on the Draft Convention by its Authors' (1960) 9 JPL 119 at 120; and E. Snyde, 'Foreign Investment Protection: A Reasoned Approach' (1963) 61 Mich LR 1087 at 1110. However, some commentators viewed it as a departure from existing law: Schwarzenberger, *ibid.*, at 154-55; I. Seidl-Hohenveldern, 'The Abs-Shawcross Draft Convention to Protect Private Foreign Investment: Comments on the Round Table' (1961) 10 JPL 100 at 101-105; S.D. Metzger, 'Multilateral Conventions for the Protection of Private Foreign Investment' (1960) 9 JPL 133 at 134-139; A. Larson, 'Recipients' Rights under an International Investment Code' (1960) 9 JPL 172; and P.O. Proehl, 'Private Investments Abroad' (1960) 9 JPL 362 at 363.

20. Wälde, *supra* note 1 at 203-205. Compare Sinclair, *supra* note 1 at 421-427.

21. The wide terms of the clause contrast with the more restrictive customary international law approach to contract protection demonstrated by the contemporary efforts to codify the rules of state responsibility for injuries to aliens. See Art. 12 of the 1961 Harvard *Draft Convention on the International Responsibility of States for Injuries to Aliens* (1961) 55 AJIL 545; and F.V. García Amador, ILC's Special Rapporteur on International Responsibility, *Fourth Report: Responsibility of the State for Injuries Caused in its Territory to the Person or Property of Aliens – Measures Affecting Acquired Rights* (1959) YBILC Vol. II.

22. See Wälde, *supra* note 1 at 205, suggesting this implicit limitation among others.

23. 1962 OECD *Draft Convention on the Protection of Foreign Property* (1963) 2 ILM 247; and 1967 OECD *Draft Convention on the Protection of Foreign Property* (1968) 7 ILM 117 [1967 Draft OECD Convention]. See *supra* Chapter 1, §1.22, on the 1967 Draft OECD

Like the Abs-Shawcross Draft Convention, the clause was understood to cover unilateral as well as contractual undertakings.[24] Whether the Organization for Economic Co-operation and Development (OECD) drafters intended the clause to depart from existing law[25] and it was meant to apply to commercial as well as governmental contracts and conduct is, however, disputed.[26] In any case, the US opposed Article 2 as too constraining on state action, an allegation that was also levelled at other provisions of the draft.[27] The convention thus failed, but the draft influenced subsequent treaty practice.[28]

§9.6 Modern treaty practice The observance of undertakings clause is not as prevalent in IIAs as other clause, such as fair and equitable treatment or expropriation provisions.[29] It is common in Dutch, German, Swiss, UK and US Bilateral

---

Convention. Similar contemporary concern for the sanctity of contracts may be found at paragraph 8 of the unanimous 1962 UNGA Resolution 1803 (XVII) on Permanent Sovereignty over Natural Resources which provided that '[f]oreign investments agreements freely entered into by, or between, sovereign states shall be observed in good faith.' See *supra* Chapter 1, §1.20, for the history of this resolution.

24. See the 1967 Draft OECD Convention's accompanying notes and comments, at Art. 2, paras 2 and 3(a) stating that the notion of property was to be understood widely. See also E. Lauterpacht, 'Drafting Conventions for the Protection of Investment,' in *The Encouragement and Protection of Investment in Developing Countries* (1962) 3 ICLQ Supp. 218 at 229.

25. See Comments, Art. 2 paras 1(a) and 3(c), stating that Art. 2 is 'an application of the general principle of *pacta sunt servanda*' and M. Brandon, 'Survey of Current Approaches to the Problem,' in *The Encouragement and Protection of Investments in Developing Countries* (1962) 3 ICLQ Supp. 1 at 10, arguing that most commentators agreed that Art. 2 reflected a general principle of international law. *Cf.* C.N. Brower, 'The Future for Foreign Investments – Recent Developments in the International Law of Expropriation and Compensation' in V.S. Cameron, ed., *Private Investors Abroad – Problems and Solutions in the International Business in 1975* (New York: Matthew Bender, 1976) at 104.

26. For the restrictive view, see Wälde, *supra* note 1 at 203-205. *Cf.* to a more expansive approach: Sinclair, *supra* note 1 at 427-433; Lauterpacht, *supra* note 24 at 31-32; and Weil, *supra* note 13 at 132.

27. Sinclair, *ibid.*, at 431-432.

28. See *supra* Chapter 1, §1.22 on the 1967 Draft OECD Convention.

29. It has been estimated that 40% of BITs contain the umbrella clause. See J. Gill, M. Gearing & G. Birt, 'Contractual Claims and Bilateral Investment Treaties: A Comparative Review of the SGS Cases' (2004) 21 JIA 397, at note 31; and OECD Working Paper, *supra* note 1 at 5. For an overview of treaty practice, see the three comprehensive studies: United Nations Centre on Transnational Corporations (UNCTC), *Bilateral Investment Treaties* (New York: United Nations, 1988) (Doc. No. ST/CTC/65); UNCTAD, *Bilateral Investment Treaties in the Mid-1990s* (New York and Geneva: United Nations, 1998) (Doc. No. UNCTAD/ITE/IIT/7); and UNCTAD, *Bilateral Investment Treaties 1995-2006* (New York and Geneva: United Nations, 2007) (Doc. No. UNCTAD/ITE/IIT/2006/5) [together *UNCTAD BIT Studies*].

Investment Treaties (BITs),[30] and is contained in the *Energy Charter Treaty* (ECT)[31] and the ASEAN *Agreement for the Promotion and Protection of Investments* (ASEAN Investment Agreement).[32] It is rare, however, in Australian, French, Italian, Japanese and Spanish BITs,[33] and it is not present in Canadian BITs, Chapter 11 of the *North American Free Trade Agreement* (NAFTA), or in the US Model BIT since 1994. The draft MAI contained two formulations of the clause in its negotiating proposals.[34]

§9.7 Placement Observance of undertakings clauses are often placed in the initial provisions of IIAs, typically within the substantive provisions on the treatment of investments.[35] Alternatively, they may be located at the end of the IIA, after the jurisdictional provisions, usually within the preservation of rights

---

30. In the 1991 UK Model BIT, the clause is at the final sentence of Art. 2 entitled 'Promotion and Protection of Investment' and reads: 'Each Contracting Party shall observe any obligation it may have entered into with regard to investments of investors of the other Contracting Party.' See, with similar wording, 1991 German Model BIT at Art. 8(2), 1986/1995 Swiss Model BIT at Art. 10, Dutch Model BIT at Art. 3(4). With regard to the US, although the US 1994 and 1998 Model BITs did not contain the umbrella clause, the majority of US BITs concluded under these models do incorporate it as do earlier BITs. See, for example, Art. II(2)(c) of Argentina-US (1991): 'Each Party shall observe any obligation it may have entered into with regard to investments'; and Art. II(2)(c), Lithuania-US (1998), containing the same wording.
31. Art. 10(1), final sentence, ECT: 'Each Contracting Party shall observe any obligations it has entered into with an Investor or an Investment of an Investor of any other Contracting Party.'
32. Art. III(3), ASEAN Investment Agreement (1987): 'Each Contracting Party shall observe any obligation arising from a particular commitment it may have entered into with regard to a specific investment of nationals or companies of the other Contracting Parties.'
33. It is found, for example at: Art. 3, France-Hong Kong (1995): 'Without prejudice to the provisions of this Agreement, each Contracting Party shall observe any particular obligation entered into with regard to investments of investors of the other contacting Party, including obligations more favourable than those of this Agreement'; Art. 3(2), Bolivia-Spain (2001): 'Cada Parte Contratante deberá cumplir cualquier obligación contractual contraída por escrito en relación con las inversiones de inversores de la otra Parte Contratante, y que sean conformes con la legislación interna de la primera Parte Contratante'; Art. 9(2), Italy-Lebanon (1997): 'Each Contracting Party shall observe any other obligation it has assumed with regard to investments in its territory by investors of the other Contracting Party'; Art. 11, Australia-China (1988): 'A Contracting Party shall, subject to its law, adhere to any written undertakings given by a competent authority to a national of the other Contracting Party with regard to an investment in accordance with its law and the provisions of this Agreement'; and Art. 2(3) last sentence, Hong Kong-Japan (1997): 'Each Contracting Party shall observe any obligation it may have entered into with regard to investments of investors of the other Contracting Party.'
34. The Annex on Country Specific Proposals of the draft MAI text provided a 'Respect Clause' as follows: 'Each Contracting Party shall observe any obligation it has entered into with regard to a specific investment of an investor of another Contracting Party'; and as 'Substantive approach to the respect clause': 'Each Contracting Party shall observe any other obligation in writing, it has assumed with regard to investments in its territory by investors of another Contracting Party. Disputes arising form such obligations shall only be settled under the terms of the contracts underlying the obligations.'
35. E.g., in UK BITs and US BITs, like Argentina-UK (1990) and Argentina-US (1991).

provision.[36] Placement might be evidence of the intended scope and effects of the clause. In particular when placed within the initial treatment provisions there is strong evidence that the clause was intended to impose substantial international obligations, separate and distinct from other IIA standards. Placement alone, however, is unlikely to prove decisive in interpreting the scope and normative effects of the clause.[37]

§9.8 Drafting variations The umbrella clause is typically short and simple in its formulation, often with an appearance of a standard provision. But its wording varies from treaty to treaty, sometimes in subtle yet important aspects potentially leading to significant differences in the scope and effect of the clause.[38] Some tribunals have recognized the importance of paying due consideration to the wording of each clause;[39] while others have tended to play down textual differences.[40] Drafting variations concern five issues in particular: duty imposed, obligation to be observed, addressee of the obligation to be observed, relationship between the obligation and its addressee, and whether or not there is reference to dispute resolution options.

First, with regard to the duty imposed, a common feature seems to be the use of mandatory language.[41] Some IIAs provide a direct duty to 'observe' or 'respect' undertakings,[42] while others provide a more indirect duty to 'guarantee' or to 'ensure' (sometimes reinforced by the word 'constantly') the observance of undertakings.[43] The latter, more indirect, formulation is arguably a less strict or, at least,

---

36. E.g., in some Swiss BITs, like Pakistan-Switzerland (1995). See *infra* §9.28 on preservation of rights clauses.
37. *SGS Société Générale de Surveillance S.A. v. Philippines* (Decision of the Tribunal on Objections to Jurisdiction, 29 Jan. 2004) [*SGS v. Philippines*] at para. 124; and *Eureko BV v. Poland* (Partial Award, 19 Aug. 2005) [*Eureko*] at para. 259. Placement will be largely irrelevant when the BIT practice of the state shows that identical language appears within the treatment obligations or the preservation of rights clause, as, for example, it does in Austrian BITs.
38. For an analysis of some drafting variations, see J.P. Gaffney & J.L. Loftis, 'The "Effective Ordinary Meaning" of BITs and the Jurisdiction of Treaty-based Tribunals to Hear Contract Claims' (2007) 8 JWIT 5 at 9-13.
39. E.g., *Noble Ventures, Inc. v. Romania* (Award, 12 Oct. 2005) [*Noble Ventures*] at para. 50.
40. E.g., *El Paso Energy International Company v. Argentina* (Decision on Jurisdiction, 27 Apr. 2006) [*El Paso Energy*] at para. 70.
41. OECD Working Paper, *supra* note 1 at 9.
42. For example, in 1991 UK Model BIT, Art. 2, entitled 'Promotion and Protection of Investment,' the final sentence reads: 'Each Contracting Party shall observe any obligation it may have entered into with regard to investments of investors of the other Contracting Party.' Sometimes the word 'adhere' is used (Art. 11. Australia-China (1988): 'A Contracting Party shall, subject to its law, adhere to any written undertakings…') which appears to be less clear and direct than the word 'observe.' In Spanish, sometimes the word 'cumplir' is used (Art. 3(2), Bolivia-Spain (2001)), but also the word 'observará,' which is closer to the English 'shall observe' (see, e.g., Art. 2(2), final sentence, of the Spanish version of Argentina-UK (1990)). In French, the expression commonly used is 'respecter.'
43. E.g., Art. 11, Pakistan-Switzerland (1995).

less precise obligation, though it is unclear if its practical effect may be radically different.[44]

Further, in some formulations the duty imposed can be regarded as an obligation of a general programmatic character without necessarily mandating strict compliance with undertakings or elevating any breaches of undertakings into treaty breaches.[45] For example, Article 2(4), Italy-Jordan (1996), provides as follows:

> Each Contracting Party shall create and maintain in its territory a legal framework apt to guarantee the investors the continuity of legal treatment, including compliance, in good faith, of all undertakings assumed with regard to each specific investor.

In *Salini Costruttori S.p.A. and Italstrade S.p.A. v. Jordan*, the tribunal noted that under this provision:

> … each contracting party did not commit itself to 'observe' any 'obligation' it has previously assumed with regard to specific investments or the investor of the other party … . It did not even guarantee the observance of commitments it had entered into with respect to investments of investors of the other Contracting Party … . It only committed itself to create and maintain a legal framework apt to guarantee the compliance of all undertakings assumed with regard to each specific investor.[46]

Other formulations qualify the duty of observance, thus narrowing the obligation provided in the clause:

> A Contracting Party shall, *subject to its law, do all in its power* to ensure that a written undertaking given by a competent authority to a national of the other Contracting Party with regard to an investment is respected.[47] [Emphasis added.]

Second, with regard to the nature of the undertaking to be observed, the majority of IIAs refer to 'obligations,' while others use the seemingly less stringent terms 'engagements' or 'commitments.' In any case, and in spite of the differences in wording, the implication is that there has been state conduct giving rise to legally binding commitments towards the foreign investment.[48] As stated by F.A. Mann, the undertaking 'may be express or implied, it may be in writing or oral. But it must be

---

44. *SGS v. Philippines, supra* note 37 at para. 119. *Cf. SGS v. Pakistan, supra* note 1 at footnote 171, considering the language is not significantly different.
45. *Noble Ventures, supra* note 39 at para. 58; and J.P. Gaffney & J.L. Loftis, *supra* note 38 at 13.
46. *Salini Costruttori S.p.A. and Italstrade S.p.A. v. Jordan* (Decision on Jurisdiction, 29 Nov. 2004) [*Salini v. Jordan*] at para. 126.
47. Art. 10, Australia-Poland (1991).
48. See Jean-Pierre Laviec, *Protection et promotion des investissements* (Paris: PUF, 1985) at 246-249. See also *CMS Gas Transmission Company v. Argentina* (Decision of the *ad hoc* Committee on the Application for Annulment of the Argentine Republic, 25 Sep. 2007) [*CMS Annulment*] at para. 89 stating that '[i]t is accepted that by obligations is meant legal obligations.'

clearly ascertainable as an obligation of the state,'[49] arising under the applicable law.[50] Some IIAs restrict the undertakings to be observed to 'written obligations.'[51]

Some IIAs refer to particular undertakings,[52] suggesting that contractual as well as specific unilateral undertakings would be covered, but that general ones contained in legislation or regulations would not. Conversely, more general undertakings would presumably be encompassed in the wider formulations referring to any undertakings,[53] although a degree of connection between the general undertaking and the relevant investment would still be required. Some IIAs, although very few, restrict the clause to contractual undertakings.[54]

Further, other IIAs use the expression undertakings with regard to 'treatment' of investments.[55] This wording suggests that the clause targets not any obligation but specifically investment protection obligations.

Third, the addressee or recipient of the undertakings is generally the 'investment,'[56] or 'investments of investors,'[57] but some IIAs refer instead to undertakings towards 'investors.'[58] The latter formulation could be narrower, as it would exclude undertakings given indirectly to a foreign investor, for example those entered into by its local subsidiary, which often qualifies as an 'investment' of the foreign investor under many IIAs, but not itself as an 'investor.' In that more narrow formulation, the foreign parent company may not be entitled to rely on the umbrella clause to claim respect for an undertaking provided not directly to it, but to its local subsidiary. This interpretation is based on a distinction between undertakings towards parent companies and subsidiaries that may not, in some cases, be easy to draw in practice. Support is found, however, in the ECT 'reader's guide' explaining the scope of the ECT umbrella clause, which refers both to undertakings with regard to 'investments' and 'investors,' as follows:

---

49. F.A. Mann, 'British Treaties for the Promotion and Protection of Investments' (1981) 52 BYIL 241 at 246.
50. See below §9.9.
51. Art. 11, Australia-Chile (1996); and Art. 9 Austria-Mexico (1998).
52. Art. III, ASEAN Agreement (1987), *supra* note 32; and Art. VII, Philippines-UK (1980).
53. Art. 11, Pakistan-Switzerland (1995); and Art. II(4), Senegal-US (1983).
54. See Art. 3(2) (final sentence), Bolivia-Spain (2001). See also Art. 2(3), Czechoslovakia-UK (1991), providing as follows: 'Investors of one Contracting Party may conclude with the other Contracting Party specific agreements … Each Contracting Party shall, with regard to investments of investors of the other Contracting Party, observe the provisions of these specific agreements ….' Austrian BITs refer to the observance of 'contractual obligations' although with respect only to 'investments approved,' i.e., contracts that have been subject to a formal approval process. This is explicit in other BITs such as Malaysia-United Arab Emirates (1991), where Art. 13(3) reads: 'Each Contracting State shall observe any obligation it may have entered into in the documents of approval of investments or the approved investment contracts by investors of the other Contracting State.'
55. Art. 3(4), Netherlands-Venezuela (1991).
56. Art. 2(2)(c), Argentina-US (1991).
57. Art. 2(2) final sentence, Argentina-UK (1990).
58. Art. 11, Australia-China (1988).

This provision covers any contract that a host country has concluded with a subsidiary of the foreign investor in the host country, or a contract between the host country and the parent company of the subsidiary.

Fourth, some IIAs speak of undertakings 'assumed'[59] or just obligations that the State may 'have' with regard to an investment.[60] But the majority use the formula 'entered into.' It has been suggested that 'entered into' would require a 'contractual element of mutual bargaining and consent/meeting of the minds,' and thus contractual but not unilateral commitments would be covered.[61] One IIA tribunal has found the term 'entered into' as sufficiently general to encompass also non-contractual undertakings.[62] The investor could argue that in investing or otherwise acting in reliance upon a unilateral undertaking, an implied agreement has been formed or 'entered into.'[63] Some IIAs refer to undertakings with regard to 'specific investments,'[64] confirming that legal obligations of a general character may not be covered unless there is a sufficiently direct link with the relevant investment.

Fifth, some IIAs, including most Indian and Mexican BITs, address the potential problem of concurrent jurisdictions (treaty arbitration and contractual or local remedies). They provide that disputes under the clause be submitted to the contract dispute resolution mechanism,[65] or that treaty remedies shall only be available in the absence of normal local judicial remedies.[66]

II   APPLICABLE LAW

§9.9 Existence of the obligation to be observed   Umbrella clauses do not specify the law applicable to determining the existence of the obligations to be observed under the clause. The question arises as to whether those matters fall under international law or the law governing the undertaking. In the context of contractual obligations, the issue is whether the clause internationalizes the contract, that is, detaches the contract from its applicable law, often the host state's law, and submits it to international law.

---

59.   Art. 8(2), Bosnia and Herzegovina-Germany (2001).
60.   Art. 12(2), Finnish Model BIT.
61.   T. Wälde & G. Ndi, 'Stabilizing International Investment Commitments: International Law versus Contract Interpretation' (1996) 31 TILJ 215 at note 94. On the expression 'entered into' as targeting consensual obligations, see *CMS Annulment, supra* note 48 at para. 95(a).
62.   In *Noble Ventures, supra* note 39 at para. 51, the tribunal found that the term 'entered into' indicated that specific, i.e., mostly contractual, undertakings rather than general undertakings were covered, but did not exclude unilateral undertakings altogether from the scope of the clause.
63.   Ben Hamida, *supra* note 1 at 60, para. 16.
64.   Art. III, ASEAN Investment Agreement (1987), *supra* note 32; and Art. VII, Philippines-UK (1980).
65.   Art. 4(3), India-Spain (1997); and Art. 9, Austria-Mexico (1998).
66.   Art. 13(2), Germany-India (1995); and Art. 8(2), Austria-India (2001).

What constitutes an undertaking or an obligation covered by the clause is normally a matter for the law of the host State, since those undertakings or obligations arise in the context of legal relationships governed by domestic law. The point was made by the tribunal in *SGS v. Philippines*[67] in applying the observance of undertakings clause of Article X(2), Philippines-Switzerland (1997):

> Whether collateral guarantees, warranties or letters of comfort given by a host State to induce the entry of foreign investments are binding or not, i.e., whether they constitute genuine obligations or mere advertisements, will be a matter for determination under the applicable law, normally the law of the host State. But if commitments made by the State towards specific investments do involve binding obligations or commitments under the applicable law, it seems entirely consistent with the object and purpose of the BIT to hold that they are incorporated and brought within the framework of the BIT by Article X(2).[68]

Undertakings or obligations may, however, in some circumstances arise autonomously from the host state law, as the use of the word 'normally' in the above quote suggests, and as was recognized by the *ad hoc* Committee in *CMS Annulment*.[69] This may in particular be the case if representations, promises, assurances or pledges are made or given by the host state to induce investment and are reasonably relied upon by an investor in making the investment.[70] Regardless of whether an undertaking is deemed to exist under the host state law, international law recognizes the existence of undertakings in certain circumstances, particularly in conditions akin to those required for the operation of the international law doctrine of estoppel. These include clear and unambiguous representations, inducement, absence of excusable state error, and reasonable good faith reliance on the part of the investor free from fault or neglect.[71] Therefore, even if under domestic law the unilateral conduct of a state does not give rise to a domestic legal obligation, or a commitment given in a contract to the investor is not legally binding under domestic law, in some circumstances the host state's conduct may give rise to an independent obligation under international law enforceable under an observance of undertakings clause.

---

67. See, generally, Chapter 2 above on applicable law.
68. *SGS v. Philippines, supra* note 37 at para. 117.
69. *CMS Annulment, supra* note 48 at para. 95(a) stating that the umbrella clause in Argentina-US (1991) 'is concerned with consensual obligations arising independently of the BIT itself (i.e., under the law of the host State or possibly under international law).'
70. See e.g., Lauterpacht, *supra* note 24 at 229, arguing as follows: 'An "undertaking" can, for example, describe the situation arising out of a general promise made by a State to accord to foreign investors a particular standard of treatment, followed by an actual investment made in reliance with that promise. There might in these circumstances be no specific contract, but the situation would constitute an undertaking given by the State to the investor.' See also 1967 Draft OECD Convention's accompanying notes and comments, Art. 2 paras 3(a), 3(a)(i) and (ii), *supra* note 23; and W.M. Reisman & M.H. Arsanjani, 'The Question of Unilateral Governmental Statements as Applicable Law in Investment Disputes' (2004) 19 ICSID Rev 328.
71. On estoppel, see D. Bowett, 'Estoppel before International Tribunals and its Relation to Acquiescence' (1957) 33 BYIL 176. See also Reisman & Arsanjani, *ibid.*, and *infra* Chapter 10, §10.27.

§9.10 Scope and effects of the obligation to be observed   A similar combination of international and domestic law (or the law of the contract), the latter being the source of law normally applicable, is pertinent to determining the scope and effects of obligations covered by the umbrella clause. The tribunal in *SGS v. Pakistan* suggested that if the umbrella clause were given its literal meaning the only applicable law would be international law. The tribunal expressed concern that such an approach would create an 'instant transubstantiation' of contracts into treaties, that is, a full internationalization of domestic contracts.[72] The tribunal in *SGS v. Philippines* criticized the tribunal's approach. It found that the observance of undertakings clause does not alter the law applicable to contract obligations, which do not become international obligations:

> But this is not what Article X(2) of the Swiss-Philippines Treaty says. It does not convert non-binding domestic blandishments into binding international obligations. It does not convert questions of contract law into questions of treaty law. In particular it does not change the proper law of the … Agreement from the law of the Philippines to international law. Article X(2) addresses not the *scope* of the commitments entered into with regard to specific investments but the *performance* of these obligations, once they are ascertained. [Emphasis in original.][73]

Similarly, in *CMS Annulment*, the *ad hoc* committee found that '[t]he effect of the umbrella clause is not to transform the obligation which is relied on into something else; the content of the obligation is unaffected, as is its proper law.'[74]

The effect of observance of undertakings clauses therefore is to make the *respect* for undertakings an obligation under the treaty. But it does not *convert* those undertakings into international obligations. It does not transform the law applicable to a particular undertaking, nor does it mean that contractual obligations under host state law are measured by international law. The host state law (or the *lex contractus*) will normally be the applicable law for determining the scope and effects of the undertakings.[75] This view is supported by international law on state responsibility, which

---

72. *SGS v. Pakistan, supra* note 1 at para. 172.
73. *SGS v. Philippines, supra* note 37 at para. 126.
74. *CMS Annulment, supra* note 48 at para. 95(c). See also J. Crawford, 'Treaty and Contract in Investment Arbitration' TDM (Provisional, Jan. 2008) at 18-21.
75. See also *Fedax N.V. v. Venezuela* (Award, 9 Mar. 1998) at para. 30 [*Fedax*], finding that Venezuelan law was relevant as the law applicable to the promissory notes, the non-payment of which the claimant submitted was a violation of *inter alia* the observance of undertakings clause under Netherlands-Venezuela (1991); and *CMS Gas Transmission Company v. Argentina* (Award, 12 May 2005) [*CMS*] at paras 115-123 and 200-227, finding that Argentine law was applicable alongside international law in a dispute concerning whether Argentina's revocation of legal and contractual commitments amounted to a violation of *inter alia* the observance of the undertakings clause of the Argentina-US BIT, and examining the scope of those commitments under Argentine law in some detail. *Cf. Eureko, supra* note 37, dissenting opinion of Jerzy Rajski (co-arbitrator), arguing that the tribunal failed to examine the questions of the existence and scope of the undertakings allegedly breached by the respondent, in violation of *inter alia* the observance of undertakings clause of Netherlands-Poland (1992)

admits that domestic law may become relevant as substantive law to the question of compliance with an international obligation and thus international responsibility. This is the case when a rule of international law, like the observance of undertakings clause, requires that the substantive legal content of the undertaking in question be determined by reference to the applicable domestic law.[76] In these cases, the international law rule incorporates the relevant domestic law obligation (to be interpreted under domestic law) to assess whether the treaty clause has been violated.

Once again, however, international law may be relevant in the case of representations made or given by the host state with regard to the scope of obligations and in the context of inducement and reliance by the investor. This is not to say that legitimate expectations generated by government representations are binding obligations which may be enforced through an umbrella clause;[77] but as stated above, in case of inducement and reliance distinct international obligations could arise, the respect of which could be so enforced. Further, there are certain issues concerning the operation of umbrella clauses to which international law has been held to apply, since umbrella clauses are international law obligations. The first issue is whether the obligation undertaken by a public entity can be imputed to the state so as to come within the scope of the umbrella clause. This is not a question of the scope of a specific obligation, on which normally there will be no international rules, but of whether given conduct is to be attributed to the state for the purposes of the IIA, on which there are international law rules.[78] Second, the issue of remedies for breach of the umbrella clause is a question of state responsibility under international law for violation of an international obligation.

III   UNDERTAKINGS COVERED

§9.11 Contractual undertakings   Umbrella clauses cover contractual undertakings entered into by the host state with respect to foreign investments or investors. Indeed, it appears from the history and early treaty practice that the clause was

---

under Polish law and focusing instead on a wrong and isolated interpretation of the terms of the contractual arrangements.

76. International Law Commission's Articles on Responsibility of States for Internationally Wrongful Acts, *Official Records of the General Assembly,* UN GAOR, 56th Sess., Supp. No. 10, UN Doc A/56/10 at 11; (2001) YBILC, Vol. II, Part Two. The Articles and commentary are *reprinted in* J. Crawford, *The International Law Commission's Articles on State Responsibility: Introduction, Text, and Commentaries* (Cambridge: Cambridge University Press, 2002) [ILC's Articles on State Responsibility]. See commentary at Art. 3, para. 7. Also see *supra* Chapter 2.

77. *CMS Annulment, supra* note 48 at para. 89 stating in relation to the application of the umbrella clause that '[a]lthough legitimate expectations might arise by reason of a course of dealing between the investor and the host State, these are not, as such, legal obligations.' See *supra* Chapter 6, §6.26.

78. See *infra* §9.15.

intended primarily to operate in relation to contractual obligations.[79] Discussions of the modern BIT practice of the UK, the US and Germany support this conclusion.[80]

IIA jurisprudence has been consistent in this regard. The first IIA case to deal with this type of clause, albeit indirectly, was *Fedax*. The tribunal held that the observance of the undertakings clause required Venezuela to honour a contractual obligation to pay some promissory notes.[81] In *SGS v. Pakistan* the tribunal interpreted the duty of observance under the clause very narrowly,[82] but still admitted that the clause operated in relation to contractual obligations.[83] In *SGS v. Philippines*, it was found that the claims for payment under a contract for the provision of custom inspection services fell within the observance of undertakings clause of Article X(2), Philippines-Switzerland (1997): 'Article X(2) includes commitments or obligations arising under contracts entered into by the host state.'[84] In *Joy Mining Machinery Ltd. v. Egypt*, the tribunal found that the clause covered 'a violation of contract rights of such magnitude as to trigger the Treaty protection.'[85] In *Salini Jordan*, the tribunal found that an observance of an undertakings clause that 'reiterated' the 'undertaking' of Jordan to be 'bound by its contractual obligations' was not present in the relevant BIT.[86] Similarly, in *Consorzio Groupement L.E.S.I. DIPENTA v. Algeria* the tribunal emphasized that observance of undertakings clauses have the effect of converting breaches of contractual obligations into treaty breaches, but that no such clause existed in the BIT at hand.[87]

IIA tribunals dealing with the Argentine crisis legislation have equally found that umbrella clauses cover contractual undertakings. In *CMS*, contractual commitments regarding the tariff regime for gas utility companies were considered obligations that Argentina was bound to respect under the observance of an

---

79. See *infra* §9.3-9.6.
80. Mann, *supra* note 49 at 245-46; K.J. Vandevelde, *United States Investment Treaties: Policy and Practice* (Boston: Kluwer Law and Taxation, 1992) at 76; M.N. Leich, 'Contemporary Practice of the United States Relating to International Law' (1990) 84 AJIL 885 at 898; and J. Karl, 'The Promotion and Protection of Foreign Investors Abroad' (1996) 11 ICSID Rev 1 at 23.
81. *Fedax, supra* note 75 at para. 29, stating: '... the Republic of Venezuela is under the obligation to honor precisely the terms and conditions governing such investment, laid down mainly in Article 3 of the Agreement [the BIT], as well as to honor the specific payments established in the promissory notes issued.'
82. See *infra* §9.13.
83. *SGS v. Pakistan, supra* note 1 at para. 172. The tribunal seemed to suggest, however, a distinction between state contracts or investment agreements, which would be covered, and ordinary commercial contracts entered into by the state or state entities, which would not (at note 175). See notes below and accompanying text.
84. *SGS v. Philippines, supra* note 37 at para. 127.
85. *Joy Mining Machinery Ltd. v. Egypt* (Award on Jurisdiction, 6 Aug. 2004) at para. 81 [*Joy Mining*].
86. *Salini v. Jordan, supra* note 46 at para. 127.
87. *Consorzio Groupement L.E.S.I.-DIPENTA v. Algeria* (Award, 10 Jan. 2005) [*L.E.S.I.-DIPENTA*] at para. 25(ii). See also the decision on the resubmitted case, *L.E.S.I. S.p.A. et ASTALDI S.p.A. v. Algeria* (Decision, 12 Jul. 2006) at para. 84(ii).

undertakings clause.[88] Similar holdings, considering undertakings contained in contracts as covered by the umbrella clause, can be found in *LG&E*, *Enron* and *Sempra*.[89] In *CMS Annulment*, the *ad hoc* committee found that '[i]n speaking of "any obligations it may have entered into with regard to investments", it seems clear that Article II(2)(c) is concerned with consensual obligations.'[90]

In *Eureko*, the clause was found to cover assurances by the Polish State Treasury regarding the continuation of the privatization of an insurance company, made in the contractual documents regarding the sale of a minority interest in that company to the claimant.[91] In *Noble Ventures*, the tribunal found that the clause applied to a privatization agreement concerning the acquisition, management, operation, and disposition of a steel mill. As to the scope of the clause in relation to contractual obligations, the tribunal stated:

> … considering the wording of Art. II(2)(c) which speaks of "any obligation [a party] may have entered into with regard to investments", it is difficult not to regard this as a clear reference to investment contracts. In fact one may ask what other obligations can the parties have had in mind as having been 'entered into' by a host state with regard to an investment. […] Article II(2)(c) would be very much an empty base unless understood as referring to contracts.[92]

The tribunal found that, apart from the wording, the inclusion of contractual undertakings in the scope of the clause also stemmed from the object and purpose of the treaty and the principle of *effet utile*.[93]

The view that contractual undertakings are covered by umbrella clauses is also supported by the majority of commentators.[94] A minority, however, would

---

88. *CMS*, *supra* note 75 at paras 296-303.
89. *LG&E Energy Corp., LG&E Capital Corp. and LG&E International Inc. v. Argentina* (Decision on Liability, 3 Oct. 2006) [*LG&E*] at paras. 170-171; *Enron Corporation Ponderosa Assets, L.P. v. Argentina* (Award, 22 May 2007) [*Enron*] at para. 274: and *Sempra, supra* note 12 at paras 309-311.
90. *CMS Annulment, supra* note 48 at para. 95(a).
91. *Eureko, supra* note 37 at paras 224-260.
92. *Noble Ventures, supra* note 39 at para. 51.
93. *Ibid.*, at para. 52: 'The object and purpose rule also supports such an interpretation. While it is not permissible, as is too often done regarding BITs, to interpret clauses exclusively in favour of investors, here such an interpretation is justified. Considering, as pointed out above, that any other interpretation would deprive Art. II (2)(c) of practical content, reference has necessarily to be made to the principle of effectiveness, also applied by other Tribunals in interpreting BIT provisions (see *SGS v. Philippines*, para. 116 and *Salini v. Jordan*, para. 95). An interpretation to the contrary would deprive the investor of any internationally secured legal remedy in respect of investment contracts that it has entered into with the host State. While it is not the purpose of investment treaties per se to remedy such problems, a clause that is readily capable of being interpreted in this way and which would otherwise be deprived of practical applicability is naturally to be understood as protecting investors also with regard to contracts with the host state generally in so far as the contract was entered into with regard to an investment.'
94. See references at note above. See also Crawford, *supra* note 74 at 19-21; Weil, *supra* note 13 at 130-132; UNCTAD, *Bilateral Investment Treaties in the Mid-1990s*, *supra* note 29 at 56; C.H. Schreuer, 'Travelling the BIT Route: Of Waiting Periods, Umbrella Clauses and Forks in

apply the much debated distinction between ordinary commercial or private law contracts and so-called state contracts or investment agreements, which derive from the state's exercise of its sovereign prerogatives and are subject primarily to administrative law.[95] These state contracts, typically concessions and licenses in the energy, mining, natural resources and infrastructure sectors, would be covered by the observance of undertakings clauses, while the former, i.e., ordinary contracts, would not.[96] This distinction, however, does not fit with the general terms of the usual observance of an undertakings clause. Such clauses apply to undertakings with regard to investments, which is a term defined in IIAs and covers many forms of contracts and contractual rights,[97] not just state contracts or investment agreements as commonly understood.[98] Further, the proponents of the distinction apparently fail to appreciate that so-called state contracts may contain 'sovereign' clauses (such as stabilization clauses) as well as ordinary commercial ones, which they would admit to be covered by the umbrella clause just by labelling the contract as a state contract.

Generally, the text of IIAs does not support a distinction between different categories of contracts or contract clauses with differing protection. The distinction would raise practical problems, given the difficulty in defining the contours of the notion of state contract and the criteria for distinguishing it from other contractual forms, considering in addition the panoply of different clauses that a contract may contain.[99] Further, as illustrated above, tribunals have found no difficulty in applying the observance of undertakings clauses to contractual obligations deriving, for example, from promissory notes and service contracts which

---

the Road' (2004) 5 JWIT 231 at 250; I.F.I. Shihata, 'Applicable Law in International Arbitration: Specific Aspects in Case of the Involvement of State Parties,' in Shihata & Wolfesohn, eds, *The World Bank in a Changing World: Selected Essays and Lectures* (The Netherlands: Brill, Leiden, 1995) at 605; R. Dolzer & M. Stevens, *Bilateral Investment Treaties* (The Hague: Kluwer, 1995) at 81-82; S.A. Alexandrov, 'Breaches of Contract and Breaches of Treaty – The Jurisdiction of Treaty-based Arbitration Tribunals to Decide Breach of Contract Claims in *SGS v. Pakistan* and *SGS v. Philippines*' (2004) 5 JWIT 555 at 566-569.

95. On the notion of state contract and the debate on the distinction see, e.g., Ch. Leben 'La théorie du contrat de l'état et l'évolution du droit international' (2004) 302 RDCADI 197; and Ch. Leben, 'L'évolution de la notion de contrats d'État' (2003) 3 Revue de l' arbitage at 629-646.

96. T. Wälde, 'International Investment under the 1994 Energy Charter Treaty: Legal, Negotiating and Policy Implications for International Investors within Western and Commonwealth of Independent States/Eastern European Countries' (1995) 29 JWT 5 at 49; and R. Happ, 'Dispute Settlement under the Energy Charter Treaty' (2002) 45 GYIL 331 at 346.

97. See *infra* §9.17.

98. The notion of 'investment agreement' can be found in some US BITs, such as Azerbaijan-US (1997).

99. See, J.-M. Jacquet, 'Contrat d'État' (1998) 565-60 J.-Cl. Droit International; Gill, Gearing & Birt, *supra* note 29 at 406; Gaffney & Loftis, *supra* note 38 at 19. The distinction was debated during the MAI negotiations and abandoned due to its practical difficulties. See OECD, *Rapports consolidés des groupes de négociations n°1 et n°2*, DAFFE/MAI(96)16, 10 Jun. 1996, at 30-31.

are not within the traditional forms of state contracts or investment agreements.[100] Some decisions, however, do seem to grant support to the view that only investment agreements or state contracts, and not other kinds of commercial contracts, are covered by umbrella clauses.[101]

§9.12 Contracts with a foreign owned company   Most umbrella clauses require state compliance with 'obligations ... entered into with regard to investments,' rather than 'investors.'[102] The question is whether a contract to which a foreign investor is not a party, for example a contract between the local subsidiary of the foreign investor and the host state, may nevertheless be considered entered into *with regard to* its investment and thus covered by and enforceable under the umbrella clause.

The issue has arisen in the arbitrations concerning claims that Argentina's crisis legislation altered the terms of the tariff regime contained in concessions and licenses for the privatized public services. In particular, although Argentina's privatization attracted many foreign investors, their investments were channelled through shareholdings in local companies that signed the relevant concession or license contracts with the state. In *CMS* the tribunal found that those concession or license contracts, to which the foreign investor claimants were not parties, could be invoked by those claimants under the umbrella clause in Article 2(2)(c), Argentina-US BIT (1991), which reads, '[e]ach Party shall observe any obligation it may have entered into with regard to investments.' Though it is not explicit in the decision, the tribunal might have relied on the literal interpretation of the umbrella clause: that Argentina entered into legal obligations under the concession and license contract which are obligations 'with regard to investments' of the claimants under the umbrella clause, thus enforceable by the shareholder claimants even if they would have not been entitled to invoke those obligations under Argentine

---

100. *Fedax, supra* note 75; and *SGS v. Philippines, supra* note 37. In *SGS v. Pakistan, supra* note 1 at note 175, the tribunal seemed to suggest, however, a distinction between contracts governed by international law and contracts governed by the host state law. The tribunal did not discuss the consequences of this distinction, although it would appear implicit in the tribunal's reasoning that international law contracts would be covered by the observance of undertakings clause while host state law contracts would not. This distinction would seem to run into the same problems as the distinction between state and ordinary contracts.

101. *El Paso Energy, supra* note 40 at paras 66-88; *Pan American Energy LLC, and BP Argentina Exploration Company v. Argentina* (Decision on Preliminary Objections, 27 Jul. 2006) [*Pan American Energy*] at paras 96-116 and *Sempra, supra* note 12 at paras 309-311. In *Noble Ventures, supra* note 39 at para. 61, the tribunal seems to hint at this distinction in arguing 'it is unnecessary for the Tribunal to express any definitive conclusion as to whether therefore, despite the consequences of the exceptional nature of umbrella clauses, Art. II(2)(c) of the BIT [the observance of undertakings clause of the Romania-US (1992)] perfectly assimilates to breach of the BIT any breach by the host State of any contractual obligation ... or whether the expression "any obligation," despite its apparent breath, must be understood to be subject to some limitation in the light of the nature and objects of the BIT.'

102. See *supra* above §9.8.

law.[103] The *ad hoc* committee in *CMS Annulment* denied that such reasoning was sufficiently clear in the award and consequently annulled this part of the award for failure to state reasons. In passing, however, the tribunal also took issue with this interpretation of the umbrella clause. It stated that the expression 'entered into' suggested that the obligations covered were consensual obligations, and typically consensual obligations are between specific obligors and obligees, which do not and cannot change by effect of the umbrella clause, considering that the content and law applicable to the obligations remains the same. The committee added that, since consensual obligations are often bilateral 'or intrinsically linked to obligations of the investment company,'[104] it would be to some extent unfair that a foreign shareholder could enforce the state's obligations and yet not be bound by the company's obligations.

Although asymmetry of obligations is a legitimate concern, a literal interpretation of the umbrella clause in *CMS* (a Standard Umbrella Clause) suggests that obligations related to investments, even if not formally undertaken towards a particular investor, could be invoked by that investor. Had treaty negotiators wanted to avoid such construction, the clause could easily have been drafted differently (for example by referring to investors rather than investments). Further, such interpretation does not seem denied by the expression 'entered into.' As explained above, the term 'entered into' is sufficiently general to encompass undertakings which target a specific investment or type or category of investment, for example when intended to attract and be relied upon by an investor in making the investment.[105] After *CMS*, tribunals dealing with Argentina's emergency legislation have clarified that Argentina's commitments relating to the tariff regime were enshrined not only in the relevant licenses and concession contracts, but also in the legal and regulatory framework, and had aimed at encouraging the investment of the claimant shareholders. Thus, such obligations were covered by the umbrella clause as being obligations *entered into* by Argentina *with regard to* those investments.[106] Similarly, the tribunal in *SGS v. Philippines* seemed to admit this possibility in observing that 'it will often be the case that the host State assumes obligations with regard to specific investments at the time of entry, including investments entered into on the basis of contracts with separate entities.'[107]

In a different context, that is, short of evidence of obligations under the contract specifically targeting certain investments, a claimant investor which is not a party to a contract may not have standing to invoke such a contract under the umbrella clause. This is clear from the awards in *Azurix Corp. v. Argentina* and

---

103. *CMS*, *supra* note 75 at paras 302-303.
104. *CMS Annulment*, *supra* note 48 at para. 95(d).
105. See above §9.8.
106. *LG&E, supra* note 89 at paras 169-175; *Enron, supra* note 89 at para. 274; *Sempra, supra* note 12 at paras 309-311. In *BG Group Plc. v. Argentina* (Final Award, 24 Dec. 2007) at paras 364-366, however, the tribunal considered that the same finding had already been made in relation to the breach of fair and equitable treatment and thus abstained from reaching a conclusion on the umbrella clause claim under the Argentina-UK BIT.
107. *SGS v. Philippines*, *supra* note 37 at para. 117.

Siemens A.G. v. Argentina, in which umbrella clause claims were rejected because the claimants were not direct parties to the underlying contract (the relevant party being the local company in which the claimants held shares).[108] These cases concerned undertakings of a commercial nature contained in the relevant contracts, thus arguably not commitments *entered into* by Argentina *with regard to* the shareholder claimants, unlike *CMS* and the other Argentine crisis cases, which concerned undertakings relating to the stability of crucial aspects of the legal and regulatory framework of the investments, marketed by Argentina to foreign investors to induce their investments.

§9.13 Unilateral undertakings The majority of umbrella clauses do not limit the 'obligations' to be observed and often refer to 'any obligations.'[109] Thus, unilateral undertakings by the host state in legislation, regulations and administrative acts would appear to be covered by the clause. In *SGS v. Pakistan*, the tribunal interpreted the term 'commitments,' the observance of which Pakistan was to 'constantly guarantee' under the observance of undertakings clause at Article 11, Pakistan-Switzerland (1995), as 'not limited to *contractual* commitments,' adding:

> The commitments referred to may be embedded in, e.g., the municipal legislative or administrative or other unilateral measures of a Contracting Party.[110]

Similarly, the tribunal in *SGS v. Philippines* adopted a broad interpretation of Article X(2), Philippines-Switzerland (1997), which provided for the observance of 'any obligation … assumed.' It ruled that the host state must observe all investment commitments, not just those in contracts.[111] The tribunal considered that the clause could cover, for example, pre-contractual unilateral undertakings such as those assumed in 'collateral guarantees, warranties or letters of comfort given by a host state to induce the entry of foreign investments.'[112] The undertakings to be observed included those assumed by the host state at the time of the entry into force of the BIT as well as thereafter.[113] In *Eureko*, the tribunal interpreted the clause mandating the observance of 'any obligations' as 'capacious,' meaning 'not only obligations of a certain type, but "any" – that is to say, all – obligations

---

108. *Azurix Corp. v. Argentina* (Award, 14 Jul. 2006) at para. 384; and *Siemens A.G. v. Argentina* (Award, 6 Feb. 2007) [*Siemens*] at para. 204.
109. See above §9.8.
110. *SGS v. Pakistan, supra* note 1 at para. 166. Art. 11, Pakistan-Switzerland (1995), states: 'Each Contracting Party shall constantly guarantee the observance of commitments it has entered into with respect to the investments or the investors of the other Contracting Party.'
111. *SGS v. Philippines, supra* note 37 at para. 115. See also *CMS, supra* note 75 at para. 303, considering that the observance clause covered 'legal and contractual obligations pertinent to the investment.'
112. *SGS v. Philippines, ibid.*, at para. 117.
113. *Ibid.*, at para. 115.

entered into with regard to investments of investors of the other Contracting Party.'[114]

Apart from specific unilateral undertakings, and depending on the wording of the clause, undertakings of a more general nature may also be included, provided that there is a sufficient connection between the general undertaking and the protected investment or investor. The point was made by the *SGS v. Philippines* tribunal responding to the concerns expressed earlier in *SGS v. Pakistan* that the clause would elevate all investment contracts to international law obligations. The tribunal found that the clause:

> ... is limited to 'obligations... assumed with regard to specific investments.' For Article X(2) to be applicable, the host state must have assumed a legal obligation, and it must have been assumed vis-à-vis the specific investment – not as a matter of the application of some legal obligation of a general character. This is very far from elevating to the international level all 'municipal legislative or administrative or to other unilateral measures of a Contracting Party.'[115]

The term 'specific' before 'investments' in the clause cited by the tribunal indicated the need for a link between the obligations and the investments. But the tribunal seems to have taken a rather restrictive interpretation requiring that the obligations be primarily directed to the relevant individual investment. The wording did not suggest that undertakings directed to a particular sector or specific category of investments, even if not specifically targeted to the investment in question, would be excluded.

Even in the absence of the term 'specific,' the typical clause referring to undertakings 'entered into,' 'with regard to,' or 'with respect to' investments requires a legally significant connection between the investments and the unilateral undertaking.[116] A threshold of any undertaking merely 'affecting' investments would provide no practical limitation. It would be satisfied by virtually any general measure having some impact on economic actors and interests. Although the existence of a legally significant connection between an investment and a unilateral undertaking must be examined case-by-case, the official notes and comments accompanying the 1967 Draft OECD Convention elaborate on this matter. They state that undertakings 'must *relate* to the property concerned; it is not sufficient if

---

114. *Eureko, supra* note 37 at para. 246.
115. *SGS v. Philippines, supra* note 37 at para. 121.
116. See *Noble Ventures, supra* note 39 at para. 51, stating that '[t]he employment of the notion "entered into" indicates that specific commitments are referred to and not general commitments, for example by way of legislative acts.' *Cf. SGS v. Pakistan, supra* note 1 at para. 166, arguing that the observance of undertakings clause in Art. 11, Pakistan-Switzerland (1995): 'while consisting in its entirety of only one sentence, appears susceptible of almost indefinite expansion.' The legally significant connection test is used by NAFTA tribunals regarding the meaning of 'relating to' in Art. 1101(1), NAFTA, which provides that Chapter Eleven '... applies to measures adopted or maintained by a Party relating to investors or investments.' See *Methanex Corporation v. United States* (Partial Award, 7 Aug. 2002) at paras 127-147.

the link is incidental,' and suggest two ways to establish a sufficient link: through the *'form* or *specific* terms in which the undertaking was couched, which identify either the property or the recipient of the undertaking,' or if it can be 'proved or presumed' that the investor 'acted in reliance on' the general undertaking.[117]

So far, the case law indicates that legislative provisions on the calculation and adjustment of utility tariffs would constitute obligations with regard to foreign investment (e.g., shareholdings acquired by foreign investors) in utility companies, in particular where the provisions were aimed at attracting such investment in the context of privatization. For example, in *CMS*, those provisions (together with more specific contractual undertakings) were found to be 'legal ... obligations pertinent to the investment'; in *LG&E*, the same tariff commitments were considered to be sufficiently related to the investment, 'by virtue of targeting foreign investors and applying specifically to their investments,' and because they were used 'to induce the entry of foreign capital to fund the privatization program.'[118] Likewise, in *Enron*, the tribunal found that the clause covered 'both contractual obligations such as payment as well as obligations assumed through law or regulation,' adding though that '"[o]bligations" covered by the "umbrella clause" are nevertheless limited by their object: "with regard to investments."'[119] It then found that Argentina's tariff commitments in the legal and regulatory framework had intended to attract the claimant's investment and thus were sufficiently specific so as to 'be with regard to' those investments.[120] A similar holding can be found in the *Sempra* award.[121]

Among the unilateral undertakings contemplated by the clause are the legal and regulatory provisions by which the host state approves or authorizes an investment, as well as national investment codes.[122] These codes establish the basic provisions on investment in the host state, with their primary purpose being the promotion or facilitation of investment. Although there are many differences among investment codes, they typically codify the provisions on admission, treatment and expropriation of foreign investment and settlement of foreign investment disputes.[123] Considering their focus on foreign investment, they are sufficiently specific to be covered by general observance of undertakings clauses. Also covered are the obligations deriving from other international instruments to

---

117. OECD Draft's accompanying notes and comments, *supra* note 24, Art. 2 paras 3(a), 3(a)(i) and (ii) [emphases in original].
118. *CMS, supra* note 75 at para. 303. See also paras 296-303. LG&E, *supra* note 89 at para. 175.
119. *Enron, supra* note 89 at para. 274.
120. *Ibid.*, at paras 275-77.
121. *Sempra, supra* note 12 at paras 311-313.
122. Ben Hamida, *supra* note 1 at 61, para. 18.
123. For a study of investment codes, see A. Parra, 'Principles Governing Foreign Investment, as reflected in National Investment Codes' (1992) 7 ICSID Rev 428. Investment codes are compiled in the series *Investment Laws of the World*, looseleaf (Dobbs Ferry, NY: Oceana, 1973).

which the host state is a party.[124] Some have suggested that observance of under-takings clauses envisage only other international treaty law obligations.[125] The tribunal in *SGS v. Philippines* rejected such a limitation, arguing that it was 'simply not there' and 'could readily have been expressed.'[126] International treaty obligations would be covered provided they are sufficiently specific to the invest-ment in question. Judicial decisions and arbitral awards might also give rise to undertakings to be observed by the host state under the clause.[127]

IV   UNDERTAKINGS ATTRIBUTABLE TO THE STATE

§9.14 State entities and attribution of obligations to the state   Observance of undertakings clauses refer, explicitly or implicitly, to the observance by each con-tracting state of undertakings entered into by 'it,' i.e., the state itself. Unless the scope of 'it' is clear from the clause or defined in the treaty,[128] the question may arise whether a particular undertaking by an entity that has a separate legal personality under national law, but which is structurally or functionally related to the state, may be attributed to the state itself for the purpose of invoking an umbrella clause.

The issue is of particular significance because investor-state contracts, the natural ground for the operation of the clause, are frequently concluded with para-statal entities rather than with government organs. If the parastatal entity then breaches its contractual commitments, the question will arise whether the investor can bring a claim against the state under the observance of undertakings clause because the contract is attributable to the state in the first place.

A different question is whether the state is liable for interfering with contracts signed by entities under its control, or even private parties, or for permitting con-trolled entities to escape their contractual obligations. This is an issue to be addressed under other treaty protections and customary international law on the attribution of conduct in breach of international law.

Some IIAs also provide specific obligations with regard to the duty of the host state to ensure that controlled entities act in conformity with the treaty.[129] For example, Article 22 of the ECT provides *inter alia*:

---

124. See UNCTAD, *Bilateral Investment Treaties in the Mid-1990s, supra* note 29 at 56.
125. See e.g., P. Peters & N. Schrijver, 'Latin America and International Regulation of Foreign Investment: Changing Perceptions' (1992) NILR 374; M. Salem, 'Le développement de la protection conventionnelle des investissements étrangers' (1986) JDI 613; and G. Gallins, 'Bilateral Investment Protection Treaties' (1984) 2 JENRL 77 at 84.
126. *SGS v. Philippines, supra* note 37 at para. 118.
127. Ben Hamida, *supra* note 1 at 60, para. 14.
128. E.g., Arts 22 and 23 of the ECT.
129. See e.g., Art. 15, Czech Republic-Singapore (1995): 'Each Contracting Party shall not inter-fere with any commitments, additional to those specified in this Agreement, entered into by nationals or companies with the nationals or companies of the other Contracting Party as regards their investments.'

Each Contracting Party shall ensure that if it establishes or maintains an entity and entrusts the entity with regulatory, administrative or other governmental authority, such entity shall exercise that authority in a manner consistent with the Contracting Party's obligations under this Treaty.[130]

The tribunal in *Alex Genin, Eastern Credit Limited, Inc. and A.S. Baltoil v. Estonia* interpreted this type of provision, contained in Estonia-US (1997), as effectively providing that state entities, in the instant case the Bank of Estonia, were bound by the treaty in the same terms as the state itself.[131] Similarly, in a NAFTA case, the equivalent provision of the NAFTA (Article 1503(2)) was considered to enshrine the principle that a 'Party cannot avoid its obligations by delegating its authority to bodies outside the core government.'[132] It appears that both decisions considered the clause as equating the state and the controlled entity for the purposes of attribution of responsibility, as do the rules of customary international law on state responsibility. However, the clause does not appear to have this meaning. Rather it could be argued that it establishes a distinct obligation of vigilance of the state over its controlled entities, and thus an independent substantive treaty standard and not simply a rule of attribution of conduct.

The issue raised at the outset of this section however still remains, which is whether a given obligation undertaken by a parastatal entity may be deemed an obligation of the state for the purposes of the umbrella clause. This issue is examined in the sections below.

§9.15 The application of international law rules of attribution Decided cases indicate that a contractual or unilateral undertaking will be covered by the umbrella clause if attributable to the state under the international law rules of attribution of conduct to the state.[133]

In *Noble Ventures*, the tribunal examined whether, for the purposes of applying the observance of an undertakings clause, the respondent state could be regarded as having entered into the contracts for the privatization of a steel mill

---

130. Another example is the French Model BIT (2005), which provides as follows: 'Pour l'application du présent Accord, il est entendu que les Parties contractantes sont responsables des actions ou omissions de leurs collectivités publiques, et notamment de leurs Etats fédérés, régions, collectivités locales ou de toute autre entité sur lesquels la Parties contractante exerce une tutelle, la représentation ou la responsabilité de ses relations internationales of sa souveraineté.'
131. *Alex Genin, Eastern Credit Limited, Inc. and A.S. Baltoil v. Estonia* (Award, 18 Jun. 2001) at para. 327.
132. *United Parcel Service of America Inc. v. Canada* (Award on Jurisdiction, 22 Nov. 2002) at para. 17.
133. See ILC's Articles on State Responsibility, *supra* note 76 in the commentaries at Arts 5 and 8. It may be argued that these rules have been developed in the context of attributing responsibility for international law breaches and are not transposable to attributing the undertaking (the contract), i.e., the legal obligation, to the state. See e.g., S.M. Perera, 'State Responsibility: Ascertaining the Liability of States in Foreign Investment Disputes' (2005) 6 JWIT 499 at 510. However the language and approach of the ILC's Articles on State Responsibility and commentaries seem to suggest that they refer to attribution of conduct generally. See below §9.17.

signed between the claimant and two Romanian entities in charge of privatizing state-owned enterprises. The tribunal stated that 'the BIT does not provide any answer to this question. The rules of attribution can only be found in general international law which supplements the BIT in this respect.'[134] Applying the ILC's Articles on State Responsibility, the tribunal found that although the entities had independent legal personality under Romanian law, they had 'acted as the empowered public institution under the Privatization Law' and thus their acts, including their contractual undertakings, were 'attributable to the Respondent for the purposes of assessment under the BIT.'[135]

In *Eureko*, the tribunal found that contractual assurances made by the Polish State Treasury regarding the continuation of the privatization of an insurance company to be undertakings of the state under international law principles, regardless of the Treasury's independent legal personality and the characterization of the contract as a civil law matter in municipal law.[136] The majority of the tribunal went on to find that non-compliance with those undertakings amounted to a breach of the observance of the undertakings clause.[137]

In *Nykomb*, the tribunal, without any detailed discussion, attributed to the state a commercial contract entered into by a wholly owned state enterprise, with governmental functions in the electricity sector in the context of claims for breach of the investment protection standards of the ECT, including the observance of an undertakings clause.[138]

In *SGS v. Pakistan*, the tribunal found that 'the "commitments" subject matter of Article 11 [the observance of undertakings clause] may, without imposing excessive violence on the text itself, be commitments of the state itself as a legal person, or of any office, entity or subdivision (local government units) or legal representative thereof whose acts are, under the law on state responsibility, attributable to the state itself.'[139]

This jurisprudence seems consistent with the general jurisprudence on the attribution of undertakings to the state for the purpose of the application of other treaty standards. In *EnCana Corporation v. Ecuador*, for example, the tribunal found that the conduct of Petroecuador, the Ecuadorian state oil company, in entering into, performing and renegotiating contracts for the exploration and exploitation of oil and gas reserves with foreign oil companies was 'attributable to Ecuador' for the purposes of the BIT.[140] This resulted from the international law principles stated in the ILC's Articles on State Responsibility, such as those attributing to the state the conduct of entities exercising governmental functions or obeying governmental instructions. Acts of Petroecuador against its contractual

---

134. *Noble Ventures, supra* note 39 at para. 68.
135. *Ibid.*, at paras 79-80.
136. *Eureko, supra* note 37 at paras 115-134.
137. *Ibid.*, at paras 244-260.
138. *Nykomb Synergetics Technology Holding AB v. Latvia* (Award, 16 Dec. 2003) at section 4.2.
139. *SGS v. Pakistan, supra* note 1 at para. 166.
140. *EnCana Corporation v. Ecuador* (Award, 3 Feb. 2006) at para. 154.

obligations could thus amount to breaches of the BIT standards of treatment.[141] In *L.E.S.I.-DIPENTA*, the tribunal, also relying on the ILC's Articles on State Responsibility, found that a contract may be attributed to the state, even if concluded by a separate entity, where the government exercises important influence over the entity and was to some extent involved in the contract negotiations.[142] In *SwemBalt AB v. Latvia*, the tribunal stated that:

> ... in the present case, we are faced with a dispute in which it is alleged that the duties and obligations of the Respondent under general international law and under the Investment Agreement [the BIT] itself have been breached. In such a case, the subdivisions of the state and the way in which each state chooses to divide the work between such subdivisions is without relevance. If the state delegates certain work to lower levels of government, be they federal, regional or municipal, it must be an obligation of the state under international law to ensure that its obligations under international law, whether general or treaty law are fulfilled by such subdivisions.[143]

This jurisprudence, therefore, stands for the proposition that international law principles apply to the attribution of undertakings to the state for the purpose of the operation of the umbrella clause. This is also the view of some commentators.[144]

§9.16 Recognition of separate personality under domestic law   In *Impregilo S.p.A v. Pakistan*, the tribunal appears to have taken a position at variance with the approach outlined in the previous section. Although the decision on this point is not entirely clear given the brevity of analysis, it appears that the tribunal found that contracts to which an independent public entity other than the state is a party are not attributable to the state, and thus are not covered by the BIT's observance of the undertakings clause.[145] The tribunal did not apply international law principles of attribution but simply relied on the separate legal personality of the entity under domestic law. It apparently considered that the claims under the clause based on contractual undertakings were to be equated with ordinary contract claims to which international law rules of attribution do not apply.[146] The decision in *Nagel v. Czech Republic* also seems to follow this line of reasoning. The tribunal was faced with

---

141.   *Ibid.*, at para. 158.
142.   *L.E.S.I.-DIPENTA, supra* note 87 at para. 19.
143.   *SwemBalt AB v. Latvia* (Decision by the Court of Arbitration 23 Oct. 2000) at para. 37.
144.   T. Wälde, 'Energy Charter Treaty-based Investment Arbitration: Controversial Issues' (2004) 5 JWIT 373 at 396-397; and Ben Hamida, and *supra* note 1 at 66, para. 29.
145.   *Impregilo, supra* note 12 at paras 220-223.
146.   *Ibid.*, at 198-219 and 262. The principle that international law rules of attribution are not operative in the case of contractual claims is well settled. See *Salini Costruttori S.p.A. and Italstrade S.p.A. v. Morocco* (Decision on Jurisdiction, 23 Jul. 2001) [*Salini v. Morocco*] at paras 59-61; *Compañía de Aguas del Aconquija S.A. and Vivendi Universal (formerly Compagnie Générale des Eaux) v. Argentina* (Decision on Annulment, 3 July 2002) at para. 96; *Consortium RFCC v. Morocco* (Decision on Jurisdiction, 16 Jul. 2001) Consortium RFCC at paras 68-69; *Consortium RFCC v. Morocco* (Arbitral Award 22 Dec. 2003) at paras 32-35; and *Cable Television of Nevis v. St. Kitts and Nevis* (Award, 13 Jan. 1997) at para. 2.17-2.27.

claims arising out of Czechoslovakia-UK (1990), including claims for breach of the observance of undertakings clause relating to a cooperation agreement signed between the investor and a state enterprise wholly owned by the respondent. The tribunal declined jurisdiction on unrelated grounds, but in *obiter dicta* indicated that the agreement was not attributable to the state, on the basis that the enterprise had separate legal personality, and that the government had not been involved in the conclusion of the contract.[147] Thus, international law rules of attribution appear not to have been considered applicable, although even if they had it is not clear that they would have led to a different result.

This was also the view of the *ad hoc* committee in the *CMS Annulment* case, where it was stated:

> The effect of the umbrella clause is not to transform the obligation which is relied on into something else; the content of the obligation is unaffected, as is its proper law. If this is so, it would appear that the *parties* to the obligation (i.e., the persons bound by it and entitled to rely on it) are likewise not changed by reason of the umbrella clause.[148] [Emphasis in original.]

Part of the doctrine seems to agree with this position, on the basis that the law applicable to the obligation is not changed by the umbrella clause, and that claims under the umbrella clause are to be equated with pure contract claims.[149] The question is whether claims under the umbrella clause are pure contract claims. It could be argued that umbrella clauses do not provide only a mechanism to enforce domestic law obligations such as contracts (unlike wide arbitration clauses under IIA). They could be said to create a distinct international obligation; even if one that incorporates a domestic law obligation in the international law standard. Domestic law (or the *lex contractus*) would be the substantive law on the question of compliance, but the scope of the treaty obligation would need to be determined under international law rules, including those on the attribution of the relevant undertaking to the state. The question would thus be, what is to be considered as part of the state for the purpose of ascertaining what undertakings the state has committed to observe under the umbrella clause? This is a matter of treaty interpretation to be determined by any relevant rules of international law, including the

---

147. *Nagel v. Czech Republic* (Award, 10 Sep. 2003) [*Nagel*] at paras 162-163.
148. *CMS Annulment, supra* note 48 at para. 95(c).
149. See Crawford, *supra* note 74 at 19. See also Y. Nouvel, 'Les entités paraétatiques dans la jurisprudence du CIRDI' in Ch. Leben, ed., *Le Contentieux arbitral transnational relative à l'investissement* (Paris: Anthemis, 2006) 25 at 50 note 85, arguing that the issue of attribution of the 'will which creates obligations' is governed by the rules of representation of the state in contractual matters on which international law has no specific rules and must refer to domestic law. This appears to be incorrect. Arts. 5 and 8 of the ILC's Articles on State Responsibility, *supra* note 76, contain rules of international law for the attribution to the state of the conduct of entities that exercise elements of governmental authority or act under the instructions, direction or control of the state, which are rules largely based on the doctrines of representation and agency. These are international law rules, even if they contain a *renvoi* to the internal law of the state to determine whether authority has been delegated to the entity or this acts under the control of the state.

rules regarding which entities should be considered to be part of the state, or what is conduct of the state for the purposes of international law.

The *Impregilo*, *Nagel* and *CMS Annulment* decisions do not appear to follow this approach. Rather, they adhere strictly to the view that since umbrella clauses do not alter the applicable law of the underlying obligation, the question of who are the parties to the obligation is by definition be judged also under that law. On policy considerations, it is clear that this approach would greatly reduce the operability of observance of undertakings clauses, considering the common phenomenon of parastatal entities that have distinct legal personality under domestic law, but which exercise elements of governmental authority in place of state organs. It has been argued that states could simply avoid umbrella clauses by causing parastatal entities to enter into foreign investment contracts.[150]

§9.17 Contract/treaty claim distinction and international rules of attribution   An argument could be made that domestic law rules on the separate personality of a state entity may apply in pure contract claims, including when brought to arbitration under a widely formulated IIA arbitration clause, but not in umbrella clause claims in which the issue is one of interpretation of the scope of a treaty obligation. In the latter, international law rules of attribution as codified by the ILC's Articles on State Responsibility would apply. This is not to say that the internal law of the state concerned would be irrelevant. For example, under Article 4 of the ILC's Articles on State Responsibility, undertakings of a governmental or commercial nature of any organ of the central government and of territorial subdivisions, whether of the legislative, executive or judicial powers, are attributable to the state. This is recognized by the ILC commentaries to the ILC's Articles on State Responsibility which state that 'the *entry into* or the breach of a contract by a State organ is nonetheless an act of the State for purposes of Article 4' [emphasis added].[151] But to determine whether a particular entity is an organ of the state, the internal law of the state concerned would be relevant, though not exclusively: a body which does in truth act as an organ of the state will be so considered under international law even if domestic law denies it that status.[152]

Further, pursuant to Articles 5 and 8 of the ILC's Articles on State Responsibility, undertakings of entities that exercise elements of governmental authority and act in that capacity in the particular instance, or give the undertaking under the instructions, direction or control of the state, are also attributable to the state. The question would be largely whether the internal law of the state has effectively conferred governmental authority to a particular entity, or whether there is evidence of instructions, directions and control by the state under domestic law. But domestic law issues – such as the classification of an entity as public or private; the state

---

150. H.-J. Schramke, 'The Interpretation of Umbrella Clauses in Bilateral Investment Treaties' (2007) 4 TDM (Provisional) at 18-21.
151. See ILC's Articles on State Responsibility, *supra* note 76, in the commentary at Art. 4 at para. 6.
152. *Ibid.*, at para. 11.

participation in, ownership of, or control over, the entity; and the domestic categorization of the act as commercial or administrative – would not be decisive criteria. They would be elements taken into account, in applying to the particular case, the international standard of 'governmental authority' or conduct under governmental 'instruction,' 'direction' or 'control,' together with other factual issues such as the history of the negotiations of the contract and its implementation.[153]

V   SUBSTANTIVE CONTENT OF THE DUTY OF OBSERVANCE

§9.18 Doctrinal debate on the substantive content of the umbrella clause   The scope of the duty of observance in umbrella clauses has been the subject of some debate.[154] For the majority of scholars, the clause imposes a substantive treaty obligation on the host state to comply with its undertakings towards investments, including contractual commitments. Any non-compliance with or breach of such undertakings, even if of a commercial nature, constitutes a violation of this treaty obligation.[155] This view is shared by commentators discussing the IIA practice of the UK, the US and Germany.[156] A minority of scholars interpret the clause more narrowly, as not targeting any commercial conduct, but as imposing a prohibition on governmental abrogation, repudiation or substantial interference with undertakings, or any other use of governmental powers to escape those undertakings. These views are based on concerns about a massive expansion of treaty cases based on contract, and unease in departing from the general international law principle that a contract breach is not *per se* a breach of international law.[157]

§9.19 The *SGS v. Pakistan* restrictive approach   The case law has been controversial. The first arbitral decision to rule directly on the substantive scope of an observance of undertakings clause, in *SGS v. Pakistan*,[158] construed the clause narrowly as one not imposing an obligation on the state to comply with undertakings. The tribunal was confronted with the clause contained in Article 11, Pakistan-Switzerland (1995), which reads: 'Either Contracting Party shall constantly

---

153. See ILC's Articles on State Responsibility, *supra* note 76, at Arts 5 and 8. On the attribution of conduct to the state in the context of investment treaty claims in general see, e.g., *Emilio Agustín Maffezini v. Spain* (Decision of the Tribunal on Objections to Jurisdiction, 25 Jan. 2000) at paras 71-89; *Emilio Agustín Maffezini v. Spain* (Award, 13 Nov. 2000) at paras 46-57; and *Consortium RFCC, supra* note 146 at paras 34-40.
154. Observance of undertakings clauses mandate that host states 'observe,' 'respect' or less frequently, 'constantly guarantee the observance of,' obligations or commitments undertaken towards investments. See *supra* §9.8.
155. See references above at note 94.
156. See references above at note 80.
157. See Happ, *supra* note 96 at 346; and Wälde, *supra* note 1.
158. As noted above the clause was only referred to indirectly in the earlier case *Fedax, supra* note 75 at para. 29.

guarantee the observance of the commitments it has entered into with respect to the investments of investors of the other Contracting Party.' The tribunal admitted that the ordinary meaning of the clause would impose an obligation on Pakistan to comply with its undertakings towards investments, including all contractual obligations, thus transforming any contract breaches into treaty breaches.[159] It rejected this reading, however, holding instead that the clause could not have this far-reaching effect.[160]

The tribunal set out five reasons for its interpretation. First, failing 'clear and convincing evidence,' it could not be assumed that the intention of the contracting parties was to attribute to Article 11 the 'far-reaching,' 'unqualified,' 'sweeping' and 'burdensome' legal consequences of treating any breach of contract as a breach of the BIT. Second, a presumption against the broad interpretation of the clause emerged also from the general principle of international law that a breach of contract 'is not, by itself, a violation of international law.' Third, the broad reading of the clause would render other substantive treaty protections superfluous, as 'there would be no real need to demonstrate a violation of those substantive treaty standards if a simple breach of contract, or municipal statute or regulation, by itself, would suffice to constitute a treaty violation.' Fourth, the expansive approach would mean that the investor could submit any contractual breaches to IIA arbitration, thus overriding contractual dispute settlement clauses. Fifth, and as a supplementary reason, the location of the clause at the end of the BIT, rather than among the substantive obligations placed in the initial articles of the BIT, suggested that Article 11 was not intended as a 'substantive "first order" standard obligation.'[161] For the tribunal, the clause could 'signal an implied affirmative commitment to enact implementing rules and regulations necessary or appropriate to give effect to a contractual or statutory undertaking,' but contract breaches would be covered only 'under exceptional circumstances,' such as a refusal to abide by a contractual arbitration provision.[162] The tribunal thus declined jurisdiction over SGS's breach of contract claims based on the observance of an undertakings clause.

§9.20 The *SGS v. Philippines* literal approach   The government of Switzerland, a Contracting Party to Pakistan-Switzerland (1995) at issue in *SGS v. Pakistan*, reacted with concern to the tribunal's narrow approach in that case with a letter to the International Centre for Settlement of Investment Disputes (ICSID) stating that it was:

> ... alarmed about the very narrow interpretation given to the meaning of Article 11 [...] which not only runs counter to the intention of Switzerland

---

159. *SGS v. Pakistan, supra* note 1 at para. 166. The tribunal did not 'see a significant difference' between the language of the clause and that of the more common and direct formulation '[e]ach Contracting Party shall observe any obligation it may have entered into with regard to investments' (*Ibid.*, at note 177).
160. *Ibid.*
161. *Ibid.*, at para. 169-70.
162. *Ibid.*, at paras 167-72.

when concluding the Treaty but is quite evidently neither supported by the meaning of similar articles in BITs concluded by other countries nor by academic comments on such provisions.[163]

The decision was also strongly criticized by commentators.[164] Further, the subsequent decision in *SGS v. Philippines* faulted it for ignoring the clause's literal interpretation, articulating no convincing reasons for its highly narrow reading and failing to give to it any clear meaning.[165] For the tribunal, the earlier *SGS v. Pakistan* decision overestimated the far-reaching effects of the clause's literal meaning. It incorrectly assumed that it would convert all undertakings into treaty obligations governed by international law. Instead, for the tribunal the clause created a treaty obligation of respect only for undertakings specific to the investment and without changing their proper law.[166] The tribunal noted that such a concept is not at all alien to customary international law. The tribunal did share the concerns regarding concurrent jurisdiction, which led it to stay proceedings pending determination of the amount payable in accordance with the contractual dispute settlement process.[167] But as far as the scope of the substantive obligation of Article X(2) was concerned, the tribunal concluded that the clause 'means what it says' and that it 'makes a breach of the BIT for the host state to fail to observe binding commitments, including contractual commitments which it has assumed with regard to specific investments.'[168] For the tribunal this textual interpretation was consistent with the intent of the contracting states and the object and purpose of the treaty to promote and protect investments. It found that the clause could cover purely commercial obligations. It required the Philippines to pay sums due under the contract.[169] The majority of commentators welcomed this decision as a more persuasive interpretation of the scope of the observance of the undertakings clause.[170]

---

163. Letter from Ambassador Marino Baldi of the State Secretariat for Economic Affairs (SECO) to Antonio Parra, ICSID's Deputy-Secretary General at the time, dated 1 Oct. 2003, *reprinted in* (2004) 19-2 Mealey's International Arbitration Quarterly Law Review, section E-1.
164. Alexandrov, *supra* note 94 at 569-572; Wälde, *supra* note 1 at 210-226; Schreuer, *supra* note 94 at 252-55; and Ben Hamida, *supra* note 1 at 73-77.
165. *SGS v. Philippines, supra* note 37 at paras 113-129. The observance of undertakings clause at issue, at Article X(2), Philippines-Switzerland (1997), reads '[e]ach Contracting Party shall observe any obligations it has assumed with regard to specific investments.'
166. *Ibid.,* at paras 121 and 126-27.
167. *Ibid.,* at paras 122-23, 136-155 and 169-176. See *infra* §9.22 for further discussion.
168. *Ibid.,* at para. 128. In reaching this conclusion the tribunal found: 'It is a conceivable function of a provision such as Article X(2) of the Swiss-Philippines BIT to provide assurances to foreign investors with regard to the performance of obligations assumed by the host State under its own law with regard to specific investments in effect to help secure the rule of law in relation to investment protection. In the tribunal's view, this is the proper interpretation of Article X(2).' *Ibid.,* at para. 126.
169. *Ibid.,* at para. 169(2).
170. *Cf.* Wälde, *supra* note 1 at 226-236, arguing that it reached a 'similar reductionist outcome' as the decision in *SGS v. Pakistan* given its decision to stay proceedings. See below §9.24.

§9.21 The governmental breach approach In *Joy Mining*, the tribunal dismissed the umbrella clause claim on unrelated grounds, but in *obiter dicta* referred to the effects of the observance of an undertakings clause in Egypt-UK (1975). The tribunal's position, while clearly departing from *SGS v. Pakistan*, and admitting that the clause imposes an obligation to comply with undertakings, provides a narrower interpretation of that obligation than *SGS v. Philippines*. The tribunal stated that:

> In this context, it could not be held that an umbrella clause inserted in the Treaty, and not very prominently, could have the effect of transforming all contract disputes into investment disputes under the Treaty, unless of course there would be a clear violation of the Treaty rights and obligations or a violation of contract rights of such magnitude as to trigger the Treaty protection, which is not the case.[171]

Thus, consistent with the approach of a minority of scholars, it seems that the tribunal rejected that mere commercial breaches of contract, as opposed to governmental types of breaches, would create international responsibility for breaches of the observance of undertakings clause.[172]

The award in *CMS* takes a similar approach. The tribunal gave meaningful substantive content to the observance of undertakings clauses, unlike *SGS v. Pakistan*, and found that Argentina had breached its obligation under the clause to observe 'legal and contractual obligations pertinent to the investment,' particularly the stabilization clauses contained in the contract.[173] The tribunal suggested, however, that the clause targets governmental interference with undertakings, rather than any commercial aspect of a contract.[174] The decisions in *Pan American Energy* and *El Paso Energy*, appear to take the same view that only governmental breaches of contracts, not commercial breaches, are covered by the umbrella clause.[175] The *Sempra* award also takes this view, though it admits that '[i]n many cases, it might be difficult to draw this distinction, as not every kind of conduct can be clearly ascribed to one or the other type.'[176] Conversely, another case concerning the Argentine crisis legislation did not refer to this distinction. In *LG&E*, the tribunal found that 'Argentina's abrogation of the guarantees under the statutory

---

171. *Joy Mining, supra* note 85 at para. 81.
172. See E. Gaillard, 'Chronique des sentences arbitrales – Centre International pour le Règlement des Différends relatifs aux Investissements (CIRDI)' (2004) JDI 135 at 181, criticizing this approach as inconsistent with the text and purpose of the observance of undertakings clause of the BIT.
173. *CMS, supra* note 75 at paras 302-303. The clause at Art. II(2)(c), Argentina-US (1991), reads '[e]ach Party shall observe any obligation it may have entered into with regard to investments.'
174. *Ibid.*, at para. 299, stating that '[p]urely commercial aspect of a contract might not be protected by the treaty in some situations, but protection is likely to be available when there is significant interference by governments or public agencies with the rights of the investor.'
175. *El Paso Energy, supra* note 40 at paras 66-88; and *Pan American Energy, supra* note 101 at paras 96-116. These decisions also seem to take the view that not all contracts, but only those of a governmental nature, would be covered by the umbrella clause.
176. *Sempra, supra* note 12 at para. 311.

framework' for the privatization of the gas industry 'violated its obligations to Claimants' investments' giving 'rise to liability under the umbrella clause.'[177] Since the case at hand concerned governmental breaches, the tribunal did not need to discuss whether commercial breaches would also be proscribed by the observance of the undertakings clause. Similarly, in *Enron*, the tribunal upheld the umbrella clause claim without referring to the commercial/governmental breach distinction.[178]

§9.22 The literal approach after *SGS v. Philippines* Faced with umbrella clause claims after the decision in *SGS v. Philippines*, the majority of tribunals have followed the literal approach contained in this decision, and thus implicitly or explicitly rejected the commercial/governmental breach distinction.

For example, in *Salini S.p.A. v. Jordan*, the tribunal declined jurisdiction because the claims were purely contractual and Italy-Jordan (1996) excluded contractual disputes from the scope of treaty arbitration. It then added:

> Of course, each State Party to the BIT between Italy and Jordan remains bound by its contractual obligations. However, this undertaking was not reiterated in the BIT. Therefore, these obligations remain purely contractual in nature and any disputes regarding the said obligations must be resolved in accordance with the dispute settlement procedures foreseen in the contract.[179]

Thus, the obligations remained purely contractual because the BIT did not provide for an observance of an undertakings clause. It could be argued that *a contrario*, in presence of such a clause, purely contractual obligations could be protected by the treaty, and contractual breaches would become treaty breaches.

The tribunal in *Eureko* makes this point expressly. Confronted with governmental rather that mere commercial conduct, it did not need to address the distinction between governmental and commercial breaches of undertakings.[180] The tribunal, however, implicitly rejected this distinction. It surveyed the existing jurisprudence and commentary on the clause and agreed with the *SGS v. Philippines* analysis. The tribunal focused on the 'not obscure' meaning of the phrase 'shall observe,' which it considered 'imperative and categorical.'[181] Together with the object and purpose of the treaty, and consistent with the principle that treaty provisions be interpreted as meaningful and effective rather than meaningless and ineffective, the tribunal found that the clause 'must be interpreted to mean something in itself.'[182] The tribunal thus held that Poland had breached the clause by failing to comply with its contractual commitment to continue the privatization of a state-owned insurance company.

---

177. *LG&E, supra* note 89 at para. 175.
178. *Enron, supra* note 89 at paras 273-77.
179. *Salini v. Jordan, supra* note 46 at para. 127.
180. *Eureko, supra* note 37 at paras 244-260.
181. *Ibid.*, at para. 246.
182. *Ibid.*, at para. 247-49.

In *Noble Ventures*, the tribunal found it unnecessary to reach a conclusion on whether the clause covered commercial as well as governmental breaches, since even according to the broadest interpretation, the claims at hand failed on the facts of the case. The tribunal's reasoning, however, lends support to a broad construction. The observance of the undertakings clause at issue reads '[e]ach party shall observe any obligation it may have entered into with regard to investments.'[183] The tribunal emphasized the importance of the formulation of the clause in the treaty, and that it was primarily directed to contracts between states and investors. It found that the clause 'was intended to create obligations, and obviously obligations beyond those specified in other provisions of the BIT itself.' On the basis of the object and purpose of the treaty and on the principle of effectiveness, the clause was 'naturally to be understood as protecting investors also with regard to contracts with the host state generally in so far as the contract was entered into with regard to an investment.' The tribunal recognized that exceptions to established rules of international law, such as those prescribing international responsibility for a breach of contract, should be interpreted restrictively. But after reviewing some other formulations of the clause in IIA practice, the tribunal concluded that the clause at hand fell in 'the category of the most general and direct formulations tending to an assimilation of contractual obligations into treaty ones.'

In *Siemens*, the tribunal rejected the claimant's umbrella clause claim because the claimant was not a party to the contract. The tribunal, however, stated in passing that the umbrella clause 'has the meaning that its terms express, namely that failure to meet obligations undertaken by one of the Treaty parties in respect to any particular investment is converted by this clause into a breach of the Treaty.'[184] Hence, for the tribunal, any breach of contract would fall within the umbrella clause.

§9.23 The correct literal and *effet utile* approach   In conclusion, the highly restrictive interpretation of the duty of observance in *SGS v. Pakistan*, not anticipated even by the most narrow doctrinal approaches, remains an isolated and probably already abandoned position. In the prevailing interpretation, the clause is understood as mandating that the state comply with its undertakings towards investments, including contractual commitments, based on the ordinary meaning of its terms. Yet the jurisprudence is not unanimous as to whether pure commercial breaches of contract, as opposed to governmental breaches, are covered by the clause. If the clause is construed as targeting governmental rather than commercial breaches then it is equated with other treaty protections. The obligation not to use governmental powers to abrogate or adversely interfere with contracts and specific unilateral undertakings towards investments is already covered by fair and equitable treatment, and possibly the obligation to ensure full protection and security. Abrogation of rights under domestic law would also likely be expropriatory.

---

183.   Art. II(c), Romania-US (1992). The relevant passages of the award (*supra* note 39) cited in the text above are at paras 51-60.
184.   *Siemens, supra* note 108 at para. 204.

Hence, the principle of effectiveness of treaty provisions would suggest a broader interpretation of the observance clause, as covering commercial as well as governmental breaches of contract. It has been argued that this would do justice to a clause that, absent clear evidence of contrary intent by the treaty parties, should be deemed to add protection to the investor.[185] Further, as admitted by the tribunal in *Sempra,* the distinction between commercial and governmental breaches is not easy to draw in practice.[186] The characterization of the nature and motives for a breach may not be therefore a reliable test and may lead to arbitrary results.[187]

VI   CONCURRENT JURISDICTIONS

§9.24   The *SGS v. Philippines* decision to stay proceedings   An investor's claim against the host state for breach of contract may be actionable as a contractual claim before the contractually agreed forum, or as a claim for breach of the observance of undertakings clause in IIA arbitration. This gives rise to the problem of overlapping and concurrent jurisdictions.

The problem was confronted by the tribunal in *SGS v. Philippines* in a claim regarding allegations of non-payment of large sums allegedly owing by the Philippines under a contract for the provision of custom inspection services. This claim was submitted both as a purely contractual claim and also as a claim for breach of Pakistan-Switzerland (1995). As to the latter, the claimant pleaded, *inter alia,* a breach of the observance of undertakings clause (Article X(2)) and of the fair and equitable treatment provision (Article IV), which the tribunal held *prima facie* constituted valid treaty claims.[188] The tribunal nevertheless noted that the essence of the claims was contractual, and that there was an unresolved issue or dispute as to the content and extent of the contractual obligation, i.e., the amount payable under the contract, which was governed by municipal law.[189] It considered that, while it could decide on these issues by applying the law of the Philippines,[190] it was more appropriate to permit the forum more specific to the parties and the dispute to determine those issues:

> At the level of jurisdiction, a claim has in its view been stated by SGS under both provisions [umbrella and FET clauses]. But, there being an unresolved dispute as to the amount payable, for the tribunal to decide on the claim in isolation from decision by the chosen forum under the CISS Agreement [the contract] is inappropriate and premature.

---

185.   See e.g. Schreuer, *supra* note 94 at 250-255; V. Zolia 'Effect and purpose of "Umbrella Clauses" in Bilateral Investment Treaties: Unresolved Issues' (2005) 2 TDM 5 at 35.
186.   *Sempra, supra* note 12 at para. 311.
187.   Crawford, *supra* note 74 at 19.
188.   *SGS v. Philippines, supra* note 37 at paras 157, 163 and 169.
189.   *Ibid.,* at paras 128 and 162.
190.   *Ibid.,* at para. 128.

The Tribunal holds that it has jurisdiction over SGS's claims under Articles X(2) and IV of the BIT, but that in respect of both provisions, SGS's claim is premature and must await the determination of the amount payable in accordance with the contractually agreed process.[191]

In relation to the observance of the undertakings clause the tribunal found that 'SGS is bound by the terms of the exclusive jurisdiction clause […] in order to establish the quantum or content of the obligation which, under Article X(2) of the BIT, the Philippines is required to observe.' Thus, the tribunal identified an admissibility impediment, on the basis of the principle of *pacta sunt servanda*, i.e., compliance with the contract which is the foundation of the claim, and implicitly that of *generalia specialibus non derogant*, i.e., deference to *fora* with more specific jurisdiction on the underlying dispute. The tribunal found, however, that international tribunals had a 'certain degree of flexibility' in dealing with questions of admissibility, and in particular of 'competing forums,' and concluded that 'justice would be best served if the Tribunal were to stay the present proceedings pending determination of the amount payable, either by agreement of the parties or by proceedings in the Philippine courts, as provided for in [the contract exclusive jurisdiction clause].'[192] The tribunal admitted that a stay may not be granted when it would cause injustice to the claimant, for example, 'if the local courts are closed ... due to armed conflict.'[193] And, in staying the proceedings, the tribunal imposed an obligation on the parties to 'expedite proceedings' before local courts, take 'all necessary measures to ensure a prompt and effective resolution of the dispute,' and to report to the tribunal every six months on the steps taken in this regard.[194] Finally, it found that the stay of proceedings could be 'lifted for sufficient cause on application by either party.'[195] The stay of proceedings was lifted by decision of 17 December 2007, when in the view of the tribunal the amount in dispute had already been determined through internal reports of the Philippines' government.[196]

§9.25 The approach to concurrent jurisdiction after *SGS v. Philippines* The decision in *SGS v. Philippines* was welcomed by some commentators,[197] while others have criticized the confusion introduced by the stay of proceedings, particularly as to when and how proceedings would be reinstated, and for undermining the effectiveness of observance of undertakings clauses.[198] These concerns

---

191. *Ibid.*, at paras 162-163.
192. *Ibid.*, at paras 170-171 and 175.
193. *Ibid.*, at paras 170.
194. *Ibid.*, at para. 176.
195. *Ibid.*
196. *SGS v. Philippines* (Order of the Tribunal on Further Proceedings, 17 Dec. 2007).
197. Z. Douglas, 'Hybrid Foundations of Investment Treaty Arbitration' (2003) 74 BYIL 151 at 288-289.
198. Wälde, *supra* note 96 at 229-332; and E. Gaillard, 'Investment Treaty Arbitration and Jurisdiction Over Contract Claims – the SGS Cases Considered,' in T. Weiler, ed., *International*

are also reflected in the partial dissent appended to the decision, which makes the point that BIT arbitration should be considered an additional option for the disgruntled investor, particularly in a case like the one at hand where the BIT was subsequent to the contract.[199]

The issue of concurrent jurisdiction did not arise in the decisions concerning claims for breaches of the observance of undertakings clause that followed *SGS v. Philippines* (i.e., *CMS*, *Eureko*, *Noble Ventures*, *LG&E*, *El Paso Energy*, *Pan American Energy*, *Sempra* and *Enron*). In *Eureko* and the Argentine cases, the claims under the observance of undertakings clauses were not reducible to pure claims for breach of contract; the undertakings allegedly not observed by the host state included unilateral regulatory undertakings, not just contractual obligations, and, even in relation to these, the claims were not for simple breaches but rather for repudiatory-type of acts. For this same reason, other seemingly genuine treaty claims were also being pursued. Similarly, in *Noble Ventures*, even if the claims under the observance of undertakings clause were contract-based, there were other treaty claims relating to conduct of the host state separate from the contract. In none of these cases was there a direct and complete overlap between the jurisdiction of the treaty tribunal and the contractual jurisdiction. It thus made sense for the treaty tribunals to exercise all aspects of their jurisdiction and permit the claimants to resolve their claims simultaneously without having to seize different tribunals with separate claims.

A stay of jurisdiction was expressly rejected in *Impregilo* and *Bayindir*.[200] These cases, however, did not concern the application of observance of undertaking clauses, but claims under other standards of treatment and for the expropriation of contract rights. Thus there was no direct overlap between the treaty and the contract claims. It may be for this reason that the tribunal in *Impregilo* found that 'it is not obvious that the contractual dispute resolution mechanisms in a case of this sort will be undermined in any substantial sense by the determination of separate and distinct Treaty Claims,'[201] and the tribunal in *Bayindir* found that '[i]n the present case, the Tribunal cannot see any compelling reason to stay the current arbitration.'[202] In any case, both tribunals underlined the practical difficulties in a stay of proceedings.[203]

There are inherent difficulties in a stay of proceedings, in particular the practicalities of determining what amounts to sufficient cause for the resumption of proceedings, or whether the claimant may be obliged to pursue one or more levels of local courts before going back to the IIA tribunal. It may be argued however that it cannot be excluded there are instances in which a stay may be appropriate.

   Investment Law and Arbitration: Leading Cases from the ICSID, NAFTA, Bilateral Treaties and Customary International Law (London: Cameron May, 2005) at 334 and 342-346.
199. *SGS v. Philippines, supra* note 37.
200. *Impregilo, supra* note 12 at paras 286-90; and *Bayindir Insaat Turizm Ticaret Ve Sanayi A. Ş. v. Pakistan* (Decision on Jurisdiction, 14 Nov. 2005) [*Bayindir*] at paras 264-273.
201. *Impregilo, ibid.,* at para. 289.
202. *Bayindir, supra* note 200 at para. 271.
203. *Impregilo, supra* note 12 at para. 290 and *Bayindir, ibid.,* at para. 272-273.

In these cases, a treaty tribunal may effectively assume the role of a court of appeal with review powers over municipal court findings on the particular matter at stake; though then the problem becomes the overlap between municipal appeals and the role of the IIA tribunal. As to the scope of the IIA tribunal's review, it would seem natural that the treaty tribunal may accord a margin of appreciation to local courts, having less competence on municipal law issues. But the treaty tribunal could not simply restrict its review to denial of justice-type of complaints. Otherwise it would appear that the stay of proceedings would effectively permit the tribunal to abdicate from its original jurisdiction over breach of contractual undertakings under the observance of undertaking clauses, and restrict its jurisdiction to violations of other treaty protections which could result from denial of justice, such as expropriation or breach of fair and equitable treatment. The additional protection that may have been intended by the observance of undertakings clauses would thus disappear.

In this context, the case law indicates that the need for or convenience of a stay of proceedings may not arise except in narrow circumstances such as those in *SGS v. Philippines*. There, the nature of the claim was purely and entirely contractual (the amount payable under contract) and fell squarely within the jurisdiction of the contractually-chosen forum. Further, and this appears as crucial, there was an underlying dispute between the parties as to the scope of the contractual obligations (as opposed to governmental action setting aside the contract).

But it is also in this type of case that the observance of an undertakings clause may really matter to the investor, as other treaty protections may not be applicable. Thus, IIA tribunals should exercise their discretion to stay proceedings with prudence, with adequate consideration of the potential injustice caused to the claimant if: (i) there is no real dispute as to the scope of the contractual obligation at play and where the government's conduct is in fact a wilful refusal to comply for whatever motives, rather than a good faith position contesting the existence of the obligation; (ii) the state interferes with the contract dispute resolution process; or (iii) the competent local courts are manifestly unable to provide relief due, for example, to declared partiality or caseload.

VII   LIMITATIONS

§9.26 Domestic law limitations   The law applicable to the existence, nature and scope of an undertaking to be respected under the observance of an undertakings clause is, in principle, the law of the host state or the law applicable to the contract.[204] The chosen applicable law governs whether, for the purposes of the operation of the clause, an undertaking may be deemed valid, existent, or otherwise applicable in given circumstances. In particular, in interpreting the scope of any given undertakings

---

204.   See *supra* §9.9 and §9.10.

clause, weight must be given to municipal law doctrines of *force majeure*, changed circumstances (*rebus sic stantibus*), non-compliance by the investor with some of the corresponding contractual obligations, commercial impracticability or frustration, police powers, '*imprévision,*' '*impossibilité sans faute,*' '*ius variandi*' or '*fait du prince,*' or any other prerogative of the state to disregard administrative law contracts (usually against the payment of compensation) or to renegotiate these contracts (usually guaranteeing their economic equilibrium).[205]

All these doctrines and legal principles may affect and thus represent potential limitations on the duty imposed by umbrella clauses because, in certain circumstances, the given undertaking would not subsist at all, would not be pertinent or applicable, or would have a different, more limited scope. Naturally, even if the observance of an undertakings clause is inapplicable, or of limited applicability in a given situation, it will still be open to a treaty tribunal to find that the conduct of the host state in those circumstances is in breach of the IIA's other provisions such as the prohibition against expropriation without compensation or fair and equitable treatment. Unlike the observance of undertakings clause, these treaty standards do not relate directly to a breach of municipal law undertakings and contracts, but set international law standards independent from domestic law.

§9.27 Observance of undertakings and stabilization clauses   It has been argued that observance of undertakings clauses embody a principle of stability in the legal framework applicable to foreign investment. That is, the clause operates as a sort of stabilization or intangibility clause freezing the law applicable to the investment and preventing the host state from altering it unilaterally.[206] This appears to be incorrect. As already set out above, umbrella clauses cannot be deemed to alter the law applicable to the underlying obligation.[207] In particular, the clause does not 'internationalize' a domestic law obligation, removing it from municipal law and subjecting it to international law. Hence, if the alteration or non-performance of an obligation by the state is licit under the applicable law, by the ordinary use of regulatory powers, or by the application, for example, of the doctrine of '*ius variandi,*' or police powers, such alteration or non-performance will not *per se* give rise to a breach of the observance of undertakings clause.

Thus, the umbrella clause is not a stabilization clause, but of course if a stabilization clause exists under the applicable domestic law it will be enforceable pursuant to the umbrella clause. Further, the state, in making certain commitments or observing certain conduct in relation to a municipal law obligation, may incur

---

205.   Ben Hamida, *supra* note 1 at paras 83-90; Mann, *supra* note 49 at 246; and Sinclair, *supra* note 1 at 432.
206.   Ben Hamida, *supra* note 1 at paras 69-79; V. Zolia 'Effect and purpose of "Umbrella Clauses" in 'Bilateral Investment Treaties: Unresolved Issues' (2005) 2 TDM at 16-25; Weil, *supra* note 13 at 130; UNCTAD, *supra* note 17 at 56, stating 'a provision of this kind ... might possibly alter the legal regime and make the agreement subject to the rules of international law'; and Leben, *supra* note 95, at 643-644.
207.   Laviec, *supra* note 48 at 249-251; and P. Mayer 'La neutralisation du pouvoir normative de l'État en matière de contrats d'État' (1985) 113 JDI 5 at 36-37. *Cf.* UNCTAD, *supra* note 17 at 56.

separate obligations under international law that may be covered by the observance of undertakings clause. For example, under international law, a state may not be able to deny the validity of a contract or a contractual obligation when it has recognized its validity and has allowed the foreign investor to perform the contract without objection.[208] In this case, even if no domestic obligation exists, a separate obligation may have arisen at the international level which would be covered by the observance of an undertakings clause. But in these circumstances, the clause protects an international law obligation, not the contract itself, which is not internationalized or detached from its applicable law.

VIII   DISTINCTION FROM OTHER CLAUSES

§9.28 Preservation of rights clause   The preservation of rights clause is a common IIA clause providing investors the right to claim the application of any rule of law more favourable than the provisions of the IIA. An example is Article 11, Argentina-UK (1990), headed 'Application of other Rules,' which reads:

> If the provisions of law of either Contracting Party or obligations under international law existing at present or established hereafter between the Contracting Parties in addition to the present Agreement or if any agreement between an investor of one Contracting Party and the other Contracting Party contain rules, whether general or specific, entitling investments by investors of the other Contracting Party to a treatment more favourable than is provided for by the present Agreement, such rules shall to the extent that they are more favourable prevail over the present Agreement.

There are many different versions of this provision. For example, in some IIAs the clause refers only to the application of a more favourable 'specific undertaking' that may have been made by the host state vis-à-vis the investor, but does not mention municipal law and international law, in contrast with the more classic clause.[209] Some IIAs contain this clause but not the observance of undertakings clause, while many other IIAs provide both clauses, sometimes in the same article.[210] Usually the clause is placed among the final provisions of the IIA, after the dispute resolution clauses; but sometimes the clause is embodied among the initial articles of the IIA establishing the substantive protections.[211]

Some authors argue that the clause operates like an observance of an undertakings clause, because the investor could claim the more favourable provisions of, for example, the municipal law or a contract, which would be incorporated in

---

208.   See e.g. *Shufeldt Claim* (1930) II RIAA 1079 at 1094. See also above at §9.11 and accompanying text.
209.   Art. 10, Argentina-France (1991).
210.   Art. X, Philippines-Switzerland (1997).
211.   Art. 2(3), Czechoslovakia-UK (1990), where the preservation of rights and the observance of undertakings clauses are two sentences in the same paragraph.

the IIA by substitution.[212] But there is nothing in the text of the formulation of this clause justifying such a conclusion. The clause, in its usual wording, simply says that in applying or enforcing the existing protections offered by the IIA, attention should be paid to any more favourable, but not unfavourable, provisions contained in domestic law or specific agreements. Thus, for example, a contractual clause providing for a mechanism to calculate compensation and resulting in a higher amount than that under the treaty's expropriation clause would need to be applied. Thus, the clause confirms that the investor may benefit from more favourable treatment, but does not add a new, specific or distinct, treaty obligation to respect commitments made. The better view is, therefore, that the preservation of rights and the observance of the undertakings clauses have different functions.

This is the position taken by the tribunal in *SGS v. Philippines* in relation to the preservation of rights clause of Philippines-Switzerland (1997). The focus of the tribunal was on the scope and effects of the observance of an undertakings clause, at Article X(2), but reference was made in passing to the preservation of rights clause at Article X(1). The tribunal stated that:

> One must begin with the actual text of Article X. It is headed 'Other Commitments.' Article X(1) is a kind of 'without prejudice' clause, providing that the legislative provisions or international law rules more favourable to an investor shall to that extent 'prevail over this Agreement.' It deals with the relation between commitments under the BIT and distinct commitments under host State law or under other rules of international law. It does not appear to impose any additional obligation or the host State in the framework of the BIT.[213]

A different view appears to have been taken in an unpublished award where a tribunal considered that the preservation of rights clause in the relevant BIT conferred jurisdiction on it to examine treaty claims arising from breach of contract.

§9.29 Wide dispute resolution clauses   Dispute resolution clauses in IIAs are often drafted in broad terms in order to provide that the investor can submit to arbitration before a treaty tribunal 'any' or 'all' disputes arising out of an investment, or simply 'investment disputes' without defining this term. Some clauses are more restrictive, providing for the possibility to submit to a treaty tribunal disputes relating to a breach of a treaty right, but also add disputes relating to an investment authorization and an investment agreement with the host state. All these clauses permit a treaty tribunal to exercise jurisdiction over disputes that do not arise out

---

212.   Ben Hamida, *supra* note 1 at 96-98.
213.   *SGS v. Philippines, supra* note 37 at para. 114, citing *Yaung Chi Oo Trading Pte. Ltd. v. Myanmar* (Award, 31 Mar. 2003) at paras 79-82, stating that the phrase 'shall prevail' used in a treaty referring to other commitments contained in other legal instruments does not have the effect of incorporating those commitments into the treaty, and thus does not give the claimant any new rights.

of, or relate to, treaty protections, but concern contractual claims or other claims based on municipal law.[214]

Thus, it has been argued that these provisions could represent disguised observance of undertakings clauses, insofar as, like these clauses, they would permit resort to treaty remedies for what would be, in effect, a contractual or municipal law claim. But there is a fundamental difference, in that purely contractual or municipal law disputes submitted to treaty arbitration under a broad treaty dispute resolution clause would be entirely governed by municipal law, or the contractual chosen law. Conversely, in disputes relating to the observance of undertakings clauses, even if the issue of compliance would equally fall to be determined under domestic law, other issues would be governed by international law.[215]

---

214. See e.g., *SGS v. Philippines, supra* note 37 at paras 130-135; and *Salini v. Morocco, supra* note 146 at para. 59. Compare *SGS v. Pakistan, supra* note 1 at paras 160-161.
215. See *supra* §9.10.

Chapter 10

Exceptions and Defences

INTRODUCTION

§10.1 Overview of exceptions and defences   This chapter covers exceptions and defences to international investment agreement (IIA) obligations. In addition to the obligation-specific exceptions addressed in previous chapters, some IIAs have general exceptions applying to all or many IIA obligations. These exceptions are used to exclude particular sectors or subject matters from IIA obligations or to permit measures necessary to meet specific objectives, including protecting essential security interests, public order, human health and the environment. Some IIAs also provide interpretive guidance regarding environmental and other types of measures. In addition to express exceptions, state responsibility for breaches of IIA obligations may be precluded under customary international law on a number of bases, including consent, *force majeure* and necessity. Finally, a number of other defences may be available, including acquiescence and estoppel.

There are myriad other reasons why an IIA claim may fail. These are not addressed in this chapter because they relate to the jurisdictional or substantive provisions of the IIA. For example, the IIA may not apply to the investor or investment in question, or the investment may not comply with local law or have been obtained through fraudulent means.[1] The IIA may not apply temporally or geographically to the state conduct at issue.[2] The IIA may have a clause denying treaty benefits.[3] Further, the IIA dispute resolution clause may provide limitations

---

1. See *Inceysa Vallisoletana, S.L. v. El Salvador* (Award, 2 Aug. 2006) and *Fraport AG Frankfurt Airport Services Worldwide v. Philippines* (Award, 16 Aug. 2007). See *supra* Chapter 2, §2.11 and §2.12.
2. See N. Gallus, *The Temporal Jurisdiction of BIT Tribunals* (London: British Institute of International and Comparative Law, forthcoming).
3. Some IIAs have denial of benefit clauses providing that benefits under the IIA may be denied where investors of non-parties own or control the investment in question. See, for example, Art. 17, US-Uruguay (2005).

to the scope of the jurisdiction of an arbitral tribunal,[4] time limits for bringing a claim may have expired or the claim may not be admissible. In addition, the conduct at issue may not be attributable to the state or, if attributable, may not breach an IIA obligation. Finally, if a contractual dispute is subject to arbitration under an IIA,[5] contractual defences may be available under the law applicable to the contract.[6]

This chapter is divided into seven parts. Part I provides an overview of express exceptions that appear in IIAs (and a type of exception in some IIAs called 'reservation') and briefly discusses the interpretation of exceptions. Security exceptions are considered in Part II, followed by Part III, which addresses general exceptions modelled on Article XX, *General Agreement on Tariffs and Trade* (GATT). Part IV discusses subject matter and obligation-specific exceptions. Part V then turns briefly to interpretive guidelines regarding the environment and other issues. Circumstances precluding wrongfulness under customary international law are addressed in Part VI. Part VII discusses other defences to claims that might be available to a respondent state.

I   EXPRESS EXCEPTIONS IN IIAS

§10.2 Introduction   The terms 'exceptions' and 'reservations' are commonly used in IIAs to exclude particular sectors or subject matters from IIA obligations. In IIA practice, express exceptions and reservations are negotiated by prospective treaty partners and incorporated into the IIA text, or accompanying annexes, protocols or letters. An express reservation in an IIA should therefore be distinguished from a reservation to a treaty, which is defined in the *Vienna Convention on the Law of Treaties* (Vienna Convention) as follows:

> ... a unilateral statement, however phrased or named, made by a State, when signing, ratifying, accepting, approving or acceding to a treaty, whereby it purports to exclude or to modify the legal effect of certain provisions of the treaty in their application to that State.[7]

In IIA treaty practice, a reservation is not a unilateral statement by one of the treaty parties. The term reservation is used in the treaty text itself to specify matters to which some or all of an IIA's obligations do not apply.

The terms exception and reservation are not used consistently in IIA treaty practice – they are often used together and interchangeably.[8] The word exception

---

4.   See *supra* Chapter 5, §5.10 *et seq.* on the application of MFN clauses to investor-state.
5.   See *supra* Chapter 9, §9.29.
6.   See *supra* Chapter 2, §2.12.
7.   Art. 2(1)(d), *Vienna Convention on the Law of Treaties*, 23 May 1969, entered into force, 27 Jan. 1980, 1155 UNTS 331, *reprinted in* (1969) 8 ILM 679 [Vienna Convention].
8.   See Art. 1108, NAFTA, and Art. 9, Canada-Peru (2006).

in IIA practice usually refers to subjects completely excluded from the treaty's scope.[9] Reservation is typically used for more specific exceptions. Although IIA practice is not consistent, the term exception is more appropriately used to apply to broad carve-outs from IIA obligations – areas in which there are, in principle, no IIA obligations. In contrast, the term reservation is more appropriately used to refer to narrower limitations to the scope of IIA obligations, for example, to exclude from the prescriptions of the IIA a specific existing law or regulation. In either case, the practical effect is the same. If there is an applicable exception or reservation, no IIA obligation exists with respect to a measure within the scope of the exception or reservation.

Some IIAs, in particular US bilateral investment treaties (BITs), refer to 'non-conforming' measures and 'non-precluded' measures. For example, Article 14(1)-(3), US-Uruguay (2005), sets out a list of non-conforming measures maintained by the state parties, which are enumerated in a series of annexes. The reference to non-conforming measures is simply another way to refer to express reservations to the treaty. Another example is Article 14(5), which provides that specific obligations (national treatment, most-favoured-nation (MFN) treatment and the provisions on senior management and board of directors) do not apply to government procurement or state subsidies and grants. In contrast, Article 18(2), on essential security interests, uses the language of non-preclusion:

> Nothing in this Treaty shall be construed: ... to preclude a Party from applying measures that it considers necessary for the fulfillment of its obligations with respect to the maintenance or restoration of international peace or security, or the protection of its own essential security interests.

Article 18(2) is an express exception for essential security interests.[10]

On the basis of the wording of this type of clause, some commentators refer to express IIA exceptions as non-precluded measure clauses (NPM clauses).[11] This expression can lead to confusion given its similarity with the language used by the International Law Commission (ILC) to refer to 'circumstances precluding wrongfulness' or state responsibility based on customary international law defences, but which operate in a different manner to treaty exceptions.[12] This

---

9. For example, Canadian IIAs expressly state that they do not apply to investments in cultural industries. See Art. 10(6), Canada-Peru (2006).
10. See *infra* Part II on security exceptions.
11. See W. Burke-White & A. Von Standen, 'Investment Protection in Extraordinary Times: The Interpretation and Application of Non-Precluded Measures Provisions in Bilateral Investment Treaties' (2008) 48 VJIL 307.
12. See *infra* Part VI. See International Law Commission's Draft Articles on Responsibility of States for Internationally Wrongful Acts, *Official Records of the General Assembly,* UN GAOR, 56th Sess., Supp. No. 10, UN Doc A/56/10 at 11; 2001 YBILC, Vol. II, Part Two. The Articles and commentary are *reprinted in* J. Crawford, *The International Law Commission's Articles on State Responsibility: Introduction, Text, and Commentaries* (Cambridge: Cambridge University Press, 2002) [ILC's Articles on State Responsibility].

chapter thus uses the terms exceptions and reservations to refer to express treaty provisions that limit the scope or applicability of substantive obligations; while the notion of preclusion is confined to customary international law defences available to a respondent state that has breached an IIA obligation.

At least five categories of exceptions and reservations can be identified in IIA treaty practice, ranging from wide (sometimes self-judging) exceptions applying to all IIA obligations, to narrowly defined reservations for specific, non-conforming measures:

- *Essential security exceptions*: IIA exceptions relating to essential security interests typically apply to all IIA obligations and sometimes use self-judging language intended to make the state in question the sole arbiter (subject to the obligation to act in good faith) of whether the exception applies and can be invoked.

- *Other general exceptions*: A small number of IIAs have general exceptions from IIA obligations for measures necessary to meet specific objectives, including public order and the protection of human, animal and plant life or health. These exceptions are typically very closely modelled on, or incorporate *mutatis mutandis*, the general exception provisions in Article XX, GATT, or Article XIV, *General Agreement on Trade and Services* (GATS).

- *Exceptions or reservations for specific sectors or types of measures*: Some IIAs exclude specific industrial sectors from IIA obligations or provide broad carve-outs for certain types of measures.[13] Others provide that certain obligations do not apply to specific categories of measures.[14]

- *Exceptions or reservations for existing non-conforming measures and amendments*: This kind of exception or reservation acts as a 'grandfathering' provision that allows for the continuation, renewal and amendment of an existing non-conforming measure, provided non-conformity does not increase.[15]

- *Exceptions or reservations for future measures*: In addition to exceptions or reservations for existing non-conforming measures, exceptions or

---

13. US and Canadian IIAs typically include exclusions for taxation measures. See Art. 16, Canada-Peru (2006), and Art. 21, US-Uruguay (2005). There are broad exceptions to Mexico's NAFTA obligations with respect to the petroleum, hydrocarbon and basic petrochemical sectors. See Mexico's schedules in Annexes I-III, NAFTA.

14. For example, US and Canadian IIAs commonly provide that the national treatment obligation does not apply to government grants and subsidies. See Art. 9(5), Canada-Peru (2006), and Art. 14(5), US-Uruguay (2005).

15. These reservations are common in US and Canadian IIAs. The practice has been for federal measures to be individually listed with a general reservation for all existing, non-conforming measures maintained by sub-national governments. The issue of reservations for existing and future measures was subject to much debate in the MAI negotiations. See 'Departures from Standstill: GATS, NAFTA and Possible Solutions for the MAI,' Note by the Chairman, 10 Mar. 1998 (DAFFE/MAI(98)5).

reservations might also be made to allow for future measures that are even more restrictive.[16]

§10.3 The interpretation of exceptions   The state party invoking an exception or reservation to an IIA obligation has the burden of proving that the exception applies and that the applicable criteria for invoking the exception are satisfied.[17] Some IIA tribunals have suggested that exceptions to IIA obligations should be interpreted narrowly and that this is consistent with the investment promotion and protection purpose of IIAs.[18] For example, the tribunal in *Canfor Corporation v. United States and Terminal Forest Products Ltd. v. United States*, referring to GATT jurisprudence, stated that exceptions in international instruments are to be interpreted narrowly.[19] Another example is the award in *Enron Corporation and Ponderosa Assets, L.P. v. Argentina* in which the tribunal, when discussing the essential security interests clause in Article XI, Argentina-US (1991), stated:

> … the Tribunal must first note that the object and purpose of the Treaty is, as a general proposition, to apply in situations of economic difficulty and hardship that guarantee the protection of the international guaranteed rights of its beneficiaries. To this extent, any interpretation resulting in an escape route from the obligations defined cannot be easily reconciled with that object and purpose. Accordingly, a restrictive interpretation of any such alternative is mandatory.[20]

Presumptions about the interpretation of exceptions, however, should be used with caution since they provide a ready-made generalized rule that may not fit in a particular case or be faithful to the intentions of treaty partners. Further, a presumption in one sense can often be counteracted by a presumption in the opposite sense. For example, the presumptions of restrictive interpretation applied by international tribunals to exceptions to treaty obligations would seem to be contradicted by the presumption of restrictive interpretation of treaty obligations as derogations of sovereignty (by way of the *in dubios mitius* principle).[21]

---

16.   See Art. 14(2), US-Uruguay (2005), providing for certain obligations not to apply to new or more restrictive measures listed in Annex II.

17.   *United Parcel Service of America Inc. v. Canada* (Separate Statement of Dean Ronald A. Cass, 24 May 2007) [*UPS Cass Separate Statement*] at para. 154. WTO Appellate Body jurisprudence on the general exceptions in Art. XX, GATT, takes a similar burden shifting approach. See *Brazil-Measures Affecting Imports of Retreaded Tyres*, WT/DS332/AB/R (adopted 17 Dec. 2007) [*Brazil-Tyres*]. For an overview of Art. XX, GATT, jurisprudence, see M. Trebilcock & R. Howse, *The Regulation of International Trade*, 3rd edn (London: Routledge, 2005).

18.   See *supra* Chapter 2, §2.29.

19.   *Canfor Corporation v. United States and Terminal Forest Products Ltd. v. United States* (Decision on Preliminary Question, 6 Jun. 2006) at para. 187.

20.   *Enron Corporation and Ponderosa Assets, L.P. v. Argentina* (Award, 22 May 2007) [*Enron*] at para. 331.

21.   See *supra* Chapter 2, §2.28 and §2.29.

A preferable approach to the interpretation of exceptions would seem to be that adopted by the Appellate Body of the World Trade Organization (WTO) in its jurisprudence on the general exceptions in Article XX, GATT, and Article XIV, GATS. The Appellate Body has stated that, general exceptions 'affirm the right of Members to pursue objectives identified in the paragraphs of these provisions even if, in doing so, Members act inconsistently with obligations set out in other provisions of the respective agreements, provided that all of the conditions set out therein are satisfied.'[22] The Appellate Body has rejected earlier GATT panel

---

22. *United States – Measures Affecting the Cross-Border Supply of Gambling and Betting Services*, WT/DS285/AB/R (adopted 20 Apr. 2005) at para. 291.
    Art. XX, GATT, headed 'General Exceptions' reads:
    'Subject to the requirement that such measures are not applied in a manner which would constitute a means of arbitrary or unjustifiable discrimination between countries where the same conditions prevail, or a disguised restriction on international trade, nothing in this Agreement shall be construed to prevent the adoption or enforcement by any contracting party of measures:
    (a) necessary to protect public morals;
    (b) necessary to protect human, animal or plant life or health;
    (c) relating to the importations or exportations of gold or silver;
    (d) necessary to secure compliance with laws or regulations which are not inconsistent with the provisions of this Agreement, including those relating to customs enforcement, the enforcement of monopolies operated under paragraph 4 of Article II and Article XVII, the protection of patents, trade marks and copyrights, and the prevention of deceptive practices;
    (e) relating to the products of prison labour;
    (f) imposed for the protection of national treasures of artistic, historic or archaeological value;
    (g) relating to the conservation of exhaustible natural resources if such measures are made effective in conjunction with restrictions on domestic production or consumption;
    (h) undertaken in pursuance of obligations under any intergovernmental commodity agreement which conforms to criteria submitted to the CONTRACTING PARTIES and not disapproved by them or which is itself so submitted and not so disapproved;
    (i) involving restrictions on exports of domestic materials necessary to ensure essential quantities of such materials to a domestic processing industry during periods when the domestic price of such materials is held below the world price as part of a governmental stabilization plan; *Provided* that such restrictions shall not operate to increase the exports of or the protection afforded to such domestic industry, and shall not depart from the provisions of this Agreement relating to non-discrimination;
    (j) essential to the acquisition or distribution of products in general or local short supply; *Provided* that any such measures shall be consistent with the principle that all contracting parties are entitled to an equitable share of the international supply of such products, and that any such measures, which are inconsistent with the other provisions of the Agreement shall be discontinued as soon as the conditions giving rise to them have ceased to exist. The CONTRACTING PARTIES shall review the need for this sub-paragraph not later than 30 June 1960.'
    Art. XIV, GATS, headed 'General Exceptions' reads:
    'Subject to the requirement that such measures are not applied in a manner which would constitute a means of arbitrary or unjustifiable discrimination between countries where like conditions prevail, or a disguised restriction on trade in services, nothing in this Agreement shall be construed to prevent the adoption or enforcement by any Member of measures:
    (a) necessary to protect public morals or to maintain public order;
    (b) necessary to protect human, animal or plant life or health;

jurisprudence on Article XX, in which panels adopted restrictive interpretations of Article XX based on panels' views of the object and purpose of the GATT. In *United States – Import Prohibition of Certain Shrimp and Shrimp Products*, the Appellate Body criticized the approach of the panel in excluding certain measures *a priori* from the scope of the Article XX exceptions, stating:

> The consequences of the interpretive approach adopted by the Panel are apparent in its findings. The Panel formulated a broad standard and a test for appraising measures sought to be justified under the chapeau; it is a standard or a test that finds no basis either in the text of the chapeau or in that of either of the two specific exceptions claimed by the United States. The Panel, in effect, constructed an *a priori* test that purports to define a category of measures which, *ratione materiae*, fall outside the justifying protection of Article XX's chapeau.[23]

The Appellate Body's general exceptions jurisprudence highlights that an exception is another treaty provision that should be interpreted in accordance with its terms, its context and in light of the object and purpose of the treaty – the ordinary rules of treaty interpretation – and not by the sole application of presumptions of restrictive interpretation one way or the other. As discussed below, rather than formalistic approaches of either restrictive or wide interpretation, in construing the meaning of 'necessary' for the purposes of the general exceptions in the GATT,the WTO Appellate Body has adopted a weighing and balancing analysis. This is arguably more in keeping with the need to balance the right of a treaty party to invoke an express exception, with ensuring the host state respects its treaty obligations.

The decision in *United Parcel Service of America Inc. v. Canada*[24] reflects this approach to the interpretation of exceptions – one that does not apply

---

    (c) necessary to secure compliance with laws or regulations which are not inconsistent with the provisions of this Agreement including those relating to:

        (i) the prevention of deceptive and fraudulent practices or to deal with the effects of a default on services contracts;

        (ii) the protection of the privacy of individuals in relation to the processing and dissemination of personal data and the protection of confidentiality of individual records and accounts;

        (iii) safety;

    (d) inconsistent with Article XVII, provided that the difference in treatment is aimed at ensuring the equitable or effective imposition or collection of direct taxes in respect of services or service suppliers of other Members;

    (e) inconsistent with Article II, provided that the difference in treatment is the result of an agreement on the avoidance of double taxation or provisions on the avoidance of double taxation in any other international agreement or arrangement by which the Member is bound.'

23.   *United States – Import Prohibition of Certain Shrimp and Shrimp Products*, WT/DS58/AB/R (adopted 6 Nov. 1998) at para. 121. The term 'chapeau' refers to the introductory part of Art. XX, GATT, providing that measures are not to be applied in a manner that would constitute a means of arbitrary or unjustifiable discrimination.

24.   *United Parcel Service of America v. Canada* (Award on the Merits, 24 May 2007) [*UPS*].

presumptions as to whether an exception to treaty obligations should be interpreted restrictively or broadly. The majority of the tribunal found that a Canadian
publications assistance program (PAP) providing postal subsidies through the
national mail service, Canada Post, to Canadian periodical publishers, fell within
the *North American Free Trade Agreement's* (NAFTA's) exceptions for measures
adopted or maintained with respect to cultural industries.[25] UPS had argued that
the cultural industries exception applied only to the cultural industries themselves
and not to delivery mechanisms. For the majority of the tribunal, however, the
language of the exception was expansive and only required that the measures were
in connection with cultural industries.[26] The tribunal accepted that the
measures at issue were rationally and intrinsically connected to assisting the
Canadian publishing industry. In particular, Canada Post was the only entity in
Canada capable of universal delivery and could do so at the least cost, thus benefiting publishers. In addition, the term cultural industries was defined to include the
distribution of periodicals, the exact aim of the PAP. In a separate statement, one
of the arbitrators found that the exception did not apply because there was no
'necessary basis connected with a cultural industry that requires Canada to structure the subsidy in the way it has chosen.'[27] In other words, there was no rational
connection between the protection of cultural industries and the exclusive use of
Canada Post as a delivery mechanism.[28] Both the majority's reasoning and that of
the separate statement exemplify a rigorous approach to the interpretation of an
IIA exception based on its text, object and purpose to elucidate whether it would
cover the measure in question.

II   SECURITY EXCEPTIONS

§10.4 Treaty practice   Most IIAs do not contain express exceptions for measures necessary for national security or the protection of essential security interests
(security exceptions).[29] The US, however, has a consistent practice of including

25. Art. 2106 and Annex 2106, NAFTA, incorporate, as between Canada and the US an exception
     for any measure adopted or maintained with respect to cultural industries. See *supra* Chapter
     4, §4.14 *et seq.*, for discussion of UPS's national treatment claim.
26. *UPS, supra* note 24 at paras 165-172.
27. *UPS Cass Separate Statement, supra* note 17 at para. 148.
28. *Ibid.*, at para. 148.
29. Austrian, Dutch, French, Swedish, Swiss, and UK BITs do not contain essential security inter-
     est exceptions. The 2003 Canadian Model BIT includes an essential security interest exception.
     Peruvian BITs with Bolivia and Paraguay also provide for general exceptions. For instance,
     Art. 3(5), Bolivia-Peru (1993), states that '[n]othing in this Treaty shall prevent a Contracting
     Party from adopting measures, if not discriminatory, for reasons of internal and external
     national security, public or moral order.' For a survey of treaty practice, see Burke-White & Von
     Standen, *supra* note 11 and the three comprehensive studies: United Nations Centre on
     Transnational Corporations (UNCTC), *Bilateral Investment Treaties* (New York: United
     Nations, 1988) (Doc. No. ST/CTC/65); UNCTAD, *Bilateral Investment Treaties in the Mid-
     1990s* (New York and Geneva: United Nations, 1998) (Doc. No. UNCTAD/ITE/IIT/7) and

essential security interest exceptions in its BITs,[30] and similar provisions occur in the BITs of some other states.[31] In addition, more recent Canadian BITs also incorporate an express security exception.[32] In BITs based on the 1992 US Model BIT, the exception reads:[33]

> This Treaty shall not preclude the application by either Party of measures necessary for the maintenance of public order, the fulfillment of its obligations with respect to the maintenance or restoration of international peace or security, or the protection of its own essential security interests.[34]

The 2004 US Model BIT, which serves as model for US-Uruguay (2005), has a slightly reformulated essential security interests provision:

> Nothing in this Treaty shall be construed:
>
> 1. to require a Party to furnish or allow access to any information the disclosure of which it determines to be contrary to its essential security interests; or
> 2. to preclude a Party from applying measures *that it considers necessary* for the fulfillment of its obligations with respect to the maintenance or restoration of international peace or security, or the protection of its own essential security interests.[35] [Emphasis added.]

UNCTAD, *Bilateral Investment Treaties 1995-2006* (New York and Geneva: United Nations, 2007) (Doc. No. UNCTAD/ITE/IIT/2006/5).

30. K.J. Vandevelde, *United States Investment Treaties: Policy and Practice* (Boston: Kluwer Law and Taxation, 1992) at 222-227.

31. Indian BITs usually include an essential security interests provision within the article on applicable law. For example, Art. 12(2), India-Sweden (2000), provides: 'Notwithstanding Paragraph 1) of this Article nothing in this Agreement precludes the host Contracting Party from taking action necessary for the protection of its essential security interests or in circumstances of extreme emergency in accordance with its laws normally and reasonably applied on a non-discriminatory basis.' See also Art. 11, India-UK (1994).

32. Canadian BITs based on the OECD model or the investment chapter of NAFTA do not have exceptions for national security. However, the 2003 Canadian Model BIT contains national security provisions that closely track the language of GATT Article XXI (National Security). The only difference is that the reference to 'relating to fissionable materials or the materials from which they are derived' in Art. XXI, GATT, is deleted and replaced with 'relating to the implementation of national policies or international agreements respecting the non-proliferation of nuclear weapons or other nuclear explosive devices.'

33. The 1992 US Model is reproduced in R. Dolzer & M. Stevens, *Bilateral Investment Treaties* (The Hague: Kluwer, 1995) at 240.

34. This clause is present in, amongst others, Albania-US (1995); Argentina-US (1991); Azerbaijan-US (1998); Bahrain-US (1999); El Salvador-US (1999); Estonia-US (1994); Congo-US (1990); Croatia-US (1996); Haiti-US (1983); and Morocco-US (1985). The BITs concluded with Egypt in 1982 and Cameroon in 1986 also include an exception for public morals.

35. Other examples in US agreements include Art. 22.2, US-Peru Trade Promotion Agreement (2006); Art. 22.2, US-Colombia (2006); Art. 23.2, US-Chile (2003); and Art. 21.2, US-CAFTA-DR FTA (2004).

As discussed below, a key difference between these two provisions is that the 2004 Model uses the phrase 'that it considers necessary' (an expression that can be found already in some pre-2004 US BITs, such as Russia-US (1992)). This language suggests that whether the exceptions clause applies or not is a self-judging determination.

Security exceptions are more common in plurilateral and multilateral agreements, including the NAFTA and the *Energy Charter Treaty* (ECT).[36] Article 24(3), ECT, provides:

> The provisions of this Treaty other than those referred to in paragraph (1) shall not be construed to prevent any Contracting Party from taking any measure which it considers necessary:
>
> (a) for the protection of its essential security interests including those
>   (i) relating to the supply of Energy Materials and Products to a military establishment; or
>   (ii) taken in time of war, armed conflict or other emergency in international relations;
> (b) relating to the implementation of national policies respecting the non-proliferation of nuclear weapons or other nuclear explosive devices or needed to fulfil its obligations under the Treaty on the Non-Proliferation of Nuclear Weapons, the Nuclear Suppliers Guidelines, and other international nuclear non-proliferation obligations or understandings; or
> (c) for the maintenance of public order.

Bilateral and regional free trade agreements (FTAs) also include security exceptions applicable to investment obligations.[37] These are placed directly into the investment chapter, as in the comprehensive security exception in the *India-Singapore Comprehensive Economic Co-operation Agreement* (India-Singapore CECA),[38] or, more commonly, included in a general chapter on exceptions

---

36. Art. 2102, NAFTA (National Security) applies to investment obligations, as do the essential security interests provisions of Art. 24, ECT (with the exception of Art. 12 (compensation for losses) and Art. 13 (expropriation)).
37. Art. 6.12, India-Singapore CECA (2005); Art. 21.3, Korea-Singapore FTA (2005); Art. 100, Chile-China FTA (2005); Art. 1602, Australia-Thailand FTA (2004); and Art. 22, FTA between the European Free Trade Association States and Lebanon (2004).
38. Article 6.12, headed 'Security Exceptions,' reads:

    '1. Nothing in this Chapter shall be construed:
        (a) to require a Party to furnish any information, the disclosure of which it considers contrary to its essential security interests; or
        (b) to prevent a Party from taking any action which it considers necessary for the protection of its essential security interests:
            (i) relating to fissionable and fusionable materials or the materials from which they are derived;
            (ii) in time of war or other emergency in international relations;
            (iii) relating to the production or supply of arms and ammunition; or

applicable to the entire agreement.[39] US FTAs also contain security exceptions with self-judging language similar to that of the 2004 US Model BIT.[40] Some other agreements incorporate Article XXI, GATT, *mutatis mutandis* together with the relevant interpretations under the WTO Agreements. A few agreements base their exception on Article XIV, GATS, which is similar to Article XXI, GATT, but includes a clause for the supply of services (in addition to goods and materials) in provisioning a military establishment.[41]

Three interpretive issues arise where an IIA has an express security exception. The most significant is the standard of review, and, in particular, whether the national security provision is self-judging. The second issue is the relationship between the security exception – an express exception to treaty obligations – and necessity as a ground for precluding responsibility under customary international law. The third issue is the scope of the security exception. Each of these issues is discussed in turn below.

       (iv) to protect critical public infrastructures, including communication, power and water infrastructures, from deliberate attempts intended to disable or degrade such infrastructures; or

    (c) to prevent a Party from taking any action in pursuance of its obligations under the United Nations Charter for the maintenance of international peace and security.

2. Nothing in this Chapter shall be construed to require a Party to accord the benefits of this chapter to an investor that is an enterprise of the other Party where a Party adopts or maintains measures in any legislation or regulations which it considers necessary for the protection of its essential security interests with respect to a non-Party or an investor of a non-Party that would be violated or circumvented if the benefits of this Chapter were accorded to such an enterprise or to its investments.

3. Paragraph 2 shall be interpreted in accordance with the understanding of the Parties on security exceptions as set out in their exchange of letters, which shall form an integral part of this Agreement.

4. This Article shall be interpreted in accordance with the understanding of the Parties on non-justiciability of security exceptions as set out in their exchange of letters, which shall form an integral part of this Agreement.'

39. See *Japan-Malaysia Economic Partnership Agreement* (2005); Korea-Singapore FTA (2005); Chile-China FTA (2005); Art. 169, *Japan-Mexico Economic Partnership Agreement* (2004); Art. 22, FTA between the European Free Trade Association States and Lebanon (2004); *Japan-Singapore Economic Partnership Agreement* (2002); and NAFTA.

40. See Art. 22.2, Australia (2004); Art. 21.2, Morocco (2004); and Art. 21.2, Singapore (2003). The Moroccan FTA adds an interpretive clause, which provides: 'For greater certainty, measures that a Party considers necessary for the protection of its own essential security interests may include, *inter alia*, measures relating to the production of or traffic in arms, ammunition, and implements of war and to such traffic and transactions in other goods, materials, services, and technology undertaken directly or indirectly for the purpose of supplying a military or other security establishment.' An exception to the usual US practice can be found in the *Agreement between the United States of America and the Hashemite Kingdom of Jordan on the Establishment of a Free Trade Area* (2000), Art. 12, which is closely modelled on Art. XXI, GATT.

41. Art. 21.3, Korea-Singapore FTA (2005); Art. 169, *Japan-Mexico Economic Partnership Agreement* (2004); and Art. XIV(2), Canada-Costa Rica (2001).

§10.5 Is the security exception self-judging?   In international case law a distinction is made between self-judging and non-self-judging security exceptions.[42] One of the best known security exceptions is Article XXI, GATT. Article XXI(b), provides, in part, that a WTO member is not prevented from:

> ... taking any action *which it considers necessary* for the protection of its essential security interests:

> (i)   relating to fissionable materials or the materials from which they are derived;
> (ii) relating to the traffic in arms, ammunition and implements of war and to such traffic in other goods and materials as is carried on directly or indirectly for the purpose of supplying a military establishment;
> (iii) taken in time of war or other emergency in international relations; ... [Emphasis added.]

No GATT or WTO panel has made a definitive interpretation of this provision and there is disagreement amongst commentators over whether the application of the exception is completely self-judging – and thus within the unilateral, subjective determination of the state – or whether the exception also has an objective content because essential security interests are defined in paras (i) to (iii) making the invocation of the exception subject to objective limits.[43] In any case, even if a tribunal finds that the state is empowered to determine whether a measure is necessary, state invocation of the exception would still be subject to the overriding obligation to perform the treaty in good faith.[44]

In a number of awards, IIA tribunals have addressed whether the security exception in Article XI, Argentina-US (1991), is self-judging.[45] This provision reads:

> This Treaty shall not preclude the application by either Party of measures necessary for the maintenance of public order, the fulfillment of its obligations with respect to the maintenance or restoration of international peace or security, or the protection of its own essential security interests.

---

42.   The International Court of Justice has considered security exceptions in *Military and Paramilitary Activities in and against Nicaragua (Nicaragua v. US)* [1986] ICJ Rep 14 [*Nicaragua*] at paras 222 and 280-282; and *Oil Platforms (Iran v. US)* [2003] ICJ Rep 161 [*Oil Platforms*] at paras 32-43 and 73-78.

43.   See M. Matsushita, T. Schoenbaum & P. Mavriodis, *The World Trade Organization: Law, Practice, and Policy*, 2nd edn (Oxford: Oxford University Press, 2006), at 594-598. See also D. Akande & S. Williams, 'International Adjudication on National Security Issues: What Role for the WTO?' (2003) 43 VJIL 365.

44.   Art. 26, Vienna Convention, *supra* note 7.

45.   *CMS Gas Transmission Company v. Argentina* (Award, 12 May 2005) [*CMS*]; *LG&E Energy Corp., LG&E Capital Corp., and LG&E International, Inc. v. Argentina* (Decision on Liability, 3 Oct. 2006) [*LG&E*]; *Enron, supra* note 20; and S*empra Energy International v. Argentina* (Award, 28 Sep. 2007) [*Sempra*].

IIA tribunals have agreed that this provision is not self-judging,[46] noting that it does not include GATT-like self-judging language (i.e. does not contain the expression 'which it considers necessary' slotted between 'measures' and 'necessary' in the above provision), and that international authorities confirm that the self-judging character of a treaty provision must be clear in order to have the exceptional effect of excluding review.[47] The absence of explicit 'which it considers' language was the basis for the International Court Justice's (ICJ's) decision denying the self-judging nature of a security exception clause in the *Nicaragua* case. The US had relied on the essential security clause in the 1956 Nicaragua-US *Treaty of Friendship, Commerce and Navigation* (FCN Treaty) against Nicaragua's claims that the US had breached the treaty by engaging in military and paramilitary activities in the territory of Nicaragua. Comparing the FCN Treaty's security clause and Article XXI, GATT, the ICJ found as follows:

> Article XXI [of the FCN Treaty] defines the instances in which the Treaty itself provides for exceptions to the generality of its other provisions, but it by no means removes the interpretation and application of that article from the jurisdiction of the Court ... . The text of Article XXI of the Treaty does not employ the wording which was already to be found in Article XXI of the General Agreement on Tariffs and Trade. This provision of GATT, contemplating exceptions to the normal implementation of the General Agreement, stipulates that the Agreement is not to be construed to prevent any contracting party from taking any action which it 'considers necessary for the protection of its essential security interests,' in such fields as nuclear fission, arms, etc. *The 1956 Treaty, on the contrary, speaks simply of 'necessary' measures, not of those considered by a party to be such.*[48] [Emphasis added.]

Further, IIA tribunals have rejected Argentina's argument that the US congressional record regarding US Senate discussions on US BIT negotiations in the 1990s was in any way conclusive in demonstrating the US intention that essential security clauses should always be considered self-judging.[49] In light of the 1986 ICJ *Nicaragua* judgment, the US (and Argentina) would probably have included that express language in the 1991 BIT had they really wanted the clause to be self-judging. Importantly, Argentina apparently provided no evidence that the self-judging issue was even discussed during the BIT negotiations, much less that it was

---

46. *CMS, ibid.*, at paras 366-373; *LG&E, ibid.*, at para. 212; *Enron, ibid.*, at paras 322-342; and *Sempra, ibid.*, at paras 364-391.
47. *Enron, ibid.*, at para. 336 and *Sempra, ibid.*, at para. 383, referring to Art. XXI, GATT; *Gabčíkovo-Nagymaros Project (Hungary v. Slovakia)* [1997] ICJ Rep 7 at paras 51-52; *Nicaragua, supra* note 42 and also Decision on Jurisdiction and Admissibility [1984] ICJ Rep 392 at para. 83; and *Oil Platforms, supra* note 42 at para. 43. The *LG&E* tribunal, *supra* note 45 at para. 213, grounds its conclusion on the fact that the US did not consider national security provisions to be self-judging until the ratification of Russia-US (1992). The Russia-US BIT, dated 17 Jun. 1992, provides for express self-judging language in para. 8 of the Protocol.
48. *Nicaragua, supra* note 42 at para. 222.
49. *CMS, supra* note 45 at para. 369; and *Enron, supra* note 20 at para. 335.

agreed to by Argentina.[50] In 1993, Kenneth Vandevelde, the US chief BIT negotiator in the 1980s, wrote on US BIT policy in the late 1980s and early 1990s and
noted that 'there was no public record that any US BIT-partner ever had been
informed that the United Sates regarded the essential security interests exception
as self-judging.'[51] Considering the rejection of the US position in *Nicaragua*, 'US
BIT-partners may well have concluded that the United States had abandoned its
claim that the essential security interests exception was self-judging.'[52]

In *Sempra,* Argentina sought to rely on a letter from an official of the US
Department of State to a former official authorizing him to testify on this self-
judging issue in another arbitration, and which stated in passing that the US
regarded security exceptions as self-judging. The tribunal accorded no probative
value to that letter: it did not record or demonstrate the agreement of the BIT-
partners on this issue at the time of signature of the treaty, nor could it be given
effect as a successive amendment of the BIT depriving treaty beneficiaries or
rights acquired under the BIT.[53]

To date, IIA tribunals have thus upheld their competence to fully review
whether the criteria for successfully invoking the security exception have been
met, without being limited to a good faith analysis.[54]

Even where the security exception is self-judging, as in the 2003 US and 2004
Canadian Model BITs, a state must still act in good faith.[55] This flows from the
fundamental obligation of *pacta sunt servanda* in Article 27, Vienna Convention,
and the duty to perform a treaty in good faith enshrined in Article 26, Vienna
Convention.[56] In *LG&E*, the tribunal suggested that a good faith review is not
significantly different from a substantive analysis as to whether the state has complied with the requirements of the exception.[57] This approach would seem to
conflate the issue of whether the state has acted in good faith in responding to a
crisis with regard to its investment protection obligations (which a tribunal could
review) with an assessment of whether the specific requirements for invoking the
exception have been met (which would be self-judging). Further, it would appear
to deprive self-judging language of *effet utile*. More consistent with this principle
is the approach taken in *Enron*, where the tribunal noted that good faith and full
substantive examination are different standards of review.[58]

Some treaties go one step further and provide expressly that security exceptions are non-justiciable, thereby seeking to avoid uncertainties as to the

---

50. *Sempra, supra* note 45 at para. 385.
51. K.J. Vandevelde, 'Of Politics and Markets: The Shifting Ideology of the BITs' (1993) 11 ITBL
     159 at 173.
52. *Ibid.,* at 175.
53. See *supra* Chapter 2, §2.30.
54. *Enron, supra* note 20 at para. 339.
55. *LG&E, supra* note 45 at para. 214; and Vandevelde, *supra* note 51 at 176.
56. Art. 26, Vienna Convention, provides: 'Every treaty in force is binding upon the parties to it
     and must be performed by them in good faith.'
57. *LG&E, supra* note 45 at para. 214.
58. *Enron, supra* note 20 at para. 339.

application of self-judging language. The exchange of letters contemplated in Article 6.12(4), India-Singapore CECA (2005), provides that:

> any decision of the disputing Party taken on such security considerations shall be non-justiciable in that it shall not be open to any arbitral tribunal to review the merits of any such decision, even where the arbitral proceedings concern an assessment of any claim for damages and/or compensation, or an adjudication of any other issues referred to the tribunal.[59]

This express language on non-justiciability would seem to make state invocation of the security exception completely immune from arbitral review, even with regard to whether it was made in good faith.

§10.6 Exception or excuse – the relationship between security exceptions and necessity In a series of IIA claims under Argentina-US (1991), Argentina has defended its measures on the basis of both the BIT's essential security interests exception and necessity under customary international law. The relationship between these two grounds of defence has not been addressed with clarity in the case law.

In *CMS, Enron* and *Sempra*, IIA tribunals applied the test of necessity in customary international law to the essential security clause of Article XI, Argentina-US (1991). For example, in *CMS*, after concluding that Article XI is not self-judging, the tribunal did not proceed to carry out a substantive examination on whether the measures complained of could be justified under that clause, apparently considering that this was already covered by the substantive examination of the customary defence of necessity.[60] Arguably, the tribunal's approach was motivated by the party's pleadings, and in particular Argentina's failure to make submissions on the substantive content of Article XI, as distinct from the customary defence of necessity and in fact conflating the two issues.[61] In *Enron*, the tribunal was more explicit in holding that since 'essential security interests' is not defined, the term takes its meaning by reference to the doctrine of necessity in customary international law.[62] According to the tribunal: 'The Treaty thus becomes inseparable from the customary law standard insofar as the conditions for the operation of state of necessity are concerned.'[63] Thus, it found that Article XI does not set out conditions different from customary law.[64] The

---

59. Art. 6.12(4) provides: 'This Article shall be interpreted in accordance with the understanding of the Parties on non-justiciability of security exceptions as set out in their exchange of letters, which shall form an integral part of this Agreement.'
60. *CMS, supra* note 45 at paras 373-374.
61. *CMS Gas Transmission Company v. Argentina* (Decision of the *Ad Hoc* Committee on the Application for Annulment of the Argentine Republic, 25 Sep. 2007) [*CMS Annulment*] at paras 122-127.
62. *Enron, supra* note 20 at para. 333.
63. *Ibid.*, at para. 334.
64. *Ibid.*, at para. 339.

tribunal in *Sempra* came to a similar conclusion.[65] In *LG&E*, the tribunal, having found that Article XI applied, stated that its conclusion was supported by the fact that Argentina satisfied the conditions for necessity under Article 25 of the ILC's Articles on State Responsibility, albeit for a limited time period.[66]

The International Centre for Settlement of Investment Dispute (ICSID) *ad hoc* committee (Committee) in *CMS* took issue with the analysis in the *CMS* award. It regretted that the *CMS* tribunal had not been 'more explicit in specifying, for instance, that the very same reasons which disqualified Argentina from relying on the general law of necessity meant that the measures it took could not be considered "necessary" for the purpose of Article XI either.' But the Committee was even more critical of the merits of the tribunal's assimilation of the Article XI and necessity analyses.[67] According to the Committee, the tribunal erred in not appreciating the conceptual difference between Article XI, an express exception to a treaty obligation, and necessity, a defence that precludes wrongfulness or responsibility. As set out by the Committee:

> Art. XI is a threshold requirement: if it applies, the substantive obligations under the Treaty do not apply. By contrast, Article 25 is an excuse which is only relevant once it has been decided that there has otherwise been a breach of those substantive obligations.[68]

The error committed by the tribunal was further explained by the Committee as follows:

> If state of necessity means that there has not been even a *prima facie* breach of the BIT, it would be, to use the terminology of the ILC, a primary rule of international law. But this is also the case with Article XI. In other terms, [...] if the Tribunal was satisfied by the arguments based on Article XI, it should have held that there had been 'no breach' of the BIT. Article XI and Article 25 thus construed would cover the same field and the Tribunal should have applied Article XI as the lex specialis governing the matter and not Article 25.
>
> If, on the contrary, state of necessity in customary international law goes to the issue of responsibility, it would be a secondary rule of international law – and this was the position taken by the ILC. In this case, the Tribunal would have been under an obligation to consider first whether there had been any breach of the BIT and whether such a breach was excluded by Article XI. Only if it concluded that there was conduct not in conformity with the Treaty would it have had to consider whether Argentina's responsibility could be precluded in whole or in part under customary international law.[69]

---

65. *Sempra, supra* note 45 at paras 375-378.
66. *LG&E, supra* note 45 at paras 245-258. ILC's Articles on State Responsibility, *supra* note 12.
67. *CMS Annulment, supra* note 61 at para. 130.
68. *Ibid.*, at para. 129.
69. *Ibid.*, at paras 133-134.

The Committee's analysis highlights that the proper interpretive approach would have been first to consider whether the IIA breach was excluded by the express exception in Article XI. If the answer was negative, and if conduct was thus not in conformity with the treaty, only then should the tribunal have determined if responsibility could be precluded in whole or part under customary international law. The Committee's approach is consistent with the proper role of exceptions and reservations to IIA obligations: if these exceptions are applicable in the circumstances of a given case, the question of breach of the IIA simply does not arise. It is only where a breach of the IIA is deemed to exist (having considered IIA obligations and their exceptions) that preclusion of responsibility under customary international law, for example necessity, becomes an issue.

The distinction between an express, treaty-based exception, and an excuse to state responsibility has important implications with respect to remedies. As the Committee highlights:

> Article XI, if and for so long as it applied, excluded the operation of the substantive provisions of the BIT. That being so, there could be no possibility of compensation being payable during that period.[70]

Partly for this reason, the Committee found that the application of Article 27, ILC's Articles on State Responsibility, by the *CMS* tribunal was another 'manifest error of law.'[71]

§10.7 The scope of the security exception   Treaty practice varies on the scope of security exceptions. Provisions based on Article XXI, GATT, include exceptions for disclosure of information and taking action pursuant to UN Charter obligations for the maintenance of international peace and security.[72] Unlike in US practice, however, these provisions typically provide an exhaustive list of what amounts to an essential security interest, which is defined as measures relating to non-proliferation of nuclear materials, traffic in arms, and war or other emergency in international relations. The reference to 'other emergency' arguably permits the broadening of essential security to catastrophic events beyond those associated with war or insurgency. However, the term is modified by the requirement that it be an emergency in 'international relations.' Emergencies with purely local effects would not appear to meet this requirement.

In contrast, the essential security interest provision in US BITs is undefined. IIA tribunals that have considered the essential security interests provision in Article XI, Argentina-US (1991), have agreed that the provision is, in principle,

---

70. *Ibid.*, at para. 146. ILC's Articles on State Responsibility, *supra* note 12.
71. *Ibid.* See *infra* §10.23 and §10.24 on Art. 27, ILC's Articles on State Responsibility.
72. See, for example, Art. 10(4), Canada-Peru (2006): '(i) relating to the traffic in arms, ammunition and implements of war and to such traffic and transactions in other goods, materials, services and technology undertaken directly or indirectly for the purpose of supplying a military or other security establishment, (ii) taken in time of war or other emergency in international relations, or (iii) relating to the implementation of national policies or international agreements respecting the non-proliferation of nuclear weapons or other nuclear explosive devices.'

broad enough in scope to include economic emergencies,[73] but have come to differing conclusions as to the degree of severity required to legitimately invoke the exception. In *CMS*, the tribunal expressly refused to limit the interpretation of 'essential security interests' to political or national security concerns, noting that situations of economic crisis might indeed pose a threat to international peace and security. The determinative issue would be the scale of the crisis triggering the application of the article. In *CMS*, *Enron* and *Sempra*, the Argentine crisis was not considered of the catastrophic magnitude required for a successful plea of necessity (and thus also for a claim of essential security interests under Article XI); by the second quarter of 2002 the Argentine economy was already recovering with respect to the worst moments of the crisis in late December 2001-early January 2002.

Conversely, in *LG&E* the tribunal found that from 1 December 2001 to 26 April 2003 Argentina was in a crisis constituting 'the highest degree of public disorder,'[74] threatening 'total collapse of the Government and the Argentine State'[75] and necessitating the enactment of measures to maintain public order and to protect essential security interests.[76] The economic, social and political conditions were therefore severe enough to trigger the protection of Article XI, and thus excuse Argentina from liability under the IIA. The Tribunal rejected the claimant's contention that Article XI is only applicable in times of war or similar circumstances. It noted:

> To conclude that such a severe economic crisis could not constitute an essential security interest is to diminish the havoc that the economy can wreak on the lives of an entire population and the ability of the Government to lead. When a State's economic foundation is under siege, the severity of the problem can equal that of any military invasion.[77]

Beyond the analysis of whether economic hardship would come within essential security exceptions, to date, as stated in the previous section, tribunals have conflated the treaty requirement that the measures be 'necessary' for the maintenance of public order or the protection of its own essential security interests, with the criteria for a successful plea of necessity in customary international law as set out in Article 25, ILC's Articles on State Responsibility. The *CMS* Committee criticized the *CMS* award in this respect as follows:

> Furthermore Article XI and Article 25 are substantively different. The first covers measures necessary for the maintenance of public order or

---

73. *CMS*, *supra* note 45 at paras 359-365; *LG&E*, *supra* note 45 at para. 238; and *Enron*, *supra* note 20 at 232.
74. On 26 Apr. 2003, Nestor Kirchner was elected as President, which the tribunal apparently considered as representing the required stability for Argentina to be deemed as having overcome the threat to its essential security.
75. *LG&E*, *supra* note 45 at para. 231.
76. *Ibid.*, at para. 226.
77. *Ibid.*, at para. 238.

the protection of each Party's own essential security interest, without qualifying such measures. The second subordinates the state of necessity to four conditions. It requires for instance that the action taken 'does not seriously impair an essential interest of the State or States towards which the obligation exists, or of the international community as a whole,' a condition which is foreign to Article XI. In other terms the requirements under Article XI are not the same as those under customary international law as codified by Article 25....[78]

An alternative to relying on the customary international law of necessity would be to draw interpretive guidance on the meaning of 'necessary' under an essential security clause from international trade law jurisprudence, as IIA security and general exceptions are typically modelled very closely on the wording used in international trade agreements (see below §10.10).

§10.8 Distinction from the war and civil disturbance clause Most IIAs contain a clause commonly referred to as a 'war and civil disturbance' clause or a 'losses due to war' clause. These clauses are discussed at Chapter 6, §6.47, above. For example, Article IV(3), Argentina-US (1991), provides:

> Nationals or companies of either Party whose investments suffer losses in the territory of the other Party owing to war or other armed conflict, revolution, state of national emergency, insurrection, civil disturbance or other similar events shall be accorded treatment by such other Party no less favorable than that accorded to its own nationals or companies or to nationals or companies of any third country, whichever is the more favorable treatment, as regards any measures it adopts in relation to such losses.

Argentina sought to rely on this clause as a defence in *CMS*, *Enron* and *Sempra*, and its equivalent in Article 4, Argentina-UK (1990), in *BG Group Plc. v. Argentina*,[79] arguing that the measures complained of in those cases had been taken in a state of 'national emergency' and were thus exempted from BIT obligations except for the national and MFN treatment prescribed in those clauses. Tribunals have rejected this argument noting that this type of clause contains no exculpatory language. For example, in *CMS* the tribunal found that:

---

78. *CMS Annulment, supra* note 61 at para. 130. ILC's Articles on State Responsibility, *supra* note 12.
79. *BG Group Plc. v. Argentina* (Final Award, 24 Dec. 2007) [*BG*]. This clause reads: 'Investors of one Contracting Party whose investments in the territory of the other Contracting Party suffer losses owing to war or other armed conflict, revolution, a state of national emergency, revolt, insurrection or riot or resulting from arbitrary action by the authorities in the territory of the latter Contracting Party shall be accorded by the latter Contracting Party treatment, as regards restitution, indemnification, compensation or other settlement, no less favourable than that which the latter Contracting Party accords to its own investors or to investors of any third State. Resulting payments shall be freely transferable.'

The plain meaning of the Article [Article IV(3) Argentina-US (1991)] is to provide a floor treatment for the investor in the context of the measures adopted in respect of the losses suffered in the emergency, not different from that applied to nationals or other foreign investors. *The Article does not derogate from the Treaty rights but rather ensures that any measures directed at offsetting or minimizing losses will be applied in a non-discriminatory manner.*[80] [Emphasis added.]

This type of provision, therefore, does not create a ground for exemption from liability; rather, it ensures that when liability does not arise for another reason (for example, due to a successful plea of military necessity) the measures still give rise to a duty to compensate losses if compensation is provided to nationals or other foreign investors. Hence this type of clause is not an exception to IIA obligations and is distinguishable from essential security interests clauses, or other exceptions clauses. As to the scope of the subject matter of the clause, its drafting suggests that it applies to situations of physical threat to property due to armed conflict and insurrection of such proportions as to constitute an emergency, and thus to losses directly occasioned by forcible action in such situations,[81] rather than to regulatory measures. However, the tribunals in *Enron* and *Sempra* observed that the clause could also cover economic emergency measures.[82]

III   GENERAL EXCEPTIONS MODELLED ON ARTICLE XX GATT OR ARTICLE XIV GATS

§10.9 Treaty practice   The use of general exceptions clauses modelled on Article XX, GATT, or Article XIV, GATS, is not common in IIAs. Canada is unique amongst Organization for Economic Co-operation and Development (OECD) states in including the exceptions in its BITs.[83] Other OECD states do not have a comparable practice. In particular, the 2004 US Model BIT does not have a general exceptions clause, although, it has a widely drafted essential security interests exception.

Until the 2003 Canadian Model BIT was approved, the general exception provision in earlier BITs was drafted as follows:[84]

Provided that such measures are not applied in an arbitrary or unjustifiable manner, or do not constitute a disguised restriction on international trade

---

80. *CMS, supra* note 45 at para. 375. See also *Enron, supra* note 20 at paras 320-321; *Sempra, supra* note 45 at paras 362-363; and *BG, supra* note 79 at paras 381-387.
81. For the application of this clause in this context, see *Asian Agricultural Products Ltd. (AAPL) v. Sri Lanka* (Final Award, 27 Jun. 1990) [*AAPL*] at para. 70; and *American Manufacturing & Trading, Inc. v. Zaire* (Award, 21 Feb. 1997) at paras 3.04, and 6.04-6.14.
82. *Enron, supra* note 20 at para. 321; and *Sempra, supra* note 45 at 363.
83. There are Art. XX-like GATT general exceptions in over twenty Canadian BITs.
84. See Annex II, Art. 24, ECT.

or investment, nothing in this Agreement shall be construed to prevent a Contracting Party from adopting or maintaining measures, including environmental measures:

(a) necessary to ensure compliance with laws and regulations that are not inconsistent with the provisions of this Agreement;
(b) necessary to protect human, animal or plant life or health; or
(c) relating to the conservation of living or non-living exhaustible natural resources if such measures are made effective in conjunction with restrictions on domestic production or consumption.[85]

The clause from the 2003 Canadian Model (used word for word in Canada-Peru (2006)) reads as follows:

Article 10
General Exceptions

1. Subject to the requirement that such measures are not applied in a manner that would constitute arbitrary or unjustifiable discrimination between investments or between investors, or a disguised restriction on international trade or investment, nothing in this Agreement shall be construed to prevent a Party from adopting or enforcing measures necessary:

(a) to protect human, animal or plant life or health;
(b) to ensure compliance with laws and regulations that are not inconsistent with the provisions of this Agreement; or
(c) for the conservation of living or non-living exhaustible natural resources.

In contrast to BITs, where general exceptions are rare, some comprehensive bilateral FTAs, particularly those between Asian states, have begun making investment obligations subject to general exceptions.[86] For example, Article 83, *Japan-Singapore Economic Partnership Agreement* (2002), provides:

1. Subject to the requirement that such measures are not applied in a manner which would constitute a means of arbitrary or unjustifiable discrimination against the other Party, or a disguised restriction on investments of investors of a Party in the territory of the other Party, nothing in this Chapter shall be construed to prevent the adoption or enforcement by either Party of measures:

(a) necessary to protect public morals or to maintain public order;
(b) necessary to protect human, animal or plant life or health;

---

85. Canada-Thailand (1998) has a more extensive general exceptions provision that includes measures for the protection of national treasures.
86. See *Japan-Singapore Economic Partnership Agreement* (2002); *India-Singapore CECA* (2005); *Japan-Malaysia Economic Partnership Agreement* (2005); and *Korea-Singapore FTA* (2005).

(c) necessary to secure compliance with the laws or regulations which are not inconsistent with the provisions of this Agreement including those relating to:

(i)   the prevention of deceptive and fraudulent practices or to deal with the effects of a default on contract;

(ii)   the protection of the privacy of the individual in relation to the processing and dissemination of personal data and the protection of confidentiality of personal records and accounts;

(iii) safety;

(d) relating to prison labour;

(e) imposed for the protection of national treasures of artistic, historic, or archaeological value;

(f) to conserve exhaustible natural resources if such measures are made effective in conjunction with restrictions on domestic production or consumption.

Another approach is to incorporate Article XIV, GATS, in relation to investments. This approach is used in the Panama-Taiwan FTA.[87]

The China-New Zealand FTA (2008) incorporates both Article XX, GATT, and Article XIV, GATS:

Article 200 General Exceptions

1. For the purposes of this Agreement, Article XX of GATT 1994 and its interpretive notes and Article XIV of GATS (including its footnotes) are incorporated into and made part of this Agreement, mutatis mutandis.

2. The Parties understand that the measures referred to in Article XX(b) of GATT 1994 and Article XIV(b) of GATS, as incorporated into this Agreement, can include environmental measures necessary to protect human, animal or plant life or health, and Article XX(g) of GATT 1994, as incorporated into this Agreement, applies to measures relating to the conservation of living and non-living exhaustible natural resources, subject to the requirement that they are not applied in a manner which would constitute a means of arbitrary or unjustifiable discrimination or a disguised restriction on trade in goods or services or investment.

3. For the purposes of this Agreement, subject to the requirement that such measures are not applied in a manner which would constitute a means of arbitrary or unjustifiable discrimination between the Parties where like conditions prevail, or a disguised restriction on trade in goods or services or investment, nothing in this Agreement shall be construed to prevent the adoption or enforcement by a Party of measures necessary to protect national works or specific sites of historical or archaeological value, or to support creative arts of national value.

---

87.   Art. 20.02(2), Panama-Taiwan (2003).

4. Nothing in this Agreement shall prevent the Parties from taking any necessary measures to restrict the illicit import of cultural property from the other Party under the framework of the United Nations Educational, Scientific and Cultural Organization ('UNESCO') Convention on the Means of Prohibiting and Preventing the Illicit Import, Export and Transfer of Ownership of Cultural Property, done at Paris on 14 November 1970. [Footnote omitted.]

§10.10 The interpretation of general exceptions   GATT and GATS-like general exceptions in IIAs raise many interpretive issues that have not been addressed to date in IIA jurisprudence. At least three possible general approaches to the interpretation of general exceptions may be identified. The first approach would be that express general exceptions are intended to provide greater regulatory flexibility to host states in pursuing the specific legitimate objectives established in the exceptions. Since inclusion of GATT and GATS-like provisions in IIAs is quite exceptional, an *effet utile* interpretation would highlight the intention of the parties to provide more regulatory space for the host state to regulate than in traditional IIAs. The second approach would be to view the exceptions as codifying the qualifications to the scope of IIA obligations recognized in the existing jurisprudence. For example, in interpreting national treatment provisions, IIA tribunals have found that host states may differentiate between investments on the basis of rational policy objectives without breaching national treatment.[88] In this view, general exceptions would provide the tribunal with explicit guidance on how to balance investment protection obligations with the legitimate objectives.

Third, general exceptions might be interpreted restrictively as providing even less regulatory flexibility to host states.[89] For example, with respect to IIA national treatment jurisprudence, it has been argued that:

> In the investment context, the broad reference to investors 'in like circumstances' has consistently enabled tribunals to balance investor interests with an unlimited list of legitimate government concerns – a list far *broader* than the exceptions in GATT Article XX.[90]

Although IIA tribunals have been reluctant to rely on WTO jurisprudence in interpreting specific investment obligations, such as national treatment,[91] with regard

---

88. See *supra* Chapter 4, §4.18.
89. One of the reasons that the International Institute for Sustainable Development did not include a GATT Article XX-like general exceptions clause in its *Model international investment agreement for Sustainable Development* was apparently because of concern that, based on GATT Art. XX jurisprudence, general exceptions in IIAs may be interpreted too narrowly. See A. Cosbey, 'The Road to Hell? Investor Protections in NAFTA's Chapter Eleven' in L. Zarsky, ed., *International Investment for Sustainable Development: Balancing Rights and Rewards* (Sterling, VA: Earthscan, 2005).
90. See N. DiMascio & J. Pauwelyn, 'Nondiscrimination in Trade and Investment Treaties: Worlds Apart or Two Sides of the Same Coin' (2008) 102 AJIL 48 at 82-83.
91. See *Methanex Corporation v. United States* (Final Award of the Tribunal on Jurisdiction and Merits, 3 Aug. 2005).

to exceptions there is a much stronger case for drawing interpretive guidance from WTO general exceptions jurisprudence, since IIA general exceptions are modelled almost word for word on Article XX, GATT. In particular, IIA tribunals should consider applicable interpretive principles drawn from WTO jurisprudence on Article XX, GATT,[92] including:

- The burden of proof that a measure falls within the exception rests on the state invoking the exception.
- The analysis under a general exceptions provision is two-tiered: (i) justification under one of the enumerated exceptions; and (ii) a determination of conformity with the requirements in the proviso or chapeau (the requirement that measures not be applied in a manner that would constitute a means of arbitrary or unjustifiable discrimination). The first tier can be broken into two further steps: (i) does the measure fall within the range of objectives permitted by the exception; and (ii) does the measure satisfy the nexus requirement of 'necessary' or 'relating to' the objective in question.
- The meaning of 'necessary' can be situated on a continuum stretching from indispensable or of absolute necessity to a contribution to achieving the objective.
- Assessing whether a measure, which is not indispensable, may nevertheless be 'necessary' involves, in every case, a process of weighing and balancing a series of factors including: (i) the relative importance of the common interests or values that the measures are intended to protect; (ii) the contribution made by the measure to achievement of the objective; and (iii) the restrictiveness and impact of the measure. In this respect, in *Brazil-Tyres*, the Appellate Body noted:

> Another key element of the analysis of the necessity of a measure under Article XX(b) is the contribution it brings to the achievement of its objective. A contribution exists when there is a genuine relationship of ends and means between the objective pursued and the measure at issue. To be characterized as necessary, a measure does not have to be indispensable. However, its contribution to the achievement of the objective must be material, not merely marginal or insignificant, especially if the measure at issue is as trade restrictive as an import ban. Thus, the contribution of the measure has to be weighed against its trade restrictiveness, taking into account the importance of the interests or the values underlying the objective pursued by it.[93]

- The proviso or chapeau to the general exception is a manifestation of the principle of good faith and the prohibition of an abuse of rights. It serves to balance the right of a state to invoke the general exception and the duty of that same state to respect the treaty rights of the other members.

---

92. See *Brazil-Tyres, supra* note 17.
93. *Ibid.*, at para. 210.

A general exception is a limited and conditional exception and subject to compliance with the chapeau.

Assuming these general principles are applied to the interpretation of general exceptions in IIAs, it remains unclear whether general exceptions in fact provide greater regulatory flexibility for host state measures that affect foreign investment and investors. With respect to relative standards of treatment, IIA tribunals have held that where there is a legitimate policy rationale for differentiating investments, not motivated by protectionism, the investments are not in like circumstances.[94] In *S.D. Myers, Inc. v. Canada*, the tribunal found that, even if the NAFTA investment chapter had Article XX-like general exceptions, the ban on PCB exports could not be justified under the chapeau of Article XX given the tribunal's finding that the ban was motivated by protectionism of the domestic PCB industry.[95] The concurring opinion expressly notes that:

> Article 1102 (National Treatment) of NAFTA is not made subject to an equivalent of Article XX (General Exceptions) of GATT. *Read in its proper context, however, the phrase 'like circumstances' in Article 1102 in many cases does require the same kind of analysis as is required in Article XX cases under the GATT.* The determination of whether there is a denial of national treatment to investors or investments 'in like circumstances' under Article 1102 of NAFTA may require an examination of whether a government treated non-nationals differently in order to achieve a legitimate policy objective that could not reasonably be accomplished by other means that are less restrictive to open trade.[96] [Emphasis added.]

With respect to breaches of a minimum standard of treatment, it is also unclear in what circumstances general exceptions would apply. On its face, if state conduct breaches the minimum standard of treatment, then it is unlikely that the conduct would be able to meet the threshold for justifying the action under the general exception. The conduct in question would have to be: (i) necessary to meet one of the three enumerated exceptions (i.e. that there was no other alternative that would reasonable meet the policy objective); (ii) not have been applied in a manner that would constitute arbitrary or unjustifiable discrimination; and (iii) not constitute a disguised restriction on international trade or investment. If a measure could be justified under the stringent requirements of a general exception provision, it is difficult to envisage a situation where it would have violated minimum standards of treatment in the first place.

Finally, with respect to expropriation, even if a measure (such as the creation of a park) is necessary for the protection of the environment, the question is whether the general exception would be interpreted as excluding the requirement to pay compensation. It would be surprising if, by effect of general exceptions,

---

94. See *supra* Chapter 4, §4.18.
95. *S.D. Myers, Inc. v. Canada* (Partial Award, 13 Nov. 2000) at para. 298.
96. *Ibid.*, Separate Concurring Opinion, at para. 129.

parties to IIAs intended to provide less protection to foreign investors that that accorded under customary international law; thus if the exception does not prevent a finding of expropriation (because the measure is a direct expropriation) presumably it cannot exclude payment of compensation. The *Multilateral Agreement on Investment* (MAI) negotiations provide support for the view that general exceptions are not intended to exclude the obligation to pay compensation: Article VI, 'General Exceptions' of the draft MAI negotiating text, provides that it does not apply to Article IV, 2 and 3 (expropriation and compensation, and protection from strife). The commentary on the text notes that the 'majority view was that the MAI should provide an absolute guarantee that an investor will be compensated for an expropriated investment.'[97] Further, thegeneral exceptions in the ECT do not apply to expropriation and compensation for losses.

Arguably many IIA obligations, such as national treatment, have implied exceptions essentially similar to a general exceptions clause. From this perspective, the inclusion of an express general exception may simply make explicit what is implied and, in practice, may not provide any greater regulatory flexibility for host states. This does not mean that a general exceptions clause is necessarily irrelevant. General exceptions may provide useful guidance to tribunals and act as a safety net against overly broad interpretations. Hence, general exceptions may be an instance of abundance of caution motivated by the concern to assist IIA tribunals account for the existing international law limitations to IIA protections; they may mitigate the risk of an overly broad interpretation of IIA obligations in a given case, which cannot then be corrected or amended considering that arbitral decisions are not subject to appeal.

IV   SUBJECT MATTER AND OBLIGATION-SPECIFIC EXCEPTIONS

§10.11 Overview   Many IIAs have exceptions or reservations for certain types of measures or subject matters. The most common are exceptions and reservations for tax measures, grants and subsidies, government procurement and prudential measures for financial services. Each state tends to have specific sectors in which there are heightened concerns about foreign ownership. For example, in the NAFTA, Mexico took a broad reservation for the hydrocarbons sector and Canada for measures relating to cultural industries.

---

97. Commentary to the MAI Negotiating Text online: <http://www1.oecd.org/daf/mai/pdf/ng/ng988r1e.pdf>.

§10.12 Tax measures   Some IIAs provide a broad express exception for all taxation measures. For example, Article 5(2), Argentina-New Zealand (1999), provides:

> The provisions of this Agreement shall not apply to matters of taxation in the territory of either Contracting Party. Such matters shall be governed by the domestic laws of each Contracting Party and the terms of any agreement relating to taxation concluded between the Contracting Parties....[98]

On its face, this provision excludes all 'matters of taxation' but does not define this expression. An alternative approach is the 'qualified exclusion model' under which taxation matters are generally excluded but subject to a small number of specific exceptions.[99] This approach is used in the ECT, the NAFTA and some IIAs.[100] For, example, the NAFTA also has a general exception for taxation measures,[101] but provides that the prohibitions on performance requirements apply to taxation measures;[102] that national and MFN treatment standards apply to some taxes, including income, capital gains or the taxable capital of corporations;[103] and that the expropriation provisions apply to taxation measures.[104] Claims with respect to expropriatory taxation, however, are subject to special review and admissibility requirements.[105] The 2004 US Model BIT and the 2003 Canadian Model BIT follow this model of a general exception and a special procedure for claims of expropriatory taxation.[106] The Canadian BIT provides that a joint decision of the taxation authorities as to whether a measure is a taxation measure is binding on a

---

98.   Art. 5(2), Argentina-New Zealand (1999).
99.   See UNCTAD, *Taxation*, UNCTAD Series on issues in international investment agreements (New York and Geneva: United Nations, 2000) (UNCTAD/ITE/IIT/16) at 37-42.
100. For example, Art. 19, Japan-Vietnam (2003), provides that taxation measures are subject to national and MFN treatment, publication obligations, fair and equitable treatment and expropriation.
101. Art. 2103(1), NAFTA: 'Except as set out in this Article, nothing in this Agreement shall apply to taxation measures.'
102. Art. 2103(5).
103. Art. 2103(4).
104. Art. 2103(6).
105. Art. 2103(6) provides: 'Article 1110 (Expropriation and Compensation) shall apply to taxation measures except that no investor may invoke that Article as the basis for a claim under Article 1116 (Claim by an Investor of a Party on its Own Behalf) or 1117 (Claim by an Investor of a Party on Behalf of an Enterprise), where it has been determined pursuant to this paragraph that the measure is not an expropriation. The investor shall refer the issue of whether the measure is not an expropriation for a determination to the appropriate competent authorities set out in Annex 2103.6 at the time that it gives notice under Article 1119 (Notice of Intent to Submit a Claim to Arbitration). If the competent authorities do not agree to consider the issue or, having agreed to consider it, fail to agree that the measure is not an expropriation within a period of six months of such referral, the investor may submit its claim to arbitration under Article 1120 (Submission of a Claim to Arbitration).' For commentary, see W. Park, 'Expropriation and Taxation in the NAFTA,' in T. Weiler, ed., *Investment Law and Arbitration: Past Issues, Current Practice, Future Prospects* (Ardsley: Transnational, 2004), at 93.
106. See Art. 21, US-Uruguay (2005), and Art. 16, Canada-Peru (2006).

tribunal. In addition, most IIAs provide an express exception to MFN treatment for obligations under international tax conventions and free trade or customs union agreements.[107]

§10.13 Subsidies and government procurement IIAs, particularly those that provide for establishment rights,[108] often clarify that IIA obligations do not extend to government procurement and subsidies or grants. The NAFTA and US and Canadian BITs follow this approach, providing that national treatment obligations do not apply to government procurement or subsidies, or government grants including government-supported loans, guarantees and insurance.[109]

§10.14 Miscellaneous exceptions IIAs have various miscellaneous exceptions, including those that allow a party to adopt reasonable measures for the protection of stakeholders in the financial services industry and to ensure the integrity and stability of a party's financial system;[110] for non-discriminatory monetary and related credit policies;[111] for certain types of WTO consistent measures;[112] and non-disclosure of information that would impede law enforcement or be contrary to privacy and confidentiality laws.

§10.15 Exceptions or reservations for non-conforming measures IIAs with establishment rights (national and MFN treatment with respect to establishment of investments) tend to have extensive reservations to national and MFN treatment, performance requirements and obligations with respect to senior management and board of directors.[113] US and Canadian BIT practice is to have three separate annexes with reservations (Annex I for existing non-conforming measures, Annex II for future measures and Annex III limiting or clarifying the application of existing measures or obligations). These annexes describe, in detail, the sector and sub-sector in which the reservation is made, the specific measures for which the

---

107. See *supra* Chapter 5, §5.27.
108. See *supra* Chapter 3, §3.8 *et seq.*
109. Art. 1108(7), NAFTA. See Art. 5(6), US-Uruguay (2005), and Art. 9(5)(b), Canada-Peru (2006). See discussion of *ADF Group Inc. v. United States* (Award, 9 Jan. 2003) at §4.24 and *UPS, supra* note 24 at paras 121-136, interpreting the government procurement exception in NAFTA. Also see *UPS Cass Separate Statement, supra* note 17 at paras 64-80, dissenting on the procurement exception issue.
110. See Arts. 10.2, 14(6) and 17, Canada-Peru (2006).
111. Art. 10(3), Canada-Peru (2006).
112. *Ibid.*, at Art. 9(4) and 10(7).
113. In contrast, in US and Canadian practice, reservations are not made for minimum standards of treatment, including expropriation.

reservation is made and a description of the non-conforming aspects of the existing measures.

V   INTERPRETIVE GUIDELINES

§10.16 Express provisions on environmental measures   Some agreements, notably the NAFTA, have interpretive statements regarding environmental measures. Article 1114, NAFTA, provides:

> Nothing in this Chapter shall be construed to prevent a Party from adopting, maintaining or enforcing any measure otherwise consistent with this Chapter that it considers appropriate to ensure that investment activity in its territory is undertaken in a manner sensitive to environmental concerns.

This type of provision is tautological as it refers to 'any measure otherwise consistent with this Chapter.' The clause while arguably providing interpretive guidance, does not provide additional regulatory flexibility for environmental measures. At most it might serve as an interpretive presumption that non-discriminatory environmental measures made in good faith do not contravene investment obligations.

§10.17 Provisions on relaxation of standards   Some IIAs have express provisions that address concerns about a so-called regulatory 'race to the bottom' by expressly providing that investment should not be encouraged by relaxing health, safety or environmental measures. Article 11, Canada-Peru (2006), provides:

> The Parties recognize that it is inappropriate to encourage investment by relaxing domestic health, safety or environmental measures. Accordingly, a Party should not waive or otherwise derogate from, or offer to waive or otherwise derogate from, such measures as an encouragement for the establishment, acquisition, expansion or retention in its territory of an investment of an investor. If a Party considers that the other Party has offered such an encouragement, it may request consultations with the other Party and the two Parties shall consult with a view to avoiding any such encouragement.

This provision is a soft obligation, the breach of which results in consultations. The *Peru-US Trade Promotion Agreement* takes a more stringent approach and provides binding obligations with respect to the enforcement of environmental and labour laws.[114]

---

114.   Online: <http://ustr.gov/Trade_Agreements/Bilateral/Peru_TPA/Section_Index.html>.

VI   CIRCUMSTANCES PRECLUDING
            WRONGFULNESS IN CUSTOMARY
            INTERNATIONAL LAW

§10.18 Circumstances precluding wrongfulness   Six circumstances are recognized under customary international law as precluding wrongfulness for conduct that would otherwise breach an international obligation: consent, self-defence,[115] countermeasures,[116] *force majeure*, distress[117] and necessity. These pleas are codified in Chapter V, Circumstances Precluding Wrongfulness, in the ILC's Articles on State Responsibility.[118] Consent, *force majeure* and necessity are the most likely pleas to arise in the IIA context and are considered in more detail below.

§10.19 Consent and waiver   Wrongfulness is precluded under customary international law if a state has validly consented to the wrongful act of another state before the act occurs or while it is occurring, provided the act remains within the limits of state consent.[119] In contrast, consent given after the conduct has occurred is a form of waiver or acquiescence.[120] The commentary to the ILC's Articles on State Responsibility notes that a waiver may apply either to the breach of the treaty

---

115.   Art. 21, ILC's Articles on State Responsibility, *supra* note 12, provides: 'The wrongfulness of an act of a State is precluded if the act constitutes a lawful measure of self-defence taken in conformity with the Charter of the United Nations.' Where a foreign investor's property is requisitioned or destroyed as a result of an act of self-defence, the plea of necessity is likely to arise.

116.   Art. 22, *ibid.*, provides: 'The wrongfulness of an act of a State not in conformity with an international obligation towards another State is precluded if and to the extent that the act constitutes a countermeasure taken against the latter State in accordance with [Articles 49 to 54].' The issue of countermeasures might arise in the context of economic boycotts that apply on the basis of nationality. The issue of countermeasures has been considered in *Archer Daniels Midland Company and Tate & Lyle Ingredients Americas, Inc. v. Mexico* (Award, 21 Nov. 2007) [*Archer Daniels*].

117.   Art. 24, *ibid.*, provides:
       '1. The wrongfulness of an act of a State not in conformity with an international obligation of that State is precluded if the author of the act in question has no other reasonable way, in a situation of distress, of saving the author's life or the lives of other persons entrusted to the author's care.
       2. Paragraph 1 does not apply if:
          (*a*) the situation of distress is due, either alone or in combination with other factors, to the conduct of the State invoking it; or
          (*b*) the act in question is likely to create a comparable or greater peril.'
       Art. 24 might arise where state agents requisition the use of an investor's equipment in order to save human lives.

118.   *Supra* note 12.
119.   Art. 20, ILC's Articles on State Responsibility, *ibid.*
120.   Art. 45(a), *ibid.*

(the primary obligation) or the consequences of the breach in terms of state responsibility (the secondary obligation).[121]

Consent and waiver raise particularly difficult conceptual issues in the context of IIAs since investment promotion and protection treaty standards benefit third parties to the treaty – investors. The customary international law principles, as codified in Articles 20 and 45(a) of the ILC's Articles on State Responsibility, specifically apply to state consent and waiver and do not address whether an investor can consent or waive its rights in relation to a wrongful act.

Home states are very unlikely to consent to or waive rights regarding breaches of an IIA by a host state and therefore, practically, this issue is unlikely to arise. If a home state consented to or waived rights with regard to host state conduct adverse to the home state's interests, wrongfulness would be precluded at the inter-state level.

The more difficult conceptual issue, however, is the effect of any home state consent or waiver on an investor's claim. This depends on the response that is given to one of the thorniest conceptual questions that arises in connection with IIA rights: what is the nature of investment protection rights under an IIA? To whom are IIA obligations owed? Based on classic public international law concepts and the model of diplomatic protection,[122] it could be argued that investment protection obligations under the IIA are ultimately owed to the home state. Even though the investor is given a specific procedural right under the IIA to enforce the host state IIA obligations, its substantive rights to investment protection are derivative – they derive from the home state's rights (the derivative rights theory). This approach is arguably reflected in the statement by the NAFTA tribunal in *The Loewen Group, Inc. and Raymond L. Loewen v. United States*, in which the tribunal stated that under Chapter Eleven, 'claimants are permitted for convenience to enforce what are in origin the rights of Party States.'[123] Viewed in this perspective, the home state could be deemed entitled to consent to an IIA breach or waive an IIA claim and thus foreclose an investor's hope for redress.

However, the classic public international law approach is increasingly called into question, for the reality is that IIAs are 'couched in terms of a direct legal relationship between the host state and the foreign investor.'[124] Under IIAs,

---

121. Crawford, *supra* note 12 at 266.
122. See *supra* Chapter 1, §1.3 on diplomatic protection.
123. *The Loewen Group Inc. and Raymond L. Loewen v. United States* (Award, 26 Jun. 2003) at para. 233. See also *Archer Daniels, supra* note 116 at paras 168-180.
124. See Z. Douglas, 'Hybrid Foundations of Investment Treaty Arbitration' (2003) 74 BYIL 151 [Hybrid Foundations] at 183. See also Z. Douglas, 'Nothing if Not Critical for Investment Treaty Arbitration: *Occidental, Eureko* and *Methanex*' (2006) 22 AI 27 [Nothing if Not Critical] at 37; O. Spiermann, 'Individual Rights, State Interests and the Power to Waive ICSID Jurisdiction under Bilateral Investment Treaties' (2004) 20 AI 179; and C. McLachlan, L. Shore & M. Weiniger, *International Investment Arbitration: Substantive Principles* (Oxford: Oxford University Press, 2007), at 60-65.

investors have complete functional control over the IIA claim. Some IIAs contain fork in the road provisions under which, if an investor litigates in municipal courts, it waives its international arbitration rights, which suggests that it is the investor who manages its rights. Further, investors may bring claims without exhausting local remedies (a traditional requirement for diplomatic protection). In addition, compensation is based on the harm suffered by the investor and does not include any independent interest of the state.[125] In *Occidental Exploration & Production Company v. Ecuador*,[126] the English Court of Appeal approved the view that: 'The functional assumption underlying the investment treaty regime is clearly that the investor is bringing a cause of action based upon the vindication of its own rights rather than those of its national State.'[127] Hence the view has arisen that IIAs provide direct rights to investors 'either from the outset, or at least (and in this event retrospectively) as and when they pursue claims in one of the ways provided.'[128] The former view would accord with a direct rights approach; the latter means that the acquisition of direct rights by the investor is contingent upon its acceptance of the offer to arbitrate contained in the IIA. As a result of this acceptance, for example by filing the request for arbitration, a 'contract' between the investor and the state is created, consisting of the agreement to arbitrate a given dispute on the basis of the standards of treatment of the IIA.[129] At that point, the investor has in its own hands the right to have its dispute resolved on the basis of the IIA, which provides the 'adjudicative standards by which the host state's conduct is assessed in the treaty arbitration.'[130] Whether a strict direct rights approach or a more nuanced contingent rights theory is adopted, a rigid public international law perspective seems incompatible with a textual analysis of IIAs and the direct right of action of aggrieved investors against the host state. Further, international law itself recognizes that non-state entities can exercise legal rights.[131] In particular, in *LaGrand*, the ICJ confirmed that a treaty may create individual rights.[132] Viewed in this way, home state consent to an IIA breach or waiver of a claim would not affect the investor's independent right to make a claim.

Assuming the investor has direct rights, a further question arises. May an investor consent to a breach of, or waive, those rights? As a practical matter, it is unlikely that an investor would expressly consent to or dispense with minimum

---

125. Hybrid Foundations, *ibid.*, at 167-185.
126. *Occidental Exploration & Production Company v. Ecuador* [2006] QB 432.
127. *Ibid.*, at para. 450 citing Hybrid Foundations, *supra* note 124 at 182.
128. *Occidental, supra* note 126 at para. 18.
129. See Hybrid Foundations, *supra* note 124 at 183 and Nothing if Not Critical, *supra* note 124 at 37. See also J. Crawford, 'Treaty and Contract in Investment Arbitration' (2008) 5 TDM at 10-11.
130. Nothing if Not Critical, *ibid.*, at 37.
131. F. Orrego Vicuña, *International Dispute Settlement in an Evolving Global Society: Constitutionalization, Accessibility, Privatization* (Cambridge: Cambridge University Press, 2004), describing treaties that provide individuals and corporate entities direct access to international courts and tribunals.
132. *LaGrand (Germany v. US)* [2001] ICJ Rep 466 and (2001) 40 ILM 1069.

standards of protection or that a state would make this request. However, there could be instances of implicit or constructive consent or waiver; thus the issue may not be moot. In this regard, the following passage in *SGS Société Générale de Surveillance S.A. v. Philippines* is of interest:

> It is, to say the least, doubtful that a private party can by contract waive rights or dispense with the performance of obligations imposed on the States parties to those treaties under international law. Although under modern international law, treaties may confer rights, substantive and procedural, on individuals, they will normally do so in order to achieve some public interest.

This statement suggests that although the investor is the beneficiary, it cannot validly consent to a breach of substantive IIA rights or waive substantive procedural rights. As the tribunal emphasizes, there may be a more general public interest in ensuring the maintenance of minimum standards of protection. Similarly, it might be considered contrary to international public policy for an investor to consent to a breach of IIA obligations, such as due process, denial of justice or protections against arbitrary or discriminatory treatment. If the rights in question are peremptory norms of general international law, consent would not be a defence to wrongfulness.[133] The contingent rights approach outlined above may be another way to address this issue at least in relation to procedural rights. As put by Zachary Douglas:

> If, however, the second conception of the investor's right is adopted, then this intuitively disturbing possibility is avoided. The investor's procedural right to have the host state's conduct adjudged according to the investment treaty standards is only perfected upon the filing of a notice of arbitration. At that point the investor is free to waive its procedural right and this of course is common practice whenever an investment treaty claim is settled and withdrawn. The substantive obligations cannot be waived by the investor because they are not directly vested.[134]

It is unclear whether and, if so, when, under this contingent rights approach an investor could waive its contingent procedural right to arbitration. In principle, it may not be able to do so until the right arises by perfecting the arbitration agreement. However, if an investor were to expressly and explicitly waive its IIA right of action in advance in a contract, the argument could be made that the renunciation embodies an implicit acceptance of the offer to arbitrate, in order for the investor to acquire its contingent rights and then bargain them away in the contract

---

133. See Art. 26, ILC's Articles on State Responsibility, *supra* note 12. The passage quoted above is at *SGS Société Générale de Surveillance S.A. v. Philippines* (Decision of the Tribunal on Objections to Jurisdiction, 29 January 2004) at para. 154.
134. Nothing if Not Critical, *supra* note 124 at 37-38.

with the state.[135] Alternatively, an estoppel against the investor may arise if the investor were to bring an IIA claim.[136]

§10.20 *Force majeure*   *Force majeure* precludes wrongfulness where the act in question is due to an irresistible force or an unforeseen event, which is beyond the control of the state and which makes it materially impossible to perform the obligations. The customary international law elements of *force majeure* are codified in Article 24, ILC's Articles on State Responsibility, as follows:

1. The wrongfulness of an act of a State not in conformity with an international obligation of that State is precluded if the act is due to *force majeure*, that is the occurrence of an irresistible force or of an unforeseen event, beyond the control of the State, making it materially impossible in the circumstances to perform the obligation.
2. Paragraph 1 does not apply if:
   (*a*) The situation of *force majeure* is due, either alone or in combination with other factors, to the conduct of the State invoking it; or
   (*b*) The State has assumed the risk of that situation occurring.

A state must satisfy three criteria: (i) the act is due to an irresistible force or of an unforeseen event; (ii) beyond the control of the state; and (iii) making it materially impossible in the circumstances to perform the obligation.[137]

Force majeure as codified in Article 24 must be distinguished from *force majeure*, frustration, *imprévision* or impossibility of performance under national or international commercial law.[138] *Force majeure* or frustration may relieve a party of its contractual obligations where the contract is governed by private law (national or international).[139] However, where public international law is the applicable contract law, *force majeure* under Article 24 may be applicable.

---

135. On the possibility of such an express waiver, see *Aguas del Tunari S.A. v. Bolivia* (Decision on Objections to Jurisdiction, 21 Oct. 2005) at paras 114 and 119; *Suez, Sociedad General de Aguas de Barcelona S.A., and InterAgua Servicios Integrales del Agua S.A. v. Argentina* (Decision on Jurisdiction, 16 May 2006) at paras 44-45; *Suez, Sociedad General de Aguas de Barcelona S.A., and Vivendi Universal S.A. v. Argentina; AWG Group Ltd. v. Argentina* (Decision on Jurisdiction, 3 Aug. 2006) at paras 44-45; and *Occidental Petroleum Corporation & Occidental Exploration and Production Company v. Ecuador* (Decision on Jurisdiction, 9 Sep. 2008) at paras 62-89.
136. See *infra* §10.27.
137. See *Sempra, supra* note 45 at para. 246.
138. Domestic and international contract law consistently excuse performance of contractual obligations where the impediment is beyond the control of the parties and was not reasonably foreseen. See the discussion in *Autopista Concesionada de Venezuela, C.A. v. Venezuela* (Award, 23 Sep. 2003) at paras 107-129; and *Nykomb Synergetics Technology Holding AB v. Latvia* (Award, 16 Dec. 2003) at section 3.8 and the rejection of contractual *force majeure*, in *CMS, supra* note 45 at para. 227. See R. Goode, H. Kronke & E. McKendrick, *Transnational Commercial Law: Text, Cases and Materials* (Oxford: Oxford University Press, 2004) on *force majeure* in international commercial law.
139. See Commentary on ILC's Articles on State Responsibility in Crawford, *supra* note 12 at 173. For a discussion of defences to contractual claims in the context of foreign investment

Force majeure should also be distinguished from necessity and supervening impossibility under Article 61, Vienna Convention. In the case of necessity, the act in question is considered voluntary – a conscious act that the state takes to safeguard an essential interest; in the case of *force majeure*, the state cannot objectively perform an obligation because of an irresistible force or unforeseen event. The essential difference is volition. Although *force majeure* precludes responsibility, supervening impossibility under Article 61, Vienna Convention,[140] allows the state to terminate, withdraw or suspend the treaty obligation. State responsibility does not arise because of the termination, withdrawal or suspension of the primary obligation.[141]

In *Asian Agricultural Products Ltd. (AAPL) v. Sri Lanka*,[142] the tribunal considered a claim with respect to the destruction of a shrimp farm during a conflict between Tamil rebels and Sri Lankan forces. The majority of the tribunal concluded that there had been a breach of full protection and security because of the failure of the Sri Lankan authorities to take precautionary measures before launching an armed attack and because the farm was destroyed while under the exclusive control of government forces. In dissent, Dr. Samuel Asante stated that:

> The Tribunal's enunciation and application of due diligence rule fails to take into account the national emergency and extraordinary conditions under which the Government mounted a strategic and highly sensitive security operation to regain its sovereign control of the area of insurgency. The Government was confronted with essentially a *force majeure* situation. Once it is conceded that the Government had a compelling sovereign duty to undertake a military operation to regain control, the timing and modalities of the security operation must surely fall within its exclusive discretion. In this regard the

---

contracts see Chapter 10, R.D. Bishop, J. Crawford & W.M. Reisman, *Foreign Investment Disputes: Cases, Materials and Commentary* (The Hague: Kluwer Law International, 2005).

140. Art. 61 (Supervening impossibility of performance) provides:

1. A party may invoke the impossibility of performing a treaty as a ground for terminating or withdrawing from it if the impossibility results from the permanent disappearance or destruction of an object indispensable for the execution of the treaty. If the impossibility is temporary, it may be invoked only as a ground for suspending the operation of the treaty.
2. Impossibility of performance may not be invoked by a party as a ground for terminating, withdrawing from or suspending the operation of a treaty if the impossibility is the result of a breach by that party either of an obligation under the treaty or of any other international obligation owed to any other party to the treaty.

141. Since the object of IIAs is the promotion and protection of investment in general, rather than the protection of specific investment, it is most unlikely that Art. 61 could ever be invoked with respect to IIAs. For example, a state could not rely on Art. 61 if it were to nationalize all foreign investment without compensation and then argue the treaty was suspended because of the disappearance of the object of the treaty.

142. *AAPL, supra* note 81.

Tribunal should be slow to second-guess the tactics and strategies of military commanders on the ground.[143]

As noted above, while situations that involve volition might give rise to the defence of necessity (as in *AAPL* in which the Sri Lankan authorities launched an armed attack), the *AAPL* situation was not one of *force majeure*, making due diligence impossible.

§10.21 Necessity as a circumstance precluding wrongfulness Where a state takes action necessary to safeguard an essential interest against a grave and imminent threat, it may invoke the principle of necessity to preclude the wrongfulness of an act not in conformity with an international obligation.[144] Article 25 of the ILC's Articles on State Responsibility is generally recognized as codifying the requirements for a plea of necessity under customary international law. In *Gabčíkovo-Nagymaros*, the ICJ relied on the then ILC's draft article on necessity (now Article 25) as an appropriate formulation of the customary international law principle and confirmed that '... the state of necessity can only be invoked under certain strictly defined conditions which must be cumulatively satisfied; and the State concerned is not the sole judge of whether those have been met.... Those conditions reflect customary international law.'[145]

Article 25 provides:

1. Necessity may not be invoked by a State as a ground for precluding the wrongfulness of an act not in conformity with an international obligation of that State unless the act:
   (a) Is the only way for the State to safeguard an essential interest against a grave and imminent peril; and
   (b) Does not seriously impair an essential interest of the State or States towards which the obligation exists, or of the international community as a whole.
2. In any case, necessity may not be invoked by a State as a ground for precluding wrongfulness if:
   (a) The international obligation in question excludes the possibility of invoking necessity; or
   (b) The State has contributed to the situation of necessity.

The article identifies four separate and cumulative requirements that a state must satisfy in order to invoke necessity. The plea of necessity is, in all respects,

---

143. *Ibid.*, 20 ILM 577 at 651-652.
144. *Gabčíkovo, supra* note 47 at paras 51-2. See the commentary on ILC's Articles on State Responsibility in Crawford, *supra* note 12 at 178-186; R. Ago, 'Addendum to the Eighth Report on State Responsibility,' UN Doc. A/CN.4/318/ADD.5-7 in (1980) YBILC, Vol. II, Part One at 19; and T. Christakis '"Nécessité n'a pas de Loi"? La nécessité en droit international,' Rapport général in *La nécessité en droit international, Colloque de Grenoble de la Société française pour le droit international* (Paris: Pedone, 2007), at 8.
145. *Ibid.*, at para. 51. Also see *Enron, supra* note 20 at para. 303.

exceptional. It can be invoked to excuse a breach of an international obligation even though the state is acting voluntarily and the party to whom the international obligation is owed is blameless.[146] As a result, it is subject to strict limitations to safeguard against its abuse. Indeed, until the IIA award in *LG&E*, no state appears to have successfully invoked the plea before an international tribunal.[147] In addition, wrongfulness may not be precluded if the act is not in conformity with an obligation arising under a peremptory norm of general international law.[148] Necessity could never excuse responsibility for acts of genocide, slavery, racial discrimination or other peremptory norms.

§10.22 IIA jurisprudence on necessity   A number of IIA awards, all in the context of claims by foreign investors against Argentina, have considered the necessity defence.[149] In these and other ongoing cases, Argentina has relied on necessity to justify the measures that it took to address the severe economic crisis it suffered starting in late 1999. The awards to date arise out of investments made by foreign investors in the Argentine gas sector in the 1990s when Argentina privatized a large number of state-owned energy utilities and created a legal and regulatory framework to attract foreign investment in this industry. In the gas sector, it created a legal regime under which gas tariffs were calculated in US dollars, converted to pesos for billing purposes, and subject to a US Producer Price Index (PPI) adjustment every six months. Due to the economic downturn, Argentina temporarily suspended the US PPI adjustment. As the economic crisis worsened, emergency legislation in early 2002 provided for the freezing of gas tariffs, the abandonment of the calculation of tariffs in US dollars and the mandatory renegotiation of utility contracts. In each case, the investor had made a major investment in gas utilities and the tribunal found that the Argentine measures breached fair and equitable treatment and the duty to observe obligations entered into with

---

146.   See the commentary on ILC's Articles on State Responsibility in Crawford, *supra* note 12 at 178.

147.   The *LG&E* tribunal based its decision on Art. XI of Argentina-US (1991) and then supported its conclusion by assessing whether Argentina satisfied the conditions for invoking necessity under Art. 25. The award states that while the Art. 25 analysis 'alone does not establish Argentina's defence, it supports the Tribunal's analysis with regard to the meaning of Art. XI' (para. 258).

148.   See Art. 26, ILC's Articles on State Responsibility, *supra* note 12 and the commentary in Crawford, *ibid.*, at 187-188.

149.   *CMS, LG&E, Sempra, supra* note 45 and *Enron, supra* note 20. For commentary on the developing jurisprudence see A. Bjorklund, 'Emergency Exceptions to International Obligations in the Realm of Foreign Investment: The State of Necessity as a Circumstance Precluding Wrongfulness' in P. Muchlinski & F. Ortino, eds, *The Oxford Handbook of International Investment Law* (Oxford: Oxford University Press, 2008); and A. Reinisch, 'Necessity in International Investment Arbitration – An Unnecessary Split in Opinion in Recent ICSID Cases?' (2007) 8 JWIT 191.

respect to the investment.[150] In *CMS*,[151] *Enron*[152] and *Sempra*,[153] the tribunals held that Argentina had failed to satisfy the conditions required to establish necessity. In contrast, in *LG&E*, the tribunal held that Argentina had proven its case under the essential security clause of Argentina-US BIT (1991) to justify its measures for a period of time. In passing, the tribunal noted that the measures would also fulfil the test of necessity for the same time-period.

While the awards differ on certain key issues of application, the IIA jurisprudence to date is consistent on the general applicable principles: Article 25 of the ILC's Articles on State Responsibility codifies customary international law with respect to necessity; the four conditions set out in Article 25 are cumulative; whether the state has met the requisite conditions is a legal and factual question to be determined by tribunal (i.e., is not self-judging); and necessity is an exceptional defence to be construed narrowly.[154]

The IIA jurisprudence on the four conditions to satisfy a successful plea of necessity is discussed next.

Condition 1 – paragraph (1)(a): Only way for the State to safeguard an essential interest against a grave and imminent peril

To date, IIA tribunals have consistently held that an economic crisis can, in principle, threaten a state's 'essential interest.'[155] In particular, what is essential is not limited to security interests – essential interests can include ecological or economic interests.[156] Further, tribunals have agreed that Argentina had suffered a severe economic crisis. Tribunals have diverged, however, on whether Argentina faced a grave and imminent peril and whether Argentina's acts were the only means available to safeguard its interests.

In *CMS, Enron* and *Sempra*, tribunals held that the economic crisis did not meet the threshold of a grave and imminent peril. In *CMS*, the tribunal considered that the economic crisis was severe but did not result in total economic and social collapse.[157] In *Enron*, the tribunal found that events were not out of control or unmanageable.[158] In *Sempra*,[159] the reasoning is identical.[160]

---

150. For a discussion of these issues see *supra* Chapter 6 on minimum standards of treatment and *supra* Chapter 9 on observance of undertakings.
151. *CMS, supra* note 45 at para. 331.
152. *Enron, supra* note 20 at para. 93.
153. *Sempra, supra* note 45 at paras 333-355.
154. *CMS, supra* note 45 at paras 315-330; *Enron, supra* note 20 at paras 304-331; *LG&E, supra* note 45 at paras 228 *et seq.*; and *Sempra, supra* note 45 at paras 334-335.
155. *LG&E, ibid.*, at para. 251.
156. *CMS, supra* note 45 at paras 319; *Enron, supra* note 20 at para. 315; *LG&E, supra* note 45 at para. 251, *Sempra supra* note 45 at paras 334-335. See also commentary on ILC's Articles on State Responsibility in Crawford, *supra* note 12.
157. *CMS, ibid.*, at para. 355. The *CMS* tribunal did not clearly distinguish between whether the economic crisis did not threaten an essential interest or whether it was not of a sufficiently significant magnitude to constitute a grave and imminent peril.
158. *Enron, supra* note 20 at para. 307.
159. *Sempra, supra* note 45 at para. 349.
160. *Ibid.*, at para. 349.

In contrast, the *LG&E* tribunal considered that Argentina:

> … faced an extremely serious threat to its existence, its political and economic survival, to the possibility of maintaining its essential services in operation, and to the preservation of its internal peace. There is no serious evidence in the record that Argentina contributed to the crisis resulting in the state of necessity. In this circumstances [sic], an economic recovery package was the only means to respond to the crisis. Although there may have been a number of ways to draft the economic recovery plan, the evidence before the Tribunal demonstrates that an across-the-board response was necessary, and the tariffs on public utilities had to be addressed.[161]

It has been argued that the reasoning in this case law regarding the existence of a grave and imminent peril is cursory and conclusionary.[162] While this may be due to the lack of convincing evidence provided by Argentina in these cases, more detailed references to such documentary evidence and/or witness or expert testimony would have been welcome, given the importance of these cases in the development of IIA jurisprudence.

Similarly, the tribunals' discussion on whether Argentina's measures were the 'only way' to address the crisis were scant and without a detailed assessment of evidence. Arguably, Argentina's evidence was of a general nature on the gravity of the crisis without specifically demonstrating why, even if this were so, the specific measures complained of needed to be taken and no alternatives existed. But tribunals could have explained this in more detail. In *CMS*, the tribunal took for granted that alternatives existed; it simply held that since other measures were available, Argentina's measures were not the only way.[163] The *Enron* tribunal's reasons were similar: 'A rather sad world comparative experience in the handling of economic crises, shows that there are always many approaches to address and correct such critical events, and it is difficult to justify that none of them were available in the Argentine case.'[164] The *Sempra* tribunal used the same analysis, almost word for word.[165] While the reasoning may be sufficient to understand the conclusion reached by the tribunals, it could have been accompanied with an evaluation of the parties' evidence to provide more clarity. Argentina's evidence is not discussed; nor is the claimants' evidence that, for example, the applicable tariff regime contained the necessary flexibility to address the situation. The result is that, except probably for the parties in dispute who knew the evidence provided, the decisions convey a sense of (perhaps undeserved) rigidity in applying this requirement of the law of necessity.[166] On the other hand, the approach

---

161. *LG&E, supra* note 45 at para. 257.
162. See Reinisch, *supra* note 149 at 199 noting that 'no detailed explanation is given.' In *Sempra, supra* note 45, the tribunal noted that the expert opinions are sharply divided.
163. *CMS, supra* note 45 at para. 323.
164. *Enron, supra* note 20 at para. 308.
165. *Sempra, supra* note 45 at para. 350.
166. See Reinisch, *supra* note 149 at 200 arguing that this case law makes it very difficult for a state to justify any specific set of measures in an economic crisis, as practically speak-

of the *LG&E* tribunal appears to frame the question as whether 'an economic recovery package was the only means to respond to the crisis,'[167] rather than addressing the necessity of the specific measures adopted. It has been argued that the better approach would be to assess whether the specific measures in question were the 'only way' to respond to the crisis in light of their potential effectiveness and proportionality in responding to the threat.[168] Whether this approach is consistent with the exceptional and inherently narrow nature of the defence of necessity is open to question.

Condition 2 – paragraph (1)(b): No serious impairment of an essential interest of the state towards which the obligation exists, or of the international community as a whole

The *CMS* and *LG&E* tribunals held that other states' rights would not be seriously impaired by the measures taken.[169] In contrast, in *Enron* and *Sempra*, the tribunals held that while there was no impairment of another state's essential interests, the interests of the claimants would be impaired by the operation of necessity.[170] The awards, however, do not explain how Article 25(1)(b) should apply in the case of IIAs, where rights are provided to non-contracting parties, namely investors.[171] In particular, the reasoning in *Enron* and *Sempra* suggest, without more elaboration, that since the investment obligations are owed to the foreign investor, essential interests of the state are somehow to be substituted with the interests of the investor. But, arguably, Article 25(1)(b) requires an evaluation of the competing public interests – not of the private interests of foreign investors. If the state has managed to satisfy the high threshold requirement that the measures are the 'only way for the State to safeguard an essential interest against a grave and imminent peril,' it is difficult to imagine a situation where the economic interests of a particular investor would outweigh the interests of the state in safeguarding its essential interests. Further, as the invocation of necessity is without prejudice to the question of compensation,[172] it may be more appropriate to satisfy a particular investor's 'essential interests' through payment of compensation.

Condition 3 – paragraph(2)(a): The international obligation in question does not exclude the possibility of invoking necessity

The defence of necessity is not available where the obligation in question explicitly or implicitly excludes its operation. For example, some humanitarian treaties applicable to armed conflict exclude reliance on military necessity.[173] In the IIA context, the question is whether the plea of necessity is unavailable

---

ing in most cases there will be a range of economic policy measures to address an economic crisis.

167. *LG&E, supra* note 45 at para. 257.
168. Reinisch, *supra* note 149 at 201.
169. *LG&E, supra* note 45 at para. 257, and *CMS, supra* note 45 at paras 325 and 358.
170. *Enron, supra* note 20 at para. 342, and *Sempra, supra* note 45 at para. 391.
171. See Reinisch, *supra* note 149 at 201-202.
172. See *infra* §10.24.
173. Commentary on ILC's Articles on State Responsibility in Crawford, *supra* note 12 at 185.

because of the object and purpose of IIAs – to promote and protect foreign investment. Some commentators suggest that such object and purpose of BITs is relevant precisely in situations in which a state is most likely to take adverse measures (i.e., in case of economic difficulties), and this would be defeated if a state is entitled to rely on the general necessity defence precisely in those situations.[174] In any case, some consideration could be given to the fact that since necessity is without prejudice to the question of compensation,[175] application of necessity does not necessarily entail complete abandonment of some measure of investment protection, hence the object and purpose of IIAs is not defeated.

The IIA case law to date appears to support the principle that IIAs should not be read as excluding the plea of necessity.[176] In *CMS*, the tribunal considered whether the object and purpose of the BIT – to protect investment from adverse government measures (often taken in times of crisis) – excluded the possibility of invoking necessity. It held that the treaty could not be read as excluding such a possibility in the case of catastrophic conditions.[177] Further, tribunals have noted that where the IIA includes an express clause addressing essential security interests, there has been an acceptance that state of necessity may be invoked.[178] In *BG*, the tribunal was more sceptical that the defence of necessity could be invoked in an IIA context, although it dismissed Argentina's defence on other grounds.[179]

Condition 4 – paragraph(2)(b): The state has not contributed to the situation of necessity

The plea of necessity is not available where the state has contributed to the situation of necessity. As noted by the tribunal in *Sempra*, this is a reflection of a general principle that a party should not be able to take 'legal advantage of its own fault'.[180] IIA tribunals addressing the claims arising from the Argentine economic crisis legislation have diverged on this issue, with the majority of tribunals finding that Argentina contributed to the crisis and therefore did not satisfy this condition. The *CMS* tribunal agreed with the ILC commentary that the contribution must be 'sufficiently substantial and not merely incidental or peripheral' and found that this was the case with regard to Argentina as the crisis had domestic and international roots, and government policies and shortcomings significantly contributed

---

174. See Reinisch, *supra* note 149 at 205.
175. See *infra* §10.24.
176. This approach is supported by the ICJ's statement in *ELSI* that unless there is clear evidence to the contrary, the court should not presume that state parties to a treaty have decided to dispense with an important rule of customary international law. In *ELSI*, the rule in question was exhaustion of local remedies. See *Elettronica Sicula S.p.A. (ELSI) (US v. Italy)* [1989] ICJ Rep 15 at para. 50.
177. *CMS, supra* note 45 at paras 353-354. In *CMS*, the tribunal noted that some treaties, such as those dealing with humanitarian issues in armed conflict, are specifically designed to apply in cases of necessity or emergency (at para. 353).
178. See *supra* §10.6 regarding the relationship between express essential security interests provisions and necessity in customary international law.
179. *BG, supra* note 79 at para. 409.
180. *Sempra, supra* note 45 at para. 353.

to the crisis.[181] In *Enron* and *Sempra*, the tribunals found that although both endogenous and exogenous factors precipitated the crisis, there was a substantial contribution by Argentina for which it should answer.[182] In contrast, the *LG&E* tribunal appears to have decided the issue on the basis of the reversal of the burden of proof, in holding that there was no serious evidence that Argentina contributed to the crisis.[183] It has been argued that the reasoning of the *CMS*, *Enron* and *Sempra* awards on the issue of contribution does not engage in any in-depth reasoning on the degree of contribution required,[184] or what facts suggested contribution, whereas the *LG&E* award does not give a reason for shifting the burden of proof to the claimant and also fails to clarify what degree of contribution is required.[185] In the context of the Argentine crisis, it may be difficult for tribunals not to find any degree of contribution by Argentina, and tribunals may have found it sufficient to deal with this issue briefly. But considering the fact that the jurisprudence on necessity is in its infancy, more analysis could have helped future tribunals address other similar situations.

§10.23 Temporal limitations on preclusion of wrongfulness   Once the circumstances giving rise to the preclusion of wrongfulness no longer exist, the duty to comply with treaty obligations is revived.[186] This is codified in Article 27, ILC's Articles on State Responsibility:

> The invocation of a circumstance precluding wrongfulness in accordance with this chapter is without prejudice to:
>
> (*a*) Compliance with the obligation in question, if and to the extent that the circumstance precluding wrongfulness no longer exists;

The commentary to the ILC's Articles on State Responsibility explains that this provision:

> … makes it clear that Chapter V has a merely preclusive effect. When and to the extent that a circumstance precluding wrongfulness ceases, or ceases to have its preclusive effect for any reason, the obligation in question (assuming it is still in force) will again have to be complied with, and the State whose earlier non-compliance was excused must act accordingly. The words 'and to the extent' are intended to cover situations in which the conditions preventing compliance gradually lessen and allow for partial performance of the obligation.[187]

---

181.   *CMS, supra* note 45 at para. 328-329.
182.   *Sempra, supra* note 45 at paras 353-354; and *Enron, supra* note 20 at paras 311-312.
183.   *LG&E, supra* note 45 at para. 257.
184.   Reinisch, *supra* note 149 at 203.
185.   Reinisch, *ibid.,* at 203.
186.   *Gabčíkovo, supra* note 47 at para. 101.
187.   Commentary on ILC's Articles on State Responsibility in Crawford, *supra* note 12 at 189.

The *CMS* and *LG&E* awards both recognized this principle. In *CMS*, the tribunal states that: 'Even if the plea of necessity were accepted, compliance with the obligation would reemerge as soon as the circumstance precluding wrongfulness no longer existed, which is the case at present.[188] The *LG&E* tribunal found that the period of crisis was from December 2001 to April 2003 and that during that time the state was exempted from liability.[189] Once the crisis was over, the obligations towards the investor reemerged.

§10.24 Compensation and preclusion of wrongfulness While a state is responsible for making reparations for wrongful acts that occurred before and after the circumstances precluding wrongfulness, the question of compensation for losses that occurred during the period of preclusion is less clear. Article 27, ILC's Articles on State Responsibility, provides:

> The invocation of a circumstance precluding wrongfulness in accordance with this chapter is without prejudice to:
> ...
> (*b*) the question of compensation for any material loss caused by the act in question.

In *Gabčíkovo-Nagymaros*, the ICJ noted that 'Hungary expressly acknowledged that, in any event, such a state of necessity would not exempt it from its duty to compensate its partner.'[190] The commentary to the ILC's Articles on State Responsibility is more nuanced. It notes that 'Paragraph (b) does not attempt to specify in what circumstances compensation should be payable. Generally the range of possible situations covered by Chapter V is such that to lay down a detailed regime for compensation is not appropriate.'[191] The *ad hoc* committee in *CMS Annulment* noted that the articles do not 'not attempt to specify in which circumstances compensation could be due, notwithstanding the state of necessity.'[192]

The commentary to the ILC's Articles on State Responsibility notes that material loss is a narrower concept than damages.[193] This might suggest a distinction between physical or material injury to assets and other forms of damages, such as lost profits or interest.[194] For example, if an investor were required to supply goods or services to the state during a situation of necessity, a tribunal might order compensation to cover the investor's costs, but not for the additional profits that it would have been able to make by selling the goods at high market prices due to the emergency situation.

---

188. *CMS, supra* note 45 at para. 382 and *LG&E, supra* note 45 at para. 226
189. *LG&E, ibid.*
190. *Gabčíkovo, supra* note 47 at para. 39.
191. Commentary on ILC's Articles on State Responsibility in Crawford, *supra* note 12 at 190.
192. *CMS Annulment, supra* note 61 at para. 147.
193. Commentary on ILC's Articles on State Responsibility in Crawford, *supra* note 12 at 190.
194. See D. Foster, 'Necessity Knows No Law! – *LG&E v. Argentina*' (2006) 9 IALR 149.

The *LG&E* tribunal found that, although Argentina would be responsible for damages for breaches of the treaty before and after the state of necessity, the damages suffered by the investor during the state of necessity should be borne by the investor, seemingly due to the application of the treaty essential security exception rather than necessity under customery international law.[195] In contrast, the *CMS* tribunal found that the plea of necessity does not exclude the duty to compensate because that would place the entire cost of the plea on the other party.[196]

VII   OTHER DEFENCES

§10.25 Acquiescence   Under customary international law, an injured state may not invoke a respondent state's treaty breach if the injured state has validly acquiesced in the lapse of the claim.[197] This principle is codified in Article 45, ILC's Articles on State Responsibility, which provide that:

> The responsibility of a State may not be invoked if:
>
> ...
>
> (*b*) the injured State is to be considered as having, by reason of its conduct, validly acquiesced in the lapse of the claim.

Although this provision applies only to states, it is likely that an IIA tribunal could apply a similar principle in the case of a foreign investor making an IIA claim.[198] In *M.C.I. Power Group L.C. and New Turbine, Inc. v. Ecuador*,[199] the tribunal, in considering an IIA claim that involved the cancellation of an operating permit, found that the investor had acquiesced in the cancellation of the permit by not seeking an administrative review of the cancellation decision.[200]

The commentary to the ILC's Articles on State Responsibility highlights that there are no clear-cut time limits to determine whether acquiescence will apply and notes that a determining criterion is undue delay:

> To summarize, a claim will not be inadmissible on grounds of delay unless the circumstances are such that the injured State should be considered as having acquiesced in the lapse of the claim or the respondent State has been seriously disadvantaged. International courts generally engage in a flexible weighing of relevant circumstances in the given case, taking into account such matters as the conduct of the respondent State and the importance of the rights involved. The decisive factor is whether the respondent State has suffered any prejudice

---

195. *LG&E, supra* note 45 at para. 264.
196. *CMS, supra* note 45 at paras 383-394.
197. Art. 45(a), ILC's Articles on State Responsibility, *supra* note 12.
198. See also I.C. MacGibbon, 'Customary International Law and Acquiescence' (1957) 33 BYIL 115.
199. *M.C.I. Power Group L.C. and New Turbine, Inc. v. Ecuador* (Award, 31 Jul. 2007).
200. *Ibid.*, at para. 302.

as a result of the delay in the sense that the respondent could have reasonably expected that the claim would no longer be pursued. Even if there has been some prejudice, it may be able to be taken into account in determining the form or extent of reparation.[201]

The reference in the commentaries to the claim not being admissible on grounds of delay might suggest that acquiescence operates as a procedural bar to the bringing of the claim, rather than as a substantive defence or preclusion of state responsibility.[202] In this respect, a distinction should be made between undue delay in presenting a claim (as a procedural bar) and the effect of the passage of time on the merits of the claim. In the latter, the claimant has, by failing to protest, arguably acquiesced in the state conduct.[203]

§10.26 Extinctive prescription and laches In addition, or as an alternative, to the principle of acquiescence, international tribunals have applied the doctrines of extinctive prescription[204] and laches[205] to bar a claim on the basis of undue delay. The NAFTA tribunal in *Grand River Enterprises Six Nations, Ltd., et al. v. United States*[206] noted that: 'The principle of extinctive prescription (bar of claims by lapse of time) is widely recognized as a general principle of law constituting part of international law, and has been accepted and applied by arbitral tribunals.'[207]

A NAFTA investment tribunal, in addressing a claimant's argument that the doctrine of laches should apply to deny a request by the US to consolidate arbitration proceedings, stated that:

Laches is an equitable defense asserted to bar the adjudication of stale claims. The doctrine is premised on the theory that a claim that is plagued with undue delay prejudices a defendant because evidence is no longer available to defend against the claim. Although Tembec defines *laches* as prohibiting

---

201. Commentary to ILC's Articles on State Responsibility in Crawford, *supra* note 12 at 269.
202. See also, *Certain Phosphate Lands in Nauru (Nauru v. Australia)* [1992] ICJ Rep 240 at 253-254, para. 32 stating that 'delay on the part of a claimant State may render an application inadmissible.'
203. R. Jennings & A. Watts, eds, *Oppenheim's International Law*, 9th edn (London: Longman, 1992), at §154.
204. See K. Hobér, *Extinctive Prescription and Applicable Law in Interstate Arbitration* (Uppsala: Iustus Förlag, 2001); C.A. Fleischhauer, 'Prescription,' in R. Bernhardt, ed., *Encyclopedia of Public International Law*, Vol. 3 (Amsterdam: North-Holland Pub. Co., 1997) at 1105; B.E. King, 'Prescription of Claims in International Law' (1934) 15 BYIL 82; B. Cheng, *General Principles of Law* (London: Stevens & Sons, Ltd., 1953) at 372-386; and *Oppenheim's International Law, ibid.*
205. See A.R. Ibrahim, 'The Doctrine of Laches in International Law' (1997) 83 VLR 647 and D.W. Bowett, 'Estoppel before International Tribunals and Its Relation to Acquiescence' (1957) 33 BYIL 176 at 183-184.
206. *Grand River Enterprises Six Nations, Ltd., et al. v. United States* (Decisions on Objection to Jurisdiction, 20 Jul. 2006). See also *Wena Hotels Limited v. Egypt* (Award, 8 Dec. 2000) at para. 106.
207. *Grand River Enterprises, ibid.*, at para. 33.

a party's 'exercise of a right that has been delayed,' the authorities cited by Tembec all refer to the application of the principle in the context of claims, and refer to cases in which tribunals have applied the doctrine to claims. The Tribunal is not convinced that under international law this doctrine is appropriately invoked by a claimant to bar a procedural request for consolidation of claims. The Tribunal notes that, in some legal systems, laches may bar requests for consolidation, as, for example, under New York law. However, the forms of equity known to Anglo-American common law do not form part of the corpus of public international law. While there is a borrowing of principles derived from domestic legal systems in public international law, this takes the form of general principles of law that do not necessarily replicate the rules of domestic law from which they derive their common origin.[208] [Footnotes omitted.]

The tribunal noted that even if it were appropriate to apply the doctrine to bar a procedural request, laches would not apply because the delay in question (12 to 18 months) was not lengthy.[209]

Some IIAs have express provisions barring claims that are not brought in a timely fashion. For example, Article 1116(2), NAFTA, provides that:

> An investor may not make a claim if more than three years have elapsed from the date on which the investor first acquired, or should have first acquired, knowledge of the alleged breach and knowledge that the investor has incurred loss or damage.

§10.27 Estoppel Estoppel operates to preclude a party from acting inconsistently where the result of the inconsistency would be to prejudice the other party. In El Salvador-Honduras *Land, Island and Maritime Frontier Dispute*,[210] a Chamber of the ICJ stated that the essential elements of estoppel include 'a statement or representation made by one party to another and reliance upon it by that other party to his detriment or to the advantage of the party making it.'[211] In *Pope & Talbot Inc. v. Canada*, the tribunal, referring to Professor Bowett's article, noted that the essential elements of estoppel are: '(1) a statement of fact which is clear and unambiguous; (2) this statement must be voluntary, unconditional, and authorised; and (3) there must be reliance in good faith upon the statement either to the

---

208. *Canfor Corporation v. United States and Terminal Forest Products Ltd. v. United States* (Order of the Consolidation Tribunal, 7 Sep. 2005) at para. 165 [Softwood Consolidation Order]. See also Ibrahim, *supra* note 205 and Bowett, *supra* note 205 at 183-184.
209. Softwood Consolidation Order, *ibid.*
210. *Land, Island and Maritime Frontier Dispute (El Salvador v. Honduras)* [1990] ICJ Rep 92 at 118, para. 63.
211. *Ibid.*, at para. 63. This case was cited with approval by the tribunal in *Philippe Gruslin v. Malaysia* (Award, 27 Nov. 2000) at paras 20.1-20.5.

detriment of the party so relying on the statement or to the advantage of the party making the statement.'[212]

Estoppel has been argued by states in a number of IIA cases.[213] In *Pope & Talbot*,[214] Canada argued that the claimant was estopped from bringing its claim as a result of the claimant's statements and conduct that it would abide by the Softwood Lumber Agreement and its implementation. The tribunal rejected Canada's argument because the investor had made no representations to Canada directly and, in any event, the representations in question did not relate to Canada's implementation of Softwood Lumber Agreement.[215] In *Siemens A.G. v. Argentina*,[216] the tribunal found that estoppel would not arise from positions taken during good faith negotiations or from compliance with law and regulations.[217] In *Pan American Energy LLC, and BP Argentina Exploration Company v. Argentina*,[218] the tribunal rejected Argentina's argument that the claimant was estopped from resorting to dispute settlement under the BIT because in a previous private contractual dispute it had argued in favour of exclusive state court jurisdiction.

Although the above discussion focuses on the use of estoppel by respondent states to defend against claims, the principle is equally applicable in investor claims against states. For example, in defining the protection of legitimate expectations as an element of fair and equitable treatment, tribunals have referred to the elements of estoppel.[219] More generally, estoppel can be applied in a broad range of circumstances to prevent states from challenging acts or transactions in the past. For example, in *ADC Affiliate Limited and ADC & ADMC Management Limited v. Hungary*, Hungary challenged the validity of various airport operation project agreements based on non compliance with local law. The tribunal stated that:

> Even if the Respondent was correct in any of its submissions on the miscellaneous points ... they would nevertheless fail on them simply because they have rested on their rights. These Agreements were entered into years ago and both parties have acted on the basis that all was in order. Whether one rests this conclusion on the doctrine of estoppel or a waiver it matters

---

212. *Pope & Talbot Inc. v. Canada* (Interim Award, 26 Jun. 2000) at para. 111; Bowett, *supra* note 205 at 176-202; *Case Concerning the Temple of Preah Vihear (Cambodia v. Thailand)* [1962] ICJ Rep 6; I. Brownlie, *Principles of Public International Law*, 6th edn (Oxford: Oxford University Press, 2003) at 616; and P. Müller & T. Cottier, 'Estoppel,' in R. Bernhardt, ed., *Encyclopedia of Public International Law*, Vol. II (Amsterdam: North-Holland Pub. Co., 1992) at 116.

213. *Pope & Talbot, ibid.*, at para. 112; *Pan American Energy LLC, and BP Argentina Exploration Company v. Argentina* (Decision on Preliminary Objections, 27 Jul. 2006) [*Pan American*] at paras 159-161; and *Siemens A.G. v. Argentina* (Award, 6 Feb. 2007) at para. 306.

214. *Pope & Talbot, ibid.*

215. *Ibid.*, at para. 112.

216. *Siemens A.G. v. Argentina* (Award, 6 Feb. 2007).

217. *Ibid.*, at para. 306.

218. *Pan American, supra* note 213 at para. 151.

219. *ADC Affiliate Limited and ADC & ADMC Management Limited v. Hungary* (Award of the Tribunal, 2 Oct. 2006) [*ADC*] at para. 475; and *International Thunderbird Gaming Corporation v. Mexico* (Arbitral Award, 26 Jan. 2006), Separate Opinion.

not. Almost all systems of law prevent parties from blowing hot and cold. If any of the suite of Agreements in this case were illegal or unenforceable under Hungarian law one might have expected the Hungarian Government or its entities to have declined to enter into such an agreement. However when, after receiving top class international legal advice, Hungary enters into and performs these agreements for years and takes the full benefit from them, it lies ill in the mouth of Hungary now to challenge the legality and/or enforceability of these Agreements.... They cannot succeed because Hungary entered into these agreements willingly, took advantage from them and led the Claimants over a long period of time, to assume that these Agreements were effective. Hungary cannot now go behind these Agreements. They are prevented from so doing by their own conduct.[220]

---

220.   *ADC, ibid.*, at para. 475.

Table of Cases

I   INTERNATIONAL INVESTMENT
     TREATY CASES

*ADC Affiliate Limited and ADC & ADMC Management Limited v.
Hungary*, ICSID Case No. ARB/03/16 (Cyprus-Hungary BIT)
(Kaplan P., Brower & van den Berg).
    Award of the Tribunal, 2 October 2006....................... 60, 369, 372-375,
382, 385, 397,
527, 528

ADF Group Inc v. United States, ICSID Case No. ARB(AF)/00/1
(NAFTA) (Feliciano P., de Mestral & Lamm).
    Award, 9 January 2003: 6 ICSID Rep 449;
    18 ICSID Rev 195 .... 185-186, 229, 236,
237, 250, 274, 276,
277, 298, 337, 426,
508

    Investor's Reply to the Counter-Memorial of the United States
    of America on Competence and Liability,
    28 January 2002... 274

AES Corporation v. Argentina, ICSID Case No. ARB/02/17
(US-Argentina BIT) (Dupuy P., Böckstiegel & Bello Janeiro).
    Decision on Jurisdiction, 26 April 2005....................... 103

Aguas del Tunari, S.A. v. Bolivia, ICSID Case No. ARB/02/3
(Netherlands-Bolivia BIT) (Caron P., Alberro-Semerena & Alvarez).
    Decision on Respondent's Objections to Jurisdiction,
    21 October 2005: 20 ICSID Rev 450........................... 69, 110, 113, 114,
117-118, 136, 514

American Manufacturing & Trading, Inc. v. Zaire, ICSID Case No.
ARB/93/1(US-Zaire BIT) (Sucharitkul P., Golsong & Mbaye).
    Award, 21 February 1997: 5 ICSID Rep 11;
    36 ILM 1534.. 59, 87, 309, 317, 500
Limited Liability Company Amto v. Ukraine, SCC
Case No. 080/2005 (ECT) (Cremades P., Runeland & Söderlund).
    Final Award, 26 March 2008.......................................   54
*Archer Daniels Midland Company and Tate & Lyle Ingredients
Americas, Inc. v. Mexico*, ICSID Case No. ARB (AF)/04/5 (NAFTA)
(Cremades P., Rovine & Siqueiros).
    Award, 21 November 2007...   510, 511
Asian Agricultural Products Ltd. (AAPL) v. Sri Lanka,
ICSID Case No. ARB/87/3 (UK-Sri Lanka BIT)
(El-Kosheri P., Goldman & Asante).
    Final Award, 27 June 1990: 4 ICSID Rep 245;
    6 ICSID Rev 526; 30 ILM 577 .... 46, 58, 85, 87, 88, 91,
                                             92, 110, 149, 194,
                                           229, 308, 309, 315,
                                           389, 396, 500,
                                           515-516
AWG Group Ltd. v. Argentina, UNCITRAL (UK-Argentina BIT)
(Salacuse P., Kaufmann-Kohler & Nikken).
    Decision on Jurisdiction, 3 August 2006......................   109, 208, 209, 514
Robert Azinian, Kenneth Davitian, & Ellen Baca v. Mexico,
ICSID Case No. ARB (AF)/97/2 (NAFTA) (Paulsson P.,
Civiletti & von Wobeser).
    Award, 1 November 1999: 5 ICSID Rep 269;
    39 ILM 537..   87, 94, 95, 240,
                                           254, 276, 297,
                                         350, 351, 354
Azurix Corp v. Argentina, ICSID Case No. ARB/01/12
(US-Argentina BIT) (Rigo Sureda P., Lauterpacht & Martins).
    Decision on Jurisdiction, 8 December 2003:
    10 ICSID Rep 416; 43 ILM 262 ....   71, 350
    Award, 14 July 2006...   109, 114, 116, 266,
                                           277, 282, 300, 302,
                                         312, 314, 345-346,
                                         352, 456-457
Bayindir Insaat Turizm Ticaret Ve Sanayi A.S, . v. Pakistan,
ICSID Case No. ARB/03/29 (Turkey-Pakistan BIT)
(Kaufmann-Kohler P., Berman & Böckstiegel).
    Decision on Jurisdiction, 14 November 2005 .... 72, 93, 104, 124, 125,
                                           183, 185, 227-228,
                                                474

Vladimir Berschader and Moïse Berschader v. Russia, SCC Case No.
080/2004 (BLEU-USSR BIT) (Sjövall P., Lebedev & Weiler).
    Award, 21 April 2006 .... 212, 214, 216, 217,
219, 318
    Separate Opinion, 7 April 2006.................................... 215
BG Group Plc. v. Argentina, UNCITRAL (UK-Argentina BIT)
(Aguilar Alvarez P., van den Berg & Garro).
    Final Award, 24 December 2007...............................72, 107, 109, 208,221,
272, 282, 285, 287,
303, 304, 306, 307,
313, 316, 346, 456,
499, 500, 521

*Iurii Bogdanov, Agurdino-Invest Ltd. and Agurdino-Chimia JSC v.
Moldova*, SCC, (USSR-Moldova BIT) (Cordero Moss).
    Arbitral Award, 22 September 2005............................ 89
Camuzzi International S.A. v. Argentina, ICSID Case No. ARB/03/7
(BLEU-Argentina BIT) (Gómez-Pinzón P., Gros Espiell & Alvarez).
    Decision of the Arbitral Tribunal on Objections to Jurisdiction,
    10 June 2005.. 209, 219
*Canfor Corporation v. United States and Terminal Forest Products
Ltd. v. United States*, (Consolidated NAFTA Arbitration, UNCITRAL
Rules) (van den Berg P., de Mestral & Robinson).
    Order of the Consolidation Tribunal,
    7 September 2005...................................... 526
    Decision on Preliminary Question, 6 June 2006......... 182, 203, 262,
337, 485

*Champion Trading Company, Ameritrade International, Inc.,
James T. Wahba, John B. Wahba and Timothy T. Wahba v. Egypt*,
ICSID Case No. ARB/02/9 (US-Egypt BIT) (Briner P., Fortier &
Aynès).
    Decision on Jurisdiction, 21 October 2003:
    19 ICSID Rev 275 93
CME Czech Republic B.V. (The Netherlands) v. Czech Republic,
UNCITRAL (Netherlands-Czechoslovakia BIT).
    Partial Award, 13 September 2001
    (Kühn P., Hándl & Schwebel): 9 ICSID Rep 121........ 96, 105, 117, 283,
295, 304, 306,
311, 337, 345,
347, 352, 369,
379, 384, 390
    Final Award, 14 March 2003 (Kühn P., Brownlie &
    Schwebel): 9 ICSID Rep 264..................................... 49, 81, 89, 96, 117,
229, 379, 384,
385, 392, 397

Separate Opinion on Final Award, 14 March 2003
(Brownlie): 9 ICSID 412...   229
Review by Svea Court of Appeal, 15 May 2003:
9 ICSID 439; 42 ILM 919...   78, 89, 96
CMS Gas Transmission Company v. Argentina, ICSID Case No.
ARB/01/8 (US-Argentina BIT) (Orrego Vicuña P., Lalonde & Rezek).
  Decision of the Tribunal on Objections to Jurisdiction,
  17 July 2003: 7 ICSID Rep 492; 42 ILM 788 ....   60, 69, 71, 102
  Award, 12 May 2005: 44 ILM 1205 ....   88, 94, 96, 106, 109,
                                                                   113, 114, 250, 264,
                                                                        271, 277, 282,
                                                                        285-289, 295,
                                                                   300-301, 303, 305,
                                                                   316, 345, 369, 388,
                                                                   417, 450, 452, 453,
                                                                   455, 456, 457, 459,
                                                                   464, 465, 469, 474,
                                                                   492, 493, 495, 498,
                                                                   500, 514, 517-524
  Decision of the *Ad Hoc* Committee on the Application
  for Annulment of the Argentine Republic,
  25 September 2007 (Guillaume P., Elaraby & Crawford):
  46 ILM 1136..   29, 78, 107, 446,
                                                                        448-451, 453,
                                                                        456, 495-497,
                                                                             499, 523

*Compañía de Aguas del Aconquija, S.A. & Compagnie Générale des
Eaux v. Argentina*, ICSID Case No. ARB/97/3 (France-Argentina
BIT) (Rezek P., Buergenthal & Trooboff).
  Award, 21 November 2000: 5 ICSID Rep 296;
  16 ICSID Rev 643; 40 ILM 426 ....   29, 70, 100, 240
  Decision on Annulment (*Compañía de Aguas del Aconquija S.A.
  and Vivendi Universal (formerly Compagnie Générale des Eaux)*),
  3 July 2002 (Fortier P., Crawford & Fernández Rozas):
  6 ICSID Rep 340; 19 ICSID Rev 89; 41 ILM 1135;
  125 ILR 58..   90, 99, 463
  Award (*Compañía de Aguas del Aconquija S.A. and
  Vivendi Universal S.A.*) (Kaufmann-Kohler P., Bernal
  Verea & Rowley), 20 August 2007...............................   102, 125, 258, 266,
                                                                   294, 295, 311-314,
                                                                   333, 340, 342, 352,
                                                                   353, 382, 384, 389,
                                                                        392, 396, 397

Consorzio Groupement L.E.S.I.- DIPENTA v. Algeria, ICSID Case
No. ARB/03/08 (Italy-Algeria BIT) (Tercier P., Faurès & Gaillard).

Award, 10 January 2005 .... 100, 452, 463
Consortium RFCC v. Morocco, ICSID Case No. ARB/00/6
(Italy-Morocco BIT) (Briner P., Cremades & Fadlallah).
    Decision on Jurisdiction, 16 July 2001 .... 463, 466
    Arbitral Award, 22 December 2003:
    20 ICSID Rev 391 .... 29, 160-161, 337,
                                        352, 463

Continental Casualty Company v. Argentina, ICSID Case No.
ARB/03/9 (US-Argentina BIT) (Sacerdoti P., Veeder & Nader).
    Decision on Jurisdiction, 22 February 2006 114
Desert Line Projects LLC v. Yemen, ICSID Case No. ARB/05/17
(Oman-Yemen BIT) (Tercier P., Paulsson & El-Kosheri).
    Award, 6 February 2008 .... 93, 134, 159, 295,
                                        343, 372

Eastern Sugar B.V. v. Czech Republic, SCC Case No. 088/2004
(Netherlands-Czechoslovakia BIT) (Karrer P., Gaillard & Volterra).
    Partial Award, 27 March 2007 .... 102, 345
    Final Award, 12 April 2007 .... 278, 290, 306
El Paso Energy International Company v. Argentina,
ICSID Case No. ARB/03/15 (US-Argentina BIT)
(Caflisch P., Stern & Bernardini).
    Decision on Jurisdiction, 27 April 2006:
    21 ICSID Rev 488 .... 60, 116, 336, 445,
                                        455, 469, 474

EnCana Corporation v. Ecuador, LCIA Case No. UN3481,
UNCITRAL (Canada-Ecuador BIT) (Crawford P., Grigera Naón &
Thomas).
    Award, 3 February 2006: 12 ICSID Rep 427;
    45 ILM 901 .... 87, 93, 105, 170, 280,
                                        336, 337, 351-353,
                                      355, 356, 361,
                                      362, 410, 462

Enron Corporation and Ponderosa Assets, L.P. v. Argentina,
ICSID Case No. ARB/01/3 (US-Argentina BIT) (Orrego
Vicuña P., Espiell & Tschanz).
    Decision on Jurisdiction, 14 January 2004:
    11 ICSID Rep 273 336
    Decision on Jurisdiction (Ancillary Claim), 2 August 2004:
    11 ICSID Rep 295 .... 103, 110
    Award, 22 May 2007 .... 106, 107, 109, 125,
                                        265, 281, 282,
                              285-287, 302, 303, 305,
                                    311, 340, 343, 344,
                                      346, 453, 456, 459,
                                      470, 474, 485,

                                                                    492-495, 498-500,
                                                                        516-520, 522
Ethyl Corporation v. Canada, UNCITRAL (NAFTA) (Böckstiegel
P., Brower & Lalonde).
    Award on Jurisdiction, 24 June 1998: 7 ICSID Rep 12;
    38 ILM 708   337
Eureko BV v. Poland, Ad Hoc (Netherlands-Poland BIT)
(Fortier P., Schwebel & Rajski).
    Partial Award, 19 August 2005: 12 ICSID Rep 335 ....   71, 97, 110, 114,
                                                                      115,290, 322, 337,
                                                                      344, 347, 350, 352,
                                                                      354, 374, 445, 450,
                                                                      453, 457, 458, 462,
                                                                          470, 474

Fedax N.V. v. Venezuela, ICSID Case No. ARB/96/3
(Netherlands-Venezuela BIT) (Orrego Vicuña P., Heth & Owen).
    Decision of the Tribunal on Objections to Jurisdiction,
    11 July 1997: 5 ICSID Rep 186; 37 ILM 1378 ....   49, 59, 66
    Award, 9 March 1998: 5 ICSID Rep 200,
    37 ILM 1391 ....   87, 450, 452, 455,
                                                                              466
Marvin Feldman v. Mexico, ICSID Case No. ARB(AF)/99/1 (NAFTA)
(Kerameus P., Covarrubias Bravo & Gantz).
    Interim Decision on Preliminary Jurisdictional Issues,
    6 December 2000: 7 ICSID Rep 327; 126 ILR 9   336
    Award, 16 December 2002: 7 ICSID Rep 341;
    126 ILR 26 ....   163, 166, 174, 183,
                                                                      184, 187, 276, 281,
                                                                          293, 294, 297,
                                                                              374, 376
Fireman's Fund Insurance Company v. Mexico, ICSID Case No. ARB
(AF)/02/1 (NAFTA) (van den Berg P., Carrillo Gamboa &
Lowenfeld).
    Decision on the Preliminary Question, 17 July 2003:
    10 ICSID Rep 213 ....   337, 348, 350, 360
Piero Foresti, Laura de Carli and others v. South Africa
(ICSID Case No. ARB(AF)/07/1) 109, 374
Fraport AG Frankfurt Airport Services Worldwide v. Philippines,
ICSID Case No. ARB/03/25 (Germany-Philippines BIT) (Fortier P.,
Cremades & Reisman).
    Award, 16 August 2007 ....   94, 134, 159, 297,
                                                                              481
GAMI Investments, Inc. v. Mexico, UNCITRAL (NAFTA)
(Paulsson P., Reisman & Lacarte Muró).
    Final Award, 15 November 2004: 44 ILM 545;
    13 ICSID Rep 177, 178, 236, 278,
                                                                      281, 296, 344, 349

Gas Natural SDG, S.A. v. Argentina, ICSID Case No. ARB/03/10
(Spain-Argentina BIT) (Lowenfeld P., Alvarez & Nikken).
    Decision of the Tribunal on Preliminary Questions on
    Jurisdiction, 7 June 2005 .... 104, 118, 208-210,
    216, 229

Generation Ukraine, Inc. v. Ukraine, ICSID Case No. ARB/00/9
(US-Ukraine BIT) (Paulsson P., Salpius & Voss).
    Award, 16 September 2003: 10 ICSID Rep 240;
    44 ILM 404 .... 72, 244, 288-289,
    298, 325, 338,
    343, 347-348,
    354, 367

Alex Genin, Eastern Credit Limited, Inc. and A.S. Baltoil v. Estonia,
ICSID Case No. ARB/99/2 (US-Estonia BIT) (Fortier P., Heth &
van den Berg).
    Award, 18 June 2001: 6 ICSID Rep 241;
    17 ICSID Rev 395 .... 87, 94, 245-246,
    270, 277, 298,
    306-307, 461

Grand River Enterprises Six Nations, Ltd., et al. v. United States,
UNCITRAL (NAFTA) (Nariman P., Anaya & Crook).
    Decision on Objections to Jurisdiction,
    20 July 2006 525

Antoine Goetz et consorts v. Burundi, ICSID Case No. ARB/95/3
(BLEU-Burundi BIT) (Weil P., Bedjaoui & Bredin).
    Award, 10 February 1999: 6 ICSID Rep 5;
    15 ICSID Rev 457 .... 72, 78, 85, 87-88,
    100-101, 135,
    333, 337, 339

Philippe Gruslin v. Malaysia, ICSID Case No. ARB/99/3
(BLEU-Malaysia BIT) (Griffith).
    Award, 27 November 2000: 5 ICSID Rep 484 .... 67-68, 94, 526

Impregilo S.p.A. v. Pakistan, ICSID Case No. ARB/03/3
(Italy-Pakistan BIT) (Guillaume P., Cremades & Landau).
    Decision on Jurisdiction, 22 April 2005:
    12 ICSID Rep 245 .... 71, 440, 463,
    465, 474

Inceysa Vallisoletana, S.L. v. El Salvador, ICSID Case No.
ARB/03/26 (Spain-El Salvador BIT) (Oreamuno Blanco
P., Landy & von Wobeser).
    Award, 2 August 2006 .... 93, 113, 134, 159,
    297, 481

International Thunderbird Gaming Corporation v. Mexico,
UNCITRAL (NAFTA) (van den Berg P., Portal Ariosa & Wälde).
    Arbitral Award, 26 January 2006 .... 245, 274, 279-283,
    294, 527

Separate Opinion of Thomas Wälde............................ 279-283, 294, 527
Judgment on Petition to Set Aside Award,
14 February 2007: 473 F. Supp.2d 80......................... 78
Jan de Nul N.V., Dredging International N.V. v. Egypt,
ICSID Case No. ARB/04/13 (BLEU-Egypt BIT)
(Kaufmann-Kohler P., Mayer & Stern).
Decision on Jurisdiction, 16 June 2006....................... 60
Joy Mining Machinery Limited v. Egypt, ICSID Case No. ARB/03/11
(UK-Egypt BIT) (Orrego Vicuña P., Weeramantry & Craig).
Award on Jurisdiction, 6 August 2004: 19 ICSID Rev 486;
13 ICSID Rep 452, 469
Ioannis Kardassopoulos (Greece) v. Georgia, ICSID
Case No. ARB/05/18 (Georgia-Greece BIT and ECT)
(Fortier P., Orrego Vicuña & Watts).
Decision on Jurisdiction, 6 July 2007 .... 54, 94, 98
Lanco International Inc. v. Argentina, ICSID Case No. ARB/97/6
(US-Argentina BIT) (Cremades P., Aguilar Alvarez & Baptista).
Preliminary Decision on the Jurisdiction of the
Arbitral Tribunal, 8 December 1998:
5 ICSID Rep 369 71
Ronald S. Lauder v. Czech Republic, UNCITRAL (US-Czech
Republic BIT) (Briner P., Cutler & Klein).
Final Award, 3 September 2001:
9 ICSID Rep 66 .... 71-72, 105, 113,
114, 254, 276, 277,
295, 300, 302, 303,
304-305, 309, 311,
337, 358

L.E.S.I. S.p.A. et ASTALDI S.p.A. v. Algeria, ICSID Case No.
ARB/05/3 (Italy-Algeria BIT) (Tercier P., Faurès & Gaillard).
Decision, 12 July 2006...................................... 67, 452, 463
*LG&E Energy Corp., LG&E Capital Corp., and LG&E International,
Inc. v. Argentina,* ICSID Case No. ARB/02/1 (US-Argentina BIT)
(de Maekelt P., Rezek & van den Berg).
Decision on Liability, 3 October 2006:
46 ILM 40... 106, 109, 264-265,
277, 281, 282,
285-287, 298, 302,
303, 305, 306, 316,
340, 344-346, 363,
364, 453, 456, 459,
469-470, 474, 492,
493, 494, 496, 498,
517-524

Link-Trading Joint Stock Company v. Moldova, UNCITRAL
(US-Moldova BIT) (Hertzfeld P., Buruiana & Zykin).
    Final Award, 18 April 2002: 13 ICSID Rep................   336, 362
The Loewen Group, Inc. and Raymond L. Loewen v. United States,
ICSID Case No. ARB(AF)/98/3 (NAFTA) (Mason P., Mikva &
Mustill).
    Decision on Hearing of Respondent's Objection to Competence
    and Jurisdiction, 5 January 2001: 7 ICSID Rep 425;
    128 ILR 339..   337
    Award, 26 June 2003: 7 ICSID Rep 442; 42 ILM 811;
    128 ILR 359..   6, 22, 151, 181,
    184, 189, 237,
    240-243, 274,
    277, 289, 363,
    511

    Decision on Respondent's Request for a Supplementary
    Decision, 6 September 2004: 44 ILM 836;
    128 ILR 420..   243
Empresas Lucchetti, S.A. and Lucchetti Peru, S.A. v. Peru, (also
known as *Industria Nacional de Alimentos v. Peru*), ICSID Case No.
ARB/03/4 (Chile-Peru BIT) (Buergenthal P., Cremades and Paulsson).
    Decision on Annulment, 5 September 2007................   29, 78
Emilio Agustín Maffezini v. Spain, ICSID Case No. ARB/97/7
(Argentina-Spain BIT) (Orrego Vicuña P., Buergenthal & Wolf).
    Decision of the Tribunal on Objections to Jurisdiction,
    25 January 2000: 5 ICSID Rep 396;
    40 ILM 1129..   112, 113, 198,
    205-217, 221,
    224, 230, 466

    Award, 13 November 2000: 5 ICSID Rep 419;
    16 ICSID Rev 248 ....   87, 94, 102, 293,
    298, 340, 350,
    466

M.C.I. Power Group L.C. and New Turbine, Inc. v. Ecuador,
ICSID Case No. ARB/03/6 (US-Ecuador BIT) (Vinuesa P.,
Greenberg & Irarrázabal).
    Award, 31 July 2007....................................   223, 285-286,
    344, 524

Metalclad Corporation v. Mexico, ICSID Case No. ARB(AF)/97/1
(NAFTA) (Lauterpacht P., Civiletti & Siqueiros).
    Award, 30 August 2000: 5 ICSID Rep 209;
    ICSID Rev 168 ....   87, 102, 117, 245,
    279, 281, 286, 287,
    291, 293, 337, 342,
    345, 346, 369, 384,

                                                              388, 389, 391, 392,
                                                                      394, 397
Review by British Columbia Supreme Court,
2 May 2001: 5 ICSID Rep 236; 125 ILR 468 ....   291-293, 346
Metalpar S.A. y Buen Aire S.A. v. Argentina, ICSID Case No.
ARB/03/5 (Chile-Argentina BIT) (Oreamuno Blanco P.,
Cameron & Chabaneix).
    Award, 6 June 2008   417
Methanex Corporation v. United States, UNCITRAL (NAFTA)
    Letter by the Claimant to the Tribunal,
    18 September 2001   274
    Second Opinion of Sir Robert Jennings,
    5 November 2002   274
    Partial Award, 7 August 2002
    (Veeder P., Christopher & Rowley) 167, 337, 350-351,
                                                                  358, 365, 366, 458

    Final Award of the Tribunal on Jurisdiction and Merits,
    3 August 2005 (Veeder P., Reisman & Rowley):
    44 ILM 1345 ....   149, 151, 167, 168,
                                                                  169, 171, 172, 173,
                                                                      187, 274, 503

Middle East Cement Shipping and Handling Co. S.A. v. Egypt,
ICSID Case No. ARB/99/6 (Greece-Egypt BIT) (Böckstiegel
P., Bernardini & Wallace).
    Award, 12 April 2002: 7 ICSID Rep 178;
    18 ICSID Rev 602 ....   85, 91, 100, 163,
                                                                      245, 345, 347,
                                                                  350, 352, 375-376,
                                                                      384, 389-390,
                                                                      391, 396, 397

Mihaly International Corporation v. Sri Lanka, ICSID Case No.
ARB/00/2 (US-Sri Lanka BIT) (Sucharitkul P., Rogers & Suratgar).
    Award, 15 March 2002: 6 ICSID Rep 308;
    17 ICSID Rev 142 ....   67, 121, 138
Mr. Patrick Mitchell v. Congo, ICSID Case No. ARB/99/7
(US-DRC BIT).
    Decision on the Application for Annulment
    of the Award, 1 November 2006
    (Dimolitsa P., Dossou & Giardina) 29, 49, 67, 78, 90
Mondev International Ltd. v. United States, ICSID Case No.
ARB(AF)/99/2 (NAFTA) (Stephen P., Crawford & Schwebel).
    Award, 11 October 2002: 6 ICSID Rep 192; 42 ILM 85;
    125 ILR 110 ....   22, 236-238,
                                                                      240-242, 246,
                                                                      270, 273, 274,
                                                                      276-278, 380

MTD Equity Sdn. Bhd. and MTD Chile S.A. v. Chile,
ICSID Case No. ARB/01/7 (Malaysia-Chile BIT) (Rigo Sureda
P., Lalonde & Oreamuno Blanco).
    Award, 25 May 2004: 12 ICSID Rep 6,
        44 ILM 91 .... 29, 85, 94, 100,
        110, 111, 113,
        114, 125, 145,
        146, 229, 264,
        265, 267, 282-285,
        296, 298, 301,
        304, 350
    Decision on Annulment, 21 March 2007
    (Guillaume P., Crawford & Ordóñez Noriega): 13
    ICSID Rep 500 .... 78, 95
William Nagel v. Czech Republic, SCC Case 49/2002
(UK-Czechoslovakia BIT).
    Award, 2003: Excerpts in 2004(1) Stockholm Arbitration Report;
    13 ICSID Rep 94, 281, 463-465
National Grid plc v. Argentina, UNCITRAL (UK-Argentina BIT)
(Rigo Sureda P., Debevoise & Garro).
    Decision on Jurisdiction, 20 June 2006 .... 112, 113, 208,
        209, 224
Noble Ventures, Inc. v. Romania, ICSID Case No. ARB/01/11
(Romania-US (1992)). (Böckstiegel P., Lever & Dupuy).
    Award, 12 October 2005 .... 110-111, 114, 115,
        150, 194, 267, 302,
        445, 446, 448, 453,
        455, 458, 461-462,
        471, 474
Nykomb Synergetics Technology Holding AB v. Latvia,
SCC Case No. 118/2001 (Energy Charter Treaty)
(Haug P., Schütze & Gernandt).
    Award, 16 December 2003 .... 54, 160, 305,
        462, 514
*Occidental Petroleum Corporation & Occidental Exploration and
Production Company v. Ecuador* (Fortier P., Williams & Stern).
    Decision on Jurisdiction, 3 August 2006 514
Occidental Exploration and Production Company v. Ecuador,
LCIA Case No. UN3467 (US-Ecuador BIT) (Orrego Vicuña
P., Brower & Sweeney).
    Final Award, 1 July 2004: 12 ICSID Rep 59 .... 105, 114, 125, 152,
        160, 165, 169, 170,
        173, 177, 178, 184,
        264, 265, 271, 277,
        279, 286, 301, 303,
        312-313, 336, 342

Judgment of English Court of Appeal,
9 September 2005, [2006] QB 432 ....   76, 95, 512
Mr. Eudoro Armando Olguín v. Paraguay, ICSID Case No. ARB/98/5
(Peru-Paraguay BIT) (Oreamuno Blanco P., Rezek & Mayora
Alvarado).
    Award, 26 July 2001: 6 ICSID Rep 164 ....   71, 337
*Pan American Energy LLC, and BP Argentina Exploration Company
v. Argentina*, ICSID Case No. ARB/03/13 (US-Argentina BIT)
(Caflisch P., Stern & van den Berg).
    Decision on Preliminary Objections,
    27 July 2006 ....   336, 417, 455, 469,
                                                                              474, 527

Parkerings-Compagniet AS v. Lithuania, ICSID Case No. ARB/05/8
(Norway-Lithuania BIT) (Levy P., Lew & Lalonde).
    Award, 11 September 2007 ....   226, 227, 230, 258,
                                                                         288, 289, 294, 312,
                                                                              345, 352, 354

Petrobart Limited v. Kyrgyz Republic, SCC Arb. No. 126/2003
(ECT) (Danelius P., Bring & Smets).
    Award, 29 March 2005: 13 ICSID Rep.........................   54, 293
Plama Consortium Limited v. Bulgaria, ICSID Case No. ARB/03/24
(ECT) (Salans P., van den Berg & Veeder).
    Decision on Jurisdiction, 8 February 2005:
    20 ICSID Rev 262; 44 ILM 721; 13 ICSID Rep 54, 110, 115, 125,
                                                                         204, 212, 213, 214,
                                                                              216, 217, 219,
                                                                                   223, 230

Pope & Talbot Inc v. Canada, UNCITRAL (NAFTA)
(Dervaird P., Greenberg & Belman).
    Statement of Claim, 25 March 1999   426
    Interim Award, 26 June 2000: 7 ICSID Rep 69;
    122 ILR 316..   22, 87, 326, 337,
                                                                       338, 341, 342, 344,
                                                                            349, 426-428,
                                                                                 526, 527
    Award on the Merits of Phase 2, 10 April 2001:
    7 ICSID Rep 102; 122 ILR 352 ....   117, 163-167,
                                                                       175-178, 180, 181,
                                                                       183, 187, 189, 229,
                                                                       236, 245, 262, 273,
                                                                            293, 294, 363
    Award in Respect of Damages, 31 May 2002:
    7 ICSID Rep 148; 41 ILM 1347; 126 ILR 127 ....   117, 118, 236
    Fourth Submission of the United States of America,
    1 Nov. 2000   273

PSEG Global Inc., and Konya Ingin Electrik Üretim ve Ticaret
Limited Şirketi v. Turkey, ICSID Case No. ARB/02/5 (US-Turkey
BIT) (Orrego Vicuña P., Fortier & Kaufmann-Kohler).
    Award, 19 January 2007 265

The Rompetrol Group N.V. v. Romania, ICSID Case No. ARB/06/3
(Netherlands-Romania BIT) (Berman P., Donovan & Lalonde).
    Decision on Respondent's Preliminary Objections
    on Jurisdiction and Admissibility, 18 April 2008......... 70
RosInvestCo UK Ltd. v. Russia, SCC Case No. Arb. V079/2005
(UK-USSR BIT) (Böckstiegel P., Steyn & Berman).
    Award on Jurisdiction, October 2007.......................... 210, 212, 215,
    219-220

Saar Papier Vertriebs GmbH v. Poland, (Germany/Poland BIT).
    Award, 1995 (not public)... 58
Saipem S.p.A. v. Bangladesh, ICSID Case No. ARB/05/07
(Italy-Bangladesh BIT) (Kaufmann-Kohler P., Schreuer & Otton).
    Decision on Jurisdiction and Recommendation on
    Provisional Measures, 21 March 2007 .... 93, 104
Salini Costruttori S.p.A. and Italstrade S.p.A. v. Jordan,
ICSID Case No. ARB/02/13 (Italy-Jordan BIT)
(Guillaume P., Cremades & Sinclair).
    Decision on Jurisdiction, 29 November 2004:
    44 ILM 573... 114, 207, 210, 211,
    216, 446, 452,
    453, 470

Salini Costruttori S.p.A. and Italstrade S.p.A. v. Morocco,
ICSID Case No. ARB/00/4 (Italy-Morocco BIT)
(Briner P., Cremades & Fadlallah).
    Decision on Jurisdiction, 23 July 2001: 6 ICSID Rep 400;
    42 ILM 609... 67, 71, 77, 93,
    463, 479

Saluka Investments BV v. Czech Republic, UNCITRAL
(Netherlands-Czechoslovakia BIT) (Watts P., Fortier & Behrens).
    Partial Award, 17 March 2006..................................... 22, 69, 114, 116,
    125-126, 236, 240,
    264, 267, 268, 270,
    272, 275-276,
    278-280, 282,
    289, 305, 306, 311,
    314, 324, 325, 344,
    358, 359, 360, 365,
    367-368

S.D. Myers, Inc. v. Canada, UNCITRAL (NAFTA)
(Hunter P., Chiasson & Schwartz).

Partial Award, 13 November 2000: 8 ICSID Rep 18;
40 ILM 1408... 87, 117, 151, 164,
165, 166, 175, 177,
185, 186, 234, 238,
246, 250, 272,
274-276, 290-292,
338, 340, 344, 345,
349, 358, 419,
424-426, 505

Mr. Franz Sedelmayer v. Russia, ad hoc (Germany-USSR BIT)
(Magnusson P., Wachler & Zykin).
Arbitration Award, 7 July 1998 .... 87, 333, 339, 341,
384, 392, 396, 397

Sempra Energy International v. Argentina,
ICSID Case No. ARB/02/16 (US-Argentina BIT)
(Orrego Vicuña P., Lalonde & Morelli Rico).
Decision on Objections to Jurisdiction,
11 May 2005..   118
Award, 28 September 2007 .... 106, 107, 118, 119,
277, 282, 285, 287,
302, 303, 305, 311,
340-342, 345, 350,
352, 385, 393, 440,
453, 455, 456, 459,
469, 472, 474,
492-496, 198-500,
514, 517-522

SGS Société Générale de Surveillance S.A. v. Pakistan,
ICSID Case No. ARB/01/13 (Swiss Confederation-Pakistan BIT)
(Feliciano P., Faurès & Thomas).
Decision of the Tribunal on Objections to Jurisdiction,
6 August 2003: 8 ICSID Rep 406; 42 ILM 1290,
129 ILR 387... 71, 77, 94, 105, 116,
437, 446, 450, 452,
454, 455, 457, 458,
460, 462, 466-468,
469, 471, 479

SGS Société Générale de Surveillance S.A. v. Philippines,
ICSID Case No. ARB/02/6 (Swiss Confederation-Philippines BIT)
(El-Kosheri P., Crawford & Crivellaro).
Decision of the Tribunal on Objections to Jurisdiction,
29 January 2004: 8 ICSID Rep 518; 42 ILM 1285;
129 ILR 444... 77, 94, 103, 104,
105, 113, 115, 125,
265, 295, 352, 355,

445, 446, 449, 450,
452-458, 460,
467-468, 470,
472, 473, 474, 475,
478, 479, 513

Order of the Tribunal on Further Proceedings,
17 December 2007 473
Waguih Elie George Siag and Clorinda Vecchi v. Egypt,
ICSID Case No. ARB/05/15 (Italy-Egypt BIT)
(Williams P., Pryles & Orrego Vicuña).
   Decision on Jurisdiction,
   11 April 2007: 46 ILM 863 .... 6, 93
Siemens A.G. v. Argentina, ICSID Case No. ARB/02/8
(Germany-Argentina BIT) (Rigo Sureda P., Brower & Bello Janeiro).
   Decision on Jurisdiction, 3 August 2004:
   12 ICSID Rep 174; 44 ILM 138 .... 113, 114, 125, 196,
197, 203, 207-210,
219, 221, 222, 223,
265, 266, 282
   Award, 6 February 2007 .... 114, 175, 182, 261,
265, 302, 303, 306,
308, 313, 318, 343,
354, 373, 381-384,
398, 457, 471, 527

Hussein Nuaman Soufraki v. United Arab Emirates,
ICSID Case No. ARB/02/7 (Italy-United Arab Emirates BIT)
(Fortier P., Schwebel & El Kholy).
   Award, 7 July 2004: 12 ICSID Rep 158 .... 93, 102
   Decision of the *Ad Hoc* Committee on the Application for
   Annulment of Mr. Soufraki, 5 June 2007
   (Feliciano P., Nabulsi & Stern)................................... 78
*Suez, Sociedad General de Aguas de Barcelona S.A., and
Vivendi Universal S.A. v. Argentina*, ICSID Case No. ARB/03/19
(France-Argentina and Spain-Argentina BITs)
(Salacuse P., Kaufmann-Kohler & Nikken)......................... 109
   Order in Response to a Petition for Transparency
   and Participation as *Amicus curiae*, 19 May 2005:
   21 ICSID Rev 342 (Spanish original);
   21 ICSID Rev 351 253
   Decision on Jurisdiction, 3 August 2006..................... 208, 210, 229, 514
*Suez, Sociedad General de Aguas de Barcelona S.A., and InterAgua
Servicios Integrales del Agua S.A. v. Argentina*, ICSID Case
No. ARB/03/17 (France-Argentina and Spain-Argentina BITs)
(Salacuse P., Kaufmann-Kohler & Nikken)......................... 109
   Decision on Jurisdiction, 16 May 2006........................ 60, 182, 203, 208,
210, 261, 514

SwemBalt AB, Sweden v. Latvia, UNCITRAL (Sweden-Latvia BIT)
(Philip P., Hober & Moller).
Decision by the Court of Arbitration,
23 October 2000 .... 87, 463

Tanmiah v. Tunisia, Arab Investment Court (Arab Investment
Agreement).
Court Decision, 12 October 2006 52
Técnicas Medioambientales TECMED, S.A. v. Mexico,
ICSID Case No. ARB (AF)/00/2 (Spain-Mexico BIT)
(Grigera Naón P., Fernández Rozas & Bernal Verea).
Award, 29 May 2003: 10 ICSID Rep 134;
19 ICSID Rev 158; 43 ILM 133 .... 100, 102, 151, 222,
245, 274, 277, 279,
280, 282, 284,
291-295, 309,
325, 337, 340,
342, 345, 346,
358, 363, 365,
369, 384, 394

Telenor Mobile Communications A.S. v. Hungary, ICSID Case No.
ARB/04/15 (Norway-Hungary BIT) (Goode P., Allard & Marriott).
Award, 13 September 2006 .... 113, 210, 212-214,
216, 219, 339, 343,
344, 350, 357

Tokios Tokelės v. Ukraine, ICSID Case No. ARB/02/18
(Lithuania-Ukraine BIT) (Weil P., Price & Bernardini).
Decision on Jurisdiction, 29 April 2004: 11 ICSID Rep 313;
20 ICSID Rev 205 .... 6, 22, 70, 94, 102,
110

Tradex Hellas S.A. v. Albania, ICSID Case No. ARB/94/2
(Böckstiegel P., Fielding & Giardina).
Final Award, 29 April 1999: 5 ICSID Rep 70;
14 ICSID Rev 197 338
United Parcel Service of America Inc v. Canada, UNCITRAL
(NAFTA) (Keith P., Cass & Fortier).
Award on Jurisdiction, 22 November 2002:
7 ICSID Rep 288 .... 22, 236, 274,
336, 461

Award on the Merits, 24 May 2007: 46 ILM 922 .... 109, 163, 164,
165, 167, 173,
179, 184, 185,
188, 487, 488,
508

Separate Statement of Dean Ronald A. Cass,
24 May 2007.. 164, 165, 167, 180,
185, 188, 485, 488,
508

Waste Management, Inc. v. Mexico (Waste Management I),
ICSID Case No. ARB(AF)/98/2 (NAFTA) (Cremades P., Highet &
Siqueiros).
    Award, 2 June 2000: 5 ICSID Rep 443........................ 277
    Dissenting Opinion of K. Highet, 2 June 2000:
    5 ICSID Rep 462... 325
Waste Management, Inc. v. Mexico (Waste Management II),
ICSID Case No. ARB(AF)/00/3 (NAFTA) (Crawford P., Civiletti &
Magallón Gómez).
    Award, 30 April 2004: 11 ICSID Rep 362; 43 ILM 967;
    132 ILR 177... 236, 238, 240, 246,
250, 251, 274, 275,
279, 281, 290, 291,
293, 325, 342, 349,
350, 353, 355, 356,
358

Wena Hotels Limited v. Egypt, ICSID Case No. ARB/98/4
(UK-Egypt BIT) (Leigh P., Fadlallah & Wallace).
    Award, 8 December 2000: 6 ICSID Rep 89;
    41 ILM 896.. 22, 29, 90-92,
96-97, 308, 309,
312-313, 345-346,
352, 368, 384,
391-393, 397, 525

    Decision on the Application by the Arab Republic
    of Egypt for Annulment, 22 January 2002.................. 78, 100
    Decision on Interpretation, 31 October 2005.............. 272, 368, 383

Yaung Chi Oo Trading Pte. Ltd. v. Myanmar,
ASEAN I.D. Case No. ARB/01/1 (Sucharitkul P., Crawford & Delon).
    Award, 31 March 2003: 8 ICSID Rep 452;
    42 ILM 540.. 52, 135, 210, 478

II   PCIJ AND ICJ CASES

Anglo-Iranian Oil Company Ltd. (United Kingdom v. Iran),
[1952] ICJ Rep 93.. 36, 196, 197, 206,
441

Barcelona Traction, Light and Power Company Limited
(Belgium v. Spain), [1970] ICJ Rep 3 ....   6, 36-39, 102, 121,
                                                                       233-234, 252
Certain German Interests in Polish Upper Silesia
(Germany v. Poland) (Merits) (1926),
PCIJ Ser. A, No. 7 ....   15, 95, 321, 322
Certain Phosphate Lands in Nauru (Nauru v. Australia),
Preliminary Objections, [1992] ICJ Rep 240   525
Continental Shelf (Libyan Arab Jamahiriya v. Malta),
[1985] ICJ Rep 13   104
Ahmadou Sadio Diallo (Republic of Guinea v. Democratic
Republic of the Congo) (Preliminary Objections,
24 May 2007), 46 ILM 712   36
Elettronica Sicula S.p.A. (ELSI) (US v. Italy),
[1989] ICJ Rep 15 ....   23, 37-39, 78, 95,
                                                                       102, 248-250, 262,
                                                                       298, 301-302,
                                                                       307-309, 312,
                                                                       373, 521
Factory at Chorzów (Germany v. Poland)
(Claim for Indemnity, Merits) (1928),
PCIJ Ser. A, No. 13 ....   15, 380-382, 395
Fisheries Jurisdiction Case (Spain v. Canada),
(Judgment, 4 December 1998), [1998] ICJ Rep 432   337
Free Zones of Upper Savoy and the District of Gex Second phase,
(Judgment, 6 December 1930) PCIJ Ser. A No. 24 and
(Judgment, 7 June 1932) PCIJ Ser. A/B No. 46   99
Gabčíkovo-Nagymaros Project (Hungary v. Slovakia)
(Judgment, 25 September 1997), [1997] ICJ Rep 7 ....   493, 516, 523
German Settlers in Poland (1923),
PCIJ Ser. B No. 6   439
Greco-Bulgarian 'Communities' Advisory Opinion (1930),
PCIJ Ser. B No. 17   99
LaGrand (Germany v. United States), [2001] ICJ Rep 466,
(2001) 40 ILM 1069.   512
Land, Island and Maritime Frontier Dispute
(El Salvador v. Honduras) (Application to Intervene, Judgment),
[1990] ICJ Rep 92   526
Mavrommatis Palestine Concessions (Jurisdiction) (1924),
PCIJ Ser. A, No. 2 ....   5, 15
Military and Paramilitary Activities In and Against Nicaragua
(Nicaragua v. US).
   Jurisdiction: [1984] ICJ Rep 392   23
   Merits: [1986] ICJ Rep 14 ....   23, 122, 128,
                                                                       492-494

Norwegian Loans (France v. Norway),
[1957] ICJ Rep 9.. 36
Oil Platforms (Iran v. US).
    Preliminary Objection: [1996] ICJ Rep 1996 256
    Merits: [2003] ICJ Rep 161 .... 492, 493
Oscar Chinn (1934), PCIJ Rep Ser A/B No. 63.................. 328
Panevezys-Saldutiskis Railway Case (1939),
PCIJ Ser. A/B, No. 76.. 5
Payment of Various Serbian Loans Issued in France;
Payment in Gold of the Brazilian Federal Loans Issued
in France (1929) PCIJ Ser. A Nos. 20/21............................ 112
Pulp Mills on the River Uruguay
(Argentina v. Uruguay)... 36
Request for the interpretation of the Judgment of November 20th,
1950, in the Asylum Case (Colombia v. Peru)
(Judgment, 27 November 1950), [1950] ICJ Rep 395 90
Rights of Nationals of the United States of
America in Morocco (France v. US) [1952]
ICJ Rep 176 .... 102, 195, 197,
247

S.S. 'Lotus' (France v. Turkey) (1927),
PCIJ Ser. A No. 10.. 80
S.S. Wimbledon (Judgment of 17 August 1923),
PCIJ Ser. A, No. 1.. 116
Temple of Preah Vihear (Cambodia v. Thailand)
(Judgment on Merits, 15 June 1962),
[1962] ICJ Rep 6... 527
Treatment of Polish Nationals and Other Persons of Polish
Origin or Speech in the Danzig (1933),
PCIJ Ser. A/B No. 44 99

III   ICSID CASES

AGIP S.p.A. v. Congo, ICSID Case No. ARB/77/1.
    Award, 30 November 1979: 1 ICSID Rep 306;
    21 ILM 726.. 378, 388
Amco Asia Corporation v. Indonesia, ICSID Case No. ARB/81/1.
    Decision on Jurisdiction, 25 September 1983:
    1 ICSID Rep 377 217-218
    Award, 20 November 1984.. 323, 376
    Decision on the Application for Annulment,
    16 May 1986: 1 ICSID Rep 509 78
    Resubmitted Case Award, 31 May 1990:
    1 ICSID Rep 569 240

Autopista Concesionada de Venezuela, C.A. v. Venezuela,
ICSID Case No. ARB/00/5.
    Decision on Jurisdiction, 27 September 2001:
    6 ICSID Rep 417   69
    Award, September 23, 2003: 10 ICSID Rep 309   514

Benvenuti and Bonfant Srl v. Congo, ICSID Case No. ARB/77/2.
    Award, 8 August 1980: 1 ICSID Rep 330;
    21 ILM 740..   327, 378, 388
Cable Television of Nevis v. St. Kitts and Nevis, ICSID Case No. ARB/95/2.
    Award, 13 January 1997: 13 ICSID Rev 328;
    5 ICSID Rep 108   463
CDC Group Plc. v. Seychelles, ICSID Case No. ARB/02/14.
    Decision of the *Ad Hoc* Committee on the Application
    for Annulment of the Republic of Seychelles,
    29 June 2005..   78
Československá Obchodní Banka, A.S. v. Slovak Republic,
ICSID Case No. ARB/97/4.
    Decision of the Tribunal on Objections to Jurisdiction,
    24 May 1999: 5 ICSID Rep 335   66
    Decision of the Tribunal on Respondent's Further and
    Partial Objection to Jurisdiction, 1 December 2000:
    5 ICSID Rep 358   95
    Award, 29 December 2004: 13 ICSID Rep..................   311, 355, 392-393
Compañiá del Desarrollo de Santa Elena, S.A. v. Costa Rica,
ICSID Case No. ARB/96/1.
    Final Award, 17 February 2000: 5 ICSID Rep 153;
    39 ILM 317..   101, 340, 369, 385

Klöckner v. Cameroon, ICSID Case No. ARB/81/2.
    Decision on Annulment, 3 May 1985:
    2 ICSID Rep 95   78

Liberian Eastern Timber Corporation (LETCO) v. Liberia,
ICSID Case No. ARB/83/2.
    Award, 31 March 1986: 2 ICSID Rep 346...................   371, 373, 378

Maritime International Nominees Establishment v. Guinea, ICSID
Case No. ARB/84/4.
    Decision on Annulment, 22 December 1989:
    4 ICSID Rep 79   78

Repsol YPF Ecuador S.A. v. Empresa Estatal Petróleos del Ecuador,
ICSID Case No. ARB/01/10.
    Award, 20 February 2004   98

Southern Pacific Properties (Middle East) Limited v. Egypt,
ICSID Case No. ARB/84/3.
    Decision on Jurisdiction, 27 November 1985:
        3 ICSID Rep 112   45
    Award on the Merits, 20 May 1992:
        3 ICSID Rep 189 ....   281-282, 297,
                                                       352, 378, 391

Vacuum Salt Products Ltd. v. Ghana ICSID Case No. ARB/92/1.
    Award, 16 February 1994: 4 ICSID Rep 329   69

IV   GATT AND WTO CASES

Brazil-Measures Affecting Imports of Retreaded Tyres,
WT/DS332/AB/R (adopted 17 December 2007) 485, 504
Canada – Autos, WT/DS139/AB/R and WT/DS142/AB/R
(adopted 19 June 2000)   421
Canada – Administration of the Foreign Investment Review Act (1984),
GATT BISD 30th Supp. 140   419
Chile – Taxes on Alcoholic Beverages, WT/DS87/AB/R and
WT/DS110/AB/R (adopted 12 January 2000)   174

EC-Measures Affecting Asbestos and Asbestos-Containing Products,
WT/DS135/AB/R (adopted 5 April 2001)   171-172
*EC-Regime for the Importation, Sale and Distribution
of Bananas* (1997), WT/DS27/AB/R
(adopted 25 September 2007) 218, 421

*Indonesia – Certain Measures Affecting the
Automobile Industry* (1998), WT/DS54/R; WT/DS55/R,
WT/DS59/R and WT/DS64/R (adopted 23 July 1998)   421

Japan – Taxes on Alcoholic Beverages, WT/DS8/AB/R,
WT/DS10/AB/R, WT/DS11/AB/R
(adopted, November 1996) 171, 174

*Korea – Measures Affecting Imports of Fresh,
Chilled and Frozen Beef,* WT/DS161/AB/R and
WT/DS169/AB/R (adopted 10 January 2001)   172

*United States – Import Prohibition of Certain Shrimp and
Shrimp Products,* WT/DS58/AB/R
(adopted 6 November 1998)   487

United States – Measures Affecting the Cross-Border
Supply of Gambling and Betting Services,
WT/DS285/AB/R (adopted 19 August 2005).....................   404, 486
United States – Section 337 of the Tariff Act of 1930
(GATT Panel, 7 November 1989)
36th Supp. BISD 345...   184, 187, 218

V   OTHER CASES AND DECISIONS

Aboilard (1905), XI RIAA 71   439
Albert Bela Root (1958), United States Foreign Claims
Settlement Commission, Decision No. Hung-1625   328
The Ambatielos Claim (Greece, United Kingdom of Great
Britain and Northern Ireland) (Final Award, 6 March 1956)
(1963), XII UNRIAA 91 ....   102, 206, 207
Amoco International Finance Corp. v. Iran (1987),
15 Iran-US CTR 189...   325, 371
Amoco International Finance Corp. v. Iran (1989),
21 Iran-US CTR 79...   378, 386
Anglo-Iranian Oil Co. Ltd. v. Jaffrate (The Rose Mary),
[1953] 1 WLR 246; 20 ILR 316..   383
Arbitration Between Valentine Petroleum & Chemical Corporation
and Agency for International Development (1967),
44 ILR 79..   376

Biloune and Marine Drive Complex Ltd. v. Ghana Investments
Centre and the Government of Ghana (Award on Jurisdiction
and Liability, 27 October 1989) 95 ILR 184.......................   107-108, 253, 328,
                                                                           342, 366, 391
Boffolo (1903), X RIAA 528   236
Booker Aquaculture Ltd. & Hydro Seafood GSP Ltd. v.
Scottish Ministers, [2003] ECR-1-7411   361
BP Exploration Company Ltd. v. Libya (1979),
53 ILR 297   24-25
British Properties in Spanish Zone of Morocco (1925),
II RIAA 615...   307, 310, 378

Case of the Former King of Greece v. Greece
(Judgment, 28 November 2002)   394
Chazen v. Mexico (1930), IV RIAA 586   359
Chevreau (1931), 27 AJIL 153   236
Corn Products Refining Company Claim (1955)
22 ILR 333..   327

*Council of Canadians et al. v. Attorney General of
Canada*, (Ontario Court of Appeal Judgment,
30 November 2006) 277 DLR (4th) 527   51

Dallal v. Iran, (Award, 10 June 1983)
3 Iran-US CTR 10..   417
Delagoa Bay Railway Case   378
*Desarrollos en Salud S.A S/Concurso preventivo/S/
Incidente de Revisión (N.V. NISSHO IWAI S.A.
(BENELUX))* (Juzgado Comercial 26, Secretaría
51, 10 November 2003) 76, 101
Deutz (1929), IV RIAA 472   439
DiRussa v. Dean Witter Reynolds, Inc. (1997),
121 F.3d 818 (2d Cir. 1997)...   78

Egypt v. Suez Canal Company (Award, 1864)....................   8
Elf Aquitaine Iran v. NIOC (1982), 11 YCA 112................   25

Faulkner (1927), 21 AJIL *349*...   14
Fedordchak Claim (1962), 40 ILR 96   327
Felix Claim (1961), 42 ILR 161   328

General Electric Company Claim (1959),
30 ILR 140...   328
George W. Cook (1927), IV RIAA 213   439
Goldenberg Case (1928), II RIAA 901   378
Gowan and Copland   327
Grimm v. Iran, (Award, February 18, 1983) 71 ILR 650....   112

Harry Roberts (1926), IV RIAA 77; 1 AJIL 357...............   14-15, 236
Hemming (1920), VI RIAA 51   439
Henke Claim (1958-II), 26 ILR 276..................................   328
Hood Corp. v. Iran, (1984) 7 Iran-US CTR 36..................   417
Hopkins (1926) IV RIAA 41; 21 AJIL 160........................   14, 236, 439
Illinois Central Railroad Company Case (1926),
IV RIAA 21   439

In the Matter of Cross Border Trucking Services
(NAFTA Chapter 20 Panel Decision,
Final Report, 6 February 2001)   162
INA Corporation v. Iran (1985) 8 Iran-US CTR 373..........   378, 379, 387, 392
*International Bank of Washington – Overseas Private
Investment Corporation: Arbitration of Dispute Involving
U.S. Investment Guaranty Program*
(Award, 8 November 1972)   361

Jaffa-Jerusalem Railway Arbitration 24
Jalapa Railroad and Power Co.
(US v. Mexico) (1948)... 440
James and Others v. United Kingdom (1986),
75 ILR 397 371
Janes (1926), IV RIAA 82.. 246
Joseph E. Davies (1927), IV RIAA 139............................. 439

Kahane (Successor)/Parisi and the Austrian State,
Case No. 131, Annual Digest 5 (1929-1930) 374
Kelo v. New London (2005), 545 US 469........................... 371
Kuwait v. American Independent Oil Company (AMINOIL)
(1982), 21 ILM 976 25

Landreau (1922), I RIAA 347... 439
LaPrade v. Kidder, Peabody & Co., 246 F.3d 702,
706 (D.C. Cir. 2001).. 78
Lena Goldfields Arbitration (1930) (1950), 56 CLQ 42 ..... 24, 80, 378
Libyan American Oil Co. (LIAMCO) v. Libya
(Award, 12 April 1977) 20 ILM 1 .... 25, 373
Lighthouses Arbitration (France v. Greece) (1956),
12 RIAA 155; 23 ILR 659.. 396

Neer (1926), IV RIAA 60 .... 14, 235-237, 270, 302
Norwegian Shipowners' Claims (Norway v. US) (1922),
1 RIAA 307... 14-15, 321, 322,
                                                                                                      324, 378

Otis Elevator Company v. Iran (1991), 84 ILR 618............ 338

Parsons (Great Britain v. United States) (1925)................. 359
Petrolane Inc. v. Iran (1991), 27 Iran-US CTR 64.............. 328
Petroleum Development Ltd. v. The Sheikh of Abu Dhabi (1951),
18 ILR 144 24-25
Phelps Dodge Corp. v. Iran (1986),
10 Iran-US CTR 121.. 391
Phillips Petroleum Company Iran v. Iran
(Award, 29 June 1989)... 342, 352
Pietrzak Claim (1962), 56 AJIL 1110 328
Rankin v. Iran (1987), 17 Iran-US CTR. 135..................... 314
Reineccius v. Bank of International Settlements,
Arbitral Tribunal of the Bank of International Settlements
(January 8, 2001) 327
*Revere Copper and Brass, Inc. and Overseas Private
Investment Corporation* (Award, 24 August 1978) 17 ILM 1321;
56 ILR 258... 41, 327-328, 438

Rudloff (1903), IX RIAA 244... 439

Ruler of Qatar v. International Marine Oil Co. (1953),
20 ILR 534.. 24-25

Sambiaggio Case (1903), X RIAA.................................... 307, 309

*Sapphire International Petroleums Ltd. v. National
Iranian Oil Co.* (1963), 35 ILR 136................................. 24-25

Saudi Arabia v. Arabian American Oil Co. (ARAMCO) (1963),
27 ILR 117.. 24-25

Saudi Arabia v. The Arabian American Oil Company (1958),
27 ILR 117.. 438

Schering Corp. v. Iran (1984), 5 Iran-US CTR 361............. 417

Sea-Land Service Inc. v. Iran (1984)
6 Iran-US CTR 149.. 359, 417

Sedco, Inc. v. National Iranian Oil Co., 10 Iran-US CTR 180,
(1986) 25 ILM 629 394

Selwyn Case (1903), IX RIAA 380..................................... 378

Shufeldt Claim (USA v. Guatemala) (Decision of the Arbitrator)
(1930), II RIAA 1079.. 98, 378, 439,
                                                                           477

*Singer Sewing Machine Company Arbitration
(United States v. Turkey)* 439

Sola Tiles, Inc. v. Iran (1987), 14 Iran-US CTR 223 378

Starrett Housing Corp. v. Iran (1983),
4 Iran-US CTR 122.. 326, 327

Starrett Housing Corp. v. Iran (Final Award) (1987),
16 Iran-US CTR 112.. 385, 389

*Tahoe-Sierra Preservation Council, Inc. v. Tahoe Regional
Planning Agency* (2002), 122 S.Ct.1465 348

*Texaco Overseas Petroleum Company (TOPCO) and California
Asiatic Oil Co. v. Libya* (1977), 104 JDI 350 (French original),
(1979) 53 ILR 389 (English translation) 24-25, 32, 438

*Tippetts, Abbett, McCarthy, Stratton and TAMS-AFFA
Consulting Engineers of Iran v. Iran* (1984),
6 Iran-US CTR 219.. 326, 327, 341, 342

Too v. Greater Modesto (1989), 23 Iran-US CTR 378........ 359

Way (1929), 23 AJIL 466.. 14

*Wilson Beimar Magne Hinojosa, Diputado Nacional contra
Eduardo Rodríguez Veltzé, Presidente Constitucional de la
República de Bolivia, y otro* (Sentencia TC 0031/2006,
10 May 2006)... 51

Youmans (1926), IV RIAA 110 246

Table of Treaties and Other Instruments

I   BILATERAL INVESTMENT TREATIES

For ease of reference, bilateral investment treaties are listed by referring to the two treaty parties in alphabetical order, followed by the date the treaty was signed (not the date of ratification). For example, *Treaty between the United States of America and the Argentine Republic Concerning the Reciprocal Encouragement and Protection of Investment* (signed 14 November 1991, entered into force 20 October 1994) is referred to as Argentina-US (1991).

Afghanistan-Turkey (2004)
    Art. 4(1) 370
Albania-Egypt (1993) 235
Albania-UK (1994) 113
    Art. 3(3) 205
Albania-US (1995) 229, 489
    Art. II(3)(b) 300
Algeria-Denmark (1999)
    Art. 2(1) 126
Algeria-Sweden (2003)
    Art. 2(4) 431
Algeria-Turkey (1997)
    Art. II(1) 135
Argentina-Australia (1995)
    Art. 1(1)(f) 411
    Art. 9(1)(a) 409
    Art. 9(1)(c) 409
    Art. 9(1)(e) 410-411
Argentina-BLEU (1990) 101
    Art. 4(1) 209

Argentina-Canada (1991)
    Art. XIII(1)(c) 410
Argentina-France (1991) 69
    Art. 3 258
    Art. 4 .... 219, 223
    Art. 5(1) 313
    Art. 5(2) 333
    Art. 10 477
Argentina-Germany (1991) 125, 221,
                                                                                         266, 313
    Art. 2(3) 299
    Art. 3 .... 209, 232
    Art. 4(1) 308
    Art. 4(2) 384
    Art. 7(1) 318
Argentina-Korea (1994)
    Art. 8(2) 205
Argentina-Mexico (1996)
    Art. 7 127
Argentina-Netherlands (1992) 123
    Art. 1(b) 68
    Art. 2 127
Argentina-New Zealand (1999) 309
    Art. 5(2) 507
Argentina-Spain (1991) 118, 207,
                                                                                         224
    Art. I(2) 93
    Art. IV(2) 206, 209
    Art. X 205
    Art. X(3) 205
Argentina-Sweden (1991)
    Art. 2(1) 126
Argentina-UK (1990) 113, 307,
                                                                                         444, 456
    Art. 1(a) 93
    Art. 2(2) 313, 445,
                                                                                         447
    Art. 3 210
    Art. 4 .... 112, 316,
                                                                                         499
    Art. 5(2) 316, 334
    Art. 8(4) 79
    Art. 11 477
Argentina-US (1991) 106, 118,
                                                                                         444, 449,
                                                                                         450, 489,
                                                                                         518

Art. I(1)(a) 65, 67
Art. II(1) 157, 201
Art. II(1)(b) 157, 299
Art. II(2)(a) 257
Art. II(2)(c) 444, 447,
                                                                       455, 469
Art. II(3) 144
Art. IV(2) 398
Art. IV(3) 158, 203,
                                                                       316, 499,
                                                                       500
Art. V 407, 411
Art. V(2) 412
Art. VII(2) 70
Art. VII(3) 70
Art. XI 485, 492,
                                                                       495, 497,
                                                                       517

Armenia-Canada (1997)
Art. V(2) 423
Art. V(2)(e) 428
Armenia-Switzerland (2003)
Art. 4(3) 160, 225
Armenia-US (1992) 123
Art. IV 409
Art. IV(1)(c) 411
Art. IV(1)(d) 409
Art. IV(1)(e) 410-411
Art. IV(1)(f) 409
Art. IV(2) 412
Asian-African Legal Consultative Committee Draft Model A (1985)
Art. 2 126-127
Art. 3(iii) 143
Asian-African Legal Consultative Committee Draft Model B (1985)
Art. 3(ii) 428
Australia-Chile (1996)
Art. 11 447
Australia-China (1988) 44
Art. X(1) 413
Art. X(1)(c) 410
Art. X(2) 411
Art. XI 444, 445,
                                                                       447
Australia-Egypt (2001) 123
Art. 3(1) 127

Art. 5.. 144
Art. 7(1).. 370
Australia-India (1999)
  Art. 1(b).. 411
  Art. 5... 144
  Art. 9(1).. 413
Australia-Peru (1995)
  Art. 1(1)(f).. 411
Australia-Poland (1991)
  Art. 10... 446
Australia-Romania (1993)
  Art. 1(b).. 410
  Art. 3(1).. 126, 130
  Art. 4.. 181, 228
  Art. 5.. 332
  Art. 7(1).. 406
  Art. 7(3).. 413
Australia-Uruguay (2001)
  Art. 3.. 126
Austria-Azerbaijan (2000).. 123
  Art. 5.. 332
  Art. 5(1).. 370, 373
  Art. 5(2)(b)... 393
  Art. 5(2)(c)... 396
  Art. 5(3).. 398
Austria-Belarus (2001)
  Art. 4(1).. 383, 395,
                                                                                            396
Austria-Belize (2001) 123
Austria-Cape Verde (1991)
  Art. 2(1).. 135
Austria-Chile (1997)
  Art. 3(2) 219, 223
Austria-Czechoslovakia (1974) 43
Austria-Egypt (2001)
  Art. 3(1) 160, 225
  Art. 4.. 332
  Art. 4(1).. 370
Austria-India (2001)
  Art. 8(2) 448
Austria-Macedonia (2001)
  Art. 6(1) 316
Austria-Mexico (1998).. 222
  Art. 9.. 447, 448
  Art. 17... 82

Austria-Oman (2001)
 Art. 4(2)(a)... 386
Azerbaijan-Finland (2003)
 Art. 4(2) 430
Azerbaijan-UK (1997)
 Art. 2(1) 130
Azerbaijan-US (1997)... 72, 454,
                   489
 Art. VI(e) 428
Bahrain-China (1999)
 Art. 2(1) 126
Bahrain-Jordan (2000)
 Art. 4(1) 370
 Art. 5... 332
 Art. 5(1) 384
Bahrain-Thailand (2002)
 Art. 6(1)(a).. 375, 384
Bahrain-US (1999).. 143, 432,
                   489
 Art. 6... 430
 Art. 7... 143
 Art. 14(2) 139
Bangladesh-BLEU (1998)
 Art. 5(3) 413
Bangladesh-Germany (1981)
 Art. 1... 130
 Art. 6(2) 412
Bangladesh-Japan (1998)
 Art. 2(2) 136
 Art. 5(1) 308
Bangladesh-Thailand (1988)
 Art. 2... 135
Barbados-Canada (1997)
 Art. VI... 336
 Art. V(2)(e)... 428
 Art. VI(2) 430
Barbados-China (1998).. 56
Belarus-Egypt (1997)
 Art. 2(1) 130
Belarus-South Korea (1997)
 Art. 2(1) 130
Belgium-Indonesia (1970)
 Art. X.. 45
Belize-UK (1982) 50
 Art. 2(1) 135

Art. 3(1) 160, 226
Benin-Germany (1978)
Art. 6(2) 412
BLEU-Burundi (1989) 339
Art. 4 333
Art. 9(5) 88
BLEU-Cameroon (1980)
Art. 2(3) 128
Art. 4(2) 370
BLEU-China (1984)
Art. 5(1)(4) 409
Art. 5(2) 413, 414
Art. 6(2) 412
BLEU-Hong Kong (1996)
Art. 1(6) 409
Art. 6(1) 407, 409
BLEU-Pakistan (1998)
Art. 7(1) 409-411
Art. 7(3) 411
Art. 7(4) 412, 413
Art. 7(5) 413
BLEU-Rwanda (1983)
Art. 2 126
BLEU-Saudi Arabia (2001)
Art. 5(1)(c) 409
Art. 5(2) 410
Art. 5(3) 412
BLEU-Singapore (1978)
Art. 3 84
Art. 6(2) 412
BLEU-Tunisia (1964) 43
BLEU-USSR (1989) 214
Art. 8(1) 318
BLEU-Venezuela (1998)
Art. 9.1 71
Bolivia-France (1989)
Art. 1(1) 93
Art. 3 .... 143, 260, 430-431
Bolivia-Germany (1987)
Art. 2(1) 126, 135
Ad Art. 3(c) 143
Bolivia-Korea (1996)
Art. 2 145
Bolivia-Netherlands (1992) 68, 118, 122
Art. 2 136

Art. 9... 71
Bolivia-Spain (2001)
    Art. 3(2) 444, 445,
    447
Bolivia-UK (1988)
    Art. 5(1) 370
Bolivia-US (1998)
    Art. VI... 430
    Art. VI(e) 428
    Annex.. 134
Bosnia and Herzegovina-Austria (2000)
    Art. 6(1) 316
Bosnia and Herzegovina-Finland (2000)
    Art. 2(1) 431
    Art. 12(2) 144
    Art. 16... 431
Bosnia and Herzegovina-Germany (2001)
    Art. 3(1) 160, 225
    Art. 8(2) 448
    Ad Art. 3(c).. 143
Bosnia and Herzegovina-Netherlands (1998)
    Art. 7.. 316
Bosnia and Herzegovina-Spain (2002)
    Art. 6(1) 316
Bosnia and Herzegovina-Sweden (2000) 395, 396
    Art. 2(1) 253
    Art. 4.. 332
    Art. 4(1) 370, 373
    Art. 4(3) 398
Bosnia and Herzegovina-UK (2002)
    Art. 5.. 332
    Art. 5(1) 375
Botswana-China (2000)
    Art. 2.. 144
Botswana-Germany (2000)
    Art. 5(a) 409
    Art. 5(c) 409
Brazil-Chile (1994).. 44
Brazil-Netherlands (1998)
    Art. 3(2) 160, 225
Brunei Darussalam-Korea (2000).. 123
Bulgaria-Croatia (1996)
    Art. 2(1) 308
Bulgaria-Cyprus (1987)
    Art. 3(1) 204, 212
    Art. 4(1) 212

Bulgaria-Finland (1997)
    Art. 2(1)   135
Bulgaria-France (1989)
    Art. 5(2)   377
Bulgaria-Thailand (2003)
    Art. 2(1)   135
Burundi-Germany (1984)
    Art. 2 ....   126, 135
Burundi Model BIT
    Art. 5(2)   413
Cambodia-France (2000)
    Art. 3 ....   260, 431
    Art. 4 ....   160, 225
Cambodia-Thailand (1995)
    Art. 3(1)   126
Cambodian Model BIT
    Art. VI   413
Cameroon-US (1986)
    Art. V(2)   412
    Art. V(2)(a)   411
Canada-Costa Rica (1998) 143, 433
    Art. V(1)   144
    Art. V(2)   144
    Art. VI   424
    Art. XIV(2)   491
Canada-Croatia (1997)
    Art. VI   422
    Art. VI(e)   428
    Art. XIV   432
Canada-Ecuador (1996)
    Art. V(2)(e)   428
Canada-Egypt (1996)
    Art. V(2)   430
    Art. V(2)(e)   428
Canada-El Salvador (1999)
    Art. VI   428
    Art. XII(7)   82
Canada-Latvia (1995)
    Art. V(2)(e)   428
Canada-Lebanon (1997)
    Art. VI(e)   428
Canada-Panama (1996)
    Art. V(2)(e)   428
Canada-Peru (2006) 123, 138
    Art. 9   482
    Art. 9(4)   508
    Art. 9(5)   484

Art. 9(5)(b).. 508
Art. 10... 501
Art. 10(2) 508
Art. 10(3) 508
Art. 10(6) 483
Art. 10(7) 508
Art. 11... 509
Art. 14(6) 508
Art. 16... 484, 507
Art. 17... 508
Annex III... 232
Canada-Philippines (1996)
    Art. V(2) 430
    Art. VI.. 423
Canada-South Africa (1995)
    Art. II... 143
    Art. V(1)(a).. 144
    Art. V(1)(b).. 144
    Art. V(2)(e).. 428
Canada-Thailand (1997) 501
    Art. II(5)... 135
    Art. V(1)(a).. 144
    Art. V(1)(b).. 144
    Art. V(2)(b).. 428
    Annex II.. 135
Canada-Trinidad and Tobago (1995)
    Art. V(2) 430
    Art. V(2)(e).. 428
Canada-Ukraine (1995)
    Art. V(2) 422
    Art. V(2)(e).. 428
Canada-Uruguay (1997)
    Art. II(1)... 130
    Art. VI.. 422
    Art. VI(3) 428
    Art. XII(7).. 82
Canada-Venezuela (1996) 407
    Art. VIII(1)(c) 410
    Art. VIII(2) 411
    Art. VIII(4)(a) 414
    Art. VIII(6) 414
Canadian Model FIPA (2003).. 48, 123,
219, 223,
232, 258,
364,
488–489,
494, 507

Art. 3.. 181, 228
Art. 5.. 255
Art. 5(3)... 255
Art. 6(1)... 144
Art. 6(2)... 139, 144
Art. 7(1)... 422
Art. 7(1)(g).. 430
Art. 7(3)... 422
Art. 7(4)... 429, 430
Art. 7(2)... 424
Art. 10.. 424, 501
Art. 13.. 334
Art. 13(5)... 336
Art. 14.. 414
Art. 14(6)... 414
Annex B.13(1)... 334
Chad-Germany (1967)
Art. 6(3)... 412
Chad-Italy (1969)
Art. VII... 45
Chile-China (1994)... 373
Art. 2(1)... 126
Art. 4... 332
Art. 4(1)(c).. 372
Art. 5... 332
Art. 6(3)... 414
Art. 6(5)... 413
Chile-Croatia (1994)
Art. 3(2)... 146
Chile-Denmark (1993).. 229
Chile-Egypt (1999) 157, 159,
                                                                                                202, 225
Art. 3(1)... 130
Art. 4(2)... 156, 181,
                                                                                                201, 228
Art. 6... 333
Chile-Germany (1991)... 123
Chile-Indonesia (1999)
Art. VI... 333
Chile-Japan (2007)
Art. 5(2)... 373
Chile-Malaysia (1992)
Art. 3(a)... 232
Art. 3(1)... 229
Chile-Nicaragua (1996)
Art. 6... 316

Chile-Tunisia (1998)
    Art. 1(2) 135
    Art. 3(1) 130
    Art. 4(2) 160, 181,
        225, 228
    Art. 5 410
    Art. 5(1)(a) 410
    Art. 5(1)(b) 409
    Art. 6 332
Chile-Turkey (1998)
    Art. 3 .... 130, 135
    Art. 5 332
    Art. 7(3) 414
    Ad Art. VII 413
Chile-New Zealand (1999)
    Art. 3 126
Chile-Tunisia (1998)
    Art. 4(2) 160, 181,
        225, 228
China-Chile (1994)
    Art. 4(1)(c) 373
China-Cote d'Ivoire
    Art. 5 316
China-Djibouti (2003)
    Art. 2(2) 308
China-Finland (1984)
    Art. 1 143
China-France (1984) 384
China-Germany (2003)
    Protocol 182, 190
China-Japan (1988)
    Art. 8(2) 414
China-Jordan (2001)
    Art. 4(1) 160, 225
    Art. 4(3) 181, 228
    Art. 5 332
    Art. 7(1)(h) 410
China-Kuwait (1985)
    Art. 6 414
    Art. 6(3) 412
    Art. 6(4) 415
China-Netherlands (2001)
    Art. 3(5) 317
    Art. 5 332
    Art. 5(1) 375
    Art. 5(2) 383

China-New Zealand (1988) 384
China-Poland (1998)
    Art. 4(1) 375
China-Romania (1994)
    Art. 2(1) 126
    Art. 3(2) 204
    Art. 4 332
China-Sri Lanka (1986)
    Art. 8(3) 415
China-Sweden (1982) 44, 56
China-Switzerland (1986)
    Art. 3(2) 145
China-Thailand (1985)
    Art. 5(1)(a) 384
    Art. 6(2) 411, 415
Chile-Indonesia (1999)
    Art. VI 333
Chile-Japan (2007)
    Art. 5(2) 373
Chile-Malaysia (1992) 146
    Art. 3(a) 232
    Art. 3(1) 229
Chile-Nicaragua (1996)
    Art. 6 316
Chile-Tunisia (1998)
    Art. 1(2) 135
    Art. 3(1) 130
    Art. 4(2) 160, 181,
                                                                                                        225, 228
    Art. 5 410
    Art. 5(1)(a) 410
    Art. 5(1)(b) 409
    Art. 6 332
Chile-Turkey (1998)
    Art. 3 .... 130, 135
    Art. 5 332
    Art. 7(3) 414
    Ad Art. VII 413
Chile-New Zealand (1999)
    Art. 3 126
Chile-Tunisia (1998) 130, 135,
                                                                                                        332, 409,
                                                                                                        410
    Art. 4(2) 160, 181,
                                                                                                        225, 228

China-Cote d'Ivoire
    Art. 5.. 316
China-Djibouti (2003)
    Art. 2(2)... 308
China-Finland (1984)
    Art. 1.. 143
China-France (1984).. 384
China-Germany (2003).. 123
    Protocol.. 182, 190
China-Japan (1988)... 156, 383
    Art. 8(2)... 414
China-Jordan (2001)
    Art. 4(1)... 160, 225
    Art. 4(3)... 181, 228
    Art. 5.. 332
    Art. 7(1)(h)... 410
China-Kuwait (1985)
    Art. 6.. 414
    Art. 6(3)... 412
    Art. 6(4)... 415
China-Netherlands (2001)... 57, 79
    Art. 3(5)... 317
    Art. 5.. 332
    Art. 5(1)... 375
    Art. 5(2)... 383
China-New Zealand (1988) 384
China-Poland (1998)
    Art. 4(1)... 375
China-Romania (1994)
    Art. 2(1)... 126
    Art. 3(2)... 204
    Art. 4.. 332
China-Sri Lanka (1986)
    Art. 8(3)... 415
China-Sweden (1982) 44, 56
China-Switzerland (1986)
    Art. 3(2)... 145
China-Thailand (1985)
    Art. 5(1)(a).. 384
    Art. 6(2) 411, 415
China-Uruguay (1993)
    Art. 6(2)... 412
Colombia-Germany (1965).. 50
Congo-US (1990).. 489
    Art. IV(2).. 411

Costa Rica-Netherlands (1999)
    Art. 12(5) 76
Costa Rica-UK (1982) 50
    Art. V(1) 370
Côte d'Ivoire-Sweden (1965) 43
Croatia-Ukraine (1997)
    Art. 2(1) 130
Croatia-US (1996) 489
Croatia-Zimbabwe (2000)
    Art. 3(1) 300
Cyprus-USSR (1997)
    Art. 2(1) 126
Cuba-Denmark (2001)
    Art. 8 408
Cuba-Ghana (1999)
    Art. 2(1) 126, 130
    Art. 5 332
Cuba-Lebanon (1995)
    Art. 2(1) 130
    Art. 2(3) 232
    Art. 3(1) 257
    Art. 3(2) 156, 181,
                                                                                                       201, 228
    Art. 5(3) 413
Cuba-Spain (1994)
    Art. 3(1) 308
Czechoslovakia-Denmark (1991)
    Art. 2 145
Czechoslovakia-Netherlands (1991) 70, 117,
                                                                                                       125, 261,
                                                                                                            385
    Art. 3(1) 257, 283,
                                                                                                       299, 306
    Art. 3(2) 311
    Art. 4 .... 407, 408
    Art. 4(d) 410
    Art. 5 .... 333, 384
    Art. 5(c) 396
    Art. 8(6) 79, 81
    Art. 9 117
    Art. 13(3) 197
Czechoslovakia-UK (1990) 464
    Art. 2(3) 477
Czechoslovakia-US (1991) 305, 385
    Art. I(d) 410

Art. II(2)(a) 254
Art. II(2)(b) 299, 301
Czechoslovakia-Spain (1990)
    Art. 6(1) 410
    Art. 6(2) 411
    Art. 6(4) 413
    Art. 6(5) 413
Czech Republic-Romania (1993)
    Art. 2(1) 130
Czech Republic-Singapore (1995)
    Art. 15 460
Czech Republic-United Arab Emirates (1994)
    Art. 2(1) 135
Danish Model BIT
    Art. 2(1) 145
    Art. 10(6) 76
Denmark-Egypt (1999)
    Art. 1 .... 409, 410
    Art. 3 260
    Art. 7 .... 406, 409
    Art. 7(1)(f) 410
Denmark-Hong Kong (1994)
    Art. 2(1) 129, 130
Denmark-Hungary (1988)
    Art. 4(1) 398
Denmark-India (1995)
    Art. 2(1) 145
    Art. 9(2)(c)(iii) 82
Denmark-Lithuania (1992)
    Art. 2 145
Denmark-Madagascar (1965) 43
Denmark-Mongolia (1996)
    Art. 2(1) 126
Denmark-Pakistan (1996)
    Art. 2(1) 145
Denmark-USSR (1993) 220
    Art. 8 215
Denmark-Vietnam (1993)
    Art. 2 145
Dutch Model BIT
    Art. 3(4) 444
Ecuador-Spain (1996) 160
Ecuador-Switzerland (1968) 50
Ecuador-US (1993) 122, 156,
160

Art. II(1)... 169, 201
Art. II(6)... 423
Egypt-Greece (1993)
Art. 3(1) 181, 228
Art. 4(c) 384
Egypt-Japan (1977).. 43
Art. 5... 332
Art. 5(2) 383
Egypt-Jordan (1996)
Art. 3(2) 181, 228
Art. 5(3) 413
Egypt-Kazakhstan (1993) 309
Egypt-Romania (1976)
Art. 1(1) 130
Art. 6... 412
Protocol... 228
Egypt-USSR (1997)
Art. 2(1) 126
Egypt-Sweden (1978) 122
Egypt-Thailand (2000)
Art. 2(1) 126
Art. 2(2) 135
Egypt-Ukraine (1992)
Art. 2... 126, 135
Egypt-UK (1975) 43, 57,
                                                                          308, 393,
                                                                          469
Art. 3(2) 181, 228
Art. 5... 384
Art. 6... 409
Egypt-US (1982)
Art. II(6).. 422
Art. III(1)(e)... 377
Art. V(2) 383
Protocol... 415
El Salvador-France (1978)... 50
El Salvador-US (1999).. 489
Eritrea-Netherlands
Art. 3(1) 308
Estonia-Czech Republic (1994)
Art. 2(1) 130
Estonia-Greece (1997)
Art. 2(1) 126
Estonia-Israel (1994)
Art. 4(1) 316

Estonia-Norway (1992)
Art. 3.. 126, 128,
                                                                                    135
Estonia-Sweden (1992)... 309
Estonia-US (1994) 489
Art. II(3)(b)... 306
Art. II(5).. 144
Art. II(6).. 423
Ethiopia-Germany (1964)
Art. 6(1) 412
Art. 6(2) 412
Ethiopia-Malaysia (1998)
Art. 4... 316
Ethiopia-Tunisia (2000)
Art. 8(1) 126
Ethiopia-Turkey (2000)
Art. 3(1) 160, 181,
                                                                                    226, 228
Finland-Kuwait (1996)
Art. 2(2) 127
Finland-Lebanon (1997)
Art. 2(2) 143
Finland-Nigeria (2005)
Art. 3(1) 138
Finland-Philippines (1998)
Art. 2(3) 143
Finland-Sri Lanka (1985)
Art. 8... 84
Finnish Model BIT
Art. 12(2) 448
France-Hong Kong (1995)
Art. 3... 444
France-Hungary (1986)... 123
Art. 9(3) 82
France-Iran (2003)
Art. 7... 415
France-Madagascar (2003)
Art. 3... 260, 431
Art. 6... 415
France-Malaysia (1975)
Art. 3... 370
France-Mexico (1998)
Art. 4... 144
France-Pakistan (1983)
Art. 5... 333

Art. 5(2) 370
France-Tunisia (1972) 43
France-Uganda (2003)
    Art. 6 415
France-Ukraine (1994)
    Art. 3 .... 260, 431
France-Venezuela (2001)
    Art. 3 .... 260, 431
France-Zimbabwe (2001)
    Art. 3 .... 260, 430,
                                                                                                431
French Model BIT 461
    Art. 4 .... 143, 260,
                                                                                                431
Gabon-Lebanon (2001)
    Art. 4 333
Gambia-Netherlands (2002)
    Art. 12(5) 76
German Model BIT (1991)
    Art. 4 384
    Art. 8(2) 444
    Ad Art. 3(c) 143
Germany-Guyana (1989)
    Art. 2(1) 134
Germany-Haiti (1973)
    Art. 6(2) 412
    Art. 6(3) 412
Germany-India (1995)
    Art. 7(4) 413
    Art. 13(2) 448
Germany-Jamaica (1992)
    Art. 2(1) 135
Germany-Kenya (1996)
    Art. 2(1) 135
    Art. 5(1) 410
Germany-Mali (1977)
    Art. 2 135
Germany-Malta (1973) 134
Germany-Nigeria (2000)
    Art. (3)(3) 299
    Ad Art. 3(c) 143
Germany-Pakistan (1959) 45, 70,405
    Art. 7 442
    Art. 11(2) 42
Germany-Papua New Guinea (1980)
    Protocol 191

Germany-Philippines (1998)
    Art. 5(3) 412
Germany-Romania (1979)
    Art. 1(1) 130
    Art. 6 412
Germany-Swaziland (1990)
    Art. 5(d) 410
Germany-Thailand (2002)
    Art. 5(2) 413
Germany-Turkey (1962)
    Art. 6(1) 412, 413
    Art. 6(2) 412
Germany-USSR (1989) 339, 397
    Art. 4 333
    Art. 4(2) 384
Germany-Zambia (1966)
    Art. 1 135
Germany-Zimbabwe (1995)
    Art. 6(2) 412
Ghana-India (2000) 228
    Art. 7(a) 409
    Art. 7(1) 413
    Art. 7(3) 411
Ghana-Switzerland (1991)
    Art. 4(1) 259
Greece-Mexico (2000)
    Art. 16 83
Greek Model BIT
    Art. 9(5) 76
Guinea-Italy (1964) 42
Haiti-UK (1985)
    Art. 4(1) 316
Haiti-US (1983) 386, 489
    Art. 1(f) 410
Hong Kong-Japan (1997)
    Art. 2(3) 444
Hong Kong-Netherlands (1992)
    Art. 1(4) 409
    Art. 1(5) 411
    Art. 6(1) 409, 413
Hong Kong-New Zealand (1995)
    Art. 3(1) 130
Hungary-India (2003)
    Art. 3(1) 131
Hungary-Netherlands (1987)
    Art. 3(2) 308

Hungary-Norway (1991).. 214
    Art. XI.. 213
Hungary-Spain (1989)
    Art. 5... 413
    Art. 5(b) 409
    Art. 5(c) 410
Hungary-Thailand (1991)
    Art. 2(1) 135
    Art. 3(1) 126
    Art. 3(2) 308
India-Ghana (2000).. 406
    Art. 4(1) 156, 181,
                                                                                       201
India-Indonesia (1999)
    Art. 4(3) 156
India-Kazakhstan (1996)... 309
India-Netherlands (1995)
    Art. 7(1) 413
India-Portugal (2000)
    Art. 5... 332
    Art. 5(2) 383, 395,
                                                                                       396
India-Spain (1997)
    Art. 4(3) 448
India-Sweden (2000)
    Art. 7(1) 413
    Art. 12(2) 489
India-Thailand (2000)
    Art. 4(1) 259
    Art. 6(1) 395
India-UK (1994) 44, 48
    Art. 11.. 489
Indonesia-Netherlands (1968)
    Art. 11.. 44-45
Indonesia-Spain (1995)
    Art. VII 411, 413
    Art. VII(a) 409
    Art. VII(c) 409
    Art. VII(i).. 410
Indonesia-Switzerland (1974)
    Protocol.. 139, 191
Indonesia-Syria (1997)
    Art. 2(2) 308
Indonesia-Thailand (1987)
    Art. 3(1) 130

Indonesia-Ukraine (1996)
    Art. 2(1).. 130
Iran-Kazakhstan (1996) 309
Iraq-Kuwait (1964) 43
Italian Model BIT (2003) 413
    Art. II(6).. 143, 144
Italy-Jordan (1996) 212, 470
    Art. 1(9) 186,
                                                                                        231
    Art. 2(4) 446
    Art. 2(8) 135
    Art. 3... 211
    Art. 9(2) 211
Italy-Korea (1989)
    Art. 1... 257
Italy-Lebanon (1997)
    Art. 9(2)... 444
Italy-Mongolia (1993)
    Art. 8... 413
Italy-Morocco (1990).. 160
    Art. 3(3) 139, 191
Italy-USSR (1989)
    Art. 2(7)... 143
Israel-Romania (1991) 386
Israel-Thailand (2000)
    Art. 2(1) 126
    Art. 5... 370, 375,
                                                                                        396
Jamaica-Netherlands (1991)
    Art. 3(6) 139, 191
Jamaica-Switzerland (1990)
    Art. 3... 139, 191
Jamaica-US (1994)
    Art. I(d)... 410
    Art. II(5).. 423
Jamaican Model BIT
    Art. 2(2) 143
    Art. 8... 143
Japan-Korea (2002).. 422
    Art. 8... 144
    Art. 10(1) 308
Japan-Malaysia (2005)... 138, 491,
                                                                                        501
    Art. 14(6) 433

Japan-Vietnam (2003).. 138, 422
    Art. 4(1)(f) 144
    Art. 8.. 143
    Art. 12.. 406
    Art. 19.. 507
Jordan-Poland (1997)
    Art. 3(1) 308
Jordan-Syria (2001)
    Art. 2(1) 130
Jordan-Tunisia (1995)
    Art. V(3) 413
Jordan-US (1997)... 143
    Art. V 415
    Art. IX.. 211
Jordan-Yemen (1996)
    Art. 2(2) 308
Kazakhstan-US (1994)
    Art. II(5).. 423
Korea-Mexico (2000)
    Art. 2(1) 130
    Art. 14(1) 82
Korea-Netherlands (2003)
    Art. 8(2) 435
    Ad Art. 4.. 415
Korea-Sri Lanka (1980)
    Art. 9... 84
Korea-Trinidad and Tobago (2002) 123
    Art. 2(3) 300
Kuwait-Netherlands (2001)
    Art. 6... 333
    Art. 6(1)(a)... 370
Kyrgyzstan-UK (1999)
    Art. 3(1) 160, 225
Kyrgyzstan-US (1993)
    Art. IV(2)... 412
Latvia-Turkey (1997)
    Art. II(1).. 135
Latvia-US (1995)
    Art. I(d)... 410
    Art. II(6).. 423
Lebanon-Netherlands (2002)
    Art. 10(5) 76
Lebanon-Switzerland (2000)
    Art. 4... 332

Lesotho-UK (1981)
    Art. 6... 414
Lithuania-Norway (1992) 226
    Art. III.. 257, 308
    Art. VI(1) 375
Lithuania-US (1998)
    Art. I(d)... 410
    Art. II(2)(c) 444
Madagascar-Norway (1966) 43
Malaysia-Sweden (1979)
    Art. 1(1) 135
Malaysia-United Arab Emirates (1991)
    Art. 2(g) 422
    Art. 13(3) 447
Malaysian Model BIT
    Art. 6(1) 413
Malta-Netherlands (1984).. 134
Marshall Islands-Taiwan (1999)
    Art. 3(1) 308
Mauritius-South Africa
    Art. 3(4)(c)... 191
Mexico-Netherlands (1998)
    Art. 8(2), Schedule 83
Mexico-Spain (1995) 222
    Art. 4(1) 284
    Art. 5(2) 384
Mongolia-Singapore (1995)
    Art. 3(1) 135
Morocco-Pakistan (2001)
    Art. 2(2) 260
Morocco-Spain (1989)
    Art. 5... 413
    Art. 5(b) 410
    Art. 5(c) 409
    Art. 6... 413
Morocco-US (1985).. 489
Mozambique-Netherlands (2001)... 123
    Art. 6... 377
Mozambique-US (1998)
    Art. VI.. 430
    Art. VI(e) 428
Myanmar-Philippines (1998).. 210
Namibia-Netherlands (2002) 123
Netherlands-Panama (2000)
    Art. 6... 333

Netherlands-Philippines (1985)
    Art. 7(1) 413
    Art. 7(3) 411
Netherlands-Poland (1992) 450-451
Netherlands-Romania (1994)
    Art. 2 .... 126, 130
    Art. 3(2) 181, 219,
                                              223, 228
    Art. 4 411
Netherlands-Sudan (1979)
    Art. XI 370
Netherlands-Suriname (2005) 123
Netherlands-Tunisia (1963) 42
Netherlands-Venezuela (1991) 59, 66,
                                              450
    Art. 3 260
    Art. 3(4) 447
    Art. 9(5) 79, 87
    Protocol 260
Nicaragua-US (1995)
    Art. VII 144
Nigeria-UK (1990)
    Art. 2(1) 135
Norwegian Model BIT (2007) 61, 124,
                                               158, 254,
                                               335
    Art. 4(3) 224
    Art. 5 255
Oman-UK (1995)
    Art. 2(1) 130
Panama-UK (1983)
    Art. 5(1) 370
Panama-US (1982) 50
                                               137, 386
    Art. 1(f) 410
    Art. II(1) 131, 138
Pakistan-Switzerland (1995) 467
    Art. 3(2) 145
    Art. 4 472
    Art. 10(2) 472
    Art. 11 .... 445, 447,
                                               457, 458,
                                               466
Paraguay-Switzerland (1992)
    Art. 3(2) 145
Paraguay-UK (1981) 50

Peru-Thailand (1991)
    Art. 2 135
    Art. 3(1) 126
    Art. 7 411
Philippines-Romania (1994)
    Art. 2(1) 128, 130
    Art. 2(2) 134
Philippines-Switzerland (1997) 159, 225
    Art. IV 157, 202
    Art. X 477
    Art. X(1) 478
    Art. X(2) 449, 452,
                                                    457, 468, 478
Philippines-UK (1980)
    Art. V(1) 370
    Art. VII 447, 448
Poland-US (1994)
    Art. 1(d) 410
Portugal-Turkey (2001)
    Art. 2(1) 126
Romania-US (1992) 471
    Art. I(1)(d) 410
    Art. II(1) 157, 201
    Art. II(2)(c) 455
    Art. III 332
    Art. IV(3) 414
Russia-US (1992) 490, 493
    Art. I(d) 410
    Art. II(3) 144
    Art. II(4) 144
    Art. IV 412
Senegal-US (1983)
    Art. II(2) 160, 431
    Art. II(4) 447
    Art. III(2) 334
Sierra Leone-UK (1981) 396
Singapore-Switzerland (1978)
    Art. 1(2) 135
Singapore-Vietnam (1992)
    Art. 3(1) 135
Sri Lanka-Switzerland (1981) 229
    Art. 6 383
    Art. 8 84
Sri Lanka-UK (1980) 46, 58,
                                                   229
    Art. 2(2) 308

Art. 4(1) 316
Art. 4(2) 315
Art. 6 409
South Africa-Turkey (2000)
Art. 3(3) 316
Swiss Model BIT (1986/1995)
Art. 10 444
Switzerland-Costa Rica (1965) 50
Switzerland-Tunisia (1961) 42
Thailand-Vietnam (1991)
Art. 3(2) 308
Trinidad and Tobago-US (1994)
Art. V(1)(a) 424
Art. VI(1)(b) 424
Art. VI (1)(c) 424
Art. VI (1)(d) 424
Art. VII 430
Art. VII (f) 430
Tunisia-US (1990)
Art. II(3) 377
Art. III(2) 398
Turkey-UK (1991)
Art. 5(1) 373
Turkey-US (1982)
Art. II(7) 422
Turkish Model BIT
Art. III(3) 143
Ugandan Model BIT
Art. 3 143
Art. 6(1) 413
UK Model BIT (1991) 57, 113,
                                                                          204, 444,
                                                                          445
Art. 11 84
UK-USSR (1989) 216
Art. 1(a) 65, 66
Art. 3 215
Art. 6(1) 415
Art. 8 215
Art. 8(1) 70, 220
UK-Vietnam (2002)
Art. 1(b) 410
Art. 5(1) 375, 383,
                                                                          393
Art. 6 409
Ukraine-US (1994) 338

Art. 1(d) 410
US Model BIT 1983
   Art. II(7) 422
US Model BIT 1994 .... 65, 299,
    444
   Art. X(1) 76
US Model BIT 2004 .... 82, 123,
    357, 364,
    489, 491,
    500, 507
   Art. 3(3) 189
   Art. 5 255
   Art. 5(3) 255
   Art. 6 334
   Art. 7(1)(a) 143
   Art. 7(4) 414
   Art. 8(3)(a) 430
   Art. 9(1) 144
   Art. 9(2) 144
   Art. 15 139
   Art. 21(2) 337
   Annex B 334, 339
US-Uruguay (2005) 82, 123,
    124, 138,
    158, 189,
    202, 231,
    489
   Art. 3 157
   Art. 5 .... 258, 259,
    308
   Art. 5(6) 508
   Art. 6 334
   Art. 7(1)(a) 409
   Art. 7(2) 412
   Art. 7(4) 414
   Art. 7(4)(a) 414
   Art. 8 422
   Art. 8(1)(g) 430
   Art. 8(2) 429
   Art. 8(3)(a) 430
   Art. 8(3)(b)(i) 429
   Art. 9(1) 144
   Art. 9(2) 144
   Art. 10 432
   Art. 11 433

        Art. 11(2)   432
        Art. 14   483
        Art. 14(2)   485
        Art. 14(5) 483, 484
        Art. 15   433
        Art. 15(1)   139
        Art. 15(2)   139
        Art. 16   318
        Art. 17   481
        Art. 18(2)   483
        Art. 21 ....   484, 507
US-Zaire (1984) 59, 422
        Art. II(4)   308
        Art. II(5)   422
        Art. IV(2)   315
        Art. IX   317
        Protocol, Art. 5   334

II OTHER INTERNATIONAL INVESTMENT AGREEMENTS

Agreement on Investment and Free Movement of
Arab Capital Among Arab Countries (1970)   43
Agreement for the Investment of Arab Capital in the
Arab States (1980) 52, 58
ASEAN Agreement for the Promotion and
Protection of Investments (1987)   52
        Art. III 447, 448
        Art. III(3)   444
        Art. IV   256
ASEAN Jakarta Protocol (1996)   52
ASEAN Framework Agreement (1998) 52, 53, 58,
                                                                                                            137, 210
        Art. 7(1)   139
Andean Investment Code (1970)   50
Australia-Thailand Free Trade Agreement (2004)
        Art. 1602   490
Australia-US Free Trade Agreement (2004)
        Art. 10.4(a)(iv)   143
        Art. 11.9(1)(a)   424
        Art. 11.9(1)(b)   424
        Art. 11.9(1)(c)   424
        Art. 11.9(1)(d)   424
        Art. 11.9(1)(e)   424
        Art. 11.9(1)(f) 428, 430

Art. 11.9(2) 429
Art. 11.9(3)(a) 429
Art. 11.9(3)(b)(ii) 424
Art. 11.9(3)(c) 424
Art. 11.9(3)(d) 423
Art. 11.9(3)(e) 423
Chapter 20 432
Bahrain-US Free Trade Agreement (2004)
Art. 10.4(a)(iv) 143
Chapter 17 432
Bolivia-Mexico Free Trade Agreement (1994) 137
Buenos Aires Protocol on the Promotion and
Protection of Investments (1994) 51, 58, 79
Canada-Chile Free Trade Agreement (1996) 137
Art. G-06 422
Art. G-06(1)(a) 424
Art. G-06(1)(b) 424
Art. G-06(1)(c) 424
Art. G-06(1)(d) 424
Art. G-06(1)(f) 428
Art. G-06(1)(g) 430
Art. G-06(2) 424
Art. G-06(3) 429
Art. G-06(6) 424
Art. G-07 144
Art. G-08(3) 430
Art. G-08(7)(a) 423
Art. G-08(7)(b) 423
Art. G-11.2 433
Art. H (Cross-Border Trade in Services) 143
Art. K (Temporary Entry for Business Persons) 143
Chapter L 432
Art. O-04 416
Art. O-04.2 416
Canada-Costa Rica Free Trade Agreement (2002)
Art. VIII(3) 143
Chapter 12 432-433
Canada-Israel Free Trade Agreement (1997)
Art. 4.8 143
Art. 8 432
Caribbean Common Market-Cuba (1997)
Art. IV 260
Caribbean-Dominican Republic Free Trade Agreement (1998)
Art. XII(iii) 409
Art. XII(iv) 410
Art. XII(3)(a) 414

Central America-Dominican Republic-US Free Trade Agreement (2004)
    Art. 21.2.. 489
    Art. 10.22(2) 82
Chile-China Free Trade Agreement (2005)
    Art. 100... 490, 491
Chile-US Free Trade Agreement (2003)...................................... 51
    Art. 10.5(1)(f) 428
    Art. 10.21(2) 82
    Art. 11.4(a)(iv)... 143
    Art. 23.2.. 489
    Annex 10-D 334
    Chapter 20 432
China-New Zealand Free Trade Agreement (2008)
    Chapter 11 (Investment).. 57, 61
    Art. 155.. 83
    Art. 200.. 502
Colombia-US Trade Promotion Agreement (2006)
    Art. 22.2.. 489
Colonia Protocol on the Reciprocal Promotion and
Protection of Investments (1994)... 51, 58
    Art. 2.. 137
    Art. 3.. 256
    Art. 3(4) 422
    Art. 9(5) 79
Colombia-Mexico-Venezuela Free Trade Agreement
(Group of Three Treaty) (1994)... 137
    Art. 17-04(1)(a) 424
    Art. 17-04(1)(b) 424
    Art. 17-04(1)(c) 424
    Art. 17-04(2)(b) 423
    Art. 17-04(3).. 429
    Art. 17-07(1)(b) 411
    Art. 17-07(1)(c) 409
    Art. 17-07(1)(e) 411
    Art. 17-07(3)(a) 414
Common Market for Eastern and Southern Africa (1994) (COMESA)
    Art. 159.. 256
Community Investment Code of the Economic Community
of the Great Lakes Countries (1982) 52
    Art. 258.. 256
    Art. 258(1)(b)... 262, 269
Costa Rica-Mexico Free Trade Agreement (1994)...................... 137
Energy Charter Treaty (1994) (ECT)... 1, 53, 82,
                                                             139, 140,
                                                             212, 254,
                                                             332

Art. 1(6) 65
Art. 5 424
Art. 5(3) 423
Art. 10 431
Art. 10(1) 160, 254,
256, 260,
299, 444
Art. 10(2) 140
Art. 10(3) 160, 186,
231, 260
Art. 10(4) 140
Art. 10(7) 219, 223
Art. 13(1) 332, 373
Art. 13(1)(a) 370
Art. 22 460
Art. 23 460
Art. 24 .... 490, 500
Art. 24(2)(b)(iii) 191
Art. 24(3) 490

European Free Trade Association States-Lebanon
Free Trade Agreement (2004)
Art. 22 .... 490, 491

ICSID Convention – Convention on the Settlement of
Investment Disputes between States and Nationals of
Other States (1965) 27-29,
45-46, 50,
51, 57, 59,
66, 69,
72-73, 80,
89, 85, 94,
96, 99,
104, 105,
217, 397,
467, 496
Art. 25 .... 67, 135
Art. 25(1) 28
Art. 26 28
Art. 27 28
Art. 42(1) 29, 82, 85,
87, 92, 101
Art. 50 29
Art. 52 78
Art. 53 60
Art. 53(1) 103
Art. 54 85

ICSID Additional Facility Rules.. 29, 85
ICSID Arbitration Rules 29, 213,
                                                                                       230
    Rule 2(3)... 44
India-Singapore Comprehensive
Economic Cooperation Agreement (2005) 57, 224,
                                                                                       261, 501
    Chapter 6 (Investment) 61, 224
    Art. 6.6... 416
    Art. 6.12... 490
    Art. 6.12(4) 495
    Art. 6.14(2) 433
    Art. 6.15... 433
    Art. 6.18... 435
Investment Agreement for the COMESA
Common Investment Area (2007)... 52
Israel-US Free Trade Agreement (1985)
    Art. 13... 423
Japan-Malaysia Economic Partnership Agreement (2005) 138, 433,
                                                                                       491, 501
Japan-Mexico Economic Partnership Agreement (2004)
    Art. 59 (Note 3) 205
    Art. 169... 491
Japan-Singapore Economic Partnership Agreement (2002)................. 491, 501
    Art. 68... 416
    Art. 75... 422
    Art. 75(1)(b).. 424
    Art. 75(1)(c).. 424
    Art. 75(1)(d).. 424
    Art. 75(1)(e).. 424
    Art. 75(1)(f) 424, 428
    Art. 75(1)(f)(i) 424
    Art. 75(1)(g).. 145
    Art. 75(1)(h).. 430
    Art. 80(1)(c).. 411
    Art. 80(1)(d).. 409
    Art. 80(1)(e).. 410
    Art. 80(1)(g).. 411
    Art. 80(3)(a).. 414
    Art. 83... 501
    Art. 83(1)(b).. 424
    Art. 83(1)(f) 424
Jordan-US Free Trade Agreement (2000)
    Art. 3... 143

Korea-Singapore Free Trade Agreement (2005)..................................... 501
    Art. 10.6.. 435
    Art. 10.12.. 415
    Art. 10.16(2) 433
    Art. 11.4.. 433
    Art. 11.5.. 433
    Art. 21.3.. 490, 491
Lomé III – Third Convention of the African, Caribbean and
Pacific Group of States and the European Economic Community
(ACP-EEC Convention) (1984)... 52
Lomé IV – Fourth Convention of the African, Caribbean and
Pacific Group of States and the European Economic Community
(ACP-EEC Convention) (1989)... 52, 256,
    262, 269

MIGA Convention – Convention Establishing the
Multilateral Investment Guarantee Agency (1985) 40, 57
    Art. 11(a)(ii)... 358
    Art. 12(d) 256
    Art. 23(b)(ii) 40
Mexico-Northern Triangle (El Salvador, Guatemala and Honduras)
Free Trade Agreement (2000)
    Art. 20-06 416
Morocco-US Free Trade Agreement (2004)
    Art. 10.8(1)(f) 428
    Art. 10.21(2) 82
NAFTA – North American Free Trade Agreement Between the
Government of Canada, the Government of Mexico and the
Government of the United States (1992)... 51, 58, 61,
    77, 102,
    149, 152,
    158, 160,
    163-164,
    166-167,
    169, 173,
    174,
    177-180,
    187, 208,
    217, 236,
    237, 240,
    242, 243,
    287, 351
    Chapter 11 .... 53, 55, 63,
    113, 117,
    151, 153,
    175, 185,

	202, 219, 223, 241, 272, 273, 342, 350, 351, 425, 444
Art. 1101	167
Art. 1101(1)	458
Art. 1102	167, 175, 183, 187, 505
Art. 1102(1)	137
Art. 1102(2)	181
Art. 1102(3)	189
Art. 1103	181, 187, 202, 225, 228, 229, 429
Art. 1104	186, 231
Art. 1105	117, 229, 234, 238, 245, 246, 254, 255, 258, 268, 272, 275, 293, 296
Art. 1105(1)	250, 253, 254, 257, 258, 272-274, 276, 277, 281, 376
Art. 1106	422
Art. 1106(1)	423, 425, 426, 427
Art. 1106(1)(a)	424, 425
Art. 1106(1)(b)	424-426, 429
Art. 1106(1)(c)	424-426, 429
Art. 1106(1)(d)	424, 425, 429
Art. 1106(1)(e)	424, 427, 429
Art. 1106(1)(f)	428, 429
Art. 1106(1)(g)	430

Art. 1106(3) 427, 429
Art. 1106(3)(a) 429
Art. 1106(3)(b) 429
Art. 1106(3)(c) 429
Art. 1106(3)(d) 427, 429
Art. 1106(4) 429
Art. 1106(6) 424, 426
Art. 1107 144
Art. 1107(1) 144
Art. 1108 482
Art. 1108(1) 138, 190
Art. 1108(1)(c) 138, 190
Art. 1108(3) 139, 190
Art. 1108(4) 191, 430
Art. 1108(7) 186, 508
Art. 1108(8) 423
Art. 1109(1)(a) 411
Art. 1110 .... 338, 353,
                                                                                         384, 507
Art. 1110(1)(a) 370
Art. 1110(1)(c) 376
Art. 1110(1) 332
Art. 1110(2) 386
Art. 1111(1) 139, 146
Art. 1111(2) 139
Art. 1114 509
Art. 1116(2) 526
Art. 1131 .... 82, 88,
                                                                                         117, 273
Art. 1136(1) 103
Art. 1503(2) 461
Chapter 16 143
Chapter 20 .... 162, 179
Art. 2001 .... 117, 273
Art. 2102 490
Art. 2103(1) 507
Art. 2103(4) 507
Art. 2103(5) 507
Art. 2103(6) 336, 507
Art. 2104 416
Art. 2106 488
Annex I 'Reservations for Existing Measures and Liberalization
Requirements' 138, 190
Annex II 'Reservations for Future Measures' 139, 190,
                                                                                         191
Annex IV 232

Annex 2106... 190, 488
New Zealand-Thailand Comprehensive Economic
Cooperation Agreement (2005) 224
Panama-Taiwan Free Trade Agreement (2003)
    Art. 20.02(2) 502
Peru-US Trade Promotion Agreement (2006) 509
    Art. 22.2.. 489
Poland-US Investment Guaranty Agreement (1989).............. 40
Singapore-US Free Trade Agreement (2003)
    Chapter 11 143
    Art. 15.8(1)(f) 428
    Art. 15.21.. 83
    Chapter 17 143

III   OTHER TREATIES

Agreement between the United Kingdom and Peru, Respecting
the Mineral Property 'La Brea y Pariñas' (1921)................... 440
Anglo-Greek Treaty of Commerce and Navigation (1886)................. 206
Belgium-US FCN Treaty (1961) 142
Charter of the United Nations (1945).................................. 10, 510
Convention for the Protection of Human Rights and
Fundamental Freedoms, Protocol No. 1 364
Covenant of the League of Nations (1919) 16, 17
Drago-Porter Convention – Hague Convention II of 1907
Respecting the Limitations of the Employment of Force for
the Recovery of Contract Debts.. 10
Economic Agreement of Bogotá (1948)............................... 23, 256,
                                                                                      441
General Treaty for the Renunciation of War (1928)............... 10
Germany-US FCN Treaty (1923) 299
Geneva Convention between Poland and Germany (1922)................. 440
Hague Convention for the Pacific Settlement of International
Disputes 1898-1899 .... 9, 10
Hague Convention for the Pacific Settlement of
International Disputes 1907.. 9, 76
    Art. 1... 9
    Art. 37.. 76
Havana Charter for an International Trade Organization (1948) 19-20, 441
    Art. 11(1)(b).. 20
    Art. 11(2) 256
IMF Articles – Amended Articles of Agreement of the
International Monetary Fund 1992....................................... 19, 148,
                                                                                      401, 403,

404 ,411,
415-417

Art. I(iv).. 401
Art. VI, Section 3... 402
Art. VII, Section 3(b).. 402
Art. VIII 148
Art. VIII, Section 2(a).. 401, 402
Art. VIII, Section 3 402
Art. XIV.. 401
Art. XIV, Section 2 .... 401, 402
Art. XXX(d)... 402
Art. XXX(f) 412
International Covenant on Civil and Political Rights (1966)............... 251
International Covenant on Economic, Social and
Cultural Rights (1966)... 251
Italy-US FCN Treaty (1948) and Supplementary
Agreement (1951).. 37, 248,
298, 307,
312
Iran-United States – Claims Settlement Declaration (1981)................ 8, 39, 59,
236, 314,
323, 325,
326, 359,
378, 385,
386, 389,
402

Iran-United States – Treaty of Amity, Economic Relations and
Consular Rights between the United States of America and
Iran (1955) 378
Art. IV(2) 389
Art. VII(1)... 417
Montevideo Convention on the Rights and Duties of States (1933)..... 17
New York Convention – Convention on the Recognition and
Enforcement of Foreign Arbitral Awards (1958).............................. 25
Nicaragua-United States FCN Treaty (1956) 41, 42,
128, 493

OECD Convention – Convention on the Organisation for Economic
Co-operation and Development (1960) 24
Organisation of Islamic Conference (1981) 52
Art. 10(1) 333
Paris Convention for the Protection of Industrial Property (1883)
Art. 2... 153
Statute of the International Court of Justice (1945).............. 35-39, 78,
80, 89, 95,
128, 195,

	247, 248,
	275, 337,
	492
Art. 38	60, 102
Art. 38(1)(c)	264
Art. 59	60
Treaty of Amity, Commerce and Navigation between Great Britain and the US (1794)	7
Treaty Establishing the European Community (Consolidated Version) (1992)	137
Art. 57(2)	416
Art. 59	416
Art. 60	416
Art. 307	416
Treaty of Asunción (1991)	50–51,
	137, 158
Vienna Convention on the Law of Treaties 1969	76, 125,
	217, 267
Art. 2(1)(a)	76, 86, 99
Art. 2(1)(d)	482
Art. 26	129, 492,
	494
Art. 27	189
Art. 31	110, 111
Art. 31(1)	110, 111,
	265
Art. 31(2)	110, 124,
	125, 219
Art. 31(3)(a)	110, 117,
	274
Art. 31(3)(b)	110, 118,
	268
Art. 31(3)(c)	99, 109,
	110
Art. 32	110
Art. 61	515
WTO Agreement on the Application of Sanitary and Phytosanitary Measures (1994)	291
WTO Agreement on Technical Barriers to Trade (1994)	291
WTO Agreement on Trade-Related Aspects of Intellectual Property (1994)	428, 429
Art. 41	291
Art. 42	291
Art. 62	291
Art. 63	291

Art. 63(1) 432
Art. 63(3) 291, 433
WTO Agreement on Trade-Related Investment Measures (1994) 1, 54,
419-421,
424, 427

WTO Doha Declaration (2001)
Para. 20 55
Para. 22 56
WTO General Agreement on Trade in Services (GATS) 1, 54-55,
138,
140-142,
173, 218,
254, 400,
403, 404,
415, 416,
421, 432,
484, 486,
491, 503

Art. II(a)... 140
Art. II(b)... 140
Art. II(c)... 140
Art. II(d)... 140
Art. III.. 148, 164,
172, 173,
291, 420
Art. III(4) 291
Art. XI.. 404, 420
Art. XII 404
Art. XIV.. 486, 500,
502
Art. XVI.. 421
Art. XVI, footnote 8 404
Art. XVI(2)(a)... 141
Art. XVI(2)(b) 141
Art. XVI(2)(c)... 141
Art. XVI(2)(d) 141
Art. XVI(2)(e)... 141
Art. XVI(2)(f) 141
Art. XVII 141, 420
Art. XXVIII(d)... 140
Art. XIX.. 141
WTO General Agreement on Tariffs and Trade (GATT) 20, 23, 54,
141, 148,
153, 168,
170–173,

	176, 184,
	187, 218,
	254, 292,
	415,
	419-421,
	482,
	484-487,
	489, 492,
	493, 497,
	500,
	502-505
Art. I(1)	199
Art. II(a)	140
Art. III	148, 164,
	173, 291,
	420
Art. III(1)	172
Art. III(2)	172
Art. III(4)	291
Art. X	291, 432
Art. X(2)	432
Art. XI	404
Art. XI(1)	420
Art. XII	404, 415
Art. XVIII:B	415
Art. XX	178,
	484-487,
	500,
	502-504
Art. XXI	489,
	491-493,
	497
Art. XXI(b)	492, 502
WTO Marrakesh Understanding on the Balance-of-Payments Provisions of the GATT (1994)	415
WTO Third Protocol to the General Agreement on Trade in Services (1995)	142

IV   OTHER INTERNATIONAL INSTRUMENTS

Convention on the International Responsibility of States for Injuries to Aliens (1961) (1961 Harvard Draft)	22, 154,
	155, 174,
	247, 329,

	358, 372, 379, 405
Art. 10	326
Art. 10(3)(a)	328, 329
Art. 10(5)	329, 405
Art. 12	442
Art. 13	246
Draft Code of Conduct on Transnational Corporations (1984) (TNC Code of Conduct)	33
Draft Convention on Investments Abroad (1959) (Abs-Shawcross Draft Convention)	21, 155, 200, 256, 264, 328, 330, 405, 442, 443
Art. I	299, 308
Art. II	154, 441
Art. III	326, 328
Art. VII	22
Draft Convention on the Protection of Foreign Property (1967 Draft OECD Convention)	30, 57, 154, 200, 256, 269, 306, 317, 442, 458
Art. 1	299, 300, 308, 309
Art. 1(a)	30, 155
Art. 1(b)	155
Art. 2	443
Art. 2(2)	443
Art. 2(3)(a)	443, 449, 459
Art. 2(3)(a)(i)	449, 459
Art. 2(3)(a)(ii)	449, 459
Art. 3	30, 326, 328, 330, 398
Art. 4	405
Art. 7	31
Art. 8	317
Draft Convention on Responsibility of States for Damages Done in Their Territory to the Person or Property of Foreigners (1929 Harvard Draft)	15, 16, 22,

	237, 239, 441
Art. 9	239, 240
Art. 10	246
Art. 11	246
Art. 12	246
Draft Convention on the Treatment of Foreigners (1929 Draft Convention)	16, 153, 154, 199-200, 237
Art. 1	153
Art. 7	153
Art. 9	153
Art. 10	153
Art. 12	153
Art. 16(8)	17
Art. 17	200
Art. 18	200
Part II	153
Draft Multilateral Agreement on Investment (MAI)	55, 137, 161, 332, 362, 444, 454, 484
Art. IV.2	506
Art. IV.2.1	331
Art. IV.3	506
ICC International Code of Fair Treatment of Foreign Investment (1948)	20-21, 154, 200, 405
Art. 4	200
International Convention for the Mutual Protection of Private Property Rights in Foreign Countries (the Köln Draft Convention)	22
Art. VII	22
International Law Commission's Articles on Responsibility of States for Internationally Wrongful Acts (ILC's Articles on State Responsibility)	99, 249, 337, 379, 392, 451, 462-463, 483, 499, 514, 520, 525

Art. 2 182,
203-204,
262, 337
Art. 3 99
Art. 4 465
Art. 5 461,
464-466
Art. 8 461,
464-466
Art. 15(1) 343
Art. 20 249,
510, 511
Art. 21 .... 249, 510
Art. 22 510
Art. 24 514
Art. 25 .... 496, 498,
516, 518
Art. 26 .... 513, 517
Art. 27 .... 497, 522,
523
Art. 36 378
Art. 44(b) 6
Art. 45 524
Art. 45(a) 510, 511,
524
International Law Commission's Draft Articles on
Most-Favoured-Nation Clauses 196, 200
Art. 5 196
Art. 7 193
Art. 8 193
Art. 9 197
Art. 9(1) 204
Art. 19 221
Art. 19(2) 186, 231
Model Clauses Relating to the Convention on the Settlement
of Investment Disputes Designed for Use in
Bilateral Investment Agreement (1969) 45
OECD Code of Liberalisation of Capital Movements (1961) 24, 155,
403
OECD Code of Liberalisation of
Current Invisible Operations (1961) 24, 155,
403
OECD Declaration and Decisions on International
Investment and Multinational Enterprises (1976) 33, 151,
155, 166

OECD Guidelines on Multinational Enterprises (1976) 33, 34
Tripartite Declaration of Principles Concerning Multinational
Enterprises and Social Policy (1978)... 33
United Nations, Charter of Economic Rights and
Duties of States (1974) 31-33, 46,
50, 269,
373, 378
United Nations, Declaration on the Establishment of a
New International Economic Order (1974) (NIEO Declaration).......... 31-33, 46,
50
United Nations, Permanent Sovereignty Over
Natural Resources, Resolution 1803 (1962)... 26, 32,
332, 377,
443
Universal Declaration of Human Rights (1948)................................... 124, 251
World Bank Guidelines on the Treatment of
Foreign Direct Investment (1992)... 49, 379,
414, 418

Index

A

Abs-Shawcross Draft Convention, *see* Table of Treaties and Other Instruments
Abuse of rights, 246-7, 280, 504
Acquiescence, 449, 481, 510, 524-5
Acquired rights, 19, 21, 25, 37, 95, 246-8, 283, 285-6, 288, 298, 321-2, 324, 350-1, 442
Administration of justice, 149, 206-7, 239-42, 244, 246, 292, 314
Administrative law, 119, 280, 454, 476
Administrative review, 57, 245, 262, 293-4, 524
Admissibility of claims, 35, 482, 503, 507
Admission, 26, 42-3, 49, 121-3, 125, 127-9, 131-41, 143, 145, 147, 150, 158, 190, 223, 399, 418
  customary international law, 121-2, 190
  distinguished from establishment, 132, 135
  domestic regulation of foreign investment, 133
  entry of personnel, 121
  General Agreement on Trade in Services (GATS), *see* Table of Treaties and Other Instruments
  granting of permits, 121, 145
  post-entry model, 128, 134-6, 143
  pre-entry model, 134, 136-7, 139, 141
  rationale, 132

senior management and offices, 144, 483, 508
  special formalities, 146
  treaty models, 134
Africa, 2, 8, 19, 26, 47, 52, 56, 109, 143-4, 191, 256, 316, 374, 428
Agreement on Trade-Related Investment Measures (TRIMS Agreement), *see* Table of Treaties and Other Instruments
Amicus curiae, 253
Applicable law, 25, 28, 75-119, 126, 144, 279, 291-2, 349-52, 447-50, 475-7
  choice of law clauses, 75, 79-80, 85-7
  domestic law, 75-7, 80-2, 86-8, 92, 94, 350-2, 449-50, 464-5, 475-6
  human rights, 109, 280
  IIA as primary source, 75, 91
  inconsistent decisions, 105
  iura novit curia, 88-9
  laws relevant to IIA disputes, 86
  meaning of applicable substantive law, 75
  precedents, 104, 106
  relevance, 75, 78, 88
  renvoi, 86, 464
  role of municipal law, 92
  sources of law/sources of international law, 75, 80, 91, 100, 102, 254, 264, 450
Arbitrary/arbitrariness, meaning of, 38, 247, 250, 302

Arbitrary measures, prohibition of, 233, 289, 424
  elements of guarantee, 300-3
  relationship with fair and equitable
    treatment, 301
  treaty practice, 299-300
Arbitration, 6-10, 24-9, 44-6, 50-4, 56-67,
    70-3, 75-80, 85-9, 100-9, 116-19,
    197-8, 204-8, 210-23, 229-30, 241-4,
    511-13
  clause, 44-6, 71, 76, 79, 82, 85, 87, 197-8,
    204-8, 210-23, 229, 437, 448, 463-5,
    467-8, 478-9
  ex aequo et bono, 76
  fork in the road, 70, 208, 217, 222,
    398, 512
  investor-state, 1-2, 6-8, 22, 39, 44-6, 51-4,
    56-9, 61, 63-5, 75-7, 204-8, 210-17,
    219-23, 229-30, 241-4, 398
  offer to arbitrate, 44, 512-13
  rules, 1, 7, 26, 29, 59, 63-5, 72-3, 79, 85-7,
    91, 100, 213, 217, 220, 230, 463-5
Argentina, 67-72, 100-4, 106-7, 111-14,
    125-7, 205-10, 221-4, 265-6, 285-7,
    409-12, 444-7, 455-7, 492-500,
    517-19, 521-4, 527
Armed conflict, 112, 158, 203, 213, 315-16,
    473, 490, 499-500, 520-1
Articles on Responsibility of States, *see* Table
    of Treaties and Other Instruments
Asia, 2, 8, 11, 47, 52-3, 56, 78, 217-18, 240,
    323, 376
Association of South East Asian Nations
    (ASEAN), 52-3, 58, 135, 137, 139,
    210, 256, 444, 447-8
  Investment Area, 52
Attribution, of responsibility to state, 40, 460-1

B

Bad faith, 236, 240, 270, 277, 279, 289, 294,
    303-4, 353, 356
Basic assumptions of investor, 283, 285
Bilateral investment treaties, *see* International
    investment agreements
Bolivia, 19, 50-1, 68-9, 71, 93, 110, 117-18,
    122, 126, 134-7, 143, 145, 260, 430-1,
    444-5, 488
Bona fides, 180
Bonds, 9, 36, 66, 132
Book value, 387, 390

Breach of contract, 94, 210, 352-6, 454, 467,
    471-2, 474, 478
Bribery, 124, 282, 297
Buenos Aires Protocol, *see* Table of Treaties
    and Other Instruments
Burden of proof, 163, 165, 176, 305, 366,
    390, 440, 504, 522

C

Calvo, 9-10, 13-14, 50, 63, 153
Calvo Clause, 9, 13
Calvo Doctrine, 10, 13, 50, 63, 153
Canada, 48, 51, 137-8, 143-4, 163-7, 179-81,
    183-6, 236, 336-8, 409-11, 421-30,
    432-3, 482-5, 487-8, 505-9, 526-7
Capital
  exporting states, 2, 57
  gains, 409-10, 507
  importing states, 2-3, 13, 16, 24, 41, 46,
    264, 377
  movements, 24, 132, 155, 402-3, 405,
    415-16
  transfers, 23, 42, 266, 400, 402-6, 408-10,
    412, 415, 417
Charter of Economic Rights and Duties of
    States, *see* Table of Treaties and Other
    Instruments
Chile, 50-1, 125-6, 130, 143-6, 156-7, 181,
    201-2, 205-7, 221-3, 228-9, 332-4,
    409-10, 413-14, 422-4, 428-30, 432-3
China, 10-11, 44, 47-8, 56-7, 61, 123, 126,
    143-5, 181-2, 190, 316-17, 332, 375,
    383-4, 409-15, 444-5
Choice of law, 24, 75-6, 79-82, 84-8, 117
Circumstances precluding wrongfulness,
    see Exceptions
Civil
  disturbance, 112, 158, 203, 316, 499
  strife, 309-11
  war, 246
Claims commissions, 2, 7-8, 14, 34-5
Codification/codify, of international invest-
    ment law, 15-16, 22, 154, 239, 309,
    329, 338, 405
  by League of Nations, 15-16
  by non-governmental initiatives, 20
Coercion, 279, 282-3, 289, 294, 323, 347
Colonia Protocol, *see* Table of Treaties and
    Other Instruments

Colonial territories, 10, 18
Compensation, *see* Expropriation, compensation
Compound interest, 383, 397
Concurrent jurisdictions, 438, 448, 468, 472-4
Conduct of investor, 286, 296
Conflict of law, 86
Contractual undertakings, *see* Observance of Undertakings
Contribution to the economic development of the host state, 67
Convention on the Protection of Foreign Property (1967 Draft OECD Convention), *see* Table of Treaties and other Instruments
Convention on the Treatment of Foreigners (1929 Draft Convention), *see* Table of Treaties and other Instruments
Convertibility, 1, 148, 377, 396, 400, 406, 411
Corruption, 24, 34, 124, 240, 297, 400
Countermeasures, 129, 510
Creeping expropriation, 323, 325, 343-4, 347, 362, 394
Current
  international transactions, 401
  invisible operations, 24, 155, 403
  Invisibles Code, *see* Table of Treaties and Other Instruments
Customary international law, 121-2, 149-50, 194, 234-5, 238-9, 250-2, 258-9, 263-4, 269-71, 306-9, 321-3, 338-9, 377-9, 481-4, 495-9, 510-11
  bilateral investment treaties (BITs), 405
  expropriation, 12-13, 26, 35, 321-3, 332, 334-5, 338-40, 343-4, 358-9, 361-2, 370, 373, 377-9, 381-2, 394-5, 505-6
  minimum standard of treatment, 2, 12-13, 16, 38, 117, 122, 149, 234-6, 238, 250-2, 254-5, 258-9, 263-5, 269-71, 273, 307-9
Czech Republic, 49, 71-2, 78, 81, 89, 96, 105, 113-14, 116-17, 125-6, 130, 229, 236, 275, 283, 337

D

Damnum emergens, 378
Date of expropriation, 368, 382, 385, 393, 395-6

Declaration on the Establishment of a New International Economic Order (NIEO Declaration), *see* Table of Treaties and Other Instruments
Decolonization, 18
Defences, 90, 99, 106, 108, 129, 138-9, 172, 190, 231, 316, 426, 481-5, 495-7, 499, 510-526
  acquiescence, 481, 524-5
  Articles on Responsibility of States, *see* Table of Treaties and Other Instruments
  burden of proof, 504, 522
  circumstances precluding wrongfulness, 482-3, 523
  compensation, 495, 523-4
  consent, 481, 511, 513
  countermeasures, 129
  distress, 510
  essential interest, of state, 499, 516, 518, 520
  estoppel, 481, 527
  extinctive prescription, 525
  force majeure, 514-6
  laches, 525-6
  necessity, 106, 316, 481, 499, 515, 519, 521, 523-4
  self-defence, 510
  supervening impossibility, 515
  temporal limitations, 522
  undue delay, 525
  waiver, 511, 513
Denial of justice, 5, 11-12, 36, 136, 237-44, 246, 251-2, 277, 301, 314, 351-2, 354, 375-6, 439, 475, 513
  and exhaustion of local remedies, 241, 301
Depoliticization, 27-8, 129
Deprivation, *see* Expropriation
Derivative rights, 511
Developing states, 19, 26, 31-3, 43, 46-9, 58, 63, 418
Diligentia quam in suis, 310
Diplomatic protection, 2-11, 13, 15, 28-9, 34-9, 235, 242, 511-12
Direct expropriation, 324, 332, 334-5, 340-2, 351, 368, 393, 395, 506
Direct rights, 403, 512
Discounted cash flow (DCF), 387-91
Discrimination, 147-52, 154, 160-2, 168-70, 174-8, 183-5, 187-9, 193-5, 198-200,

251-2, 289-91, 301, 304-7, 373-4,
    486-7, 501-2
application of host state law, 252
arbitrary or unreasonable distinctions, 233,
    252, 289
domestic law, 77, 154, 250, 252, 289, 304
effects-based analysis, 306
human rights, 148, 251-2, 289, 304, 360
intent, 152, 174-6, 183, 289-90, 304, 306, 374
most-favoured-nation treatment, 193,
    195-6, 233
national treatment, 147-8, 150-2, 154-5,
    158, 160-4, 168-70, 174-5, 177-8,
    180-1, 183-5, 187-9, 191, 193, 224,
    290, 305-7
nationality-based discrimination, 147-8,
    150-2, 161-2, 164, 168-70, 174-8,
    181, 183-4, 187-9, 193, 233, 251-2,
    289-91, 304, 306-7
non-discrimination in international
    economic law, 147
race, 251, 289, 304
sex, 251, 289, 304
Discriminatory measures, prohibition of, 233,
    307
elements of guarantee, 300-1, 304-6
overlap with national and MFN treatment
    clauses, 306-7
relationship with fair and equitable
    treatment, 301
treaty practice, 299-300
Dispute resolution, 2, 8, 20, 28, 43-4, 59,
    71-2, 75-7, 111, 113, 207, 210-12,
    216, 224, 474-5, 477-9
claims commissions, 7-8, 34-5
contractual, 44, 77, 448, 474-5, 479
international arbitration, 8, 44, 75-6, 397
International Centre for the Settlement of
    Investment Disputes
investment treaties and instruments, 44-6,
    58-9, 70-3
most-favoured-national treatment, 205-222
Distress, 510
Domestic content, 1, 422-6, 429
Domestic law, 27-9, 75-82, 85-9, 91-101,
    153-4, 158-9, 260-1, 317-8, 346-7,
    350-2, 375, 434, 449-51, 462-5, 475-9
applicable law, 75-7, 80-2, 86-9, 92, 94,
    350-2, 449-50, 465, 475-6

discrimination, 77, 154, 251-2, 289-90, 304
existence of investment, 77, 92-3, 95-9
expropriation, 77, 96, 269, 346-8, 350-2,
    354, 367-9, 374-5, 379, 476, 478
fair and equitable treatment, 77, 94, 146,
    245, 250, 260-1, 269-71, 280, 283,
    286, 289-90, 304, 351, 471, 476
limitations to the role, 97
national treatment, 135, 153-4, 159-60, 420-1
observance of undertakings, 437, 449-51,
    465, 476-7, 479
relationship to international law, 86-102
renvoi, 86, 95, 97, 464
subsequent changes, 98
Draft Convention on Investments Abroad
    (Abs-Shawcross Draft Convention),
    see Table of Treaties and Other
    Instruments
Draft OECD Convention, *see* Table of
    Treaties and Other Instruments
Draft Statutes of the Arbitral Tribunal for
    Foreign Investment and the Foreign
    Investment Court (ILA Statute), *see*
    Table of Treaties and Other
    Instruments
Drago Doctrine, 10
Drago-Porter Convention, 10
In dubio mitius, 116, 217, 267
Due diligence, 236-8, 246, 251, 277, 288,
    298, 307, 309-10, 315, 515-16
Due process, 12, 15, 238, 240-2, 244-9,
    251-2, 259, 267, 271, 275-8, 280, 293,
    321-2, 329-31, 375-6, 431-3
Duress, 295, 385, 387

E

Economic crisis/financial crisis, 59, 302, 357,
    400, 415-6, 498, 517-21
Economic development, 21, 33, 48-9, 66-7,
    125, 135, 137, 232, 266, 299, 371, 418
Ecuador, 50-1, 76, 87, 93, 98, 105, 122, 125,
    152, 160, 169-70, 285-6, 336, 462,
    512, 524
Effet utile, 111, 114, 290, 306, 453, 471, 494,
    503
Egypt, 8, 10-11, 43, 45-7, 126-7, 130, 156-7,
    181, 201-2, 228, 308-9, 332-3, 345-6,
    368, 383-4, 409-10

Emergency, 101, 103, 106-7, 109, 112-13, 139, 158, 203, 208, 315-16, 324, 456, 489-90, 497, 499-500, 517
Energy Charter Treaty (ECT), *see* Table of Treaties and Other Instruments
Entry, 4, 47, 58, 65, 121-2, 127-8, 131-7, 139-44, 146, 154, 158-9, 191, 222-3, 232, 345, 456-7
   investment, 47, 58, 65, 121-2, 127-8, 131-7, 139-40, 142-4, 154, 158-9, 191, 222-3, 233, 317, 456-7, 459
   investors, 47, 65, 121-2, 127, 131-2, 134, 136-7, 139-40, 143, 146, 158-9, 222-3, 232, 459
   personnel, 121, 140, 142-3
   post-entry model, 128, 134-6, 143
   pre-entry model, 134, 136-7, 139, 141, 144, 146
Environment, protection of the, 323, 505
Essential interest, of the state, 499, 516, 520
Essential security interests, 90, 151, 372, 481, 483-5, 488-95, 497-500, 521
Establishment, 1, 17, 27, 31, 121-3, 127-9, 131-46, 154, 156-9, 190, 201-3, 223-4, 404, 422-3, 490-2, 508-9
   customary international law, 121-2, 190, 491, 510
   distinguished from admission, 132
   domestic regulation of foreign investment, 133
   entry of personnel, 121, 142
   General Agreement on Trade in Services, 1, 138, 140, 142, 404
   granting of permits, 121, 145
   performance requirements, 1, 133-4, 422-3, 508
   post-entry model, 128, 134-6, 143
   pre-entry model, 134, 136-7, 139, 141, 144, 146
   rationale, 132
   rights, 1, 17, 31, 47, 122, 127, 132-7, 140-2, 144-6, 154, 157-9, 201-2, 223, 404, 423, 508
   senior management and offices, 144
   special formalities, 146
   treaty models, 134
Estoppel, 98, 271, 279-80, 449, 481, 514, 525-7
European Court of Human Rights (ECtHR), 280, 364, 394

Ex aequo et bono, 76, 275
Exceptions, 56-7, 111, 133-4, 137-41, 149-50, 155, 157, 178-9, 186, 189-90, 194, 231-3, 319, 414-15, 422-4, 481-509
   distinction from treaty reservations, 482-5
   environmental measures, 501-2, 509
   essential security interests, 481, 483-5, 488-95, 498, 500
   future measures, 139, 190, 484-5, 508
   General Agreement on Tariffs and Trade (GATT), 415, 482
   general exceptions, 178, 189, 231, 415, 481-2, 484-8, 499-506
   government procurement, 167, 186, 190, 423, 426, 483, 506, 508
   interpretation, 111, 129, 190, 235, 290, 482-3, 485-8, 493, 503, 505-6
   interpretive guidelines, 482, 509
   necessity, relationship with, 495-497
   non-conforming measures, 57, 138, 190, 231, 484, 508
   non-precluded measures, 483
   presumptions, 111, 485, 487-8
   public order, 329, 481, 484, 486, 489-90, 492, 498, 501
   relaxation of standards, 509
   security exceptions, 482-4, 488, 490-2, 494-5, 497-8
   self-judging, 484, 490-5
   subject matter, 137, 140, 157, 213, 482, 500, 506
   subsidies, 167, 190, 423, 484, 488, 506, 508
   tax measures, 506-7
   war and civil disturbance clause, distinction from, 499
Excuse, *see* Defences
Exhaustion of local remedies, 6, 28, 208, 217, 241-3, 301, 347, 521
Expropriation, 12-15, 18-20, 22-4, 26-7, 32-3, 35-6, 38-43, 130-1, 212-16, 219-20, 321-398, 410-11, 505-8
   breach of contract, 352-6
   burden of proof, 366, 390
   case-by-case analysis, 344, 366
   compensation, *see* Compensation for Expropriation
   conditions for lawful expropriation, 321, 360, 367, 369, 396

compensation, 377-98
due process, 375-6
non-discrimination, 373-5
public purpose, 370-3
contractual undertakings, 369, 377, 443, 475
creeping, 323, 325, 343-4, 347, 362, 394-5
customary international law, 12-13, 26, 35,
38, 41, 149, 194, 321-3, 334-5, 338-9,
358, 360-1, 377-9, 381-2, 394-5, 400
date of the expropriation, 368-9, 373, 375,
381, 385, 393-4, 396-7
debt contracts, 355
deprivation, the requirement for, 327, 344-7
direct, 22, 57, 70, 244, 262, 323-4, 328,
332, 334-5, 340-3, 351, 368, 376, 379,
393, 395
discrimination, 42, 77, 148, 194, 246, 322,
328, 362, 373-4, 400, 505
domestic law, relationship with, 351-2
due process, 15, 244, 246, 321-2, 329-31,
350, 366, 369, 375-6, 380, 398, 431
effect of a finding of expropriation, 368
effects-based approach, 326, 341, 374
environment, 10, 49, 130, 323, 331, 335,
357, 361, 505
exceptions, 56-7, 194, 319, 336, 341, 490,
505-7, 509
forced sales, 327
form, 325, 327, 338-41, 343, 352, 356, 395
human health, 361
illegal, 297, 346, 359, 369, 379-82, 385,
394-6
indirect, 131, 297, 322-5, 327-8, 332,
334-5, 338-9, 341-3, 346-7, 350-1,
357, 362, 367-9, 393-5
intent, 262, 327, 341-3, 374, 507
judicial review, 375, 377, 398
legitimate expectations, 335, 341, 350-1,
357, 364, 367, 384
lump sum agreement, 34-5, 379
management or control of business
enterprise, 327
measures, meaning of, 182, 203-4, 337-8
model BITs, 61, 334
nationalization, 18-19, 26, 325, 332-4, 338,
342, 371, 373, 398
object of the deprivation, 348
omission, 262, 337-8, 343
opinio juris, 360

partial, 22, 35, 69, 322-4, 337-8, 345,
347-50, 410, 505
payments under statutory obligations, 356
permanence, 345
police powers, 325, 328, 331, 340-2, 344,
358, 360, 363, 366
proportionality, 358, 363-4
public health, order, safety order or
morality, 329, 335, 357-60, 364
public purpose/public interest condition,
321-2, 330, 333, 340, 350, 366,
369-73, 380, 394
regulation, 323-4, 331, 334, 336, 339, 341,
348-51, 357, 360-1, 364, 366-7
regulatory purpose, 342
requisition, 324, 327, 342
scientific evidence, 365
scope of, 36, 93, 96, 194, 212, 214, 219-20,
335-6, 338-9, 351, 360, 370, 385, 475
standard of review, 363
tantamount to expropriation, 331, 334, 339,
347, 355
taxation, 325, 327, 331-3, 336-7, 356-8,
361-2, 392, 507
title to expropriated property, 369
transparency, 49, 130-1, 399, 411, 431
treaty practice, 22, 41-2, 194, 332, 370,
375, 377, 393, 395, 398, 405, 443
Expropriation, compensation
actual investment, 391-2
amount, 377-8, 380-1, 385, 387-8, 390-3,
395-8
arm's length transaction, 392
asset value, 386
Charter of Economic Rights and Duties of
States, 378
compound interest, 383
convertibility, 377, 396
customary international law, 378
date for determining compensation, 377,
393-4
delay, 395-6
discounted cash flow (DCF), 387-91
fair market value, 377-9, 383-9, 391-3
freely usable currency, 396
full reparation, 381, 394-5
going concern value, 386, 388
Hull Rule, 18, 30, 377-9, 383
illegal expropriation, 379, 381-2, 385, 394

interest, 377, 380, 382-3, 392-3, 396-7
liquidation value, 390
lump sum settlements, 379
market capitalization, 392
most-favoured-nation treatment, 385
net book value (NBV), 390-1
Permanent Sovereignty Over Natural
    Resources, 377
prompt, adequate and effective compensa-
    tion, 377, 379, 383-4
reductions, 392-3
replacement value, 386-7, 390
restitution, 380, 383
standard for compensation, 377-9, 380,
    382-3, 385
third party offer to purchase, 390, 392
transferability, 377, 395-6
treaty practice, 383-4
valuation methods, *see* Valuation methods
Extinctive prescription, 525
Extraordinary losses, 233, 235, 315
Extraterritorial jurisdiction, 10-11

F

Fair and equitable treatment, 22, 94, 111, 114,
    123-5, 131-2, 233-5, 238-9, 244-6,
    250, 253-80, 283-7, 289-301, 303-4,
    311-14, 430-1
  Art., 1105(1), NAFTA 113, 117, 146, 229,
    232, 238-9, 245-6, 250, 253-5, 257-8,
    268, 272-7, 287, 292-3, 296, 351
  autonomous meaning, 264-5, 308
  bad faith, 270, 277, 279, 289, 294, 303-4
  baseline of investment protection, 255
  coercion, 279, 283, 289, 294
  conduct of foreign investor, 296-8
  customary international law, 111, 117, 149,
    234-5, 238-9, 254, 258-9, 263-4, 266,
    269-71, 273, 277, 290, 308-9, 312
  discrimination, 77, 154, 233, 246, 267, 279,
    289-91, 301, 304, 306
  domestic law, 77, 94-5, 146, 244-5, 250,
    260-1, 270-1, 280, 283, 286, 289, 304,
    351, 471, 476
  early treaty practice, 22, 255
  favourable conditions, 114, 123, 130-2,
    266-7, 295-6
  general characteristics, 275

good faith, 111, 129, 246, 265-7, 271, 274,
    277, 279-80, 284, 294, 304, 443, 527
harassment, 279, 289, 294-5, 314
impairment, 262
independent treaty standard, 264-5, 270, 272
intent, 262, 277, 289-90, 306, 472
interpretive approaches, 263-75
legitimate expectations, *see* Legitimate
    expectations
meaning of treatment, 261, 263
minimum standard of treatment, 22, 30,
    117, 149, 234-6, 238, 245-6, 250,
    253-5, 258-9, 261, 263-5, 268-74,
    276-9, 290, 308-9
misrepresentation by foreign investor,
    297, 351
non-discrimination, 77, 267, 279, 289
reliance, 265, 279, 283, 286-7, 294, 296-7
rule of law, 131, 234, 255, 267, 279, 292,
    296, 303
scope, 149, 205, 262, 277-8, 292, 304,
    312-13, 351, 475-6
stable and predictable (stability and pre-
    dictability), 132, 271, 280, 286-9, 314
subjective, 275-6, 306
threats, 279, 294
transparency, 124, 131, 245, 262, 269, 275,
    278-80, 284, 289, 291-4, 296,
    407, 431
treaty practice, 22, 123, 255, 257, 264, 268,
    290, 299, 443
Fair market value, 377-80, 383-9, 391-3
Financial crisis/economic crisis, 59, 302, 357,
    400, 415-16, 498, 517-21
Force majeure, 476, 481, 510, 514-16
Foreign direct investment (FDI), 3, 40, 43,
    48-9, 56, 58, 62-3, 127, 133, 135, 137,
    140, 147, 323, 379, 414-5, 418-19
Foreign investment insurance, 39-40
  Multilateral Investment Guarantee Agency
    (MIGA), 40
Fork in the road, 70, 208, 217, 222, 398, 512
France, 3, 14, 26, 32, 36, 43, 50, 69, 80, 112,
    143-4, 260, 333, 370, 415, 430-1
Fraud, 282, 297
Free trade agreement (FTAs), 1, 51, 53, 57,
    61, 82-3, 137, 142, 151, 158, 202, 238,
    258, 272, 334, 336, 411, 416, 422,
    428, 432, 435, 444, 488, 490-1, 501

Freely usable currency, 411-2

Friendship, Commerce and Navigation
     Treaties (FCN Treaties), 23, 37-8, 41,
     46, 57, 128, 142, 200, 248-9, 256,
     298, 307-8, 493

Full protection and security, 117, 233, 235,
     238, 253-4, 257-9, 263, 268-9, 272-3,
     278, 287, 308-9, 311-14, 471, 515

G

General Agreement on Tariffs and Trade
     (GATT), 20, 141, 148, 199, 254, 415,
     482, 493

General Agreement on Trade in Services
     (GATS), 1, 54, 138, 140, 142, 173,
     218, 254, 400, 404, 421

General exceptions, *see* Exceptions

General principles of law (of international
     law), 25, 79, 80-1, 87, 102, 247, 254,
     271, 279-80, 293, 310, 321, 335, 364,
     370, 525-6

Generalia specialibus non derogant, 473

Germany, 8-9, 15, 42, 45, 56, 123, 125-6,
     130, 134-5, 143, 190-1, 299, 384, 397,
     409-10, 412-13, 448

Going-concern, 386, 388

Good faith, 25, 27, 98, 102, 110-11, 129, 145,
     246-7, 265-7, 277, 279-81, 355-7,
     365-6, 370-3, 494-5, 526-7

Good governance, 49, 131, 234, 279

Government procurement, 53, 56, 167, 186,
     190, 341, 423, 426, 483, 506, 508

Grotius, 4, 24-5, 439

Gunboat diplomacy, 9

H

Hague Convention, 9-10, 76

Harassment, 279, 289, 294-5, 314, 328

Harvard Draft Convention on Responsibility
     of States for Damage done in their
     Territory to the Person or Property of
     Foreigners (1929 Harvard Draft), 15,
     22, 239, 246, 411

Harvard Draft Convention on the International
     Responsibility of States for Injuries to
     Aliens (1961 Harvard Draft), 22,
     154-5, 174, 246-7, 326, 328-9, 358,
     372, 379, 405, 442

Havana Charter, 19-20, 256, 441

Health, 36, 123-4, 158, 171, 178, 182, 228,
     329, 335, 357-8, 361, 364, 424, 486,
     501-2, 509

Hull Rule, 18, 30

Human rights, 64-5, 107-9, 124, 148,
     251-3, 263, 280, 289, 304, 360,
     364, 371

I

Illegal expropriation, *see* Expropriation

Inconsistent decisions, 64, 105, 293

India, 44, 48, 57, 61, 82, 144-5, 156, 224,
     395-6, 411, 413, 416, 433, 435, 448,
     489-90

Indirect expropriation, 131, 297, 322-5, 327,
     334-5, 338-9, 341-3, 346-7, 350-1,
     357, 362, 367-9, 393-5

Insurance, 24, 39-40, 42, 97, 195, 298, 328,
     337, 347, 350, 354, 374, 403-4, 453,
     462, 470

Insurrection, 112, 158, 203, 246, 315-16,
     499-500

International capital movements, 402

International Centre for the Settlement of
     Investment Disputes (ICSID), 27-9,
     40-2, 44-6, 50-1, 59-61, 66-7, 72-3,
     77-8, 80, 82, 85, 91-2, 99-101, 103-6,
     197-8, 322-4

   Additional Facility Rules, 29, 85

   annulment, 29, 78, 89

   arbitration, 27-9, 46, 72, 82, 85, 100, 103

   Arbitration Rules, 29, 213, 230

   convention, *see* Table of Treaties and Other
        Instruments

International Chamber of Commerce (ICC),
     17, 20-1, 47, 61, 73, 86, 154, 200,
     297, 397, 404-5

International Code of Fair Treatment for
     Foreign Investments (ICC Code), *see*
     Table of Treaties and Other
     Instruments

International Court of Justice (ICJ), 23, 35-9,
     42, 60, 78, 80-90, 95, 102-4, 121-2,
     128, 195-7, 206-7, 247-8, 256, 264,
     275, 337, 411, 492-3, 512, 525-7

   Investment disputes before the ICJ, 35-9

International economic law, 14, 33, 121,
     147-8, 152, 194, 198, 291, 400, 432

International Institute for Sustainable
Development (IISD), 59, 63-4, 108,
116, 252-3, 361, 416, 503
International investment agreements (IIAs),
1-4, 23, 41, 55-8, 60-6, 66, 121-2,
125-30, 132-7, 139-46, 149, 156, 193,
198-8, 225-9, 233-5, 252, 322-3,
332-9, 399, 404-17, 422-4, 427-32,
443-8, 481-5
1970s and, 1980s 31, 46-8, 50, 52, 57, 133,
378, 418, 494
1990s, 47-9
Africa, 52-3
Asia, 52-3
asymmetrical economic and political
relationship, 43-4
China, 156, 332
Critiques, 63-4
dispute settlement, 64, 141, 198
Energy Charter Treaty, 1, 53-4
expanding network, 57-8
fork in the road, 398
historical developments, 1-73
India, 156, 332, 435
investment promotion effects, 62-3
investor-state arbitration, 1, 141
jurisprudence, 40
Latin America, 50-1
Multilateral Agreement on Investment
(MAI), 55
new models, 61
North American Free Trade Agreement
(NAFTA), 1, 232, 255, 332, 428, 507
obligations, 41, 64, 121, 129, 141, 149,
193, 233, 252-3, 322, 437, 507
origins, 41
preamble, 122-4
renegotiation, 61
scope of application, 65-9
investment, 65-8
investors, 68-9
structure, 1, 198
titles, 121-2
treaty interpretation, *see* Interpretation
treaty obligations, 129
treaty practice, 122, 156, 255, 332, 398,
437
treaty shopping, 198
International Law Commission's Articles
on State Responsibility, *see*

Table of Treaties and Other
Instruments
International Monetary Fund (IMF), 1, 19, 48,
148, 400-4, 406, 409-12, 414-7
Articles of Agreement, *see* Table of
Treaties and Other Instruments
International Trade Organization (ITO),
19-20, 256, 401
Interpretation, 75-7, 79-81, 83, 105-7, 109-19,
124-6, 169-71, 216-17, 264-9, 272-4,
337-9, 453, 455-8, 467-9, 471-2,
485-8
adjudicative function, 119
approached, 205, 210
by the contracting states, 117
in dubio mitius, 116, 217, 267
effet utile, 111, 114, 290, 306, 453, 471,
494, 503
ejusdem generis, 112, 204-5, 207
expressio unius, 111-12
in favorem validitatis, 217
general exceptions, 482, 485-7, 503, 505-6
generalia specialibus non derogant, 473
literal, 128, 151, 455-6, 467-8, 471
methods of interpretation, 111, 115, 125
object and purpose, 110-15, 125, 128-9,
265-7, 453, 468, 471, 485, 487-8
ordinary meaning, 110-11, 265, 267,
467, 471
preambles, 113, 115-16, 124-5, 266
presumptions, 111-12, 216, 485, 487
pro-investor or pro-state, 113
process of applying proper law, 109-10
rules on treaty interpretation, 110
travaux préparatoires, 113, 254
treaty titles, 124
Vienna Convention on the Law of Treaties,
76, 111, 118, 124-5, 217, 265, 267-8
Investment, 1-3, 17-33, 35-73, 75-87, 91-100,
121-59, 193-205, 222-31, 250-7,
265-73, 276-94, 331-9, 341-58,
403-16, 441-50, 452-63
contribution to the economic development
of the host state, 67
insurance, 39-40, 42, 97, 298, 347,
350, 403
protection, 1-2, 4-7, 9-11, 18-23, 27-30,
34-45, 47-8, 51-6, 122-4, 126-9,
252-7, 266-9, 277-9, 307-14, 441-5,
511-12

Investment treaty arbitration, 2, 7, 44, 46, 48, 53, 59-65, 67, 77-8, 86, 97, 105, 119, 152, 473, 511
  advent of treaty based arbitration, 44
  fork in the road, 512
  host state courts, 13, 72
  institutional arbitration, 73,
  jurisdiction, 44-6, 60, 77, 198, 473-4, 511
  most-favoured-nation treatment, 205-222
  notification, 46
  'trigger' letter, 71
  waiver, 13
Investments, defining scope of covered investment, 65-8
Investor, defining scope of covered investors, 68-9
Iran, 8, 10-11, 19, 36, 39, 314, 325-8, 342, 358-9, 377-9, 385-7, 389, 391-2, 402, 417, 441
Iran-United States Claims Tribunal, 8, 39, 59, 323, 326, 358, 377, 402, 417

J

Jay Treaty, 7
Judicial review, 292, 375, 377, 398
Jurisdiction, of tribunals under IIAs, 70-3, 210-5

K

Kompetenz-Kompetnz, 224

L

Labour, 33, 47, 123-4, 144, 173, 329, 331, 428, 486, 502, 509
Laches, 525-6
Lapse of time, 390, 525
Latin America, 2, 8-9, 11, 13, 19, 46, 50, 460
Lauterpacht, 27, 377-8, 381, 384, 440-1, 443, 449
Lawful expropriation, 321, 369, 381-2, 396
Legitimate expectations/reasonable expectations, 98, 104, 255, 277-83, 285-8, 292-3, 296-7, 335, 341, 350-1, 357, 363-4, 367, 384, 451, 527
  assessing, 283, 286, 288, 296, 341, 350
  good faith, 277, 279-81, 357, 527

  reliance on host state conduct/reasonable reliance, 283, 286, 297
  stability and predictability of legal framework/stable and predictable, 280, 287
Less favourable treatment, *see* Most-favoured-nation treatment and National treatment
Letters of comfort, 449, 457
Lex contractus, 450, 464
Lex situs, 92, 350-1
Lex specialis, 91, 100, 382, 496
Like circumstances, *see* Most-favoured-nation treatment and National treatment
Like products, 153, 164, 168, 170-3
Liquidation value, 390
Lost profits, 378, 381, 389, 523
Lucrum cessans, 378
Lump sum agreements, 34-5, 379

M

Margin of appreciation, 178, 315, 365, 370-1, 373, 475
Market capitalization, 392
Measure, meaning of, 337
Mercado Común del Sur/Common Market of the South (MERCOSUR), 50-1, 58, 79, 137, 158, 422
Mexico, 9-10, 13-14, 18, 51, 53, 82-3, 87, 137, 162-3, 222, 236, 239-40, 245, 283-4, 325, 336-7
Minimum standard of treatment, 11-16, 22-3, 30, 148-9, 153, 234-9, 245-7, 250-5, 258-9, 261, 263-5, 268-74, 276-9, 290, 307-9, 505
  abuse of rights, 246-7
  arbitrariness, 38, 238, 246-7, 250, 252
  arbitrary measures (prohibition of), 233, 289
  content, 33, 117, 148-9, 234-5, 259, 270-1, 274, 277, 279
  continued relevance, 235
  denial of justice, 12, 237-9, 244, 246, 252, 277
  discrimination, 148, 238, 246, 251-2, 279, 289-90, 307, 505
  discriminatory measures (prohibition of), 151, 233, 307
  due diligence, 236-8, 246, 277, 307, 309

due process, 12, 238, 244-6, 252, 259, 271, 276-8, 321, 431
early jurisprudence, 11, 14
efforts to codify, 15
exceptions, 17, 149, 153, 235, 290, 505
expropriation, *see* Expropriation
extraordinary losses, 235
fair and equitable treatment, 22, 30, 117, 149, 233-5, 238, 245-6, 250, 253-5, 258-9, 261, 263-5, 268-74, 276-9, 290, 308-9
Hull Rule, 18, 30
human rights, 148, 251-3
more favourable treatment clauses, 235
opinio juris, 149, 264, 271
preservation of rights clauses, 65, 84, 91, 235, 317, 319, 445, 477-8
principle and rationale, 193, 233
protection and security obligations, 307, 309
treatment in accordance with international law, 234-5, 253-4, 258, 272
unreasonable or unjustifiable measures (prohibition of), 303-4
Moral damages, 314, 343
Morocco, 11, 29, 61, 67, 71, 77, 82, 102, 139, 160, 191, 195, 197, 409-10, 413, 463
Most-favoured-nation, 4, 19, 72, 105, 111, 122, 148, 186, 193-233
application to investor state arbitration, 84, 158
assessment of IIA jurisprudence, 216-22
basic treaty, 197, 204, 220
beneficiary state, 196, 204, 231
clauses, 105, 186, 193, 195-9, 201-2, 204-5, 216, 219-21, 224, 233
comparator, 203, 233
comparisons of treatment, 181
de facto analysis, 182-3
definition, 195-6, 412
ejusdem generis, 112, 204-5, 207
exceptions, 111, 231
forms of MFN, 198-9
granting state, 195-6, 231
historical background, 198
less favourable treatment, 196, 215, 227, 229-30
like circumstances, 201-2, 225, 227, 230

opinio juris, 194
overlap with clauses prohibiting discriminatory measures, 306-7
presumption, 205, 216
principle and rationale, 193, 233
protectionist intent or motive, 152, 164, 174-5, 183
public health, order or safety, 228
purpose, 122, 195, 227, 373
relative standard, 193, 233
reservations, 191, 231, 483
scope of application, 194-5, 196, 205, 213, 222-5
similarities with national treatment analysis, 224
special legal relationships, 227
standard of compensation, 322
standard of treatment, 193, 233
subject matter of MFN treatment, 197, 204
treatment, 4, 19, 122, 148, 186-7, 193-205, 207, 209, 211-13, 215, 217-19, 221, 223-7, 229-31, 233, 483
meaning of, 203
treaty-based obligation, 193-4
treaty practice/provisions, 122, 198-9, 201, 215-6, 412
Multilateral Agreement on Investment (MAI), 55, 161, 323, 331, 506
Multilateral Investment Guarantee Agency (MIGA), 27, 40, 57, 129, 256, 358
Municipal law, *see* Domestic law

N

National claims commissions, 34
National law, *see* Domestic law/municipal law
National security, 17, 133, 137, 488-93, 498
National treatment, 17, 19-20, 33, 134-5, 137-9, 147-192, 199-201, 224-8, 230-1, 290, 305-7, 419-23, 503, 505-6
analysis, 19, 148, 150-2, 159, 161-5, 167-74, 177-8, 180, 183, 224-7, 230, 233, 297, 306-7, 377, 505
application, 135, 150-1, 154, 156, 158-60, 163-4, 171, 184, 188, 225, 423
best in-state treatment, 188-9
best out-of-state treatment, 188
best treatment, 186-8

burden of proof, 163, 165, 176

comparator, 149-50, 156, 158-65, 168-70, 181, 187, 201, 224, 226, 233

competitive relationship, 152, 164-5, 167-8, 171-4, 176, 226

definition, 138, 150-1

de facto/de jure discrimination, 152, 154, 174, 176-7, 183

domestic law, 136, 153-4, 159, 420

economic sector, 163-5, 169, 174, 226

exceptions, 17, 57, 134, 137-9, 149-50, 153, 155, 157, 189-90, 231, 422-3, 484-5, 488, 503, 505-6, 508

historical background and development, 152

less favourable treatment, 150-1, 156, 159, 162-4, 167, 170, 172, 174-5, 177-89, 224, 227-8, 230, 423

like circumstances, 137, 150-1, 156-74, 176-7, 179, 181, 183, 185, 187-9, 201, 225-8, 230, 307, 503, 505

non-discrimination international economic law, 147-8

obligations, 54, 122, 134-5, 137-9, 144, 148-51, 155-6, 158-9, 175, 201, 290, 420, 422-3, 483-4, 503, 508

opinio juris, 149

overlap with clauses prohibiting discriminatory measures, 233

performance requirements, 133-4, 147, 233, 405, 419, 421-3, 427, 508

pre-entry and post-entry models, 158

proportionality, 178

protectionist intent or motive, 152, 164, 174

provisions, 17, 19, 33, 52-3, 134, 149-55, 158-61, 172-3, 181, 188, 227-8, 290-1, 306-7, 316, 377, 503

public health, order, safety, 158, 182

purpose, 122, 144, 150-2, 154, 162-5, 168-9, 171-2, 174-5, 177, 179, 191, 227, 273, 488

regulatory purpose, 162-3, 165, 175, 177, 342

relative standard, 148, 159, 193, 233, 290

relevant factors, 164

reservations, 18, 138-9, 150, 159, 189-91, 231, 290, 483-5, 508

sequence of analysis, 162

standard of treatment, 13, 18, 33, 43, 122, 148-9, 153, 159, 181, 188-9, 193, 228, 233, 236, 290, 505

  application to sub-state units, 188

  best or average treatment, 186-7

  comparisons of treatment, 183-4

  de facto analysis, 182-3

  less favourable treatment, 159, 181, 188, 228

  meaning of treatment, 182

  treaty provisions, 181, 228

treaty-based obligation, 149-50

treaty practice, 42, 122, 134, 149, 155-6, 190, 201, 290, 377, 488

Nationality-based discrimination, 147-8, 150-2, 161-2, 164, 168-70, 174-8, 181, 183-4, 187-9, 193, 233, 251-2, 289-91, 304, 306-7

Nationalization, *see* Expropriation

Necessity, as a circumstance precluding wrongfulness, 482, 510, 516-7

  compensation, 523-4

  jurisprudence, 517-23

  requirements for a plea, 516-22

  temporal limitations, 522-3

Negative listing, 137-8, 141

Net book value (NBV), 390-1

Netherlands, 42, 44, 56-7, 68, 70-1, 76, 79, 81, 117-18, 122-3, 125-7, 181, 332-3, 383-5, 407-11, 413

Nicaragua, 9, 23, 41-2, 122, 128, 144, 316, 422, 492-4

Non-derogation clause, 235, 317-8

Non-discrimination, *see* Discrimination

North American Free Trade Agreement (NAFTA), 1, 51, 53, 82, 137, 151, 202, 238, 272, 336, 411, 444, 488

Norway, 14-15, 32, 36, 43, 53, 124, 126, 128, 135, 213-14, 226, 257, 308, 321, 375

O

Obiter dictum, 242

Object and purpose of IIAs, *see* International Investment Agreements

Obligation of conduct and result, 249, 375-6

Observance of undertakings, 22, 25, 233, 269, 319, 354, 377, 406, 437-480, 518

applicable law, 25, 319, 377, 437, 447,
    449-50, 454, 465, 476-7
attribution, 460, 462, 464-6
concurrent jurisdictions, 438, 472
contracts international law, 438-40
contractual undertakings, 443, 447, 451-2,
    459, 475
distinction from other clauses, 477
domestic law, 434, 449-51, 464-5, 476,
    478-9
drafting variations, 445-8
history and early treaty practice, 440-1
limitations, 438, 442, 476
literal approach, 467-8, 470-2
pacta sunt servanda, 437-8, 473
placement, 444-5
principle and rationale, 438
scope and effect, 438, 445, 450-1
separate personality, 465
stabilization clauses, 454, 469, 476
state entities, 452, 460-1
substantive content, 233, 469
treaty practice, 377, 437, 441, 443
umbrella clause, 437-8
unilateral undertakings, 447-8, 457, 459
Opinio juris, 149, 194, 264, 271, 360
Ordinary meaning, *see* Interpretation
Organization for Economic Co-operation and
    Development (OECD), 2, 23-4, 30-1,
    33-4, 53, 55, 57-8, 151, 154-5, 166,
    175, 193, 200, 255-6, 269, 299-300,
    330, 400, 403-5, 442-3, 500
  1967 OECD Draft Convention, *see*
    Convention on the Protection of
    Foreign Property in Table of Treaties
    and Other Instruments
  Capital Movements Code, *see* Table of
    Treaties and Other Instruments
  Current Invisibles Code, *see* Table of
    Treaties and Other Instruments
  Declaration on International Investment
    and Multinational Enterprises, *see*
    Table of Treaties and Other
    Instruments
  Guidelines on Multinational Enterprises,
    see Table of Treaties and Other
    Instruments
  National Treatment Instrument, *see* Table
    of Treaties and Other Instruments

P

Pacta sunt servanda, 217, 271, 437-8, 441,
    443, 473, 494
Partial expropriation, 323, 348-50
Performance requirements, 1, 133-4, 147, 186,
    233, 399, 401, 403, 405, 407, 409,
    411, 417-431, 507-8
  de facto, 423, 426
  de jure, 426
  domestic content, 1, 422-6, 429
  establishment rights, 133-4, 423, 508
  exceptions, 134, 414, 422-3, 426, 507-8
  General Agreement on Trade in Services
    (GATS), 1, 400, 404, 415, 421
  justification, 147, 419
  national treatment, 134, 147-8, 233, 404,
    419-23, 426, 508
  sales of goods, 425, 427
  sourcing, 418, 424
  subsidies, 423, 429
  technology transfer, 418
  trade balancing, 418, 424, 429
  Trade-related investment measures
    (TRIMs), 1, 418-22, 424
  treaty practice, 134, 398, 422, 431
Permanent Court of International Justice
    (PCIJ), 5, 15, 80, 89, 99, 102, 112,
    116, 321-2, 328, 380-1, 439
Permanent Sovereignty Over Natural
    Resources, 26, 31-2, 332, 377, 443
Philippines, 77, 94, 103-5, 115, 134, 159,
    265, 295, 355, 411-13, 423, 445-50,
    452-8, 467-70, 472-5, 477-9
Physical protection, 309-13
Poland, 15, 40, 58, 71, 95, 97, 290, 308,
    321-2, 347, 354, 375, 380, 410,
    439-40, 445-6
Police powers, 325, 328-9, 331, 340-2, 344,
    358-60, 363, 366, 372, 476
  burden of proof, 366
  environment, 357-8, 361
  health, 329, 357-8, 361
  proportionality, 358, 363
  public order and morality, 358
  scientific evidence, 365
  standard of review, 363
  tax/taxation, 361-2
  transparency, 366

Positive listing, 138, 141
Post-entry/pre-entry, *see* Entry
Post-establishment/pre-establishment, *see*
    Establishment
Preamble(s), 21, 27, 41, 65, 110, 113-16,
    121-5, 218, 266-7, 287, 295, 442
Precedent(s), 39, 60, 75, 102-6, 207, 213,
    267, 394
Preclusion of wrongfulness, *see* Defences
Preservation of rights, 65, 84, 91, 235, 317,
    319, 444-5, 477-8
  distinction from observance of under-
    takings clause, 477
Promotion and encouragement obligations,
    126-7, 129-30
  favourable conditions, 128, 130
Proper law, *see* Applicable law
Proportionality, 109, 178, 250, 267, 358,
    363-5, 520
Protection and security obligations, 235, 307,
    309-11, 313-14
  administration of justice, 314
  background, 307
  legal protection, 311
  level of host state resources, 310
  physical protection, 309-11, 313
  treaty practice, 308-9
Protectionist, *see* Most-favoured-nation treat-
    ment and National treatment
Public health, 158, 182, 228, 335, 357-8, 364
Public interest, *see* Expropriation, public
    purpose
Public order and morality, *see* Exceptions;
    Expropriation
Public purpose, *see* Expropriation
Publication, *see* Transparency

R

Race/racial, 4, 150, 238, 246, 251, 275,
    289-90, 304, 360, 373-4, 509, 517
Ratione materiae, 297, 487
Rebus sic stantibus, 476
Renvoi, 86, 95, 97, 464
Reparation, 2, 5, 15, 99, 229, 354-5, 369,
    379-81, 394-5, 523, 525
Replacement value, 386-7, 390
Requisition, 15, 37-8, 248-9, 312, 315, 324,
    327, 342, 510

Res inter alios acta, 196
Reservations, to IIA obligations, 482-5
Restitution, 102, 112, 315-16, 380, 383,
    409, 499
Returns, *see* Transfer of funds
Revolution, 7, 39, 112, 158, 203, 315-16, 499
Root, Elihu, 11-2, 80, 328, 440-1
Russia, 13-14, 53, 65, 87, 144, 210, 212,
    214-16, 220, 318, 333, 341, 397, 410,
    412, 493

S

Safeguard, 139, 177, 335, 408, 415-16,
    515-18, 520
Safety, 103, 123-4, 158, 179, 335, 357-8, 361,
    364, 429, 487, 502, 506, 509
Schwebel, Stephen, 24, 26-7, 37-9, 61,
    248-50, 267, 270, 332, 352, 439-41
Security exceptions, 482-4, 488-92, 494-5,
    497-8
  necessity, relationship with, 495-7
  scope, 482, 484, 497
  self-judging, 484, 490-2, 494-5
  treaty practice, 484, 488, 497
  war and civil disturbance clause, distinction
    from, 499
Self-defence, 510
Self-judging, 113, 118, 372-3, 484, 490-5,
    518
Shihata, Ibrahim, 27-8, 40, 49, 85, 121, 129,
    133, 137, 454
Source(s) of law, *see* Applicable law, Spain
Special drawing rights, 412
Special formalities, 146
Sri Lanka, 46, 58, 67, 84-5, 121, 138, 149,
    194, 229, 308-9, 315-16, 383, 389,
    409, 415, 500
Stabilization clauses, 98, 288, 357, 413, 454,
    469, 476
Standard of review, 179, 363, 365, 491
Standstill, 138, 190, 484
State contract(s), 25, 75, 80, 98, 228, 355,
    440-1, 452, 454-5, 460
State entities, 452, 460-1, 465, 512
State responsibility (Articles on
    Responsibility of States), *see* Table of
    Treaties and Other Instruments
Stay of proceedings, 473-5

Stockholm Chamber of Commerce (SCC),
  73, 86
Subrogation, 40, 42, 65
Subsidy/subsidies, 167, 190, 356, 423, 429,
  483-4, 488, 506, 508
Substantial deprivation, *see* Expropriation
Sustainable development, 59, 61, 63-4, 108,
  116, 123-4, 252, 361, 416, 503

T

Tax/taxation measures, 154, 331-2, 336-7,
  362, 484, 506-7
Technology transfer, 31, 123, 418, 423, 428-9
Third party offer to purchase, 392
Trade-related investment measures (TRIMs),
  1, 54, 418-21, 422, 424
Transfer of funds, 19, 23, 39, 399-417
  additional investment, 409
  balance of payments, 400, 403-4, 415
  capital gains, 408-10
  capital movement, 402
  compensation payments, 407
  convertibility, 406
  current transactions, 402, 404
  delay, 402, 406, 413
  early investment instruments, 404
  exchange, 400, 406, 411-13, 415, 417
  freely usable currency, 411-12
  General Agreement on Trade in Services
    (GATS), 400, 403-4, 415
  International Monetary Fund (IMF), 19,
    400-4, 412, 415
  jurisprudence, 39, 402, 417
  non-monetary transfers, 411
  Organization for Economic Co-operation
    and Development (OECD), 403-5
  payments, 400, 402-5, 407, 411, 415
  proceeds from sale or liquidation/proceeds
    of sale, 403, 405, 407-8, 410
  profits, 399, 402, 405
  reinvestment, 409
  remittances by foreign employees, 407, 410
  restrictions, 39, 399-400, 404, 406-7,
    413, 417
  returns, 407
  scope of transfer rights, 406
  temporary derogation, 415
  treaty practice, 398, 405, 412

types of transfers, 407
Transparency, 49, 55-6, 63, 102, 124, 130-1,
  180, 238, 245-6, 253, 262, 269,
  278-80, 291-4, 399, 431-3
  administration obligation, 291-4
  administrative rulings, 291, 420, 431-2
  comment obligation, 292
  due process, 238, 244-5, 275, 278, 289,
    293, 366, 431, 433, 435
  fair and equitable treatment, 124, 132, 245,
    262-3, 269, 275, 278-80, 284, 289-94,
    296, 406, 431
  notification, 291-2, 433
  publication, 291, 431-3
  treaty practice, 254, 398, 431
Treatment, *see* Most-favoured-nation treatment, minimum standard of treatment
  and National treatment
Treaty, *see* International investment
  agreements

U

Ultra vires, 98, 250
Umbrella clause, *see* Observance of
  Undertakings
Undertakings, *see* Observance of
  Undertakings
Undue delay, 30, 240, 395-7, 524-5
Unilateral acts, 118, 279
Unilateral undertakings, 447-8, 457-9,
  461, 471
United Kingdom/UK, 43-4, 50, 57-8,
  65-6, 112-3, 130-1, 149, 160, 194,
  203-6, 210-12, 215-20, 225-6, 268,
  315-6, 370-1, 409-10, 440-1, 443-5,
  447-8
United Nations, 3, 26-7, 41, 49, 56-9, 122,
  133, 156, 193, 200-1, 255-7, 332, 405,
  428, 443, 488-9
  Centre on Transnational Corporations
    (UNCTC), 30, 41, 122, 156, 201, 257,
    325, 332, 405, 443, 488
  Charter of Economic Rights and Duties of
    States, 31
  Code of Conduct on Transnational
    Corporations, 33
  Commission on International Trade Law
    (UNCITRAL), 59, 73, 82, 213

United States/US, 6-9, 22-3, 38-9, 46-7, 61,
149, 172, 236-7, 247, 273-4, 326-8,
330, 337, 416-17, 485-7, 525-6
Unreasonable or unjustifiable measures,
prohibition of, 303-4
elements of guarantee, 303-4
relationship with fair and equitable
treatment, 301

V

Valuation methods, 377, 383, 385-7, 392
actual investment, 391-2
arm's length transaction, 392
asset value, 386
discounted cash flow (DCF), 387
going concern value, 386-91
liquidation value, 390
market capitalization, 392
net book value (NBV), 390
reductions, 392
replacement value, 386-7
third party offer to purchase, 392
de Vattel, Emmerich, 4
Venezuela, 9, 49-51, 59, 66, 69, 71, 79, 82,
87, 260, 409-11, 414, 423-4, 450,
452, 514
Vienna Convention on the Law of Treaties
(VCLT), *see* Table of Treaties and
Other Instruments

W

Waiver, 13, 244, 283, 510-14, 527

War, 3, 8, 10-11, 23, 90, 112, 148, 158, 203,
246, 252, 315-16, 328, 359, 490-2,
497-9
World Bank, 19, 27-8, 40, 48-9, 62, 80, 137,
379, 387-8, 401, 414, 418, 454
World Bank Guidelines on the Treatment of
Foreign Direct Investment, *see* Table
of Treaties and Other Instruments
World Trade Organization (WTO), 1, 54-6,
128, 138, 140-2, 170-4, 218, 254,
291-2, 400, 404, 414-5, 418-22,
428-9, 485-7, 491-2, 503-4
Agreement on Technical Barriers to Trade
(TBT Agreement), *see* Table of
Treaties and Other Instruments
Agreement on the Application of Sanitary
and Phytosanitary Measures (SPS
Agreement), *see* Table of Treaties and
Other Instruments
Agreement on Trade-Related Investment
Measures (TRIMs Agreements), *see*
Table of Treaties and Other
Instruments
Appellate Body, 485-6
Doha Declaration, *see* Table of Treaties and
Other Instruments
General Agreement on Tariffs and Trade
(GATT), *see* Table of Treaties and
Other Instruments
General Agreement on Trade in Services
(GATS), *see* Table of Treaties and
Other Instruments
Working Group on the Relationship
between Trade and Investment